Frommer's®

National Parks
of the
American West

4th Edition

by Don & Barbara Laine

with Jack Olson, Eric Peterson & Shane Christensen

WILEY

Wiley Publishing, Inc.

Published by:
Wiley Publishing, Inc.
111 River St.
Hoboken, NJ 07030-5774

ISBN 0-7645-4362-8

Editor: Alexis Lipsitz Flippin
Production Editor: M. Faunette Johnston
Cartographer: Elizabeth Puhl
Photo Editor: Richard Fox
Production by Wiley Indianapolis
Composition Services

Front cover photo: Bryce Canyon, Utah
Back cover photo: Bighorn rams in Yellowstone National Park

For information on our other products and services or to obtain technical support, please contact our Customer Care Department within the U.S. at 800/762-2974, outside the U.S. at 317/572-3993 or fax 317/572-4002.

Wiley also publishes its books in a variety of electronic formats. Some content that appears in print may not be available in electronic formats.

Manufactured in the United States of America

5   4   3   2   1

Note: Please be advised that travel information is subject to change at any time. This is especially true of prices. The publisher and the authors have endeavored to provide useful information in this publication, but we suggest that you write or call ahead for confirmation when making your travel plans. The publisher and authors cannot be held responsible for the experiences of readers while traveling. National parks are, by their very nature, potentially hazardous places. In visiting any of the places or doing any of the activities described herein, readers assume all risk of injury or loss that may accompany such activities. The publisher and the authors disavow all responsibility for injury, death, loss, or property damage that may arise from a reader's visit to any of the places or participation in any of the activities described herein, and the publisher and the authors make no warranties regarding the competence, safety, and reliability of outfitters, tour companies, or training centers described in this publication.

Contents

List of Maps

Authors

Don and Barbara Laine have written about and traveled extensively throughout the Rocky Mountains and the Southwest. They are the authors of Frommer's guides to Utah, Colorado, and Montana and Wyoming, as well as *Frommer's Zion & Bryce Canyon National Parks, Frommer's Yosemite & Sequoia/Kings Canyon National Parks,* and *Frommer's Rocky Mountain National Park;* and are contributing authors to *Frommer's Texas.*

Jack Olson, a longtime resident of Denver, wanders the Rockies and the entire country as a freelance photographer and writer. He writes travel articles for AAA magazines and his photos may be seen in such publications as *Backpacker, Audubon, Sierra,* and *National Geographic Books.*

Eric Peterson is a Denver-based freelance writer who has authored *Frommer's Montana & Wyoming* and *Frommer's Yellowstone & Grand Teton National Parks;* and contributed to *Frommer's Texas, Frommer's Yosemite & Sequoia/Kings Canyon National Parks,* and *Frommer's Colorado.* He also writes for several Colorado-based business and entertainment periodicals, makes a mean chicken chile, and takes as many weekend treks into the Rockies as possible.

A California native, **Shane Christensen** has written travel guides throughout the American Southwest, as well as books covering destinations in Europe, Latin America, and the Caribbean. He is coauthor of *Frommer's Argentina & Chile.* Shane is also a Foreign Service Officer and currently works as Special Assistant to Ambassador Zalmay Khalilzad at the U.S. Embassy in Kabul, Afghanistan.

Acknowledgments

The authors offer sincere thanks to the following park rangers and other employees of the National Park Service who have reviewed chapters, provided information and tips, answered questions, and generally helped us assure the accuracy of the following chapters:

Arches, Diane Allen; **Badlands,** Marianne Mills; **Big Bend,** David Elkowitz; **Black Canyon of the Gunnison,** Paul Zaenger; **Bryce Canyon,** Cheryl Schreier; **Canyonlands,** Paul Henderson; **Capitol Reef,** Riley Mitchell; **Carlsbad Caverns,** Bridget Eisfeldt; **Channel Islands,** Yvonne Menard and Lisa Porto; **Crater Lake,** Marsha McCabe; **Custer State Park,** Craig Pugsley; **Death Valley,** Vicki Wolfe; **Devils Tower,** Christine Czazasty; **Glacier,** Amy Vanderbilt and Tony Clark; **Grand Canyon,** Maureen Olprogge; **Grand Teton,** Jackie Skaggs; **Great Basin,** Betsy Duncan-Clark; **Great Sand Dunes,** Carol Sperling; **Guadalupe Mountains,** Doug Buehler; **Jewel Cave,** Karen Rosga; **Joshua Tree,** Joe Zarki; **Lassen Volcanic,** Narissa Willever; **Little Big Horn,** Ken Woody; **Mesa Verde,** Tessy Shirakawa; **Mojave,** Linda Slater; **Mount Rainier,** Patti Wold; **Mount Rushmore,** Jim Popovich; **North Cascades,** Joyce Brown; **Petrified Forest,** Michael Stuckey; **Point Reyes,** John Dell'osso; **Redwood,** Carol McCall; **Rocky Mountain,** Dick Putney; **Saguaro,** Melanie Florez; **Sequoia/Kings Canyon,** Lisa Ann Carrillo; **Theodore Roosevelt,** Bruce Kaye; **Waterton,** Janice Smith; **Wind Cave,** Phyllis Cremonini; **Yellowstone,** Cheryl Matthews & Jim Williams; **Yosemite,** Raye Santos; **Zion,** Ron Terry.

Also thanks to Becki Lewis, **Xanterra Parks & Resorts;** Mona & Tom Mesereau, **Mesereau Public Relations;** and Floydeen Kendall, Forest Recreation Management, **Black Hills National Forest.**

An Invitation to the Reader

In researching this book, we discovered many wonderful places—hotels, restaurants, shops, and more. We're sure you'll find others. Please tell us about them, so we can share the information with your fellow travelers in upcoming editions. If you were disappointed with a recommendation, we'd love to know that, too. Please write to:

Frommer's National Parks of the American West, 4th Edition
Wiley Publishing, Inc. • 111 River St. • Hoboken, NJ 07030-5774

The following abbreviations are used for credit cards:

AE	American Express	V	Visa
DC	Diners Club	MC	MasterCard
DISC	Discover		

Frommers.com

Now that you have the guidebook to a great trip, visit our website at **www.frommers.com** for travel information on more than 3,000 destinations. With features updated regularly, we give you instant access to the most current trip-planning information available. At Frommers.com, you'll also find the best prices on airfares, accommodations, and car rentals—and you can even book travel online through our travel booking partners. At Frommers.com, you'll also find the following:

- Online updates to our most popular guidebooks
- Vacation sweepstakes and contest giveaways
- Newsletter highlighting the hottest travel trends
- Online travel message boards with featured travel discussions

Other Great Guides for Your Trip:

Introduction: Enjoying the Parks
Without the Crowds

The National Park Service seems to be walking a tightrope. The service really has two missions, and they sometimes seem to run in opposition to each other. Its first mission is to preserve some of America's most unique and important natural areas for future generations; the second is to make these places available for the enjoyment of all Americans. Because the number of visitors to our national parks has grown tremendously over the years, some of the busiest parks, including the Grand Canyon, Yosemite, Zion, and Yellowstone, are now searching for ways to make both of these goals reality.

Park Service officials have often said that the real source of congestion in the most heavily visited parks is not the number of people but rather the number of cars. (You don't go to a national park hoping to get caught up in a traffic jam, do you?) As a result, those parks with yearly attendance in the millions are now putting together plans to limit vehicle traffic within their boundaries.

If all of this leads you to despair that you can't have a true "wilderness" experience in one of the national parks of the American West, banish the thought. Even in a park as crowded as Yosemite, there are places where you can completely escape the crowds, where you'll be able to walk among the trees and hear nothing but the sound of your own footsteps. All it takes is a little effort and planning, and that's where this book can help.

Our authors have talked to the rangers, hiked the trails, and taken the tours, all the while asking, "How can our readers avoid the crowds?" In each of the following chapters, you'll find a section giving you straightforward, practical advice on just how to do this. Sure, if you're an outdoors iron man (or woman), you can avoid the crowds by taking off on the most strenuous backcountry hikes, but not everyone is made of iron. So we've searched for secluded trails that can be hiked by the average person (not just the ones you'll see on the covers of *Outside* magazine); scenic drives where you won't get caught in bumper-to-bumper traffic; and points where, with only minimum effort, you'll be afforded spectacular views without feeling as if you're packed into Times Square on New Year's Eve.

We've also discovered that *when* you go is as important as *where* you go. Since most of the West's national parks and monuments are busiest in July and August, you can avoid many of the people by going in April or September, especially if you can go just before or just after the times when schools are generally out for summer vacation. Remember that most national parks are open year-round, though services are sometimes limited during the off season. In fact, many are great places to go in winter for skiing and exploring, and these are also times when you're less likely to feel mobbed. The hoodoos of Bryce Canyon, for example, are just as strikingly beautiful when they're snow-covered, and you won't be jostling with nearly as many people at the viewpoints.

The last thing we've discovered (though it's not a very big secret) is that there are many hidden gems among the national parks and monuments of the American West. Everyone knows about Mount Rainier and Carlsbad Caverns but not always about the less-visited parks, such as Great Basin in Nevada, Great Sand Dunes in Colorado, the Channel Islands in California, Little Bighorn Battlefield in Montana, Jewel Cave in the Black Hills of South Dakota, and the Guadalupe Mountains in Texas. These are places of great beauty or historical significance, but they're often overlooked because of their remoteness or simply because they're relatively new to the national park system.

As we all explore these parks and monuments, we should remember that they have been set aside not only for our enjoyment, but also to be preserved for future generations. Let our gift to tomorrow's park visitors be that we have almost no impact on the beauty around us, and if anything, we leave it cleaner than we found it.

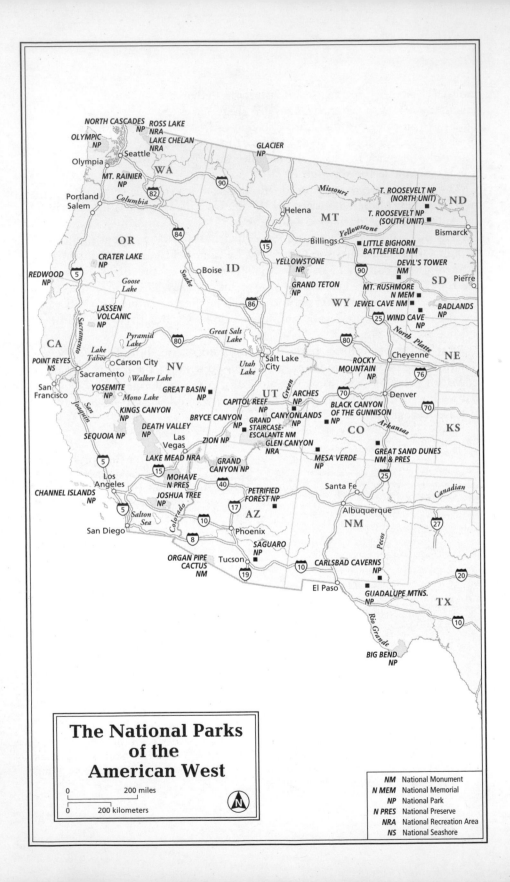

The National Parks of the American West

0   200 miles

0   200 kilometers

NM	National Monument
N MEM	National Memorial
NP	National Park
N PRES	National Preserve
NRA	National Recreation Area
NS	National Seashore

JUST THE FACTS:

Planning Your Trip to the National Parks of the American West

N THIS CHAPTER, WE'VE TRIED TO GIVE YOU ALL THE GENERAL INFORmation you will need to help plan your trip to the national parks of the western United States. The individual park chapters that follow will be able to answer your more specific questions.

The Parks Without the Crowds—Some General Tips

It's not easy to commune with nature when you're surrounded by hordes of fellow visitors. For each park, we've discussed the best times of year to go and listed certain areas, trails, and sites that are less visited than the others. For really specific information, you can find park use statistics at www.aqd.nps.gov/ stats. Beyond that, here are a few general guidelines.

◆ **Avoid the high season.** For most parks in the West, this especially means July and August; but anytime schools are not in session, parks are crowded with families on vacation. Spring and fall in many of these national parks offer mild weather, vibrant plant and animal life, and relatively empty trails and roads. The exception (as least as far as crowds are concerned) is college spring break, which is usually in March or April, when some parks,

such as Big Bend, get unbelievably crowded.

◆ **Walk away if you find yourself in a crowd.** It sounds simple, but often when a scenic overlook is crowded, you'll find an equally good view that is completely empty just a short stretch down the road or trail.

◆ **Visit popular attractions at off-peak hours,** especially early in the morning or late in the afternoon. You'll be surprised at how empty the park is before 9 or 10am. Dawn and dusk are also often the best times to see wildlife. You can avoid waits and crowds at restaurants by eating at off-peak hours—try lunch at 11 and dinner at 4—and campers using public showers will often find them jammed first thing in the morning and just before bedtime, but deserted the rest of the day.

◆ **Don't forget winter.** You may not see wildflowers, and some roads and areas may be closed, but many

Planning a Trip Online

A world of information is available on the Internet—in fact, you may find yourself inundated with almost *too* much information. In each of the following chapters we include pertinent websites, but a few stand out.

The National Park Service's website, **www.nps.gov**, has general information on the national parks, monuments, and historic sites, as well as individual park maps that can be downloaded in a variety of formats. The site also contains a link to every individual park's website, and those often contain links to nearby attractions and other useful information.

Another useful website for anyone interested in the outdoors is **www.recreation.gov**, a partnership among federal agencies that can link you to information on national parks, national forests, Bureau of Land Management sites, Bureau of Reclamation sites, Army Corps of Engineers sites, and National Wildlife Refuges.

Finally, those planning to travel with a dog or cat should check out **www.petswelcome.com**, a site that provides tips on traveling with pets, as well as lists of lodgings that accept pets, kennels for temporary pet boarding, and veterinarians to call in an emergency.

national parks are wonderful places to ski, snowshoe, or snowmobile or just admire the snowy landscape.

◆ Finally, **remember that some parks are rarely crowded,** and we've made a special effort to include information about many of them in this book. Generally, the more difficult a park is to get to, the fewer people you'll encounter there. And many of the smaller parks remain essentially undiscovered while offering scenery and recreation opportunities that rival or even surpass the big-name parks. Consider out-of-the-way parks such as Great Basin, as well as one of America's newest national parks, Black Canyon of the Gunnison.

Information

Doing your homework can help you make the most of your trip; it can also help you avoid the crowds. For park brochures and general planning information, contact each park directly, at the addresses included in each of the following chapters.

Planning a National Park Itinerary

Even though distances seem vast in the western United States, it's possible to visit more than one of the national parks there in a single trip. In fact, people often combine visits to Yellowstone and Grand Teton, Yosemite and Sequoia, and Zion and Bryce Canyon.

The parks of the California desert (Death Valley, Joshua Tree, and Mojave Preserve) can be knitted into a nice itinerary that might even leave you time to stop off in the resort town of Palm Springs. A popular trip for families is a drive through Badlands National Park and the Black Hills of South Dakota, all the way through Devils Tower to Yellowstone. It's not a small stretch, but it's doable if you have more than a week.

Although it can be a lot of fun to combine several national parks in your vacation trip, try not to make the all-too-common mistake of attempting to see everything there is to see in too short a period of time. Be realistic about how much you want to see at each park, and create an itinerary that lets you thoroughly enjoy one or two aspects of a park rather than just glimpsing every corner as you speed by. And try to schedule a little relaxation time, especially for trips of more than a week—perhaps loafing in the campground one afternoon, or lounging by the motel swimming pool.

Visitor Centers

Your first stop at any national park should be the visitor center. Not only will you learn the why of the park, but you'll also get timely information such as road and trail closures, safety issues, and the schedule for upcoming ranger programs. Visitor center hours usually vary by season; most are open daily from 8am until 6 or 7pm in summer, closing earlier at other times.

Fees & Permits

Though fees have increased in the past few years, visiting a national park is still a bargain—a steal compared to the prices you'd pay to visit a theme park or even go to a movie. Entry fees, ranging from nothing at Guadalupe to $20 at Yosemite and other high-profile parks, are usually charged per private vehicle (for up to 1 week), regardless of how many visitors are stuffed inside. Those arriving on foot or by bicycle often pay lower per-person fees. Some parks offer passes good for unlimited visits to the same park for 12 months.

Special Passes. There are several passes that offer discounts or completely free admission to as many different parks as you care to visit.

If you plan to visit a number of national parks and monuments within a year—and by "a number" we really mean only five or six—a **National Parks Pass,** which costs $50, will save you a bundle. The passes are good at all properties under the jurisdiction of the National Park Service, but not at sites administered by the Bureau of Land Management, National Forest Service, or other federal or state agencies. The National Parks Pass provides free entrance for the pass holder and all vehicle occupants to National Park Service properties that charge vehicle entrance fees, and for the pass holder, spouse, parents, and children for sites that charge per-person fees. The passes can be purchased at park entrance stations and visitor centers, or by mail order (© **888/GO-PARKS;** www.nationalparks.org).

> *To preserve and protect . . . and to provide for the enjoyment of park visitors.*
> —**National Park Service Organic Act, 1916**

North to Alaska!

Although this book looks closely at the national parks in the American West of the continental United States, we need to point out that another destination not included here has some of the country's most beautiful and pristine national parks: Alaska. In fact, more than two-thirds of America's national park acreage is in our northernmost state, encompassing huge areas of wilderness and near-wilderness, with few roads, buildings, or even airplane landing strips.

Most of the Alaska parks are challenging, both to get to and then to explore. One exception is **Denali National Park,** which provides visitors with easy access to genuine wilderness. Denali has sweeping tundra vistas, abundant wildlife, and North America's tallest mountain—20,320-foot Mount McKinley. But what makes this park unique is that its accessibility hasn't spoiled the natural experience. That's because the only road through the park is closed to the public. To see Denali, you must ride a bus. The grizzly bears and other animals are still there to watch, and their behavior remains more normal than that of the animals seen in the more visitor-affected and vehicle-intensive parks such as Yellowstone and Yosemite.

Another recommended Alaska experience is **Glacier Bay National Park,** a rugged wilderness the size of Connecticut that can be seen only by boat or plane. Created by a receding glacier, this bay is a work in progress, where you'll see a vast variety of flora and fauna, including grizzly bears, mountain goats, seals, and especially whales, including humpback whales breaching—leaping all the way out of the water.

Other national parks in Alaska include **Katmai,** the site of a phenomenal volcanic eruption in 1912 and now an excellent place to see relatively close up the huge Alaska brown bear as it devours a seemingly endless supply of red salmon. **Kenai Fjords National Park,** a remote area of mountains, rocks, and ice, is the spot to see a vast array of sea lions, otters, seals, and birds. And **Wrangell–St. Elias National Park,** which at over 8 million acres is by far the largest unit in the National Park Service's system, consists of numerous rugged mountains and glaciers, plus some fascinating history from its early copper mining days.

The above parks, plus a number of other national parks, monuments, and preserves, are explored fully in *Frommer's Alaska* by Charles P. Wohlforth, a lifelong resident of Alaska.

Also available at park service properties, as well as other federal recreation sites that charge entrance fees, is the **Golden Age Passport,** for those 62 and older, which has a one-time fee of $10 and provides free admission to all national parks and monuments, plus a 50% discount on camping fees. The **Golden Access Passport,** free for blind or permanently disabled U.S. citizens, has the same benefits as the Golden Age Passport, and is available at all federal recreation sites that charge entrance fees.

Available from U.S. Forest Service, Bureau of Land Management, and Fish and Wildlife areas is the **Golden Eagle Pass.** At a cost of $65 for 1 year from the date of purchase, it allows the bearer, plus everyone traveling with him or her in the same vehicle, free admission to all National Park Service properties plus other federal recreation sites that charge fees. The National Parks Pass discussed above can be upgraded to Golden Eagle status for $15.

Backcountry Permits. At most national parks, it is necessary to obtain a backcountry permit to stay overnight in the park's undeveloped backcountry. Some parks have even more restrictions. To be safe, if you intend to do any backpacking, look in the individual park chapter or contact the park's backcountry office in advance. In some cases, it may be possible to obtain a permit by mail; in most cases, you must appear in person the day before your trip. Some parks charge for backcountry permits, while others are free, and some restrict the number of permits issued.

Other Permits. Hunting is not allowed in national parks, but fishing often is, and you will usually need a state fishing license. Licenses are generally available at local sporting-goods stores and offices of states' game and fish departments. Fees vary for state residents and nonresidents, for various time periods, and sometimes by location within the state, but you can usually get a nonresident 1-day license for $5 to $10 and a 5- to 7-day nonresident license for $15 to $20.

In some parks (Yellowstone and Grand Teton, for example), you will need a special permit to go boating. In others you may need a special permit for crosscountry skiing. Check the individual park chapters for details on these and other permits that might be required.

Getting a Campsite

Although a growing number of national park campgrounds accept campsite reservations, many still do not. If you plan to camp and are heading to a first-come, first-served campground, the first thing to do upon arrival is to make sure a site is available. Campsites at major park campgrounds fill up early in summer, on weekends, and during other peak times, such as school holidays. A reservation, or an early morning arrival at a campground

(sometimes as early as 7 or 8am), is the best defense against disappointment. In each chapter, we've indicated whether a campground tends to fill up especially early, and whether or not reservations are accepted.

The **National Park Service Reservation Center** (© 800/365-2267; http://reservations.nps.gov) provides reservations for National Park Service campgrounds at many popular parks, including Channel Islands, Death Valley, Glacier, Grand Canyon, Joshua Tree, Mount Rainier, Rocky Mountain, Sequoia–Kings Canyon, Yosemite, and Zion. Campground reservations are also available for another group of parks including Arches, Big Bend, Black Canyon of the Gunnison, Bryce Canyon, and Lassen Volcanic, through the **National Recreation Reservation Service** (© 887/444-6777; www.reserveusa.com), which also takes reservations for many national forests.

Maps

When you arrive at a national park site, you'll receive a large, four-color brochure that has a good map of the park on it; and of course, you also have the maps in this book. If you plan to do some serious hiking, especially into backcountry and wilderness areas, these won't be enough, however. What you'll really need are detailed topographic maps.

Topo maps can usually be ordered in advance from the individual park bookstores, which are discussed in the following chapters. Those published by National Geographic Maps/Trails Illustrated are especially useful, and can be ordered directly from the publisher (© 800/962-1643; http://national geographic.com/trails). Most topo maps retail for about $10.

Tips for RVers

Many people prefer to explore the national parks in an RV—a motor home, truck camper, or camper trailer—especially in the warm months. One advantage to this type of travel is that early morning and early evening are among the best times to be in the parks if you want to avoid crowds and see wildlife. Needless to say, it's a lot more convenient to experience the parks at these times if you're already there, staying in one of the park campgrounds.

Carrying your house with you also lets you stop for meals anytime and anywhere you choose, and makes it easy to take care of individual dietary needs. RVing also means you don't have to worry about sleeping on a lumpy mattress, and you won't need to spend time searching for a restroom—almost all RVs have some sort of bathroom facilities, from a full bathroom with tub/shower combination to a Porta Potti hidden under a seat.

There are disadvantages, of course. If you already own an RV, you know what you had to pay for it. And even if you rent, you probably won't save a lot of money. Renting a motor home will probably end up costing almost as much as renting a compact car, staying in moderately priced motels, and eating in family-style restaurants and cafes. That's because the motor home will go only one-third as far on a gallon of gas as your compact car will, and they're expensive to rent. Some of the fancier private campgrounds now charge as much for an RV site with utility hookups as you'd expect to pay in a cheap motel.

Other disadvantages include the limited facilities in national park campgrounds (although they are being upgraded to the point where camping purists are starting to complain). Even in most commercial campgrounds the facilities are less than you'd expect in moderately priced motels. And parking is often limited in national parks, especially for motor homes and other large vehicles. However, since most people are driving in the parks between 10am and 5pm, the solution is to head out on the scenic drives either early or late in the day, when there's less traffic. It's nicer then, anyway.

If you'll be traveling in the park in your RV and want to make it obvious that your campsite is occupied, carry something worthless to leave in it, such as a cardboard box with "Site Taken" clearly written on it. You can usually find a rock to weigh it down.

Because many of the national park campsites are not level, carry four or five short boards, or leveling blocks, that can be placed under the RV's wheels. You can buy small, inexpensive levels at RV and hardware stores. You'll discover that not only will you sleep better if your rig is level, but your food won't slide off the table and the refrigerator will run more efficiently.

Renting an RV. If you're flying into the area and renting an RV when you arrive, choose your starting point carefully; not only do you want to keep your driving to a minimum—you'll be lucky to get 10 miles per gallon of gas—but rental rates vary depending on the city in which you pick up your RV, so do some research before you commit to a particular starting point. Rates are generally highest in midsummer, between $1,000 and $1,100 per week. The nation's largest rental company is **Cruise America** (✆ **800/327-7799** or 480/464-7300; fax 480/464-7321; www.cruiseamerica.com), with outlets in most major western cities. RV rentals in many western states are also available from **El Monte RV** (✆ **888/337-2214** or 562/483-4956; www.elmonte.com). Information on additional rental agencies, as well as tips on renting, can be obtained from the **Recreation Vehicle Rental Association,** 3930 University Dr., Fairfax, VA 22030 (✆ **703/591-7130;** fax 703/591-0734; www.rvra.org).

Tips for Traveling with Kids

The **Junior Ranger Programs** offered at most parks give kids the chance to earn certificates, badges, and patches for completing certain projects, such as tree or animal identification, or answering questions in a workbook. It's a good way to learn about the national parks and the resources that the Park Service protects. Also, many parks offer special discussions, walks, and other ranger-led activities for children.

Tips for Travelers with Disabilities

The National Park Service has come a long way in the past dozen or so years in making the parks more accessible for visitors with disabilities. Most parks have accessible restrooms, and many have at least one trail that is wheelchair accessible—the Rim Trail at Bryce Canyon is a prime example. In addition, as campgrounds, boat docks, and other facilities are being upgraded, improvements are being made to make them more accessible. Some parks now have campsites designed specifically for those in wheelchairs, and park amphitheaters can usually accommodate wheelchair users.

But perhaps just as important as upgrades in facilities is the prevailing attitude on the part of National Park Service personnel that these parks are for the public—the entire public—and they are going to do whatever it takes to help everyone enjoy his or her park experience. Those with special needs are encouraged to talk with park workers, who can usually assist, such as by opening locked gates to get vehicles closer to scenic attractions, or simply by pointing out trails with the lowest grades or with portable toilets that are accessible.

One note on service dogs: Seeing Eye and other service dogs are not considered pets, and are permitted anywhere in the parks. However, because of potential problems with wildlife or terrain (sharp rocks on some trails can cut dogs' paws), it's best for those taking service dogs into the parks to discuss their plans with rangers beforehand.

Many of the major car-rental companies now offer hand-controlled cars for drivers with disabilities, and can provide those vehicles with advance notice. **Wheelchair Getaways** (✆ **800/642-2042** or 859/873-4973; www.wheelchairgetaways.com) rents specialized vans with wheelchair lifts and other features for visitors with disabilities, with outlets in most western states.

And don't forget your **Golden Access Passport** (see "Fees & Permits," above). It is free and will grant you free admission to most national parks and a 50% discount on many park services and facilities.

Tips for Travelers with Pets

National parks as well as other federal lands administered by the National Park Service are not pet-friendly, and those planning to visit the parks should consider leaving their pets at home. Pets are almost always prohibited on hiking trails, in the backcountry, and in buildings, and must always be on a leash. Essentially, this means that if you take your dog or cat into the parks, they can be with you in the campgrounds and inside your vehicle, and you can walk them in parking areas, but that's about it. It's no fun for either you or your pet.

Aside from regulations, though, you need to be concerned with your pet's well-being. Pets should never be left in closed vehicles, where temperatures can soar to over 120°F (49°C) in minutes, resulting in brain damage or death, and no punishment is too severe for the human who subjects a dog or cat to that torture.

Those who do decide to take pets with them into these parks despite these warnings should take the pets' leashes, of course; carry plenty of water (pet shops sell clever little travel water bowls that won't spill in a moving vehicle); and bring proof that the dogs or cats

Special Tip for Pet Owners

Although pets are not permitted on the trails or backcountry in practically all national parks, those traveling with their dogs can hike with them over miles of trails administered by the U.S. Forest Service and Bureau of Land Management, adjacent to many parks.

have been vaccinated against rabies. Flea and tick spray or powder is also important, since fleas that may carry bubonic plague have been found on prairie dogs and other rodents in some parks.

Protecting Your Health & Safety

First of all, don't forget that motor vehicle accidents cause more deaths in the parks every year than anything else. Scenic drives are often winding and steep; take them slowly and carefully. And no matter how stunning the snow-capped peak you may glimpse off to the side, keep your eyes on the road.

When out on the trails, even for a day hike, keep safety in mind. The wild, untouched nature of these parks is what makes them so exciting and breathtakingly beautiful—but along with wildness comes risk. The national parks are not playgrounds, nor are they zoos. The animals here are truly untamed and sometimes dangerous. This doesn't mean that disaster could strike at any time, but it does mean that visitors should exercise basic caution and common sense at all times, respecting the wilderness around them and always following the rules of the park.

Never feed, bother, or approach animals. Even the smallest among them can carry harmful, sometimes deadly, diseases, and feeding them is dangerous not only to yourself, but to the animals too, who (like us) will happily eat what their bodies can't handle. In addition, wild animals' dependence on human handouts can lead to unpleasant confrontations, which often result in rangers having to relocate or kill the animal. As the Park Service reminds us, "A fed bear is a dead bear."

In some parks where there are bears and mountain lions it's often a good idea to make noise as you hike, to make sure you don't accidentally stumble upon and frighten an animal into aggression. Also, follow park rules on food storage when in bear country. Photographers should always keep a safe distance when taking pictures of wildlife—the best photos are shot with a telephoto lens.

It's equally important for your safety to know your limitations, to understand the environment, and to take the proper equipment when exploring the park. Always stop at the visitor center before you set out on a hike. Park staff there can offer you advice on your hiking plans and supply you with pamphlets, maps, and information on weather conditions or any dangers, such as bear activity or flash flood possibilities on canyon hikes. Once out on the trail, hikers should always carry sufficient water and, just as important, remember to drink it. Wear sturdy shoes with good ankle support and rock-gripping soles. Always keep a close eye on any children in your group, and never let them run ahead.

Since many park visitors live at or near sea level, one of the most common health hazards is **altitude sickness,** caused by the high elevations of many of the parks in this book. Symptoms include headache, fatigue, nausea, loss of appetite, muscle pain, and lightheadedness. Doctors recommend that, until you are acclimated, which can take several days, the best remedy is to consume light meals and drink lots of liquids, avoiding those with caffeine or alcohol.

So You Like a Mystery?

Author Nevada Barr spins a good yarn. A former National Park Service ranger, she writes what she knows—the settings for her mysteries are national parks, and her detective, Anna Pigeon, is a ranger. Anna joined the Park Service after her actor husband was killed in New York City, and she now finds safety in solitude. But occasionally someone breaks into her aloneness, such as the time she enjoyed a brief liaison with an FBI agent she met during a bizarre murder investigation at Lake Superior. Anna loves wild country, and her work often takes her into strange situations. It's fascinating to envision the parks as described through Anna's eyes, first as she patrols the backcountry of Guadalupe Mountains on horseback— is the killer really a mountain lion as the tracks imply, or something more sinister—or when she strives to uncover the cause of inexplicable deaths amid the ruins at Mesa Verde. The "accident" that befalls a spelunker in the depths of Carlsbad Caverns takes the reader into subterranean territory, and the tense situation that develops among the small group of isolated firefighters during the aftermath of a raging forest fire at Lassen Volcanic National Park is riveting. Each book takes place in a different park, so you can sample a variety of environments: arid deserts, forested mountains, deep cold lakes, dark caves, teeming islands—wherever there's a national park, there just might be a mystery from Nevada Barr's pen. Try one.

It's a good idea to take frequent sips of water, as well.

One proven method of minimizing the effects of high altitudes is to work up to them. For instance, on a visit to southern Utah, go to lower-elevation Zion National Park for a day or two before heading to the higher mountains of Bryce Canyon.

A waterborne hazard is *Giardia*, a parasite that wreaks havoc on the human digestive system. If you pick up this pesky hanger-on, it may accompany you on your trip home. The best solution is to carry all the water you'll need (usually a gallon a day). If you need additional water from the parks' lakes and streams, it should be boiled for 3 to 6 minutes before consumption.

Hiking Tips

Don't venture off on any extensive hike, even a day hike, without the following gear: a compass, a topographical map, bug repellent, a whistle, and a watch. In many western parks, sunglasses, sunscreen, and wide-brimmed hats are also considered essential. To be on the safe side, you should keep a **first-aid kit** in your car or luggage, and have it handy when hiking. At a minimum, it should contain butterfly bandages, sterile gauze pads, adhesive tape, an antibiotic ointment, pain relievers, alcohol pads, and a knife with scissors and tweezers.

Planning a Backcountry Trip

Here are some general things to keep in mind when planning a backcountry trip:

◆ **Permits** In many parks, overnight hiking and backcountry camping require a permit.
◆ **Camping Etiquette & Special Regulations** Follow the basic rules of camping etiquette: Pack out all your trash, including uneaten food and used toilet paper. Camp in

> *Surely the great United States of America is not so poor we cannot afford to have these places, nor so rich we can do without them.*
> —Newton Drury, National Parks Service Director, 1940–1951

obvious campsites. If pit toilets are not available, bury human waste in holes 6 inches deep, 6 inches across, and at least 200 feet from water and creek beds. When doing dishes, take water and dishes at least 200 feet from the water source, and scatter the wastewater. Hang food and trash out of reach of wildlife, use bear-proof containers, or follow other park rules to keep wildlife from human food.

◆ **Shoes** Be sure to wear comfortable, sturdy hiking shoes that will resist water if you're planning an early season hike.

◆ **Sleeping Bags** Your sleeping bag should be rated for the low temperatures found at high elevations. Most campers are happy to have a sleeping pad.

◆ **Water** If you're not carrying enough water for the entire trip, you'll also need a good water purifying system, since that seemingly clear stream is filled with a bacteria likely to cause intestinal disorders.

◆ **Your Pack** The argument rages about the merits of old-fashioned external-frame packs and the newer, internal-frame models. Over the long run, the newer versions are more stable and allow you to carry greater loads more comfortably; however, they also cost more. The key issue is finding a pack that fits well, has plenty of padding, a wide hip belt, and a good lumbar support pad.

Protecting the Environment

Not long ago, the rule of thumb was to "leave only footprints"; these days, we're trying to do better and not leave even footprints. It's relatively easy to be a good outdoor citizen—just use common sense. Pack out all trash; stay on designated trails; be especially careful not to pollute water; don't disturb plants, wildlife, or archaeological resources; don't pick flowers or collect rocks; and, in general, do your best to have as little impact on the environment as possible. Some hikers go further, carrying a small trash bag to pick up what others may have left. As the Park Service likes to remind us, protecting our national parks is everyone's responsibility.

ARCHES NATIONAL PARK

by Don & Barbara Laine

*[handwritten note: * in park - 1 campground fills early - others near though!]*

ATURAL STONE ARCHES AND FANTASTIC ROCK FORMATIONS, SCULPTED as if by an artist's hand, are the defining features of this park, and they exist in remarkable numbers and variety. Just as soon as you've seen the most beautiful, most colorful, most gigantic stone arch you can imagine, walk around the next bend and there's another—bigger, better, and more brilliant than the last. It would take forever to see them all, with more than 2,000 officially listed and more being discovered, or "born," every day.

Just down the road from Canyonlands National Park, Arches is more visitor-friendly, with relatively short, well-maintained trails leading to most of the park's major attractions. It's also a place to let your imagination run wild. Is Delicate Arch really so delicate? Or would its other monikers (Old Maid's Bloomers or Cowboy Chaps) be more appropriate? And what about those tall spires? You might imagine they're castles, giant stone sailing ships, or the petrified skyscrapers of some ancient city.

Exploring the park is a great family adventure. The arches seem more accessible and less forbidding than the spires and pinnacles at Canyonlands and most other western parks. Some think of arches as bridges, imagining the power of water that literally cuts a hole through a solid rock. Actually, to geologists there's a big difference. Natural bridges are formed when a river cuts a channel, while the often bizarre and beautiful contours of arches result from the erosive force of rain and snow, freezing and thawing, as it dissolves the "glue" that holds sand grains together and chips away at the stone.

Although arches usually grow slowly—*very* slowly—occasionally something dramatic happens. Like that quiet day in 1940 when a sudden crash instantly doubled the size of the opening of Skyline Arch, leaving a huge boulder lying at its feet. Luckily, no one (at least no one we know of) was standing underneath it at the time. The same thing happened to the magnificently delicate Landscape Arch in 1991, when a slab of rock about 60 feet long, 11 feet wide, and 4½ feet thick fell from the underside of the arch. It's hard to believe that such a thin ribbon of stone can continue hanging on at all.

Spend a day or a week here, exploring the terrain, watching the rainbow of colors deepen and explode with the long rays of the setting sun, or glimpsing ribbons of moonlight on tall sandstone cliffs. Be on the lookout for mule deer, cottontail rabbits, and the bright green collared lizard as they go about the task of desert living. And let your imagination run wild among the Three Gossips, the Spectacles, the Eye of the Whale, the Penguins, the Tower of Babel, and the thousands of other statues, towers, arches, and bridges that await your discovery in this remarkable sandstone playground.

Avoiding the Crowds. This is a very popular park, and you should expect to find crowded parking areas and full campgrounds daily from March through October, with the peak month being August. The quietest months are December, January, and February, but it can be cold then. Those wanting to avoid crowds might gamble on Mother Nature and visit in November or late February, when days might be delightfully sunny and just a bit cool, or bitterly cold, windy, and awful. As with most popular parks, avoid visiting during school vacations if possible.

Just the Facts

GETTING THERE & GATEWAYS

The entrance to the park is 5 miles north of Moab, Utah, on U.S. 191. To get there from Salt Lake City, about 230 miles away, follow I-15 south to Spanish Fork; then take U.S. 6 southeast to I-70; follow that east to Crescent Junction, where you'll pick up U.S. 191 south. From Grand Junction, Colorado, take I-70 west until you reach Crescent Junction, and then go south on U.S. 191.

The Nearest Airport. The closest major airport is **Walker Field,** in Grand Junction, Colorado (© 970/244-9100; fax 970/241-9103; www.walkerfield.com), about 125 miles east of Moab. Airlines

operating at Walker Field include **America West Express,** with daily service to Phoenix; **Delta/SkyWest,** with daily service to Salt Lake City; and **United Express,** with daily service to Denver. Rental cars are available from Avis, Budget, Enterprise, Hertz, National, and Thrifty. A list of toll-free numbers is in the appendix.

GROUND TRANSPORTATION

The easiest way to get from Salt Lake City to Moab is with **Airport Rapid Konnection** (© 888/655-7433 or 801/328-9920; fax 801/328-4490; www.goark.com), which charges $49 each way.

Rentals (standard passenger cars, vans, and four-wheel-drive vehicles) are available from **Thrifty** (© 800/847-4389 or 435/259-7317) and **Farabee 4WD Rentals** (© 888/806-5337 or 435/259-7494), which is also the local agent for **Budget.** Four-wheel-drive vehicles are also available from **Slickrock Jeep Rentals** (© 435/259-5678) and **Castle Rock Jeep Rentals** (© 435/259-5432).

INFORMATION

Contact the **Superintendent, Arches National Park,** P.O. Box 907, Moab, UT 84532-0907 (© 435/719-2299; www.nps.gov/arch).

Books, maps, and videos on Arches as well as Canyonlands National Park and other southern Utah attractions can be purchased from the nonprofit **Canyonlands Natural History Association,** 3031 S. U.S. 191, Moab, UT 84532 (© 800/840-8978; fax 435/259-8263; www.cnha.org). Some publications are available in foreign languages, and a variety of videos can be purchased in either VHS or PAL formats. For more detailed descriptions of the park's hiking trails and backcountry roads, purchase *Exploring Canyonlands and Arches National Parks* (Falcon Press, 1997) by Bill Schneider, at the visitor center or by contacting the Canyonlands Natural History Association.

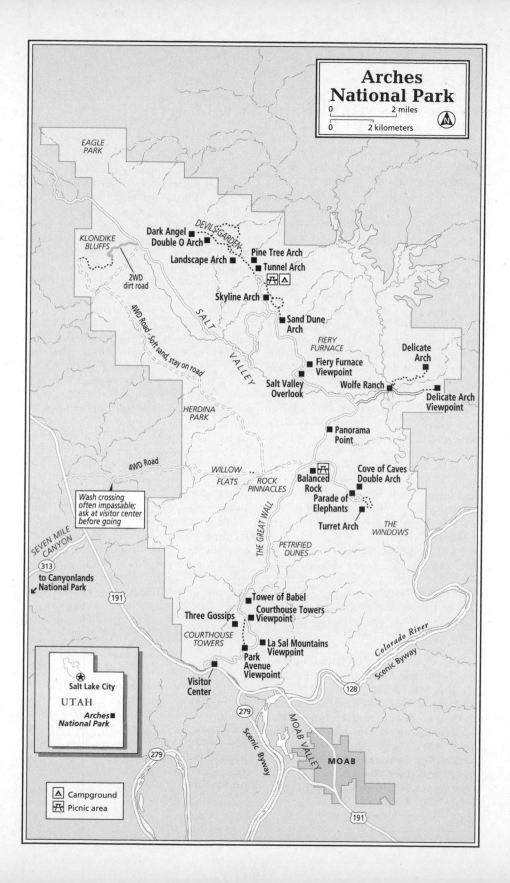

Arches National Park

0 — 2 miles
0 — 2 kilometers

EAGLE PARK

KLONDIKE BLUFFS

DEVILS GARDEN

Dark Angel
Double O Arch
Landscape Arch
Pine Tree Arch
Tunnel Arch
Skyline Arch
Sand Dune Arch

2WD dirt road

4WD Road - Soft sand stay on road

SALT VALLEY

FIERY FURNACE

Delicate Arch

Fiery Furnace Viewpoint
Salt Valley Overlook
Wolfe Ranch
Delicate Arch Viewpoint

HERDINA PARK

4WD Road

Panorama Point

Wash crossing often impassable; ask at visitor center before going

WILLOW FLATS

ROCK PINNACLES

Balanced Rock

Cove of Caves
Double Arch

Parade of Elephants

Turret Arch

THE WINDOWS

THE GREAT WALL

PETRIFIED DUNES

SEVEN MILE CANYON

313
to Canyonlands National Park

191

Tower of Babel
Courthouse Towers Viewpoint

Three Gossips

COURTHOUSE TOWERS

La Sal Mountains Viewpoint

Park Avenue Viewpoint

Visitor Center

Colorado River
Scenic Byway

128

279

Salt Lake City
UTAH
Arches National Park

Scenic Byway

MOAB VALLEY

MOAB

279

191

△ Campground
⛺ Picnic area

Tips from a Park Ranger

A "good family park" is how Arches' chief of interpretation Diane Allen describes this national park. "What makes Arches special is its variety of rock formations and the ease of accessibility," she says. "You can see quite a bit even if you have only a few hours."

Allen says that 2 hours is about the minimum amount of time needed to tour the scenic drive, stopping at the viewpoints and taking a few short walks, but 1 to 1½ days would give you a pretty good look at the park. She suggests you start your park experience at the **visitor center** to find out about guided hikes and other ranger-led activities, and then get out on the trails early in the day, while it's still cool. **The Devils Garden Trail** provides a variety of experiences, Allen says, and is a fairly easy hike to scenic **Landscape Arch.** She says that hikers should carry and drink plenty of water—rangers recommend a gallon per person each day—because in this extremely arid climate dehydration and heat problems can be fatal. If at the end of the day you have a slight headache and feel a bit lethargic and grouchy, it's likely because you didn't drink enough water.

Although park visitors will of course want to see the park's arches—**Delicate Arch** has practically become the symbol for the state of Utah—Allen says that Arches National Park is more than arches. "There are many other formations—spires, pinnacles, natural bridges, and great walls," she says, adding that the park is a prime example of Colorado Plateau vegetation. "We've got a little bit of everything: wildflowers, cactus, pinyon, juniper, a few riparian areas; and if you want to learn about geology, it's all exposed, easy to see."

The park is busiest between March and October, with August usually registering the most visitors. Summers are hot, and spring and fall are very pleasant. One way to avoid crowds, Allen says, is to visit in winter—"You can get fantastic hiking days in February, but keep in mind that days are shorter then." The other proven way to avoid crowds, even at the height of the summer, is to get out onto the trails early in the day. "It's a much more pleasant time to be in the park," she says. "It's cooler, you have a better chance of seeing wildlife, and there are fewer people."

You can also ask rangers for suggestions on lesser-used trails. Allen says she likes the **Tower Arch Trail,** which is more of a primitive experience where you are less likely to see a lot of other hikers.

For advance area information, contact the **Grand County Travel Council,** P.O. Box 550, Moab, UT 84532 (✆ **800/ 635-6622** or 435/259-8825; fax 435/259-1376; www.discovermoab.com). Once you arrive, stop at the **Moab Information Center,** located in the middle of town at the corner of Main and Center streets and open daily 8am to 9pm in the summer, with shorter winter hours.

The **Arches National Park Visitor Center,** located just inside the entrance gate, has maps, brochures, and other information. A museum tells you all you need to know about arch formation and other features of the park, and there is a short orientation program in the auditorium.

FEES & PERMITS

Entry for up to 7 days costs $10 per private vehicle or $5 per person on foot or bike. A $25 annual pass is also available; it's good for Arches and Canyonlands national parks as well as Natural Bridges and Hovenweep national monuments. Campsites cost $10 per night. Required permits for overnight trips into the backcountry, available at the visitor center, are free.

SPECIAL REGULATIONS & WARNINGS

Ground fires are not permitted; grills are provided in the campground (see below), but you must bring your own firewood. Be aware that although the desert terrain appears hardy, it is easily damaged. Rangers ask that hikers stay on trails and be careful around the bases of arches and other rock formations.

SEASONS & CLIMATE

Summer days are hot, often reaching 100°F (38°C), and winters can be cool or cold, dropping below freezing at night, with snow possible. The best time to visit, especially for hikers, is in the spring or fall, when daytime temperatures are usually between 60° and 80°F (16°C and 27°C) and nights are cool. Spring winds, although not usually dangerous, can be gusty, particularly as they whip through an arch, so hold on to your hat.

SEASONAL EVENTS

An Easter sunrise service takes place annually.

If You Have Only 1 Day

Arches is one of the easiest national parks to see in a day if that's all you can spare. A **scenic drive** offers splendid views of countless natural rock arches and other formations, and several easy hikes open up additional scenery. The drive is 18 miles one-way, plus 5 miles for a side trip to the Windows and 4½ miles for a side trip to Delicate Arch.

Start out by viewing the short slide show at the **visitor center,** and then ask rangers for their suggestions for a short hike, so you can get a close-up view of some of the arches. Possibilities include the short, easy hike to **Double Arch** and the longer and sometimes hot hike to **Delicate Arch.** If you're up for a more strenuous excursion, and the timing's right, join one of the ranger-guided hikes to **Fiery Furnace,** one of the most colorful areas of the park.

Exploring the Park by Car

You can see many of the park's most famous rock formations through your car windows, although we strongly urge you to get out and explore on foot. You have the option of walking short distances to a number of viewpoints, or stretching your legs on a variety of longer hikes (see "Day Hikes," below). The main road is easy to navigate, even for RVs, but parking at some viewpoints is limited. Please be considerate and leave trailers at the visitor center parking lot or in a campground.

After leaving the visitor center, drive north past the Moab Fault to the overlook parking for **Park Avenue,** a solid rock "fin" that reminded early visitors of the New York skyline. From here, your next stop is **La Sal Mountain Viewpoint,** where you look southeast to the La Sal Mountains, named by early Spanish explorers who thought the snow-covered mountains looked like huge piles of salt. In the overlook area is a "desert scrub" ecosystem, composed mostly of blackbrush, with some sagebrush, saltbush, yucca, and prickly pear cactus, all plants that can survive in sandy soil with little moisture. The area's wildlife includes the black-tailed jackrabbit, rock squirrel, kangaroo rat, coyote, and several species of lizards.

Continuing on the scenic drive, you begin to see some of the park's major formations at **Courthouse Towers,** where large monoliths such as Sheep Rock, the Organ, and the Three Gossips dominate the landscape. Leaving Courthouse Towers, watch for the **Tower of Babel** on the east (right) side of the road, then proceed past the "petrified" sand dunes to **Balanced Rock,** a huge boulder weighing about 3,600 tons, perched on a slowly eroding pedestal.

Continuing, you'll soon take a side road east (right) to **The Windows.** Created when erosion penetrated a sandstone fin, they can be seen via a short walk from the parking area. Also in this area are **Turret Arch** and the **Cove of Caves.** As erosion continues in the back of the largest cave it may eventually become an arch. A short walk from the parking lot takes you to **Double Arch,** which looks exactly like what the name implies. From the end of this trail you can also see the delightful **Parade of Elephants.**

Return to the main park road, turn north (right), and drive to **Panorama Point,** with an expansive view of Salt Valley and the Fiery Furnace, which can really live up to its name at sunset.

Next, turn east (right) off the main road onto the Wolfe Ranch Road and drive to the **Wolfe Ranch** parking area. A very short walk leads to what's left of this 100-year-old ranch. If you follow the trail a bit farther, you'll see some **Ute petroglyphs.** More ambitious hikers can continue for a moderately difficult 3-mile round-trip excursion to **Delicate Arch,** with a spectacular view at trail's end. If you don't want to take this hike, you can still see this lovely arch, albeit from a distance, by getting back in your car and continuing down the road for 1 mile and walking a short trail to the **Delicate Arch Viewpoint.**

Returning to the park's main road, turn north (right) and go to the next stop, the **Salt Valley Overlook.** The various shades and colors in this collapsed salt dome have been caused by varying amounts of iron in the rock, as well as other factors.

Continue now to the viewpoint for **Fiery Furnace,** which offers a dramatic view of colorful sandstone fins. From here, drive to a pullout for **Sand Dune Arch,** located down a short path from the road, where you'll find shade and sand, a good place for kids to play, along with the arch. The trail also leads across a meadow to **Broken Arch** (which isn't broken at all; it just looks that way from a distance).

Back on the road, continue to **Skyline Arch,** which doubled in size in 1940 when a huge boulder tumbled out of it. The next and final stop is the often crowded parking area for the **Devils Garden Trailhead.** From here you can hike to some of the most unique arches in the park, including **Landscape Arch,** among the longest natural rock spans in the world.

From the trailhead parking lot, it's 18 miles back to the visitor center.

Organized Tours & Ranger Programs

From March through October, rangers lead **guided hikes** into the Fiery Furnace area twice daily, by reservation. Cost is $6 per adult and $3 per child over 6, and reservations must be made in person up to 7 days in advance. As you hike along, a ranger describes the desert plants, points out hard-to-find arches, and discusses the geology and natural history of the Fiery Furnace. Also see the section on the Fiery Furnace under "Day Hikes," below. Also from March through October, rangers lead daily nature walks from various park locations. **Evening campfire programs,** from April through October, cover topics such as rock art, geological processes, and wildlife. Check the schedule at the visitor center and on bulletin boards throughout the park.

Historic & Man-Made Attractions

Although not many have left their mark in this rugged area, a few intrepid Ute Indians and pioneers have spent time here. Just off the Delicate Arch Trail is a **Ute petroglyph panel** that includes etchings of horses and bighorn sheep. Also, near the beginning of the trail is **Wolfe Ranch.** Disabled Civil War veteran John Wesley Wolfe and his son Fred moved here from Ohio in 1898, and in 1907 were joined by John's daughter Flora, her husband, and their two children. They left in 1910, after which John's cabin was destroyed by a flash flood. The cabin used by Flora's family survived and has been preserved by the Park Service. You'll see the cabin, a root cellar, and a corral.

Day Hikes

Most trails here are short and relatively easy, although because of the hot summer sun and lack of shade, it's wise to wear a hat and carry plenty of water on any jaunt expected to last more than1 hour.

SHORTER TRAILS

Balanced Rock Trail

0.3 mile RT. Easy. Access: Balanced Rock parking area on the east side of the main park road.

This short, easy walk is perfect for visitors who want to get out and stretch their legs and incidentally get a great close-up view of the huge and precariously perched Balanced Rock. The loop takes you around the formation. The 0.16 mile round-trip is wheelchair accessible.

Broken Arch

1 mile RT. Easy. Access: At the end of Devils Garden Campground.

This easy hike, with little elevation change, traverses sand dunes and slickrock to the arch. Watch for the rock cairns, in some places poorly defined, marking the path through the arch. A little farther along is a connecting trail to **Sand Dune Arch,** about 0.5 miles out and back. At the end of the loop you have a 0.25-mile walk along the paved campground road back to your car.

Double Arch

0.25 mile one-way. Easy. Access: Double Arch parking area, in Windows section of the park.

This easy walk, with very little elevation change, leads you to the third-largest arch opening in the park—don't be fooled by how small it looks from the parking area. Along your way, look for the **Parade of Elephants,** off to the left. Once there, you can go a little farther and climb right up under the arch—just be very careful not to disturb the delicate desert vegetation or natural features. To the right of Double Arch are several alcoves that may one day become arches. If you're visiting in spring, look for the **sego lily,** Utah's state flower. It has three lovely cream-colored petals with a reddish-purple spot fading to yellow at the base.

Park Avenue

1 mile one-way. Easy. Access: Park Ave. or Courthouse Towers parking areas.

This easy downhill hike takes you into the canyon through scattered Utah juniper, single-leaf ash, blackbrush, and, in spring, wildflowers that sprinkle the sides of the trail with color. **Courthouse Towers, Tower of Babel, Three Gossips,** and **Organ Rock** can all be seen from the park road, but it's not nearly as awe-inspiring as actually walking among them. Have a friend provide a ride to the starting point so the trip is all downhill, or start at the **Courthouse Towers** end and make the 320-foot climb first, so the return to your vehicle is downhill.

Sand Dune Arch

0.3 mile one-way. Easy. Access: Sand Dune Arch parking area.

This is an easy walk through low shrubs and grasses to the arch, which is hidden among and shaded by rock walls, with a naturally created giant sandbox below. Please resist the temptation to climb onto the arch and jump down into the sand—not only is it dangerous, but it can damage the arch. Just before reaching **Sand Dune Arch** a trail cuts off to the left that leads to **Broken Arch,** adding 1.2 miles to your hike. Those who try this detour should watch for mule deer and kit foxes, which inhabit the grassland along the way.

Skyline Arch

0.2 mile one-way. Easy. Access: Skyline Arch parking area.

This is an easy walk along a flat, well-defined trail, with a view of Skyline Arch dominating the horizon. On a cold November night in 1940, a large boulder fell from the opening of this arch, doubling its size.

Windows Primitive Loop

1 mile loop. Easy. Access: Windows parking area.

This easy, fairly flat hike leads to three massive arches, two of which appear to be almost perfectly round windows. It's a busy trail, but you'll find fewer people if you hike early or late in the day. On your way to **North Window,** take a short side trip to **Turret Arch.** Once you reach North and South Windows, take the loop around back and see for yourself why they are sometimes called Spectacles— the scene almost looks like a sea monster poking its large snout up into the air.

LONGER TRAILS

Delicate Arch

1.5 miles one-way. Moderate to strenuous. Access: Wolfe Ranch parking area.

Climbing about 480 feet, this hike is considered by many to be the park's best and most scenic, though complicated by slippery slickrock, no shade, and some steep drop-offs along a narrow cliff. Your efforts are rewarded with a dramatic,

spectacular view of **Delicate Arch.** Along the way, you'll see the **John Wesley Wolfe Ranch** and have an opportunity to take a side trip to a **Ute petroglyph panel** that includes drawings of horses and what may represent a bighorn sheep hunt.

When you get back on the main trail, watch for **collared lizards,** bright-green foot-long creatures with stripes of yellow or rust and a black collar. Feeding mostly in the daytime, they particularly enjoy insects and other lizards, and can stand and run on their large hind feet in pursuit of prey. Continuing along the trail, watch for **Frame Arch,** off to the right. Its main claim to fame is that numerous photographers have used it to "frame" a photo of Delicate Arch in the distance. Just past Frame Arch, the trail gets a little weird, having been blasted out from the cliff.

Should you choose to not take this hike, consider driving to the **Delicate Arch Viewpoint Trail,** which provides an ideal location for a photo, preferably with the arch highlighted by a clear blue sky. From the parking area it is about a 5-minute walk to the viewpoint.

Devils Garden

7.2 miles RT. Easy to strenuous. Access: Devils Garden parking area.

The whole Devils Garden loop is a fairly long, strenuous, and difficult hike, from which you can see 15 to 20 arches and some exciting scenery. Be sure to take plenty of water, and don't hurry.

You don't have to go the entire way to see some unusual formations. Just 0.25 mile from the trailhead, a spur takes off to the right down a little hill. Here a left turn takes you to **Pine Tree Arch,** and turning right brings you to **Tunnel Arch.**

After returning to the main trail, stay to the left, and soon you'll reach the turnoff to **Landscape Arch,** a long (306 ft.), thin ribbon of stone that is one of the most beautiful arches in the park. This is about a 2-mile round-trip, but is an absolute must-see during a visit to Arches National Park. Geologically speaking,

Landscape Arch is quite mature and may collapse any day. Almost immediately after passing Landscape Arch, look to your right for **Wall Arch.** From here the trail is less well defined but marked by cairns.

After another 0.25 mile, a side trip to the left has two spurs leading to **Partition Arch,** which you could see earlier behind Landscape Arch, and **Navajo Arch.** The spurs take you right up under the arches. Navajo Arch is shaded, providing a good spot to stop and take a breather while absorbing the view.

Once back on the main trail, which gets rougher and slicker as you hike, it's 0.5 mile to the strange **Double O Arch,** where one arch stands atop another. Now you've reached another junction, whose left spur leads to the **Dark Angel,** a dark sandstone spire reaching toward the heavens from the desert floor. The right spur takes you on to the **primitive loop,** a difficult trip through a dramatic desert environment with some drop-offs and narrow ledges. There is just one major arch along this part of the trail, **Private Arch,** located on a short spur to the right. You'll have the primitive loop almost to yourself, as most people turn back at Double O Arch rather than tackle this more difficult trail.

Fiery Furnace

2 miles RT. Moderate to strenuous. Access: Fiery Furnace parking area.

This is a difficult and strenuous hike to some of the most colorful formations in the park. The name comes not from the summer heat, but rather from the rich reddish glow the rocks take on at sunset.

Guided hikes are given twice daily from March through October (see "Organized Tours & Ranger Programs," above). You can choose to head out on your own (permits required, fee not known at press time) for an off-trail adventure, but special restrictions apply, so you must first talk with a ranger at the visitor center. Trails aren't marked, so unless you are experienced in the Fiery Furnace, it's best to join a guided hike.

Tower Arch

1.7 miles one-way. Strenuous. Access: Follow Salt Valley Rd. for 7.1 miles, turn left toward Klondike Bluffs, and go 1.5 miles to the Tower Arch Trailhead. (Be careful not to take the left turn just before the Klondike Bluffs Rd. as it is a difficult four-wheel-drive road.)

This is a short but rugged hike on a primitive trail. It starts with a steep incline to the top of the bluff and proceeds up and down, with great views of the Klondike Bluffs to the right. Beware of the slickrock that makes up part of the trail, and watch for the cairns leading the way. The hardest part is near the end, where you struggle uphill through loose sand. Your reward is a grand sight: the immense **Tower Arch** standing among a maze of sandstone spires. Climb up under it for a soothing view while you take a much-deserved break. In spring, the majestic, snowcapped **La Sal Mountains** can be seen to the east through the arch opening.

Exploring the Backcountry

There are no designated backcountry trails or campsites, and very little of the park is open to overnight camping, but backcountry hiking is permitted. Ask park rangers to suggest routes. No fires are allowed, and hikers must carry their own water and practice low-impact hiking and camping techniques. Those planning to be out overnight need to get free backcountry permits, available at the visitor center.

Other Sports & Activities

Although Arches National Park and the surrounding public lands offer plenty for the do-it-yourselfer, some 50 local outfitters offer excursions of all kinds just outside the park, from rugged mountain-bike treks to relatively comfortable four-wheel-drive adventures. You can also rent a canoe or take a guided boat trip on the Colorado River, which follows the park's southeast boundary.

The chart below lists some of the major companies that can help you fully enjoy this beautiful country, including those that rent equipment and will shuttle you and/or your vehicle to or from trailheads. They are all located in Moab (zip code 84532). Advance reservations are often required, and it's best to check with several outfitters before deciding which best fits your needs. When making reservations, be sure to ask about the company's cancellation policy, just in case.

Biking. Bikes are prohibited on all trails and off-road in the backcountry. They are, however, permitted on the scenic drive, although the 18-mile dead-end road is narrow and winding in spots, and can be crowded with motor vehicles during the summer.

Mountain bikers also have the option of tackling one of several four-wheel-drive roads (see the "Four-Wheeling" section, below). Cyclists can get information, as well as rent or repair bikes at **Slickrock Cycles,** 94 W. 415 N. Main St. (© 800/825-9791 or 435/259-1134). Bike rentals start at about $35 per day. In addition to the companies listed in the chart below, bike shuttle services are available from **Acme Bike Shuttle** (© 435/260-2534), **Coyote Shuttle** (© 435/259-8656), **Moab Outback** (© 435/259-2667), and **Roadrunner Shuttle** (© 435/259-9402). Several local companies (see the "Outfitters" chart, at right) also offer guided mountain-bike tours, with rates of about $80 for a half day and $95 for a full day, including bike rental. Multiday biking/camping trips start at about $550 for a 3-day excursion.

Boating, Canoeing & Rafting. Although there are no bodies of water actually in Arches National Park, the Colorado River follows the park's boundary along its southeast edge, and river-running is a wonderful change of pace from hiking over the park's dry, rocky terrain. You can travel down the river in a canoe, kayak, large or small rubber raft (with or without a motor), or a speedy, solid jet boat.

Do-it-yourselfers can rent kayaks or canoes for $25 to $35 for a half day and $30 to $45 for a full day, or rafts from $50 to $85 for a half day and $65 to $115 for a full day. Half-day guided river trips cost from $35 to $45 per person; full-day trips are usually $40 to $60. Multiday rafting expeditions, which include meals and camping equipment, start at about $150 per person for 2 days. Jet-boat trips, which cover a lot more river in a given amount of time, start at $60 for a half-day trip, with full-day trips about $85. Children's rates are usually about 20% lower. Some companies also offer sunset or dinner trips. See the "Outfitters" chart at right.

Public boat-launching ramps are opposite Lion's Park, near the intersection of U.S. 191 and Utah 128; at Take-Out Beach, along Utah 128 about 10 miles east of its intersection with U.S. 191; and at Hittle Bottom, also along Utah 128, about 23.5 miles east of its intersection with U.S. 191. The **Colorado Basin River Forecast Center** (© 801/539-1311; www.cbrfc.gov) provides information on river flows and reservoir conditions statewide.

Four-Wheeling. Although Arches hasn't nearly as many four-wheel-drive opportunities as in nearby Canyonlands National Park, it has a few—but check first with rangers on possible road closures and conditions that make the routes impassable. One possibility is the 17-mile road from Klondike Bluffs to Willow Flats, which is best driven from north to south because of soft sand on steep grades. Turn west off the main park road 1 mile south of Devils Garden Trailhead, and follow the road up through the Salt Valley about 7.7 miles to the turnoff for Klondike Bluffs. The next 17 miles, heading into high desert terrain and opening up panoramas of surrounding mountains and red rock formations, are strictly for four-wheelers. The route also passes Eye of the Whale Arch, views of Elephant Butte (the highest point in the park at 5,653 ft.), and the imposing Courthouse Towers. Also

Outfitter	4WD	Bike	Boat	Horse	Rent	Shuttle
Adrift Adventures 378 N. Main St., Box 577 © 800/874-4483, 435/259-8594 www.adrift.net	Yes	No	Yes	Yes	No	No
Canyon Voyages Adventure Co. 211 N. Main St., Box 416 © 800/733-6007, 435/259-6007 www.canyonvoyages.com	Yes	No	Yes	No	Yes	No
Dreamrides 59 E. Center St., Box 1137 © 888/662-2882, 435/259-6419 www.dreamride.com	No	No	Yes	No	No	No
Moab Rafting Co. Box 801 © 800/746-6622, 435/259-7238 www.moab-rafting.com	No	No	Yes	No	No	No
Navtec Expeditions 321 N. Main St., Box 1267 © 800/833-1278, 435/259-7983 www.navtec.com	Yes	No	Yes	No	Yes	No
Nichols Expeditions 497 N. Main St. © 800/648-8488, 435/259-3999 www.nicholsexpeditions.com	No	Yes	No	No	Yes	No
OARS Canyonlands Tours 543 N. Main St. © 800/342-5938, 435/259-5865 www.oarsutah.com	Yes	No	Yes	No	No	No
Pack Creek Ranch U.S. 191, S. of Moab, Box 1270 © 435/259-5505 www.packcreekranch.com	No	No	No	Yes	No	No
Tag-A-Long Expeditions 452 N. Main St. © 800/453-3292, 435/259-8946 www.tagalong.com	Yes	No	Yes	No	Yes	No
Western River Expeditions 1371 N. U.S. 191 © 888/622-4097, 435/259-7019 www.westernriver.com	No	No	Yes	No	Yes	Yes

seen along the route are drifting sand dunes and the red rock Marching Men formation. The road brings you out at the Balanced Rock parking area.

Rock Climbing. Technical climbing is permitted in some areas of the park, but only for experienced climbers. In addition, it is prohibited on many of the park's best-known arches, as well as Balanced Rock and a few other locations. Information is available from park rangers.

Camping

INSIDE THE PARK

Located at the north end of the park's scenic drive, **Devils Garden Campground** is Arches' only developed campground. The sites are nestled among rocks, with plenty of pinyon and juniper trees. In the summer, the campground fills early, so if you don't have a reservation, contact **National Recreation Reservation Service** (© 877/444-6777; www.reserve usa.com), be sure to get to the visitor center by 7:30am.

NEAR THE PARK

More than a dozen commercial campgrounds can be found in and around Moab. Located at the junction of U.S. 191 and U.S. 313, **Arch View Camp Park,** U.S. 191 (P.O. Box 1496), Moab, UT 84532 (© **800/813-6622** or 435/259-7854; www.archviewresort.com), offers all the usual RV hookups, showers, and other amenities you'd expect in a first-class commercial RV park, plus great views into the park. Arch View has a

Campground	Elev.	Total Sites	RV Hookups	Dump Station	Toilets	Drinking Water
Inside Arches						
Devils Garden	5,355	52	No	No	Yes	Yes
Inside Canyonlands						
Willow Flat	6,200	12	No	No	Yes	No
Squaw Flat	5,100	26	No	No	Yes	Yes
Near Canyonlands						
Dead Horse Point	5,600	21	21	Yes	Yes	Yes
Near Monticello						
Mountain View RV Park	7,000	35	29	Yes	Yes	Yes
Newspaper Rock	6,000	8	No	No	Yes	No
In and Near Moab						
Arch View Camp Park	5,000	85	54	No	Yes	Yes
Canyonlands Campground & RV Park	4,000	144	113	Yes	Yes	Yes
Moab KOA	5,000	154	73	Yes	Yes	Yes
Moab Valley RV & Campground	4,000	134	92	Yes	Yes	Yes
Spanish Trail	4,200	73	60	No	Yes	Yes

grassy tent area, trees throughout the park, a convenience store, a swimming pool, playground, and propane, gasoline, and diesel sales. There are also six log cabins ($30–$35 for two).

Canyonlands Campground & RV Park, 555 S. Main St., Moab, UT 84532 (© **800/522-6848** or 435/259-6848; www. moab-utah.com/canyonlands/rv.html), is surprisingly shady and quiet given its in-town location, and is convenient to Moab's restaurants and shopping. On-site is a convenience store with food and some RV supplies. There are also six cabins ($35 for two).

The **Moab KOA,** 3225 S. U.S. 191, Moab, UT 84532 (© **800/562-0372** for reservations, or 435/259-6682; fax 435/ 259-8703), located about 3 miles south of Moab, has trees and great views of the La Sal Mountains. It has a miniature

golf course, game room, two playgrounds, cable TV hookups, and a convenience store with RV supplies and propane. About half of the sites are for tents only. There are also one- and two-room cabins ($42–$55 double).

On the north side of Moab, near the intersection of U.S. 191 and Utah 128, is **Moab Valley RV & Campground,** 1773 N. U.S. 191, Moab, UT 84532 (© **435/259-4483;** fax 435/259-4469; www.moabvalley rv.com). All sites offer great views of the surrounding rock formations. The park accommodates practically any size RV in its extra large pull-through sites, and provides cable television connections on full RV hookups. There are trees and patches of grass for both tenters and RVers. You can refuel at the convenience store that sells propane, groceries, and RV and camping supplies. Dogs are permitted

Showers	Fire Pits/ Grills	Laundry	Public Phone	Reserve	Fees	Open
No	Yes	No	No	Yes	$10	Year-round
No	Yes	No	No	No	$5	Year-round
No	Yes	No	No	No	$10	Year-round
No	Yes	No	Yes	Yes	$13	Year-round
Yes	No	Yes	Yes	Yes	$17–$20	May–Oct
No	Yes	No	No	No	Free	Year-round
Yes	Yes	Yes	Yes	Yes	$20–$30	Year-round
Yes	Yes	Yes	Yes	Yes	$21–$24	Year-round
Yes	Yes	Yes	Yes	Yes	$25–$30	Mar–Oct
Yes	Yes	Yes	Yes	Yes	$24–$26	Mar–Oct
Yes	No	Yes	Yes	Yes	$24–$28	Year-round

in RV sites, but not in tent sites or cabins. There are 12 cabins ($39–$49 for two) that offer comfortable beds, air-conditioning, and TVs, but still require a walk to the bathhouse; six new cottages have private bathrooms ($60 for two). Smoking is not permitted in the cabins and cottages.

Just south of Moab is **Spanish Trail RV Park and Campground,** 2980 S. U.S. 191, Moab, UT 84532 (✆ **800/787-2751** or 435/259-2411; fax 435/259-2410; www.moab.net/spanishtrail), with spacious sites accommodating big RVs, some shaded sites, and scenic views. It offers cable TV hookups, volleyball, horseshoes, and a convenience store with RV supplies.

You'll also find campgrounds at nearby Canyonlands National Park (see "Camping," in chapter 8) and in areas under the jurisdiction of the U.S. Forest Service, Bureau of Land Management, and Utah state parks. The **Mountain View RV Park** in Monticello (included in the campground chart here) is discussed in chapter 8. Also, check at the **Moab Information Center** or with the **Grand Country Travel Council** (see "Information," above).

Where to Stay

There are no lodging facilities inside the park.

Moab is the nearest town to Arches (5 miles south). Room rates are generally highest from mid-March through October, and sometimes drop by up to half in the winter.

Most visitors are here for the outdoors and don't plan to spend much time in their rooms; as a result, many book into one of the fully adequate chain and franchise motels, including **Super 8,** on the north edge of Moab at 889 N. Main St. (✆ 435/259-8868), the town's largest lodging; **Days Inn,** 426 N. Main St.

(✆ 435/259-4468); **Comfort Suites,** 800 S. Main St. (✆ 435/259-5252); **Motel 6,** 1089 N. Main St. (✆ 435/259-6686); **Sleep Inn,** 1051 S. Main St. (✆ 435/259-4655); **Ramada Inn,** 182 S. Main St. (✆ 435/259-7141); **Best Western Canyonlands Inn,** 16 S. Main St. (✆ 435/259-2300); and **Best Western Greenwell Inn,** 105 S. Main St. (✆ 435/259-6151). Rates for two in standard rooms are generally less than $120 in all of the above. Chain motel toll-free phone numbers are listed in the appendix. Also see the **cabins** at Arch View Camp Park, Canyonlands Campground & RV Park, Moab KOA, and Moab Valley RV & Campground, under "Camping," above.

Aarchway Inn

1551 N. U.S. 191, Moab, UT 84532. ✆ **800/341-9359** or 435/259-2599. Fax 435/259-2270. www.aarchwayinn.com. 97 units. A/C TV TEL. Mar–Oct $89–$108 double; $150–$170 suite; lower rates Nov–Mar. Rates include continental breakfast. AE, DC, DISC, MC, V.

This two-story property, just 2 miles from the entrance to Arches National Park, has large rooms with great views, decorated in Southwestern style. Most rooms contain two queen-size beds; eight family units also have a queen hide-a-bed. There are a variety of suites, including a honeymoon suite; all have refrigerators, microwave ovens, and whirlpool tubs. Facilities include a large outdoor heated pool, courtyard with barbecue grills, indoor hot tub, exercise room, bike storage, coin-operated laundry, conference rooms, and gift shop. There are also two apartments, with full kitchens and 46-inch TVs (call for rates). The entire facility is nonsmoking.

Bowen Motel

169 N. Main St., Moab, UT 84532. ✆ **800/874-5439** or 435/259-7132. Fax 435/259-6641. www.bowenmotel.com. 40 units. A/C TV TEL. $65–$75 double; off-season 40% less. Rates include continental breakfast. AE, DC, DISC, MC, V.

This family-owned and -operated motel offers fairly large, comfortable, clean, basic rooms with attractive wallpaper, a king or one or two queen-size beds, and shower/tub combos. Some units have a refrigerator and microwave; and two family rooms sleep up to six each. The original structure was built in the 1940s, with an addition made in 1978; a major renovation was completed in 1993–94. Facilities include an outdoor heated swimming pool. Several restaurants are within easy walking distance.

Cali Cochitta Bed & Breakfast

110 S. 200 E., Moab, UT 84532-2606. ℂ **888/ 429-8112** or 435/259-4961. Fax 435/259-4964. www.moabdreaminn.com. 5 units, including 1 cottage. A/C TV. $95–$150 double spring–fall; about $20 less in winter. Rates include full breakfast. AE, MC, V.

For a delightful escape from the hustle and bustle of Moab, head to the Cali Cochitta (Aztec for "House of Dreams"), a handsomely restored late-1800s Victorian home, with great views of the surrounding mountains and red rock formations. The spacious guest rooms have queen-size beds, handsome wood furnishings (including many antiques), and cotton robes. The suite has queen and double beds in two rooms and offers wonderful views. The little cottage, adjacent to the main house, is perfect for two singles traveling together; each of the two bedrooms has a twin bed and a bathroom. Our favorite room here is the romantic "Cane," which has a high queen-size mahogany sleigh bed and French glass doors. Modem hookups are available in one room, the cottage, and the dining room. Breakfasts include a hot entree (often prepared with herbs from the inn's garden), plus fresh muffins or other baked goods, fruit, and beverages. Bike storage and guest laundry facilities are available. The entire inn is nonsmoking.

The Lazy Lizard International Hostel

1213 S. U.S. 191, Moab, UT 84532. ℂ **435/ 259-6057.** Fax 435/259-1122. www.lazylizard hostel.com. 25 dorm beds, 10 private rooms, 8 cabins; total capacity 65 persons. A/C. $9 dorm bed; $22 private room; from $27 cabin; $6 per person camping space. Showers $2 for nonguests. Hostel membership not necessary. MC, V.

Located on the south side of town behind the A-1 self-storage units, this hostel offers exceptionally clean, comfortable lodging at bargain rates for those willing to share. The main house, which is air-conditioned, has basic dorm rooms plus two private rooms. A separate building contains four additional private rooms, which look much like older motel units. The best facilities are the cabins, constructed of real logs and with beds for up to six. There's also a camping area (no hookups). Everyone shares the bathhouses, and there's a phone in the main house. Guests also have use of a fully equipped kitchen; living room with TV, VCR, and movies; whirlpool; self-service laundry; gas barbecue grill; and picnic tables. Groups should inquire about the nearby houses, which can be rented by the night ($100–$220 for 14–30 people).

Red Stone Inn

535 S. Main St., Moab, UT 84532. ℂ **800/772-1972** or 435/259-3500. Fax 435/259-2717. www.moabredstone.com. 52 units. A/C TV TEL. Summer $60–$75 double; winter $30–$35 double; slightly higher in Sept and during special events. Rollaway beds $5 extra. AE, DISC, MC, V. Pets permitted with $5 fee.

This centrally located motel is comfortable, clean, quiet, and an especially good choice for mountain bikers. The exterior gives the impression that these are cabins, and the theme continues inside as well, with attractive knotty-pine walls decorated with colorful posters and maps of area attractions. Rooms are a bit on the small side, although perfectly adequate and spotlessly maintained. All rooms have kitchenettes with microwaves, 10-cup coffeemakers (with coffee supplied), and refrigerators. Three handicapped-accessible rooms have combination shower/tubs, while the rest have showers only. There's a 24-hour self-service laundry, a covered picnic area with tables and gas barbecue grills, and a bike work stand and bike wash station. Bikes are permitted in the rooms. There is no swimming pool on the premises, but guests have access to an outdoor heated pool at another motel across the street.

Sunflower Hill Bed & Breakfast Inn

185 N. 300 E., Moab, UT 84532. © **800/ 662-2786** or 435/259-2974. Fax 435/259-3065. www.sunflowerhill.com. 12 units. A/C TV. Mar to mid-Nov and holidays $135–$195 double; mid-Nov to Feb $90–$140 double. Rates include full breakfast and evening refreshments. AE, DISC, MC, V. Children under 10 accepted by prior arrangement only.

This country-style retreat, 3 blocks off Main Street on a quiet dead-end road, offers elegant rooms and lovely outdoor areas, and is our choice for a relaxing escape. The rooms are individually decorated—for instance, the Garden Suite boasts a colorful garden-themed mural—and have handmade quilts on the beds. Deluxe rooms have jetted tubs and private balconies. The popular French Bedroom includes a hand-carved antique bedroom set from France, a stained-glass window, vaulted ceiling, white lace curtains, and a large whirlpool tub and separate tiled shower.

The substantial breakfast buffet includes homemade breads and fresh-baked pastries, honey-almond granola, fresh fruits, and a hot entree such as a garden vegetable frittata, blueberry pancakes, or asparagus quiche. The inn also offers a guest laundry. The grounds are grassy and shady, with fruit trees and flowers in abundance. Guests enjoy a year-round outdoor hot tub, swing, picnic table, and barbecue. Smoking is not permitted.

Where to Dine

There are no restaurants inside the park.

NEAR THE PARK

In addition to the restaurants discussed below, those looking for a foot-stompin' good time and a Western-style dinner will want to make their way to the **Bar-M Chuckwagon Live Western Show and Cowboy Supper,** 7 miles north of Moab on U.S. 191 (© **800/214-2085** or 435/ 259-2276; www.barmchuckwagon.com). The Bar M has an indoor, climate-controlled dining room, and diners go through a supper line to pick up sliced roast beef or barbecued chicken, baked potatoes, baked beans, cinnamon applesauce, buttermilk biscuits, dessert, and nonalcoholic beverages. Vegetarian meals can be prepared with advance notice, and beer and wine coolers are available. After dinner, a stage show entertains with Western-style music, jokes, and down-home silliness from the Bar-M Wranglers. The grounds, which include a small Western village and gift shop, open at 6:30pm, with gunfights starting at 7pm, dinner at 7:30pm, and the show following supper. The Bar-M is usually open from spring to early fall, but closed Sundays and Tuesdays; call for the current schedule. Supper and show cost $20 for adults, $10 for children 4 to 10. Reservations are strongly recommended.

Buck's Grill House

1393 N. U.S. 191, about 1½ miles north of town. © **435/259-5201.** Main courses $5.95–$20. DC, DISC, MC, V. Daily 5:30pm–closing. Closed Dec–Jan. AMERICAN WESTERN.

This popular restaurant, among the area's best places for steak, also offers a number of other choices to suit a variety of palates. The dining room's subdued

Western decor is accented by exposed wood beams and Western and scenic paintings by local artist Pete Plastow. There's a delightful patio out back complete with a rock wall, shade trees, and a waterfall for peaceful alfresco dining. The adventurous will likely enjoy one of our top choices here—the buffalo meatloaf, with black onion gravy and mashed potatoes. We also recommend the prime rib and the artichoke ceviche (artichoke marinated with tomatoes, onions, and peppers, and topped with mozzarella). Southwestern dishes include grilled chicken tacos, buffalo chorizo tacos, and duck tamale with grilled pineapple salsa. All breads and other baked items are made in-house. Buck's offers full liquor service and a good wine list, and serves a variety of Utah microbrews.

Center Cafe

60 N. 100 W. © **435/259-4295.** Dinner reservations recommended. Main courses $14–$28 at dinner. DISC, MC, V. Daily 5:30pm–closing (time varies). Closed Dec to early Feb. CONTEMPORARY AMERICAN.

Not really a cafe at all, this fine small restaurant, with white tablecloths, a stone fireplace, rich wood colors, and a bright, contemporary look, is the place to come for innovative seafood selections, plus a variety of meat, pasta, and vegetarian dishes. The menu changes seasonally but always includes fresh seafood such as oven-roasted monkfish with black olive vinaigrette and orzo pasta, or salmon Wellington with a pinot noir sauce. We also recommend the pan-seared lamb loin with roasted garlic flan and the grilled Black Angus beef tenderloin with soft polenta, caramelized onion, and Gorgonzola. There's also patio dining, and full liquor service is available.

Eddie McStiff's

57 S. Main St. (in McStiff's Plaza, just south of the information center). © **435/259-2337.** Fax 435/259-3022. www.eddiemcstiff.com. Main courses $7–$19; pizza $4.50–$20. DISC, MC, V. Daily 11:30am–midnight. Shorter hours in winter. AMERICAN.

This bustling, somewhat noisy brewpub is half family restaurant and half tavern, with a climate-controlled garden patio as well. In the restaurant dining room, you'll find Southwest decor and paintings by local artists, while the tavern looks just as a tavern should: long bar, low light, and lots of wood. The menu changes seasonally to accommodate sports enthusiasts in spring and fall, Europeans and families in summer. There's always a wide range of appetizers, salads, and half-pound Black Angus beef burgers, plus grilled steaks, pasta, and Southwestern dishes. You'll find a good choice of sandwiches at lunch. Among the specialties are grilled salmon filet and house-smoked St. Louis–style barbecued ribs. At least a dozen fresh-brewed beers are on tap at any given time and can also be purchased to go in six-packs, 22-ounce bottles, and half-gallon refillable growlers. Mixed drinks, wine, and beer are sold in the dining room with food only; beer can be purchased with or without food in the tavern. (You must be at least 21 to enter the tavern.)

Moab Brewery

686 S. Main St. © **435/259-6333.** www.the moabbrewery.com. Main courses $5.95–$19. AE, DISC, MC, V. Daily 11:30am–10pm summer; 11:30am–9pm winter. ECLECTIC.

Fresh handcrafted ales brewed on-site, along with a wide variety of steaks, sandwiches, salads, soups, vegetarian dishes, and assorted house specialties, are served at this open, spacious microbrewery/restaurant on the south side of town. It's popular with families, who gobble down basic American fare such as burgers and fresh fish. The adventuresome can choose from the more exotic selections, such as the margarita chicken dinner, smoked portobello mushroom pasta, or the popular St. Louis smoked ribs. The huge dining room is decorated with light woods, outdoor sports equipment—including a hang glider on the ceiling—and local artwork. Patio dining is available.

You can sample the brews—from German-style unfiltered wheat ale to easy-drinking American ale—at the separate bar. The brewery usually has about half a dozen of its beers available on tap at any given time. There's a gift shop plus beer-to-go in half-gallon jugs in insulated carriers. Beer is sold in the bar; in the restaurant, diners can purchase beer, wine, or mixed drinks.

Moab Diner

189 S. Main St. (2 blocks south of Center St.). © **435/259-4006.** Main courses $3.50–$13. MC, V. Daily 6am–10:30pm. Closes earlier in winter. AMERICAN/SOUTHWESTERN.

Late risers can get breakfast—among the best in town—all day here, with all the usual egg dishes, biscuits and gravy, six kinds of omelets, and a spicy breakfast burrito. The decor is definitely diner, but the place does have lots of green plants. Hamburgers, sandwiches, and salads are the offerings at lunch, of course, and for dinner there's steak, shrimp, and chicken, plus liver and onions. In addition to ice cream, you can get malts and shakes, plus sundaes with seven different toppings. No alcoholic beverages are served.

Poplar Place Restaurant & Pub

11 E. 100 N. © **435/259-6018.** Main courses $6.75–$14; pizza $12–$19. MC, V. Daily 11:30am–10pm. Reduced hours in winter. MEXICAN/ITALIAN.

This two-story corner pub has been a busy lunch and dinner stop for locals since it opened in 1972, serving lots of pizzas, pasta, sandwiches, soups, and Mexican dishes. We enthusiastically recommend the popular homemade pizzas, which come with either a tomato or Alfredo sauce and your choice of toppings; several specialty pizzas are also listed. Or try one of the popular house specialties: chicken Parmesan and shrimp scampi. Mexican selections include chicken or pork burritos with green chile sauce, and what the Poplar Place calls a "Popco": a cross between a taco and a fajita, with chicken, beef, or crab. Dine inside or out on the new patio. Full liquor service is available in addition to a good selection of wine, Utah microbrews, and Guinness Stout on tap.

Sunset Grill

900 N. U.S. 191. © **435/259-7146.** Fax 435/259-7626. www.moab-utah.com/sunsetgrill. Main courses $9.95–$21. AE, DISC, MC, V. Daily 5–10pm. AMERICAN.

Perched on a hill at the north edge of Moab, this fine restaurant offers the best sunset views in town. Once the home of Moab area miner Charles Steen, the Sunset Grill contains four tastefully decorated dining rooms and three patios. A favorite of locals celebrating special events, the restaurant serves aged USDA Choice steaks, hand-cut in-house, plus such treats as grilled Colorado lamb chops in mint butter and served with a port-wine peppercorn sauce; and grilled Atlantic salmon filet, prepared with an Asian hoisin glaze and served in a light soy-sherry cream sauce. Texas-style prime rib sells out often, so get here early if it's your first choice. The menu also includes a number of chicken dishes, Colorado lamb, and several pasta selections. Utah microbrews, some 30 wines, and full liquor service are offered.

Picnic & Camping Supplies

The best grocery store in town is **City Market,** 425 S. Main St. (© **435/259-5181**). You can pick up sandwiches from the deli, assemble your own salad at the salad bar, or choose fresh-baked items from the bakery. The store also sells fishing licenses, money orders, and stamps; offers photo finishing and Western Union services; and has a pharmacy. For camping supplies and equipment for hiking, biking, and other outdoor activities, try **Red Canyon Outfitters,** 23 N. Main St. (© 435/259-3353); **Moab** **Outdoors General Store,** 702 S. Main St. (© 435/259-5731); or **Gearheads,** 471 S. Main St. (© 435/259-4327).

Nearby Attractions

Many visitors to Arches also spend time at nearby Canyonlands National Park, which is discussed in chapter 8.

3

BADLANDS NATIONAL PARK

by Jack Olson

IT'S A STRANGE AND SEEMINGLY COMPLICATED PLACE. FROM THE ragged ridges and saw-toothed spires to the wind-ravaged desolation of Sage Creek Wilderness Area, Badlands National Park is an awe-inspiring sight and an unsettling experience. Few leave here unaffected by the vastness of this geologic anomaly, spread across 381 square miles of moonscape.

The Sioux Indians who once traversed this incredible land named it *mako sica,* or "land bad." Early French-Canadian trappers labeled it *les mauvaises terres a traverser,* or "bad lands to travel across."

Steep canyons, towering spires, and flat-topped tables are all found among Badlands buttes. Despite their apparent complexity, the unusual formations of the Badlands are essentially the result of two basic geologic processes: deposition and erosion.

The layered look of the Badlands comes from sedimentary rocks composed of fine grains that have been cemented into a solid form. Layers with similar characteristics are grouped into units called formations. The bottom formation is the **Pierre Shale,** deposited 68 million to 77 million years ago during the Cretaceous period, when a shallow, inland sea stretched across the present-day Great Plains. The black mud of the sea floor hardened into shale, leaving fossil clamshells and ammonites that today confirm a sea environment. The sea eventually drained away, and the upper layers of shale were weathered into soil, now seen as yellow mounds.

The **Chadron Formation,** deposited 32 million to 37 million years ago during the Eocene epoch, sits above the Pierre Shale. By this time, a flood plain had replaced the sea, and each time the rivers flooded, they deposited a new layer of sediment on the plain. Alligator fossils indicate that a lush, subtropical forest covered the region. However, mammal fossils dominate. The Chadron is best known for its large, elephant-like mammals called titanotheres.

Some of the sediment carried by rivers and wind was volcanic ash, the product of eruptions associated with the creation of the Rocky Mountains. This ash mixed with river and stream sediments to form clay stone, the main material from which Badlands buttes are constructed. After the Eocene epoch, the climate began to dry and cool, and tropical forests gave way to open savanna. Rivers deposited the **Brule** and **Sharps formations** during the Oligocene epoch from 26 million to 32 million years ago, and today these formations contain the most rugged peaks and canyons of the Badlands.

Actually, the impressive serrated ridges and deep canyons of the Badlands did not exist until about 500,000 years ago, when water began to cut through the layers of rock, carving fantastic shapes into what had been a flat floodplain. Once again, the ancient fossil soils, buried for millions of years, became exposed. That erosion continues, and every time it rains, or snow melts in spring, more sediment is washed from the buttes in this ongoing work of sculpting the earth. On average, the buttes erode an inch a year; scientists believe that the buttes will be gone in another 500,000 years.

In addition to its scenic wonders, the Badlands are one of the richest Oligocene fossil beds known to exist. Remains of three-toed horses, dog-sized camels, saber-toothed cats, giant pigs, and other species have been found here, all dating from 25 million to 35 million years ago.

Flora & Fauna. Largely a mixed-grass prairie, the park contains 56 different types of grasses, most of which are native species, including green needlegrass and buffalo grass. Wildflowers, including curlycup gumweed and pale purple coneflower, add color, with the best wildflower displays in June and July. What you won't find here are many trees.

Wildlife to watch for includes bison, Rocky Mountain bighorn sheep, pronghorns, and mule deer. Darting in and out of the grass are desert and eastern cottontail rabbits. Prairie dogs thrive here; a prairie dog town is just 5 miles down Sage Creek Rim Road. You might also see a prairie rattlesnake slithering through the grass, plus several nonpoisonous snake species.

Avoiding the Crowds. The vastness of the park means that overcrowding is usually not a problem. Entrance stations, visitor centers, park concessions, and the Loop Road can become busy during the height of the summer season, especially in July and August, but most roads, trails, and services are not overtaxed any time of the year.

As with most other national parks, those wishing to avoid crowds should visit during the shoulder seasons of April to May and September to October. If you must go in summer, visit early in the day when the numbers of people are lowest and the sun hasn't begun to scorch the earth. Dawn and dusk are ideal times to photograph the unearthly beauty of the park, and are also the best times to see wildlife.

Just the Facts

GETTING THERE & GATEWAYS

Located in extreme southwestern South Dakota, Badlands National Park is easily accessed by car either on **S. Dak. 44** east of Rapid City, or off **I-90** at Wall or Cactus Flat. Westbound I-90 travelers take Exit 131 south (Cactus Flat) onto S. Dak. 240, which leads to the park boundary and the **Ben Reifel Visitor Center** at Cedar Pass. This road becomes **Badlands Loop Road,** the park's primary scenic drive. After passing through the park, S. Dak. 240 rejoins I-90 at Exit 110 at Wall. Eastbound travelers do the reverse, beginning in Wall and rejoining I-90 at Exit 131.

The Nearest Airport. Rapid City **Regional Airport** (© **605/394-4195**), located 10 miles southeast of Rapid City on S. Dak. 44, provides direct access to the Badlands, Black Hills, and Mount Rushmore. **Northwest, Delta/Skywest,** and **United Express** serve the airport with daily flights to Minneapolis, Salt Lake City, and Denver. Car-rental companies at the airport include **Avis, Budget, Hertz, National,** and **Thrifty.** Toll-free

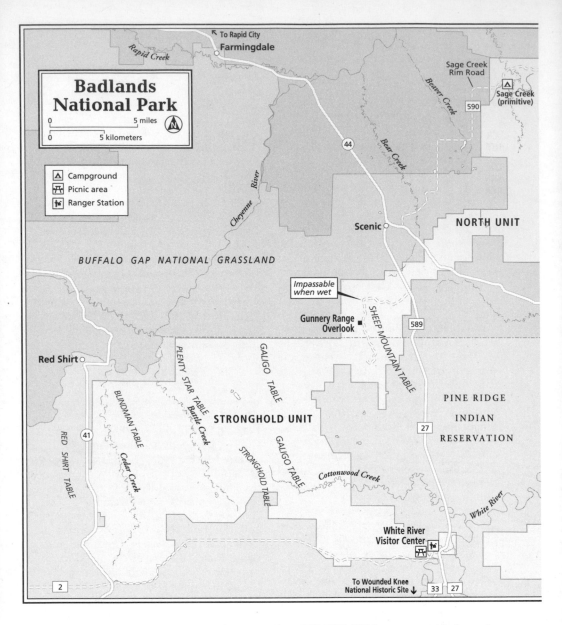

Badlands National Park

0 ——————— 5 miles
0 ——————— 5 kilometers

△ Campground
🅿 Picnic area
👁 Ranger Station

To Rapid City
Farmingdale

Rapid Creek

Sage Creek
Rim Road

△ Sage Creek
(primitive)

Beaver Creek

590

44

Bear Creek

Cheyenne River

Scenic ○

NORTH UNIT

BUFFALO GAP NATIONAL GRASSLAND

Impassable
when wet

**Gunnery Range
Overlook** ■

SHEEP MOUNTAIN TABLE

589

Red Shirt ○

PLENTY STAR TABLE

GALIGO TABLE

BLINDMAN TABLE

RED SHIRT TABLE

41

Cedar Creek

Battle Creek

STRONGHOLD UNIT

GALIGO TABLE

STRONGHOLD TABLE

Cottonwood Creek

PINE RIDGE

INDIAN

RESERVATION

27

White River

**White River
Visitor Center**
🅿👁

2

To Wounded Knee
National Historic Site ↓

33   27

numbers for airlines and car-rental agencies are listed in the appendix.

For Badlands National Park information, contact Badlands National Park, P.O. Box 6, Interior, SD 57750 (© 605/ 433-5361; www.nps.gov/badl).

For information about the area, contact **South Dakota Tourism,** 711 E. Wells Ave., Pierre, SD 57501-5070 (© **800/SDAKOTA** or 605/773-3301;

fax 605/773-3256; www.travelsd.com); or the **Black Hills, Badlands & Lakes Association,** 1851 Discovery Circle, Rapid City, SD 57701 (© **605/355-3600;** www.blackhillsbadlands.com).

The National Park Service makes available a wide variety of brochures on topics including geology, prairie grasses, backpacking, biking, wildlife, plants, and use of horses in the park. You can pick up these brochures at the park visitor centers and ranger stations. In addition, *The Prairie Preamble,* published by the

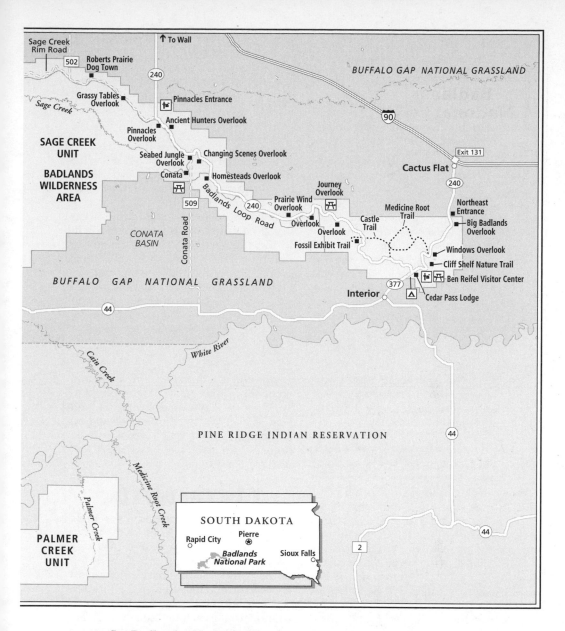

nonprofit **Badlands Natural History Association,** P.O. Box 47, Interior, SD 57750 (✆ **605/433-5489;** www.nps.gov/ badl/exp/bnha.htm), provides up-to-date information on visitor center hours, park programs, camping, and hiking trails.

Visitor centers are located at Cedar Pass and White River. The **Ben Reifel Visitor Center** at Cedar Pass is open year-round and features exhibits on the park's natural and cultural history. The **White River Visitor Center** is open June through late August only, and includes exhibits about Oglala Sioux history.

Park entry costs $10 per passenger vehicle (up to 7 days) or $5 per person on foot or bike. Members of the Oglala Sioux tribe pay half price. Camping

Tips from the Chief of Interpretation

Badlands National Park's 244,000 acres of stark scenery deserve special attention on any visitor's itinerary, according to the park's chief of interpretation, Marianne Mills.

"This park is larger than all of the other National Park Service units in the Midwest combined," Mills notes. "We have a great diversity of stories that converge here—the fossils, the prairie grasses and wildlife, Lakota history, pioneer history, and homesteading. It's all here waiting to be explored."

Mills suggests no less than 2 days to fully experience the park. "Visitors to the Badlands should at least experience a night in the park. The air is so clear here that the stars shine."

She also advises visiting in the spring or fall. "The grasses are just greening in spring, the birds are migrating, and the prairie animals are giving birth to their young. In the fall, the canyons and the ravines are filled with beautiful golden colors, the birds are migrating . . . and you can enjoy an uncrowded hike, a bike ride, or just a solitary experience."

costs $10 per site per night at the Cedar Pass Campground in summer; $8 in winter. Camping at Sage Creek Primitive Campground is free.

SPECIAL REGULATIONS & WARNINGS

Water in the Badlands is too full of silt for humans to drink and will quickly clog a water filter. When hiking or traveling in the park, always carry an adequate supply of water. Drinking water is only available at the Cedar Pass area, the White River Visitor Center, and the Pinnacles Ranger Station. No campfires are allowed. Climbing Badlands buttes and rock formations is allowed, but can be extremely dangerous due to loose, crumbly rock. Unpaved roads in the park can become dangerous in winter and during thunderstorms, when surfaces may become extremely slippery.

SEASONS & CLIMATE

Badlands weather is often unpredictable. Heavy rain, hail, and high, often damaging winds are possible, particularly during spring and summer. Lightning strikes are common. Summer temperatures often exceed 100°F (38°C),

so sunscreen, a broad-brimmed hat, and plenty of drinking water are essential to avoid severe sunburn, dehydration, and heat stroke. Winter travelers should be aware of approaching storms and be prepared for sleet, ice, heavy snow, and blizzard conditions.

If You Have Only 1 Day

It's relatively easy to explore the highlights of the North Unit of Badlands National Park in a day or less. (Most visitors spend an average of 3–5 hr.) A few miles south of the park's northeast entrance (the closest entrance to I-90), is the **park headquarters,** open year-round, which includes the Ben Reifel Visitor Center, Cedar Pass Lodge, and a campground, amphitheater, and dump station. After stopping at the visitor center exhibits, bookstore, and information desk, and after watching an orientation video (which we recommend), it's time to hit the trail.

The visitor center is located within 5 miles of several trailheads, scenic overlooks, and three self-guided nature trails. Each of the seven trails in the area offers an opportunity to view some of the formations for which the Badlands is famous. The **Fossil Exhibit Trail** is wheelchair accessible. The **Cliff Shelf Nature Trail** and the **Door Trail** are moderately strenuous and provide impressive glimpses of Badlands formations. But none are longer than 1 mile, and any one of them can be hiked comfortably in less than an hour. (See "Day Hikes," below.)

Leading directly from the visitor center is the 30-mile **Badlands Loop Road,** the park's most popular scenic drive. Angling northwest toward the town of Wall, it passes numerous overlooks and trailheads, each of which commands inspiring views of the Badlands and the prairies of the Buffalo Gap National Grassland. Binoculars will increase your chances of spotting bison, pronghorn, bighorn sheep, and coyote.

The paved portion of the Loop Road ends at the turnoff for the Pinnacles Entrance. Beyond this point the road becomes the **Sage Creek Rim Road,** a 30-mile gravel road, at the end of which is the **Sage Creek Campground.** Five miles west of the end of the pavement, a visit to the **Roberts Prairie Dog Town** gives you a chance to watch black-tailed prairie dogs "barking" their warnings and protecting their "town."

If You Have More Time

Those staying overnight have more opportunities to explore the park at a leisurely pace, taking advantage of some of the other trails, such as the **Castle Trail,** which connects the Fossil Exhibit Trail and Window Fossil Exhibit Trail, and **Notch Trail.** You could also take in some of the park's summer evening ranger programs.

Organized Tours & Ranger Programs

In addition to these suggestions, look at "Other Sports & Activities," below.

Motor Coach Tours. A number of charter bus park tours and "step-on" guide services throughout the area are available.

Gray Line of the Black Hills, P.O. Box 1106, Rapid City, SD 57709 (✆ **800/ 456-4461** or 605/342-4461; www.black hillsgrayline.com), offers bus tours of the area, with prices from $30 to $50. Tours are also available, at similar rates, from **Jack Rabbit Charter & Tours,** 301 N. Dakota Ave., Sioux Falls, SD 57104 (✆ **800/678-6543** or 605/336-3339; fax 605/336-1444; www.jackrabbitlines.com).

Ranger Programs. A limited schedule of naturalist-led walks and programs generally begins in mid-June, becoming more frequent as visitation increases. Check the activities board at the Ben Reifel Visitor Center or campground bulletin boards for times, locations, and other details. Activities vary each year, but often include the following:

- ◆ **Evolving Prairie Walk.** Generally conducted in the early evening, this 60-minute, 1-mile stroll introduces visitors to the paleontology, prairie, and people of the Badlands. Participants meet at the Ben Reifel Visitor Center.
- ◆ **Fossil Talk.** Generally slated for midmorning and late afternoon, this program allows participants to join a naturalist for a 20-minute discussion on the geological history and fossil resources of the White River Badlands. It's wheelchair accessible and meets at the Fossil Exhibit Trail.
- ◆ **Evening Program.** Begins at 9pm. These 45-minute amphitheater programs cover topics such as paleontology, geology, the prairie, and the area's human history. The program is wheelchair accessible and meets at the Cedar Pass Campground amphitheater.

Day Hikes

Numerous hiking trails provide a closer look at the Badlands for those adventurous enough to leave the comfortable confines of their vehicles. All developed trails start from parking areas within

> I've been about the world a lot and pretty much over our own country; but I was totally unprepared for that revelation called the Dakota Badlands . . . Let sculptors come to the Badlands. Let painters come. But first of all the true architect should come. He who could interpret this vast gift of nature in terms of human habitation so that Americans on their own continent might glimpse a new and higher civilization certainly, and touch it and feel it as they lived in it and deserved to call it their own. Yes, I say the aspects of the Dakota Badlands have more spiritual quality to impart to the mind of America than anything else in it made by man's God.
>
> —Frank Lloyd Wright, in a letter to a friend following his 1935 visit to the Badlands

5 miles of the Ben Reifel Visitor Center at Cedar Pass.

Castle Trail

5 miles RT. Moderate. Access: Trailheads are at the Fossil Exhibit Trail and at the Door Trail parking area.

Winding more than 5 miles through the mixed-grass prairie and badlands, this is the longest developed trail in the park and runs parallel to some interesting Badlands formations. The trail is fairly level and connects the Fossil Exhibit Trail and the Doors and Windows parking area. Just walking this trail a short distance from the Door Trail parking area brings the hiker close to outstanding formations. It's possible to make this a loop, if you follow the signs and turn off onto the well-marked Medicine Root Trail. The trail is not heavily used, making it an ideal spot to escape the crowds, but it can be treacherous during and just after a heavy rain.

Cliff Shelf Nature Trail

0.5 mile RT. Moderate. Access: 0.5 miles north of the Ben Reifel Visitor Center.

This popular trail takes you through a "slump" area where a good supply of water supports an oasis of green, which stands out in contrast to the stark badlands formations. A self-guided brochure can be purchased on the trail. The trail includes some steep sections and boardwalk stairs. Its parking lot cannot accommodate RVs towing other vehicles.

Door Trail

0.6 mile RT. Moderate. Access: 2 miles northeast of the Ben Reifel Visitor Center.

This trail winds through some of the "baddest" of the Badlands. The first 100 yards to a beautiful view at "The Door" are mostly downhill and accessible, with assistance, to those in wheelchairs. A self-guided brochure can be purchased at this point on the trail. The more rugged section takes off to the right of the viewing area; striped posts mark the way, indicating where to stop and read the trail brochure.

Fossil Exhibit Trail

0.25 mile RT. Easy. Access: 5 miles northwest of the Ben Reifel Visitor Center.

This easy boardwalk loop will give you an idea of what animal life was like 30 million years ago. A self-guided brochure can be purchased at the trailhead. Wheelchair accessible.

Notch Trail

1.5 miles RT. Moderate. Access: The north end of the Door Trail parking area.

This trail takes you up a wash between the buttes, then up a 45-degree angle wood/rope ladder, a climb that may rattle those afraid of heights. Follow the wash to the "Notch"; the payoff is a striking view overlooking the Cliff Shelf area and the White River Valley.

Saddle Pass Trail

0.25 mile RT. Moderate to strenuous. Access: This trail branches off the Castle Trail just west of its intersection with the Medicine Root Trail, and leads to the Badlands Loop Rd.

In less than 0.25 mile, this trail rises steeply 200 feet from the bottom of the Badlands Wall to the top, connecting with the Castle and Medicine Root trails. It's impassable after rains, however, so ask about trail conditions at the visitor center before you set out.

Window Trail

0.25 mile RT. Easy to moderate. Access: The trailhead is at the center of the Door Trail parking area.

A 100-yard trail leads to a spectacular view through a "window," or opening, in the Badlands Wall. Wheelchair accessible.

Exploring the Backcountry

The park encompasses the largest prairie wilderness in the United States, where expansive grasslands make cross-country travel unique. Vast ranges of classic badlands provide rugged, challenging terrain for even skilled hikers. Wildlife is close and abundant. Best of all, it's never crowded and hikers often have hundreds of acres to themselves.

Unlike many national parks in the West, the Badlands has no formal system of backcountry permits or reservations. Let friends and relatives know when you depart and when you expect to return. Rangers at the Ben Reifel Visitor Center can assist in planning a safe, enjoyable excursion by offering directions, safety tips, maps, and information sheets.

When planning your backcountry hike, examine past, present, and forecasted weather carefully. With even a small amount of precipitation, some trails can become slick and impassable. Carry water if you think you could be out for as little as a half-hour. Cross-country hikers are encouraged to carry a map, compass, and water, and to wear or carry appropriate clothing. No campfires are allowed. All overnight backcountry hikers should discuss their route with a park ranger before departure.

Spring and fall may be the best times to experience the Badlands backcountry. Days are often pleasant and nights are cool. In summer, temperatures often exceed 100° and pose health hazards. Avoid heat sickness by drinking plenty of water and avoiding the midday sun. Only the hardiest hikers attempt winter backpacking trips. Severe winter temperatures coupled with strong winds and sudden blizzards make backcountry survival difficult for those unprepared. Winter hikers should speak with a ranger at the Ben Reifel Visitor Center before setting out.

Other Sports & Activities

Aerial Tours. If you want to see the Badlands from above, you have two options: helicopter or hot-air balloon. **Badger Helicopters** (© 605/433-5322 or 608/254-4880) takes off near the park's east entrance (take I-90, Exit 131) between mid-May and mid-September. Call for current rates.

If you're looking for a hot-air-balloon adventure, call **Black Hills Balloons,** P.O. Box 210, Custer, SD 57730 (© 800/568-5320 or 605/673-2520; www.rapidnet.com/~balloons), which offers flights over the Badlands and Black Hills year-round.

Biking. Off-road biking is not allowed in the park, but the Loop Road is accessible to bikes. (There are even bike racks at the Ben Reifel Visitor Center.) The 22-mile route from Pinnacles Overlook to the Ben Reifel Visitor Center is mostly downhill (though there are several steep passes to climb). Many bikers ride along Sage Creek Rim Road, past the prairie dog town, to spectacular views of the Badlands wilderness. During summer, though, car traffic is heavy and the temperatures hot. There are no bike rentals available in the park.

Horseback Riding. Several companies offer guided trail rides through the backcountry of the Badlands (and the Black Hills), including family-run **Dakota Badland Outfitters,** P.O. Box 85, Custer, SD 57730 (✆ **605/673-5363** winter; 605/673-2999 or 605/574-2525, ext. 812 summer; www.ridesouthdakota.com). Call for rates, activities, and reservations.

Camping

A chart summarizing facilities at campgrounds in the Badlands and Black Hills area is in chapter 6.

INSIDE THE PARK

Camping is available inside Badlands National Park at either the Cedar Pass Campground or the Sage Creek Primitive Campground, on a first-come, first-served basis. Both campgrounds are suitable for both tents and RVs, and offer scenic views but little shade. Campfires are not permitted. **Cedar Pass Campground** is located just off the Loop Road and has an amphitheater and the Night Sky Interpretive Area. **Sage Creek Primitive Campground** is located at the end of Sage Creek Rim Road, a gravel road that begins at the point where the park's Loop Road turns toward the Pinnacles Entrance. Access may be limited in winter due to impassable roads.

Backcountry camping is also permitted (see "Exploring the Backcountry," above).

NEAR THE PARK

Badlands Ranch and Resort is much more than a campground. Here, in addition to the amenities noted in the campground chart in chapter 6, you'll find a barbecue area with gas grills, pool, whirlpool, playground, good fishing, rock hunting, and trail rides. For details, see the "Where to Stay" section, below.

Where to Stay

INSIDE THE PARK

Cedar Pass Lodge Cabins

Badlands National Park, P.O. Box 5, Interior, SD 57750. ✆ **605/433-5460.** Fax 605/433-5560. 22 cabins. A/C TEL. $53–$58 double. AE, DISC, MC, V. Closed Oct 15 to mid-Mar.

The Cedar Pass Lodge, adjacent to the Ben Reifel Visitor Center, offers somewhat rustic but comfortable cabins in a great location. This is the spot to be to see the Badlands at dawn and dusk—an incredible experience.

NEAR THE PARK

The closest lodging outside the park is in the tiny community of Interior. Wall, north of the park, and Rapid City, 55 miles to the west on I-90, offer hundreds of hotel and motel rooms, as well as quaint bed-and-breakfasts. Reliable chains in Wall include **Best Western Plains Motel,** 712 Glenn St., Wall, SD 57790 (✆ **605/279-2145**), charging $52 to $108 double; **Days Inn,** 10th Ave., Wall, SD 57790 (✆ **605/279-2000**), charging $47 to $84 double; and **Super 8 Motel,** 711 Glenn St., Wall, SD 57790 (✆ **605/279-2688**), with rates of $42 to $78 double. A list of toll-free numbers appears in the appendix.

Accommodations in Rapid City and the Mount Rushmore area are listed in chapter 6.

Rates vary by season, with the highest rates in summer, and some properties close for several months in winter.

IN INTERIOR

Badlands Ranch and Resort

S. Dak. 44 (HCR 53, P.O. Box 3), Interior, SD 57750. ✆ **877/433-5599** or 605/433-5599. Fax 605/433-5598. www.badlandsranchand resort.com. 7 cabins, 4 motel units, 35 RV hookups; large lodge space for up to 35. A/C TV. $62–$72 cabin, $52–$56 motel room, $12 RV hookups, $88–$150 lodge room; $500 for

The Famous Wall Drug Store

You'll see the signs offering "free ice water" at the Wall Drug Store at 510 Main St. in Wall, which is about 8 miles north of Badlands National Park on S. Dak. 240 and I-90. And you'll see them almost everywhere you go throughout the Black Hills region, all telling you how many miles it is to the small town of Wall and its eponymous drugstore. In fact, there are now more than 3,000 of these signs, all over the world. The advertising gimmick saved what used to be a small-town drugstore in an isolated community from bankruptcy during the Great Depression. But

Dorothy and Ted Hustead's gimmick also turned their little establishment into a block-long Old West emporium that now draws crowds from all over the United States and the world. You can buy pancakes or doughnuts (some of the best in the state, in fact), American Indian crafts, books, jewelry, and Western apparel, and watch the animated "cowboy band" perform every 15 minutes. Do you want a "genuine" jackalope? Yes, they've got those too. Oh, and the ice water is still free. Want to know more? Go to **www.walldrug.com**.

entire lodge; rates are negotiable during winter months. Breakfast is included in the lodge room rates only. AE, DISC, MC, V. From the park, head west on S. Dak. 44 approximately 6 miles toward Interior; when you go past the KOA Campground, look for the marked turnoff that leads to the resort's grounds.

This friendly, year-round resort, which opened in 1997, is located on 1,000 picturesque acres with views of the Badlands and plenty of wildlife to see. In addition to the several accommodations options, there is also a campground (see "Camping," above). The resort offers a pool and a hot tub, plus nightly bonfires and cookouts with entertainment, two fishing lakes, and horseback trails (moonlight trail rides can also be arranged). If you wish, the owners can also help arrange guided tours of the area's attractions and the adjoining American Indian reservation. Cabins and motel units are comfortable and well maintained. Rooms in the lodge are more plush—we suggest the delightful top-floor honeymoon suite, which has a sunroom, whirlpool, and great views of the Badlands.

Where to Dine

INSIDE THE PARK

Cedar Pass Lodge Restaurant

Cedar Pass Lodge. © **605/433-5460.** Main courses $5–$9. AE, DISC, MC, V. Open daily for all meals, call for hours. Closed late Oct to mid-Apr.

Located near the Ben Reifel Visitor Center in the park's North Unit, the lodge's restaurant (the only dining choice inside the park) has a full menu ranging from buffalo burgers to steaks and trout, as well as ice-cold soft drinks, beer, and wine for superb after-hike refreshments.

NEAR THE PARK

In Interior, the **Wooden Knife Cafe,** at the junction of S. Dak. 44 and S. Dak. 377, on Interior's east side (© **605/433-5463;** www.woodenknife.com), is home to what it calls its "world-famous Wooden Knife Indian Fry Bread," plus other authentic American Indian dishes, burgers, chicken, and old-fashioned scoop ice cream. It's an inexpensive place to stop for a quick meal.

Several other eating places are located in the communities surrounding Badlands National Park, including Interior and Wall (see the sidebar "The Famous Wall Drug Store," above). Establishments in Rapid City and the communities surrounding Mount Rushmore are listed in chapter 6.

Picnicking in the Park

Badlands National Park has two designated picnic areas, though you're likely to see people munching at nearly every overlook and trailhead in the park.

Conata Picnic Area is located on Conata Road, just south of Dillon Pass and the Badlands Loop Road in the North Unit. It has tables, trash cans, and pit toilets. Camping and fires are not allowed, and there is no drinking water available.

Big Foot Picnic Area is located near Big Foot Pass on the Badlands Loop Road in the North Unit, about 7 miles northwest of the Ben Reifel Visitor Center. It also has tables and pit toilets, but no drinking water. Camping and fires are not allowed.

Nearby Attractions

Beyond the boundaries of Badlands National Park are several other areas and sites that you may wish to visit, including **Mount Rushmore National Memorial, Wind Cave National Park, Jewel Cave National Monument, Custer State Park,** and **Crazy Horse Memorial.** All are discussed in chapter 6.

4

BIG BEND NATIONAL PARK

by Don & Barbara Laine

AST AND WILD, BIG BEND NATIONAL PARK IS A LAND OF EXTREMES, diversity, and a few contradictions. Its rugged terrain harbors thousands of species of plants and animals—some seen almost nowhere else on earth. A visit to the park can be a hike into the sun-baked desert, a float down a majestic canyon-land river, or a trek in mountains where bears and mountain lions rule.

Geologists tell us that this area was once covered by an inland sea. As it dried up, sediments of sand and mud turned to rock. Tectonic plates collided and mountains were created; further upheaval occurred later from volcanic eruptions. It took millions of years of geologic activity and subsequent erosion to form the delightful canyons and rock formations we marvel at today. These rock formations—with their wonderful hues of red, orange, yellow, white, and brown—have created a unique and awe-inspiring world of immense and rugged beauty. This is not a fantasyland of delicate shapes and intricate carvings, such as Bryce Canyon in Utah, but a powerful and dominating landscape. Although the greatest natural sculptures can be seen in the park's three major river canyons—the Santa Elena, Marsical, and Boquillas—throughout Big Bend you'll find spectacular and majestic examples of what nature can do with

this mighty yet malleable building material we call rock.

Visitors to Big Bend National Park encounter not only a geologic wonder, but also a wild, rugged wilderness, populated by myriad desert and mountain plants and animals, ranging from box turtles and black-tailed jackrabbits to funny-looking javelina and powerful black bears and mountain lions. The park is considered a birders' paradise, with more species than at any other national park. It's also a wonderful spot to see wildflowers and the colorful display of cactus blooms.

For hikers, the park offers a tremendous variety of trails, from easy walks to rugged backcountry routes that barely qualify as trails at all. There are also opportunities to let the Rio Grande do the work, carrying watersports enthusiasts on rafts, canoes, and kayaks through canyons carved into 1,500 feet of solid rock. Adventurers with 4WDs enjoy exploring the backcountry roads, and history buffs enjoy a number of historical attractions and cultural experiences.

Avoiding the Crowds. Average annual visitation is just over 300,000. Although the park is relatively uncrowded much of the year, there are several periods when lodging and campgrounds are full: college spring break (usually the second and third weeks in Mar), Easter weekend, Thanksgiving weekend, and the week between Christmas and New Year's Day. Park visitation is generally highest in March and April, and lowest in August and September.

Although the park's visitor centers, campgrounds, and other developed facilities may be overburdened during the busier times, visitors can still be practically alone simply by seeking out lesser-used hiking trails. Discuss your hiking skills and expectations with rangers, who can offer advice on the best areas to get away from the crowds.

Just the Facts

GETTING THERE & GATEWAYS

Big Bend National Park is not really close to anything except the Rio Grande and Mexico. There is no public transportation to or through the park.

Park headquarters is 108 miles southeast of the town of Alpine via Tex. 118 and 69 miles south of Marathon via U.S. 385. There is train and bus service to Alpine, where you'll also find car rentals and the nearest hospital to the park. For information, contact the **Alpine Chamber of Commerce** (© **800/561-3735** or 915/837-2326; www.alpinetexas.com).

From El Paso, 323 miles northwest of the park, take I-10 east 121 miles to Exit 140, follow U.S. 90 southeast 99 miles to Alpine, then turn south on Tex. 118 for 108 miles to park headquarters.

The Nearest Airport. The nearest airport is **Midland International** (© **432/560-2200;** www.midlandinternational. com), 225 miles north, serviced by **American Eagle, Continental,** and **Southwest Airlines.** From the airport, located between Midland and Odessa,

take I-20 west about 50 miles to Exit 80 for Tex. 18, which you follow south about 50 miles to Fort Stockton. There take U.S. 385 south 125 miles through Marathon to park headquarters. Car rentals are available from the major national companies. Toll-free numbers for airlines and car-rental agencies are given in the appendix.

INFORMATION

For information, contact the **Superintendent,** P.O. Box 129, **Big Bend National Park,** TX 79834 (© **432/477-2251;** www.nps.gov/bibe).

The free park newspaper, *The Big Bend Paisano,* published seasonally by the National Park Service, is a great source of current information on seminars, new or special publications, suggested hikes, kids' activities, and local facilities, with telephone numbers inside and outside the park.

Books, maps, and videos are available from **Big Bend Natural History Association,** P.O. Box 196, Big Bend National Park, TX 79834 (© **432/477-2236;** www. bigbendbookstore.org). The *Official Big Bend National Park Handbook* (Washington, D.C.: Department of the Interior, 1983) by the Division of Publications, National Park Service, is a good introduction to the what and why of the park, describing in detail the terrain, flora, fauna, and human history of the area. Several booklets produced by the Park Service detail improved and unimproved roads and hiking trails. A particularly good hiking guide is *Hiking Big Bend National Park* (Helena, Montana: Falcon Press, 1996) by Laurence Parent. Those planning backpacking trips will also want to get the appropriate topo maps, which, along with the publications discussed above, are available at the park's visitor centers or by mail from the Big Bend Natural History Association.

For information on nearby attractions, as well as places to stay and eat, contact the **Big Bend Area Travel Association** (© **877/244-2363;** www. visitbigbend.com).

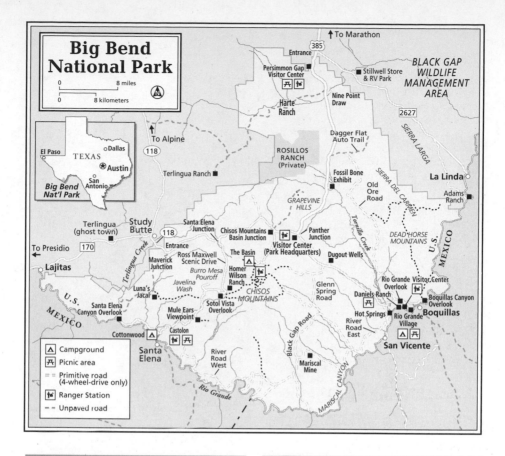

Big Bend National Park

0   8 miles
0   8 kilometers

TEXAS
- El Paso
- Dallas
- Austin
- San Antonio
- Big Bend Nat'l Park

To Marathon

Entrance 385

Persimmon Gap Visitor Center

Stillwell Store & RV Park

BLACK GAP WILDLIFE MANAGEMENT AREA

Nine Point Draw

Harte Ranch

2627

SIERRA LARGA

To Alpine 118

Dagger Flat Auto Trail

ROSILLOS RANCH (Private)

Terlingua Ranch

Fossil Bone Exhibit

Old Ore Road

La Linda

Adams Ranch

SIERRA DEL CARMEN

GRAPEVINE HILLS

Terlingua (ghost town)

Study Butte 118

Santa Elena Junction

Chisos Mountains Basin Junction

Panther Junction

Visitor Center (Park Headquarters)

Dugout Wells

DEAD HORSE MOUNTAINS

Tornillo Creek

Rio Grande Visitor Center

To Presidio 170

Entrance

Ross Maxwell Scenic Drive

The Basin

Homer Wilson Ranch

Daniels Ranch

Rio Grande Village Overlook

Boquillas Canyon Overlook

Lajitas

Maverick Junction

Burro Mesa Pouroff

CHISOS MOUNTAINS

Glenn Spring Road

Boquillas

Javelina Wash

Luna's Jacal

Sotol Vista Overlook

Hot Springs

Rio Grande Village

River Road East

Santa Elena Canyon Overlook

Mule Ears Viewpoint

Castolon

Santa Elena

River Road West

San Vicente

Cottonwood

Mariscal Mine

Rio Grande

MARISCAL CANYON

U.S. MEXICO

Terlingua Creek

Legend:
- △ Campground
- 🛆 Picnic area
- = = Primitive road (4-wheel-drive only)
- Ranger Station
- - - Unpaved road

VISITOR CENTERS

The park has four visitor centers. **Panther Junction Visitor Center** (open daily year-round) is centrally located at park headquarters; **Persimmon Gap Visitor Center** (open most of the year) is at the north entrance to the park on U.S. 385; **Rio Grande Village Visitor Center** (open Nov–Apr) is on the river in the eastern part of the park; and **Chisos Basin Visitor Center** (open year-round) is in the Chisos Mountains in the middle of the park, at 5,401 feet in elevation.

All visitor centers provide information, backcountry permits, books, and maps, and also have exhibits; a particularly impressive display on mountain lions can be seen at Chisos Basin. At **Castolon,** near the river in the southwest end of the park, there is a visitor contact station. Bulletin boards with schedules of ranger programs, notices of animal sightings, and other visitor information are located at each of the visitor centers and the contact station.

FEES & PERMITS

Entry into the park for up to a week costs $15 per passenger vehicle, and $5 per person on foot or bicycle. Camping costs $10 per night in the three developed campgrounds. There's a concession-operated RV campground at Rio Grande Village, with full hookups, costing $18. A free camping permit, available at any visitor center, is required for all backcountry camping; free permits are also required for all river-float trips (see "Camping" and "River Running," later in this chapter).

SPECIAL REGULATIONS & WARNINGS

Watch for wildlife along the roads, particularly javelina, reptiles, deer, and rabbits, and especially at night when they may be blinded by your vehicle's headlights and freeze in the middle of the road. Of course, feeding wildlife is prohibited, not only to minimize the

Tips from a Park Ranger

"This park has something for everyone," says David Elkowitz, Big Bend's chief of interpretation and visitor services. High among the park's assets, he says, is its variety of activities, including both easy day hikes and extended backpacking trips, great bird-watching, wildlife viewing, river running, and camping.

Big Bend is not a good choice for a quick visit, and Elkowitz recommends that people spend at least 3 days. "Be prepared for long distances, and don't expect all the amenities you might find in other places," he says.

Although Big Bend is one of America's lesser-used national parks, Elkowitz says that it does get busy occasionally, particularly during spring break time, usually March and early April, when college students arrive en masse to hit the trails. The hottest months are May and June, he says, adding that the heat of July and August is usually tempered by afternoon thunderstorms. September is among the slowest times in the park, and it can be very nice, although still hot. "October is a great time, still quiet and a bit cooler," he says.

Elkowitz advises summer visitors to avoid hiking in the desert, but it's a "good time to visit the higher and cooler Chisos Mountains, which offer camping and miles of good trails." Here it can be 20° cooler than on the river. He also recommends hiking into the high country from October through December to see the beautiful fall colors. On the other hand, the desert is a "wonderful choice for fall and winter hiking into remote areas, with few, if any, other visitors."

risk of injuries to park visitors, but also because it's bad for the animals.

The Basin Road Scenic Drive into the Chisos Mountains has sharp curves and steep grades and is not recommended for trailers longer than 20 feet or RVs longer than 24 feet. The **Ross Maxwell Scenic Drive** to Castolon is okay for most RVs and trailers but can present a problem for vehicles with insufficient power to handle the steep grade. These roads require extra caution by all users— drivers of motor vehicles, pedestrians, and bicyclists. Horses are not permitted on any paved roads in the park.

Desert heat can be dangerous. Hikers should carry at least 1 gallon of water per person per day; wear a hat, long pants, and long sleeves; and use a good sunscreen. Don't depend on springs as water sources, and avoid hiking in the middle of the day in summer. Early mornings and evenings are best for both comfort and sightseeing. Talk to rangers about your plans before heading out; they can help you plan a hike in accordance with your ability and time frame. Check with rangers about weather forecasts—sudden summer thunderstorms are common and can cause flash flooding in usually dry washes and canyons.

Swimming is not recommended in the Rio Grande, even though it may look tantalizingly inviting on a hot summer day. Waste materials and waterborne microorganisms have been found in the river and can cause serious illness. Also, strong undercurrents, deep holes, and sharp rocks in shallow water are common. Should you decide to swim in spite of these warnings, be sure to wear a life jacket.

Wood or ground fires are prohibited in the park, and caution is advised when using camp stoves, charcoal grills, and cigarettes. Smoking is prohibited on all trails. Check at the visitor centers for current drought conditions and for any special restrictions that may be in effect when you visit.

SEASONS & CLIMATE

Weather here is generally mild to hot, although because of the vast range of elevations—from about 1,800 feet at the eastern end of Boquillas Canyon to 7,825 feet on Emory Peak in the Chisos Mountains—conditions can vary greatly throughout the park at any given time. Essentially, the higher you go, the cooler and wetter you can expect it to be, although no section of the park gets a lot of precipitation.

Summers here are hot, often well over 100°F (38°C) in the desert in May and June, and afternoon thunderstorms are common from July through September. Winters are usually mild, although temperatures occasionally drop below freezing, and light snow is possible, especially in the Chisos Mountains. Fall and spring are usually warm and pleasant.

If You Have Only 1 Day

Big Bend National Park is huge, and you can't hope to see all of it in 1 day or even 2. It's best to allow at least 3 days, essentially devoting 1 day each to the desert, river, and mountains. If you have a limited amount of time in the park, however, the best choice is to start with the **Chisos Basin** and see the mountains in the middle of the park. Take the short, easy **Window View Trail,** a self-guided nature trail (see "Day Hikes," below) that discusses the flora and fauna of the Chisos Mountains. Then head back down and drive the **Ross Maxwell Scenic Drive** (see "Exploring the Park by Car," below) through the Chihuahuan Desert to the Rio Grande. If time allows, hike into **Santa Elena Canyon** (see "Day Hikes," below), one of the most beautiful canyons in the

park. Finally, take in a ranger program at one of the park amphitheaters.

Exploring the Park by Car

The park has several paved roads—one goes through the park and others take you to different sections. In addition, there are several roads requiring high clearance or 4WD vehicles (see "Backcountry Driving," later in this chapter).

The park has two scenic drives, both with sharp curves and steep inclines and not recommended for certain RVs and trailers (see "Special Regulations & Warnings," above).

The 7-mile **Chisos Basin Drive** climbs up Green Gulch to Panther Pass before dropping down into the Basin. Near the pass there are some sharp curves, and parts of the road are at a 10% grade. The views are wonderful any time of the year, and particularly when the wildflowers dot the meadows, hills, and roadsides. The best month for wildflowers is usually October, after the summer rains.

When you've breathed your fill of clear mountain air, head back down and turn west toward the **Ross Maxwell Scenic Drive** through the Chihuahuan Desert and finally to the Rio Grande. This drive winds through the desert on the west side of the Chisos Mountains, providing a different perspective. Afterward, it passes through Castolon and then continues along and above the river to **Santa Elena Canyon.** Here you should park and hike the trail, which climbs above the river, offering great views into the steep, narrow canyon (see "Day Hikes," below).

Another worthwhile drive, recommended for all vehicles, begins at **Panther Junction Visitor Center** and goes to Rio Grande Village, a distance of 20 miles. From the visitor center, head southeast through the desert toward the high mountains that form the skyline in the distance. The first half of the drive passes through desert grasses, which are finally making a comeback after severe

Keeping the Wild in Wildlife, or How to Avoid an Unpleasant Encounter

The signs and warnings are everywhere: "THIS IS BEAR AND MOUNTAIN LION COUNTRY," and although one of the thrills of visiting Big Bend National Park is the opportunity to see wildlife, for the safety of both the human visitors and the park's wildlife, these animals should always be viewed from a distance. Rangers say that since the 1950s there have been more than 1,000 sightings of mountain lions in the park, and numerous sightings of black bears. Although the vast majority of encounters have been relatively uneventful—albeit definitely something to tell the neighbors about when you get home—four people have been attacked by mountain lions in the park. Fortunately, all recovered from their injuries; unfortunately, it was considered necessary to kill the mountain lions.

Hikers, especially in the Chisos Mountains, should be especially careful to minimize the danger of an encounter. First, discuss your hiking plans with park rangers to see if there have been any recent mountain lion sightings where you plan to hike. Don't hike alone, especially at dawn or dusk. Watch children carefully—never let them run ahead. If you do end up face-to-face with a mountain lion, rangers offer these tips: Don't run, but stand your ground, shout, wave your arms, and try to appear as large as possible. If you have children with you, pick them up. If the mountain lion acts aggressively, throw stones, and try to convince it that not only are you not prey, but also that you may be dangerous. Then report the incident to a ranger as soon as possible.

The other animal you may see is one of the estimated 10 to 20 black bears that currently live in the Chisos Mountains. Bears are attracted to food, and the best way to avoid an unwanted encounter with a bear is to keep a clean camp. Park rangers recommend that you store all foodstuffs, cooking utensils, and toiletries in a hard-sided vehicle. Food storage lockers are available for hikers and campers in the Chisos Mountains. Always dispose of garbage properly in the receptacles provided. If you do see a bear, keep a safe distance; do not approach or follow it, and of course, never attempt to feed a bear. If a bear approaches you, scare it away by shouting, waving your arms, or throwing rocks or sticks. Watch for cubs—you never want to be between a mother bear and her cubs. Report any sightings of bears to a ranger.

Bears and mountain lions aren't the only wild animals in the park. Many visitors see javelinas (officially known as collared peccaries), which look a bit like their rather distant relative, pigs, and are very nearsighted. A group of 10 to 20 are often seen in and near Rio Grande Village Campground. Some of them have learned to recognize the crinkling sound of potato chip bags, and will run toward the sound in hopes of a snack. Although javelinas are not aggressive, they are easily frightened, and could inflict some damage with the javelin-sharp tusks from which they get their name. Please help to protect these wild animals: Never actively feed them and always practice proper food storage.

Also deserving of mention are the park's poisonous snakes, scorpions, spiders, and centipedes, which are most active during the warmer months. Rangers advise that you watch carefully where you put your feet and hands, and use flashlights at night. Hikers may want to consider wearing high boots or protective leggings. It's also a good idea to check your shoes and bedding before use. Although few find these creatures cute or cuddly, they are an important part of the park ecosystem, and should be respected and protected—by avoiding them whenever possible.

overgrazing in the decades before the establishment of the park in 1944. Recovery is slow in this harsh climate, but it is beginning to revegetate.

As you progress farther into the desert, the elevation gradually decreases, and the grasses give way to lechugilla and ocotillo stalks, cacti, and other arid-climate survivors. To the south is the long, rather flat **Chilicotal Mountain,** named for the chilicote, or mescal-bean bushes, growing near its base. The chilicote's poisonous red bean is used in Mexico to kill rats. Several miles farther the River Road turns off and heads southwest toward Castolon, more than 50 miles away. This primitive road is for high-clearance vehicles only.

If you feel adventurous, take the **Hot Springs** turnoff about a mile beyond the Tornillo Creek Bridge. It follows a rough wash to a point overlooking the confluence of Tornillo Creek and the Rio Grande. A trail along the riverbank leads to several springs. The foundation of a bathhouse is a remnant of the town of Hot Springs, which thrived here about 20 years before the park was established, and continued as a concession for another 10 years.

Back on the paved road, you'll soon pass through a short tunnel in the limestone cliff, after which is a parking area for a short trail to a viewpoint overlooking Rio Grande Village. It's just a short drive from here to **Rio Grande Village,** your destination, where you can take a 0.75-mile nature trail ending at a high point above the Rio Grande that offers terrific views up and down the river, as well as some great bird-watching opportunities.

Organized Tours & Ranger Programs

Park ranger naturalists offer a variety of programs year-round. Illustrated evening programs take place at the **Chisos Basin amphitheater** in summer. From November through April, evening programs are offered regularly in the amphitheater at

Rio Grande Village and occasionally at Cottonwood Campground. Subjects include the park's geology, plants, animals, and human history. Rangers also offer guided **nature walks** and occasionally lead **driving tours.** Workshops are also planned on subjects such as adobe construction or photography. Look for weekly schedules on the bulletin boards scattered about the park.

The **Big Bend Natural History Association** (see "Information," earlier in this chapter) offers a variety of seminars, ranging from 1-day workshops starting at $40, to multiday programs starting at $80. Subjects could include black bears, archaeology, bats, birds, cacti, and wildflowers. A 1-day introductory overview covers the plants, animals, geology, and history of the park. In recent years there have also been multiday photography workshops by noted nature photographer Jim Bones.

Historic & Man-Made Attractions

There is evidence that both prehistoric American Indians and later Apaches, Kiowas, and Comanches occupied this area. Throughout the park you can find **petroglyphs, pictographs,** and other signs of early human presence, including ruins of **stone shelters.** Pictographs can be found along the Hot Spring Trail (see "Day Hikes," below), and along the river. Watch for **mortar holes** scattered throughout the park, sometimes a foot deep, where American Indians would grind seeds or mesquite beans.

Also within the park boundaries are the remains of several early-20th-century communities, a mercury mine, and projects by the Civilian Conservation Corps (see below).

The **Castolon Historic District,** located in the southwest section of the park just off the Ross Maxwell Scenic Drive, includes the remains of homes and other buildings, many stabilized by the National Park Service, that were constructed in the early 1900s by

Mexican-American farmers, Anglo settlers, and the U.S. Army. The first is the **Alvino House,** the oldest surviving adobe structure in the park, dating from 1901. Nearby is **La Harmonia Store,** built in 1920 to house cavalry troops during the Mexican Revolution, but never actually used by soldiers because the war ended. Two civilians then purchased the building, converting it to a general store. The store continues to operate, selling snacks, groceries, and other necessities.

The village of **Glenn Springs,** located in the southeast section of the park and accessible by dirt road off the main park highway, owes its creation to having a reliable water source in an otherwise arid area. It was named for a rancher called H. E. Glenn, who grazed horses in the area until he was killed by American Indians in the 1880s. By 1916 there were several ranches, a factory that produced wax from the candelilla plant, a store, a post office, and a residential village divided into two sections—one for Anglos and the other for Mexicans. But then Mexican bandit-revolutionaries crossed the border and attacked, killing and wounding a number of people, looting the store, and partially destroying the wax factory. Within 3 years the community was virtually deserted. Today, the spring still flows, and you can see the remains of several adobe buildings and other structures.

Remains of a small health resort can be seen at the **Hot Springs,** accessible by hiking trail or dirt road, along the Rio Grande west of Rio Grande Village in the park's southeast section. Construction of the resort was begun in 1909 by J. O. Langford, who was forced to leave during the Mexican Revolution. Langford returned, however, and completed the project in the 1920s, advertising the Hot Springs as "The Fountain of Youth that Ponce de León failed to find." Today you'll see the ruins of a general store/post office, other buildings, and a foundation that fills with natural mineral water, at about 105°F (41°C), creating an almost natural hot tub.

To get to the **Marsical Mine** you will likely need a four-wheel-drive or high-clearance vehicle. Located in the south-central part of the park, it is most easily accessed by River Road East, which begins 5 miles west of Rio Grande Village. The mine operated on and off between 1900 and 1943, producing 1,400 76-pound flasks of mercury, which was almost one-quarter of the total amount of mercury produced in the United States during that time. Mining buildings, homes, the company store, a kiln, foundations, and other structures remain, in what is now a National Historic District.

Also in the park you can see some excellent examples of the work done by the **Civilian Conservation Corps** in the 1930s and early 1940s. These include stone culverts along the Basin Road, the Lost Mine Trail, and several buildings, including some stone-and-adobe cottages that are still in use at the Chisos Mountain Lodge.

Day Hikes

SHORTER TRAILS

Boquillas Canyon Trail

1.4 miles RT. Moderate. Access: End of Boquillas Canyon Rd.

This hike, a good choice for those who want to see some of the area's birds, begins by climbing a low hill and then drops down to the Rio Grande, ending near a shallow cave and huge sand dune. There are good views of the scenic canyon and the Mexican village of **Boquillas,** across the Rio Grande.

Burro Mesa Pour-Off

1 mile RT. Easy. Access: Parking area at the end of Burro Mesa spur road, about 12 miles down the Ross Maxwell Scenic Dr. on the west (right).

This short hike takes you to the bottom of a desert pour-off. The beginning of the trail is a well-marked path, but as you turn into Javelina Wash it becomes less obvious, so watch for the lines of rocks pointing the way. The trail has an elevation gain of about 60 feet. The pour-off is a long, narrow chute that is usually dry, but the extensive cut gives testimony to the power of rushing water after a heavy summer rain. Don't attempt to climb to the top from here; it is quite hazardous. There is an easier way for those with good route-finding skills: See "Top of Burro Mesa Pour-Off," below.

Chihuahuan Desert Nature Trail

0.5 mile RT. Easy. Access: Dugout Wells Picnic Area, 6 miles east of Panther Junction.

A good introduction to the flora of the Chihuahuan Desert, this is an easy stroll along a relatively flat gravel path with signs describing the plants you see along the way.

Chisos Basin Loop Trail

1.6-miles loop. Easy. Access: Chisos Basin Trailhead.

This fairly easy walk climbs about 350 feet into a pretty meadow and leads to an overlook that offers good views of the park's mountains, including **Emory Peak,** highest point in the park at 7,825 feet.

Hot Springs Trail

1 mile RT. Easy. Access: End of improved dirt road to Hot Springs, off road to Rio Grande Village.

An interpretive booklet available at the trailhead describes the sights, including a historic health resort and homestead (see "Historic & Man-Made Attractions," above), along this easy loop. Fairly substantial **ruins** remain of a general store/post office, other buildings, and a foundation that fills with natural mineral water, at about 105°F (41°C), creating an inviting hot tub. Also along the trail are **pictographs** left by ancient American Indians, and panoramic views of the Rio Grande and Mexico.

Panther Path

50 yards RT. Easy. Access: Panther Junction Visitor Center.

This is a short walk through a **garden of cacti** and other desert plants. A booklet discussing the park's plant life is available at the trailhead.

Rio Grande Village Nature Trail

0.75 mile RT. Easy. Access: Southeast corner of Rio Grande Village Campground, across from site 18.

A good choice for sunrise and sunset views, this self-guided loop nature trail (booklet available at the trailhead) climbs from the surprisingly lush river floodplain about 125 feet into desert terrain and up a hilltop that offers excellent panoramic views.

Santa Elena Canyon

0.8 mile one-way. Moderate. Access: End of Ross Maxwell Scenic Dr.

You may get your feet wet crossing a broad creek on this trail, which also takes you up a series of steep steps. But it's one of the most scenic short trails in the park, leading along the canyon wall (with good views of rafters on the Rio Grande), and continuing down among the boulders along the river. Interpretive signs describe the canyon environment. Beware of flash flooding as you cross the Terlingua Creek, and skip this trail altogether if the creek is running swiftly.

Top of Burro Mesa Pour-Off

1.8 miles one-way. Moderate. Access: Trailhead parking about 7 miles down the Ross Maxwell Scenic Dr. on the west (right).

This moderate hike takes you through some narrow rocky gorges to the top of the Burro Mesa Pour-Off. The trail may not be well marked, so it's a good idea to carry a topographical map and compass. As you hike along the now-dry washes, you'll realize that the rock cairns marking the trail are quickly scattered when water floods through them. There is a gradual decline of about 525 feet to the top of this desert waterfall, where the drainage drops suddenly and precipitously from the wash where you stand to the one below. Do not chance this hike in stormy weather or you might get washed away with the rock cairns.

Tuff Canyon

0.75 mile RT. Easy. Access: Ross Maxwell Scenic Dr., 5 miles south of Mule Ears Overlook access road.

This easy trail leads into a narrow canyon, carved from soft volcanic rock called tuff, with several canyon overlooks.

Window View Trail

0.3 mile RT. Easy. Access: Chisos Basin Trailhead.

Level, paved, and wheelchair accessible, this self-guided nature trail (a brochure is available at the trailhead) runs along a low hill and has a great variety of plant life. In addition, it offers magnificent sunset views through the Window, a V-shaped opening in the mountains to the west.

LONGER TRAILS

Chimneys Trail

4.8 miles RT (to the chimneys). Moderate. Access: Ross Maxwell Scenic Dr., 1.2 miles south of the Burro Mesa Pour-Off access road.

This flat trail through the desert follows an old dirt road to a series of chimney-shaped rock formations. American Indian **petroglyphs** can be seen on the southernmost chimney, and nearby are **ruins of rock shelters**. Those who want to extend this hike can continue to a **desert spring,** although the trail is difficult to follow after the Chimneys and a topographical map is highly recommended.

Grapevine Hills Trail

2.2 miles RT. Easy. Access: 6 miles down the unpaved Grapevine Hills Rd.

An easy walk, this trail follows a sandy wash through the desert, among massive granite boulders, ending at a picturesque **balancing rock.** There is an elevation change of about 240 feet.

Lost Mine Trail

4.8 miles RT. Moderate. Access: Chisos Basin Rd. at Panther Pass.

This self-guided nature trail (a booklet is available at the trailhead) is a popular mountain hike that climbs about 1,100 feet. It was built in the early 1940s by the Civilian Conservation Corps—evidence of their rock work can still be seen. Along the way, the trail climbs through **forests of pinyon, juniper, and oak,** and offers splendid views. Those with limited time or ambition don't have to hike all the way—some of the trail's best views are about 1 mile from the trailhead, from a saddle where you can look out over a pretty canyon to the surrounding mountains and even deep into Mexico.

Mule Ears Spring Trail

3.8 miles RT. Moderate. Access: Mule Ears Overlook parking area, along the Ross Maxwell Scenic Dr.

This relatively flat desert trail crosses several arroyos and then follows a wash most of the way to Mule Ears Spring. It offers great views of unusual rock formations, such as the **Mule Ears,** and ends at a **historic ranch house and rock corral.**

Pine Canyon Trail

4 miles RT. Moderate. Access: End of unpaved Pine Canyon Rd. (check on road conditions before going).

With a 1,000-foot elevation gain, this trail takes you from desert grasslands, dotted with sotols, into a pretty canyon with dense stands of pinyon, juniper, oak, and finally bigtooth maple and ponderosa pine. At the higher elevations you'll also see **Texas madrones**—evergreen trees whose smooth reddish bark is shed each summer. At the end of the trail is a **200-foot cliff,** which becomes a picturesque waterfall after heavy rains. At the cliff's base you're likely to see the delicate yellow flowers of **columbine,** a member of the buttercup family.

Slickrock Canyon

10 miles RT. Moderate. Access: Main Park Rd., about 12 miles west of Panther Junction, at Oak Creek Bridge.

This hike follows Oak Creek northwest to a small, scenic canyon, passing along the south edge of Slickrock Mountain. This is not a marked trail but rather a route through sand and gravel washes, and a topographical map is helpful. Hikers in this deep canyon will find desert plants such as mesquite and creosote bush, and possibly tracks of coyotes, javelinas, and mountain lions.

Window Trail

5.2 miles RT. Moderate. Access: Chisos Basin Trailhead.

A scenic trail through Oak Creek Canyon, this hike involves descending about 800 feet to the base of the **Window,** a V-shaped opening in the mountains that frames panoramic desert scenes. Following the Oak Creek drainage, it provides a good chance to see deer, javelina, rock squirrels, and a variety of birds.

Exploring the Backcountry

The park offers numerous possibilities for backpacking, both on established and marked hiking trails and on relatively unmarked hiking routes following washes, canyons, or abandoned rough dirt roads dating from the late 1800s. In all, the park has more than 150 miles of designated trails and routes. Cross-country hiking is also permitted. Because many trails and hiking routes are hard to follow, rangers advise that hikers carry detailed 7.5-minute topographical maps and compasses.

Campers can use numerous designated backcountry campsites and are also allowed to camp in desert areas. The required free permits must be obtained in person, no more than 24 hours in advance. In the high Chisos Mountains, backcountry campers must stay at designated campsites and carry special permits, available on a first-come, first-served basis. These campsites are often difficult to obtain during the park's busiest times—Thanksgiving and Christmas holidays and college spring-break season (usually Mar or early Apr).

Ground fires are prohibited throughout the park. Rangers warn that backcountry water availability is spotty and changeable, and advise backpackers to carry enough water for their entire trip.

Other Sports & Activities

A local company that provides equipment rentals, shuttle services, and a variety of guided adventures both in the park and the general area is **Desert Sports** (© **888/989-6900** or 432/371-2727; www.desertsportstx.com), located on FM 170, 5 miles west of the junction of FM 170 and Tex. 118.

Backcountry Driving. Big Bend has a number of unimproved roads requiring high-clearance vehicles and sometimes four-wheel-drive. Many have roadside campsites. Get details on current road conditions from rangers before setting out, and pick up the useful backcountry road guide, available at visitor centers. All overnight trips require backcountry permits. **Texas River and Jeep Expeditions** (© **800/839-7238** or 432/371-2633; www.texasriver.com) offers four-wheel-drive tours of the area, including trips into the national park. The most popular trip costs $55 per person for 3 hours. The nearest four-wheel-drive rentals are in Alpine, Texas, 108 miles northwest of the park.

Horseback Riding. Horses are permitted on most dirt roads and many park trails (check with rangers for specifics), and may be kept overnight at many of the park's primitive road campsites, although not at the developed campgrounds. The **Government Springs**

Campsite, located 3½ miles from Panther Junction, is a primitive campsite with a corral that accommodates up to eight horses. It can be reserved up to 10 weeks in advance (✆ **432/477-2251,** ext. 158). Those riding horses in the park must get free stock use permits, which should be obtained in person up to 24 hours in advance at any of the park's visitor centers.

Although there are no commercial outfitters offering guided rides in the park as of this writing, there are opportunities for rides just outside the park on private land, at nearby Big Bend Ranch State Park. **Big Bend Stables** (✆ **800/ 887-4331** or 432/371-2212), and **Lajitas Stables** (✆ **888/508-7667** or 432/424-3238; www.lajitasstables.com), offer a variety of guided trail rides, lasting from 1 hour to all day to 5 days. Some trips follow canyon trails; others visit ancient American Indian camps, ghost towns, or abandoned mines. They can also take you to see pictographs, fossils, and petrified wood. Both stables are under the same management, and the company also has access to facilities in Mexico. Rates are $25 for a 1-hour ride, $58 for a 4-hour ride, and $110 for a full day in the saddle. Multiday trips are usually about $140 to $175 per day, and include all meals and camping equipment, as well as the horse. Novice riders and children 4 and up are welcome.

Mountain Biking. Bikes are not permitted on hiking trails but are allowed on the park's many established dirt roads. Mountain bikes are available for rent from **Desert Sports** (see above), starting at about $30 per day. The company also offers 1-day and multiday guided trips, including a combination mountain-biking and float trip in the park—3 days for $450.

River Running. The Rio Grande follows the southern edge of the park for 118 miles, and extends another 127 miles downstream as a designated Wild and Scenic River. The river offers mostly fairly calm float trips, but does have a few sections of rough white water during high-water times. It can usually be run in a raft, canoe, or kayak. Either bring your own equipment or rent equipment near the park (none is available in the park), or take a trip with one of several local river guides under permit by the National Park Service. *Note:* The water can be quite low in summer, so call ahead if this is an important part of your visit.

Those planning trips on their own must obtain free permits at a park visitor center, in person only, no more than 24 hours before the trip. Permits for the lower canyons of the Rio Grande Wild and Scenic River are available at the **Persimmon Gap Visitor Center,** when it's open, and at a self-serve permit station located at **Stillwell Store and RV Park,** 7 miles from the park's north entrance on FM 2627. Permits for the section of river through Santa Elena Canyon can also be obtained at the **Barton Warnock Environmental Education Center** 1 mile east of the community of Lajitas, Texas, about 20 miles from the park's west entrance. Park rangers, however, strongly advise that everyone planning a river trip check with them beforehand to get the latest river conditions. A river-running booklet, with additional information, is available at park visitor centers and from the **Big Bend Natural History Association** (see "Information" under "Just the Facts," earlier in this chapter).

Rafts, inflatable kayaks, and canoes can be rented from several local companies. Rafts typically cost about $25 per person per day (with a three-person minimum), inflatable kayaks cost about $40 per day, and canoes cost about $50 per day. There are discounts for multiday rentals. You can also take guided river trips, with rates of about $60 per person for a half-day float to $130 for a full day. Multiday trips are also available.

Companies to check with include **Desert Sports** (see above); **Far Flung Adventures** (© 800/359-4138 or 432/371-2489; www.farflung.com); **Rio Grande Adventures** (© 800/343-1640 or 432/371-2567; www.riograndeadventures.com); and **Texas River and Jeep Expeditions** (© 800/839-7238 or 432/371-2633; www.texasriver.com).

Big Bend River Tours (© 800/545-4240 or 915/371-3033; www.bigbendrivertours.com) offers several especially interesting river trips, ranging from a delightful half-day float for about $65 per person to 10-day excursions for about $1,600 per person. Among the company's most popular trips is the 21-mile float through beautiful Santa Elena Canyon, which offers spectacular scenery and wonderful serenity, plus the excitement of running a challenging section of rapids called the **Rockslide.** There are often opportunities to see javelinas, coyotes, beavers, wild burros, golden eagles, and peregrine falcons. The canyon can be explored on a day trip (about $135 per person), a 2-day trip (about $300 per person), or a 3-day trip (about $450 per person), with rates varying based on the number of people making the trip. The longer trips include a stop in a side canyon with waterfalls and peaceful swimming holes. Big Bend River Tours also offers guided canoe and inflatable kayak trips, provides a shuttle service, and rents equipment.

Wildlife Viewing & Bird-Watching. Big Bend National Park has an absolutely phenomenal variety of wildlife. About 450 species of birds may be found here over the course of the year—that's more than at any other national park and nearly half of all those found in North America. At last count, there were also about 75 species of mammals, close to 70 species of reptiles and amphibians, and more than three dozen species of fish.

This is the only place in the United States where you'll find the **Mexican long-nosed bat,** listed by the federal government as an endangered species. Other endangered species that make their homes in the park include the **black-capped vireo** (a small bird) and the **Big Bend gambusia,** a tiny fish that we hope prospers and multiplies—its favorite food is mosquito larvae.

Birders consider Big Bend National Park a key bird-watching destination, especially for those looking for some of America's more unusual birds. Among the park's top bird-watching spots are Rio Grande Village and Cottonwood campgrounds, the Chisos Basin, and the Hot Springs. Species to watch for include the colorful **golden-fronted woodpecker,** which can often be seen year-round among the cottonwood trees along the Rio Grande; and the rare **colima warbler,** whose range in the United States consists solely of the Chisos Mountains at Big Bend National Park. Among the hundreds of other birds that call the park home, at least part of the year, are scaled quail, spotted sandpipers, white-winged doves, greater roadrunners, lesser nighthawks, white-throated swifts, black-chinned hummingbirds, broad-tailed hummingbirds, acorn woodpeckers, northern flickers, western wood-pewees, ash-throated flycatchers, tufted titmice, bushtits, cactus wrens, canyon wrens, loggerhead shrikes, Wilson's warblers, and Scott's orioles.

Mammals you may see in the park include desert cottontail rabbits, black-tailed jackrabbits, rock squirrels, Texas antelope squirrels, Merriam's kangaroo rats, coyotes, gray foxes, raccoons, striped skunks, mule deer, and white-tailed deer. There are occasional sightings of mountain lions, usually called panthers here, most commonly in the Green Gulch and Chisos Basin areas. Four attacks on humans are known to have occurred in the park (see the special section titled "Keeping the Wild in Wildlife, or How to Avoid an Unpleasant Encounter," earlier in this chapter). Black bears, which were frequently seen in the area until about

1940, were mostly killed off by local ranchers, who saw them as a threat to their livestock. With the protection provided by national park status, however, they began to return in the mid-1980s, and have now established a small population.

A number of reptiles inhabit the park, including some poisonous snakes, such as **diamondback, Mojave, rock, and black-tailed rattlesnakes,** plus the **trans-pecos copperhead** (see "Keeping the Wild in Wildlife, or How to Avoid an Unpleasant Encounter," earlier in this chapter). Fortunately, it is unlikely you will see a rattler or copperhead, since they avoid both the heat of the day and busy areas. You are more apt to encounter nonpoisonous **western coachwhips,** which are often seen speeding across trails and roadways. They're reddish, sometimes bright red, and among America's fastest snakes; sometimes they're called "red racers." Other nonpoisonous snakes that inhabit the park include Texas whipsnakes, spotted night snakes, southwestern black-headed snakes, and black-necked garter snakes.

Among the lizards you may see scurrying along desert roads and trails is the **southwestern earless lizard**—adult males are green with black-and-white chevrons on their lower sides, and often curl their black-striped tails over their backs. You'll also see various **whiptail lizards** in the desert, but in the canyons and higher in the mountains, watch for the **crevice spiny lizard,** which is covered with scales and has a dark collar. Although rare, **western box turtles** inhabit the park, as well as several types of more common **water turtles.**

Camping

A free camping permit, available at any visitor center, is required for use of the primitive backcountry roadside and backpacking campsites.

INSIDE THE PARK

The park runs three developed campgrounds, and an RV park is operated by a concessionaire. Reservations are available for Chisos Basin and Rio Grande Village campgrounds through the **National Recreation Reservation Service** (© 877/444-6777; www.reserveusa.com).

Rio Grande Village Campground is the largest. It has numerous trees, many with prickly pear cacti growing up around them, and thorny bushes everywhere. Sites are either graveled or paved and are nicely spaced for privacy. They often fill up by 1pm in winter (the high season). One area is designated a "No Generator Zone." Separate but within walking distance is **Rio Grande Village RV Park,** a concessionaire-operated RV park with full hookups. It looks like a parking lot in the midst of grass and trees, fully paved with curbs and back-in sites (no pull-throughs). Tents are not permitted. A small store has limited camping supplies and groceries, a coin-operated laundry, showers for a fee, propane, and gasoline.

Chisos Basin Campground, although not heavily wooded, has small pinyon and juniper trees and well-spaced sites. The campground is nestled around a circular road in a bowl below the visitor center. The access road to the campground is steep and curved, so take it slowly.

Cottonwood Campground is named for the huge old cottonwood trees that dominate the scene. Sites in this rather rustic area are gravel and spacious, within walking distance of the river. There are pit toilets.

NEAR THE PARK

About 7 miles east of the park's north entrance on FM 2627 is **Stillwell Store and RV Park,** HC 65, Box 430, Alpine, TX 79830 (©/fax **432/376-2244**), a casual RV park in desert terrain. There are two areas across the road from each other. The west side has full hookups, while the east has water and electric only, but the east side also features horse corrals and plenty of room for horse trailers. There is also almost unlimited space for tenters, who are charged $5 per person. The park office is at the Stillwell Store, where you can get groceries, limited camping supplies, and gasoline. A small museum (donations accepted) features exhibits from the Stillwell family's pioneer days.

About 3 miles from the west entrance to the park is **Terlingua Oasis RV Park,** part of the Big Bend Motor Inn complex at the junction of Tex. 118 and FM 170 (P.O. Box 336, Terlingua, TX 79852; ℂ 800/848-BEND or 432/371-2218). This park offers pull-through and back-in sites, grassy tent areas, gasoline and diesel fuel, a restaurant (see "Where to Dine," below), a convenience store, and a gift shop.

Where to Stay

INSIDE THE PARK

Chisos Mountains Lodge

Chisos Basin, Big Bend National Park, TX 79834-9999. ℂ **432/477-2291.** www.chisos mountainslodge.com. 72 units. $79–$84 double (rates lower in summer). AE, DC, DISC, MC, V. Pets accepted.

The lodge offers a variety of accommodations from simple motel rooms to historic stone cottages. Motel rooms are small and simply decorated but well maintained. They have two double beds, air-conditioning, tub/shower combos, and terrific views of the Chisos Mountains, but no telephones or TVs. The **Casa Grande Motor Lodge,** part of the Chisos Mountains Lodge, offers somewhat larger motel rooms, attractively furnished, with tiled bathrooms and tub/shower combos, most with two beds. Each room has a private balcony and air-conditioning.

Built by the Civilian Conservation Corps in the 1930s, the six delightful stone cottages are our choice, each with stone floors, front patio, wooden furniture, three double beds, and shower

only. Book as far in advance as possible. The lodge units are the least expensive accommodations and are a bit more rustic. They have one double and one single bed, a tiled bath, tub/shower combo, wood furnishings, painted brick walls with Western and/or Southwestern art, and good views.

NEAR THE PARK

Big Bend Motor Inn

Junction of Tex. 118 and FM 170 (P.O. Box 336), Terlingua, TX 79852. ℂ **800/848-BEND** or 432/371-2218. Fax 432/371-2555. 86 units. A/C TV TEL. $75–$85 double; $125–$145 suite with kitchen. AE, DC, DISC, MC, V.

About 3 miles from the west entrance to the park, this standard American motel offers simple but comfortable rooms, most with one king bed or two queen-size beds. Some have kitchenettes, and two units each have a bedroom, a living room, and a kitchen. There are also a few smaller rooms with one queen bed.

Chisos Mining Co. Motel

On FM 170 about ¾ mile west of Tex. 118 (P.O. Box 228), Terlingua, TX 79852. ℂ **432/ 371-2254.** www.cmcm.cc. 28 units including 9 cabins. A/C. $47–$65 double. MC, V.

This is an attractive, homey, well-maintained motel. The rooms have tub/shower combos; some have TVs. Cabins, also with shower/tub combos, have fully equipped kitchens but no TVs. There's a curio shop on the premises, and next door the **Hungry Javelina** offers speedy takeout for breakfast and lunch.

Mission Lodge

Junction of Tex. 118 and FM 170 (P.O. Box 336), Terlingua, TX 79852. ℂ **800/848-BEND** or 432/371-2218. Fax 432/371-2555. 36 units. A/C TV TEL. $65–$75 double. AE, DC, DISC, MC, V.

Located across the street from the Big Bend Motor Inn, and owned by the same people, the Mission Lodge is

Campground	Elev.	Total Sites	RV Hookups	Dump Station	Toilets	Drinking Water
Inside the Park						
Chisos Basin	5,401	63	No	Yes	Yes	Yes
Cottonwood	2,169	31	No	No	Yes	Yes
Rio Grande Village	1,850	100	No	Yes	Yes	Yes
Rio Grande Village RV Park	1,850	25	25	No	Yes	Yes
Near the Park						
Terlingua Oasis	2,480	175	125	No	Yes	Yes
Stillwell Store and RV Park	2,600	80+	80	Yes	Yes	Yes

smaller, simpler, and less expensive but is still clean and well maintained. Rooms have one queen-size bed and a tub/shower combo.

Where to Dine

INSIDE THE PARK

Chisos Mountains Lodge Restaurant

Chisos Basin, Big Bend National Park. ℂ **432/477-2291.** Main courses $6.25–$16. AE, DC, DISC, MC, V. Daily 7am–8pm. AMERICAN.

Good food at reasonable prices, plus the best location in the area, is the draw here. The dining room is simply but attractively decorated, with good views from the large windows. The menu changes periodically but generally includes steak, pork chops, roast turkey, baked trout, and sandwiches, plus specials such as chicken fajitas and a vegetarian dish. Hikers and others on the move can order a "traveler's lunch" to be picked up the next morning.

NEAR THE PARK

Big Bend Motor Inn Restaurant & Convenience Store

Junction of Tex. 118 and FM 170, Terlingua. ℂ **432/371-2483.** Main courses $4–$12. AE, DC, DISC, MC, V. Daily 6am–10pm. MEXICAN/AMERICAN.

This cafe-style restaurant offers basic Mexican and American fare such as sandwiches and burgers, burritos and tacos, and one of the best breakfasts in the area—try the breakfast burrito or biscuits and gravy. You can also get full dinners such as chicken fried steak as well as Mexican combination plates.

Ms. Tracy's Cafe

West side of Tex. 118, Study Butte; 2 miles west of the park entrance. ℂ **432/371-2888.** Breakfasts, sandwiches, and Mexican items $3.50–$8.95; main dinner courses $8.95–$17. DISC, MC, V. Mid-Nov to Apr daily 7am–9pm; May to mid-Nov daily 7am–5pm. AMERICAN/MEXICAN.

This somewhat funky roadside cafe has a decidedly Western look, with cattle skulls, cowboy chaps, and other Old West memorabilia, but it's actually owned and operated by a Manchester, England, transplant, who sometimes pays homage to her homeland by serving one British item, such as a shepherd's pie, as a lunch special. Other than that, Ms. Tracy's is pure Texas, with beef and buffalo burgers, a variety of sandwiches, a few salads, and a variety of surprisingly good Mexican dishes including burritos, tamales, and quesadillas. Breakfasts feature American and Southwestern standards. Full dinners, served only in winter, vary nightly

Showers	Fire Pits/ Grills	Laundry	Public Phone	Reserve	Fees	Open
No	Yes	No	Yes	Yes	$8	Year-round
No	Yes	No	No	No	$8	Year-round
No	Yes	No	No	Yes	$8	Year-round
Yes	No	Yes	Yes	No	$15	Year-round
Yes	Yes	Yes	Yes	Yes	$9–$21	Year-round
Yes	Yes	Yes	Yes	Yes	$14–$16	Year-round

depending on Ms. Tracy's mood, but often include steak Diane, a fish of the day, vegetarian items, and specialties such as chicken veronique—sautéed chicken breast with white wine tarragon sauce and white grapes.

Picnic & Camping Supplies

Inside the park, limited groceries and camping supplies are available at Chisos Basin, Rio Grande Village, Castolon, and Panther Junction. There is also a gift shop in the lodge at the Basin. Gasoline is available at Rio Grande Village and Panther Junction only, so check your gas gauge before heading out, as everything in this park is pretty far from everything else. Minor car repairs are available at Panther Junction.

Outside the north entrance to the park, southeast about 7 miles on FM 2627, is **Stillwell Store and RV Park** (© **432/376-2244**), where you'll find groceries, limited camping supplies, and gasoline. Just outside the west entrance to the park, in Study Butte/ Terlingua, you'll find several gas stations, car repair, a convenience store, and a liquor store. Also in the Study Butte/Terlingua area is **Desert Sports** (see above), with rental equipment, bike and boat parts and supplies, maps, and guidebooks.

Nearby Attractions

On the west side of Big Bend National Park, just beyond the communities of Study Butte and Terlingua, are three worthwhile side trips. Heading west, the first you'll encounter is the **Barton Warnock Environmental Education Center,** 1 mile east of Lajitas on FM 170 (© **432/424-3327;** www.tpwd.state.tx. us/park/barton). Named for botanist and author Dr. Barton Warnock, the center is operated by Texas Parks & Wildlife. It features exhibits on the geology, archaeology, human history, and especially the flora and fauna of the Big Bend area, with a museum plus 2½ acres of desert gardens with a self-guided walk among the various plants of the Chihuahuan Desert. There is also a gift shop/bookstore. Gates are open daily year-round from 8am to 4:30pm; admission costs $4 for adults, $1.50 for children 6 to 12, and is free for children under 6.

Continuing west, you enter **Big Bend Ranch State Park,** P.O. Box 2319, Presidio, TX 79845 (© **432/229-3416;** www. tpwd.state.tx.us), which covers some 290,000 acres of Chihuahuan Desert wilderness along the Rio Grande. Perhaps even more remote and rugged than Big Bend National Park, this mostly undeveloped state park (also called Big Bend Ranch Natural Area on some signs) contains two mountain ranges, extinct volcanoes, scenic canyons, a wide variety of desert plants, and wildlife including javelina, mountain lions, deer, coyotes, a variety of lizards, several poisonous snakes, and numerous birds including golden eagles and peregrine falcons. There is also a small herd of Texas longhorn cattle, a reminder of the property's ranching days. Several outfitters offer river trips as well as mountain biking and hiking excursions in the state park. See "Other Sports & Activities," earlier in this chapter.

The 50-mile **Farm Road 170** between Lajitas and Presidio goes through the park, providing a wonderful scenic drive for 28 miles along the Rio Grande, and also offering access to several put-in and take-out points for rafts and canoes. The road is winding and hilly in places, with no shoulders and a maximum speed limit in most places of 45mph. It meanders along the Rio Grande, passing among hillsides dotted with mesquite, yucca, ocotillo, prickly pear cactus, and a variety of desert shrubs. There are pullouts with picnic tables (protected from the weather by fake American Indian teepees). Although paved, the road is subject to flash floods and rock slides, so we do not recommend it during or immediately after heavy rains.

The park also has several miles of roads that require high-clearance four-wheel-drive vehicles, and about 30 miles of hiking and backpacking trails, with trailheads along FM 170. There are also a number of primitive camping areas. Those planning trips into the park can get permits and information (including a very good trail guide) at Barton Warnock Environmental Education Center (see above), Fort Leaton State Historical Park (see below), or the **ranch administrative offices,** just west of Fort Leaton State Historical Park, where

a small interpretive center has displays on the region's ranching heritage, a gift shop and bookstore, and public showers. Entrance fees are $3 for anyone 12 and older (free for children under 12), and everyone must also pay a $3 activity fee. Those driving through the park on FM 170 are not required to pay the entrance fee and can get out of their vehicles to look around, but should generally stay within sight of their vehicles.

Just west of Big Bend Ranch State Park is **Fort Leaton State Historic Site,** 4 miles east of Presidio on FM 170 (© **432/229-3613;** www.tpwd.state.tx.us/park/fortleat), a restored fort and trading post that is best known for the violence perpetrated both by and toward its residents. It was built by Benjamin Leaton in 1848, just after the end of the Mexican-American War, wherein the United States acquired most of the Southwest from Mexico. Leaton had been working as a "scalphunter"—killing American Indians for the governments of several Mexican states—and built the adobe fortress for his family and employees and to use as a base of operations for a trading business. It was said at the time that part of this business included encouraging area bands of Apaches and Comanches to steal livestock from Mexican settlements, which they would trade to Leaton for guns and ammunition. Leaton, considered a generally unsavory character, was known locally as *un mal hombre*—Spanish for a bad man.

After his death in 1851, Leaton's widow married Edward Hall, who moved into the fort, from which he operated a freight business. Hall borrowed a large sum of money from a former associate of Leaton, John Burgess, and when in 1864 Hall could not repay the loan, Burgess foreclosed on the fort, which had been used as collateral. Hall refused to leave and was subsequently murdered, supposedly by Burgess, who then moved his family into the fort. Burgess ran a very successful freight business from the fort until 1875, when he himself was murdered by Bill Leaton, Ben Leaton's youngest son, in retaliation for the death of Bill Leaton's stepfather, Edward Hall, in 1864.

Despite this bloody chain of events, the remaining members of the Burgess family lived in the fort until 1926, when it was abandoned and began to fall into ruin. It was donated to the state in 1968 and has been partially restored so today's visitors can get a good sense of what life was like at a trading-post fort in the untamed frontier of the 19th century. Twenty-five rooms are open to the public, either by guided (45–60 min.) or self-guided tours. The guided tours are especially good, since you get the guide's perspective on the building's violent past.

Fort Leaton State Historic Site includes a museum, with exhibits on the human history of the area—from the prehistoric American Indians who farmed here in the 15th century to the Spanish and Mexican colonizers who followed, and finally the Anglo Americans who arrived in the mid-1800s, including, of course, those who built and lived in Fort Leaton. The park holds periodic living-history demonstrations, such as how to make adobe bricks, blacksmithing, 19th-century cooking, and the like. The historic park is open daily from 8am to 4:30pm, except Christmas Day. Admission costs $2 for adults or $1 for children 6 to 12, and is free for those under 6.

5

BLACK CANYON OF THE GUNNISON NATIONAL PARK

by Don & Barbara Laine

ARLY AMERICAN INDIANS AND, LATER, UTES AND ANGLOS AVOIDED the Black Canyon of the Gunnison, believing that no human could survive a trip through its depths. Now, the deepest and most spectacular 14 miles of this 48-mile canyon comprise one of America's newest national parks.

The Black Canyon, which had been a national monument since 1933, became a national park on October 21, 1999. In a statement issued after the bill signing ceremony, Pres. Bill Clinton called it a "true natural treasure," adding, "Its nearly vertical walls, rising a half-mile high, harbor one of the most spectacular stretches of wild river in America."

The Black Canyon ranges in depth from 1,730 feet to 2,700 feet. Its width at its narrowest point (cleverly called "The Narrows") is only 40 feet at the river. This deep slash in the earth was created through 2 million years of erosion, a process that's still going on—albeit slowed by the damming of the Gunnison River above the park. At 30,300 acres, the Black Canyon is among the smallest of America's national parks.

Most visitors view the canyon from the **South Rim Road,** site of the visitor center, or the lesser-used **North Rim Road.** Short paths branching off both roads lead to splendid viewpoints with signs explaining the canyon's unique geology.

The park has hiking trails along both rims and backcountry hiking routes down into the canyon, and offers excellent trout fishing for ambitious anglers willing to make the trek to the canyon floor. It also provides an abundance of thrills for the experienced rock climbers who challenge its sheer canyon walls. In winter, much of the park is closed to motor vehicles, but it's a delight for cross-country skiers and snowshoers.

The Black Canyon shares its eastern boundary with **Curecanti National Recreation Area,** which offers boating and fishing on three reservoirs, as well as hiking and camping.

Avoiding the Crowds. Although overcrowding has not been much of a problem in the past, with about 200,000 people visiting each year, visitation is expected to increase now that the Black

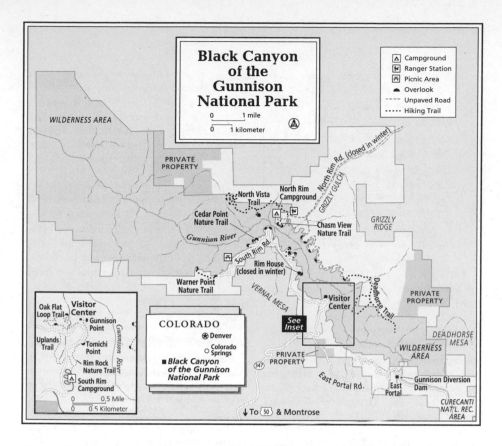

**Black Canyon
of the
Gunnison
National Park**

0   1 mile

0   1 kilometer

Campground
Ranger Station
Picnic Area
Overlook
Unpaved Road
Hiking Trail

WILDERNESS AREA

PRIVATE
PROPERTY

North Rim Rd. (closed in winter)

GRIZZLY GULCH

North Vista
Trail

North Rim
Campground

GRIZZLY
RIDGE

Cedar Point
Nature Trail

Chasm View
Nature Trail

Gunnison River

South Rim Rd.

Rim House
(closed in winter)

Warner Point
Nature Trail

VERNAL MESA

Visitor
Center

Deadhorse Trail

PRIVATE
PROPERTY

See
Inset

DEADHORSE
MESA

Oak Flat
Loop Trail

Visitor
Center

Gunnison
Point

Uplands
Trail

Tomichi
Point

COLORADO

Denver

Colorado
Springs

Gunnison River

Rim Rock
Nature Trail

South Rim
Campground

■ *Black Canyon
of the Gunnison
National Park*

PRIVATE
PROPERTY

347

WILDERNESS
AREA

East Portal Rd.

East
Portal

Gunnison Diversion
Dam

0   0.5 Mile

0   0.5 Kilometer

↓ To 50 & Montrose

CURECANTI
NAT'L. REC.
AREA

Canyon has gained national park status. Summer is the busiest time, with more than half the park visitors arriving between Memorial Day and Labor Day. December through February is the quietest time. Those seeking solitude should visit before Memorial Day and after Labor Day. Although winter can be beautiful, park access is limited.

Just the Facts

GETTING THERE & GATEWAYS

The park is located on Colo. 347, 6 miles north of U.S. 50. To reach the south rim, travel east 8 miles from Montrose on U.S. 50 to the well-marked turnoff. To reach the north rim from Montrose, drive north 21 miles on U.S. 50 to Delta, east 31 miles on Colo. 92 to Crawford, then south on an 11-mile access road.

The Nearest Airports. The Montrose Regional Airport, 2100 Airport Rd. (✆ **970/249-3203**), off U.S. 50, 2 miles northwest of Montrose, is served by America West and United Express, with rental cars from Budget, Dollar, Enterprise, and Thrifty.

A bigger airport is **Walker Field** in Grand Junction (✆ **970/244-9100;** www.walkerfield.com), about 75 miles northwest of the park. Located about a mile north of I-70 Exit 31 (Horizon Dr.), on the north side of Grand Junction, Walker Field has commercial flights connecting Grand Junction with most major cities. Airlines operating at Walker Field include **America West Express,** with daily service to Phoenix; **Delta/Skywest,** with daily service to Salt Lake City; and **United Express,** with daily service to Denver. Rental cars are available from **Alamo, Avis, Budget, Enterprise, Hertz, National,** and **Thrifty.**

> No other canyon in North America combines the depth, narrowness, sheerness, and somber countenance of the Black Canyon.
>
> —Geologist Wallace Hansen, who mapped the canyon in the 1950s

Toll-free reservations numbers for airlines and car rental companies are listed in the appendix.

INFORMATION

For information on both the national park and the adjacent Curecanti National Recreation Area, contact **Black Canyon of the Gunnison National Park/Curecanti National Recreation Area,** 102 Elk Creek, Gunnison, CO 81230 (© 970/641-2337); or the **South Rim Visitor Center** (© 970/249-1914, ext. 23; www.nps.gov/blca). A bookstore at the South Rim Visitor Center, operated by the Western National Parks Association, offers a variety of publications, including the very useful *South Rim Driving Tour Guide,* which was published by the association.

For information on other area attractions, lodging, and dining, contact the **Montrose Visitors** and **Convention Bureau,** 1519 E. Main St. (P.O. Box 335), Montrose, CO 81402 (© 800/873-0244 or 970/240-1414; www.visitmontrose. net); or stop at the **Montrose Visitor Center** (© 970/249-1726) in the **Ute Indian Museum,** 17253 Chipeta Dr., on the south side of town off U.S. 550. Information on federal lands in the area, including those under the jurisdiction of the Bureau of Land Management, is available at the **Public Lands Center,** 2505 S. Townsend Ave., Montrose, CO 81401 (© 970/240-5300), which is open year-round Monday through Friday.

VISITOR CENTERS

The park's **South Rim Visitor Center** is open year-round, except on winter federal holidays; the **North Rim Ranger Station** is open intermittently in summer but closed at other times.

FEES & PERMITS

Admission for up to 7 days costs $7 per vehicle or $4 per person on foot or bike. Camping costs $10 per night for basic sites; $15 for sites with electric hookups. Required backcountry permits are free.

SPECIAL REGULATIONS & WARNINGS

Visitors are warned to not throw anything from the rim into the canyon, since even a single small stone thrown or kicked from the rim could be fatal to people below. Visitors are also advised to supervise children very carefully— many sections of the rim have no guardrails or fences.

Unlike at most national parks, leashed pets are permitted on some of the shorter rim trails (check with rangers), but are specifically prohibited on others and are not permitted in the inner canyon or wilderness areas.

SEASONS & CLIMATE

Temperatures and weather conditions often vary greatly between the canyon rim and the canyon floor, and it gets progressively hotter as you descend into the canyon. Average summer temperatures range from highs of 60° to 90°F (16°C–32°C), with summer lows dropping to 30° to 50°F (–1°C–10°C). In winter, highs range from 20° to 40°F (–7°C–4°C), with lows from 0°F to 20°F (–18°C–7°C). Brief afternoon thunderstorms are fairly common in the summer. The South Rim Road usually remains open to the visitor center through the winter, but the North Rim Road is often closed by snow between December and March.

If You Have Only 1 Day

It's fairly easy to see a great deal here in a short amount of time, especially if you stick to the South Rim. First, stop at the visitor center to see the exhibits and get an understanding of how this phenomenal canyon was created. Then, from the visitor center, drive 6 miles (one-way) to the end of South Rim Drive, stopping at the overlooks. Finally, take off on one of the rim hiking trails, such as the easy **Cedar Point Nature Trail** or the somewhat more challenging **Warner Point Nature Trail** (see "Day Hikes," below). If you'll be camping in the park or staying nearby, you might plan to attend the evening ranger program.

Exploring the Park by Car

The park's 7-mile (one-way) **South Rim Drive** provides an excellent and fairly easy way to see much of the park. There are about a dozen overlooks along the drive, and in most cases you'll be walking from 140 feet to about 700 feet to reach the viewpoints from your vehicle.

Among the not-to-be-missed overlooks are **Gunnison Point,** behind the visitor center, which offers stunning views of the seemingly endless walls of dark rock, capped by a pinkish rock layer; and the **Pulpit Rock Overlook,** which provides a splendid view of the rock walls and about 1½ miles of the Gunnison River, some 1,770 feet down. Farther along the drive is **Chasm View,** where you can see the incredible power of water, which here cut through more than 1,800 feet of solid rock. Near the end of the drive, be sure to stop at **Sunset View,** where there's a picnic area and a short (140 ft.) walk to a viewpoint, which offers distant views beyond the canyon as well as of the scenic canyon (but not the river). And, if your timing is right, you might be treated to a classic western sunset, in all its red-and-orange glory.

Organized Tours & Ranger Programs

A variety of **ranger-conducted programs,** which might include nature walks, geology talks, and evening campfire programs, are presented from Memorial Day through mid-September on the South Rim (check at the visitor center for the current schedule). During the winter, guided snowshoe walks and moonlight cross-country ski tours are usually offered on the South Rim when snow conditions are right (stop at the visitor center or call ahead for information and reservations).

Day Hikes

Trails on the monument's rims range from short, easy walks to moderate-to-strenuous hikes of several miles; hiking below the rim is mostly difficult and not recommended for those with a fear of heights. Permits are not needed for hiking rim trails, but free backcountry permits are required for all treks below the rim.

SOUTH RIM TRAILS

Cedar Point Nature Trail

0.7 mile RT. Easy. Access: Cedar Point Trailhead, along South Rim Rd.

With signs along the way describing the plants you'll see, this sunny trail not only offers a painless botany lesson, but at the end provides breathtaking views of the Gunnison River, 2,000 feet down, as well as the **Painted Wall,** at 2,250 feet considered the tallest cliff in Colorado.

Oak Flat Loop Trail

2 miles RT. Moderate to strenuous. Access: Near the visitor venter.

Dropping slightly below the rim, this trail offers excellent views into the canyon, while also taking you through a grove of aspen, past Gambel oak, and finally through a forest of aspen, Gambel oak, and Douglas fir. Be aware that the trail is narrow in spots and a bit close to steep drop-offs.

Rim Rock Nature Trail

1 mile RT. Moderate. Access: Near the entrance to the South Rim Campground's Loop C.

Following the rim along a relatively flat path, this trail leads to an overlook, providing good views of the Gunnison River and the canyon's sheer rock walls. A pamphlet available at the trailhead describes plant life and other points of interest.

Warner Point Nature Trail

1.5 miles RT. Moderate. Access: High Point Overlook at the end of South Rim Rd.

This trail offers a multitude of things to see, such as mountain mahogany, pinyon pine, Utah juniper, and other area flora; distant mountains and valleys; and the Black Canyon and its creator, the Gunnison River 2,722 feet below. A trail guide is available at the trailhead.

NORTH RIM TRAILS

Chasm View Nature Trail

0.3 mile RT. Moderate. Access: End of the North Rim Campground loop.

Starting in a pinyon-juniper forest, this trail heads to the rim for good views of the canyon and the river; you'll also have a good chance of seeing swallows, swifts, and raptors.

Deadhorse Trail

5 miles RT. Easy to moderate. Access: Kneeling Camel Overlook.

Actually an old service road, this trail offers a good chance of seeing various birds, plus views of **Deadhorse Gulch** and the **East Portal area** at the southeast end of the park.

North Vista Trail

7 miles RT. Moderate to strenuous. Access: North Rim Ranger Station.

Offering some of the best scenic views in the Black Canyon, this trail also provides hikers with a good chance of seeing red-tailed hawks, white-throated swifts, Clark's nutcrackers, and ravens. You might also be lucky enough to spot a peregrine falcon. The trail goes through a pinyon-juniper forest along the canyon's rim about 1.5 miles to **Exclamation Point,** which offers an excellent view into the canyon. Up to this point the trail is rated moderate, but it continues another 2 miles (rated strenuous) to **Green Mountain,** where you'll find broad, panoramic vistas.

Exploring the Backcountry

Experienced hikers in excellent physical condition may want to hike down into the canyon. Although the canyon has no maintained or marked trails, rangers can help you plot out several recommended routes. Free permits are required. A limited number of campsites are available for backpackers.

The most popular inner canyon hike is the strenuous **Gunnison Route,** which branches off the South Rim's Oak Flat Loop Trail (see above) and meanders down the side of the canyon to the river. Eighty feet of chain help keep you from falling on a stretch about a third of the way down. This hike has a vertical drop of 1,800 feet and takes 4 to 5 hours.

Other Summer Sports & Activities

Biking. Although bikes are not permitted on any park trails, this is still a popular destination for bikers, who travel the **South Rim Road** to the various overlooks and trailheads. There are also plenty of mountain biking opportunities outside the park. You can obtain maps, information, bike repairs, and accessories in

Montrose at **Cascade Bicycles,** 25 N. Cascade Ave. (© **970/249-7375**).

Climbing. The sheer vertical walls and scenic beauty of the Black Canyon make it an ideal and popular destination for rock climbers, but—and we cannot emphasize this too strongly—this is no place for beginners. These cliffs require a great deal of experience and the best equipment. Free permits are required, and prospective climbers should discuss their plans first with park rangers.

Fishing. Dedicated anglers can make their way to the Gunnison River at the bottom of the canyon in a quest for **brown** and **rainbow trout.** East Portal Road (open only in summer) provides access to the upstream section of the river from adjacent Curecanti National Recreation Area. The stretch of the Gunnison River located within the park has been designated as Gold Medal Waters; only artificial lures are permitted, and other special rules apply (check with park rangers). A Colorado fishing license is required.

Watersports. Mostly, don't do it! Through the park, the Gunnison River is **extremely dangerous,** for both swimmers and rafters (it's considered unraftable). Sections of river west of the park are more suitable; information is available from the Public Lands Center office in Montrose (see "Information," above). The only exception is for experienced kayakers, who find the river an exhilarating challenge. Free permits are required.

Wildlife Viewing. The park is home to a variety of wildlife, and you're likely to see chipmunks, ground squirrels, badgers, marmots, and mule deer. Although not frequently seen, there are also black bear, cougars, and bobcats, and you'll probably hear the lonesome high-pitched call of coyotes at night. The peregrine falcon can sometimes be spotted along the cliffs, and you may also

In September 1949, Ed Nelson accomplished what practically everyone considered impossible: He was the first man to boat through the Black Canyon of the Gunnison. Amazingly, he accomplished this feat in a 5-pound collapsible boat, using Ping-Pong paddles for oars!

see red-tailed hawks, turkey vultures, golden eagles, and white-throated swifts.

Winter Sports

When the South Rim Road is closed by winter snows, the Park Service plows only to the South Rim Visitor Center, leaving the rest of the park the domain of cross-country skiers and snowshoers. The South Rim Road makes a great trail, running about 6 miles from the visitor center into the park; and, 0.2 mile beyond the visitor center, the Vernal Mesa Ski Trail loops off the road, providing another 1.5 miles for cross-country skiers and snowshoers.

Camping

There are campgrounds on both rims, usually open from May through October, with a limited water supply hauled in by truck. The campgrounds have pit toilets, but no showers. The **South Rim Campground,** which rarely fills, has 89 sites (23 of which have electric hookups), but the **North Rim Campground,** with only 13 basic sites, does occasionally fill up. Sites are available on a first-come, first-served basis, and cost is $10 per night for basic sites and $15 for sites with electric hookups. Reservations available through the **National Recreation Reservation Service** (© **877/444-6777;** www. reserveusa.com).

Campgrounds with hot showers and RV hookups are available in Montrose. Our choice is the **Hangin' Tree R.V. Park,** 17250 U.S. 550 S., Montrose, CO

81401 (℃ **970/249-9966;** hangintree@ rmi.net), which is open year-round. It has grassy tent sites and large pull-through RV sites, a self-service laundry, a convenience store, and a 24-hour gas station. Its 25 sites run $16 to $24 a night and major credit cards are accepted.

Where to Stay

NEAR THE PARK

There is no lodging inside the park; the nearest facilities are in Montrose. In addition to the properties discussed below, Montrose has a **Comfort Inn,** 2100 E. Main St., Montrose, CO 81401 (℃ **970/240-8000**), charging $60 to $99 double; **Days Inn,** 1655 E. Main St., Montrose, CO 81401 (℃ **970/249-3411**), with rates of $37 to $67 double; **Holiday Inn Express Hotel & Suites,** 1391 S. Townsend Ave., Montrose, CO 81401 (℃ **970/240-1800**), which accepts pets and charges $99 to $149 double; and **Super 8,** 1705 E. Main St., Montrose, CO 81401 (℃ **970/249-9294**), with double rates from $49 to $78. National toll-free reservations numbers are listed in the appendix.

Best Western Red Arrow Motor Inn

1702 E. Main St. (P.O. Box 236), Montrose, CO 81402. ℃ **800/468-9323** (direct) or 970/ 249-9641. www.bestwestern.com/redarrow. 60 units. A/C TV TEL. $62–$115 double. Rates include continental breakfast. AE, DC, DISC, MC, V.

Those seeking the reliability and familiar surroundings of a major chain motel will like the Red Arrow. Occupying a large two-story building near the east end of town, it offers spacious rooms, most with queen beds, plus refrigerators, coffeemakers, bathrobes, and hair dryers. Anyone traveling with a laptop will appreciate the two-line phones with dataports and voice mail. A handful of "spa rooms" have large whirlpool tubs. Amenities include a solarium with a hot tub and fitness center, seasonal heated outdoor pool, playground, guest laundry, conference space for 360, and courtesy airport transportation.

Lathrop House Bed & Breakfast

718 E. Main St., Montrose, CO 81401. ℃ **970/ 240-6075.** www.lathrophouse.com. 5 units (3 with bathroom). A/C TV. $79 double shared bathroom, $89–$99 double private bathroom. Rates include full breakfast and evening wine and cheese. DC, DISC, MC, V. Suitable for children 14 and older.

The handsome Victorian architecture and historic flavor may lead you to the Lathrop House for your first visit, but the service—okay, it's really pampering—and the delightful breakfasts will bring you back. Listed on the National Register of Historic Places, this home was built in 1902 by the Lathrops, a prominent Montrose family that owned the local hardware store and also the first automobile in Montrose. Like many of Colorado's historic homes, it had fallen into disrepair and its days looked numbered when it was rescued by innkeeper Cindy K. Crosman in the 1980s. Following a major restoration, it opened for business in the fall of 1998.

Today's guests will find an attractive three-story home typical of those built by the West's well-to-do citizenry of 100 years ago. There are four rooms on the second floor and one on the third, each one different. For instance, the J. V. Lathrop Room has Victorian decorations such as an ornate mirror and antique sewing machine converted to a sink, plus masculine touches including a set of elk antlers over the king-size bed, and a deer head on the opposite wall. It contains a half bath (toilet and sink only) and shares a shower. A favorite of honeymooners, the colorful Emma Lathrop Room has hand-stenciled designs on the ceiling and walls, a queen-size canopy bed, a pleasant sitting area, a fireplace, a private deck, a washer and dryer, and a bathroom with shower only (no tub). Breakfasts are especially memorable—candlelit and somewhat elegant, with fresh fruit, home-baked breads and muffins, and hot entrees such as banana-stuffed French toast, breakfast burritos, or steak and eggs. Smoking is not permitted.

Western Motel

1200 E. Main St. (at Stough Ave.), Montrose, CO 81401. © **800/445-7301** or 970/249-3481. www.westernmotel.com. 28 units. A/C TV TEL. $52–$64 double, $85–$115 family units; lower rates in winter. Rates include continental breakfast May–Sept. AE, DC, DISC, MC, V. Pets accepted ($5 fee).

A one-story white stucco building with a two-story annex, this attractive independent motel, renovated in late 1999, offers clean, comfortable rooms that are a tad larger than average, with some homey touches, and most have queen-size beds. A few two- and three-room family units are available, and most rooms have door-front parking. VCRs are available to rent, and there's free coffee in the lobby. Facilities include a seasonal heated outdoor swimming pool, plus a hot tub and sauna.

Where to Dine

NEAR THE PARK

In addition to the Montrose restaurants discussed below, Montrose has a **Starvin' Arvin's,** a regional-chain family restaurant, located at 1320 S. Townsend Ave. (© **970/249-7787**), that's open daily from 6am to 10pm.

Glenn Eyrie Restaurant

2351 S. Townsend Ave. © **970/249-9263.** Reservations recommended. Main courses $12–$30. AE, DC, DISC, MC, V. Tues–Sat 5–9pm. CONTINENTAL/AMERICAN.

This small, cozy restaurant is lodged in a colonial farmhouse on the south end of town. In summer, guests can dine inside or outdoors in the garden; in winter,

folks seek tables near the cozy central fireplace. Just about everything is made in-house, including rolls, jams, and sauces; and many items are grown on the grounds—fruits, herbs, and greens. Owner-chef Steve Schwathe changes the menu frequently to reflect the seasons and availability of fresh ingredients, but choices might include whole rack of lamb, which is grilled, then slow-baked, and served with a sauce of tomato, rosemary, and garlic; or steak Diane, a butterflied beef tenderloin steak that is flamed tableside in a mustard, applejack brandy, and cream sauce, and served with mushrooms and artichoke hearts. The restaurant also offers fresh seafood selections and vegetarian dishes.

The Whole Enchilada

44 S. Grand Ave., near W. Main St. © **970/ 249-1881.** Main courses $3.75–$8.50 at lunch, $5.75–$14 at dinner. AE, DISC, MC, V. Mon–Thurs 11am–9pm; Fri–Sat 11am–10pm. MEXICAN.

Come to this local favorite for well-prepared Mexican fare, such as burritos, tostadas, fajitas, and tacos. Those seeking a bit more adventure might opt for enchiladas Acapulco (corn tortillas stuffed with chicken, black olives, almonds, and cheese); or from the "Not for Gringos" section of the menu, the El Paso chimichanga (a fried flour tortilla filled with beef and jalapeños and smothered in green-chile sauce). A variety of burgers are also available. The restaurant is locally famous for its margaritas, and a delightful outdoor patio is open in summer.

Picnic & Camping Supplies

A good bet for those seeking groceries, deli sandwiches, baked goods, or a buy-by-the-pound salad bar is one of the two **City Market** grocery stores in Montrose. There's one at 128 S. Townsend Ave. and another at 16400 S. Townsend Ave. For information, call © **970/249-3405.**

THE BLACK HILLS:
Mount Rushmore National Memorial, Wind Cave National Park, Jewel Cave National Monument & Custer State Park

by Jack Olson

CHISELED IN GRANITE HIGH ON A PINE-CLAD CLIFF IN SOUTH DAKOTA'S fabled Black Hills are the portraits of four of America's greatest leaders. Since 1941, George Washington, Thomas Jefferson, Abraham Lincoln, and Theodore Roosevelt have gazed quietly across the Great Plains and a land they did so much to mold.

Most of the 2.7 million people who visit each year spend but a short hour or two at the memorial, maybe eating a sandwich, then moving on to Yellowstone National Park or some other "major" destination. But those with the time and inclination will discover much to enjoy at Mount Rushmore and the other attractions of the Black Hills. Within an hour's drive of Mount Rushmore, you will find not only Wind Cave National Park and Jewel Cave National Monument, but also Custer State Park and the Crazy Horse Memorial—a work in progress that will be far larger than Mount Rushmore. And if you are willing to get off the beaten path—something that relatively few visitors do—you will find a backcountry dotted with trails through the region's pine forests, a virtually untrammeled wilderness where you can escape the crowds for days, or perhaps just an hour.

Geologists predict the presidents will continue their earthly vigil at **Mount Rushmore National Memorial** for many centuries, eroding less than 1 inch every 10,000 years. Although major changes aren't predicted for the giant faces anytime soon, return visitors to the base of the mountain will discover greatly improved facilities.

Thanks to the Mount Rushmore Preservation Fund—one of the most successful public-private fundraising partnerships for the National Park Service to date—$56 million in improvements await travelers at the base of the sculpture, including new theaters, viewing terraces, interpretive exhibits, walking trails, and concession facilities.

As the "crown jewel" of South Dakota's state park system, **Custer State Park** offers 73,000 acres of prime Black Hills real estate, the largest and most diverse population of wildlife, the best accommodations and facilities, and the

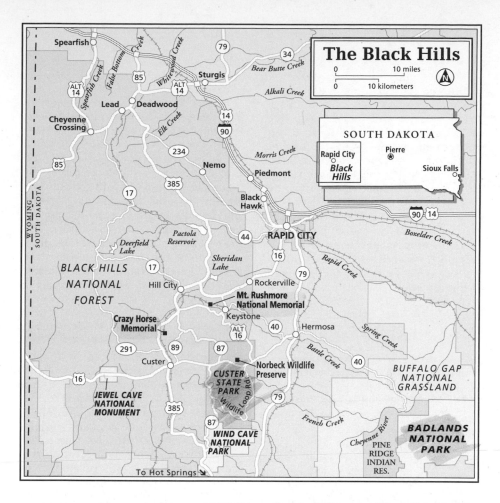

most memorable natural resources of any park in the state.

Located east of the town of Custer, the park is home to four resorts, four fishing lakes, wildlife loops, campgrounds, scenic drives, and granite spires so impressive that they make you want to get out of the car and walk the forest floor. With rolling meadows and foothills, pine forests, and the giant fingerlike granite spires of the Needles, Custer State Park is a must on any Black Hills itinerary.

Even after more than 100 years since the establishment of the park, there is still something to discover in the darkened depths of **Wind Cave National Park.** Although the cave formations here are generally not as ornate as those in some of the West's other caves, such

as Carlsbad Caverns, Wind Cave has its share of fairyland-style decorations, including popcorn, shimmering needle-shaped crystals, and an abundance of formations called "box work," which sometimes looks like fine lace. With 107 miles of mapped passageway, Wind Cave is one of the longest caves in the world. And, with each succeeding expedition, the interconnecting network of known passages continues to grow, sometimes by a few paces, other times by several hundred feet. Barometric wind studies conducted by the U.S. Geological Survey estimate that only 5% of the total cave has been discovered.

But there's a great deal more to Wind Cave than just its underground geological wonders. Aboveground, 28,295 acres of rolling prairie and ponderosa pine forests are ablaze with wildflowers and teeming with wildlife. Bison and antelope graze on the park's lush grasslands while prairie dogs watch from the relative safety of their "towns." In the fall, elk can be heard "bugling" throughout the confines of the park; and overhead, hawks, eagles, and vultures float on the thermal currents that rise from the rocky ridges of the Black Hills.

In the limestone labyrinth that rests below the Black Hills, **Jewel Cave National Monument** offers a mysterious, mazelike network of caverns and passageways, filled with rare specimens and beautiful jewel-like crystals that have yet to be fully explored.

Just the Facts

GETTING THERE & GATEWAYS

Rapid City is the most popular gateway to the Black Hills and its bountiful selection of national and state parks, monuments, and memorials.

The most direct route to the Black Hills by car is I-90. To reach **Mount Rushmore,** take Exit 57 to U.S. 16 (Mt. Rushmore Rd.) and continue approximately 23 miles southwest of Rapid City to the memorial entrance.

Custer State Park, between Mount Rushmore and Wind Cave National Park, is accessible via S. Dak. 79 and S. Dak. 36 from the east, U.S. 16A from the north and west, and S. Dak. 87 from the north and south.

Wind Cave National Park is best accessed via U.S. 385 north of Hot Springs, South Dakota, or S. Dak. 87 from Custer State Park, which shares its southern boundary with Wind Cave's northern perimeter. It's about an hour's drive south from Mount Rushmore.

The Crazy Horse Memorial is 5 miles north of Custer on U.S. 16/385.

Jewel Cave National Monument, the westernmost of the sites discussed in this chapter, is just off U.S. 16, 13 miles west of Custer.

The Nearest Airport. Rapid City Regional Airport (© 605/394-4195; www.rcgov.org/Airport/pages), located 10 miles southeast of Rapid City on U.S. 44, provides direct access to the Black Hills and Mount Rushmore. **Northwest Airlines, Delta/Skywest,** and **United Express** serve the airport with daily flights to Minneapolis, Salt Lake City, and Denver. Car-rental agencies at the airport include **Avis, Budget, Hertz, National,** and **Thrifty.** You'll find a list of toll-free numbers in the appendix.

INFORMATION

For information on Mount Rushmore, contact the **Superintendent, Mount Rushmore National Memorial,** P.O. Box 268, Keystone, SD 57751-0268 (© **605/574-2523;** www.nps.gov/moru). For information about **Custer State Park,** contact the park at HC83, Box 70, Custer, SD 57730-9705 (© **605/255-4515;** www.custer statepark.info). To get information about Wind Cave, contact the **Superintendent, Wind Cave National Park,** RR1, Box 190, Hot Springs, SD 57747-9430 (© **605/745-4600;** www.nps.gov/wica). For details on Jewel Cave, contact the **Superintendent, Jewel Cave National Monument,** RR1, Box 60 AA, Custer, SD 57730 (© **605/ 673-2288;** www.nps.gov/jeca). To get information about Crazy Horse, contact the **Crazy Horse Memorial,** Avenue of the Chiefs, Crazy Horse, SD 57730-9506 (© **605/673-4681;** www.crazy horsememorial.org).

For information about the entire area, contact **South Dakota Tourism,** Capitol Lake Plaza, 711 E. Wells Ave., Pierre, SD 57501-5070 (© **800/SDAKOTA** or 605/ 773-3301; fax 605/773-3256; www.travel sd.com); or the **Black Hills, Badlands & Lakes Association,** 1851 Discovery Circle, Rapid City, SD 57701 (© **605/355-3600;** www.blackhillsbadlands.com).

Summer days in the Black Hills are often sunny with temperatures in the 80s, so a broad-brimmed hat and sunscreen are advised. Temperatures often drop rapidly after sunset, particularly in the mountains. In the fall, sunny skies and crisp temperatures can make for pleasant traveling conditions, though snowstorms may occur as early as September at higher elevations.

Winter daytime temperatures average 20 ° to 40 °F (-6°C–4°C), and icy roads are common. Even in spring, weather can often be cold and wet.

Visiting Mount Rushmore National Memorial

Widely regarded as one of the manmade wonders of the world, Mount Rushmore is as much a work of art as it is an engineering marvel. Its creator, sculptor Gutzon Borglum, wanted to symbolize in stone the very spirit of a nation and, through four of its most revered leaders—George Washington, Thomas Jefferson, Abraham Lincoln, and Theodore Roosevelt—the country's birth, growth, preservation, and development. A half century after its completion, Mount Rushmore remains one of America's most enduring icons.

In 1924, Borglum visited the Black Hills, looking for a place to carve a lasting legacy for himself and the nation. The artist hoped to locate a mountain with a suitable mass of stone, as well as a southeasterly exposure that would take advantage of the sun's rays for the greatest portion of the day. He decided on a rock outcropping named Mount Rushmore.

Inclement weather and lack of funds frequently stalled progress on the memorial. All told, the monument was completed at a cost of about $1 million during 6½ years of work over a 14-year period.

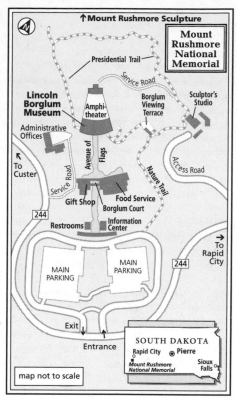

Plaster Portraits. Having studied under the master sculptor Auguste Rodin in Paris, Borglum understood art. When he arrived at Rushmore in 1925, Borglum was 58 years old and had already created a full roster of memorials to famous Americans, including Gen. Philip Sheridan, Gen. Robert E. Lee, and Pres. Abraham Lincoln. Relying on his independent study of the four presidents, as well as life masks, paintings, photographs, and descriptions, Borglum created plaster sketches of the men. These sketches became the models for the memorial, and copies of each president's likeness were always on display on the mountain as a guide for the workmen.

Using a method of measurement called "pointing," Borglum taught his crews to measure the models, multiply by 12, and transfer the calibrations to the mountain carving. Using a simple ratio of 1:12, 1 inch on the model would equal 1 foot on the mountain.

Borglum and his dedicated crew used dynamite to carve more than 90% of the memorial. Powdermen became so skilled in the use of dynamite that they could grade the contours of the cheeks, chin, nose, and eyebrows to within inches of the finished surface. Skilled drillers used bumper bits and pneumatic drills to complete each portrait, leaving the surfaces of the presidents' faces as smooth as a concrete sidewalk. Up close, the pupils of each of the presidents' eyes are actually shallow recessions with projecting shafts of granite. From a distance, this unlikely shape makes the eyes sparkle. Several men were injured while working at Mount Rushmore, but miraculously, no one was killed during its construction.

As work neared completion in March 1941, Borglum died in a Chicago hospital at age 74. His son, Lincoln, carried on the work for another 6 months, but that work was soon interrupted by the winds of war. On October 31, as war clouds rumbled over Europe, the younger Borglum and his crew turned off the drills for good and removed the last scaffolding from the sculpture, returning the mountain to the eternal silence from which it had been awakened in 1927.

The untiring effort of the Borglums and their determined cadre of influential supporters resulted in a work of art for the ages. George Washington, the most prominent figure in the group, symbolizes the birth of a republic founded on the principle of individual liberty; Thomas Jefferson, who managed to fund the Louisiana Purchase and balance the federal budget, signifies the growth of the United States; Abraham Lincoln, the Great Emancipator, imparts the strength of character responsible for preserving the union in the throes of the bloody Civil War; and Theodore Roosevelt, the "Trust Buster" and friend of the common man, embod-

ies the American spirit of independence, strength, and a love of the rugged wilderness.

Avoiding the Crowds. Peak visitation at Mount Rushmore is during June, July, and August. Mount Rushmore is very popular. The best time to visit is September and October, with April and May as alternatives. Although spring months can be wet and cold, the Hills' dry weather patterns make fall visits ideal. The varied mix of trees and plant life found in the alpine meadows and creek-carved canyons also makes the Black Hills a popular destination for avid "leaf-peepers."

If possible, view the sculpture at daybreak, when the golden orb of the sun crawls out of the morning mist of the badlands. Few vacationers are stirring at sunrise, making it among the best times to enjoy a more contemplative and less crowded experience. And there may be no finer setting for breakfast than the park's Buffalo Dining Room, which affords a commanding view of the presidents.

ESSENTIALS

Visitor Center. Mount Rushmore is open 24 hours a day, year-round. The **Information Center,** located just inside the entrance to the memorial, is open daily (except Christmas) from 8am to 5pm in winter, and 8am to 10pm in the summer. The **Lincoln Borglum Museum** maintains the same hours. This outstanding museum contains 5,200 square feet of exhibits, a bookstore operated by the Mount Rushmore History Association, and two 125-seat theaters. One interactive display features the dynamite blasting used to carve the mountain. This is an educational experience not to be missed, and the museum also features some of the best views of the sculptures.

Fees. Mount Rushmore remains one of the few popular parks that have managed to avoid an entrance fee. However,

Tips from the Park Superintendent

Mount Rushmore has undergone a great many changes recently, according to Superintendent Don Striker, who says, "The Lincoln Borglum Museum provides an interpretive experience unequaled in western national park areas." Striker says that interactive displays depict sculptor Gutzon Borglum and his crew at work. There's also a large mural on the history of the United States that helps visitors understand why these four presidents were selected for the monument.

The Presidential Trail is a favorite of visitors, according to Striker, who adds, "This trail allows visitors to get close to the carving to better understand the scale of the sculpture." He adds that it also offers extraordinary views. "Our ranger program in the evening, with the lighting of the memorial, is a popular, patriotic experience," Striker says.

you will have to pay an $8 fee for parking, which is funding the parking structure at the memorial. National Park, Golden Eagle, Golden Age, and Golden Access passes are not accepted for the parking fee, but because it's an annual ticket, you can come back later for no extra charge. Limited free parking is available near the sculptor studio as you arrive at Rushmore from Keystone. Expect a short walk up stairs if you park here. This walk can be strenuous, though, for those with breathing, leg, or foot problems. The fee parking might be a better choice.

Special Regulations & Warnings. Visitor access is prohibited within a restricted area around the Mount Rushmore sculpture. In other areas of the park, rock climbing and hiking are permitted.

Useful Publications. The National Park Service has a number of informational pamphlets and other materials at the Information Center as you enter the memorial. A variety of books, maps, and videos are sold in the bookstore located in the Lincoln Borglum Museum.

IF YOU HAVE ONLY 1 DAY

Unlike many of the larger national park units in the country, a complete visit to Rushmore may be accomplished in 2 to 3 hours. Even with its repertoire of interpretive exhibits, trails, and theaters, the park can be fully explored and appreciated in a fraction of the time of many of its western counterparts.

Particularly in the high-visitation summer months, the park is best placed at the beginning or end of a visitor's daily itinerary. Excellent light at daybreak, coupled with its scenic setting and great breakfasts in the Buffalo Dining Room, make Mount Rushmore hard to beat for the first stop of the day. The patriotic ranger program and dramatic lighting ceremony, held nightly at 9pm from mid-May through September, also make the memorial inspiring at night.

EXPLORING THE PARK BY CAR

Although Mount Rushmore is best enjoyed on foot, many visitors overlook an impressive view of the sculpture that is best reached by car. After leaving the park's parking lot, turn right on S. Dak. 244 and proceed west then northwest around the memorial. Less than a mile from the parking lot you'll discover the proud profile of George Washington in the upper-right corner of your windshield. While surveying the scene, keep an eye out for the Rocky Mountain goats that frequent the memorial and the Black Elk Wilderness Area to the west.

ORGANIZED TOURS & RANGER PROGRAMS

Mount Rushmore offers a variety of excellent interpretive programs, including the following:

- A 30-minute **Nature Walk** leads to the Sculptor's Studio, with frequent stops to discuss the area's flora, fauna, and geology. The walking tour ends at the historic studio in time for the Studio Talk.
- The 15-minute **Studio Talk** (summer only) at the 1939 Sculptor's Studio examines techniques used by the artist to carve the memorial, as well as the original tools and plaster models employed in its construction.
- **Amphitheater Programs** are extremely popular and often patriotic. Depending on the timing of your visit, you could be treated to a solemn ceremony, a full-fledged celebration, or a musical presentation.
- A **regular 30-minute program** at the amphitheater includes a talk and movie about the memorial, which coincides with its dramatic lighting ceremony. (The sculpture is illuminated nightly for 1–2 hr. year-round). The program begins at 9pm from mid-May through September and at 8pm in the fall.
- A 13-minute **film** narrated by noted reporter and South Dakotan Tom Brokaw is shown continuously at the visitor center and museum. Painting a broad overview of the memorial's history, construction, and subjects, the movie gives visitors a greater understanding of the colossal carving.

HISTORIC BUILDINGS & OTHER ATTRACTIONS

The 1939 **Sculptor's Studio** played an important role in the final years of the construction of Mount Rushmore. Today, the spacious studio and the artist's models it houses are integral to understanding how Borglum and his drill-dusty crew carved the sculpture from Black Hills granite.

Located on the walkway between the Concession Building and the Lincoln Borglum Museum, the **Avenue of Flags** features the official flags of all U.S. states, territories, districts, and commonwealths, arranged in alphabetical order. The flags serve as a patriotic, colorful frame to Mount Rushmore.

DAY HIKES

The **Presidential Trail** begins near the main viewing terrace, then proceeds west through the ponderosa pines to the talus slope at the base of the sculpture. The trail is 0.6 mile long, and a large portion of it is accessible to travelers with disabilities. The other portion of the trail consists of many steps, and depending on which direction a visitor walks, the trail can be a steep climb. The boardwalk circles the southeastern slope of the mountain before arriving at the Sculptor's Studio. In addition to decreasing crowding on the memorial's viewing terraces, this new trail takes visitors into the woods and affords new vantage points from which to view the four presidents.

ROCK CLIMBING

Although climbing on the Mount Rushmore sculpture and within the restricted zone adjacent to the sculpture is prohibited, much of the park is open to climbing. The park is known internationally as a world-class sports climbing area, with its massive spires and large rock faces nestled amid tall ponderosa pines.

Visiting Custer State Park

Custer State Park is one of the largest state parks in the Lower 48, and because of its unique historical, cultural, and natural resources it attracts many visitors. If

Crazy Horse Memorial

Known by locals as the "Fifth Face" in the Black Hills, the sculpture of the legendary Lakota Chief Crazy Horse began with the dedication of the work on June 3, 1948. More than a half century later, work continues on what is expected to be the world's largest sculpture. The chief's nine-story-high face has been completed, and work has begun on carving the 22-story-high horse's head.

Begun by the late sculptor Korczak Ziolkowski (pronounced jewel-*cuff*-ski), and carried on by his widow, sons, and daughters, the mountain sculpture memorial is dedicated to all American Indians.

"My fellow chiefs and I would like the white man to know the red man has great heroes, too," Sioux Chief Henry Standing Bear wrote Ziolkowski in 1939, inviting him to create the mountain memorial. Seven years later, the sculptor agreed and began carving the colossal work.

When the sculpture is completed, Crazy Horse will sit astride his mount, pointing over his stallion's head to the sacred Black Hills. So large is the sculpture (563 ft. high) that all four presidents on Mount Rushmore would fit in Crazy Horse's head.

Visitors driving by the site on U.S. 16/385, 5 miles north of the town of Custer, might hear dynamite blasts, a surefire signal that work on the mountain carving is progressing. When night blasts are detonated, they tend to be among the most impressive events in the Black Hills.

In addition to viewing the carving in progress and watching an audiovisual display about the work, visitors may stop at the **Indian Museum of North America** at Crazy Horse, which is home to one of the most extensive collections of American Indian artifacts in the country. The museum's gift shop features authentic American Indian crafts.

For more information, go to the Crazy Horse Memorial website: **www. crazyhorsememorial.org**.

you want to avoid the crowds, the best times to visit are from May to mid-June and September through October. Spring offers a reawakening of the grasslands and the birth of cinnamon-colored bison calves, as well as elk, deer, antelope, and other wildlife. Fall beckons the change of colors in every canyon and ravine, as well as the bugling of bull elk as they search for mates.

ESSENTIALS

Visitor Centers. The **Peter Norbeck Visitor Center,** located between the State Game Lodge and the Coolidge Inn Store on U.S. 16A, offers brochures, interpretive exhibits, and a variety of educational items.

The **Wildlife Station Visitor Center,** located on the southeast part of the Wildlife Loop, has shade, information, exhibits, and educational items.

Fees. Contact the park for current **entrance fees.** Modern **campsites** cost $16 per unit per night; semimodern campsites are $14; basic campsites are $7.

Special Regulations & Warnings. The park's biggest attraction may be its 1,500 head of bison. Remember that all animals in the park are wild and can be dangerous. Bison are extremely fast and can be lethal if provoked, so give them plenty of space.

Campers and hikers should never drink water from lakes, streams, or springs.

Useful Publications. The **South Dakota Game, Fish and Parks Department** provides a number of helpful brochures for the park, available at the Peter Norbeck Visitor Center and at park headquarters. The park's newspaper, *Tatanka,* provides information on the park's resorts and activities. The newspaper is available at each park entrance station, the visitor center, and park headquarters.

IF YOU HAVE ONLY 1 DAY

Of all the state and federal parks in South Dakota, Custer State Park may be the most difficult to see in a day. Three scenic drives, numerous hiking trails and nature walks, historic sites, wildlife loops, resorts, and some of the most spectacular scenery in the West tend to slow you down.

If you have only a day, try the 18-mile **Wildlife Loop** (described below), and then stop at the observation deck of the **Mount Coolidge Fire Tower** and the historic **Gordon Stockade.** If time permits, take a hike, perhaps on the popular trail to the **Cathedral Spires.**

EXPLORING THE PARK BY CAR

For a first-class sightseeing excursion, pick any of the park's three scenic drives: the Needles Highway, the Wildlife Loop Road, or the Iron Mountain Road. When driving through the park, it's important to keep an eye on the road and not your watch. Winding roads generally keep travel at 25 miles per hour or less.

Be aware: Tunnels on Iron Mountain Road (U.S. 16A) are 12 feet, 2 inches high and 13 feet, 2 inches wide. Tunnels on the Needles Highway/Sylvan Lake Road (S. Dak. 87) are as low as 10 feet, 7 inches and as narrow as 8 feet, 4 inches.

Needles Highway. This is a mesmerizing 14-mile journey through pine and spruce forests, meadows surrounded by birch and quaking aspen, and giant granite spires that reach to the sky. Visitors pass the picturesque waters of Sylvan Lake, through tunnels, and near a unique rock formation called the "Needle's Eye."

Wildlife Loop Road. This 18-mile drive takes you through open grasslands and pine-clad hills—an area that is home to most of the park's wildlife, including pronghorn, bison, white-tailed and mule deer, elk, coyote, begging wild burros, prairie dogs, eagles, hawks, and other birds. Stop by the Wildlife Station Visitor Center on the southeast part of the loop for information and exhibits. There are unpaved side roads off the Wildlife Loop Road that offer a quiet outdoor experience, in contrast to the main road in the summer. For example, one circle drive starts near the Wildlife Station Visitor Center. Take Park Road #3, then right on Park Road #4, right again on Park Road #5, and one more right on Park Road #2, which will take you back to the Wildlife Loop Road and the Wildlife Station.

Iron Mountain Road. Although only a portion of this scenic roadway rests in Custer State Park, it ranks as a must-see on any South Dakota visit. The winding road runs between Mount Rushmore and the junction of U.S. 16A and S. Dak. 36. Along the route are wildfire exhibits, wooden "pig-tail" bridges, pullouts with wonderful views, and tunnels that frame the four presidents at Mount Rushmore.

DAY HIKES

Custer State Park is home to a wide variety of hiking experiences ranging from short nature walks to backcountry treks. A 22-mile segment of the South Dakota Centennial Trail, the **Harney Peak Summit Trail,** extends through the park. The **Cathedral Spires Trail** is also a popular choice. Be aware that some trails are also open to mountain bikers and horseback riders.

Visiting Wind Cave National Park

For several centuries, American Indians have told stories of holes in the Black Hills through which the wind would blow and howl. But the first recorded

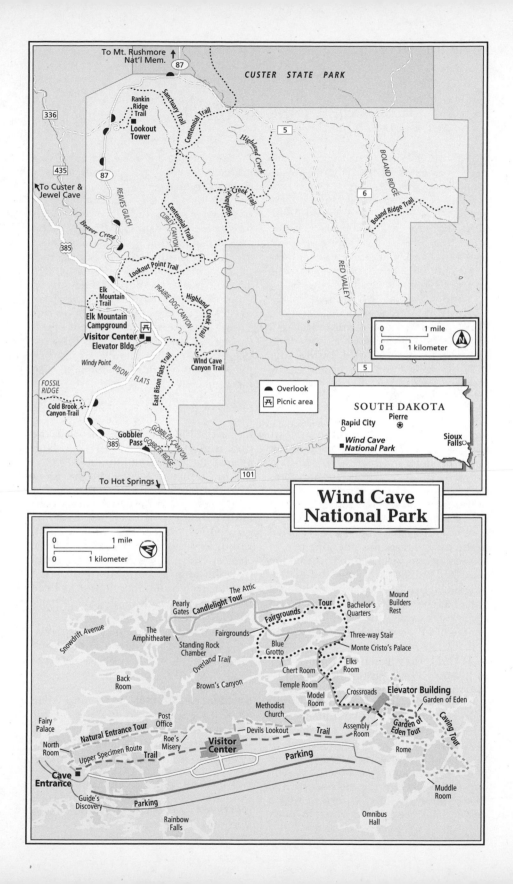

Wind Cave National Park

Top map (surface):

To Mt. Rushmore Nat'l Mem.
87
CUSTER STATE PARK
336
Rankin Ridge Trail
Sanctuary Trail
Centennial Trail
Lookout Tower
5
Highland Creek
BOLAND RIDGE
435
87
6
Boland Ridge Trail
REAVES GULCH
Centennial Trail
Highland Creek Trail
To Custer & Jewel Cave
Beaver Creek
CURLEY CANYON
385
Lookout Point Trail
RED VALLEY
Elk Mountain Trail
PRAIRIE DOG CANYON
Highland Creek Trail
Elk Mountain Campground
Visitor Center
Elevator Bldg.
Windy Point
BISON FLATS
Wind Cave Canyon Trail
5
East Bison Flats Trail
Overlook
Picnic area
FOSSIL RIDGE
Cold Brook Canyon Trail
GOBBLER CANYON
SOUTH DAKOTA
Rapid City
Pierre
Gobbler Pass
385
GOBBLER RIDGE
Wind Cave National Park
Sioux Falls
To Hot Springs
101

0   1 mile
0   1 kilometer
N

Bottom map (cave):

0   1 mile
0   1 kilometer

The Attic
Pearly Gates
Candlelight Tour
Fairgrounds
Tour
Bachelor's Quarters
Mound Builders Rest
Snowdrift Avenue
The Amphitheater
Fairgrounds
Three-way Stair
Standing Rock Chamber
Blue Grotto
Monte Cristo's Palace
Overland Trail
Elks Room
Back Room
Brown's Canyon
Chert Room
Temple Room
Crossroads
Elevator Building
Garden of Eden
Fairy Palace
Post Office
Methodist Church
Model Room
Garden of Eden Tour
Caving Tour
North Room
Natural Entrance Tour
Roe's Misery
Devils Lookout
Trail
Assembly Room
Rome
Upper Specimen Route
Trail
Visitor Center
Parking
Cave Entrance
Guide's Discovery
Parking
Muddle Room
Rainbow Falls
Omnibus Hall

Tips from an Insider

Former Wind Cave National Park Superintendent Jimmy Taylor loves this park.

"This is truly an amazing park," says Taylor. "You can see and hear wildlife here. We have 300 to 400 head of elk, more than 300 bison, 35 antelope, two highways, and two all-weather gravel roads that make this park very accessible and suitable to the family sedan."

Wind Cave is "an intimate park" where road-weary travelers can put the brakes on and enjoy plant and animal life at its best, Taylor says. Visitors often settle back and just watch prairie dogs building their "towns" or bison grazing on the prairie grasses. In fall, Taylor says there's nothing quite like the sound of a lonely bull elk bugling from a rocky ridge in the park.

And beneath this remarkable place, says Taylor, is an underground wilderness whose depths have only been guessed at, and whose complexity we are only beginning to understand.

"Imagine," the superintendent says, "that only a few hundred feet underground there are spaces people have never seen, and perhaps may never see. Think that every time someone crawls through a hole or peeks into the next opening, they may literally be the first person in the history of mankind who has ever seen it."

discovery of Wind Cave came in 1881 when brothers Jesse and Tom Bingham were lured to the cave by a whistling noise. As the legend goes, the wind was rushing from the cave entrance with such force that it blew Tom's hat right off his head.

A few days later, when Jesse returned to the cave to show this phenomenon to friends, he was surprised to find that the wind had shifted directions and his hat was sucked into the cave. A hundred years later, we know that the direction of the wind is related to the difference in atmospheric pressure between the cave and the surface.

J. D. McDonald was the first person to attempt to establish a tourist attraction at Wind Cave, complete with stagecoach transportation, a hotel, and a gift shop. He did this primarily because there were no valuable mineral deposits in the cave to mine. But "ownership" of the cave came into question, and the matter soon entered a courtroom. The controversy caught the attention of the Department of the Interior, which decided in December 1899 that no party had a claim to Wind Cave. In 1901, the department withdrew all the land around the cave from homesteading.

On January 9, 1903, president Theodore Roosevelt signed the bill that established Wind Cave as America's seventh national park, and the first one created to protect the underground resources of a cave. In 1913 and 1914, the American Bison Society assisted in reestablishing a bison herd at Wind Cave, through the donation of 14 head from the New York Zoological Society. Also arriving in the park were 21 elk from Wyoming and 13 pronghorn antelope from Alberta, Canada. Today, Wind Cave is home to 350 bison, as well as large herds of elk and antelope.

Avoiding the Crowds. With more than 28,000 acres, 2 paved highways, 2 all-weather gravel roads, 10 excellent trails, backcountry camping, and plenty of room to roam, avoiding the crowds in Wind Cave National Park is a cinch.

July and August are the busiest months. Annual visitation averages 800,000, and about 100,000 people participate in a cave tour each year. When planning daily itineraries, include Wind Cave in either the early morning or late afternoon, when visitation is lowest and wildlife is most active. Buy your cave tour tickets early in the day.

ESSENTIALS

Visitor Center. The visitor center (located right off U.S. 385), which is open daily year-round (except New Year's Day, Thanksgiving, and Christmas), has books, brochures, exhibits, and slide programs about the cave and other park resources. Cave tour information and tickets are available, and schedules of activities, including talks and nature walks, are posted.

Fees & Permits. Wind Cave National Park does not charge an entrance fee. It does, however, charge a fee for cave tours, ranging from $6 ($2 with a Golden Age Passport) for a simple guided tour ($3–$4.50 for children 6–16, children under 6 are free) to $20 for a 4-hour introduction to basic caving techniques.

Camping in Elk Mountain Campground costs $12 per night from mid-May through mid-September, and $6 per night during the rest of its season; all camping is on a first-come, first-served basis. Backcountry camping is allowed with a free permit, which must be picked up in person at the visitor center.

Special Regulations & Warnings. The danger of wildfire is usually high year-round. Build fires only in the campground and only in fire grills or camp stoves. Never leave a fire unattended. Off-road driving is prohibited. Watch for rattlesnakes and black widow spiders, especially around prairie dog burrows.

Cave tour pathways may be uneven or wet and slippery. Watch your step and wear low-heeled, nonslip shoes. A jacket, sweater, or sweatshirt is recommended for protection from the cave's 53°F (12°C) temperature. If you have breathing, heart, or walking problems, or are claustrophobic, consult with a ranger before taking a tour. The cave's delicate formations are easily broken or discolored by skin oils, so please don't touch them. Smoking, food, and drink are prohibited in the cave.

Useful Publications. The National Park Service publishes a variety of informational handouts on topics such as park history, hiking, camping, geology, wildlife, bird life, prairie grasses and ecosystems, and environmental concerns. In addition, the park produces *Passages,* a free visitor newspaper that is available at the visitor center.

IF YOU HAVE ONLY 1 DAY

Even with more than 44 square miles of forest, grasslands, and quiet canyons, visitors can appreciate most of the highlights of Wind Cave National Park in a day or less. You'll have time for a cave tour and a drive through the park to view the bison and elk. If you have time, then get out on one of the park's hiking trails.

ORGANIZED CAVE TOURS

The park offers five cave tours during the summer season and one tour the remainder of the year. Adventurous cavers should consider the two tours that are limited to 10 people each; these will definitely take them away from the crowds.

The Garden of Eden Tour. Entering and leaving Wind Cave by an elevator, this 1-hour tour takes participants past representative cave features. It's the park's least strenuous tour, climbing 150 stairs.

Natural Entrance Tour. Beginning at the walk-in entrance to the cave and leaving by elevator, this moderately strenuous 75-minute tour has 300 stairs (though most of these are down) and

Deadwood: The Wildest & Woolliest Town in the West

There was a time when it wasn't safe to walk the cobblestone streets of the Black Hills' original sin city. But that was a thousand gunfights and barroom brawls ago, when Deadwood was known as the wildest, wickedest, woolliest town in the West; where Wild Bill Hickok was gunned down and where Calamity Jane Canary claimed she could outdrink, outswear, and outspit any man.

Today, the sounds of slot machines and streetside barkers have replaced the sporadic gunshots, crunching blows, and general rowdiness of a century ago, when miners, gamblers, and painted ladies all searched for their pot of gold. They found gold, of course, but seldom retained it.

The city's merchants, bankers, and saloonkeepers, however, cleverly invested their money in beautiful Victorian buildings and residences that today stand as testament to a richer time.

Although Deadwood was labeled "a disaster" by historic preservation officials just over a decade ago, the town is alive and kicking today. This is due to a great extent to limited stakes gambling, approved by South Dakota voters in 1989 to generate money to restore and preserve this mile-high community. The $5 maximum bet was raised to $100 in 2000.

Now, state and national historic preservation officials call Deadwood's metamorphosis "a miracle." Brick streets, period lighting, and colorful trolleys greet visitors, who spend hours ducking in doorways and trying their luck in the town's 85—yes, 85—gambling halls. In addition to gambling, Deadwood has some of the best restaurants and hotels in the state.

For more information on accommodations, walking tours, museums, attractions, special events, and gambling packages, contact the **Deadwood Chamber of Commerce & Visitor Bureau** (© 800/999-1876; www.deadwood.org), or stop by the History and Information Center in the classic train depot at 3 Siever St.

leads visitors through the middle of the cave, with an abundance of "box work"—thin blades of calcite that project from the cave's walls and ceiling in a honeycomb pattern.

Fairgrounds Tour. This includes some of the larger rooms found in the developed area of the cave. Participants view many cave formations, including box work. The tour enters and exits by elevator. This moderately strenuous excursion has 450 stairs and lasts 90 minutes.

Candlelight Tour. This is one of the most popular tours, especially for children 8 and over. Trekking through a less-developed, unlighted section of the cave, tour participants each carry a candle bucket and experience the cave by candlelight. Shoes with nonslip soles are required; no sandals are allowed. This tour is limited to 10 people (minimum age is 8). This strenuous tour covers 1 mile of rugged trail and lasts 2 hours. Reservations, available no more than 1 month before the tour, are strongly advised (© 605/745-4600).

Caving Tour. You can also explore Wind Cave away from the established trails. On this 4-hour adventure, visitors are introduced to basic, safe caving practices. You need to wear old clothes and gloves, since much of the tour is spent crawling. Long pants, long-sleeve shirts, and sturdy, lace-up boots or shoes with nonslip soles are a must. The park provides hard hats, lights, and kneepads. Do not bring jewelry, watches, or other valuables. This tour is limited to 10 people and the minimum age is 16. (Signed consent forms from a parent or guardian are required for 16- and 17-year-olds.) Reservations, which are available 1 month before the tour, are required (℃ **605/745-4600**).

Tours for People with Disabilities. The visitor center and the cave are accessible to people with limited mobility. Call ahead (℃ **605/745-4600**) to make special arrangements or inquire about a special tour at the information desk. Some areas of the cave are accessible to wheelchairs. Fees are charged for special services.

EXPLORING THE PARK BY CAR

Wind Cave National Park is not just about a cave. The rolling prairies of western South Dakota run smack into the ponderosa pine forests of the Black Hills in the park, and its roadways provide access to some of the best wildlife viewing opportunities in the region. Bison, pronghorn, elk, and other wildlife abound in this rugged preserve, and you'll be able to see many of them as you drive down through Custer State Park on S. Dak. 87 to Wind Cave. The combination of Wind Cave National Park and the adjoining Custer State Park presents a most attractive introduction to the Black Hills. Several scenic roadways lead through the Black Hills to Wind Cave. Roadside sightseers will find the Wildlife Loop Road, Iron Mountain Road, and Needles Highway particularly enjoyable. All of these are in Custer State Park, just north of Wind Cave National Park, and are described in the preceding section.

Warning: Tunnels on Iron Mountain Road (U.S. 16A) are 12 feet, 6 inches high and 13 feet, 6 inches wide. Tunnels on the Needles Highway/Sylvan Lake Road (S. Dak. 87) are as low as 10 feet, 8 inches and as narrow as 8 feet, 7 inches.

RANGER PROGRAMS

Park rangers provide a number of **talks** and programs at Wind Cave. Topics range from local wildlife, plants, and geology to area history and spelunking and cave surveying. **Campfire programs** are conducted most evenings during the summer months. There is a 2-hour ranger-guided **prairie hike** conducted daily in the morning during the summer. Check with the visitor center for times and locations.

DAY HIKES

More than 30 miles of trails crisscross the park's backcountry. Several can be combined to create round-trip hikes, or you may want to leave the trails and hike a ridgeline, explore a canyon, or trek across an open prairie bordered by ponderosa pine. Backcountry camping is permitted in the northwestern portion of the park with a free permit, available at the visitor center or either of the Centennial trailheads.

Park handouts also provide information on more than a half-dozen other trails ranging from 1.4 miles to 8.6 miles.

Centennial Trail

6 miles one-way. Moderate. Access: Along S. Dak. 87, 0.7 mile north of its intersection with U.S. 385.

Wind Cave provides the southern terminus for the 110-mile-long Centennial Trail, built in honor of South Dakota's centennial in 1989. The trail leads through the heart of the Black Hills before ending at Bear Butte State Park near Sturgis. A 6-mile section of the Centennial Trail is in the park, where it crosses the prairie, climbs the foothills and forested ridges, and also provides access to the wetter, riparian habitat of **Beaver Creek.**

Elk Mountain Nature Trail

0.5 mile one-way. Easy. Access: Elk Mountain Campground.

This interpretive trail explores an eco-tone, or meeting zone, where prairie and forest converge. Booklets are available at the trailhead.

Rankin Ridge Nature Trail

0.75 mile RT. Moderate. Access: Rankin Ridge parking lot.

This loop trail leads to the highest point in the park, and is one of Wind Cave's most popular. You can stop at the lookout tower, about halfway around the loop. Booklets are available at the trailhead.

Visiting Jewel Cave National Monument

The exploration of Jewel Cave began in about 1900 when two South Dakota prospectors, Frank and Albert Michaud, and a companion, Charles Bush, happened to hear wind rushing through a hole in the rocks in Hell Canyon. After enlarging the hole, they discovered a cave full of sparkling crystals. The entrepreneurs filed a mining claim on the "Jewel Lode," but they found no valuable minerals, so they attempted to turn the cave into a tourist attraction. The business was never a success, but the cave's uniqueness did attract attention, and in 1908 Pres. Theodore Roosevelt established Jewel Cave National Monument to protect this remarkable natural wonder.

A half-century later, exploration of the cave intensified. Led by the husband and wife team of Herb and Jan Conn, spelunkers discovered new wonders and explored and mapped miles of passageways.

When first asked to consider a trek below the surface, the Conns were reluctant. But after their first excursion into the underworld, the couple could not be turned away. In more than 2 decades of spelunking in Jewel Cave, the Conns logged 708 trips into the cave and 6,000 hours of exploration and mapping. Their efforts proved that Jewel Cave was among the most extensive and complex cave ecosystems in the world, filled with scenic and scientific wonders.

The explorers discovered chambers with exquisite calcite crystals and other rare specimens. One room mapped by the Conns, the Formation Room, is now a highlight of the Park Service tours. They also found rooms as large as 150 feet by 200 feet, passageways as long as 3,200 feet, and a place where the cave wind blows at speeds of 32 miles per hour. In 1980, after discovering more than 65 miles of passageways, the Conns retired, and a new generation of spelunkers have pushed the known boundaries of the cave to well over 125 miles.

When the Conns said, "We are still just standing on the threshold," they could not have known how accurate they were. Studies by the U.S. Geological Survey have since attempted to determine the amount of passageways in the cave by measuring the volume of air leaving or entering the cave, depending on the barometric pressure outside. Conclusions of those studies indicate that known passageways at Jewel Cave constitute less than 5% of what actually exists in the quiet darkness below the Black Hills.

Only Mammoth Cave in Kentucky and Optimisticeskaja in the Ukraine are longer than Jewel Cave. Explorations of Jewel Cave in 1997 moved the cave from fourth- to third-longest, surpassing Holloch Cave in Switzerland.

Known for its calcite nailhead and dogtooth spar crystal, Jewel Cave is home to a variety of rare and unusual cave formations. The Cave's hydromagnesite "balloons," fragile silvery bubbles that look as if they might pop any minute, have been found in just a handful of other caves. Scintillites, reddish rocks coated with sparkling clear quartz crystals, were unknown until they were discovered in Jewel Cave. One particularly intriguing mineral, gypsum, combines with time and the ceaseless presence of seeping water to assume the shapes of flowers, needles, spiders, and cottony beards that sway from the heat of an explorer's lamp.

Avoiding the Crowds. The highest visitation at Jewel Cave occurs in June, July, and August. With 1,274 acres above the surface and annual visitation of approximately 140,000, Jewel Cave is rarely overcrowded, even at the height of the tourist season. However, because space on some scenic tours is limited and more than 90,000 park visitors participate in a cave tour annually, visitors should anticipate a wait to be able to enter the cave. If you want to keep your wait to a minimum, arrive early in the morning or late in the day.

ESSENTIALS

Visitor Center. The visitor center has books and brochures, and park rangers can assist travelers in planning their visit, pointing out special interpretive programs, and answering questions about the park's cultural, historical, and geologic resources. Up-to-date cave information and tour tickets also are available at the visitor center, which is open daily year-round.

Fees. There is no entry fee for the national monument, but you'll pay for cave tours. The Scenic and Candlelight tours cost $8 ($4 for children ages 6–16); the Spelunking tour is $27. Reservations can be made by calling ✆ **605/673-2288, ext. 1220.** Golden Age and Golden Access Passport holders pay reduced tour fees.

Special Regulations & Warnings. Low-heeled, rubber-soled shoes are highly recommended because trails can be slippery; some stair-climbing is required on each tour. A jacket, sweater, or sweatshirt will keep you comfortable in the 49°F (9°C) year-round temperature of the cave. Persons with respiratory or heart problems or who have been recently

Tips from the Chief of Interpretation

"**J**ewel Cave is one of the most structurally complex caves in the world and it is still being explored," according to Chief of Interpretation Karen Rosga. "This is not a cave that has been fully mapped, and it's probable that it will not be fully explored in any of our lifetimes." She adds, "To this point, we have been very successful in developing a visitor experience that allows people to enjoy the cave in a relatively pristine state."

For travelers with children over 6, Rosga recommends the "adventurous experience" of a candlelight tour into the cave, the park's Junior Ranger Program, and the variety of surface programs that augment the cave tours.

Fall, winter, and spring are ideal times to visit Jewel Cave National Monument, Rosga says. Even with arctic blasts on the surface, temperatures within the cave are constant at 49°F (9°C), with humidity averaging 98%. "In the middle of winter, it can actually be quite pleasant in the cave," says Rosga.

hospitalized or have a fear of heights or confined spaces should talk with a park ranger before selecting a tour. Damaging or even touching cave formations is prohibited because of the fragile and irreplaceable nature of the formations. Pets and smoking are not allowed in the cave. Cameras are permitted on cave tours, but tripods are not.

Useful Publications. The National Park Service publishes brochures covering a variety of topics, such as bats, birds, wildflowers, surface trails, spelunking tours, and the history and exploration of the cave.

IF YOU HAVE ONLY 1 DAY

This is a small monument—only 2 square miles aboveground—and exploring the highlights is possible in a fraction of a day. Allow 2 to 4 hours for a trip to the visitor center, a scenic cave tour, and a walk on one of the monument's surface trails.

CAVE TOURS

Visitors can have an adventure in Jewel Cave by taking any of the park's ranger-guided tours. Tickets for the Scenic Tour or Candlelight Tour must be purchased at the visitor center on the day of the tour. Reservations for the Spelunking Tour are strongly encouraged. Call ☏ **605/673-2288,** ext. 1220, for advance reservations. It's also a good idea to contact the monument before visiting to determine whether special hours, activities, or tour schedules are being observed.

Scenic Tour. This ½-mile, 80-minute tour visits chambers decorated with calcite crystals and colorful stalactites, stalagmites, and draperies. The loop tour begins at the visitor center with an elevator ride into the cave. Tour participants take a paved, lighted path and climb up and down more than 700 stairs on this moderately strenuous journey into the underground wilderness. The tour, which is offered year-round, is conducted several times daily from May to September and is limited to 30 persons.

Candlelight Tour. This ½-mile, 105-minute tour follows in the footsteps of early Jewel Cave explorers. Tour participants see the cave's calcite-coated passageways lighted by old-style candle lanterns. This round-trip tour starts at the cave's historic entrance in Hell Canyon, is moderately strenuous with many steep stairs, and requires much bending and stooping. Long pants and sturdy, closed-toe shoes are highly recommended. The

tour is offered several times daily from mid-June through Labor Day and is limited to 25 persons. (Definitely call ahead to find out if it will be offered when you are in the area.) Children under age 6 are not allowed.

Spelunking Tour. This physically and mentally challenging ½-mile, 3- to 4-hour tour gives participants a taste of modern-day cave crawling in a wild, undeveloped portion of Jewel Cave. The round-trip tour begins at the visitor center with an elevator ride into the cave. Old clothes, kneepads, and gloves are recommended; ankle-high laced boots with lug soles are required. The park supplies hard hats and headlamps. To qualify for the tour, participants are required to crawl through an 8½-by-24-inch concrete block tunnel. This tour is offered daily (12:30pm) from mid-June through mid-August; the limit is five persons (here's your chance to avoid the crowds). Children under 16 are not allowed; 16- and 17-year-olds must have a parent or guardian's written permission. You can (and should) reserve your place on a tour in advance by calling ☏ **605/673-2288,** ext. 1220.

RANGER PROGRAMS

In addition to the cave tours (see above), during the summer season, a number of special interpretive programs take place at the visitor center, including ranger talks, demonstrations, and guided walks. Check at the visitor center for specifics.

DAY HIKES

Travelers to Jewel Cave should also take time to experience life in the world aboveground by taking a nature hike (there are two hiking trails), enjoying a picnic, or searching out the plants and animals that inhabit the rugged hills and canyon country of the Black Hills.

In the stillness of the ponderosa pine forest that blankets the park are live mule deer, white-tailed deer, elk, porcupines, coyote, squirrels and chipmunks, and several species of birds, including golden eagles and hawks. Plants of both the prairie and the hills grow here, and in summer, wildflowers paint the landscape.

Some park trails were damaged by the Jasper Fire in August 2000, so check at the visitor center or with a park ranger for current conditions.

Canyons Trail

3.5 miles RT. Easy to moderate. Access: Visitor center.

This loop trail provides views of the limestone palisades of Hell Canyon and Lithograph Canyon, and offers a chance of seeing some of the deer, birds, and wildflowers that live in the ponderosa pine forest through which the trail winds. If you want to experience a part of the Canyon Trail without going the entire distance, you might try the 1.5-mile round-trip between the visitor center and the historic area of the cave.

Walk on the Roof

0.25 mile RT. Easy. Access: Visitor center.

While visiting the "roof" of Jewel Cave on this self-guided interpretive walk, you'll learn how the monument's surface and subsurface resources interact. Interpretive trail guides for this walk are available at the information desk in the visitor center.

Guided Tours

A number of charter bus park tours and guide services throughout the area are available. **Gray Line of the Black Hills,** P.O. Box 1106, Rapid City, SD 57709 (© **800/456-4461** or 605/342-4461; www. blackhillsgrayline.com) offers bus tours of the area. **Jack Rabbit Charters & Tours,** 301 N. Dakota Ave., Sioux Falls, SD 57104 (© **800/678-6543** or 605/336-3339; www.jackrabbitlines.com) offers 1-day and extended tours. **Golden Circle Tours Inc.,** P.O. Box 454, Custer, SD 57730 (© **877/811-4349** or 605/ 673-4349; www.goldencircletours.com),

offers guided van tours of the area. Its office is located on U.S. 16A, 1 mile east of Custer. The company rents cars and vans as well.

Sports & Activities

Aerial Tours. If you want to see the Black Hills from above, contact **Black Hills Balloons,** P.O. Box 210, Custer, SD 57730 (© **800/568-5320** or 605/673-2520; www. rapidnet.com/~balloons), which offers flights over the Black Hills, as well as Badlands National Park and Devils Tower National Monument, year-round.

Biking. The Black Hills region has more than 6,000 miles of fire trails, logging roads, and other undeveloped roads, and it is quickly becoming a top spot for mountain biking. **Custer State Park** is a prime spot for mountain biking—most park trails and roads are open to bikers. (The Legion Lake Resort in Custer State Park rents mountain bikes; see the complete listing under "Where to Stay," below.)

Fishing. Rainbow trout are stocked at **Horsethief Lake,** below Mount Rushmore, where there is a Forest Service campground (see "Camping," below). **Center** and **Stockade lakes** in Custer State Park are also good fishing spots. Many streams in this area, including **Grizzly Bear Creek,** behind Mount Rushmore, have good fishing for brook trout. You'll need a fishing license, available at sporting-goods stores and many convenience stores.

Horse-Packing Trips. Several companies offer guided trail rides through the backcountry of the Black Hills, including family-run **Dakota Badland Outfitters,** P.O. Box 85, Custer, SD 57730 (© **605/673-5363** winter; 605/673-2999 or 605/574-2525, ext. 812, summer; www.ridesouthdakota.com). Call for rates, activities, and reservations.

Snowmobiling. The upper Black Hills have hundreds of miles of groomed snowmobile trails, and many guest ranches and resorts, such as **Deadwood Gulch Resort** (see "Where to Stay," below), rent snowmobiles to their guests. You can get more information on trails and companies that rent snowmobiles from South Dakota Tourism (see "Information," earlier in this chapter).

Camping

Although there are no campgrounds within the boundaries of Mount Rushmore National Memorial or Jewel Cave National Monument, there are several campgrounds in Custer State Park and another campground in Wind Cave National Park, plus those in the Black Hills National Forest and privately operated campgrounds. Many commercial campgrounds offer free shuttle services, nightly entertainment, pools, convenience stores, and horseback riding. Reservations are recommended. Choice spots are often filled by midmorning, so arriving at popular campgrounds early in the day is advised.

For more information on camping opportunities, contact South Dakota Tourism (see "Information," earlier in this chapter). For information on National Forest Service campgrounds, contact the **Forest Supervisor,** Black Hills National Forest, RR2, P.O. Box 200, Custer, SD 57730 (℅ **605/673-9200;** www.fs.fed.us/r2/blackhills), or contact **Forest Recreation Management, Inc.,** 111 Elm St., Hill City, SD 57745 (℅ **605/574-4402;** www.forestrecreation management.com).

INSIDE WIND CAVE NATIONAL PARK

Located in the pine forests 1 mile north of the park visitor center, **Elk Mountain Campground** has shady sites suitable for tents and recreational vehicles. The campground fee is $12 per night per site mid-May through mid-September and $6 per night per site the remainder of its season, when water is turned off.

Park rangers give campfire programs at the amphitheater in the summer. **Backcountry camping** is also permitted (contact the park office for details), and backcountry campers are encouraged to practice low-impact camping and hiking techniques.

INSIDE CUSTER STATE PARK

Campgrounds here require park entrance fees as well as camping fees.

Each campsite at Custer State Park has a gravel or paved camping pad, drinking water and showers, and a picnic table, and all campgrounds but Center Lake have flush toilets. About 200 campsites throughout the park may be reserved beginning in January, while other sites are available on a first-come, first-served basis.

Campsites range from modern to primitive. Group camping is available at two campgrounds; the French Creek Horse Camp is designated specifically for campers with horses.

For information and reservations contact **Custer State Park,** HC 83, Box 70, Custer, SD 57730 (℅ **800/710-2267** or 605/255-4515).

Blue Bell Campground is located in a mature stand of ponderosa pine near French Creek, not far from the site where Lt. Col. George Armstrong Custer and his 7th Cavalry discovered gold in 1874. It offers easy access to the Wildlife Loop Road, horseback riding, stream fishing, and fabulous hiking.

Game Lodge Campground is another of Custer State Park's fine campgrounds. This one was designed for larger RVs, but tent campers will find cool, shady sites and an occasional bison along the banks of Grace Coolidge Creek. It's located near the park's Peter Norbeck Visitor Center and the State Game Lodge.

Legion Lake Campground is centrally located in Custer State Park, with fishing, boating, and hiking opportunities right at your doorstep. Historic sites are within walking distance, as is the Legion Lake Resort across the highway.

You'd probably have to camp in Yosemite Valley to get a better view than the one at **Sylvan Lake Campground.** This mountain retreat is located just off the incredible Needles Highway, near 7,242-foot **Harney Peak,** the highest point between the Rockies and the Swiss Alps, and affords visitors the best in Black Hills hiking and mountain climbing. Its campsites fill quickly, so make your reservations early; all sites are reservable.

The park's other three campgrounds are **Center Lake,** 5 miles northeast of the junction of U.S. 16A and S. Dak. 87; **Grace Coolidge,** 13 miles east of Custer on U.S. 16A; and **Stockade Lake,** located just inside the park's western boundary on U.S. 16A.

Reservations are accepted at Game Lodge, Legion Lake, Blue Bell, Stockade North, Sylvan Lake, and French Creek Horse Camp. It's first-come, first-served at Grace Coolidge, Center Lake, and Stockade South.

INSIDE THE BLACK HILLS NATIONAL FOREST

You can make **National Forest camping reservations** by calling © 877/444-6777 or online at www.reserveusa.com. Below are just two of 19 campgrounds in the Black Hills National Forest of South Dakota and Wyoming.

Horsethief Lake Campground, only a mile west of Mount Rushmore, offers scenic sites adjacent to picturesque Horsethief Lake. At a 5,000-foot elevation, 28 sites are for tents, travel trailers, and RVs, while 8 sites are for tents only. Sites not reserved (50% can be reserved) fill quickly, so you need to claim yours early in the day.

Roubaix Lake Campground, off U.S. 385 on FDR 255, is nestled in a ponderosa pine forest next to scenic Roubaix Lake, which offers great fishing and swimming at a 5,500-foot elevation. Spaces fill fast; some can be reserved.

COMMERCIAL CAMPGROUNDS

A variety of privately operated campgrounds provide all the usual RV hookups and other services.

American Presidents Resort, 1 mile east of Custer on Hwy. 16A, P.O. Box 446, Custer, SD 57730 (© 605/673-3373; www.presidentsresort.com), is a perfect home base for touring the southern Black Hills. The campground's 40-by-60-foot heated pool is popular, as are its free miniature golf and horseshoes. The campground, with 70 sites, also has a store and fishing nearby. A 10% discount is offered on reservations made before May 15. Also available are 44 full-service cabins, some with kitchens, that sleep from 2 to 12 people and a 15-unit motel (call for rates).

Berry Patch Campground, 1860 E. North St. (I-90 at Exit 60), Rapid City, SD 57701 (© 800/658-4566 or 605/341-5588; berrypat@rapidnet.com), is the easiest campground to reach on and off I-90; it's also clean and friendly. Full hookups and drive-throughs complement its heated pool, store, nightly movie, and game room.

Big Pine Campground, R.R. 1, P.O. Box 52, Custer, SD 57730 (© 800/235-3981 for reservations, or 605/673-4054; www.bigpinecampground.com), secluded from traffic noises, offers level, naturally shaded sites; fireplaces and wood; and a store, game room, playground, hiking, and horseshoes.

Miners RV Park, P.O. Box 157, Keystone, SD 57751 (© 800/727-2421 or 605/666-4638; www.blackhills.com/minersresort), in the heart of the former mining town of Keystone, is close to numerous attractions and only a stone's throw from Mount Rushmore National Memorial. The campground and its adjacent 43-unit motel offer cool shade and a gurgling brook, as well as a store, gas, ice, gifts, restaurant, heated pool, and hot tub. Take a fun walk down Keystone's Main Street while you're here.

Campground	Total Sites	RV Hookups	Dump Station	Toilets	Drinking Water
Inside Badlands National Park					
Cedar Pass	110	No	Yes	Yes	Yes
Sage Creek	15	No	No	Yes	No
Near Badlands National Park					
Badlands Ranch and Resort	35	Yes	No	Yes	Yes
Inside Wind Cave National Park					
Elk Mountain	75	No	No	Yes	Yes
Inside Custer State Park					
Blue Bell	35	No	No	Yes	Yes
Center Lake	71	No	No	Yes	Yes
Game Lodge	59	No	Yes	Yes	Yes
Grace Coolidge	26	No	No	Yes	Yes
Legion Lake	25	No	No	Yes	Yes
Stockade Lake	85	No	No	Yes	Yes
Sylvan Lake	40	No	No	Yes	Yes
Inside Black Hills National Forest					
Horsethief Lake	36	No	No	Yes	Yes
Roubaix Lake	56	No	No	Yes	Yes
Private Campgrounds in the Black Hills					
American Presidents	70	Yes	No	Yes	Yes
Berry Patch	130	Yes	Yes	Yes	Yes
Big Pine	90	Yes	Yes	Yes	Yes
Miners	28	Yes	No	Yes	Yes
Mount Rushmore KOA	500	Yes	Yes	Yes	Yes
Rapid City KOA	255	Yes	Yes	Yes	Yes
Whistler Gulch	127	Yes	Yes	Yes	Yes

*Campground opening and closing dates can vary from year to year.

Mount Rushmore KOA, P.O. Box 295, Hill City, SD 57745 (✆ **800/562-8503;** www.mtrushmorekoa.com), part of the Palmer Gulch Resort, is among the best campgrounds in the region. With 500 sites and 55 Kamping Kabins, two pools and spas, a water slide, American Indian dancers, movies, miniature golf, fishing, hayrides, a restaurant, tours, and car rentals, this is what many commercial campgrounds want to be when they grow up.

Rapid City KOA, P.O. Box 2592, Rapid City, SD 57709 (✆ **800/KOA-8504** or 605/348-2111; rckoa@aol.com), is conveniently located on Rapid City's eastern flank. This large KOA offers a free pancake breakfast and a grand pool and spa. Bus tours and car rentals are available, and great shopping,

Showers	Fire Pits/ Grills	Laundry	Public Phone	Reserve	Fees	Open*
No	Yes	No	Yes	No	$10	Year-round
No	Yes	No	No	No	Free	Year-round
Yes	Yes	Yes	Yes	Yes	$12	Year-round
No	Yes	No	Yes	No	$6–$12	Apr–Oct
Yes	Yes	Yes	Yes	Yes	$16	May 1–Oct 1
Yes	Yes	No	Yes	No	$14	May 1–Sept 15
Yes	Yes	Yes	Yes	Yes	$16	May 1–Nov 1
Yes	Yes	No	Yes	No	$16	May 1–Oct 1
Yes	Yes	No	Yes	Yes	$16	May 1–Sept 15
Yes	Yes	No	No	Yes	$16	May 1–Sept 5
Yes	Yes	Yes	Yes	Yes	$16	May 1–Sept 15
No	Yes	No	No	Yes	$18–$20	Closed winter
No	Yes	No	Yes	Yes	$16–$18	Year-round (13 sites)
Yes	Yes	Yes	Yes	Yes	$25.50–$33.95	May 15–mid-Oct
Yes	Yes	Yes	Yes	Yes	$32–$35	Year-round
Yes	Yes	Yes	Yes	Yes	$17–$22	May 10–Oct 1
Yes	Yes	Yes	Yes	Yes	$26	Apr 15–Oct 15
Yes	Yes	Yes	Yes	Yes	$25–$60	May 1–Oct 1
Yes	Yes	Yes	Yes	Yes	$26–$59	Apr 15–Oct 15
Yes	Yes	Yes	Yes	Yes	$20–$30	May 1–Oct 1

sightseeing, and Rushmore Plaza Civic Center are nearby.

Whistler Gulch Campground, 235 Cliff St., Hwy. 85 S., Deadwood, SD 57732 (© **800/704-7139** or 605/578-2092; www. deadwood.com/whistler), is nestled in one of Deadwood's famous mining gulches. The campground offers 100 full-service RV sites and secluded tent sites. Facilities include a heated swimming pool, a sport court, and a small store. The town trolley takes visitors to Deadwood's casinos and historic sites.

Where to Stay

There are no accommodations at Mount Rushmore, Wind Cave, or Jewel Cave; but inns, hotels, motels, lodges, and bed-and-breakfasts are plentiful in nearby Black Hills communities and parks. Custer State Park has four popular lodges; reservations are strongly recommended, especially in summer months. In fact, for popular destinations such as Custer State Park, it's best to call 6 months to a year in advance of your visit. In addition to the properties listed below in Rapid City, Nemo, and Deadwood, you'll find accommodations in Keystone and Hill City (especially convenient to Mount Rushmore), as well as in Custer and Hot Springs (more convenient to Jewel Cave and Wind Cave, respectively). If you're continuing west, you might also consider lodging in Newcastle, Wyoming, 25 miles west of Jewel Cave National Monument.

For information on accommodations in the Black Hills, contact either the South Dakota Department of Tourism or the Black Hills, Badlands & Lakes Association (see "Information," earlier in this chapter).

IN RAPID CITY

Abend Haus Cottages and Audrie's B&B

23029 Thunderhead Falls Rd., Rapid City, SD 57702-8524. © **605/342-7788.** www.audries bb.com. 9 units. TV. $115–$175 double. Rates include full breakfast. No credit cards. Couples only (no children). Located 7 miles west of town on U.S. 44.

Set on the banks of a rippling trout stream, Audrie's is a perfect choice for those couples seeking a romantic and luxurious escape during their visit to the Black Hills. The spacious cottages and suites ooze old-world charm, with European antiques, private hot tubs, fireplaces, and patios. Among the cottages, an excellent choice is the Yuletide Haus, made of hand-peeled lodgepole pine logs, with a king-size bed, refrigerator, microwave, CD and tape player, and TV with VCR. More upscale is Moonlight Lodge, a 1,100-square-foot log cabin that boasts a king bed, handsome river rock gas fireplace, refrigerator and

microwave, and entertainment center complete with a 53-inch large-screen TV. Smoking is not permitted.

Hotel Alex Johnson

523 6th St., Rapid City, SD 57701. © **800/ 888-2539** or 605/342-1210. Fax 605/342-7436. www.alexjohnson.com. 143 units. A/C TV TEL. Apr to mid-Oct $106–$160 double, $350–$400 suite; mid-Oct to Mar $69–$89 double, $350–$400 suite. AE, DC, DISC, MC, V.

This finely restored hotel, listed on the National Historic Register, has a Germanic Tudor mixed with Lakota Sioux atmosphere on the inside, with a Germanic Tudor exterior. The furniture was handcrafted in Rapid City to replicate the hotel's original 1928 furnishings. It contains an Irish pub, gift shop, and highly recommended restaurant, **The Landmark,** that's open for breakfast, lunch, and dinner.

Rushmore Plaza Holiday Inn

505 N. 5th St., Rapid City, SD 57701. © **605/ 348-4000.** Fax 605/348-9777. 205 units. A/C TV TEL. Winter $71–$89 double; summer $109–$129 double. AE, DC, DISC, MC, V.

This eight-story atrium hotel with a pool and waterfall offers all the spaciousness and amenities you would expect in a top-rated modern hotel. It also has a relaxing piano lounge and exercise facilities and is close to downtown shopping, dining, and entertainment.

IN CUSTER

Bavarian Inn Motel

U.S. 16/385 N., Custer, SD 57730. © **800/ 657-4312** or 605/673-2802. www.custer-sd. com/bavarian. 64 units, 1 condo. A/C TV TEL. $39–$78 single; $55–$108 double; $65–$159 suite. AE, DISC, MC, V.

The Bavarian Inn's location 1 mile north of downtown is convenient to many of the Black Hills' most popular attractions, including Mount Rushmore, Crazy Horse Memorial, and

Custer State Park. There's a restaurant (German/American) and lounge on-site, plus heated indoor and outdoor pools, a tennis court, a sauna and hot tub, and a game room.

IN DEADWOOD

The Bullock Hotel

633 Historic Main St., Deadwood, SD 57732. © **800/336-1876** or 605/578-1745. Fax 605/578-1382. www.bullockhotel.com. 36 units. A/C TV TEL. $34–$159 double, varied by seasons. AE, DISC, MC, V.

This is the finest hotel in South Dakota. You'll find turn-of-the-20th-century surroundings complemented by modern amenities. There's also 24-hour gambling, a full-service bar, and a quaint restaurant called **Bully's.** For a special treat, try one of the Jacuzzi suites. Keep an eye out for the hotel's namesake, legendary lawman Seth Bullock, whose ghost has a habit of reappearing here.

Deadwood Gulch Resort

U.S. 85 S., 1 mile from Historic Main St. (P.O. Box 643, Deadwood, SD 57732). © **800/695-1876** or 605/578-1294. Fax 605/578-2505. www.deadwoodgulch.com. 96 units. A/C TV TEL. Oct–June 15 $45–$85 double; June 16–Sept 5 $99–$200 double; Sept 6–30 $65–$85 double. AE, DC, DISC, MC, V.

With a comfortable hotel, three casinos, a convention center, bars, a creekside restaurant, outdoor recreation, a 24-hour hot tub, and heated pools, this resort is a good home base for those exploring the area as well as a destination to enjoy for its own merits. The attractive modern rooms have one or two queen-size beds, and minisuites are also available. There's a convenience store and gas station, and trolley service to historic Main Street is available. In the summer, the resort has mountain-bike rentals; in the winter, you can rent snowmobiles, and special events are on offer year-round.

INSIDE CUSTER STATE PARK

Custer State Park is home to four rustic resorts that offer lodging, dining, and a wealth of recreational opportunities in the heart of the Black Hills.

The **State Game Lodge & Resort** (© **605/255-4541**), located on U.S. 16A near the park's main visitor center, served as the "Summer White House" for Presidents Calvin Coolidge and Dwight D. Eisenhower. The stone and wood lodge features stately rooms, motel units, and pine-shaded cabins, as well as meeting and banquet facilities. The lodge offers an excellent Buffalo Jeep Safari Ride into the backcountry and a Safari Ride cookout dinner tour.

The **Sylvan Lake Resort** (© **605/574-2561**), on S. Dak. 87 in the northeast corner of Custer State Park, overlooking scenic Sylvan Lake and the Harney Range, features cozy lodge rooms and rustic family cabins. The lodge is also close to a number of outdoor activities, including hiking, swimming, fishing, boating, and rock climbing.

The **Blue Bell Lodge & Resort** (© **605/255-4531**), located on S. Dak. 87, just before the turnoff for the Wildlife Loop Road (if you are traveling south), is among western South Dakota's best-kept secrets. The retreat has an Old West flavor, with handcrafted log cabins (our choice for the best place to stay in the park) scattered around a lodge with a dining room, lounge, and meeting room. A general store, gift shop, and gasoline station are located on-site, and fishing is available nearby. The Blue Bell also offers hayrides, chuck-wagon cookouts, and trail rides.

The **Legion Lake Resort** (© **605/255-4521**), located near the junction of the Needles Highway (S. Dak. 87 and U.S. 16A), dates from 1913 and features cottages nestled in the pines near the lakeshore. A dining room, a store, paddle boats, and mountain bikes are available at the resort, and the 110-mile Centennial Trail passes through the Legion Lake area.

Rates at these lodges range from around $85 for a sleeping cabin at Legion Lake in the high season to $350 for a four-bedroom cabin at the State Game Resort. The more facilities and amenities, the more you pay. Most of the resorts open in late April or May and close down in September or late October; a few cabins are kept open for winter visitors. These fill quickly, and some people call 6 months in advance for reservations. For more information or to make reservations at any of Custer State Park's resorts, contact **Custer State Park Resort Co.,** HC 83 Box 74, Custer, SD 57730 (© **800/658-3530**).

Where to Dine

Dining in the Black Hills tends to be a casual affair, but the selection can be excellent, ranging from homemade pies and ranch-raised buffalo to hearty steaks and succulent pheasant. "Summer" means Memorial Day through Labor Day.

Inside the Parks. The only full-service dining for all meals within the National Park Service properties in the Black Hills is the Buffalo Dining Room at Mount Rushmore (see below). Wind Cave and Jewel Cave have vending machines. The four resorts at Custer State Park offer dining facilities that non-guests may enjoy as well; all offer what we might call upscale family dining, with mostly American fare at relatively moderate prices (see the individual resort descriptions under "Where to Stay," above).

In addition to the restaurants listed below, you might consider two establishments in Custer, which is east of Jewel Cave National Monument, west of Custer State Park, and northwest of Wind Cave National Park. The **Bavarian Inn,** at the junction U.S. 385 and U.S. 16 (© 605/673-4412), serves American and German dishes at reasonable prices, with live music most nights. The **Chief Restaurant,** 140 Mount Rushmore Rd. (© 605/673-4402), offers family-style

dining, with choices ranging from prime rib and steaks to pizza and buffalo burgers.

AT MOUNT RUSHMORE NATIONAL MEMORIAL

Buffalo Dining Room

At Mount Rushmore National Memorial. © **605/574-2515.** www.rushmoregifts.com. Breakfast items $3.50–$6.50; lunch and dinner entrees $6–$8. AE, DISC, MC, V. Summer daily 7am–8pm; other times of the year daily 8am–4pm (though hours may vary during the off season). AMERICAN.

Every day, visitors to the Black Hills dine with presidents at Mount Rushmore's fabled Buffalo Dining Room. Operated by Xanterra Parks and Resorts, the memorial's concessionaire, the dining room serves a wide array of food year-round in one of the world's most famous settings. Scrambled eggs, hash browns, homemade biscuits and sausage gravy, and country-fried steak, with coffee, tea, or milk, are a deal at $3.95. What's especially nice about the place is that most choices retain a homemade taste, not something you can say about all national park fare. The buffalo stew is excellent; you'll also find burgers, hot dogs, chicken, pot roast, spaghetti, baked fish, ham steaks, great pies and fudge, and monumental scoops of ice cream.

IN KEYSTONE

The Ruby House Restaurant and Red Garter Saloon

126 Winter St., Keystone. © **605/666-4404.** Lunch entrees $6–$10; dinner entrees $9–$20. DISC, MC, V. Summer daily for 3 meals, 8am–9:30pm. STEAK/SEAFOOD/BUFFALO/ELK.

Steaks, seafood, game, and other specialties are served in a richly appointed Victorian dining room. If you've never tried buffalo, order one of the steaks or burgers here—they're similar to very lean beef, but pricier. This is a quiet stop in a tumultuous town.

IN HILL CITY

The Alpine Inn

225 Main St., Hill City. ℭ **605/574-2749.** Lunch entrees $2–$7; dinner entrees $7–$9. No credit cards. Summer Mon–Sat 11am–2:30pm and 5–10pm; winter Mon–Sat 11am–2:30pm and 5–9:30pm. Closed Sun. STEAKS.

The Alpine Inn remains a favorite among most locals and all carnivores. This is a steak place, and steak is what the restaurant does well. The lack of a wide selection of entrees is mitigated by a choice of more than 30 desserts, most of which are homemade and all of which are delectable. An attractive porch overlooks the bustle of downtown.

IN RAPID CITY

Botticelli Ristorante Italiano

523 Main St., Rapid City. ℭ **605/348-0089.** Lunch entrees $5.50–$9; dinner entrees $8.50–$23. AE, MC, V. Mon–Fri 11am–2:30pm; Mon–Thurs 5–10pm; Fri–Sat 5–11pm; Sun 5–9pm. ITALIAN.

In business only since the late 1990s, Botticelli has quickly become a culinary hot spot. Featuring a wide selection of creamy pastas and delightful chicken and veal dishes, the fare smacks of northern Italy. Even though Botticelli is set in the heart of cattle country, the fresh seafood specials and other non-beef items are generally the best choices. There's also a fine wine selection.

Firehouse Brewing Co.

610 Main St., Rapid City. ℭ **605/348-1915.** Lunch entrees $5–$8; dinner entrees $5–$18. AE, DC, DISC, MC, V. Summer Sun–Thurs 11am–11pm, Fri–Sat until midnight; other times of the year Sun–Thurs 11am–9pm, Fri–Sat until 10pm. CONTINENTAL/PUB FARE.

The entire brewing process is visible behind glass in this classic, renovated fire station. Burgers, buffalo, and chicken wings are favorites, but we also recommend the Reuben sandwich, the bean soup offered in fall, and the

desserts, such as the Big Cookie—a freshly baked white and dark chocolate mix the size of a dinner plate that is topped with two large scoops of French vanilla ice cream and served with melba sauce on the side. Live entertainment is offered on a large, heated patio Wednesday through Saturday nights in the summer.

Fireside Inn

On S. Dak. 44, 6 miles west of Rapid City. ℭ **605/342-3900.** Dinner entrees $12–$35. AE, DISC, MC, V. Daily 5–9pm. STEAKS/SEAFOOD/PASTA.

Bean soup is a great starter, but the Fireside Inn has made a name for itself with its excellent prime rib and intimate fireside setting. Relax with refreshments on a spacious new patio before checking out the 20-ounce Cattlemen's Cut. Or you might want to sample the fresh salmon or the delicious chicken Wellington. The New York steak is among the best in the business.

Golden Phoenix

2421 W. Main St., Rapid City. ℭ **605/348-4195.** Lunch entrees $4.95–$5.25; dinner entrees $6–$10. AE, DC, DISC, MC, V. Daily 11am–10pm. CHINESE.

A relaxed atmosphere with reasonable prices, quick service, and convenient parking make this a good choice in Rapid City. There is a wide selection of Chinese dishes, but it's hard to beat the Mongolian beef, sesame chicken, or Hunan shrimp.

IN PIEDMONT

Elk Creek Steakhouse & Lounge

I-90 at Exit 46, Piedmont. ℭ **605/787-6349.** Dinner entrees $4.50–$29. AE, DISC, MC, V. Mon–Thurs 5–10pm; Fri–Sat 5–11pm; Sun 4:30–10pm. STEAKS/SEAFOOD/PASTA/CHICKEN.

Steak's the thing at Elk Creek, and the buffalo steaks are excellent. The special duchess potatoes are wonderful, and the chef's special—a rib-eye served on an English muffin, topped with broccoli, mock crab, and a hollandaise-cheese sauce—is wicked. The lounge features a live band on Saturday and Sunday nights.

IN DEADWOOD

Deadwood Social Club

On the 2nd floor of Saloon No. 10, 657 Main St. 𝄌 **800/952-9398.** Reservations appreciated but not required. Lunch entrees $2.50–$11; dinner entrees $9–$22. AE, MC, V. Summer weekends 11:30am–10pm, weekdays 11:30am–9pm; other times of the year 11:30am–9pm. Closed Sun Oct–Apr. STEAKS/PASTA.

A warm atmosphere is made even cozier with light jazz and blues in the background and one of South Dakota's largest wine selections in the cellar. Pasta dishes, such as the popular rigatoni con pollo, are exquisite. The tenderloin and rib-eye are each served with grilled vegetables and roasted New England potatoes, then topped with a special demiglace. On the lighter side, Mother's Enchiladas are a favorite.

Jakes

Atop the Midnight Star, 677 Main St., Deadwood. 𝄌 **800/999-6482** or 605/578-3656. www.themidnightstar.com. Reservations recommended. Dinner entrees $16–$29. AE, DC, DISC, MC, V. Summer Sun–Fri 5–10pm, Sat 5–11pm; other times of the year Sun–Thurs 5:30–9:30pm, Fri 5–10pm, Sat 5–11pm. NEW AMERICAN.

Before dining, browse handsomely displayed costumes worn by Kevin Costner in his feature films, including *The Postman, Dances with Wolves,* and *Tin Cup.* Kevin and partners Carla and Francis Caneva own Jakes, which features some of the most unique food in the region. Seasonal dishes include salmon, elk, chicken, duck, lamb, and buffalo, and a different chef's featured selection is part of the menu every night. Appetizers can range from escargot to buffalo carpaccio. There is also an excellent wine list.

BRYCE CANYON NATIONAL PARK & GRAND STAIRCASE– ESCALANTE NATIONAL MONUMENT

by Don & Barbara Laine

WELCOME TO A MAGICAL LAND, A PLACE OF INSPIRATION AND SPECtacular beauty where thousands of intricately shaped hoodoos stir the imagination as they stand in silent watch.

Hoodoos, geologists tell us, are simply pinnacles of rock, often oddly shaped, left standing after millions of years of water and wind erosion have carved away softer or more-protected rock. But perhaps the truth really lies in a Paiute legend. These American Indians, who lived in the area for several hundred years before being forced out by Anglo pioneers, told of a "Legend People" who lived here in the old days; for their evil ways they were turned to stone by the powerful Coyote, and even today they remain frozen in time.

Whatever the cause, Bryce Canyon is unique. Its intricate and often whimsical formations are smaller and on a more human scale than the impressive rocks seen at Zion and Canyonlands national parks, and it's far easier to explore than the huge and sometimes intimidating Grand Canyon. Bryce is comfortable and inviting in its beauty; we feel we know it simply by gazing over the rim.

Although the colorful hoodoos grab your attention first, it isn't long before you notice the deep amphitheaters that enfold them, with their cliffs, windows, and arches—all colored in shades of red, brown, orange, yellow, and white— that change and glow with the rising and setting sun. Beyond the rocks and light are the other faces of the park: three separate life zones, each with its own unique vegetation, changing with elevation; and a kingdom of animals, from the busy chipmunks and ground squirrels to stately mule deer and their archenemy, the mountain lion.

Human exploration of the Bryce area likely began with the Paiutes, and it's possible that trappers, prospectors, and early Mormon scouts may have visited here in the early to mid-1800s, before Maj. John Wesley Powell conducted the first thorough survey of the region in the early 1870s. Shortly after Powell's exploration, Mormon pioneer

Tips from a Park Insider

"**A** lot of people think this is one of America's prettiest parks," says former park ranger Dave Mecham. "The hoodoos are what people come to see—that's what made Bryce famous—and it's the most popular thing."

Bryce Amphitheater has the best scenery in the park, in Mecham's opinion. "It's the place in the park where everything's coming together geologically to carve hoodoos at their best," he says. He particularly enjoys the **Rim Trail** that runs along the edge of the canyon, and highly recommends the section between Inspiration and Bryce points, with perhaps the very best view from **Upper Inspiration Point,** which is 300 to 400 yards south of Inspiration Point.

Mecham calls Bryce Canyon a "morning park," because the views are much better illuminated by early morning light than at any other time of day. He recommends spending at least 1 night at or near the park. "If you're spending the night close by, I think it would be a big mistake to miss sunrise."

Getting up early is also the best way to avoid crowds, according to Mecham, since most people don't get to the view points or out onto the trails until about 10am. The other way to avoid crowds is to walk away from them. Mecham says that you're not likely to see anyone at all on the park's two backcountry trails at the south end of the park, but avoiding crowds even in the park's most popular areas often takes only a short walk.

"Sunset Point is the busiest place in the park, especially in midsummer at midday," he says. "You finally get a parking spot, then walk out to a very crowded vantage point, where you're standing shoulder to shoulder and it's real hectic. But if you take a 5-minute walk south along the rim trail toward Inspiration Point, you'll leave the crowds immediately—they just cluster at those views."

Mecham says September and October are probably the best times to visit. "It's still busy," he says, "but less crowded on trails." If you *really* want to avoid people, you'll feel you have the park all to yourself if you visit midweek in the middle of the winter. "We plow the roads so people can drive to the view points and photograph the canyon with snow on it, and the people who ski or snowshoe will enjoy it the most," he says, adding, "Skiing is at its best in January and February, when it's really cold."

Ebenezer Bryce and his wife, Mary, moved to the area and tried raising cattle. Although they stayed only a few years, Bryce left behind his name and his oft-quoted description of the canyon as "a helluva place to lose a cow."

Avoiding the Crowds. Although Bryce Canyon receives only two-thirds the number of annual visitors that pour into nearby Zion National Park, Bryce can still be crowded, especially during its peak season from mid-June to mid-September. If you must visit then, try to hike some of the lesser-used trails (ask rangers for recommendations), and get out onto the trails as soon after sunrise as possible.

A better time to visit, if your schedule allows, is spring or fall. If you don't mind a bit of cold and snow, the park is practically deserted in the winter—a typical January sees some 22,000 to 25,000 visitors, while in August there are well over 10 times that number—and the sight of bright red hoodoos capped with fresh white snow is something you won't soon forget.

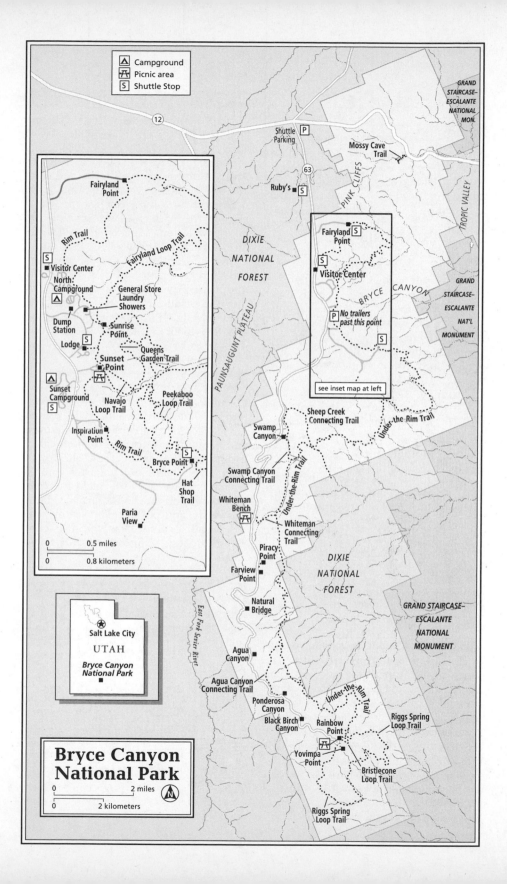

△ Campground
🏕 Picnic area
Ⓢ Shuttle Stop

GRAND
STAIRCASE-
ESCALANTE
NATIONAL
MON.

Shuttle
Parking Ⓟ

12

Mossy Cave
Trail

Ⓟ Shuttle
Parking

63

Ruby's Ⓢ

PINK CLIFFS

TROPIC VALLEY

DIXIE
NATIONAL
FOREST

BRYCE CANYON

Fairyland
Point Ⓢ

Ⓢ

Visitor Center

GRAND
STAIRCASE-
ESCALANTE
NAT'L
MONUMENT

Ⓟ No trailers
past this point

Ⓢ

see inset map at left

Fairyland
Point

Rim Trail

Fairyland Loop Trail

Ⓢ Visitor Center

North
Campground △

General Store
Laundry
Showers

Dump
Station

Sunrise
Point

Ⓢ

Lodge

Queens
Garden Trail

Sunset
Point

△

Peekaboo
Loop Trail

Sunset
Campground

Ⓢ

Navajo
Loop Trail

PAUNSAUGUNT PLATEAU

Sheep Creek
Connecting Trail

Swamp
Canyon

Under-the-Rim Trail

Inspiration
Point

Rim Trail

Swamp Canyon
Connecting Trail

Under-the-Rim Trail

Bryce Point Ⓢ

Hat
Shop
Trail

Whiteman
Bench

Whiteman
Connecting
Trail

Paria
View

Piracy
Point

DIXIE
NATIONAL
FOREST

0   0.5 miles
0   0.8 kilometers

Farview
Point

Natural
Bridge

GRAND STAIRCASE-
ESCALANTE
NATIONAL
MONUMENT

East Fork Sevier River

Agua
Canyon

Salt Lake City

Agua Canyon
Connecting Trail

UTAH

Ponderosa
Canyon

Under-the-Rim Trail

Bryce Canyon
National Park
■

Black Birch
Canyon

Rainbow
Point

Riggs Spring
Loop Trail

Yovimpa
Point

Bristlecone
Loop Trail

Bryce Canyon
National Park

0   2 miles
0   2 kilometers

Ⓝ

Riggs Spring
Loop Trail

Just the Facts

Situated in the mountains of southern Utah, the park is crossed from east to west by Utah 12, with the bulk of the park, including the visitor center, accessed by Utah 63, which turns south off Utah 12 into the main portions of the park. U.S. 89 runs north to south, west of the park, and Utah 12 heads east to Tropic and eventually Escalante.

From Salt Lake City, it's about 250 miles to the park. Take I-15 south about 200 miles to Exit 95, head east 13 miles on Utah 20, south on U.S. 89 for 17 miles to Utah 12, and east 17 miles to the park entrance road. The entrance station and visitor center are 3 miles south of Utah 12.

From St. George, about 135 miles southwest of the park, travel north on I-15 10 miles to Exit 16, then head east on Utah 9 for 63 miles to U.S. 89, north 44 miles to Utah 12, and east 17 miles to the park entrance road.

From Cedar City (I-15 exits 57, 59, and 62), about 80 miles west of the park, take Utah 14 west 41 miles to its intersection with U.S. 89 and follow that north 21 miles to Utah 12, then east 17 miles to the park entrance road.

A couple of other handy driving distances: Bryce is 83 miles east of Zion National Park, 160 miles north of the North Rim of the Grand Canyon, and 245 miles northeast of Las Vegas, Nevada.

The Nearest Airport. Bryce Canyon Airport (© **435/834-5239**), located several miles from the park entrance on Utah 12, has charter service from **Bryce Canyon Airlines** (© **800/979-5050** or 435/834-5341). Car rentals are available from **Hertz** (© **800/654-3131** national reservations, or locally at 866/866-6616, ext. 7195).

You can also fly into St. George or Cedar City and rent a car at either of their airports.

Contact **Superintendent, Bryce Canyon National Park,** P.O. Box 170001, Bryce Canyon, UT 84717 (© **435/834-5322;** www.nps.gov/brca). It's best to write at least a month before your planned visit, and ask for a copy of the national park newspaper, *Hoodoo,* which contains a map of the park, plus information on hiking, weather, ranger-conducted activities, and current issues.

If you want more details, you can order books, maps, and videos from the nonprofit **Bryce Canyon Natural History Association,** Box 170002, Bryce Canyon, UT 84717 (© **888/362-2642** or 435/834-4600; fax 435/834-4102; www.nps.gov/brca/nhamain).

Located at the north end as you enter the park, the visitor center has exhibits on the geology and history of the area and presents a short introductory video program. Rangers answer questions, offer advice, and provide backcountry permits. You can also pick up free brochures and buy books, maps, videos, postcards, and posters. The visitor center is open daily year-round except Thanksgiving, Christmas, and New Year's days.

Entry into the park (for up to 7 days) costs $20 per private vehicle, which includes unlimited use of the park shuttle (when it's operating). A $30 annual pass is available; and campsites cost $10 per night.

Backcountry permits, which cost $5 and are available at the visitor center daily until 8pm, are required for all overnight trips into the backcountry, and backcountry camping is permitted on only two trails, with details at the visitor center.

Although most visitors to Bryce Canyon enjoy an exciting vacation without serious mishap, accidents can occur. The most common injuries are sprained, twisted, and broken ankles. Park rangers strongly recommend that hikers, even those just out for short day hikes, wear sturdy hiking boots with good traction and ankle support.

Another concern in the park in recent years has been **bubonic plague,** which, contrary to popular belief, is treatable with antibiotics if caught early. The bacteria that causes bubonic plague has been found on fleas in prairie dog colonies in the park, so you should avoid contact with wild animals, especially prairie dogs, squirrels, and other rodents. Those taking pets into the park should dust them with flea powder. Avoiding contact with infected animals will greatly minimize the chances of contracting this holdover from the Dark Ages, but caution is still necessary. Symptoms, which generally occur from 2 to 6 days after exposure, may include high fever, headache, vomiting, diarrhea, and swollen glands. Anyone showing these symptoms after visiting the park should get medical attention immediately—the plague can be fatal if not treated promptly.

Backcountry hikers should carry water. Campfires are not permitted in the backcountry.

With elevations ranging from 6,620 feet to 9,115 feet, Bryce Canyon is cooler than southern Utah's other, lower-elevation parks. From May through October, daytime temperatures are pleasant—usually from the low 60s to the upper 80s—but nights are quite cool, dropping into the 40s even at the height of summer. Afternoon thunderstorms are common in July and August. In winter, days are generally clear and crisp, with high temperatures often reaching the 40s, and nights are cold, usually in the single digits or teens, and sometimes dipping well below zero. Snow is common in winter, but the roads to the view points are plowed.

In addition to the nightly campfire/amphitheater programs, the park has a monthly **star-watching program.** Check at the visitor center for the details and current schedule.

If You Have Only 1 Day

What makes this park so attractive is that there are ways to see a good deal of Bryce in a short amount of time.

Start at the **visitor center** and watch the short video program that explains some of the area's geology. Then drive the 18-mile (each way) dead-end **park road,** stopping at view points to gaze down into the canyon (see "Exploring the Park by Car," below); visit the most popular view points on the **Bryce Canyon Shuttle;** or hop on the **Bryce Canyon Scenic Tours & Shuttle** van for a 1½- to 2-hour guided tour, complete with lively commentary (see "Organized Tours & Ranger Programs," below).

Whichever way you choose to get around, make sure you spend at least a little time at **Inspiration Point,** which offers a splendid (and yes, inspirational) view into **Bryce Amphitheater** and its hundreds of statuesque pink, red, orange, and brown hoodoo stone sculptures. After seeing the canyon from the top down, it's time to get some exercise, so walk at least partway down the **Queen's Garden Trail.** If you can spare 3 hours, hike down the Navajo Loop Trail and return to the rim via Queen's Garden Trail (see "Day Hikes," below). Those not willing or physically able to hike into the canyon can enjoy a leisurely walk along the **Rim Trail,** which provides spectacular views down into the canyon, especially just after sunrise and about an hour before sunset. That evening, try to take in the **campground amphitheater program.**

Exploring the Park by Car

The park's **18-mile scenic drive** (one-way) follows the rim of Bryce Canyon, offering easy access to a variety of views into the fanciful fairyland of stone sculptures below. Trailers, not allowed on the road, must be left at one of several parking lots. Because all overlooks are on your left as you begin the drive, it's best to avoid crossing traffic by driving all the way to the end of the road and stopping at the overlooks on your return. Allow 1 to 2 hours.

After leaving the visitor center, drive the length of the 18-mile road to **Yovimpa and Rainbow Point overlooks,** which offer expansive views of southern Utah, Arizona, and sometimes even New Mexico. From these pink cliffs you can look down on a colorful platoon of stone soldiers, standing at eternal attention. A short loop trail from Rainbow Point leads to an **1,800-year-old bristlecone pine,** believed to be the oldest living thing at Bryce Canyon.

From here, drive back north to **Ponderosa Canyon Overlook,** where you can gaze down from a dense forest of spruce and fir at multicolored hoodoos, and then continue to **Agua Canyon Overlook,** with some of the best color contrasts in the park. Looking almost straight down, watch for a hoodoo known as **The Hunter,** with a hat of green trees.

Now continue on to **Natural Bridge,** actually an arch carved by rain and wind, spanning 85 feet. From here, continue to **Farview Point,** with a panoramic view to the distant horizon and the Kaibab Plateau at the Grand Canyon's North Rim. Next, pass through **Swamp Canyon,** and continue until you hit a turnoff from the main road on the right.

This turnoff leads to three overlooks, the first of which is **Paria View,** looking off to the south of the White Cliffs, carved into light-colored sandstone by the Paria River. To the north of Paria View, you'll find **Bryce Point,** a splendid stop for seeing the awesome **Bryce Amphitheater,** the largest natural amphitheater in the park, as well as distant views of the Black Mountains to the northeast and Navajo Mountain to the south. From here it's just a short drive to **Inspiration Point,** which offers views similar to those at Bryce Point plus the best view in the park of the **Silent City,** a sleeping metropolis of stone.

Now return to the main road and head north to **Sunset Point,** where you can see practically all of Bryce Amphitheater, including the aptly named **Thor's Hammer** and the 200-foot-tall cliffs of **Wall Street.**

Continue north to a turnoff for your final stop at **Sunrise Point,** where there's an inspiring view into Bryce Amphitheater. This is the beginning of the **Queen's Garden Trail,** an excellent choice for even a quick walk below the canyon rim.

Seeing the Park by Shuttle

In recent years, congestion has been increasing along the park's only road, making a drive through the park a less than pleasurable experience. To alleviate this, a **shuttle service** is now in effect from mid-to-late May to September, between 7am and dark. Visitors can park their cars at the parking and boarding area at the intersection of the entrance road and Utah 12, 3 miles from the park boundary, and ride the shuttle into the park. Those staying in the park at Bryce Canyon Lodge or one of the campgrounds can also use the shuttle, at no additional charge (see "Fees," earlier in this chapter). The shuttle has stops at various viewpoints, as well as Ruby's Inn, Ruby's Campground, the visitor center, Sunset Campground, and Bryce Canyon Lodge, running every 10 to 15 minutes.

Organized Tours & Ranger Programs

Park rangers present a variety of free programs and activities. **Evening programs,** which may include a slide show, take place most nights at campground amphitheaters. Topics vary, but may include such subjects as the animals and plants of the park, geology, and man's role in the park's early days. Rangers also give **half-hour talks** on similar subjects several times daily at various locations in the park, and lead **hikes and walks,** including a moonlight hike (reservations required) and a wheelchair-accessible 1-hour canyon rim walk. Schedules are posted on bulletin boards at the visitor center, general store, campgrounds, and Bryce Canyon Lodge.

Once or twice a week, spring through fall, usually in the evening, a free **talk** is given on the patio of Bryce Canyon Lodge. Topics include lodge history, the geology of the area, and discussion of some trails. Check at the lodge for the current schedule.

Bryce Canyon Scenic Tours (© 800/432-5383 or 435/834-5200; www.bryce tours.com) offers 1½- to 2-hour tours year-round, leaving from Bryce Canyon Resorts next to the shuttle parking area outside the park entrance. A general tour, stopping at several viewpoints, costs $26 for adults, $12 for children 5 to 15, and is free for children under 5. Sunrise/sunset and other specialized tours are also available.

For a bird's-eye view of the canyon and its numerous formations, contact **Bryce Canyon Airlines & Helicopters** (ask for the flight desk at Ruby's Inn; © 435/834-5341). Tours last from less than 20 minutes to more than an hour, and the longer trips include surrounding attractions. Prices start at $60 per person, with discounts for families and groups.

Several national **adventure tour operators** offer guided biking, hiking, and backpacking trips near the park, and other companies offer more traditional tour packages. Operators offering a variety of classic or multisport tours of the area include **Backroads** (© 800/462-2848; www.backroads.com), **The World Outdoors** (© 800/488-8483, www.theworldoutdoors.com), and **Timberline Adventures** (© 800417-2453; www.timbertours.com).

Historic & Man-Made Attractions

Although early American Indians and 19th-century pioneers spent some time in what is now Bryce Canyon National Park, they left little evidence. The park's main historic site is the handsome sandstone and ponderosa pine **Bryce Canyon Lodge,** built by the Union Pacific Railroad and opened in 1924. Much of it has been faithfully restored to its 1920s appearance.

Day Hikes

One of the wonderful things about Bryce Canyon is that you don't have to be an advanced backpacker to really get to know the park. But those looking for a challenge won't be disappointed, either.

All trails below the rim have at least some steep grades, so you should wear hiking boots with a traction tread and good ankle support to avoid ankle injuries, the most common accidents in the park. During the hot summer months you'll want to hike either early or late in the day, always keeping in mind that it gets hotter the deeper you go into the canyon. Bryce's rangers do not rate hiking trails as to their difficulty, saying that what is easy for one person may be difficult for another. Ratings here are provided by the authors and other experienced hikers, and are entirely subjective.

The Best of Two Great Trails

A great choice for getting down into the canyon and seeing the most with the least amount of sweat is to combine the **Navajo Loop Trail** with the **Queen's Garden Trail.** The total distance is just under 3 miles, and most hikers take from 2 to 3 hours. It's best to start at the Navajo Loop trailhead at Sunset Point and leave the canyon on the less steep Queen's Garden Trail, returning to the rim at Sunrise Point, 0.5 mile north of the Navajo Loop trailhead.

SHORTER TRAILS

Bristlecone Loop

1 mile RT. Easy. Access: Rainbow Point parking area at the end of the scenic drive.

An easy walk entirely above the canyon rim, this trail traverses a subalpine fir forest. Here you'll find more bristlecone pines than along the other park trails. It takes just 45 minutes to 1 hour to complete the loop, which has an elevation change of 100 feet.

Hat Shop Trail

3.8 miles RT. Strenuous. Access: Bryce Point Overlook.

This is a strenuous hike with a 900-foot elevation change. Leaving the rim, you'll drop quickly to the Hat Shop, so-named because it consists of hard gray "hats" perched on narrow reddish brown pedestals. The trail offers close-up views of gnarled ponderosa pine and Douglas fir, as well as distant panoramas across the Aquarius Plateau toward the Grand Staircase–Escalante National Monument. This trail is also

the beginning of the Under the Rim Trail (see "Exploring the Backcountry," below).

Mossy Cave Trail

0.8 mile RT. Easy. Access: Along Utah 12, about 3½ miles east of the highway's intersection with Utah 63.

This often-overlooked trail located outside the main part of the park offers an easy and picturesque 45-minute walk. The trail follows an old irrigation ditch up a short hill to a shallow cave, where seeping water nurtures the cave's moss. Just off the trail you'll also see a small **waterfall.** Elevation gain is 150 feet. Hikers will usually get their feet wet, and should be careful when crossing the ditch.

Navajo Loop Trail

1.4 miles RT. Moderate. Access: Trailhead signpost at the central overlook point at Sunset Point.

This trail descends from the canyon rim 521 feet to the bottom of the canyon floor and back up again. Traversing graveled switchbacks, it affords terrific views of several impressive formations, including the towering skyscrapers of **Wall Street,** the awesome **Twin Bridges,** and the precariously balanced **Thor's Hammer.** The round-trip on this trail takes 1 to 2 hours.

Queen's Garden Trail

0.9 mile one-way. Easy to moderate. Access: South side of Sunrise Point.

This short trail, which drops 320 feet below the rim, takes you down into **Bryce Amphitheater,** with rest benches near the formation called Queen Victoria. At the beginning of the descent, keep an eye cocked to the distant views so you won't miss **Boat Mesa, the Sinking Ship, the Aquarius Plateau,** and **Bristlecone Point.** As you plunge deeper into the canyon, the trail passes some of the park's most fanciful formations, including majestic **Queen Victoria** herself, for whom the trail and this grouping of hoodoos were named, plus the **Queen's Castle** and **Gulliver's Castle.** The round-trip takes 1 to 2 hours.

LONGER TRAILS

Fairyland Loop

8 miles RT. Strenuous. Access: Fairyland Point Overlook, off the park access road north of the visitor center; also accessible from Sunrise Point.

From Fairyland Point this strenuous but little-traveled trail descends into **Fairyland Canyon,** then meanders up, down, and around **Boat Mesa,** crosses **Campbell Canyon,** passes Tower Bridge junction—a short 200-yard side trail takes you to the base of **Tower Bridge**—and begins a steady climb to the **Chinese Wall.** About halfway along the wall, the trail begins the serious ascent back to the top of the canyon, finally reaching it near Sunrise Point. To complete the loop, follow the Rim Trail back through juniper, manzanita, and Douglas fir to Fairyland Point. The loop has an elevation change of 900 feet.

Peekaboo Loop

6.8 miles RT. Strenuous. Access: Bryce Point Overlook parking area.

Open to hikers, mules, and horses, the Peekaboo Loop winds among hoodoos below Bryce and Inspiration points and has an elevation change of 800 feet. It has several fairly steep inclines and descents, but the views make all the effort worthwhile. You can see far to the east beyond Bryce Canyon toward the Aquarius Plateau, Canaan Mountain, and the Kaiparowits Plateau; or enjoy the closer prospect of the **Wall of Windows, the Three Wisemen, the Organ,** or the **Cathedral.** Various connecting trails make Peekaboo easily adaptable. *Note:* Horse use is heavy from spring to fall, and hikers should step aside as horseback riders pass them on the trail.

Rim Trail

5.5 miles one-way. Easy to moderate. Access: North trailhead is at Fairyland Point, south trailhead is at Bryce Point; also accessible from Sunrise, Sunset, and Inspiration points, and numerous other locations in between.

The Rim Trail, which does not drop into the canyon but offers splendid views from above, meanders along the rim for more than 5 miles, with a total elevation change of 550 feet. It includes a 0.5-mile section between two overlooks—**Sunrise** and **Sunset**—that is suitable for wheelchairs. Overlooking **Bryce Amphitheater,** the trail offers excellent views almost everywhere and is a good choice for an early morning or evening walk, when you can watch the changing light on the rosy rocks below.

Sheep Creek Trail

3–5 miles one-way. Easy to moderate. Access: Trailhead sign and parking area 5 miles south of the visitor center.

This trail takes you down into the canyon bottom, and if you follow the extension, right out of the park into the **Dixie National Forest.** The first mile is on the rim, but then the trail descends the Sheep Creek draw below pink limestone cliffs toward the canyon bottom, traversing part of the Under the Rim Trail along its way. Watch signs carefully; the route can be confusing. The trail has up to a 1,250-foot elevation change.

Exploring the Backcountry

For die-hard hikers who don't mind rough terrain, Bryce has two backcountry trails, usually open in the summer only. The truly ambitious can combine the two trails for a weeklong excursion. Permits, which cost $5 and are available at the visitor center, are required for all overnight trips into the backcountry.

Riggs Spring Loop

8.8-mile loop. Moderate to strenuous. Access: South side of parking area for Rainbow Point.

This hike can be completed in 4 or 5 hours, or can be more comfortably done as a relaxing overnight backpacking trip. The trail goes through a deep forest, but also provides breathtaking views of the huge **Pink Cliffs** at the southern end of the plateau. It has an elevation change of 1,675 feet.

Under the Rim Trail

22.6 miles one-way. Moderate. Access: East side of the parking area for Bryce Point Overlook.

This moderately strenuous trail runs between Bryce and Rainbow points, and offers the full spectrum of views of Bryce Canyon's scenery. Since the trail runs below the rim, it is full of steep inclines and descents, with an overall elevation change of 1,500 feet. Allow 2 to 3 days to hike the entire length. There are five camping areas along the trail, plus a group camp area.

Other Summer Sports & Activities

Biking & Mountain Biking. Bikes are permitted only on the park's established roads, which are generally narrow, winding, and crowded with motor vehicles during the summer. However, you'll find plenty of mountain biking opportunities just outside the park in the Dixie National Forest. For information, stop at the national forest's **Red Canyon Visitor Center** (usually open daily early May to early Oct), along Utah 12 about 10½ miles west of the Bryce Canyon National Park entrance road (© **435/676-2676**); or contact the Powell District office of the **Dixie National Forest,** 225 E. Center St. (P.O. Box 80), Panguitch, UT 84759 (© **435/676-9300;** www.fs.fed.us/dxnf).

Horseback Riding. To see Bryce Canyon the way early pioneers did, you need to look down from a horse or a mule.

Canyon Trail Rides, P.O. Box 128, Tropic, UT 84776 (© **435/679-8665;** www.canyonrides.com), offers a close-up view of Bryce's spectacular rock formations from the relative comfort of a saddle, and welcomes first-time riders. Canyon Trail Rides has a desk inside Bryce Lodge. A 2-hour ride to the canyon floor and back costs $30, including tax, per person, and a half-day trip farther into the canyon costs $45 per person. Rides are offered, weather permitting, April through November. Riders must be at least 7 years old for the 2-hour trip and at least 8 for the half-day ride, and riders can weigh no more than 220 pounds.

Guided rides are also provided by **Ruby's Scenic Rim and Outlaw Trail Rides** (© **800/679-5859** or 435/834-5280), at Ruby's Inn, at similar rates; in addition, Ruby's offers a full-day ride with lunch for $79. Ruby's will also board your horse (call for rates).

Wildlife Watching. The park has a variety of wildlife, ranging from **mule deer,** which seem to be almost everywhere, to the often-seen **golden-mantled ground squirrel** and **Uinta chipmunk.** Occasionally visitors catch a glimpse of a **mountain lion,** most likely on the prowl in search of a mule deer dinner; elk and **pronghorn** may be seen at higher elevations. Also in the park are black-tailed jackrabbits, coyotes, striped skunks, and deer mice.

The **Utah prairie dog,** now listed as a threatened species, is actually a rodent. It inhabits park meadows in busy colonies, and can be fascinating to watch. However, be sure to keep your distance because its fleas may carry disease (see "Special Regulations & Warnings," earlier in this chapter).

Of the many birds in the park, you're bound to hear the rather obnoxious call of the **Steller's jay.** Other birds often seen include violet-green swallows, common ravens, Clark's nutcrackers, American robins, red-shafted flickers, dark-eyed juncos, and chipping sparrows. Watch for white-throated swifts as they perform their exotic acrobatics along cliff faces. The park is also home, at least part of the year, to peregrine falcons, red-tailed hawks, golden eagles, bald eagles, and great horned owls.

The **Great Basin rattlesnake,** although pretty, should be given a wide berth. Sometimes growing to more than 5 feet long, this rattler is the park's only poisonous reptile. Fortunately, like most rattlesnakes, it is just as anxious as you are to avoid a confrontation. Other reptiles you may see in the park are the mountain short-horned lizard, the tree lizard, the side-blotched lizard, and the northern sagebrush lizard.

Winter Sports & Activities

Bryce is beautiful in the winter, when the white snow settles over the red, pink, orange, and brown hoodoos.

Snowshoes may be used anywhere in the park except on cross-country-ski tracks. **Cross-country skiers,** meanwhile, will find several marked, ungroomed trails (all above the rim), including the **Fairyland Loop Trail,** which leads 1 mile through a pine and juniper forest to the Fairyland Point Overlook. From here you can take the 1-mile **Forest Trail** back to the road, or continue north along the rim for another 1.2 miles to the park boundary. There are also connections to ski trails in the adjacent national forest.

Although the entire park is open to cross-country skiers, rangers warn that it's impossible to safely ski the steep trails leading down into the canyon. Stop at the visitor center for additional trail information, and go to **Ruby's Inn,** just north of the park entrance (© **435/834-5341**), for information on cross-country-ski trails and snowmobiling opportunities outside the park. Ruby's grooms over 30 miles (50km) of ski trails and also rents ski equipment. Use of the trails is free; ski rentals cost $7 for a half day and $10 for a full day.

Camping

INSIDE THE PARK

Typical of many of the West's national park campgrounds, the two facilities at Bryce offer plenty of trees with a genuine "forest camping" experience and easy access to trails, but limited facilities. **North Campground** is our top choice—it's closer to the Rim Trail, making it easier to rush over to catch those amazing sunrise and sunset colors, plus you can also reserve a spot through the **National Recreation Reservation Service** (© **877/444-6777;** www.reserveusa.com). But we wouldn't turn down a site at **Sunset Campground.** Try to get to the park early to claim a site (usually by 2pm in the summer). Showers ($2) are located at a general store in the park, although it's a healthy walk from either campground. The Park Service also operates an RV dump station ($2 fee) in the summer.

The general store near the Sunrise Point parking area has a coin-operated laundry and a snack bar, plus bundles of firewood, food and camping supplies, and souvenirs. There are tables on a covered porch along one side of the building.

NEAR THE PARK

Just outside the park is **Ruby's Inn RV Park & Campground,** Utah 63 (P.O. Box 22), Bryce, UT 84764 (© **800/468-8660** or 435/834-5301, Nov–Mar 435/834-5341; fax 435/834-5481; www.rubysinn.com; credit cards accepted), along the park's shuttle route. It has shaded campsites, an adjacent lake and horse pasture, a swimming pool, a game room, horseshoes, and a store with groceries and RV supplies.

Bryce Canyon Pines, milepost 10, Utah 12 (P.O. Box 64000-435, Bryce, UT 84764; © **800/892-7923** or 435/834-5441; fax 435/834-5330; www.brycecanyon motel.com; credit cards accepted), is part of a motel/restaurant/store/campground complex about 3½ miles west of the park entrance road. The

Campground	Elev.	Total Sites	RV Hookups	Dump Station	Toilets	Drinking Water
Inside the Park						
North	7,700	105	No	No	Yes	Yes
Sunset	8,000	111	No	No	Yes	Yes
Near the Park						
Bryce Canyon Pines	7,600	39	26	No	Yes	Yes
Bryce Pioneer Village	7,600	55	15	Yes	Yes	Yes
King's Creek (USFS)	8,000	34	No	Yes	Yes	Yes
Red Canyon (USFS)	7,400	37	No	Yes	Yes	Yes
Ruby's Inn RV Park	7,600	227	127	Yes	Yes	Yes
Kodachrome Basin SP	5,800	27	No	Yes	Yes	Yes

campsites, set back from the highway behind a gas station and store, are interspersed among ponderosa pines and junipers, with wildflowers and grasses. Campers have access to the motel swimming pool across the street. Those not camping here can get showers for $2.50.

Bryce Pioneer Village, 80 S. Main St. (Utah 12; P.O. Box 119), Tropic, UT 84776 (© **800/222-0381** or 435/679-8546; fax 435/679-8607; www.bpvillage. com; credit cards accepted), is a small motel/cabins/campground combination in nearby Tropic, with easy access to several restaurants. Dump station use costs $3; and showers are available to noncampers for $2.

King's Creek Campground, in the Powell District of the Dixie National Forest (mailing address P.O. Box 80, Panguitch, UT 84759; © **435/676-9300;** www.fs.fed.us/dxnf), is located above Tropic Reservoir, with graded gravel roads and sites nestled among tall ponderosa pines. The reservoir has two boat ramps and good trout fishing. From the intersection of Utah 63 and Utah 12, head west on Utah 12 about 2½ miles to the access road, turn south (left) and follow signs to Tropic Reservoir for about 7 miles to the campground.

About 9½ miles west of the park is another Dixie National Forest campground, **Red Canyon Campground**

(same contact information as King's Creek Campground, above). Set among the trees along the south side of Utah 12, it offers terrific views of the red rock formations across the highway, although there is a bit of road noise. Showers cost $2, whether you're staying in the campground or not.

Kodachrome Basin State Park, about 22 miles southeast of Bryce Canyon National Park, has an attractive campground with sites scattered among unusual rock "chimneys" and pinyon and juniper trees.

Where to Stay

INSIDE THE PARK

Bryce Canyon Lodge

Bryce Canyon National Park, UT. © **435/834-5361.** Information and reservations: Xanterra Parks & Resorts, 14001 E. Iliff Ave., Suite 600, Aurora, CO 80014. © **888/297-2757** or 303/297-2757. Fax 303/297-3175. www. brycecanyonlodge.com. 110 units in motel rooms and cabins; 3 suites and 1 studio in lodge. TEL. $110–$115 motel double; $120–$125 cabin; $102–$135 lodge unit. AE, DISC, MC, V. Closed Nov–Mar.

This is the perfect place to stay while you explore Bryce Canyon National Park,

Showers	Fire Pits/ Grills	Laundry	Public Phone	Reserve	Fees	Open
No	Yes	No	No	No	$10	Year-round
No	Yes	No	No	No	$10	May–Sept
Yes	Yes	Yes	Yes	Yes	$16–$24	Mar–Nov
Yes	No	No	No	Yes	$10–$16	Year-round
No	Yes	No	No	No	$8	Memorial Day–Sept
Yes	Yes	No	No	No	$9	May–Sept
Yes	Yes	Yes	Yes	Yes	$16–$26	Apr–Oct
Yes	Yes	No	Yes	Yes	$14	Year-round

letting you watch the play of changing light on the rock formations throughout the day. The handsome sandstone and ponderosa-pine lodge, which opened in 1924, contains desks in the lobby for horseback riding and other activities, and a gift shop that offers everything from postcards and souvenirs to a fine selection of American Indian pawn jewelry. The luxurious lodge suites are wonderful, with white wicker furniture, ceiling fans, and separate sitting rooms. The motel units, on the other hand, are simply pleasant, modern motel rooms, with two queen-size beds and either a balcony or a patio. The best choice is one of the historic cabins, restored to their 1920s appearance. They're not large, but they have two double beds, high ceilings, stone (gas-burning) fireplaces, and log beams—you might call the ambience "rustic luxury." There is no swimming pool. Try to reserve 4 to 6 months in advance.

NEAR THE PARK

Best Western Ruby's Inn

Utah 63 at the entrance to Bryce Canyon (P.O. Box 1), Bryce, UT 84764. © **800/468-8660** or 435/834-5341. Fax 435/834-5265. www. rubysinn.com. 369 units. A/C TV TEL.

June–Sept $96–$150 double; Apr–May and Oct $67–$120 double; Nov–Mar $46–$85 double; family suites $85–$150 year-round. AE, DC, DISC, MC, V. Pets accepted.

This large Best Western provides most of the beds for tired hikers and canyon gazers visiting the park. The lobby is among the busiest places in the area, with an ATM, a small liquor store, car rentals, a beauty salon, a 1-hour film processor, and tour desks where you can arrange excursions of all sorts, from horseback and all-terrain-vehicle rides to helicopter tours. Near the lobby are a restaurant; a Western art gallery; a huge general store that sells souvenirs, cowboy hats, camping supplies, and groceries; and a U.S. post office. Outside are two gas stations.

Spread among nine separate buildings, the modern motel rooms contain art depicting scenes of the area, wood furnishings, and shower/tub combos. Some even have whirlpools. Services include a concierge and courtesy transportation from the Bryce Airport; facilities include two indoor pools, one indoor and one outdoor whirlpool, a sun deck, nature and cross-country ski trails, a game room, a business center, conference rooms, and two coin-operated laundries.

Bryce Canyon Pines

Utah 12 (3 miles west of intersection with park entry road; P.O. Box 64000-43, Bryce, UT 84764). © **800/892-7923** or 435/834-5441. Fax 435/834-5330. www.brycecanyonmotel. com. 51 units. A/C TV TEL. Summer $65–$85 double; $95–$125 kitchenettes and suites. Lower rates in winter. AE, DC, DISC, MC, V.

A modern motel with a Western flair, the Bryce Canyon Pines offers well-maintained rooms with light-colored wood furnishings, a table and two padded chairs, and two queen-size beds in most rooms. Some units have fireplaces (wood supplied free in winter), some have fully stocked kitchenettes, and one has its own whirlpool tub. There's a covered, heated swimming pool, and an adjacent restaurant (see "Where to Dine," below).

Bryce Canyon Resorts

13500 E. Utah 12 (P.O. Box 640006), Bryce, UT 84764. © **800/834-0043** or 435/834-5351. Fax 435/834-5256. www.brycecanyonresorts. com. 70 units. A/C TV TEL. Summer $85–$95 double. Lower rates at other times. MC, V. Small pets accepted for a $5 fee.

This attractive property is a somewhat elegant change of pace from the Western and Southwestern decor found in most other lodgings in the area. It also has a good location, adjacent to the main parking area for the Bryce Canyon shuttle, at the intersection of Utah highways 12 and 63.

The spacious rooms are Victorian in style, with drapes and bed coverings in royal purples and reds, and solid wood furniture stained a rich mahogany. Each contains one king- or two queen-size beds, a table with two upholstered chairs, two sinks, a shower-tub combo, an ample closet, and better-than-average lighting. There are also some renovated historic cabins (which don't have air-conditioning) and cottages with kitchenettes. On the property are an indoor pool and sauna, a campground, and a restaurant.

Bryce Country Cabins

320 N. Utah 12 (P.O. Box 141), Tropic, UT 84776. © **888/679-8643** or 435/679-8643. Fax 435/679-8989. www.brycecountrycabins. com. 8 units. A/C TV TEL. Summer $65–$75 double; lower rates at other times. DC, MC, V.

There's something neat about bedding down in a log cabin during a national park vacation, but there's also something very appealing about hot showers and warm beds. Bryce Country Cabins offers both, with six recently constructed log-style cabins and a historic two-room pioneer cottage, set on a 20-acre farm. The grounds surrounding the cabins and cottage are nicely landscaped, and you get views out over the national park, although we wish the units were farther back from the highway. The intriguing part of the facility, though, is the farm behind the buildings, where cattle graze in the fields and the chickens think they own the place.

The comfortable cabins have knotty pine walls and ceilings, exposed beams, and ceiling fans. Each has two queen-size beds, a table with two chairs, a coffeemaker, and a private porch. Bathrooms have showers only. The cottage, built in 1905, has two spacious rooms with country-style decor, each with its own entrance. Both have two queen-size beds and full bathrooms with shower/tub combos. The cottage's two rooms can be rented together or individually.

Bryce Pioneer Village

80 S. Main St. (Utah 12; P.O. Box 119), Tropic, UT 84776. © **800/222-0381** or 435/679-8546. Fax 435/679-8607. www.bpvillage.com. 62 units. A/C TV TEL. Summer $55–$75 double, $55–$85 cabins and kitchenette units; winter $30 double (call for availability and rates for other units). AE, MC, V. Closed Nov–Mar. Pets accepted in cabins.

This is a good choice for those seeking a comfortable night's rest at a reasonable rate. The small, no-frills motel rooms in a modular building have showers only, but they're clean and comfortable and have walk-in closets. Cabins, which were relocated from inside the national park, are more interesting. Most are small but cute, with one queen bed plus a twin bed, a chair, and a small bathroom with a corner shower but no tub. Several others, which have been renovated within the past few years, are much larger, with two queen beds, attractive floral-print wallpaper, and average-size bathrooms with shower/tub combinations. Two rooms contain three queen beds each. On the property are two hot tubs, a picnic area, and a small curio shop. Just outside the motel office you can see the cabin where Ebenezer and Mary Bryce, for whom the national park is named, lived in the late 1870s.

Bryce Point Bed & Breakfast

61 N. 400 W. (P.O. Box 96), Tropic, UT 84776-0096. © **888/200-4211** or 435/679-8629 (voice/fax). 6 units. TV. $70 double; $90–$120 honeymoon cottage. Rates include full breakfast. MC, V.

Each room in Lamar and Ethel LeFevre's bed-and-breakfast is named for and decorated in the style of one of the couple's children. For instance, son Les is a firefighter, so the Les and Dela room contains fire-fighting memorabilia and photos; son Lynn is in the airline industry, so you'll find airplane mementos in Lynn and Karen's room. In addition to memorabilia, most rooms offer beautiful views of Bryce Point through large picture windows. All rooms have queen or king beds and private bathrooms (showers only); and all have TV/VCR combos, with free use of the LeFevre's video collection. The honeymoon cottage is beautifully furnished in country style, with a gas fireplace in the living room, full kitchen, washer and dryer, and a king bed in the spacious bedroom. Breakfasts are full, satisfying, and homemade, with selections such as bacon and eggs with pancakes and apple cider syrup. All guests have

use of a large enclosed hot tub. The B&B is entirely nonsmoking.

Bryce View Lodge

Utah 63 across from Best Western Ruby's Inn (P.O. Box 64002), Bryce, UT 84764. © **888/279-2304** or 435/834-5180. Fax 435/834-5181. www.bryceviewlodge.com. 160 units. A/C TV TEL. $44–$60 double. AE, DC, DISC, MC, V. Pets accepted.

This basic modern American motel gets our vote for the best combination of economy and location. It consists of four two-story buildings, set back from the road and grouped around a large parking lot and attractively landscaped area. Rooms are simple but comfortable, recently refurbished, and quiet. Guests have access to the amenities across the street at Best Western Ruby's Inn (see above).

Canyon Livery Bed & Breakfast

50 S. 660 W. (P.O. Box 24), Tropic, UT 84776-0024. © **888/889-8910** or 435/679-8780. Call for fax. www.canyonlivery.com. 5 units. A/C. Apr–Oct $75–$95 double; Nov–Mar $65–$75 double. Rates include full breakfast. MC, V.

The homey touches and personal attention make this B&B an attractive alternative to the standard motel. The rooms are simply but attractively decorated, with handmade quilts on the queen beds. Two rooms are dedicated to women pioneers and have brass beds; two have handmade wooden beds and are dedicated to male pioneers; and the fifth is Western style, with a wonderful high arched window providing terrific views of the night sky. Breakfasts include a hot dish, homemade breads, and fresh fruits. All rooms have windows facing the national park, and the three upstairs rooms have private balconies. Each has its own entrance, and there is a corral if you happen to bring your horse ($5 a day extra, plus food). Smoking is not permitted.

Foster's

Utah 12 (mailing address: Star Route, Panguitch, UT 84759), Bryce, UT. © **800/475-4318** or 435/834-5227. Fax 435/834-5304. fosters@color-country.net. 52 units. A/C TV TEL. Summer $54 double; winter $45 double. AE, DISC, MC, V. 1½ miles west of the national park access road turnoff.

Clean and economical lodging is what you'll find at Foster's. A modular unit contains small rooms, each with either one queen-size or two double beds and decorated with posters showing scenery of the area; bathrooms have showers only. Also on the grounds are a restaurant (see "Where to Dine," below) and a grocery store (open 7am–10pm, closed Oct–Feb) with a rather nice bakery.

World Host Bryce Valley Inn

199 N. Main St., Tropic, UT 84776. © **800/442-1890** or 435/679-8811. Fax 435/679-8846. www.brycevalleyinn.com. 65 units. A/C TV TEL. May–Oct $55–$60 double; Nov–Apr $36–$44 double. AE, DISC, MC, V. 8 miles east of the park entrance road. Pets accepted for a fee.

These simply decorated, basic motel rooms offer a clean, economical choice for park visitors. Rooms, all of which have shower/tub combos and light-colored walls, are furnished with either one or two queen beds. One suite has two queens and a hide-a-bed. The motel has a 24-hour coin-operated laundry. The **Hungry Coyote Restaurant & Saloon** (see "Where to Dine," below) serves basic American grub. A gift shop on the premises offers a large selection of American Indian arts and crafts, handmade gifts, rocks, and fossils.

Where to Dine

INSIDE THE PARK

Bryce Canyon Lodge

Bryce Canyon National Park. © **435/834-5361.** Reservations required for dinner. Breakfast $3.95–$7.95; lunch $5.75–$7.95; dinner $8.95–$21. AE, DC, DISC, MC, V. Daily 6:30–10am, 11:30am–3pm, and 5:30–9pm. Closed Nov–Mar. AMERICAN.

It's worth coming here just for the delightful mountain lodge atmosphere, with two large stone fireplaces, American Indian weavings and baskets, a huge 45-star 1897 American flag, and large windows looking out on the park. But the food's good, too, and reasonably priced considering that this is the only real restaurant actually in the park. The menu is subject to change, but at dinner it's likely to include excellent slow-roasted prime rib au jus and fresh mountain trout. There are usually several vegetarian items also available, such as lasagna and black bean stuffed pepper. Ask about the lodge's specialty ice creams and desserts, such as the exotic (and very tasty) wild "Bryceberry" bread pudding and the excellent caramel apple cheesecake. At lunch you'll usually find trout, burgers, sandwiches, stews, and salads. All the usual American selections are offered for breakfast, and an excellent breakfast buffet is usually available. The restaurant will pack lunches to go, and offers full liquor service.

NEAR THE PARK

Bryce Canyon Pines

Utah 12 about 3 miles west of the intersection with the park entry road. © **435/834-5441.** www.brycecanyonmotel.com. Sandwiches $3.95–$7.95; full dinners $9.95–$19. AE, DC, DISC, MC, V. Daily 6:30am–9:30pm (may close slightly earlier in spring and fall). Closed mid-Nov to mid-Mar. AMERICAN.

A country cottage–style dining room, with an old wood stove and white eyelet-trimmed curtains, is a good setting for the wholesome American food served here. Especially popular for its traditional breakfasts, the restaurant is also known for its homemade soups and pies. Both sandwiches and full dinners are available at lunch and dinner. Recommended are the hot sandwiches, the Utah trout, and the 8-ounce tenderloin steak. Beer and wine are available.

Canyon Diner

Just north of the park entrance on Utah 63, in the Ruby's Inn complex, Bryce Canyon. © **435/ 834-5341.** www.rubysinn.com. Reservations not accepted Individual items $2.50–$6; meals $5–$9.50. AE, DISC, MC, V. Daily 6:30am–10pm. Closed Nov–Mar. AMERICAN.

This fast-food restaurant is a great place to fill up the kids without going broke. Breakfasts, served until 11am, include bagels and several egg croissants; for lunch and dinner, you can get hoagies, burgers, hot dogs, particularly good stuffed potatoes, fresh-made pizza, a broiled chicken sandwich, and salads. We especially recommend the Piccadilly (English-style) chips. Specialties include bratwurst with homemade sauerkraut and a halibut fish-and-chips basket. On a hot day, try a basic salad complemented by a filling malt or milkshake. No alcohol is served.

Foster's Family Steak House

Utah 12 about 1½ miles west of the park entrance road. © **435/834-5227.** Reservations not accepted. Breakfast and lunch items $1.75–$6; main dinner courses $9–$20. AE, DISC, MC, V. Mar–Nov daily 7am–10pm; Dec–Feb daily 3–10pm. STEAK/SEAFOOD.

The simple Old West decor here provides the appropriate atmosphere for a family steakhouse, popular for its slow-roasted prime rib and steamed Utah trout. Foster's also offers several steaks (including a 14-oz. T-bone), sandwiches, a soup of the day, and homemade Western-style chili with beans. All the pastries, pies, and breads are baked on the premises. Bottled beer is available.

Hungry Coyote Restaurant & Saloon

199 N. Main St. (Utah 12; 8 miles east of the park entrance road), at the World Host Bryce Valley Inn, Tropic. © **435/679-8822.** www. brycevalleyinn.com. Breakfast $3.95–$6.95; dinner main courses $7–$21. AE, DISC, MC, V. Daily 6:30–11am and 5–10pm; reduced hours in winter. AMERICAN/WESTERN.

The Old West is still king here; look around at the rough wood walls, old ranch tools, kerosene lanterns, and warnings that patrons must "check your gun with the waitress." Beef eaters will savor the thick 20-ounce T-bone, the most expensive item on the menu. You can also get pork chops, grilled chicken breast, or the popular local trout. The restaurant has full liquor service.

Ruby's Inn Cowboy's Buffet and Steak Room

Utah 63, the Ruby's Inn complex, Bryce. © **435/834-5341.** www.rubysinn.com. Reservations not accepted. Buffets: breakfast $8.50 adults and $6 children 3–12; lunch $9 adults and $7 children; dinner $15 adults and $7.50 children. Main courses $3.95–$14 breakfast and lunch, $5.95–$20 dinner. AE, DC, DISC, MC, V. Summer daily 6:30am–10pm; winter daily 6:30am–9pm. STEAK/SEAFOOD.

The busiest restaurant in the Bryce Canyon area, Ruby's moves 'em through with buffets at every meal, plus a well-rounded menu and friendly service. The breakfast buffet offers more choices than you'd expect, including scrambled eggs, fresh fruit, several breakfast meats, potatoes, pastries, and cereals. At the lunch buffet, you'll find country-style ribs, fresh fruit, salads, soups, vegetables, and breads. The dinner buffet features charbroiled thin-sliced rib-eye steak and other meats, pastas, potatoes, and salads. Regular menu dinner entrees include prime rib, slow-roasted baby-back ribs, breaded-and-grilled southern Utah rainbow trout, broiled chicken breast, burgers, and salads. In addition to the large, Western-style dining room, an outdoor patio is open in good weather. Full liquor service is available.

Picnic & Camping Supplies

A small store inside the national park has groceries, camping supplies, and snacks, all at surprisingly low prices. Just outside the park, the huge general store in Ruby's Inn (see "Where to Stay," above) offers camping supplies, groceries, Western clothing, and souvenirs.

For excursions throughout the area, the **Best Western Ruby's Inn,** on Utah 63 just north of the Bryce Canyon National Park entrance (see "Where to Stay," above), is practically a one-stop entertainment center.

Directly across Utah 63 from the motel are **Old Bryce Town Shops,** operated by Ruby's Inn, which are open from mid-May through September. Here you'll find a rock shop, souvenir shops, a Christmas store, and an opportunity to buy that genuine cowboy hat you've been wanting. There's a trail especially for kids where they can search for arrowheads, fossils, and petrified wood; you can also try your hand at panning for gold. Nearby, **Bryce Canyon Country Rodeo** has bucking broncos, bull riding, calf roping, and all sorts of rodeo fun in a 1-hour program from Memorial Day weekend through mid-September, Monday through Saturday evenings at 7pm. Admission is $7 for adults and $4 for children under 12.

Grand Staircase–Escalante National Monument

Covering about 1.9 million acres, this vast area of red-orange canyons, mesas, plateaus, and river valleys became a national monument by presidential proclamation in 1996. Known for its rugged beauty, it contains a combination of geological, biological, paleontological, archaeological, and historical resources. In announcing the creation of the monument, President Clinton proclaimed, "This high, rugged, and remote region was the last place in the continental United States to be mapped; even today, this unspoiled natural area remains a frontier, a quality that greatly enhances the monument's value for scientific study."

Unlike most other national monuments, almost all of this vast area is undeveloped—it has few all-weather roads, only one maintained hiking trail, and two small campgrounds. But for the adventurous there are miles upon miles of dirt roads and practically unlimited opportunities for hiking, horseback riding, mountain biking, and camping.

The national monument can be divided into three distinct sections: The **Grand Staircase** of sandstone cliffs—including five life zones from Sonoran desert to coniferous forests—is the southwest section; the **Kaiparowits Plateau,** a vast, wild region of rugged mesas and steep canyons, is the center section; and the **Escalante River Canyons,** a delightfully scenic area containing miles of interconnecting river canyons, is the northern section.

JUST THE FACTS

Getting There. The national monument covers an area almost as big as the states of Delaware and Rhode Island combined, with Bryce Canyon National Park to the west, Capitol Reef National Park along the northeast edge, and Glen Canyon National Recreation Area along the east and part of the south sides.

Access is via Utah 12 along the monument's northwest edge, from Kodachrome Basin State Park and the communities of Escalante and Boulder; and via U.S. 89 to the southern section of the monument, east of the town of Kanab.

Information & Visitor Centers. Stop at the **Escalante Interagency Office,** on the west side of Escalante at 755 W. Main St. (Utah 12) (© **435/826-5499**); or contact the Bureau of Land Management's **Kanab Visitor Center,** 745 E. U.S. 89, Kanab, UT 84741 (© **435/644-4680;** www.ut.blm.gov/monument), open daily from late March to mid-November.

Fees, Regulations & Safety. There is no charge to enter most of the monument; those planning overnight trips into the backcountry should obtain permits (free at press time) at either of the offices listed above. **Calf Creek Recreation Area**

charges $2 for day use and $7 for camping; camping at Deer Creek costs $4. Regulations are similar to those on other public lands, and, in particular, forbid damaging or disturbing archaeological and historic sites.

The main safety concern is water—either too little or too much. This is generally very dry country, so those going into the monument should carry plenty of drinking water. On the other hand, thunderstorms can turn the monument's dirt roads into impassable mud bogs in minutes, stranding motorists. Potentially fatal flash floods through narrow canyons can catch hikers by surprise. *The upshot:* Everyone planning trips into the monument should check first with one of the offices listed above on current and anticipated weather and travel conditions.

SPORTS & ACTIVITIES

Hiking, Mountain Biking & Horseback Riding. Located about 15 miles northeast of Escalante via Utah 12, the **Calf Creek Recreation Area** has a campground (see "Camping," below) and a picnic area with fire grates, tables, drinking water, and flush toilets. Well shaded, it lies along a creek at the bottom of a narrow, high-walled rock canyon.

The best part of the recreation area is the moderately strenuous 5.5-mile round-trip hike to **Lower Calf Creek Falls.** A sandy trail leads along **Calf Creek,** past beaver ponds and wetlands, to a beautiful waterfall cascading 126 feet down a rock wall into a tree-shaded pool. You can pick up an interpretive brochure at the trailhead.

Even though the Calf Creek Trail is the monument's only officially marked and maintained trail, there are numerous unmarked cross-country routes ideal for hiking, mountain biking, and horseback riding. We strongly recommend that hikers stop at the Interagency Office in Escalante or the Bureau of Land Management office in Kanab to get recommendations on hiking routes and to purchase topographical maps.

Among the popular and relatively easy-to-follow hiking routes is the footpath to **Escalante Natural Bridge.** It repeatedly crosses the river, so be prepared to get wet up to your knees. The easy 2-mile (one-way) hike begins at a parking area at the bridge that crosses the Escalante River near Calf Creek Recreation Area, 15 miles northeast of the town of Escalante. From the parking area, hike upstream to Escalante Natural Bridge, on the south side of the river. The bridge is 130 feet high and spans 100 feet. From here you can continue upstream, exploring side canyons, or turn around and head back to the parking lot.

Also starting at the Utah 12 bridge parking area is a hike downstream to **Phipps Wash.** Mostly moderate, this hike goes about 1.5 miles to the mouth of Phipps Wash, which enters the river from the west. On a northside drainage of Phipps Wash you'll find **Maverick Natural Bridge;** by climbing up the south side you can get to **Phipps Arch.**

Hiking the national monument's **slot canyons** is very popular, but we can't stress too strongly that you make sure to check on flood potentials before starting out. One challenging and very strenuous slot canyon hike is through **Peek-a-boo** and **Spooky canyons,** which are accessed from the Hole-in-the-Rock Road (see "Sightseeing & Four-Wheeling," below). Stop at the Escalante Interagency Office for precise directions.

Sightseeing & Four-Wheeling. This is one of America's least-developed large sections of public land, offering a wonderful opportunity for exploration by the adventurous. Be aware, though, that roads inside the monument are dirt that becomes mud, and often impassable, when it rains.

One particularly popular road is the **Hole-in-the-Rock Scenic Backway,** which is partly in the national monument and partly in the adjacent Glen Canyon

National Recreation Area. Like most roads in the monument, this should be attempted in dry weather only. Starting about 5 miles northeast of Escalante off Utah 12, this clearly marked dirt road travels 57 miles (one-way) to the Hole-in-the-Rock, where Mormon settlers in 1880 cut a passage through solid rock to get their wagons down a 1,200-foot cliff to the canyon floor and Colorado River below.

About 12 miles in, the road passes by the sign to **Devil's Rock Garden,** an area of classic red-rock formations and arches, where you'll also find a picnic area (about 1 mile off the main road). The road continues across a plateau of typical desert terrain, ending at a spectacular scenic overlook of Lake Powell. The first 35 miles of the scenic byway are relatively easy (in dry weather) in a standard passenger car, but then it gets a bit steeper and sandier, and the last 6 miles of the road require a high-clearance 4WD vehicle. Allow about 6 hours round-trip, and make sure you have plenty of fuel and water.

Another recommended drive in the national monument is the **Cottonwood Canyon Road,** which runs from Kodachrome Basin State Park south to U.S. 89, along the monument's southern edge, a distance of about 46 miles. The road is sandy and narrow, and washboard in places, but usually passable for passenger cars in dry weather. It mostly follows Cottonwood Wash, with good views of red-rock formations plus distant panoramas from hilltops. Unfortunately, views through the canyon are marred by two power lines, which make photography a challenge—though in all fairness, we should acknowledge that the road would not exist at all if not for the power lines.

About 10 miles east of Kodachrome Basin State Park is a short turnoff from Cottonwood Canyon Road that leads to **Grosvenor Arch.** This magnificent stone arch, with an opening 99 feet wide, was named for National Geographic Society founder and editor Gilbert H. Grosvenor, and is well worth the trip.

Wildlife Viewing & Bird-Watching. The isolated and rugged terrain offers a good habitat for a number of species, such as desert **bighorn sheep** and mountain lions. As for birds, more than 200 species have been spotted, including **bald eagles, golden eagles, Swainson's hawks,** and **peregrine falcons.** The best areas for seeing wildlife are along the Escalante and Paria rivers and Johnson Creek.

CAMPING

Backcountry camping is permitted in most areas of the monument with a permit (free at press time), available at the Interagency office in Escalante and the BLM office in Kanab. There are also two designated campgrounds. **Calf Creek Recreation Area,** about 15 miles northeast of the town of Escalante via Utah 12, has 13 sites and a picnic area. Open year-round, the tree-shaded campground often fills by 10am in summer. Located in a scenic, steep canyon along Calf Creek, surrounded by high rock walls, the campground has a volleyball court and offers access to an interpretive hiking trail (see "Hiking, Mountain Biking & Horseback Riding," above). It has drinking water and restrooms with flush toilets, but no showers, RV hookups or dump station, or garbage removal. In addition, from November through March, water is turned off and only vault toilets are available. To reach the campground, vehicles ford a shallow creek. The campground is not recommended for vehicles over 25 feet long. Campsites cost $7 per night; day use is $2 per vehicle.

The national monument's other designated campground is **Deer Creek,** located 6 miles east of the town of Boulder along the scenic Burr Trail Road. It has four primitive sites and no drinking water or other facilities; camping costs $4 per night.

8

CANYONLANDS NATIONAL PARK

by Don & Barbara Laine

TAH'S LARGEST NATIONAL PARK, CANYONLANDS IS A RUGGED HIGH desert of rock, with spectacular formations and gorges carved over the centuries by the park's primary architects, the Colorado and Green rivers. This is a land of extremes, of vast panoramas, dizzyingly deep canyons, dramatically steep cliffs, broad mesas, and towering red spires.

The most accessible part of Canyonlands is the Island in the Sky District, in the northern section of the park between the Colorado and Green rivers, where a paved road leads to sites such as Grand View Point, overlooking some 10,000 square miles of rugged wilderness. Island in the Sky also has several easy to moderate trails offering sweeping vistas of the park. A short walk provides views of Upheaval Dome, which resembles a large volcanic crater but may actually have been created by the crash of a meteorite. For the more adventurous, the 100-mile White Rim Road takes experienced mountain bikers and those with high-clearance four-wheel-drive vehicles on a winding loop tour through a vast array of scenery.

The Needles District, in the park's southeast corner, has only a few view points along the paved road, but it offers numerous possibilities for hikers, backpackers, and those with high-clearance 4WD. Named for its tall, red-and-white-striped rock pinnacles, this diverse district is home to impressive arches, including the 150-foot-tall Angel Arch, as well as grassy meadows and the confluence of the Green and Colorado rivers. Backcountry visitors to the Needles District will also find ruins and rock art left by prehistoric American Indians some 800 years ago.

Most park visitors don't get a close-up view of the Maze District, which lies on the west side of the Green and Colorado rivers, but instead see it off in the distance from Grand View Point at Island in the Sky, or Confluence Overlook in the Needles District. That's because it's inhospitable and practically inaccessible. You'll need a lot of endurance and at least several days to see even a few of its sites. Hardy hikers can visit Horseshoe Canyon in 1 day, where they can see the Great Gallery, an 80-foot-long rock art panel.

The park is also accessible by boat, which is how explorer Maj. John Wesley Powell first saw the canyons in 1869,

Tips from a Park Ranger

"**A** wilderness of rock," is how Paul Henderson, Canyonlands' chief of interpretation, describes the park, adding that it contains some of the most remote country left in the Lower 48. "There's some wonderful opportunities here to find solitude that don't exist in too many other places," Henderson adds.

"Island in the Sky District receives the highest visitation and has the most extensive front-country road system, so it's a place where folks that aren't equipped for a backcountry adventure can still get a good feeling for what this park is all about," he says. "There's a paved road system, and you can have a really good experience in half a day."

However, Henderson says that Island in the Sky is not only for the pavement-bound. "The premier opportunity at Island in the Sky is the White Rim Road," he says, "a network of old mining roads and cowboy trails that make about a 100-mile trip—it's one of the premier mountain-biking trips in the country."

The Needles District, he says, is not a good place to cycle, but it has absolutely first-rate options for hiking, backpacking, and four-wheeling. "Needles is pretty rough country, with some classic four-wheel-drive roads that for the most part are not for novice four-wheel-drivers." He adds, "I cringe when I see somebody in a brand-new $35,000 rig and it's probably the first time they've locked it into four-wheel-drive."

The park's third district, the Maze, is very rough backcountry, Henderson says, and certainly not for everyone. It is, however, a great destination if you don't want to see many people. "In August 1997, we had about 40,000 people at Island in the Sky, about 20,000 at Needles, and 546 at the Maze."

when he made his first trip down the Green to its confluence with the Colorado, and then even farther downstream, eventually to the Grand Canyon. River access is from the towns of Moab and Green River; local companies offer boat trips of various durations.

You'll find a fascinating mixture of mountain and desert animals in Canyonlands that varies depending on the time of year and particular location within the park. The best times to see most wildlife are early and late in the day, especially in the summer when the midday sun drives all Canyonlands residents in search of shade. Throughout the park you'll probably hear, if not see, coyotes, and it's likely you'll spot white-tailed antelope squirrels and other rodents scampering among the rocks. Watch for the elusive and rather antisocial bighorn sheep along isolated cliffs, where you might also see a golden eagle or a turkey vulture soaring above the rocks in search of prey. In the little pools of water that appear in the slickrock after rainstorms, you're likely to see tadpole shrimp—1-inch-long crustaceans that look as though they would be more at home in the ocean. Among the cottonwoods and willows along the rivers you'll find a variety of wildlife: deer, beaver, an occasional bobcat, and various migratory birds.

Avoiding the Crowds. Although Canyonlands does not get nearly as crowded as most other national parks, the more popular trails can be busy at certain times. Spring and fall see the most visitors, but summer has recently become popular, despite scorching temperatures. Those who seriously want to avoid humanity should visit from November through mid-March, when the park is practically deserted, though some trails

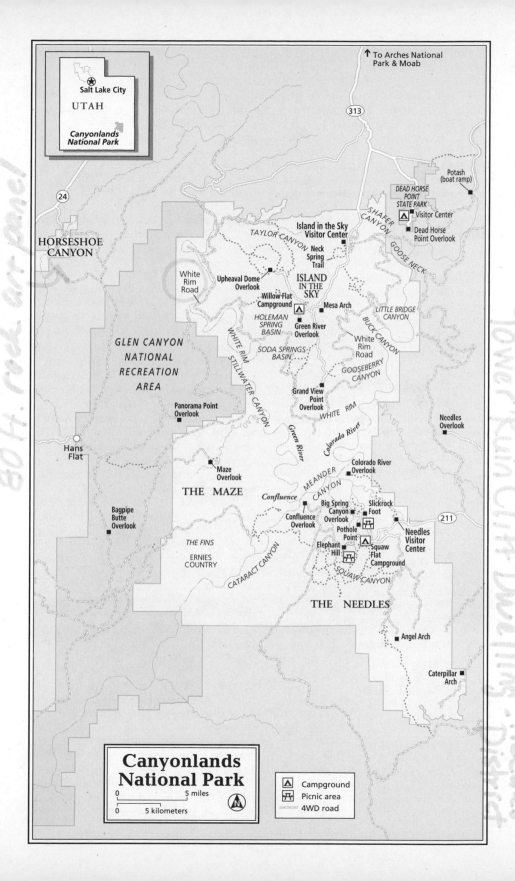

Canyonlands National Park map. Text labels visible on the map:

Inset map: Salt Lake City, UTAH, Canyonlands National Park

To Arches National Park & Moab

313

Potash (boat ramp)

DEAD HORSE POINT STATE PARK, Visitor Center, Dead Horse Point Overlook

SHAFER CANYON, GOOSE NECK

24

HORSESHOE CANYON

TAYLOR CANYON

Island in the Sky Visitor Center

Neck Spring Trail

White Rim Road

Upheaval Dome Overlook

Willow Flat Campground

ISLAND IN THE SKY

Mesa Arch

LITTLE BRIDGE CANYON

Green River Overlook

BUCK CANYON

White Rim Road

HOLEMAN SPRING BASIN

GLEN CANYON NATIONAL RECREATION AREA

SODA SPRINGS BASIN

GOOSEBERRY CANYON

WHITE RIM CANYON

STILLWATER CANYON

Grand View Point Overlook

WHITE RIM

Panorama Point Overlook

Needles Overlook

Hans Flat

Green River

Colorado River

Maze Overlook

THE MAZE

Confluence

MEANDER CANYON

Colorado River Overlook

Bagpipe Butte Overlook

Confluence Overlook

Big Spring Canyon Overlook

Slickrock Foot

Pothole Point

211

Needles Visitor Center

THE FINS

ERNIES COUNTRY

Elephant Hill

Squaw Flat Campground

CATARACT CANYON

SQUAW CANYON

THE NEEDLES

Angel Arch

Caterpillar Arch

Canyonlands National Park

0   5 miles
0   5 kilometers

Campground
Picnic area
4WD road

(margin, vertical text) 80 ft. rock. air onnel

(margin, vertical text) Tower Ruin Cliff Dwelling · Needles District and 4WD roads may be inaccessible. College spring-break time—usually from mid-March through April—can be especially busy, and any other school vacation usually brings more visitors as well. Hiking in the early morning—often the best time to hike anyway—is a good way to beat the crowds any time of year.

One thing that makes the backcountry experience here especially pleasant, even during the park's busiest times, is that the number of permits for overnight trips is limited (and often sold out well in advance). If you're willing to hike, bike, or drive far enough, you're guaranteed that you won't be sharing the trail or road with a lot of other people.

Just the Facts

There are no lodgings, restaurants, or stores inside the park. Most visitors use Moab as a base camp.

GETTING THERE & GATEWAYS

For directions to Moab, see "Getting There & Gateways," in chapter 2.

To get to the Island in the Sky Visitor Center from Moab (about 34 miles away), take U.S. 191 (which runs north-south through eastern Utah from Wyoming to Arizona) north to Utah 313, which you follow south into the park.

To reach the Needles Visitor Center from Moab, leave U.S. 191 at Utah 211 south of Moab, and head west into the park. It's about 75 miles.

Getting to the Maze District is a bit more interesting. From Moab take U.S. 191 north, then go west for about 11 miles on I-70, crossing Green River, and then take Utah 24 south. Watch for signs and follow two- and four-wheel-drive dirt roads east into the park.

The detached Horseshoe Canyon area of the park is about 120 miles from Island in the Sky. To get there by two-wheel-drive vehicle, again follow I-70 west from Green River to U.S. 24, and

then go south about 24 miles to the Horseshoe Canyon turnoff (near the WATCH FOR SAND DRIFTS sign), where you turn left. Follow this maintained dirt road for about 30 miles to the canyon's west rim, where you can park. This is the trailhead for the hike to the Great Gallery (see "Day Hikes," below).

The Nearest Airport & Renting a Car. See the "The Nearest Airport" and "Ground Transportation" sections in chapter 2.

INFORMATION

Contact the **Superintendent, Canyonlands National Park,** 2282 S. West Resource Blvd., Moab, UT 84532-3298 (© 435/719-2313; www.nps.gov/cany). You can get additional information from the **Moab Information Center** (see "Information," in chapter 2).

Canyonlands Natural History Association offers a number of helpful books and maps for sale (see "Information," in chapter 2). A couple of very good guides to hiking and off-roading are *Exploring Canyonlands and Arches National Parks* (Helena, Montana: Falcon Press, 1997) by Bill Schneider, and *Canyon Country Off-Road Vehicle Trails, Canyon Rims and Needles Areas* (Moab, Utah: Canyon Country Publications, 1990) by F. A. Barnes.

VISITOR CENTERS

Canyonlands National Park operates two visitor centers: **Island in the Sky Visitor Center,** in the northern part of the park, and **Needles Visitor Center,** in the southern section. In both, you can get advice from rangers as well as maps and free brochures on hiking trails.

FEES & PERMITS

Entry into the park (for up to 7 days) costs $10 per private vehicle or $5 per person on foot or bike. The camping fee at Squaw Flat Campground in the

Needles District is $10; camping at Willow Flat Campground in the Island in the Sky District costs $5.

Backcountry permits, available at either visitor center, are required for all overnight stays in the park, except at the two established campgrounds. Permit reservations can be made in advance (© 435/259-4351). Permits for overnight four-wheel-drive and mountain-bike trips are $30, while those for overnight backpacking trips are $15. The permit for white-water boating through Cataract Canyon is $30; flat-water boating costs $20.

There is also a $5 day-use fee for those visitors bringing motor vehicles, horses, or mountain bikes on roads into Salt Creek/Horse Canyon and Lavender Canyon in the Needles District.

SPECIAL REGULATIONS & WARNINGS

Backcountry hikers must pack out all trash, and wood fires are prohibited. Canyonlands National Park is not a good place to take pets. Dogs, which must be leashed at all times, are prohibited in public buildings, on all trails, and in the backcountry. This includes four-wheel-drive roads—dogs are not permitted even inside your vehicle. In addition to the regulations, you should be aware that because of its extreme heat and rough terrain, this park can be extremely hazardous to pets.

Indeed, the varied terrain at Canyonlands can be brutal not just for pets, but for people too. The main safety problem at Canyonlands is that people underestimate the hazards. It's important that you know your own limitations as well as the limitations of your vehicle and other equipment. Rangers warn hikers to carry at least 1 gallon of water per person per day, to be especially careful near cliff edges, to avoid overexposure to the intense sun, and to carry maps when going off into the backcountry. During lightning storms, avoid lone trees, high ridges, and cliff edges. Four-wheel-drive-vehicle operators should carry extra food and emergency equipment. Also, anyone going into the backcountry should let someone know where they're going and when they plan to return. Traveling alone in Canyonlands is not a good idea.

SEASONS & CLIMATE

Summers here are hot, with temperatures sometimes exceeding 100°F (38°C). Winters can be cool or cold, dropping well below freezing at night. The best time to visit, especially for hikers, is in the spring or fall, when daytime temperatures are usually from 60° to 80°F (16°C–27°C), and nights are cool. Late summer and early fall visitors should be prepared for afternoon thunderstorms.

If You Have Only 1 Day

Canyonlands is not an easy place to see in a short period of time. In fact, if your schedule permits only a day, skip the Needles and Maze districts entirely, and drive directly to the **Island in the Sky Visitor Center.** After looking at the exhibits, drive to several of the overlooks, stopping along the way for a short hike or two. Make sure you get to the **Grand View Point Overlook,** at the south end of the paved road. Among the best trails for a quick trip is the **Grand View Trail,** which starts at the overlook and is especially scenic in late afternoon. Allow about 1½ hours for this easy 2-mile walk. Also recommended is the **Upheaval Dome Overlook Trail,** which should take about a half-hour, and brings you to a mile-wide crater of mysterious origins.

Perhaps a better choice for a quick visit to the park, especially for those with a bit of extra cash, is to take a guided trip by four-wheel-drive vehicle or raft. See the "Organized Tours & Ranger Programs" and "Outfitters Based in Moab" sections, below.

Exploring the Park by Car

No driving tour has yet been designed to show off Canyonlands National Park. The Island in the Sky District has about 20 miles of paved highway, some gravel roads accessible to two-wheel-drive vehicles, and several view points. The Needles District only has 8 miles of paved roads. Many (but not all) of Needles' view points and trailheads are accessible only by high-clearance 4WD vehicles or plain old foot power. The Maze District has only two main roads, neither of them paved. Both lead to trailheads.

Of course, if you happen to have a serious 4WD, and if you are equally serious about doing some hard-core four-wheeling, this is the park for you. See "Other Sports & Activities," below. Because of the constantly changing conditions of dirt roads, we strongly suggest that you discuss your plans with rangers before setting out.

Organized Tours & Ranger Programs

In summer, rangers offer evening **campfire programs** at Squaw Flat and Willow Flat campgrounds, and also frequently give short morning talks at the Island in the Sky Visitor Center and at Grand View Point.

Canyonlands by Night (✆ 800/394-9978 or 435/259-5261; www.canyonlands bynight.com) offers an evening river trip, operating spring through fall, that combines a sunset boat ride with stories of outlaws, rock formations, and a sound-and-light show against the backdrop of the canyon walls. The office and dock are just north of Moab at the Colorado River Bridge. Dutch oven dinners in a covered patio, with live country-western entertainment, precede the boat trip. Cost for the boat trip and dinner is $40 for adults, $25 for children 6 to 12, and $9 for kids 2 to 5. Reservations are recommended.

Many of Canyonlands' most spectacular sections are difficult to get to, to say the least. One solution is to take to the air. **Slickrock Air Guides, Inc** (✆ 435/259-6216; fax 435/259-2226; www.slickrock airguides.com) offers 1-hour scenic flights over Canyonlands National Park and Dead Horse State Park (about $100) and 2½-hour flights that take in Canyonlands and Monument Valley (about $200).

If helicopters are your bag, contact **Arches & Classic Helicopter Services** (✆ 435/259-4637; www.moab-utah.com/archeshelicopter.html). Half-hour charter flights start at $80 per person with a five-person minimum.

Historic & Man-Made Attractions

This land was once the domain of prehistoric American Indians, who constructed their buildings out of the region's rock, hunted deer and bighorn sheep, and left numerous drawings on rock walls. Most of the park's archaeological sites are in the Needles District. They include the well-preserved cliff dwelling called **Tower Ruin,** high on a cliff ledge in Horse Canyon; and an easy-to-reach **ancient granary,** near the Needles Visitor Center, accessible on the short self-guided Roadside Ruin Trail. Throughout the park you'll also find evidence of more modern peoples—the trappers, explorers, and cowboys of the 19th century.

In Horseshoe Canyon, a separate and remote section of the park on the west side of the Green River, you'll find the **Great Gallery,** one of the most fantastic rock art panels in the Southwest. More than 80 feet long, the panel contains many red-and-white paintings of what appear to be larger-than-life human figures. The paintings are believed to be at least 2,000 years old.

Day Hikes

Conditions along these trails can be tough in summer: little shade, no reliable water sources, and temperatures soaring to over 100°F (38°C). Because of this, rangers strongly advise that hikers carry at least 1 gallon of water per person per day, along with sunscreen, a hat, and all the usual hiking and emergency equipment. Ideally, if you expect to do some serious hiking, try to plan your trip for the spring or fall, when conditions are much more hospitable.

All hikers should be careful on the many trails that cross slickrock, a general term for any bare rock surface. As the name implies, it can be slippery, especially when wet. Also, because some of the trails may be confusing, hikers attempting the longer ones should take good topographical maps, available at park visitor centers and at stores in Moab.

The following are some of the park's many hiking possibilities, arranged by district; check with rangers for other suggestions.

ISLAND IN THE SKY DISTRICT

SHORTER TRAILS

Grand View Trail

1 mile one-way. Easy. Access: Grand View Point Overlook at the south end of the paved road.

At the trailhead, stop and read the sign that points out all the prominent features you can see, such as the **Totem Pole,** the confluence of the **Colorado and Green rivers,** and the **White Rim Trail.** Although this is a fairly flat and easy trail to hike, you should watch carefully for the cairns, since some are on the small side. And always stay back from the cliff edge. This trail is especially beautiful at sunset, when the panorama seems to change constantly with the diminishing angle of sunlight.

Mesa Arch Trail

0.5 mile RT. Easy. Access: The trailhead is along a paved road about 6 miles south of the visitor center.

This is a self-guided nature walk through an area of pinyon and juniper trees, mountain mahogany, cactus, and a plant called Mormon Tea, from which Mormon pioneers made their hot drinks. The trail's main scenic attraction is the **Mesa Arch,** made of Navajo sandstone. It hangs precariously on the edge of a 500-foot cliff, framing a spectacular view of nearby mountains.

Upheaval Dome Overlook

0.4 mile one-way. Moderate. Access: The trailhead is at the end of Upheaval Dome Rd.

This hike to the overlook has a few steep inclines. Upheaval Dome doesn't fit with the rest of the Canyonlands' terrain—it's the result not of gradual erosion like the rest of the park, but rather of a dramatic deformity in which rocks have been pushed into a dome-like structure. At one time it was theorized that the dome was formed by a hidden volcano, but now experts say the cause may have been a meteorite that struck the earth some 60 million years ago. Hiking another 0.5 mile takes you to a second overlook, closer to the Dome, but with a less panoramic view.

Whale Rock Trail

0.5 mile one-way. Moderate. Access: The trailhead is about 4 miles down Upheaval Dome Rd.

This trail provides breathtaking 360-degree views of the Island in the Sky District. It's a climb of 300 feet up a slickrock trail with handrails. Wander around on top a bit and study the varied formations; to those with some imagination, the outcrop you just climbed resembles a whale.

LONGER TRAILS

Gooseberry Trail

2.7 miles one-way. Moderate. Access: Island in the Sky Picnic Area, about 11 miles south of the visitor center.

Although the beginning of this trail is so steep it looks like a cliff, don't be deterred. True, it drops 1,400 feet over the course of the hike, and most of that (1,300 ft.) in the first 1.5 miles. But the trail is well made, and with a little care is quite safe. As you gingerly hike down the switchbacks—be careful of the loose sand—you get superb views of the White Rim Country. Once down in Gooseberry Canyon, it's nearly a level walk out to the road. When you decide you're ready to face the climb back to the top, be sure to take lots of rest stops to admire the varying scenery.

Lathrop Trail

6.8 miles one-way. Strenuous. Access: The trailhead is about 1.5 miles south of the visitor center along paved road.

The first 2.5 miles of this trail are on top of the mesa, but then it meanders down into the canyon, descending about 1,600 feet to the White Rim Road. This strenuous hike traverses steep terrain and loose rock—and remember, you have to climb back up to your car, unless you have been able to arrange for someone to meet you at the road. As you hike down the slope, you get grand views of **Lathrop Canyon** and occasional glimpses of the **Colorado River.** It is possible to continue down to the river from the road (another 4 miles each way), but check with rangers about the feasibility of an overnight trip before attempting it.

Neck Spring Trail

5 miles RT. Moderate to strenuous. Access: The trailhead is about 0.5 mile south of the visitor center along paved road.

This fairly strenuous hike follows the paths that animals and early ranchers

created to reach water at two springs. You'll see water troughs, hitching posts, rusty cans, and the ruins of an old cabin. Because of the water source, you'll encounter types of vegetation not usually seen in the park, such as maidenhair ferns and gambel oak. The water also draws wildlife, including mule deer, bighorn sheep, ground squirrels, and hummingbirds. Climbing to the top of the rim, you get a beautiful view of the canyons and even the **Henry Mountains,** some 60 miles away.

Syncline Loop Trail

8.3 miles RT. Strenuous. Access: Upheaval Dome Picnic Area at the end of Upheaval Dome Rd.

This is a long, hot day hike over one of only three loop trails in the Island in the Sky District. Be sure to start early and carry plenty of water. The trail drops 1,300 feet, and is best hiked clockwise so you take the steepest part going down, into **Upheaval Canyon.** Along the way, you'll follow dry washes, climb small hills and steep canyon sides, cross part of the Syncline Valley, pass **Upheaval Dome,** traverse some slickrock, and finally hit an area of lush vegetation.

NEEDLES DISTRICT

Hiking trails here are generally not too tough, but keep in mind that slickrock can live up to its name and that there is generally little shade.

SHORTER TRAILS

Roadside Ruin Trail

0.3 mile RT. Easy. Access: The trailhead is just over 0.5 mile west of the visitor center along paved road.

This self-guided nature walk leads to an ancient granary, probably used by the Ancestral Puebloans some 700 to 1,000 years ago to store corn, nuts, and other foods. For 25¢ you can get a brochure at the trailhead that discusses the plants along the trail. Although flat, this trail can be muddy when wet.

Slickrock Foot Trail

2.4 miles RT. Moderate. Access: The trailhead is about 6½ miles from the visitor center, almost at the end of the road.

View points along this trail show off the stair-step topography of the area, from its colorful canyons and cliffs to its flat mesas and striped needles.

LONGER TRAILS

Confluence Overlook Trail

5.5 miles one-way. Moderate to strenuous. Access: Big Spring Canyon Overlook.

This hike has steep drop-offs and little shade, but the hard work is worthwhile—it shows off splendidly the many colors of the Needles District, and also offers excellent views into the Maze District of the park. The climax is a spectacular view overlooking the confluence of the **Green and Colorado rivers** in a 1,000-foot-deep gorge. This hike can be done as a day hike (allow 4–6 hr.) or quite pleasantly as an overnight hike.

Elephant Hill–Druid Arch Trail

5.4 miles one-way. Moderate. Access: Elephant Hill Trailhead at end of graded gravel road, drivable in most 2-wheel-drive passenger cars, although those in large vehicles such as motor homes will want to avoid it.

A number of interconnecting trails lead into the backcountry from this trailhead. The hike to Druid Arch, though not difficult, challenges hikers with steep drop-offs, quite a bit of slickrock, and a 1,000-foot increase in elevation. But the effort is worth the views, as you hike through narrow rock canyons, past colorful spires and pinnacles, and up the steep climb to the bench just below the huge **Druid Arch,** its dark rock somewhat resembling the stone structures of Stonehenge.

Squaw Canyon— Big Spring Canyon Loop

7.5-mile loop. Strenuous. Access: Squaw Flat Campground.

This hike over steep slickrock winds through woodlands of pinyon and juniper, offering views along the way of the Needles rock formations for which the district is named, plus nearby cliffs and mesas as well as distant mountains. Watch for wildflowers from late spring through summer. The hike can be completed in about half a day, but several backcountry campsites make it available to overnighters.

MAZE DISTRICT

Getting to the trailheads in the Maze District involves rugged four-wheel-drive roads; rangers can help you with directions.

The 3-mile **Maze Overlook Trail** is not for beginning hikers or anyone with a fear of heights, and is quite steep in places, requiring the use of your hands for safety. At the trailhead you get a fine view of the many narrow canyons that inspired this district's name; then the trail descends 600 feet to the canyon bottom.

The 12-mile **Harvest Scene Loop** (difficult, 7–10 hr. or overnight) leads over slickrock and along canyon washes—watch for the cairns to be sure you don't wander off the trail—to a magnificent example of rock art.

Other trailheads lie in what is known as the **Doll House Area.** Check with a ranger for current trail conditions and difficulty.

HORSESHOE CANYON

This detached section of the park was added to Canyonlands in 1971 mainly because of its **Great Gallery,** an 80-foot-long rock art panel with larger-than-life human figures, which dates from 2000 B.C. to A.D. 500. The Horseshoe Canyon Unit is some 120 miles (one-way) from

Island in the Sky, and has only one road in (see "Getting There & Gateways," above). From the parking area it's a 6.5-mile round-trip hike to see the rock art. The hike begins with a 1.5-mile section down an 800-foot slope to the canyon floor, where you then turn right and go 1.75 miles to the Great Gallery. There is no camping in Horseshoe Canyon, but just outside the park boundary primitive camping is available on Bureau of Land Management property on the rim.

Exploring the Backcountry

You'll find many opportunities for backpacking in Canyonlands National Park, although hikers will often be sharing trail/road combinations with four-wheel-drive vehicles and mountain bikes. Additional information is provided below.

Other Sports & Activities

Canyonlands is a park that begs to be explored—if you've come to Utah for mountain biking, hiking, four-wheeling, or rafting, this is the place. The region holds a few surprises, too, from ancient American Indian dwellings and rock art to dinosaur bones.

Unlike most national parks, the backcountry at Canyonlands is not only the domain of backpackers. Here, rugged four-wheel-drive and mountain-bike roads, as well as rivers navigable by boat, lead to some of the park's most scenic areas. Primitive campsites, strategically located throughout the backcountry, are available to all visitors, regardless of their mode of transport. Just be sure to make your backcountry campsite reservations well in advance—up to a year ahead for the more popular areas. You can get reservation forms and detailed information by mail, phone, or from the park's website (see "Information," above).

OUTFITTERS BASED IN MOAB

Although this area offers plenty for the do-it-yourselfer, some 50 local outfitters offer excursions of all kinds, from lazy canoe rides to hair-raising jet-boat and four-wheel-drive adventures. The chart below lists some of the major companies that want to help you fully enjoy this beautiful country. All are located in Moab (zip code 84532). Advance reservations are often required, and it's best to check with several outfitters before you decide on one. In addition to asking about what you'll see and do and what it will cost, it doesn't hurt to make sure the company is insured and has the proper permits with the various federal agencies. Also ask about its cancellation policy, just in case.

Boating, Canoeing & Rafting. After spending hours in the blazing sun looking at mile upon mile of huge red sandstone rock formations, it's easy to get the idea that Canyonlands National Park is a baking, dry, rock-hard desert. Well, it is. But both the Colorado and Green rivers run through the park, and one of the most exciting ways to see the park and surrounding country is from river level.

You can travel into the park in a canoe, kayak, large or small rubber raft (with or without motor), or speedy, solid jet boat. Do-it-yourselfers can rent kayaks or canoes for $25 to $35 for a half day and $30 to $45 for a full day, or rafts from $50 to $85 for a half day and $65 to $115 for a full day. Half-day guided river trips cost from $35 to $45 per person; full-day trips are usually $40 to $60. Multiday rafting expeditions, which include meals and camping equipment, start at about $150 per person for 2 days. Jet-boat trips, which cover a lot more river in a given amount of time, start at $60 for a half-day trip, with full-day trips about $85. Children's rates are usually about 20% lower. Some companies also offer sunset or dinner trips. **Sheri Griffith Expeditions** even has a 5-day, 4-night "Expedition in Luxury," at $1,745 per person, which pampers you with gourmet food served with white tablecloths, fine wines, and your every need anticipated.

The Colorado and Green rivers meet in the park, and both are fairly calm before the confluence. But after the confluence the Colorado becomes serious white water; at this point you will most likely want to be on a guided raft trip.

One fantastic canoe trip is along the Green River. Canoeists usually start in or near the town of Green River (put in at Green River State Park or at Mineral Bottom, just downstream) and spend about 2 days to get to the Green's confluence with the Colorado, where they can arrange to be picked up by a local outfitter.

Public boat-launching ramps in the Moab area are opposite Lion's Park, near the intersection of U.S. 191 and Utah 128; at Take-Out Beach, along Utah 128 about 10 miles east of its intersection with U.S. 191; and at Hittle Bottom, also along Utah 128, about 24 miles east of its intersection with U.S. 191. Information on river flows and reservoir conditions statewide can be obtained from the **Colorado Basin River Forecast Center** (© 801/539-1311; www.cbrfc.gov).

Four-Wheeling. Unlike most national parks, where all motor vehicles and mountain bikes must stay on paved roads, Canyonlands has miles of rough, four-wheel-drive roads where mechanized transport is king. Keep in mind that we're talking serious four-wheeling here, where most roads require high-clearance short-wheelbase vehicles. Many of these roads also require the skill that comes only from experience, so it's usually a good idea to discuss your plans with rangers before putting your high-priced vehicle on the line. Four-wheelers must stay on designated 4WD roads, but here the term *road* can mean anything from a graded, well-marked

two-lane gravel byway to a pile of loose rocks with a sign that says "that-a-way." Many of the park's Jeep roads are impassable during heavy rains and for a day or two after.

Local companies offering four-wheel-drive rentals include **Thrifty** (© 800/THRIFTY or 435/259-7317), **Farabee's 4WD Rentals** (© 888/806-5337 or 435/259-7494), and **Slickrock Jeep Rentals** (© 435/259-5678). Rates are usually $100 to $135 per day, with some mileage included.

The best four-wheel-drive adventure in Canyonlands' Island in the Sky District is the **White Rim Road,** which runs some 100 winding miles and affords spectacular and ever-changing views, from broad panoramas of rock and canyon to close-ups of red and orange towers and buttes. A high-clearance 4WD is essential. Expect the journey to be slow, lasting 2 to 3 days, although with the appropriate vehicle it isn't really difficult. There are primitive campgrounds along the way, but reservations on this popular route should be made well in advance.

Four-wheeling on one of many exciting routes in the Needles District can be an end in itself or simply a means to get to some of the more interesting and remote hiking trails and camping spots. Four-wheelers will find one of their ultimate challenges on the **Elephant Hill Jeep Road,** which begins at a well-marked turnoff near Squaw Flat Campground. Although most of the 10-mile trail is only moderately difficult, the stretch over Elephant Hill itself near the beginning can be a nightmare, with steep, rough slickrock, drifting sand, loose rock, and treacherous ledges. Coming down the hill there is one switchback that requires you to back to the edge of a steep cliff before continuing ahead. This is also a favorite of mountain bikers, although bikes will have to be walked on some stretches over an abundance of sand and rocks. The route offers views of numerous rock

Outfitter	4WD	Bike	Boat	Horse	Rent	Shuttle
Adrift Adventures 378 N. Main St., Box 577 © 800/874-4483, 435/259-8594 www.adrift.net	Yes	No	Yes	Yes	No	No
Canyon Voyages Adventure Co. 211 N. Main St., Box 416 © 800/733-6007, 435/259-6007 www.canyonvoyages.com	Yes	No	Yes	No	Yes	No
Dreamrides 59 E. Center St., Box 1137 © 888/662-2882, 435/259-6419 www.dreamride.com	No	Yes	No	No	No	No
Moab Rafting Co. Box 801 © 800/746-6622, 435/259-7238 www.moab-rafting.com	No	No	Yes	No	No	No
Navtec Expeditions 321 N. Main St., Box 1267 © 800/833-1278, 435/259-7983 www.navtec.com	No	Yes	No	Yes	No	Yes
Nichols Expeditions 497 N. Main St. © 800/648-8488, 435/259-3999 www.nicholsexpeditions.com	No	Yes	No	No	Yes	No
OARS Canyonlands Tours 543 N. Main St. © 800/342-5938, 435/259-5865 www.oarsutah.com	Yes	No	Yes	No	No	No
Pack Creek Ranch U.S. 191, S. of Moab, Box 1270 © 435/259-5505 www.packcreekranch.com	No	No	No	Yes	No	No
Red River Canoe Co. 702 S. Main St. © 800/753-8216, 435/259-7722 www.redrivercanoe.com	No	No	Yes	No	No	No
Rim Tours 1233 S. U.S. 191 © 800/626-7335, 435/259-5223 www.rimtours.com	No	Yes	No	No	Yes	No
Sheri Griffith Expeditions 2231 S. U.S. 191, Box 1324 © 800/332-2439, 435/259-8229 www.griffithexp.com	No	Yes	Yes	Yes	Yes	No

Outfitter	4WD	Bike	Boat	Horse	Rent	Shuttle
Tag-A-Long Expeditions 452 N. Main St. ℂ 800/453-3292, 435/259-8946 www.tagalong.com	Yes	No	Yes	No	Yes	Yes
Tex's Riverways 691 N. 500 W., Box 67 ℂ 435/259-5101	No	No	No	Yes	No	Yes
Western River Expeditions 1371 N. U.S. 191 ℂ 888/622-4097, 435/259-7019 www.westernriver.com	No	No	Yes	No	Yes	Yes
Xtreme Adventure Tours N. U.S. 191 ℂ 435/259-3906 www.xtremeadventuretours.com	Yes	No	No	No	Yes	No

formations, from striped needles to balanced rocks, plus steep cliffs and rock "stairs." Side trips can add another 30 miles. Allow from 8 hours to 3 days.

For a spectacular view of the Colorado River, the **Colorado River Overlook Road** can't be beat. This 14-mile round-trip is popular with four-wheelers, backpackers, and mountain bikers. Considered among the park's easiest 4WD roads, the first part is very easy indeed, accessible by high-clearance two-wheel-drives, but the second half has a few rough and rocky sections that require four-wheel-drive. Starting at the Needles Visitor Center parking lot, the trail takes you past numerous panoramic vistas to a spectacular 360-degree view of the park and the Colorado River some 1,000 feet below.

Biking. Road bikes are of little use in Canyonlands, except for getting to and from trailheads, view points, visitor centers, and campgrounds in the Island in the Sky and Needles districts. Although bikes of any kind are prohibited on hiking trails and cross-country in the backcountry, they are permitted on designated two- and four-wheel-drive roads. This means that mountain bikers have

many possibilities here, although they will find themselves sharing dirt roads with motor vehicles and hikers. Some of the four-wheel-drive roads have deep sand in spots that can turn into quicksand when wet—so you may find that mountain biking, while certainly a challenge, is not as much fun as you'd expect. It's wise to talk with rangers about conditions on specific roads before setting out.

Among popular rides are the **Elephant Hill and Colorado River Overlook Jeep roads,** both in the Needles District. The 100-mile **White Rim Road,** in the Island in the Sky District, also makes a great mountain-bike trip (allow at least 4 days), especially for bikers who can arrange for an accompanying 4WD vehicle to carry water, food, and camping gear. See "Four-Wheeling," above. For information on where to get advice, bike rentals and repairs, equipment, and bike shuttle services, see the "Biking" section in chapter 2.

Camping

For details on the following campgrounds, see the campground chart in chapter 2.

INSIDE THE PARK

The park has two developed camp-grounds, both set among rugged rocks. **Willow Flat Campground** is in the Island in the Sky District, and **Squaw Flat Campground** is in the Needles District. Primitive campsites are also available throughout the park for four-wheelers, boaters, mountain bikers, and back-packers (see "Exploring the Backcoun-try," above).

NEAR THE PARK

Near Island in the Sky, the campground at scenic **Dead Horse Point State Park** (P.O. Box 609, Moab, UT 84532-0609; © 435/259-2614; www.stateparks.utah. gov) has electric hookups, and accepts reservations from mid-March to mid-October with a $7 processing fee (© 800/322-3770). The **Newspaper Rock Camp-ground** (contact the Bureau of Land Management, P.O. Box 7, Monticello, UT 84535; © 435/587-1500; www.ut.blm. gov), located along the road to the Nee-dles District, offers primitive camping. Additional camping facilities are available on nearby public lands administered by the Bureau of Land Management and U.S. Forest Service; check at the **Moab Information Center,** located in Moab at

the corner of Main and Center streets, or contact the **Moab Area Travel Council,** P.O. Box 550, Moab, UT 84532 (© **800/635-6622** or 435/259-8825; fax 435/259-1376; www.discovermoab.com or www. canyonlands-utah.com). There are also over a dozen commercial campgrounds in and around Moab.

Near the Needles District of the park are several commercial campgrounds in the town of Monticello, along U.S. 191, about 15 miles south of the intersection of U.S. 191 and the park entry road. These include **Mountain View RV Park,** along the north edge on Monticello at 632 N. Main St. (P.O. Box 910), Mon-ticello, UT 84535 (© **435/587-2974**), a well-maintained campground with grassy sites, some trees, and cable TV hookups.

Accommodations, Dining & Picnic & Camping Supplies

There are no facilities for lodging, din-ing, or buying supplies inside Canyon-lands National Park. The nearest town to the park is Moab. For information on restaurants, hotels, and supply stores in Moab, see the "Where to Stay," "Where to Dine," and "Picnic & Camping Sup-plies" sections in chapter 2.

9

CAPITOL REEF NATIONAL PARK

by Don & Barbara Laine

CAPITOL REEF NATIONAL PARK IS ONE OF THOSE UNDISCOVERED GEMS, its rangers quietly going about the business of protecting and interpreting its natural wonders and historic sites while visitors flock to its more famous neighbors, Bryce Canyon and Zion.

But when people do stumble across this park, they are often amazed. Capitol Reef not only offers spectacular southern Utah scenery, but it also has a unique twist and a personality all its own.

The geologic formations here are incredible, if not downright peculiar. This is a place to let your imagination run wild, where you'll see the commanding Castle; the tall, rust-red Chimney Rock; the silent and eerie Temple of the Moon; and the appropriately named Hamburger Rocks, sitting atop a white sandstone table. A spectacular palette of colors paints Capitol Reef's canyon walls, which is why some Navajos called the area "The Land of the Sleeping Rainbow."

Capitol Reef is more than brilliant rocks and barren desert, however. Here the Fremont River has helped create a lush oasis in an otherwise unforgiving land. Cottonwood, willow, and other trees fill its banks. In fact, 19th-century pioneers found the land so inviting that they established the community of Fruita, planting orchards that have been preserved by the National Park Service.

Because of differences in geologic strata, elevation, and water availability in different sections of the park, you'll find a variety of ecosystems and terrain, along with a variety of possible activities. There are trails for hiking; roads for mountain biking and four-wheel-drive touring; lush fruit orchards; rich, green cottonwood groves and desert wildflowers; an abundance of songbirds; and a surprising amount of wildlife, from lizards and snakes to the bashful ring-tailed cat (which isn't a cat at all, but a member of the raccoon family). You'll also find thousand-year-old petroglyphs left behind by the ancient Fremont and Ancestral Puebloan peoples, and other traces of the past left by the more recent Utes and Southern Paiutes. This was both a favorite hideout for Wild West outlaws and a home for industrious Mormon pioneers, who planted orchards while their children learned

Tips from a Park Ranger

Thanks to the geology of the Waterpocket Fold, the park has a lot of variety—in elevation, landscape, and terrain, according to Riley Mitchell, Capitol Reef's chief of interpretation.

"This tilted layer cake of geologic strata formed a variety of different microhabitats as it eroded," he says. "There's an immense desert wilderness, but within that you've got perennial streams that have created a very rich riparian habitat, where prehistoric and historic people settled."

Capitol Reef is still relatively unknown, he says, and hasn't changed much since *Outside* magazine sang its praises as one of America's eight most undervisited national parks—"parks as they were meant to be." Mitchell says, "When people stop here on their way to one of Utah's better-known national parks, they're usually pleasantly surprised."

The park is known for its wonderful colors, and Mitchell says you can see them practically everywhere. "At sunset along Utah 24 and along the Scenic Drive you'll find a brilliant spectrum of colors—you can see them right from your car."

"The Frying Pan Trail is one of my favorite hikes," he says. "It's well marked, easy to get to, and you get wonderful views from the top as you hike along the crest of the Waterpocket Fold." Mitchell adds that another benefit to the trail is that it provides access to the spectacular spur trail to Cassidy Arch.

The dirt roads in the park can be a bit rugged, but most are accessible by two-wheel-drive, high-clearance vehicles, she says. However, Mitchell advises that a four-wheel-drive vehicle makes exploring the remote areas of the park easier and less worrisome in bad weather.

Given a choice, Mitchell would probably visit in the spring or fall, because it's a bit cooler. But, he adds, "summer's beautiful too, because wildflowers are in bloom and the orchards are open for fruit picking."

the three R's and studied the Bible and the Book of Mormon in the one-room Fruita Schoolhouse.

The name Capitol Reef conjures up images of a tropical shoreline—an odd choice for a park composed of cliffs and canyons in landlocked Utah. But many of the pioneers who settled the West were former seafaring men, and they extended the traditional meaning of the word *reef* to include these seemingly impassable rock barriers. They added *Capitol* to the name because the huge white rounded domes of sandstone reminded them of the domes of capitol buildings.

To be accurate, the park should probably be called the Big Fold. When the earth's crust uplifted some 60 million years ago, creating the Rocky Mountains, most of this uplifting was relatively even. But here, through one of those fascinating quirks of nature, the crust wrinkled into a huge fold. Extending 100 miles, almost all within the national park, it's known as the Waterpocket Fold.

Avoiding the Crowds. Although Capitol Reef receives only about 600,000 visitors annually, it can still be busy, especially during its peak season, which lasts from April through September. For this reason, the best time to visit is fall, particularly in October and November, when temperatures are usually warm enough for comfortable hiking and camping, but not so high as to send you constantly in search of shade. You also don't have to be as worried about flash floods

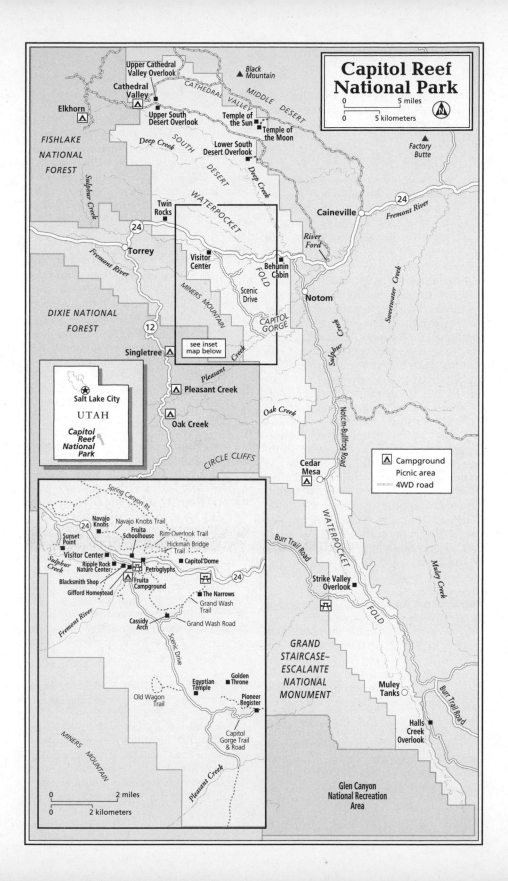

Capitol Reef National Park

0 — 5 miles
0 — 5 kilometers

Upper Cathedral Valley Overlook
Cathedral Valley
Elkhorn
Upper South Desert Overlook
Black Mountain
Temple of the Sun
Temple of the Moon
Factory Butte
Lower South Desert Overlook

FISHLAKE NATIONAL FOREST

Deep Creek
SOUTH DESERT
Deep Creek

Sulphur Creek

WATERPOCKET

Twin Rocks
Caineville
Fremont River
24

24
Torrey
Fremont River
Visitor Center
River Ford
Behunin Cabin
FOLD
Notom

MINERS MOUNTAIN

DIXIE NATIONAL FOREST

12
Scenic Drive
CAPITOL GORGE

Singletree

see inset map below

Pleasant Creek
Pleasant Creek

Oak Creek

Oak Creek

Sulphur Creek

Sweetwater Creek

Notom-Bullfrog Road

WATERPOCKET

CIRCLE CLIFFS

Cedar Mesa

⛺ Campground
🌲 Picnic area
═══ 4WD road

Burr Trail Road

Strike Valley Overlook

Muley Creek

FOLD

GRAND STAIRCASE-ESCALANTE NATIONAL MONUMENT

Muley Tanks

Burr Trail Road

Halls Creek Overlook

Glen Canyon National Recreation Area

Utah inset
⭐ Salt Lake City
UTAH
Capitol Reef National Park

Inset map below

Spring Canyon Rt.

Navajo Knobs
Navajo Knobs Trail
Fruita Schoolhouse
Rim Overlook Trail
24
Sunset Point
Hickman Bridge Trail
Visitor Center
Capitol Dome
Ripple Rock Nature Center
Petroglyphs
24
Blacksmith Shop
Fruita Campground
Gifford Homestead
Sulphur Creek
The Narrows
Grand Wash Trail
Cassidy Arch
Grand Wash Road
Fremont River
Scenic Drive
Egyptian Temple
Golden Throne
Old Wagon Trail
Pioneer Register
MINERS MOUNTAIN
Capitol Gorge Trail & Road
Pleasant Creek

0 — 2 miles
0 — 2 kilometers

through narrow canyons as you do during the July-through-September thunderstorm season.

Just the Facts

The park is about 121 miles northeast of Bryce Canyon National Park, 204 miles northeast of Zion National Park, 224 miles south of Salt Lake City, and 366 miles northeast of Las Vegas, Nevada.

It straddles Utah 24, which connects with I-70 to both the northeast and the northwest. Coming from the east along I-70, take Exit 147 and follow Utah 24 southwest to the park. Traveling from the west along I-70, there are two options: Take Exit 48 for Sigurd and follow Utah 24 east to the park; or take Exit 85 for Fremont Junction, then Utah 72 south to Loa, where you pick up Utah 24 east to the park.

Those coming from Bryce Canyon National Park can follow Utah 12 northeast to its intersection with Utah 24 at the small town of Torrey, and turn right (east) to Capitol Reef. If you're approaching the park from Glen Canyon National Recreation Area, take Utah 276 (from Bullfrog Basin Marina) or Utah 95 (from Hite Crossing) north to the intersection with Utah 24, and follow that west to the park.

The Nearest Airport. The closest major airport is **Walker Field,** located about 200 miles east in Grand Junction, Colorado (© **970/244-9100;** fax 970/241-9103; www.walkerfield.com), which has direct flights or connections from most major cities on **America West Express, Delta/Skywest,** and **United Express.**

Renting a Car. Car rentals are available at the Grand Junction airport from **Avis, Budget, Enterprise, Hertz, National, and Thrifty.** Toll-free reservations numbers are given in the appendix.

Contact **Capitol Reef National Park,** HC 70 Box 15, Torrey, UT 84775 (© **435/425-3791;** www.nps.gov/care). Books and maps are available from the nonprofit **Capitol Reef Natural History Association,** Capitol Reef National Park, HC 70, Box 15, Torrey, UT 84775 (© **435/425-3791,** ext. 113 or 115).

The park **visitor center** is located on the Scenic Drive at its intersection with Utah 24. A path connects it to the campground, passing the historic blacksmith shop, orchards, and a lovely shaded picnic ground. There are exhibits on the geology and history of the area, and a 10-minute slide show on the park. Rangers answer questions and provide backcountry permits. You can also pick up free brochures and buy books, maps, videos, postcards, and posters.

The **Ripple Rock Nature Center,** located about ¾ mile south of the visitor center along the Scenic Drive, offers exhibits and activities especially for children. It's open during the summer only.

Entry into the park (for up to 7 days) costs $5 per vehicle or $2 per person on foot or bike. Camping in the main campground costs $10 per night; the two primitive campgrounds are free. Free **backcountry permits** (available at the visitor center) are required for all overnight hikes.

Although most visitors to the park enjoy a wonderful vacation without mishap, problems can occur. Hikers need to carry plenty of water, especially in summer. A major concern is weather: Afternoon thunderstorms in July, August, and September can bring flash floods, which fill narrow canyons suddenly and without warning. Steep-walled Grand Wash and Capitol Gorge can be particularly hazardous and should be avoided whenever storms are threatening.

Because wildlife refuse to follow park rules regarding wildlife diet, campers should be careful of where and how they store food, and dispose of garbage promptly.

ATVs are not permitted in the park.

SEASONS & CLIMATE

Because of its higher elevation, Capitol Reef doesn't get as hot as some of the other Southwestern parks, but summer temperatures can be uncomfortably warm on the trail. Winters can be very pleasant—snow falls occasionally but doesn't usually last, and temperatures are often in the 50s. Late winter and spring are often windy.

Depending on the weather, the Scenic Drive sometimes closes, most frequently in late summer during flash flood season but occasionally in winter due to snow. When it's closed, you can still access a network of trails from Utah 24 and get to the picnic area and campground.

If You Have Only 1 Day

Because Capitol Reef is such a compact park, it's fairly easy to see a lot in a short amount of time. Although the ideal situation would be to spend 2 or 3 days in the park, it is quite possible to have an enjoyable time with just half a day or so. Because there are no food services in the park (except fruit in season), you'll want to pack a picnic lunch.

Start at the **visitor center,** and watch the short slide show explaining the park's geology and early history. Then head out on the paved 25-mile round-trip **Scenic Drive** (described below), stopping along the way for a short hike, perhaps the easy walk up the Grand Wash. In the historic pioneer community of **Fruita,** near the beginning of the Scenic Drive, you can wander among the orchards, where you're likely to see deer. Then visit the historic **Gifford Farmhouse,** where you can get a taste of the daily life of Fruita's Mormon settlers and purchase replicas of pioneer era household items and crafts. Then hike one of the shorter trails in the Fruita area before going to see the **Fruita Schoolhouse** and some of the park's **petroglyphs.** In the evening, try to take in a ranger program at the **amphitheater.**

Exploring the Park by Car

Capitol Reef is relatively easy to see from the comfort of your automobile. From the visitor center, the **Scenic Drive** leads about 12½ miles south into the park. Pick up a copy of the free Scenic Drive brochure at the entrance station, then set out, stopping at view points to gaze up and out at the array of colorful cliffs, monoliths, and commanding rock formations.

If the weather is dry, drive down the gravel **Capitol Gorge Road** at the end of the paved Scenic Drive for a look at what many consider to be the park's best scenery. It's a 5-mile round-trip drive. If you're up for a short walk, the relatively flat 2-mile (round-trip) **Capitol Gorge Trail,** which starts at the end of Capitol Gorge Road, takes you to the historic **Pioneer Register,** a rock wall where traveling pioneers "signed in" (see "Day Hikes," below).

Another dry-weather driving option is the **Grand Wash Road,** a maintained dirt road that is subject to flash floods, but in good weather offers an easy route into a spectacular canyon. Along the 2-mile round-trip you'll see **Cassidy Arch,** named for famed outlaw Butch Cassidy, who, at least by some accounts, hid out in this area.

Utah 24, which crosses Capitol Reef from east to west, also has several view points offering a good look at some of the park's best features, such as the monumental **Capitol Dome,** which resembles the dome of a capitol building; the striking **Chimney Rock;** the aptly named **Castle;** the historic **Fruita Schoolhouse;** and some **petroglyphs** left by the prehistoric Fremont people (see "Historic & Man-Made Attractions," below).

Organized Tours & Ranger Programs

Park rangers present a variety of free programs and activities from the spring through fall. **Campfire programs** take place most evenings at the outdoor amphitheater at Fruita Campground. Topics vary, but could include the animals and plants, geology, and human history of the area. Rangers also lead **walks,** and give **short talks** on a variety of subjects, such as the history of the pioneer Fruita Schoolhouse and the Gifford Farmhouse. Schedules are posted on bulletin boards at the visitor center and campground.

Historic & Man-Made Attractions

Throughout the park you'll find evidence of human presence. The Fremont people lived along the river as early as A.D. 700, staying until about A.D. 1300. Primarily hunters and gatherers, the Fremonts also grew corn, beans, and squash to supplement their diet. Their dwellings were pit houses, which were dug into the ground; the remains

> The colors are such as no pigments can portray. They are deep, rich, and variegated; and so luminous are they, that light seems to flow or shine out of the rock.
> —Geologist C. E. Dutton, 1880

of one can be seen from the **Hickman Bridge Trail.** Many Fremont petroglyphs (images carved into rock) and pictographs (images painted on rock) are still visible on the canyon walls. If we could understand them, they might tell us why these early Americans left the area, a puzzle that continues to baffle archaeologists. The most easily accessible site is located 1½ miles east of the visitor center along Utah 24. There is a sign near the parking area and a short path to the petroglyph panels, which contain some of the most interesting images in the park.

Prospectors and other travelers passed through the **Capitol Gorge** section of the park in the late 1800s, leaving their names on the **Pioneer Register,** reached via a 2-mile round-trip walk (see "Day Hikes," below).

Mormon pioneers established the community of **Junction** (later named Fruita) in 1880. Now a historic district listed on the National Register of Historic Places, the orchards those settlers planted continue to flourish, tended by park workers who invite you to sample the "fruits" of their labor. Nearby is a historic blacksmith shop. The tiny **Fruita Schoolhouse,** built in 1896, was a church, social hall, and community meeting hall in addition to a one-room schoolhouse. The school closed in 1941, and was restored in 1984. It's furnished with old wood and wrought-iron desks, a wood stove, a chalkboard, and textbooks. A hand bell used to call students to class still rests on the corner of the teacher's desk.

Also in the Fruita district, the **Gifford Farmhouse,** built in 1908, is typical of rural Utah farmhouses of the early 1900s. Renovated and furnished by the Capitol Reef Natural History Association, the home is located off the Scenic Drive about 1 mile south of the visitor center, and is open from April through September. The home's former kitchen is a gift shop, selling reproductions of the household tools, toys, and utensils used by Mormon pioneers, plus crafts, jams and jellies, dried fruits, historic postcards, and books.

Day Hikes

Trails through the park offer sweeping panoramic views of colorful cliffs and domes, eerie journeys through desolate, steep-walled canyons, and cool walks along the tree-shaded Fremont River. Watch carefully for petroglyphs and other reminders of this area's first inhabitants. This is also the real Wild West, little changed from the way cowboys, bank robbers, settlers, and prospectors found it in the late 1800s. One of the best things about hiking here is the combination of scenic beauty, prehistoric American Indian rock art, and Western history you'll discover.

Among the last areas in the continental United States to be explored, Capitol Reef has many parts that remain practically unknown, perfect for those who want to see this rugged country in its natural state. Several local companies offer guide and shuttle services, including **Wild Hare Expeditions,** P.O. Box 750194, Torrey, UT 84775 (© **888/304-HARE** [4273] or 435/425-3999; www.color-country.net/~thehare). Wild Hare offers mountain bike and four-wheel-drive tours (see below), as well as hiking and backpacking tours. Located in the Best Western Capitol Reef Resort complex, a mile west of the park entrance, Wild Hare Expeditions' shop, called **"The Hare Lair,"** rents snowshoes ($7 per day), bikes (see below), bike racks, tents, sleeping bags, and backpacks; repairs bikes; and sells bike accessories, climbing equipment, backcountry clothing and gear, and maps. Call for current hours.

SHORTER TRAILS

Capitol Gorge Trail

1 mile one-way. Easy. Access: End of the Capitol Gorge dirt road.

This is a mostly level walk along the bottom of a narrow canyon. Looking up at the tall, smooth walls of rock conveys a strong sense of what the pioneers must have seen and felt 100 years ago when they moved rocks and debris to drive their wagons through this canyon. The trail leads past the **Pioneer Register,** where early travelers carved their names.

Fremont River Trail

1.25 mile one-way. Easy to moderate. Access: Fruita Campground.

This self-guided nature trail is quite easy (and wheelchair accessible) for the first 0.5 mile as it meanders past the orchards along the river, but it becomes increasingly strenuous thereafter. The path climbs to an overlook of the lovely valley. Part of the trail is steep, with long drop-offs.

Goosenecks Trail

0.1 mile one-way. Easy. Access: Panorama Point Turnoff on Utah 24, 3 miles west of the visitor center, then 1 mile on a gravel access road.

This short walk affords great views of **Sulphur Creek Canyon.** It's a good trail for those with little time because it offers both sweeping panoramic views of the geology of **Waterpocket Fold** and close-ups of interesting rock formations.

Hickman Bridge Trail

1 mile one-way. Moderate. Access: Hickman Bridge parking area on Utah 24, 2 miles east of the visitor center.

Starting at the Fremont River, this self-guided nature trailheads into the desert, ascending several short steep hills to **Hickman Natural Bridge,** which has an opening 133 feet wide and 125 feet high. The trail has a 400-foot elevation gain.

Sunset Point Trail

0.3 mile one-way. Easy. Access: Panorama Point Turnoff on Utah 24, 3 miles west of the visitor center, then 1 mile on a gravel access road.

This hike affords panoramic views of cliffs and domes, which are most dramatic around sunset.

LONGER TRAILS

Cassidy Arch Trail

1.75 miles one-way. Strenuous. Access: Grand Wash Trailhead, via Scenic Dr. and Grand Wash Rd.

This trail offers spectacular views as it climbs steeply from the floor of Grand Wash to high cliffs overlooking the park. From the trail you'll also get several perspectives of Cassidy Arch, a natural stone arch named for outlaw Butch Cassidy, who is believed to have occasionally used the Grand Wash as a hideout.

Chimney Rock Trail

3.5 miles RT. Moderate to strenuous. Access: Chimney Rock parking area on Utah 24, 2 miles west of the visitor center.

This trail begins with a strenuous climb up switchbacks to the more moderate loop trail on top. It affords views of Chimney Rock from both below and above, plus panoramic views of the **Waterpocket Fold** and surrounding areas.

Cohab Canyon Trail

1.75 miles one-way. Moderate to strenuous. Access: Across from Fruita Campground.

After the first 0.25 mile, which is rather strenuous, this trail levels out a bit and has fewer steep grades. It climbs to a hidden canyon above the campground, and has two short side trails leading to overlooks. From the overlooks you get good views of the **Fremont River, historic Fruita,** and **the campground.**

Fremont Gorge Overlook Trail

2.25 miles one-way. Strenuous. Access: Blacksmith shop.

A strenuous climb to 1,000 feet above the Fremont River, this trail rewards you with a great view into the Fremont Gorge at the end. The middle of the hike, across Johnson Mesa, is fairly easy.

The trail also affords good views of **Fruita** and the escarpment of the **Waterpocket Fold.**

Frying Pan Trail

3 miles one-way. Strenuous. Access: Across from the Fruita Campground or Grand Wash parking area.

This strenuous but scenic trail, which links Cohab and Cassidy Arch trails, follows the ridge of the Waterpocket Fold escarpment, with a number of climbs up and down canyons and over slickrock. You'll get good views of **Miners Mountain** to the southwest, rugged canyons to the side, and the **Grand Wash** below near the end of the trail.

Golden Throne Trail

2 miles one-way. Strenuous. Access: Capitol Gorge parking area.

A strenuous climb from the bottom of the gorge to the top of the cliffs at the base of the Golden Throne, this trail provides several panoramic vistas, good spots to stop to catch your breath. The Golden Throne is a large formation of Navajo sandstone that glows golden-yellow in the light of the setting sun.

Grand Wash Trail

2.25 miles one-way. Easy. Access: Grand Wash parking area, or on Utah 24 east of the visitor center.

This is a relatively easy hike along a narrow wash bottom with sheer rock walls on both sides. The trail shows the phenomenal power of water, as it winds between tall polished walls of stone, scoured smooth by the force of flash floods.

Old Wagon Trail

3.5 miles RT. Strenuous. Access: West side of Scenic Dr. near end.

This 1,000-foot climb up the east flank of **Miners Mountain** is certainly strenuous, but it affords spectacular and unusual views of the **Waterpocket Fold escarpment.** This hike is best done late in the day when the cliffs are lit by the setting sun.

Rim Overlook Trail

2.25 miles one-way. Strenuous. Access: Hickman Bridge parking area on Utah 24 east of the visitor center.

After a strenuous 1,000-foot climb, hikers are rewarded with good views of **Fruita** and vistas to the south.

Exploring the Backcountry

The park offers a variety of backpacking opportunities, including the 15-mile round-trip **Upper Muley Twist** route, which follows a canyon through the Waterpocket Fold and offers views of arches and narrows, and panoramic vistas from the top of the fold; and the 22-mile round-trip **Halls Creek Narrows,** which follows Halls Creek through a beautiful slot canyon (where you may have to wade or swim). **Free backcountry permits** (available at the visitor center) are required for all overnight hikes. Backcountry hikers should discuss their plans with rangers before setting out, since many of these routes are prone to flash floods.

Other Sports & Activities

Four-Wheel-Drive Touring & Mountain Biking. As in most national parks, bikes and 4WD vehicles are restricted to established roads, but Capitol Reef has several such "established" roads— actually little more than dirt trails—that provide exciting opportunities for those using 4WD or pedal-power. However, use of ATVs is not permitted anywhere in the park.

The only route appropriate for road bikes is the **Scenic Drive,** described above, but both the Grand Wash and Capitol Gorge roads (see "Exploring the Park by Car," above), plus three longer backcountry roads, are open to mountain bikes as well as four-wheel-drive vehicles. Be aware that rain can make the roads impassable, so it's best to check on current conditions before setting out.

One recommended trip is the **Cathedral Valley Loop.** It covers about 60 miles on a variety of road surfaces, including dirt, sand, and rock, and requires the fording of the Fremont River, where water is usually 1 to 1½ feet deep. The rewards are beautiful, unspoiled scenery, including bizarre sandstone monoliths and majestic cliffs, in one of the park's more remote areas. There's a small primitive campground (see "Camping," below). Access to this loop is from Utah 24, just outside the park, 11¾ miles east of the visitor center via the River Ford Road, or 18½ miles east of the visitor center on the Caineville Wash Road.

Mountain-bike and four-wheel-drive **tours** into the national park and surrounding areas are provided by **Wild Hare Expeditions** (see above). Full-day tours, including lunch, cost $75 to $100; a variety of other guided trips, including multiday excursions, are offered as well. The company rents mountain bikes at $20 for a half day and $30 for a full day, with discounts for those taking guided tours and for multiday rentals. Four-wheel-drive tours are also available from **Hondoo Rivers and Trails** (see "Horseback Riding," below), including multiday trips to petroglyph and pictograph sites in the area. Those wanting to go four-wheel-drive touring on their own can rent a 4WD for about $75 per day, at **Thousand Lakes RV Park & Campground;** and ATV guided tours and rentals (call for current rates and schedules) are available from **Wonderland Inn.** See "Camping," below, for contact information for both businesses.

Horseback Riding. Horses are welcome in some areas of the park but prohibited in others; check at the visitor center for

Especially for Kids

In addition to the **Junior Ranger Program** (see "Tips for Traveling with Kids," in chapter 1), kids from third through eighth grades can become **Junior Geologists** by joining a ranger on a field trip (usually held once each week in summer). Families are invited to borrow a **Family Fun Pack,** containing park-related games and activities, at the visitor center and the **Ripple Rock Nature Center** (see "Visitor Centers," earlier in this chapter).

details. **Capitol Reef Trail Rides,** at the Best Western Capitol Reef Resort in Torrey (see below), P.O. Box 375, Bicknell, UT 84715 (© **435/425-3761**), offers a variety of rides in the area, ranging from 1 hour ($25) to all day. First-time riders are welcome, minimum age is 8, and maximum weight is 230 pounds. Several cookout rides and other special activities are available; call for information.

Horseback trips are also offered by **Hondoo Rivers and Trails** (P.O. Box 98, Torrey, UT 84775; © **800/332-2696** or 435/425-3519; fax 435/425-3548; www. hondoo.com). Their goal is to provide comfortable and informative backcountry experiences for small groups. Scheduled trips include 1- to 5-day excursions into the backcountry of Capitol Reef National Park, nearby Boulder Mountain, and the canyons of Grand Staircase–Escalante National Monument. Trail rides are aimed at wildflower or wildlife viewing. Day trips start at $75; multiday trips begin at $875; custom tours can also be arranged.

Wildlife Viewing. Summer in Capitol Reef is hot and sometimes stormy, but it's a good season for wildlife viewing. In particular, many species of **lizards** make their home in the park; you will probably catch a glimpse of one warming itself on a rock. The western whiptail, eastern fence, and side-blotched lizards are the most common, but the most attractive is the collared lizard, which is usually colored turquoise with yellow speckles.

Watch for **deer** and **marmots** in Fruita, especially along the path between the visitor center and Fruita Campground. This area is also where you're likely to see **chipmunks** and **white-tail antelope squirrels.** Although they're somewhat shy and only emerge from their dens at night, the **ring-tailed cat,** a member of the raccoon family, also calls the park home; as do **bighorn sheep, bobcat, cougar, fox,** and **coyote.**

If you keep your eyes to the sky you may see a **golden eagle, Cooper's hawk, raven,** or any of the many other types of birds attracted by the park's variety of habitats. Year-round residents include chukars, common flickers, yellow-bellied sapsuckers, horned larks, canyon wrens, rock wrens, American robins, ruby-crowned kinglets, starlings, and American kestrels. In warmer months you're also likely to see yellow warblers, red-winged blackbirds, western tanagers, northern orioles, violet-green swallows, white-throated swifts, and black-chinned hummingbirds. Bird-watching is particularly good along the Fremont River Trail in the spring and early summer.

Camping

INSIDE THE PARK

The pleasant **Fruita Campground,** located along the Scenic Drive, 1 mile south of the visitor center, has shade trees and modern restrooms, and is within walking distance of the Fruita School and other historic attractions.

Capitol Reef also has two primitive campgrounds. **Cedar Mesa Campground,** in the southern part of the park, is reached by going east of Utah 24 about 9 miles to Notom-Bullfrog

Road, which you take about 23 miles south (the first 10 miles are now paved) to the campground. The road may be impassable in wet weather. **Cathedral Valley Campground** is in the northern part of the park, about 35 miles from the visitor center (get directions at the visitor center). *Note:* Access roads to Cathedral Valley Campground require a high-clearance or four-wheel-drive vehicle at all times and may be completely inaccessible in bad weather.

Backcountry camping is permitted in much of the park with a free permit, available at the visitor center.

NEAR THE PARK

There are several commercial campgrounds in the community of Torrey, about 5 miles west of the park entrance, and an attractive U.S. Forest Service campground not too far away.

At **Sandcreek RV Park & Hostel,** 540 Utah 24 (P.O. Box 750276), Torrey, UT 84775 (© **877/425-3578** or 435/425-3577; www.sandcreekrv.com), you'll find RV sites with full hookups, plus grassy tent sites, not to mention great views in all directions. Trees have been planted and will provide shade as they grow. There are horseshoe pits, a gift shop and espresso bar, and a hostel (see "Where to Stay," below).

Also in Torrey is **Thousand Lakes RV Park & Campground,** Utah 24 (P.O. Box 750070), Torrey, UT 84775 (© **800/355-8995** for reservations, or 435/425-3500; fax 435/425-3510; www.thousandlakesrv park.com). In addition to the usual amenities, this campground offers good views of surrounding rock formations, plus some shade trees. RV sites are gravel; tent sites are grass. The campground also has a convenience store, a coin-op laundry, horseshoes, an outdoor heated pool, barbecues, and jeep rentals (call for rates). The campground has five camping cabins ($29), which involve a walk to the bathhouse; and three deluxe cabins ($55) with their own bathrooms, one of which

sleeps five and has a kitchen. In addition, Western dinners are offered Monday through Saturday.

Wonderland RV Park, at the junction of Utah 24 and 12 (P.O. Box 67), Torrey, UT 84775 (© **800/458-0216** or 435/425-3345; www.capitolreefwonderland.com), is a delightful campground, protected from the highway by a row of trees, with mostly open, grassy sites (although young and mostly small trees do their best to provide some shade) and all the usual commercial campground amenities. In addition, Wonderland offers guided ATV tours and ATV rentals (call for rates). Just across the street are groceries and a full service deli.

Those looking for a forest camping experience on the west side of the national park will like **Singletree Campground,** on Utah 12 about 16 miles south of Torrey (Teasdale Ranger District of the Dixie National Forest, Box 90, Teasdale, UT 84773; © **435/425-3702;** reservations 877/444-6777; www.reserveusa.com). Located in a forest of tall pines, this campground has standard individual campsites ($10) plus six multiple-family sites ($20). All sites are paved, and many offer distant panoramic views of the national park. Near two of the large multiple-family sites, you'll find a horseshoe pit and volleyball court.

Where to Stay

There are no lodging facilities in the park itself, but the town of Torrey, just west of the park entrance where Utah 12 meets Utah 24, can take care of most needs.

NEAR THE PARK

In addition to the properties discussed below, Torrey has a **Days Inn,** 675 E. Utah 24 (at Utah 12; © **435/425-3111**), and a **Super 8,** 600 E. Utah 24 (near the intersection of Utah 24 and Utah 12; © **435/425-3688**). Also see the information on cabins at **Thousand Lakes RV**

Campground	Elev.	Total Sites	RV Hookups	Dump Station	Toilets	Drinking Water
Fruita	5,500	70	0	Yes	Yes	Yes
Cedar Mesa	5,400	5	0	No	Yes	No
Cathedral Valley	7,000	6	0	No	Yes	No
Sandcreek	6,840	24	12	Yes	Yes	Yes
Singletree	8,200	31	0	Yes	Yes	Yes
Thousand Lakes	6,840	67	58	Yes	Yes	Yes
Wonderland	6,980	33	33	Yes	Yes	Yes

Park & Campground under "Camping," above. Motel chains' toll-free reservation numbers are listed in the appendix.

Austin's Chuck Wagon Lodge & General Store

12 W. Main St. (P.O. Box 750180), Torrey, UT 84775. © **800/863-3288** or 435/425-3335. Fax 435/425-3434. www.austinschuckwagon motel.com. 24 units. A/C TV. New units $64 double, older units $42 double; cabins $110 first 4, $6 each additional person, maximum 6; family suite $125 first 4, $6 each additional person, maximum 8. AE, DISC, MC, V. Closed Nov–Feb.

This attractive family-owned and -operated motel offers a wide range of options. The well-maintained property includes newer, modern motel rooms, with Southwestern decor, phones, satellite TV, and two queen-size beds; and older, somewhat rustic units, which have knotty pine walls, one queen bed, and no phones. Also available is a family suite, which has a large living room with a queen sofa bed, a kitchen with microwave but no stove, and three bedrooms. Our choice here, however, is one of the plush but still Western-style cabins, which were completed in 2000. Measuring 576 square feet, each cabin has two bedrooms (each with a queen-size bed), a living room with a queen-size sofa bed, a complete kitchen, a full bathroom with shower/tub combo, satellite TV, a covered porch, and a small yard with a barbecue grill and a picnic table. The grounds are attractively landscaped, with a lawn and large trees, and facilities include an outdoor pool and whirlpool. Located on the property are a grocery store/bakery/deli, coin-op laundry, and beauty salon.

Best Western Capitol Reef Resort

2600 E. Utah 24 (P.O. Box 750160), Torrey, UT 84775. © **888/610-9600** or 435/425-3761. Fax 435/425-3300. www.bwcapitolreef.com. 100 units. A/C TV TEL. June–Sept $99 double, $119–$139 suite; Oct–May $59–$79 standard double; $69–$119 suite. AE, DC, DISC, MC, V.

Located a mile west of the national park entrance, this attractive Best Western is one of the closest lodgings to the park. Try to get a room on the back side of the motel, where you'll be rewarded with fantastic views of the area's red-rock formations. Standard units have either one king or two queen beds and hair dryers. Minisuites have a king bed and a queen sofa sleeper, plus a coffeemaker, refrigerator, microwave, and wet bar; full suites add a separate sitting room for the sofa sleeper, a second TV and telephone, a jetted tub, and a patio. The outdoor heated pool, whirlpool, and sun deck are situated out back, away from road noise, with glass wind barriers and spectacular views. There's also a tennis/basketball court, horseback trail rides, and mountain bike rentals. The motel restaurant serves breakfast and dinner daily year-round.

Showers	Fire Pits/ Grills	Laundry	Public Phone	Reserve	Fees	Open
No	Yes	No	Yes	No	$10	Year-round
No	Yes	No	No	No	Free	Year-round
No	Yes	No	No	No	Free	Year-round
Yes	Yes	Yes	Yes	Yes	$10–$19	Apr to mid-Oct
No	Yes	No	No	Yes	$10–$20	mid-May to Oct
Yes	Yes	Yes	Yes	Yes	$13–$19	Apr to late Nov
Yes	Yes	Yes	Yes	Yes	$18	Apr–Oct

Boulder View Inn

385 W. Main St. (Utah 24), Torrey, UT 84775. © **800/444-3980** or 435/425-3800. 12 units. A/C TV TEL. $50 double. Rates include continental breakfast. AE, DISC, MC, V.

This attractive, modern motel is a bargain for those who just want a good night's sleep without a lot of frills. Guest rooms are large and comfortable, with combination shower/tubs, queen or king beds, tables with chairs, and a Southwestern motif. The inn has no swimming pool, and smoking is not permitted.

Capitol Reef Inn & Cafe

360 W. Main St. (Utah 24), Torrey, UT 84775. © **435/425-3271.** www.capitolreefinn.com. 10 units. A/C TV TEL. $48 double. AE, DISC, MC, V. Closed Nov–Mar.

This older, Western-style motel—small, beautifully landscaped, and adequately maintained—offers guest rooms that are both homey and comfortable. The furnishings are handmade of solid wood. Only one unit has a combination shower/tub; the others have showers only. Facilities include a playground, 10-person whirlpool tub, and lovely desert garden and kiva. Adjacent, under the same ownership, are an excellent restaurant (see "Where to Dine," below) and a gift shop that sells American Indian crafts, guidebooks, and maps.

Sandcreek RV Park & Hostel

540 Utah 24, 5 miles west of the park entrance (P.O. Box 750276), Torrey, UT 84775. © **877/425-3578** or 435/425-3577. www.sandcreekrv.com. Hostel $10–$12 per person. MC, V. Closed mid-Oct to Mar.

This hostel, in a handsome log building, consists of one large room in which everyone—both men and women—sleeps, bunkhouse style. It offers sleeping space for eight, a TV, a microwave, high ceilings, and a porch with tables and chairs. The walls, high ceiling, and beams are of Ponderosa pine, and the bunk beds are made of logs. Hostellers share the bathhouse with campers (see "Camping," above), and linens are available. You'll also find an espresso bar, laundry, horseshoe pits, and a natural stone and petrified wood labyrinth (sort of like a maze), that leads to a quiet meditation area. In addition, a gift shop features handmade deer antler jewelry, and you can often see the jeweler (who is also the hostel's owner/manager) at work.

Skyridge Inn Bed and Breakfast

950 East Utah 24, just east of its intersection with Utah 12 (P.O. Box 750220), Torrey, UT 84775. © and fax **435/425-3222.** www.skyridgeinn.com. 6 units. A/C TV/VCR TEL. Apr–Oct $115–$172 double; Nov–Mar $104–$155 double. Rates include breakfast and evening hors d'oeuvres. AE, MC, V.

This combination bed-and-breakfast and art gallery offers a delightful alternative to the standard motel. The three-story contemporary inn has six distinctive units, each with private bathroom, hair dryers, robes, CD player, and coffee service. Rooms are decorated with an eclectic mix of antiques, folk sculpture, and contemporary art. Two rooms have private decks with hot tubs, while another features a two-person whirlpool tub and private deck.

An impressive fireplace, decorated with over 30 pounds of roofing nails, sits in the shared gallery/gathering room, which also contains books, games, CDs, and movies available for guest use. There is also an outdoor hot tub available to all guests. The inn is set on 75 acres, with its own hiking trails and spectacular views of the national park and Boulder Mountain. Full breakfasts include homemade granola, fresh-baked coffee cake, muffins, or cinnamon rolls, and a hot entree such as Southwest frittatas, pecan griddle-cakes, or apple-stuffed croissants along with fresh fruit. Smoking is permitted outside on decks or porches.

Wonderland Inn

Junction of Utah 24 and 12 (P.O. Box 67), Torrey, UT 84775. ✆ **800/458-0216** or 435/425-3775. Fax 435/425-3212. www.capitolreef wonderland.com. 50 units. A/C TV TEL. Summer $58–$68 double, $76 suite; winter $36–$44 double, $68 suite. AE, DC, DISC, MC, V.

If you want panoramic views in all directions, this is the place to come. Built in 1990, this modern motel is perched high on a hill and set back from the highway, which not only provides great views but also makes it peaceful and quiet. Built, owned, and managed by Ray and Diane Potter and family, the property is especially well kept. Standard motel rooms have two queen-size beds or one king, along with typical modern motel decor and some genuine wood touches. Suites have king-size beds, large Jacuzzi tubs, and private balconies. Facilities include a combination indoor/outdoor heated swimming pool, tanning room, whirlpool, sauna, beauty salon, gift shop, and restaurant (open daily year-round, with a popular breakfast buffet in summer).

Where to Dine

There are no dining facilities inside the park.

NEAR THE PARK

In addition to the restaurants discussed below, you'll find good restaurants, open year-round, at both the Best Western Capitol Reef Resort and the Wonderland Inn (see "Where to Stay," above).

Brink's Burgers Drive-In

165 E. Main St., Torrey. ✆ **435/425-3710.** Most items $1.50–$4.50. MC, V. Daily 11am–9pm. Closed in winter. BURGERS/SANDWICHES.

This nonfranchise fast-food restaurant serves good burgers and crunchy English-style fries in a cafelike setting and at outdoor picnic tables. In addition to better-than-average burgers, choices include a garden burger, chicken and fish selections, cheese sticks, onion rings, zucchini slices, breaded mushrooms, and spicy potato wedges. A wide variety of ice-cream cones and thick milkshakes are also available; no alcohol is served.

Cafe Diablo

599 W. Main St., Torrey. ✆ **435/425-3070.** www.cafediablo.net. Main courses $16–$29. MC, V. Daily 5–10pm. Closed mid-Oct to late Apr. SOUTHWESTERN.

Looks are deceiving. What appears to be a simple small-town cafe in a converted home is in fact a very fine restaurant, offering innovative beef, pork, chicken, seafood, and vegetarian selections, many created with a Southwestern flair. The menu varies, but could include pumpkin-seed-crusted local trout served with cilantro-lime sauce and wild rice pancakes; medallions of local lamb marinated with sage and rosemary and served with potato roulade, asparagus, and mint sauce; or baby-back pork ribs slow roasted in a chipotle, molasses, and rum glaze. Pastries and ice creams, all made on the premises, are spectacular, and beer—both microbrewed and regular—plus wines and tequilas are available. There's also patio dining, with heaters for those chilly evenings.

Capitol Reef Inn & Cafe

360 W. Main St. © **435/425-3271.** Main courses $4.25–$7.50 breakfast, $5.50–$8.50 lunch, $5–$16 dinner. AE, DISC, MC, V. Daily 7–9pm. Closed Nov–Mar. AMERICAN.

A local favorite, this restaurant offers fine, fresh, and healthy dining that's among the best you'll find in Utah. Famous for its locally raised trout, the cafe is equally well known for its

10-vegetable salad served with all dinner entrees. Vegetables are grown locally, and several dishes, such as spaghetti, an excellent fettuccine primavera, and shish kebabs, can be ordered vegetarian or with various meats or fish. Steaks and chicken are also served. The atmosphere is casual, marked by comfortable seating, American Indian rugs and crafts, and large windows. The restaurant offers an extensive wine list, plus domestic and imported beers.

Picnic & Camping Supplies

In addition to groceries, **Austin's Chuck Wagon Lodge & General Store,** at 12 W. Main St. in Torrey (**435/425-3288**), has a bakery, a full-service deli, a large selection of organic fruits and vegetables, a coin-operated laundry, and a hair salon. Austin's is closed December through February.

10

CARLSBAD CAVERNS NATIONAL PARK

by Don & Barbara Laine

O NE OF THE LARGEST AND MOST SPECTACULAR CAVE SYSTEMS IN THE world, Carlsbad Caverns National Park comprises more than 100 known caves that snake through the porous limestone reef of the Guadalupe Mountains. Fantastic and grotesque formations fascinate visitors, who find every shape imaginable (and unimaginable) naturally sculpted in the underground—from frozen waterfalls to strands of pearls, soda straws to miniature castles, draperies to ice-cream cones.

Formation of the caverns began some 250 million years ago, when a huge inland sea covered this region. A reef formed, and then the sea disappeared, leaving the reef covered with deposits of salts and gypsum. Eventually, uplifting and erosion brought the reef back to the surface, and then the actual cave building began. Rainwater seeped through cracks in the earth's surface, dissolving the limestone and leaving hollows behind. With the help of sulfuric acid, created by gases released from oil and gas deposits farther below ground, the cavern passageways grew, sometimes becoming huge rooms.

Once the caves were hollowed out, nature's artistry took over, decorating the rooms with a vast variety of fanciful formations. Very slowly, water dripped down through the rock into the caves, dissolving more limestone and absorbing the mineral calcite and other materials on its journey. Each drop of water then deposited a tiny load of calcite, gradually creating the cave formations that lure visitors to Carlsbad Caverns each year.

Although American Indians had known of Carlsbad Cavern for centuries, it wasn't discovered by settlers until ranchers in the 1880s were attracted by sunset flights of bats emerging from the cave. The first reported trip into the cave was in 1883, when a man supposedly lowered his 12-year-old son into the cave entrance. A cowboy named Jim White, who worked for mining companies that collected bat droppings for use as fertilizer, began to explore the main cave in the early 1900s. Fascinated by the formations, White shared his discovery with others, and soon word of this magical underground world spread.

Carlsbad Cave National Monument was created in October 1923. In 1926, the first electric lights were installed,

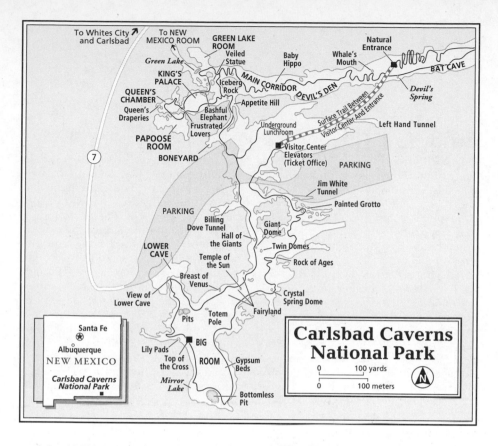

Carlsbad Caverns National Park

Santa Fe
Albuquerque
NEW MEXICO
Carlsbad Caverns National Park

and in 1930 Carlsbad Caverns gained national park status.

Underground development at the park has been confined to the famous Big Room, one of the largest and most easily accessible of the caverns, with a ceiling 25 stories high and a floor large enough to hold more than 6 football fields. Visitors can tour parts of it on their own, aided by an excellent portable audio guide, and explore other sections and several other caves on guided tours. The cave is also a summer home to about 250,000 Mexican free-tailed bats, which hang from the ceiling of Bat Cave during the day, but put on a spectacular show each evening as they leave the cave in search of food, and again in the morning when they return.

In addition to the fascinating underground world, the national park has a scenic drive, interpretive nature trail, and backcountry hiking trails through the Chihuahuan Desert.

Avoiding the Crowds. The park is open year-round. Crowds are thickest in summer and on weekends and holidays year-round, so visiting on weekdays between Labor Day and Memorial Day is the best way to avoid them. January is the quietest month.

Visiting during the park's off season is especially attractive because the climate in the caves stays the same regardless of the weather above. The only downside to an off-peak visit is that you won't be able to see the bat flights. The bats head to Mexico when the weather starts to get chilly, usually by late October, and don't return until May. There are also fewer guided cave tours off season. The best time to see the park might well be September, when you can still see the bat flights but there are fewer visitors than during the peak summer season.

Tips from an Insider

"If you can only see one thing here, see the Big Room in Carlsbad Cavern," advises Bridget Eisfeldt, the park's public affairs specialist. "Allow an hour and a half, and if you have more time and are in good physical condition, take the Natural Entrance Route into the cave, which has a 750-foot descent and is a bit strenuous."

The potential for scientific discoveries from caves is tremendous, Eisfeldt says, adding that research is underway in Lechugilla Cave that may eventually provide a cure for certain types of cancer. "They're collecting microscopic life forms—bacteria that survive without sunlight and secrete an enzyme that appears to be able to kill breast cancer cells without harming healthy human cells."

Eisfeldt says that park visitors should not miss out on the aboveground attractions, such as the evening bat flight, and the 9½-mile scenic drive, which provides panoramic views of the surrounding desert. "A good time to take the drive is late afternoon or early evening after the visitor center has closed and before the bat flight program has begun," Eisfeldt says, adding that "it's usually cooler then, too." She also suggests a picnic at Rattlesnake Springs, a "birders' paradise," she calls it, and adds that those who want to experience the Chihuahuan Desert without any crowds should consider hiking the park's backcountry, which is done by less than 1% of the park's visitors.

Just the Facts

GETTING THERE & GATEWAYS

The main section of the national park, with the visitor center and entrance to Carlsbad Cavern, is about 30 miles southwest of the city of Carlsbad via U.S. 62/180 and N. Mex. 7. From Albuquerque drive east on I-40 for 59 miles to Clines Corners, and turn south on U.S. 285 for 216 miles to the city of Carlsbad. For the caverns, continue southwest 23 miles on U.S. 62/180 to White's City, and go about 7 miles on N. Mex. 7, the park access road, to the visitor center. From El Paso drive east 150 miles on U.S. 62/180 to White's City, and then 7 miles on N. Mex. 7 to the visitor center.

The Nearest Airport. Air travelers can fly to **Cavern City Air Terminal** (© 505/887-1500), at the south edge of the city of Carlsbad, which has commercial service from Albuquerque with **Mesa Airlines** (© 505/885-0245), plus Hertz car rentals.

The nearest major airport is **El Paso International** (© 915/772-4271) in central El Paso just north of I-10, with service from **American, America West, Continental, Delta, Southwest, Frontier,** and **Aerolitoral** (© 800/237-6639); and car rentals from most major companies. Toll-free numbers are given in the appendix.

INFORMATION

Contact the **Superintendent, Carlsbad Caverns National Park,** 3225 National Parks Hwy., Carlsbad, NM 88220 (© 505/785-2232; www.nps.gov/cave). Those arriving in the city of Carlsbad before going to the park can get brochures, maps, and other information at the **National Park Service's Administrative Office and Bookstore,** at 3225 National Parks Hwy. (at the intersection with West Pecan St.). It's open Monday through Friday from 8am to 4:30pm.

Because the park's backcountry trails may be hard to follow, rangers strongly recommend that those planning any serious aboveground hiking obtain topographical maps. An excellent book for hikers is *Hiking Carlsbad Caverns and Guadalupe Mountains National Parks* (Helena, Montana: Falcon Press, 1996) by Bill Schneider, which was published in partnership with the Carlsbad Caverns–Guadalupe Mountains Association and is keyed to the Trails Illustrated topographical map of the park. Contact the visitor center's bookstore or the **Carlsbad Caverns–Guadalupe Mountains Association** (see "Visitor Center," below).

VISITOR CENTER

The park visitor center is open daily 8am to 7pm from Memorial Day to Labor Day; and self-guided cave tours can be started from 8:30am to 5pm. The rest of the year the visitor center is open from 8am to 5:30pm, with self-guided cave tours from 8:30am to 3:30pm. Tour times and schedules may vary during slower times in the winter. The park is closed on Christmas Day.

At the visitor center are displays depicting the geology and history of the caverns, bats and other wildlife, and a three-dimensional model of Carlsbad Cavern. You can also get information about the tours available and other park activities, both below- and aboveground. There is a well-stocked bookstore, operated by the **Carlsbad Caverns–Guadalupe Mountains Association,** 727 Carlsbad Caverns Hwy., Carlsbad, NM 88220 (© **505/785-2486;** www.ccgma. org).

Attached to the visitor center is a family-style restaurant (see "Where to Dine," later in this chapter) and a gift shop (© **505/785-2281**) that offers the usual souvenir items such as postcards and sweatshirts, plus film and a variety of gift items including handmade American Indian crafts. Another gift shop is located in the Underground Rest Area (see "Where to Dine," later in this chapter).

FEES & RESERVATIONS

Admission to the visitor center and aboveground sections of the park is free. The basic cavern entry fee, which is good for 3 days and includes self-guided tours of the Natural Entrance and Big Room, is $6 for adults, $3 for children 6 to 15, and free for children under 6. Holders of Golden Eagle, Golden Age, Golden Access, and National Parks passes, plus their immediate families, are admitted free. An audio tour of the two self-guided routes is available for a $3 rental fee.

Reservations are required for all guided tours. In addition to tour fees, you will need a general cave admission ticket for all guided cave tours, except those to Slaughter Canyon Cave and Spider Cave. Holders of Golden Age and Golden Access passports receive 50% discounts on tours. The King's Palace guided tour costs $8 for adults, $4 for children 6 to 15, and is free for children ages 4 and 5 with an adult— younger children are not permitted. Guided tours of Left Hand Tunnel, limited to those 6 and older, cost $7 for adults and $3.50 for children 6 to 15. Guided tours of Spider Cave, Lower Cave, and Hall of the White Giant are limited to those 12 and older, and cost $20 for adults and $10 for youths 12 to 15. Slaughter Canyon Cave tours, for those 6 and older, cost $15 for adults and $7.50 for children 6 to 15.

You can make reservations for cave tours up to 3 months in advance by phone or via the Internet (© **800/967-CAVE** [2283] or 301/722-1257; http:// reservations.nps.gov).

SPECIAL REGULATIONS & WARNINGS

As you would expect, damaging the cave formations in any way is prohibited. Even touching the formations, walls, or ceilings of the caves can damage them. This is not only because many of the features are delicate and easily broken, but also because skin oils will discolor the rock and disturb the mineral deposits that are necessary for growth.

All tobacco use is prohibited underground. In addition, food, drinks, candy, and chewing gum are not allowed on the underground trails. Please do not throw coins or other objects into the underground pools.

Cave visitors should wear flat shoes with rubber soles and heels because of the slippery paths. Children under 16 must remain with an adult at all times while in the caves. Strollers are not allowed in the cave, so child backpacks are a good idea, but beware of low ceilings and doorways along the pathways.

Flash photography is not permitted at the evening Bat Flight programs.

Pets are not permitted in the caverns, on park trails, or in the backcountry, and because of the hot summer temperatures pets should not be left unattended in vehicles. There is a kennel (© 505/785-2281) available at the visitor center. It has cages in an air-conditioned room, but no runs, and is primarily used by pet owners for periods of 3 hours or so while they are on cave tours. Pets are given water, but not food, and there are no grooming or overnight facilities. Reservations are not necessary; cost is $4 per pet.

SEASONS & CLIMATE

The climate aboveground is warm in the summer, with highs often in the 90s (30s Celsius) and sometimes exceeding 100°F (38°C), and evening lows in the mid-60s (upper teens Celsius). Winters are mild, with highs in the 50s and 60s (10s and mid-teens Celsius) in the day and nighttime lows usually in the 20s and 30s (low negatives Celsius). Summers are known for sudden intense afternoon and evening thunderstorms; August and September see the most rain. Underground it's another story entirely, with a year-round temperature that varies little from its average temperature of 56°F (13°C), making a jacket or sweater a welcome companion.

SEASONAL EVENTS

A "bat flight breakfast," planned from 5 to 7am on the second Thursday in August, encourages visitors to watch the bats return to the cavern after their night of insect-hunting. Park rangers prepare breakfast for early morning visitors for a small fee and then join them to watch the early morning return flight. Call the park for details.

If You Have Only 1 Day

Those with only 1 day to spend at Carlsbad Caverns National Park can see quite a bit if they organize their time well. First, stop at the **visitor center** to look at the exhibits and check out that day's tours and programs. If you would like to take any guided tours later in the day, it's best to buy tickets now. Then head into the main cave through the steep **Natural Entrance Route,** and continue on a self-guided tour of the **Big Room.** For those not wishing to follow the steep switchback trail into the Natural Entrance, and anyone with health concerns, an elevator is also available in the visitor center that will deliver you easily and safely to the Big Room.

You'll finish your Big Room tour at the elevators near the **Underground Rest Area,** so pick up a sandwich there or take the elevator up to the surface, where you can dine in the restaurant at the visitor center or drive out to **Rattlesnake Springs** for a picnic lunch. (Rattlesnake Springs is a picnic area with tables, grills, drinking water, and restrooms. It's located along the access road to Slaughter Canyon Cave.) After lunch, take the **King's Palace Guided Tour** (for which you wisely purchased tickets earlier). Then walk the nature trail outside the visitor center and drive the 9½-mile **Walnut Canyon Desert Drive.** If possible, try to get back to the amphitheater at the cave's Natural

Entrance by dusk to see the nightly **bat flight** (mid-May to Oct only), when thousands of bats leave the cave for a night of insect-hunting.

Exploring the Park by Car

No, you can't take your car into the caves, but it won't be totally useless here, either. For a close-up as well as panoramic view of the Chihuahuan Desert, head out on the **Walnut Canyon Desert Drive,** a 9½-mile loop. You'll want to drive slowly on the one-way gravel road, both for safety and to thoroughly appreciate the dramatic scenery. Passenger cars can easily handle the tight turns and narrow passage, but the road is not recommended for motor homes and cars pulling trailers. Pick up an interpretive brochure for the drive at the visitor center bookstore.

Organized Tours & Ranger Programs

In addition to the cave tours, which are discussed below, rangers give a talk on bats at sunset each evening from Memorial Day through mid-October at the cavern's Natural Entrance (times change; check at the visitor center or call © 505/785-3012). They also offer a variety of demonstrations, talks, guided nature walks, and other programs daily. Especially popular are the climbing programs, where rangers demonstrate caving techniques. In recent years there have also been a series of stargazing programs presented by graduate students from New Mexico State University. A schedule of ranger-led activities is posted at the visitor center.

Historic & Man-Made Attractions

Although this park is devoted primarily to the work of nature, observing human activities in the caves is also part of the Carlsbad Caverns National Park experience. Throughout the main cavern

you'll see evidence of human use (and misuse) of the caves. Those taking the guided Lower Cave tour will see historical artifacts left by early cave explorers, including members of a 1924 National Geographic Society expedition.

Cave Exploration

Carlsbad Cavern (the park's main cave), Slaughter Canyon Cave, and Spider Cave are open to the general public. Experienced cavers with professional-level equipment can request permission to explore 10 of the park's other caves.

Most park visitors head first to Carlsbad Cavern, which has elevators, a paved walkway, and an Underground Rest Area. A 1-mile section of the Big Room self-guided tour is accessible to those in wheelchairs (no wheelchairs are available at the park), though it's best to have another person to assist. Pick up a free accessibility guide at the visitor center.

MAIN CARLSBAD CAVERN ROUTES

Most visitors see Carlsbad Cavern by taking the following three trails, all of which are lighted, paved, and have handrails. However, the Big Room is the only one of the three that's considered easy.

The formations along these trails are strategically lit to display them at their most dramatic. The odd tints of green and yellow that may appear in your photos are caused by the various types of electric lighting used, and not by your film processor.

Big Room Self-Guided Tour

1¼-mile loop. Easy. Access: Visitor center elevator to Underground Rest Area or via the Natural Entrance Route (see below).

Considered the one essential of a visit to Carlsbad Caverns National Park, this easy trail meanders through a massive chamber—it isn't called the Big Room for nothing—where you'll see some of the park's most spectacular formations and likely be overwhelmed by the enormity of it all. Allow about 1½ hours.

King's Palace Guided Tour

¾-mile loop. Moderate. Access: Visitor center elevator to Underground Rest Area.

This ranger-led walk wanders through some of the cave's most scenic chambers, where you'll see wonderfully fanciful formations in the King's Palace, Queen's Chamber, and Green Lake Room. Watch for the delightful Bashful Elephant formation between the King's Palace and Green Lake Room. Along the way, rangers discuss the geology of the cave and early explorers' experiences. Although the path is paved, the 80-foot elevation change makes this more difficult than the Big Room trail.

Natural Entrance Route

1¼ miles. Moderate to strenuous. Access: Outside the visitor center.

This moderately strenuous hike takes you into Carlsbad Cavern on the same basic route used by its early explorers. You leave the daylight to enter a big hole, and then descend more than 750 feet into the cavern on a steep and narrow switchback trail, moving from the "twilight zone" of semidarkness to the depths of the cave, which would be totally black without the electric lights conveniently provided by the Park Service. The self-guided tour takes about 1 hour and ends near the elevators, which can take you back to the visitor center. However, it is strongly recommended that from here you proceed on the Big Room Self-Guided Tour, which is described above, if you have not already been there.

CAVING TOUR PROGRAMS IN CARLSBAD CAVERN

Ranger-led tours to these less-developed sections of Carlsbad Cavern provide more of the experience of exploration and genuine caving than the above routes over well-trodden trails. These caving tours vary in difficulty, but all include a period of absolute darkness or "blackout," which can make some people uncomfortable. Because some tours involve walking or crawling through tight spaces, people who suffer from claustrophobia or who have other health concerns should discuss specifics with rangers before purchasing tickets.

See below for age restrictions and required equipment. Rangers provide headlamps and helmets on some tours. All tours must be reserved and have individual fees in addition to the general entrance fee. Tours are sometimes fully booked weeks in advance, so reserve early.

Hall of the White Giant

½ mile one-way. Strenuous. Access: Starts at the visitor center.

If you want a strenuous, 3- to 4-hour trip where you crawl through narrow, dirty passageways and climb up slippery rocks, this tour is for you. The highlight is, of course, the huge formation called the White Giant. Only those in excellent physical condition should consider this tour; children must be at least 12. Four AA batteries for the provided headlamp and sturdy hiking boots are required, and kneepads, gloves, and long pants are strongly recommended.

Left Hand Tunnel

½ mile one-way. Easy. Access: Starts at the visitor center near the elevator.

The easiest of the caving tours, this one allows you to actually walk (rather than crawl) the entire time! Hand-carried lanterns (provided by the Park Service) light the way, and the trail is dirt but relatively level. You'll see a variety of formations, fossils from Permian times, and pools of water. Ages 6 and up. The tour takes about 2 hours.

Lower Cave

1 mile RT. Moderate. Access: Starts at the visitor center near the elevator.

This 3-hour trek involves descending or climbing over 50 feet of ladders, and an optional crawl. It takes you through an area that was explored by a National Geographic Society expedition in the 1920s, and you'll see artifacts from that and other explorations. In addition, you'll encounter a variety of formations, including cave pearls, which look a lot like the pearls created by oysters and can be as big as golf balls. Ages 12 and up. Four AA batteries are required for the provided headlamp; sturdy hiking boots and gloves are recommended.

OTHER CAVING TOURS

It takes some hiking to reach the other caves in the park, so carry drinking water, especially on hot summer days. Children under 16 must be accompanied by an adult; other age restrictions apply as well. Each tour includes a period of true and total darkness or "blackout." There are tour fees for both, but a general cave admission ticket is not required. Tours are popular and are frequently fully booked, so call a few months ahead for reservations.

Slaughter Canyon Cave

1¼ miles RT (plus ½-mile hike to and from cave). Moderate. Access: The cave is about a 45-min. drive from Carlsbad and is reached via U.S. 62/180, going south 5 miles from White's City, to a marked turnoff that leads 11 miles to a parking lot. Tours meet and depart from the cave entrance located ½ mile west of the parking lot.

Discovered in 1937, this cave was mined for bat guano (used as fertilizer) until the 1950s. It consists of a corridor 1,140 feet long with many side passageways. This excellent guided tour lasts about 2½ hours, plus at least another half-hour to hike up the steep trail to the cave

entrance. No crawling is involved, although the smooth flowstone and old bat guano on the floor can be slippery, so good hiking boots are recommended. You'll see a number of wonderful cave formations, including the crystal-decorated Christmas Tree, the 89-foot-high Monarch, and the menacing Klansman. Ages 6 and up. Participants must take D battery flashlights.

Spider Cave

1-mile loop (plus ½-mile hike to and from cave). Strenuous. Access: Meet at the visitor center and follow a ranger to the cave.

Very strenuous, this tour is ideal for those who want the experience of a rugged caving adventure as well as some great underground scenery. Highlights include climbing down a 15-foot ladder, squeezing through very tight passageways, and climbing on slippery surfaces—all this after a fairly tough half-mile hike to the cave entrance. But it's worth it. The cave has numerous beautiful formations—most much smaller than those in the Big Room—and picturesque pools of water. Ages 12 and up. Participants need four AA batteries for the provided headlamps, and good hiking boots. Kneepads, gloves, and long pants are strongly recommended.

WILD CAVING

Experienced cavers with the proper gear can request permits from the park's **Cave Resources Office** (© 505/ **785-3107**) to enter one of several undeveloped caves in the park on their own. In addition, Ogle Cave is open to experienced vertical cavers on ranger-led trips. Applications should be submitted at least 1 month ahead of time. There is a $15 fee for entry into Ogle Cave; permits for other caves are free. Further information is available from the Cave Resources Office.

Other Sports & Activities

Hiking & Backpacking. Most of the hiking here is done underground, but there are opportunities for hiking on the earth's surface as well. The park's busiest trail is the **Nature Trail,** a fairly easy, 1-mile paved loop that begins just outside the visitor center and has interpretive signs describing the various plants of the Chihuahuan desert.

About a half dozen other trails wander through the park's 30,000 acres of designated wilderness. These **backcountry trails** are usually poorly marked—rangers strongly recommend that hikers carry topographical maps, which can be purchased at the visitor center. Watch for rattlesnakes, especially in warmer months. Lighting fires and entering backcountry caves without permits are prohibited. Obtain a free permit at the visitor center for overnight hikes.

Backcountry trails include the 3.5-mile (one-way) **Guano Road Trail,** with an elevation change of 710 feet; the 6-mile (round-trip) **Rattlesnake Canyon Trail,** with an elevation change of 670 feet; the 6-mile (one-way) **Slaughter Canyon Trail,** which has an elevation change of 1,850 feet; the 11-mile (one-way) **Yucca Canyon Trail,** with a 1,520-foot elevation change; the 11.8-mile (one-way) **Guadalupe Ridge Trail,** with an elevation change of 2,050 feet; the 3.5-mile (one-way) **Juniper Ridge Trail,** with an 800-foot elevation change; and the 1.5-mile (one-way) **Ussery Trail,** which has an elevation change of 2,500 feet. Backcountry camping is permitted (with a free permit) on all of the above trails except Guano Road. Additional trail information is available from park rangers.

Horseback Riding. Most of the backcountry trails are open to those on horseback. A small corral is available, with advance arrangements. Contact the park **Resource Management Office** (© 505/785-3091).

Wildlife Viewing & Bird-Watching. At sunset, from Memorial Day through mid-October, a crowd gathers at the Carlsbad Cavern Natural Entrance to watch hundreds of thousands of bats take off for the night. All day long the **Mexican free-tailed bats,** which spend their winters in Mexico, sleep in the cavern, and then strike out on an insect hunt each night. An amphitheater in front of the Natural Entrance provides seating, and ranger programs are held each evening (exact times vary; check at the visitor center or call © 505/785-3012) during the bats' residence at the park. The most bats are seen in August and September, when baby bats born earlier in the summer join their parents, along with migrating bats from the north, on the nightly forays. Early risers can also see the return of the bats just before dawn. Flash photography is not permitted, as it may disturb the bats.

Bats aren't the only wildlife at Carlsbad Caverns, however. The park has a surprising number of **birds**—more than 300 species—many of which are seen in the Rattlesnake Springs area. Among species you're likely to see are turkey vultures, red-tailed hawks, scaled quail, killdeer, mourning doves, lesser nighthawks, black-chinned hummingbirds, vermilion flycatchers, canyon wrens, northern mockingbirds, black-throated sparrows, and western meadowlarks. In addition, each summer several thousand cave swallows build their mud nests on the ceiling just inside the Carlsbad Cavern Natural Entrance. (The bats make their home farther back in the cave.)

Among the park's **larger animals** are mule deer and raccoons, which are sometimes spotted near the Natural Entrance at the time of the evening bat flights. The park is also home to porcupines, hog-nosed skunks, desert cottontails, black-tailed jackrabbits, rock squirrels, and the more elusive ringtails, coyotes, and gray fox. These are sometimes seen in the late evenings along the park entrance road and the Walnut Canyon Desert Drive. In recent years there have also been a few sightings of mountain lions and bobcats.

Camping

There are no developed campgrounds or vehicle camping of any kind inside the national park. Backcountry camping, however, is permitted in some areas. (See the description of backcountry trails under "Hiking & Backpacking," above.) Pick up free permits at the visitor center.

The closest camping is **White's City RV Park,** 17 Carlsbad Cavern Hwy. at N. Mex. 7 (P.O. Box 128), White's City, NM 88268 (© **800/228-3767** or 505/785-2291; www.whitescity.com), located in the White's City complex at the east edge of the park boundary, about 7 miles east of the visitor center. In addition to RV sites with hookups and shade shelters, the campground has practically unlimited tent camping in a grassy area with picnic tables and some trees. Because the campground is part of the White's City complex, with its motels, restaurants, and other services, campers have access to the pool, an ATM, a convenience store, a liquor store, and a gift shop.

A good choice in the city of Carlsbad is **Carlsbad RV Park & Campground,** 4301 National Parks Hwy., Carlsbad, NM 88220 (© **888/878-7275** or 505/885-6333; www.carlsbadrvpark.com). This tree-filled campground offers pull-through sites large enough to accommodate big rigs with slide-outs, as well as tent sites and sites for everything in between. Some sites have cable TV hookups. There's an indoor heated pool, a game room, a playground, and a meeting room with kitchen. A convenience store sells groceries, gifts, and RV supplies.

Especially for Kids

Children usually love the self-guided walk through the main cavern's **Big Room,** with its many bizarre and beautiful shapes, especially when they're encouraged to let their imaginations run wild. Younger children, however, are often bored on the **King's Palace Guided Tour** because it has several stops, and everyone must remain with the group. (Children under 4 are not permitted on the King's Palace tour.) Families with children at least 6 years old (and preferably a bit older) enjoy the **Slaughter Canyon Cave** tour, which has some spectacular formations and gives the feeling of exploring a wild cave.

Those who will be exploring the city of Carlsbad and other area attractions may want to use as a base camp **Brantley Lake State Park,** P.O. Box 2288, Carlsbad, NM 88221 (© **505/457-2384**). Located 12 miles north of the city of Carlsbad via U.S. 285, and then 4½ miles northeast on Eddy County Road 30, this quiet and relaxing park is almost 40 miles from the Carlsbad Caverns Visitor Center. Activities include boating, swimming, and fishing on the 2,800-acre lake, as well as bird-watching. The park also has boat ramps, picnic tables, two playgrounds, and exhibits on the 19th-century community of Seven Rivers, considered one of the West's wildest towns, which now lies at the bottom of the lake. Day use fee is $4 per vehicle. There are 51 developed RV campsites (48 with only water and electric hookups, three with water, electric, and sewer), plus primitive camping along the lakeshore for 20 to 50 RVs or tents, depending on the lake level. Rangers

Campground	Elev.	Total Sites	RV Hookups	Dump Station	Toilets	Drinking Water
Carlsbad RV Park & Campground	3,110	136	95	Yes	Yes	Yes
Brantley Lake State Park	3,300	51+	51	Yes	Yes	Yes
White's City RV Park	3,630	80+	80	Yes	Yes	Yes

present programs in the campground Saturday evenings during the summer. Reservations, for a $10 charge (in addition to the campsite fee), are available from spring through early fall by calling © 877/664-7787 or on the Web at www. icampnm.com.

Where to Stay

There are no accommodations within the park. The closest are at White's City, which contains a variety of businesses under one management, including lodging, dining, shops, a museum, a gas station, and an RV park.

The next closest services are in and near the city of Carlsbad. Here you'll find several chain and franchise motels. Those located on the southwest edge of the city, on the road to Carlsbad Caverns, include **Comfort Inn,** 2429 W. Pierce St., Carlsbad, NM 88220-3515 (© 505/887-1994), with rates for two of $65 to $79; **Days Inn,** 3910 National Parks Hwy., Carlsbad, NM 88220 (© 505/887-7800), with rates for two of $69 to $89; **Quality Inn,** 3706 National Parks Hwy. (P.O. Box 5037), Carlsbad, NM 88220 (© 505/887-2861), with rates for two of $60 to $80; and **Super 8 Motel,** 3817 National Parks Hwy., Carlsbad, NM 88220 (© 505/887-8888), charging $50 to $60 for two. Toll-free reservation numbers are given in the appendix.

For additional information on area lodging, contact the **Carlsbad Chamber of Commerce,** P.O. Box 910, Carlsbad, NM 88220 (© 800/221-1224 or 505/887-6516; fax 505/885-1455; www.chamber. caverns.com), or at the chamber's visitor center at 302 S. Canal St. in Carlsbad.

Best Western Cavern Inn

17 Carlsbad Cavern Hwy. at N. Mex. 7, White's City, NM 88268. © **800/228-3767** direct, or 505/785-2291. www.whitescity.com. 105 units. A/C TV TEL. May 15–Sept 14 $75–$105 double; Sept 15–May 14 $65–$95 double. AE, DC, DISC, MC, V. Pets accepted ($10 fee).

This motel and its associated properties (all the facilities in White's City discussed in this chapter are under the same management) are the most convenient places to stay during your visit to Carlsbad Caverns. Rooms are spacious, with Southwestern decor and either two queen-size beds or one king. About half have whirlpool tubs. Most folks dine and drink at the complex's Velvet Garter Saloon and Restaurant or pick up a quick meal at nearby Fast Jack's (see "Where to Dine," below). The White's City arcade contains a post office, a small grocery store, a gift shop, a museum, and a theater. Set between the Cavern Inn and its neighbor properties are two swimming pools, two hot tubs, and a tennis court.

Best Western Stevens Inn

1829 S. Canal St., Carlsbad, NM 88220. © **800/730-2851** direct, or 505/887-2851. www.cavemen.net/stevens. 202 units. A/C TV TEL. $69–$99 double. Rates include full breakfast. AE, DC, DISC, MC, V. Pets accepted ($10 fee).

Well-landscaped gardens surround this handsome property, composed of several buildings spread across spacious grounds. All the rooms have Southwestern decor and coffeemakers, and most have two queen beds. Some units, with

Showers	Fire Pits/ Grills	Laundry	Public Phone	Reserve	Fees	Open
Yes	Yes	Yes	Yes	Yes	$19–$24	Year-round
Yes	Yes	No	Yes	Yes	$8–$18	Year-round
Yes	Yes	Yes	Yes	Yes	$18–$23	Year-round

peaked ceilings to make them feel even larger, also have back-door patios. There are some wheelchair-accessible rooms with roll-in showers. The motel has a restaurant (see "Where to Dine," below), room service, courtesy airport transportation, guest laundry, 24-hour front desk, swimming pool, and playground.

Holiday Inn

601 S. Canal St., Carlsbad, NM 88220. © **800/742-9586** direct, or 505/885-8500. holidayinn1@carlsbadnm.com. 100 units. A/C TV TEL. $75–$90 double. AE, DC, DISC, MC, V. Pets accepted.

A handsome New Mexico Territorial-style building houses this first-rate full-service hotel in downtown Carlsbad, where guests can unwind in an attractive outdoor heated swimming pool, sauna, and whirlpool. There's also an exercise room and playground, a self-service laundry, and courtesy transportation. The large rooms are decorated in Southwestern motif and have coffee-makers. Some wheelchair-accessible rooms have roll-in showers. The hotel restaurant serves breakfast and dinner.

Where to Dine

INSIDE THE PARK

There are two concessionaire-operated restaurants at the park (© **505/785-2281**). A family-style full-service restaurant at the **visitor center** serves three meals daily. It offers standard breakfasts such as bacon and eggs, hot cakes, sweet rolls, and Spanish omelets. For lunch and dinner you'll find a variety of sandwiches, beef burgers, a veggie burger, and a few Mexican items. The menu also includes chicken-fried steak, a garden salad with breast of chicken, and daily specials. Prices are in the $3 to $8 range. The restaurant is open 8:30am to 4:30pm most of the year, with longer hours from Memorial Day through mid-August and on Labor Day weekend.

The **Underground Rest Area,** located inside the cavern 750 feet below ground, contains a cafeteria-style eatery offering fast food such as sandwiches, pizza, and burritos. Prices are in the $3 to $6 range. There is also a gift shop, with a variety of items including post-cards, sweatshirts, and film. Concession hours are coordinated with cave hours (see "Just the Facts," above).

NEAR THE PARK

The Flume

Best Western Stevens Inn, 1829 S. Canal St., Carlsbad. © **505/887-2851.** Lunch $4–$8; dinner $8–$20. AE, DC, DISC, MC, V. Mon–Sat 6am–10pm; Sun 6am–9pm. AMERICAN.

This relatively elegant restaurant has comfortable seating, candlelight, wall sconces, and chandeliers. For breakfast and lunch you can choose from a good selection of American favorites. The dinner menu includes a variety of steaks, seafood such as the New Orleans shrimp plate, and chicken, including a house specialty, teriyaki chicken breast. Dinners for light eaters are also available.

Larez Restaurant

1524 S. Canal St., Carlsbad. © **505/885-5113.** Main courses $3–$10. AE, DC, DISC, MC, V. Mon–Fri 11am–1:45pm and 4:30–8:45pm. MEXICAN.

Authentic Mexican food prepared personally by restaurant owner Dora Larez is what you'll get here, and be prepared to wait a little for it because items are prepared from scratch. Decor is unpretentious—cafelike, simple, and clean. The food is tasty and not excessively spicy. Try the guacamole salad with homemade chips for an excellent appetizer. The menu includes a variety of Mexican specialties such as chimichangas, a chile relleno plate, a green-chile plate, and a taco plate. A good choice is the Larez deluxe plate, which includes an enchilada, tamale, asado, taco, rice, beans, chile relleno, green chile, and guacamole salad. American dishes include a chicken strip plate, steak finger plate, and a green-chile cheeseburger. Takeout is available.

Velvet Garter Saloon and Restaurant

26 Carlsbad Hwy., White's City. © **505/785-2291.** www.whitescity.com. Main courses $8–$15. AE, DC, MC, V. Daily 4–9pm. AMERICAN.

This comfortable family-style restaurant, with a separate saloon, has two beautiful stained-glass windows portraying the caverns and the Guadalupe Mountains, as well as other works of Western art and assorted Old West touches. The menu includes steaks, chicken, and fish; there's also a salad bar. Nearby, Fast Jack's (same address and phone as above) serves three meals daily, with various breakfast items, burgers, sandwiches, and a few full meals, with prices from $3 to $6.

Picnic & Camping Supplies

The closest grocery store to the national park is the convenience store located at the **Texaco gas station** in the White's City complex, at the intersection of U.S. 62/180 and N. Mex. 7, about 7 miles from the visitor center. You'll find a good variety of stores in the city of Carlsbad, including an **Albertson's grocery store** at 808 N. Canal St., at its intersection with West Church Street (© **505/885-2161**), which has a well-stocked deli and bakery.

Nearby Attractions

Many visitors to Carlsbad Caverns also spend time at nearby Guadalupe Mountains National Park, which is discussed in chapter 20.

CHANNEL ISLANDS NATIONAL PARK

by Eric Peterson

RUSTED WINDMILL WATCHES OVER SCORPION RANCH ON THE EASTERN end of Santa Cruz Island, a reminder of man's impact on even our wildest places. It is but one of a staggering array of archaeological and historic sites found in this national park. But the Channel Islands are still defined more by the sea and the wind than anything else. On land, the dry grasses and shrubs remain constantly in motion, mimicking the white-capped water of the Santa Barbara Channel that separates the islands from the mainland. These waters contain a diversity of life matched by few places on earth.

Although it is one of America's least-visited national parks, the Channel Islands offer plenty of reasons to keep visitors coming back. Opportunities for sea kayaking and hiking are numerous, you'll find plants and animals that live nowhere else, and archaeological remains serve as reminders of long-vanished cultures. It's also a draw for underwater explorers from all over—twice as many people come here to explore the waters around the islands than ever set foot on the shore.

Channel Islands National Park encompasses the five northernmost islands of an eight-island chain: Santa Barbara, Anacapa, Santa Cruz, Santa Rosa, and San Miguel. (Santa Catalina, San Clemente, and San Nicolas are not included in the park.) Not limited to the islands themselves, the park also encompasses 1 nautical mile of ocean around each island, and the 6 nautical miles around each island have been designated a national marine sanctuary. The smallest of the park's islands, tiny Santa Barbara, lives a solitary existence off by itself. The four northern islands are clustered in a 40-mile-long chain. During the last ice age, before the continental ice sheets melted and vaulted the level of the sea upward, these islands were actually connected as one huge island that geologists now call Santarosae.

Although it was once theorized that the Channel Islands broke off of the California coast some 600,000 years ago, geologists now believe that the three northwesternmost islands in the park, Santa Cruz, Santa Rosa, and San Miguel, are an extension of the southern traverse range of Baja California and were never connected to the mainland. Anacapa and Santa Barbara are both products of underwater volcanic activity.

Flora & Fauna. The isolation of the Channel Islands has allowed a diverse array of life to develop and evolve, prompting some biologists to dub them the "North American Galápagos." Most of the differences from mainland species are in size, shape, or color variation. Perhaps the most curious of the islands' former inhabitants was the pygmy mammoth, only 4 to 6 feet tall, that roamed over Santarosae during the Pleistocene era—fossilized remains have been found on San Miguel and Santa Rosa.

Other island species, however, have survived. Like the mammoth, the **Santa Cruz gopher snake, island spotted skunk,** and **island fox** (the latter are two of the islands' three endemic mammal species) have all evolved to be smaller than their mainland relatives. Weighing just 4 pounds, the island fox is actually the smallest fox species in North America. Like Darwin's finches in the Galápagos, the islands' native birds also show marked adaptation: The **Santa Cruz Island scrub jay** displays "gigantism"—it is one-third larger and a deeper blue than mainland jays, and the **orange-crowned warbler** and **rufous-sided towhee** have oversize body parts.

But the diversity of animal life on the islands is outdone by the vast array of native plant life. One of the most spectacular of the islands' plants is the **yellow coreopsis,** or "tree sunflower," which can be found on all five islands as well as the mainland. Other species of plants live nowhere else on earth—the islands support 43 endemic varieties of plants. Like the pygmy mammoth, Santa Rosa's endemic **Torrey pine** population dates from the Pleistocene era, though a remnant mainland subspecies survives at Torrey Pines State Reserve north of La Jolla, California.

Marine life around the islands, however, easily wins the diversity award. The islands are the meeting point of two distinct marine ecosystems: The cold, nutrient-rich waters of Northern California swirl together with the warmer, clearer currents of Baja California. Everything from microscopic plankton to the largest creature ever to live on earth, the blue whale, calls these waters home. Orcas and great white sharks, anemone and abalone, lobsters and starfish, plus dozens of varieties of fish, live in the tide pools, kelp forests, and waters surrounding the islands. Six varieties of seal and sea lions beach themselves on San Miguel, four of which breed here, making it one of the largest seal and sea lion breeding colonies in the United States. The islands are also the most important seabird nesting area in Southern California.

Avoiding the Crowds. Unlike many of the more popular (and more easily accessible) national parks, crowds are rarely a problem on any of the islands. In a given year, about 350,000 people stop in at the park visitor center and 300,000 go into the park waters, but only about 60,000 actually set foot on the islands themselves. Although visitors rarely number above 80 a day to any given island, the open section of Anacapa (the closest and most popular day-trip destination) is so small that it may be difficult, though still possible, to completely separate yourself from the flock. As for the other four islands in the park, you should have no trouble finding a secluded picnic spot or overlook. Santa Barbara Island is the least crowded, Santa Rosa allows for backcountry beach camping, and San Miguel is the most remote (it takes 5 hr. to get there by boat) and the wildest.

Just the Facts

GETTING THERE & GATEWAYS

Most people travel to the islands by boat from **Ventura,** but even though there are no park fees, getting there is expensive—anywhere from $32 to $100 per person, the higher price being for a

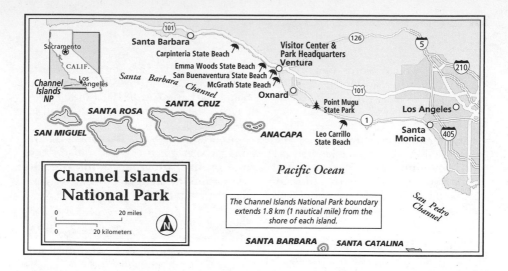

trip by air to Santa Rosa. If you fly, you may leave from the **Camarillo** airport. Anacapa, 14 miles out, is closest to the mainland, about a 1-hour boat ride.

The Nearest Airport. The closest major airport to the Channel Islands is **Los Angeles International Airport (LAX)** (✆ 310/646-5252; www.lawa.org). It's served frequently by all major airlines, with connections to almost anywhere you want to go. Los Angeles is 96 miles southeast of Santa Barbara; Ventura is 30 miles southeast of Santa Barbara. All major **car-rental** companies have vehicles at LAX. Toll-free numbers for airlines and car rental companies are listed in the appendix.

Getting to the Islands by Boat. Island Packers, next to the visitor center at 1867 Spinnaker Dr. (✆ 805/642-7688 for recorded information, or 805/642-1393 for reservations; www.islandpackers. com), is one of the park's two concessionaires for boat transportation to and from the islands. They will take you on a range of regularly scheduled excursions, from 3½-hour nonlanding tours of the islands to full-day excursions, as well as transport you to and from the islands for overnight trips. Prices start at $24 per person for the nonlanding tours and $32 to $62 for the full-day excursions. Island Packers also arranges specialty trips to the islands—primarily sea kayaking and snorkeling. Private yachts and commercial dive and tour boats also visit the park on a regular basis. Specializing in dive trips, the second boat concessionaire is **Truth Aquatics** (✆ 805/962-1127; www.truthaquatics. com). They leave from Santa Barbara Harbor and charge $79 for a 1-day round-trip to San Miguel, Santa Rosa, or Santa Cruz; overnight live-aboard trips are also available. The trips take about 3 hours each way.

If You Have Your Own Boat. If you want to take your own boat, check with the mainland visitor center. Access to the islands is prohibited in some places and difficult in others—going ashore often requires a skiff, raft, or small boat:

- You may land without a permit on East Anacapa, Santa Barbara, and east Santa Cruz between Prisoner's Harbor and Valley Anchorage.
- West Anacapa, except the beach at Frenchy's Cove, is closed to the public to protect nesting brown pelicans.
- Access to middle Anacapa requires a ranger escort.
- Landings and beach use on Santa Rosa and San Miguel do not require a permit; inland hiking excursions are also allowed on Santa Rosa. Special closures may exist; contact the park for up-to-date information.
- To land on the private western portion of Santa Cruz, boaters must obtain a permit from **The Nature**

Conservancy, Santa Cruz Island Preserve, 201 Mission Dr., 4th floor, San Francisco, CA 94105 (© **949/263-0933;** www.tnccalifornia.org/preserves/santacruz). A fee is charged, no overnight stays are permitted, and it may take 10 or 12 days to process the request. Applications are available from the mainland visitor center or by contacting the Nature Conservancy directly.

Getting to the Islands by Air. If you want to get to Santa Rosa in a hurry, **Channel Islands Aviation,** 305 Durley Ave., Camarillo, CA 93010 (© **805/987-1678;** www.flycia.com), will fly you there from Camarillo in one of its small, fixed-wing aircraft (around $100 per adult round-trip).

INFORMATION

Contact the **Superintendent, Channel Islands National Park,** 1901 Spinnaker Dr., Ventura, CA 93001 (© **805/658-5730;** fax 805/658-5799; www.nps.gov/chis).

For information on Ventura, try the **Ventura Visitors & Convention Bureau,** 89 S. California St., Suite C, Ventura, CA 93001 (© **800/333-2989** or 805/648-2075; www.ventura-usa.com).

VISITOR CENTERS

The main visitor center for the islands is actually on the mainland, in Ventura Harbor, where you'll also find the park headquarters. Visit the **Channel Islands National Park Headquarters and Visitor Center,** 1901 Spinnaker Dr., Ventura, CA 93001 (© **805/658-5730**), to get acquainted with the various programs and individual personalities of the islands through maps and displays. Although a wide variety of publications are available, among the most helpful are the free handouts focusing on the individual islands. The center is open daily from 8:30am to 5pm, only closing for Christmas and Thanksgiving. There

is a second visitor center in Santa Barbara, 113 Harbor Way, 4th floor, Santa Barbara, CA, 93109 (© 805/884-1475), that is open daily from 11am to 6pm.

Anacapa and **Santa Barbara** also have smaller visitor centers, and rangers run interpretive programs both on the islands and at the mainland visitor center year-round.

FEES

There are no entrance fees for the park, but you should consider the cost of getting to the islands when planning your budget. There is a nightly $10 per site charge for camping on all five islands; you must make reservations (see the "Camping" sections for each island, below).

SPECIAL REGULATIONS & WARNINGS

The relative inaccessibility of these islands makes preplanning a must. The boat concessionaires are often booked a month or so in advance, so be sure to make reservations. Also, remember that once on the islands, you can't go back to your car, so bring anything you might need (including water, food, and equipment if you're camping). If you're camping, bring a good tent—if you don't know the difference between a good and a bad tent, the island wind will gladly demonstrate.

SEASONS & CLIMATE

Although the climate is mild with little variation in temperature year-round, the weather on the islands is always unpredictable. Thirty-mile-an-hour winds can blow for days, or sometimes a fog bank will settle in and smother the islands for weeks at a time. Winter rains can turn island trails into mud baths. In general, plan on wind, lots of sun (bring sunscreen), cool nights, and the possibility of hot days. Water temperatures are in

Which Island Should You Visit?

Even if you have a few days to visit the Channel Islands, odds are you're only going to visit one or two islands on a given trip, so figuring out which ones to devote your time to may be your most important planning decision. It all depends on what you want to do. Here's a summary of activities available at each island. For more detailed information, see the individual island sections later in this chapter.

ANACAPA. Families with children will probably want to start with Anacapa, but will want to be especially cautious when near the island's unfenced cliff edges. There are more **organized activities** here than on the other islands, and the crossing to Anacapa is the shortest—an important consideration when dealing with potentially seasick youngsters. If you're interested in **sea kayaking,** Anacapa's scores of sea caves also make it your best bet. Though much smaller than its huge neighbor Santa Cruz, Anacapa has several times more caves, many of which can be entered by kayak.

SANTA CRUZ. It may have fewer caves than Anacapa, but Santa Cruz, the largest of the islands, is still a good choice for sea kayakers—the island's **Valdez Cave** (or Painted Cave) is the largest and deepest sea cave in the world. The Nature Conservancy owns much of Santa Cruz, and you must apply for permission to visit the portions of the island they manage (see "Getting There & Gateways," above). **Backcountry enthusiasts** take note: Landing at Prisoner's Harbor here allows for the most challenging hikes in the park.

SANTA ROSA. This is probably your best bet if you want to visit one of the islands for more than a day. (It's relatively big, so there's more to explore.) Those interested in **ranching history** and *vaqueros* (Mexican cowboys) will probably want to visit Santa Rosa. Santa Rosa's hundreds of undisturbed **archaeological sites** (please leave them undisturbed) also may attract anthropology buffs and others interested in Chumash culture. (The Chumash were the American Indians who inhabited all four of the islands.) Those interested in **endemic plant life** will probably also enjoy a visit. Though a century of ranching has wreaked havoc on the island's traditional landscape, the prehistoric **stand of Torrey pines** is spectacular—this particular species grows in only one other spot on earth (near San Diego).

SAN MIGUEL. If adventure is what you're after, the choice is pretty simple: The ranger-led 15-mile trek to Point Bennett offers the most visible wildlife and greatest diversity of scenery among the park's hikes. San Miguel is also your best choice if you want to **observe wildlife**—as many as 35,000 seals and sea lions gather at Point Bennett, seabirds nest on Prince Island in the mouth of Cuyler Harbor.

SANTA BARBARA. This is the smallest of the island chain, not to mention one of the most **distant and solitary.** After a 3-hour boat trip, you'll be completely free to hike this tiny island as alone as you might ever care to be.

the 50s and 60s year-round. Also be aware that inclement weather or sea conditions can cause concessionaires to cancel trips on the day of the excursion, so it's a good idea to have a plan B just in case.

From January through March, **gray whales** can be viewed from the islands as they pass by on their annual 10,000-mile migration from their warmer breeding grounds off the coast of Baja California to their cold-water feeding grounds in the Arctic Ocean. **Blue and humpback whales** can be seen in the waters off the islands between June and October.

If You Have Only 1 Day

Each of the islands is distinct. If you only have a day, Anacapa and east Santa Cruz are the closest to the mainland and the easiest to get to. The bad side: They're the most crowded (though crowded is a relative term here).

Exploring the Islands

EXPLORING ANACAPA

Sitting only 14½ nautical miles off the Ventura coast, tiny Anacapa has historically been the most visited of the park's islands. (Santa Cruz recently overtook it in terms of visitation.) Referring to Anacapa as an island, however, is somewhat misleading—it is actually a chain of three small islets—East, Middle, and West Anacapa—inaccessible to each other except by boat. Seen from shore, the flat landscapes of East and Middle Anacapa stand out in sharp contrast to West Anacapa's twin peaks.

Anacapa is the only island in the chain to keep anything resembling its original name—Anacapa is actually a corruption of the Chumash word **Eneepah,** meaning island of deception or mirage, and on a foggy or hot day it is easy to see why: Tricks of light make the island's cliff walls seem enormous or almost nonexistent; 40-foot-high **Arch Rock,** a natural offshore bridge, can seem to dominate the eastern end of the island or barely emerge from the water.

At only 1 square mile, Anacapa is probably not the best choice for people who need a lot of room to roam. To cramp things even more, only East Anacapa is completely open to the public. Visitors to Middle Anacapa must be accompanied by a park ranger.

Visitors interested in seeing the island's marine life up close may want to opt for a trip to **Frenchy's Cove** on West Anacapa instead of visiting East Anacapa. Unlike most of the mainland tide pools, the island's tide pools remain in pristine condition, housing thriving marine communities. Only the beach at Frenchy's Cove is open to visitors, though. The rest of West Anacapa is closed to protect the nesting areas of the endangered brown pelican—the islet houses the largest breeding rookery for the bird on the West Coast.

Seabirds are easily the island's most abundant wildlife. Because of the island's relative lack of predators, thousands of birds nest on the island, including the endangered brown pelican, rare xantus murrelets, and western gulls. Cormorants, scoter ducks, and black oystercatchers can also be seen plying the air and waters above and around the island. (In 2003, the park successfully removed nonnative rats from Anacapa in the largest-scale rodent eradication program on any island in the world. The island is now free of rats, and the seabirds are thriving.)

The island also harbors a community of California sea lions and harbor seals. The animals rest and breed on Anacapa's rocky shores and feed in the kelp forests surrounding the island. Overlooks at **Cathedral Cove, Pinniped Point,** and **Inspiration Point** offer visitors excellent views of them.

Although most of the year the island is covered with scrubby brownish vegetation, winter rains bring the island's vegetation to vibrant life—the bright blossoms of the yellow coreopsis, or "tree sunflower," are often so numerous that they can be seen from the mainland.

Organized Tours & Ranger Programs. Despite its confines, Anacapa is the most visitor-friendly island in the park: Rangers, volunteers, and concessionaire-employed naturalists lead guided nature walks daily during the summer, and self-guided trail booklets are available at the visitor center on the island.

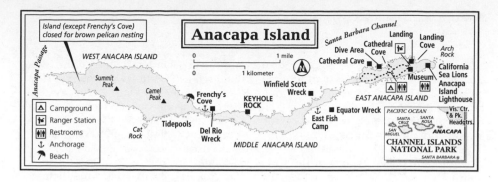

Every Tuesday and Thursday from Memorial Day through Labor Day, rangers plunge into the kelp forest off the island with a video camera. The rangers allow visitors to view the undersea world on the monitor on the island's landing dock (or on a large screen in the mainland visitor center).

Historic & Man-Made Attractions. In 1853, the steamer *Winfield Scott* grounded and sank off the coast of Middle Anacapa (remains of the wreck can still be seen off the north coast of the islet), prompting the government to build a 50-foot tower supporting an acetylene beacon.

In 1932, the U.S. Lighthouse Service replaced the tower with the present **lighthouse** and facilities on East Anacapa. The fully automated lighthouse still used the original handmade Fresnel lens until 1990, when a more modern lighting system was installed—the original lead crystal lens is now on display in the island's visitor center. The lighthouse is still operated by the U.S. Coast Guard, but visitors are warned *not to approach the building*—the foghorn can leave permanent hearing damage. Special ranger-led tours are available.

Today the other lighthouse service buildings house the visitor center and ranger residences. A churchlike building actually houses two 55,000-gallon water tanks that supply fresh water for the residences and fire fighting. It was designed to resemble a Spanish mission to discourage snipers who used to take potshots at the wooden tanks.

Day Hikes. The 2-mile, figure-eight **Loop Trail** on East Anacapa serves up plenty of great views and is a good introduction to the island's natural history. Follow signs from the boat-landing area to the trailhead. A pamphlet describing the island's most significant features is available in the small visitor center. Naturalists also lead guided nature walks daily during the summer.

Camping. Camping is allowed on East Anacapa year-round, but don't bring more than you're able to carry up the 154-stair, half-mile trail from the landing cove. The campground has seven sites and a capacity of 30 people. The campsites are primitive; there is no shade, and food and water are not available. Pit toilets are provided. No fires are allowed, but cooking is permitted on enclosed, backpack-type stoves. Bring earplugs and steer clear of the foghorn. There is a nightly $10 per campsite charge, and a reservation is required (✆ **800/365-CAMP** [2267]; http://reservations.nps.gov). Campground reservations fill quickly, so be sure to call well in advance.

EXPLORING SANTA CRUZ

By far the biggest of the islands—nearly 100 square miles—Santa Cruz is also the most diverse. It has huge canyons, year-round streams, beaches, cliffs, the highest mountain in the Channel Islands (2,400 ft.), abandoned cattle and sheep ranches, and American Indian Chumash village sites.

The pastoral **central valley** that separates the island's two mountains is still being created by a major earthquake fault. The island also hosts seemingly endless displays of flora and fauna, including 650 species of plants, nine of which are endemic; 140 land bird species; and a small group of other land animals, including the island fox. Lying directly between cold northern and warm southern waters, the waters off the island contain a marine community representing 1,000 miles of coastline.

Originally called **Limuw** by the Chumash (who believed the island was the site of their creation, before they took to the mainland via the mythological Rainbow Bridge), Santa Cruz gained its present moniker after a priest's staff was accidentally left on the island during the Portola expedition of 1769. A resident Chumash found the cross-tipped staff and returned it to the priest, inspiring the Spaniards to dub the island **La Isla de Santa Cruz,** or the Island of the Sacred Cross.

Much of the island is still privately owned: The Nature Conservancy holds the western three-quarters. In 1997 the Park Service took over the eastern end from the Gherini family, which had operated a sheep ranch here. Most visitors come to **Scorpion Ranch** and **Smuggler's Ranch** on the Park Service's land. Unfortunately, the island's ranching heritage has left its mark on the land— the island has been badly overgrazed by feral sheep. From 1998 to 2003, the island's feral sheep population was shipped off the island to spend the rest of their years at an Oregon conservancy; the vegetation is now showing signs of recovery. Much of the most beautiful land is on Nature Conservancy property, which includes Santa Cruz's lush Central Valley and the islands' highest peaks.

On December 5, 1997, the island was doused with more than 12 inches of rain. Floodwaters crested at nearly 4 feet, effectively destroying the campground— it has since been restored. However, a great deal of restoration work continues at the Scorpion Ranch area.

It's difficult, but not impossible, to get access to the more pristine Conservancy land; Island Packers runs occasional trips to **Prisoner's Harbor.** At one point, it was possible to arrange stays at Christy Ranch on the windswept west end of the island and visits to the Main Ranch in the Central Valley, but at press time the ranches were under restoration, and access needed to be arranged before arrival. Contact the **Nature Conservancy** (© 949/263-0933) for up-to-date information.

Valdez Cave (also known as Painted Cave for its colorful rock types, lichens, and algae) is the largest and deepest known sea cave in the world. The huge cave stretches nearly a quarter of a mile into the island and is nearly 100 feet wide. The entrance ceiling rises 160 feet, and in the spring, a waterfall tumbles over the opening. Located on the northwest end of the island, the cave can only be entered via dinghy or kayak. See "The Extra Mile: Exploring the Coastline & Waters Off the Channel Islands," later in this chapter.

Historic & Man-Made Attractions. After more than a century of ranching, Santa Cruz has acquired its fair share of historic buildings, including adobe ranch houses, barns, blacksmith and saddle shops, wineries, and a chapel. The ranch house and adobe bunkhouse at **Scorpion Ranch** are private residences today, just as they were in the early 20th century. All around Scorpion Ranch, fascinating ranch and farm implements, some dating back decades, speckle the landscape. The Park Service has plans to include some in a visitor center on the island. Also planned is an interpretive center in the historic buildings.

Day Hikes. Most hikes in the national parkland of Santa Cruz begin at Scorpion Ranch. The easiest and shortest is the **Historic Ranch Walk.** The ranch area is visible from the beach. This hike is basically the beginning leg of all the hikes described below, so if you are planning to take one of those, you don't really need to allocate much additional time for this hike.

The hike up to **Cavern Point** leads you to the bluffs northwest of Scorpion Harbor, providing spectacular views of the north coast of the island. Between

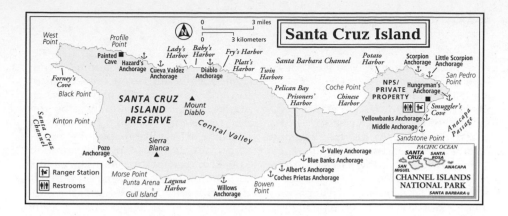

January and March, this is an excellent vantage from which to spot **migrating gray whales.** Follow the main trail from the beach through the ranch area. Beyond the ranch, look for the first side canyon on your right (west). Follow the signed trail through the eucalyptus grove and up the side of the canyon to Cavern Point. Avoid the unstable cliff ledges at the top and return to Scorpion Beach by following the trail to the east. At 2 miles round-trip, the hike is rated moderate to difficult due to a 200-yard uphill climb, uneven terrain, and loose rock.

A little longer than the Cavern Point Hike, the hike up to the **Potato Harbor Overlook** also provides magnificent coastal views. Head past the ranch about 0.75 mile until you come to a big break in the eucalyptus trees. A trail sign marks the spot. Follow the old road on the right (west) until you reach the bluff trail to Potato Harbor Overlook. Avoid cliff edges, and return the way you came. The round-trip is 4 miles and is rated moderate due to a 1-mile uphill climb.

For another coastal view, you can head up to **Scorpion Bluffs.** Approximately 100 feet past the ranch area, before the eucalyptus grove, head left (east) on the road/trail across the streambed to the base of Smugglers Road. At the top of the road, follow the trail that goes along the bluffs. Avoid cliff ledges, and return the way you came. The round-trip is 2 miles and is rated moderate for its 300-foot elevation gain.

Your best chance to see the endemic island jay is to head up **Scorpion Canyon.** Follow the main road/trail though the ranch area and into the eucalyptus grove. The trail will eventually wind in and out of an old streambed before reaching the first oak tree after approximately 1½ miles. You may continue up the streambed, but the terrain is rocky and uneven.

For those with a little more time, the hike to **Smugglers Cove** is a nice way to spend a day. At 7 miles round-trip, though, it is not recommended for visitors with time constraints. Easy to follow, the hike follows Smugglers Road all the way from Scorpion Ranch to the white sand and cobblestone beaches of Smugglers Cove. If the Park Service has not removed all of them by your visit, you may see a few feral pigs left over from the island's ranching days. Because of the 600-foot elevation gain over many uphill sections, the hike is rated strenuous.

There are also numerous hikes through the Nature Conservancy property, many beginning at Pelican Bay. Often the hikes are led by a Nature Conservancy naturalist who points out natural and historical highlights. For information, contact the **Nature Conservancy** at © 949/263-0933.

Camping. Camping is allowed at the Scorpion Ranch Campground on the east end of Santa Cruz year-round. All gear must be carried about a half-mile to the numerous sites. The campsites are primitive; there is plenty of shade, and potable water is available (but no food). Pit toilets are provided. Cooking is permitted on enclosed backpack-type stoves, and open fires are allowed only on the beach from December to May. There is a nightly $10 per campsite charge. A reservation is required and can be obtained at the park visitor center or from Biospherics, Inc. (© 800/365-CAMP [2267]; http://reservations.nps.gov). There is no camping allowed on Nature Conservancy land (the western 75% of the island).

EXPLORING SANTA ROSA

Windy Santa Rosa was California's only singly owned, entirely private island until it was purchased by the National Park Service for $30 million in the 1980s from the Vail and Vickers ranching company. In 1998, the company ceased all cattle operations, ending nearly 2 centuries of ranching on the islands that now form the national park.

The second-largest island in the park, Santa Rosa displays widely different landscapes: After decades of ranching, rolling nonnative grasslands cover about 85% of the island, but high mountains with deep canyons are also present. A unique **coastal marsh** on the east end of the island is among the most extensive freshwater habitats found on any of the Channel Islands.

As with Santa Cruz, the island's size allows for a fantastic variety of life. Although the impact of ranching has been severe, native plant species still survive, primarily in the rocky canyons and upper slopes. Santa Rosa is home to a large concentration of endangered plant species, 34 of which occur only on the islands. **Torrey pines** grow only in two places. One is on Santa Rosa, in two ancient groves near Bechers Bay. (They also grow on the mainland near San Diego.) The island's vast grasslands provide prime habitat for 195 **bird species;** shore birds and waterfowl prefer the marshy terrain on the island's eastern tip.

Santa Rosa is also home to the diminutive **island fox,** a tiny cousin of the gray fox that has become nearly fearless as it has evolved in the predator-free island environment. The recovery of California's golden population nearly wiped out the fox population on San Miguel in recent years, however, leading to a captive breeding program on both that island and Santa Rosa; park biologists are keeping a close eye on the situation.

The **kelp beds** that surround the island function as an invaluable nursery for the sea life that feeds the Channel Islands' marine mammals and seabirds.

Historic & Man-Made Attractions. The Chumash lived on **Wima** (their name for the island) until they were moved to mainland missions around 1820. Through radiocarbon dating, scientists have been able to date human use of the island back 13,000 years, making Santa Rosa an invaluable archaeological resource. More than 500 largely undisturbed **archaeological sites** have been recorded, and visitors are asked to be especially careful not to disturb any sites that they encounter. In 1959 archaeologist Philip Orr discovered an individual we now refer to as Arlington Woman. Lacking evidence of a traditional burial site, scientists believe she was killed accidentally some 13,000 years ago, possibly while gathering food. The bones of the Arlington Woman may be the oldest human remains found in the United States.

The island also provides an important fossil record. A fossilized pygmy mammoth skeleton carbon-dated at 12,000 years old was discovered on the island in 1994. It is the most complete specimen ever discovered.

The island also provides insights into a more modern culture, with the buildings and other remains of a **cattle ranch,** owned by the Vail and Vickers Company, that operated here from 1902 until 1998 with little changes except for the addition of modern-day vehicles.

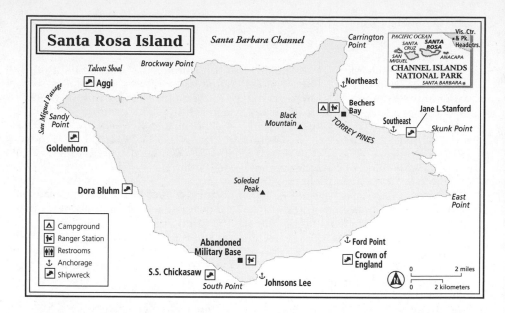

Day Hikes. Because of its large size, Santa Rosa offers a diverse array of possible hikes. To get to all the trailheads, follow signs from the boat-landing area.

The primitive **Cherry Canyon Trail** provides excellent opportunities to see inland island wildlife, plus sweeping views of the interior of the island. The trail is 4 miles round-trip and is rated moderate.

The **Lobo Canyon Trail** descends through Lobo Canyon to a Chumash Village site and then on to an excellent tide-pooling area. Unlike most mainland tide pools, the Channel Islands' intertidal zones have not been destroyed by human impact on their fragile habitats. The hike is 10 miles round-trip and is rated moderate.

The hike to the island's endemic stand of **Torrey pines** is 5 miles round-trip and has unbelievable views, and **East Point Trail** is a strenuous 12-mile round-trip that also allows for more views of these rare trees, as well as the brackish marsh at the island's eastern tip.

Camping. Camping is allowed in Water Canyon on Santa Rosa's northeast end year-round. All gear must be carried 1½ miles from the pier on Bechers Bay. The campground is provided with water and chemical toilets, and each of the 15 sites has its own picnic table and windbreak. There is a nightly $10 charge per campsite for the campground; the required reservations can be obtained from Biospherics, Inc. (© **800/365-CAMP** [2267]; http://reservations.nps.gov).

Beach camping is also permitted on a limited number of beaches around the island at certain times of the year. Although the winds will definitely test your tent, this is a good option for sea kayakers and divers who don't want to lug their equipment all the way into Water Canyon. A free permit is necessary, and can be obtained by calling © **805/658-5711.**

EXPLORING SAN MIGUEL

People often argue about what's the wildest place left in the Lower 48. They bat around places such as Montana, Colorado, and Idaho. Curiously, no one ever thinks to consider San Miguel, the farthest west of the Channel Islands. They should, for this 9,500-acre island is a wild, wild place. Lying west of the influence of Point Conception, the wind blows constantly here, and the island can be shrouded in fog for days at a time. Human presence is definitely not the status quo.

Visitors land at **Cuyler Harbor,** a half moon–shaped cove on the island's east end. Arriving here is like arriving on earth the day it was made: perfect sand, outrageously blue water, seals basking on the offshore rocks. The island's **caliche forest** appears otherworldly. Created by caliche (calcium carbonate) sand castings of a once-living forest, today all that remains are these natural stone sculptures.

As it did on most of the other islands in this chain, a long history of ranching nearly destroyed native vegetation. The removal of the imported grazing animals, though, has given the island's recovery a major boost. Today many native species are reclaiming their ancestral lands.

Though widely hunted during the 19th century, the island's seal and sea lion populations have clearly recovered and can be seen on ranger-guided hikes. At certain times of the year—June is often the best—as many as 35,000 animals, including California sea lions, northern elephant seals, and northern fur seals, occupy the beach at **Point Bennett,** making it one of the largest concentrations of wildlife in the world. The Guadalupe fur seal and Stellar sea lion, former island residents, are also occasionally spotted. Harbor seals haul out on other island beaches.

Prince Island, just outside the mouth of Cuyler Harbor, is an important nesting area for western gulls, brown pelicans, cormorants, and Cassin's auklets. And San Miguel's inland bird species can once again count the peregrine falcon among their number. After years of decimation by the pesticide DDT, the falcon has been reintroduced to the island and is now nesting successfully.

The waters around San Miguel are the richest but most dangerous of all the islands—the island is exposed to wave action from all sides. Harsh sea conditions have resulted in a fair number of shipwrecks in the surrounding waters, including the luxury liner *Cuba,* which went under on September 8, 1923. Fortunately, everyone on board was rescued, along with $2.5 million in gold and silver bullion.

Swimming among the wrecks are a wide variety of sea mammals: In addition to the pinnipeds (seals and sea lions), dolphins, porpoises, gray whales, orcas, and even blue whales can sometimes be seen off the island's shore.

The boat concessionaires' schedule to San Miguel is sporadic in summer and almost nonexistent in winter, so call ahead.

Historic & Man-Made Attractions. Like Santa Rosa, San Miguel has more than 500 Chumash archaeological sites.

The island also holds the remains of the earliest modern structure on any of the islands. In the 1850s Capt. George Nedever established a sheep, cattle, and horse ranch on the island. The **adobe** he built is barely visible today.

In the 1930s, Herbert and Elizabeth Lester became the island's caretakers. During his time on the island, Herbert became known as "the King of San Miguel." After being asked to leave San Miguel during World War II by the navy, which owned the island, Herbert committed suicide in 1942. Both he and Elizabeth are buried on San Miguel. Today only a few fence posts and small piles of rubble near the trail mark the **Lester Ranch Complex.** Technically the navy still owns San Miguel, though the Park Service manages it.

Day Hikes. Outside of the Cuyler Harbor/Lester Ranch Area, hikes on San Miguel must be led by a ranger. There are three trails, all of which meet at Lester Ranch. Due to terrain, length, and the tiring effects of walking in all that wind, all three are rated moderately strenuous.

If you don't feel up to a serious trek, you can still make the relatively easy walk from the landing at Cuyler Harbor to Cabrillo Monument and Lester Ranch, the starting point for the three official hikes.

The first trail heads north to **Harris Point,** allowing marvelous views of Prince Island to the east and Simonton Cove to the west. Taking the trail southeast from Lester Ranch will lead you to **Cardwell Point.**

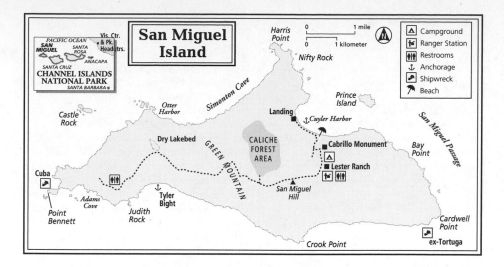

San Miguel's most popular hike, though, is the 7-mile round-trip trek along the **Point Bennett Trail** to the aforementioned caliche forest.

For those with more time and stamina, consider following the trail all the way to Point Bennett, a 15-mile round-trip. Camping along the trail is forbidden. The diversity of scenery and wildlife on view is seemingly endless for those hikers hardy enough to endure the wind and weather. After crossing San Miguel Hill, the trail passes the caliche forest. From the caliche forest, the trail heads west to Point Bennett, passing south of the island's other peak, Green Mountain. At the end of the trek, the barking of sea lions will signal your arrival at Point Bennett, where as many as 35,000 pinnipeds can congregate.

Note: San Miguel Island was used as a bombing range for the U.S. Navy between 1948 and 1970. Live ordnance is still occasionally uncovered by shifting sand, so it is extremely important to *stay on established trails.*

Camping. Camping is allowed on San Miguel year-round, though camping dates are subject to the availability of the San Miguel Island ranger. Located 1 mile south of Cuyler Harbor, between Cabrillo Monument and the old Lester Ranch complex, the campground has nine primitive sites and a capacity of 30 people. The hike to the campground includes a steep climb up Nidever

Canyon—keep this in mind before packing your accordion. There is a pit toilet and basic wind shelter at each site, but food and water are not available. No fires are allowed, but cooking is permitted on enclosed backpack-type stoves. Be sure to bring a strong tent, sleeping bag, and waterproof clothes—the wind is often fierce, and damp fog can set in for days.

There is a nightly $10 charge per site for camping, and a reservation is required. Reservations can be obtained at the park visitor center or from Biospherics, Inc. (✆ **800/365-CAMP** [2267]; http://reservations.nps.gov). Campground reservations fill up quickly, so be sure to call well in advance.

EXPLORING SANTA BARBARA

Lonely, lonely Santa Barbara. As you come upon the island after a typical 3-hour crossing, you'll think that someone took a single, medium-size grassy hill, ringed it with cliffs, and plunked it down in the middle of the ocean. In terms of land, there's just not a lot here. Even the Chumash eschewed living on the island because of its lack of fresh water. But the upside is that, of all the islands, Santa Barbara gives you the best sense of what it's like to be stranded on a desert isle, surrounded by the immense Pacific Ocean.

The island's deserted appearance is somewhat misleading. During the 1920s, farming, overgrazing, intentional

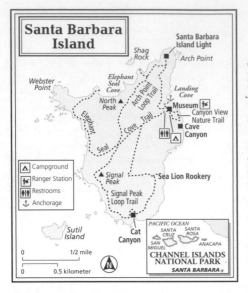

Santa Barbara Island

Shag Rock
Santa Barbara Island Light
Arch Point
Webster Point
Elephant Seal Cove
North Peak
Landing Cove
Arch Point Loop Trail
Museum
Canyon View Nature Trail
Cave Canyon
Cove Trail
Elephant Seal
Campground
Ranger Station
Restrooms
Anchorage
Signal Peak
Sea Lion Rookery
Signal Peak Loop Trail
Sutil Island
Cat Canyon
PACIFIC OCEAN
SANTA CRUZ
SANTA ROSA
SAN MIGUEL
ANACAPA
CHANNEL ISLANDS NATIONAL PARK
SANTA BARBARA
0   1/2 mile
0   0.5 kilometer

burning by island residents, and the introduction of rabbits all but destroyed the island's native vegetation. To survive the island conditions, plants must be tolerant of salt water and wind—and unfortunately, perfectly suited to this type of environment is the Santa Barbara ice plant.

Originally imported from South Africa in the early 1900s, the nonnative ice plant survives by capturing moisture from sea breezes and subsequently leaches salt into the soil, raising the soil's salt concentration. This has wreaked havoc on the natural ecosystem, virtually taking over much of the island. Through their resource management program, however, the Park Service is taking steps to eradicate nonnative species from the islands.

Other than the **landing cove,** there's no access to the water's edge. (The snorkeling in the chilly cove is great.) You can hike the entire 640-acre island in a few hours, then spend some time staring out to sea. You won't be let down. The cliffs and rocks are home to elephant seals (weighing up to 6,000 lb.) and sea lions that feed in the kelp forests surrounding the island. Because of the island's small size, the barking of sea lions can be heard almost everywhere. The **Sea Lion Rookery, Webster Point,** and **Elephant Seal Cove** all provide excellent overlooks from which to observe the animals. Be sure to stay at least 100 yards away, particularly from January through July during pupping time—young animals may become separated from their mothers if disturbed.

Santa Barbara's cliffs and rocks are home to swarms of seabirds such as you'll never see on the mainland, including western gulls, endangered brown pelicans, and the world's largest colony of xantus murrelets. Inland species include the horned lark, orange-crowned warbler, and house finch, all endemic subspecies found only on Santa Barbara Island.

There's also a tiny **museum** chronicling island history. *Note:* Island Packers and Truth Aquatics only schedule boats to Santa Barbara between April and November. (See "Getting to the Islands by Boat," earlier in this chapter, for more information.)

Day Hikes. Hiking the short **Canyon View Nature Trail** is a good introduction to Santa Barbara, but since it's such a small island, it's not that difficult to hike all three of the island's main trails (they only come to 5.5 miles combined). All trails begin and end at the campground and visitor center.

The **Elephant Seal Cove Trail** heads southwest from the visitor center to the west coast of the island, and then heads up by Webster Point, a favorite beach for sea lions and elephant seals, and then up to Elephant Seal Cove.

The **Arch Point Loop Trail** heads north from the visitor center to Arch Point, the northernmost tip of the island. It then turns south, following the island's northwestern bluffs before turning inland and crossing the Elephant Seal Cove Trail. Once across the Elephant Seal Cove Trail, the trail becomes the **Signal Peak Loop Trail** and continues southwest and up Signal Peak. It then follows the bluffs around the southern portion of the island, cutting inland briefly to bypass Cat Canyon. Once on the southeastern side of the island, the trail heads up to Sea Lion Rookery where it heads inland to the middle of the island and then north back to the visitor center.

Camping. Camping is allowed on Santa Barbara year-round. Note, though, that all gear must be carried up the 131 steps to the campground, located approximately ¼ mile inland. The eight campsites are primitive; there are pit toilets, but food, water, and shade are not available. No fires are allowed, but cooking is permitted on enclosed back-pack-type stoves. There is a nightly $10 per site charge for camping, and a reservation is required. Permits can be obtained at the park visitor center or from Biospherics, Inc. (© **800/365-CAMP** [2267]; http://reservations.nps. gov); campground reservations fill up quickly, so be sure to call in advance.

The Extra Mile: Exploring the Coastline & Waters Off the Channel Islands

Sea Kayaking. One of the best ways to explore the fascinating coastline of the islands is by kayak. **Island Kayakers** (© 805/390-8213; www.islandkayakers. com) leads small group tours by sea kayak to Santa Cruz and Anacapa. The trips allow you to explore sea caves and rock gardens. Channel crossing by charter boat, brief lessons, and lunch are included. Fares generally run $150 per person.

Aquasports (© **800/773-2309** or 805/968-7231; www.islandkayaking.com) and **Paddle Sports** (© **805/899-4925;** www.kayaksb.com), headquartered in Ventura and Santa Barbara respectively, lead similar trips (starting at $165 per day per person), or trips can be arranged through Island Packers or Truth Aquatics (see "Diving," below).

Diving. Half of Channel Islands National Park is underwater. In fact, twice as many visitors come annually to dive the waters than ever set foot on the

islands. Scuba divers come here from all over the globe for the chance to explore stunning kelp forests, ship-wrecks, and underwater caves, all with the best visibility in California. Every-thing from sea snails and urchins to orcas and great white sharks call these waters home.

Truth Aquatics in Santa Barbara (© **805/962-1127;** www.truthaquatics. com) is the best provider of single- and multiday dive trips to all the islands, with 1-day trips beginning at $79.

Ventura Dive & Sport (© **805/650-6500;** www.venturadive.com) also leads trips, including their "Discover Pro-gram," which allows novice and uncer-tified divers to explore the waters accompanied by an instructor. They also have a well-stocked sales and rental department that delivers to Ventura-harbored boats free of charge.

Channel Islands Scuba (© **805/644-3483;** www.channelislandsscuba.com) and **Pacific Scuba** (© **805/984-2566;** www.pacificscuba.com) also lead regu-lar trips, as do boats from San Pedro and other Southern California ports.

Where to Stay in Ventura

Although there are no accommoda-tions other than camping available on any of the islands (see the "Camping" sections for each island, above), the town of Ventura, the launching point for most island trips, has lots of options. The Nature Conservancy used to allow stays at Christy Ranch on the windswept west end of Santa Cruz, but at press time the ranch was under restoration and access was restricted. Contact the **Nature Conservancy** (© 949/263-0933) for up-to-date information.

In addition to the lodgings dis-cussed below, chain motels in the area include the **Best Western,** 708 E. Thompson Blvd. (© **805/648-3101**), $69 to $99 double; and **Motel 6,** 2145 E. Harbor Blvd. (© **805/643-5100**), $55 to $70 double. Toll-free reservation num-bers are given in the appendix.

Bella Maggiore Inn

67 S. California St. (½ block south of Main St.), Ventura, CA 93001. ✆ **800/523-8479** or 805/652-0277. Fax 805/648-5670. 24 units. TV TEL. $75–$175 double; $150 suite. Rates include full breakfast and afternoon refreshments. AE, DISC, MC, V.

European elegance pervades the Bella Maggiore, an intimate Italian-style inn whose simply furnished rooms (some with fireplaces, balconies, or bay window seats) overlook a romantic courtyard or roof garden. Breakfast is served around the patio fountain, an intimate spot known to non-guests as **Nona's Courtyard Cafe.** Nona's also serves breakfast and lunch daily (and dinner Wed–Sun). Be sure to ask the innkeeper about midweek specials.

Clocktower Inn Hotel

181 E. Santa Clara St. (1 block north of Thompson Blvd.), Ventura, CA 93001. ✆ **800/727-1027** or 805/652-0141. Fax 805/643-1432. www.clocktowerinn.com. 50 units. $109–$129 double. AE, DC, DISC, MC, V.

The Clocktower Inn is a good choice for families—it's within walking distance of the beach and Ventura pier. Integrating a 1940s firehouse (now the lobby) and adjacent clock tower when it was built in 1985, the establishment manages to gracefully blend reliable convenience with Southern California flair, the end result being one of the better motels in Ventura. All rooms come with a 25-inch color TV and spacious bathrooms, and many have fireplaces and private balconies. An Italian restaurant onsite serves lunch and dinner and is home to a better-than-average bar.

La Mer European Bed & Breakfast

411 Poli St. (west of City Hall), Ventura, CA 93001. ✆ **805/643-3600.** Fax 805/653-7329. www.lamerbnb.com. 5 units. $95–$195 double. Rates include full breakfast and complimentary wine in room. AE, DISC, MC, V. No children.

Perfect for a romantic getaway, La Mer is an 1890 Victorian Cape Cod–style home with a spectacular view of the ocean from the parlor, breakfast room, and two of the five units, each of which is furnished with European flair. The rooms, each named for a Channel Island, are cozy and recently refurnished with plush queen beds and televisions with DVD players. Two of the rooms have Jacuzzi tubs. The innkeepers can arrange special packages, including cruises to Anacapa Island, country carriage rides, therapeutic massages, and picnic lunches.

Ventura Beach Marriott

2055 Harbor Blvd., Ventura, CA 93001. ✆ **805/643-6000.** Fax 805/653-2509. www.marriott.com. 285 units. $129–$159 double. DC, DISC, MC, V.

Just 1½ blocks from the beach, this former Clarion was gutted and underwent a $9.5 million transformation into a plush Marriott property in 2002. The rooms are a cut above that of the average chain, centered about an interior courtyard with a pool and Jacuzzi. There is a restaurant and lounge onsite, not to mention the business center, bike rentals, and coin-op washers and dryers.

Where to Dine in Ventura

There is no food available on any of the islands in the national park; however, there are several recommendable places in Ventura.

Andria's Seafood Restaurant and Market

1449 Spinnaker Dr. (in Ventura Harbor Village). ✆ **805/654-0546.** www.andriasseafood.com. Main courses $7–$15. No credit cards; ATM cards accepted. Sun–Thurs 11am–9pm; Fri–Sat 11am–10pm. SEAFOOD.

Set aside your inevitable reservations at seeing the fast-food decor here and proceed to the counter to place your order—Andria's has been voted Ventura County's best seafood restaurant for over a decade (it doubles as a fresh seafood market). The fish goes directly from the ocean into the deep-fat fryer (charbroiled selections are also available) and onto your plate, with only a short stint on the boat in between. The food isn't fancy, but it's fresh, and the outdoor harborside seating is pleasant.

Jonathan's at Peirano's

204 E. Main St. © **805/648-4853.** Main courses $17–$26. AE, MC, V. Tues–Sat 11:30am–2pm; Tues–Sat 11:30–2:30 and Tues–Sun 5:30–9:30pm. MEDITERRANEAN.

Inhabiting the first commercial building in Ventura County (1877), Jonathan's is the sleek anchor of the west end of downtown Ventura. Proprietors Jonathan and Sharon Enabnit are seasoned veterans of the restaurant industry and it shows, from the main dining room's design, replete with redbrick, columns, and a Douglas fir floor, to the sumptuous selection of pastas, stews, and entrees from Italy, Spain, Portugal, Morocco, and other Mediterranean locales. Among the specialties are a spicy cioppino (with a pinch of saffron!), almond-crusted halibut, and rack of lamb with a Greek chile sauce. There are also excellent wine and martini lists (including the tequila-based "margatini") and decadent desserts. Next door is **J's,** a casual tapas bar also under the Enabnit umbrella.

Rosarito Beach Cafe

692 E. Main St. (at Fir St.). © **805/653-7343.** Main courses $10–$19. AE, MC, V. Tues–Sat 11:30am–2pm; Tues–Thurs and Sun 5:30–9pm, Fri–Sat 5–10pm. MEXICAN.

This cafe really packs them in. You can dine inside the 1938 Aztec-revival moderne building or on its welcoming outdoor patio. The superb Baja-style cuisine borrows tangy elements from the Caribbean. It has a culinary sophistication rare in modest Ventura. Make sure to try the delicious handmade tortillas.

The Sportsman

53 California St. (½ block south of Main). © **805/643-2851.** Main courses $10–$30. AE, DISC, MC, V. Mon–Thurs 11am–9:30pm; Fri 11am–10pm; Sat 9am–2pm and 5–10pm; Sun 9am–2pm and 4–10pm. AMERICAN.

You might walk right by the inconspicuous facade of Ventura's oldest restaurant. Like the intriguingly retro lettering on its awning, the interior hasn't changed a lick since it opened in 1950: plush leather booths, brass lamps, wood-paneled bar, giant trophy swordfish on the back wall, and light kept at dimness levels normally reserved for planetariums. The Sportsman looks "fancy," but is quite affordable (especially at breakfast and lunch), and they serve up fine hearty omelets, burgers, steaks, and other grilled items. Or you can wet your whistle with $3.50 well drinks from the bar.

Yolie's Fresh Mex Grill

26 S. Garden St. (corner of Main, west of Mission). © **805/652-0338.** www.yoliesmexgrill.com. Main courses $5–$13. AE, DC, DISC, MC, V. Mon–Thurs 11am–9pm; Fri–Sat 11am–10pm; Sun 10am–9pm. MEXICAN.

This colorful cantina's funny moniker is a nickname of the proprietor, Yolanda, and the place is better than its nondescript business-park exterior leads you to believe. Yolie's offers an impressive fresh salsa bar (authentic and delicious) as well as an admirable beer, margarita, and tequila menu. The patio and dining room are festooned with rainbow serapes and sombreros; the kitchen quickly sends out traditional combination plates (as well as lighter and/or vegetarian adaptations). The fajitas, especially the California chicken variety, are some of the coast's best.

Picnic & Camping Supplies

Food is not available on any of the islands, so you'll need to bring a picnic lunch and water for day trips and enough food and water (1 gal. a day per person) if you are camping. Picnic supplies can be bought at the **Von's** grocery store at 2433 Harbor Blvd. (© 805/642-6761) in Ventura; the **Village Market** (© 805/644-2970) in Ventura Harbor Village is another source. The **Sports Chalet** in Oxnard, 1885 Ventura Blvd. (© 805/485-5222), is the best area choice for picking up any camping essentials you forgot to pack.

12

CRATER LAKE NATIONAL PARK

by Jack Olson

TO MANY PEOPLE, SOUTHERN OREGON MEANS ONE THING: CRATER Lake. It's the deepest lake in the country, but more important, it's astoundingly beautiful. Visitors to the area haven't the slightest hint of the awesome grandeur that lies ahead as they approach the rim of the caldera, which makes the lake's appearance 1,000 feet below all the more stunning.

With Mount Shasta, Mount Lassen, the Trinity Alps, and the Marble Mountains just to the south of the Oregon/California border, it's hard to get excited about the low peaks of southern Oregon. Evidence of past volcanic activity is less vertical here, but more dramatic. Mount Mazama, in which Crater Lake is located, once stood as tall as its neighbors to the south, but 7,700 years ago it erupted with almost unimaginable violence, a blast estimated as 42 times greater than that of Mount St. Helens. When it had finished erupting, the volcano collapsed in on itself, forming a vast caldera 6 miles wide and almost 4,000 feet deep. Within 500 years, the caldera filled with water to become today's Crater Lake. The sapphire-blue lake's surface is at the base of 1,000- to 2,300-foot cliffs that rise to a total elevation of more than 8,000 feet.

The lake has no inlet or outlet streams and is fed solely by springs, snowmelt, and rainfall. Evaporation and ground seepage keep the lake at a nearly constant level. Because it is so deep, it rarely freezes over entirely, despite long, cold winters. The high elevation of the caldera rim and heavy winter snowfalls mean that the busy summer season here is short.

Whites first encountered Crater Lake when, in 1853, gold prospectors searching for a lost gold mine stumbled upon the lake's rim. The American Indian tribes of the region, who held the lake as sacred, had never mentioned its existence to the first explorers and settlers. But, by 1886, explorers had made soundings and established its depth at 1,996 feet, making it the deepest lake in the United States. Sonar soundings later set the depth at 1,943 feet. In 1902, the lake was designated a national park.

"I came, I saw, I left," could be the motto of most of the 500,000 visitors each year, who, from mid-July to mid-September, ride dutifully around the Rim Road and then move on. If you're looking to interact with the landscape on a more personal level, however, you have some options, such as road biking around the Rim Road or day hiking to the summits of several peaks, including that of 764-foot Wizard Island in the middle of the lake, not to mention superb cross-country skiing and snowshoeing opportunities in winter.

The Pacific Crest Trail passes through the park, with a 6-mile stretch on the west side of the lake. Wildlife is mostly limited to the lowlands surrounding the caldera, although at the summit you can see hawks, eagles, and many types of birds and small mammals. In addition, the spotted owl has been found nesting within the park boundaries. The forested slopes provide refuge for deer, elk, porcupine, and rabbit, and trout and salmon live in the lake.

Avoiding the Crowds. It's hard to avoid crowds here when the snows have melted. Given the area's harsh winters, most visitors come during the relatively short "summer" season between late June and the end of September. However, since many day visitors drive from cities some distance from the park, the Rim Road is not crowded early in the morning. Circle the lake before 10am and you can easily pick your view point. The best advice is to stay longer than the single day that 90% of the visitors allot to the park. Once you've seen and appreciated the lake (take the lake cruise early before the crowds form), go off and hike some of the less-trampled paths. Several of the longer trails will lead you to fabulous and relatively uninhabited view points. Especially recommended are the Dutton Creek, Garfield Peak, and Mount Scott trails (see "Day Hikes," below).

Just the Facts

GETTING THERE & GATEWAYS

There are three ways into Crater Lake National Park, the most convenient being from the west and south on Ore. 62, which runs through the southwest corner of the park.

To get to the park's west entrance, drive northeast from Medford 75 miles on Ore. 62.

To get to the park's south entrance from Klamath Falls, travel north on U.S. 97, then northwest on Ore. 62; the total distance is 60 miles.

To get to the park's north entrance from Roseburg, take Ore. 138 east; the total distance to Rim Drive is approximately 92 miles. (This entrance is open only during summer.)

If you're arriving in winter, call the Crater Lake National Park Headquarters for road information (© 541/594-3000). From October to May, access to the park by the northern route is frequently limited by snow, so expect delays.

The Nearest Airports. Area airports include **Rogue Valley International** (© 541/772-8068), in Medford, which is served by Horizon Air, United, and United Express airlines with car rentals from Avis, Budget, Hertz, and National. The **Klamath Falls Airport** (© 541/883-5372) is served by Horizon Airlines; Budget, Enterprise, and Hertz rent cars here. The toll-free reservation numbers are given in the appendix.

INFORMATION

Contact **Crater Lake National Park,** P.O. Box 7, Crater Lake, OR 97604 (© 541/594-3000; fax 541/594-3010; www.nps.gov/crla) for the free park guide, *Crater Lake Reflections,* which has a good summary of most of the park's trails, accommodations, and seasons. You can obtain a catalog of books and maps about the park from the **Crater Lake Natural History Association,** P.O. Box 157, Crater Lake, OR 97604 (© 541/594-3111; www.nps.gov/crla/nha.htm).

VISITOR CENTERS

The park has two visitor centers. **Steel Information Center,** south of the lake at an outdoor amphitheater; details are posted daily at the visitor centers. The talks start at 9pm from late June through July, and at 8:30pm from August to Labor Day.

The most famous Crater Lake tour is the guided boat tour that leaves Cleetwood Cove every 45 minutes or so, daily from late June through mid-September, from 10am to the last shove-off at 4:00pm. Remember, there is a steep trail down to the boat landing. The tour docks briefly at Wizard Island and glides past the Phantom Ship before heading back to the Cleetwood Dock. Take a jacket because weather here can change rapidly. Tickets are available at the trail-head. Adult tickets are $19 and children 3 to 11 are $12.

Sometimes the wait for the boat ride can be as long as 1½ hours. Purchase your ticket and then go off and do some hiking. Come back, and your boat will be waiting when you make it to the dock. Also, keep in mind that if you do get off the boat on Wizard Island, you might have to wait until somebody gets off an arriving boat so you can get on for the return trip. Boat capacity is limited, and people have on occasion been stuck on the island for several hours.

Historic & Man-Made Attractions

In addition to the Crater Lake Lodge, which you might want to take a look at even if you don't spend the night, the Sinnott Memorial Overlook has evidence of past travels through, and visits to, this area by numerous people over the last 150 years. If you're lucky, you might find some wagon tracks, whose faint impressions can be found here and there throughout the outer perimeters of the park. Ask the rangers at the visitor center to suggest trails where you might be able to see them.

Day Hikes

Annie Creek Canyon

1.7 miles RT. Easy. Access: Via the Mazama Campground Trailhead, between the D and E loops of the campground.

This is a scenic walk through old-growth forest and wildflower meadows, which serves as a nice little break from all the ancient volcanic starkness going on up at the rim. There is an elevation gain of about 200 feet.

Castle Crest Wildflower Trail

0.5 mile RT. Easy. Access: Park headquarters in Mazama Village.

Summer is short on the rim of Crater Lake, so when the snow finally melts, wildflowers burst forth with nearly unrivaled abandon. This trail meanders through one of the best displays of wildflowers in the park. Late July and early August are the best wildflower periods. Although this trail is judged "easy," be careful of slick rocks, which must be traversed along the way. Hiking boots, or shoes with good tread, are helpful. There is an elevation gain of about 100 feet.

Cleetwood Cove Trail

2.2 miles RT. Strenuous. Access: North side of the lake, 4½ miles east of the North Junction.

This is the only trail down to the shore of Crater Lake, and it stays busy with those trying to get to the water or to Cleetwood Cove to take the boat tour. Because the trail leads downhill, many visitors are lured into thinking that this is an easy trail. It's not! The climb 700 feet back up from the water to the rim is strenuous and steep.

Godfrey Glen

1 mile RT. Easy. Access: 1½ miles past the Mazama Village Entrance, on the right side of the road.

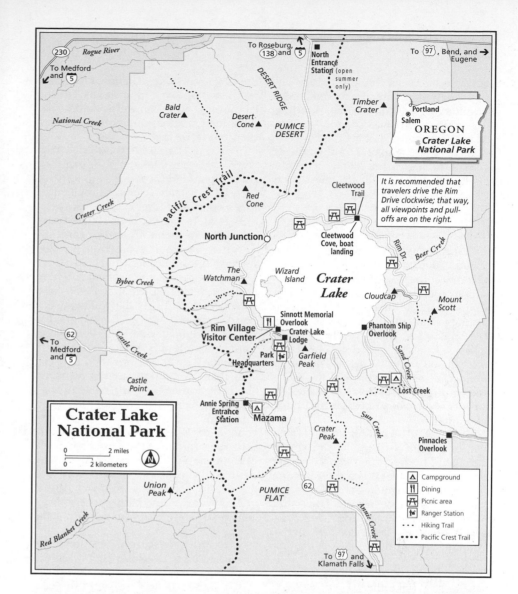

off Ore. 62, is open daily year-round and contains park headquarters. You can talk to a ranger and find out about local weather forecasts and general park information, purchase books and maps, and watch an 18-minute film. The **Rim Village Visitor Center,** along the southern edge of the caldera rim, is open daily from June through September. Here you can obtain general park information, and books, videos, and maps. In addition, there is a short, paved trail leading from the visitor center to the Sinnott Overlook, which offers a fine view of the lake and several interpretive exhibits.

Entrance into the park costs $10 per vehicle; an annual National Park Pass costs $50. Camping in Mazama Campground is $16 per tent site, and $19 to $21 per RV site. Camping in the Lost Creek Campground is $10 per site. Backcountry camping requires registration, but no fee.

No, you may not climb into the caldera. The only access to the lake is through the Cleetwood Cove Trail. And after getting a view of some of the steep and sharp-looking volcanic boulders lining the trip down, you won't want to try.

Fire prevention is of such a concern in this park that smoking on the trails is prohibited, much less building a fire anywhere other than in the pits at the designated camping sites.

At Crater Lake there are basically two seasons. The main tourist season lasts from mid-June, when most of the park's facilities open, through September. The busiest months are July and August. Summer temperatures in southern Oregon can get pretty scorching in the lower elevations, sometimes hovering near the 100°F (38°C) mark. The upper elevations (including most of the park) remain slightly cooler, but even the lake's rim can get pretty hot and dusty in summer.

In the winter, snowfall up to 44 feet deep buries the park, making it virtually impassable to everyone save skiers and snowshoers. Roads along the lake rim are left unplowed and are open to the non-car travelers exclusively. The winter season generally includes fall and spring, stretching from late October to mid-June or even early July.

If You Have Only 1 Day

Most people enter the park's west and south entrances on Ore. 62. Bypass the Mazama Village area unless you need to load up on snacks, and stop at the **Steel Information Center** for a preview of what lies ahead.

At this point, provided you have the stamina to hike down to the lakeshore, it might be a good idea to head for the requisite boat trip to Wizard Island before it gets too late in the day and consequently too crowded at the boat dock. The first boat leaves at 10am.

Drive north, clockwise around the rim from the Rim Village entrance, to the **Cleetwood Cove Trailhead** (the only trail in the park that leads to the lakeshore), approximately 5 miles past the junction of the northern route to the Pumice Desert.

The trip down Cleetwood Cove Trail is for the muscles in the front of your thighs, and the trip back is for your calves. It's a steep, strenuous trail, equal to a climb of 65 flights of stairs, or an elevation change of about 700 feet over 1 mile's distance. Consider carefully whether you are in good enough shape to make the 1-mile climb back up before you head down to the boat dock. There are benches along the way, if you have to rest (you will). At the trailhead is a concessionaire who sells tickets for the guided boat ride. The tour takes approximately 1¾ hours before you arrive back on shore, provided that you don't lay over on Wizard Island when the boat stops there during the tour.

It's perfectly fine to explore **Wizard Island** for a while, climbing the 700 feet to its summit on the Wizard Island Trail, and then catching the next boat back. You might want to eat lunch on the beach at Cleetwood Cove before you head back up the trail. After all, this is the only area of the park where you can get next to the water, so why not take advantage?

After the boat trip, it's time for the **Rim Drive.** Go clockwise toward the **Cloudcap Overlook** turnoff, for a brief drive to the 2,000-foot views of the lake and, farther off on the horizon to the south, Mount Scott and Mount Shasta. Make a short stop to admire pretty **Vidae Falls;** there may be lovely wildflowers blooming along the cascade. Then keep heading clockwise. You'll eventually approach a turnoff to view **The Pinnacles,** an area of unique rock formations. These spires are the remnants of fumaroles that formed in hot volcanic debris from the great eruption of Mount Mazama.

The road back to the rim terminates at a junction with another great view point, the **Phantom Ship Overlook.** The "ship" is an ornate piece of eroded basalt jutting up from the lake that sometimes seems to be sailing when the wind is whipping up the water just right. You might want to skip this if you took the boat ride and got an up-close look.

Return to the Rim Village for the last stop of the day, a little walk to the **Rim Village Visitor Center** and down the path to the **Sinnott Overlook,** which has new exhibits that tell you about the lake and the geology of this volcano.

You can get a cup of coffee at the Rim Village Cafeteria, or sit back and watch the sun go down with a meal at the Crater Lake Lodge (see "Accommodations," below), just east of the visitor center. (Be sure to call ahead for reservations. Way ahead.)

If you skipped the boat ride, you'll have time for a short hike. Two of the easy, short trails in the park are the Annie Creek Canyon and Godfrey Glen trails, which begin around Mazama Village. A third is the Castle Crest Wildflower Trail, which begins at the Steel Information Center. None of these trails are over 2 miles (see "Day Hikes," below).

If You Have More Time

Even though most summer visitors come into the park's west or south entrances, you can still access Crater Lake from the north. And it's a shame to miss these northern perimeter lands; the sands of the Pumice Desert are otherworldly when wildflowers are scattered across its flat canvas. If you have the time, it might be worthwhile to detour north when driving in from the south, just to see this area. From the south entrance, it adds only an extra 15 miles or so, depending on how far out toward the north entrance station you want to drive.

If you'd rather spend any extra time you have outside your car, try hiking a section of the moderate to strenuous Pacific Crest Trail listed under "Longer Trails," below.

The Crater Lake Rim Drive

Exploring the park by car is de rigueur for most people. There are 33 miles of the famous Rim Drive, with more than 30 overlooks lining this summertime-only two-lane road, and a couple of spur roads that lead to spectacular spots in the southeastern section of the park. Allow 2 hours to complete the drive; more time if you plan to enjoy any of the many trails and overlooks that are accessible from it. Gasoline is available only at Mazama, and then only from late May to mid-October. Otherwise, gasoline should be purchased in Medford, Roseburg, or any of the other outlying communities.

It's best to travel clockwise on Rim Drive because all the lake view points are located on the inside, or right side, of the road as you drive that way, so entering and exiting the view points is easier. There are also some view points on the outside of the ring that provide views of mountain scenery away from the lake.

Organized Tours & Ranger Programs

There are numerous ranger-led programs and tours in the summer. From the Rim Village, 15-minute talks are given several times daily at the Sinnott Memorial Overlook (below the visitor center). Check the park newspaper, bulletins boards, or at the visitor center for the current program schedule.

At Mazama Campground, there are evening programs on a variety of topics

This trail is a very easy walk through an old-growth forest and alpine meadows overlooking the Annie Creek Valley (also now accessible by trail). You'll cross Munson Creek at Duwee Falls before you head back to the car. It's a good walk for kids, with lots of possibilities to see deer, elk, rabbits, and grouse.

Watchman Peak

1.4 miles RT. Moderate. Access: 3¾ miles northwest of Rim Village on West Rim Dr.

With a historic fire lookout perched on its summit, the Watchman is one of the high points on the rim of the caldera. A short but steep (655-ft. elevation gain) hike leads to the top for an outstanding view of the lake with the conical Wizard Island rising from the deep blue of the foreground. This is the shortest climb you can make along the rim of the caldera.

Wizard Island

2 miles RT. Easy to moderate. Access: Take the Cleetwood Cove Trail (see above) and then the boat tour, disembarking on the island.

Though it is small, Wizard Island is a great temptation to many Crater Lake visitors. The island, with its steep volcanic cone rising from the deep, is fun to explore for a few hours, and this trail climbs 765 feet up to the island's summit. To spend some time here, take an early boat tour, get off on the island, and return on a later boat. Because most of the hiking is on jagged lava rock, be sure to wear sturdy boots.

LONGER TRAILS

Bald Crater/Boundary Springs

20 miles RT. Easy to moderate. Access: Via the Rim Dr. to northwest of the Rim Village area; continue to the Northern Park Junction of the Rim Dr. and the northern access road; from here, it's 3 miles down the northern access road to the trailhead on the left.

The ashy, flat, and rolling Pumice Desert stretches to the north along the trail as you travel some 3-odd miles toward the 8,763-foot summit of the Red Cone, a miniature Mount Mazama before it collapsed and created the caldera that holds the lake. The plains give way to ancient forests interspersed with fields of wildflowers. At the junction of the Pacific Crest Trail and the Bald Crater Trail, turn right to head for another miniature Mount Mazama experience: Bald Crater Peak. The peak is about 2 miles south of some fine campsites at the end of the Bald Crater Trail, along Boundary Springs, near the headwaters of the beautiful Rogue River.

Crater Peak

6 miles RT. Easy to moderate. Access: From park headquarters, head east around the Rim Dr. The trailhead is now located at the Vidae Falls Picnic Area.

This beautiful little walk takes you to a peak that is also a crater. How? The summit of this hike is the rim of yet another little volcanic cone to the south of the once huge Mount Mazama.

The trail begins with an uphill stroll through 2 miles of alpine forest and meadow, before reaching the steep final 0.5 mile to the summit of Crater Peak, with its full panoramic vistas of Sun Mountain, Maklaks, and Scoria to the south, and the rim of Crater Lake to the north. To the west lies Arant Point, near Mazama, and to the east the Grayback Ridge. All of them combine to form an incredible view. Early in the morning or late in the evening, you may see deer or elk.

Discovery Point

2.6 miles RT. Easy to moderate. Access: West end of the Rim Village parking area.

This trail, like most trails around the rim, provides brilliant views of the vast lake and Wizard Island below, ending after a short climb at an overlook where John Hillman, one of the first European explorers of the area, first witnessed the beauty of Crater Lake in 1853.

Dutton Creek

4.8 miles RT. Easy to moderate. Access: West end of the Rim Village parking area.

If you think the whole volcano experience is about ash and pumice, check out the old-growth forest of hemlocks, fir, and pine located on the sometimes-vertiginous Dutton Creek Trail. This is also the section of the Pacific Crest Trail that leads the long-distance hiker up to the rim. But for short-timers heading south, it provides an opportunity to get away from the crowds and see something besides a volcano's mouth. That something might be a deer or an elk as you hike down this narrow, heavily forested valley along Dutton Creek, before reaching the junction with the Pacific Crest Trail and getting ready for the climb back the way you came.

Garfield Peak

3.4 miles RT. Moderate to strenuous. Access: East end of Rim Village parking area.

Sure the view from the Rim Village borders on sublime, but this is even better. You'll leave most of the crowds behind, get in a good hike, and treat yourself to an even more breathtaking (literally, since the hike starts above 7,000 ft.) view of the lake by hiking to the summit of 8,054-foot Garfield Peak, which lies just east of the Rim Village. The route gains all of its 1,010 feet of elevation in a short 1.5 miles of nearly constant switchbacks. From the summit, the entire lake is visible below, including the island called Phantom Ship, which is hard to see from the Rim Village. To the south, Mount Shasta can be seen.

Mount Scott

5 miles RT. Strenuous. Access: 14 miles east of park headquarters on East Rim Dr. and across the road from Cloudcap Junction.

If the trail to Garfield Peak had a few too many other hikers on it for your tastes, try this trail to the top of 8,929-foot Mount Scott. This is the highest point within Crater Lake National Park, and the trail is longer and steeper and entails more elevation gain (1,480 ft.) than the trail up Garfield Peak. The views from the summit are the most far-reaching in the park, encompassing not only the entire lake but also such surrounding peaks as Mount Thielsen, Mount Shasta, and Mount McLoughlin, as well as the vast expanse of Klamath Lake to the south.

Pacific Crest Trail Section

33 miles one-way. Moderate to strenuous. Access: Via Mazama Village. Approximately ¼ mile west of the village, the trailhead is on the left.

For those who want to chalk up this particular section of the Pacific Crest Trail, which stretches along the west coast from the Mexican to Canadian border, there's a lot to chalk up. The trail essentially bisects the park, with only one section that follows the rim for views of the lake. Otherwise, you're pretty much out there in the flatlands.

From the trailhead, the path follows the base of the mountain's curve to the west for views of the mountain's slow climb to its rim to your right, and the rolling high desert plains to your left. At the northern end of the walk, before crossing into the vast Pumice Desert, there is an opportunity to circle back to the rim at North Junction.

Pumice Flat

6 miles RT. Easy to moderate. Access: 3 miles south of Mazama Village on Ore. 62.

This is the southern equivalent of the park's northern Pumice Desert area. This dusty trail takes you through gently rolling pumice and ash plains littered with sharp volcanic rocks, before intersecting the Pacific Crest Trail for the loop to Mazama. You can also simply return on the shorter route back to the trailhead where you started.

Stuart Falls

11 miles RT. Easy to moderate. Access: 3 miles south of the Mazama Village park entrance on Ore. 62.

Stuart Falls is really outside the park's boundaries, but the trailhead isn't. There's a nice contrast as you climb down to the dusty and volcanically beautiful Pumice Flats before heading into the Red Blanket Valley after the junction with the Pacific Crest Trail. You'll begin to notice a bare trickle of water turning into a creek turning into a much bigger creek that ends up as a fine crashing mist of spray known as Stuart Falls. Folks have been known to take a rest in Stuart Fall's fine white spray before heading back up the steep and often parched trail.

Other Summer Sports & Activities

Biking. The 33-mile circuit of Crater Lake is one of the most popular road-bike trips in the state, despite the heavy car traffic. Although it would seem at first that this would be an easy trip, numerous ups and downs (especially on the east side of the lake) turn it into a demanding ride. Keep in mind that there are more hills on the east side, but there are also more views. An alternative is to do the 21-mile out and back ride from the Rim Village to the Cleetwood Cove Trailhead (and maybe add on a boat tour of the lake). There are no bike rentals available in the park, but Diamond Lake Resort rents them in the summer. (See "Where to Stay & Dine," below).

Fishing. Anglers occasionally try for rainbow trout and kokanee salmon near the boat dock or from Wizard Island, but because fishing in the lake generally isn't very good, we suggest you stick to sightseeing and hiking in the park. However, fly-fishing in stream outside the park is pretty good—stop at the fly-fishing shop at Steamboat Inn (see "Where to Stay & Dine," below).

Swimming. Although Crater Lake is too deep to ever reach a truly comfortable temperature (even in the summer), plenty of people take the plunge and do a few quick strokes to cool down after hiking the Cleetwood Cove Trail or after exploring Wizard Island. But this is an informal activity, and there are no facilities for swimmers.

Winter Sports & Activities

Cross-Country Skiing. The **Diamond Lake Nordic Center,** 4 miles north of the park on Ore. 138 (© **800/733-7593**), offers Crater Lake ski tours that include a Sno-Cat ride. The Nordic Center has 8 miles of groomed trails and over 50 miles of marked backcountry trails. They also rent cross-country skis and boots. Maps of ski areas are available at the Steel Information Center at park headquarters.

Without a doubt, the **rim** of Crater Lake National Park offers some of the best cross-country skiing in the country. Not only are there numerous views of sapphire-blue Crater Lake 1,000 feet below you, but the views to the west and south take in Mount McLoughlin, Mount Shasta, and countless ridges and seemingly endless forest vistas as well.

The **ultimate ski tour** is the 30- to 33-mile circuit of the lake. Although this route has been done in a single day by racers, most skiers take 3 days and enjoy the views along the way. Because the weather is better and there's still plenty of snow, March and April are the most popular months. The route is very straightforward, although you may have to do some route finding on the northeast side of the lake. Be sure to get a backcountry permit for overnight trips and check weather forecasts and avalanche danger.

The **West Rim Trail,** which follows Rim Drive, is the most popular day skiing area. By mid-October the road is unplowed and the snow cover turns it into an excellent trail that requires a little climbing. It's best done in good weather and good snow conditions. Consult a park ranger for snow conditions before heading out.

The **East Rim Trail** is not nearly as popular as the West Rim Trail for the simple reason that it is between 4.25 and 5.4 miles to the first view of the lake (depending on where you start). This trail also has a lot more ups and downs. So, why would you want to start on this section at all? To stay out of the wind, that's why. If, after driving all the way up here, there's a gale-force wind blowing up the west slopes, you really don't have much choice. Never set out, though, without checking with the rangers at park headquarters to find out about avalanche conditions and other dangers.

Snowmobiling. During winter months, snowmobiling is allowed, but only on the north entrance road up to its junction with Rim Drive. (Snowmobiles are not allowed on Rim Dr.) You cannot drive snowmobiles on any park trails, either. Snowmobile rentals are available from Diamond Lake Resort from $80 to $190 depending on the time period rented and $75 to $135 double for guided tours. See "Where to Stay & Dine," below.

Snowshoeing. With its jewel of a lake for a centerpiece and views that extend all the way to Mount Shasta in California, Crater Lake National Park is a natural magnet for snowshoers. The **West Rim Trail** is the most popular route (just as it is for cross-country skiing), but snowshoers have the advantage of being able to go where few skiers can. Before you head out, discuss possible routes with the rangers and ask about avalanches and other potential dangers.

If you've never snowshoed before, you can give it a try at Rim Village, where 90-minute guided snowshoe hikes are offered weekends at 1pm from late November through March.

Camping

Within Crater Lake National Park, there are only two campgrounds, one large and one small. No reservations are taken.

Mazama Village Campground ($16 per tent and $17 per RV per night) has 198 sites available, with drinking water, a dump station, restrooms, a public phone, and fire pits. It's at Mazama Village off Ore. 62. There is also a general store and an adjacent post office. It's open from June through mid-October.

Lost Creek Campground ($10 per night) has 16 sites for tents only. It is located on the southeastern section of the park, on the spur road to The Pinnacles. It's open from mid-July to mid-September.

Where to Stay & Dine

INSIDE THE PARK

Aside from the Crater Lake Lodge Dining Room (see below), places to eat in the park are limited to the snack bar at the Rim Village Cafeteria and Gift Shop and the grocery store in the Mazama Village.

Crater Lake Lodge

1211 Ave. C, White City, OR 97503. © **541/ 830-8700.** Fax 541/830-8514. www.craterlake lodges.com. 71 units. $123–$238 double. MC, V. Closed mid-Oct to mid-May.

Perched on the edge of the rim overlooking Crater Lake, this lodge was completely rebuilt in 1995 and has since become the finest national park lodge in the Northwest. Not only are the views breathtaking, but also the amenities are modern without sacrificing the rustic atmosphere that visitors expect in a mountain lodge. Among the lodge's few original features are the stone fireplace and ponderosa pine–bark walls in the Great Hall. Slightly more than half the guest rooms overlook the lake, and although most of the rooms have modern bathrooms, there are eight rooms with claw-foot bathtubs. The very best rooms are the corner ones on the lake side of the lodge. As at other national park lodges, reservations should be made as far in advance as possible.

The lodge's dining room serves creative Northwest cuisine and provides views of both Crater Lake and the Klamath River basin. Reservations are strongly recommended.

Mazama Village Motor Inn

1211 Ave. C, White City, OR 97503. ✆ **541/ 830-8700.** Fax 541/830-8514. www.craterlake lodges.com. 40 units. $103 double. MC, V. Closed Nov–May.

Though the Mazama Village Motor Inn isn't on the rim of the caldera, it's just a short drive away. The modern motel-style guest rooms are housed in 10 steep-roofed buildings that look much like traditional mountain cabins. A laundry, gas station, and general store make Mazama Village a busy spot in the summer.

NEAR THE PARK

Since the park is so isolated, there are few options in the small, surrounding communities for accommodations and dining outside of the following.

Diamond Lake Resort

Diamond Lake, OR 97731. ✆ **800/733-7593** or 541/793-3318 (RV Park). www.diamondlake. net. 92 units. TV. $79 motel double; $90 studio housekeeping for 2; $150–$225 cabins; lower rates in winter. AE, DISC, MC, V.

Located on the shores of Diamond Lake 5 miles from the park's north entrance, this resort has long been a popular family vacation spot, and with Mounts Thielsen and Bailey flanking the lake,

it's one of the most picturesque settings in the Oregon Cascades. The variety of accommodations provides plenty of choices, but our favorites are the lake-front cabins, which are large enough for a family or two couples, with great views of the lake and mountains. If you want to do your own cooking, you'll find kitchenettes in both the cabins and the studios. Lodge guests and campers can dine at the resort's dining room, cafe, and pizza parlor—all family-type places with standard American menus and moderate prices. Boat, mountain-bike, and horse rentals are available, and there's a small sandy beach and a bumper-boat area. In winter the resort is most popular with snowmobilers but also attracts a few cross-country skiers. There's a 160 unit Diamond Lake RV Park nearby in summer, with full hookups and prices beginning at $20.

Prospect Historical Hotel and Motel

391 Mill Creek Dr., Prospect, OR 97536. ✆ **800/944-6490** or 541/560-3664. Fax 541/ 560-3825. www.prospecthotel.com. 24 units. $50–$150 double. Hotel room rates include breakfast. DC, DISC, MC, V.

This hotel, located in the tiny hamlet of Prospect, 34 miles from Crater Lake's Rim Village, is a combination vintage/ modern hotel. The old (1889) hotel is a big white building with a wraparound porch on which sit several bent-willow couches. The small rooms are furnished with antiques and have a country styling that gives them a bit of charm. The motel rooms are modern and clean and have TVs and telephones, and some also have kitchenettes. The elegant seasonal dining room is well known for its excellent meals, ranging from $16 to $20. Although the menu of innovative American and regional dishes changes periodically, it will likely include entrees such as slow roasted whiskeyed prime rib, lemon dill roasted salmon, or a very special lasagna.

Steamboat Inn

42705 N. Umpqua Hwy., Steamboat, OR 97447-9703. © **800/840-8825** or 541/498-2230. Fax 541/498-2411. www.the steamboatinn.com. 19 units. $145 double cabins; $185–$190 cottages and houses; $265 suite. MC, V.

Located roughly midway between Roseburg and Crater Lake, this inn on the bank of the North Umpqua River is by far the finest lodging on the North Umpqua. The beautiful gardens, luxurious guest rooms, and gourmet meals attract people looking for a quiet getaway in the forest and a base for hiking and biking. If you aren't springing for one of the suites, which have their own soaking tubs overlooking the river, your best bet will be stream-side rooms, which are referred to as cabins but really aren't. These have all been recently renovated, have gas fireplaces, and open onto a long deck that overlooks the river. The hideaway cottages are more spacious but don't have river views and are ½ mile from the lodge (and the dining room). Dinners—innovative American cuisine with main courses of beef, fish, poultry, lamb, or pork, at a fixed price of $40—are elaborate multicourse affairs served in a cozy dining room, and breakfast is available all day. There's also a fly-fishing shop on the premises. Anglers congregate here in the fall.

Union Creek Resort

56484 Ore. 62, Prospect, OR 97536. © **866/560-3565.** Fax 541/560-3339. www.unioncreek oregon.com. 22 units. $40–$50 double room in lodge; $55–$95 cabin for 2–6 people. MC, V.

Located almost across the road from the Rogue River Gorge, this rustic resort has been catering to Crater Lake visitors since the early 1900s and is listed on the National Register of Historic Places. Tall trees shade the grounds of the resort, which is right on Ore. 62 about 23 miles from Rim Village. Accommodations include both lodge rooms and very basic cabins (many of which have kitchenettes), and most have been updated in recent years. Across the road from the cabins and lodge building is Beckie's Café, which serves home-style meals and is best known for its pies. This is the best and closest option outside the west entrance to Crater Lake National Park.

13

DEATH VALLEY NATIONAL PARK & MOJAVE NATIONAL PRESERVE

by Eric Peterson

IN 1994, DEATH VALLEY NATIONAL MONUMENT BECAME DEATH VALLEY National Park. The forty-niners, whose suffering gave the valley its name, would've howled at the notion. To them, several four-letter words other than "park" would've come to mind: gold, mine, heat, lost, dead.

Americans looking for gold in California's mountains in 1849 got lost in the parched desert here trying to avoid the severe snowstorms in the nearby Sierra Nevada. One person perished along the way, and the land became known as Death Valley. Little about the valley's essence has changed today. Its mountains stand naked, unadorned. The bitter waters of saline lakes evaporate into bizarre razor-sharp crystal formations. Jagged canyons jab deep into the earth. The ovenlike heat, the frigid cold, and the driest air imaginable combine to make this one of the world's most inhospitable locations.

Death Valley is raw, bare earth, the way things must've looked before life began. Here, earth's forces are exposed to view with dramatic clarity; just looking out on the landscape, you'll find it impossible to know what year, or century, it is. It's no coincidence that many of Death Valley's topographical features

are associated with hellish images: Funeral Mountains, Furnace Creek, Dante's View, Coffin Peak, and Devil's Golf Course. But the valley can be a place of serenity as well.

Human nature being what it is, it's not surprising that people have long been drawn here to challenge the power of Mother Nature. The area's first foray into tourism was in 1925, a scant 76 years after the forty-niners' harrowing experiences. It probably would've begun sooner, but the valley had been consumed by lucrative borax mining since the late 1880s, when teamsters drove 20-mule-team wagons filled with borax through the dusty landscape. This white compound is used as a cleaning agent, preservative, and flux; in fireproofing; and as a water softener.

In one of his last official acts, Pres. Herbert Hoover signed a proclamation designating Death Valley a national monument in February 1933. With the stroke of a pen he not only authorized the protection of a vast and wondrous land but also helped to transform one of the earth's least hospitable spots into a popular tourist destination.

The naming of Death Valley National Monument came at a time when Americans were discovering the romance of the desert. Land that had previously been considered hideously devoid of life was now being celebrated for its spare beauty; places that had once been feared for their harshness were now being admired for their uniqueness.

In 1994, when U.S. President Clinton signed the California Desert Protection Act, Death Valley National Park became the largest national park outside Alaska, with more than 3.3 million acres. Though remote, it's one of the most heavily visited parks, and in the summer, you're likely to hear less English spoken than German, French, and Japanese.

Flora & Fauna. Most of Death Valley's climate zones are harshly limiting to plants and animals, but are diverse nevertheless. Within the park, elevations range from 282 feet below sea level (Badwater, the lowest point in the Western Hemisphere) to 11,049 feet above sea level (Telescope Peak, blanketed by snow during winter and early spring). Little sign of life is found at the lowest elevations; any groundwater is highly saline and supports only algae and bacteria. One notable exception is the unique and endangered **desert pupfish,** an ancient species that has slowly adapted to Death Valley's increasingly harsh conditions. You can see the tiny fish in the marshes of Salt Creek, halfway between Furnace Creek and Stovepipe Wells, where a boardwalk lined with interpretive plaques allows you an up-close look.

Hardy desert shrubs such as **mesquite, creosote,** and **arrowweed** flourish at the mouths of canyons, where enough fresh water is channeled from the mountains to support these miserly plants. You have to look closely to see the surprising number of small mammals and birds that live at the lower elevations (sea level to 4,000 ft.); **rabbits, rodents, bats, snakes, roadrunners,** and even **coyotes** all get by on very little water. At the higher elevations, where **pinyon** and **juniper** woodlands blanket the slopes, animals are more plentiful and can include **bobcats** and the elusive **bighorn sheep.** Above 10,000 feet, look for small stands of **bristlecone pine,** the planet's longest-lived tree; some specimens on Telescope Peak are more than 3,000 years old.

Avoiding the Crowds. You may think that no one would plan a vacation in a 120°F plus (49°C plus) remote desert, but Death Valley is full year-round. Summer is when primarily Europeans visit, and many are disappointed when the thermometer doesn't soar to record-breaking heat. North Americans tend to avoid the hottest season and crowd Death Valley on weekends and school holidays the rest of the year. December and January are the quietest months (with the exception of Christmas week and Martin Luther King Jr. Day weekend). The following advice will help ease the crush during your visit.

◆ Make all accommodations reservations as far in advance as you can, at least 2 or 3 months ahead. Facilities are limited inside the park, and Death Valley's isolation makes it time-consuming to locate elsewhere. Those planning to set up in one of the "first-come, first-served" camping areas should try to claim a site between 9am and noon.

◆ Avoid visiting on weekends and during school vacation periods, and plan to enjoy the most popular activities early in the day, since crowds start building up around 10am. An alternative, particularly on summer days, is to wait until crowds dissipate around 4pm. Remember, the sun doesn't set until after 7pm between June and September and it stays hot well past midnight.

◆ With the help of a high-clearance four-wheel-drive vehicle you'll find a whole world of hidden valleys and ghost towns, mountainous sand dunes, and remote canyons that are inaccessible to most of Death Valley's visitors. Check the Park Service's official map, where roads are clearly marked according to how passable they are.

Just the Facts

GETTING THERE & GATEWAYS

There are several routes into the park—all involve crossing one of the steep mountain ranges that isolate Death Valley. The most common access route from Los Angeles and points south is via Calif. 127 from I-15 at the town of Baker; from Death Valley Junction, Calif. 190 leads to the park's center. From Las Vegas, Nev. 160 and 372 lead to Shoshone at the intersection of Calif. 178 and 127, which is just 27 miles south of Calif. 190. Perhaps the most scenic entry is via Calif. 190 from the west, reached from Calif. 14 and U.S. 395 by taking Calif. 178 from Ridgecrest. To access the same route from the north, pick up Calif. 190 directly from U.S. 395 at Olancha. You can also approach the park from Nevada by taking Nev. 374 from Beatty, located on U.S. 95.

The Nearest Airport. The nearest airport is Las Vegas's **McCarran International Airport,** 5757 Wayne Newton Blvd. (✆ **702/261-5211;** www.mccarran. com), with regularly scheduled flights from practically all major airlines, and vehicles from all major rental agencies. See the appendix for toll-free phone numbers. In addition, **Allstate** (✆ **800/ 634-6186** or 702/736-6147) is a local company that rents standard cars and four-wheel-drive vehicles.

It's a 2½-hour drive from Vegas to Death Valley. A four-wheel-drive vehicle is recommended for backcountry travel, and you'll need one to access 2 of the 10 campgrounds (see "Camping," below).

INFORMATION

Contact the **Superintendent, Death Valley National Park,** Death Valley, CA 92328 (✆ **760/786-3200;** www.nps.gov/ deva). Be sure to pick up the official *Guide for the Visitor,* a newspaper-style free handout listing most of the park basics. It's available at ranger stations and the Furnace Creek Visitor Center (see below). Also, it's not a bad idea to ask a ranger about tips for avoiding heat exhaustion and on high-temperature auto care.

The **Death Valley Natural History Association,** P.O. Box 188, Death Valley, CA 92328 (✆ **800/478-8564**), operates the park bookstores; contact them for their latest publications list and catalog.

VISITOR CENTERS

Park headquarters are at the **Furnace Creek Visitor Center** (✆ **760/786-3200**), open daily year-round in Furnace Creek, 15 miles inside the eastern park boundary on Calif. 190. You'll find well-done interpretive exhibits and an hourly slide program as well as an extensive bookstore. There's also a museum, a bookshop, and an information center at **Scotty's Castle** (✆ **760/786-2392**), open daily year-round (see "Historic & Man-Made Attractions," below).

There are ranger stations that collect fees and can provide you with information at **Stovepipe Wells** (✆ **760/786-2342**) and **Grapevine** (✆ **760/786-2313**), as well as in Beatty, Nevada (✆ **775/ 553-2200**).

FEES

Entry into the park for up to 7 days costs $10 per car (or $5 per person on foot, motorcycle, or bike). Be sure to keep the receipt handy for the duration of your stay, since you'll be required to show it when passing the entry checkpoint near Scotty's Castle (Grapevine).

There are 10 campgrounds within park boundaries. Four are free; overnight fees elsewhere range from $10 to $16.

SPECIAL REGULATIONS & WARNINGS

It isn't called Death Valley for nothing, but there's little chance that you'll encounter any life-threatening situations, especially if you carefully follow commonsense safety tips. You'll find these and many more in brochures available at the park's visitor centers.

- **Always carry a supply of water for everyone,** including your car. Dehydration is your most urgent concern, particularly in summer, when temperatures routinely reach 120°F (49°C) and higher at the arid lower elevations. Recommended minimum amounts are 1 gallon per person per day and twice that if you're planning strenuous activity. Drink often, whether you feel thirsty or not, and be alert for the signs of dehydration: dizziness, headache, and cold, clammy skin. It's a good idea to stow several gallons for the car, even though radiator water is available from tanks placed at strategic points (uphill climbs) along the main roads.
- **Always carry sunscreen and protective clothing,** including a wide-brimmed hat and sunglasses.
- **When driving, turn off your air-conditioning** on uphill grades if your car begins overheating. In the event that your car overheats, keep the engine running and turn the car into the breeze. While the car idles, pour sufficient water over the radiator to cool it before removing the cap and refilling the radiator water.
- **Be alert for wildlife on the road** and don't let yourself be distracted by the scenery. Single-car accidents are the number-one cause of death in Death Valley, and they can occur summer or winter, daylight or nighttime. Many long miles of roads run through the park; though well paved, they often have sharp curves, dips, and steep downhill grades. If your tires wander off the edge of the pavement at high speed, don't jerk the wheel, which can cause you to skid out of control. Instead, gradually slow down until it's safe to bring all four tires back onto the road.

SEASONS & CLIMATE

Although Death Valley is undeniably one of the world's driest deserts, altitudes range from 282 feet below sea level to over 11,000 feet above; therefore, **desert** doesn't always equal **hot.** From June to September, temperatures in the valley can soar above 120°F (49°C), making the mountain sections of the park a welcome relief with temperatures in the 70s and 80s. But from November to February, when valley temperatures are comfortable in the 60s and 70s, many higher areas are frigid and snowy.

SEASONAL EVENTS

The weeklong **Death Valley 49'ers Encampment** is held the second week in November. It features a fiddlers' contest, a burro flapjack race, square dancing, tours, a Western art show, and a golf tournament. Contact the visitor center for current information.

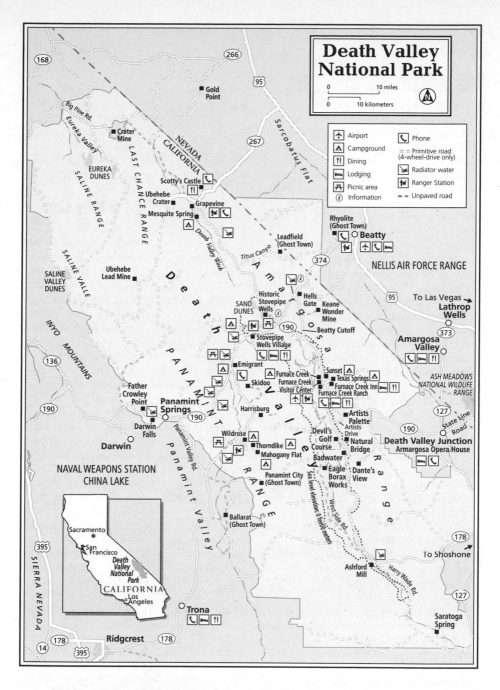

Death Valley National Park

✈ Airport	📞 Phone
△ Campground	== Primitive road (4-wheel-drive only)
🍴 Dining	🔧 Radiator water
🛏 Lodging	🏛 Ranger Station
🏕 Picnic area	-- Unpaved road
ⓘ Information	

If You Have Only 1 Day

The distances inside Death Valley National Park are enormous, so the following is merely a guideline. If there's a destination you don't want to miss,

you'll have to pass up some of the other sites in the interest of time.

If you have only 1 day and want to get a sampling of the park's best-loved spots, start at the **Furnace Creek Visitor Center,** located at the center of the action in

Furnace Creek (see "Visitor Centers," above). View the **slide show** (shown continuously throughout the day) for an overview of the park and a taste of the things you won't get a chance to see. This advice holds even for visitors with several days; there's always something you'll have to miss. Step over to the center's museum for a look at the 10-by-20-foot **relief map** of the park, which will give you a feel for where your destinations are in the context of the whole region, including the all-important elevation factor. If you have time, check out the tiny **Borax Museum,** housed in an old miners' boardinghouse at nearby Furnace Creek Ranch. Admission is free.

Scotty's Castle is a must-see for most people, but you need to plan ahead because of the popularity of ranger-guided house tours. Even if you want to explore only the grounds, remember that the castle is 53 miles north of Furnace Creek, an hour's drive each way. A good plan is to make the castle your first activity after breakfast, avoiding the crowds and freeing up the afternoon for seeing other sites or squeezing in a short hike. Easily reached spots are **Artists Palette, Harmony Borax Works, Badwater, Devil's Golf Course, Zabriskie Point,** and **Dante's View.**

If the weather is agreeable, replace one or two of these attractions with a short hike (such as **Mosaic Canyon, Sand Dunes,** or the **Salt Creek Nature Trail**)—for details, see "Day Hikes," below. Just after the junction where Calif. 190 turns west toward the Sand Dunes and Stovepipe Wells, you'll pass the **Devil's Cornfield,** where arrowweed bushes grow in unusual clumps resembling corn stalks. There's a turnout where you can park to view this strange landscape and plant, which got its name because American Indians used the stalks to make arrow shafts.

Because each gateway to Death Valley has its own features, visitors with time limitations can maximize their experience by choosing a different entrance and exit route. If you drove in on Calif. 127 through Death Valley Junction, try leaving via the scenic route west through the Panamint Valley. If you entered from the Panamint side, try following Calif. 178 south from Furnace Creek, across the Black Mountains and Greenwater Valley, to pick up Calif. 127 at Shoshone.

Exploring the Park by Car

Death Valley National Park is crisscrossed by a network of roads, ranging from washboard remnants of old mining days to well-maintained highways built during the 1930s. You'll find that most of the popular destinations, as well as the five major entry routes, have superior-quality roads suitable for all passenger vehicles as well as trailers and motor homes. One exception is the Emigrant/Wildrose Canyon pass between Calif. 190 and Calif. 178, sections of which are rough, narrow, and winding; vehicles over 25 feet are prohibited at all times, and other drivers may want to consult a ranger about current road conditions before attempting the unpaved section south of Wildrose.

The park is ideal for viewing by car. Conservationists are adamant that the parade of vehicles detracts from the valley's natural beauty and preservation, but this feature does help make the park more accessible to those with limited time to traverse the vast distances involved (and limited ability to withstand the often grueling weather). Some of the most beautiful sites have handy access roads, vista turnouts, or loop drives to facilitate viewing. These include **Artists Palette,** where the 9-mile one-way Artists Drive takes you through a colorful display hidden from the main road. Over millions of years, mineral deposits have created brilliant swaths of color across the low, rocky hills. There's a scenic overlook at the beginning of the drive as well as a parking area farther ahead in case you want to stop and scramble amid the pink, blue, red, orange, and green patches.

South of Artists Drive, Calif. 178 takes you past several of Death Valley's highlights, which best illustrate this environment of low-elevation extremes. **Devil's Golf Course,** accessible by a short spur of graded dirt road, sets your car right in the middle of a forbidding landscape created by salt and erosion on a lake bed that dried up about 2,000 years ago. The results are spikes, pits, craters, and jagged ridges stained brown and smoothed by human feet near the parking area; walk just 2 minutes in any direction and you'll see the salty white surface in its natural state.

About 5 miles south of this is **Badwater,** whose simple name indicates the lowest, hottest, and (curiously) wettest spot on the valley floor. At 279 feet below sea level, Badwater is the lowest spot in the park accessible by auto and is marked by permanent spring-fed pools. The water at first seemed like relief to early travelers—until they tasted the amounts of chloride, sodium, and sulfate. It isn't poisonous, however, and is home to beetles, soldier fly larvae, and a snail that slowly adapted to these harsh conditions.

A similar site is 25 miles north on Calif. 190: **Salt Creek,** home to the **Salt Creek pupfish,** found nowhere else on earth. You can glimpse this little fish, which has made some amazing adaptations to survive in this arid land, from a wooden boardwalk nature trail. In spring, a million pupfish might be wriggling in the creek; but by summer's end only a few thousand remain.

Your car will also take you all the way to two of the best lookout points around, both along Calif. 190 southeast of Furnace Creek. Before sunrise, photographers set up their tripods at **Zabriskie Point,** 5 miles southeast of Furnace Creek off Calif. 190, and aim their cameras down at the pale mudstone hills of Golden Canyon and the great valley beyond. The panoramic view is magnificent.

Another grand park vista is at **Dante's View,** located 25 miles south of Furnace Creek via Calif. 190 and Dante's View Road, a 5,475-foot point looking out over the shimmering Death Valley floor backed by the high Panamint Mountains.

Nearly everyone takes the scenic drive up Scotty's Castle Road to visit the park's major man-made attraction, **Scotty's Castle** (see below). While you're there, it's worth taking the 15-minute drive to **Ubehebe Crater,** 9 miles west of the Castle, the otherworldly pockmark from a volcanic explosion 3,000 years ago. You'll know that you're close when the landscape begins to darken from layers of cinders that were spewed from the half-mile crater. A convenient loop road takes you up to the most scenic lip. A few explanatory signs grace the parking area, and there's a hiking path (for those willing to brave the often-gusting winds) to an even more dramatic overlook and a field of smaller craters.

Organized Tours & Ranger Programs

In addition to providing hourly **Scotty's Castle** "Living History" tours (see below), Death Valley rangers keep busy giving lectures, group discussions, and film presentations. The topics are varied, and for those eager to get their shoes dusty, several hikes and guided walks are conducted seasonally, with themes such as Moonlight Meander and Canyon Secrets. Contact park headquarters for a seasonal schedule of day and evening events; nearly all programs (except for year-round Scotty's Castle tours) cease between mid-May and early October.

Historic & Man-Made Attractions

Scotty's Castle, the Mediterranean hacienda in the northern part of the park, is unabashedly Death Valley's premier attraction. Visitors are wowed by the elaborate Spanish tiles, well-crafted furnishings, and innovative construction with ahead-of-its-time solar water heating. Even more compelling is the colorful history of this villa in remote Grapevine Canyon, brought to life by park rangers dressed in 1930s clothing. Construction of the "castle"—more officially, Death Valley Ranch—began in 1922. It was to be a winter retreat for Chicago millionaire Albert Johnson. The insurance tycoon's unlikely friendship with prospector/cowboy/spinner-of-tall-tales Walter Scott put the $2.3-million structure on the map and captured the public's imagination. Scotty greeted visitors and told them fanciful stories from the early mining days of Death Valley.

The 50-minute guided tour of Scotty's Castle is excellent, both for its inside look at the mansion and for what it reveals about the eccentricities of Johnson and Scotty. Tours depart about every 20 minutes (hourly in the winter) from 9am to 5pm; they fill up quickly, so arrive early for the first available spots (there's an $8 fee for adults). During busy periods, you may have to wait an hour or more, perusing the gift shop or relaxing in the snack bar. There's also a self-guided walking tour (excluding the interiors); the pamphlet *A Walking Tour of Scotty's Castle* leads you on an exploration from stable to pool, from bunkhouse to powerhouse. Organized groups (only) can reserve tour times by calling © **760/786-2392.**

In 2000, Congress passed a bill that returned 7,000 acres (including about 300 in the Furnace Creek area) in and around the park to the Timbisha Shoshone, an American Indian tribe that inhabited the area for thousands of years before it became a national monument. This represents the first time that a tribal homeland has been established within the boundaries of a national park, and nearly 50 tribal members now live in the valley year-round. The bill banned casinos, but the future of the Timbisha Shoshone's homeland might include a cultural center, lodging, and homes

for tribal members. For up-to-date information, contact the **Timbisha Shoshone Tribe** at © **760/786-2374.**

For yet another side of the human experience here, visit the **Harmony Borax Works,** located 1 mile north of Furnace Creek off Calif. 190, via a short spur road and a very short trail—a rock-salt landscape as tortured as you'll ever find. Death Valley prospectors called borax "white gold," and though it wasn't exactly a glamorous substance, it was a profitable one. From 1883 to 1888, more than 20 million pounds of it were transported from the Harmony Borax Works, and borax mining continued in Death Valley until 1928. A short trail with interpretive signs leads past the ruins of the old borax refinery and some outlying buildings.

Transport of the borax was the stuff of legends, too. The famous 20-mule teams hauled the huge loaded wagons 165 miles to the rail station at Mojave. (To learn more about this colorful era, visit the Borax Museum at Furnace Creek Ranch, near the park visitor center.) Other remnants of human industry are the **Eagle Borax Works** ruins, 20 miles south of Furnace Creek via Badwater Road and the unpaved dirt West Side Road, and the **Wildrose Charcoal Kilns,** 39 miles south of Stovepipe Wells off Emigrant Canyon Road, where vast amounts of charcoal were manufactured for use on the lucrative silver mining in neighboring Panamint Valley. Located near the Wildrose campground, the road to the kilns is partially paved and precariously twisted; vehicles over 25 feet are prohibited.

Day Hikes

There are routes to suit all levels of expertise and at varying elevations. Wherever you hike, never forget to carry enough water; even in seemingly mild weather conditions, hikers can become dehydrated quickly. Park rangers can provide topographical maps, current weather conditions, and detailed directions to each trailhead.

SHORTER TRAILS

Eureka Dunes

1 mile RT. Moderate. Access: Located in the Eureka Sand Dunes National Natural Landmark Area, at the end of South Eureka Rd.

This area is approachable only from the remote north end of the park and by rutted dirt and gravel roads subject to washout, so travel to this area requires a sturdy vehicle in good condition. The dunes, however, are magnificent, the tallest and oldest in North America. The whole family will enjoy hiking here, spotting dune grass and wildflowers or the tracks of lizards and rodents. (Tread lightly, however, as this area is home to myriad endangered and threatened plant species.) The view from atop the highest dune (700 ft.) takes in the splendid contrast of creamy sand against the layer-cake band of nearby rock, and small avalanches of sand create the trademark "singing" peculiar to such dunes.

Keane Wonder Mine Trail

2 miles RT. Strenuous. Access: Located past the parking area and the old mill site; the mine is 20 miles north of Furnace Creek via Daylight Pass Cutoff and then after 3 miles of graded dirt road.

A rocky mountainous trail climbs steeply to the site of this successful gold mine, passing along the way the solid, efficient wooden tramway that carried ore out of the mountain. The trail obeys an old miner's adage that the best way up a mountainside is the straightest, even if the most strenuous—but you'll be rewarded with spectacular views of the park and substantial artifacts from the mining operation. The many mine tunnels and shafts are fascinating though potentially deadly; cave-ins, rattlesnakes, poisonous gases, and abandoned explosives lead the list of reasons

to keep your distance. If this hike seems too challenging, try the Keane Wonder Spring trail, below.

Keane Wonder Spring Trail

2 miles RT. Easy. Access: The trailhead leads away from the Keane Wonder parking area in a northerly direction, away from the steeper mine hike.

This trail undulates gently across an alluvial fan and follows the pipeline from the spring that supplied water for the gold-mining operation. The smell of sulfur and piping calls of birds signal your arrival at the spring, which lies slightly uphill of the trail. A short walk beyond leads to cabin ruins and a mine shaft.

Mosaic Canyon

2.4 miles RT. Moderate. Access: Located at the end of a short, graded dirt road just east of Stovepipe Wells via Calif. 190.

This short stroll requires a bit of rock scrambling into a canyon where water has polished the marble rock into white, gray, and black mosaics. The first mile is very easy, suitable for every skill level, and children will love running their hands over the water-smoothed rock walls. More adventurous climbers can continue up a series of chutes and dry waterfalls in the latter half of the hike.

Natural Bridge Canyon

1 mile RT. Moderate. Access: Located 15 miles south of Furnace Creek via Badwater Rd. and a 2-mile unpaved spur road suitable for passenger vehicles.

This short walk takes you into a colorful narrow canyon. The loose gravel underfoot makes for a tiring walk, but it's less than 0.5 mile to the distinctive formation that gives the canyon its name: a rock bridge overhead, formed when rushing waters cut through softer lower layers.

Salt Creek Nature Trail

0.5 mile RT. Easy. Access: Salt Creek is located 14 miles north of Furnace Creek via Calif. 190 or 13 miles east of Stovepipe Wells, then down a 1-mile graded dirt spur road.

A leisurely hike on a wooden boardwalk leads you along the unique salt marshes, passing a myriad of unusual plants along the way. In the spring, watch also for the amazingly adaptive Salt Creek pupfish flashing about in the shallow water.

Sand Dunes

2 miles RT. Easy. Access: 3 miles north of Calif. 190 via Scotty's Castle Rd.; it's indicated with a signed turnoff and has picnic tables and a restroom.

Although not as majestic as the remote Eureka Dunes in northern Death Valley, these golden mounds off Scotty's Castle Road are easy to reach and fun to romp around on. There's no formal trail—simply explore to your heart's content; kids especially will enjoy a barefoot romp on the fine sand dotted with stands of mesquite. Don't forget an adequate supply of water; in the midday sun, the dunes get very hot.

Titus Canyon

3 miles RT. Easy. Access: Located up a signed dirt road off Scotty's Castle Rd. (about 15 miles north of Calif. 190) that leads to the mouth of Titus Canyon, where a road for 4WD vehicles continues through to Nev. 374; the trail begins at the point where the road becomes one-way coming toward you (from Nevada).

As you hike, watch for vehicle traffic coming one-way from the other direction. The canyon's rock walls are an amateur geologist's dream—layers of orange and black volcanic sediment streaked with threads of gleaming white calcite. Though you can augment this easy hike by continuing through the canyon, there's a broad pullout from

the road at 1.5 miles; it's a good place to enjoy the view, and perhaps a picnic, before returning the way you came.

Little Hebe Crater Trail

1.5 miles RT. Moderate. Access: The trailhead leads up from the parking area for Ubehebe Crater, which is 7 miles northwest of the Grapevine Ranger Station.

You get to the crater via a steep but plain trail that leads from the parking area, up to the crater's lip, around some of the contours, and past several lesser craters. Black cinders and volcanic fragments cover the desolate countryside surrounding Ubehebe Crater, which erupted as recently as 1,000 years ago. Fierce winds can hamper your progress, but you'll get an exhilarating feeling, as though you're visiting another planet. High-top boots or shoes are recommended for the pebbly path.

LONGER TRAILS

Golden Canyon Trail

4.6 miles RT. Easy to moderate. Access: The parking lot for Golden Canyon along Calif. 178, about 2 miles south of the Furnace Creek Inn.

This trail's proximity to Furnace Creek, plus its varying degrees of difficulty, make it especially popular. Start by hiking along the once-paved route that allowed cars to drive into the canyon, but was destroyed by flash flooding. Soon you'll be scrambling around the "badlands," yellowed hills of mud and silt deposited by ancient lakes. Those with more stamina can continue past towering Manly Beacon (a sandstone formation), across gullies and washes, and then steeply up to Zabriskie Point for panoramic views of the forbidding badlands. *Note:* If you hike beyond Manly Beacon, be sure to pick up a map at one of the park's visitor centers—it is extremely easy to lose your bearings in this area.

Grotto Canyon

4 miles RT. Moderate to strenuous. Access: 2½ miles east of Stovepipe Wells on Calif. 190.

This route is marked by deep "grottos" in the rocks (smooth hollows formed by erosive floodwaters). The first mile follows a rugged gravel road up the canyon's alluvial fan; if you have an off-road vehicle, drive this portion as far as the wash. Continue on foot from there, as the canyon narrows and you begin to encounter the grottos, beyond which waterfalls trickle. The cool hidden grottos are a nice place to stop for a snack, sheltered from the sun.

Jayhawker Canyon

4.2 miles RT. Moderate. Access: Off Calif. 190, just west of the Emigrant Ranger Station.

This obscure, out-of-the-way route follows the path of a desperate group of pioneers attempting to find a way out of Death Valley in 1849. The footing is treacherous in this debris-filled canyon, and several forks and tributaries can distract you from staying in the main wash. At the end of the route lies a spring marking the Jayhawkers' camp, also a popular stopping place for the native Shoshone. Boulders in the area are marked with petroglyphs depicting bighorn sheep, along with the initials of several pioneers scratched into the rocks.

Telescope Peak Trail

14 miles RT. 8,130 ft.–11,049 ft. Strenuous. Access: Mahogany Flat Campground, past the Wildrose Charcoal Kilns (only experienced drivers with high-clearance 4WD vehicles should attempt the road).

A grueling 3,000-foot climb ultimately leads to the 11,049-foot summit, where you'll be rewarded with the view described thusly by one pioneer: "You can see so far, it's just like looking through a telescope." Snow-covered in winter, the peak is best climbed from May to November. Consult park rangers for current conditions and detailed advice—and *never attempt this climb alone*.

Wildrose Peak Trail

8.4 miles RT. 6,890 ft.–9,060 ft. Strenuous. Access: Wildrose Charcoal Kilns, usually accessible by passenger vehicles (check with park rangers for road conditions).

Mostly comprised of steady and unrelenting ascents, this steep hike has several level portions for rest stops. And you'll need them since you'll be climbing over 2,000 feet on the way to the 9,060-foot summit. Marvelous views along the way present the stark Panamint Range, a bird's-eye view of Death Valley, and panoramas of the Sierras on the western horizon. It's unwise to attempt this hike in winter or without obtaining a topographical map from the ranger station.

Other Sports & Activities

Biking. Because 94% of the park is federally designated wilderness, cycling is allowed only on roads used by motor vehicles and not on hiking trails. Weather conditions between May and October make bicycling at the lower elevations dangerous at times other than early morning.

There are no bike rentals available in the park, and given the park's isolation, the only practical option is to bring your own. You'll need a pretty rugged mountain bike to do most of these routes.

Good choices are **Racetrack** (28 miles one-way), **Greenwater Valley** (30 miles one-way, mainly level), **Cottonwood Canyon** (20 miles one-way), and **West Side Road** (40 miles one-way, fairly level with some washboard sections). **Artists Drive** is 9 miles long, paved, with some steep uphill stretches. A favorite is **Titus Canyon** (28 miles on a one-way hilly road—it has some very difficult uphill and downhill stretches).

Camping

Death Valley offers little variety to those seeking conventional accommodations, but campers (tent, trailer, and RV) can expect to find similar comforts to most other desert parks. You should take special care, however, when selecting a campground. Although most locations are closed seasonally to protect visitors from the harshest elements (only five campgrounds are open year-round), there's always a risk of unseasonably hot temperatures at the none-too-shady campgrounds on the valley floor, as well as early or late snow at remote mountain sites. Always inquire with the park ranger about current conditions before setting up camp.

Emigrant Campground is located 9 miles southwest of Stovepipe Wells on Calif. 190. **Furnace Creek Campground** (which has $40 group sites, which can be reserved), located just north of the Furnace Creek Visitor Center, has showers nearby (for a fee) from a strained water supply. (During peak times, there are quotas.) **Mahogany Flats Campground,** 38 miles south of Stovepipe Wells, off Trona-Wildrose Road, can only be reached by four-wheel-drive vehicle. It has pit toilets but no other facilities. **Mesquite Spring Campground** is 5 miles south of Scotty's Castle on Grapevine Road. The **Panamint Springs Resort** (✆ 775/482-7680), located 30 miles west of Stovepipe Wells on Calif. 190, operates a commercial campground with 40 spaces (12 with RV utility hookups) for $25 per night for full RV hookups ($15 for dry RV sites), and $12 for a tent campsite. **Stovepipe Wells Campground** has 190 spaces with 14 RV hookups and pay showers, charging $10 for a campsite or $22 if you want an RV utility hookup.

The huge **Sunset Campground,** located just ¼ mile east of the Furnace Creek Ranch, has nearby showers (from a limited supply, for a fee). **Texas Spring,** in the same area as Sunset Campground, has 92 sites and 2 group sites. The fee is $12 per site for an individual site. **Thorndike Campground,** which is 37 miles south of Stovepipe Wells and 1 mile from Mahogany Flats Campground, off the Trona-Wildrose Road, is accessible only by four-wheel-drive vehicle. It has eight primitive campsites with pit toilets but no other facilities.

Campground	Elev.	Total Sites	RV Hookups	Dump Station	Toilets	Drinking Water	
Emigrant	2,100	10	No	No	Yes	Yes	
Furnace Creek	−196	136	No	Yes	Yes	Yes	
*Mahogany Flat**	8,200	10	No	No	Yes	No	
Mesquite Spring	1,800	30	No	Yes	Yes	Yes	
Panamint Springs Resort	N/A	40	12	No	Yes	Yes	
Stovepipe Wells	Sea level	190	14	Yes	Yes	Yes	
Sunset	−190	1,000	No	Yes	Yes	Yes	
Texas Spring	Sea level	92	No	Yes	Yes	Yes	
*Thorndike**	7,800	6	No	No	Yes	No	
Wildrose	4,100	23	No	No	Yes	Yes	

* Road not passable for trailers, campers, or motor homes. Passenger cars not advised; four-wheel-drive vehicle may be necessary.

Wildrose Campground, located 30 miles south of Stovepipe Wells off the Trona-Wildrose Road, has pit toilets and drinking water.

Campsite **reservations** for Furnace Creek and the group sites at Texas Spring are available from the **National Park Reservation Service** at © **800/ 365-CAMP** (2267) or online at **http:// reservations.nps.gov.** Payment can be made by Discover Card, MasterCard, Visa, check, or money order. For reservations at privately owned **Panamint Springs,** call © 775/482-7680.

Where to Stay

INSIDE THE PARK

Furnace Creek Inn

Calif. 190, 1 mile south of Furnace Creek Visitor Center (P.O. Box 1), Death Valley, CA 92328. © **760/786-2345.** www.furnacecreekresort. com. 66 units. A/C TV TEL. Oct–May $240–$365 double; closed mid-May to mid-Oct. AE, DC, DISC, MC, V.

The Furnace Creek Inn is exceptional and exceptionally expensive, a 1920s resort whose charm has been successfully preserved. Like an oasis in the middle of stark Death Valley, the inn's red-tiled roofs and sparkling, spring-fed pool hint at the elegance within, where the deluxe rooms and suites have every modern amenity. Stroll the lush palm-shaded gardens before sitting down to a meal in the elegant dining room, where the food is excellent but the formality—no jeans, shorts, or T-shirts at dinnertime—a bit out of place for such a rugged location. Tennis on lighted courts and nearby golf and horseback riding are available; there's even a shuttle from the Furnace Creek private airstrip. *Note:* The property was expected to be closed during summer 2004, but it could well reopen during the summer months in 2005. If it does, look for lower rates in summer.

Furnace Creek Ranch

On Calif. 190, adjacent to the Furnace Creek Visitor Center (P.O. Box 1), Death Valley, CA 92328. © **760/786-2345.** Fax 760/686-2514. www. furnacecreekresort.com. 224 units. A/C TEL. $105–$174 per unit. AE, DC, DISC, MC, V.

Though the Furnace Creek Ranch is run by the same folks who maintain the

Showers	Fire Pits/ Grills	Laundry	Public Phone	Reserve	Fees	Open
No	No	No	Yes	No	No	Year-round
Nearby (fee)	Yes	Nearby	Yes	Yes**	$10–$16/$40	Year-round
No	Yes	No	No	No	No	Mar–Nov
No	Yes	No	No	No	$10	Year-round
Yes	Yes	No	Nearby	Yes	$12/$25	Year-round
Nearby (fee)	Yes	No	Yes	No	$10/$22	Oct–Apr (full hookups year-round)
Nearby (fee)	No	No	No	No	$10	Oct–Apr
Nearby (fee)	Yes	No	Yes	No	$12	Oct–Apr
No	Yes	No	No	No	No	Mar–Nov
No	Yes	No	No	No	No	Year-round

** Reservations can be made Oct 15–Apr 15 only.

elegant Furnace Creek Inn, the ranch is more down to earth, with rustic cottages and motel rooms that are great for families. Amenities include a spring-fed pool, the world's lowest 18-hole golf course, tennis and basketball courts, a playground, and a selection of dining options (see below).

Panamint Springs Resort

Calif. 190, 30 miles west of Stovepipe Wells (P.O. Box 395), Ridgecrest, CA 93555. © **775/ 482-7680.** www.deathvalley.com. 14 units, 1 cottage. A/C. $65–$79 double, $139 cottage. DISC, MC, V.

The privately owned Panamint Springs Resort, across the Panamint Range and about a 45- to 60-minute drive west from Furnace Creek, is a bit off the beaten path, not just geographically but also philosophically. A welcome change from the touristy overtones of Death Valley, this truly charming rustic motel has plain but clean rooms as well as a full-service restaurant that serves breakfast, lunch, and dinner. Featuring traditional American fare, dinner is priced at $10 to $24.

Stovepipe Wells Village

Calif. 190 at Stovepipe Wells, Death Valley, CA 92328. © **760/786-2387.** Fax 760/786-2389. 83 units. A/C. $75–$95 double. AE, DC, DISC, MC, V.

The truly budget-conscious opt for Stovepipe Wells Village, where 83 modest air-conditioned motel rooms (sans phones and TVs) surround a small pool. About 23 miles northwest of Furnace Creek, Stovepipe Wells has a general store, Internet kiosk, saloon, and dining room (see below). The rates are the same year-round, and rooms have two twin beds, two double beds, or one king.

NEAR THE PARK

Because accommodations in Death Valley are limited, you might consider the money-saving (but inconvenient) option of spending a night in one of the gateway towns. **Lone Pine,** on the west side of the park, is a good choice, with a wide selection of lodging and great Western views and charm. **Beatty, Nevada,** and **Shoshone, California,** both have inexpensive lodgings. Each is about an hour's drive from the park's center, but accommodations are limited to unremarkable motels. In Death Valley Junction, the restored **Amargosa Opera House and Hotel** (© **760/852-4441;** www.amargosa-opera-house.com) offers 14 air-conditioned rooms in a historic out-of-the-way place, 30 miles from Furnace Creek. Credit cards (AE, MC, V) are accepted, and room rates are $45 to $60 double. Operas are staged on Saturdays from October to May, with additional shows on Mondays from February through March.

Where to Dine

INSIDE THE PARK

There aren't many restaurants inside the park, and most of them serve basic American fare, but here's a rundown.

There are three dining options at the **Furnace Creek Ranch,** all relatively informal. The best and most economical is the **Forty Niner Cafe,** a diner with better-than-average food and a widely varied menu. It's open daily from 7am to 9pm. The adjacent **Wrangler Steakhouse** offers an all-you-can-eat buffet for breakfast (6–9am) and lunch (11am–2pm). The prices are higher than average, but the buffet is a good choice for families with hearty eaters. From 5:30 to 9:30pm, the Wrangler reverts to table service, grilling steaks, ribs, and other satisfying specialties; the servings are generous, but the dinners pricey. At the golf course, the **19th Hole Bar & Grill** serves sandwiches and pub fare from October to May. All these places accept major credit cards (AE, DC, DISC, MC, V).

The dining room at the **Furnace Creek Inn** (© **760/786-2345**) is elegant, and the menu features elements of several continental and regional cuisines. The peaceful setting and attentive service can be a welcome (though pricey) treat during otherwise exhausting travels through the park. Breakfast, lunch, and dinner are served. The Sunday buffet brunch, served from mid-October to mid-May, is truly decadent. Reservations are necessary. The dining room serves breakfast and dinner year-round, but closes from 2:30 to 5:30pm daily and does not serve lunch from mid-May to mid-October. Major credit cards (AE, DC, DISC, MC, V) are accepted.

The restaurant at **Stovepipe Wells** (© 760/786-2604) is kind of a cross between a camp dining room and a casual cafe. It's open daily 7am to 2pm and 6:30 to 10pm and accepts major credit cards (AE, DC, DISC, MC, V). Other choices are a snack bar at **Scotty's Castle** and a rustic (and affordable) burgers-and-beer cafe at **Panamint Springs.**

Helpful hint: Meals and groceries are exceptionally costly inside the park because of its remote location. If possible, consider bringing a cooler with some snacks, sandwiches, and beverages to last the duration of your visit. Ice is easily obtainable, and you'll also be able to keep water chilled.

NEAR THE PARK

Too far away for a round-trip excursion once you're in Death Valley, **The Mad Greek** (© 760/733-4354) in Baker is a restaurant you must stop at on the way there or home. At the junction of I-15 and Calif. 127, this roadside treasure is an ethnic surprise beloved by many. White tiles and Aegean-blue accents complement a menu of traditional Greek specialties such as souvlaki, spinach-and-feta spanakopita, stuffed grape leaves, green salad with tangy feta, exquisite pastries, and even Greek beer. The mile-long menu also includes traditional road fare, such as hamburgers and hot sandwiches.

Picnic & Camping Supplies

Within park boundaries, **Furnace Creek Ranch** has a market carrying a fairly wide selection of groceries and ice; propane is available at the adjacent service station. **Stovepipe Wells** offers ice, limited groceries, propane, and white gas.

Outside the park, if you want to stock up before entering, groceries and supplies are available in the towns of **Baker, Beatty, Shoshone, Pahrump,** and **Ridgecrest.** For visitors approaching on U.S. 395 from the south, Ridgecrest is your best choice—it's a sizable city with chain grocery stores, fast-food restaurants, and a selection of gas stations. If you're coming from Las Vegas, however, the booming **Pahrump** is the place to stop, with a pair of good-sized grocery stores to fill most travelers' needs.

A Nearby Desert Wonderland: Mojave National Preserve

To most Americans, the eastern Mojave is that vast, bleak, interminable stretch of desert to be crossed as quickly as possible along California's I-15 and I-40. But just southeast of Death Valley National Park, this national preserve is what many consider to be the crown jewel of the California desert.

This is a hard land to get to know—it has no accommodations or restaurants, few campgrounds, and only a handful of roads suitable for the average passenger vehicle. But hidden within this natural fortress are some true gems—its 1.6 million acres include the world's largest Joshua tree forest; abundant wildlife; spectacular canyons, caverns, and volcanic formations; tabletop mesas; and a dozen mountain ranges.

It's ironic that the eastern Mojave owes much of its appearance to water—canyons carved by streams, mineral-encrusted dry lake beds, and mountains whose colorful layers represent sandstone deposited in ancient oceans—for today the landscape is distinguished primarily by its extreme dryness. The climate changed dramatically following the end of the last ice age, about 10,000 years ago; around this time the first humans are believed to have migrated into the area. Lakes fed by glacial runoff supported fish, mammoths, camels, and diverse vegetation. When traditional food such as bison and antelope diminished, the inhabitants adapted a lifestyle better suited to the arid climate, ultimately relying on small game and plants.

The European invasion started in the 18th century, when Spanish missionaries and explorers ventured north from Mexico; but in the 19th century American pioneers arrived, crossing the Mojave on their way west to the coast. Then in 1883 the railroad arrived, boosting existing mining and ranching operations.

By the 1970s, environmentalists had become gravely concerned with the region's protection. Destructive off-road use, the theft of rare desert plants, the plunder of archaeological sites, and the killing of threatened desert tortoises all endangered the delicate ecological balance. Then in 1994 President Clinton signed the California Desert Protection Act, creating Mojave National Preserve.

Thus far, the Mojave's elevated status hasn't attracted hordes of sightseers, and devoted visitors are happy to keep it that way. Unlike a fully protected national park, the national preserve designation allows hunting, and continued grazing and mining within the preserve's boundaries are sore spots for ardent preservationists.

Flora & Fauna. There's much more life in the Mojave Desert than the human eye can immediately discern. Many animals are well camouflaged and/or nocturnal, but if you tread lightly and keep your eyes sharpened, the experience is rewarding. Wildlife includes the hopping kangaroo rat, ground squirrels, cottontails and jackrabbits, bobcats, coyotes, lizards, snakes, and the threatened desert tortoise. Consider

yourself lucky to spot elusive bighorn sheep or shy mule deer. Migrating birds that stop off in the Mojave are met by permanent residents such as quail, pinyon jays, sparrows, noisy cactus wrens, and the distinctive roadrunner.

You're certain to see familiar desert plants such as the fragrant creosote bush, several varieties of cacti (including the deceptively fluffy-looking cholla, or "teddy bear"), and several strains of yucca. On and around Cima Dome grows the world's largest and densest **Joshua tree forest.** Botanists say that Cima's Joshuas are more symmetrical than their cousins elsewhere in the Mojave. The dramatic colors of the sky at sunset provide a breathtaking backdrop for Cima's Joshua trees, some more than 25 feet tall and several hundred years old.

Other desert flora include therapeutic Mormon tea, cliff rose, aromatic blue sage, desert primrose, and cats-claw; these flowering plants are among many that make the spring wildflower season a popular time to visit. Junipers, seed-bearing pinyons, and scrub oaks are found in the preserve's higher elevations.

JUST THE FACTS

Getting There. I-15, the major route between Los Angeles and Las Vegas, extends along the northern boundary of the preserve. I-40, the major route between southern California and Arizona, is the southern access route.

Common entry points include **Kelbaker Road,** which bisects the preserve from Baker at the north, through Kelso in the south. There are Kelbaker exits from both I-15 and I-40. The **Essex Road** exit from I-40, 25 miles east of Kelbaker Road, is the access point for **Providence Mountains State Recreation Area** (Mitchell Caverns) and two other campgrounds. The **Cima Road** exit from I-15 in Mountain Pass leads into the center of the preserve.

The town of **Nipton,** technically outside preserve boundaries but a common

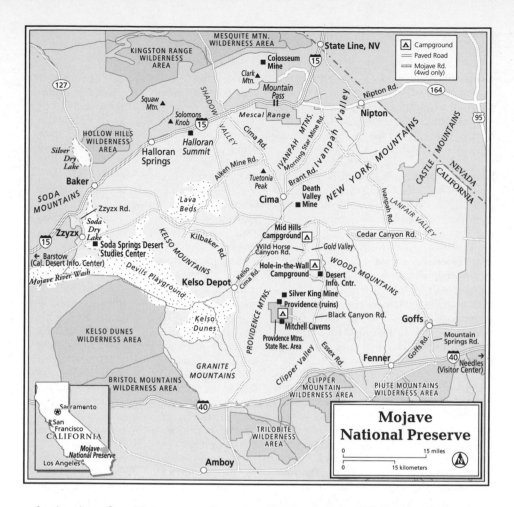

Mojave National Preserve

destination for Mojave travelers, is reached via Nipton Road from I-15, within sight of the Nevada border.

The nearest airport is Las Vegas's **McCarran International,** discussed earlier in this chapter.

Information & Visitor Centers. Contact the **Superintendent, Mojave National Preserve,** 222 E. Main St., Suite 202, Barstow, CA 92311 (✆ **760/255-8801;** www.nps.gov/moja).

The best source for up-to-date weather conditions and a free map is the **Mojave National Preserve-Baker Information Center,** 72157 Baker Blvd. (under the "World's Tallest Thermometer"), Baker, CA 92309 (✆ **760/733-4040),** which offers a superior selection of books. Additional information and maps are available inside the preserve at the **Hole-in-the-Wall**

Ranger Station (✆ **760/928-2572),** generally open weekends from 10am to 2pm (as staffing allows).

Fees & Warnings. Entry into the preserve is free. Campsites cost $12. A constant threat in the desert is **dehydration.** Rangers recommended drinking 1 gallon of water per person per day, or twice that if you're planning strenuous activity.

Seasons & Climate. Mojave National Preserve's 1.6 million acres lie in the high desert, with elevations from 1,000 feet to nearly 8,000 feet. Although December to February can be windy and cold with a dusting of snow, summers often see blistering temperatures exceeding 100°F (38°C). The best time to visit is between March and May, when temperatures are mild and wildflowers are in bloom. October and November have comfortable weather and very few visitors. The area gets precious little rainfall, but what does occur (usually during winter) can begin suddenly and cause flash flooding.

Seasonal Events. Best between February and May, the **wildflower viewing** is dependent on weather conditions such as rainfall, sunshine, and temperatures, but you can bet on seeing the brilliant blooms somewhere in the preserve each year. The information centers can help direct you to the flowers currently in bloom, and 24-hour recorded information on prime viewing sites is available between March and May from the **Payne Foundation Wildflower Hot Line** at ✆ **818/768-3533;** or online at **www. theodorepayne.org.**

EXPLORING THE MONUMENT BY CAR

At the risk of discouraging you from leaving your car to really experience the Mojave, we must admit that **Kelbaker Road** provides an excellent opportunity to sample the preserve with a minimal expenditure of time or trouble. The well-paved two-lane road, bisecting the preserve north to south between I-15 and I-40, takes about 1 hour one-way without stops.

You'll drive through the eerie blackened landscape of **lava beds** and **cinder cones,** visit the elegant but empty **Kelso Depot,** and see the towering golden mounds of **Kelso Dunes.** This 45-square-mile formation of magnificently sculpted sand dunes is famous for its "booming," a low rumble emitted when small avalanches or blowing sands pass over the underlying layer. Geologists speculate that the extreme dryness of the East Mojave Desert, combined with the wind-polished, rounded nature of the sand grains, has something to do with the musicality. Sometimes the low rumbling resembles a Tibetan gong; other times it sounds like a 1950s doo-wop musical

group. After the Kelso Dunes you'll end your trip with views of the **Granite Mountains,** where erosion has removed all but the most resilient chunks of extraordinarily hard rock, leaving piles of rosy-hued boulders that are alternately smooth and jagged.

Leading northeast from Kelso Depot, the **Kelso-Cima Road** provides another scenic diversion, running alongside railroad tracks to the tiny town of **Cima** (Spanish for "summit"), at the foot of a geological oddity called **Cima Dome,** an almost perfectly rounded landform rising 1,500 feet above the desert. The dome is a batholith, created by molten rock that, unlike its volcano cousin, stopped rising below the surface. This unusual formation is blanketed by majestic Joshua trees. The community of Cima consists of a tiny U.S. post office and a ramshackle market. (Don't be fooled by its boarded-up appearance.) Be prepared for the many heart-stopping dips in the Kelso-Cima Road; they're a favorite with young back-seat passengers.

Visitors with four-wheel-drive vehicles or especially rugged two-wheel drives can explore the **Wildhorse Canyon Road,** looping from Mid Hills to Hole-in-the-Wall, at the preserve's heart. In 1989, this short route was declared the nation's first official "Backcountry Byway," an honor that federal agencies bestow on America's most scenic back roads. The 11-mile horseshoe-shaped route crosses wide-open country dotted with cholla and, in season, delicate purple, yellow, and red wildflowers. Dramatic volcanic slopes and flat-top mesas tower over the low desert.

ORGANIZED TOURS & RANGER PROGRAMS

The Park Service holds evening ranger programs intermittently at Hole-in-the-Wall campground, but they're excellent and worth planning a stop around. These programs might include talks on the endangered desert tortoise or the area's violent geological history, or an evening slide program. Guided walks and hikes are also offered, such as guided hikes to Kelso Dunes or Banshee Canyon. Contact one of the information centers listed above for the current schedule.

The only organized attraction is **Mitchell Caverns,** contained in a state recreation area within the national preserve. Rangers lead regular tours of these rock rooms, where you'll see marvelous stalactites, stalagmites, and other limestone formations, plus archaeological artifacts from the area's early human inhabitants. The caves, which maintain an almost constant temperature of 65°F (18°C), provide a welcome respite during hot weather. Tours are given daily between Labor Day and Memorial Day weekdays at 1:30pm, and weekends/holidays at 10am, 1:30pm, and 3pm. In summer, tours are Saturday and Sunday only at 1:30pm. Cost is $3 for adults, $1 for kids 6 to 16, and free for those under 6. Tours are limited to 25 people and fill quickly, so arrive early to ensure a spot. For information, call ✆ **661/942-0662.** *Note:* Additional tours are often added without notice during periods of high demand. To check last-minute schedules or find out whether a particular tour is sold out, call the visitor center (✆ **760/928-2586**).

HISTORIC & MAN-MADE ATTRACTIONS

In the days of steam trains, the town of Kelso was a critical watering spot for locomotives. Built in 1924, the elegant **Kelso Depot** is Spanish Revival style, with the requisite red-tile roof and graceful arches. At its peak, during World War II, the town supported 2,000 residents, and the depot's diner, the **Beanery,** served customers 24 hours a day. Once slated for demolition, the Kelso Depot is now boarded up, but the National Park Service is refurbishing the building for use as the preserve's visitor center; the dedication is slated for fall 2004.

Skirting the preserve's northern boundary is the charming whistle-stop town of **Nipton.** Founded in 1885, Nipton was a true ghost town nearly a century later, when Los Angeles transplants Jerry and Roxanne Freeman began restoring its dilapidated buildings. At its height, Nipton was at the center of Mojave industry, providing railroad access for miners and ranchers, and silent film star Clara Bow was a frequent visitor. Call ✆ **760/856-2335** for additional information on Nipton.

At the preserve's western boundary, on the shores of the stark white Soda Dry Lake, is **Soda Springs/Zzyzx** (a cryptic name, pronounced *zeye*-zix, that's puzzled generations of motorists). Reached by taking the Zzyzx Road exit from I-15 and carefully negotiating a 4-mile rocky dirt road, the springs have a colorful history. In addition to being an important watering hole for those crossing the desert, the site was an American Indian camp, a military outpost, a wagon station, the headquarters of a Hollywood radio evangelist, and a once-trendy health resort (sporting the fanciful name of Zzyzx Mineral Springs). The springs are still active, feeding the elegant pools left over from the resort's heyday and supporting an entire ecosystem of wildlife at the lake bed's edge. You can stroll among the buildings, now used by the California State University's Desert Studies Center, and learn more about the area's history at an unstaffed visitor center.

Throughout the preserve are remnants of the historic **Mojave Road,** a popular 19th-century wagon route to the West Coast. Check with preserve rangers for tips on where to find sections of the old road.

DAY HIKES

In addition to the preserve's marked and maintained hiking trails, many hikers create their own routes using the abundant dirt roads crisscrossing the area. Some are so poor that they're passable only by high-clearance off-road vehicles, so there's little or no traffic.

There are several good hiking areas along **New York Mountains Road,** west of Ivanpah Road (itself unpaved and rough), an area of mine ruins, ranch structures, and cool pine-studded canyons. Several sections of the historic **Mojave Road** are also great for hiking but can be reached only by four-wheel-drive vehicles; remains of a wagon route stretch from Piute Wash beyond the eastern boundary of the preserve, through Cedar Canyon and past the lava beds, all the way to Zzyzx Springs on Soda Dry Lake at the western edge. When you're hiking in the backcountry, please respect private lands, which are not always well marked.

SHORTER TRAILS

Kelso Dunes Trail

3 miles RT (to the dunes). Moderate. Access: A parking area 8 miles south of the Kelso Depot.

These are the second-highest dunes in California, covering 45 square miles and reaching 700 feet high. The dunes are visible from Kelbaker Road, and 3 miles of graded dirt road lead to a parking area, where several interpretive signs give information on dunes ecology. Follow the trail out past the vegetation, then ramble to your heart's content, trying to spot examples of the many plants and animals that live in the seemingly barren dunes. Among them are rodents, kit foxes, lizards, sand verbena, and desert primrose, which color the dunes with brilliant blooms of yellow, white, and pink in springtime. *Note:* Climbing the soft dunes requires time and exertion, but tumbling back down is the fun reward.

Mary Beal Nature Trail

0.5 mile Easy. Access: Providence Mountains State Recreation Area Visitor Center, on Essex Rd., 16 miles northwest of I-40.

Suitable for all ages, the path winds past examples of the diverse plant and animal life found in the Mojave. Named for a prominent naturalist who spent 50 years exploring this desert, the trail has numbered posts keyed to a brochure (25¢) from the visitor center.

LONGER TRAILS

Mid Hills/Hole-in-the-Wall Trail

2 miles RT to 8 miles one-way. Easy to strenuous. Access: Hole-in-the-Wall Picnic Area.

Stretching between the two campgrounds, this maintained trail can be hiked in part or full. The entire hike is a grand tour of canyons and tabletop mesas, large pinyon trees, and colorful cacti; it's an all-day, one-way undertaking if you can arrange a car shuttle, and is much more enjoyable in the downhill direction from Mid Hills to Hole-in-the-Wall. If you're not up for a long day hike, the 2-mile hike from Hole-in-the-Wall Campground to Banshee Canyon offers an easier alternative. From Hole-in-the-Wall, the initial segment of the trail offers the most adventure; climbers descend through a vertical chute in the rock using a series of metal rings. Even with handholds, the climb requires agility and concentration—don't try it if you have any doubts.

Teutonia Peak Trail

4 miles RT. Moderate. Access: On Cima Rd. between I-15 and the town of Cima.

This trail leads to an excellent view of Cima Dome, an unusual volcanic formation, from the top of Teutonia Peak (600 ft. higher than the trailhead), and to panoramic views of the surrounding desert. You'll walk among Joshua trees, Mojave yucca, and cholla "teddy bear" cactus. Near the summit, the trail is faint but marked with cairns—small piles of stones. This land is leased for grazing, and the hiking trail encounters two ranch gates: Be sure to close them as you pass through.

BIKING

Opportunities are as extensive as the preserve's hundreds of miles of lonesome dirt roads. The 140-mile-long historic **Mojave Road,** a rough four-wheel-drive route, bisects the preserve east to west and visits many of the most scenic areas in the East Mojave; sections of this road make excellent bike tours, but you'll definitely need a mountain bike. Prepare well—the Mojave's dirt roads are rugged routes surrounded by miles of desert wilderness. There are no bike rentals in the park.

CAMPING

There are three established campgrounds in the preserve, all open year-round on a first-come, first-served basis. None have showers, laundry facilities, or RV hookups, though the Hole-in-the-Wall Campground has a dump station.

The **Mid Hills Campground,** with 26 sites, is in a woodland of pinyon and juniper and offers outstanding views. It is located 35½ miles northwest of Essex, off Black Canyon Road. This mile-high camp is the coolest in the East Mojave. Pit toilets, fire grates, and drinking water are provided, but there are no public telephones. Cost is $12 per night.

Nearby **Hole-in-the-Wall Campground** is perched above two dramatic canyons, 25½ miles northwest of Essex, on Black Canyon Road, near the Mid Hills Campground. There are 37 sites for $12 per site per night. You'll find pit toilets, drinking water, public phones, fire grates, and a dump station.

Warning: The washboard dirt road between the Mid Hills and Hole-in-the-Wall campgrounds might be too jarring for many two-wheel-drive passenger cars.

The sites at **Providence Mountain State Recreation Area** (© 760/928-2586)

Especially for Kids

There's a lot for kids to enjoy in Mojave, from scrambling on sandy Kelso Dunes to exploring Mitchell Caverns, which resemble an *Indiana Jones* movie set. You can show them lava beds so similar to the moon's surface that U.S. astronauts once trained here, or make a contest of finding familiar shapes and profiles in the jagged Granite Mountains.

are adjacent to the Mitchell Caverns Visitor Center. There are only six first-come, first-serve sites, for $10 each per night. You'll find flush toilets, drinking water, public telephones, and fire grates.

A highlight of the East Mojave is camping in the open desert all by your lonesome; at press time **backcountry camping** was fairly unregulated, requiring no registration. Campfires are prohibited outside of designated fire grates; backcountry campers need to pack out all trash, and take care not to set up in a gully or dry wash subject to flash flooding. It's advisable to contact an information center before establishing camp. And please respect private lands.

In addition to the campgrounds in the preserve, 30 acres of camping space are available in a privately owned campground in Nipton, in the open desert beyond the town's historic B&B inn (double rates are about $70). Other facilities include hot tubs, showers, drinking water, two cabin tents ($60 per night), and four RV hookups ($20). For information call © **760/856-2335** or surf over to **www.nipton.com.**

14

DEVILS TOWER NATIONAL MONUMENT

by Don & Barbara Laine

RISING 1,267 FEET ABOVE THE BELLE FOURCHE RIVER BELOW, THE stone stump of Devils Tower greets visitors miles before they arrive. Established in 1906 by Pres. Theodore Roosevelt as the country's first national monument, Devils Tower is well off the beaten path in extreme northeast Wyoming, but it's well worth the trip.

Col. Richard I. Dodge, who commanded a military escort for a U.S. Geological Survey party that visited the Black Hills in 1875, is credited with giving the formation its name. In his book *The Black Hills,* written the year after his journey, Dodge described Devils Tower as "one of the most remarkable peaks in this or any other country."

The steep-sided mass of igneous rock rises abruptly from the grasslands and pine forests, and remains one of the Black Hills' most conspicuous geologic features. Movie buffs will recognize the tower as the landing site of an alien spaceship in Steven Spielberg's 1977 Oscar-winning film *Close Encounters of the Third Kind,* starring Richard Dreyfuss, François Truffaut, and Teri Garr.

Geology. Although the 50-million-year-old tower is composed of hard igneous rock, much of the other exposed rock within the 1,347-acre monument is made of soft sediments from the warm shallow seas of the Mesozoic era. These colorful bands of rock encircling the igneous core include layers of sandstone, shale, mudstone, siltstone, gypsum, and limestone.

The story of Devils Tower's geology is but one chapter in the history of the Black Hills. Even now, after extensive study and detailed geologic mapping, the origins of Devils Tower are still being debated by modern scientists. Of the several theories on the formation of the tower, the most popular suggests that it is the result of volcanic activity in the early Tertiary period, some 50 million years ago. Scientists believe that a mass of molten rock forced its way upward from below the surface of the Earth, forming an inverted, cone-shaped structure beneath layers of sedimentary rock in what is now northeastern Wyoming. As the molten rock slowly cooled, it cracked and fractured, creating one of the most striking features of the monument, its polygonal columns. Most of the columns are five-sided, but others are four- or six-sided. The largest columns measure 15

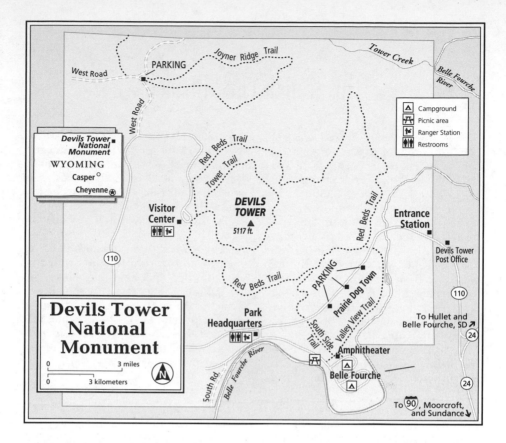

Devils Tower
National
Monument
WYOMING
Casper °
Cheyenne ⊛

Campground
Picnic area
Ranger Station
Restrooms

Joyner Ridge Trail

Tower Creek

Belle Fourche River

West Road

PARKING

West Road

Red Beds Trail

Tower Trail

DEVILS TOWER
▲
5117 ft.

Visitor Center

Red Beds Trail

110

Entrance Station

Devils Tower Post Office

Red Beds Trail

Red Beds Trail

PARKING

Prairie Dog Town

110

Devils Tower
National
Monument

0   3 miles
0   3 kilometers

Park Headquarters

South Side Trail

Valley View Trail

Amphitheater

Belle Fourche

To Hullet and Belle Fourche, SD ↗
24

South Rd.

Belle Fourche River

To ⑨⓪, Moorcroft, and Sundance ↓

24

---

to 20 feet in diameter at their base and gradually taper upward to about 10 feet in diameter at the summit.

Over centuries, the gentle waters of ancient streams and rivers carried away sedimentary layers, leaving the more erosion-resistant igneous rock behind. Today the tower appears to sit quietly on the crest of a wooded hill, but its base is actually the top of the unexposed magma, covered with fallen columns and soil.

American Indian Legend. American Indians have their own name for Devils Tower. The Lakota call it *Mato Tipila*, or Grizzly Bear Lodge, and descendants of several American Indian nations of the Great Plains share similar legends of how the prominent butte was formed.

According to the Kiowa version of the tale, seven sisters watch with horror as their brother is turned into a bear. The sisters run from him, to the stump of a large tree, which beckons them to climb on. (In other versions, they run to a large, flat stone.) When they do, the stump rises up into the sky, and the bear, unable to climb up the stump to reach the sisters, scores it with its claws. The sisters are then raised into the sky, becoming the seven stars of the Big Dipper.

What inspired the imagination of American Indians also attracts their reverence. In deference to the religious significance of the tower to many tribes, the National Park Service has requested that climbing of the tower be voluntarily suspended during the month of June so that ceremonies may be conducted without interference.

First Ascent. As a battle to preserve the monument from commercial encroachment was being waged in 1893, two local ranchers decided it was time someone made the first recorded climb to its summit.

Tips from a Park Insider

Former Devils Tower National Monument superintendent Deb Liggett has seen much of what the National Park Service has to offer. After a stint at Everglades National Park, she moved to the superintendent's post in northeastern Wyoming. In late 1997, the career Park Service employee transferred to Alaska. She says her 3½ years at Devils Tower will always stay with her: "I have a friend who says that Devils Tower is like a piece of sculpture—perfect in every light and from every angle. I think that's really true. The tower can be quite dramatic."

In 2002, more than 400,000 travelers visited this national monument—almost as many people as live in the state of Wyoming. Liggett says visitors, particularly photo buffs, prefer the light in early morning or at dusk. With the surrounding forest and decreased crowds, she notes that fall can be a perfect time to visit. Whenever you choose to stop at Devils Tower, she says you'll probably be pleased.

"The tower often creates its own shadows and its own weather, with terrific thunder and lightning storms in the summer," she says. "People often come to Devils Tower as a lark—as a quick trip between Rushmore and Yellowstone. I think they have a classic park experience. They are definitely pleasantly surprised by their discovery."

William Rogers and Willard Ripley planned for months before making their first attempt on the southeast face on July 4, 1893. As the date approached, the pair began distributing handbills offering such amenities as ample food and drink, daily and nightly dancing, and plenty of grain for horses. The flyers also touted the feat as the "rarest sight of a lifetime."

Rogers and Ripley used a wooden stake ladder for the first 350 feet of the climb. As more than 1,000 spectators watched, the pair made the harrowing climb in about an hour, raised Old Glory, then sold pieces of it as mementos of the occasion. Thereafter, the tower became a popular place for Independence Day family gatherings. At the annual affair in 1895, Mrs. Rogers used her husband's ladder to become the first woman to reach the summit.

On Top of the Tower. From its base, most visitors would surmise that the top of Devils Tower is a flat, barren pinnacle. As the 1,500 climbers who make it to the peak each year will attest, the top of the tower isn't that much different than the countryside that surrounds it— except that it's said you can see five states.

The summit is actually slightly domed with a few small outcroppings and is covered with prairie grasses, prickly pear cactus, currant and gooseberry bushes, and native big sage, thanks to prairie falcons and turkey vultures that nest in the tower's columns and deposit seeds on top. A number of animals also have been spotted on the crown of Devils Tower, including rattlesnakes, pack rats, and the cute red squirrels that have slithered and scampered up the cracks and fissures.

At the top, climbers may sign a register and record any unusual aspect or oddity of their adventure. More than 50,000 signatures have been gathered since records of tower climbs were first kept in 1937. In that time, climbers have used more than 220 routes to the top; in 1941 world-record holding parachutist George Hopkins jumped from an airplane to the cap of the tower, then lost his escape rope and was stranded on top for 6 days.

Avoiding the Crowds. Traffic patterns at the monument are similar to those of national park areas throughout the West. Expect the highest visitation from June through August, with lower visitation in the shoulder months of April to May and September to October; the lowest visitation is during winter. Parking is limited in summer.

If you visit during the summer, stop at the tower early in the day, or take in a fireside ranger talk when crowds have thinned in the evening. Be advised that each year during the second week in August a huge motorcycle rally takes place in nearby Sturgis, South Dakota. Attendance may significantly increase during that period.

Just the Facts

GETTING THERE & GATEWAYS

Because of its remote location, Devils Tower is best accessed by private vehicle. The monument entrance is 33 miles northeast of Moorcroft, Wyoming; 27 miles northwest of Sundance, Wyoming, via U.S. 14 (travel to the immediate area on I-90). Scheduled airlines serve Gillette, Wyoming (regional commuter service), and Rapid City, South Dakota, where cars may be rented. For information on the Rapid City airport and rental car options, see chapter 3, "Badlands National Park."

INFORMATION

Contact **Devils Tower National Monument,** P.O. Box 10, Devils Tower, WY 82714-0010 (© **307/467-5283;** www.nps. gov/deto). The **Devils Tower Natural History Association,** P.O. Box 37, Devils Tower, WY 87214-0037 (© **307/467-5283**), operates a bookstore at the monument's visitor center and offers a variety of publications.

VISITOR CENTER

Open from early April through late November only, the visitor center is located 3 miles from the monument's entrance, with exhibits about the tower's history and geology.

FEES

There is an entrance fee of $8 per vehicle or $3 per person on foot, motorcycle, or bike. Camping costs $12 per night.

SPECIAL REGULATIONS & WARNINGS

Do not feed, chase, or disturb prairie dogs; they bite and may carry diseases. Abandoned prairie dog holes are often homes to black widow spiders and rattlesnakes. Disturbing any wildlife or gathering items such as rocks or flowers is prohibited. Also see "Climbing the Tower," below.

SEASONS & CLIMATE

The monument is open year-round. The climate and seasons at Devils Tower echo those in the Black Hills region. Summer days can be hot and dry, although thunderstorms are not uncommon; evenings and early mornings are usually damp

A dark mist lay over the Black Hills, and the land was like iron. At the top of the ridge I caught sight of Devils Tower upthrust against the gray sky as if in the birth of time the core of the earth had broken through its crust and the motion of the world was begun. There are things in nature that engender an awful quiet in the heart of man; Devils Tower is one of them.

—N. Scott Momaday, Pulitzer Prize–winning author of *House Made of Dawn* and cool. Spring weather is often chilly and rainy, while in fall weather is often pleasant but can be cool, and often cold at night. Winters are usually cold, but snow and sunlight can combine to create incredible pictures of the landmark.

If You Have Only 1 Day

You can experience much of what Devils Tower has to offer in less than a day. Rangers recommend that you allow 2 to 4 hours to walk a trail, stop at the visitor center, and view the prairie dogs.

Surrounded by ponderosa pines and bathed in blue sky, the towering rock obelisk is visible for miles, and it's easy to imagine the reaction of the first lonely American Indian scouts and French fur trappers who stumbled upon this stunning geologic anomaly a few centuries ago.

Home to the feisty black-tailed **prairie dog,** the grounds of Devils Tower National Monument are perfect for picnicking and viewing wildlife. You can watch the sociable prairie dogs in their colony, or "town," just inside the park's east entrance station. The critters excavate elaborate networks of underground passageways, then guard their burrows with warning "barks" when predators such as hawks, eagles, bullsnakes, coyote, red fox, and mink come too close. Walk the leisurely **Valley View Trail,** or savor a picnic lunch among the wildflowers at the monument's picnic area on the banks of the sleepy Belle Fourche River.

Climbing the Tower

Climbers must register with a ranger before starting and upon their return; otherwise, there are no permits or requirements for climbing the tower. Be prepared for sudden storms; carry rain gear and a flashlight. Rockfall is common, so helmets are advised. Ask a ranger for additional safety and climbing information. A voluntary climbing ban is observed each June out of respect for American Indian religious ceremonies that are held on Devils Tower at that time.

Organized Tours & Ranger Programs

A variety of talks, walks, and other activities are scheduled, mostly in summer. Check at the visitor center for locations and times.

Interpretive Talks. Meet a park ranger in front of the visitor center for bear tales and interpretive talks about climbing, geology, and Tower trivia. Programs last about 20 minutes and are wheelchair accessible.

Tower Walk. Meet a park ranger in front of the visitor center and enjoy a lively walk as the sun rises above the tower. Good walking shoes and water are recommended. These guided walks last about an hour and a half and end on the Tower Trail (see "Day Hikes," below).

Evening Programs. Learn more about America's first national monument by the glow of a campfire. Join a park ranger in the monument's amphitheater each evening from Memorial Day through Labor Day. During inclement weather, programs may be moved to the picnic shelter.

Cultural Program Series. During the summer, Devils Tower plays host to scholars, artists, and performers who bring their expertise to the monument, including American Indian storytellers, musicians, historians, costumed interpreters, photographers, poets, and astronomers.

Day Hikes

Devils Tower will announce itself (through your windshield) miles before you arrive. In fact, you may drive to within a few hundred yards of the tower, but the real highlight of any visit to Devils Tower is the park's trails; get out and enjoy them. Pets are not allowed on trails.

The paved 1.3-mile **Tower Trail,** rated easy, goes all the way around the tower, offering close-up views of the tower on fairly level ground. Wayside exhibits tell the Devils Tower story.

There are several other trails: **Red Beds Trail,** 3 miles; **Southside Trail,** 0.6 mile; **Joyner Ridge Trail,** 1.5 miles; **Valley View Trail,** 0.6 mile (combine Southside and Valley View for 1.2 miles). Since none of the trails get very crowded, these are a good way to examine the terrain around the monument, including the pine forest and the prairie dog town, and avoid some of the summer crowds.

Camping

Located a mile from the monument's headquarters, **Belle Fourche Campground** is open from April through October. Its 30 sites accommodate RVs (up to 35 ft. long) and tents on a first-come, first-served basis. Each campsite has a cooking grill, table, and nearby drinking water. There are no showers, RV hookups, or dump station. Sites costs $12 per night, and there are three group sites, which cost $2 per person per night, with a six-person minimum. The adjacent Valley View Trail skirts a giant prairie dog town. The campground's amphitheater offers excellent interpretive ranger programs.

Those looking for a commercial campground with RV hookups, hot showers, and all the usual amenities will find the **Devils Tower KOA,** P.O. Box 100, Devils Tower, WY 82714 (© **800/KOA-5785** or 307/467-5395; www.devils towerkoa.com), just outside the monument entrance. Open from May through September, it offers 56 RV sites, 100 tent sites, and 11 camping cabins (which share two bathhouses and other campground facilities). Rates for two adults are $24 to $45 in hookup sites, $21 for tents, and $52 for cabins (DISC, MC, V). Amenities include a heated pool, self-service laundry, game room,

cafe, two gift shops, horseback rides, twice-weekly rodeos June through August, hayrides, and a nightly showing of *Close Encounters of the Third Kind,* which was filmed in part at Devils Tower.

Accommodations & Dining

There are no lodging facilities or restaurants within the monument boundaries.

NEAR THE PARK

Recommended in Sundance is the **Best Value Inn Bear Lodge,** 218 Cleveland St., on Wyo. 14 at Business Loop I-90 (P.O. Box 912), Sundance, WY 82729 (© **888/315-2378** or 307/283-1611; fax 307/283-2537). It offers 32 well-maintained basic motel rooms (all with TV, TEL, A/C), which rent for about $65 per night (double occupancy) during the summer and fall, and a bit less in winter and spring. Major credit cards (AE, DISC, MC, V) are accepted. A 32-ton native stone fireplace greets guests in the Western-style lobby, where you can have free coffee. Its location in the center of town, across the street from two restaurants and the community's museum, is convenient. Another good choice is the **Best Western Inn at Sundance,** 2719 E. Cleveland, at I-90 Exit 189 (P.O. Box 927), Sundance, WY 82729 (© **800/238-0965** or 307/283-2800; fax 307/283-2727), which offers everything you would expect from a top-notch Best Western, at rates of $79 to $109 in summer, and much lower prices from fall through spring.

There are two moderately priced restaurants, open year-round, across the street from the Best Value Inn Bear Lodge: **Aro Restaurant,** at 205 Cleveland St. (© **307/283-2000**), is open from 7am to 10pm in summer, with slightly shorter hours in winter. It serves a home-style American menu of sandwiches, burgers, and steak, plus a few Mexican dishes, with lunch prices from $2.50 to $6.95 and dinner prices from $5.95 to $17. At 101 N. 3rd

St., **Higbee's Café** (© **307/283-2165**) advertises "erratic" hours, but generally serves breakfast and lunch Monday through Friday, plus dinner on Wednesdays. It offers homemade soups and a variety of sandwiches, with most prices from $4.50 to $5.50, and breakfast is served anytime the restaurant is open.

In Hulett, try the **Motel Pioneer,** 3 blocks north of downtown on Wyo. 24, mailing address: P.O. Box 389, Hulett, WY 82720 (© **800/231-6335** or 307/467-5656; fax 307/467-5688; www.hulett.org/motelpioneer). Several units have kitchenettes or refrigerators. Double rates are about $50 year-round; major credit cards (AE, DISC, MC, V) are accepted. Rooms are clean and well maintained, and most have two beds—either two doubles or a double and a single. There are also two large family units with four beds each. Public tennis courts are next door, and a golf course is across the highway. It's 9 miles to the national monument entrance from here. A grocery store is located about 3 blocks from the motel.

15

GLACIER NATIONAL PARK & WATERTON LAKES NATIONAL PARK

by Jack Olson

MAJESTIC AND WILD, THIS VAST PRESERVE BECKONS VISITORS WITH stunning mountain peaks (many covered year-round with glaciers), verdant mountain trails that cry out for hikers, and a huge diversity of plant and animal life. Every spring, Glacier is a postcard come to life: Wildflowers carpet its meadows; bears emerge from months of hibernation; and moose, elk, and deer play out the drama of birth, life, and death. The unofficial mascot in these parts is the grizzly, a refugee from the high plains.

Here you'll see that nature is at work as well: The glaciers are receding (the result of global warming, some say) and avalanches have periodically ravaged Going-to-the-Sun Road, the curving, scenic 50-mile road that bisects the park. For the time being, the park is intact and very much alive, a treasure in a vault that opens to visitors.

Named in honor of the slow-moving glaciers that carved awe-inspiring valleys throughout this expanse of nearly 1 million acres, Glacier National Park exists because of the efforts of George Bird Grinnell, a 19th-century magazine publisher and cofounder of the Audubon Society. Following a pattern established with Yellowstone and Grand Teton, Grinnell lobbied for a national park to be set aside in the St. Mary region of Montana, and in May 1910 his efforts were rewarded. Just over 20 years later, it became, with its northern neighbor Waterton Lakes National Park in Canada, Glacier-Waterton International Peace Park—a gesture of goodwill and friendship between the governments of two countries.

If your time is limited, simply motor across Going-to-the-Sun Road, viewing the dramatic mountain scenery. Visitors with more time will find diversions for both families and hard-core adventurers; while some hiking trails are suitable for tykes, many more will challenge those determined to conquer and scale the park's tallest peaks. The park's lakes, streams, ponds, and waterfalls are equally engaging. Travelers board cruise boats to explore the history of the area; recreational types can fish, row, and kayak.

However, to truly experience Glacier requires slightly more effort, interest, and spunk than a drive through—abandon the pavement for even the shortest and easiest hiking trail and you'll discover a window into Glacier's soul.

Avoiding the Crowds. The simplest way to leave the crowds behind is to avoid visiting the park in its peak season, from mid-June to Labor Day (Aug is the busiest month). Late September and October, when the fall colors light up the park, are excellent months to visit. A highlight is the display put on by the larch trees throughout the western portions of the park. Entire hillsides turn a bright yellow, fading to a dull orange glow as the month of October wanes.

If visiting in the off season isn't possible, consider the following: Because most people congregate in close proximity to the major hotels, find a trailhead that is equidistant from two major points and head for the woods. If you must drive, to make the trip more enjoyable (and traffic-free), journey across the Going-to-the-Sun Road before 8:30am; you'll be astounded at the masterful job Mother Nature does of painting her mountains. You can always see more wildlife in the early morning (or just before dark).

Just the Facts

GETTING THERE & GATEWAYS

Glacier National Park is located in the northwest corner of Montana, on the Canadian border. The closest cities with airline service are **Kalispell,** 29 miles southwest of the park, and **Great Falls,** 143 miles southeast. If you're driving, the easiest ways to reach the park are from **U.S. 2** and **U.S. 89.**

Among the park's entrances are those at West Glacier, Camas Road, St. Mary, Many Glacier, Two Medicine, and Polebridge. Access is primarily at either end of Going-to-the-Sun Road: at West Glacier on the southwest side and St. Mary on the east.

From the park's western boundary, you may enter at Polebridge to access Bowman and Kintla lakes or take Camas Road to Going-to-the-Sun Road.

The following east-side entrances are primarily designed to access specific places and may not necessarily take you into the heart of the park: Essex, East Glacier, Two Medicine, Cut Bank, and Many Glacier.

Visitor entrance passes are sold at the West Glacier, Two Medicine, Many Glacier, Polebridge, and St. Mary Park entrances. Entrance is severely restricted during winter months when most of Going-to-the-Sun Road is closed. (See "Seasons & Climate," below.)

The Nearest Airports. Glacier Park International Airport, north of Kalispell at 4170 U.S. 2 (© **406/257-5994**), is serviced by Northwest, Delta, Big Sky, and Horizon; these airlines also serve **Great Falls International Airport** (© **406/727-3404**). Avis, Budget, Hertz, and Alamo/National have counters at Kalispell's airport; Hertz, Avis, and Alamo/National have counters at Great Falls International Airport; Enterprise and Budget will also deliver rental cars. Toll-free reservations numbers for airlines and car-rental companies are given in the appendix.

By Rail. Amtrak's Empire Builder (© **800/872-7245**), a Chicago-Seattle round-trip route, makes stops between May 1 and October 1 at East Glacier and year-round at West Glacier and Essex.

INFORMATION

Contact the **Superintendent, Glacier National Park,** West Glacier, MT 59936 (© **406/888-7800;** fax 406/888-7808; www.nps.gov/glac). A vast array of publications can be obtained from the **Glacier Natural History Association,** P.O. Box 310, West Glacier, MT 59936 (© **406/888-5756;** fax 406/888-5271; www.glacierassociation.org).

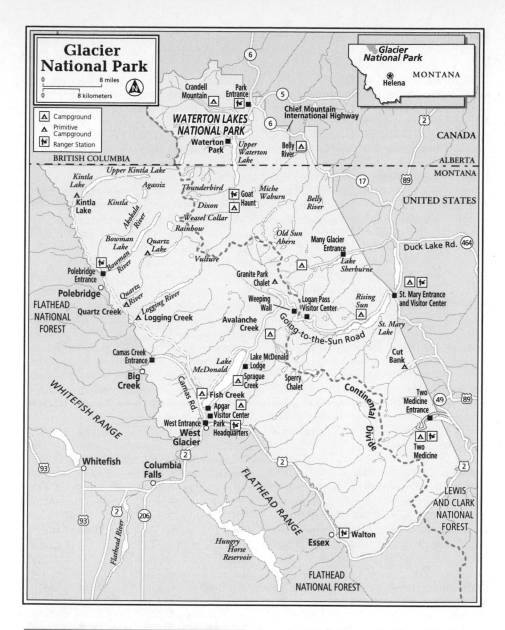

Glacier National Park

0   8 miles
0   8 kilometers

- △ Campground
- ▲ Primitive Campground
- ⌂ Ranger Station

Glacier National Park

MONTANA
Helena

WATERTON LAKES NATIONAL PARK

Crandell Mountain
Park Entrance
Chief Mountain International Highway

CANADA

Waterton Park
Upper Waterton Lake
Belly River

BRITISH COLUMBIA
ALBERTA
MONTANA

Upper Kintla Lake
Kintla Lake
Agassiz
Thunderbird
Goat Haunt
Miche Wahurn
Belly River

UNITED STATES

Kintla Lake
Kintla
Dixon
Weasel Collar
Rainbow

Akokala River
Bowman Lake
Quartz Lake
Vulture
Old Sun Ahern
Many Glacier Entrance

Duck Lake Rd. 464

Bowman River
Quartz River
Polebridge Entrance

Lake Sherburne

St. Mary Entrance and Visitor Center

Polebridge
Granite Park Chalet

FLATHEAD NATIONAL FOREST
Quartz Creek
Logging River
Logging Creek
Weeping Wall
Logan Pass Visitor Center
Rising Sun

Quartz River

Avalanche Creek
Going-to-the-Sun Road
St. Mary Lake

Camas Creek Entrance
Big Creek
Lake McDonald
Lake McDonald Lodge
Sprague Creek
Sperry Chalet

Cut Bank

WHITEFISH RANGE
Camas Rd.
Fish Creek
Apgar
Visitor Center
West Entrance
Park Headquarters
West Glacier

Continental Divide

Two Medicine Entrance

Two Medicine

Whitefish
Columbia Falls

FLATHEAD RANGE

LEWIS AND CLARK NATIONAL FOREST

Flathead River

Hungry Horse Reservoir
Essex
Walton

FLATHEAD NATIONAL FOREST

VISITOR CENTERS

For up-to-date information on park activities, check in at visitor centers located at Apgar, Logan Pass, and St. Mary; a center staffed by info-givers from Travel Alberta is located at **West Glacier**. St. Mary is open from mid-May through mid-October; **Logan Pass,** from mid-June through mid-October; and **Apgar,** from late April through October (and weekends during the winter). Park information may also be obtained from the **Two Medicine, Polebridge,** and **Many Glacier** ranger stations or park headquarters.

FEES

A vehicle pass good for 7 days costs $20. An individual pass for walk-ins and bike riders, also good for 7 days, is available for $5. An annual park pass costs $25. A separate entrance fee is charged for visitors to Waterton Lakes National Park.

Camping fees are $12 to $17 per night at the park's drive-in campgrounds.

SPECIAL REGULATIONS & WARNINGS

Biking. Bikes are restricted to established roads, bike routes, or parking areas, and are not allowed on trails. Restrictions apply to the most hazardous portions of Going-to-the-Sun Road during peak travel times from around mid-June to Labor Day; call ahead to find out when the road will be closed to bikers. During low-visibility periods of fog or darkness, a white front light and a back red reflector are required.

Boating. Although boating is permitted on some of Glacier's lakes, motor size is restricted to 10 horsepower on most. A detailed list of other regulations is available at park headquarters and staffed ranger stations. Park rangers may inspect or board any boat to determine regulation compliance.

Fishing. A fishing license is not required within the park's boundaries; however, there are guidelines, so check with rangers at visitor centers or ranger stations for regulations. Also, keep in mind since the eastern boundary of the park abuts the Blackfeet Indian Reservation, you may find yourself fishing in their territorial waters. To avoid a problem, purchase a $10 use permit from businesses in the gateway towns; the permit covers fishing, hiking, and biking in the reservation. Fishing outside the park in Montana waters requires a state license; check in at a local fishing shop to make certain you're within the laws.

Horses. Although visitors may bring their own horses and pack animals into the park, restrictions apply to private stock. A free brochure detailing regulations regarding horseback riding is available from the Park Service.

Vehicles. RVs and other vehicles longer than 21 feet or wider than 8 feet are prohibited on the 24-mile stretch of Going-to-the-Sun Road between Avalanche Campground and Sun Point on St. Mary Lake. Snowmobiling is prohibited in the park.

SEASONS & CLIMATE

Glacier is magnificent at any time of the year, but some roads are closed and park access is limited in the winter. By far the most popular time to visit is during the summer, when Going-to-the-Sun Road is fully open; in summer months sunrise is around 5am and sunset is nearly 10pm, so you have plenty of time for exploring. The shoulder seasons of spring and fall are equally magnificent, with budding wildflowers and variegated leaves and trees, but these sights can only be viewed from the park's outer boundaries and a limited stretch of the scenic highway.

In winter, Glacier shuts itself off from much of the motorized world. The Going-to-the-Sun Road, which is generally fully open only from early June to mid-October, is usually plowed from West Glacier to the head of Lake McDonald. U.S. 89 provides access to the St. Mary area. The North Fork Road from Columbia Falls is open for winter travel to the North Fork area and the Polebridge Ranger Station. Temperatures sometimes plummet to -30°F (-34°C), so appropriate dress for those conditions is essential.

If You Have Only 1 Day

If you have a limited amount of time to spend in Glacier, the best way to experience the park's full beauty is to drive **Going-to-the-Sun Road,** the 50-mile road that bisects the park between West Glacier and St. Mary. Points of interest are clearly marked and correspond to the park brochure, *Points of Interest Along the Going to the Sun Road,* available at visitor centers.

Remember that the road gains more than 3,400 feet in 32 miles, and is very narrow in places. Visitors with a fear of heights might consider a guided van tour (see "Organized Tours & Ranger Programs," below).

Just a short drive from West Glacier is **Lake McDonald,** the largest body of water in the park, and numerous turnouts along the way present opportunities to photograph the panoramic views of the lake with its mountainous backdrop. **Sacred Dancing Cascade** and **Johns Lake** are visible by taking an easy 0.5-mile hike from the roadside through a red cedar/hemlock forest. You'll often see moose and waterfowl. The **Trail of the Cedars** is a short, wheelchair-accessible boardwalk trail thickly carpeted in vibrant, verdant hues. All hiking trails mentioned below are described in the "Day Hikes" section.

Almost exactly halfway along Going-to-the-Sun is **The Loop,** an excellent vantage point for views of **Heaven's Peak.** Just 2 miles farther is the **Bird Woman Falls Overlook,** an outlook for falls located across the valley. **The Weeping Wall,** a wall of rock that does, in fact, weep groundwater profusely in the summer, is a popular subject for photographers.

At the 32-mile mark from West Glacier is **Logan Pass,** one of the park's most highly trafficked areas and the starting point for the hike to **Hidden Lake,** one of the park's most popular. There's a visitor center here, atop the Continental Divide.

As you head downhill, you'll reach the turnout for **Jackson Glacier,** the most easily recognizable glacier in the entire park, followed by **Sunrift Gorge** and **Sun Point,** which are accessible via two short trails that present opportunities to view wildlife.

Exploring the Park by Car

Because of the massive mountains that surround visitors to Glacier National Park, it is impossible to drive through the park without drawing comparisons

Picnicking Tips

The best picnicking spot on the Going-to-the-Sun Road is at **Sun Point,** which is also the trailhead for the 1.6-mile round-trip to Baring Falls, a trail that follows the shoreline of the lake. From the picnic area the views across the lake to the mountains are unrivaled. Even better: Be there at sunrise.

to Grand Teton. Perhaps the most significant difference is that here one drives among the mountain peaks; at Teton the mountains are viewed from a distance, unless you're willing to head for the hiking trails.

Going-to-the-Sun Road is by far the most driver-friendly avenue on which to enjoy the park and see some of the more spectacular views. Consult the previous section, "If You Have Only 1 Day," for an idea of what you'll see along this road.

You can easily circumnavigate the lower half of the park in 1 long day, without traveling at warp speed. Along the way, you'll experience Glacier's splendor and get a bird's-eye view of Big Sky country in the process. After a leisurely breakfast in West Glacier, you'll be in East Glacier in plenty of time for lunch at the Glacier Park Lodge (see "Where to Stay," later in this chapter) and at St. Mary or Many Glacier for dinner. To complete a counterclockwise loop from West Glacier, take U.S. 2 along the park's southern boundary to Essex and East Glacier, then north to St. Mary.

The road between West Glacier and East Glacier, which is approximately 57 miles, is a well-paved, two-lane affair that winds circuitously around the western and southern edges of the park and follows the Middle Fork of the Flathead River. In the summertime, the fluorescent orange blobs you'll see on the river below are inner tubes and white-water rafts filled with the hordes that travel the river every summer. As you descend to the valley floor, you'll drive through beautiful, privately owned Montana ranch- and farmland. Shortly after entering the valley, look to the north and admire the park's massive peaks—spires as beautiful as any on the planet. The Goat Lick parking lot, on U.S. 2 just east of Essex, gets you off the beaten path and provides a view into a canyon carved by the Flathead River; if you have time, take the short hike down to the stream.

Beyond East Glacier, as you head northwest on Mont. 49 and west toward Two Medicine, you'll notice that the earth appears to fall off. The contrast is inescapable—mountains tower in the west, but to the east the Hi-Line begins, sporting a horizon that extends so far and so flat as to seemingly lend credence and legitimacy to the Flat Earth Society. But round a corner on the Two Medicine Road and suddenly you'll find yourself faced with three mountains (Appistocki Peak, Mt. Henry, and Bison Mountain) bare of vegetation but as red as their Southwest counterparts. The difference here is that the crevasses are filled with snow, even in mid-August. Ten miles later, continuing the route northward on U.S. 89, you'll come across a wide panorama of mountain peaks, valleys, ridges, and forested mountains that truly characterize Glacier's personality. Conclude the bottom half of your long loop by winding downward from these high elevations to the village of St. Mary. Not a bad day's drive!

There are two ways to see the park's western boundary and to access the Polebridge area, in the north; one is slow and uncomfortable, the other slightly faster and less uncomfortable. The **North Fork Road** (Mont. 486) from Columbia Falls takes about an hour to negotiate. It's a sometimes-paved (mostly gravel and pothole-filled) stretch that follows the North Fork of the Flathead River; spectacular views ameliorate the condition of the drive. Not much is there besides water

and scenery, but the area around Polebridge is a popular spot for the outdoor crowd—an excellent location to experience Montana's natural beauty without modern-day distractions such as telephones and TVs.

The **Inside North Fork Road,** just north of Apgar, also runs to Polebridge. However, it's totally unpaved, takes an hour longer, and is much harder on driver, passenger, and equipment. Unless you are a glutton for punishment, take the faster route and spend that extra hour relaxing on a riverbank.

Organized Tours & Ranger Programs

Ranger-guided activities and evening campfire and slide-show programs are offered daily throughout the park. The park's *Glacier Explorer* publication—free upon entering the park and also available at visitor centers—is a thorough source for days, times, and locations of various educational programs. Local tribal members provide programs highlighting **American Indian culture and history.** Most programs are free, although those including boat trips may include a minimal charge.

Glacier Park Boat Co. offers narrated boat tours from Lake McDonald, St. Mary, Two Medicine, and Many Glacier from mid-June to mid-September. These "scenicruises" combine the comfort of an hour-long lake cruise with a short hike or picnic to create an unforgettable Glacier experience. Spectacular views of Lake McDonald sunsets, the awe-inspiring Grinnell Glacier, and the panoramic rugged cliffs ringing St. Mary Lake are just a few of the possible photo opportunities you may have while enjoying a cruise. The boats typically depart every hour, usually seven times each day (although schedules are subject to change in late season or if the weather is inclement), and ticket prices top out at $12. For a complete listing of prices and departure times, contact

Glacier Park Boat Co., P.O. Box 5262, Kalispell, MT 59903 (℄ 406/257-2426; www.glacierparkboats.com). Listed below are seasonal phone numbers for cruises at the following locations: **Lake McDonald** (℄ 406/888-5727), **Many Glacier** (℄ 406/226-4467), **Two Medicine** (℄ 406/732-4480), and **St. Mary** (℄ 406/732-4430).

Unique **"Jammer" coach tours** are given along Going-to-the-Sun Road and north to Waterton. Thirty-three classic bright-red coaches from the 1930s, long identified with Glacier, are now in service after a restoration project that began in 1999. Their drivers provide insightful commentary about the park and its history, and you don't have to worry about how close you may be to the edge of the often-precipitous road! For schedules, contact **Glacier Park Inc.** (℄ 406/892-2525).

Historical-cultural 25-passenger **motor coach tours** of the Going-to-the-Sun Road conducted by knowledgeable guides from the Blackfoot Nation originate from East Glacier, Browning, and St. Mary. The reasonable rates start at $40 for a 6-hour trip. Contact **Suntours** (℄ 800/786-9220).

Scenic **helicopter tours** of Glacier are offered by **Eagle Aviation** (℄ 406/755-2612), **Glacier Heli Tours** (℄ 800/879-9310), and **Kruger Helicopters** (℄ 406/387-4565). Prices are $90 and up, depending on the destination, length of the trip, and the number of passengers. All are located within 2 miles of West Glacier off U.S. 2.

The **Glacier Institute** conducts field classes in the summer that examine Glacier's cultural and natural resources. These 1- to 5-day courses include instruction, transportation, park fees, and college credit. Instructors are highly skilled in their area of expertise, bringing to each course an intimate knowledge of the region and subject matter. The classroom is Glacier National Park and—during the park's off season—other areas in northwest

Photo Tips

The adventurous shutterbug will find that the best photo ops occur early in the morning, regardless of location. Near bodies of water, the sunrise provides an unrivaled multitude of oranges, blues, and yellows. Then, as the earth warms, lakes are transformed to fog-covered valleys, creating a mystical photographic opportunity.

One of the most picturesque spots is the west end of St. Mary Lake; not only does sunrise paint the lake orange and yellow, it paints the mountains red and orange. A close runner-up is the view west from an overlook across St. Mary Lake to Wild Goose Island in the foreground and the peaks and glaciers at the west end of the lake. Logan Pass, when it's carpeted with wildflowers, is not to be missed.

Late-day photos of the Garden Wall from west of Logan Pass are also very dramatic.

Montana. Previous courses have covered alpine wildflowers, Glacier's grizzlies, weather systems, and nature photography. Contact the institute for a copy of their current catalog at 137 Main St., P.O. Box 7457, Kalispell, MT 59904 (℄ 406/755-1211; www.glacier institute.org). Prices range from $50 to $400 per course.

Finally, **Glacier Wilderness Guides,** P.O. Box 330, West Glacier, MT 59936 (℄ 800/521-RAFT for reservations, or 406/387-5555; fax 406/387-5656; www. glacierguides.com), organizes backpacking trips into the Glacier National Park backcountry. They have been the exclusive backpacking guide service in the park since 1983. See "Exploring the Backcountry," below.

Day Hikes

With more than 700 miles of maintained trails, the park is best explored by hiking. Because most of these trails are rather short, you might also wish to check out "Exploring the Backcountry," below. Many of the longer trails described there can be done fully (or at least partially) in a day, and are likely to take you farther off the beaten path and away from the crowds.

Trail maps are available at outdoor stores in Whitefish and Kalispell as well as at visitor centers and the major ranger stations at each entry point. **Glacier Park Inc.** (© **406/892-2525**) operates a **hiker's shuttle** that makes regular stops at popular trailheads.

Before striking off into the wilderness, however, check with the nearest visitor center or ranger station to determine the accessibility of your destination, trail conditions, and recent bear sightings. It can be a bummer when, 10 miles into the trip, a ranger turns you back.

The Park Service asks you to stay on trails to keep from eroding the fragile components of the park. Also, snowbanks shouldn't be traversed, especially the steeper ones. You should have proper footwear and rain gear, enough food, and, most important, enough water, before approaching any trailhead. A can of **pepper spray** can also come in handy when you're in grizzly habitat (if you plan on hiking in Canada, be sure the bear spray is

> Give a month to this precious reserve. The time will not be taken from the sum of your life. Instead of shortening, it will indefinitely lengthen it and make you truly immortal.
>
> —John Muir, naturalist and conservationist

USEPA-approved). Contact **Canadian Customs** (© **204/983-3500** or 506/636-5064) for regulations. See "Exploring the Backcountry," below, for further relevant information.

LAKE MCDONALD AREA

Trail of the Cedars Nature Trail

0.25 mile RT. Easy. Access: Across from the Avalanche Campground Ranger Station.

This level trail, consisting of a wheelchair-accessible boardwalk, offers a respite from the crowds in a forested area. There are interpretive signs along the way.

Trout Lake

8.4 miles RT. Moderate. Access: North end of Lake McDonald, 1½ miles west on Lake McDonald Rd.

This is a good workout if you're moping around Lake McDonald Lodge sipping coffee and skipping rocks off the lake. This hike is straight up and straight down. The trail takes you from the north end of Lake McDonald to the foot of Trout Lake and back.

LOGAN PASS AREA

Hidden Lake Nature Trail

1.5 miles one-way. Easy to moderate. Access: Logan Pass Visitor Center.

This trail climbs 460 feet and requires more spunk than others in the area, yet it's still not too hard. It's a popular trail, but if you hike all the way to the lake, you'll be able to avoid some of the crowds. This is an interpretive nature trail, with several signs along the way that point out what you are seeing.

The Loop

8 miles RT. Moderate. Access: Along Going-to-the-Sun Rd., about halfway between Avalanche Campground and Logan Pass Visitor Center.

Not considered easy mainly because of its altitude gain, The Loop is a popular hiking trail that winds up to Granite Park Chalet and back. Many people use it as a continuation of the Highline Trail, but this is the section to do if you're short on time (the Highline Trail is 7.6 miles one-way to the chalets, but not nearly as steep as the Loop). If you want to spend the night in one, contact **Glacier Wilderness Guides** for reservations (℡ **800/521-7238**). (See the descriptions of the chalets under "Camping," below.)

Sun Point Nature Trail

1.4 miles RT. Easy. Access: 9 miles west of St. Mary at Sun Point parking area.

This walk on gentle slopes presents commanding views of Baring Falls.

MANY GLACIER AREA

Iceberg Lake

9.5 miles RT. Moderate. Access: Starts at a trailhead in a cabin area east of the Swiftcurrent Coffee Shop and Campstore.

This beautiful hike traverses flower-filled meadows to a jewel of a high lake backed against a mountain wall. Even in summer, there may be snow on the ground and ice floating in the lake. Look for mountain goats or bighorn sheep on the cliffs above. And, as in many of the park's backcountry areas, keep an eye out for the grizzlies.

Swiftcurrent Lake Nature Trail

2.4 miles RT. Easy. Access: Picnic area ½ mile west of the hotel turnoff.

This is a fun hike along the shore, through the woods, and near a marsh, so you may see deer and birds—keep an eye out for blue grouse. If you have time, continue on the trail as it circles Lake Josephine, another easy hike, adding 2.8 miles to the trip. Dramatic Mount Gould towers above the far end of the lake. Midsummer wildflowers can be spectacular. A longer, 10.4-mile round-trip trail to Grinnell Glacier, the park's largest, is also accessed from this area.

TWO MEDICINE AREA

Appistoki Falls

1.2 miles RT. Easy. Access: The Mt. Henry Trailhead.

This trail, with an elevation gain of only 260 feet, climbs through a forest of fir and spruce, then runs along Appistoki Creek before ending at an overlook that provides views of a scenic 65-foot waterfall.

Running Eagle Falls

0.3 mile one-way. Easy. Access: 1 mile west of the Two Medicine entrance.

Hardly even a hike, the easiest trail in the area is to Running Eagle Falls along a path that winds through a heavily forested area to a large, noisy waterfall. The path is wheelchair-accessible.

Twin Falls Trail

3.8 miles one-way. Easy. Access: Two Medicine Campground.

The most popular hiking path in this area is the one to Twin Falls, which originates at the campground. Hikers may walk the entire distance to Twin Falls on a clearly identified trail, or boat across Two Medicine Lake to the foot of the trailhead, and hike the last mile.

Exploring the Backcountry

Depending upon your point of view, negotiating the backcountry may translate to a leisurely stroll or a tortuous experience in the high country. Choices range from 4-mile day hikes to multiday treks, so you'll need to consider your experience and fitness level before heading out. Then, locate a park map that presents trails and campsites in the area you want to explore.

Backcountry campgrounds have maps at the entrance to show you the location of each campground, the pit toilet, food preparation areas, and, perhaps most important, food storage areas. In addition, you can obtain a free loan of bear-resistant food containers at most backcountry permit issuing stations. If you fish while camping, it's recommended you exercise catch-and-release to avoid attracting wildlife in search of food. If you eat the catch, be certain to puncture the air bladder and throw the entrails into deep water at least 200 feet from the nearest campsite or trail. When backpacking in Glacier, especially in the high country, it's important to remember to pack as lightly as possible and make sure you're aware of the trail's degree of the ascent. And remember the cardinal rule: Pack it in, pack it out. No exceptions.

Wherever you decide to go, remember that you must secure a backcountry permit before your trip. Advance reservations can be made (© 406/888-7800).

A Guided Backcountry Trip. Many folks like to stand back and let someone else make all the arrangements, leaving themselves free to concentrate on the hiking experience itself. If this seems like your kind of trip, then you may wish to consider the services of **Glacier Wilderness Guides,** the exclusive backpacking guide service in Glacier National Park. For a price, they will put together any kind of trip; they have several regularly scheduled throughout the season, from the end of June through the beginning of September. These include a 3-day "taste" of the park for $315 per person, and an entire week in the wilderness for $630 per person. Add $10 per day if you want them to provide a backpack, tent, sleeping bag, and pad. Custom trips run $130 a day per person, with a four-person minimum. They'll even organize a trip where you spend the day hiking and the night cuddled in a comfy inn inside the park or in the Granite Park Chalet (see "Camping," below).

Their main office is located 1½ miles west of West Glacier on U.S. 2. (A second office is in West Glacier itself, behind the Glacier Highland Motel, across from the Amtrak depot.) For information and reservations, contact the company at P.O. Box 330, West Glacier, MT 59936 (© **800/521-RAFT** for reservations, or 406/387-5555; fax 406/387-5656; www.glacierguides.com).

KINTLA LAKE AREA

Kintla Lake to Upper Kintla Lake

12 miles one-way. Moderate. Access: Kintla Lake Campground.

Skirting the north shore of Kintla Lake above Polebridge for about 7 miles, before climbing a couple hundred feet, this stretch of the Boulder Pass hike is a breeze. However, once you hit Kintla Creek you may want to reconsider going any farther. With 12 miles under your belt at this point, climbing 3,000 feet may not seem like a great idea. The trail, once it breaks into the clear, offers views of several peaks, including Kinnerly Peak to the south of Upper Kintla Lake.

POLEBRIDGE AREA

Bowman Lake

7.1 miles one-way. Moderate. Access: Bowman Lake Campground; follow Glacier Rte. 7 to Bowman Lake Rd., just north of Polebridge, then follow the signs to Bowman Lake Campground.

This trail (14 miles to Brown Pass) is similar to the Kintla Lake hike in difficulty, and, like the Kintla Lake Trail, passes the lake on the north. After a hike through rolling hills sheathed in foliage, the trail climbs out of reach for anyone not in top shape, ascending 2,000 feet in less than 3 miles to join the Kintla Lake Trail at Brown Pass. A left turn takes you back to Kintla Lake (23 miles), a right takes you to Goat Haunt at the foot of Waterton Lake (9 miles).

Quartz Lake

12 miles RT. Moderate. Access: Bowman Lake Picnic Area; cross the bridge over Bowman Creek and you're on your way.

The loop runs up and over an 1,800-foot ridge and down to the south end of

Lower Quartz Lake. From there it's a level 3-mile hike to the west end of Quartz Lake, then it's 6 miles back over the ridge farther north (and higher up) before dropping back to Bowman Lake. An interesting aspect of this trail is evidence of the Red Bench Fire of 1988, which took a chunk out of the North Fork area.

LOGAN PASS AREA

Highline Trail

11.9 miles one-way (including The Loop). Moderate. Access: Granite Park Chalet.

This relatively easy hike gains a mere 200 feet in elevation over 7.6 miles. It begins at the Logan Pass Visitor Center and skirts the Garden Wall at heights of over 6,000 feet to Granite Park Chalet. Give yourself plenty of time for the return hike to Logan Pass. Or, rather than retracing your steps, continue on from the chalet to The Loop, the aptly named section of Going-to-the-Sun Road. The trail actually terminates here (an additional 3.5 miles), although you'll need to plan for a shuttle back to your car. (It's also possible to continue all the way to Upper Waterton Lake, but if you do this, you should allow 3 days for the trip.)

TWO MEDICINE AREA

Pitamakan Pass Trail

6.9 miles one-way. Moderate. Access: Two Medicine Campground.

This trail presents several options: You can take one or two long day hikes, or you can use it as the jumping-off point for an extended trip. From the trailhead, the path winds to Old Man Lake and a campground, and then up 2,400 feet to Pitamakan Pass. At this point, your options are to return via the same trail or to continue to Dawson Pass, through Twin Falls, and then back to the campground, which adds about 10 miles to the trip and completes the loop. Alternately, you could head north on the Cut Bank or Nyack Creek trails, which will add days to your trip.

Other Summer Sports & Activities

Boating. With all of this water around, it only makes sense that boat rentals would also be available, as they are. At Apgar and Lake McDonald you will find kayaks, canoes, rowboats, and motorboats; gas-powered outboard motors of 10 horsepower or less are permitted at Two Medicine Lake and Bowman Lake. You can also rent kayaks, canoes, rowboats, and electric motorboats at Two Medicine. At Many Glacier you can rent kayaks, canoes, and rowboats. For details call **Glacier Park Boat Co.** at ✆ **406/257-2426** or browse www.glacierparkboats.com.

Fishing. The crystal-clear mountain streams and lakes of Glacier are home to many native species of trout. Anglers looking to hook a big one should try the North Fork of the Flathead for cutthroat and any of the three larger lakes in the park (Bowman Lake, St. Mary Lake, and Lake McDonald) for lake trout and cutthroat. For equipment or sage advice, or to schedule a guided foray ($250 for two people for a half day), contact **Lakestream Flyshop** in Whitefish (✆ **406/862-1298;** www.lakestram.com).

Horseback Riding. One alternative to overstressing your muscles on hiking trails is to saddle up Old Paint and take an Old West approach to transportation. Horseback riding at East Glacier is provided by **Glacier Gateway Outfitters** (✆ **406/226-4408**), located a stone's throw from the front door of the lodge; they offer hourly ($25) and full-day rides ($175) into the nearby wilderness. **Mule Shoe Outfitters** (✆ **406/888-5555;** www.mule-shoe.com) offers similar rides from corrals at Lake McDonald, Apgar, and the Many Glacier Corral.

Kayaking. Most kayaking in the pa involves passages across lakes; the r popular are Bowman Lake and Lake McDonald. Inquire at any ranger station for details and conditions (for rentals, see "Boating," above).

Mountain Climbing. The peaks of Glacier Park rarely exceed elevations of 10,000 feet, but don't let the surveyors' measurements fool you. Glacier has some incredibly difficult climbs, and you must inquire at a visitor center or ranger station regarding climbing conditions and closures. In general, the peaks are unsuitable except for experienced climbers or those traveling with experienced guides; park administration does not recommend climbing because of the unstable nature of the rock.

Rafting & Float Trips. Though the waters that are actually in the park don't lend themselves to white-water rafting, the boundary forks of the Flathead River are some of the best in the northwest corner of the state. For just taking it easy and floating along in the summer sun, the North Fork of the Flathead River stretching from Polebridge to Columbia Falls and into Flathead Lake is ideal. The same may be said for the Middle Fork of the Flathead, which forms the southern border of the park.

For white-water voyagers, the North Fork of the Flathead River (classes II and III) and the Middle Fork (class III) are the best bets. Inquire at any ranger station for details and conditions, since flow rates change dramatically as snow melts or storms move through the area.

The Middle Fork is a little more severe and isn't the sort of river you enjoy with an umbrella drink in hand. The names of certain stretches of the Middle Fork are terror-inspiring in themselves (the Narrows, Jaws, Bonecrusher) and to assuage that terror, several outfitters offer expert, sanctioned guides.

Montana Raft Company, a division of Glacier Wilderness Guides (see "Exploring the Backcountry," above), offers rafting trips in the Glacier area. The trips range from half-day trips for $41 per person, full-day excursions for $75 per person, 2-day trips for $267 per person, to 3½-day outings for $410 per person; the 3½-day trip includes a day hike in Glacier National Park. Their prices include all necessary equipment and food. They also offer daily raft trips, inflatable kayaks, and fly-fishing from drift boats. Other companies offering similar services at similar prices include **Great Northern Whitewater,** P.O. Box 270, West Glacier, MT 59936 (© **800/735-7897** or 406/387-5340; www.gnwhitewater.com); **Glacier Raft Company,** P.O. Box 210, West Glacier, MT 59936 (© **800/235-6781** or 406/888-5454; www.glacierraftco.com); and **Wild River Adventures,** P.O. Box 272B, West Glacier, MT 59936 (© **800/700-7056** or 406/387-9453; www.riverwild.com).

Winter Sports & Activities

All unplowed roads become trails for snowshoers and cross-country skiers, who rave about the vast powdered wonderland that exists here. Guided trips into the backcountry are a great way to experience the park in winter, or you can strap on a pair of snowshoes and explore it on your own. *Note:* Snowmobiles are prohibited in the park.

Snowshoeing & Cross-Country Skiing. Glacier has an abundance of cross-country-ski trails, the most popular of which is the **Upper Lake McDonald Trail** to the Avalanche picnic area. This 8-mile trail offers a relatively flat route up Going-to-the-Sun Road with views of McDonald Creek and the mountains looming above the McDonald Valley.

For the advanced skier, the same area presents a more intense trip that heads northwest in a roundabout fashion to the Apgar Lookout. This 10½-mile trip may be a little more than the beginner bargains for.

The most popular trail on the east side is the **Autumn Creek Trail** near Marias Pass. However, avalanche paths cross this area, so inquire about weather conditions before setting out. Yet another popular spot is in Essex along the southern boundary of the park at the **Izaak Walton Inn.**

Camping

INSIDE THE PARK

Two ways to spend your evenings at the park are inside the hotel lounge looking across a martini at the folks in the campground, and vice versa. For those who prefer the latter, Glacier offers 13 campgrounds, 8 of which are accessible by paved road.

Most campgrounds are available on a first-come, first-served basis. Fish Creek and St. Mary campgrounds may be reserved through the **National Park Service Reservation System** (© 800/ **365-CAMP** or 301/722-1257; http:// reservations.nps.gov). Most campgrounds have restrooms with flush toilets and cold running water.

Fish Creek is on the west side of Lake McDonald; **Many Glacier** is in the northeast part of the park; **Rising Sun** is on the north side of St. Mary Lake; **St. Mary** is on the east side of the park; and **Two Medicine** is at the southeast part of the park near East Glacier. **Sprague Creek,** near the West Glacier entrance, offers a paved road but does not allow towed vehicles or vehicles longer than 21 feet.

Despite its proximity to the center of the hotel and motel activity, the **Many Glacier Campground** is a well-forested, almost secluded campground that provides as much privacy in a public area as you'll see anywhere. The campground has adequate space for recreational vehicles and truck/camper combinations, but space for vehicles pulling trailers is limited. It is a veritable mecca for tent campers.

Apgar Campground is located at the bottom of Lake McDonald, near the West Glacier Entrance and the Apgar Visitor Center. The **Avalanche Campground** may be the nicest of all because it is situated in the bottom of the valley, 4 miles north of Lake McDonald on Going-to-the-Sun Road in a heavily treed area that is also immediately adjacent to the creek. Of its 87 sites, 50 are suitable for RVs.

Bowman Lake Campground is located at the end of a primitive dirt road in the northwest section of the park (accessed through the Polebridge entrance). It's not recommended for RVs. The bad news about the **Cut Bank Campground** road is that it's not paved. The good news is it's only 5 miles from the pavement of U.S. 89 to the ranger station and campground, which are located in the southeast portion of the park between St. Mary and Two Medicine. Still more good news is that the unpaved road deters many from heading into the outback to this campground, which sits in the shadow of Bad Marriage and Medicine Wolf mountains. The campground was only recently reopened after being rebuilt, so is still relatively undiscovered; the road, and campground, are best suited to recreational vehicles 21 feet or shorter.

Fish Creek Campground is located 2 miles from Apgar, on the western shore of Lake McDonald. **Kintla Lake Campground** is located in the northwest section of the park, reached by primitive dirt roads through the Polebridge entrance station, so it is not recommended for RVs. **Logging Creek** is a primitive campground reached by dirt roads, just beyond Quartz Creek; and **Quartz Creek** is another primitive campground, accessed by dirt roads through the Polebridge entrance.

Sprague Creek Campground is located on the eastern shore of Lake McDonald. No towed trailers or vehicles longer than 21 feet are allowed. **St. Mary Campground** is located just outside the town of St. Mary. **Rising Sun Campground,** located 6 miles west of St. Mary, is close to the public showers at Rising Sun Motor Inn.

Campground	Total Sites	RV Hookups	Dump Station	Toilets	Drinking Water
Inside the Park					
Apgar	192	No	Yes	Yes	Yes
Avalanche	87	No	Yes	Yes	Yes
*Bowman Lake**	48	No	No	Yes	Yes
*Cut Bank**	19	No	No	Yes	Yes
Fish Creek	180	No	Yes	Yes	Yes
*Kintla Lake**	13	No	No	Yes	Yes
*Logging Creek**	8	No	No	Yes	Yes
Many Glacier	110	No	Yes	Yes	Yes
*Quartz Creek**	7	No	No	Yes	Yes
Rising Sun	83	No	Yes	Yes	Yes
Sprague Creek	25	No	No	Yes	Yes
St. Mary	148	No	Yes	Yes	Yes
Two Medicine	99	No	Yes	Yes	Yes
Near the Park					
Y Lazy R	40	Yes	Yes	Yes	Yes
Johnson's of St. Mary	115	Yes	Yes	Yes	Yes
Glacier Campground	160	Yes	Yes	Yes	Yes
Lake Five Resort	45	Yes	Yes	Yes	Yes

* Campground accessible only by narrow dirt roads. RVs not recommended.

The **Two Medicine Campground** is situated in the shadows of major mountains near three lakes and a stream. It is a forested area that has beautiful sites, plenty of shade, and opportunities to wet a fishing line or dangle your feet in cool mountain water.

Backcountry Camping. If it's the backcountry you're bent on seeing, Glacier has 66 backcountry campgrounds. Fortunately, many are at lower elevation, so inexperienced backpackers have an opportunity to take advantage of them. For an accurate depiction of your itinerary's difficulty, and advice on what may be needed, check with rangers in the area you contemplate visiting. One of the main dangers is running into a bear. Visitors planning to camp overnight in Glacier's backcountry must stop at a visitor center or ranger station and obtain a backcountry use permit. Backcountry permits may be reserved in advance (see "Exploring the Backcountry," above). Permits are only good for the pre-arranged dates and locations, with no more than 3 nights allowed at each campground. Certain campgrounds have a 1-night limit. There are separate fees for advance reservations ($20 per permit) and backcountry camping ($4 per person per night).

Backcountry camping permits may be obtained in person from the visitor centers at Apgar, Waterton Townsite, and St. Mary, or the ranger stations at Many Glacier, Two Medicine, and Polebridge. During summer months permits may be obtained no earlier than 24 hours before your trip.

Showers	Fire Pits/ Grills	Laundry	Public Phone	Reserve	Fees	Open
No	Yes	No	Yes	No	$14	Early May to mid-Oct
No	Yes	No	No	No	$14	Mid-June to Labor Day
No	Yes	No	No	No	$12	Mid-May to mid-Sept
No	Yes	No	No	No	$12	Early June to late Sept
No	Yes	No	Yes	Yes	$17	Early June to Labor Day
No	Yes	No	No	No	$12	Mid-May to mid-Sept
No	Yes	No	No	No	$12	July to Labor Day
Yes**	Yes	No	Yes	No	$14	Late May to late Sept
No	Yes	No	No	No	$12	July to Labor Day
Yes**	Yes	No	Yes	No	$14	Late May to mid-Sept
No	Yes	No	No	No	$14	Mid-May to late Sept
No	Yes	No	Yes	Yes	$17	Late May to late Sept
No	Yes	No	Yes	No	$14	Late May–late Sept
Yes	Yes	Yes	Yes	Yes	$15/$18	June to mid-Sept
Yes	Yes	Yes	Yes	Yes	$18/$25/$28	Apr–Oct
Yes	Yes	Yes	Yes	Yes	$18/$24	Mid-May to Sept
Yes	Yes	Yes	Yes	Yes	$25/$30	Early May to mid-Oct

** Public showers located nearby, for a fee.

Winter Backcountry Camping. Though snow camping isn't for everyone, it's a great way to see the park in winter and to complement a winter excursion. Permits are required for all overnight trips but, due to lower demand, there is no fee to reserve one up to 7 days in advance. There are a few rules that do take effect beginning each November 20, so double-check at visitor centers for details.

Chalets. Two of the park's most popular destinations, Granite Park and Sperry Chalets, are National Historic Landmarks built by the Great Northern Railway between 1912 and 1914. The former is a basic hiker's shelter, while Sperry is a full-service chalet.

For information on **Granite Park Chalet,** contact **Glacier Wilderness Guides/Montana Raft Company** (© 800/ 521-7238 or 406/387-5654; www.glacier guides.com). This company handles the reservations for Granite Park Chalet, a backcountry hikers' hut, and operates guided hikes into the Glacier backcountry (see "Exploring the Backcountry," above). The chalet has 12 rooms (all with single bunk beds), and sleeps two to six per room. The chalet is pricey if you just stay overnight ($66 per person per night, with an additional $10 per person linen charge; there's no running water or other facilities); you may get better value by going on an organized trip.

Sperry Chalet, a rustic backcountry chalet, is accessible by trail only. It operates from mid-July through mid-September. Services include overnight accommodations and full meal service for a double rate of $255. Reservations are required. For information and reservations call (✆ **888/345-2649** or 406/387-5654; www.sperrychalet.com), or write: **Belton Chalets,** P.O. Box 188, West Glacier, MT 59936.

NEAR THE PARK

IN EAST GLACIER

Y Lazy R

P.O. Box 146, East Glacier, MT 59434. ✆ **406/226-5573.** 10 tent sites, 30 RV sites. $15 tent, $18 full hookup.

Situated just off U.S. 2, this campground is conveniently located within walking distance of East Glacier and is the closest to town with laundry facilities. Plan to arrive early if you want to snag one of the few sites with trees. This place is a great value and an ideal place to plant the RV before heading off to explore the region. The same owners also operate Firebrand Campground 3 miles west of East Glacier with 10 tent and 20 RV sites at the same prices.

IN ST. MARY

Johnson's of St. Mary

St. Mary, MT 59417. ✆ **406/732-4207** campground, or 406/732-5565 cafe. 50 tent sites, 65 RV sites. $18 tent; $25 RV with electricity and water only, $28 full hookup; $20 motor home, no hookup.

From April through September (depending on the weather) this is where you want to camp if you can get a spot. With showers ($3) and a Laundromat, campers both inside the park and out come to St. Mary for a good meal at Johnson's Cafe, where homemade American grub is served family style, with serving dishes placed daily on each table for breakfast, lunch, and dinner. Lunches here include burgers, sandwiches, and homemade soup (most

items $3.50–$6.50), and dinners usually include your choice of entrees such as fried chicken (the Sun special), trout, sirloin or T-bone steak, or pork chops, with prices from $10 to $18.

IN WEST GLACIER

Glacier Campground

P.O. Box 447, 12070 U.S. 2, West Glacier, MT 59936. ✆ **888/387-5689** or 406/387-5689. 80 tent sites, 80 RV sites, 5 cabins. $18 tent; $20–$24 RV; $30–$40 cabin.

One mile west of West Glacier on U.S. 2 is the closest campground outside the park. Set amid a forested area overgrown with evergreens, it's a quiet, comfortable place to retreat under the shade of the trees, especially on hot summer days. Most sites have water and electric hookups; the rest are perfect for tent camping. Five rather primitive cabins are also available, but furnishings are modest: electricity, beds with mattresses, and use of the campground's bathhouse. Recreational facilities include volleyball, horseshoes, and a basketball court; also on the premises are a Cajun restaurant, a Laundromat, and a small general store.

Lake Five Resort

540 Belton Stage Rd., West Glacier, MT 59936. ✆ **406/387-5601.** www.lakefiveresort.com. 9 cabins, 6 tepee lodges, 45 sites with electricity and water (14 of which have sewer hookups). $75–$125 cabin; $30–$40 tepee; $25–$30 site.

Located 3 miles west of West Glacier and ¾ mile from U.S. 2, this cabin and campground arrangement is an alternative to potentially crowded park campgrounds, but is still close to the park itself. The resort is situated on a 235-acre lake. Seven of the nine cabins are on the lakefront; all are equipped with bathrooms and showers.

Where to Stay

INSIDE THE PARK

With only one exception, Glacier Park Inc. (GPI) operates all of the hostelries in Glacier National Park, which fall into two different categories. Lake McDonald Lodge, Glacier Park Lodge, and Many Glacier Hotel are first-tier properties that have been popular destinations since early in the 20th century; Swiftcurrent Motor Inn is typical of the casual motel-style properties at the other end of the spectrum that provide good accommodations for less money. Although the lodges have a certain stately charm, don't expect in-room hot tubs or even air-conditioning. The structures may have been constructed to withstand natural disasters, but little thought was given to interior soundproofing. So if you're an eavesdropper, you'll be in heaven; if you're a light sleeper, bring earplugs. Although all of the lodges are adequately comfortable, their greatest attribute, aside from the architecture, may be their location in one of the most stunning natural settings in the world.

Reserve well in advance; July and August dates may fill before the spring thaw. For more information on the GPI-operated properties and to make reservations, contact **Glacier Park Inc.,** P.O. Box 2025 Columbia Falls, MT 59912 (© **406/892-2525;** fax 406/892-1375; www.glacierparkinc.com).

Apgar Village Lodge

Apgar Village, Box 398, West Glacier, MT 59936. © **406/888-5484.** Fax 406/888-5273. www.westglacier.com. 28 cabins, 20 motel rooms. TV. $90–$227 cabin; $71–$98 double motel room. DISC, MC, V. Closed early Oct to Apr.

The Apgar Village Lodge is located on the south end of Lake McDonald and is one of two lodgings located in Apgar Village. A less expensive alternative to the park's GPI-owned properties, the log-and-frame cabins have a rustic charm but lack in-room amenities.

Glacier Park Lodge

Glacier National Park, MT 59936. © **406/892-2525.** Fax 406/892-1375. www.glacierparkinc.com. 154 units. TEL. $145–$205 double; $399 suite. AE, DC, DISC, MC, V.

Actually just outside the southeast entrance at East Glacier, this is the flagship inn of the park, an imposing timbered lodge that stands as a stately tribute to the Great Northern Railroad and its early attempts to lure tourists to Glacier. The carefully manicured lawn and ever-blooming wildflowers frame the grounds in colors spectacular enough to rival the mountain backdrop. The interior features massive Douglas fir pillars, some 40 inches in diameter and 40 feet tall. In fact, stand in the middle of the lobby and look up—beams carved from massive trees are the structural supports for the entire building. Skylights, wrought-iron chandeliers, and a desk hewn from a 36-inch-diameter log add to the Old West flavor.

Rooms are well furnished, but showers are elbow-banging small, and sinks are significantly smaller than those found in today's modern hotels and motels. A wooden deck outside the lounge provides an excellent spot for cocktails, reading, or a late-afternoon snooze. A glass-enclosed breezeway connects the main building to the west wing; the oak chaise lounges found there are an ideal spot from which to watch a sunrise. There's even an immaculately groomed executive-style 9-hole golf course. The **Trading Post** offers traditional souvenirs, as well as nicely crafted American Indian artwork and clothing. While here, plan to spend an evening around the fireplace as members of the Blackfeet tribe recount their history and culture.

Lake McDonald Lodge

Glacier National Park, MT 59936. © **406/892-2525.** Fax 406/892-1375. www.glacierparkinc.com. 62 units in lodge and motel, 38 cottage units. TEL. $149 lodge room; $96–$109 motel unit; $96–$149 cottage. DISC, MC, V.

The Lake McDonald Lodge feels like a genuine mountain lodge. Although this two-story building doesn't have the same towering ceilings and open spaces as other park hotels, it has a warm, cozy feel inspired by its wood construction. Lodge rooms, located on the second and third floor of the lodge (no elevator), are pleasantly decorated and have a historic feel, while the motel units are simply well-maintained motel rooms. The well-preserved cottages are located in multi-unit cottage buildings in a wooded area. Situated on the shore of the park's largest lake, the lodge provides a marvelous central base for exploring the western part of the park. The lodge is a center for boating activity; scenic cruises depart daily and canoe rentals are popular. Common lounging areas are furnished with heavy couches, sofas, and chairs that surround a stone fireplace. The lodge houses a dining room, gift shop, and lounge; a coffee shop, post office, and sundries store are also on the grounds. The entire lodge is nonsmoking.

Many Glacier Hotel

Glacier National Park, MT 59936. © **406/892-2525.** Fax 406/892-1375. www.glacierparkinc.com. 216 units. TEL. $106–$195 double; $230 suite. DISC, MC, V.

This alpine-style hotel may be the most photographed building in the park. When you arrive at Many Glacier after driving along the park's interior road from Babb, it comes slowly into view, as picturesque as a Swiss chalet and almost as inviting as the turquoise blue waters of Swiftcurrent Lake. Built in 1915 by the Great Northern Railway, this is the largest hotel in the park and our top choice for a place to stay. Its chalet-style architecture fits right in with the alpine environment that surrounds it. In August, after the huckleberries ripen, you can almost count on seeing grizzly bears on the slopes of the mountain across the road from the hotel.

Rooms, decorated in keeping with the hotel's historic roots, are located in the main lodge around the balconies overlooking the lobby or in the adjoining annex. We like the lakeside rooms, for their views of Swift Current Lake. Those who plan to use the room as a place to crash at the end of the day can save money by booking one of the smaller rooms without a view. A dining room, coffee shop, gift shop, and lounge are all located in the hotel; nightly performances begin midsummer. All units are nonsmoking.

Rising Sun Motor Inn

Glacier National Park, MT 59936. © **406/892-2525.** Fax 406/892-1375. www.glacierparkinc.com. 63 units. TEL. $92–$105 double; $96 cottage. AE, DISC, MC, V.

Located 6½ miles from St. Mary, just off Going-to-the-Sun Road, the Rising Sun is a complex made up of a restaurant, a motor inn, cottages, a camp store, a gift shop, and a service station. The basic motel rooms are just that—basic but uninspiring motel rooms—that are completely adequate for a good night's rest and in an excellent location for those who want to explore the eastern side of the park from Going-to-the-Sun Road. The cottage rooms (half of a duplex) are more interesting, but a bit on the rustic side. All units here are nonsmoking.

Swiftcurrent Motor Inn

Glacier National Park, MT 59936. © **406/892-2525.** Fax 406/892-1375. www.glacierparkinc.com. 88 units and cabins (most cabins without private bathroom). $92–$105 double in motor inn; $45 double in cabin. DISC, MC, V.

The appeal here is for those satisfied with modest prices and decor—primarily active types interested in spending lots of time exploring the backcountry trails. Like Many Glacier, which is just up the street, the inn is set against a mountain backdrop in what is considered a hiker's paradise. Motel rooms here have standard motel decor—functional but nothing special; cabins are a bit more interesting, with one or two bedrooms, and perhaps a bathroom (communal facilities are nearby). There's also a coffee shop/restaurant on the premises. All units are nonsmoking.

Village Inn

Glacier National Park, MT 59936. ✆ **406/892-2525.** Fax 406/892-1375. www.glacierparkinc.com. 36 units. $109–$177 double. DISC, MC, V.

Not to be confused with Apgar Village Lodge (see above), the Village Inn is the smallest of the properties operated by GPI in Glacier. Located in Apgar Village, the inn is near the general store, cafes, and boat docks. Like its counterparts throughout the park, the Village Inn is comfortably outfitted with modest furnishings, making it a cozy and convenient place to sleep. All 36 rooms are located on two floors of the inn and 12 of them have kitchenettes. Second-level rooms have the same lake views as those downstairs, but have less people traffic. Though you won't find a dining room on the property, the restaurants of Lake McDonald and Apgar are all close by. Close to the Apgar corral and the docks of Lake McDonald, not to a plethora of hiking trails, Apgar Village bustles with activity during the summer.

NEAR THE PARK

If the convenience of staying on Glacier's back porch is important to you, the following are your best bets. However, you'll find a greater variety of accommodations in surrounding communities not necessarily classified as gateway towns, especially if you're willing to travel as far as Whitefish, Kalispell, or Columbia Falls. These places might be more in line with your needs if the park is merely a 1- or 2-day part of your vacation.

IN EAST GLACIER

Backpacker's Inn

P.O. Box 94, East Glacier, MT 59434. ✆ **406/226-9392.** 16 beds in 3 cabins. $8–$10 per person in single-sex dorms; $20 for 1 person and $30 for 2 in private cabin. DISC, MC, V. Closed mid-Oct to Apr.

Low-cost sleeping accommodations for those willing to share bathroom facilities are what you pay for, and what you get, at this dorm-style hostel.

Brownies Grocery and AYH Hostel

P.O. Box 229, East Glacier, MT 59434. ✆ **406/226-4426** or 406/226-4456. 12 units (all with shared bathroom). AYH members $13–$26 or $35 family room; nonmembers $15–$29 or $35 family room. Family rooms sleep 2–6. MC, V. Closed Oct to early May, depending on the weather.

Reservations are recommended at this popular combination grocery store/hostel, which offers comfortable rooms at extremely affordable prices. Dorm and family rooms are located on the second floor of a rustic, older log building with several common rooms for guests to share, including a porch, kitchen, bathrooms, and laundry. A bakery and deli (and Internet access) have been added to the grocery; there's a restaurant next door.

Jacobson's Cottages

120 Mont. 49 (P.O. Box 454), East Glacier, MT 59434. ✆ **888/226-4422** or 406/226-4422. Fax 406/226-4425. 12 cottages. TV. $55–$75 double. AE, DISC, MC, V. Closed Nov–Apr.

Located in a nicely wooded area, these quaint cottages are small but comfortable. All have cable TV and one has a kitchen. Entertainment and good food are nearby, with the Restaurant Thimbleberry a half block down the street and Two Medicine a 12-mile drive. The cottages are available seasonally, and reservations are recommended.

Mountain Pine Motel

Mont. 49, East Glacier, MT 59434. ℭ **406/ 226-4403.** 25 units and 2 houses. TV TEL. $58–$64 double. AE, DC, DISC, MC, V.

This property is a one-story, 1950s-type remodeled motel that provides clean, well-furnished rooms in a shaded, timbered area just off the main highway. Most standard rooms have two queen-size beds, reading chairs and table, chest, and bathrooms with tub-shower combinations. Considering the fact that rooms here are about a third as expensive as at the park hotels, this is an excellent alternative.

IN ESSEX

Izaak Walton Inn

290 Izaak Walton Inn Rd., Essex, MT 59916. ℭ **406/888-5700.** Fax 406/888-5200. www. izaakwaltoninn.com. 33 units plus 4 caboose cottages. $88–$128 double, $160–$180 suite, $525–$545 caboose with a 3-night minimum stay. MC, V.

Built in 1939 by the railway, this historic Tudor lodge once served as living quarters for rail crews who serviced the railroad. Located just off U.S. 2 on the southern boundary of Glacier Park, the Izaak Walton is now extremely popular with tourists and locals alike, many of whom choose to travel via Amtrak train, which stops a mere 100 yards from the front door of the lodge. Both lodge rooms and the converted cabooses offer comfortable and attractive lodging, with wood-paneled walls and various Western touches. And who can pass up the opportunity to sleep in a caboose? During winter months this inn is a popular jumping-off spot for cross-country skiers; photo seminars are offered year-round.

Paola Creek Bed & Breakfast

P.O. Box 97, West Glacier, MT 59936. ℭ **888/ 311-5061** or 406/888-5061. Fax 406/ 888-5063. www.paolacreek.com. 5 units. $140–$170 double. MC, V. Closed Oct–Apr.

This handcrafted log home, nestled between Glacier National Park and the Great Bear Wilderness, features a relaxing Great Room with river rock fireplace, a library, and a large dining room with a stunning view. Rooms are very western in appearance, with log walls, log-beamed ceilings, attractive quilts on the beds, and lots of mountain lodge-style decorations. In the summer, it's a refined base of operations for hiking, biking, and river activities; the huge breakfasts can fuel just about anyone for a day in the outdoors.

IN POLEBRIDGE

North Fork Hostel and Square Peg Ranch

80 Beaver Dr., Polebridge, MT 59928. ℭ **406/ 888-5241.** www.nfhostel.com. 12 bunks, 2 cabins, 2 log homes. $15 bunk, $30 cabin, $65 log home. AE.

Formerly called the Quarter Circle MC Ranch and located inside the park, this lodge was moved to its present location near Polebridge in the late 1960s, and is ideal for the back-to-nature traveler. It now sits within a stone's throw of the North Fork of the Flathead River and right across the river from Glacier National Park. Accommodations are rustic, with a mountain cabin feel—there's no electricity in Polebridge, so lighting is powered by kerosene and propane, and heat is from an old-fashioned wood stove. There are separate facilities for men and women, as well as couples' accommodations, washrooms with hot showers, and clean outhouses. There are also several small cabins suitable for families. Hostel guests should bring linens or sleeping bags (sheets are available for rent) and flashlights. The Square Peg

Ranch offers two rustic log homes, with similar decor to the hostel, and a few bare-bones tepees and campsites for $10 a night. The log homes have solar-heated showers, or guests can use the hostel showers, and there are outhouses. The hostel and cabins have complete kitchen facilities, and the former has a relaxing 6-foot-long claw-foot bathtub. Equipment rentals and Internet access are also available here.

Polebridge Mercantile and Cabins

P.O. Box 280042, Polebridge, MT 59928. ☎ **406/888-5105.** www.members.tripod.com/ polebridge. 4 cabins. $35–$45 cabin. MC, V.

If you can make the trek up the gravelly North Fork Road, then give these bare-bones cabins a try. There is no electricity and no running water in the lower-priced cabins, let alone bedding—it's bring your own sleeping bag at the Merc—which is also home to a fantastic bakery. Each cabin has a propane cooking stove and lights, and the views out over the west side of Glacier National Park make the price tag a steal, especially if you brought the kids. This may sound like an adventure in hell, but Polebridge is a happening spot in the summer when all the river rats and seasonal residents converge for whopping good times and tall tales about running rapids and climbing peaks.

IN ST. MARY

St. Mary Lodge

U.S. 89 and Going-to-the-Sun Rd., St. Mary, MT 59417. ☎ **800/368-3689** or 406/732-4431. Fax 406/732-9265. www.glcpark.com. 124 units, including 57 hotel rooms, 48 lodge rooms and suites, and 19 cabins and cottages. TEL. $85–$135 double hotel, $145–$325 cabin or cottage, and $160–$230 lodge room or suite. AE, DISC, MC, V.

Situated at the St. Mary end of Going-to-the-Sun Road, this lodge is another member of the minority of park properties that aren't managed by GPI. The main lodge and attendant rooms are standard Montana fare, with tasteful Western lodgepole furnishings. Lodging is in three different areas in close proximity to the center of the complex; lodge and motel rooms are nicely done motel-style units that may have two single beds or a queen. Rooms are tiny but are furnished with stylish lodgepole pine beds, tables, and brass reading lamps. Bathrooms are small, self-contained units with showers. Nicer units are in the Glacier cabins, which boast living areas with dining tables, kitchenettes with microwaves and minifridges, and queen beds in a separate sleeping area. The most expensive units here are the Pinnacle Cottages, newly constructed cabins perched on a bluff across the highway from the main complex that afford views of Going-to-the-Sun Road and St. Mary Lake. (All rooms have phones; most have TVs and air-conditioning.)

IN WEST GLACIER

Glacier Wilderness Resort

P.O. Box 295, West Glacier, MT 59936. ☎ **406/888-5664.** www.glacierwildernessresort.com. 10 lodges. TEL. $175–$200 per lodge per night. 5-night minimum stay. MC, V.

Surrounded by Forest Service lands, the lodges at this year-round resort are as private as you can get. Each lodge is a "home," done in modern Western decor, complete with a stereo, satellite TV, a VCR, and a hot tub on the front porch. Families will find the two-bedroom lodges to their liking, and kids can play outdoors during the day (there are 23 undeveloped acres) and at the Recreation Center, with diversions such as foosball, pool, and video games. There is a new indoor year-round heated pool. Hiking trails abound and some even come upon some surprising waterfalls. For a summer stay, reservations should be made before March.

Great Northern Chalets

12127 U.S. 2, West Glacier, MT 59936. ✆ **800/735-7897** or 406/387-5340. Fax 406/ 387-9007. www.gnwhitewater.com. 5 units. $197–$280 double. AE, DISC, MC, V.

This small, family-oriented resort located near West Glacier offers log chalets that have balconies facing landscaped flower gardens and a pond, with mountain views in the distance. Three types of chalets are offered, the largest being a beautifully furnished two-story, two-bedroom unit with three queen beds, a full bathroom upstairs, and a half bathroom downstairs. Smaller chalets have one large upstairs bedroom with two queen beds, and a downstairs level with a full-size sleeper sofa and a kitchen with service for six. A 16-foot indoor hot tub spa is on the property, as are a volleyball court that doubles as a sandbox for children and a pond that is used for fly-fishing instruction.

Vista Motel

11955 U.S. 2 East (P.O. Box 90), West Glacier, MT 59936. ✆ **406/888-5311.** Fax 406/888-9027. 25 units, including 5 cabins. TV. $65–$120 double. AE, DISC, MC, V. Closed late Sept to Apr.

Perched atop a hill at the west entrance to Glacier National Park, the Vista boasts tremendous views of the mountains. Accommodations are not memorable, but the modern motel rooms are clean and comfortable, the cabins can easily house a family, and there's an outdoor heated pool.

West Glacier Motel

200 Going-to-the-Sun Rd., West Glacier, MT 59936. ✆ **406/888-5662.** www.westglacier. com. 32 units. Motel rooms $73 double, cabins $121–$140. AE, DISC, MC, V.

Formerly the River Bend Motel, this property has two locations. Half of the units are in West Glacier on the Going-to-the-Sun Road, about 1 mile from the park entrance, and a second set of units is 1 mile away on forested grounds with panoramic views of the park. This 1950s-style motel is equipped with TV sets despite the fact that there is virtually no reception unless it happens to be your lucky day. However, the prices can't be beat during peak season, and rates drop dramatically in mid-September. The Western-style cabins are better suited for families; they come with two or three queen beds and fully equipped kitchens.

Where to Dine

INSIDE THE PARK

Food options inside the park are primarily limited to dining rooms operated by GPI. They're convenient, however, and you're almost always assured of friendly service from a staff of 20-something college students from around the country. Credit cards accepted at all GPI properties include American Express, Diners Club, Discover, MasterCard, and Visa. Breakfasts range from $4.50 to $9, lunch entrees are $6 to $10, and most dinner entrees $10 to $25.

You'll find above-average food served at above-average prices in the dining rooms at the major properties. Glacier Park Lodge has the **Great Northern Steak & Rib House,** which has Western decor and a menu of beef, barbecued ribs, fish, and chicken, plus a full breakfast buffet; and **The Sunset Lounge,** which offers a bar menu of sandwiches and appetizers. At Lake McDonald Lodge you'll find **Russell's Fireside Dining Room,** which has a hunting-lodge atmosphere with rough-hewn beams and hunting trophies and specializes in American standards, including beef tenderloin, roast duckling, seared mountain trout, roast turkey, Alaskan salmon, and steaks; there's also a full breakfast buffet. Also at Lake McDonald Lodge is the **Stockade Lounge,** which serves a bar menu of sandwiches and appetizers, and **Jammer Joe's,** a pizzeria/family restaurant.

Many Glacier Hotel has the **Ptarmigan Dining Room,** which has Swiss decor in keeping with the lodge, emphasizing spectacular mountain views, and serves continental and Swiss cuisine plus a breakfast buffet. Many Glacier also has the **Swiss Room and Interlaken Lounge,** with a bar menu of sandwiches and appetizers, and **Heidi's,** a fast-food counter known for its huckleberry frozen yogurt. The dining rooms open with the park and close sometime in September, depending on the facility. At each dining room, breakfast is served from 6:30 to 9:30am; lunch from 11:30am to 2pm; and dinner from 5:30 to 9:30pm. Coffee and snack shops open either at 7 or 8am and close at 9pm. All of the above restaurants are nonsmoking.

The alternatives include second-tier restaurants in close proximity to the hotels, most of which are comparable to chain restaurants in both quality and price. The **Two Dog Flats Grill** at the Rising Sun Motor Inn serves "hearty American fare"; the Swiftcurrent Motor Inn restaurant is the **Italian Gardens Ristorante.** Lunch and dinner feature combinations of salads, sandwiches, pasta dishes, and "create your own" pizzas. At Apgar you'll find a deli and a family dining arrangement.

NEAR THE PARK

The gateway cities have a number of good restaurants, and you'll find many more choices in Whitefish and Kalispell.

IN EAST GLACIER

Whistle Stop, 1020 Mont. 49 (© **406/ 226-9292**), may serve up the very best breakfasts in the area, with reasonable prices (mostly in the $5–$10 range). Omelets and huckleberry French toast are specialties; the omelets come in seven different styles, including a Spanish omelet with chorizo, lots of peppers, tomatoes, onions, and spinach.

Definitely an eye-opener. They're also known for barbecued ribs and chicken. Try their huckleberry pie.

The **Snowgoose Grille,** located in St. Mary Lodge (see "Where to Stay," above), is the high-priced alternative. Breakfasts start at $4.75 for a stack of flapjacks and run to $9.25 for steak and eggs; an all-you-can-eat buffet is $9 for adults. The ambience is upscale for these parts—a glass-enclosed dining room with views of the mountains and the creek. Lunch entrees include typical restaurant sandwiches with fancy names such as the "Garden Wall," filled with such diverse items as turkey and buffalo steak; prices range from $6 to $9. The dinner menu features home-smoked Prime rib and wild game specials; main courses run $12 to $28. The St. Mary Lodge also has the **Curly Bear Café,** plus pizza, ice cream, espresso, pastry, and fudge facilities.

Glacier Village Restaurant

304–308 Mont. 2, East Glacier. © **406/226-4464.** Breakfast items $4–$8; main courses $2–$9 lunch, $6.50–$19 dinner. MC, V. Daily 6:30am–9:30pm. Closed Oct–Apr. AMERICAN.

This family-owned, seasonal restaurant is one of the few full-service dining establishments in the area that serves three meals, starting with breakfast at 6:30am. Portions are healthy and prices are moderate, with standards such as yummy pancakes made from home-made batter. The restaurant's impressive menu includes dishes such as pork chops with huckleberry sauce, buffalo, and huckleberry items galore.

Restaurant Thimbleberry

1112 Mont. 49, East Glacier. © **406/226-5523.** Breakfast items $3–$7; main courses $4.50–$8 lunch, $9–$15 dinner. DISC, MC, V. Daily 6:30am–10pm. Closed Oct to mid-May. AMERICAN.

Locally famous for their incredible pies, the Thimbleberry also serves great omelets for breakfast, sandwiches and salads for lunch, and an excellent cornmeal-dusted St. Mary's Lake whitefish for dinner. Serving self-described "slow food," this is a good choice for vegetarians or those looking for something other than a Montana steak or hamburger. And if you've never had fry bread, then the Thimbleberry is the place to try it.

Serrano's

29 Dawson Ave., East Glacier. © **406/226-9392.** Reservations recommended. Main courses $9–$15. AE, DISC, MC, V. Daily 5–10pm. Closed Oct–Apr. MEXICAN.

Perhaps the area's best restaurant, Serrano's is just off the highway at the center of town. Serrano's has an outstanding local reputation, so don't be surprised if you encounter masses of people in its dining room and on its outdoor deck during the height of summer. You can expect hearty portions of Mexican food, plus an ample selection of imported beers and microbrews, and a full bar featuring margaritas.

IN POLEBRIDGE

Northern Lights Saloon

Polebridge. © **406/888-5669.** Reservations not accepted. Main courses $9–$13. MC, V. Memorial Day weekend to Sept 15 daily 4–10pm; Sept 15 to Memorial Day weekend Fri–Sat 4–9pm, Sun 9am–3pm. Bar open later. AMERICAN/ECLECTIC.

When people don't mind traveling over 30 miles of bumpy gravel road, when they don't blink an eye as they hit yet another gaping pothole and lose a hubcap or bend a rim, they must know something you don't about wherever it is they're going—in this case, the Northern Lights Saloon. This small restaurant, located squarely in the middle of nowhere, attracts summer crowds that often have to wait patiently outside for a table to clear, in anticipation of the well-prepared and reasonable gourmet specials and fresh strawberry-rhubarb pie.

Picnic tables, a volleyball net, and the peaks of Glacier Park are there to make the wait as painless as possible. You won't find a place with more character or a friendlier staff.

IN WEST GLACIER

Glacier Highlander Restaurant

U.S. 2, West Glacier. © **406/888-5427.** Breakfast items $3–$6.50; main courses $5–$7 lunch, $5–$19 dinner. AE, DISC, MC, V. Daily 7am–10pm. Closed mid-Nov to Mar. AMERICAN.

This may be the spot to satisfy your sweet tooth; a baker is on hand, so the pies are well worth the stop, and the cinnamon rolls are breakfast giants. The Highland Burger is, by any standard, a great hunk of beef, and the fresh trout is a dinner specialty.

Heaven's Peak Dining and Spirits

12130 U.S. 2, West Glacier. © **406/387-4754.** Dinner main courses $12–$22. All credit cards accepted. Daily 5–10pm. AMERICAN.

This restaurant, in a massive log building, has a wonderful atmosphere, with a huge deck that overlooks a beautiful sculpted rock garden and manicured lawns. The only negative is that there's a bit too much road noise, but the beautiful views into Glacier National Park help compensate. The chef uses only fresh ingredients; gardens have been planted to provide vegetables and fruit. Dinners here are especially healthy—you won't find anything deep-fried on the menu—and include the highly recommended fresh fish, as well as pasta, chicken, buffalo (another of our favorites), beef, and roast duck. *Note:* At the time of this writing, dinner hours had been temporarily scaled back to Friday to Sunday only, but the proprietors expected to return to daily operation by 2004.

Picnic & Camping Supplies

East Glacier. In East Glacier are a gas station, a post office, several gift shops, and a small market with a limited supply of fresh meats and produce as well as beer and wine and a modest supply of fishing and camping accessories.

West Glacier. A gas station, general store, Laundromat, photo shop, rafting companies, post office, and gift shop are located in West Glacier, as are a bar and restaurant.

St. Mary. The **St. Mary Country Market** (© 406/732-4431) at the St. Mary Lodge will never be confused with a metropolitan area supermarket, but it's the closest thing you will find in any of the park gateway cities except Kalispell, which is 80 miles due west. Fresh produce, canned goods, and beverages, including beer and wine, will be found here, but you can expect to pay tourist-town prices. There's also a post office.

A Side Trip to Waterton Lakes National Park

It's worth finding the time to explore the upper regions of this area. From St. Mary, head north to visit Waterton Lakes National Park, Glacier's northern Canadian counterpart. You'll be rewarded with different yet equally beautiful scenery and a touch of European culture.

Located in Alberta, Canada, Waterton is the place where the Canadian mountains meet the rolling prairie; hence, it has an incredible variety of flowers and animals. As you travel along the high ridge you'll see meadows and boggy areas that are ideal habitat for moose; later, you'll find yourself surrounded by lakes, as the Canadian Rockies fill the horizon. The area is also a haven for elk, mule deer, and bighorn sheep, and both grizzly and black bears are found in the park.

JUST THE FACTS

Getting There. From the eastern entrance of Glacier National Park at St. Mary, drive north through Babb, which is barely a whistle-stop, until you reach the intersection of Mont. 17—it's very well marked. Head northwest to the Canadian border, where Mont. 17 becomes Alberta Hwy. 6. *Remember:* You need proof of citizenship to cross the border—a passport or a copy of your birth certificate will do. Head down into the valley until you reach the park entrance on your left.

Visitor Information. The park's **Visitor Reception Centre** is just inside the park, on the same road you used coming in (© 403/859-5133; www.parkscanada.gc.ca/waterton).

Fees & Permits. Park entrance costs Can$5 (about $3.50) per person, at a maximum of Can$13 ($8.75) per vehicle; an annual pass is Can$42 ($29). Day hiking does not require a permit, but backcountry overnight trips do, at a cost of Can$6 ($4.20) per person per day.

A BRIEF HISTORY

Compared with its counterparts in the Lower 48, Waterton is a tiny park; the total size is only 203 square miles. However, the park has great historical significance: Based on more than 200 identified archaeological sites, historians think that Aborigines first populated the area 11,000 years ago.

In modern times, Waterton Lakes became a national park about 6 years before oil was discovered here. (Oil and mineral exploration was allowed in Canada's national parks during the system's infancy.) It was set aside as a national park in 1895, thanks to the efforts of a local rancher. Then in 1932, following an initiative by the Rotary Clubs of Alberta and Montana, Waterton Lakes and Glacier national parks were designated the world's first **International Peace Park,** and have since come to represent the need for cooperation between nations where sharing resources and ecosystems is possible. The areas were designated Bio-Sphere Reserves by the UNESCO Man and Bio-Sphere Program, in order to provide information about the relationships between people and the environment. The two parks were jointly designated a UNESCO World Heritage Site in 1995.

EXPLORING THE PARK

Unlike most "park centers"—essentially a smattering of restaurants, souvenir shops, and gas stations clustered around the primary lodging—Waterton Village actually is a village. As you cruise the perimeter of the lake headed for Waterton Village, you'll pass three large lakes, the habitat of bald eagles that are often seen perched atop the snags of dead trees. The park bears a striking resemblance to Grand Teton in that its attractions spread out across a narrow valley floor; however, the valley is narrower and peaks surround three-fourths of it, so the overall effect is cozier but equally dramatic.

By most standards, it's also windier here, though locals say that they don't acknowledge the wind unless there are whitecaps in the restroom toilets at the Prince of Wales Hotel (see "Where to Stay," below).

Hiking, cruising the lake, or just doing nothing are ideal pastimes in this neck of the woods. Most of the 120 miles of trails are easily accessible from town and range in difficulty from short strolls to steep treks for overnight backcountry enthusiasts.

DAY HIKES

The park is a popular destination for European, Canadian, and American hiking fanatics. For nearly 20 years, the 10.8-mile **Crypt Lake Trail** has been rated as one of Canada's best hikes—except for those prone to seasickness, since the trailhead is reached by taking a 2-mile boat ride across Upper Waterton Lake. Contact **Waterton InterNation Shoreline Cruises** (© **403/859-2362**) for details regarding the boat shuttle. After that, the trail leads past Hellroaring Falls, Twin Falls, and Burnt Rock Falls,

before reaching Crypt Falls and a passage through a 60-foot rock tunnel. The elevation gain is 2,300 feet, but veterans say the hike is doable in 3 hours, one-way.

A second extended tour starts at the marina and heads south across the international boundary to **Goat Haunt,** Montana, an especially popular trip because of the sightings of bald eagles, bear, bighorn sheep, deer, and moose, as well as numerous unusual geologic formations.

The **International Peace Park Hike,** a free guided trip that follows Upper Waterton Lake, is held on Saturdays from the end of June through the end of August. Participants meet at the Bertha Trailhead in the morning and spend the day on an 8.5-mile trail with U.S. and Canadian rangers. At the end of the trail, hikers return via boat to the main dock. Adult fare is Can$15 ($11); children's fare Can$6 to Can$8 ($4.20–$5.60).

CAMPING

At the west end of the village is **Townsite Campground,** a Parks Canada–operated facility with 235 sites that's an especially popular jumping-off spot for campers headed into the park's backcountry. Prices range from Can$16 ($11) to Can$24 ($17); half of the sites have electricity and sewage disposal. Also available on the premises are kitchen shelters, washrooms, and shower facilities. The site is perched right on the lake, so views are excellent and trails await evening strollers.

There are 10 designated **wilderness campgrounds** with dry toilets and surface water, some of which have shelters.

WHERE TO STAY

For complete lodging information, contact **central reservations** for the Waterton area (© **800/215-2395;** www. trailofthegreatbear.com).

Although the Prince of Wales Hotel (see below) is clearly the flagship in these woods, alternate arrangements can be made at **Kilmorey Lodge** (© 888/859-8669). This cozy country inn on Emerald Bay, at the north end of the lake, has a comfortable, historic ambience, with antique furnishings and down comforters on the beds. It also has a dining room and lounge on the premises. Standard doubles are Can$108 ($76). The **Waterton Lakes Lodge** (© 888/985-6343 or 403/859-2150; www.watertonlakes lodge.com), which opened in 1997, has a great location in the heart of Waterton Village. The lodge offers lake and mountain views, and some rooms have fireplaces, whirlpool tubs, and kitchenettes. Other facilities include a health center spa and indoor pool. Basic lodge doubles start at Can$215 ($151) in summer; the facility is closed December through April.

The Prince of Wales Hotel

Waterton Lakes National Park, AB T0K 2M0. © **403/859-2231,** or 406/892-2525 in winter. Fax 403/859-2630. www.glacierparkinc.com. 87 units. TEL. Can$179–Can$399 (US$125–US$279) double, Can$599 (US$419) suite. MC, V. Closed Oct–Apr.

The Prince of Wales compares with the finest park hostelries in Montana and Wyoming. Built in 1927 by the Great Northern Railway, the hotel boasts soaring roofs, gables, and balconies that convey the appearance of a giant alpine chalet. Rooms, though small, have aged well, with dark-stained, high-paneled wainscoting and heavily upholstered chairs. Bathrooms have European-style tubs with wraparound curtains; one look at the wash basins, and you'd surmise guests were Lilliputian-size when the hotel was first constructed.

The lobby, like many of the old railroad hotels, is wood, wood, and more wood—in this case accented by tufted furniture and carpeting. Two-story-high windows overlook the lake and village, only minutes away by footpath. If you don't spend the night at the Prince of Wales, at least stop in for a traditional British high tea, served afternoons from 2 to 5pm. All in all, the experience is very European—the gift shop even sells china and crystal.

WHERE TO DINE

All of the village's restaurants and retail outlets are within a 4-block area around Waterton Avenue (which the locals call Main St.). So despite the fact that many buildings aren't numbered, you'll have no problem finding places to eat or shop.

The **Bighorn Grill** (© 403/859-2150) at the Waterton Lakes Lodge offers casual dining (mostly beef and seafood) and spectacular views. The **Royal Stewart Dining Room** (© 403/859-2231) serves breakfast, lunch, dinner (mostly continental and English fare), and tea in the lobby of the Prince of Wales Hotel.

You'll find luxurious surroundings, and slightly higher prices, at **Kootenai Brown Dining Room** (© 403/859-2211) at the Bayshore Inn, considered the luxury spot on the lake. The order of the day is steaks, chicken, rack of lamb, and the occasional seafood entree (main courses cost $9–$19); the dining room is also open for breakfast and lunch.

New Frank's Restaurant (© 403/859-2240), located on Waterton's main street, serves both conventional Western fare that includes beef, chicken, and spaghetti, and a Chinese menu that includes an all-you-can-eat evening buffet, as well as breakfast and lunch.

16

GRAND CANYON NATIONAL PARK

by Shane Christensen

THE FIRST THING YOU NOTICE ABOUT THE GRAND CANYON IS ITS SIZE. At 277 river miles long, roughly 4,000 feet deep, and an average of 10 miles across, it's so big that even the breezes seem to draw a deep breath at the rims. But it's far more than an enormous gulch. In the past 6 million years, while the river or rivers that would eventually become the Colorado River were carving the main canyon, runoff from the rims cut hundreds of side canyons that funnel like capillaries into the larger one. As the side canyons deepened and spread, they gradually isolated buttes and mesas that tower thousands of feet above the canyon floor. Early cartographers and geologists noticed similarities between these rock pinnacles and some of the greatest works of human hands. They called them temples and shrines, and named them after Far Eastern deities such as Brahma, Vishnu, and Shiva.

The canyon not only inspires reverence but tells the grandest of stories. Half the earth's history is represented in its rocks. The oldest and deepest rock layer, the Vishnu Formation, began forming 2 billion years ago, before aerobic life forms even existed. The different layers of sedimentary rock that piled up atop the Vishnu Formation tell of landscapes that changed like dreams. They speak of mountains that really did move, eroding away into nothingness; of oceans that poured forth across the land before receding; of deserts, swamps, and rivers the size of the Mississippi—all where the canyon now lies. The very evolution of life is illustrated by the fossils in these layers.

Many of the latest products of evolution—more than 1,500 plant and 400 animal species—still survive at the canyon today. If you include the upper reaches of the Kaibab Plateau (on the canyon's North Rim), this small area of northern Arizona includes zones of biological life comparable to ones found as far south as Mexico and as far north as Alaska. The species come in every shape, size, and temperament, ranging from tiny ant lions dwelling in the canyon floor to 1,000-pound elk roaming the rims. And for every species there is a story within the story. Take the Douglas fir, for example. Once part of a forest that covered both rims and much of the canyon, this tree has endured since the last ice age on shady, north-facing slopes beneath the South Rim—long after the sun-baked rim itself became too hot and inhospitable.

A number of different Native American tribes have lived in or around the canyon, and the Navajo, Havasupai, Kaibab Paiute, Hopi, Zuni, and Hualapai tribes still dwell in this area. The Hopi still regard the canyon as their place of emergence and the place to which their dead return. Their predecessors left behind more than 3,000 archaeological sites and artifacts as old as 10,000 years.

In the 1500s Spanish missionaries and gold-greedy explorers passed through the area, but it wasn't until the 1800s that white people began settling here. Prospectors clambered through the canyon in search of precious minerals, and some of them stayed after their mines, plagued by high overhead costs, shut down. The first tourists followed, and began flooding the area after the railroad linked Grand Canyon Village to Williams, Arizona, in 1901.

When Theodore Roosevelt visited here in 1903, the canyon moved him to say, "Leave it as it is. You cannot improve on it. The ages have been at work on it, and man can only mar it. What you can do is to keep it for your children, your children's children . . . as the one great sight which every American . . . should see." Roosevelt did his part to back up his words, using the Antiquities Act to declare Grand Canyon a national monument in 1908. Congress established Grand Canyon National Park in 1919.

Although designated a "park," Grand Canyon still has a daunting, even ominous side. Visitors, no matter how many times they enter it, must negotiate with it for survival. One look at the clenched jaw of a river guide as he or she rows into Lava Rapids will remind you that the canyon exacts a heavy price for mistakes, the most common of which is to underestimate it. Try to escape, and it becomes a prison, with walls 4,000 feet high. The canyon's menace reminds us that we still haven't completely conquered nature. It even has its own symbols: the rattlesnake's warning; the elegant symmetry of the black widow; the seductive, lilylike flower of the deadly sacred datura.

Clearly, you can suffer here, but reward is everywhere. It's in the spectrum of colors: The Colorado River, filled with runoff from a recent rain in the Painted Desert, runs blood red beneath slopes of orange Hakatai shale; cactus flowers explode in pink, yellow, and red; and lichens paint rocks orange, green, and gray, creating art more striking than the works in any gallery. It's in the shapes, too—the spires, amphitheaters, temples, ramps, and cliffs—and in the shadows that bend across them before lifting like mist. It's in the myriad organisms and their individual struggles for survival. Perhaps most of all, it's in the constancy of the river, which reminds us that all things break down, wash away, and return to the earth in time.

Avoiding the Crowds. Maureen Oltrogge, the public affairs officer for Grand Canyon National Park, offers this straightforward advice for people wanting to avoid the crowds at the park: "Prime season is July and August. Try to visit at another time. If you can't come during the off season, we recommend that you come before 10am or after 2pm, so that you can avoid both the lines at the entrance gates and the parking problems inside the park."

Oltrogge's advice applies to both rims. She points out that because the North Rim lacks facilities for large numbers of people, it sometimes feels as crowded as the South Rim, despite having roughly one-eighth the visitation. Outside of spring break and midsummer, however, crowds should not be a big issue on either rim.

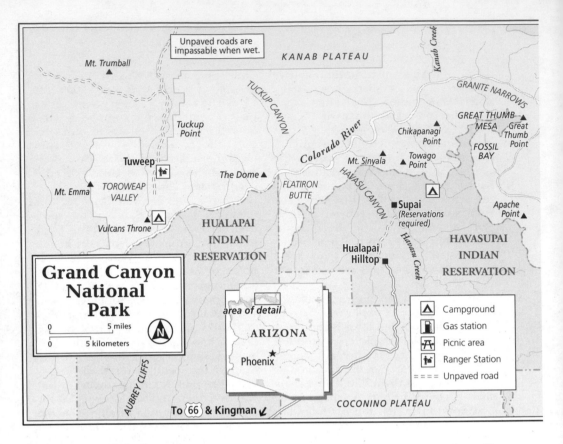

The map shows **Grand Canyon National Park** with a scale of 5 miles / 5 kilometers. Labeled features include: Mt. Trumball, Unpaved roads are impassable when wet., KANAB PLATEAU, Kanab Creek, TUCKUP CANYON, Tuckup Point, GRANITE NARROWS, Chikapanagi Point, GREAT THUMB MESA, Great Thumb Point, Tuweep, Mt. Sinyala, Towago Point, FOSSIL BAY, Colorado River, The Dome, Mt. Emma, TOROWEAP VALLEY, FLATIRON BUTTE, HAVASU CANYON, Supai (Reservations required), Apache Point, Vulcans Throne, HUALAPAI INDIAN RESERVATION, Havasu Creek, Hualapai Hilltop, HAVASUPAI INDIAN RESERVATION, area of detail, ARIZONA, Phoenix, AUBREY CLIFFS, To 66 & Kingman, COCONINO PLATEAU.

Legend:
- Campground
- Gas station
- Picnic area
- Ranger Station
- ==== Unpaved road

Just the Facts

GETTING THERE & GATEWAYS

The nearest cities to the South Rim of the Grand Canyon are Flagstaff, Arizona, 78 miles south of Grand Canyon Village on U.S. 180; and Williams, Arizona, 59 miles south on Ariz. 64.

The closest small town to the park is Tusayan, Arizona, 1 mile south of the south entrance gates on Ariz. 64. The closest substantial town to the North Rim is Kanab, Utah, 78 miles northwest of Grand Canyon National Park on U.S. 89A.

The Nearest Airports. Many travelers fly to **Phoenix/Sky Harbor International Airport** (℃ **602/273-3300**), 220 miles from the South Rim, or to **McCarran International Airport** (℃ **702/261-5743**) in Las Vegas, 263 miles from the North Rim. Both airports are served by the major airlines and car-rental companies. See the appendix for toll-free numbers.

For those who would like to fly closer than Phoenix or Las Vegas, **America West Express** (℃ **800/235-9292**) has daily jet service connecting Phoenix/Sky Harbor International Airport and **Flagstaff Pulliam Airport.** Closer still is **Grand Canyon National Park Airport** (℃ **928/638-2446**) in Tusayan, 1½ miles outside the park entrance. **Air Vegas** (℃ **800/255-7474** or 702/736-3599) and **Scenic Airlines** (℃ **800/634-6801** or 702/638-3300) both offer daily service between Las Vegas and Grand Canyon National Park Airport.

By Rail. Amtrak (℃ **800/872-7245** or 928/774-8679) regularly stops in downtown Flagstaff, where lodging, rental cars, and connecting bus service are available, and in Williams, where lodging and connecting rail service (on the historic Grand Canyon Railway) are available.

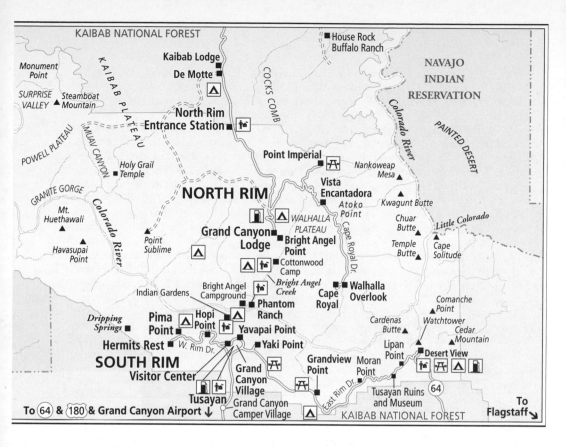

The **Historic Grand Canyon Railway** (℡ 800/843-8724) offers daily service linking Williams and Grand Canyon Village. Pulled by historic steam engines during the summer, the train leaves Williams in the morning and returns in late afternoon.

By Bus. Open Road Tours (℡ 800/766-7117) has bus service linking Flagstaff with Grand Canyon National Park. To reach either Flagstaff or Williams by bus, you can also use **Greyhound** (℡ 800/231-2222). From mid-May to mid-October, daily bus service between the North and South rims is available on the **Trans-Canyon Shuttle** (℡ 928/638-2820). The adult fare is $65 one-way, $110 round-trip.

GROUND TRANSPORTATION

Renting a Car. Most major car-rental companies have offices in Flagstaff. See the appendix for the toll-free numbers.

Exploring the Park Without a Car. Once at the South Rim, you can ride the park's **free shuttles** from March 1 through November 30 (year-round on the loop serving Grand Canyon Village). Three shuttle routes together serve marked stops throughout Grand Canyon Village, and at Mather Point, Yavapai Point, Yaki Point, and along Hermits Rest Route. When the shuttles run, Hermits Rest Route and Yaki Point (including the South Kaibab Trailhead) are closed to most private vehicles.

When the shuttles don't meet your needs, you can call **Fred Harvey's 24-hour taxi service** (℡ 928/638-2822).

INFORMATION

Contact **Grand Canyon National Park,** P.O. Box 129, Grand Canyon, AZ 86023 (℡ 800/638-7888; www.nps.gov/grca), for a free copy of the *Grand Canyon Trip Planner.* Those who want more in-depth information can buy books, maps, and videos from the Grand Canyon Association, P.O. Box 399, Grand Canyon, AZ 86023 (© **800/858-2808;** www.grand canyon.org). Among the hundreds of books written on the Grand Canyon, several stand out. For a discussion of the human history of the Grand Canyon, try *Living at the Edge: Explorers, Exploiters and Settlers of the Grand Canyon Region* (Grand Canyon Association, 1998), by Michael F. Anderson. In *An Introduction to Grand Canyon Geology* (Grand Canyon Association, 1999) author L. Greer Price explains the geology of the Grand Canyon in terms anyone can understand.

Call © **928/638-7888** for recorded weather information.

FEES & PERMITS

Admission to Grand Canyon National Park costs $20 per private vehicle and $10 for those on foot or bicycle. The receipt is good for a week and includes both rims. You can make advance reservations for campsites at Mather Campground (on the South Rim) and at the North Rim Campground by calling © **800/365-CAMP** (2267).

Permits are required for all overnight camping in the backcountry. This includes all overnight stays below the rims (except in the cabins and dorms at Phantom Ranch) and on parkland outside of designated campgrounds.

Backcountry permits for the month desired go on sale on the first of the month, 4 months earlier. For example, permits for all of May go on sale January 1; permits for June go on sale February 1, and so on. At press time, fees were $10 per permit plus $5 per person per night camped below the rim, or $5 per group per night camped above the rim. You can get a **Backcountry Permit Request Form** by ordering the free Backcountry Trip Planner from the park. To do this, call the park's main extension at © **800/638-7888** and choose the "backcountry information" option; or write to Grand Canyon National Park, P.O. Box 129, Grand Canyon, AZ 86023. Or, you can download a form and instructions from www.nps.gov/grca.

You can fax in your Backcountry Permit Request Form to **928/638-2125** no earlier than the date the permits become available; or mail it with a postmark no earlier than the date the permits become available. The park receives many more permit requests than it can fill, so it's a good idea to put in your request as soon as permits become available. No requests are taken by phone. However, the **Backcountry Information Center** (© **928/638-7875**) at the Maswik Transportation Center across the railroad tracks from Maswik Lodge, does answer questions over the telephone Monday through Friday from 1 to 5pm Arizona time.

INFORMATION CENTERS

Completed in the fall of 2000 near Mather Point, the Canyon View Information Plaza was designed to orient visitors arriving at the park via a new light rail system. Though the rail system has not yet been built, the Information Plaza has the streamlined appearance of a modern transportation hub, with ample room for pedestrians and no automobile parking lots. Outdoors in the landscaped plaza, kiosks provide basic information on tours, trails, canyon overlooks, cycling, and other topics. The main South Rim visitor center is inside the long, glass-fronted building known as **Canyon View Center.** Here, you'll find additional displays on the canyon and the Colorado Plateau, an information desk, and an area for ranger presentations. There's also a large bookstore at the plaza, and ample restrooms. To reach the plaza you'll need to take a free shuttle, walk, or park a short distance away at Mather Point.

The **Yavapai Observation Station,** ⅔ mile west of Canyon View Center on Yavapai Point, has an observation room where you can see and identify many of the monuments in the central canyon. Rangers here frequently lead interpretive programs.

The **Desert View Contact Station,** 26 miles east of Grand Canyon Village, is small and staffed by volunteers. It sells books and provides information on the canyon.

Located 3 miles west of Desert View, **Tusayan Museum** has an information desk staffed by rangers in addition to displays on the area's indigenous peoples.

Historic **Kolb Studio,** located on the rim at the west end of Grand Canyon Village, houses a small bookstore and an art gallery with free exhibits.

The **North Rim Visitor Center** has a small bookstore and information desk staffed by rangers, volunteers, and employees of the **Grand Canyon Association.**

SPECIAL REGULATIONS & WARNINGS

It's illegal to remove any resources from the park. These can be anything from flowers to broken pottery fragments. Even seemingly useless articles such as bits of metal from the canyon's old mining operations have historical value and are protected by law.

Fires are strictly prohibited except at North Rim, Desert View, and Mather campgrounds. In the backcountry, use a small camp stove for cooking.

SEASONS & CLIMATE

The climate at Grand Canyon varies greatly not only from season to season but from point to point. At over 8,000 feet in elevation, the North Rim is by far the coldest, dampest part of the park. Its temperatures run about 30° (-1°C) cooler than at the canyon-bottom Phantom Ranch more than 5,000 feet below, and 7° cooler than the South Rim, roughly 1,000 feet below. It averages 25

inches of precipitation per year, compared to just 8 inches at Phantom Ranch and 16 inches on the South Rim.

The North Rim doesn't open until mid-May, so your only choice in early spring is the South Rim, where daily highs average 60°F and 70°F (16°C and 21°C) in April and May, respectively. Travelers should be prepared for late-winter storms, which occasionally bring snow to the rim. Spring is an ideal time to hike the inner canyon, with highs in April averaging 82°F (28°C).

In summer, the rims seldom become unbearably hot. Summer highs are usually in the 80s (mid-20s Celsius) on the South Rim and in the 70s (lower 20s Celsius) on the North Rim. The Inner Gorge, on the other hand, can be torrid, with highs in July averaging 106°F (41°C). Localized thunderstorms frequently drench the park in late July and August, the wettest month of the year, when nearly 2¼ inches of rain fall on the South Rim. On the North Rim, nights can be nippy even during July, when low temperatures average a chilly 46°F (8°C).

After the thunderstorms taper off in mid-September, fall is a great time to be anywhere in the park. Highs on the South Rim average 76°F (24°C) in September, 65°F (18°C) in October, and 52°F (11°C) in November. The North Rim has highs of 69°F (21°C) in September and 59°F (15°C) in October. (It closes in mid-Oct.) The Inner Gorge remains hot in September, but cools off considerably, to an average high of 84°F (29°C), in October. The first winter storms can hit the North Rim as early as mid-October.

In winter, the North Rim is closed, and drivers to the South Rim should be prepared for icy roads and occasional closures there as well. When the snow isn't falling, the South Rim warms up nicely, with average highs of 41°F (5°C) in January. Hiking trails remain open during winter but are often snow-packed and icy.

For 3 weeks every September, world-renowned musicians gather for the **Grand Canyon Music Festival.** Most of the offerings are chamber-music concerts, and all are at the acoustically superb Shrine of the Ages Auditorium next to Park Headquarters. Tickets for the 7:30pm concerts are available in advance through **Grand Canyon Music Festival,** P.O. Box 1332, Grand Canyon, AZ 86023 (© **800/997-8285;** www.grandcanyonmusicfest.org).

For up-to-date information on other special events, consult the park's newspaper, *The Guide.*

If You Have Only 1 Day

After stopping at one of the **information centers** to get your bearings, hike a short distance down the **Bright Angel** or **North Kaibab trails** in the morning. (If the weather is hot or if your condition is not top-notch, a rim trail may be preferable.) At midday, attend a ranger presentation; times and locations are printed in *The Guide.* Later in the day, go on a scenic drive. On the South Rim, your best choice on the first day would be **Desert View Drive,** which remains open to cars year-round and offers expansive views of the central and eastern canyon. On the North Rim, travel the **Cape Royal Road.** To complete your scenic drive, watch sunset from **Lipan Point** on the South Rim or from **Cape Royal** on the North Rim. The scenic drives and corridor trails are detailed later in this chapter.

Exploring the Park by Car

Hermits Rest Route

This 8-mile road from Grand Canyon Village to Hermits Rest is open to private cars only in Dec–Feb, months when the shuttles aren't running.

Your first stops are at **Trailview 1 and 2.** Looking north from these view points, you can see straight down the side canyons that formed on either side of the Colorado River along the Bright Angel fault. Below, you may spot lush vegetation growing around a spring. This area is Indian Garden, where Havasupai Indians once farmed.

The next stop, **Maricopa Point,** overlooks the old Orphan Mine, which produced some of the richest uranium ore anywhere during the 1950s and 1960s. Below and to the west, you can see the metal framework from the tramway used to move ore to the rim from 1956 to 1959.

At the **Powell Memorial,** you'll find a memorial to John Wesley Powell, the one-armed Civil War veteran thought to be the first white person to float through the canyon. From atop the memorial, you can get an especially fine view 60 miles southeast to the San Francisco peaks, including Humphreys Peak, which at 12,643 feet is the highest point in Arizona.

Because the next stop, **Hopi Point,** projects far into the canyon, its tip is the best place on Hermits Rest Route to watch the sunset. As the sun drops, its light will play across four of the canyon's loveliest temples. The flat mesa almost due north of the point is Shiva Temple. The temple southwest of it is Osiris; the one southeast of it is Isis. East of Isis is Buddha Temple.

The next stop, **Mohave Point,** is a great place to observe some of the Colorado River's most furious rapids. Farthest downstream (to your left) is Hermit Rapids. Above it, you can make out the top of the dangerous Granite Rapids. Just above Granite Rapids, you can make out the bottom of Salt Creek Rapids. As you look at Hermit Creek Canyon and the rapids below it, you can easily visualize how floods washed rocks from the side canyon into the Colorado River, forming the natural dam that creates the rapids.

Next you'll come to **The Abyss,** where the steep canyon walls drop 2,600 feet to the base of the Redwall Limestone.

Three thousand feet below the next stop, **Pima Point,** you'll see some of the

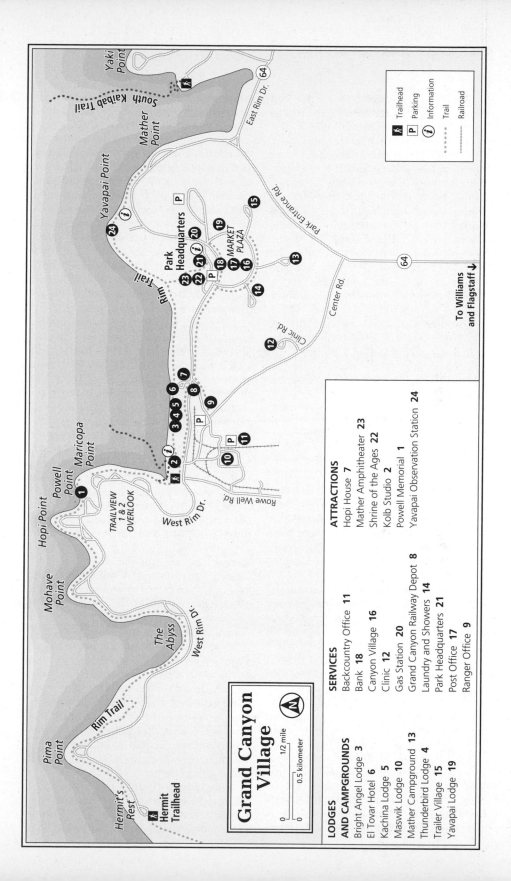

Grand Canyon Village

N

0 _____ 1/2 mile
0 _____ 0.5 kilometer

LODGES
AND CAMPGROUNDS
Bright Angel Lodge **3**
El Tovar Hotel **6**
Kachina Lodge **5**
Maswik Lodge **10**
Mather Campground **13**
Thunderbird Lodge **4**
Trailer Village **15**
Yavapai Lodge **19**

SERVICES
Backcountry Office **11**
Bank **18**
Canyon Village **16**
Clinic **12**
Gas Station **20**
Grand Canyon Railway Depot **8**
Laundry and Showers **14**
Park Headquarters **21**
Post Office **17**
Ranger Office **9**

ATTRACTIONS
Hopi House **7**
Mather Amphitheater **23**
Shrine of the Ages **22**
Kolb Studio **2**
Powell Memorial **1**
Yavapai Observation Station **24**

Legend: K Trailhead   P Parking   i Information   ···· Trail   ┼┼┼┼ Railroad

Yaki Point
South Kaibab Trail
Mather Point
Yavapai Point
East Rim Dr.
64
Park Entrance Rd.
Park Headquarters
MARKET PLAZA
Center Rd.
Clinic Rd.
64
To Williams and Flagstaff →
Rim Trail
Maricopa Point
Powell Point
Hopi Point
Mohave Point
The Abyss
West Rim Dr.
Rim Trail
Pima Point
Hermit's Rest
Hermit Trailhead
TRAILVIEW 1 & 2 OVERLOOK
West Rim Dr.
Rowe Well Rd.

foundations and walls from the old Hermit Camp, a tourist destination built in 1912 by the Santa Fe Railroad.

Before descending to Hermit Camp, tourists took a break at the next stop, **Hermits Rest.** In this 1914 building, Mary Colter celebrated the "hermit" theme by building what resembled a crude rock shelter, with stones heaped highest around the chimney. Inside, Colter covered the ceiling above the large fireplace with soot, so that the room had the look of a cave warmed by fire. Nearby are restrooms and a snack bar selling sweets, chips, soda, and sandwiches.

Highlights: Closed to cars during high season, the overlooks are quieter than those on the Desert View Drive and afford excellent river views.

Drawbacks: Occasional long waits for buses.

Desert View Drive

Allow a half day for this 25-mile scenic drive on Ariz. 64, which connects the South Entrance Rd. with Desert View.

The first stop, **Yavapai Point,** features some of the most expansive views both up and down the canyon. A historic observation station here has huge plate glass windows overlooking the canyon, along with interpretive panels identifying the major landmarks.

People entering the park from the south generally catch their first glimpse of the canyon from the next stop, **Mather Point.** It's a clamorous place with one redeeming feature: a canyon view. (There's no such thing as a bad canyon view.) You can park here and walk to the South Rim's new visitor center at the **Canyon View Information Plaza.**

Yaki Point, the first stop located off Ariz. 64, is accessible by car only when the shuttles aren't running. It's a great place to see the monuments of the central canyon, including Wotan's Throne, Vishnu Temple, and Zoroaster Temple. Two trails are also easy to spot from here. To the north, the South Kaibab Trail descends in switchbacks below Skeleton Point. Meanwhile, the Tonto Trail meanders across the broad blue-green terrace known as the Tonto Platform.

The next stop, 7,406-foot-high **Grandview Point,** is one of the highest spots on the South Rim. In the 1890s, one of the canyon's early prospectors, Pete Barry, built a trail from Grandview Point to nearby Horseshoe Mesa, where he mined copper. He then built cabins and a dining hall on the mesa, and a hotel a short distance from Grandview Point. Today only a trace of the hotel's foundation remains, but the trail is still used, and Horseshoe Mesa still bears the remnants of Barry's mines.

Next you'll come to **Moran Point,** named for landscape painter Thomas Moran. This is the best place from which to view the tilting block of rock known as "The Sinking Ship." Stand at the end of the point and look southwest at the rocks level with the rim. The "Sinking Ship" appears to be "submerged" in the horizontal layers of Coronado Butte (in the foreground). It's part of the Grandview Monocline, a place where rocks have bent in a single fold around a fault line.

Next comes **Tusayan Pueblo,** built in the 12th century by the ancestral Pueblo people. Among the 3,500 documented archaeological sites in and around the Grand Canyon, this may have been the last one abandoned. A self-guided tour takes you around the pueblo. Built in 1932, the adjoining Tusayan Museum celebrates the traditions of the area's Native American tribes.

Don't miss the next stop, **Lipan Point.** With views far down the canyon to the west, it's a great place to catch the sunset. It also overlooks the Colorado River where the river makes two sweeping curves to form an enormous S. Just downstream of the S, the river begins cutting through the 2 billion-year-old Vishnu Formation, and the steep-walled Inner Gorge begins.

Like Lipan Point, the next stop, **Navajo Point,** offers fine views of the Grand Canyon Supergroup, a formation of igneous and sedimentary rocks that have eroded altogether in many other parts of the canyon. The long, thin streaks of maroon, gray, and black, which tilt at an angle of about 20 degrees, are layers of this formation.

The last stop on the Desert View Drive is **Desert View,** where you'll find the Watchtower, a 70-foot-high, historic stone building that was modeled after towers found at ancient pueblos such as Mesa Verde and Hovenweep. Atop the Watchtower is an enclosed observation deck, which at 7,522 feet is the highest point on the South Rim. The rim at Desert View offers spectacular views of the eastern canyon.

If you take the Desert View Drive shuttle, be aware that the buses stop only at Mather, Yavapai, and Yaki Points.

Highlights: Spectacular views of both the central and the eastern canyon.

Drawbacks: Packed parking lots in summer.

North Rim: Cape Royal Drive

From the Grand Canyon Lodge on the North Rim, it's best to go the length of the scenic drive 23 miles directly to Cape Royal, on the Walhalla Plateau, then make your stops on the way back to the lodge. That way, you can do the short hikes near Cape Royal while your legs are fresh, and stop at the picnic areas, closer to the lodge, on your way back. Allow a half day to a day for this drive.

Start your driving tour at **Cape Royal,** where a gentle, paved 0.3 mile (each way) trail passes a natural bridge, Angel's Window, carved into a rock peninsula along the rim. The trail ends at the tip of Cape Royal, with views of the looming butte known as Wotan's Throne.

Your next stop may be at the **Cliff Springs Trail,** a 0.5-mile walk that ends at a small spring. (See "Day Hikes," below.)

From the next stop, **Walhalla Overlook,** you can follow with your eyes the tan line of Unkar Creek as it snakes down toward Unkar Delta. The soil and abundant water at the delta made for excellent farming for the ancestral Pueblo people, who occupied the canyon through about A.D. 1175. Many of these people migrated seasonally to dwellings such as the two small pueblos across the street from this overlook.

The next stop, **Roosevelt Point,** is one of the best places in the Canyon to see the confluence of the gorge of the Little Colorado River with the Grand Canyon. They meet at nearly a right angle, unusual in that most tributaries enter at close to the same direction as the larger rivers.

By starting your driving tour of the Walhalla Plateau early in the day, you can reach the next stop, **Vista Encantadora,** in time for a late picnic on one of several tables with canyon views.

From there you can finish your driving tour by taking the 3-mile spur from the Cape Royal Road to **Point Imperial,** which at 8,803 feet is the highest point on the North Rim. It's also the best place on either rim to view the northeastern end of the park.

Highlights: Sparse crowds and lovely views of the eastern canyon.

Drawbacks: The Colorado River is not visible as often on this drive as on the South Rim drives. Also, there's no shuttle on the north rim, so you must do all the driving yourself.

Organized Tours & Ranger Programs

The park offers a host of ranger programs whose schedule changes seasonally. A typical schedule includes guided hikes and walks, kids' programs, and discussions of geology, native species, and natural and cultural history. Evening programs are scheduled nightly. In winter, the South Rim cuts back on its programs and the North Rim is closed. For an up-to-date schedule, consult the park newspaper, *The Guide.*

Guided Hikes & Trips. The nonprofit **Grand Canyon Field Institute** schedules dozens of backpacking trips and outings ranging in length from 2 to 9 days.

Some explore broad subjects such as ecology; others hone narrow skills such as orienteering or slot-canyon photography. Each is guided by an expert on the topics covered. Because the courses vary greatly, the Field Institute assigns a difficulty level to each and tries to help participants find ones suited to their skill levels, fitness levels, and interests. For more information, call © **928/638-2485;** write to P.O. Box 399, Grand Canyon, AZ 86023; or check out the website at **www.grandcanyon.org/fieldinstitute**.

Bus Tours. Of the many private companies that offer bus tours, **Fred Harvey** has the most extensive schedule. Among the choices are East Rim (Desert View) and West Rim (Hermits Rest) tours ($28 and $16, respectively, for adults; under 16 free), sunset tours to Hopi or Mojave Point ($12), sunrise tours ($12) to one of several rim stops, and all-day outings ($34) that combine two of the shorter tours. Unlike the drivers on the free shuttles, Fred Harvey drivers narrate the tours. Don't believe everything they say. Though they mean well and offer some valuable information, they were not hired for their command of natural science and history. (Just be glad you don't have distracted professors driving the bus.) For advance reservations, call © **888/297-2757.** Once at the canyon, visit the transportation desks at Yavapai, Maswik, or Bright Angel lodges, or call © **928/638-2631,** ext. 6015.

Open Road Tours (© 800/766-7117) offers 1-day guided canyon tours that depart from Flagstaff at 9:30am and return by 5:30pm. The cost is $69 for adults; $35 for 11 and under.

Historic & Man-Made Attractions

Most of the historic buildings on the South Rim are concentrated in **Grand Canyon Village,** a National Historic District. Hermits Rest, on Hermits Rest Rout, and The Watchtower, on the Desert View Drive, are also of historical significance (see "Exploring the Park by Car," above).

More than a half dozen of these historic buildings were designed by Mary Colter, a Minneapolis schoolteacher who began decorating the shops that sold American Indian art along the Santa Fe Railroad line in 1902. As both a decorator and a self-trained architect, Colter later designed these Grand Canyon landmarks: Hopi House (1905), The Lookout (1914), Hermits Rest (1914), Phantom Ranch (1922), Watchtower (1932), and Bright Angel Lodge (1935). Colter's work drew heavily on the architectural styles of Native Americans and Spanish settlers in the Southwest. Another historic building, the El Tovar Hotel (1905), was designed by Charles Whittlesey in a style reminiscent of a northern European hunting lodge.

On the North Rim, Grand Canyon Lodge, built in 1928, is included on the National Register of Historic Places.

Day Hikes

There's no better way to enjoy the canyon than by actually walking down into it, watching the vegetation and rock layers change as you descend. The experience is far more rewarding than merely looking down from the rims.

Unfortunately, hiking below the rims can be dangerous, especially at midday during summer. Changes in temperature and elevation can make hiking difficult even in ideal conditions. The jarring descent can strain your knees; the climb back out will test your lungs and heart. If it's hot out or you aren't up to climbing, consider walking on one of the rim trails. If nothing else, this will help you move away from the crowds at the overlooks. The rim trails are especially peaceful in the forests on the North Rim.

First-time hikers in the canyon should consider one of the **corridor trails:** North Kaibab, South Kaibab, and

Bright Angel. Well maintained and easy to follow, these are regularly patrolled by park rangers. Each has at least one emergency phone and pit toilet. Drinking water is available at several sources along both the Bright Angel and North Kaibab trails, but not on the South Kaibab. Wherever you hike, carry plenty of water and food, and check with the rangers about the availability of additional water along the trail. Eat and drink regularly. Wear sunscreen, sunglasses, and protective clothing. If you hike into the canyon, allow yourself twice as much time for the trip out as for the descent.

RIM TRAILS: SOUTH RIM

West Rim (Hermits Rest) Trail & South Rim Trail

8 miles on West Rim Trail to Hermits Rest, 2.1 miles on South Rim Trail to Mather Point. Easy to moderate. Access: Grand Canyon Village, along the rim behind the El Tovar Hotel. Water sources at Grand Canyon Village, Hermits Rest, Park Headquarters, Yavapai Point, and Canyon View Information Plaza.

From Grand Canyon village, you can follow the rim trail 8 miles west to Hermits Rest or 1.5 miles northeast to Yavapai Point

West Rim (Hermits Rest) Trail. Walking instead of driving along the rim is a great way to see the canyon while putting some elbow room between yourself and the crowds at the overlooks. The trail travels parallel to Hermit Road and passes through all the same scenic overlooks described in the driving tour. The 1.3-mile stretch from the Village to Maricopa Point is paved, with one 200-vertical-foot climb. Past Maricopa Point, the trail planes off somewhat and the pavement ends. For the rest of the way to Hermits Rest, the "trail" becomes a series of footpaths that meander through pinyon-juniper woodland along the rim (when not crossing overlooks).

Sagebrush roots and loose rocks make for tricky footing, but the scenery is lovely, and the crowds thin as you move farther west.

Because 16 miles might be too much hiking for 1 day, I recommend hiking out on this trail from Grand Canyon Village and taking the shuttle back (Mar–Nov). By hiking out, you can avoid revisiting the same overlooks on the shuttle ride back—the shuttles stop at every turnout while en route to Hermits Rest, but only stop at Mohave Point and Hopi Point on their way back to Grand Canyon Village.

South Rim Trail. This smooth, paved trail connects Grand Canyon Village and Mather Point, 2.1 miles away. Around the lodges, the path is a flat sidewalk teeming with people. The crowds dissipate somewhat between the east edge of the village and Yavapai Point. Near Yavapai Point you'll find many smooth flat rocks along the rim—great places from which to contemplate the canyon. **Yavapai Point** has a historic observation station overlooking the canyon. Passing Yavapai Point, you can walk another 0.6 miles to Mather Point on a portion of the park's new Greenway, which closely parallels the rim. If you grow fatigued during your walk, you can catch a shuttle back to Grand Canyon Village from Mather or Yavapai points.

RIM TRAILS: NORTH RIM

Cape Final Trail

2 miles one-way. Easy. Access: An unmarked dirt parking area off the Cape Royal Rd., 5 miles south of Roosevelt Point.

This relatively flat, boulder-free trail is a good choice for a first hike in the backcountry. It meanders through ponderosa pine forest on an old Jeep trail, ending at Cape Final, where you'll have partial views of the northern canyon and Juno Temple.

Cliff Springs Trail

0.5 mile one-way. Moderate. Access: A small pullout ⅓ mile north of Cape Royal on the Cape Royal Rd.

Both scenic and fairly short, this hike is perfect for active families. This dirt trail seems to head into forest away from the canyon, but it soon descends into a narrow, rocky side canyon that drains into the larger one—a reminder that the Walhalla Plateau is a peninsula. It hugs the north wall of the side canyon, passing under limestone overhangs, in light colored green by the canopies of box elder trees. The springs drip from one of these overhangs, where mosses carpet fissures in the rock It is not suggested to drink spring water as it's not potable. A waist-high boulder marks the end of the trail.

Ken Patrick Trail

10 miles one-way. Strenuous. Access: From the south side of the parking area for Point Imperial or from the parking area for the N. Kaibab Trail (on the N. Rim entrance road, 2 miles north of Grand Canyon Lodge).

This steeply rolling trail travels through ponderosa pine and spruce-fir forest between the head of Roaring Springs Canyon and Point Imperial. Starting at the North Kaibab end, the first mile of the trail has been pounded into dust by mules. The path becomes very faint about 4 miles in, after passing the trailhead for the old Bright Angel Trail. Past the Cape Royal Road, the trail descends into, then climbs out of, a very steep drainage overgrown with thorn-covered New Mexican locust. Although challenging, the 3-mile section between the Cape Royal Road and Point Imperial is also the prettiest stretch, skirting the rim of the canyon above upper drainages of Nankoweap Creek. You'll see plenty of scarlet bugler, identifiable by its tubular red flowers with flared lower petals, as well as a number of Douglas firs interspersed among the ubiquitous ponderosa pines.

The Transept Trail & Bright Angel Point Trail

Bright Angel Point Trail 0.25 mile each way. Transept Trail 1.5 miles Easy. Access: Behind Grand Canyon Lodge.

To familiarize yourself with the North Rim, start with these trails, which are different sections of the same pathway. At the bottom of the stairs behind Grand Canyon Lodge, the Bright Angel Point Trail goes to the left, while the Transept Trail goes right.

The **Bright Angel Point Trail,** which is paved, travels a quarter-mile to the tip of a narrow peninsula dividing Roaring Springs and Transept canyons. It passes a number of craggy outcroppings of Kaibab Limestone, around which the roots of wind-whipped juniper trees cling like arthritic hands. The trail ends at 8,148-foot-high Bright Angel Point.

The **Transept Trail** ventures northeast along the rim of Transept Canyon, connecting the lodge and the North Rim Campground. Passing through old-growth ponderosa pine and quaking aspen, it descends into, then climbs out of, three shallow side drainages, with ascents steep enough to take the breath away from people unaccustomed to the altitude. Approximate round-trip hiking time for this trail is 1½ hours.

Widforss Trail

5 miles one-way. Moderate. Hiking time approximately 6 hours round-trip. Access: A dirt road ¼ mile south of the Cape Royal Rd. Follow this road about ¾ mile to the parking area, which is well marked.

Named for landscape painter Gunnar Widforss, this trail skirts the head of Transept Canyon before venturing south to Widforss Point. For the first 2 miles, the trail undulates through ponderosa pine and spruce-fir forest, with spruce-fir on the shady side of each drainage. Past the head of Transept Canyon, the trail heads south through a stand of old-growth ponderosa, some of which have been singed by forest fires.

The trail reaches the rim again at Widforss Point, where you'll have a view of five temples. Near the rim are a picnic table and several good campsites. This is a self-guided hike. Brochures can be obtained at the trailhead.

CANYON TRAILS

Because of the huge elevation changes on the canyon trails, none should be called easy. (More people are rescued off the Bright Angel Trail, generally considered the "easiest" trail into the canyon, than off any other trail.) In general, please note that rating a trail easy, moderate, or difficult oversimplifies the situation; for this reason, we've avoided doing so below. For example, among the wilderness trails, the **Hermit Trail** is fine for many day hikers going to Santa Maria Spring, but it becomes more rugged and harder to follow beyond that point; this trail offers day hikes that vary in distance up to 12 miles. The **Tonto Trail** is often easy to walk on, but has little water or shade. It's always a good idea to discuss your plans and your experience with a ranger before setting out on a hike.

SOUTH RIM CORRIDOR TRAILS

Bright Angel Trail

4.7 miles to Indian Garden, 7.8 miles to Colorado River, 9.3 miles to Bright Angel Campground. Access: Just west of Kolb Studio, near Grand Canyon Village. 6,860 ft. at trailhead; 3,800 ft. at Indian Garden; 2,450 ft. at Colorado River. Water sources at One-and-a-Half-Mile House (seasonal), Three-Mile House (seasonal), Indian Garden, Colorado River (purify before drinking), Bright Angel Campground.

Both Native Americans and early settlers recognized this as a choice location for a trail. First, there's an enormous fault line that creates a natural break in the cliffs. Then there's the water—more of it than anywhere on the South Rim.

On a day hike, follow the switchbacks below Grand Canyon Village to One-and-a-Half-Mile House or Three-Mile House, each of which has shade, an emergency phone, and drinking water (seasonally). The Park Service, which responds to hundreds of emergency calls on this trail every year, discourages many day-hikers from going past One-and-a-Half-Mile House.

If you continue on the trail past Three-Mile House, you begin a long descent to the picnic area near the spring at Indian Garden, where lush vegetation will surround you and large cottonwood trees provide shade. At 4.6 miles and more than 3,000 vertical feet from the rim, Indian Garden is dangerously deep for many people. However, a few well-prepared day-hikers may wish to hike an additional 1.5 miles past Indian Garden on the relatively flat (in this area) Tonto and Plateau Point trails. The Plateau Point Trail eventually dead-ends at an overlook of the Colorado River 1,300 feet below.

South Kaibab Trail

6.3 miles to Colorado River, 7.3 miles to Bright Angel Campground. Access: At Yaki Point (Ariz. 64, East Rim Dr., 5 miles east of Grand Canyon Village). 7,260 ft. at trailhead; 2,450 ft. at Colorado River. Water sources at Colorado River and Bright Angel Campground.

Unlike the Bright Angel Trail, which follows natural routes into the canyon, the South Kaibab was built using dynamite and hard labor. And unlike the Bright Angel Trail, which stays near creek beds for much of the distance to the Colorado River, the South Kaibab Trail travels on ridgelines with expansive views. Because the South Kaibab has no water and little shade, it is best for descending. Bright Angel Trail is a safer trail for most hikers.

For a good day hike, follow the trail as it makes a series of switchbacks through the upper rock layers, down the west side of Yaki Point. Below the Coconino Sandstone, the trail heads north to Cedar Ridge, a platform that has pit toilets and a hitching post for mules. Shaded by pinyon and juniper trees, it affords expansive views down side canyons to the east and west. This is an excellent place for day-hikers to picnic and rest before hiking the 1.5 miles and 1,500 vertical feet back out.

NORTH RIM CORRIDOR TRAIL

North Kaibab Trail

2.7 miles to Supai Tunnel, 4.7 miles to Roaring Springs, 6.8 miles to Cottonwood Campground, 14.4 miles to the Colorado. Access: On North Rim entrance road, 2 miles north of Grand Canyon Lodge. 8,250 ft. at North Kaibab Trailhead; 5,200 ft. at Roaring Springs; 4,080 ft. at Cottonwood Campground; 2,400 ft. at Colorado River. Water sources at Roaring Springs (seasonal), Bright Angel Creek, Cottonwood Campground (seasonal), Phantom Ranch, Bright Angel Campground.

Less crowded than the South Rim corridor trails, this one begins at a parking area off the North Rim entrance road, 2 miles north of Grand Canyon Village. It starts with a long series of switchbacks through thickly forested terrain at the head of Roaring Springs Canyon. The first major landmark is Supai Tunnel. At 2.7 miles from the trailhead, and with seasonal water, shade, and restrooms available, this is an excellent turnaround point for day-hikers. Beyond the tunnel, the trail descends in relatively gradual switchbacks through the bright red Supai Formation rocks, then crosses a bridge over a creek bed. Past the bridge, the trail travels along the south wall of Roaring Springs Canyon, on ledges atop cliffs of Redwall Limestone. A spire known as "The Needle" marks the point where the trail begins its descent of the Redwall cliffs. Roaring Springs, the water source for both rims, becomes audible just above the confluence of Bright Angel and Roaring Springs canyons. A 0.2-mile-long spur trail descends to the springs. In the lush vegetation around it, you'll find drinking water (seasonally), shade, and picnic tables. Roughly 5 miles and 3,000 vertical feet below the rim, this is the farthest a day-hiker should go.

WILDERNESS TRAILS

Rangers are seldom encountered on the wilderness trails, which are not maintained by the park. These boulder-strewn trails have all but washed away in some places; in others, they descend steeply through cliffs.

Two South Rim wilderness trails, the Grandview and Hermit trails, work well for day hikes. Day-hikers often descend 2,600 vertical feet on the **Grandview Trail** to Horseshoe Mesa (avoid when wet or icy). This trail does not provide direct access to the Colorado River. Another option is to follow the **Hermit Trail** to Santa Maria or Dripping Springs (via a spur on the Dripping Springs Trail). Other South Rim wilderness trails include the Tanner, New Hance, Boucher, and South Bass. North Rim wilderness trails include the Bill Hall, Thunder River, Deer Creek, North Bass, and Nankoweap.

Other Sports & Activities

Fishing. There's great trout fishing in the Colorado River just upstream of the National Park, between Glen Canyon Dam and Lees Ferry. For advice on fishing this area, contact **Lees Ferry Anglers Guides and Fly Shop** (© 800/962-9755 or 928/355-2261), at Cliff Dwellers Lodge, about 2½ hours north of Flagstaff on U.S. 89A. Before you can fish in or near the park, you'll need an Arizona Fishing Permit and trout stamp, available at Lees Ferry Anglers or at the **Canyon Village Marketplace** (© 928/638-2262) in Grand Canyon Village.

Biking. Inside the park, cyclists are required to stay on roads, many of them narrow and crowded, and they are not allowed on the new section of Greenway. On the South Rim, the best riding is on the Hermits Rest Route when the road is closed to most cars. At these times, you'll still have to watch out for tour buses, shuttles, and an occasional private vehicle. You can mountain bike on trails in the Kaibab

National Forest, which borders the park on both rims.

Cross-Country Skiing. When snow sticks on the South Rim, you can cross-country ski at the **Grandview Nordic Center** in the Kaibab National Forest near Grandview Point. To get there, drive east toward Desert View on Ariz. 64. About 1¾ miles past the Grandview Point turnoff, turn right on the road to the Arizona Trail. The Forest Service has marked three loops in this area, each meandering through meadows and ponderosa pine forest. For more information call the **Kaibab National Forest Tusayan Ranger District Office** at © **928/638-2443.**

White-Water Rafting. White-water raft trips inside the park generally last from 3 to 14 days and must be booked well ahead of time. Although most trips begin at Lees Ferry, Arizona, the end points vary. Some companies allow for partial trips by picking up or dropping off passengers at various points in the canyon (most often at Phantom Ranch).

All the companies operating in Grand Canyon run excellent trips, though all are subject to the whims of the Colorado River and the storms that move through the canyon. For about $225 per day, all provide food, portable toilets, and some camping equipment, as well as access to parts of the inner canyon that are difficult, if not impossible, to reach on foot. Among them are some of the most beautiful places on earth.

For a list of companies offering both motorized and oar-powered river trips through the canyon, contact the park directly or log on to www.nps.gov/grca.

Tamer Alternatives. Aramark-Wilderness River Adventures, 50 S. Lake Powell Blvd., Page, AZ (© **800/528-6154** or 928/645-3279), offers half-day smoothwater raft trips from the base of Glen Canyon Dam to Lees Ferry, where the companies floating into Grand Canyon begin their trips. Cost for the half-day

trip is $59 for adults, $49 for 12 and under. This company also runs whitewater trips (© **800/992-8022**).

Grand Canyon Airlines (© **866/235-9422** or 928/638-2463) offers a half-day trip (really a full day when you factor in bus rides to and from the rafting site), plus round-trip transportation (totaling 290 miles) from Grand Canyon National Park Airport in Tusayan, 1½ miles south of the park's south entrance. Cost for this 12-hour tour is $111 ($61 for 12 and under).

One-day trips through the westernmost part of Grand Canyon are available through **Hualapai River Runners** (© **928/769-2210**), P.O. Box 246, Peach Springs, AZ 86434. These trips (in sturdy, rubber motorized rafts), which cost $265 per person, begin with rapids in the lower Granite Gorge of Grand Canyon and end on the still waters of Lake Mead. Family discounts are offered.

Overflights. Six companies at Grand Canyon National Park Airport in Tusayan currently offer scenic airplane or helicopter rides over the canyon. With more than 600,000 people taking air tours over the canyon every year, the flights, which generate a great deal of noise in parts of the park, have become a politically charged issue.

The following companies offer air tours originating from Tusayan: **Papillon Grand Canyon Helicopters** (© **800/528-2418** or 928/638-2419; www.papillon.com); **Air Grand Canyon/Sky Eye Air Tours** (© **800/247-4726** or 928/638-2686; www.airgrandcanyon.com); **AirStar Airlines** (© **800/962-3869** or 928/638-2139; www.airstar.com); **AirStar Helicopters** (© **800/962-3869** or 928/638-2622); **Grand Canyon Airlines** (© **800/528-2413** or 928/638-2407; www.grandcanyonairlines.com); and **Kenai Helicopters** (© **800/541-4537** or 928/638-2764; www.flykenai.com).

Prices for air tours vary, but the airplane flights, by and large, last longer and cost less. Most airplane tours remain airborne for 40 to 50 minutes, at costs ranging from $75 to $89 per person; most helicopter tours fly for 30 minutes, at costs of $99 to $115. The planes also cover more ground, crossing the canyon near Hermits Rest and returning along the East Rim, near Desert View. The helicopter tours, meanwhile, usually fly out and back in the same corridor near Hermits Rest. (Some do go for the full loop.)

Mule Rides. The prospect of descending narrow trails above steep cliffs on animals hardly famous for their intelligence might make you nervous. Once on the trail, however, you'll soon discover that the mules are no more enthralled by the idea of falling than you are. Although the mules walk close to the edges, there has never been a fatal accident on a Fred Harvey mule ride.

From the South Rim, you can take a 12-mile round-trip day ride to Plateau Point, or purchase 1- or 2-night packages that go to the bottom of the canyon and include lodging and meals at Phantom Ranch. Because the rides are strenuous for both riders and mules, the wranglers strictly adhere to the following requirements: You must weigh less than 200 pounds fully dressed, be at least 4 feet, 7 inches tall, speak English, and not be pregnant.

Costs range from $129 for the Plateau Point trip to $494 for the 2-night package (which is offered Nov 1–Mar 31 only). Trips to Phantom Ranch fill up 23 months in advance, so make your reservations early. Starting on the first of the month you can make reservations for the next 23 months. For advance reservations call © 888/297-2757. For possible openings the next day, call the **Bright Angel Transportation Desk** at © 928/638-2631, ext. 6015.

On the North Rim, mule rides are through a small, family-run outfit, **Canyon Trail Rides.** The company offers two types of rim rides and two canyon rides (none of which go to Phantom Ranch), at prices ranging from $20 to $95 (credit cards not accepted). Riders must be at least 12 to go on the all-day ride. No one over 200 pounds is allowed on the canyon rides; for the rim rides, the limit is 220 pounds. All riders must speak English.

The mule rides on the North Rim tend to fill up later than those on the South Rim. To sign up, visit the **Canyon Trail Rides** desk (open daily 7am–6pm) at Grand Canyon Lodge, or call © 928/638-9875. The off-season number is © 435/679-8665 and the Web address is www.canyonrides.com.

Horseback Riding. For horseback riding near the South Rim, go to **Apache Stables** (© 928/638-2891; www.apachestables. com), based outside the south entrance station to Grand Canyon National Park. This is a great family activity. Children as young as 8 are allowed on the 1-hour trail rides, which, like the 2-hour ones, loop through the Kaibab National Forest near the stables. Apache Stables also offers a 4-hour ride east through the forest to near Grandview Point. Prices for the rides, running mid-March through the end of November, range from $31 to $96.

On the North Rim, **Allen's Guided Tours** (© 435/644-8150) offers horseback rides from 8am to 6pm Monday through Saturday from May 15 through September 15. Departing from a corral ¼ mile south of Jacob Lake on Ariz. 67, the tours travel on gentle terrain in the Kaibab National Forest. Prices range from $25 for an hour to $65 for full day.

Camping

INSIDE THE PARK

You can make reservations for campsites in the Mather and North Rim campgrounds by calling © 800/365-2267 (301/722-1257 when calling from outside the U.S.); or online at www. reservations.nps.gov.

Inside the park on the South Rim, 26 miles east of Grand Canyon Village on

Ariz. 64, you'll find **Desert View Campground** (no phone). At dusk, the yips of coyotes drift over this campground in pinyon-juniper woodland at the eastern edge of the park. Elevated, cool, and breezy, the peaceful surroundings offer no clue that the bustling Desert View Overlook is within walking distance. The floor of the woodland makes for smooth tent sites, the most secluded being on the outside of the loop drive. The only drawback: The nearest showers are 28 miles away at Camper Services. During high season, this first-come, first-served campground usually fills up by noon.

Near Grand Canyon Village on the South Rim is **Mather Campground** (© 800/365-2267 or 928/638-7851). Despite having 319 sites in a relatively small area, this remains a pleasant place. Pinyon and juniper trees shade the sites, spaced just far enough apart to afford some privacy. The Aspen and Maple loops are the most roomy. Also, don't stay too near the showers, located in the Camper Services building next to the campground. If you're too close, you'll have hundreds of campers tramping past your site.

For RV drivers on the South Rim, there's **Trailer Village** in Grand Canyon Village (P.O. Box 699), Grand Canyon, AZ 86023 (advance reservations: © 888/297-2757; same-day reservations and campground questions © 928/638-2631, ext. 6035), offering full hookups. The neighbors are close, the showers far (½ mile) away, and the vegetation sparse. However, a few sites at the end of the numbered drives have grass, shade trees, and one neighbor-free side. You can catch a shuttle bus at a stop near the campground.

Inside the park on the North Rim, the **North Rim Campground** (© 800/365-2267 for advance reservations or 928/638-9239 for campground questions) is 44 miles south of Jacob Lake on Ariz. 67. Shaded by old-growth ponderosa pines and situated alongside Transept Canyon (part of Grand Canyon), this is a delightful place to spend a few days. The 1.5-mile-long Transept Trail links the campground to Grand Canyon Lodge, and the North Rim General Store is within walking distance. The most spectacular sites are the rim sites, which open onto the canyon. These cost an extra $5 but are worth it, being some of the prettiest anywhere. Showers (cost: $1.25 for 5 min.) are within walking distance.

With only 83 sites, the North Rim Campground fills up for much of the summer. If you show up without a reservation only to find the SORRY, CAMPGROUND FULL sign on the entry booth, don't be afraid to ask if there have been any cancellations—you might just end up with a campsite. The best time to ask about openings is 8am, when sites made available by the previous night's cancellations go up for sale. The campground is open May 15 to October 15, with a limited number of sites remaining open until after mid-October until the first snowfall.

NEAR THE PARK: SOUTH RIM

Just outside the park is **Grand Canyon Camper Village** in Tusayan, 1 mile south of the park entrance on Ariz. 64 (P.O. Box 490, Grand Canyon, AZ 86023-0490; © 928/638-2887). This campground's advantage is its location, within easy walking distance of Tusayan's stores and restaurants. Its disadvantages are its relatively narrow (average width: 27 ft.) campsites and the noise from the nearby Grand Canyon National Park Airport. The restrooms are clean, and showers cost 75¢ for 6 minutes. There's also a playground and a gravel basketball court.

Ten X Campground (© 928/638-2443) is 2 miles south of Tusayan on Ariz. 64. Large, wooded campsites make this the most peaceful campground within 20 miles of the South Rim. With plenty of distance between you and your neighbors, it's a great place to linger over a

Campground	Rim	Total Sites	RV Hookups	Dump Station	Toilets	Drinking Water
Cameron Trading Post RV Park	South	48	48	Yes	No	Yes
Demotte Park Campground	North	23	No	No	Yes	Yes
Desert View Campground	South	50	No	No	Yes	No
Diamond Creek Campground	South	open tent camping	No	No	Yes	No
Flintstone Bedrock City	South	unlimited tent sites	27	Yes	Yes	Yes
Grand Canyon Camper Village	South	300	250	Yes	Yes	Yes
Jacob Lake Campground	North	53	No	No	Yes	Yes
Kaibab Lake Campground	South	72	No	No	Yes	Yes
Kaibab Camper Village	North	130	70	Yes	Yes	Yes
Mather Campground	South	323	No	Yes	Yes	Yes
North Rim Campground	North	87	No	Yes	Yes	Yes
Ten X Campground	South	70	No	No	Yes	Yes
Trailer Village	South	84	84	Nearby	Yes	Yes
Tuweep	North	11	No	No	No	No

* $12 two-person tent, $14 electric hookup, $16 water/electric, $2 each additional person.
** $26 full hookup, $24 water/electric, $22 electric, $18 tent sites, $20 tepees.
*** $22 hookups, $12 dry sites, $12 tent sites, $65 cabin-style rooms.

fire. All sites have fire pits and grills, and the campground host sells wood. Later, you'll find the soft, needle-covered floor perfect for sleeping. This campground, which is first-come, first-served, does sell out. If you're driving up from Flagstaff or Williams, consider snagging a site before going to the canyon for the day. Open May to September.

NEAR THE PARK: NORTH RIM

Kaibab Camper Village is 0.5 mile west of Ariz. 67, just south of Jacob Lake. Mailing address only: P.O. Box 3331, Flagstaff, AZ 86003 (© **800/525-0924;** Mon–Fri 8am–5pm) or 928/526-0924 when closed; www.canyoneers.com). Compared to most South Rim RV parks, where sagebrush is often the largest plant in sight, this is like a fairy tale. Ponderosa pine trees tower above the campsites, making this easily the prettiest RV park in the Grand Canyon area. Tent campers will also be comfortable here, especially if they pay the extra $3 for one of the improved sites, which have sand rings and views of tiny Jacob Lake. The use of generators is forbidden, so everyone can enjoy the quiet.

Showers	Fire Pits/ Grills	Laundry	Public Phone	Reserve	Fees	Open
No	No	No	Yes	Yes	$15	Year-round
No	Yes	No	No	No	$10	Mid-May to mid-Oct
Yes	No	No	No	No	$12 per site	Mid-May to mid-Oct
No	Yes	No	No	No	$10 per person	Closed in the winter
Yes	No	Yes	Yes	Yes	*	Year-round
Yes	Yes	No	Yes	Yes	**	Year-round
Yes	Yes	No	No	No	$12	Mid-May to mid-Oct
No	Yes	No	No	No	$12	May—Oct
Yes	No	No	Yes	Yes	***	May 15—Oct 15
Yes	Yes	Yes	No	Mar—Nov	$15-$20	Year-round
Nearby	Yes	Nearby	Yes	Yes	$15	May 15—Oct 15
No	Yes	No	No	No	$10	Apr—Sept
Nearby	Yes	No	Nearby	Yes	$25	Year-round
No	Yes	No	No	No	No charge	When roads are passable

The campground recently added two showers ($1.50 for 5 min.).

DeMotte Park Campground (no phone) is a Forest Service campground 5 miles north of the park boundary on Ariz. 67. If you come here, bundle up for the night. It's 8,760 feet high, in spruce-fir forest, so you're sure to be cool. The road through the campground curves sharply and some of the spaces are small, so this place may not work for large RVs.

Just north of Jacob Lake on U.S. 89A and nestled into rolling hills covered with ponderosa pine forest, **Jacob Lake Campground** (no phone) is a beauty of a Forest Service campground. Towering pines shade sites only a short drive from Jacob Lake Inn (where you'll find a gas station, store, restaurant, and motel). Sites are available on a first-come, first-served basis.

Where to Stay

INSIDE THE PARK

Lodging inside the park is handled by **Xanterra Parks and Resorts,** P.O. Box 699, Grand Canyon, AZ 86023

(© **888/297-2757;** fax 928/638-9810; www.xanterra.com). Beginning the first of the month, you can reserve a room for the next 23 months. For example, on January 1, 2004, you can reserve rooms through the end of December 2006. Because the concessionaire allows cancellations without penalty up to 48 hours in advance, you can sometimes grab a room at the last minute, even at the busiest times, by directly calling the Xanterra switchboard (© **928/638-2631**). This is also the number to call to contact lodging guests on the South Rim. The phone number for the **Grand Canyon Lodge** on the North Rim is © **928/638-2611.** The hotels do not have street addresses. When you enter the park, you will receive a map locating all the hotels. Xanterra accepts American Express, Diners Club, Discover, MasterCard, and Visa as payment for lodging. Only El Tovar and Yavapai East (at Yavapai Lodge) have air-conditioning. Children under 16 stay free with their parents.

SOUTH RIM

Bright Angel Lodge & Cabins

© **928/638-2631** (main switchboard) or 888/297-2757 (reservations only). Fax 303/297-3175. 34 units (10 with sink only, 10 with sink and toilet, 14 with bathroom); 55 cabin rooms. TV (most rooms) TEL. $55 with sink only; $58 with sink and toilet only; $70 standard, with bathroom; $83 historic cabins; $107–$130 historic rim cabins; $245 rim-side Bucky O'Neill Suite, with fireplace. AE, DC, DISC, MC, V.

Guests of Bright Angel Lodge stay in tightly clustered buildings and historic cabins near the rim west of the main lodge. In the 1930s, The Fred Harvey Co. needed to develop new, affordable lodging for the many visitors who had begun driving to the canyon. At the company's request, Mary E. Jane Colter designed both the lodge and the cabins alongside it. The cabins were built around several historic buildings, including the area's

first post office and the Bucky O'Neill Cabin, the oldest continually standing structure on the rim.

Low-end accommodations start with clean, spare rooms in two long buildings adjacent to Bright Angel Lodge. At $55 a night, the "hiker rooms" are the least expensive in the park. Each has a bed and desk but no television or private bathroom. Other lodge rooms have double beds and toilets but no showers. Still others are appointed like standard motel rooms, only with showers instead of tubs.

Rooms in the historic cabins cost only about $10 more than the most expensive lodge rooms and are worth the extra money. Most of these free-standing cabins house two guest rooms, have many windows, and are bright inside. Buses often stop near the cabins on the Village Loop Road; the cabins near the rim are slightly quieter. At the high end of the price range are the 12 rim-side cabins, which have partial views of the canyon and cost from $107 to $130. Costing $245, the luxurious Bucky O'Neill Cabin boasts a fireplace and canyon views. The rim-side cabins tend to fill up far in advance. The lodge has two restaurants (reviewed later in this chapter).

El Tovar Hotel

© **928/638-2631** (main switchboard) or 888/297-2757 (reservations only). Fax 303/297-3175. 78 units. A/C TV TEL. Standard $120–$140; deluxe rooms $185; suites $210–$295. AE, DC, DISC, MC, V.

With its European hunting-lodge style, the El Tovar is a dark, cool counterpoint to the warm, pueblo-style buildings of Mary Colter. Completed in 1905 to accommodate tourists arriving on the Santa Fe Railroad, the El Tovar, situated a few yards from the rim, casts a long shadow over Grand Canyon Village. A pointed cupola sits like a witch's cap above its three stories of Oregon pine and native stone, and spires rise above an upstairs deck. The building's interior is as unforgettable as the outside. Moose and elk heads hang on varnished walls, dimly lit by copper chandeliers. Take away the modern-day tourists and the El Tovar looks much as it did at its inception, when it offered luxuries such as a music room, art classes, and a roof garden.

The hotel remains the most luxurious at the canyon and is the only one to offer room service and a nightly turndown. If the hotel isn't busy, ask to see a few rooms before settling in; they vary in size and shape. The hotel's "deluxe rooms" are larger than the "standard rooms," but the most stunning accommodations by far are the four "view suites," each of which has a sitting room and a private deck overlooking the canyon. These suites, which cost $295, often fill up a year or more in advance.

The hotel restaurant (reviewed later in this chapter) occupies a stunning dining room with views of the canyon.

Maswik Lodge

© **928/638-2631** (main switchboard) or 888/ 297-2757 (reservations only). Fax 303/297- 3175. 278 units. TV TEL. Maswik South $80; Maswik North $125. Winter rate $66. AE, DC, DISC, MC, V.

Built in the 1960s, Maswik Lodge is in a wooded area, a 5-minute walk from the rim. If you're not up to walking, you can catch a shuttle directly in front of the lodge. Most of the guest rooms are in 16 two-story wood-and-stone buildings known as Maswik North and South. Most Maswik North rooms have vaulted ceilings, private balconies, and forest views, making them among the most pleasant in the park. Rooms in Maswik South are 5 years older, are a bit smaller, and have less pristine views. With only one window each, they can also be hot during midsummer. However, the Maswik South rooms were renovated in 2001, and their low cost—$45 less than Maswik North—makes them a good value despite their shortcomings.

Maswik is especially good for families, and all rooms offer two queen-size beds. You can dine at the lodge's cafeteria (reviewed later in this chapter).

Thunderbird & Kachina Lodges

© **928/638-2631** (main switchboard) or 888/ 297-2757 (reservations only). Fax 303/297- 3175. 55 units at Thunderbird, 49 at Kachina. TV TEL. Park side $122; canyon side $132. AE, DC, DISC, MC, V.

Fans of 1960s-era dormitory architecture will admire the flat roofs, decorative concrete panels, and metal staircases on the buildings' exteriors, and the brick walls inside. The rooms (identical at both lodges) are surprisingly pleasant, with wall-to-wall windows on one side. Most of the upstairs units on the more expensive "canyon side" have at least a partial view of the canyon. Check-in for the Thunderbird is at the Bright Angel Lodge; for the Kachina, it's at the El Tovar.

Yavapai Lodge

© **928/638-2631** (main switchboard) or 888/ 297-2757 (reservations only). Fax 303/297- 3175. 358 units. TV TEL. $95 Yavapai West; $108 Yavapai East. Winter rate $66. AE, DC, DISC, MC, V.

The largest lodge at the canyon, Yavapai is a mile from the historic district but close to Bank One, the post office, and the Canyon Village Marketplace. Built between 1970 and 1972, Yavapai resembles a Route 66 motor lodge. The rooms are in 10 single-story buildings known as Yavapai West and 6 two-story wood buildings known as Yavapai East. Most rooms in Yavapai West have cinder-block walls, and all are compact, but they do afford guests the benefit of driving to the door. Even so, it's worth the extra $13 for Yavapai East's larger units, with king beds, air-conditioning, and many with forest views. The lodge has a cafeteria, which is reviewed later in this chapter.

CANYON BOTTOM

Phantom Ranch

© **928/638-2631** (main switchboard) or 888/297-2757 (reservations only). Fax 303/297-3175. 7 4-person cabins, 2 cabins for up to 10 people, 4 dorms of 10 people each. $28 dorm bed; $72 cabins (for 2). $11 for each additional person. Most cabins are reserved as part of mule-trip overnight packages. AE, DC, DISC, MC, V.

Accessible only by rafting down the Colorado River, or by hiking or riding a mule to the bottom of Grand Canyon, Phantom Ranch is the only park lodging below the canyon rims, and it sometimes sells out on the first day of availability—more than 23 months ahead. To reserve a spot, call as early as possible. (See directions for Xanterra lodges, above.) If you arrive at the canyon without a reservation, contact the **Bright Angel Transportation Desk** (© **928/638-2631,** ext. 6015) for information about openings the next day.

The reason for the booked slate? Clean sheets never felt better than at the bottom of the Grand Canyon, cold beer never tasted this good, and a hot shower never felt so, well, miraculous. Phantom Ranch is the only place below the rims inside the park that has these amenities.

The ranch's nine evaporatively cooled cabins are a simple pleasure. Famous Grand Canyon architect Mary Colter designed four of them using rocks from the nearby Bright Angel Creek. Connected by dirt footpaths, they sit, natural and elegant, alongside picnic tables and under the shade of cottonwood trees. Inside each cabin, there's a desk, concrete floor, and 4 to 10 bunk beds, as well as a toilet and sink. A shower house for guests is nearby.

Although most of Phantom Ranch was completed in the 1920s and '30s, four 10-person dorms, each with its own bathing facilities, were added in the early 1980s. Used mostly by hikers, these are ideal for individuals and small groups looking for a place to bed down; larger groups are better served by reserving cabins, which provide both privacy and a lower per-person price than the dorms.

In the late afternoon, many guests and hikers from the nearby Bright Angel Campground gravitate to the canteen, which sells snacks when not serving meals (see full review later in this chapter).

NORTH RIM

Grand Canyon Lodge

© **928/638-2611** (main switchboard) or 888/297-2757 (reservations only). Fax 303/297-3175. 208 units. TEL. $92 Frontier Cabin; $91 motel room; $101 Pioneer Cabin; $106 Western Cabin; $116 Rim-View Cabin. AE, DC, DISC, MC, V.

Although Union Pacific Railroad built the lodge in 1928, the train never came closer than Cedar City, Utah. After burning in 1932, the lodge reopened in 1937 and now blends almost seamlessly with the landscape. In its expansive lobby, a 50-foot-high ceiling absorbs sound like the forest floor. Beyond it, the octagonal Sun Room has three enormous picture windows opening onto the canyon. Two long decks with imitation-hickory chairs flank the Sun Room, overlooking the canyon. The lodge also houses a saloon, a snack bar, a meeting room, and an excellent dining room (reviewed later in this chapter).

The 140 cabins come in four types, all with private bathrooms. With wicker furniture, gas fireplaces, bathtubs, and small vanity rooms, the Western Cabins and Rim Cabins are the most luxurious. The Western Cabins cost $10 less than the four Rim Cabins, which have stunning views of Bright Angel Canyon. The Rim Cabins generally fill up on their first day of availability, nearly 2 years in advance.

The two other types—Pioneer and Frontier—are far more rustic. Tightly clustered along the rim of Transept Canyon, they have walls and ceilings of exposed logs, electric heaters, and showers instead of bathtubs. The Frontier Cabins have one guest room while the Pioneer Cabins have two adjoining rooms. An insider's tip: If your reservations are for a Frontier or Pioneer cabin, ask for one that overlooks Transept Canyon. The lodge may be able to accommodate you, and there's no extra charge for the view.

A few motel rooms are also available, yet their atmosphere doesn't compare to the cabins.

OUTSIDE THE PARK

NEAR THE NORTH ENTRANCE

Jacob Lake Inn

Jacob Lake (junction of hwy. 67 and 89A), AZ 86022. © **928/643-7232.** Fax 928/643-7235. www.jacoblakc.com. 12 motel units, 27 cabins, all with showers only. May 14–Nov 31 $72–$90 double; Dec 1–May 13 $52 double. AE, MC, V. $10 extra for pets.

In 1922, Harold and Nina Bowman bought a barrel of gas and opened a gas "stand" near the present-day site of the Jacob Lake Inn. Seven years later they built this inn at the junction of highways 67 and 89A (44 miles from the North Rim). Today Jacob Lake Inn is the main hub of activity between the North Rim and Kanab, Utah, and encompasses a bakery, soda fountain, gift shop, restaurant, and gas station.

Lodgers can choose between motel units and cabins. The rooms in the front building are not nearly as peaceful as the rooms and cabins behind the lodge. Built in 1958, the motel rooms in back are solid and clean, but most people prefer the rustic cabins. The cabin floors creak, the guest rooms (from one to three per cabin) are cramped, and most smell like soggy pine needles. In other words, they're exactly how cabins should be. Unfortunately, two have been lovingly restored and therefore ruined.

Kaibab Lodge

HC 64, Box 30 (26 miles south of Jacob Lake on Hwy. 67), Fredonia, AZ 86022. © **928/638-2389** (May 15–Nov 1); 800/525-0924 or 928/526-0924 (rest of year). Fax 928/638-9864. www.canyoneers.com. 29 units. $85–$99 double. DISC, MC, V.

Located 26 miles south of Jacob Lake on Highway 67, the main lodge here feels as warm and comfortable as a beloved summer camp. It has an open-framed ceiling and enormous pine beams that date from its construction in the 1920s. Perhaps because the guest rooms lack phones and all but two lack televisions, guests tend to congregate in the Adirondack-style chairs in front of the 5-foot-wide fireplace, in the small television room, or at the tables across from the counter that doubles as front desk and beer bar.

Each cabinlike building houses 2 to 4 of the 24 guest rooms, which sleep from two to five people. The rooms are spare but clean, with paneling of rough-hewn pine. One luxury room, added in 1999, has a queen bed, microwave, refrigerator, and coffeemaker. Because the walls of the older units are very thin, it's best to share a cabin with friends. The rooms open onto the broad expanse of DeMotte Park, one of the large, naturally occurring meadows on the Kaibab Plateau. The restaurant serves mediocre food.

NORTHEAST OF THE PARK

The Marble Canyon area, at the northeast tip of the park (though it's closer to the north entrance than the east entrance), is a great place to stop if you're driving from rim to rim. In addition to Lees Ferry Lodge, you can find pleasant accommodations in the Marble Canyon area at **Cliff Dwellers Lodge** (© **800/433-2543**), 9 miles west of Navajo Bridge on North Hwy. 89A (HC 67-30), Marble Canyon, AZ 86036. Another reliable option is **Marble Canyon Lodge** (© **800/726-1789** or 928/355-2225), a quarter mile west of Navajo

Bridge on Highway 89A, Marble Canyon, AZ 86036. Rates at both lodges are $60 to $70 double.

Lees Ferry Lodge

4 miles west of Navajo Bridge on N. Hwy. 89A (HC 67-Box 1), Marble Canyon, AZ 86036. (Located in the tiny "Arizona designated place" of Vermilion Cliffs.) ℂ **800/451-2231** or 928/355-2230. www.leesferrylodge.com. 10 units. A/C. Rates vary from $56–$82 depending on the number of people per room. MC, V. Pets allowed.

Some of the best porch-sitting anywhere can be enjoyed outside the low sandstone buildings of this sleepy roadside lodge, a popular stopping place for trout fishers. Although the hotel sits close to the road, traffic is slow at night, and the overall effect is restful. Paintings of wildfowl, trout, and flowers grace the small, rustic rooms. The only things not relaxing are the showers, which erupt like Old Faithful, only less faithfully. Comparable accommodations can be found a few miles away at Cliff Dwellers Lodge, but the restaurant here surpasses other area eateries.

EAST OF THE PARK

Cameron Trading Post Motel

54 miles north of Flagstaff on Hwy. 89 (P.O. Box 339), Cameron, AZ 86020. ℂ **800/338-7385** or 928/679-2231. Fax 928/679-2350. www.camerontradingpost.com. 66 units. A/C TV TEL. June 1–Oct 15 $89–$119 double; Oct 16–Dec 31 $59–$79; Jan 1–Feb 28 $49–$69; Mar 1–May 31 $69–$89. AE, DC, DISC, MC, V. Pets allowed.

The rooms at Cameron Trading Post Motel are among the most stylish in the Grand Canyon area. Each features its own unique, Southwestern-style furnishings, many of them handmade by the motel's staff. The motel's Hopi building borders a terraced garden with stone picnic tables, a fountain, and a large grill. There's also a restaurant and an immense trading post on the premises.

TUSAYAN

Tusayan is located about 1 mile south of the park. A chain hotel with doubles ranging from $75 to $135 in Tusayan is **Grand Canyon Rodeway Inn Red Feather Lodge** (ℂ **800/228-2000** or 928/638-2414) on Highway 64.

Best Western Grand Canyon Squire Inn

P.O. Box 130 (1½ miles south of the park on Hwy. 64), Grand Canyon, AZ 86023. ℂ **800/622-6966** or 928/638-2681. Fax 928/638-2782. www.grandcanyonsquire.com. 250 units. A/C TV TEL. Apr 1–Oct 31 $105–$185 double; Nov 1–Mar 31 $65–$135; $150–$225 suite year-round. AE, DC, DISC, MC, V.

There's a lot to do at this hotel, which prides itself on being the only full-service resort at Grand Canyon. You'll find two restaurants (including the town's best, The Coronado Room, reviewed later in this chapter), two bars, tennis courts, a beauty shop, an exercise room, and an outdoor swimming pool. The kids will love the family recreation center, which features bowling and video games.

At $15 to $25 extra, the deluxe rooms are spacious, thick-walled, and quiet; they're among the most comfortable in town. The standard rooms are no larger than the rooms at the other area motels, but they do offer hair dryers and coffeemakers.

Grand Canyon Quality Inn and Suites

P.O. Box 520 (on Hwy. 64, 1 mile south of the park entrance, next to the IMAX Theater), Grand Canyon, AZ 86023. ℂ **800/221-2222** (reservations only) or 928/638-2673. Fax 928/638-9537. www.grandcanyonqualityinn.com. 232 units. A/C TV TEL. Apr 1–Oct 20 $118–138 double; Oct 21–Mar 31 $78 double. AE, DC, DISC, MC, V.

In summer, guests here sun themselves around the large outdoor swimming pool and hot tub. In winter, they head for the hotel's atrium, where tropical plants and palm trees shade an 18-foot-long spa with a waterfall. As the area's hot tubs go, this one is the grandest, with jets to massage every aching joint. When the guests finally finish soaking, they find themselves occupying some of the most pleasant accommodations in town, including a number of rooms with private decks and refrigerators. Some of the rooms bordering the atrium have only tiny windows to the outside (and larger ones facing the atrium). Ask for a room with a large exterior window if dark rooms bother you.

Grand Hotel

P.O. Box 33319 (on Hwy. 64, 1½ miles south of the park entrance), Grand Canyon, AZ 86023. © **888/634-7263** or 928/638-3333. Fax 928/638-3131. www.gcanyon.com. 121 units. A/C TV TEL. High season $139 standard, $149 balcony; low-season $99 standard, $109 balcony. AE, DISC, MC, V. No pets.

Tusayan's newest hotel is also its most stylish. Modeled after a lodge of the Old West, the hotel's lobby features an enormous fireplace, hand-woven carpets, and hand-oiled, hand-painted goatskin lanterns. The rooms are considerably less grand than the lobby, however, and perhaps not large enough to justify their high prices. The choicest rooms have balconies facing away from the highway and cost an extra $10. The hotel restaurant (reviewed later in this chapter) features Navajo dancing most nights.

Holiday Inn Express

P.O. Box 3245 (on Hwy. 64, 1½ miles south of the park entrance), Grand Canyon, AZ 86023. © **928/638-3000.** www.gcanyon.com. 197 units. A/C TV TEL. Mar 15–May 30 $89–$109; June 1–Oct 15 $99–$139; Oct 15–Mar 14 $69–$89. $159 suite year-round. Rates include continental breakfast. AE, DC, DISC, MC, V.

Decorated in a Southwestern motif, the rooms at this 1995 motel still feel crisp and new. Come morning, you can enjoy a free continental breakfast in a sun-soaked dining area. The Holiday Inn Express also operates 32 two-room suites, each with a different theme, in a building adjacent to the larger property.

7-Mile Lodge

P.O. Box 56 (1½ miles south of park entrance on Hwy. 64), Grand Canyon, AZ 86023. © **928/638-2291.** Reservations not accepted. 20 units. A/C TV. High season $68 double; low season $48 double ($7 for extra person). AE, DISC, MC, V.

Instead of taking reservations, the owners of this motel start selling spaces at around 9am and usually sell out by early afternoon. If you need a reasonably priced place to stay, think about stopping here on your way *into* the park. Don't be put off by the motel's cramped office; the rooms are actually quite comfortable and large enough to hold two queen beds. Built in 1984, they have 2-inch doors and walls thick enough to muffle the noise of planes from the nearby airport.

WILLIAMS

Williams is located 59 miles south of the park. It has one expensive chain hotel that we recommend: **Best Western Inn of Williams** (© **928/635-4400**), 2600 Rte. 66. Rates run about $70 to $130 double.

Two recommended midprice chain hotels in Williams are **Quality Inn Mountain Ranch** Resort (© **928/635-2693**), 6701 E. Mountain Ranch Rd. (8 miles east of Williams off I-40, Exit 171); and **Holiday Inn** (© 928/635-4114), 950 N. Grand Canyon Blvd., off I-40, Exit 163. Other midprice chain hotels include **Days Inn** (© **928/635-4051**), 2488 W. Rte. 66; **Econo Lodge** (© **928/635-4085**), 302 E. Rte 66; and **Fairfield Inn by Marriott** (© **928/635-9888**), 1029 N. Grand Canyon Blvd., off I-40 Exit 163. Doubles at these hotels usually run about $45 to $105.

In addition to the properties described below, a recommended B&B

in Williams is the **Terry Ranch Bed and Breakfast** (© 800/210-5908 or 928/635-4171), 701 Quarterhorse Rd. (near Rodeo Rd.), with room rates of $139 to $172 double. A recommended, inexpensive motel in Williams is **El Rancho Motel** (© 928/635-2552), 617 E. Route 66, with rooms costing $30 to $60 double.

Inexpensive chain hotels include **Travelodge** (© 928/635-2651), 430 E. Rte. 66; **Motel 6 East** (© 928/635-4464), 720 W. Rte. 66; **Motel 6 Premier** (© 928/635-9000), 831 W. Rte. 66; **Howard Johnson Express** (© 800/720-6614 or 928/635-9561), 511 N. Grand Canyon Blvd., off I-40 Exit 163; and **Super 8** (© 928/635-4700), 2001 Bill Williams Ave. Doubles average about $35 to $90.

Fray Marcos Hotel

235 N. Grand Canyon Blvd., Williams, AZ 86046. © **800/843-8724** or 928/635-4010. Fax 928/635-2180. www.thetrain.com. 196 units. A/C TV TEL. Mar 16–Oct 15, $121 double; Oct 16–Mar 15, $89 double. AE, DISC, MC, V.

Named for a Franciscan monk, this sprawling hotel replaces the original Fray Marcos Hotel, which now houses a gift shop and the museum for the Grand Canyon Railway. In the lobby of the new hotel, oil paintings of the Grand Canyon adorn the walls, and cushy chairs surround a flagstone fireplace. Next to the lobby, Spenser's Lounge offers simple dining and drinks from behind a 100-year-old bar. The hotel has an indoor pool and an exercise room.

Thanks to the success of the Grand Canyon Railway, the hotel grew rapidly in the late 1990s. A 300-seat restaurant, Max and Thelma's, was built nearby, and the hotel more than doubled the number of guest units. Rooms are fairly spartan. Although this is a nice hotel providing good service, it does feel less intimate and more commercial than other area lodges.

Mountain Country Lodge B&B

437 W. Rte. 66, Williams, AZ 86046. © **800/973-6210** or 928/635-4341. www.thegrandcanyon.com/mclodge/index.htm. 9 units. A/C TV. Double $59–$119 for walk-ups; $39–$119 for Internet bookings. Rates include breakfast.

From the outside, this 1909 house on Route 66 in downtown Williams seems like an unlikely place for luxury. The surprise comes when you open the door to a guest room. Decorated in seemingly random themes such as "Alaska," "Route 66," and "Lavender," the nine recently refurbished guest units all have plush sofas or easy chairs, TVs with VCRs, refrigerators, and charming decor. "The Cowboy Room," for example, has metal cutouts of cowboys, a replica of a sign from an old general store, and linens that look like denim. If you take advantage of the Internet booking discount, this lodge is a great value.

Red Garter Bed and Bakery

P.O. Box 95 (137 W. Railroad Ave.), Williams, AZ 86046. © **800/328-1484** or 928/635-1484. www.redgarter.com. 4 units, all with private bathroom, 1 with shower only. TV. $85–$125. Rates include continental breakfast. DISC, MC, V. Closed Dec–Jan.

In the early 1900s this Victorian Romanesque building had a brothel upstairs, a saloon downstairs, and an opium den in the back. The innkeeper, John Holst, has worked hard to preserve both the building, built in 1897, and its colorful history. Each of the four rooms has custom-made moldings, a 12-foot-high ceiling, a ceiling fan, and antique furnishings. The Best Gals' Room overlooks Route 66 and is the largest and most luxurious of the four. Its two adjoining rooms were once reserved for the brothel's "best gals," who would lean out of the double-hung windows to flag down customers. This unusual B&B boasts "more than 100 years of personal service."

Sheridan House Inn

460 E. Sheridan Ave., Williams, AZ 86046. © **888/635-9345** or 928/635-9441. Fax 928/635-1005. www.thegrandcanyon.com/sheridan. 8 units. TV TEL. $145–$210 double. Rates include full breakfast and dinner. AE, DISC, MC, V. Ask about pets in advance.

This inn bristles with bronze sculptures and shimmers with original paintings. Most guest rooms offer brass beds, glass-topped coffee tables, TVs, stereos, VCRs, and refrigerators stocked with cold drinks; the Aspen has a fireplace, impressionist paintings, and a large marble bathroom with separate shower and tub. Outside, under the ponderosa pines at the end of a quiet, dead-end street (a short walk from downtown Williams), the seasonal hot tub awaits. Making the setting all the more enjoyable are the friendly innkeepers, Steve and Evelyn Gardner, who serve a three-course dinner in addition to breakfast.

FLAGSTAFF

Flagstaff is located 78 miles south of Grand Canyon village. A recommended, expensive chain hotel in Flagstaff is **Radisson Woodlands Hotel Flagstaff** (© **928/773-8888**), 1175 W. Rte. 66. Another is **Little America** (© **800/352-4386** or 928/779-7900), 2515 E. Butler (off I-40 Exit 198). Other options include **AmeriSuites** (© **928/774-8042**), 2455 S. Beulah (north of I-40 Exit 195B); **Flagstaff Hilton Garden Inn** (© **928/226-8888**), 350 W. Forest Meadows; and **Residence Inn by Marriott** (© **928/526-5555**), 3440 Country Club Dr. Rooms at these hotels cost from $70 to $170.

A recommended mid- to high-price chain hotel in Flagstaff is the **Holiday Inn Flagstaff** (© **928/714-1000**), 2320 E. Lucky Lane (off I-40 Exit 198). Other midprice options include **Quality Inn Flagstaff** (© **928/774-8771**), 2000 S. Milton (near I-40 Exit 195); **Best Western Kings House Motel** (© **928/774-7186**), 1560 E. Rte. 66; **Best Western Pony**

Soldier Inn & Suites (© 928/526-2388), 3030 E. Rte. 66; **Econo Lodge** (© 928/774-7326), 914 S. Milton Rd. (near I-40 Exit 195); **Days Inn Route 66** (© 928/774-5221), 1000 W. Rte. 66; **Days Inn East** (© 928/527-1477), 3601 E. Lockett (near I-40 Exit 201); **Days Inn I-40** (© 928/779-1575), 2735 S. Woodlands Village Blvd. (near I-40 Exit 195); **Fairfield Inn by Marriott** (© 928/773-1300), 2005 S. Milton (near I-40 Exit 195); **Hampton Inn** (© 928/526-1885), 3501 E. Lockett (near I-40 Exit 201); **Hampton Inn and Suites** (© 928/913-0900), 2400 S. Beulah Blvd. (north of I-40 Exit 195); **Travelodge** (© 928/779-6944), 2200 E. Butler (off I-40 Exit 198); and **La Quinta Inn & Suites** (© 928/556-8666), 2015 S. Beulah Blvd. (north of I-40 Exit 195). Rates for these hotels usually run $50 to $125.

One good, inexpensive chain hotel is **Super 8** (© 928/526-0818), 3725 N. Kasper Ave. (on Rte. 66, 1 mile west of I-40 Exit 201), Flagstaff, AZ 86004. Other inexpensive chain hotels include **Howard Johnson Inn** (© 928/526-1826), 3300 E. Rte. 66; **Motel 6** (© 928/774-1801), 2010 E. Butler (off I-40 Exit 198); **Motel 6** (© 928/779-3757), 2745 S. Woodlands Village Blvd. (near I-40 Exit 195); **Ramada Limited** (© 928/779-3614), 2350 E. Lucky Lane (off I-40 Exit 198); **Ramada Limited West** (© 877/703-0291), 2755 S. Woodlands Village Blvd.; **Econo Lodge Lucky Lane** (© 928/774-7701), 2480 E. Lucky Lane (off I-40 Exit 198); **Rodeway Inn East** (© 928/526-2200), 2650 E. Rte. 66; **Travelodge Flagstaff** (© 928/526-1399), 2610 E. Rte. 66. Rates for these motels usually run $35 to $65.

For toll-free numbers, see the appendix.

In addition to the properties described below, a recommended B&B in Flagstaff is **Jeanette's Bed and Breakfast** (© 800/752-1912 or 928/527-1912), 3380 E. Lockett Rd.; double $115 to $145. Another is **Fall Inn To Nature** (© 888/920-0237), 8080 N. Colt Dr.; double $65 to $95.

Comfi Cottages

1612 N. Aztec St., Flagstaff (another location at 710B W. Birch), AZ 86001. © **888/ 774-0731** or 928/774-0731. Fax 928/773-7286. www.comficottages.com. 8 cottages in different locations in Flagstaff. TV TEL. $120–$260 double. Add $10 per person, per night, if more than 2 people. Rates include breakfast. DISC, MC, V. Inquire about pets.

In the 1970s Pat Wiebe, a nurse at the local hospital, began purchasing small homes in Flagstaff. Today she rents out eight of these quaint cottages, most built in the 1920s and '30s. Wiebe has modernized them somewhat, adding thermostat-controlled fireplaces, televisions, VCRs, and washer/dryers. There's also a lovely new property at 710 W. Birch, with upstairs and downstairs units resembling contemporary town homes. In every unit you'll find fresh-cut flowers, antiques, cupboards stocked with breakfast foods, and rag dolls from her personal collection.

Hotel Weatherford

23 N. Leroux, Flagstaff, AZ 86001. © **928/779-1919.** Fax 928/773-8951. www.weatherford hotel.com. 8 units (3 with shared bathrooms). High season $45–$70; low season $35–$45. AE, DC, DISC, MC, V. Parking behind the hotel.

Constructed in 1898, this hotel in historic downtown Flagstaff has antiques-filled common areas, several delightful bars (including one with a wraparound balcony), and a popular restaurant (reviewed later in this chapter). The guest rooms, only five of which have private bathrooms, are varied and eccentric, with eclectic antiques in each. They have transoms and Pullman windows for ventilation. The main advantage to this hotel is its lively atmosphere. However, the atmosphere can become a drawback when the hotel bars get too noisy. If you're staying here, rest up in advance, and plan on joining the party. For the least noise, get the Zane Gray Room; it's at the end of the building farthest from the upstairs bar. Note that rooms offer few amenities beyond a bed and a heater.

The Inn at 410 Bed & Breakfast

410 N. Leroux St., Flagstaff, AZ 86001. © **800/ 774-2008** or 928/774-0088. Fax 928/ 774-6354. www.inn410.com. 9 units. A/C. $145–$205 double. Rates include full breakfast. MC, V.

Peering into each of the rooms at this inn is like flipping the pages in an issue of *House & Garden*. Each expertly decorated room is daringly different, yet tasteful. Collectively, they make this 1894 home owned by Sally and Howard Krueger one of the most stunning B&Bs anywhere. One room, Monet's Garden, is reminiscent of a French country garden, complete with impressionist paintings brushed upon the walls. Our favorite, the Conservatory, captures the sophistication and artistry of the great masters, an elegant tribute to the beauty of music and literature. An antique secretary and classic armchairs distinguish the sitting area, with a violin and music stand complementing the theme. The room has a four-poster bed, rich burgundy carpet, and 19th-century formal draperies set against a backdrop of music-themed artwork. A gourmet Southwestern breakfast, served at your table, includes juice, fresh fruit, a homemade pastry, and a nonmeat entree. Everything is baked from scratch, and the owner has even published a cookbook.

KANAB, UTAH & FREDONIA, ARIZONA

Kanab and Fredonia are located about 78 miles northwest of the park. Kanab has two pleasant, midprice to expensive chain hotels: **Holiday Inn Express** (© **435/644-8888**), 815 E. Hwy. 89; and **Best Western Red Hills** (© **435/ 644-2675**), 125 W. Center St. There's also a delightful chain hotel 19 miles north of Kanab, en route to Zion National Park: **Best Western Thunderbird Resort** (© **888/848-6358** or 435/648-2203), located at the junction of highways 89 and 9 (P.O. Box 5536), Mt. Carmel Junction, Utah 84755. Rates range from about $85 to $110 double.

Clean, inexpensive rooms can be found at **Crazy Jug Motel** (© 928/643-7752), 465 S. Main St. (Hwy. 89A), Fredonia; at the **Blue Sage Motel and RV Park** (© 928/643-7125), 330 S. Main St. (Hwy. 89A), Fredonia; and at **Aiken's Lodge** (© 435/644-2625), 79 W. Center St., Kanab. Prices for doubles run about $25 to $54.

Parry Lodge

89 E. Center St., Kanab, UT 84741. © **800/748-4104** or 435/644-2601. Fax 801/644-2605. www.infowest.com/parry. 89 units. A/C TV TEL. May 1–Oct 31 $45–$70 double, $70 family room; Nov 1–Apr 30 $35–$50 double, $50 family room. AE, DISC, MC, V. Pets $5.

Many of the older rooms (known as "movie units") in this 1929 colonial-style lodge display plaques bearing the names of stars who stayed in them while filming Westerns (Dean Martin, Gregory Peck, and Sammy Davis Jr. among others). The movie units are smaller and closer to Center Street than the motel's newer rooms, but they're far more charming (if you want a bathtub, you'll need to take a newer unit). Most have tile bathroom floors and classic American furnishings inside, and they're shaded by trees. Open from April 1 through October 30, the lodge's restaurant serves good breakfasts.

Treasure Trail Motel

150 W. Center St., Kanab, UT 84741. © **800/603-2687** (reservations only) or 435/644-2687. Fax 435/644-2754. www.treasuretrailmotel.com. 29 units (6 with showers only). A/C TV TEL. May 15–Oct 31 $40–$58 double; Nov 1–May 14 $32–$44 double. AE, DC, DISC, MC, V. 1 small pet per room, $5.

Built in the 1950s and '60s, this family-run motel recalls the days when enormous gas guzzlers that were not SUVs prowled the American West. The showers, which predate today's water-saving plumbing, slam you like fire-hose spray; surrounded by lounge chairs and beached flotation toys, the swimming pool calls to mind a 5¢ postcard; and the gaudy neon motel sign would look right at home in a Rat Pack movie. Best of all, the motel remains clean, comfortable, and relatively quiet. The corner units in the older, one-story building have space to spare and feel as solid as pyramids. Consider having a picnic in the large garden with red rock benches.

Viola's Garden Bed and Breakfast

250 N. 100 W., Kanab, UT 84741. © **435/644-5683.** www.violas-garden.com. 5 rooms, each with private bathroom (shower only in 4 rooms). A/C. $90–$150 double. Rates include gourmet breakfast. DISC, MC, V. Older children welcomed.

In 1912, a sheep rancher named James Swapp built this home using a $640 kit from the Sears Roebuck catalog. All the components of the home, including pre-cut beams, siding, roofing, and paint, were delivered by train from Chicago to Marysvale, Utah, then carried an additional 200-odd miles on a buckboard wagon to Kanab. Today, Swapp's granddaughter, Nileen, and her husband, Von Whitlock, welcome guests to a very comfortable B&B in the home. Two guest rooms—the English Garden Room and the Rose Garden—are in the original home; the other three are in an addition. The nicest, the English Garden Room, has a fully tiled shower, dormers, a Victorian-style bed, and best of all, a private second-story balcony.

Where to Dine

INSIDE THE PARK

SOUTH RIM

Arizona Steakhouse

At Bright Angel Lodge. © **928/638-2631.** Reservations not accepted. Entrees $15–$21. AE, DC, DISC, MC, V. Daily 4:30–10pm. Closed in winter. STEAKS AND SEAFOOD.

Lining up before this restaurant's 4:30pm opening isn't a bad idea. Instead of arriving after sunset to find an hour's wait, you can watch the changing colors through the long, canyon-facing windows. Or, when the days are longer, finish the meal in time to step outside for the evening's show. Either way, make sure you land a table because the Arizona Room dishes up the most consistently tasty dinners on the South Rim. Entrees include broiled or blackened hand-cut steaks, mustard and rosemary crusted prime rib, succulent baby-back ribs, marinated chicken breast, and pan-seared salmon with melon salsa. To accompany your meal, you can choose from a variety of California wines.

Bright Angel Restaurant

Located in Bright Angel Lodge. ℂ **928/638-2631.** Reservations not accepted. Breakfast $5.25–$7.40; lunch $7–$10; dinner $7–$16. AE, DC, DISC, MC, V. Daily 6am–10pm. AMERICAN.

Though this restaurant recently removed the words "coffee shop" from its name, it still serves average American coffee shop food. The breakfast fare, including omelets, French toast, and pancakes, is not bad. At lunch, the burgers, hot sandwiches, and large salads usually pass muster. At dinnertime, the restaurant supplements the lunch menu by adding palatable entrees such as grilled New York strip steak, chicken Alfredo, and stuffed shells.

This is a good, casual place for families, who can dine here without worrying much about the children's behavior. The games on the **kids' menu** should distract the small fry until the French fries arrive.

El Tovar Restaurant

In the El Tovar Lodge. ℂ **928/638-2631,** ext. 6432. Reservations accepted for dinner only. Breakfast $3.70–$10; lunch $6.95–$15; dinner entrees $17–$25. AE, DC, DISC, MC, V. Daily 6:30–11am, 11:30am–2pm, and 5–10pm. CONTINENTAL.

More than 100 years after opening its doors, this restaurant remains a unique dining experience. Best of all is the stunning room—walls of Oregon pine

graced with murals depicting the ritual dances of four American Indian tribes and banks of windows at the north and south ends.

At dinner, a Southwestern influence spices the Continental cuisine, which includes steak, chicken, fish, and pasta dishes. One tasty appetizer is the black bean soup. For an entree, meat eaters will enjoy the flame-broiled peppercorn-crusted filet mignon in roasted garlic sauce. Meanwhile, vegetarians can munch on some Clesan-Du-Klish (Native American vegan blue-corn tamales). Expect large portions.

The El Tovar accepts reservations for dinner only, but it's also open for breakfast and lunch. If you're traveling on a budget or prefer the dinner menu at the Arizona Room (as many do), try dining here during non-dinner hours, when you can enjoy the lovely surroundings for just a dollar or two more than you'd spend at the other canyon restaurants. At breakfast, be sure to sample the coffee, the best on the South Rim, and order the eggs Benedict with smoked salmon.

Maswik & Yavapai Cafeterias

Located at Maswik and Yavapai lodges, respectively. ℂ **928/638-2631.** No reservations. Breakfast $2–$5.25; lunch and dinner $2.25–$7. AE, DC, DISC, MC, V. Maswik daily 6am–9pm; Yavapai daily 6am–10pm (may fluctuate seasonally; Yavapai sometimes closes in low season). CAFETERIA.

For the price of a burger, fries, and a soft drink at the Tusayan McDonald's, you can eat a full meal at either Maswik or Yavapai cafeterias. The food costs about the same at either cafeteria, but there are key differences between the two. Maswik more closely resembles a food court, where meals come complete with side dishes. One station serves Mexican fare, another has hot sandwich plates, a third offers spaghetti and burgers, and a fourth serves barbeque chicken and steak. At Yavapai you can mix and match from a variety of stations, picking up a piece of fried chicken from one, a slice of pizza from another, a dish of mashed potatoes from another. For $2.25, you can also assemble your own dinner salad at the salad bar. Compared with Maswik's food, Yavapai's fare (especially the turkey potpie) tastes less institutional. If you're hungry for a burger, however, go to Maswik, where the meat is grilled instead of fried.

INSIDE THE CANYON

Phantom Ranch

Inside the canyon ½ mile north of the Colorado River on the North Kaibab Trail. To order meals more than 1 day in advance, call ☎ **303/297-2757;** to order meals for the next day, contact the Bright Angel Transportation Desk at ☎ 928/638-2631, ext. 6015. Reservations required. Steak dinner $28; stew $19; vegetarian $19; sack lunch $9; breakfast $16. AE, DC, DISC, MC, V (for advance reservations, AE, DISC, MC, V only). STEAKS.

At the bottom of the Grand Canyon, whether you get there by mule or on foot, pretty much anything tastes good. Every evening, just three options are offered: a steak dinner at 5pm, a vegetarian dinner at 5pm, and a hearty beef stew at 6:30pm. The vegetarian plate consists of lentil loaf and the side dishes to the steak dinner: vegetables, cornbread, baked potato, and salad. With all three dinners, the dessert is chocolate cake.

The family-style, all-you-can-eat breakfasts provide ample calories for people hiking out of the canyon. Heaping platters of eggs, bacon, and pancakes are laid out on the long tables in the canteen. The only disappointment is the sack lunch, whose meager offerings (bagel, summer sausage, apple, peanuts, raisins, pretzels, cookies, and apple juice) don't seem worth the $8.50 price. Pack your own lunch and, if necessary, supplement it with snacks from the canteen.

Because the number of meals is fixed, hikers and mule riders must reserve them ahead of time through Xanterra (see number above) or at the Bright Angel Transportation Desk. As a last resort, inquire upon arrival at Phantom Ranch to see whether any meals remain.

NORTH RIM

Café on the Rim

In the west wing of Grand Canyon Lodge. ☎ **928/638-2611.** Reservations not accepted. Breakfast $1.85–$4.80; lunch and dinner $2.75–$7. Daily 7am–9pm. CAFETERIA.

The cafe serves the best pizza on the North Rim, or so the joke goes. That speaks well for the pizza, which could just as easily—and no less truthfully—be called the worst. At $2.75 to $3.25 a slice, it's an economical alternative to firing up the camp stove, though not an ethereal experience. The snack bar also serves burgers, calzones, salads, made-to-order sandwiches, and breakfasts. If all you desire is good coffee and a muffin, stop by the saloon, where an espresso bar operates daily from 7 to 10am.

Grand Canyon Lodge Dining Room

At Grand Canyon Lodge. ☎ **928/638-2611,** ext. 160. Reservations required for dinner, not accepted for breakfast and lunch. Breakfast $2.50–$9; lunch $4.75–$9.50; dinner $14–$25. AE, DC, DISC, MC, V. Daily 6:30–10am, 11:30am–2:30pm, and 4:45–9:30pm. CONTINENTAL.

Long banks of west- and south-facing windows afford views of Transept Canyon and help warm this room, where the high, open-framed ceiling absorbs the clamor of diners. This is, without question, one of the most scenic dining rooms anywhere. Now, thanks in part to a food and beverage director from Utah's posh Deer Valley resort, the cuisine pleases diners nearly as much as the surroundings do.

At dinner, try the pasta Lydia—fresh asparagus and potatoes tossed in pesto sauce with bow-tie pasta. Other excellent choices are the pan-seared Atlantic salmon topped with blueberry chardonnay sauce, and the Four Corners lime chicken—a sautéed chicken breast with artichokes and capers in white wine sauce. The restaurant also offers steaks, prime rib, and salmon, as well as a varied wine list.

The lunch menu consists mostly of burgers, sandwiches, and salads. At breakfast, a full buffet costs under $9, but the most delectable choice may be the artichoke and asiago cheese omelet.

Because of the volume of diners, the staff here does not accept reservations for window seats. However, they can often accommodate customers who are willing to wait outside the restaurant.

OUTSIDE THE PARK

NORTHEAST OF THE PARK

Lees Ferry Lodge Vermilion Cliffs Bar & Grill

4 miles west of Navajo Bridge on Hwy. 89A, Marble Canyon, AZ. ℂ **928/355-2231.** Breakfast $4.50–$8; lunch $5.50–$12; dinner $8–$22. Daily 6am–9pm. AMERICAN.

After rigging boats for trips down the Colorado, many river guides come to this remote restaurant, and not just for the 130 types of bottled beer. They also come for nicely prepared steaks, chicken, and fish, and for imaginative sandwiches such as the "Turkey in a Straw"—sliced turkey breast, sauerkraut, and Swiss cheese grilled on sourdough bread and served with Thousand Island dressing. It's the most delectable food for miles around, served by a low-key, friendly staff.

TUSAYAN

Cafe Tusayan

Located next to the Rodeway Inn, 1½ miles south of the park on Hwy. 64, Tusayan. ℂ **928/638-2151.** Reservations not accepted. Breakfast $3.75–$9.25; lunch $5.95–$9.95; dinner $8.95–$17. MC, V. Daily 7am–9pm during high season; hours vary during low season. AMERICAN/SOUTHWESTERN.

Since opening Cafe Tusayan in spring 1999 in a space formerly occupied by Denny's, the restaurant's owners have wisely kept the menu small. They serve a few varieties of salads; appetizers such as jalapeño poppers and sautéed mushrooms; and a half dozen entrees,

including salmon with herb butter, baked chicken, and stroganoff. Perhaps because the chefs are able to focus on just a few dishes, the food ranks among the best in Tusayan. However, the servers tend to lose focus when busy, and the decor screams "chain restaurant."

Canyon Star Restaurant

In the Grand Hotel on Hwy. 64 (1½ miles from the park's south entrance), Tusayan. ℂ **888/ 634-7263** or 928/638-3333. Reservations not accepted. Breakfast $4.50–$8.95; lunch $3.95–$11; dinner entrees $13–$23. Daily 7:30–10am, 11am–2pm, and 5–9pm. AE, DISC, MC, V. REGIONAL.

The entertainment at this sprawling restaurant seems designed to give foreign tourists exactly what they hope to find in the American West. Most nights, a lonesome cowboy balladeer and spiritual Native American dancers take turns performing for the visitors. In case anyone gets bored with the show, video clips of the canyon play constantly on monitors above the dance floor. The distractions—especially the dances, which can be captivating—are more than enough to make a person forget the food, even the mesquite-smoked barbecue.

Coronado Dining Room

In the Best Western Grand Canyon Squire Inn (1½ miles south of the park on Hwy. 64), Tusayan. ℂ **928/638-2681,** ext. 4419. Reservations accepted. Entrees $14–$25. AE, DC, DISC, MC, V. Daily 5–10pm. CONTINENTAL.

This restaurant serves tasty steaks, chicken, and seafood, with a few Southwestern dishes thrown in. The most delicious entree may be the elk tournedos—broiled elk tenderloin medallions served with cornbread timbale and finished with a roasted shallot demi-glace. The nattily attired waiters, combined with the high-backed wooden chairs and the dimly lighted metal chandeliers, make the surroundings more formal than at other area eateries. This is the premier restaurant in Tusayan, which, considering the competition, is not that mean a feat.

FLAGSTAFF

Brewer Street Brewery

11 S. Beaver St., Flagstaff. © **928/779-0079.** Lunch and dinner items $7.50–$9.25. AE, DISC, MC, V. Sun–Thurs 11:30am–11pm; Fri–Sat 11:30am–midnight. AMERICAN.

This upscale whistle-stop cafe was the first microbrewery in Flagstaff. Potbelly stoves and railroad artwork decorate the high-spirited dining room, with an open-view kitchen and popular bar attached. Pub-style platters include bratwurst sausages, crunchy Cajun catfish, a number of sandwiches, and wood-fired pizzas. It doesn't make a whole lot of sense to come here without trying one of the fresh brews, as well! Among the best are raspberry ale, Indian pale ale, and Railhead red ale (the most popular brew among locals).

Charly's

In the historic Hotel Weatherford, 23 N. Leroux, Flagstaff. © **928/779-1919.** Lunch $5.75–$9.95; dinner entrees $7.95–$19. AE, DC, DISC, MC, V. Daily 11am–11pm (10pm in winter). SOUTHWESTERN/AMERICAN.

Charly's is spacious and cool, both inside, where the 12-foot-high ceilings of the Hotel Weatherford provide breathing room, and on the sidewalk, a favorite place for summertime dining. Besides steaks and burgers, the restaurant offers a number of vegetarian dishes and salads that make for perfect light dining. It also has 20 beers on tap, and is one of the town's more festive nightspots.

Cottage Place

126 West Cottage Ave., Flagstaff. © **928/774-8431.** Reservations recommended. Dinner $20–$28; chateaubriand for 2, $60. AE, MC, V. Tues–Sun 5–9:30pm. COUNTRY FRENCH.

The quiet serenity of Flagstaff's most elegant restaurant is ideal for special occasions, a wonderful spot to peacefully celebrate your vacation to the Southwest. Original artwork decorates three rose-colored rooms, where soft conversations are heard from the candlelit tables. Chateaubriand (for two) is Executive Chef/Owner Frank Branham's signature dish, served with fresh vegetables, garlic Duchess potatoes, and tomato Provençal. All entrees are served with soup du jour, green salad, and fresh breads. A number of fish and seafood selections accompany the meat choices. Service is refined, and the restaurant's impressive selection of wines has earned *Wine Spectator's* Award of Excellence most years over the past decade. A six-course tasting menu is offered Thursday through Saturday with or without matching wines.

Josephine

503 N. Humphreys, Flagstaff. © **928/779-3400.** Reservations accepted. Lunch $7.25–$8.75; dinner entrees $15–$19. AE, DISC, MC, V. Mon–Sat 11am–2:30pm and 5:30–9pm; closed Sun. AMERICAN.

This modern American bistro opened in 2002 in the historic Milton Clark house, previously home to Chez Marc restaurant. The simple, creative menu offers dishes ranging from marinated lamb meatloaf to cilantro pesto halibut or grilled vegetables with couscous. At lunch, an uncommon but recommended choice is the Lebanese hummus and baba ghanouj platter, served with warm pita bread and a Mediterranean salad. Josephine's also serves a small selection of pizzas and calzones, washed down with a delicious glass of fresh lemonade. This is a great place to meet friends, and service is friendly and informal.

Macy's European Coffee House Bakery & Vegetarian Restaurante

14 S. Beaver St., Flagstaff. © **928/774-2243.** Reservations not accepted. Main courses $3–$8. No credit cards. Sun–Thurs 6am–8pm; Fri–Sat 6am–10pm. VEGETARIAN/BAKED GOODS.

Macy's may not be able to save the world, but its fine vegetarian food, fresh pastries, and great coffee encourage people to slow down and smell the latte. It's a place where vegans are welcomed, where bikes lean against the building, and where the staff will (literally) carry your meal across a busy street for you. In addition to the standard menu items such as tempeh tuna and "tofurkey" (tofu made to taste like, but not too much like, turkey) sandwiches, Macy's serves daily specials, including a pasta of the day. Live music is offered all evenings but Monday, which is chess night.

Pasto

19 E. Aspen Ave., Flagstaff. © **928/779-1937.** Reservations suggested. Dinner $8.95–$17. AE, MC, V. Sun–Thurs 5–9pm; Fri–Sun 5–9:30pm. ITALIAN.

This excellent restaurant bills its fare as "fun" Italian dining, but "rare" might be more apropos. It's unusual to find Italian food this rewarding in a town where the closest thing to Little Italy is Little America. Popular dishes include the black bean ravioli, which has zesty Southwestern accents, and the pan-seared chicken breast braised in an orange-garlic basil sauce. If you're still hungry after the main course, dip into the one and only dish that the owner prepares: the tiramisu.

WILLIAMS

Cruisers Cafe 66

233 W. Rte. 66, Williams. © **928/635-2445.** Reservations not accepted. Lunch/dinner $7.95–$18. AE, DISC, MC, V. Daily 4–9:30pm (may vary seasonally). AMERICAN.

Built in an old Route 66 gas station, this restaurant (formerly Tiffany's), is jammed with gas-station memorabilia, including stamped glass, filling-station signs, "Sky Chief" gas pumps, and photos of classic stations. Served up with plenty of napkins as well as drinks in unbreakable plastic mugs, the roadhouse-style food will fuel you for days to come. Start with the sampler of appetizers—wings, chicken strips, mozzarella sticks, and fried mushrooms—served on

a real automobile hubcap. The burgers are delicious, but the best choice, if you really want to fill up, is the baby-back ribs.

Pine Country Restaurant

107 N. Grand Canyon Blvd., Williams. © **928/635-9718.** Reservations accepted. Breakfast $2.95–$5.25; lunch $4.50–$6.25; dinner $6.95–$12. Daily 5:30am–9pm. AMERICAN.

Many locals who dine at this no-frills, mom-and-pop restaurant in downtown Williams eat their pie first. One taste of any of this restaurant's 31 varieties of fresh-baked pie, including unusual varieties such as banana–peanut butter and strawberry–cream cheese, will convince you that the pie-eaters have their priorities straight. But pie is just a slice of the offerings. Dinner entrees such as roast beef, pork chops, and fried shrimp cost under $7 and taste like meals your mother should have made. The lunch menu consists of mostly burgers and hot sandwiches.

Rod's Steak House

301 E. Rte. 66, Williams. © **928/635-2671.** $9–$29. AE, DISC, MC, V. Daily 11:30am–9:30pm. Closed 1st 2 weeks of Jan and on Sun Oct–Feb. STEAKS.

If you're a steak lover, brake for the cow-shaped sign on Route 66 as you would for real livestock. This landmark restaurant, sprawling across a city block between the highway's east- and west-bound lanes, has hardly changed since opening in 1946. Printed on a paper cutout of a cow, the menu is still only about 6 inches across—more than enough space for its laconic descriptions of the restaurant's offerings. You can choose nonsteak items such as "beef liver grilled onions and bacon" and "jumbo fantail shrimp tempura battered"; or prime rib in three sizes, from the 9-ounce "ladies lite cut" to the 16-ounce "cattleman's hefty cut." But the stars of the menu are the mesquite-broiled steaks that have made this place a hit for a half-century.

KANAB & FREDONIA

Houston's Trails End Restaurant

32 E. Center St., Kanab. ✆ **435/644-2488.** Breakfast $4.20–$8.50; lunch $4.95–$9.50; dinner $4.95–$19. AE, DISC, MC, V. Daily 6am–10pm. Closed mid-Nov to Mar 15. STEAKS, BURGERS, SEAFOOD.

For a taste of Kanab's traditional fare, head for Houston's. While country music plays, waitresses wearing toy (we hope) sidearms serve up meaty courses such as the house special, a chicken-fried steak, and baby-back ribs slathered in barbecue sauce. The soup is made fresh daily, as are the enormous yeast rolls that come with each dinner. Breakfast includes a choice of omelets, and lunch consists primarily of burgers and sandwiches.

Nedra's Café

Hwy. 89A, Fredonia. ✆ **928/643-7591.** Reservations not accepted. Breakfast items $3.25–$8.50, lunch and dinner $3.25–$16. AE, DISC, MC, V. Mon–Thurs 8am–10pm, Fri–Sun 7am–10pm (may vary in winter). MEXICAN.

Because this restaurant in Fredonia, Arizona, serves hearty Mexican food at a moderate price, it's a great place to fill up after completing a North Rim backpacking trip. In addition to enchiladas, tostadas, burritos, and tacos, Nedra's serves less-common Mexican dishes such as *carnitas* (seasoned roast pork topped with fresh cilantro and green onions) and *machaca* (shredded beef cooked with tomatoes, onion, green chiles, cilantro, and egg). In Kanab you'll find a similar restaurant, **Nedra's Too,** but the tastiest Mexican fare in that community is at **Escobar's Mexican Restaurant** (✆ **928/644-3739**), 373 E. 300 S.

Rocking V Café

97 W. Center St., Kanab. ✆ **435/644-8001.** Reservations accepted. Main lunch items $6–$9.50. Main dinner items $9–$21. V, MC. Daily 11:30am–9:30pm. ECLECTIC.

In 2000, Vicky Cooper left her stressful job as a TV news reporter to open this eclectic cafe, easily the best restaurant in Kanab. If you're here at dinnertime, start with the bruschetta—a house-baked focaccia topped with freshly sliced Roma tomatoes, slivered garlic, basil, and olive oil. Then, indulge in the chicken and mushroom Alfredo—a creamy Alfredo sauce atop spinach fettuccine, sautéed mushrooms, and grilled chicken. Or try the charbroiled filet mignon encrusted with portobello mushrooms and surrounded with a thyme port demi-glace. Finish with the raspberry almond torte. The restaurant, which also serves lunch, occupies a glass-fronted 1892 building that has seen duty as a general store, mortuary, grocery, and bank. The wine cellar is in the safe, which seems to make sense in Utah.

Picnic & Camping Supplies

If possible, stock up on your camping items at a grocery store in a large city such as Flagstaff. In general, prices are lowest in Flagstaff and rise steadily as you near the canyon, peaking at the **Canyon Village Marketplace** inside the park on the South Rim, in Market Plaza at Grand Canyon Village (✆ **928/638-2262**). Also on the South Rim is **Desert View General Store,** at Desert View off Ariz. 64 (✆ **928/638-2393**). On the North Rim is the **North Rim General Store** (✆ **928/638-2611,** ext. 270), adjacent to North Rim Campground.

Outside the park, in Tusayan, is **Tusayan General Store,** 1 mile south of the park entrance on Ariz. 64 (✆ **928/638-2854**). Williams has a **Safeway,** 637 W. Rte. 66 (✆ **928/635-0500**). In Cameron try **Simpson's Market,** at the junction of U.S. 89 and Ariz. 64, next to the Chevron (✆ **928/679-2340**). In Kanab you'll find **Glazier's Food Town,** 264 S. 100 E. (✆ **435/644-5029**); and **Honey's Jubilee Foods,** 260 E. 300 S. (✆ **435/644-5877**). There are four large supermarkets in Flagstaff: **Albertson's,** 1416 E. Rte. 66 (✆ **928/773-7955**); **Basha's,** 2700 Woodlands Village Blvd. (✆ **928/774-3882**); **Basha's,** 1000 N. Humphreys St. (✆ **928/774-2101**); and **Fry's,** 201 N. Switzer Canyon Dr. (✆ **928/774-2719**).

GRAND TETON NATIONAL PARK

by Eric Peterson

 VERY TIME YOU FOCUS YOUR CAMERA IN GRAND TETON, THE FRAME will likely be centered on one of its many stately peaks. As a whole, the towering mountains of the Teton Range define this park, unlike neighboring Yellowstone, distinguished by its

pastiche of thermal features and subtle beauty. You'll still see wildlife—eagles and osprey along the Snake River; moose and, if you're lucky, a black bear in the vicinity of the Jackson Lake Junction; and pronghorn on the valley floor—but it is the landscape that makes Grand Teton.

Compared with the undulations of Yellowstone, Grand Teton presents two vistas: a long, wide valley bordered on all sides by vertical peaks. If possible, once you enter the park, make a beeline for the summit of Signal Mountain, near Jackson Lake. There you will have a commanding 360-degree view that will put the park and surrounding areas in perspective. It's also the viewpoint from which some of the most famous early photos of the park were taken.

From the Jackson Point Overlook on Signal Mountain, you'll see a valley floor that was once covered with a freshwater sea and later thousands of tons of ice; to the west are views of a mountain formation towering more than a mile overhead.

Consider this: The tops of the Tetons, which sit on a 40-mile-long fault, were displaced by 30,000 feet of movement of the earth's crust over the last 13 million years—the valley floor dropped by 24,000 feet as the mountains shot up 6,000 feet. They were thrust skyward by massive geological upheaval. The canyons that punctuate the mountains were carved by ice-age glaciers, which also gouged out hundreds of lakes in the park.

One advantage of Grand Teton is that it's significantly easier to navigate than Yellowstone, in part because the park is smaller and activity centers are closer to each other. Jackson Lake and the Snake River, prime recreational areas for anglers and boaters, are only short distances from the hiking trails and campsites. Though less stately than the more famous Old Faithful Inn, Jackson Lake Lodge is quite appealing and comfortable in its own right.

The first homesteaders began arriving in the area in the 1880s. Many discovered, though, that the frigid winters and short growing season made it difficult—indeed, virtually impossible—to eke out a living, so they abandoned the area. By 1907 cattle ranchers discovered that wealthy Eastern hunters were attracted to the area as a vacation site, and the dude-ranching industry secured its first foothold in Jackson Hole, the great valley that runs the length of the Tetons on the east side.

When cattle interests learned of a movement to convert privately owned grazing land on the valley floor into a national park, a rancorous tug-of-war began. Congress had designated the area south of Yellowstone National Park the Teton Forest Reserve in 1897 and attempted to create a larger sanctuary in 1918; however, local opposition defeated the measure. In 1923, a more well-reasoned and successful attempt was made to preserve the area for future generations when Maud Noble, a conservation-minded entrepreneur, and a group of other concerned locals, aided by Yellowstone Superintendent Horace Albright, prepared a plan for setting aside a portion of the Jackson Hole as a national recreation area. Congress first set aside 96,000 acres of mountains and forests (excluding Jackson Lake) as a national park in 1929.

John D. Rockefeller Jr. got into the act by establishing the Snake River Land Company, which became the vehicle through which he anonymously accumulated more than 35,000 acres of land between 1927 and 1943. His goal was to donate the property for an enlarged park, but opponents in Congress prevented the government from accepting his gift.

Finally, in 1950, the feds and the locals reached a compromise: The government agreed to reimburse Teton County for revenue that would have been generated by property taxes, and to honor existing leaseholds, and present-day Grand Teton National Park was born.

Avoiding the Crowds. Most of the travelers who visit Grand Teton are also visiting Yellowstone on the same trip—and this means that when winter closes in on Yellowstone, the crowds abandon both parks. Since Grand Teton usually holds out against winter a bit longer than the higher plateau to the north, you may enjoy a wonderful, traffic-free visit in early June and late October at Grand Teton. But I emphasize the word *may:* Snow can fall as early as September.

Another off-season risk, in addition to unpredictable snowfall, is that it's sometimes harder to get around. In the spring, higher trails are still blocked by snow or the mud that follows it. This soggy season can last well into June. In the fall, temperatures can drop at night, and icy winds sometimes blow.

In spring, however, wildflowers are particularly dynamic, filling the meadows and hillsides with vast arrays of color. In the fall, golden aspens rustle amid the evergreens, and the thinning crowds provide a respite for both visiting humans and resident wildlife. In some streams, this is the best time for angling. It's cheaper, too: Motels drop their rates during the off-season.

If crowds make you claustrophobic, the key months to avoid are July and August. But most of the people who come through the gates in midsummer go only to the developed campgrounds and lodges at Colter Bay, Jenny Lake, Jackson Lake, and Signal Mountain; to the lakes and views accessible by car; and to the short paths that stay within view of the visitor center. If you have the energy to hike up into Cascade Canyon and beyond, you'll see an entirely different landscape. And, of course, summer is a beautiful time of year, with wildflowers blooming well into July, and wildlife always in evidence.

Just the Facts

GETTING THERE & GATEWAYS

The park is essentially the east slope of the Tetons and the valley below, so if you drive to it, you enter from the south,

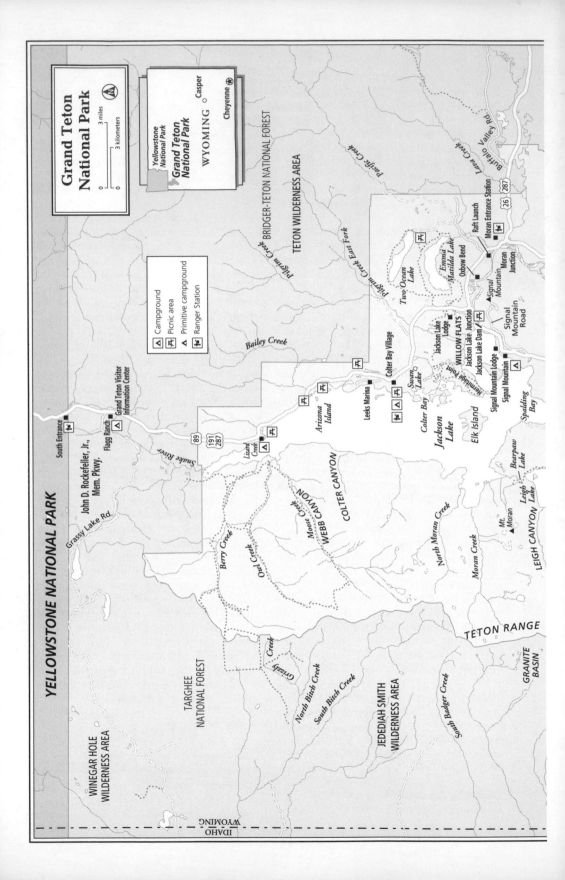

Grand Teton National Park

3 miles

3 kilometers

WYOMING

Casper

Cheyenne

Yellowstone National Park

Grand Teton National Park

YELLOWSTONE NATIONAL PARK

BRIDGER-TETON NATIONAL FOREST

TETON WILDERNESS AREA

Pilgrim Creek

Pilgrim Creek East Fork

Pacific Creek

Buffalo Valley Rd.

Lava Creek

287

26

Moran Entrance Station

Raft Launch

Moran Junction

Oxbow Bend

Emma Matilda Lake

Two Ocean Lake

Signal Mountain

Jackson Lake Lodge

WILLOW FLATS

Jackson Lake Junction

Jackson Lake Dam

Signal Mountain Road

Signal Mountain Lodge

Signal Mountain

Colter Bay Village

Swan Lake

Colter Bay

Hermitage Point

Leeks Marina

Arizona Island

Jackson Lake

Elk Island

Spalding Bay

Bailey Creek

Campground

Picnic area

Primitive campground

Ranger Station

South Entrance

John D. Rockefeller, Jr., Mem. Pkwy.

Flagg Ranch

Grand Teton Visitor Information Center

Grassy Lake Rd.

Snake River

89

191

287

Lizard Creek

Moose Creek

WEBB CANYON

COLTER CANYON

Berry Creek

Owl Creek

Grizzly Creek

North Bitch Creek

South Bitch Creek

North Moran Creek

Moran Creek

Mt. Moran

Bearpaw Lake

Leigh Lake

LEIGH CANYON

TETON RANGE

GRANITE BASIN

South Badger Creek

JEDEDIAH SMITH WILDERNESS AREA

TARGHEE NATIONAL FOREST

WINEGAR HOLE WILDERNESS AREA

IDAHO

WYOMING

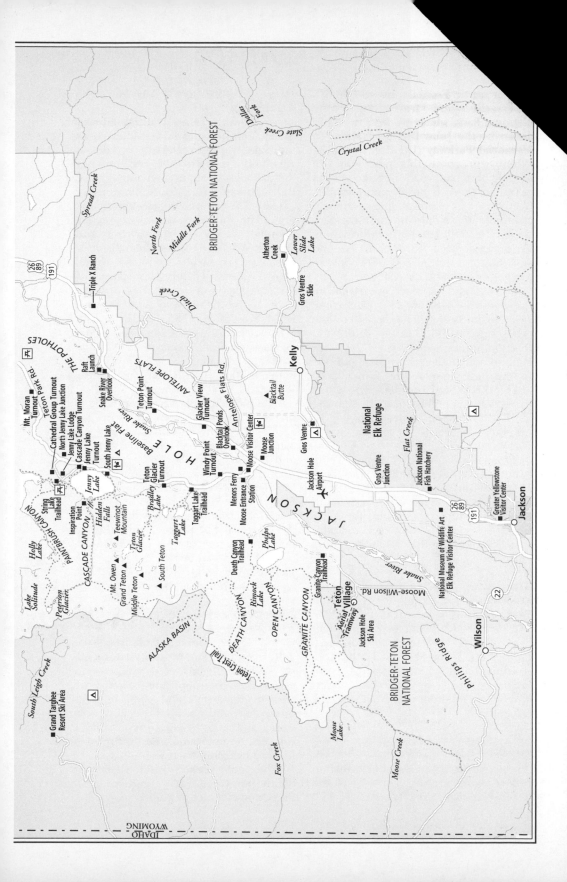

Maps

...he north, you can ...om Yellowstone ...s linked to Grand ... **Rockefeller, Jr.,** ...U.S. 89/191/287). When you come this way, you will already have paid your entrance to both parks, so there is no entrance station, but you can stop at **Flagg Ranch,** approximately 5 miles north of the park boundary, and get park information. From December to March, Yellowstone's south entrance is open only to snowmobiles and snow coaches.

You can also approach the park from the east, via U.S. 26/287. This route comes from Dubois, 55 miles east on the other side of the Absaroka and Wind River mountains, and crosses Togwotee Pass, where you'll get your first and one of the best views of the Tetons from above the valley. Travelers who come this way can continue south on U.S. 26/89/191 to Jackson without paying an entrance fee, though they are within the park boundaries.

Finally, you can enter Grand Teton from Jackson in the south, driving about 12 miles north on U.S. 26/89/191 to the Moose turnoff and the park's south entrance. Here you'll find the park headquarters and visitor center, and a small community that includes dining and shops.

The Nearest Airport. Inside the southern boundary of Grand Teton National Park, **Jackson Hole Airport** (✆ 307/733-7682) is clearly the most convenient airport, served by American, Continental Express, Delta, SkyWest (Delta Connection), and United Express. Most major car-rental companies have outlets here. For toll-free numbers, see the appendix.

INFORMATION

To receive park maps and information before your arrival, contact **Grand Teton National Park,** P.O. Drawer 170, Moose, WY 83012 (✆ **307/739-3600;** www.nps.gov/grte).

The **Grand Teton Natural History Association** provides information about the park through retail book sales at park visitor centers; you can also buy these books by mail. Contact them at P.O. Drawer 170, Moose, WY 83012 (✆ **307/739-3403;** www.grandtetonpark. org). The following books are recommended: *Teton Trails* by Katy Duffy and Darwin Wile and *Grand Teton National Park,* both available from the Grand Teton Natural History Association; *A Guide to Exploring Grand Teton National Park,* Linda Olson and Tim Bywater, RNM Press, Box 8531, Salt Lake City, UT 84108; and *An Outdoor Family Guide to Yellowstone and Grand Teton National Parks,* Lisa Gollin Evans, The Mountaineers, 1001 SW Klickitat Way, Seattle, WA 98134.

The **Jackson Hole Chamber of Commerce** provides information on just about everything in and around Jackson. Along with the U.S. Forest Service and National Park Service, representatives of the chamber can be found at the informative **Greater Yellowstone Visitor Center,** 532 N. Cache, about 3 blocks north of the town square with a view of the National Elk Refuge. For information on lodging, events, and activities, contact the chamber at P.O. Box 550, Jackson, WY 83001 (✆ **307/733-3316;** www.jacksonholechamber.com).

VISITOR CENTERS

Grand Teton National Park has three visitor centers. The **Moose Visitor Center** is a half-mile west of Moose Junction at the southern end of the park. It's the park headquarters, and offers exhibits on geology and natural history, a bookstore, and audiovisual programs. You can pick up maps and permits for boating and backcountry trips.

The **Jenny Lake Visitor Center** at South Jenny Lake has maps, publications, and a geology exhibit.

The **Colter Bay Visitor Center,** the northernmost of the park's visitor centers, provides permits, information audiovisual programs, and a bookstore. This is also the home of the **Indian Arts Museum.**

Finally, there is an information station at the **Flagg Ranch** complex, which is approximately 5 miles north of the park's northern boundary.

FEES & PERMITS

There are no park gates on U.S. 26/89/191, so the views are free as you pass through the park on that route, but if you want to get off the highway and explore, you'll pay $20 per automobile for a 7-day pass (admission is good for both Yellowstone and Grand Teton). If you expect to visit the parks more than once a year, buy a $40 annual permit.

Fees for **camping** in Grand Teton are $12 per night at all the park campgrounds. You must have a permit to sleep in the backcountry. See "Exploring the Backcountry," later in this chapter, for more information.

SPECIAL REGULATIONS & WARNINGS

It is unlawful to approach within 100 yards of a bear or within 25 yards of other wildlife. Feeding any wildlife is illegal.

SEASONS & CLIMATE

A popular song once romanticized "Springtime in the Rockies," but what the rest of the world calls **spring** is likely to be chilly and spitting snow or rain here. Trails are still clogged with snow and mud. Cold and snow may linger into April and May, though temperatures are generally warming. The average daytime readings are in the 40s and 50s, gradually increasing into the 60s and 70s by early June. A warm jacket, rain gear, and water-resistant walking shoes are advised.

Summer is finally underway in mid-June, with wildflowers starting to bloom in May in the lower valleys and plains, and in July in the higher elevations. Temperatures are typically 75°F to 90°F (24°C–32°C) in the lower elevations and are especially comfortable because of the lack of humidity. Nights, however, will be cool, even during the warmest months, with temperatures dropping into the low 40s (single digits Celsius), so you'll want to include a light jacket in your wardrobe. Summer thunderstorms are common.

As **fall** approaches and temperatures remain mild but begin to cool, you'll want to have an additional layer of clothing. The first heavy snows typically fall by November 1 and continue through March or April.

Winter is a glorious season here, though it's not for everyone—it can get very cold. But the air is crystalline, the snow is powdery, and the skiing is fantastic. You'll need long johns, heavy shirts, vests and coats, warm gloves, and thick socks to combat daytime temperatures hovering in single digits and sub-zero overnights. If you drive in the park's vicinity in the winter, always carry sleeping bags, extra food, flashlights, and other safety gear.

If you're planning on visiting Yellowstone as well as Grand Teton and are considering making your trip to the parks before the middle of June, think about beginning your exploration in Grand Teton before working north to Yellowstone. Elevations here are slightly lower and snow melts earlier so that accumulations on trails are reduced, and temperatures are more moderate.

ROAD OPENINGS

Teton Park Road opens to conventional vehicles and RVs around May 1. The **Moose-Wilson Road** opens to vehicles about the same time. Roads close to vehicles on November 1 and open for snowmobiles in mid-December, though they never close for nonmotorized use.

If You Have Only 1 Day

A 1-day trip around this park is not unreasonable, given its size, and you can complete a loop that encompasses many major attractions without having to retrace your steps. Although this 1-day itinerary assumes you are entering Grand Teton from the north, possibly after visiting Yellowstone, you could just as easily begin your itinerary in Jackson, 13 miles south of the Moose Entrance Station.

Begin at the south entrance of Yellowstone National Park, driving through the **John D. Rockefeller, Jr., Memorial Parkway** on U.S. 89/181/287 past the **Flagg Ranch Information Station.** As you drive south, you'll find yourself skirting the northern shore of Jackson Lake, with a view of **Mount Moran** to the west, and, farther south, the towering **Cathedral Group.**

Colter Bay Village on the northeast shore of Jackson Lake is one of the park's busiest spots. Several popular hiking trails start here. If you turn right at Colter Bay Junction and go another half-mile, you'll be at the **Colter Bay Visitor Center;** stop here if you wish to take in the interesting **Indian Arts Museum** (© 307/739-3594).

The **Lakeshore Trail** begins at the marina entrance and runs along the harbor for an easy 2-mile round-trip. It's level, paved, shady, and wheelchair-accessible, offering you your best opportunity for a hike in this area if you don't have much time. The Douglas firs and pine trees here are greener and healthier than the lodgepole pines you see at higher elevations in Yellowstone.

A few minutes' drive south of Colter Bay, you'll pass **Jackson Lake Lodge** and then **Jackson Lake Junction,** where a right turn puts you on **Teton Park Road,** the beginning of a 43-mile loop tour. You'll be driving parallel to the mountain range with its 13,770-foot centerpiece, Grand Teton. You'll see lakes, created by glaciers thousands of years ago, bordering a sagebrush valley inhabited by pronghorn and elk.

Just 5 miles down the road along Jackson Lake, a left-hand (east) turn will take you up **Signal Mountain,** where you'll have a 360-degree view of the valley. You might want to grab a quick lunch at Signal Mountain Lodge, a friendly lakeside eatery with a beautiful view. Then continue south on Teton Park Road to **South Jenny Lake.** If you have time, go to the other side (it's a 2-mile hike) and make the short climb to **Hidden Falls.** Otherwise, your best bet for a day hike in this area is the **Moose Ponds Trail** (see "Day Hikes," below).

When you leave South Jenny Lake, you'll drive a flat, sagebrush stretch to Moose, the southernmost of the park's service centers. One half-mile before Moose Junction is the **Moose Visitor Center.** While you're in Moose, you might visit the **Menor/Noble Historic District** and the **Chapel of the Transfiguration.**

Coming out of Moose, take a left (north) on U.S. 26/89/191, which crosses the open flats above the Snake River to Moran Junction. The best views along this road are the **Glacier View Turnout** and the **Snake River Overlook,** both of which are right off the road and well marked. At Moran Junction, turn left for a final 5-mile drive back to Jackson Lake Junction, past **Oxbow Bend,** a great spot for wildlife watching.

If You Have More Time

A 1-day whirlwind tour of Grand Teton is far from ideal. Like Yellowstone, this park demands a visit of 2 days or more. An extended stay allows for some relaxed hiking, picnicking, and sightseeing—you'll gain a greater appreciation for the park and the area's culture and history.

As with the short tour in the previous section, we begin at the northern end of the park. But you could just as easily start exploring from the southern end near

Jackson. From Jackson, it's 13 miles to the Moose Entrance Station, another 7 miles to the Jenny Lake Visitor Center, another 12 miles to the Jackson Lake Junction, and 5 more miles to Colter Bay.

JACKSON LAKE & THE NORTH END OF THE PARK

Many people enter Grand Teton National Park from the north end, emerging from Yellowstone's south entrance with a 7-day park pass that is good for admission to Grand Teton as well. Yellowstone is connected to Grand Teton by a wilderness corridor called the **John D. Rockefeller, Jr., Memorial Parkway** through which the highway runs for 8 miles, over the Snake River, past meadows sometimes dotted with elk, along the shores of Jackson Lake, and through forests.

In the parkway, not far from Yellowstone, you'll pass the recently modernized **Flagg Ranch Resort** (see "Where to Stay," later in this chapter), with gas, restaurants, lodging, and other services. In the winter, this is a busy staging area for the snow-coach and snowmobiling crowd.

Giant **Jackson Lake,** a huge expanse of water filling a deep gouge left 10,000 years ago by retreating glaciers, dominates the north end of the park. Though it empties east into the Snake River, curving around in the languid **Oxbow Bend**—a favorite wildlife-viewing float for canoeists—the water from Jackson Lake eventually turns south and then west through Snake River Canyon and into Idaho. Stream flow from the dam is regulated both for potato farmers downstream in Idaho and for rafters in the canyon, so, for better or ill, we have an irrigation dam in a national park. Elsewhere on the lake, things look quite natural, except when water gets low in the fall.

As the road follows the east shore of the lake from the north, the first development that travelers encounter is

Leeks Marina, where boats can launch, gas up, and moor from mid-May to mid-September. There are numerous scenic pullouts along the lake, some good for picnics.

Just south of Leeks is **Colter Bay,** a busy outpost of park services that offers a visitor center, a general store, a laundry, two restaurants, a boat launch, boat rentals, and tours. Colter Bay has lots of overnight options, from cabins to old-fashioned tent camps to a trailer park. You can take pleasant short hikes in this area, including a walk around the bay or out to **Hermitage Point** (see "Day Hikes," below).

The **Indian Arts Museum** (© 307/739-3594) at the Colter Bay Visitor Center is worth a visit, though it is not strictly about the Native American cultures of this area. The artifacts are mostly from Plains Indian tribes, but there are also some Navajo items from the Southwest. The collection includes moccasins, pipes, shields, dolls, and war clubs sometimes called "skull crackers." Visiting American Indian artists work in the museum all summer long and sell their wares on-site. Admission is free.

From Colter Bay the road swerves east and then south again past Jackson Lake Lodge. Numerous trails emanate from here, both to the lakeshore and east to **Emma Matilda Lake.** The road then comes to **Jackson Lake Junction,** where you can either continue west along the lakeshore or go east to the park's Moran Entrance Station. If you go out through the Moran entrance, you are still in the park and may turn south on U.S. 26/89/191 and drive along the Snake River to Jackson, making the most of your journey within the park's borders.

But if you're here to enjoy the park, you should turn right (west) on **Teton Park Road** at Jackson Lake Junction. After only 5 miles, you will arrive at **Signal Mountain.** Like its counterpart at Colter Bay, this developed recreation area, on Jackson Lake's southeast shore, offers camping sites, accommodations in cabins and multiplex units, two restaurants, and a lounge with one of the few televisions in the park. If you need to stock up with gas or food, do so at the small convenience store here. Boat rentals and scenic cruises of the lake are also available.

If you turn east instead of west off Teton Park Road at Signal Mountain, you can drive up a narrow, twisty road to the **top of the mountain,** 700 feet above the valley, where you'll have a fine view of the ring of mountains—Absarokas, Gros Ventres, Tetons, and Yellowstone Plateau—that create the Jackson "Hole." Note also the potholes created in the valley's hilly moraines left by retreating glaciers. Below the summit, about 3 miles from the base of the hill, is **Jackson Point Overlook,** a paved path 100 yards long leading to the spot where the Hayden Expedition's photographer William Henry Jackson shot his famous wet-plate photographs of Jackson Lake and the Tetons more than a century ago—proof to the world that such spectacular places really existed.

Looking for a hideaway? On the right (west) side of the road between Signal Mountain and North Jenny Lake Junction, approximately 2 miles south of the Mount Moran Turnout, is an unmarked, unpaved road leading to **Spalding Bay.** It's a sheltered little campsite and boat launch area with a primitive restroom. There isn't much space if others have beaten you there, but it's a great place to be alone with great views of the lake and mountains. An automobile or SUV will have no problem with this road, taking it slowly. You'll pass through brush and forest and might spot a moose.

JENNY LAKE & THE SOUTH END OF THE PARK

Continuing south along Teton Park Road, you move into the park's southern half, where the tallest peaks rise abruptly above a string of smaller lakes strung together in the foothills—**Leigh Lake,** the appropriately named **String Lake,** and **Jenny Lake,** many visitors' favorite. At North Jenny Lake Junction you can take a turnoff west to Jenny Lake Lodge. The road then continues as a one-way scenic loop along the lakeshore before rejoining Teton Park Road about 4 miles later.

Beautiful **Jenny Lake** gets a lot of traffic throughout the summer, both from hikers who circumnavigate the lake on a 6-mile trail and from more sedentary folks who pay for a boat ride across the lake to Hidden Falls and the short steep climb to **Inspiration Point** (see "Day Hikes," below). The parking lot at **South Jenny Lake** is often jammed, and there can be a long wait for the boat ride, so you might want to get there early in the day. Or you can save your money by taking the 2-mile hike around the lake—it's level and easy. There is also a tents-only campground, a visitor center, and a general store. You'll have to buy a ticket and wait in line for the trip across the lake in a powerboat that holds about 30 people. Hours and prices change from year to year, but generally, the hours are from 8am to 6pm, with boats leaving every 20 minutes. The trip costs about $7 round-trip for adults, $5 for children 7 to 12, and free for children under 6. One-way trips cost $5 for adults and $3 for children (free for those under 6). Contact **Jenny Lake Boating Company** (© 307/733-9227) for more information.

South of the lake, Teton Park Road crosses open sagebrush plains with never-ending views of the mountains. You'll pass the Climbers' Ranch and some trailheads for enjoyable **hikes to Taggart Lake** and elsewhere. Look closely in the sagebrush for the shy pronghorn, an antelope-like creature. This handsome animal, with tan cheeks and black accent stripes, can spring along at up to 60 mph. If you wander in the sagebrush here, you may encounter a badger, a shy but mean-spirited creature that sometimes comes out of its hole in the morning or at twilight.

The **Teton Glacier Turnout** presents a view of a glacier that grew for several hundred years until, pressured by hotter summer temperatures in the past century, it reversed direction, and began retreating.

The road arrives at the park's south entrance—again, actually well within the park's boundaries—and the **Moose Visitor Center,** which is also park headquarters and the only year-round visitor center here.

Just behind the visitor center is **Menors Ferry.** Bill Menor had a country store and operated a ferry across the Snake River at Moose back in the late 1800s. The ferry and store have been reconstructed, and you can buy items like those once sold here. Also in the area is the **Chapel of the Transfiguration.** In 1925 this chapel was built in Moose so that settlers wouldn't have to make the long buckboard ride into Jackson. It's still in use for Episcopal services from spring to fall, and it's a popular place for weddings, with a view of the Tetons through a window behind the altar.

Dornan's is a small village area just south of the visitor center on a chunk of private land owned by one of the area's earliest homesteading families. There are a few shops and a semigourmet grocery store, a collection of nice rental cabins that sleep four to six ($155–$230 in the summer), a post office, a bar with occasional live music, and even a first-rate wine shop.

THE EAST SIDE OF THE PARK

At Moose Junction, just east of the visitor center, drivers can rejoin the highway and either turn south to Jackson and the Gros Ventre turn, or cruise north up U.S. 89/26/191 to Moran Junction. This 18-mile trip is the fastest route through Grand Teton National Park, and, being farther from the mountains, offers views of a broader mountain tableau.

The junction of U.S. 89 with **Antelope Flats Road** is 1¼ miles north of the Moose Junction. The 20-mile route

beginning here is an acceptable biking route. It's all on level terrain, passing by the town of Kelly and the Gros Ventre campground before looping back to U.S. 26/89/191 at the Gros Ventre Junction to the south. If you continue straight on Antelope Flats Road, you'll reach the **Teton Science School** (see "Organized Tours & Ranger Programs," later in this chapter) at the road's end, about a 5-mile trip.

Less than a mile farther along U.S. 26/89/191, on the left, **Blacktail Ponds Overlook** offers an opportunity to see how beavers build dams and the effect these hardworking creatures have on the flow of the streams. The area is marshy early in summer, but it's still worth the quarter-mile hike down to the streams where the beaver activity can be viewed more closely.

Two miles farther along U.S. 89 brings you to the **Glacier View Turnout,** which offers views of an area that 140,000 to 160,000 years ago was filled with a 4,000-foot-thick glacier. The view of the gulch between the peaks offers vivid testimony of the power of the glaciers that carved this landscape. Lower **Schwabacher Landing** is at the end of a 1-mile, fairly well-maintained dirt road that leads down to the Snake River; you'll see the turnoff 4½ miles north of Moose Junction. The road winds through an area filled with glacial moraine (the rocks, sand, gravel, and so forth that were left behind as glaciers passed through the area) left over from several different ice ages. At the end of the road is a popular launch site for float trips and fly-fishing. It's also an ideal place to retreat from the crowds. Don't be surprised to see bald eagles, osprey, moose, river otter, and beaver, which regularly patrol the area.

The **Snake River Overlook,** approximately 4 miles down the road beyond the Glacier View Turnout, is the most famous view of the Teton Range and the Snake River, immortalized by Ansel Adams. From this overlook you'll also see at least three separate, distinctive,

200-foot-high plateaus that roll from the riverbed to the valley floor, a vivid example of the power of the glaciers and ice floes as they sculpted this area.

A half-mile north of the Snake River Overlook is the newly repaved road to **Deadman's Bar,** a peaceful clearing on the riverbank. Many float trips launch here and there is a limited amount of fishing access.

Cunningham Cabin, 1¾ miles north of Deadman's Bar, is a nondescript historic site at which homesteaders Pierce and Margaret Cunningham built their ranch in 1890. By 1928, they had been defeated by the elements and sold out to Rockefeller's Snake River Land Co. You can visit it at any time.

If you head down the highway in the other direction (south) from Moose Junction on U.S. 26/89/191 you can turn east on the **Gros Ventre River Road** 5 miles before you reach Jackson and follow the river east into its steep canyon—a few miles past the little town of Kelly you'll leave the park and be in **Bridger-Teton National Forest.**

In 1925, a huge slab of mountain broke off of the north end of the Gros Ventre Range on the east side of Jackson Hole, a reminder of nature's violent and unpredictable side. The slide left a gaping open gash in the side of Sheep Mountain, sloughing off nearly 50 million cubic yards of rock and forming a natural dam across the Gros Ventre River half a mile wide. Two years later, the dam broke, and a cascade of water rushed down the canyon and through the little town of Kelly, taking several lives. The town of **Kelly** is a quaint and eccentric community with a large number of yurts. Up in the canyon formed by the Gros Ventre River, is a roadside display with photographs of the slide area and a short nature walk from the road down to the residue of the slide and **Lower Slide Lake.** Here, signs identify the trees and plants that survived or grew in the slide's aftermath.

Organized Tours & Ranger Programs

The **Grand Teton Lodge Company** (© **800/628-9988** or 307/543-2811; www. gtlc.com) runs half- and full-day bus tours of Grand Teton ($30 adults, $15 children) and Yellowstone ($50 adults, $30 children) from mid-May to mid-October, weather permitting.

The excellent **Teton Science School,** P.O. Box 68, Kelly, WY 83011 (© **307/ 733-4765;** www.tetonscience.org), offers a curriculum for students of all ages, from integrated science programs for junior high kids to adult seminars covering everything from botany to astronomy. Classes take place at the newly renovated Stokes Family Learning Center in Kelly, and younger students can stay on-site in log cabins for some of the programs. The school's **Wildlife Expeditions** (© **307/773-2623;** www. wildlifeexpeditions.org) offers tours that bring visitors closer to the park's wildlife. These trips range from a half-day to a week, covering everything from bighorn sheep to the wolves of Yellowstone.

Within the park, there are several interesting ranger programs. These range from a ranger-led, 3-mile hike from the Colter Bay Visitor Center to Swan Lake to a relaxed evening chatting with a ranger on the back deck of the Jackson Lake Lodge, with the Tetons as a dramatic backdrop and spotting scope for watching moose and birds. There are numerous events during the summer at Colter Bay, South Jenny Lake, and the Moose Visitor Center. Check the daily schedules in the park's newspaper, *The Teewinot,* which you can pick up at any visitor center.

At the Taggart Lake trailhead, there are **wildflower walks** led by rangers who can tell you the difference between lupine and larkspur, daily in June and July, and guided morning hikes to Hidden Falls from Jenny Lake (you take the boat across the lake), among other activities.

At Colter Bay, you can climb aboard a boat for an afternoon **fire and ice cruise,** during which a ranger will talk about volcanics, glaciers, and fires that have shaped, reshaped, and colored the landscape. There are programs on American Indian art and culture, lakeshore strolls with rangers, and evening gatherings at the Colter Bay amphitheater in which rangers teach about park wildlife.

Youngsters 8 to 12 can join **Young Naturalist programs** at Colter Bay or Jenny Lake and learn about the natural world for 2 hours while hiking with a ranger. Sign-ups are at the visitor centers (the fee is a mere $1), and the kids will need basic hiking gear.

There are also evening campfire gatherings at the Gros Ventre, Jenny Lake, Signal Mountain, Lizard Creek, and Colter Bay campground amphitheaters, on a variety of park-related topics.

Day Hikes

COLTER BAY AREA

Lakeshore Trail

2 miles RT. Easy. Access: Marina entrance.

Originating in the Colter Bay area, this short jaunt starts at the marina and leads out to pebble beaches on the west side of Jackson Lake. The trail is wide and shady, and views of the entire Teton Range leap out at you from across the lake when you arrive at the end of the trail.

TRAILS FROM THE HERMITAGE POINT TRAILHEAD

The **Hermitage Point Trailhead** near the marina is the starting point for an interesting variety of trips ranging from 1 to 9 miles. With careful planning, it's possible to start the day with a hike beginning at Colter Bay that leads past **Cygnet Lake** across **Willow Flats** to Jackson Lake Lodge (where you can stop for lunch). Then, after a break, take the same path and return to Colter Bay in

time for the evening barbecue. All told, that's 10 miles round-trip.

When choosing your route, keep in mind that the three trails running through this same forested part of the Colter Bay area—Heron Pond Trail, Swan Lake Trail, and Hermitage Point Loop—have virtually identical foliage and terrain. The numerous options can be confusing, so carry a map.

Hermitage Point Loop

8.8 miles RT. Moderate. Access: Swan Lake/ Heron Pond trail intersection.

This trail goes through a thickly forested area to the isolated Hermitage Point, a peninsula jutting into Jackson Lake, from which you can look across the bay to the Signal Mountain Lodge. If you're seeking solitude, this is an excellent place to find it, though you should check with rangers before leaving—this is bear country.

Heron Pond Trail

3 miles RT. Easy. Access: Hermitage Point Trailhead.

If you take this trail in the early morning, you will be more likely to see the beavers that live in the pond. This is bear territory, as well as a home for Canada geese, trumpeter swans, and moose. Wildflowers are part of the show in the early summer—look for lupine, gilia, heartleaf arnicas, and Indian paintbrush. The first 200 yards of the trail are steep, but after reaching the top of a rise, it levels out and has only moderate elevation gains from that point on.

Swan Lake Trail

3 miles RT. Easy. Access: Hermitage Point Trailhead.

Finding swans at Swan Lake requires a trip to the south end where a small island offers them isolation and shelter for nests. From Swan Lake, it's only 0.3 mile through a densely forested area to the intersection with the trail to Heron

Pond. Hermitage Point is 3 miles from this junction along a gentle path that winds through a wooded area that is a popular bear hangout.

Willow Flats

5 miles one-way. Easy. Access: Horse corrals at Colter Bay.

An alternative to mountainous, forested trails, this trip from Colter Bay to Jackson Lake Lodge takes you across marshy flats where you'll have an excellent view of the Tetons and a good chance of seeing moose and other wildlife. You begin by skirting the sewage ponds at Colter Bay (sorry), then pick up a trail east to Cygnet Lake. Instead of looping back to Colter Bay, you take a spur that crosses Pilgrim Creek going east across the flats. You can hike in either direction, but drop a car at each end if you don't want to double back on foot.

JACKSON LAKE LODGE AREA

Christian Pond Trail

1 mile RT. Easy. Access: 200 yards south of the entrance to Jackson Lake Lodge. It's unmarked, so look carefully.

This trail begins with a half-mile walk through a grassy, wet area to a pond with nesting trumpeter swans and other waterfowl. You can circle the pond, adding another 3 miles to the trip. In May and June, this is a great wildflower walk, but also prime habitat for bears, so check with rangers first. The south end of the pond is covered with little grassy knolls upon which the birds build their nests and roost, and beavers have constructed a lodge here too. It's a restful sanctuary but one often infested with gnats and mosquitoes.

Signal Mountain Summit Trail

8 miles RT. Moderate. Access: Near the entrance to the Signal Mountain Lodge, or 1 mile (by car) up Signal Mountain Rd. to a pond on the right.

This up-and-down trail gives you a few fine hours of solitude with views of the mountains, wildflowers, and, at the end, a grand panorama of the glacially carved valley. After negotiating a steep climb at the beginning of the trail, you'll come upon a broad plateau covered with lodgepole pines, grassy areas, and seasonal wildflowers. Cross a paved road to a lily-covered pond, and just beyond you'll choose from two different trails—take the right one up (ponds, wildlife, maybe moose and bear) or the left one down (open ridges with views).

TWO OCEAN & EMMA MATILDA LAKE TRAILS

You can come to these lakes from the east or west: From the west you'd begin at the Grand View Point Trailhead, 1 mile north of Jackson Lake Lodge; or at the Christian Pond Trailhead, just east of Jackson Lake Lodge. From the east, you'd go up Pacific Creek Road, 4 miles east of Jackson Lake Junction on the road to the Moran entrance. There is a pullout for Emma Matilda Lake 2 miles up this road, or you can go a half-mile farther, take a left on Two Ocean Lake Road, and go to the Two Ocean Lake trailhead parking lot, with trails leading to both lakes.

Emma Matilda Lake Trail

12 miles RT. Easy to moderate. Access: Emma Matilda Lake Trailhead on Pacific Creek Rd. or trailhead off Two Ocean Lake Rd. north of Jackson Lake–Moran Rd.

Circumnavigating this lake is a pleasant, up-and-down journey with great views of the mountains and a good chance of seeing wildlife. The hike winds uphill for 0.5 mile from the parking area to a large meadow favored by mule deer. The trail follows the northern side of the lake through a pine forest 400 feet above the lake, and then descends to an overlook where you'll have panoramic views of the Tetons, Christian Pond, and Jackson Lake. The trail on the south side of the lake goes through a densely forested area populated by Englemann spruce and subalpine fir. Be watchful and noisy because this is grizzly bear country. It's possible to branch off onto the Two Ocean Lake Trail along the northern shore of the lake.

Two Ocean Lake Trail

5.7 miles RT. Easy. Access: Two Ocean Lake Trailhead on Two Ocean Lake Rd., or Grand View Point Trailhead.

Take your time and take a picnic on this delightful, underused trail around Two Ocean Lake. You can start at either end, but I recommend a side trip up Grand View Point, which will add about 2.5 miles. You'll be rested for this climb because the walk around the lake is fairly level. The variety of habitat—marshes, lakes, woodlands, and meadows—means you'll see birds, wildflowers, butterflies, and possibly beaver, elk, deer, and moose. There are great views of the Tetons, too, but for the best vistas you need to take the trip up to Grand View Point, a climb that will take you from lodgepole to fir to a hilltop of arrowleaf balsamroot, with its large, yellow flowers. You'll look down on lakes, meadows, and volcanic outcrops, and in the distance you'll gaze at the Tetons, the Mount Leidy Highlands, and Jackson Lake. It's possible to branch off onto the Emma Matilda Lake Trail at the east end of Two Ocean Lake.

JENNY LAKE AREA

Amphitheater Lake Trail

9.6 miles RT. Strenuous. Access: Lupine Meadows Trailhead. From the Moose Entrance Station on Teton Park Rd., drive 6⅔ miles to the Lupine Meadows Junction and follow signs to the trailhead; if you're coming from Jenny Lake, the trailhead is at the end of a road less than 1 mile south of South Jenny Lake.

Here's a trail that can get you up into the high mountains and out in a day, if you're in good shape and acclimated to the altitude (you'll climb 3,000 ft.). You'll cross glacial moraines and meadows quilted with flowers, and enter forests of fir and lodgepole and whitebark pine

(a bear food—be alert!). Finally you clear the trees and come into an amphitheater of monstrous rock walls topped by Disappointment Peak, with the Grand and Teewinot in view. Surprise Lake and Amphitheater Lake sit in this dramatic setting, with a few gnarled trees struggling to survive on the slopes.

Cascade Canyon Trail

4.5 miles one-way. Moderate to strenuous. Access: Inspiration Point.

For those who have time to go a little farther, Cascade Canyon Trail is the most popular in the park. You can begin the hike from South Jenny Lake, but you can also shave 2 miles off each way by riding the boat service across the lake and beginning your hike at the Boat Dock (see "Jenny Lake & the South End of the Park," earlier in this chapter). At this point, you're only a steep 1-mile hike from Inspiration Point (see the "Hidden Falls & Inspiration Point Trail," below), which is as far as many visitors go. From here, you make a brief steep climb to the glacially rounded canyon, where the trail levels out and you're in a wonderland of wildflowers and waterfowl and busy pikas. On a nice day, the warblers will be singing and you may see moose and bear. If you want to go farther once you reach forks of North and South Cascade Canyon, follow either the South Fork to Hurricane Pass, or the North Fork to Lake Solitude. These are overnight trips.

A less taxing alternative to the Cascade Canyon trip mentioned above is a detour to **Moose Ponds,** which begins on the Inspiration Point trail. The ponds, located 2 miles from either west or east boat docks, are near the south end of the lake, and are alive with birds. The area near the base of Teewinot Mountain, which towers over the area, is populated with elk, mule deer, black bears, and moose. The trail is flat (at lake level), short, and easy to negotiate in 1 to 1½ hours. The best times to venture forth are in early morning and evening.

Hidden Falls & Inspiration Point Trail

1.8–5.8 miles RT. Moderate. Access: East or West Shore Boat Dock.

Many people cross Jenny Lake, either by boat or on foot around the south end, and then make the short, forest-shaded uphill slog to Hidden Falls (less than 1 mile of hiking if you take the boat; 5 miles round-trip if you walk around), which tumbles down a broad cascade. Some think that's enough, and don't go another steep half-mile to Inspiration Point. Up there you get a great view of Jenny Lake below, and you can see the glacial moraine that formed it. If you're only going to these two overlooks, we recommend a relaxed and easy hike around the south end of the lake.

Jenny Lake Loop Trail

7 miles. Easy to moderate. Access: Trailhead at East Shore Boat Dock.

Another lake to circumnavigate, following the shore. You can cut the trip in half by taking the Jenny Lake Boat Shuttle from the East Shore Boat Dock to the West Shore Boat Dock. The lake has a pastoral setting at the foot of the mountain range, providing excellent views throughout the summer. *Warning:* This is one of the most popular spots in the park; to avoid crowds, travel early or late in the day. The trails to Hidden Falls, Inspiration Point, and the Moose Ponds branch off this trail on the southwest shore of the lake. The trails to String and Leigh lakes branch off this trail on the northern shore of Jenny Lake.

Exploring the Backcountry

Grand Teton may seem small compared with Yellowstone, but it has more than 250 miles of backcountry trails that provide good opportunities for solitude and adventure. You must have a permit from the Park Service to sleep in the backcountry—the permits are free, but reservations are not. The permit is valid only on the dates for which it is issued.

There are two methods of securing permits: They may be picked up at park visitor centers the day before you start your trip, or you can make a reservation for a permit in advance of your arrival, for a $15 fee. Reservations are only accepted from January 1 to May 15, by writing the **Permits Office,** Grand Teton National Park, P.O. Drawer 170, Moose, WY 83012, or by faxing 307/739-3438.

Remember that this region has a short summer and virtually no spring. Although the lower-elevation areas of the park are open in May, some of the high country trails may not be clear of snow or high water before late June or early July. Look in the "Backcountry Camping" brochure available at the visitor center for approximate dates when specific campsites will be habitable.

Perhaps the most popular backcountry trail in Grand Teton is the 19.2-mile **Cascade Canyon Loop,** which starts on the west side of Jenny Lake, winds northwest 7.2 miles on the **Cascade Canyon Trail** to Lake Solitude and the Paintbrush Divide, then returns on the 10.3-mile-long **Paintbrush Trail** past Holly Lake. It is one of the most rigorous hikes in either park because of gains in elevation—more than 2,600 feet—rocky trails, and switchbacks through loose rock and gravel that can become slippery, especially in years when snow remains until the middle of summer on the north-facing side of Paintbrush Divide.

Rangers recommend the hike for several reasons, the most noteworthy of which is unsurpassed scenery. Moose and black bears inhabit this part of the park, so hikers are cautioned to be diligent about making noise. There's also the possibility of sighting harlequin ducks, since they nest near the trail in Cascade Creek. You'll see many types of wildflowers, large stands of whitebark pine trees, and an almost unimaginable array of bird life.

Though it adds 5.1 miles to the trip (one-way), a detour west from the Cascade Canyon Trail to **Hurricane Pass** will reward you with a view from the foot of **Schoolroom Glacier.** If it's an extended trip you're after, head west into the Jedediah Smith Wilderness on a trail that eventually crosses into Idaho. This trail doesn't stop anytime soon—you can actually continue trekking all the way to Alaska.

If you're unable to complete the hike in 1 day, you can trek 7.2 miles on the Cascade Canyon Trail to **Solitude Lake** and return via the same trail. If you can afford a 2-day trip, camping zones are 6 miles west of the trailhead on the Cascade Canyon Trail and 8.7 miles northwest on the Paintbrush Canyon Trail at Holly Lake. Be sure to get a reservation.

Perhaps the quickest way to get up high in these mountains for a backcountry foray is to hitch a ride up **Rendezvous Mountain** on the Jackson Hole Ski Resort Tram. This puts you at 10,450 feet in **Bridger-Teton National Forest,** just south of the park, and ready to embark north toward the park's Middle Fork Cutoff. From here you can head down into Granite Canyon to Phelps Lake, or go north along the **Teton Crest Trail** to Fox Creek Pass (over 8 difficult miles from the tram) and **Death Canyon** and beyond. If you are hardy enough to make it to **Death Canyon Shelf,** a wildflower-strewn limestone ledge that runs above Death Canyon toward **Alaska Basin,** you'll have an extraordinary high-altitude view of the west side of the Tetons' biggest peaks. If you are on an extended backcountry trip, you can continue north to Hurricane Pass, where you can come back down to the valley floor by way of Cascade Canyon.

This kind of backcountry trip is really an expedition, and requires skill and experience. Go over any such plans with park rangers, who can help you evaluate your ability to take on such a challenge.

Other Summer Sports & Activities

Biking. This is no bicyclist's paradise; bikes are banned from hiking trails in the park. On the paved roads below, the problem is safety—huge RVs careen about, and some roads have only narrow shoulders. Teton Park Road has been widened somewhat, but traffic is heavy here; road bikers should try **Antelope Flats,** beginning at a trailhead 1 mile north of Moose Junction and going east. Sometimes called **Mormon Row,** this paved route crosses the flats below the Gros Ventre Mountains, past old ranch homesteads and the small town of Kelly. It connects to the unpaved **Shadow Mountain Road,** which actually goes outside the park into national forest, climbing through the trees to the summit. Total distance is 7 miles, and the elevation gain is 1,370 feet; you'll be looking at Mount Moran and the Tetons across the valley.

Mountain bikers have a few more options: Try **Two-Ocean Lake Road** (reached from the Pacific Creek Rd. just north of Moran Junction) or the **River Road,** a 15-mile dirt path along the Snake River's western bank. (Bison use it, too, and you'd be smart to yield.) Ambitious mountain bikers may want to load their overnight gear and take the **Grassy Lake Road,** once used by American Indians, west from Flagg Ranch on a 50-mile journey to Ashton, Idaho.

A map that shows bicycle routes is available from the Park Service at visitor centers, or from **Adventure Sports** at Dornan's in the town of Moose (© 307/733-3307), which is inside the boundaries of Grand Teton National Park. You can also rent mountain bikes here.

Boating. If you bring your own boat, you must register it: For human-powered craft, it's $5 for 7 days, or $10 for a year permit; motorized skippers pay $10 for 7 days and $20 for an annual permit, which you can buy at the Colter Bay and Moose visitor centers. Boat and canoe rentals, tackle, and fishing licenses are available at Colter and **Signal Mountain** (rental fees of $21 per hr. for motorboats include permits); sailboat tours are also available at the latter. The **Jenny Lake Boating Company** (© 307/733-9227) runs shuttles to the west side of Jenny Lake and offers scenic cruises.

Motorized boats are allowed on Phelps, Jackson, and Jenny lakes, but on Jenny Lake the motor can't be over 10 horsepower. Only human-powered vessels are permitted on Emma Matilda, Two Ocean, Taggart, Bradley, Bearpaw, Leigh, and String lakes. Rafts, canoes, dories, and kayaks are allowed on the Snake River within the park. No boats are allowed on Pacific Creek or the Gros Ventre River.

Scenic cruises of Jackson Lake are conducted daily, and breakfast and dinner cruises are twice weekly, both leaving from the **Colter Bay Marina** from May through September. You'll travel to Elk Island, where they cook up a pretty good meal: trout and steak for dinner, or trout and eggs for breakfast. The scenic trips are 1½ hours long and cost $16 adults, $8 for kids; the meal cruises are twice that length and run $28 (breakfast) or $46 (dinner) for adults and $17 or $27 for kids.

Additionally, you can rent kayaks and canoes at **Adventure Sports** at Dornan's in the town of Moose (© **307/733-3307**), which is within the boundaries of Grand Teton National Park.

Climbing. The Tetons have a strong allure for climbers, even inexperienced ones, perhaps because you can reach the tops of even the highest peaks in a single day. The terrain is mixed, with snow and ice year-round—knowing how to self-arrest with an ice axe is a must—and the weather can change suddenly. The key is to get good advice, know your limitations, and if you're not already skilled, take some lessons and hire a guide at the local climbing schools. A pair of long-standing operations offers classes and guided climbs of Grand Teton: **Jackson Hole Mountain Guides** in Jackson (© **800/239-7642** or 307/733-4979; www.jhmg.com) and **Exum Mountain Guides** in Moose (© **307/733-2297**; www.exumguides. com). Expect to pay around $300 to $400 for a guided climb or $100 for a class. Those who need to practice their moves on a rainy day should try the

Teton Rock Gym, at 1116 Maple Way in Jackson (© **307/733-0707**). The **Jenny Lake Ranger Station** (© **307/739-3343**; open only in summer) is the center for climbing information; climbers are encouraged to stop in and obtain information on routes, conditions, and regulations.

Fishing. The lakes and streams of Grand Teton are popular fishing destinations. Jackson, Jenny, and Phelps lakes are loaded with lively cutthroat trout, whitefish, and mackinaw (lake) trout. Jackson has produced some monsters weighing as much as 50 pounds, but you're more likely to catch fish under 20 inches, fishing deep with trolling gear from a boat during hot summer months.

The Snake River runs for about 27 miles in the park, and has cutthroat and whitefish up to about 18 inches. It's a popular drift-boat river for fly-fishers. If you'd like a guide who knows the holes, try **Jack Dennis Fishing Trips** (© **307/733-3270**) or **Triangle X-Osprey Float Trips** (© **307/733-5500**). **Westbank Anglers** (© **307/733-6483**) is another full-service fly shop that sells gear and organizes trips in Jackson Hole. As an alternative, stake out a position on the banks below the dam at **Jackson Lake,** where you'll have plenty of company and just might snag something. You'll need a Wyoming state fishing license, and you'll have to check creel limits, which vary from year to year and place to place.

Float Trips. One of the most effective and environmentally sound (not to mention relaxing) methods of viewing wildlife in Grand Teton is aboard a floating watercraft that silently moves downstream without disturbing the animals. The park's 27-mile stretch of river is wonderful for wildlife, with moose, eagles, and other animals coming, like you, to the water's edge. Most of the commercial float operators in the park run from mid-May to mid-September (depending on weather and river flow conditions). These companies offer

5- to 10-mile scenic floats, some with early-morning and evening wildlife trips. Try **Solitude Float Trips** (© 307/ 733-2871); **Barker-Ewing Float Trips** (© 800/365-1800); **Grand Teton Lodge Company** (© 307/543-2811); **Signal Mountain Lodge,** in Grand Teton National Park (© 307/543-2831); and **Flagg Ranch Float Trips** (© 307/543-2861).

Horseback Riding. The **Grand Teton Lodge Company** offers tours from stables next to popular visitor centers at Colter Bay and Jackson Lake Lodge. Choices are 1- and 2-hour guided trail rides daily aboard well-broken, tame animals. An experienced rider may find these tours too tame; wranglers refer to them as "nose-and-tail" tours. In Jackson, try **Jackson Hole Trail Rides** (© 307/ 733-6992), **Snow King Stables** (© 307/ 733-5781), **Spring Creek Ranch Riding Stables** (© 800/443-6139), or the **Mill Iron Ranch** (© 307/733-6390). Rates usually run about $25 an hour, and many trips include a meal.

Winter Sports & Activities

Park facilities pretty much shut down during the winter, except for a skeleton staff at the Moose Visitor Center, and the park shows no signs of becoming the winter magnet for snowmobilers or backcountry skiers that Yellowstone is. That may be just as well—you can enjoy some quiet, fun times in the park without the crowds.

Skiing. You can ski flat or you can ski steep in Grand Teton. The two things to watch out for are hypothermia and avalanches. As with climbing, know your limitations, and make sure you're properly equipped. Check with local rangers and guides for trails that match your ability. Among your options is the relatively easy **Jenny Lake Trail,** starting at the Taggart Lake Parking Area, about 9 round-trip miles of flat and scenic trail that follows Cottonwood Creek. A more difficult ski is the **Taggart Lake–Beaver Creek Loop,** about a 3-mile route that

has some steep and icy pitches coming back. About 2 miles of the **Moose-Wilson Road**—the back way to Teton Village from Moose—is unplowed in the winter, and is an easy trip through the woods. You can climb the windy unplowed road to the top of **Signal Mountain** and have some fun skiing down. There is an easy ski trail from the Colter Bay Ranger Station area to **Heron Pond;** it's about 2.6 miles, with a great view of the Tetons and Jackson Lake. Get a ski trail map from the visitor centers.

Skiers who come to Jackson Hole are usually after the hard, steep stuff at the Jackson Hole Ski Resort, but a growing contingent of backcountry telemark skiers ski off Teton Pass and out of the ski resort boundaries.

Snowmobiling. Snowmobiling is another popular winter option. The **Continental Divide Snowmobile Trail** in Grand Teton is groomed, providing access to trails in the nearby **Bridger-Teton National Forest,** the area to the immediate east of Grand Teton National Park, and into Yellowstone.

For snowmobile rentals in Jackson, contact **Leisure Sports** (© 307/733-3040) or **Wyoming Adventures** (© 800/ 637-7147).

In the winter, **Flagg Ranch Resort** (see "Where to Stay," below) is a base for snowmobiling in between Grand Teton and Yellowstone, but given its isolation from the rest of Grand Teton during these months (and the fact that the accommodations are no longer open during winter), we don't recommend that you base yourself there.

Note: Legal wrangling over whether to ban snowmobiling in the parks is ongoing. You can get up-to-date information by calling © 307/344-2580 or visiting **www.nps.gov.**

Camping

INSIDE THE PARK

The campground chart below lists amenities for each campground in the *last to fill!*

spaces gone by noon

Campground	Total Sites	RV Hookups	Dump Station	Toilets	Drinking Water
Inside the Park					
Colter Bay	350	No	Yes	Yes	Yes
Colter Bay Trailer Village	112	Yes	Yes	Yes	Yes
Gros Ventre	372	No	Yes	Yes	Yes
*Jenny Lake**	51	No	No	Yes	Yes
Lizard Creek	60	No	No	Yes	Yes
Signal Mountain	86	No	Yes	Yes	Yes
Near the Park					
Flagg Ranch	172	Yes	Yes	Yes	Yes
Snake River Park KOA	80	Yes	Yes	Yes	Yes
Teton Village KOA	148	Yes	Yes	Yes	Yes
Wagon Wheel	32	Yes	Yes	Yes	Yes

* Tents only are allowed here.

park. All the park-run campgrounds except Jenny Lake can accommodate tents, RVs, and trailers, but none have utility hookups. Jenny Lake Campground, a tents-only area with 49 sites, is situated in a quiet, wooded area near the lake. You have to be here first thing in the morning to get a site.

The largest campground, **Gros Ventre,** is the last to fill, if it fills up at all—probably because it's located on the east side of the park, a few miles from Kelly on the Gros Ventre River Road. It has 360 sites, a trailer dump station, a tents-only section, and no showers. If you arrive late in the day and you have no place to stay, go here first.

Signal Mountain Campground, with views of the lake and access to the beach, is another popular spot that fills first thing in the morning. It has 86 sites overlooking Jackson Lake and Mount Moran, as well as a pleasant picnic and boat launch. No showers or laundry, but there's a store and service station nearby.

Colter Bay Campground and Trailer Village has 350 sites, some with RV hookups, showers, and a launderette. The area has access to the lake but is far enough from the hubbub of the village

to offer a modicum of solitude; spaces are usually gone by noon.

Lizard Creek Campground, at the north end of Grand Teton National Park near Jackson Lake, offers an aesthetically pleasing wooded area near the lake with views of the Tetons, bird-watching, and fishing (and mosquitoes; bring your repellent). It's only 8 miles from facilities at Colter Bay and has 60 sites that fill by 2pm.

A concessionaire-operated campground is located at the **Flagg Ranch Resort** complex on the John D. Rockefeller, Jr., Memorial Parkway. The area, situated in a wooded area next to the parkway, has 121 sites for RVs and campers, showers, and a launderette.

NEAR THE PARK

There are several places to park the RV or pitch a tent around Jackson Hole, and a few of them are reasonably priced and not too far from the park. Some of your best bets are either out of Jackson or way out of Jackson. Most campgrounds are open from late spring to early fall.

In Jackson, the **Wagon Wheel Campground** (© 307/733-4588) is about 5 blocks north of Town Square at the

Showers	Fire Pits/ Grills	Laundry	Public Phone	Reserve	Fees	Open
Yes	Yes	Yes	Yes	No	$12	Mid-May to late Sept
No	Yes	Yes	Yes	Yes	$27–$40	Mid-May to late Sept
No	Yes	No	Yes	No	$12	Early May to Oct
No	Yes	No	Yes	No	$12	Late May to late Sept
No	Yes	No	Yes	No	$12	Early June to early Sept
No	Yes	No	Yes	No	$12	Mid-May to Oct
Yes	Yes	Yes	Yes	Yes	$22/$40	Mid-May to late Sept
Yes	Yes	Yes	Yes	Yes	$31/$45	Mid-Apr to mid-Oct
Yes	Yes	Yes	Yes	Yes	$33/$44	May to mid-Oct
Yes	Yes	Yes	Yes	Yes	$24/$45	Mar–Oct

Wagon Wheel Motel. The **Teton Village KOA** (© **307/733-5354**), 12 miles northwest of Jackson, has 148 sites. Also away from the crowds, the **Snake River Park KOA Campground** is also on U.S. 89, 10 miles south of town (© **307/733-7078**), and has 80 sites.

Where to Stay

INSIDE THE PARK

Grand Teton doesn't have a lot of lodging options, but what's there is varied. You can get information about or make reservations for Jackson Lake Lodge, Jenny Lake Lodge, and Colter Bay Village through the **Grand Teton Lodge Company,** Box 240, Moran, WY 83013 (© **800/628-9988** or 307/543-3100; www. gtlc.com). For Signal Mountain Lodge, contact **Signal Mountain Lodge Co.,** Box 50, Moran, WY 83013 (© **307/543-2831;** www.signalmountainlodge.com).

Grand Teton National Park properties have in-room telephones, but none have in-room televisions or air-conditioning. You'll find televisions in the lounge areas at the Jackson Lodge, Signal Mountain Resort, and Flagg Ranch.

COLTER BAY VILLAGE AREA

Colter Bay Village

P.O. Box 240, Moran, WY 83013. © **800/628-9988** or 307/543-3100. www.gtlc.com. 166 units. $74–$139 log cabin; $37 tent cabin. AE, DC, MC, V. Closed late Sept to late May.

You might call this the people's resort of Grand Teton. Its simpler lodgings, lower prices, and lively, inclusive atmosphere seem particularly suited to families. Situated on the eastern shore of Jackson Lake, 35 miles north of Jackson, Colter Bay Village is a full-fledged recreation center. Guest accommodations are in roughly built log cabins perched on a wooded hillside; they are clean and simply furnished with area rugs on tile floors, beamed ceilings, and copies of pioneer furnishings—chests, oval mirrors, and extralong bedsteads with painted headboards. The simple bathrooms have stall showers, and some singles share bathrooms. If you want to take a trip back to the early days of American auto travel, when car-camping involved unwieldy canvas tents on slabs by the roadside, you can spend an inexpensive night in "tent cabins"

Bring your sleeping bags and sleep on squeaky bunks, and stop that giggling because there's another tent nearby with equally thin walls and small children trying to settle down. The shared shower/bathroom is just down the road.

Jackson Lake Lodge

P.O. Box 240, Moran, WY 83013. © **800/628-9988** or 307/543-3100. www.gtlc.com. 385 units. $120–$210 double; $146–$210 cottage; $385–$550 suite. AE, DC, MC, V. Closed mid-Oct to mid-May.

Much the way Old Faithful Inn or the Lake Hotel capture historic eras of Yellowstone tourism, Jackson Lake Lodge epitomizes the architectural milieu of the period when Grand Teton became a park. That era was the 1950s, an era of right angles, flat roofs, and big windows. While not as distinctive, the lodge is more functional and comfortable than its northern counterparts. The setting is sublime, overlooking Willow Flats, the lake in the distance, and towering over it, without a stick in the way, the Grand Teton and Mount Moran. You don't even have to go outside to see this impressive view—the lobby has 60-foot-tall windows. Add to that a good restaurant, comfortable rooms, and easy access from Jackson, only 35 miles away. Guest rooms are in the three-story main lodge and in cottages scattered about the property, some of which have large balconies and mountain views. Lodge rooms are spacious and cheery, and most offer double beds and newly tiled bathrooms. There is a large outdoor swimming pool, a cocktail lounge, full-course dining in the **Mural Room** (reviewed under "Where to Dine," below), and lighter fare at the **Pioneer Grill.**

SIGNAL MOUNTAIN AREA

Signal Mountain Lodge

P.O. Box 50, Moran, WY 83013. © **307/543-2831.** www.signalmountainlodge.com. 79 units. TEL. $95–$235 double. AE, DISC, MC, V. Closed late Oct to early May.

Signal Mountain has a different feel, and different owners, from the other lodgings in Grand Teton. What they all have in common is the Teton view, and this lodge, located right on the banks of Jackson Lake, may have the best. For one, it's got lakefront retreats that you can really inhabit, with stoves, refrigerators, and foldout sofa beds for the kids. Other accommodations, mostly free-standing cabins, come in a variety of flavors, from motel-style rooms in four-unit buildings set amid the trees to family bungalows with decks, some enjoying beach frontage. The carpeted cabins feature handmade pine furniture, electric heat, covered porches, and tiled bathrooms; some have fireplaces.

The registration building has a small TV viewing area, a gift shop, and outdoor seating on a deck overlooking the lake. A restaurant (the **Peaks,** reviewed under "Where to Dine," below) and coffee shop that serve average food share a separate building with a small lounge and gift shop. Recreational options include cycling, rafting, water-skiing, and fishing, but note that boat rentals are expensive here. A convenience store and gas station are on the property.

JENNY LAKE AREA

Jenny Lake Lodge

Box 240, Moran, WY 83013. © **800/628-9988** or 307/543-3300. www.gtlc.com. 37 units. $459 double; $620–$661 suite. Rates include breakfast, dinner, and activities. AE, DC, MC, V. Open June to mid-Oct.

Though it's located 20 miles from Jackson Airport, this small resort prides itself on its seclusion and tranquillity. It also has an award-winning restaurant. The Lodge is a hybrid of mountain lake resort and dude ranch, with activities such as horseback riding and bicycling. Accommodations are in rustic, pitched-roof log cabins fronted by a long, pillared porch. Each cabin has been named for a resident flower and most have forest views; some can see the lake. The luxurious interiors contain bright braided rugs, dark wood floors, beamed ceilings, log furniture with cowhide upholstery, and tiled combination bathrooms. Rooms have one queen, one king, or two double beds.

The lodge functions primarily as a dining establishment (the **Jenny Lake Lodge Dining Room** is reviewed under "Where to Dine," below) and caters to an older, affluent clientele. The style here is an odd mixture of peaceful rusticity and occasional reminders of class and formality (jackets for men are "appreciated").

NEAR THE PARK
FLAGG RANCH VILLAGE AREA

Like Grant Village in Yellowstone, Flagg Ranch offers travelers the full gamut of services: cabins, tent and RV sites, an above-average restaurant (at the Flagg Ranch Resort), and a gas station. Until a ban on snowmobiling was recently reinstated, it was a popular jumping-off spot for snowmobilers during winter months. However, it's situated in a stand of pines in the middle of nowhere, and there's not much to do in the immediate vicinity except watch the Snake River pass by.

Flagg Ranch Resort

P.O. Box 187, Moran, WY 83013. © **800/443-2311** or 307/543-2861. www.flaggranch.com. 92 cabins, 171 RV sites. $139–$149 double. AE, DISC, MC, V. Closed Nov–Mar.

A few years ago this resort just outside Yellowstone National Park was showing its age—the sort of place a hunter would rent a drafty room to collapse in after a few days in the woods. Not anymore: It's all fixed up, transformed into an all-seasons resort on the Snake River with log-and-luxury ambience. The newest accommodations are duplex and fourplex log cabins constructed in the 1990s that feature king-size beds, spacious sitting areas with writing desks and chests of drawers, wall-to-wall carpeting, and bathrooms with tub-shower combinations and separate vanities.

Call in advance about winter lodging. Due to the on again, off again ban on snowmobiling in the park, winter lodging may or may not be available. In the summer, there is plenty to do, however: float trips, horseback rides, and excellent fishing in Polecat Creek or the Snake River. The new lodge is a locus of activity, with its fireplace, dining room (reviewed under "Where to Dine," below), gift shop, espresso bar and pub, convenience store, and gas station.

IN JACKSON

Clustered together near the junction west of downtown where Wyo. 22 leaves U.S. 26/89 and heads north to Teton Village is a colony of chain franchises, including **Motel 6,** 600 S. U.S. 89 (© **307/733-1620**), and the not-just-numerically superior **Super 8,** 750 S. U.S. 89 (© **307/733-6833**). Also in the vicinity is the more expensive **Days Inn,** at 350 S. U.S. 89 (© **307/733-0033**), with private hot tubs and fireplaces; and the **Red Lion Inn,** at 930 W. Broadway (© **307/734-0035**). High season prices for the motels start around $90 and top out over $300. You can find toll-free numbers and websites for major chain hotels in the appendix.

Jackson Hole Lodge

420 W. Broadway, Jackson, WY 83001. © **800/604-9404** or 307/733-2992. Fax 307/739-2144. www.jacksonholelodge.com. 59 units. $109–$134 double; $189–$304 condo. AE, DC, DISC, MC, V.

Though it sits near one of the busiest intersections in Jackson, and is packed into a small space, this lodge is quiet and well designed. The indoor pool is not just for splashing—you can swim its 40-foot length, sit in one of the whirlpools, take a sauna, or lounge outside on the sun deck. If you're traveling with kids, your best bet is the condo lodgings, with two upstairs bedrooms, a full kitchen, and a living room with fold-out couch.

Rusty Parrot Lodge and Spa

175 N. Jackson, Jackson, WY 83001. © **800/ 458-2004** or 307/733-2000. www.rustyparrot. com. 31 units. $309–$355 double; $600 suite. Rates include full breakfast. AE, DC, DISC, MC, V.

The name sounds like an out-of-tune jungle bird, but since 1990 the Rusty Parrot has demonstrated excellent pitch, cultivating a country lodge and spa right in the heart of busy Jackson. Located across from Miller Park, the Parrot is decorated in the new-Western style of peeled log, with an interior appointed with pine furniture and river rock fireplaces. One very attractive lure is The **Body Sage spa,** where you can get yourself treated to all sorts of massages, wraps, and facials. The breakfast that comes with your room includes omelets, fresh pastries, fruits, cereals, and freshly ground coffee.

Trapper Inn

235 N. Cache, Jackson, WY 83001. © **800/ 341-8000** or 307/733-2648 for reservations. www.trapperinn.com. 54 units. $107–$171 double; $179–$231 suite. AE, DC, DISC, MC, V.

The employees here are among the most helpful in Jackson. Just 2 short blocks from downtown Jackson, the Trapper is hard to miss if you're walking north on Cache from the Town Square—on the left side of Cache you'll notice the bronze Trapper guy on the sign. Though the decor is undistinguished, the rooms are luxuriously spacious. They come with miniature refrigerators, microwaves, and coffeemakers; laundry facilities and an indoor/ outdoor hot tub are also on hand.

Virginian Lodge

750 W. Broadway, Jackson, WY 83001. © **800/ 262-4999** or 307/733-2792. Fax 307/733-4063. www.virginianlodge.com. 170 units. $95–$109 double; $125–$185 suite. AE, DC, DISC, MC, V.

It's not brand new, it's not a resort, and it doesn't have a golf course, but the Virginian is actually one of the better motels in Jackson. Located on the busy Broadway strip, the courtyard seems a world away and the prices remain reasonable, All in all, it's a busy, cheerful place to stay. A large outdoor pool is open seasonally, and you can get a room with a private Jacuzzi. Kids can romp in the arcade, and parents can relax in the **Virginian Saloon.**

Wort Hotel

50 N. Glenwood, Jackson, WY 83001. © **307/ 733-2190.** www.worthotel.com. 60 units. $165–$275 double; $325–$550 suite. AE, DISC,MC, V.

Located on Broadway just off the town square, the Wort's Tudor-style two-story building was largely rebuilt after a 1980 fire. Opened in the early 1940s by the wife and son of Charles Wort, an early-20th-century homesteader, it has an older style, both in the noisy and relaxed **Silver Dollar Bar** and the quiet, formal dining room. (There's a more bustling coffee shop next to it.) The rooms aren't Tudor at all—the Wort labels them "New West" and has totally renovated each of them since New Year's 2000. Brass number plates and doorknobs welcome you into comfortable, air-conditioned guest rooms with modern decor, thick carpeting, and armoires.

A warm, romantic fireplace graces the lobby; another fireplace and a huge hand-carved mural accent a mezzanine sitting area, providing a second hideaway. The famous bar itself is inlaid with 2,032 silver dollars, the most precious piece of furniture rescued from the fire.

NEAR JACKSON

Amangani

1535 NE Butte Rd., Jackson, WY 83002 (on top of East Gros Ventre Butte). © **877/734-7333** or 307/734-7333. www.amangani.com. 40 units. $700–$1,100 double. AE, DC, DISC, MC, V.

Chopped into the side of East Gros Ventre Butte, Amangani's rough rock exterior blends in so well that the lights from its windows and pool appear to be glowing from within the mountain. The style is understated and rustic, but every detail is expensively done. Owner Adrian Zecha has resorts like this around the world, from Bali to Bora Bora; and although the designs are tailored to the landscape, the approach is the same: personal service, luxury, and all the little touches—such as CDs in every bedroom, cashmere throws on the day beds, and slate and redwood walls. There's an outdoor pool, tennis courts, a health center, and an on-site restaurant, the **Grill,** that serves steaks, seafood, and regional organic foods.

Bentwood Inn

4 miles W of Jackson on Teton Village Rd., P.O. Box 561, WY 83001. ℭ **307/739-1411.** www. bentwoodinn.com. 5 units. $195–$325 double. Rates include complimentary full breakfast and evening cocktails. AE, DISC, MC, V.

This B&B is an architectural marvel. Built from 200-year-old timber cleared from Yellowstone to make room for a rest area, the inn is a 6,000-square-foot log mansion with an amazing 43 corners. The rooms, all with remote-controlled gas fireplaces, private balconies, and Jacuzzi tubs, are extensions of the innovative design, with touches equally urban and rural, from ornate tilework to longhorn skulls above the bed. Innkeepers Bill and Nell Fay (the former designed the inn himself) pay a great deal of attention to detail and it shows: One room is pet-friendly, the breakfasts are simultaneously hearty and gourmet, and the fridge is always stocked with a wide range of soft drinks and libations.

Spring Creek Ranch

1800 Spirit Dance Rd. (on top of the East Gros Ventre Butte), P.O. Box 4780, Jackson, WY 83001. ℭ **800/443-6139** or 307/733-8833. 125 units. A/C TV TEL. $210 double; $375–$1,200 condo. AE, MC, V.

Atop East Gros Ventre Butte, 1,000 feet above the Snake River and minutes from the airport and downtown Jackson, this resort commands a panoramic view of the Grand Tetons and 1,500 acres of land populated by deer, moose, and the horses at its riding facility in the valley below. Though it seems a little less exclusive now that Amangani has opened next door, Spring Creek still has a lot going for it. The rooms are divided among four buildings with cabinlike exteriors and have fireplaces, Native American floor and wall coverings, refrigerators, coffeemakers, and balconies with views of the Tetons. Most rooms have king- or queen-size beds, and the studio units boast kitchenettes. In addition to its own rooms, the resort arranges accommodations in the privately owned condominiums that dot the butte—large, lavishly furnished, and featuring completely equipped kitchens. The resort also has a pool, two tennis courts, and a concierge.

IN TETON VILLAGE

Although lodging in the town of Jackson tends to be a little cheaper in the winter than in the summer, at Teton Village the ratio is reversed—rooms by the ski hill get more expensive after the snow falls.

Alpenhof Hotel

3255 W. McCollister Dr., Teton Village, WY 83025. ℭ **800/732-3244** or 307/733-3242. www.alpenhoflodge.com. 42 units. $92–$238 double; $183–$538 suite. AE, DC, DISC, MC, V. Closed Nov.

This Swiss chalet–style hostelry has a prize location only 50 yards from the ski resort tram. Four stories tall, with a pitched roof and flower boxes on the balconies, the hotel combines an old-world atmosphere with excellent service. The dining room and deluxe accommodations were recently upgraded with brightly colored alpine fabrics and handcrafted European furnishings; rooms have tiled bathrooms with big, soft towels. Two junior suites have kitchenettes, five rooms have fireplaces, and four rooms have a shared deck that you access via an outside staircase. Economy rooms offer double or queen beds. Your choices for dinner include award-winning and expensive continental fare served in the **Alpenhof** dining room; or pork, game, and pasta, which are staples in the bistro-style loft.

Hostelx

Box 546, Teton Village, WY 83025. ℭ **307/733-3415.** Fax 307/739-1142. www.hostelx. com. $50–$60 double. MC, V.

If you came to Wyoming to ski, not to lie in the lap of luxury, get yourself a room at Hostelx and hit the slopes. Called "the soul of Jackson Hole," it's a great bargain for skiers who don't need the trimmings, but it's not a dormitory, either—the comfortable private rooms are above the caliber of a roadside motel, with king-size beds that hold up to four people. Hostelx also has a good place to prep your skis, a library, and a common room with a fireplace, where ski movies run in the winter. You can walk to the **Mangy Moose** (reviewed below) and other fun spots, and nobody will be able to tell you apart from the skiers staying at the Ritz.

Snake River Lodge & Spa

7710 Granite Loop Rd. (Box 348), Teton Village, WY 83025. ℭ **800/445-4655** or 307/732-6000. www.snakeriverlodge.com. 135 units. May to early June and Sept to mid-Dec $169–$299 double, $300–$900 suite; June to mid-Sept $229–$329 double, $450–$1,050 suite; mid-Dec to Apr $340–$380 double, $450–$1,250 suite. AE, MC, V.

Major renovations were completed here in 2003, and this perpetually changing establishment appears to have gained some stability under the ownership of RockResorts. Wooden walls, stone floors and fireplaces, and a stuffed bison accent the main reception area. The main lodge provides lodging where classy overshadows rustic, with exposed wooden-beam ceilings, down comforters, and luxurious furnishings. There are three levels of suites, from oversized versions of the standard rooms to three-bedroom versions with top-of-the-line kitchens, good sound systems, and Jacuzzi tubs. Two restaurants are located on the mezzanine level: **Gamefish** serves regional game and seafood, and the bar and grill offers a place to unwind with just about any beer you can think of (including microbrews), pool tables, and sports on television. The 17,000-square-foot **Avanyu Spa** features everything from hydrotherapy to free weights. Winter visitors can ski directly to a locker room with whirlpool and sauna, and drop their skis off for an overnight tune-up.

Teton Mountain Lodge

3385 W. Village Dr. (P.O. Box 564), Teton Village, WY 83025. ℭ **800/801-6615** or 307/734-7111. Fax 307/734-7999. www.tetonlodge. com. 129 units. $199–$319 room or studio; $249–$1,200 suite. AE, DC, DISC, MC, V.

The newest lodging option in Teton Village—at least until the long-awaited Four Seasons opens—the refined Teton Mountain Lodge opened in 2002 with a nice variety of contemporary Western rooms. Lodge studios have Murphy beds and full kitchens, while the lodge rooms have a queen or king, a sofa sleeper, and two doubles, but no kitchen. There are also spacious one-, two-, and three-bedroom suites that essentially combine one or more rooms and a studio. The decor includes attractive wood furnishings, black-and-white prints, and stone fireplaces. The property is luxurious but not overbearing, and its slope-side location can't be beat. The lodge offers winter ski packages as well as summertime white-water ones.

Teton Pines Resort

3450 N. Clubhouse Dr., Jackson, WY 83001. ℭ **800/238-2223** or 307/733-1005. www. tetonpines.com. 14 units. Summer $395–$750 suite; rest of year $100–$675 suite. AE, MC, V.

Arnold Palmer and Ed Seay designed the challenging 18-hole golf course attached to this luxury resort. Don't expect to improve your handicap, but do expect to soothe your frustrations in the comfortable rooms, which feature his-and-her bathrooms, one with tub, one with shower. The resort offers a range of activities, including tennis, diving, and fly-fishing. (Some activities have extra fees.) The Jackson Hole Ski Resort is 5 minutes away. The **Pines Restaurant,** serving contemporary American cuisine, is one of the better places to eat in Jackson, though pricey.

Where to Dine

INSIDE THE PARK

COLTER BAY

John Colter Cafe Court

Across from the visitor center and marina in Colter Bay Village. © **307/543-2811.** Breakfast $3–$6; lunch $5–$8; dinner $6–$14. DISC, MC, V. Daily 6am–10pm. Closed Oct–Apr. DELI/FAST FOOD.

These are the two sit-down restaurants in the village (though there's also a snack shop in the grocery store). Three meals are served daily during the summer months. The **deli** serves sandwiches, chicken, pizzas, salads, and soup, with prices that range from $4.50 for an individual pizza to $13 for a chicken dinner. The **Chuckwagon Steak and Pasta House's** breakfast menu features a vast, scrumptious all-you-can-eat buffet. Lunch is soup, salad, and hot sandwiches; dinner is a buffet featuring entrees like trout, lasagna, pork chops, beef stew, and New York strip steaks. The ambience is very casual.

JACKSON LAKE JUNCTION

The casual dining choice at the Jackson Lake Lodge is the **Pioneer Grill;** entrees are light and less expensive than those at the Mural Room (see below). The **Blue Heron** lounge (also at Jackson Lake Lodge) is one of the nicest spots in either park to enjoy a cocktail.

Signal Mountain Lodge

At Signal Mountain Resort. © **307/543-2831.** Breakfast $4–$9; lunch $6–$9.50; dinner $10–$27. AE, DISC, MC, V. Summer daily 7–10am and 11:30am–10pm. SANDWICHES/MEXICAN/ECLECTIC.

There are actually three places to eat here, each serving delicious food in the friendliest style in the park. The fine dining room and lounge are the **Peaks** and **Deadman's Bar,** respectively, and the **Trapper Grill** supplements the top-notch fare with sandwiches and Mexican entrees. Dishes at the Peaks include chicken potpie, pasta, and veal saltimbocca. When the bargain-hunting folks who work for the park's concessionaires head out for dinner, though, chances are good they'll land here and order the mountainous Nachos Supreme from the bar menu. This nutritionist's nightmare—melted cheddar and Jack cheese with spicy beef or chicken served on a bed of corn chips topped with sour cream—will satisfy the appetite of three or four hungry adults. The bar has one of three televisions in the park and is equipped with cable for sports nuts, so the crowd tends to be young and noisy.

The Mural Room

Jackson Lake Lodge. © **800/628-9988.** Breakfast buffet $10, lunch $6–$13, dinner $17–$27. AE, MC, V. Summer daily 7–9:30am, noon–1:30pm, and 5:30–9:30pm. BEEF/WILD GAME.

Jackson Lake's main dining room is quiet and fairly formal, catering to a more sedate crowd as well as corporate groups; it's also more expensive than other park restaurants. The floor-to-ceiling windows provide stellar views across a meadow that is moose habitat, to the lake and the Cathedral Group. Walls are adorned with hand-painted Western murals. Dinner may be a grand, five-course event that includes a shrimp cocktail, French onion soup, and Caesar salad, followed by an entree of Idaho trout, buffalo prime rib, vegetable lasagna, or rack of lamb.

JENNY LAKE

Jenny Lake Lodge Dining Room

Jenny Lake Lodge. ℂ **307/543-3300.** Fixed-price breakfast $16; lunch $6–$13; fixed-price dinner $50, not including alcoholic beverages. AE, MC, V. Summer daily 7:30–9am, noon–1:30pm, and 6–9pm. CONTINENTAL.

The finest meals in either park are served here, where a Cordon Bleu–trained chef creates culinary delights for guests (who have included U.S. presidents in the past). All three daily meals are appetizing, but the six-course dinner is the bell-ringer. Guests choose from appetizers such as chilled lobster salad, smoked sturgeon ravioli, or buffalo mozzarella and plum tomato salads; entrees include roasted pheasant, prosciutto-wrapped veal, or buffalo tenderloin. Desserts are equally decadent. Price is no object for guests, since meals are included in the room charge.

NEAR THE PARK

The Bear's Den

At Flagg Ranch, John D. Rockefeller, Jr., Pkwy. ℂ **800/443-2311.** Breakfast $3–$8; lunch $4–$9; dinner $13–$26. AE, DISC, MC, V. Summer 7am–1:30pm and 5–9pm; closed Nov–Mar. AMERICAN.

The food at this oasis is better than what is typically found in what most refer to as a "family restaurant," and servings are generous. The dinner menu includes fish, chicken, and beef dishes, as well as home-style entrees such as ranch beef stew and chicken potpie. The ambience is nice as well; wooden chairs and tables with colorful upholstery liven up this newly constructed log building.

Mangy Moose

Teton Village. ℂ **307/733-4913.** Reservations for larger parties recommended. Main dinner courses $11–$26. AE, MC, V. Daily 5:30–10pm. AMERICAN.

Coming off the slopes at the end of a hard day of skiing or snowboarding, you can slide right to the porch of this ski area institution. Good luck getting a seat inside, but if you like a lot of noise and laughter and tasty dishes such as buffalo meatloaf and Wyoming trout, be patient—it beats getting into your car and driving elsewhere. The decor matches the pandemonium: It looks like an upscale junk shop, with bicycles, old signs, and, naturally, a moose head or two hanging from the walls and rafters. The restaurant offers typical Wyoming fare (steak, seafood, and pasta), a good salad bar, and a smattering of Mexican dishes.

Nora's Fish Creek Inn

5600 W. Wyo. 22, Wilson. ℂ **307/733-8288.** Breakfast $5–$8; lunch $4–$9; dinner $12–$21. AE, DISC, MC, V. Mon–Fri 6am–1:30pm; Sat–Sun 7am–1:30pm; Wed–Sun 5–9:30pm. AMERICAN.

If you want to hang with the locals and you like to eat a lot, Nora's is the place to go—especially at breakfast, when they have pancakes and huevos rancheros that practically overflow the huge plates. Prices are inexpensive compared with those at any of the other restaurants in town. You still get as many coffee refills as you like. Dinner is fish, fish, and more fish, such as fresh Idaho trout.

Stiegler's

Teton Village Rd. at the Aspens. ℂ **307/733-1071.** Reservations recommended. Main courses $18–$30. AE, MC, V. Tues–Sun 5:30–9:30pm. AUSTRIAN/CONTINENTAL.

Austrian cuisine isn't exactly lurking beyond every street corner waiting to be summoned with a Julie Andrews yodel, but Jackson Hole has two options, both at this address: Stiegler's Restaurant or Stiegler's Bar. Since 1983, Stiegler's has been confusing, astonishing, and delighting customers with such favorites as the Bauern Schmaus (a "farmer's feast" that includes pork and bratwurst) and the less-perplexing venison St. Hubertus. You'll recognize the desserts, at least: apple strudel and chocolate bread pudding. Peter Stiegler, the Austrian chef, invites you to "find a little *Gemütlichkeit*"—the feeling you get when you're surrounded by good friends, good food, and, of course, good beer.

IN JACKSON

Billy's Giant Hamburgers

West side of Town Square. ℂ **307/733-3279.** Lunch and dinner main courses $4–$6. AE, MC, V. Daily 11:30am–10pm. Closed Nov. BURGERS.

If you take a wrong turn while entering the posh Cadillac Grille (reviewed below), you find yourself in this cramped '50s-style lunch booth and counter shop—and you might just stay. Big, juicy burgers are what you'll get, cooked right in front of you. You can actually sit here and order from the Cadillac Grille, perhaps a Maine lobster and a fine sauvignon blanc, or go for a giant cheeseburger with a pile of fries on the side.

The Blue Lion

160 N. Millward St. ℂ **307/733-3912.** Reservations recommended. Main courses $15–$28. AE, DC, MC, V. Summer daily 5:30–10pm; winter daily 6–10pm. CONTINENTAL.

In the fast-moving, high-rent world of Jackson dining, the Blue Lion stays in the forefront by staying the same. On the outside, it's a two-story blue clapboard building across from the town park—it looks like a comfy family home. On the inside, it's soft light in intimate rooms and unhurried meals of elegant food. The menu features rack of lamb and the usual (in Jackson) wild-game specialties, such as grilled elk loin in a

peppercorn sauce. Fresh fish is flown in for dishes such as the herb-encrusted rainbow trout.

The Cadillac Grille

55 N. Cache St. ℂ **307/733-3279.** Reservations recommended. Lunch $5–$18; dinner $16–$29. AE, MC, V. Daily 11am–3pm and 5:30–10pm. Closed Nov to mid-Dec. CALIFORNIA ECLECTIC.

Neon and a hip menu give this restaurant a trendy air that attracts see-and-be-seen visitors more than locals. The chefs work hard on presentation, but they also know how to cook a wide-ranging variety of dishes, from fire-roasted elk tenderloin to pancetta-crusted Alaskan halibut. The wine list is equally long and varied. The menu in this Art Deco restaurant changes regularly, but the place itself is one of Jackson's longer-lived establishments.

Jedediah's House of Sourdough

135 E. Broadway. ℂ **307/733-5671.** Reservations not accepted. Breakfast $5–$9; lunch $5–$8; dinner $8–$19. AE, DC, DISC, MC, V. Year-round daily 7am–2pm; summer 5:30–9pm. AMERICAN.

You feel as if you've walked into the kitchen of some sodbuster's log cabin home when you enter Jedediah's, with good reason—the structure dates from 1910. Bring a big appetite for breakfast, and a little patience—you may have to wait for a table, then you may have time to study the interesting old photos on the wall as you wait for your food. But it's worth it, especially for the rich flavor of the sourjacks, a stack of sourdough pancakes, served with blueberries. The 'Diah's omelette is a big three-egg concoction stuffed with bacon, onions, and cheddar cheese and served with a side of potatoes. During summer months, Jedediah's also serves dinner: steaks, barbecued chicken, trout, and the like.

Koshu Wine Bar

200 W. Broadway in the back of the Jackson Hole Wine Company. © **307/733-5283.** Reservations not accepted. Main courses $12–$18; brunch courses $6–$11. AE, MC, V. Tues–Sat 6pm–midnight; Sun 11am–2pm and 6–10pm. Bar open later. Closed Mon. ECLECTIC.

A relatively new entry in Jackson's frenetic dining scene, the Koshu Wine Bar has quickly emerged as one of the hippest restaurants in town. Both locals and tourists crowd the small, sleek dining room for ingenious Asian fusion creations. The ever-changing menu reads "Asian inspired food," but the Far East is just a starting point, as the chef melds dozens of other influences into dishes such as tamarind pork with coconut milk, green onions, and rice; sweet miso-marinated black cod with spinach and mushrooms; and a terrific ahi sashimi.

Nani's Genuine Pasta House

242 N. Glenwood St. © **307/733-3888.** Reservations suggested. Dinner main courses $12–$30. Daily 5–10pm. MC, V. ITALIAN.

At Nani's the setting is simple, but the food is extraordinary. There are two menus: a *carta classico* featuring pasta favorites such as *amatriciana* (tomato, onion, pancetta, and freshly ground black pepper) and mussels in wine broth; and a menu that features a region of Italy, with dishes such as veal Marsala and stuffed swordfish. Your only problem with this restaurant might be finding it—it's tucked away behind a rather run-down motel.

Old Yellowstone Garage

175 Center St. © **307/734-6161.** Main courses $15–$36. AE, DISC, MC, V. Tues–Sun 6–10pm. ITALIAN.

Since relocating west from Dubois in 2000, the Old Yellowstone Garage has continued its 10-year tradition of serving up delectable Italian in a casual Western atmosphere. The self-dubbed "slow food" served here includes starters such as *cozze mie* (mussels in a garlic–white wine sauce), calamari, and antipasti plates. The dinner menu includes risotto (prepared differently every day), the San Remo (deep-fried zucchini stuffed with mascarpone), and slow-cooked lamb shank, a wintertime favorite. Wood-oven pizzas round out the menu (and *are* the menu on Sun), the specialty being the *pizze bianca,* with homemade cheeses and fresh herbs. All of this is served up in a room with hardwood floors, big windows, tables, and booths, marked simply on the outside with the letters OYG.

Pato

680 S. Broadway. © **307/739-9191.** Reservations recommended. Main courses $14–$28. AE, MC, V. Sun–Thurs 5:30–9pm; Fri–Sat 5:30–10pm. Closed last 2 weeks of both May and Nov. CONTEMPORARY FUSION.

Serving cuisine "from places that are warm," Pato opened in 2001 in the converted house formerly occupied by the Lame Duck. The name (*pato* is Spanish for "duck") might be similar, but the food goes beyond the Lame Duck's traditional Chinese. The influences are Cuban, Mexican, Vietnamese, and Mediterranean. The seasonally rotating menu might include starters like a rich gazpacho or citrus-tinged scallop and shrimp ceviche. Entrees like jalapeño-encrusted halibut and mahmahi tacos round out the menu. The dining room is contemporary, with ochre walls and offbeat fine art depicting animals. Three bonuses: a view of the Tetons in the distance (this is the only eatery in town with one), regular two-for-one early-bird specials, and Latin dance parties on Friday nights.

Rendezvous Bistro

380 S. Broadway. © **307/739-1100.** Reservations recommended. Main courses $9–$20. AE, MC, V. Daily 5:30–10:30pm. Closed mid-Apr to mid-May. AMERICAN/SEAFOOD.

Taking over a building that once housed a Denny's franchise, the Rendezvous opened in 2001 and garnered a fast local following. It's easy to see why: The place is contemporary yet casual, the food is affordable but very good, and the service is well above average. Climb into one of the intimate booths and order a dozen oysters on the half shell and slurp away, but save some room for a main course, such as grilled New York strip or whole Maine lobster. It might sound formal, but it's really not—the beauty is that the food is top-notch, but the atmosphere is laid-back and friendly.

Snake River Grill

Town Square, Jackson. © **307/733-0557.** Reservations recommended. Dinner $20–$40. AE, DC, MC, V. Daily 5:30–10pm. Closed Nov and Apr. CONTEMPORARY AMERICAN.

This is a popular drop-in spot for locals, including some of the glitterati who sojourn in the area—Harrison Ford and Uma Thurman have been spotted. It's an award-winning restaurant for both its wine list and its menu, which features regular fresh fish dishes (ahi tuna is a favorite), crispy pork shank, and some game entrees such as venison chops and Idaho trout. From a wood-burning oven come pizzas with exotic ingredients such as duck sausage or eggplant with portobello mushrooms. The front-room dining area overlooks the busy Town Square, but a more private, romantic room is located in the back.

Sweetwater Restaurant

85 King St. © **307/733-3553.** Reservations recommended. Lunch $5–$8; dinner $13–$22. AE, DISC, MC, V. Daily 11am–3pm and 5:30–10pm, shorter hours in winter. AMERICAN.

Though this little log restaurant serves American fare, it does so in a decidedly offbeat way. The eclectic menu includes, for example, a Greek salad, a Baja chicken salad, and a cowboy grilled roast beef sandwich. The dinner menu is just as quirky; try the unique smoked buffalo carpaccio before diving into the giant grilled salmon filet. Vegetarians will want to sample the roasted veggies and polenta with a balsamic glaze.

Nearby Attractions

It's not exactly nature's way, but the U.S. Fish & Wildlife Service makes sure that the elk at the **National Elk Refuge,** just north of Jackson on U.S. Hwy. 26/89 (© 307/733-9212; www.nationalelk refuge.fws.gov), eat well during the winter by feeding them alfalfa pellets. It keeps them out of the haystacks of area ranchers, and creates a beautiful tableau on the flats along the Gros Ventre River: Thousands of elk, some with huge antler racks, dot the snow for miles. Though the elk are absent in the summer, there is still plenty of life on the refuge, including, most recently, a quite visible mountain lion and cubs.

Each winter from mid-December until March, the Fish & Wildlife Service offers **horse-drawn sleigh rides** that weave among the elk refuge. Rides early in the winter will find young, energetic bulls playing and banging heads; in late winter, when the animals are fed, the scene is more placid. Rides embark from the **National Museum of Wildlife Art** (across the highway from the refuge) between 10am and 4pm on a first-come, first-served basis. Tickets for the 45-minute rides cost $13 for adults and $9 for children 6 to 12, and can be purchased at the museum. A $15 combination pass gives you access to the sleigh ride and the museum.

18

GREAT BASIN NATIONAL PARK

by Don & Barbara Laine

REAT BASIN NATIONAL PARK, LOCATED ALONG THE UTAH-NEVADA border, provides an intimate glimpse of a vast, rugged section of America, with ample opportunities for outdoor (and underground) adventures. A region of desert, valleys, mountains, lakes, and streams, North America's Great Basin includes Nevada, Utah, and parts of California, Oregon, and Idaho. It received its name because the rainwater that falls here has no outlet to the sea.

Founded in 1986, this park not only looks out at the Great Basin's expanse of desert and mountains from the summit of 13,063-foot Wheeler Peak, but also descends beneath the earth's surface for a subterranean tour among the intricately and delicately formed stalactites, stalagmites, and other exotic formations in the unreal world of Lehman Caves.

Hiking trails abound, through rugged pine and aspen forests, or above the tree line to a moonlike world of barren, windswept rocks. Camping in the park is a delight, with quiet campgrounds, plenty of trees, and splendid scenery. The park contains forests of bristlecone pine—a species scientists believe are the oldest living trees on earth—as well as pinyon, juniper, spruce, fir, pine, and aspen. You'll see wildflowers such as yellow aster and Parry's primrose during the summer, and watch for mule deer, bighorn sheep, squirrels, and golden eagles.

Like most of the American West's national parks, Great Basin offers ample activities to keep you busy for at least a week, and it is strongly suggested that you plan to spend at least 1 full day in the park. For the best park experience, try to allow at least 3 full days to provide enough time to tour Lehman Cave and explore the scenic drive, and to hike to the bristlecone pine forest and perhaps to one of the park's high-mountain lakes.

Because of its remoteness—Great Basin isn't near any other popular tourist destinations or even along a route to one—you'll find it relatively quiet and uncrowded, similar to what you would have found 30 or 40 years ago in America's loved-to-death parks such as Yosemite and Grand Canyon. Although Great Basin National Park is in Nevada, many visitors are Utah residents on long-weekend excursions from Salt Lake City. Visitors to the national

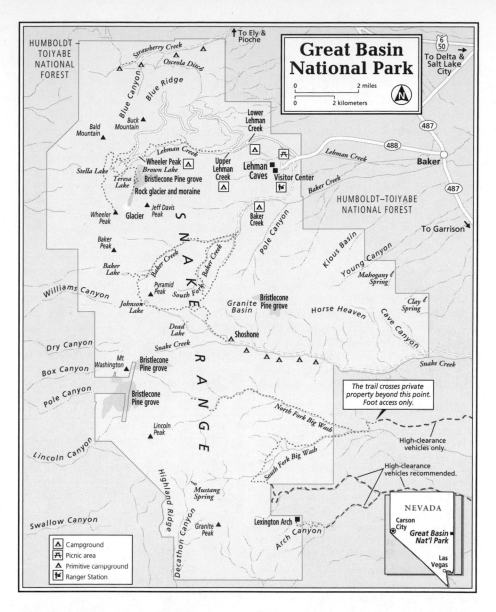

Great Basin National Park

parks of Arizona and Utah who start their trips in Las Vegas, Nevada, can easily add Great Basin to their driving loop, either at the beginning or end.

Avoiding the Crowds. Because Great Basin National Park is seemingly in the middle of nowhere, it receives far fewer visitors than most other national parks. However, it isn't deserted. During the relatively busy summer season you'll need to arrive at the visitor center early for your cave tour tickets (or purchase them in advance), and don't count on finding a campsite if you arrive late in the day, especially on weekends. The busiest times are on Memorial Day weekend and from July through Labor Day. Although the park is quieter in spring, weather can be a problem, with snow in the higher elevations. The park has its lowest visitation in January and February, but that is also when it will be the coldest and snowiest. For those who

Tips from a Park Insider

Anne Hopkins Pfaff, who worked as a park ranger at Great Basin National Park for a number of years, says that during her time at Great Basin she enjoyed both the park and the surrounding desert. "It's a gorgeous area," she says. "I like the remoteness."

Asked what she especially likes about the 77,100-acre park, Pfaff replies, "The variety of vegetation and habitats, and the views—especially the views that include both Wheeler Peak and out across the Great Basin, such as you get from Mather Overlook." This park, she says, "is one of America's real treasures, where you can get out on the trails and not see another human being." Pfaff says that as far as national parks go, Great Basin's campgrounds offer minimal services, and although many visitors thoroughly enjoy this aspect, others miss their creature comforts, such as hot showers and RV hookups.

Pfaff says she's impressed by the bristlecone pines—their age and their beauty—and considers a hike to the bristlecone pine forest among the park's top experiences. Also on her list of things all visitors should do are touring Lehman Caves and taking the Wheeler Peak Scenic Drive. If she were to come to the park as a visitor, it would be in September, she says, "when the crowds are gone and the weather is usually beautiful—not too hot at the lower elevations but not yet snow-covered in the upper elevations."

can arrange it, the best time to visit is from just after Labor Day through the end of September, when there are fewer people and the weather is beautiful—with warm days and crisp, cool nights. Early October is also usually nice,
but check the weather reports—you could find yourself in an early winter snowstorm.

Just the Facts

GETTING THERE & GATEWAYS

Great Basin National Park is 5 miles west of the small town of Baker, Nevada; 70 miles southeast of Ely, Nevada; 385 miles east of Reno, Nevada; 286 miles north of Las Vegas, Nevada; 200 miles north of St. George, Utah; and 234 miles southwest of Salt Lake City, Utah.

From points in west-central Utah, take U.S. 50 west just across the state line into Nevada, go south on Nev. 487 to the village of Baker, and then go west on Nev. 488 into the park. From St. George, take I-15 north to Cedar City; continue north on Utah 130 to Minersville; take Utah 21 west through Milford to the Nevada state line, where it becomes Nev. 487, which you follow to Baker; and then take Nev. 488 west to the park.

If coming from Las Vegas, follow U.S. 93 north to U.S. 50, which you take east to Nev. 487, where you turn south to Baker, and then follow Nev. 488 into the park.

From Ely and Reno, Nevada, follow U.S. 50 east to Nev. 487, and follow directions above.

The Nearest Airports. The closest major airports are **McCarran International Airport** in Las Vegas, Nevada (© **800/261-5704** or 702/261-5211; www.mccarran.com) and **Salt Lake City International Airport** (© **801/575-2400;** www.slcairport.com) in Salt Lake City, Utah. Both are served by most major airlines and national car rental agencies, whose toll-free numbers are included in the appendix.

INFORMATION

Contact the **Superintendent, Great Basin National Park,** 100 Great Basin National Park, Baker, NV 89311-9700 (© **775/234-7331;** www.nps.gov/grba). Be sure to ask for a copy of the park's excellent newspaper-style guide, **Bristlecone,** which includes a map, current activities and costs, and nearby services.

Those who want to buy maps and books can contact the nonprofit **Great Basin Association,** Baker, NV 89311 (© **775/234-7270;** www.nps.gov/grba/gbnha/gba.htm).

VISITOR CENTER

The visitor center, located on Nev. 488 at the northeast corner of the park, is where you'll buy tickets for cave tours. It contains the Great Basin Association's bookstore, brochures and other free information, and exhibits on the park's geology, history, flora, and fauna. In addition, a slide show provides an introduction to the park.

The park is open every day of the year, but the visitor center and cave are closed Thanksgiving, Christmas, and New Year's Day.

FEES

Park entry is free. The 90-minute cave tour costs $8 for adults, $4 for those under 12; the 60-minute tour costs $6 for adults, $3 for those under 12; the 30-minute tour fee is $2 for adults and free for kids under 12. Golden Age and Golden Access cardholders pay half the adult rates. Cave tour tickets can be purchased by phone (© **775/234-7331,** ext. 242) from 24 hours to 30 days in advance. Camping costs $10 per night; use of the dump station costs $3.

SPECIAL REGULATIONS & WARNINGS

Although backcountry permits are not required, those planning to go into the backcountry are encouraged to register

at the visitor center, where they will also receive information on the latest backcountry conditions and regulations. Hikers going to the top of 13,063-foot Wheeler Peak may develop symptoms of altitude sickness (headache, nausea), in which case they should turn back immediately. Vehicles are also sometimes affected by the elevation and steep roads, and the Wheeler Peak Scenic Drive, which leads to several trailheads, is not recommended for motor homes over 24 feet long and vehicles pulling trailers.

For regulations and advice concerning Lehman Caves, see "Organized Tours & Ranger Programs," below.

SEASONS & CLIMATE

Although open year-round, the above-ground activities are limited during the winter by deep snow and bitter cold. The cave, which has a year-round temperature of 50°F (10°C) and humidity of 90%, can be visited at any time. Outdoors, conditions are tied to elevation, which ranges from 6,825 feet at the visitor center to 13,063 feet at Wheeler Peak. Hiking trails at lower elevations are usually free of snow from late spring through early fall, but snow is possible at any time above 10,000 feet. Summer thunderstorms are common during the afternoon but can occur any time.

If You Have Only 1 Day

In some ways, the Great Basin is actually two parks: the caverns and the mountains. Because of the frequency of afternoon thunderstorms in the summer, it is usually best to do outdoor activities early in the day. Therefore, those with only 1 day at the park should spend the morning on the **Wheeler Peak Scenic Drive,** possibly allowing time to hike at least part of one of the trails. Then, after a picnic lunch or sandwich from the cafe, take a **cave tour** (it's best to purchase tickets in advance; see "Fees," above), see the exhibits and programs in the **visitor center,** and take a walk along the **Mountain View Nature Trail.**

Exploring the Park by Car

The **Wheeler Peak Scenic Drive** runs 12 miles one-way. The road is paved, but steep (about an 8% grade) and winding, as it ascends over 3,000 feet from the visitor center, at 6,825 feet elevation, to the base of Wheeler Peak, at almost 10,000 feet. Along the way, there are pullouts where you can stop to take in views of the Great Basin and Wheeler Peak. At the first pullout, a short walk brings you to the remnants of an 18-mile aqueduct built in 1890 to carry water from Lehman Creek to a gold mining operation. The road ends at Wheeler Peak Campground, where several hiking trails begin. The road is not recommended for motor homes over 24 feet or vehicles pulling trailers, and it is usually closed by snow (except for the first 3 miles) from fall through spring.

Organized Tours & Ranger Programs

The only way to see **Lehman Caves** is on a guided tour led by a park naturalist, who points out the intricately formed stalactites, stalagmites, draperies, and shields that have been created by the oozing and dripping of water. Although Lehman lacks the vastness of the caves at Carlsbad Caverns National Park in New Mexico (see chapter 10, "Carlsbad Caverns National Park"), it makes up for that in the number of beautiful formations it squeezes into this small space, and the fact that Lehman can be seen easily and fairly quickly. In addition, Lehman Caves possess formations called **shields,** rarely seen in other caves. These consist of two roughly circular halves that look like flattened clamshells. Scientists have yet to agree on how the shields are formed.

Cave tours begin near the visitor center and are given daily year-round (call for schedules), except on Thanksgiving, Christmas, and New Year's Day. A part of the tour is accessible to those in wheelchairs, with assistance. Adults must accompany all children under 16, and children under 5 are not permitted on the 90-minute cave tour. The temperature in Lehman Caves is 50°F (10°C) year-round, so a jacket or sweater is advised. Because the path is often wet, good traction shoes with rubber soles are strongly recommended. Since some passageways are narrow, items such as fanny packs, purses, backpacks, and the like are prohibited, although handheld cameras are permitted.

Although the park's main ranger-led activity is the Lehman Caves tour, during the summer rangers also lead guided nature walks and hikes and present other programs. These change each year, but recent programs have included a 1.4-mile hike (one-way) to the bristlecone pine grove. Rangers usually present short talks several times daily at the visitor center, and evening campfire programs at Wheeler Peak and Upper Lehman campgrounds, with subjects such as the night sky, gold prospecting, and the area's bat population. One-hour programs for children, who must be accompanied by adults, have also been scheduled in recent years.

Historic & Man-Made Attractions

Throughout the park are reminders of the region's mining days, and along several trails you will see the ruins of miners' cabins, mining equipment, and mine shafts and tunnels (which are dangerous and should not be entered). Just outside the visitor center is the historic **Rhodes Cabin,** which dates from the period 1920 to 1932, when Clarence Rhodes and his wife, Beatrice, were custodians of the property for the U.S. Forest Service. The cabin, constructed of Englemann spruce and white fir, was one of nine tourist cabins built in the 1920s, along with a log lodge, a dining room, a dance hall, and a swimming tank. This particular cabin was rented to tourists until 1933, and from then until

1936, it was used as the home of the national monument custodian and his family. It was then used for storage before being restored by the Park Service.

Day Hikes

There are a wide variety of trails, ranging from easy walks to challenging, high-altitude hikes. Higher-elevation areas may be closed by snow from late October until mid-June, and afternoon thunderstorms are common during July and August. Exposed ridges should be avoided during lightning storms. Hikers should also be aware that they may be sharing trails with rattlesnakes, which have the right-of-way.

Because of loose rock and steep grades on some trails, sturdy hiking boots with good ankle support are recommended. Hikers also need to carry plenty of water—usually 1 gallon per person per day. Park rangers emphasize that although the rocky alpine sections of the park at its highest elevations may appear rugged, they are quite fragile. Plants grow slowly, and even under the best of conditions their survival rate is low. Therefore, hikers should be diligent about staying on trails and having the least impact possible on the land.

SHORTER TRAILS
Alpine Lakes Loop

3 miles RT. Easy to moderate. Access: Just north of Wheeler Peak Campground.

With an elevation gain of only about 400 feet, this is a relatively easy and accessible trail, especially popular with families. However, keep in mind that those not accustomed to the 10,000-foot elevation may find any activity tiring. The loop can be hiked in either direction, passing through forests of spruce and pine trees, as well as meadows dotted with colorful wildflowers. Teresa and Stella Lakes are shallow and clear, and the reflections of snowcapped peaks are often seen in their smooth surfaces.

Bristlecone Pine Trail

4.6 miles RT. Easy to moderate. Access: Near the Wheeler Peak parking area.

Those who want to take a relatively easy hike through a unique forest will enjoy this trail. It goes through a grove of bristlecone pines and then on to a view of an ice field and what is believed to be a rock glacier—a rock-covered permanent mass of ice moving very slowly downhill. Distance to the bristlecone pine grove is 1.4 miles one-way, and the ice field is another 0.9 mile. During summer, rangers often lead hikes to the bristlecone grove. Elevation is about 10,000 feet.

Lexington Arch

1.7 miles one-way. Moderate. Access: About 18 miles south of the visitor center off a dirt road; ask park rangers for specific directions and current road conditions.

This six-story arch is a bit out of the way, but the splendidly framed views through its 75-by-120-foot opening prove an ample reward. After driving into Utah and then following a dirt road, you will find yourself hiking a sunny path that takes you past wildflowers, mountain mahogany, fir, and pinyon. The easy-to-follow trail ends at the arch, which is unique because it has been carved from limestone, not sandstone as is usually the case in the American West. Some geologists believe it is not really an arch, but a natural bridge; the difference being that arches are formed by wind, rain, and ice, while bridges are created by the eroding force of streams and rivers.

Mountain View Nature Trail

0.4 mile RT. Easy. Access: Outside the visitor center.

This is a self-guided loop, with a brochure available at the visitor center that provides information on plants, animals, and geology. The short trail is popular among those with 20 to 30 minutes to wait before their guided cave tour.

Baker Creek Trail

6 miles one-way. Moderate to strenuous. Access: End of Baker Creek Rd.

Following Baker Creek, this trail leads to Baker Lake, climbing from about 8,000 feet in elevation to over 10,500 feet. It passes through meadows and forests, past pinyon, juniper, aspen, and pine, changing with the elevation. It's a good choice for wildlife viewing; you are likely to see mule deer, rock squirrels, and a variety of birds. Anglers often stop to catch a trout in the creek (see "Fishing," below), and the trail provides excellent views of the surrounding peaks. Along the way you pass the remains of a miner's log cabin before reaching picturesque Baker Lake.

Johnson Lake Trail

3.6 miles one-way. Moderate to strenuous. Access: End of Snake Creek Rd.

This rugged trail follows an old mining road, with an elevation gain of about 1,000 feet, before arriving at Johnson Lake, named for Alfred Johnson, who mined and processed tungsten here in the early part of the 20th century. The Johnson Lake Trail can be combined with the Baker Creek Trail to produce a loop, starting with the Baker Creek Trail and descending along Snake Creek. Parts of this loop are difficult to follow, and topographical maps and good mountaineering skills are needed.

Lehman Creek Trail

3.4 miles one-way. Easy. Access: Connects Upper Lehman Creek Campground with Wheeler Peak Campground.

Although there is a 2,100-foot elevation change along this trail, it's an easy downhill walk for those who start at Wheeler Peak Campground and have a vehicle waiting at Lehman Creek Campground. The trail mostly follows a bluff above Lehman Creek, crossing through several separate life zones and offering views of a wide variety of plant life, from sagebrush and cactus to forests of aspen, spruce, pinyon, and tall Douglas fir. Along the way you will also see mountain mahogany and, if your timing's right, an abundance of wildflowers.

Wheeler Peak Summit Trail

8.6 miles RT (from campground). Strenuous. Access: Begins at Summit Trailhead, about 0.5 mile from Wheeler Peak Campground, or from the campground via Alpine Lakes Loop Trail, which intersects with Summit Trail.

Those looking for stupendous panoramic vistas should consider this strenuous trail, which begins as a relatively gentle walk through a forest of pine, becoming considerably steeper as it reaches the tree line. Eventually you find yourself on the summit, at an elevation of 13,063 feet, the second-highest point in Nevada. During its 3,000-foot ascent, the trail passes through several plant communities, including forests of Englemann spruce and pine, before climbing above the tree line. This is generally an all-day hike, and rangers advise starting early so you're off the summit by the time afternoon thunderstorms appear. Hikers are also advised to carry plenty of drinking water, extra clothing, and rain gear.

Exploring the Backcountry

There are numerous opportunities for backcountry hiking in the park, but few maintained trails. The most commonly used routes follow river valleys or ridgelines. Topographical maps, available at the visitor center, are essential; and although backcountry permits are not required, rangers strongly recommend that those planning to go into the backcountry register and discuss their plans with park staff before setting out.

Backcountry camping is permitted in most areas, although not within ¼ mile of most trails, in bristlecone pine forests, in Wheeler Peak and Lexington Day Use Areas, or within 100 feet of a water source. Backcountry campers are encouraged to use backpacking stoves;

campfires are permitted below 10,000 feet elevation only, and you are not allowed to burn any wood from the bristlecone pine tree. Trash, including toilet paper, should be packed out, and human waste should be buried at least a half-foot deep and no less than 100 feet from water sources.

Other Summer Sports & Activities

Biking. Although biking is permitted only on designated motor vehicle roads, the park has miles of dirt roads, many of which receive little traffic. Bikers should check with rangers about which roads are open and their current condition.

Educational Programs. The Great Basin Association (see "Information," earlier in this chapter) presents programs and seminars throughout the summer. Schedules change, but past programs have included archaeology field trips, hands-on American Indian craft making, and astronomy. Most programs are free, although donations are appreciated. Contact the Great Basin Association for current information.

Fishing. The park's small, clear mountain streams provide good but somewhat challenging fishing for rainbow, brook, and brown trout. Anglers over 11 will need a Nevada fishing license, available in Baker.

Horseback Riding. Some of the backcountry trails are open to horseback riding; check with park rangers.

Wildlife Viewing. Almost every visitor to Great Basin National Park will see wildlife, whether it be some of the many mule deer that frequent the campgrounds, meadows, and creek sides; or birds such as the pinyon jays, western tanagers, and Clark's nutcrackers. Park visitors should also watch for golden eagles, bighorn sheep, bobcats, and small mammals including rock squirrels, wood rats, and marmots.

Especially for Kids

In addition to **The Great Basin Junior Ranger Program,** families are invited to stop at the visitor center and borrow a **Family Adventure Pack,** which offers activity ideas and equipment, such as a hand lens, compass, string, and pencils. Rangers also lead various walks, hikes, and other activities that are suitable for children, including some specifically geared to kids.

Winter Sports

Although there are no designated cross-country ski trails, once snow falls—sometimes as early as October—the park becomes a winter playground, especially at higher elevations. You can use cross-country skis or snowshoes on many of the trails and several roads, although it's best to talk with rangers about your plans before setting out so you can avoid trails that might be too steep for your ability. In lean snow years you may have to hike a bit from parking areas to snow that's right for skiing, but there's almost always plenty of snow at the higher elevations.

One favorite cross-country ski trip is up **Baker Creek Road,** which leads to Baker Creek Campground, and then on up the Baker Creek Trail for a while before heading back. Those particularly skilled and in good physical condition might ski the 4-mile trail from **Upper Lehman Creek Campground** up to **Wheeler Peak Campground.** The trail climbs about 2,100 feet. Although Wheeler Peak Campground is technically closed from about mid-October through mid-June, skiers are welcome to spend the night.

There are no snowshoe or cross-country ski rentals available in the park or nearby.

Camping

INSIDE THE PARK

The park has four developed campgrounds—Lower Lehman Creek, Upper Lehman Creek, Baker Creek, and Wheeler Peak—with a total of just over 100 sites. They have lots of trees, pit toilets, and picnic tables. Those with large RVs will want to arrive as early in the day as possible, since there are only a limited number of sites that can easily accommodate rigs over 25 feet.

One campground is open year-round, while the others are open from spring through fall, weather permitting. There are also some primitive campsites available along **Strawberry Creek** in the far northern reaches of the park, and along **Snake Creek** in the southern half of the park. These sites have tables and fire grates, but no drinking water. There are a few pit toilets along Snake Creek, but no toilets along Strawberry Creek.

Backcountry camping is also permitted; see the section "Exploring the Backcountry," above. The park has an RV dump station (near the visitor center) but no hookups or showers. The park's only public telephone is at the visitor center, which is not within walking distance of any campgrounds. All campsites are on a first-come, first-served basis.

NEAR THE PARK

The **Border Inn RV Park**, on U.S. 50/6 at the Nevada–Utah border about 13 miles northeast of the national park (P.O. Box 30, Baker, NV 89311; © **775/234-7300**) has 22 gravel pull-through RV sites with full hookups, plus shower and laundry facilities. Showers are free for registered campers; $3 for others. There's also a motel and restaurant (see below).

Where to Stay

There are no lodging facilities in the park, but the tiny community of Baker, 5 miles east of the park entrance, has several places to stay. You can get additional information on the Baker businesses discussed below, as well as other facilities, from the **Great Basin Business & Tourism Council**'s website, www.greatbasinpark.com. Otherwise, park visitors will find services in Ely, Nevada, 70 miles west; and Delta, Utah, about 100 miles east. Both Ely and Delta also have a variety of restaurants, plus fuel, groceries, and camping supplies.

NEAR THE PARK

The Border Inn

U.S. 50/6 at the Nevada-Utah border, 13 miles northeast of the national park (P.O. Box 30, Baker, NV 89311). © **775/234-7300.** 29 units. A/C TV TEL. $30–$40 double. AE, DISC, MC, V. Pets accepted.

This comfortable motel has basic rooms and 12 kitchenette units in Utah, and a restaurant with a bar and slot machines a few feet away in Nevada. The wood-paneled rooms are simply but

Campground	Elev.	Total Sites	RV Hookups	Dump Station	Toilets	Drinking Water
Border Inn RV Park	5,300	22	Yes	Yes	Yes	Yes
Lower Lehman Creek	7,500	11	No	No	Yes	Yes
Upper Lehman Creek	7,800	24	No	No	Yes	Yes
Baker Creek	8,000	32	No	No	Yes	Yes
Wheeler Peak	9,950	37	No	No	Yes	Yes

attractively furnished. There are a coin-operated laundry and VCR and videotape rentals. Gasoline and diesel fuel are available. Also see "Where to Dine," below.

Silver Jack Motel and Gift Shop

Downtown Baker, 5 miles east of the national park (P.O. Box 166, Baker, NV 89311). © **775/234-7323.** www.greatbasinpark.com. 7 motel units, 2 cabins. A/C TV. Motel $38–$45 double; cabins $57–$60 double. DISC, MC, V. Closed mid-Nov to mid-Mar. Pets accepted.

This well-maintained family-owned and -operated motel is the closest lodging to the national park. Basic motel rooms have either one or two double beds, and one unit has two double beds plus a twin bed in a separate room. Some units have shower-tub combinations, while others have showers only. There is an attractive patio with a fountain where guests sit, chat, and watch the hummingbirds. The attached gift shop offers local art and high-quality crafts, and several restaurants are across the street (see below). The separate cabins are several blocks away. One, with a kitchenette, sleeps two; the other, with a full kitchen, sleeps up to seven.

Where to Dine

INSIDE THE PARK

The only food services in the park are the visitor center's cafe and gift shop (© **775/234-7221**), open from April through October. Your choices here include light breakfasts, soup and sandwich lunches, and snack items, including excellent homemade ice cream sandwiches.

NEAR THE PARK

The Border Inn

U.S. 50/6 at the Nevada-Utah border, 13 miles northeast of the national park. © **775/234-7300.** Lunch $2.25–$5.95; dinner $6.45–$11. AE, DISC, MC, V. Kitchen open daily 6am–10pm; bar and store open daily 24 hr. Closed Christmas Day. AMERICAN.

Good burgers and chicken-fried steak are served at this roadside restaurant, which also specializes in homemade soups and baked items. The dining room is large and open, with a bar along one side. There are also slot machines, video games, a pool table, a gift shop, a convenience store, an ATM, and a gas station with diesel fuel.

T&D's Country Store, Restaurant & Bar

Corner of Elko and Main, downtown Baker. © **775/234-7264.** Sandwiches and meals $3.95–$8.95; large pizzas $11–$18. DISC, MC, V. Summer hours: restaurant Mon–Thurs 11am–10pm, Fri–Sat 7am–10pm, Sun 7am–9pm; store daily 8am–7pm in summer. Shorter hours in winter. AMERICAN/MEXICAN.

The restaurant is located in a bright and cheery sunroom attached to the small grocery store. It's known for its pizzas, deli sandwiches, homemade salsa and chips, and big steak and chicken

Showers	Fire Pits/ Grills	Laundry	Public Phone	Reserve	Fees	Open
Yes	No	Yes	No	No	$15	Year-round
No	Yes	No	No	No	$10	Year-round
No	Yes	No	No	No	$10	May 15–Oct 15
No	Yes	No	No	No	$10	May 15–Sept 15
No	Yes	No	No	No	$10	June 15–Sept 15

burritos. The restaurant also serves burgers, steak sandwiches, pita sandwiches, a good selection of vegetarian items, and several more elaborate meals, including barbecued ribs and an Asian chicken salad. Breakfast is served only during the summer. There is a full bar, with several beers on tap, and a surprisingly good stock of wines available by the glass. There is also a large-screen TV in a separate sports lounge. You can get your food items to go, and there is a full liquor store, propane, videotape rentals, camping and fishing gear, plus Nevada hunting and fishing licenses.

Picnic & Camping Supplies

In addition to the snacks available at the cafe and gift shop in the park, you can find take-out food, ice, and packaged liquor at **T&D's Country Store, Restaurant & Bar** in Baker. At **The Border Inn,** along U.S. 50/6 at the Nevada-Utah border, there's a small convenience store. Both properties are listed above.

19

GREAT SAND DUNES NATIONAL MONUMENT & PRESERVE

by Don & Barbara Laine

ERE IN SOUTHERN COLORADO, FAR FROM ANY SEA OR EVEN A MAJOR desert, is a startling sight—a huge expanse of sand, piled nearly 750 feet high. The towering dunes—the tallest on the continent—seem incongruous here, out of place in a

land best known for the aptly named Rocky Mountains. But here they are, some 30 square miles of light brown sand dunes, restlessly grasping at the western edge of the Sangre de Cristo Mountains. (Sangre de Cristo is Spanish for "Blood of Christ"; the name comes from the deep red color reflected onto the snowcapped mountains by the setting sun.)

The dunes were created over thousands of years by southwesterly winds blowing across the San Luis Valley. They were formed when streams of water from melting glaciers carried rocks, gravel, and silt down from the mountains. Accumulating on the valley floor, the sand was picked up by the wind and carried toward the mountains.

Even today, the winds are changing the face of the dunes. So-called "reversing winds" from the mountains pile the dunes back upon themselves, building them higher and higher. Though it's physically impossible for sand to be

piled steeper than 34 degrees, the dunes often appear more sheer because of deceptive shadows and colors that change with the light: gold, pink, tan, sometimes even bluish.

Great Sand Dunes became a national monument by presidential proclamation in 1932, but in recent years concerns over the possible effects on the dunes and the monument's ecosystem from water usage just outside the monument, as well as other issues, inspired an effort to expand the site and give Great Sand Dunes national park status. In fall of 2000 Congress passed and President Bill Clinton signed legislation that expands the former 38,659-acre national monument into a new national park and preserve covering some 150,000 acres.

The national park designation will take effect when the purchase of the adjacent 100,000-acre **Baca Ranch** is completed. (It remained pending in mid-2003.) In addition, some additional lands previously under the administration of the U.S. Forest Service have been added to the new national park and preserve. Hunting will be permitted in the preserve, but not the park, and both will be administered jointly by the National Park Service.

Avoiding the Crowds. Overcrowding has not been a major problem at Great Sand Dunes—in recent years, the monument has received fewer than 300,000 visitors annually, compared to more than three million at Rocky Mountain National Park, just a half day's drive to the north. But it's expected that national park status and the additional acreage and attractions will produce an increase in visitation (at least that's what area motel and restaurant owners are hoping for). Therefore, we suggest that to avoid possible crowds you try to visit at times other than during school vacations—early fall can be especially pleasant here—and that holiday weekends also be avoided. Memorial Day weekend is particularly busy, with limited parking and traffic congestion. If you do happen to visit on a busy day, a hike along Sand Ramp Trail (see "Day Hikes," below) usually gets you away from the crowds.

Just the Facts

GETTING THERE & GATEWAYS

From Alamosa, there are two main routes to Great Sand Dunes: east 14 miles on U.S. 160, then north on Colo. 150; or north 14 miles on Colo. 17 to Mosca, then east on Six Mile Lane to the junction of Colo. 150.

The Nearest Airports. The **Alamosa San Luis Valley Regional Airport** (✆ 719/589-6444), about 1 mile off U.S. 285, on the south side of the city, has service to and from Denver with **Great Lakes Aviation.** Car rentals are available at the airport from **Budget** and a local company, **L&M Automobile Rental** (✆ 719/589-4651). Toll-free reservation numbers for

airlines and national car rental companies are listed in the appendix.

INFORMATION

Contact Great Sand Dunes National Monument & Preserve, 11500 Colo. 150, Mosca, CO 81146-9798 (✆ **719/378-6300;** www.nps.gov/grsa).

For information on other area attractions, lodging, and dining, contact the **Alamosa Visitor Information Center,** Cole Park (Chamber Dr. at 3rd St.), Alamosa, CO 81101 (✆ **800/258-7597** or 719/589-4840; fax 719/589-1773; www.alamosa.org).

VISITOR CENTER

The visitor center (✆ **719/378-6399**) has exhibits on dune formation and life in the dunes, a bookstore, and a short video shown throughout the day. It's open daily year-round, except Christmas and New Year's Day.

FEES & PERMITS

Admission to the monument for up to 7 days costs $3 per person (free for those under 17). Camping costs $12 per night.

SPECIAL REGULATIONS & WARNINGS

Although summer air temperatures are very pleasant, sand temperatures can soar to 140°F (60°C), so park officials strongly advise that shoes be worn when hiking in the dunes. Also, summer thunderstorms are fairly common and hikers are advised to leave the dunes quickly when lightning threatens to avoid the chance of being struck.

Pets are permitted throughout the monument and preserve but must be leashed, and officials ask that owners clean up after their pets. They also warn that the sand in the dunes can be very hot and will burn the pads on dogs' feet, so they suggest dune hiking with pets early or late in the day, when the sand is cooler.

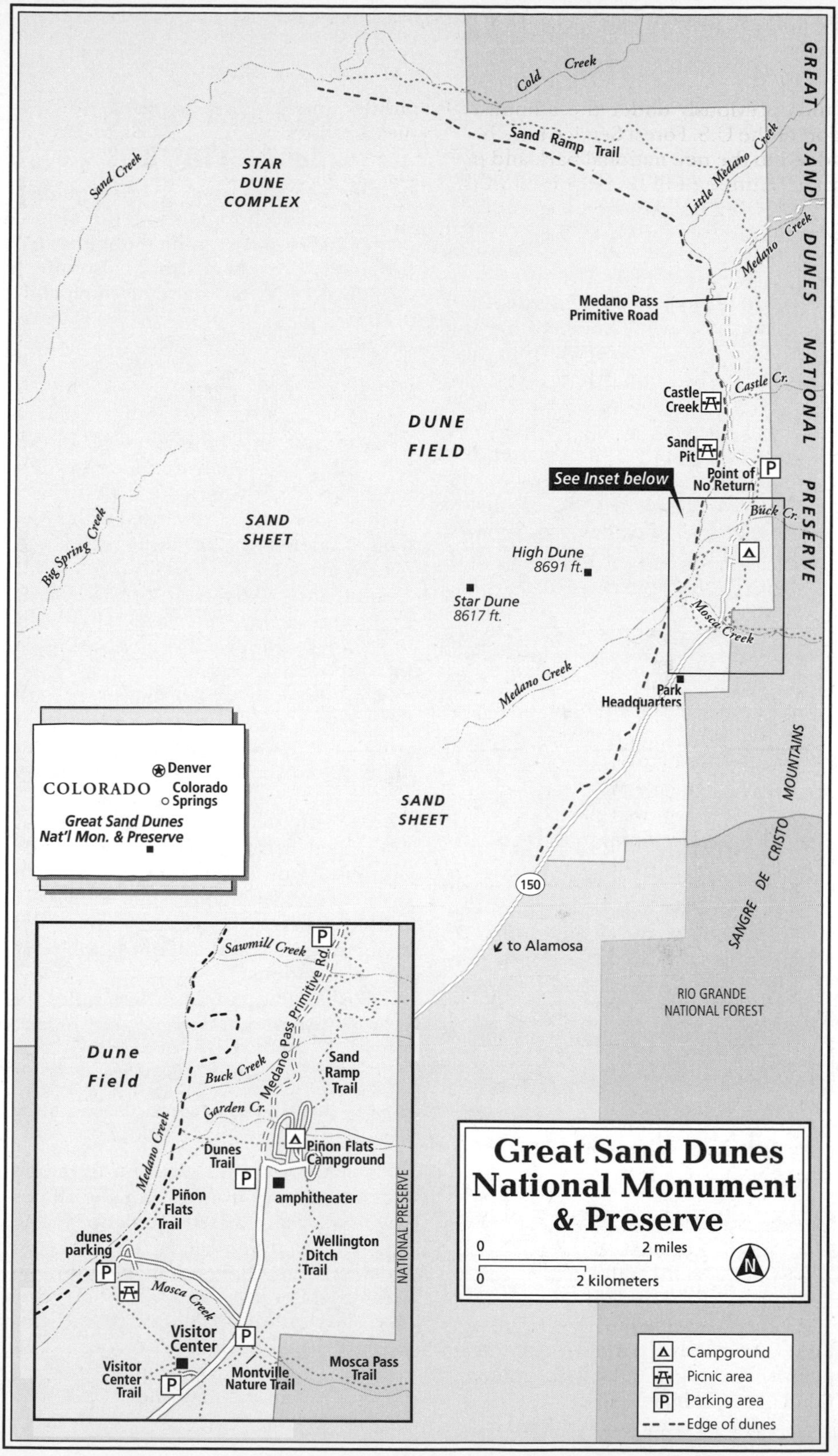

Great Sand Dunes National Monument & Preserve
GREAT SAND DUNES NATIONAL PRESERVE
Cold Creek
Sand Ramp Trail
Sand Creek
STAR DUNE COMPLEX
Little Medano Creek
Medano Creek
Medano Pass Primitive Road
Castle Creek
Castle Cr.
Sand Pit
DUNE FIELD
See Inset below
Point of No Return
Buck Cr.
SAND SHEET
High Dune 8691 ft.
Star Dune 8617 ft.
Big Spring Creek
Mosca Creek
Medano Creek
Park Headquarters
COLORADO
Denver
Colorado Springs
Great Sand Dunes Nat'l Mon. & Preserve
SAND SHEET
SANGRE DE CRISTO MOUNTAINS
150
to Alamosa
RIO GRANDE NATIONAL FOREST
Sawmill Creek
Medano Pass Primitive Rd
Dune Field
Buck Creek
Sand Ramp Trail
Garden Cr.
Medano Creek
Dunes Trail
Piñon Flats Campground
amphitheater
Piñon Flats Trail
dunes parking
Wellington Ditch Trail
NATIONAL PRESERVE
Mosca Creek
Visitor Center
Visitor Center Trail
Montville Nature Trail
Mosca Pass Trail
0 2 miles
0 2 kilometers
Campground
Picnic area
Parking area
Edge of dunes

SEASONS & CLIMATE

Pleasant summers and cool to cold winters are the rule here. Daytime summer temperatures average 70°F to 80°F (21°C–27°C), with nighttime lows often dropping into the 40s and low 50s (single digits Celsius). Thunderstorms are common in July and August. High winds can be expected at any time and are often especially ferocious from April through early June, when northeast winds have been clocked at over 90 mph. From fall through spring, expect moderate daytime temperatures; winter days can see daytime temperatures in the 40s, but winter nights are usually below freezing, and often below zero. Snowfall averages a bit over 3 feet annually, with March being the snowiest month.

SEASONAL EVENTS

The "Friends of the Dunes" host a variety of events each summer, including castle building and kite-flying contests, musical events, and workshops. Contact the visitor center for details.

If You Have Only 1 Day

Great Sand Dunes is fairly easy to see in a day or less. First stop at the visitor center for a look at the exhibits (and an explanation of how these dunes were and are being formed), and then drive to a parking area and walk into the dunes. If time permits, also walk one of the shorter trails, such as the Montville Nature Trail or Visitor Center Trail.

Exploring the Park by Car

Although you will use your vehicle to get to the visitor center, dunes, and a few spots where you'll get good views, the Great Sand Dunes environment is best explored on foot, or special wheelchair (see "Day Hikes," below).

Organized Tours & Ranger Programs

In the summer, rangers offer guided nature walks, short talks at the visitor center patio, and evening amphitheater programs. Great Sand Dunes also offers a Junior Ranger program, in which children complete various activities to earn badges.

Day Hikes

You can hike anywhere you want in the sand dunes, although there are no designated trails. If you make it all the way to the top, you'll be rewarded with spectacular views of the dunes and the nearby mountains. It usually takes about 1½ hours to get to the crest of a 750-foot dune and back to the base. Hiking in the dunes is especially pleasant on a moonlit night.

Until recently, wheelchair users were pretty much limited to seeing the dunes from their motor vehicles and parking areas because the loose sand made access to the dunes nearly impossible for conventional wheelchairs. But now two wheelchairs specially designed for over-sand travel, with large, inflatable tires, are available for loan at the visitor center. A helper is needed to push the chair, and the chairs are not suitable for very large adults.

The monument also has miles of more conventional trails.

Medano Creek to Castle Creek

5 miles RT. Moderate. Access: Dunes parking area.

This route, which leads north along the face of the dunes from the dunes parking area, follows Medano Creek upstream to a spot where the dunes are so steep that they avalanche into the creek.

Montville Nature Trail

0.5 mile RT. Easy. Access: Parking area on the east side of the main park road, just past the visitor center.

This pleasant walk—especially nice on hot days—runs along shady Mosca Creek, through the lower part of Mosca Canyon, offering dramatic views of the dunes from several high points. A guide for the nature trail is available at the visitor center.

Mosca Pass Trail

7 miles RT. Strenuous. Access: Same as Montville Nature Trail, above.

This challenging hike, which climbs 1,463 feet into the mountains, passes through forests of pinyon, juniper, aspen, spruce, and fir to a grasslands near the top of the pass, and offers good chances of seeing quite a bit of wildlife. *Note:* Rangers say that each year hikers report seeing bears and mountain lions along this trail.

Piñon Flats Trail

1.5 miles RT. Easy. Access: Campground or dunes parking area.

This convenient trail runs through a grassy area, connecting the campground with the dunes parking area.

Sand Ramp Trail

22 miles RT. Moderate. Access: Campground, near site 62.

Those looking for a longer hike than most of those at Great Sand Dunes can escape any crowds that happen to be in the monument by following this trail along the northern edge of the dunes, crossing Little Medano Creek and Cold Creek. A pleasant half-day jaunt can be accomplished by hiking the first 3 miles and then turning around and heading back.

Visitor Center Trail

0.5 mile RT. Easy. Access: visitor center.

This fairly level, wheelchair-accessible loop features exhibits on the area's natural and human history.

Wellington Ditch Trail

2 miles RT. Easy. Access: Loop 3 of the campground (park in the amphitheater parking area).

This level trail offers good views of the dune field. Part of the trail follows an irrigation ditch that was hand-dug by a 1920s homesteader named Wellington.

Exploring the Backcountry

Backpacking is permitted throughout the monument, and there are backcountry campsites along the Sand Ramp Trail. The required free backcountry permits are available at the visitor center.

Other Summer Sports & Activities

Fishing. Although this is not a prime fishing destination, anglers with a Colorado fishing license can fish Sand Creek and Medano Creek. Medano is stocked with Rio Grande cutthroat trout, and is catch-and-release only.

Horseback Riding. Horseback riding is permitted in some areas of the monument; contact the visitor center for information.

Four-wheeling. Driving in the dunes or off-road in any section of the monument is specifically prohibited, but those with 4WDs can get wonderful views of the dunes and access the national preserve on the Medano Pass Primitive Road, which takes off from the main park road near the amphitheater and heads north out of the monument. This rugged road, which has a lot of deep sand, is closed by winter snow from November through April.

Wildlife Viewing. Among the specialized animals that survive in this unusual environment are the **Ord's kangaroo rat,** a creature that never drinks water, plus several insects found nowhere else on earth, including the **Great Sand Dunes tiger beetle**. Among more common wildlife you're apt to see are Rocky Mountain elk, mule deer, coyotes, black-tailed and white-tailed jackrabbits, desert cottontail rabbits, golden-mantled ground squirrels, and Colorado chipmunks. Just outside the monument look for bison. More than 150 species of **birds** have been sighted in the monument, including both golden and bald eagles, ravens, white-throated swifts, broad-tailed hummingbirds, Lewis' woodpeckers, Say's phoebes, violet-green swallows, yellow-rumped warblers, black-headed grosbeaks, and chipping sparrows. Prime bird-watching areas include the Montville and Wellington Ditch trails, and you're also likely to see all kinds of wildlife along Medano Creek, which is located along the base of the dunes and usually flows in spring and early summer.

Camping

The shady **Piñon Flats Campground,** with an abundance of pinyon and juniper trees, offers great views of the dunes and nearby mountains. It has 88 sites and is open year-round. There are picnic tables, fire grates, flush toilets, and drinking water, but no showers or RV hookups. Campsites are assigned on a first-come, first-served basis, and cost $12 per night.

Where to Stay & Dine

There are no lodging or dining facilities in the park, so your base for exploring Great Sand Dunes will likely be Alamosa (zip code 81101), where there are a number of motels and a small but adequate variety of restaurants. In addition to the attractive Cottonwood Inn &

Gallery (discussed below), reliable chains in Alamosa include the **Best Western Alamosa Inn,** 1919 Main St. (© **800/459-5123** or 719/589-2567), with a restaurant that serves three meals daily; **Comfort Inn,** 6301 U.S. 160 (© **719/587-9000**); **Holiday Inn,** 333 Santa Fe Ave. (© **719/589-5833**); and **Super 8,** 2505 Main St. (© **719/589-6447**). All have rates for two that are mostly in the $65 to $95 range. Toll-free reservation phone numbers are listed in the appendix.

You'll find a number of restaurants along Alamosa's Main Street. We especially like the Mexican food at **Oscar's Restaurant,** 710 Main St. (© **719/589-9230**), open daily 11am to 9pm (slightly shorter hours in winter), with prices from $4.50 to $9.95. We also recommend the restaurant at the **Best Western Alamosa Inn** (see above).

The Cottonwood Inn & Gallery

123 San Juan Ave., Alamosa, CO 81101. © **800/955-2623** or 719/589-3882. www. cottonwoodinn.com. 10 units. TEL. $60–$125 double. Rates include full breakfast. AE, DC, DISC, MC, V. Located 3 blocks north of Main St. Pets accepted in 2 apt suites with $50 deposit.

This delightful bed-and-breakfast has a distinctly artsy orientation. Innkeeper Deborah Donaldson has decorated the common areas and bedrooms as a gallery of regional art, much of which is for sale. The Cottonwood is composed of two main buildings and a carriage house. The 1908 neo-colonial two-story bungalow has five guest rooms, furnished largely in Arts and Crafts style. Each room is unique: The Rosa Room has queen and single beds to accommodate small families, along with children's books and stuffed animals, while the Blanca Room weds Southwestern decor with Art Deco motifs. Three of these five units have bathrooms with showers only; the other two have bathrooms with shower/tub combos. Adjacent to the bungalow is a 1920s fourplex with four apartment suites, each with a kitchen and claw-foot tub with shower conversion. Located between the two main buildings is a cobblestone courtyard with a hot tub. The carriage house, also in the courtyard, has a queen bed and private bathroom. Full homemade breakfasts often feature regional specialties, such as fresh fruit crepes with Mexican chocolate and whipped cream. Smoking is not permitted.

Picnic & Camping Supplies

For groceries and other necessities, head to Alamosa and stop at **City Market,** 131 Market St. (© **719/589-2492**); or **Safeway,** 1301 Main St. (© **719/587-3075**). You'll find a variety of camping supplies plus groceries and just about everything else you might want at the **Wal-Mart SuperCenter,** 3333 Clark Ave., Alamosa (© **719/589-9071**).

20

GUADALUPE MOUNTAINS NATIONAL PARK

by Don & Barbara Laine

ONCE IT WAS A LONG REEF POKING UP THROUGH THE OCEAN, THEN IT became a dense forest. Today, Guadalupe Mountains National Park is a rugged wilderness of tall Douglas firs and almost lush vegetation rising out of a vast desert. Here you will find numer-

ous hiking trails, panoramic vistas, the highest peak in Texas, plant and animal life unique in the Southwest, and a canyon that many believe is the prettiest spot in all of Texas.

As you approach from the north, the mountains seem to rise gradually from the landscape, but seen from the south they stand tall and dignified. El Capitan, the southern tip of the reef escarpment, watches over the landscape like a sentinel. In the south-central section of the park, Guadalupe Peak, at 8,749 feet the highest mountain in Texas, provides hikers with incredible views of the surrounding mountains and desert.

The 86,416-acre park has several separate sections. Park headquarters and the visitor center are at Pine Springs, along the park's southeast edge, where you'll also find a campground and several trailheads, including one with access to the Guadalupe Peak Trail, the park's premier mountain hike. Nearby, a short dirt road leads to historic Frijole Ranch, with a museum and more trailheads. A horse corral is nearby for those

with the forethought to bring their own mounts. The McKittrick Canyon section of the park, near its northeast corner, may be the most beautiful spot in Texas, especially in fall, when its oaks, maples, and other trees produce a spectacular show of color. A day-use area only, McKittrick Canyon has a delightful (though intermittent) stream, a wide variety of plant and animal life, several trailheads, and historic buildings. Along the park's northern boundary, practically in New Mexico, is the secluded and forested Dog Canyon.

Particularly impressive is Guadalupe Mountains National Park's vast variety of flora and fauna. You'll find species here that don't seem to belong in west Texas, such as the maple and oak trees that produce the fall colors in McKittrick Canyon, and even black bears and red squirrels, which are usually only found much farther north. Scientists say these seemingly out-of-place plants and animals are leftovers from a time when this region was cooler and wetter. As the climate changed and the desert spread,

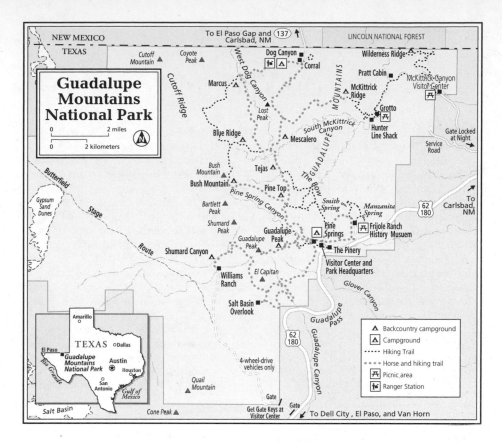

Guadalupe
Mountains
National Park

0   2 miles
0   2 kilometers

Legend:
▲ Backcountry campground
△ Campground
····· Hiking Trail
···· Horse and hiking trail
☉ Picnic area
☒ Ranger Station

some species were able to survive in these mountains, where conditions remained somewhat cooler and moister. At the base of the mountains, at lower elevations, you'll find desert plants such as sotol, agave, and prickly pear cactus; but as you start to climb, especially in stream-nurtured canyons, expect to encounter ponderosa pine, ash, walnut, oak, and ferns. Wildlife abounds, including mule deer, elk, and all sorts of birds and snakes.

Avoiding the Crowds. Guadalupe Mountains National Park is one of America's lesser-visited national parks, with attendance of only about 200,000 each year. This is partly because it is primarily a wilderness park, where you'll have to tackle rugged hiking trails to get to the best vistas. But it's also out of the way and somewhat inconvenient—the closest lodging is 35 miles away from the park's main section. In fact, about the only time the park might be considered even slightly crowded is during spring-break time at Texas and New Mexico colleges, usually in March, when students bring their backpacks and hit the trails. Quite a few families visit during summer, although the park is not usually crowded even then, and visitation drops considerably once schools open in late August.

An exception is McKittrick Canyon, renowned throughout the Southwest for its beautiful fall colors, at their best in late October and early November. The one road into McKittrick Canyon will be busy then, but once you get out on the trails, you can distance yourself from others.

Just the Facts

GETTING THERE & GATEWAYS

Located on the border of New Mexico and Texas, the park is 55 miles southwest of Carlsbad, New Mexico, along

Tips from a Park Ranger

"This is essentially a hiking park," says Rich McCamant, the park's former chief of interpretation. He says the park's two main attractions, which he recommends to all visitors, are the hike to the top of Guadalupe Peak and the colors in McKittrick Canyon, either the trees in fall or the wildflowers in spring.

McCamant says that those without the time or desire to hike the strenuous Guadalupe Peak Trail should consider the more moderate Smith Springs Loop Trail or Devil's Hall Trail.

"This is a park you can visit any time of year and have a good experience," McCamant says, although he adds that many consider October to have the best weather, while spring can be windy.

McCamant says there are five species of rattlesnakes in the park, but visitors probably won't see any, and in the history of the park there have been no reported rattlesnake bites. "The biggest threat here is the sun," he says. "Hikers really need to carry a gallon of water per day, and drink it."

He also warns that because many of the trails have a lot of loose rock, good hiking boots are essential. The other thing he wants park visitors to keep in mind is that there is no gasoline or other services close to the park, so you should have plenty of fuel and anything else you might need.

U.S. 62/180. From Albuquerque, drive east on I-40 for 59 miles to Clines Corners, and turn south on U.S. 285 for 216 miles to the city of Carlsbad, then head southwest 55 miles on U.S. 62/180 to the park entrance at Pine Springs. From El Paso, drive northeast 110 miles on U.S. 62/180 to Pine Springs.

The Nearest Airport. Air travelers can fly to **Cavern City Air Terminal** (© 505/887-1500), at the south edge of the city of Carlsbad, which has commercial service from Albuquerque with **Mesa Airlines** (© 505/885-0245), plus Hertz car rentals.

The nearest major airport is **El Paso International** (© 915/772-4271; www.elpasointernationalairport.com) in central El Paso just north of I-10, with service from **American, America West, Continental, Delta, Southwest, Frontier,** and **Aerolitoral** (© 800/237-6639); and with car rentals from most major companies. Toll-free numbers are given in the appendix.

Contact **Guadalupe Mountains National Park,** HC 60, Box 400, Salt Flat, TX 79847-9400 (© **915/828-3251;** www.nps.gov/gumo). Books and maps can be ordered from the **Carlsbad Caverns–Guadalupe Mountains Association,** 727 Carlsbad Caverns Hwy., Carlsbad, NM 88220 (© **505/785-2232,** ext. 480; www.caverns.org).

Those arriving in the city of Carlsbad before going to the park can get a variety of brochures, maps, and other information at the **National Park Service's Administrative Office and Bookstore,** at 3225 National Parks Hwy. (at its intersection with West Pecan St.). It's open Monday through Friday from 8am to 4:30pm.

Because the park's backcountry trails often crisscross each other and can be confusing, rangers strongly recommend that those planning any serious hiking carry topographical maps. An excellent book for hikers is *Hiking Carlsbad Caverns and Guadalupe Mountains National*

Parks (Falcon Press, 1996) by Bill Schneider, which was published in partnership with the Carlsbad Caverns–Guadalupe Mountains Association and is keyed to the Trails Illustrated topographical map of the park. Also very useful is a shorter and less expensive guide, *Trails of the Guadalupes* (Environmental Associates, 1992), by Don Kurtz and William D. Goran. These are available at the visitor center's bookstore or from the Carlsbad Caverns–Guadalupe Mountains Association.

A small seasonal park newspaper contains pertinent up-to-the-minute information for visitors. It is available free at the visitor center.

VISITOR CENTERS

Park headquarters and the main visitor center are located at Pine Springs just off U.S. 62/180. There are three other access points along this side of the park: Frijole Ranch, about 1.5 miles east of Pine Springs and a mile north of the highway; McKittrick Canyon (day use only), about 7 miles east and 4 miles north of the highway; and Williams Ranch, about 8 miles south of Pine Springs and 8 miles north of the highway on a four-wheel-drive road.

The **Pine Springs Visitor Center,** open daily year-round except Christmas, has natural history exhibits, a bookstore, and an introductory slide program. **McKittrick Canyon** has a visitor contact station with outdoor exhibits and an outdoor slide program on the history, geology, and natural history of the canyon.

On the north side of the park is **Dog Canyon Ranger Station** at the end of N. Mex. 137, about 70 miles from Carlsbad and 110 miles from park headquarters. Information, restrooms, and drinking water are available.

FEES & PERMITS

An entrance fee of $3 per person 16 years or older, which is good for 7 days, is charged (collected at trailheads). Camping at developed campgrounds costs $8 per night. Backcountry camping is free, but a permit is required. Corrals are available for those who bring their horses to ride in the park; although use is free, permits are required. All permits are available at the Pine Springs Visitor Center and Dog Canyon Ranger Station, and must be requested in person, either the day before or the day of use.

SPECIAL REGULATIONS & WARNINGS

Visitors to McKittrick Canyon, a day-use area, must stay on the trail; entering the stream is not permitted. The McKittrick Canyon **entrance gate** opens at 8am daily and closes at 4:30pm during standard time and at 6pm when daylight saving time is in effect.

Neither wood nor charcoal fires are allowed anywhere in the park. Horses are prohibited in the backcountry overnight.

SEASONS & CLIMATE

In general, summers in the Guadalupe Mountains are hot with highs in the 80s and 90s (mid-20s and lower 30s Celsius) and lows in the 60s (teens Celsius). Winters are mild with highs in the 50s and 60s (lower teens Celsius) and lows in the upper 20s and 30s (just below zero Celsius), but there can be sudden and extreme changes in the weather at any time. In winter and spring, high winds can whip down the mountain slopes in gusts reading 100 mph, and on hot summer days, thunderstorms can blow up quickly. The sun is warm even in winter, and summer nights are generally cool no matter how hot the afternoon. Clothing that can be layered is best, comfortable and sturdy walking/hiking shoes are a must, a hat and sunscreen are highly recommended, and plenty of drinking water is essential for hikers.

McKittrick Canyon's beautiful display of fall colors usually takes place between early October and mid-November. It varies, however, so call before going.

If You Have Only 1 Day

This park is best explored over a period of 2 or 3 days, with at least 1 day devoted to the visitor center, historic attractions, and trails in the Pine Springs section, and another full day allotted to McKittrick Canyon. Those with additional time could then head over to the park's third section, Dog Canyon.

Those who have only 1 day can still see quite a bit but will need to decide on either Pine Springs or McKittrick Canyon. If it's fall and the colors are right, drive to the **McKittrick Canyon Visitor Contact Station,** look at the exhibits, and hike the **McKittrick Canyon Trail** to the historic **Pratt Lodge.** If it's not fall, or if you don't care about fall colors, go directly to the **Pine Springs Visitor Center,** see the exhibits, and hike one of the trails—the **Guadalupe Peak Trail** for the ambitious or the **Devil's Hall Trail** for those who prefer less physical exertion.

Exploring the Park by Car

The Guadalupe Mountains are not the place for the vehicle-bound. There are no paved scenic drives traversing the park; roads here are simply means of getting to historical sites and trailheads.

Organized Tours & Ranger Programs

On summer evenings, rangers offer programs at the campground amphitheater.

Historic & Man-Made Attractions

The Pinery was one of 200 stations along the 2,800-mile Butterfield Overland Mail Coach Route. The stations provided fresh mules every 20 miles and a new coach every 300 miles, to maintain the grueling speed of 5 mph 24 hours a day. John Butterfield had seen the need for overland mail delivery between the eastern states and the West Coast, so he designed a route and the coaches, and acquired a federal contract to deliver the St. Louis mail to San Francisco in 25 days. In March 1857 this was a real feat. The Pinery commemorates his achievement.

Named for nearby stands of pine, the Pinery had abundant water and good grazing. It was a high-walled rock enclosure with a wagon repair shop, blacksmith shop, and three mud-roofed rooms where passengers could get a warm meal, if they had time. The first mail coach came through on September 28, 1858. It continued until August 1859, when the route was abandoned for a new road that better served the West's military forts.

Located in McKittrick Canyon, **Pratt Lodge** was built by Wallace E. Pratt in 1931–32, from stone quarried at the base of the Guadalupe Mountains, using heart-of-pine from east Texas for rafters, collar beams, and roof supports. Pratt, a geologist for the Humble Oil Co. (now Exxon), and his family came for summer vacations when the heat in Houston became unbearable. He finally retired here in 1945. Soon after, he and his family built a second house, **Ship on the Desert,** outside the canyon. In 1957, the Pratts donated 5,632 acres of their 16,000-acre ranch to the federal government to begin the national park. In addition to the grand stone lodge, there are several outbuildings, stone picnic tables, and a wonderful stone fence.

Williams Ranch house rests at the base of a 3,000-foot rock cliff on the west face of the Guadalupe Mountains. The 7½-mile access road, navigable only by high-clearance 4WDs, follows part of the old Butterfield Overland Mail Route for about 2 miles. The road crosses private land and has two locked metal gates for which you must sign out keys at the visitor center.

It's not clear exactly who built the house and when, but it's believed to have been built around 1908, and that the first inhabitants for any significant period of time were almost certainly Henry and Rena Belcher. For almost 10 years, they maintained a substantial ranch here, running up to 3,000 head of longhorn cattle. Water was piped from Bone Spring down the canyon to holding tanks in the lowlands. James Adolphus Williams acquired the property around 1917, and with the help of an American Indian friend, ranched and farmed the land until he moved to New Mexico in 1941. After Williams's death in 1942, Judge J. C. Hunter bought the property, adding it to his already large holdings in the Guadalupes.

Another historic site is **Frijole Ranch,** which was a working ranch from the 1870s until 1972. Inside the ranch house is a museum with exhibits on the cultural history of the Guadalupe Mountains, including information on the prehistoric American Indians, the Mescalero Apaches who came later, the Spanish conquistadors, and ranchers of the 19th and 20th centuries. On the grounds are several historic buildings, including a schoolhouse.

Day Hikes

This is a prime hiking park, with more than 80 miles of trails that range from easy walks to steep, strenuous, and sometimes precarious adventures.

SHORTER TRAILS

Indian Meadow Nature Trail

0.6 mile RT. Easy. Access: Dog Canyon Campground; walk south from the water fountain.

This exceptionally easy stroll follows a series of numbered stops keyed to a free brochure, available at the trailhead. You'll learn about the native vegetation and cultural history of the area as you ramble along a virtually level dirt path in a lovely meadow.

McKittrick Canyon Nature Trail

0.9 mile RT. Easy to moderate. Access: McKittrick Canyon Visitor Center.

An ideal way to discover the variety of plants and animals that inhabit the canyon, this trail has some steep climbs. Read the numerous interpretive signs along the path, telling you all you wanted to know about, for example, why rattlesnakes are underappreciated and how cacti supply food and water for wildlife.

Pinery Trail

0.75 mile RT. Easy. Access: The trailhead is by the Pine Springs Visitor Center; or from the parking area on U.S. 62/180, located ½ mile north of the visitor center entrance road.

A paved trail, accessible by wheelchair, the Pinery Trail gives visitors a brief introduction to the low-elevation environment at the park. The interpretive signs discuss both the plants along the trail and the history of the area. About 0.25 mile from the visitor center, the trail leads to the ruins of an old horse-changing station, left over from the Butterfield Stage Route (see "Historic & Man-Made Attractions," above).

Smith Spring Loop

2.3 miles RT. Easy to moderate. Access: The north edge of the Frijole Ranch and Museum.

The Smith Spring Loop begins in the dry desert and climbs 440 feet to the lush oasis of Smith Spring. The first part of the trail, which takes you to Manzanita Spring, is easy and navigable by people with mobility impairments. If you take this walk in the evening, you might catch a glimpse of an elk, deer, or other wildlife coming to the spring for water. After Manzanita Spring, the trail begins the climb to Smith Spring, following a good example of a desert riparian zone along Smith Canyon. Look for the damage caused by a lightning fire in 1990, and how the desert environment has recovered, even improved. Smith

Spring itself is a magnificent oasis, with enough water seeping out to form a small waterfall and stream. Here you'll find maidenhair fern, bigtooth maple, chinquapin oak, and Texas madrone—all in the middle of the Chihuahuan Desert. Although lush, the area is fragile, so please remain in the designated area to preserve the ecosystem.

LONGER TRAILS

El Capitan Trail

9.4 miles one-way. Moderate to strenuous. Access: Williams Ranch.

This trail, which offers little shade, climbs over 1,500 feet and takes a long day to complete, including the drive to Williams Ranch, which requires a four-wheel-drive vehicle (see "Historic & Man-Made Attractions," above). This is the only trail into the remote western part of the Guadalupe Mountains. The incredible scenery along the first 2 miles more than makes up for the long, slow, and usually hot climb up Shumard Canyon, an elevation gain of over 1,300 feet. Stop occasionally to look back down the canyon to the west, and ahead toward Shumard Peak and the impressive escarpment of the Guadalupes. After Shumard Canyon the hike takes you 3 miles around El Capitan, keeping in the shadow of the escarpment and climbing another 200 feet. After about 5 miles, the Salt Basin Overlook loop takes off to the right, and you stay to the left, gradually dropping down into Guadalupe Canyon, where you meet the other end of the lower Salt Basin Overlook loop. From here the last 3.4 miles of the trail are fairly easy, level walking to Pine Springs. The trail can also be hiked out and back from Pine Springs, an arduous 18.8-mile overnight hike, which is why many hikers get lifts from friends to the ranch and hike back to Pine Springs. An alternative you may consider is to hike from Pine Springs to the Salt Basin Overlook Trail, hike around it, and then head back to Pine Springs, a trip of 11.3 miles.

Guadalupe Peak Trail

4.2 miles one-way. Strenuous. Access: Pine Springs Campground.

This trail is strenuous, climbing almost 3,000 feet, but the views from the 8,749-foot-high Guadalupe Peak are magnificent. The peak is the highest in the park and the state of Texas. If you have only 1 day to explore this park, and you are an average or better hiker, this is the hike you should choose. Start early, take plenty of water, and be prepared to work. When you've gone about halfway, you'll see what seems to be the top not too far ahead, but beware: This is a false summit. Study the changing life zones as you climb from the desert into the higher-elevation pine forests—this will take your mind off your straining muscles and aching lungs. A mile short of the summit, a campground lies in one of the rare level spots on the mountain. If you plan to spend the night, anchor

Campground	Elev.	Total Sites	RV Hookups	Dump Station	Toilets	Drinking Water
Pine Springs	5,840	39	0	No	Yes	Yes
Dog Canyon	6,320	13	0	No	Yes	Yes
Carlsbad RV Park & Campground	3,110	136	95	Yes	Yes	Yes
Brantley Lake State Park	3,300	51+	51	Yes	Yes	Yes
White's City RV Park	3630	80+	80	Yes	Yes	Yes

your tent strongly—the winds can be ferocious up here, especially in spring.

From the summit, the views are stupendous. To the north are Bush Mountain and Shumard Peak, the next two highest points in Texas, with respective elevations of 8,631 and 8,615 feet. The Chihuahuan Desert stretches to the south, interrupted only by the Delaware and Sierra Diablo mountains. This is one of those "On a clear day you can see forever" spots—sometimes all the way to 12,003-foot-high Sierra Blanca, near Ruidoso, New Mexico, 100 miles north.

Lost Peak

3 miles one-way. Moderate. Access: Dog Canyon Trailhead.

A moderate hike you can probably complete in a half day, Lost Peak is especially good near dawn or dusk when you may see wild turkey, deer, and other wildlife. A lightning-caused fire scorched the area in 1994, and although many plants have been recovering, the loss of the tall trees will be felt for a long time. After leaving the trailhead, follow the Tejas Trail up Dog Canyon on a gradual climb for about 1.5 miles. Just before reaching Dog Canyon Springs, the trail starts to switchback up the west side of the canyon to a ridgeline, offering great views back to the campground. If you continue all the way to the peak, the next 1.5 miles climbs about 1,100 feet, the steepest section of the trail. There's no sign for the peak and it's easy to hike on by, so watch your topographical map

carefully—the peak is just a bit to the right of the trail. After scrambling up to the summit for a panoramic view, head back down the trail. The total elevation change is 1,420 feet.

McKittrick Canyon

5.1 miles one-way. Moderate to strenuous. Access: McKittrick Canyon Trailhead.

McKittrick Canyon is one of the most famous scenic areas in Texas, and this trail explores the length of it. The first 2.3 miles to the Pratt Lodge are easy, the following 1.2 miles to the Grotto gain 340 feet in elevation and are considered moderate, and the strenuous climb to the Notch rises 1,300 feet in 1.6 miles. Even so, this is one of the most popular hikes in the park, though not everyone makes it to the Notch.

The canyon is forested with conifers and deciduous trees. In fall the maples, oaks, and other hardwoods burst into color, painting the world in bright hues set off by the rich variety of the evergreens. The stream in the canyon, which appears and disappears several times in the first 3 miles of the trail, is a unique, permanent desert stream, with reproducing trout. Hikers may not drink from, wade in, fish, or disturb the stream in any way.

The first part of the trail is wide and seems flat, crossing the stream twice on its way to Pratt Lodge, which is wonderfully situated at the convergence of North and South McKittrick canyons. About a mile from the lodge a short

Showers	Fire Pits/ Grills	Laundry	Public Phone	Reserve	Fees	Open
No	No	No	Yes	No	$8	Year-round
No	No	No	Yes	No	$8	Year-round
Yes	Yes	Yes	Yes	Yes	$19–$24	Year-round
Yes	Yes	No	Yes	Yes	$8–$18	Year-round
Yes	Yes	Yes	Yes	Yes	$18–$23	Year-round

spur veers off to the left to the Grotto, a recess with odd formations that look like they belong in a cave. This is a great spot for lunch at one of the stone picnic tables. Continuing down the spur trail to its end, you reach the Hunter Line Cabin, which served as temporary quarters for ranch hands of the Hunter family. Beyond the cabin, South McKittrick Canyon has been preserved as a Research Natural Area with no entry. Return to the main trail and continue toward the Notch, or head back down the canyon to your vehicle. In another 0.5 mile, the trail begins to switchback up the side of South McKittrick Canyon for the steepest ascent in the park, until it slips through the Notch, a distinctive narrow spot in the cliff. Sit down and rest while you absorb the incredible scenery. The view down the canyon is magnificent, and dazzling in autumn. You can see both Hunter Line Cabin and Pratt Lodge in the distance. Remember to start down in time to reach your vehicle well before the gate is locked.

Exploring the Backcountry

A variety of possibilities exist for backpacking. It's always best to discuss your plans with rangers before heading out into the backcountry to find out about current trail conditions and to decide on the trail or trails you want to take. The required free backcountry campsite permits can be obtained no more than 24 hours in advance at the Pine Springs Visitor Center or Dog Canyon Ranger Station. Also, see "Camping," below.

The Bowl

13-mile loop. Strenuous. Access: Pine Springs Campground.

This hike climbs 2,546 feet in elevation if you go to the top of Hunter Peak. Because this is primarily an overnight hike, you'll camp either at Pine Top, about 4.2 miles down the trail and a bit

off it to the left, or at Tejas Campsite about 5.5 miles along. The trail crosses a dry wash, follows the Tejas Trail up a hill, has a fairly level stretch, and then starts the climb up to Pine Top, rising 2,000 feet over 3 miles of switchbacks. The view from the top of the escarpment is breathtaking. The trail then continues through a magnificent pine forest—watch for elk along the way. There are some old water tanks and a pipe running along the trail in spots, left over from a water system used by ranchers years ago. You can take a side trip to the top of Hunter Peak for another incredible view before heading back down.

Other Sports & Activities

Horseback Riding. About 60% of the park's trails are open to horses for day trips, although horses are not permitted in the backcountry overnight. There are **corrals** at Frijole Ranch (near Pine Springs) and Dog Canyon (see "Fees & Permits," above). Each set of corrals contains four pens that can accommodate up to 10 horses. No horses or other pack animals are available for hire in or near the park. Park rangers warn that horses brought into the park should be accustomed to steep, rocky trails.

Wildlife Viewing & Bird-Watching. Because of the variety of habitats, and also because these canyons offer some of the few water sources in western Texas, Guadalupe Mountains National Park offers excellent wildlife viewing and bird-watching. **McKittrick Canyon** and **Frijole Ranch** are considered among the best wildlife viewing spots, but a variety of species can be seen throughout the park. Those spending more than a few hours will likely see mule deer, and the park is also home to a herd of some 50 to 70 elk, which are sometimes observed in the higher elevations or along the highway in winter. Other **mammals** include raccoons, striped and hog-nosed skunks, gray foxes, coyotes, gray-footed chipmunks, Texas antelope squirrels, black-tailed jackrabbits, and desert cottontails. Black bears and mountain lions are also known to live in the park, but are seldom seen.

About two dozen varieties of **snakes** make their home in the park, including five species of rattlesnakes. There are also numerous **lizards,** which are usually seen in the mornings and early evenings. These include the collared, crevice spiny, tree, side-blotched, Texas horned, mountain short-horned, and marbled whiptail. The most commonly seen is the prairie lizard, which is identified by the light-colored stripes down its back.

More than 200 species of **birds** spend time in the park, including peregrine falcons, golden eagles, turkey vultures, and wild turkeys. You are also likely to encounter rock wrens, canyon wrens, black-throated sparrows, common nighthawks, mourning doves, rufous-crowned sparrows, mountain chickadees, ladder-backed woodpeckers, solitary vireos, and western scrub jays.

Camping

INSIDE THE PARK

There are two developed vehicle-accessible campgrounds in the park. **Pine Springs Campground** is near the visitor center and park headquarters just off U.S. 62/180. There are 18 spaces for RVs, 20 very attractive tent sites, and 2 group campsites. There is usually a campground host on duty. About ½ mile inside the north boundary of the park is **Dog Canyon Campground,** accessible from N. Mex. 137. Here there are 9 tent sites and 4 RV sites. Although reservations are not accepted, you can call ahead to check on availability of sites (© 915/828-3251). Camp stoves are allowed, but wood and charcoal fires are prohibited.

The park also has 10 designated backcountry campgrounds, with from 2 to 8 sites each. Be sure to pick up free

permits at the Pine Springs Visitor Center or Dog Canyon Ranger Station the day of or the day before your backpacking trip. No drinking water is available in the backcountry, and all trash, including toilet paper, must be packed out. Fires are strictly prohibited; use cookstoves only. You can only camp in designated campgrounds.

NEAR THE PARK

The closest commercial campgrounds are across the state line in New Mexico, at **White's City RV Park** in White's City, and **Carlsbad RV Park** and **Brantley Lake State Park** in Carlsbad. For further information on these campgrounds, see "Camping" in chapter 10, "Carlsbad Caverns National Park."

Where to Stay

There are no accommodations within the park. The nearest are 35 miles northeast at **White's City,** New Mexico, and 55 miles northeast in **Carlsbad,** New Mexico. For information, see "Where to Stay" in chapter 10.

Where to Dine

There are no restaurants within the park, although about 5 miles northeast of the park visitor center on U.S. 62/180, the **Nickel Creek Cafe** (© 915/828-3295) serves breakfast and lunch from Monday through Saturday, 7am to 2pm, with prices from $2 to $5.95.

The next closest dining possibilities are in **White's City,** New Mexico, 35 miles from the park, and in **Carlsbad,** New Mexico, 55 miles from the park. See "Where to Dine" in chapter 10.

Picnic & Camping Supplies

The closest grocery store to the national park is the convenience store located at the Texaco gas station in the **White's City complex,** at the intersection of U.S. 62/180 and N. Mex. 7, about 35 miles from the visitor center. You'll find a good variety of stores in the city of Carlsbad, including an **Albertson's** grocery store at 808 N. Canal St., at its intersection with West Church Street (© **505/885-2161**), which has a well-stocked deli and bakery.

Nearby Attractions

Many visitors to Guadalupe Mountains also spend time at nearby Carlsbad Caverns National Park, which is discussed in chapter 10.

JOSHUA TREE NATIONAL PARK

by Eric Peterson

T JOSHUA TREE NATIONAL PARK, THE TREES THEMSELVES ARE MERELY the starting point for exploring the seemingly barren desert. Viewed from the roadside, the dry land only hints at hidden vitality, but closer examination reveals a giant mosaic of an

ecosystem, intensely beautiful and complex. From lush oases teeming with life to rusted-out relics of man's attempts to tame this wilderness; from low plains of tufted cacti to mountains of exposed, gnarled rock; the park is much more than a tableau of the curious tree for which it's named.

The Joshua tree is said to have been given its name by early Mormon settlers (circa 1850)—its upraised limbs and bearded appearance reminded them of the prophet Joshua leading them to the promised land. It's not really a tree, but a variety of yucca, a member of the lily family.

Joshua Tree National Park's name is fitting, for here the peculiar tree reaches the southernmost boundary of its range. The park straddles two desert environments: The mountainous, Joshua tree–studded Mojave Desert forms the northwestern part of the park, while the hotter, drier, and lower Colorado Desert, characterized by a wide variety of desert flora such as cacti, ocotillo, and native California fan palms, comprises the

park's southern and eastern sections. Between them runs the "transition zone," displaying characteristics of each.

The area's geological timeline is fascinating, stretching back almost 2 billion years. Eight million years ago, the Mojave landscape was one of rolling hills and flourishing grasslands; horses, camels, and mastodons abounded, with saber-toothed tigers and wild dogs filling the role of predator. Displays at the Oasis Visitor Center show how climactic, volcanic, and tectonic activity created the park's signature cliffs and boulders and turned Joshua Tree into the arid desert you see today. Human presence has been traced back nearly 10,000 years with the discovery of the Pinto culture, and you can see evidence of more recent habitation throughout the park in the form of American Indian rock art. Miners and ranchers began coming in the 1860s, but the boom went bust by the turn of the 20th century. Then a Pasadena doctor by the name of James Luckie, treating World War I veterans suffering from respiratory and heart

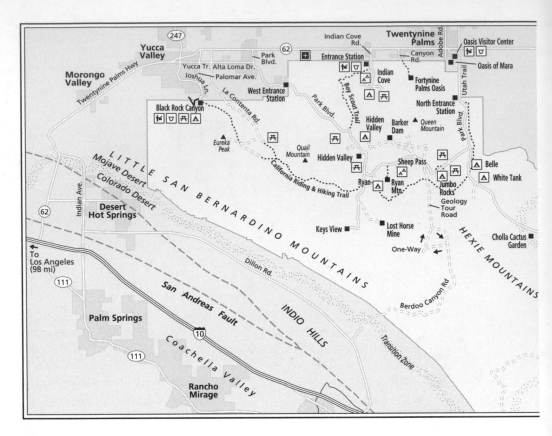

ailments caused by mustard gas, prescribed the desert's clean, dry air—and modern interest in the area was born.

During the 1920s, a worldwide fascination with the desert emerged, and cactus gardens were much in vogue. Entrepreneurs hauled truckloads of desert plants into Los Angeles for quick sale or export, and souvenir hunters removed archaeological treasures. Incensed that the beautiful Mojave was in danger of being picked clean, Pasadena socialite Minerva Hoyt organized the desert conservation movement and successfully lobbied for the establishment of Joshua Tree National Monument in 1936.

In 1994, under provisions of the federal California Desert Protection Act, Joshua Tree was "upgraded" to national park status and expanded to nearly 800,000 acres.

Flora. The eastern half of the park is typical of the lower Colorado Desert, dominated by the abundant and fragrant **creosote** bush, a drought-resistant survivor that releases secretions into the surrounding soil to inhibit competing seedlings. Adding interest to the arid land are small stands of spidery, tenacious **ocotillo,** a split personality that drops its leaves in times of drought, making it appear dry and spindly. But when the rains come, the ocotillo can sprout bushy leaves in a few days, and its flaming blooms atop leafy green branches bear little resemblance to its dormant alter ego.

Most people associate desert plants with cacti, which are indeed here in abundance. One of the more unusual members of the cactus family is the **Bigelow cholla cactus** ("teddy bear" or "jumping" cactus). Cholla's fine needles appear soft and fluffy from afar, but the folks who have accidentally gotten a clump stuck to their skin or clothing know the truth about these deceptively barbed spines. Most of the park's points of interest lie in the higher, slightly cooler and wetter Mojave desert, the special habitat of the burly **Joshua tree,** which displays huge white flowers

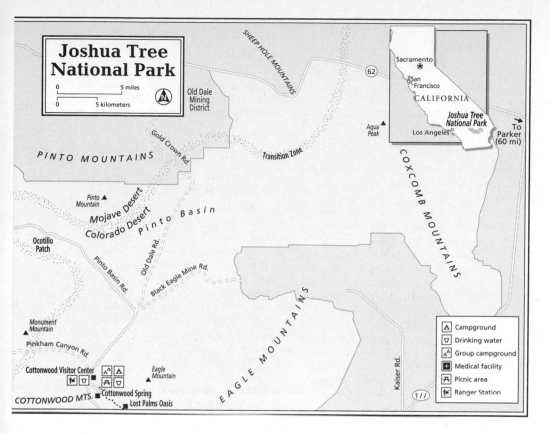

Joshua Tree National Park

following a good rainy season. Early pioneers (and many ignorant modern campers) tried to chop down the "trees" for firewood, only to discover that what resembled trunks were actually fireproof stalks. Five **fan palm** oases (in both climate zones) flourish in areas where water is forced to the surface along fault lines.

Wildflower lovers, take note: The Joshua Tree area has traditionally been an excellent place to view nature's springtime bonanza. In addition to the flowering plants discussed above, the desert is home to sand verbena, desert dandelion, evening primrose, and dozens more varieties, some so tiny that you must crouch down to make out their brightly colored petals—veteran viewers call these "belly flowers."

Fauna. One of the more wonderful aspects of the Joshua Tree desert is the way this seemingly harsh and barren landscape slowly reveals itself to be richly inhabited. From the black-tailed **jackrabbits** abundant at the Oasis of

Mara and throughout the park to **bobcats** and **cougars** prowling around less-traveled areas, the desert teems with life.

Some other frequently spotted residents: the **roadrunner,** a member of the cuckoo family with long, spindly legs and that telltale gait; the **coyote,** a fearless scavenger who'll openly trot along the road in search of food (*Beware:* They'll eat tennis shoes or picnic trash as eagerly as they eat rabbits or young tortoises); and **bighorn sheep,** most often seen atop the rocky hills they ascend with sharp cloven hooves. Perhaps the most unusual animal is the **desert tortoise,** a slow-moving burrow dweller not often seen by casual visitors. The tortoises, which can live more than 50 years, are a protected threatened species, and you're prohibited from touching or interfering with them in any way. A poignant exception to this is if you encounter a tortoise on the road in danger of being hit—you're permitted to pick it up gently with two hands and, holding it level, carry it off the road, placing it in the same direction as it was traveling.

Avoiding the Crowds. Joshua Tree Chief of Interpretation Joe Zarki is often consulted for advice on the park's natural flora and fauna. But he also offers the following valuable tips for maximizing your enjoyment even during the most crowded months:

- Joshua Tree's greatest volume occurs in spring, when temperatures are moderate and wildflowers are blooming. From March to May, the number of monthly visitors ranges from 150,000 up. (The unofficial record is 233,000 in Apr 1995.) Compared to summer, which sees 60,000 to 70,000 people each month, these figures are staggering. October and November are also popular, with numbers around 100,000. If you can, time your visit outside of these crowded periods—if not, try to visit during the week to avoid the crush of weekenders from nearby Los Angeles, and stay away during spring break.
- Choose to enjoy the more popular activities (such as designated nature trails and easy hiking routes) before 9 or 10am. Most people see the park between 10am and 4pm, so the evening hours can also offer some respite from crowds, and the sun sets after 7pm from May to September. In addition, you'll enjoy cooler temperatures during the morning and evening hours.
- Campers eager to stake their claim in the campground of their choice need to be diligent during springtime crowding, since it's first-come, first-served at all but two of the park's campgrounds. (Black Rock Canyon and Indian Cove take reservations.) Generally, it's best to arrive between 9am and noon to snatch an available space. The campsites near popular rock-climbing areas (Hidden Valley, Jumbo Rocks, Indian Cove) fill first. If

you're staying over a weekend in peak season, try to claim your site Friday morning, before weekenders arrive.

Just the Facts

GETTING THERE & GATEWAYS

There are three roads into the park. The most commonly used is the **West Entrance Station,** on Park Boulevard in the town of Joshua Tree along Calif. 62. The **North Entrance Station** at the end of Utah Trail in the town of Twentynine Palms, on Calif. 62, 40 miles north of its junction with I-10, is also a popular gateway to the park. On the southern side of the park is the **Cottonwood Visitor Center,** about 25 miles east of Indio along I-10.

The Nearest Airport. The closest airport is the **Palm Springs International Airport,** 3400 E. Tahquitz Canyon Way (✆ **760/318-3800**), served by Alaska, American, America West, Continental, Delta/Skywest, and United; with car rentals from Alamo, Avis, Budget, Dollar, Enterprise, and Hertz. See the appendix for their toll-free phone numbers.

INFORMATION

Contact the **Superintendent, Joshua Tree National Park,** 74485 National Park Dr., Twentynine Palms, CA 92277 (✆ **760/367-5500;** www.nps.gov/jotr). A terrific website with abundant info on the park and surrounding communities is **www.desertgold.com**.

In addition to the complimentary newspaper-style *Joshua Tree Guide,* published by the Joshua Tree National Park Association, the following publications might prove helpful: Robert Cates's *Joshua Tree National Park: A Visitors Guide* (Chatsworth, California: Live Oak Press, 1984), and John Krist's *50 Best Short Hikes in California Deserts* (Berkeley: Wilderness Press, 1995). Order them from the **Joshua Tree National Park Association,** 74485 National Park Dr.,

Twentynine Palms, CA 92277 (© **760/ 367-5525;** www.joshuatree.org).

Your best source of information in the park is the large and well-stocked Park Service's **Oasis Visitor Center,** 74485 National Park Dr., Twentynine Palms, CA 92277, on the road to the North Entrance Station. The **Cottonwood Visitor Center,** at the south end of the park, houses a gift shop/bookstore and an interpretive exhibit on the area's wildlife. The privately run **Park Center,** 6554 Park Blvd., Joshua Tree, CA 92252, is near the West Entrance Station in Joshua Tree. In addition to providing official visitor materials and information, this center has a supply/gift shop, a deli, and an art gallery.

Admission to the park is $10 per car (valid for 7 days). Four of the nine developed campgrounds charge fees of $10 for individual sites, more for group sites. Backcountry camping is free, but registration is required.

In addition to the standard national park regulations designed to protect fragile ecosystems, keep these in mind while enjoying Joshua Tree:

◆ Dehydration is a constant threat in the desert; even in winter, carry plenty of drinking water and drink regularly even if you don't feel thirsty. Recommended minimum supplies are 1 gallon per person per day or twice that if planning strenuous activity. Water is available only at five park locations: Cottonwood Springs, the Black Rock Canyon Campground, the Indian Cove Ranger Station, West Entrance, and the Oasis Visitor Center. Some of the water is

dispensed via a coin-operated fountain—bring plenty of quarters.

◆ Sections of the park (identified on the official map) contain abandoned mines and associated structures. Use extreme caution in the vicinity, watching for open shafts and prospect holes. Supervise children closely and never enter abandoned mines.

◆ There's potential flash flooding following even brief rain showers, so avoid drainage areas and be especially observant of road conditions at those times.

Joshua Tree National Park's nearly 800,000 acres straddle two distinct desert climates—the eastern half of the park is hot, dry, Colorado Desert; while most points of interest lie in the higher, slightly cooler and wetter Mojave Desert. The Mojave will occasionally get a dusting of snow in winter, but neither section sees more than 3 to 6 inches of annual rainfall. Winter temperatures are in the comfortable 50s or 60s (lower teens Celsius) during the day and often approach freezing overnight; summer days can blaze past 100°F (38°C) at noon, and even nighttime offers little relief in August and September, when lows are still in the 80s (upper 20s Celsius). At the park's higher elevations, however, the summer climate is much more bearable.

Best between February and May, the springtime **wildflower viewing** is dependent on rainfall, sunshine, and temperatures, but you can depend on seeing the brilliant blooms somewhere in the park each year. Rangers lead interpretive walks to the best displays, and 24-hour recorded information on prime viewing sites (updated at least weekly during the Mar–May wildflower season) is available from the **Payne Foundation**

Wildflower Hot Line at © 818/768-3533 or online at **www.theodorepayne.org.**

If You Have Only 1 Day

An excellent first stop is the main **Oasis Visitor Center,** located alongside the Oasis of Mara, also known as the Twentynine Palms Oasis. For many generations the native Serrano and Chemehuevi tribes lived at this "place of little springs and much grass." Get maps, books, and the latest in road, trail, and weather conditions before beginning your tour, and stroll the short, paved nature trail through the oasis behind the center—it provides an introduction to the park's flora, wildlife, and geology.

From the Oasis Center, drive south to **Jumbo Rocks,** which captures the complete essence of the park: a vast array of rock formations, a Joshua tree forest, and the yucca-dotted desert open and wide. Check out the many boulders that appear to resemble humans, dinosaurs, monsters, cathedrals, and castles; if you're visiting with kids, it's a great way to put their imaginations to work. Stroll among the giant rock piles and observe the rock climbers who travel from around the world to practice their craft here—they're one of the park's most distinctive features.

At Cap Rock Junction, the main park road swings north toward the **Wonderland of Rocks,** 12 square miles of massive jumbled granite. This curious maze of stone hides groves of Joshua trees, trackless washes, and several small pools of water. To the south is the road that dead-ends at mile-high **Keys View.** You get a panoramic view of the park from this wind-whipped overlook; several informative plaques explain the topography you're seeing and provide some insight into the delicate desert ecosystems found in the park.

Don't miss the contrasting Colorado Desert terrain found along Pinto Basin Road—to conserve time, simply plan to exit the park via this route, which ends up at I-10. You'll pass both the **Cholla Cactus Garden** and spindly **Ocotillo**

Patch on your way to vast Pinto Basin, a barren lowland surrounded by austere mountains and punctuated by trackless sand dunes. Then continue to **Cottonwood Springs,** which has a cool, palm-shaded oasis and groves of mature cottonwood trees.

Try to participate in a ranger-led tour or hike (see below). You'll learn to appreciate the park in a short amount of time, for the rangers here are as exuberant about their patch of wilderness as they are well informed.

Exploring the Park by Car

There are two main roads through the park, and by driving them both you'll be able to see virtually every feature that distinguishes Joshua Tree; there are even a couple of easy opportunities to stop and stretch your legs.

Park Boulevard loops through the high northern section between the North Entrance Station in Twentynine Palms and the West Entrance Station in Joshua Tree. Along the drive, which takes about 45 minutes one-way, you'll get an eyeful of the spectacular rock formations and oddly shaped Joshua trees. Stop at one of the well-marked interpretive trails along the way (see "Day Hikes," below), but don't miss the detour to **Keys View,** one of the most popular spots in the park. A paved road leads to this mile-high mountain crest, where a series of plaques describe the land below and a panoramic view that encompasses both the highest (Mount San Gorgonio) and the lowest (Salton Sea) points in Southern California.

Pinto Basin Road bisects the park from top to bottom, forking away from Park Boulevard near the North Entrance Station and winding down to the Cottonwood Entrance off I-10. Driving it, you'll pass from the higher Mojave Desert into the lower Colorado Desert, across the "transition zone" snaking through the middle of the park, a fascinating melting pot where the two climates are both represented. Stop to marvel at the Cholla Cactus Garden (see

"Day Hikes," below) or the Ocotillo Patch, where this spidery, tenacious desert shrub sports flaming red blooms following spring rains. At the park's southern end you can explore the lush Cottonwood Spring or see relics of World War II training maneuvers (see "Historic & Man-Made Attractions," below). Driving from end to end takes between 45 and 60 minutes.

Organized Tours & Ranger Programs

A multitude of ranger-led seminars and guided hikes are offered. They change annually, but might include topics such as "Sketching the Sunrise (or Sunset)," "Birding for Beginners," "Stars Over Joshua Tree," and "Meteors," as well as guided hikes on many of the park's popular trails. Throughout the wildflower blooming season, and especially during Easter week, special walks visit the most abundantly flowering areas.

The Park Service also conducts guided tours of the historic **Desert Queen Ranch** (see below). From approximately November to May, tours are given several times daily ($5 adults, $2.50 kids 6–11). Contact the visitor center for a seasonal schedule; tours are given much less frequently during the hot summer. Plan to arrive early—these events are popular and groups are limited to 25.

Historic & Man-Made Attractions

Miners and ranchers began coming in the 1860s, including the McHaney brothers, who established the **Desert Queen Ranch.** Later on, former Rough Rider Bill Keys acquired it, and lived there until his death in 1969. Many of the ranch structures have been restored to their Keys-era condition, painting a compelling picture of how one hardy family made a home in the unforgiving

desert. Admittance is limited to official Park Service tours (see above).

You can find petroglyphs near **Barker Dam,** where an easy 1.1-mile loop hiking trail leads to a small artificial lake framed by the Wonderland of Rocks. After scrambling a bit to get atop the dam, you'll find a sandy path leading to the "Disneyland Petroglyph" site. Its wry name stems from the fact that a movie crew once retraced the ancient rock carvings to make them more visible to the camera, thus defacing them forever. If you investigate the cliffs along the remainder of the trail, however, you're likely to find some untouched drawings depicting animals, humans, and other aspects of desert life as interpreted by long-ago dwellers. You'll see additional petroglyphs along the 18-mile **Geology Tour Road,** a sandy and lumpy dirt road accessible only by four-wheel-drive vehicles or hardy mountain bikers.

During World War II, George S. Patton trained over a million soldiers in desert combat at several sites throughout the Mojave and Colorado deserts. Tank tracks are still visible in the wilderness around the former Camp Young, near Cottonwood Springs. The **Camp Young Memorial** marker is 1 mile east of Cottonwood Springs Road, just before the park entrance; an informational kiosk there gives details of the training maneuvers and daily camp life. To learn more, you can visit the **General Patton Memorial Museum** (© 760/227-3483) in Chiriaco Summit, on I-10 about 5 miles east of the Cottonwood Entrance. The museum contains an assortment of memorabilia from World War II and other military glory days, as well as displays of tanks and artillery; it's open daily from 9:30am to 4:30pm (except Thanksgiving and Christmas) and admission is $4 ($3.50 for seniors 62 and older and free for children under 12).

Hikes

The good news about Joshua Tree: Its natural wonders are accessible to everyone, not just to the extreme outdoor adventurer. Nowhere is this more apparent than in the diversity of hiking and nature trails, which range from a half-mile paved nature trail (ideal for even strollers and wheelchairs) to trails of 15-plus miles requiring strenuous hiking and backcountry camping.

SHORTER TRAILS

Barker Dam Nature Trail

1.1 miles RT. Easy. Access: Barker Dam parking area.

This sandy path leads to a small lake—formed in a natural rock basin by an artificial dam—a relic of the ranchers who used such "tanks" to water their stock. Signs along the way describe some of the plant and animal life found here, including migratory wildfowl that use this as a watering hole on their journeys. After scrambling up the dam, you'll come to some petroglyph sites (see "Historic & Man-Made Attractions," above).

Cap Rock Nature Trail

0.4 mile RT. Easy (paved). Access: Cap Rock parking area.

Climbers gather here, and they're as interesting to watch as the short, informative trail leading from the parking lot. In between identifying different desert plants along the path, test your footing on some of the rocks to get a feel for the climbing experience.

Cholla Cactus Garden Nature Trail

0.25 mile RT. Easy. Access: Middle of the park, about halfway between the north and south entrances.

This trail winds through an unusually dense concentration of Bigelow cholla, one of the desert's more fascinating residents. Often called "teddy bear cactus" for its deceptively fluffy appearance, cholla is also nicknamed "jumping cactus" for the ease with which its barbed spines stick to the clothing and skin of anyone who passes too close. Any ranger

can tell you horror stories of people who've tripped into a cholla bush and emerged porcupine-like and suffering—but please don't let that stop you from enjoying this pretty roadside diversion.

Cottonwood Springs Nature Trail

1 mile RT. Easy. Access: Cottonwood Campground.

The trail leads through rolling desert hills long inhabited by Cahuilla Indians. Signs along the way relate how they used native plants in their everyday lives; the trail culminates at lush Cottonwood Springs. The prolific underground water source supports thick groves of cottonwood and palm trees, plus the birds and animals that make them home.

Desert Queen Mine

1.5 miles RT. Easy to moderate. Access: Reached via a dirt road leading from Park Blvd., opposite the Geology Tour Rd.

The "trail" meanders and forks through the ruins of a gold mine that yielded several million dollars' worth of ore between 1895 and 1961. Building ruins, steel machinery parts, and sealed mine shafts dot the hillsides and ravine; there's a signboard at the overlook with information about mine operations.

Fortynine Palms Oasis

3 miles RT. Strenuous. Access: End of Canyon Rd. in Twentynine Palms (outside the park, down Canyon Rd.).

This hike begins with a steep, harsh ascent to a ridge fringed with red-spined barrel cacti. Down the other side, a rocky canyon contains the spectacular oasis whose fan palm and cottonwood tree canopy shades clear pools of green water. Plants, birds, and other wildlife are abundant in this miniature ecosystem, and the scorched trunks of trees bear witness to past fires that have nourished rather than destroyed the life here. Beware of rattlesnakes in the shaded brush around the oasis.

Hidden Valley Nature Trail

1-mile loop RT. Easy. Access: A paved spur near the Hidden Valley picnic area.

This trail is fun for kids and adults who like rock climbing and intrigue. You can see sport climbers surrounding the small valley, which is reputed to have been a hideout for 19th-century cattle rustlers. Signs posted along the trail talk about the area's geology and history. The trail is relatively level, though there's some easy boulder scrambling along the route.

High View Nature Trail

1.3 miles RT. Moderate. Access: Dirt road turnoff immediately before the entrance to Black Rock Campground at the northwestern edge of the park.

This well-maintained and popular trail involves a steady, moderately steep climb to one of Joshua Tree's many spectacular vistas. Alternately rocky and sandy, numbered signposts mark the trail, keyed to a leaflet that, unfortunately, is often unavailable from the Black Rock Ranger Station. Benches are found at intervals and also at the summit.

Mastodon Peak Trail

3 miles RT. Moderate. Access: Cottonwood Spring or Cottonwood Campground.

Well-worn and scenic, this is the longest loop trail in the park, offering great views of the Eagle Mountains and the nearby Salton Sea. For history buffs, it also passes an old gold mine, long since abandoned. There is a small amount of elevation gain, about 400 feet on the way to the 3,371-foot summit of Mastodon Peak.

Oasis of Mara Nature Trail

0.5 mile RT. Easy (paved). Access: Behind the Oasis Visitor Center.

Leading into a miniature ecosystem of palm trees, small ponds, and abundant animal life, this incredibly easy path is lined with interpretive signs. It's a great place to start your first visit to Joshua Tree and an excellent introduction to the centuries of human inhabitants who used the oasis to sustain life.

Pine City

3 miles RT. Easy. Access: Begin at the same trailhead for Desert Queen Mine.

This path takes you to a cluster of boulder formations and sandy washes. Pinyon trees thrive in the moisture provided by these natural drainage courses, and its pine nuts were a food source for early inhabitants. Birds now gather in the trees and bighorn sheep are occasionally found among the rocks.

Ryan Mountain

3 miles RT. Strenuous. Access: A marked parking area along Park Blvd.

A constant, steep climb (almost 1,000 ft.) leads to the best panoramic views in the park, encompassing snowcapped mountain peaks, broad tree-dotted valleys, and dark volcanic mounds. Ascending through a juniper and pinyon pine woodland, the trail is mostly rocky, well-maintained, and easy to follow—you'll likely spot rock climbers to the west of the mountain.

Skull Rock Nature Trail

0.5 mile RT. Easy. Access: Jumbo Rocks Campground (Loop E).

Leading to another unusually anthropomorphic rock formation, the trail meanders through boulders, desert washes, and a rocky alleyway. Watch for the "ducks" (small stacks of rocks) that mark the pathway. The official trail ends at the main road, but a primitive trail continues on a mile-long loop across the street.

LONGER TRAILS

Boy Scout Trail

16 miles RT. Moderate. Access: Keys West backcountry board, 6½ miles east of the West Entrance Station.

From the trailhead, you progress downhill, through picturesque, sandy washes lined with oak and pine trees. Traveling through a variety of terrain, this trail can also be taken one-way, in either direction. The latter portion skirts a rocky mountainside, then finishes through open desert, ending up at the Indian Cove Ranger Station and backcountry board.

California Riding and Hiking Trail

35 miles RT. Easy to strenuous. Access: There are 6 access points along the trail's path; your best bet is to consult with park rangers and obtain a topographical map to help you stay on track.

In general, it's easier to travel from west to east since the western sections are at higher elevations. Marked by distinctive brown posts stenciled with "CRH," the many miles of this trail pass through distinct areas of the park, from pinyon/juniper forests to flat, lower desert terrain. It takes 2 to 4 days to hike the trail in its entirety, but you can also hike it in sections ranging from 4.4 to 11 miles.

Lost Horse Mine

4 miles RT. Moderate. Access: End of a dirt road leading from Keys View Rd., 2½ miles south of its junction with Park Blvd.

This trail leads to the ruins of the area's most successful mining operation. Well-preserved remnants include the steam engine that powered the machinery, a winch for lowering equipment into the mine, settling tanks, and stone building foundations. The trail, actually an old wagon road, winds gradually up through rolling hills; once there, you can take an additional short, steep hike to the hilltop behind the ruins for a fine view into the heart of the park. Hikers with children should keep a watchful eye around the mine ruins.

Lost Palms Oasis

7.5 miles RT. Moderate. Access: Park at Cottonwood Spring, accessible by paved road just beyond the Cottonwood Campground.

This long trail leads through sandy washes and rolling hills to the oasis overlook, then a steep, rugged, and strenuous trail continues on to the canyon bottom. Whether or not you're up to the entire challenge, the beauty of birdsong and rustling palms echoing through the canyon make this a special hike. Lost Palms is the park's largest oasis; look closely for elusive bighorn sheep in the remote canyon bottom.

Other Sports & Activities

Biking. Because most of Joshua Tree National Park is designated wilderness, special care must be taken not to damage the fragile ecosystem. That means bicycles are restricted to roads, none of which have bike lanes. This effectively puts biking out of reach for most casual pedalers. If you're into mountain biking, though, and up to a challenge, there are miles of unpaved roads ripe for exploration. Distraction from cars is rare, particularly on four-wheel-drive roads such as the 18-mile **Geology Tour Road,** which begins 2 miles west of Jumbo Rocks. Dry lake beds contrast with towering boulders along this downhill, sandy and lumpy dirt road; you can stop to see a Joshua tree woodland, abandoned mines, and American Indian petroglyphs.

A short but rewarding ride starts at Covington Flats, accessible only by unpaved (two-wheel-drive okay) La Contentata Road in the town of Joshua Tree. From the picnic area, ride west to Eureka Peak, 4 miles away through lush high desert vegetation such as extralarge Joshua trees, junipers, and pinyons. The road is steep near the end, but your reward will be a panoramic view of Palm Springs to the south, the Morongo Basin to the north, and the jagged mountain ranges of the park in between. For other bike-friendly unpaved and four-wheel-drive roads, consult the park map available at all visitor centers. There are no bike rentals available in the park, so you'll have to bring your own.

Especially for Kids

Joshua Tree National Park is a great place for the kids — they'll see unusual plants and animals, learning just enough to stimulate their imaginations but not so much they zone out. From identifying familiar everyday shapes in rock formations to investigating the mysterious "teddy bear" cactus, the possibilities are endless. Parents must exercise caution, with regard to the weather and other dangers. Bring plenty of water, sunscreen, and protective clothing for children, and keep a close eye (if not grip) on them at all times to avoid their straying into perilous desert terrain (prickly cacti, steep rocks, or abandoned mine shafts).

Start by taking the kids on a designated nature trail (listed in the free *Joshua Tree Guide* and indicated by roadside signs). The park's 11 nature trails have numerous plaques along the way to help your family interpret the rocks, plants, and other characteristics you'll see in the context of their geological history and significance to animal and human desert dwellers. They're all short (0.25- to 1.3-mile loops) and relatively flat, making them ideal for most visitors. Three of these (**Oasis of Mara, Bajada Trail,** and **Cap Rock**) are even paved and wheelchair-accessible.

The Park Service is eager for younger visitors to learn nature appreciation and conservation. Available at the park's visitor centers, the **Junior Ranger** publication offers several "games" (thinly veiled educational activities) for kids, ranging from sketching rock formations and plants to quizzes on the park's facilities. If your youngster is interested enough to complete five of the activities, rangers at the Oasis and Cottonwood visitor centers will reward him or her with an official Junior Ranger badge.

Rock Climbing. During most of the year, visitors to the park can observe rock climbers scurrying up, down, and across the many geological formations in the northwestern quadrant. Joshua Tree is one of the sport's premier destinations, with more than 4,000 individually rated climbs.

Spectacular geological formations have irresistible names such as **Wonderland of Rocks** and **Jumbo Rocks**—lovers of Stonehenge and Easter Island will delight in bizarre stacks with names such as **Cap Rock** (for the single flat rock perched atop a haphazard pile) or **Skull Rock** (where the elements have worn an almost-human countenance into a boulder arrangement). But human hands had nothing to do with nature's sculptural artistry here; these fantastic formations are made of quartz monzogranite, once a molten liquid forced upward that cooled before reaching the surface. Tectonic stresses fractured the rocks, and as floods eventually washed away the ground cover and exposed the monzonite, natural erosion wore away the weakened sections, creating the bizarre shapes and piles you see today. Climbers of every skill level travel here from around the world, drawn by the otherworldly splendor of rock piles worn smooth by the elements.

Hidden Valley is another good place to watch enthusiasts from as far away as Europe and Japan scaling sheer rock faces with impossible grace. Climbers sometimes practice bouldering—working on strength and agility on smaller boulders within jumping distance of the ground. You can try some bouldering to sample the high-friction quartz monzogranite; even tennis shoes seem to grip the rock surface.

If you'd like to learn the sport of rock climbing from scratch, it's easier than you think. The folks at (aptly named) **Uprising** (© 888/254-6266 or 760/320-6630; www.uprising.com) in Palm Springs have accredited, experienced climbing guides who'll orchestrate your entire excursion, starting with detailed instruction on rock-climbing basics. Later, the guide will lead each climb, setting up ropes for belay and rappelling, then guiding students every step of the way. All-day excursions range from $100 to $115 per person in groups of three or larger, $150 each for two people, or $225 for private instruction. The company operates year-round, and the prices include all necessary gear.

Camping

There are nine developed drive-in campgrounds in the park, and at this writing, you can only make reservations for individual sites at Black Rock Canyon and Indian Cove (© 800/365-CAMP [2267]; http://reservations.nps. gov). You can make group camping reservations (sites accommodate 10–70 people) at the same number. **Belle Campground,** located on Pinto Basin Road 9 miles south of Twentynine Palms, has chemical toilets. **Black Rock Canyon Campground** is in the northwest corner, at the head of the 35-mile California Riding and Hiking Trail (to reach it you have to leave the park boundaries), and is the most developed campground. There is also a visitor center here. **Cottonwood Campground** is in the southern portion of the park, near the Cottonwood Visitor Center. **Hidden Valley Campground,** located 14 miles south of Joshua Tree, California, is on the main park road. **Indian Cove** is just inside park boundaries west of Twentynine Palms; like at Black Rock there are many hiking trails leading farther into Joshua Tree, but no roads. **Jumbo Rocks Campground,** so named for its—surprise!—jumbo rocks, is 11 miles south of Twentynine Palms. **Ryan Campground,** 16 miles southeast of Joshua Tree, California, is reached via Park Boulevard. **Sheep Pass group camp,** a few miles east of Ryan Campground, has group sites only. **White Tank Campground** is 2 miles beyond the Belle

Campground	Total Sites	RV Hookups	Dump Station	Toilets	Drinking Water
Belle	18	No	No	Yes	No
Black Rock Canyon	100	No	Yes	Yes	Yes
Cottonwood	62 individual, 3 group	No	Yes	Yes	Yes
Hidden Valley	39	No	No	Yes	No
Indian Cove	101 individual, 13 group	No	No	Yes	Yes
Joshua Tree Lake RV & Campground (private)	49	No	Yes	Yes	Yes
Jumbo Rocks	125	No	No	Yes	No
Ryan	31	No	No	Yes	No
Sheep Pass	No individual, 6 group	No	No	Yes	No
White Tank	15	No	No	Yes	No

* Reservations can be made (by mail) for group sites.

Campground. There are no showers or laundry facilities at any of the campgrounds, and you can only make fires in the fire pits provided at each campsite.

The park also allows **backcountry camping** in the wilderness areas; regulations include mandatory registration at 1 of 12 boards (see the Park Service map for locations). Park honchos recommend backcountry enthusiasts buy "Trails Illustrated's" topographic map of the park (available through the park association) before embarking on a backpacking trip.

Outside of the park boundaries, there are a few commercial campgrounds. One of the best is the **Joshua Tree Lake RV & Campground,** located 5 miles north of Calif. 62 on Sunfair Road near the town of Joshua Tree (© **760/ 366-1213**). It has a fishing lake (with bass, bluegill, and catfish), a dump station, and a small convenience store, but no hookups. Showers cost $3.

Where to Stay

Aside from camping, there are no overnight accommodations available within the boundaries of Joshua Tree National Park.

Best Western Gardens Motel

71487 Twentynine Palms Hwy., Twentynine Palms, CA 92277. © **800/528-1234** or 760/367-9141. Fax 760/367-2584. 84 units. A/C TV TEL. $79–$95 double. Rates include continental breakfast. AE, DC, DISC, MC, V.

Located on the main highway at the western end of town, the stucco-clad Best Western Gardens might be a predictable representative of this motel chain, but it's also more reliable than many of the funky roadside places you'll pass. Kept sparkling clean and recently refurbished, the Best Western even has some two-room suites whose extra sleeping area and kitchenette are perfect for families. Three rooms have hot tubs, plus the motel has a fitness room, heated outdoor pool, and whirlpool.

Harmony Motel

71161 Twentynine Palms Hwy., Twentynine Palms, CA 92277. © **760/367-3351.** www. harmonymotel.com. 6 units, 1 cabin. A/C. $70– $80 double; $100 cabin. AE, MC, V.

	Showers	Fire Pits/ Grills	Laundry	Public Phone	Reserve	Fees	Open
	No	Yes	No	No	No	No	Year-round
	No	Yes	No	No	Yes	$10	Year-round
	No	Yes	No	No	No*	$10–$25	Year-round
	No	Yes	No	No	No	No	Year-round
	No	Yes	No	No	Yes*	$10–$35	Year-round
	Yes		Yes	Yes	No	Yes	$7 plus $2/person
	No	Yes	No	No	No	No	Year-round
	No	Yes	No	No	No	No	Year-round
	No	Yes	No	No	Yes*	$25	Year-round
	No	Yes	No	No	No	No	Year-round

Jeffrey Jones, a Venice Beach–based artist, took over this weathered roadside motel in 2002 and treated it as his own personal canvas. A self-described "found object and assemblage" artisan, Jones gutted the rooms and inserted a unique aesthetic that merges form and function. Now bare of carpet, the basic rooms are peaceful and comfortable with woven mats, odds and ends Jones uncovered in the desert, and other touches of "rustic Zen." There is a communal kitchen and an attractive outdoor pool, and—like the Joshua Tree Inn, below—this place has some serious rock history: U2 stayed here after recording *The Joshua Tree.*

Joshua Tree Inn

61259 Twentynine Palms Hwy., Joshua Tree, CA 92252. © **760/366-1188.** Fax 760/366-3805. www.joshuatreeinn.com. 10 units. A/C. $75–$145 double; $135 cottage. Rates include continental breakfast. AE, DISC, MC, V.

Not all local lore has to do with pioneering miners and ranchers—and one former motel, now a gracious B&B, boasts of a more recent rock 'n' roll history. Built in the 1950s, the Joshua Tree Inn has been the choice of the Rolling Stones, the Flying Burrito Brothers, and the cast of *Saturday Night Live.* The lobby is decorated with posters of folk singer/songwriter Gram Parsons, who died of a drug overdose here in 1973, and one of the rooms is dedicated to his memory. Legends aside, the low-slung adobe-style inn and cottages are basic but charming, surrounding a large pool near the west entrance of Joshua Tree National Park, though set back far enough from the main highway to escape most of the traffic noise. New ownership took over in 2002 and planned to convert the formerly frilly country inn–themed motel into one decorated with rock posters and psychedelic art.

Oasis of Eden Inn & Suites

56377 Twentynine Palms Hwy., Yucca Valley, CA 92284. © **800/606-6686** or 760/365-6321. Fax 760/365-9592. www.oasisofeden.com. 40 units. A/C TV TEL. $59–$199 double (higher costs are for "theme" rooms). Rates include continental breakfast. AE, DC, DISC, MC, V.

It may look like a plain roadside motel on the outside, but the Oasis of Eden has surprises waiting behind its doors. If you think the name makes it sound like a good place for illicit liaisons, wait till you see one of the 14 "theme rooms," each with a whirlpool and VCR. The Oasis of Eden is a less-grand cousin to San Luis Obispo's famous Madonna Inn; here you can go back to the heyday of Elvis and sleep in a bed shaped like a '59 Cadillac in the '50s Room, revisit Caesar's Palace in the marble-pillared Roman Suite, or return to your vine-swinging roots in the popular Jungle Room—ask about their special romance packages. There are also 26 standard rooms, all with air-conditioning and some with kitchenettes. As motels go, this one's a cut above, offering 24-hour complimentary coffee and tea; a heated outdoor pool and spa; in-room dataports; and juice, granola, yogurt, and fresh fruit at no extra charge.

29 Palms Inn

73950 Inn Ave., Twentynine Palms, CA 92277. © **760/367-3505.** Fax 760/367-4425. www.29palmsinn.com. 19 units. A/C TV. Sept–June $70–$125 double; July–Aug $50–$125 double. Midweek discounts sometimes apply. Rates include morning coffee and muffins. AE, DC, DISC, MC, V.

The closest you can stay to the Joshua Tree National Park entrance is the 29 Palms Inn. This rustic, family-run inn dates from the 1920s and consists of adobe cottages and old frame cabins scattered among 70 acres of the Oasis of Mara, the other side of which holds the main visitor center for the park. It has gradually been discovered by Hollywood celebrities in need of a low-key resort dedicated to the art of relaxation. The grounds are quite lovely, including lawns frequented by ducks from the nearby pond and shaded by the namesake 29 original palms. Behind the simple pool is the inn's restaurant, one of the best in town (see "Where to Dine," below). Included with the room are morning coffee and fresh-baked muffins around the pool patio. The cottages are all unique; most have a fireplace or wood stove and patio or deck, but all have evaporative coolers for the sweltering summer. There's also a three-bedroom, two-bathroom guesthouse available for $140 to $235 a night and a historic adobe home for $210 to $295.

Where to Dine

There are no restaurants in the park.

NEAR THE PARK

You can't be anywhere in the Southwest without seeing a Mexican restaurant, and the Morongo Basin is no exception. Although none can compare to true south-of-the-border authenticity, you'll find tasty, traditional fare such as saucy enchiladas, bulging burritos, layered tostadas, and plenty of crispy chips and salsa. The locals favor **Edchada's,** 56805 Twentynine Palms Hwy. in Yucca Valley (© 760/365-7655), so much that a second restaurant recently opened in Twentynine Palms, at 73502 Twentynine Palms Hwy. (© 760/367-2131). Both Edchada's are open daily from 11am to 9pm and have a full cocktail bar; they take credit cards (AE, DISC, MC, V), and vegetarian dishes are available. Also in Twentynine Palms is **Ramona's,** 72115 Twentynine Palms Hwy. (© 760/367-1929), a tiny family-run place with vinyl tablecloths, piñatas, and its own local following. Ramona's serves beer and wine only and is open Monday to Saturday from 11am to 8pm; credit cards are accepted (DISC, MC, V). A good family diner is the circus-themed **Carousel Cafe,** 72317 Twentynine Palms Hwy., Twentynine Palms (© 760/367-3736), a friendly octagonal joint with great burgers and hearty breakfasts, as well as a variety of steaks at dinner. It's open daily from 6am to 9pm and takes all major credit cards (AE, DC, DISC, MC, V).

29 Palms Inn

73950 Inn Ave., Twentynine Palms. © **760/ 367-3505.** Reservations recommended for dinner. Lunch entrees under $6; full dinners $9–$18. AE, DC, DISC, MC, V. Daily 11am–2pm and 5–9pm (until 9:30pm Fri–Sat). AMERICAN.

A favorite spot for local artists to display their works, this restaurant is tucked away behind its namesake hotel's postage stamp–size pool and consists of a paneled dining room whose large, hospitable bar sports a vaguely nautical Polynesian theme. The reasonably priced meals here enjoy their own fame, separate from the hotel's, and deservedly so. Starting with fresh vegetables from the inn's garden (which flourishes in this fertile oasis) and quality meat, poultry, and fresh fish, the kitchen sends out simple meals accented with zesty condiment inventions (such as their citrus-tinged mustard/herb salad dressing). Lunch choices include fluffy quiche du jour, creamy soups, crunchy salads, and tostadas, plus a variety of hot and cold sandwiches—call ahead if you'd like to have a sack lunch prepared for a day in the park. Dinner is more robust, featuring grilled meats and fish, seafood sautéed in butter and garlic, and whimsical specials such as Cat Ballou Drunk Steak. The evening ambience is further enhanced by the white-plumed barn owls cavorting among the palm canopy.

Pappy and Harriet's Restaurant & Saloon

Pioneertown Rd., Pioneertown. © **760/365-5956.** Reservations recommended. Main courses $7–$20. AE, DISC, MC, V. Thurs 5–10pm; Fri–Sat 10am–1am; Sun 10am–10pm. Located 4 miles N of Yucca Valley via Pioneertown Rd. TEX-MEX/BARBECUE.

Pappy and Harriet's motto, "Best food in the desert . . . no brag, just fact," might seem a bit over-the-top, but you can definitely make a case for their succulent, mesquite-grilled chicken and steaks and just-right enchiladas. Dr̶ are served in mason jars, pa̶ serve as napkins, and the atmosphere of the grand, old-fashioned Western bar would best be described as rough around the edges. But truth be told, the joint has been a favorite of Southern California musicians for decades, including the legendary Gram Parsons and, more recently, rockers who have used the stage as a recording studio. There's live music every night Pappy and Harriet's is open, from 7 to 11pm.

CAFES

Whether you crave the jolt of a cup of java or a fix of bohemian coffeehouse culture, you won't find the Morongo Basin lacking. **Crossroads Cafe and Tavern,** 61715 Twentynine Palms Hwy. (© **760/366-5414**), offers fresh coffee flown in from Olympia, Washington, fresh fruit smoothies, fresh fish, plus a renowned menu of hot and cold gourmet sandwiches—try the Grilled Coyote: chicken and portobello mushrooms, capped with balsamic mayo. For entertainment, Crossroads offers live music on Saturday nights (usually folk, jazz, or blues). There's also a patio with great views of the Milky Way, far away from the light pollution of the big city. Credit cards are not accepted, and the cafe closes during the hot summer.

Picnic & Camping Supplies

General Stores. If you need camping (or climbing or hiking) gear, visit **Rio Desert Ranch Market,** 73544 Twentynine Palms Hwy., Twentynine Palms (© **760/367-7814**), a general store carrying a limited selection of gear, including boots, cookstoves and fuel, ice chests, and hats. Or check out the **Park Center,** 6554 Park Blvd., Joshua Tree (© **760/366-3448**), near the west entrance to the park; in addition to gift items and work by local artisans, it carries a limited selection of common

items such as water bottles and clothing. A more comprehensive outfitter is 15 minutes away: **Jernigan's Sporting Goods,** 56845 Twentynine Palms Hwy., Yucca Valley (© **760/365-1828**), is in a shopping mall behind Denny's and can help you with everything from tents and lanterns to serious climbing gear and a dozen brands of heavy-duty hiking boots.

Serious Gear. Experienced climbers needing backpack or climbing equipment might want to step into **Nomad Ventures,** 61795 Twentynine Palms Hwy. (© **760/366-4684**), an outfitter conveniently located on the way to the park's west entrance. Open daily, it rents and sells climbing shoes, and sells packs, harnesses, and other necessities of the sport.

Picnic Supplies. Need provisions for picnicking or camping? You can stock up on the way into Yucca Valley, where **Kmart, Wal-Mart, Von's,** and **Stater Brothers** loom large on Highway 62, along with every fast-food joint you can imagine. Once you're in Twentynine Palms, though, try the **Plaza Market** (© **760/367-3464**), across from the chamber of commerce in the Historic Plaza on the northwest corner of Adobe and Two Mile roads. This friendly local market is convenient to the park's north entrance. A good place to pick up sandwiches, salads, and other prepared lunch foods is the **Wonder Garden Café,** 73511 Twentynine Palms Hwy. (© **760/367-2429**), a downtown coffeehouse, deli, and gourmet food emporium popular among locals. You might also try the **Park Center** in the town of Joshua Tree. In addition to being the visitor center for the West Entrance Station, the Park Center has a deli/bakery/coffee bar ready to pack up easy lunches.

22

LASSEN VOLCANIC NATIONAL PARK

by Don & Barbara Laine, with Eric Peterson

STASHED IN THE NORTHEASTERN CORNER OF CALIFORNIA, LASSEN Volcanic National Park is a remarkable reminder that North America is still evolving and that the ground below is alive with the forces of creation and sometimes destruction. Lassen Peak is the southernmost volcano in the Cascade Mountain Range, a chain that also includes Mount St. Helens and stretches all the way north to British Columbia.

Though the 10,457-foot Lassen Peak is dormant, the surrounding landscape is still very much alive. The peak last awakened in May 1914, beginning a cycle of eruptions that spit lava, steam, and ash until 1921. The eruption climaxed in 1915 when Lassen blew its top, sending up a 6-mile-high mushroom cloud of ash that was seen from hundreds of miles away. The peak itself has been dormant for more than three-quarters of a century, but the park's geothermal features still boil with ferocious intensity; boiling springs, fumaroles (vents for volcanic steam and gases), and mud pots are all still very active to this day. Volcanologists, however, cannot predict when any of the volcanoes in the area will erupt again, but they are fairly sure such an event will eventually take place.

Until then, the park gives you an interesting chance to watch a landscape recover from the destruction brought on by an eruption. To the north of Lassen Peak is the aptly named Devastated Area, a swath of volcanic scars steadily repopulating with conifers. Forest botanists have revised their earlier theories that forests must be preceded by herbaceous growth after watching the Devastated Area immediately revegetate with a diverse mix of eight conifer species, four more than were present before the blast.

The 106,000-acre park is a place of great beauty. The flora and fauna are an interesting mix of species from the Cascade Range, stretching north from Lassen; species from the Sierra Nevada, stretching south; and species from the Basin Range, to the east. The resulting blend accounts for an enormous diversity of plants: 715 distinct species have been identified in the park. Though it's snowbound in winter, Lassen is an important summer feeding ground for black bears and transient herds of mule deer.

In addition to the dozens of volcanoes and geothermal features, Lassen Volcanic National Park includes 150 miles of hiking trails, more than 50 beautiful lakes, large meadows, cinder cones, lush forests, cross-country skiing, and great backcountry camping. In fact, three-quarters of the park is designated wilderness.

The Lassen area was inhabited by four groups of American Indians before the arrival of Europeans. The Atsugewi, Maidu, Yana, and Yahi all used portions of the park as their summer hunting grounds. The white man's diseases and encroachment into their territory quickly decimated their population. By the turn of the 20th century, they were thought to be gone from the wilds of the Lassen area. In 1911, however, a nearly naked American Indian man was discovered by butchers at a slaughterhouse in Oroville. When they couldn't communicate with him, the sheriff locked the man in a cell.

News of the "Wild Man" found a receptive audience among anthropologists at the University of California at Berkeley, who quickly rescued the man. Ishi, as he came to be known, turned out to be the last of the Yahi tribe and lived at the university's Museum of Anthropology for 5 years before succumbing to tuberculosis. Ishi, through sharing his knowledge with anthropologist Alfred Kroeber and others, is responsible for much of what's known about Yahi culture in California.

Avoiding the Crowds. Crowds? Forget it. Lassen is one of the least-visited national parks in the contiguous 48 states. Unless you're here on July 4 or Labor Day weekend, you won't encounter anything that could rightly be called a crowd. Even then, you can escape simply by skipping the popular sites, such as Bumpass Hell, Lassen Peak, and the Sulphur Works, and heading a few miles down any of the backcountry trails.

Just the Facts

GETTING THERE & GATEWAYS

Part of the reason Lassen Volcanic National Park is one of the least visited national parks is its remoteness. The most foolproof route is to take Calif. 44 east from Redding (via I-5), which leads to the park's northwest entrance. A shortcut if you're coming from the south along I-5 is Calif. 36 in Red Bluff, which leads to the park's southwest entrance.

If you're arriving from the east via I-80, take the U.S. 395 turnoff at Reno and head to Susanville. Depending on which end of the park you're shooting for, take either Calif. 44 (to the northwest entrance) or Calif. 36 (to the southwest entrance) from Susanville.

Calif. 89 leads to the Park Road, which crosses the park in a 29-mile half-circle, with entrances and visitor contact stations at either end.

Most visitors enter the park at the **Southwest Entrance Station,** drive through the park, and leave through the **north entrance,** or vice versa. Three other entrances lead to remote portions of the park. **Warner Valley** and **Juniper Lake** are reached from the south on the road from Chester. **Butte Lake** entrance is reached by a dirt road from Calif. 44 between Calif. 89 and Susanville.

The Nearest Airport. The closest airport is **Redding Municipal Airport,** 6751 Woodrum Circle (© **530/224-4320**), served by **Horizon Air** and **United Express,** with car rentals from **Avis** and **Hertz** (see the appendix for toll-free reservation numbers). The closest major airports are in Sacramento and Reno.

INFORMATION

Contact the **Superintendent, Lassen Volcanic National Park,** P.O. Box 100, Mineral, CA 96063-0100 (© **530/595-4444;** www.nps.gov/lavo). *Peak Experiences* is a free, handy little newspaper listing activities, hikes, and points of interest. Also useful is Robert and Barbara Decker's *Road Guide to Lassen Volcanic National Park* (Decker Press, 1997), which gives a tour of the park from a motorist's viewpoint. These and other books, plus maps and videos, are available from the **Lassen**

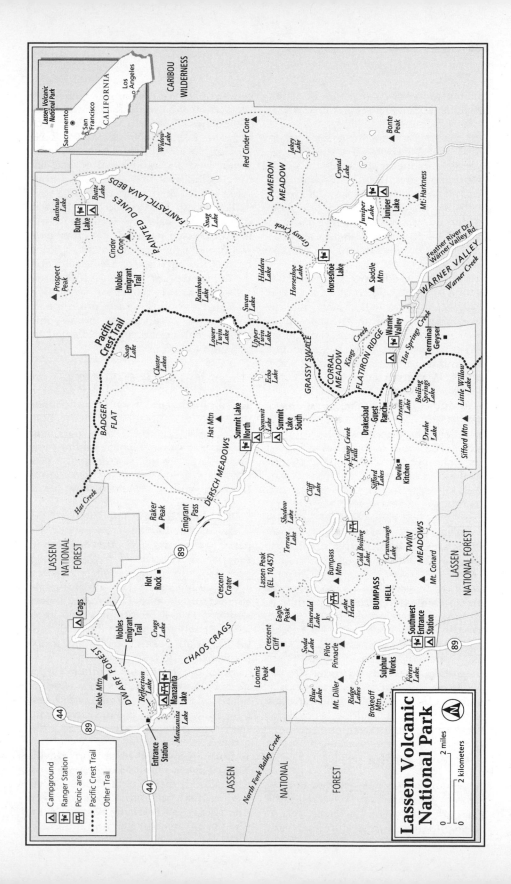

Lassen Volcanic National Park

CALIFORNIA

Lassen Volcanic National Park

Sacramento
San Francisco
Los Angeles

CARIBOU WILDERNESS

Willow Lake
Red Cinder Cone
Jakey Lake
Bonte Peak
Crystal Lake
CAMERON MEADOW
Mt. Harkness
Bathtub Lake
Butte Lake
Juniper Lake
Juniper Lake
Snag Lake
PAINTED DUNES
FANTASTIC LAVA BEDS
Cinder Cone
Hidden Lake
Horseshoe Lake
Horseshoe Lake
Saddle Mtn
Prospect Peak
Rainbow Lake
Feather River Dr./ Warner Valley Rd.
Nobles Emigrant Trail
Swan Lake
Grassy Creek
WARNER VALLEY
Warner Creek
Pacific Crest Trail
Lower Twin Lake
Upper Twin Lake
Echo Lake
GRASSY SWALE
CORRAL MEADOW
FLATIRON RIDGE
Warner Valley
Terminal Geyser
Soap Lake
Cluster Lakes
Kings Creek
Hot Springs Creek
BADGER FLAT
Drakesbad Guest Ranch
Dream Lake
Boiling Springs Lake
Little Willow Lake
Hat Creek
Hat Mtn
Summit Lake North
Summit Lake
Summit Lake South
Kings Creek
Kings Creek Falls
Drake Lake
Sifford Mtn
DERSCH MEADOWS
Sifford Lakes
Devils Kitchen
Raker Peak
Cliff Lake
Emigrant Pass
Shadow Lake
LASSEN NATIONAL FOREST
89
Terrace Lake
Cold Boiling Lake
Crumbaugh Lake
TWIN MEADOWS
Mt. Conard
LASSEN NATIONAL FOREST
Hot Rock
Crescent Crater
Lassen Peak (EL. 10,457)
Bumpass Mtn
BUMPASS HELL
Crags
Crags Lake
Eagle Peak
Emerald Lake
Lake Helen
Nobles Emigrant Trail
Crescent Cliff
Soda Lake
Southwest Entrance Station
CHAOS CRAGS
Loomis Peak
Pilot Pinnacle
Sulphur Works
Forest Lake
89
DWARF FOREST
Table Mtn
Reflection Lake
Manzanita Lake
Manzanita Lake
Blue Lake
Mt. Diller
Ridge Lakes
Brokeoff Mtn
44
89
Entrance Station
North Fork Bailey Creek
LASSEN
NATIONAL
FOREST
44

Legend:
△ Campground
🏚 Ranger Station
🏕 Picnic area
•••• Pacific Crest Trail
⋯⋯ Other Trail

2 miles
0
2 kilometers

Loomis Museum Association (© 530/595-3399; www.lassenloomis.info).

The visitor center is just inside the **north entrance** at the Loomis Museum. The Loomis Museum (open daily late May–late Sept.) provides interpretive displays, ranger-led walks, and informational leaflets. The Loomis Museum also has exhibits, and informational videos are shown.

The **park headquarters** in Mineral, located on Calif. 36, southwest of the park, offers information and publications Monday to Friday (except holidays) year-round. There are additional ranger stations at Summit Lake, and also in the more isolated reaches of the park at Warner Valley, Juniper Lake, and Butte Lake.

At press time, the **Southwest Information Station,** just inside the southwest entrance, was slated for demolition in late 2004. The plan calls for a bigger and better year-round visitor center to open at the same spot in 2007.

Entry into the park for up to a week costs $10 per vehicle or $5 per person on foot, motorcycle, horse, or bike. Camping fees range from $10 to $16. Anyone spending the night in the backcountry must obtain a free wilderness permit.

Because of the dangers posed by the park's thermal features (specifically boiling water), always remain on trails in active areas and heed warning signs. Fires are allowed in campgrounds only. And remember that warm clothing is needed year-round.

The park is in one of the colder areas of California, and temperatures at night can drop below freezing at any time. Blanketing the area with an average of 500 inches of snow a year, winter can begin in late October, and Park Road can be closed until mid-June. Even in summer, you should be prepared for the possibility of rain and snow, and in some years you might even see snowbanks lining the Park Road into July. Winter, however, shows a different and beautiful side of Lassen that more people are starting to appreciate. Since most of the park is over a mile high and the highest point is 10,457 feet, snow accumulates in incredible quantities. (It's also a good thing to think about if you intend to stay in the area—some medical conditions can be affected by this high elevation.)

If You Have Only 1 Day

The highlights of Lassen are, of course, the **volcanoes** and their offshoots: boiling springs, fumaroles, mud pots, and so on. You can see many of the most interesting sites in a day, making it possible to visit Lassen as a short detour from I-5 or U.S. 395 on the way to or from Oregon.

Bumpass Hell, a 1.5-mile walk off the Park Road in the southern part of the park, is the largest geothermal site in the park—16 acres of bubbling mud pots cloaked in a stench of rotten egg–smelling sulfur. The colorful name comes from an early Lassen area homesteader guide, K. V. Bumpass, who lost a leg after falling though thin earth into boiling mud during one of his tours. Don't make the same error.

Sulphur Works is another stinky, steamy example of Lassen's residual heat. Two miles from the southwest park entrance, the ground hisses with seething gases escaping from the ground.

Boiling Springs Lake and **Devil's Kitchen** are two of the more remote geothermal sites; they're in the Warner Valley section of the park, usually accessed from the Feather River Drive/Warner Valley Road near the small town of Chester.

Exploring the Park by Car

The **Park Road** crosses the park in a half-circle with entrance stations at either end, and it is usually open from mid-June through early November. Most visitors enter the park at the Southwest Entrance Station, drive through the park, and leave through the northwest entrance, or vice versa.

The 29-mile tour through this rugged yet captivating region should take no more than a couple of hours, though it's a good idea to factor in a few more hours to hike up Lassen Peak or explore the Devastated Area and Bumpass Hell. If there's still time left, make an effort to stop at Sulphur Works near Mineral (about 2 miles from the southwest entrance), an acrid, noisy cauldron of steam vents that let off a mighty pungent odor.

Organized Tours & Ranger Programs

Free interpretive programs are offered daily in summer, highlighting everything from flora and fauna to cultural history and volcanic processes. Junior Ranger programs are also offered to kids; check park bulletin boards (or the park's website) for a current schedule.

From January to early April, a park ranger leads free 1½- to 2-hour snowshoe hikes across Lassen's snow-packed hills. The tours take place on Saturday afternoons at 1:30pm at the Lassen Chalet, located at the park's southwest entrance. You must be at least 8 years old, warmly dressed, and wearing boots. Snowshoes are provided free of charge on a first-come, first-served basis, though a $1 donation is requested for upkeep. For details, call park headquarters at © 530/595-4444.

Day Hikes

Most Lassen visitors drive through in a day or two, see the geothermal hot spots, and move on. That leaves 150 miles of trails and expanses of backcountry to the few who take the time to get off-road.

Bumpass Hell Trail

1.5 miles one-way. Moderate. Access: The well-marked trailhead is just off the Park Rd. in the southern part of the park.

This walk leads you to the middle of the largest geothermal site in the park—16 acres of bubbling mud pots cloaked in a stench of sulfur. Stay on the wooden boardwalks that safely guide you past the pyrite pools, steam vents, and noisy fumaroles.

Cinder Cone Trail

4 miles RT. Moderate. Access: Butte Lake Campground.

Black and charred, Cinder Cone is almost barren of life, but surrounded by picturesque dunes of multihued volcanic ash. If 4 miles seems too short, you can extend this hike by heading in about 8 miles from Summit Lake on the Park Road, or else diverting to the east side of Butte Lake.

Lassen Peak Trail

2.5 miles one-way. Strenuous. Access: 7 miles from the southwest entrance on the Park Rd.

This climb to the top of Lassen Peak is among the most popular hikes in the park. Two-and-a-half miles may seem like a short distance, but the trail is steep and generally covered with snow until late summer. At 10,457 feet in elevation, though, you'll get a view of the surrounding wilderness that's worth every step of the way. On clear days you can see south all the way to Sutter Buttes near Yuba City and north into the Cascades. The round-trip takes about 4 to 5 hours, and often takes longer for those unaccustomed to high elevation.

Manzanita Lake Trail

1.5 miles RT. Easy. Access: Loomis Museum.

This trek runs along the shoreline of pretty Manzanita Lake, which is 2 miles inside the northwest entrance to the park. It's easy to get to by car, and an easy hike for almost anyone. (If you want to do a bit more distance, you can hike around Reflection Lake as well.)

Nobles Emigrant Trail

11 miles RT. Easy. Access: Northwest entrance.

One of the park's easiest longer hikes is this scenic trail that passes though an old-growth forest, past Chaos Jumbles (pink-hued rocks shaken from nearby volcanoes 300 years ago), and into Lassen's Dwarf Forest, a bizarre region of stunted trees.

Pacific Crest Trail

17 miles one-way. Moderate. Access: Via the Warner Valley Rd. or by a long hike from Hat Lake.

This is a small section of the famed Pacific Crest Trail, which runs some 2,650 miles from Mexico to Canada. The most scenic section of the trail in the park is the 5-mile segment south of Drakesbad that leads toward the park's boundary via Boiling Springs Lake. For information on the entire Pacific Crest Trail, contact the **Pacific Crest Trail Association,** 5325 Elkhorn Blvd., PMB 256, Sacramento, CA 95842 (© **916/ 349-2109;** www.pcta.org).

Paradise Meadow

3.5 miles RT. Moderate. Access: Hat Lake parking area, off Calif. 89 between Emigrant Pass and the Summit Lake campgrounds.

This hike rises at a steady grade along a creek, eventually coming to a series of small waterfalls and a picture-perfect meadow with outstanding wildflower displays during midsummer.

Summit Lake Trail

1.5 miles RT. Easy. Access: Accessible from either of the Summit Lake campgrounds.

This is another walk around a pristine alpine lake that's often frequented by deer in the evening.

Summit Lake to Echo and Twin Lakes

8 miles RT. Moderate. Access: The longer version of the trail breaks off from the midpoint of the Summit Lake Trail (see above).

A popular day or overnight hike, this trek passes several pretty lakes and wildflower-filled meadows on the way to Lower Twin Lake. After you pass the first moderately steep crest, the rest of the hike is less strenuous. Camping is allowed at Twin Lakes, but not Echo Lake.

Other Summer Sports & Activities

Canoeing & Kayaking. Paddlers can take canoes, rowboats, and kayaks on any of the park lakes except Reflection, Emerald, Helen, and Boiling Springs. Motors, including electric motors, are prohibited on all park waters. Lakes accessible from the Park Road include Manzanita and Summit. You can get to Butte Lake in the northeast section of the park on a gravel road from Calif. 44. Juniper Lake can be reached from a gravel road in the southeast section of the park.

Winter Sports & Activities

The Park Road usually closes to cars in November due to snow, and most years it doesn't open until June, so winter recreationists have their run of the area. Snowmobiles are forbidden.

Cross-Country Skiing & Snowshoeing. Trails of all skill levels leave from Manzanita Lake at the north end of the park and Lassen Chalet at the south. There are heated bathrooms and running water at the chalet and Loomis Plaza. Popular trips are the trails to Sulphur Works. More advanced skiers and snowshoers can make the trek to Lake Helen.

You can also ski the popular 30-mile course of the Park Road in an overnight trek, but doing this involves a long car shuttle. For safety reasons, the park requires all skiers to register at the

Lassen Chalet or Loomis Ranger Station before heading into the backcountry, even for a day trip, and a free backcountry permit is required for overnight camping.

Sledding. During winter, heavy snows close Park Road, but the southwest entrance is kept open, allowing access to Lassen Chalet, and the north entrance provides access to the Loomis Ranger Station. On weekends, you can bring snow toys, kids, and picnic baskets and enjoy the slopes.

Camping

Car campers have their choice of eight park campgrounds with over 400 sites. Reservations are available for Manzanita Lake and Summit Lake campgrounds through the **National Recreation Reservation Service** (© 877/444-6777; www. reserveusa.com). Sites do fill up on weekends, so if you don't have a reservation, your best bet is to get to the park early Friday to secure a spot. There are no RV hookups at the park, but you'll find them at nearby private campgrounds, as well as Hat Creek Resort and Lassen Mineral Lodge (see "Where to Stay," below).

By far the most "civilized" campground in the park is at **Manzanita Lake,** where you'll find flush toilets and a camper store. There is also the **Crags Campground,** about 5 miles away, which is much more basic, with vault toilets. Farther into the park along Park Road are the **Summit Lake Campgrounds,** on the north and south ends of Summit Lake, where you'll find flush toilets in the north campground and vault toilets in the south campground. It's a pretty spot, often frequented by deer, and is a launching point for some excellent day hikes. In the southern end of the park is **Southwest Campground,** a walk-in camp directly adjacent to the Lassen Chalet parking lot.

The remote entrances to Lassen have their own campgrounds: **Warner Valley, Butte Lake,** and **Juniper Lake** campgrounds. All three are reached via dirt

roads, and Warner Valley and Juniper Lake are not recommended for trailers.

Backcountry camping is allowed in much of the park, and traffic is light. Ask about closed areas when you get your free wilderness permit, which is issued at the visitor stations and required for anyone spending the night in the backcountry. Fires and dogs are prohibited in the backcountry.

If park campgrounds are full, myriad campgrounds are available in surrounding **Lassen National Forest,** so you'll find a site somewhere. For information, contact the Forest Supervisor's Office, 2550 Riverside Dr., Susanville, CA 96130 (© 530/257-2151).

Where to Stay

INSIDE THE PARK

Drakesbad Guest Ranch

At the end of the Warner Valley Rd. from Chester, in the southern part of the park. (California Guest Services, 2150 Main St., Ste. 5, Red Bluff, CA 96080.) © **530/529-9820** or 530/529-1512. www.drakesbad.com. 19 units. $225–$270 double. Rates include all meals. DISC, MC, V. Open 1st week June to mid-Oct, weather permitting.

The only lodge operating in Lassen Park is Drakesbad, hidden in a high mountain valley and surrounded by meadows, lakes, and streams. The 100-year-old Drakesbad is famous for its rustic cabins, lodge, and steaming thermal swimming pool, fed by a natural hot spring and open 24 hours. Horseback riding is also a big draw. The ranch is as deluxe as only a facility with very little electricity and no phones can be, with quilts on every bed, propane heaters for warmth, and kerosene lamps for light. Daily housekeeping service is provided. Food here is hearty American fare, with an emphasis on fresh fruits and vegetables, and often creative variations on standard dishes. Breakfast and lunch are buffets (sack lunches are also available), and dinners are served at the table. The lodge is extremely popular

Campground	Elev.	Total Sites	RV Hookups	Dump Station	Toilets	Drinking Water
Butte Lake	6,100	101	No	No	Yes	Yes
Crags	5,700	45	No	No	Yes	Yes
*Juniper Lake***	6,792	18	No	No	Yes	No
Manzanita Lake	5,890	179	No	Yes	Yes	Yes
Southwest	6,700	21	No	No	Yes	Yes
Summit Lake (North)	6,695	46	No	No	Yes	Yes
Summit Lake (South)	6,695	48	No	No	Yes	Yes
*Warner Valley***	5,650	18	No	No	Yes	Yes

* Not recommended for trailers since approach is via a dirt road.
** Campgrounds usually open in June or July and close in September, but weather can affect these dates; call park headquarters for actual dates.

and open for only 5 months, so reservations are booked as far as 2 years in advance (Feb is a good time to call to take advantage of cancellations).

NEAR THE PARK

The Bidwell House

1 Main St. (P.O. Box 1790), Chester, CA 96020. ℂ **530/258-3338.** www.bidwellhouse.com. 14 units (12 with private bathroom), 1 cottage. $75–$180 double. Rates include full breakfast. MC, V.

In 1901, Gen. John Bidwell, a California senator who made three unsuccessful bids for the presidency, built a country retreat and summer home for his beloved young wife, Annie. After her death, when Chester had developed into a prosperous logging hamlet, the building, with its farmhouse-style design and spacious veranda, was converted into the headquarters for a local ranch.

Today, the house sits at the extreme eastern end of Chester, adjacent to a rolling meadow. The lake is visible across the road, and inside, Ian and Kim James maintain one of the most charming B&B inns in the region. Seven of the rooms have whirlpool tubs, and three offer wood-burning stoves. The cottage (which sleeps up to six) has a kitchenette. The gourmet omelets are a breakfast favorite.

Hat Creek Resort

Calif. 44/89 (P.O. Box 73), Old Station, CA 96071. ℂ **530/335-7121.** Fax 530/335-7031. hatcreekresort@juno.com. 17 units. $55–$125 double. AE, MC, V. Motel open year-round; cabins open May–Oct.

A haven for hunters and anglers (many of whom make their reservations years in advance), this quiet resort, 11 miles northeast of Lassen Volcanic National Park, features housekeeping cabins and motel rooms situated alongside Hat Creek. The small cabins have double beds, showers only, and kitchens with dishes and basic cooking utensils. (There's a grocery store and deli next door.) The motel rooms are spacious, basic units with queen beds and tub/shower combos. Wagon rides are offered on summer weekends, and the Pacific Crest Trail runs through the property. Also in the resort are an RV park with 52 sites ($21 with full hookups) and a horse hotel ($15; bring your own hay). A restaurant, the **Coyote Grill,** is adjacent to the property.

Lassen Mineral Lodge

Calif. 36 E. (P.O. Box 160), Mineral, CA 96063. ℂ **530/595-4422.** Fax 530/595-4452. www.minerallodge.com. 20 units. $70–$95 double; lower rates in winter. AE, DISC, MC, V.

Showers	Fire Pits/ Grills	Laundry	Public Phone	Reserve	Fees	Open
No	Yes	No	No	No	$14	June–Sept**
No	Yes	No	No	No	$10	June–Sept**
No	Yes	No	No	No	$10	June–Sept**
Yes	Yes	Yes	Yes	Yes	$16	June–Sept**
No	Yes	No	Yes	No	$14	Year-round
No	Yes	No	No	Yes	$16	June–Sept
No	Yes	No	No	Yes	$14	June–Sept
No	Yes	No	No	No	$14	June–Sept

A mere 9 miles south of the park's southern entrance, this family-owned and -operated lodge (established in 1896) offers a homey atmosphere in a delightful forested setting. The motel-style rooms, constructed in the 1940s, are renovated on a near-annual basis and are reliably clean. Most rooms have king or queen beds; several larger rooms also have two twin beds and kitchenettes, making them a good choice for families. In summer, the lodge is almost always bustling with guests and customers who venture into the gift shop, general store, and full-service restaurant and bar (see "Where to Dine," below); and there's good fishing within walking distance. Also on the property is a full-service RV park and campground (call for current rates).

Mill Creek Resort

On Calif. 172 (3 miles south of Calif. 36), Mill Creek, CA 96061. © **888/595-4449** or 530/595-4449. www.millcreekresort.net. 9 cabins. $60–$85 cabin. No credit cards. Pets accepted.

Set deep in the forest, the Mill Creek is a rustic mountain retreat that is well off the beaten path. A homey country general store and coffee shop serve as the resort's center, a good place to stock up on food while exploring Lassen

Volcanic National Park. The basic housekeeping cabins, available on a daily or weekly basis, are clean, cute, and furnished with rustic wooden lodgepole beds. All of the cabins have kitchens.

The Weston House

Red Rock Rd., 1½ miles south of Calif. 44 off Shingletown Ridge Rd. (P.O. Box 276), Shingletown, CA 96088. © **530/474-3738.** www.westonhouse.com. 6 units (2 share a bathroom). $145–$215 double. Rates include full breakfast. MC, V.

Located 19 miles west of Lassen's northwest entrance, The Weston House is a modern B&B with a spectacular location. Sumptuous views of the upper Sacramento Valley abound, from each room as well as from the massive redwood deck with a lap pool and whirlpool tub. The rooms are uniquely decorated with antiques and art. The most luxurious unit is spacious Jennifer's Room, with a full private bathroom, queen-size and twin beds, sofa and love seat, television and VCR, wet bar, wood stove, and patio. The gourmet breakfast menu might include frittatas or croissant French toast, accompanied by fresh fruit and beverages. The entire inn is nonsmoking.

Where to Dine

INSIDE THE PARK

The only sit-down restaurant in the park (besides the Drakesbad Guest Ranch; see "Where to Stay," above) is the **Lassen Chalet** (© 530/595-3376), which serves basic American breakfasts plus sandwiches and burgers for lunch or an early supper. At the park's southwest entrance, it's open late May to early October, daily from 9am to 6pm in mid-summer, closing at 4pm at the beginning and end of the season. There's also a snack bar, with sandwiches, hot dogs, and the like, at the **Manzanita Lake Camper Store** (© 530/335-7557), at the park's north entrance, open late May to early October, daily from 8am to 8pm in midsummer, 9am to 4pm at the beginning and end of the season.

NEAR THE PARK

Restaurant choices in the area are limited, and the best approach may be to either stay at a B&B or lodge that offers meals or book a room (or stay at a campsite) where you can prepare your own. See "Where to Stay" and "Camping," above.

There are, however, a few eateries fairly close to the park, primarily in Chester and on the shores of Lake Almanor. From the south entrance, the closest restaurant is the **Lassen Mineral Lodge** (see "Where to Stay," above), which serves basic American fare—try the barbecued pork ribs—plus a few

Italian, Mexican, and vegetarian items, with both indoor and outdoor dining, in a picturesque setting. You can also head southeast on Calif. 36 to Chester and dine at the **Knotbumper,** 274 Main St. (© 530/258-2301), one of the area's better restaurants, which serves eclectic gourmet lunches and dinners. Another local favorite in Chester is the **Kopper Kettle,** Main and Myrtle streets (© 530/258-2698), specializing in breakfast fare and pancakes that fill up the entire plate.

On the Lake Almanor Peninsula, **Tantardino's,** 401 Ponderosa Dr. (© 530/596-3902), is a time-tested pizzeria and Italian restaurant. A great lunch spot (and prime rib spot on Friday evenings) is **BJ's BBQ & Deli,** 3881 Hwy. A-13 (© 530/596-4210). For a fancy dinner, locals head to the **Lake Almanor Inn,** 3965 Hwy. A-13 (© 530/596-3910), for steaks, seafood, and pasta dishes.

Picnic & Camping Supplies

The **Manzanita Lake Camper Store** (© 530/335-7557), at the park's north entrance, is a good place to stock up on groceries, ice, firewood, and basic outdoor gear. It also sells gasoline. At the southern end of the park, you'll find just about everything you need for your outdoor adventure in the old-fashioned general store at **Lassen Mineral Lodge,** on Calif. 36 in Mineral (see "Where to Stay," above). In Old Station, try the store at **Rim Rock Ranch Resort,** 13275 Calif. 89 (© 530/335-7114), where you'll also find an assortment of cabins and motel rooms.

23

MESA VERDE, CANYON DE CHELLY, CHACO & OTHER ARCHAEOLOGICAL SITES OF THE FOUR CORNERS REGION

by Don & Barbara Laine

ITH ALMOST 5,000 ARCHAEOLOGICAL SITES, MESA VERDE National Park is the largest archaeological preserve in the United States. Among the sites are some of the largest cliff dwellings in the world as well as mesa-top pueblos, pit houses, and kivas (subterranean rooms used for meetings and religious ceremonies)—all of which were built by the Ancestral Puebloans (also called the Anasazi). The sites here tell the story of an 800-year period (A.D. 500–1300) during which these people shifted from a seminomadic hunter-gatherer lifestyle to a largely agrarian way of life centered around large communities in cliff dwellings.

Mesa Verde must have looked inviting to the Ancestral Puebloans, whose descendants are such modern Pueblo tribes as the Hopi, Zuni, and Acoma. On the mesa's north side, 2,000-foot-high cliffs form a natural barrier to invaders. The mesa slopes gently to the south, and erosion has carved numerous canyons, most of which receive abundant sunlight and have natural overhangs for shelter.

The Ancestral Puebloans became especially adept at surviving here. The mesa tops were covered with loess, a red, wind-blown soil good for farming. And while water was scarce, it could seep into the sandstone overhangs where they eventually made their homes. For food, they farmed beans, corn, and squash; raised turkeys; foraged in the pinyon-juniper woodland; and hunted for game such as cottontail rabbits and deer. They wove sandals and clothing from yucca fibers, and traded for precious stones and shells, which they used to make jewelry.

To the visitor today, however, their most impressive accomplishments are the multistoried cliff dwellings, which were largely ignored until ranchers Charlie Mason and Richard Wetherill chanced upon them in 1888. Looting of artifacts followed their discovery until a

What's in a Name?

The prehistoric inhabitants of the ancient villages of the Four Corners region have long been known as the Anasazi. That word is being phased out, however, in favor of the term Ancestral Puebloans because modern American Indians who trace their roots to the Ancestral Puebloans consider the word Anasazi demeaning. *Anasazi* is a Navajo word that means, at least according to some sources, "enemy of my people," as the Navajos considered the Ancestral Puebloans their enemies. Some are also using the term ancient Pueblo people.

Denver newspaper reporter's stories aroused national interest in protecting them. The 52,000-acre site was declared a national park in 1906—it's the only U.S. national park devoted entirely to the works of humans.

Lightning-caused fires blackened about 58% of the park during the summers of 2000 and 2002, closing the park for several weeks each summer. Officials said that although the park's pinyon-juniper forests were severely burned, none of the major archaeological sites were damaged, and, in fact, the fires revealed some sites that park workers did not know existed.

The **Cliff Palace,** the park's largest and best-known site, is a four-story apartment complex with stepped-back roofs forming courtyards for the dwellings above. Accessible by guided tour only, it is reached by a quarter-mile downhill path. Its towers, walls, and kivas are all set back beneath the rim of a cliff. Another ranger-led tour takes visitors up a 32-foot ladder to explore the interior of **Balcony House.** Each of these tours is given only in summer and into fall.

Two other important sites—**Step House** and **Long House,** both on Wetherill Mesa—can be visited in summer only. Rangers lead tours to **Spruce Tree House,** another of the major cliff-dwelling complexes, only in winter, when other park facilities are closed; during the summer you can see Spruce Tree House on your own.

For reasons as yet not understood, these cliff homes were only fully occupied for about a century; their residents left about 1300.

Although Mesa Verde is the largest and probably the most impressive archaeological site in the Four Corners region, it is not the only one. In fact, archaeologists say that from about 700 to 1,000 years ago this area was teeming with busy communities. Following the discussion of Mesa Verde is a quick look at some of the other important archaeological attractions in the region.

Avoiding the Crowds. With 600,000 visitors annually, Mesa Verde seems packed at times. But park officials point out that the numbers are much lower just before and after the summer rush. They say that June 15 to August 15 is the high summer visitation period, and that if people visit during the first 2 weeks of June or the last 2 weeks of August, they'll see fewer crowds.

Another way to beat the crowds is to make the 12-mile drive to Wetherill Mesa. In one recent year only 5% of the park's visitors—just over 30,000 people—ventured to the mesa, which has some of the park's most interesting archaeological sites. The third and perhaps best way to beat the crowds is to hike one of the backcountry trails. As one former park ranger told us, "With our backcountry closed to camping, our hiking trails aren't used very much, and these are great ways for people to get away."

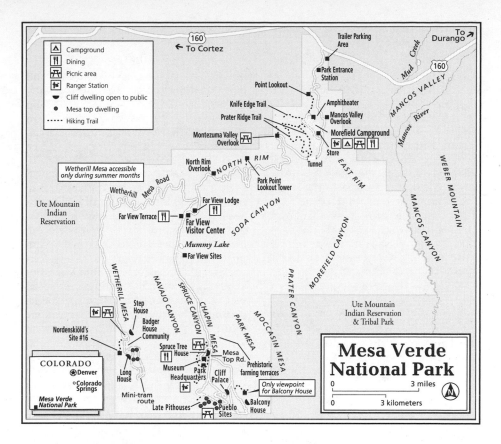

Legend:
- ⌂ Campground
- ⟡ Dining
- ⊞ Picnic area
- ⟟ Ranger Station
- ⌐ Cliff dwelling open to public
- ● Mesa top dwelling
- ····· Hiking Trail

Mesa Verde National Park

0 ————— 3 miles

0 ————— 3 kilometers

Just the Facts

GETTING THERE & GATEWAYS

Mesa Verde National Park is in southwestern Colorado, just under 400 miles southwest of Denver and 252 miles northwest of Albuquerque. The park entrance is located on U.S. 160, 10 miles east of the town of Cortez and 6 miles west of Mancos.

From Cortez, U.S. 491 (formerly U.S. 666) runs north to Monticello, Utah (and on to Salt Lake City), and south to Gallup, New Mexico (on I-40). U.S. 160 runs east through Durango to Walsenburg and I-25, and west through the Four Corners area into Arizona. Colo. 145, north to Telluride and Grand Junction, intersects U.S. 160 at the east end of town.

The Nearest Airport. Cortez Municipal Airport (✆ 970/565-7458), about 3 miles southwest of town off U.S. 491 and U.S. 160, is served by **Great Lakes Airlines** (✆ 970/565-9510), which offers daily service between Cortez and Denver, and has rental cars from **Enterprise** and **Budget** (✆ 970/565-9168). Toll-free reservation numbers are in the appendix.

INFORMATION

Contact **Mesa Verde National Park,** P.O. Box 8, Mesa Verde N.P., CO 81330 (✆ 970/529-4465; www.nps.gov/meve). For advance information on southwestern Colorado, contact the **Mesa Verde Country Visitor Information Bureau,** P.O. Box HH, Cortez, CO 81321 (✆ 800/253-1616; www.mesaverdecountry.com); and when you get in the area, stop at the **Colorado Welcome Center at Cortez,** Cortez City Park, 928 E. Main St. (✆ 970/565-4048).

For more in-depth background, *The Story of Mesa Verde* (1980, Mesa Verde Museum Association) written by Gil Wenger, a former chief archaeologist at the park, summarizes the natural and human histories of this area, tracing developments in the Ancestral Puebloan culture. In *Indians of the Mesa Verde* (Mesa Verde Museum Association), author Don Watson attempts to re-create a year (1268) in the life of the Ancestral Puebloans at Cliff Palace. These books and others are available from the **Mesa Verde Museum Association,** P.O. Box 38, Mesa Verde, CO 81330 (© **800/305-6053** or 970/529-4445; www.mesaverde.org).

VISITOR CENTERS

The **Far View Visitor Center,** 14 miles southwest of the park entrance, is the only place that sells tickets for the ranger-guided hikes. There's an information desk, an impressive display of American Indian art, and a small bookstore. It's open only during the summer.

The staff at the small **Morefield Ranger Station** in Morefield Village also provide park information. It's open in summer only, usually during the afternoon and early evening.

The **Chapin Mesa Archaeological Museum** (open year-round) has dioramas and interpretive displays on Pueblo culture, a ranger-staffed information desk, and a bookstore.

FEES

Entry for up to 7 days costs $10 per vehicle, and there are also fees for guided tours (see "Organized Tours & Ranger Programs," below).

GETTING AROUND

The Park Service operates a **minitram** in the Wetherill Mesa area during the summer season. Leaving from the parking area, it takes you to the main archaeological sites, a real time-saver since your only other choice is to hike; cars aren't permitted in this area beyond the parking area.

SPECIAL REGULATIONS & WARNINGS

To protect the many archaeological sites, the Park Service has outlawed backcountry camping and off-trail hiking. It's also illegal to enter cliff dwellings without a ranger present. Similarly, all artifacts and archaeological sites are protected by federal law.

The Wetherill Mesa Road cannot accommodate vehicles longer than 25 feet. Cyclists must have lights to pedal through the tunnel on the entrance road.

SEASONS & CLIMATE

With an average annual precipitation of just 18 inches, Mesa Verde remains dry despite being between 6,000 feet and 8,572 feet high. June is the driest month, with ⅔ inch of rain; and August is the wettest, with 2 inches. The park typically receives 80 inches of snow in a season. Summer temperatures tend to be about 10° cooler than in the nearby Montezuma Valley. Even during July, the hottest month, highs average an easily bearable 87°F (30°C) and nighttime lows dip into the mid-50s (lower teens Celsius). In winter, temperatures on the mesa can sometimes be 10° warmer than in the valley. This happens during calm, clear periods when cold air is trapped in the lowlands. Daytime highs on the mesa average in the low 40s (single digits Celsius) in December, January, and February.

Because winter storms often continue well into March, spring tends to come late. Warm autumns, however, are not uncommon. In April, average temperatures are 5° cooler than in October with 60s (teens Celsius) for highs and 30s (single digits Celsius) for lows.

Throughout the summer, American Indian artists demonstrate their crafts at various locations in the park, and in August, Hopi dancers perform at **Chapin Mesa Amphitheater.** Contact the park for exact dates.

If You Have Only 1 Day

If you have only a day to spend at the park, stop first at the Far View Visitor Center to buy tickets for a late-afternoon tour of either **Cliff Palace** or **Balcony House**—visitors are not allowed to tour both on the same day. Then travel to the **Chapin Mesa Museum** for a look at the history behind the sites you're about to see. From here, walk down the trail behind the museum to **Spruce Tree House.** Lunch at Spruce Tree Terrace, then take the **Mesa Top Loop Road.** Cap your day with the guided tour. If time permits, you may wish to stop at **Far View Sites** on your way out of the park.

Exploring the Park by Car

The main scenic drive in the park is the **Mesa Top Loop Road.** Each of the 10 stops along this 6-mile loop either overlooks cliff dwellings or is a short walk from mesa-top dwellings. The sites date from A.D. 675 to A.D. 1275 and include structures from the Basket Maker and three Pueblo periods. By reading the interpretive panels at each site, you can learn about the developments in architecture and the changes in Pueblo culture during those periods. Highlights include the **Square Tower House Viewpoint,** where binoculars are handy in spotting the myriad cliff dwellings in this canyon; **Sun Point Pueblo,** where a tunnel links a kiva—a subterranean room used in ceremonies—to a lookout tower; and the mysterious **Sun Temple,** a D-shaped structure that may have been a shrine or community gathering area.

On your way back to the Far View Visitor Center, consider stopping at the **Far View Sites Complex,** located 1 mile south of the Far View Visitor Center; six sites are within walking distance, including what seems to be the remains of an ancient reservoir.

Organized Tours & Ranger Programs

Three of the park's spectacular cliff dwellings—Cliff Palace, Balcony House, and Long House—can only be visited during ranger-guided tours. Tickets ($2.50) go on sale daily at 8am at the Far View Visitor Center. Visitors may tour Long House and either Cliff Palace or Balcony House on the same day, but may not tour both Cliff Palace and Balcony House in 1 day. (We suggest that first-time visitors with only 1 day to spend here tour Cliff Palace, the largest site in the park)

Departing every half-hour between 9am and 6pm, the **Cliff Palace** tour involves a 100-vertical-foot descent to the dwelling and a same-height climb to exit. In between, you'll have to scale four 10-foot-high ladders. The effort is well worth it. With 151 rooms and 23 kivas, Cliff Palace is the largest cliff dwelling in the Southwest and one of the largest in the world. Especially striking is the original red-and-white wall painting that remains inside a four-story tower.

Merely reaching the 45-room **Balcony House,** the most fortresslike of the Mesa Verde dwellings, will make you appreciate the agility of the Ancestral Puebloans, who used hand and footholds and log ladders to scale the cliffs. During the tour, you'll descend 90 vertical feet of stairs, climb 32- and 20-foot-long ladders, and slip through a narrow 12-foot-long crawl space. When you do reach the dwelling, you'll be standing on a level stone floor 700 feet above the floor of Soda Canyon. The Puebloans dumped tons of fill inside

15-foot-high stone retaining walls below this floor, creating a level surface on which to build. Tours run every half-hour between 9am and 5pm.

Some people remember the **Long House** tour for its half-mile walk, the flight of 52 stairs, and the two 15-foot-high ladders they have to negotiate. Others will recall the dwelling itself, with its 21 kivas and 150 rooms stretching across a long alcove in Rock Canyon. At its center is a large plaza where the community gathered and danced. Granaries are tucked like mud dauber nests into two smaller alcoves (one above the other) to the rear of the large one. Tours meet at the minitram depot on Wetherill Mesa and run regularly from 10am to 4pm.

The Cliff Palace tours run from mid-April to mid-November, a few weeks longer than the season for Balcony House. Wetherill Mesa, site of Long House, is open only from Memorial Day weekend through Labor Day. To replace these attractions during the off season, the park offers ranger-guided tours of Spruce Tree House, a self-guided area in summer. Call the park to find out the exact opening and closing dates for its tours.

In addition to the ranger-guided tours, park concessionaire Aramark offers **comprehensive half- and full-day guided tours** from spring through early fall, leaving from Morefield Campground and Far View Lodge. Transportation is provided, and full-day tours include lunch. Rates for half-day tours are $34 to $37 for adults and $23 to $26 for children from 5 to 17; full-day tours are $56 to $61 for adults, $44 to $49 for children 5 to 17 (both tours are free for kids under 5). Get details at the campground or lodge or from **Aramark,** P.O. Box 277, Mancos, CO 81328 (✆ **800/449-2288** or 970/533-1944; www.visitmesaverde.com).

Day Hikes

Although none of the trails to the Mesa Verde sites are strenuous, the 7,000-foot elevation can make the treks tiring for visitors who aren't used to the altitude.

SHORTER TRAILS ON CHAPIN MESA

Spruce Tree House

0.25 mile one-way. Easy. Access: Chapin Mesa Museum.

Open from 8:30am to 6:30pm daily during summer, this paved trail descends from behind Chapin Mesa Museum to Spruce Tree House, a dwelling with 130 rooms and 8 kivas. Because Spruce Tree House sits in an 89-foot-deep alcove, this is the best-preserved dwelling at Mesa Verde. Rangers are here to answer questions during high season. Off season, they guide tours here. The trail is accessible to the mobility-impaired, although they may require assistance on some of its grades.

ON WETHERILL MESA

Badger House Community Trail

0.75 mile RT. Easy. Access: Wetherill Mesa parking area.

This tour, accessible to travelers with disabilities, visits mesa-top sites on Wetherill Mesa. Usually uncrowded, the paved trail is accessible from one of three minitram stops or by making a longer walk from the parking area. The 12-stop self-guided tour details 600 years of history.

Nordenskiold's Site no. 16 Trail

2 miles RT. Easy. Access: Wetherill Mesa parking area.

Begin this quiet hike by taking the minitram to its trailhead, or by making a longer walk from the parking area. Mostly flat, the dirt trail descends over rocks for the last few yards before it reaches an overlook of Site no. 16, a 50-room cliff dwelling that was occupied for most of the 13th century. On the way, the self-guided tour identifies many of the plants in the area.

Step House

0.5 mile RT. Moderate. Access: Wetherill Mesa parking area.

This loop descends roughly 75 feet of stairs and switchbacks to Step House, a cliff dwelling that dates from A.D. 1226. Three Modified Basket Maker pit houses dating from A.D. 626 are found to the left of Step House (as you look toward it). A set of prehistoric stone stairs climbs from these dwellings toward a break in the cliffs.

NEAR MOREFIELD CAMPGROUND

Knife Edge Trail

1.5 miles RT. Easy. Access: Near Morefield Village.

This trail follows the old Knife Edge Road, the only automobile route into the park until a tunnel was blasted between Prater and Morefield canyons in 1957. Now, during wet years, wildflowers brighten the old roadbed, which hugs the side of Prater Ridge on one side and drops off all the way to the Montezuma Valley on the other. A self-guided tour identifies many of the plant species along the trail. From the end of this trail, you can watch the sun set behind Sleeping Ute Mountain.

Point Lookout Trail

2.3 miles RT. Moderate. Access: Near Morefield Village.

This trail rises in tight switchbacks from the northeast corner of the campground to the top of Point Lookout, a monument conspicuous from near the park's entrance. It then traverses the top of this butte to a stunning overlook of the Montezuma Valley. Sheer drops in several places make this trail unsuitable for small children.

Prater Ridge Trail

7.8 miles RT. Moderate. Access: Near Morefield Village.

This loop rises 700 feet from the campground's west side to the top of Prater Ridge. Once atop the ridge, the trail forks, looping around the top of the mesa and opening onto views of the Montezuma and Mancos valleys and the La Plata Mountains. A cutoff trail halves the mesa-top loop, which zigzags around a number of side canyons. Because the trail is faint in places where it crosses the sandstone, some route-finding skills may be necessary. Fire in the summer of 2000 damaged the area, leaving almost no shade along the trail.

LONGER TRAILS ON CHAPIN MESA

Three backcountry trails on Chapin Mesa are open to day hikers. Before hiking the Petroglyph Point and Spruce Canyon trails, register at the trailhead, where a booklet for the self-guided tour on the Petroglyph Point Trail can be borrowed or purchased for 50¢. No registration is required for the Soda Canyon Overlook Trail.

Petroglyph Point Trail

2.8 miles RT. Moderate. Access: A short distance down the paved trail to Spruce Tree House site, just below the Chapin Mesa Museum and Chief Ranger Station.

This loop trail travels just below the rim of a side canyon of Spruce Canyon. It eventually reaches Petroglyph Point, one of the park's most impressive panels of rock art. Just past the petroglyphs, the trail climbs to the rim. It stays on the relatively flat rimrock for its return to Chapin Mesa Museum.

Soda Canyon Overlook Trail

1.5 miles RT. Easy. Access: A pullout on the Cliff Palace Loop Rd.

This trail crosses the rim from a parking area on the Cliff Palace Loop Road to overlooks of Soda Canyon and Balcony House. To view Balcony House, go right when the trail forks.

Spruce Canyon Trail

2.1 miles RT. Moderate. Access: Same as Pet-roglyph Point Trail.

This loop descends 500 feet into a trib-utary of Spruce Canyon. Turning to the north, it travels up the bed of Spruce Canyon before climbing in steep switch-backs to the rim. It reaches the rim near the park's picnic area, a short walk from Chapin Mesa Museum. The vege-tation along the bottom of the canyon includes Douglas firs and ponderosa pines, which flourish in the moist, cool canyon-bottom soil. Damaged by fire in 2002, the exit area of the trail has little shade in the afternoon.

Camping

The impressive **Morefield Campground,** c/o Aramark, P.O. Box 277, Mancos, CO 81328 (© **800/449-2288** or 970/ 533-1944; www.visitmesaverde.com), located 4 miles past the entrance station on the park's entrance road, is among the largest in the national park system. Its 435 sites line four loop roads on the gently sloping floor of Morefield Canyon. For tent campers, the sites on Navajo Loop afford extra privacy. Though lower than the others, this loop is free of RVs and cuts into dense clus-ters of gambel oak.

If you prefer panoramic vistas, head for Hopi Loop, where the campsites are higher and less wooded than the others, affording views down the canyon. At dusk on most nights, mule deer browse in the bushes around many campsites. RVers will find 15 water-electric hookups. Show-ers cost $1 at Morefield Village, just out-side the campground entrance, where a self-serve laundry is also available. The campground has toilets, drinking water, and public phones. The fee is $25 for 1 of the 15 RV hookup sites, $19 for non-hookup sites. The campground is closed from late October through late April (call ahead for exact dates). Reservations are accepted for the basic sites, although almost never needed, but not for the sites with RV hookups.

Where to Stay

INSIDE THE PARK

Far View Lodge

C/o Aramark, P.O. Box 277, Mancos, CO 81328. © **800/449-2288** or 970/533-1944. www.visitmesaverde.com. 150 units. $82–$134 dou-ble. Closed Nov–Mar. AE, DC, DISC, MC, V. Pets accepted with a deposit.

This is our first choice for lodging when visiting Mesa Verde National Park, but we have to admit that the rooms are nothing special—what you're paying for here is the location. You can save an hour or more each day by staying here and not commuting to the park, and this should free up time for relaxing in the captain's chairs on the private deck of your room, from which you'll see as far as New Mexico on a clear day. Located in 17 buildings scattered across the hilltop, the rooms are basic, and don't have TVs or phones. Each unit has a convex ceiling, Southwestern decor, and either one queen-size bed or two doubles. What are called deluxe rooms also have refrigerators and coffeemak-ers. All rooms are nonsmoking. The lodge's restaurant is reviewed below.

NEAR THE PARK

Summer is the busy season, and that's when you'll pay the highest lodging rates. In addition to the properties dis-cussed below, you'll find comfortable, reasonably priced lodging in Cortez (zip code 81321) at: **Best Western Sands,** 1120 E. Main St. (© **970/565-3761**), with double rates of $45 to $89; **Best Western Turquoise Inn & Suites,** 535 E. Main St. (© **800/547-3376** [direct] or 970/565-3778), with rates for two from $64 to $149; **Comfort Inn,** 2321 E. Main St. (© **970/565-3400**), which charges $59 to $109 for two; **Days Inn,** 430 N.

Colo. 145 (© **970/565-8577**), with double rates of $55 to $100; and **Super 8,** 505 E. Main St. (© **970/565-8888**), with rates of $46 to $76 double. National toll-free reservations numbers for these chains are listed in the appendix.

Anasazi Motor Inn

640 S. Broadway, Cortez, CO 81321. © **800/ 972-6232** or 970/565-3773. www.anasazi motorinn.com. 87 units. A/C TV TEL. $55–$71 double. AE, DC, DISC, MC, V. Pets accepted.

This attractive independent motel offers spacious Southwest-decorated rooms with either one king-size bed or two queens, plus an outdoor heated swimming pool, hot tub, sand volleyball court, restaurant with American cuisine, and lounge. Large murals—one of pueblo sites, the other of American Indian dances—add color to cinderblock buildings. Many of the ground-floor rooms have patios.

Holiday Inn Express

2121 E. Main, Cortez, CO 81321. © **800/626- 5652** or 970/565-6000. www.coloradoholiday. com. 100 units. A/C TV TEL. $79–$149 double. Rates include continental breakfast. AE, DC, DISC, MC, V. Pets accepted.

The thousands of flowering plants on the grounds of this family-owned and -operated hotel draw travelers like nectar draws hummingbirds. Once on the hotel grounds, guests flit between luxuries—a 15-station fitness center, an indoor swimming pool, a hot tub, and the margaritas and draft beer at **Ko Ko's Friendly Pub**—or they simply relax in one of the comfortable and spotlessly clean Southwest-decor guest rooms, most of which have views of Mesa Verde or Sleeping Ute Mountain. Standard rooms have two queen-size beds or one king, and several suites have been specially designed for kids—in addition to having a king-size bed for the parents, a microwave, and a refrigerator, each comes with a partitioned area for the

kids that's modeled after a Western fort, with bunk beds and a separate TV with VCR and a game station.

Travelodge

440 S. Broadway, Cortez, CO 81321. © **800/ 578-7878** or 970/565-7778. Fax 970/565- 7214. 42 units. A/C TV TEL. $42–$79 double. Rates include continental breakfast. AE, DISC, MC, V. Pets accepted with deposit.

A good choice for the budget-conscious, this well-maintained Travelodge has flower boxes decorating the buildings, plus a heated outdoor swimming pool, whirlpool, and guest laundry. Most of the attractive modern American motel-style rooms have good quality queen beds, and a few have kings. You'll find tub/shower combos in 31 rooms, showers only in the rest. There's also in-room coffee.

Where to Dine

INSIDE THE PARK

Reservations are not accepted at any of the restaurants within the park, which are all operated by **Aramark** (© **800/ 449-2288** or 970/533-1944; www.visit mesaverde.com). In addition to the restaurants discussed below, a cafe at the Morefield Campground serves an all-you-can-eat pancake breakfast when the campground is open.

Far View Terrace

Across from the Far View Visitor Center. © **800/ 449-2288** or 970/533-1944. Main courses $4.95–$9.95. Daily 6:30am–9pm. Closed late Oct to mid-Apr. AE, DISC, MC, V. AMERICAN/ REGIONAL.

This food court offers a variety of foods, cafeteria-style, with a wide-ranging menu that includes pancakes and eggs at breakfast; and salads, sandwiches, burgers, pizzas, and Southwestern dishes at lunch and dinner—the Navajo taco is a specialty. While dining, you can see as far as New Mexico through a long bank of windows.

Metate Room

Far View Lodge, across from Far View Visitor Center, 17 miles down the park entrance road. ☎ **970/529-4423.** Main courses $9.95–$27. AE, DISC, MC, V. Daily 5–9:30pm. Closed late Oct to mid-Apr. SOUTHWESTERN.

The best and by far the most expensive restaurant in the park, the Metate Room specializes in Southwestern and American Indian–inspired dishes. Try the oven-roasted chicken breast with green-chile stuffing, served on tangy salsa; a mixed grill of lamb, pheasant, and buffalo; or chorizo-stuffed mushrooms topped with jack cheese. The restaurant displays high-quality American Indian rugs and pottery, which you might not notice, given the breathtaking views from the windows.

Spruce Tree Terrace

Across from Chapin Mesa Museum. Most items $3.95–$7.95. AE, DISC, MC, V. Daily 9am–6pm mid-Apr to Oct; shorter hours Nov to mid-Apr. AMERICAN.

Although hamburgers, cheeseburgers, and hot dogs dominate the menu at this fast-food cafeteria, deli-style sandwiches, tossed salads, yogurt, and ice cream are also available. Sit in the Southwestern-style dining area, or take your food out onto the deck.

NEAR THE PARK

Homesteaders Restaurant

45 E. Main St., Cortez ☎ **970/565-6253.** www.thehomesteaders.com. Main courses $3.40–$6 lunch, $4.60–$16 dinner. AE, DISC, MC, V. Mon–Sat 11am–9:30pm. AMERICAN/MEXICAN.

A rustic, Old West atmosphere pervades this popular family restaurant, with lots of wood, historic photos, and pioneer memorabilia. The menu has a good selection of home-style American basics, with charbroiled beef including burgers,

T-bones, and top sirloins. Those wanting a bit more zip might try the Southwestern steak—top sirloin smothered with salsa, green chiles, and cheese. We also suggest the barbecued baby-back ribs and the old-fashioned dinners, such as thin-sliced roast beef or deep fried catfish filet. Several Mexican standards are also offered, as well as salads and vegetarian items. Smoking is not permitted.

Main St. Brewery and Restaurant

21 E. Main, Cortez. ☎ **970/564-9112.** Reservations not accepted. Main courses $6.95–$18. AE, MC, V. Daily 3pm–midnight. AMERICAN.

Modern thin-bladed fans mince the air under a stamped-tin ceiling, and fanciful murals splash color above subdued wood paneling. The pleasant contrasts found in the decor carry over to the menu. In addition to brewpub staples such as fish and chips, pizza, and bratwurst, you'll find steaks and prime rib plus a vegetarian skewer plate and Rocky Mountain trout on the menu. The beers brewed here complement the food. We especially recommend the hoppy, slightly bitter "Pale Export" and the porter. Smoking is not permitted.

Nero's

303 W. Main St., Cortez. ☎ **970/565-7366.** http://subee.com/neros/home.html. Main courses $6.95–$21. Reservations recommended in summer. AE, MC, V. Daily 5–10pm; closed Sun in winter. ITALIAN/AMERICAN.

Among our favorite places for a good meal in southwestern Colorado, Nero's is a small, homey restaurant with a Southwestern art-gallery decor that doubles its capacity in summer with an outdoor patio. The innovative entrees prepared by chef Richard Gurd include house specialties such as the cowboy steak (a charbroiled sirloin seasoned with a spicy steak rub) and the mushroom ravioli (with Alfredo sauce, sautéed spinach, sun-dried tomatoes, mushrooms, and pecans). All told, there's an excellent selection of beef,

Kokopelli: Casanova or Traveling Salesman?

Of the many subjects of rock art found in the West, one claims both a name and a gender: He's Kokopelli, and he's been found in ruins dating as early as A.D. 200 and as late as the 16th century. The consistency of the depictions of him over a wide geographic area indicates that Kokopelli was a well-traveled and universally recognized deity of considerable importance. The figure is generally seen as hunchbacked and playing a flute. His image is still used by potters, weavers, and painters, as well as for decoration on jewelry and clothing. Kokopelli has never been an evil character, although he's frequently been a comic one.

Until quite recent times, legends of Kokopelli were still current among the Pueblo peoples of the Four Corners area. Although the many stories differ in detail, almost all connect Kokopelli to a fertility theme. Sometimes he's a wandering minstrel with a sack of songs on his back; other times he is greeted as a god of the harvest.

The Hopi of First Mesa seem to identify him with an unethical guide of Spanish friars searching for the Seven Cities of Cibola in 1539. This guide was more interested in making passes at Hopi maidens than in searching for the fabled cities, according to legend, and Hopi men consequently shot him with arrows and buried him under a pile of rocks. Another Hopi village holds Kokopelli to be a sort of traveling salesman who traded deerskin shirts and moccasins for brides. Yet another Hopi legend has him seducing the daughters of a household and sewing shirts, while his wife chased the men.

The Hopi also make kachina dolls of Kokopelli, and one of his wife, Kokopelli-mana, both of which are sold to tourists. As with most kachina dolls, there was also a real-life kachina dancer, who used to make explicit gestures to female tourists and missionaries—until the visitors found out what the gestures meant. Many early peoples welcomed Kokopelli around corn-planting time, and married women, hoping to conceive, sought his blessing. Single maidens, however, fled in panic.

---

plus seafood, chicken, veal, and homemade pasta. Smoking is not permitted in the dining room, but is allowed at the bar.

Picnic & Camping Supplies

Inside the park, a general store in Morefield Village sells camping supplies and groceries from late April through late October. In nearby Cortez, **City Market,** 508 E. Main (© **970/565-6504**), with a deli, bakery, and excellent salad bar, sells everything you might want for a picnic or family outing, including fishing licenses.

Nearby National Monuments & Archaeological Sites

The major archaeological center of the United States, the Four Corners area—where the states of Colorado, New Mexico, Arizona, and Utah meet—is surrounded by a vast complex of ancient villages that dominated this entire region a thousand years ago. Here among the reddish-brown rocks, abandoned canyons, and flat mesas, you'll discover another world, once ruled by the Ancestral Puebloans (Anasazi), and today largely the domain of the Navajo.

HOVENWEEP NATIONAL MONUMENT

Preserving some of the most striking and isolated archaeological sites in the Four Corners area, **Hovenweep** is the Ute word for "deserted valley." Its inhabitants apparently left the area around 1300, and even today it's often overlooked by tourists, who instead flock to its more famous neighbor, Mesa Verde. Hovenweep contains six separate sites, and is noted for mysterious, 20-foot-high sandstone towers, some of them square, others oval, circular, or D-shaped. The towers have small windows up and down their masonry sides, and remain solid today. Archaeologists have suggested their possible function as everything from guard or signal towers, celestial observatories, or ceremonial structures, to water towers or granaries.

A visitor center, with exhibits, restrooms, and drinking water, is located at the **Square Tower Site,** the most impressive and best preserved of the sites. The **Square Tower Loop Trail** winds among the stone structures and provides excellent views of the stone buildings as well as the surrounding countryside. The other five sites are difficult to find, and you'll need to stop at the visitor center to obtain detailed driving directions and check on current road conditions before setting out.

The **Hovenweep Campground,** with 30 sites, is open year-round. It has flush toilets, drinking water, picnic tables, and fire pits, but no showers or RV hookups. Cost is $10 per night. Reservations are not accepted, but you'll probably be able to get a site; the campground rarely fills, even during the peak summer season.

Regulations are much the same here as at most National Park Service properties, with an emphasis on being careful to not damage archaeological sites. Dogs must be leashed and are not permitted on trails. Summer temperatures can reach over 100°F (38°C), and water supplies are limited, so take your own and carry a canteen even on short walks.

Gnats can be a nuisance in late May and June, and bug repellent is advised.

The visitor center is open daily from 8:30am to 4:30pm year-round, but may be closed for short periods while the ranger is on patrol. Trails are open from sunrise to sunset. Admission for up to 1 week costs $6 per vehicle. The monument straddles the Colorado-Utah border, 40 miles west of Cortez. From Cortez, take U.S. 160 south about 4 miles to County Rd. G, and go 41 miles into Utah and to the monument.

For information, contact **Hovenweep National Monument,** McElmo Route, Cortez, CO 81321 (© **435/719-2100** or 970/562-4282; www.nps.gov/hove).

UTE MOUNTAIN TRIBAL PARK

If you liked Mesa Verde, but would have enjoyed it more without the company of so many fellow tourists, you'll *love* the Ute Mountain Tribal Park (P.O. Box 109, Towaoc, CO 81334; © **800/847-5485** or 970/565-3751, ext. 330). Set aside by the Ute Mountain tribe to preserve its heritage, the 125,000-acre park—which abuts Mesa Verde National Park—includes hundreds of surface sites and cliff dwellings that compare in size and complexity with those in Mesa Verde, as well as wall paintings and ancient petroglyphs.

Accessibility to the park is strictly limited to guided tours. Full- and half-day tours begin at the Ute Mountain Museum and Visitor Center at the junction of U.S. 491 and U.S. 160, 20 miles south of Cortez. Mountain-biking and backpacking trips are also offered. No food, lodging, gasoline, or other services are available within the park. The half-day tours are fairly easy, with all sites a short walk from the roadway. The full-day tours are for individuals in good physical shape, and include a 3-mile walk on unpaved trails and climbing five ladders.

Charges for tours in your vehicle cost $20 per person for a half day, $40 per person for a full day; it's $8 extra per

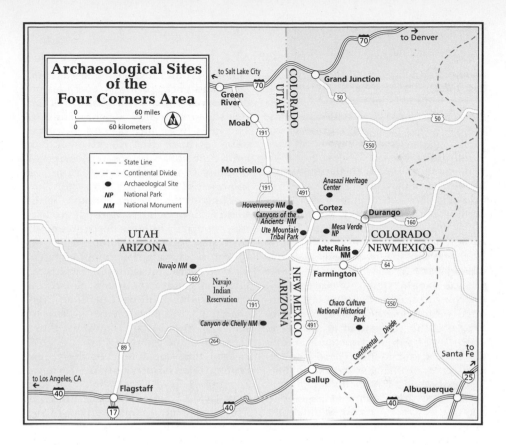

to Denver

to Salt Lake City

Grand Junction

Green River

Moab

UTAH

COLORADO

Monticello

Anasazi Heritage Center

Hovenweep NM

Cortez

Durango

Canyons of the Ancients NM

Mesa Verde NP

Ute Mountain Tribal Park

UTAH

ARIZONA

COLORADO

NEWMEXICO

Aztec Ruins NM

Navajo NM

Farmington

Navajo Indian Reservation

NEW MEXICO

ARIZONA

Chaco Culture National Historical Park

Canyon de Chelly NM

Continental Divide

to Santa Fe

to Los Angeles, CA

Flagstaff

Gallup

Albuquerque

person to go in the tour guide's vehicle. Reservations are required. Professional photography and dogs are not permitted. The tribal park has a primitive **campground** ($12 per vehicle).

ANASAZI HERITAGE CENTER

When the Dolores River was dammed and McPhee Reservoir created in 1985, some 1,600 ancient archaeological sites were threatened. Four percent of the project costs were set aside for archaeological work, and over two million artifacts and other prehistoric items were rescued. The largest share are displayed in this fine museum. Located 10 miles north of Cortez, it is set into a hillside near the remains of 12th-century sites.

Operated by the Bureau of Land Management, the center emphasizes visitor involvement. Children and adults are invited to examine corn-grinding implements, a loom and other weaving materials, and a re-created pit house.

You can touch artifacts 1,000 to 2,000 years old, examine samples through microscopes, use interactive computer programs, and engage in video lessons in archaeological techniques.

A half-mile trail leads from the museum to the **Dominguez and Escalante Ruins,** atop a low hill, with a beautiful view across the Montezuma Valley.

The center is at 27501 Colo. 184, Dolores, CO 81323 (☏ **970/882-5600;** www.co.blm.gov/ahc). It's open March through October, daily from 9am to 5pm; November through February, daily from 9am to 4pm; and closed major winter holidays. Admission (collected Mar–Oct only) is $3 for adults, free for those 17 and under.

CANYONS OF THE ANCIENTS NATIONAL MONUMENT

The 164,000-acre Canyons of the Ancients National Monument, located west of Cortez, contains numerous archaeological sites—what some claim is the highest density of archaeological sites in the United States—including the remains of villages, cliff dwellings, sweat lodges, and petroglyphs going back at least 700 years, and possibly as much as 10,000 years.

The monument includes **Lowry Pueblo,** an excavated 12th-century village that is located 26 miles from Cortez via U.S. 491, on County Road CC, 9 miles west of Pleasant View. This pueblo, which was likely abandoned by 1200, has standing walls from 40 rooms plus 9 kivas (circular underground ceremonial chambers). A short, self-guided interpretive trail leads past a kiva decorated with geometric designs, and continues to the remains of a great kiva, which, at 54 feet in diameter, is among the largest ever found. There is also a picnic area, drinking water, and toilets.

Canyons of the Ancients is managed by the Bureau of Land Management, and at this writing has no visitor center or even contact station. Those wishing to explore the monument are strongly advised to contact or preferably stop first at the Anasazi Heritage Center (see above) for information, including directions and current road conditions.

CANYON DE CHELLY NATIONAL MONUMENT

It's hard to imagine narrow canyons less than 1,000 feet deep being more spectacular than the Grand Canyon, but in some ways Canyon de Chelly is just that. Gaze down from the rim at an ancient cliff dwelling as the whinnying of horses and clanging of goat bells drifts up from below, and you will be struck by the continuity of human existence. For more than 2,000 years people have called these canyons home, and today there are more than 100 prehistoric dwelling sites in the area.

The monument consists of two major canyons—**Canyon de Chelly** (which is pronounced canyon de *shay* and is derived from the Navajo word *tségi*, meaning "rock canyon"), and **Canyon del Muerto** (Spanish for "Canyon of the Dead")—and several smaller canyons. The canyons extend for more than 100 miles through the rugged slickrock landscape of northeastern Arizona, draining the seasonal runoff from the snowmelt of the Chuska Mountains.

Canyon de Chelly's smooth sandstone walls of rich reds and yellows contrast sharply with the deep greens of corn, pasture, and cottonwood on the canyon floor. Vast stone amphitheaters form the caves in which the Ancestral Puebloans built their homes, and as you watch shadows and light paint an ever-changing canyon panorama, it's easy to see why the Navajo consider these canyons sacred ground.

Your first stop should be the **visitor center,** which is open daily May through September from 8am to 6pm (on daylight saving time) and October through April from 8am to 5pm. In front of the visitor center is an example of a traditional crib-style hogan, a hexagonal structure of logs and earth that Navajo use as both home and ceremonial center. Inside, a small museum acquaints visitors with the history of Canyon de Chelly, and there's often a silversmith demonstrating Navajo jewelry-making.

From here most people tour the canyon by car. Each of the rim drives is around 20 miles in each direction, and with stops each can easily take 2 hours.

The **North Rim Drive** overlooks Canyon del Muerto. From view points, you'll see **Ledge Ruin,** which was occupied between A.D. 1050 and 1275, and nearby, a lone kiva (circular ceremonial building) that was reached by means of toeholds cut into the soft sandstone cliff wall. **Antelope House,** once home to from 20 to 40 people, takes its name from the Navajo paintings of antelopes on a nearby cliff wall, believed to have been done in the 1830s. Farther along the drive you'll see the most spectacular archaeological site in the canyon:

Named for two mummies found in burial urns, **Mummy Cave** is actually a giant amphitheater consisting of two caves, believed to have been occupied from A.D. 300 to 1300. There's a three-story structure similar to dwellings at Mesa Verde, and altogether there are 80 rooms. The final stop on the North Rim Drive is at the **Massacre Cave Overlook,** where Spanish troops in 1804 killed about 120 Navajo.

The **South Rim Drive** climbs slowly but steadily along the South Rim of Canyon de Chelly, and at each stop you're a bit higher above the canyon floor. From overlooks you'll see rugged canyons, the junction of Canyon del Muerto and Canyon de Chelly, and the **Junction Ruin,** with 10 rooms and 1 kiva. It was occupied from around 1100 until the Ancestral Puebloans disappeared shortly before 1300. Also visible is **First Ruin,** perched precariously on a long narrow ledge, with 22 rooms and 2 kivas. Farther along is the **White House Overlook,** which provides the only opportunity for descending into Canyon de Chelly without a guide or ranger (see below). The next stop is at **Sliding House Overlook,** offering a view of ruins built on a narrow shelf that appear to be sliding down into the canyon. Inhabited from about 900 until 1200, Sliding House contained between 30 and 50 rooms. The final stop on the South Rim is one of the most spectacular, providing a view of monumental **Spider Rock,** twin towers that rise 800 feet from the canyon floor.

The **White House Ruins Trail,** the only trail into the canyon you can take without a guide, descends 600 feet to the canyon floor, crosses Chinle Wash, and approaches the White House Ruins. These buildings were constructed both on the canyon floor and 50 feet up the cliff wall in a small cave. One of the largest ruins in the canyon, it contains 80 rooms and was inhabited between 1040 and 1275. Notice the black streaks on the sandstone walls above the White House Ruins. These streaks were

Photo Tip

The best time to see and photograph the ruins along the North Rim Drive is in the morning, when they're bathed in sunlight.

formed by seeping water that reacted with the iron in the sandstone. Iron is what gives the walls their reddish hue. Ancestral Puebloan artists chipped away at this black patina to create petroglyphs. Though you cannot enter the ruins, you can get close enough for a good look. You're not allowed to wander off this trail, and please respect the privacy of those Navajo living here. It's a 2.5-mile round-trip hike and takes about 2 hours. Be sure to carry water.

Access to the floor of Canyon de Chelly is restricted, and in order to enter the canyon **you must be accompanied by either a park ranger or an authorized guide** (unless you're on the White House Ruins Trail). **Navajo guides** will lead you into the canyon on foot or in your own or their four-wheel-drive vehicle, and there are also guided horseback tours. Check at the visitor center for fees and other details.

The cottonwood-shaded **Cottonwood Campground,** near the visitor center, has 96 sites, a dump station, toilets, fire pits, and no fee. There is water in summer but not in winter. Reservations are not accepted.

To get to Canyon de Chelly from Cortez, follow U.S. 160 south and west 76 miles into Arizona to U.S. 191, which you take south 62 miles to Chinle, where you turn east to enter the park.

The park is open daily year-round; admission is free.

For information contact **Canyon de Chelly National Monument,** P.O. Box 588, Chinle, AZ 86503 (© **928/674-5500;** www.nps.gov/cach).

NAVAJO NATIONAL MONUMENT

Located 30 miles west of Kayenta and 110 miles northwest of Canyon de Chelly, Navajo National Monument encompasses three of the best-preserved Ancestral Puebloan cliff dwellings in the region: Betatakin, Keet Seel, and Inscription House. It's possible to visit both Betatakin and Keet Seel, but fragile Inscription House is closed to the public.

The name Navajo National Monument is a bit misleading. Although the Navajo people inhabit the area now, it was the Ancestral Puebloans who built the cliff dwellings. The Navajo arrived centuries later. The Ancestral Puebloan who lived here, in Tsegi Canyon, are considered the ancestors of today's Hopi and other Pueblo peoples.

They began abandoning their well-constructed homes around the middle of the 13th century for reasons unknown. Tree rings suggest that a drought in the latter part of the 13th century prevented the Ancestral Puebloans from growing sufficient crops. However, in Tsegi Canyon there's another theory for the abandonment. The canyon floors were usually flooded each year by spring and summer snowmelt, which made farming quite productive; but in the mid-1200s weather patterns changed and streams running through the canyons began cutting deep into the soil, forming deep, narrow canyons, which lowered the water table and made farming much more difficult.

Your first stop should be the **visitor center,** which has informative displays on the Ancestral Puebloan and Navajo cultures, including numerous artifacts from Tsegi Canyon. You can also watch several short films or a slide show, and there is a shop that sells Navajo and Pueblo arts and crafts. The center is open daily from 8am to 5pm. (*Note:* The state of Arizona does not recognize daylight saving time, but the Navajo Nation, where Navajo National Monument is located, does.) The visitor center is closed on Thanksgiving, Christmas, and New Year's Day.

Betatakin, which means "ledge house" in Navajo, is the only one of the three ruins that can be seen easily. Built in a huge amphitheater-like alcove in the canyon wall, Betatakin was occupied only from 1250 to 1300, and at its peak may have housed 125 people.

The 1-mile round-trip paved **Sandal Trail** runs from the visitor center through a wooded area to overlooks of Betatakin. Although wheelchair-accessible, it's a bit steep and manual wheelchair users will need assistance for the return trip. The strenuous 5-mile round-trip **hike to Betatakin** itself is led by a ranger, takes about 6 hours, and involves descending more than 700 feet to the floor of Tsegi Canyon, and later hiking back up to the rim. This hike is conducted from late May through early September and leaves from the visitor center. Hikers should carry 2 quarts of water. This popular hike is limited to 25 people per tour; many people line up at the visitor center an hour or more before the center opens.

Keet Seel, which means "broken pieces of pottery" in Navajo, has a much longer history than Betatakin, with occupation beginning as early as A.D. 950 and continuing until 1300. At one point Keet Seel may have housed 150 people.

The 17-mile round-trip hike to Keet Seel is quite strenuous. Hikers may stay overnight at a primitive campground near the ruins. You must carry enough water for your trip, since none is available along the trail. Only 20 people a day are given permits, and the trail is open only from Memorial Day to Labor Day. Permits are available in advance (call the monument office).

There is a free, shady **campground** with 31 small sites, available year-round on a first-come, first-served basis, plus an overflow area containing about a dozen more (open in summer only).

From Cortez, follow U.S. 160 south and west 137 miles into New Mexico and Arizona, to Ariz. 564, which leads north 9 miles to the monument.

For information, contact **Navajo National Monument,** HC-71, Box 3, Tonalea, AZ 86044-9704 (✆ **928/672-2700;** www.nps.gov/nava). The park is open daily year-round. Admission is free.

CHACO CULTURE NATIONAL HISTORICAL PARK

A combination of a stunning setting and well-preserved ruins makes the dusty drive to Chaco Canyon well worth the trip. Whether you come from the north or south, you drive in on a graded (and sometimes muddy) dirt road that seems to add to the authenticity and adventure of this remote New Mexico experience.

When you finally arrive, you walk through stark desert country that seems perhaps ill-suited as a center of culture. However, the ancient Ancestral Puebloan people (the group here are also called Chacoans) successfully farmed the lowlands and built elaborate public buildings, which connected with other Chacoan sites over a wide-ranging network of roads.

What's particularly interesting is how changes in architecture chart the area's cultural progress. These changes began in the mid-800s, when the Chacoans started building on a larger scale than they had previously. They used the same masonry techniques that people had used in smaller villages in the region—walls one stone thick with generous use of mud mortar—but their stone buildings contained multiple stories, with rooms several times larger than in the previous stage of their culture. Within a century, six large structures were underway. This pattern of a single large building with oversized rooms, surrounded by conventional villages, caught on throughout the region. New communities built along these lines sprang up. Old villages built similarly large structures. Eventually there were more than 150 of them, most closely tied to Chaco by an extensive system of roads.

This progress led to Chaco becoming the ceremonial and economic center of the San Juan Basin by A.D. 1000, when from 2,000 to 5,000 people may have lived in some 400 settlements in and around Chaco. As masonry techniques advanced through the years, walls rose more than four stories high. Some of these are still visible today.

Chaco's decline after 1½ centuries of success coincided with a drought in the San Juan Basin between A.D. 1130 and 1180, but anthropologists still argue vehemently over why the site was abandoned. Many believe that an influx of outsiders may have brought new and troubling influences—one controversial theory maintains that cannibalism existed at Chaco, practiced either by the Ancestral Puebloans themselves or by invaders, such as the Toltecs of Mexico. Most, however, agree that for some reason the people of Chaco drifted away and that today their descendants live among the region's Pueblo people, including the Hopi, Zuni, Acoma, and Zia.

Exploring the ruins and hiking are the most popular activities here. A series of monumental ruins stand within 5 or 6 miles of each other on the broad, flat, treeless canyon floor. Plan to spend at least 3 to 4 hours here, driving to and exploring the different structures. A one-way road from the visitor center loops up one side of the canyon and down the other.

You may want to focus your energy on **Pueblo Bonito,** one of the largest prehistoric dwellings ever excavated in the Southwest. It contains giant kivas and 800 rooms covering more than 3 acres. The **Pueblo Alto Trail** is a pleasant hike that takes you up on the canyon rim so you can see the ruins from above—in the afternoon, with thunderheads building, the views are spectacular. For cyclers, there's a map that shows trails open to biking, which is an excellent way to traverse the vast expanse while experiencing the quiet of these ancient dwellings.

Other ruins accessible directly from the auto road or via short walks are Chetro Ketl, Pueblo del Arroyo, Kin Kletso, Casa Rinconada, Hungo Pavi, and Una Vida. Backcountry hikes (2–5 hr.) are required to reach some ruins; they include Penasco Blanco, Tsin Kletsin, Casa Chiquita, and Wijiji.

Most ruins are on the north side of the canyon. **Chetro Ketl** had some 500 rooms, 16 kivas, and an impressive enclosed plaza. **Pueblo del Arroyo** was a four-story, D-shaped structure, with about 280 rooms and 20 kivas; **Kin Kletso** had three stories, 100 rooms, and 5 kivas. **Una Vida,** a short walk from the visitor center, was one of the first Chacoan buildings constructed and has been left only partially excavated; it had 150 rooms and 5 kivas. **Casa Rinconada,** on the south side of the canyon, is the largest "great kiva" in the park, and is astronomically aligned to the cardinal directions and the summer solstice. It may have been a center for the community at large, used for major spiritual observances.

Aerial photos show hundreds of miles of roads connecting these towns with the Chaco structures, one of the longest running 42 miles straight north toward Salmon Ruin and Aztec Ruins (see below). Settlements were spaced along the road. These roads were not simple trails worn into the stone by foot travel, but engineered highways 30 feet wide with a berm of rock to contain the fill. Where the road went over flat rock, walls were built along the sides of it. It is this road network that leads some scholars to believe Chaco was the center of a widespread, unified society.

The Chacoans' trade network, as suggested by artifacts found here, stretched from California to Texas and south into Mexico. Seashell necklaces, copper bells, and the remains of macaws were found among Chaco artifacts. Some of these items are displayed in the museum at the visitor center.

The visitor center, with a bookstore and a museum showing films on Ancestral Puebloan culture, is open daily year-round. Ranger-guided walks and campfire talks are available in the summer at the visitor center, and this is also where you can get self-guiding trail brochures.

Gallo Campground, located within the park, is quite popular with hikers. It's located about 1 mile east of the visitor center; fees are $10 per night. The campground has 48 sites (2 group sites are also available), with fire grates (bring your own wood or charcoal), central toilets, nonpotable water, and no shade. Drinking water is available only at the visitor center. The campground cannot accommodate trailers over 30 feet.

This is an isolated area, and there are **no services** available within or close to the park—no food, gas, auto repairs, firewood, lodging (besides the campground), or drinking water (other than at the visitor center) are available.

The primary entrance is off U.S. 550 and San Juan County Roads 7900 and 7950. To get to Chaco from Santa Fe, take I-25 south to Bernalillo (Exit 242), then U.S. 550 northwest through Cuba to mile marker 112. Turn left onto San Juan County Road 7900 (paved) for 5 miles, and turn right for 16 miles on dirt San Juan County Road 7950 to the park entrance. This road is fine in dry weather but dangerous when it rains, and often flooded where arroyos cross it. The route is well marked, and the trip takes about 3½ to 4 hours. Farmington is the nearest population center, and it's still a 75-mile, 1½-hour drive to the park. Head east on U.S. 64 to Bloomfield and turn right onto U.S. 550. Three miles south of the Nageezi Trading Post (the last stop for food, gas, or lodging), turn onto San Juan County Road 7900 and proceed as above.

Whichever way you come, call ahead to inquire about **road conditions**

(© 505/786-7014) before leaving the paved highways. The dirt roads can get extremely muddy after rain or snow, and afternoon thunderstorms are common in late summer.

For information, contact **Superintendent, Chaco Culture National Historical Park,** P.O. Box 220, Nageezi, NM 87037-0220 (© **505/786-7014;** www.nps.gov/chcu).

Admission for up to 7 days costs $8 per vehicle.

AZTEC RUINS NATIONAL MONUMENT

What's most striking about these ruins is the central kiva, which visitors can enter. The ruins of this 450-room pueblo, left by the Ancestral Puebloans 7 centuries ago, are located along the Animas River, 14 miles northeast of Farmington in the town of Aztec. Early Anglo settlers, convinced that the ruins were of Aztec origin, misnamed the site. Despite the fact that this pueblo was built long before the Aztecs of central Mexico lived, the name persisted.

The influence of the Chaco culture is strong at Aztec, as evidenced in the pre-planned architecture, the open plaza, and the fine stone masonry. But a later occupation shows signs of Mesa Verde influence. This second group of settlers, who lived here from about 1200 to 1275, remodeled the old pueblo and built others nearby, using techniques less elaborate and decorative than the Chacoans.

Aztec is best known for its **Great Kiva,** the only completely reconstructed great kiva in existence. About 50 feet in diameter, with a main floor sunken 8 feet below the surface of the surrounding ground, this circular ceremonial room rivets the imagination.

Allow 1 to 2 hours to visit Aztec Ruins National Monument, including time to take the 0.25-mile self-guided trail, see the exhibits in the visitor center, and watch the 25-minute video that helps explain the history of the native cultures in the area. The visitor center displays some outstanding examples of Ancestral Puebloan ceramics and basketry, as well as such finds as an intact Pueblo ladder, and an empty case where a warrior's remains were once displayed. (They were subsequently removed out of deference to the Pueblo people's sensibilities.)

There is no camping at the monument.

Aztec Ruins is approximately ½ mile north of U.S. 550 on Ruins Road (County Rd. 2900) on the north edge of the city of Aztec. Ruins Road is the first street immediately west of the Animas River bridge on U.S. 550.

For information, contact **Aztec Ruins National Monument,** 84 County Rd. 2900, Aztec, NM 87410 (© **505/334-6174;** www.nps.gov/azru). Admission is $4 per person (children under 17 are admitted free), good for up to 7 days. The visitor center is open daily from 8am to 5pm year-round; the monument grounds are open the same hours from Labor Day to Memorial Day, but open until 6pm from Memorial Day to Labor Day. The monument is closed Thanksgiving, Christmas, and New Year's Day.

MOUNT RAINIER NATIONAL PARK

by Jack Olson

N SUMMER WEEKENDS, WHEN "THE MOUNTAIN IS OUT," AS THE LOCALS say, busloads of noisy tourists descend on Mount Rainier, camcorders whirring and cameras clicking. But for anyone willing to expend a little bit of energy to get away from the roadside crowds, this mountain, which dominates the Puget Sound and western Washington skyline for miles around, has many secrets to share: mountain goats and marmots, streaming waterfalls, ominous walls of ice deep in the rain forest, and thousand-year-old trees set against subalpine meadows teeming with summer wildflowers.

Should you visit on a wet, dreary October day, you may theorize that Mount Rainier was named for its climatological proclivities. In fact, Capt. George Vancouver named it in 1792 for his friend Rear Adm. Peter Rainier (who never laid eyes on the mountain). The region's native people had been calling it Tahoma, or other variations, for centuries, however, and the name remained (and some might say still remains) contentious up until the early 19th century. Nevertheless, the mountain is known as Rainier to most people, while a sprawling city to the northwest, Tacoma, wound up with the American Indian name. Rainier was finalized as the name when the park was established in 1899.

Native peoples hunted deer, elk, and mountain goat and gathered huckleberries on its lower slopes for thousands of years. Today, Mount Rainier is a symbol of the wild Northwest, providing constant reassurance of the beauty that lies beyond the sprawl of suburbia.

Although most of the mountains in the West were seen as obstacles by the early pioneers, 14,410-foot Mount Rainier so captivated early settlers that as early as the 1850s, less than a decade after Seattle was founded, aspiring mountaineers were heading for its snowcapped slopes. In 1857, an army lieutenant, August Valentine Kautz, climbed to within 400 feet of the summit; and in 1870, Gen. Hazard Stevens and Philemon Van Trump made the first recorded complete ascent of the mountain (trapped near the summit at dark, they survived the night huddled in ice caves formed by sulfurous steam vents, with the steam providing enough heat to keep them from freezing to death). In 1884, James and Virinda Longmire opened the mountain's first

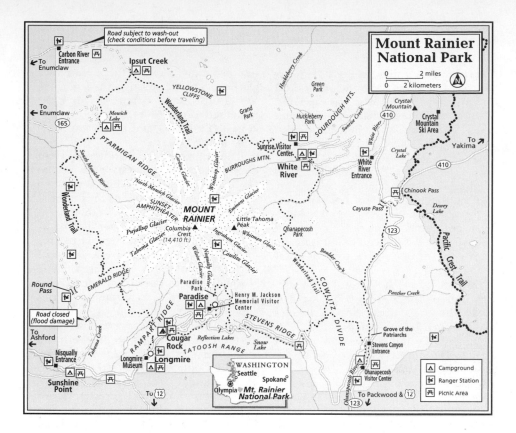

Mount Rainier
National Park

0   2 miles
0   2 kilometers

Carbon River
Entrance
←To
Enumclaw

Ipsut Creek

YELLOWSTONE
CLIFFS

Green
Park

Crystal
Mountain

To
← Enumclaw

Mowich
Lake

Wonderland Trail

Grand
Park

Huckleberry
Park

Huckleberry Creek

SOURDOUGH MTS.

Sunrise Creek

White River

Crystal
Mountain
Ski Area

To ↗
Yakima

PTARMIGAN RIDGE

Carbon Glacier

Winthrop Glacier

BURROUGHS MTN.

Sunrise Visitor
Center

White
River

White
River
Entrance

Crystal
Lake

North Mowich Glacier

SUNSET
AMPHITHEATER

MOUNT
RAINIER

Emmons Glacier

Chinook Pass

Dewey
Lake

Wonderland
Trail

South Mowich River

Puyallup Glacier

Columbia
Crest
(14,410 ft.)

Little Tahoma
Peak

Whitman Glacier

Ohanapecosh
Park

Cayuse Pass

Tahoma Glacier

Ingraham Glacier

Wilson Glacier

Cowlitz Glacier

Boulder Creek

Round
Pass

EMERALD RIDGE

Paradise
Park

Paradise

Nisqually Glacier

Henry M. Jackson
Memorial Visitor
Center

Panther Creek

COWLITZ DIVIDE

Pacific Crest Trail

Road closed
(flood damage)

To
Ashford

RAMPART RIDGE

STEVENS RIDGE

Grove of the
Patriarchs

Nisqually
Entrance

Tahoma Creek

Cougar
Rock

Reflection Lakes

TATOOSH RANGE

Snow
Lake

Stevens Canyon
Entrance

Sunshine
Point

Longmire
Museum

Longmire

WASHINGTON

Seattle

Spokane

Ohanapecosh
Visitor Center

△ Campground

⊡ Ranger Station

☇ Picnic Area

Olympia Mt. Rainier
National Park

To Packwood &

To 12

hotel, at a spot that now bears their name. In 1899, Mount Rainier became the nation's fifth national park, and by 1916, the trail system now known as the Wonderland Trail was completed, forming a loop nearly 100 miles long around the mountain.

Because of its massive system of glaciers and unpredictable weather, Mount Rainier is an unforgiving peak. Dozens of climbers throughout the years have died on its slopes, yet each year about 10,000 climbers set out for the summit of this dozing volcano. Only about half of them ever reach the top, however. The rest are turned back by bad weather, altitude sickness, exhaustion, and hazardous glacial crossings. This is not a mountain to be treated lightly.

Although the mountain is a magnet for climbers, these adventurers make up only a tiny fraction of the two million visitors who come to the park each year. This mountain is really all about hiking through subalpine meadows, the main activity pursued by the vast majority of park visitors, most of whom visit during the short summer season (July–Sept in the higher elevations).

Scenic idylls through flower-strewn meadows aside, the Cascades are not dead, they're just sleeping. This fact was driven home with the eruption of Mount St. Helens on May 18, 1980. But what of Mount Rainier? Snow and glaciers notwithstanding, Rainier has a heart of fire. Steam vents at the mountain's summit are evidence of that. Though this volcanic peak has not erupted for more than 150 years, it could erupt again at any time. Some scientists believe that Rainier's volcanic activity occurs in 3,000-year cycles; if this holds true, we have another 500 years (give or take) to go before another big eruption. So go ahead and plan that trip. Probably only the scenery will blow you away.

Terrain. According to local legend, Martha Longmire, who helped found the first hotel in the area, was supposed to have exclaimed, "This must be what paradise is like," upon her first visit to the subalpine meadows that now bear that name. It is these meadows, now the site of the seasonal Paradise Inn and the Henry M. Jackson Memorial Visitor Center, that are the most popular spots in the park. Wildflowers cover the slopes here, and the vast bulk of the mountain rises so steeply overhead that it is necessary to strain one's neck to gaze up at the summit.

Mount Rainier lies toward the southern end of the Washington Cascades. Here, the crags of the North Cascades are replaced by a volcanic landscape of rolling hills punctuated by Mount Rainier, Mount St. Helens, and to the east, Mount Adams and Goat Rocks: the latter but a remnant of an ancient volcano, the former, a snow cone as impressive as Mount Rainier.

It is said that Rainier makes its own weather, and more often than not, it isn't what people consider good weather. Rising more than 2 miles above the surrounding landscape, Mount Rainier interrupts the eastward flow of moisture-laden air that comes in off the Pacific Ocean. Forced upward into the colder altitudes, this moist air drops its load of water on the mountain. At lower elevations on the west side this moisture falls as rain, which creates a **rain forest** in the Carbon River Valley. However, at higher elevations, the mountain's precipitation falls as snow. On average, about 680 inches of snow falls each winter at Paradise on Mount Rainier, but in the winter of 1971–72, 1,122 inches (94 ft.) of snow were recorded at Paradise, setting a world annual snowfall record.

Mount Rainier is the single most glaciated mountain in the contiguous 48 states. So much snow falls here each winter that it can't melt over the short summer months. Each year the snow accumulates, eventually compressing into ice that adds to the mountain's **glaciers.** There are 26 named glaciers on Mount Rainier and another 50 unnamed ones. Among these are the largest (Emmons) and the lowest (Carbon) in the Lower 48.

These glaciers in turn feed a half dozen rivers. The Muddy Fork of the **Cowlitz River** and the **White River** take their names from the color that the glacial flour (silt) imparts to them. Fortunately, the **Carbon River** is not as black as its name implies. The river instead takes its name from the coal deposits found in the area. The **Nisqually,** the **Puyallup,** and the Cowlitz all retain names given to them centuries ago by the region's American Indian tribes. All of these rivers eventually flow westward to the Puget Sound, with the exception of the Cowlitz, which flows into the Columbia River.

Surrounding the national park are four different **national forests:** Mount Baker, Snoqualmie, Wenatchee, and Gifford Pinchot. Within these national forests are seven wilderness areas and thousands of miles of logging roads and trails.

Flora & Fauna. In a national park, where animals need not fear hunters, you often get unexpected chances to encounter wildlife up close and personal, sometimes whether you want to or not. Yes, **cougars** live in this park, as do **black bears,** but neither is seen very often. Much more commonly spotted large mammals are the park's deer, elk, and mountain goats. **Deer,** mostly black-tailed, are the most frequently spotted. **Elk,** much larger and more majestic in stature, are less in evidence than the deer, but can sometimes be seen in the Sunrise area in the summer and throughout the eastern regions of the park during the autumn. **Mountain goats,** which are actually not goats but rather a longhaired relative of the antelope, keep to the rocky cliffs above alpine and subalpine meadows during the summer.

Perhaps the most entertaining and enviable of the park's wild residents are its **marmots.** These largest members of the squirrel family spend their days nibbling wildflowers in subalpine meadows, and stretching out on rocks to bask in the sun. In meadows throughout the park, these chubby creatures seem oblivious to human presence, contentedly grazing only steps away from hikers.

Marmots share these subalpine zones with **pikas,** tiny relatives of rabbits, that are more often heard than seen. Living among the jumbled rocks of talus slopes, pikas skitter about their rocky domains calling out warnings with a high pitched beep that is surprisingly electronic in tone.

Monkeyflowers, elephant's heads, parrot's beaks, bear grass: they represent just a small fraction of the variety of **wildflowers** to be found on the slopes of Mount Rainier. This mountain's subalpine meadows are among the most celebrated in the Northwest and the world. Although not as colorfully named as the flowers mentioned above, lupines, asters, gentians, avalanche lilies, phlox, heather, and Indian paintbrush all add their own distinctive splashes of color to these slopes in summer.

The meadows at Paradise are much wetter than those at Sunrise, which lie in a rain-shadow zone and consequently are relatively dry. In the northwest corner of the park, the **Carbon River Valley** opens out to Puget Sound and channels moisture-laden air into its valleys. As a result, this valley is a rain forest where tree limbs are draped with moss and lichen, and where Douglas fir and western red cedar grow to enormous proportions. However, it is in the southeast corner of the park, in the **Grove of the Patriarchs** near the Stevens Canyon Park Entrance, that some of the oldest trees stand—Douglas firs more than 1,000 years old and western red cedars more than 25 feet in circumference.

Avoiding the Crowds. On a sunny summer weekend it is sometimes necessary to park more than a mile away from Paradise and walk on forest trails and the road to the meadows. You can avoid the crowds by **visiting in the spring or fall.** Keep in mind that in May Paradise and Sunrise will still be snow-covered and most park roads will be closed; weather may still be unsettled. Even in June, Paradise may remain snow-covered and some park roads may be closed. Also, the rainy season starts in mid- to late October and keeps going until early summer.

Perhaps the best tip, if you're traveling in busy months, is to **visit on weekdays** rather than weekends. You might also consider avoiding the Sunrise and Paradise areas altogether, heading instead to the **more remote sections** of the park, such as the Carbon River area in the northwest section, or the Denman Falls/Gobblers Knob area in the southwest. Both are accessible, at least part of the way, by car and provide the same sorts of stunning vistas you get at Sunrise and Paradise. The Carbon River Road is subject to flood closures; check with park staff. The Westside Road, which leads to the Denman Falls area (open summer only), is closed due to flood damage 3 miles up, so you will have to do some hiking (be sure to check at the ranger station for the latest info).

Otherwise, a good plan is to arrive at either Sunrise or Paradise early in the day—before 10am—spend an hour checking out the visitor center, and then hightail it out to a trail. Likewise, people generally leave the park between 4 and 6pm, so if you can arrange to arrive at a visitor center around 5pm (with the idea of staying put for an hour or so), you can avoid a lot of the traffic.

Finally, you might try reversing this advice, hitting Sunrise at sundown. Most park visitors are leaving via the Nisqually Entrance in the park's southwest corner late in the day; you'll be heading in the opposite direction.

Just the Facts

Unlike its cousin across the Puget Sound, Olympic National Park, no roads completely encircle Rainier; the northwest corner of the park, for example, is only accessible through one entrance.

The **Nisqually Entrance** (also known as the Nisqually-Longmire Rd.) in the southwest corner of the park is the park's main entrance. Just to the west on Wash. 706 is **Ashford,** where most of the area's accommodations and services are to be found. A few miles farther west is **Elbe,** where a few more choices can be located.

However, at the park's northeast corner, the **White River Entrance,** off Wash. 410, provides easier access from Seattle and points north if your goal is only the Sunrise area. The town closest to this entrance is **Greenwater,** which also provides some overnight options.

In the northwest corner, the **Carbon River Entrance** is off Wash. 165. **Enumclaw** offers motels, restaurants, and fuel.

At the southeast corner, the **Stevens Canyon Entrance,** off Wash. 123 from U.S. 12, provides access from Yakima. **Packwood** and **Randle,** both located south of the park on U.S. 12, are two of the larger towns in the nearby area. You'll find some recommendable accommodations in Packwood.

During the summer it is also possible to enter the park from the east on Wash. 410, which also leads to Yakima by way of Chinook Pass. Entering this way gives you the option of heading north to the White River Entrance and Sunrise, or south to Stevens Canyon.

In winter, only the Nisqually Entrance is open.

The Nearest Airport. The nearest airport is the **Seattle-Tacoma International Airport** (© 206/433-5388), 70 miles northwest of the park (allow about 2 hr. on I-5, Wash. 7, and Wash. 706 to the Nisqually Entrance). The airport is served by practically all major airlines and car-rental companies, whose toll-free numbers are in the appendix.

Contact the **Longmire Museum, Mount Rainier National Park,** Tahoma Woods, Star Route, Ashford, WA 98304 (© 360/569-2211; www.nps.gov/mora). The park publishes a free newspaper, the *Tahoma,* available at all visitor centers, which gives current information about park activities.

When you arrive, stop at one of the park's four visitor centers. The **Longmire Museum** (© 360/569-2211, ext. 3314) is located just inside the park beyond the Nisqually Entrance and is the welcoming center for the park. The **Henry M. Jackson Memorial Visitor Center** (© 360/569-2211, ext. 2328), near Paradise Meadows, main visitor center. The **Ohanapecosh Visitor Center** (© 360/569-6046), off Wash. 123 in the southeast corner of the park, is near the Stevens Canyon Entrance. The center is open in the summer only.

The **Sunrise Visitor Center,** off Wash. 410, past the White River Entrance (© 360/663-2425), is in the northeast section of the park. It's open in the summer only.

Entry into the parks for up to 7 days costs $10 per vehicle. Camping costs $10 to $15 per night, depending on the campground and season.

The main thing to remember in the heavily visited spots in the subalpine portions of the park is to stay on the trails and stay off the wildflowers. Off-trail trampling erodes the thin, loam topsoil that supports the fragile vegetation.

Be sure to boil any water taken from the park's rivers, as it has been known to carry *Giardia,* the little bug of the mighty intestinal disorder.

Don't even think about heading for a day climb anywhere near the upper altitudes of Rainier without checking in at a ranger station or employing a guide. Steep snowfields can become slippery in the sun or contain unstable ice bridges. Remember, people die in the high altitudes every year.

Additionally, there are some risks the National Park Service wants visitors to be aware of: Mud flows, glacial outburst floods, and falling rocks are hazards that may be encountered here.

SEASONS & CLIMATE

Summer is the warmest and driest time of the year, with frequent fog banks rolling in late and early in the day, and temperatures ranging from the upper 40s to the low 80s (10s to mid-20s Celsius). The spring and fall are cool and drizzly, with occasional days of warm weather late in the spring and early in the fall. The greatest rainfall comes in January and December, with daytime temperatures in the 40s (10s Celsius). Weather is generally going to get colder and nastier the higher up you go, and of course, there is lots of snow in the higher elevations. This snow can linger well into the summer, even at popular Paradise.

It's important that you dress in layers for a day visit, as you may encounter any type of weather. It can go from warm to cool very quickly as you climb in altitude. Rain can come in suddenly, so rain gear is a good precaution.

Park Highlights

Longmire, just inside the Nisqually Entrance, is the park's oldest developed area, the site of the historic hotel, which opened in 1899. Here you'll find the old

Mount Rainier National Park Headquarters, the National Park Inn, which houses a year-round lodge and restaurant. There's also a museum, a general store, a wilderness information center, and a post office. Although it sounds as if this must be a small city, it is actually quite compact and rarely very crowded. Other important features of the area are the Trail of the Shadows, Historic District Walking Trail, and a Transportation Exhibit.

Paradise, in the south-central portion of the park, is a subalpine meadow and one of the most popular areas for visitors. Nearby you'll find the Henry M. Jackson Memorial Visitor Center, the park's main visitor center, a gracefully curving stone and concrete structure that houses a snack bar and the only public showers in the park. Interesting exhibits on geology, glaciers, and the local flora and fauna are here. Paradise is also the site of the Paradise Inn (open mid-May to early Oct), a historic mountain lodge.

Ohanapecosh, off Wash. 123 in the park's southeast corner, offers scenic views of the Ohanapecosh River near the small visitor center located here. Inside, look for exhibits focusing primarily on the old-growth forest ecosystem that surrounds this particular area of the park. The 188-site Ohanapecosh Campground is here, as well as several good, short hikes.

At 6,400 feet, **Sunrise,** in the northeast part of the park, is the highest point to which you can drive in the park. This is the second most popular spot in the park. You'll find displays and naturalist-led walks, a snack bar/restaurant, and interpretive programs on the subalpine and alpine ecosystems. You can also look at the glaciers up close with free telescopes. The visitor center here is open daily from July through mid-September, when the roadway is open.

The **Carbon River area,** in the northwest corner, provides access to the most heavily forested area in the park. The jury is still out as to whether the terrain is actually lowland forest or temperate rain forest. Check road conditions before visiting; this road is subject to washouts. Trails here lead into the backcountry and connect with the **Wonderland Trail.** A separate road (Wash. 165) reaches the Mowich Lake area, open to the lake in summer only.

If You Have Only 1 Day

Most folks who make Mount Rainier a day trip are coming from the **Seattle** area, and they work their way around to Sunrise from the southwest corner of the park, driving first through **Longmire** to **Paradise,** then **Ohanapecosh,** and on to **Sunrise.** But, Sunrise being named what it is, you might want to go the other way around to get the best daylight, in which case you'll want to enter on Wash. 410 at the park's northeast corner. If you're coming from the south or from Yakima, you'll want to adjust your entry point and itinerary accordingly. The day-tripper will probably not be able to visit the Carbon River area in the northwest if you want to see Paradise and Sunrise. But Carbon River also makes a great 1-day visit.

It might be a bit pedestrian, but if you want to get the whole flavor of what Mount Rainier is about, you will probably want to do the normal route and head into the park via the Longmire Entrance in late summer. You get old-growth forests, subalpine meadows blooming with flowers, and a look at the rocky scree underneath the Emmons and Winthrop glaciers. If you'd rather avoid lines of cars later in the day (and who doesn't?), get a jump on things early in the morning. By noon, Rainier is going to be packed, especially on weekends.

For an 80-mile trip, start out at the **Nisqually Entrance** on Wash. 706, and check out the **Longmire Museum** for exhibits on American Indian culture, European exploration, and the area's natural history, as well as the local flora and fauna. If you've already been driving a bit, take a walk on the excellent 0.7-mile **Trail of the Shadows** across

from the National Park Inn. The trail passes by the mineral springs that once hosted the early hotel, as well as a cabin (reconstructed) built by one of the Longmires in 1888. Don't drink the mineral water; it will make you very sick.

Next is an up-close-and-personal look at the fantastic burst of colors in **Paradise's** fields of brilliant paintbrush, anemones, and gentians. But first, visit the **Henry M. Jackson Memorial Visitor Center** and figure out what you're looking at. It might be the Nisqually or Wilson glacier hanging over your head. For a more up-close view of the Nisqually Glacier, take the 1.2-mile (1-hr. round-trip) **Nisqually Vista Trail** from the visitor center. Otherwise, there are numerous trails leading from the parking lot that will allow you to create your own wildflower stroll. Please stay on the trails to protect these wildflowers.

From Paradise, head east toward the **Stevens Canyon Entrance,** with your next goal a short hike along the **Grove of the Patriarchs** at Ohanapecosh. This 1.3-mile walk, one of the most popular in the park, is famous for its absolutely huge Douglas fir and western red cedar, located on a small island accessible by a bridge across the beautiful Ohanapecosh River. If you have time, take the **Hot Springs Nature Trail,** which begins at the visitor center, a quick 0.4-mile jaunt where you will see a shallow hot spring alongside the trail as you gaze down at a meadow of lush grass. Other worthy stops are at Reflection Lakes and Box Canyon along the Stevens Canyon Road.

Finally, wind your way through forests of fir, cedar, and hemlock on the way to **Sunrise.** The big, snowcapped mountain in your rearview mirror to the south is Mount Adams, equal in beauty to Mount Rainier, but more remote. This side of the mountain is glacier-packed, so check out **Emmons Vista** for excellent views of Little Tahoma and the Emmons glacier, or take the 1.5-mile **Sunrise Rim Trail,** which also leads away from the day lodge. For a close-up view, use the telescopes at the visitor center.

If You Have More Time

The best way to explore the park is on foot, and if you have more than 1 day you'll be able to get out on the trails. And the mother of all park trails is the **Wonderland Trail,** which, as it winds its labyrinthine route around the entire mountain (most folks plan 10 days to 2 weeks to do this one), takes you through any section of the park you might be interested in. There's no law that says you can't do a small portion of the Wonderland Trail, though. Since it's accessible from all the major park centers, you can do a piece as a day hike (see "Hikes," below).

The least visited sections of the park are really some of the best, including the incredibly beautiful **Carbon River** area northwest of the mountain. But, like many things in life, the good things take a little more effort. Still, if you have the time, go there. The Carbon River basin contains a temperate rain forest. The only other temperate rain forest in the United States is on the Olympic Peninsula, making the Carbon River area a unique jewel of an ecosystem. The Carbon River Road is very susceptible to flood damage and may not be passable to vehicles. Check with park staff before driving out.

Organized Tours & Ranger Programs

Gray Line Tours of Seattle (✆ 800/426-7532 or 206/624-5077; www.graylineofseattle.com) offers regularly scheduled bus tours into the park from mid-spring through mid-fall, departing daily at 8am from the Convention Center in downtown Seattle. Cost for a 1-day tour is $44 per person; the Seattle Classic tour with a Mt. Rainier overnight costs from $338 per person.

Ranger-led tours, discussions, and seminars take place or begin at Longmire, Ohanapecosh, Paradise, and Sunrise visitor centers.

At **Longmire,** short history talks are offered daily in summer. There are evening programs at Cougar Rock Campground.

At **Ohanapecosh,** there are several ranger-led hikes and walks along popular trails almost daily, as well as evening programs during July and August devoted to natural and cultural history and resources.

From **Paradise,** there are daily walks to view wildflowers and glaciers. Park naturalists also roam the area answering questions.

From the **Sunrise** area, there are daily ranger-led walks. During July and August there are evening campfire programs at White River Campground.

Programs change each year and season. Check at a visitor center for specific programs and times during your visit.

Hikes

Some trails, especially those near Sunrise and Paradise, are packed throughout the summer. However, many forest trails offer significant solitude. Trails in the northwest corner, near the Carbon River Entrance, are relatively quiet. The Carbon River road is recommended for high clearance vehicles only. This road is known to wash out, so prior checking of road conditions is advised. Mowich Lake sees more weekend foot traffic since the road there is open in the summer.

For current information on trail availability or closures, call the **Wilderness Information Center** (✆ 360/569-HIKE) in summer, or the Longmire Museum (✆ **360/569-2211,** ext. 3314) year-round.

In addition to the trails discussed below, a section of the famed Pacific Crest Trail skirts the park's eastern edge. This trail runs some 2,650 miles from Mexico to Canada. For information on the entire Pacific Crest Trail, contact the **Pacific Crest Trail Association,** 5325 Elkhorn Blvd., PMB no. 256, Sacramento, CA 95842-2526 (✆ **916/349-2109;** fax 916/349-1268; www.pcta.org).

ALL THE WAY AROUND MOUNT RAINIER

Wonderland Trail

93 miles RT. Allow 10–14 days. Strenuous. Access: This hike can be started from Longmire, Paradise, Sunrise, Mowich Lake, or Carbon River.

With varying degrees of difficulty, this 93-mile loop circles Mount Rainier, with numerous connecting trailheads, and is the mother of all trails in the park. To some, it's a northwest rite of passage to make this loop through some of the most stunning vistas in the continental United States. Think hard and plan ahead before you try to take it all at once. You'll probably want to leave yourself about 2 weeks' time to make the whole loop. There are more things to see on this trail than you can name. But, of course, expect to find yourself traveling through subalpine meadows, glacial streams, mountain passes, valley forests, and an ultimate summit point of 6,500 feet at Panhandle Gap. There are many backcountry camping spots along the way that provide water in the summer, but be sure to purify every drop. In the interest of planning shorter trips, keep in mind that you can connect with this trail from any of the spokelike trails that crisscross and touch the trail throughout the park, allowing you to set up a hiking mileage and time schedule all your own. It's possible for 1 day's elevation gain to be as much as 7,000 feet.

LONGMIRE AREA

Although the Westside Road is closed 3 miles up, the **Lake George and Gobblers Knob Lookout Trail** is open.

Carter Falls Trail

2.2 miles RT. Easy. Access: 100 yards downhill from the Cougar Park Campground on the road to Paradise.

This trail passes a wooden pipeline that once carried water, which generated electricity for Longmire. Go past Carter Falls about 50 yards for a look at the second falls, the zany Madcap Falls. This trail is part of the Wonderland Trail and takes you to Paradise to the east, or Indian Henry's to the west.

Rampart Ridge Trail

4.6 miles RT. Moderate. Access: Across the road from the Longmire Museum.

This is a somewhat steep trail at first (the elevation gain is 1,339 ft.), before you arrive at the top of an ancient lava flow called the Ramparts, which offers panoramic views of the Nisqually Valley to the south, Mount Rainier to the north, and, to the west, the site of the massive Kautz Creek Mudflow of 1947. It's also your connection with many of the other trails in the area, including the Van Trump, Comet, and Christine Falls trails.

Trail of Shadows Nature Trail

0.7 mile RT. Easy. Access: Across the road from the Longmire Museum.

This short, level loop trail is a highly enjoyable walk through the forest around Longmire Meadow. It takes you past the former site of the Longmire Springs Hotel, as well as an old log cabin that's the oldest man-made structure in the park. Don't drink from the springs.

Van Trump Park & Comet Falls Trail

5.6 miles RT. Moderate. Access: Below Christine Falls Bridge on the road to Paradise.

This steep trail (total elevation gain of 2,200 ft.) leads through beautiful old-growth forest to scenic Comet Falls, the second highest falls in the park at 320 feet. Another mile uphill takes you to beautiful views of the Nisqually, Van Trump, and Kautz glaciers. This is a popular trail in the summer, but can be dangerous in early summer due to flooding and steep, icy slopes; stop in at the ranger station and ask for information on trail conditions before heading up.

PARADISE AREA

Alta Vista

1.75 miles RT. Easy. Access: Jackson Visitor Center parking lot.

This popular day hike meanders through subalpine meadows along a trail that leads to the top of an overlook of Paradise Meadows, Mount Adams, and Mount St. Helens to the south. There's a 600-foot elevation gain.

Bench & Snow Lakes Trail

2.5 miles RT. Easy to moderate. Access: Stevens Canyon Rd., 1½ miles east of Reflection Lakes.

You can catch both lakes on this trail of gradual ups and downs over low ridges before reaching Bench Lake after 0.75 mile, then continuing another 0.5 mile to Snow Lake, with beautiful views of beargrass and meadow flowers. The round-trip takes about an hour, with a 700-foot elevation gain.

Dead Horse Creek Trail

2.5 miles RT. Easy to moderate. Access: The northern end of the Jackson Visitor Center parking lot.

The Dead Horse Trail serves as a conduit to the Moraine and Glacier Vista trails, as well as provides beautiful views of the Nisqually Glacier to your left as you head up the ridge. You will be rewarded with especially dramatic views if you take the Moraine Trail spur to the left, 0.75 mile up the path.

Nisqually Vista Trail

1.2 miles RT. Easy. Access: Henry M. Jackson Memorial Visitor Center.

This interpretive trail leads across rolling terrain, with a 200-foot elevation gain, to explore the high country flowers, with views of the Nisqually Glacier.

Skyline Loop Trails

5.8–6.5 miles RT. Moderate. Access: To the left of the Paradise Ranger Station, next to the restrooms.

These trails are a good choice for high-elevation hiking, without going all the way to the top of Mount Rainier. They're sort of extended versions of all the trails that surround Paradise, offering lots of beautiful subalpine meadows and close-up views of the Nisqually Glacier, one of the most visible and beautiful glaciers in the park. At Panorama Point, there is a pit toilet for a quick stop before the trail begins to loop back around to the southeast. At the top of this loop, you may have to traverse some snow. There's a 1,700-foot elevation gain. On the way back, check out the views of Mount Adams and Mount St. Helens.

SUNRISE & NORTHEASTERN AREAS

Berkeley Park/Grand Park Trail

13 miles RT. Strenuous. Access: Branches off the Sourdough Ridge Trail (described below).

Head for the high tableland meadows and wildflower and green field bonanza at Grand Park. Please stay on the trails to protect fragile vegetation. Bring plenty of water—there's none up here. Head out of the Sunrise parking lot to the Sourdough Ridge Trail, where the view is the most scenic and the road the easiest. At 6,700-foot Frozen Lake, descend toward Berkeley Park, keeping right with the trail to Mystic Lake. Berkeley Camp is 4 miles from Sunrise, and it's another 2.5 miles, mostly uphill, to the Plateau of Grand Park.

Burroughs Mountain Trail

6 miles RT. Moderate to strenuous. Access: Branches off the Sunrise Rim Trail (described below).

If you can't handle the snow, you might not want to take this trail. It's ice-ax territory, sometimes until early August, so come prepared. Follow the Sunrise Rim Trail, which begins on the south side of the Sunrise Visitor Center parking lot, to Shadow Lake and Sunrise Campground, and to a sharp upturn toward the First Burroughs Peak at 7,000 feet. Beyond this point, you're in a delicate tundra climate, one of the few in the Lower 48. It's possible to take the Frozen Lake Trail at First Burroughs and make a loop back to Sunrise, if you don't feel like climbing anymore. However, should you decide to head up the remaining 400 vertical feet, you'll be treated to fantastic views of Mount Rainier and the Emmons and Winthrop glaciers. Total elevation gain is 1,200 feet.

Glacier Basin Trail

6.5 miles RT. Moderate to strenuous. Access: Past the White River Campground Entrance Station, in the upper area of the White River Campground.

Watch for rusting machinery on this journey through a part of the park that wasn't always so protected. You'll see remnants of an old mining operation from the late 1800s in this glacial valley. Follow an old road up past the headwaters of the White River. After 1 mile, veer to the left for beautiful views of the Emmons Glacier. Beyond the junction of the trail with the Burroughs Mountain Trail, you'll arrive at Glacier Basin Camp. Look for climbers making the ascent to the summit here, along a secondary route. Elevation gain is 1,700 feet.

Mount Fremont Trail

5.6 miles RT. Moderate. Access: The north end of the Sunrise Visitor Center parking lot.

From the trailhead you climb for about 0.3 mile along this popular trail through the surrounding meadows, then follow Sourdough Ridge to the left toward Frozen Lake. At the end of the lake, take the fork to the right for the easy 1.3-mile hike to the Fremont Lookout, from where you can get excellent glimpses of the surrounding Cascades.

On a clear day you might even be able to see Seattle. Elevation gain is 900 feet.

Naches Peak Trail

3.5 miles RT. Easy. Access: Take the Pacific Crest Trailhead located near Tipsoo Lake to a junction with the Naches Peak Loop Trail. (There is also a wheelchair-accessible path at Tipsoo Lake, near the Pacific Crest Trailhead junction.)

This is another popular hike, with stunning views from the top of Naches Peak of the meadows and lakes stretching toward Rainier's icy summit. From the Pacific Crest Trailhead (see the intro to the "Hikes" section, above), head south, traversing the east side of the Naches Peak. There's the junction with the loop that can be taken back to Tipsoo Lake, or continue ahead 0.5 mile to Dewey Lake, where there are good campsites. Elevation gain is 500 feet.

Palisades Lake Trail

7 miles RT. Easy to moderate. Access: Sunrise Visitor Center.

This is a pretty popular trail, so don't expect to get away from other hikers. However, if you're out for a fairly invigorating stroll through forest and meadowlands, this is a good one, with only small rises and falls in elevation as you wander past small alpine lakes towards a rock outcropping called, appropriately enough, the Palisades. There are also good wilderness campsites a little farther on at Dick's Lake and Upper Palisades Lake, though they tend to be crowded in the summertime.

Sourdough Ridge Nature Trail

1.5 miles RT. Easy. Access: Sunrise Visitor Center parking lot.

This loop provides you with a brief glimpse of what's on the longer Sourdough Ridge Trail, described below. This is a self-guided tour of the summer wildflowers and subalpine meadows that's quite popular, and good for kids.

Sourdough Ridge/Dege Peak Trail

4.2 miles RT. Easy to moderate. Access: Sunrise Visitor Center.

From the trailhead, climb to a ridge top and turn east beneath the gaze of Antler Peak, after which you'll cruise along the ridge for wonderful views of Rainier to the south and the brilliant greens of the Yakima parklands below. At the top of Dege Peak, look south for close-up views of the Cowlitz Chimneys and farther-off views of snowcapped Mount Adams.

Summerland Trail

8.5 miles RT. Easy to moderate. Access: Past the White River Entrance, on the way to the Sunrise or the White River areas.

If you want to see some mountain goats, take this trail to Panhandle Gap, about 1.5 miles past the end of the 4-mile, one-way entrance into the Frying Pan Glacier area. This trail can host hundreds of hikers on a peak summer day, so beware. And please stay on the trails to avoid trampling the wildflowers. It's a 3.5-mile graded walk through mature forests before entering the Frying Pan Creek area, where the scenery opens up into the brushy upper Frying Pan Valley. From there it's a 0.5-mile steep climb to the spectacular Summerland Meadows. The total elevation gain is 1,500 feet.

Sunrise Rim Trail

5.2 miles RT. Easy to moderate. Access: Sunrise Visitor Center.

This is another nature trail with many interpretive signs to tell you what to look for as you gaze up at Mount Rainier to the north. About 1.5 miles into the trail, you'll arrive at Shadow Lake, and just beyond, the walk-in Sunrise Campground. With a little more effort, you can hike south to the glacier overlook and be awed by the blue-white overhangs of Emmons Glacier and on to the first Burroughs Mountain.

OHANAPECOSH AREA

Grove of the Patriarchs Trail

1.3 miles RT. Easy. Access: Just west of the Stevens Canyon Entrance on Stevens Canyon Rd.

This short, level, and very popular trail follows the Ohanapecosh River before crossing over a bridge to an island of incredibly huge, thousand-year-old Douglas firs and western red cedars. Even though it's well traveled, it's still a pretty awe-inspiring place, if you can manage to find a little silence in which to meditate on the grandeur of the trees.

Silver Falls Trail

2.7 miles RT. Easy. Access: Ohanapecosh Visitor Center; start at the far end of the "B" Loop of the Ohanapecosh Campground.

This trail, a fairly level one, is popular with families. It winds its way through old-growth forests and over a bridge above the pristine waters of the Ohanapecosh River facing the falls that give the area its name. The misty falls themselves drop 75 feet. Across the bridge below the falls is the return trail to the Ohanapecosh Campground.

NORTHWESTERN RAINIER

In 1999, the Carbon River Road reopened after years of storm damage. This is a very flood-prone area and the road opens and closes periodically. For all trails listed below, remember that the road may end at the park boundary 5 miles from the Ipsut Creek Campground. Be sure to call the **Park Information Line** (© **360/569-2211**) for information before taking any of the northwest Rainier trips.

Storm damage notwithstanding, all trails in the northwestern section of the park can best be reached by driving to the end of the Ipsut Creek Campground Road (or as close as possible) and connecting with the Wonderland Trail, or driving in on the Mowich River Road (Wash. 165). Access to the Wonderland

Trail along this corner of the park by car, unlike those on the southern and northeastern side, is limited. The Carbon Glacier, Rainforest, Mystic Lake, Moraine Park, Mowich Lake, and Tolmie Peak trails can all be reached via the Carbon River Road and the Mowich Lake Road by car, or by the Wonderland Trail on an extended hike.

Carbon Glacier & Moraine Park Trails

6–11 miles RT (depending on route). Moderate to strenuous. Access: The end of the road at the Ipsut Creek Campground.

You begin this hike toward Moraine Park on the Wonderland Trail, the first 3 miles of which are a gentle uphill grade as they parallel the beautiful glacial waters of the Carbon River. Subsequently, the trail crosses the river on a suspension bridge just below the lower edge of the Carbon Glacier. Take a right turn on the Wonderland Trail at its junction with the Northern Loop, and the trail will lead you to the edge of this, the lowest and seemingly most monstrous glacier in the Lower 48. The trail then becomes a series of steep switchbacks that lead you through the neighboring forest to Moraine Park. Along the way, you'll pass several campsites (Carbon River, Dick Creek, and farther along, Mystic Lake). The elevation gain is 1,200 to 3,300 feet, depending on the route you take.

Mystic Lake Trail

15.8 miles Moderate to strenuous. Access: First, take the trail to Moraine Park, then continue to Mystic Lake.

To reach Mystic Lake, you must first hike to the narrow, subalpine valley of Moraine Park, a moderate to strenuous trip. When Mystic Lake is included in the hike, the entire round-trip distance becomes 15.8 miles with elevation gains of 3,900 feet. Beyond the park, the trail goes over two small, wooded ridges, and then descends a short distance to Mystic

Lake. The trail was named by two early naturalists who claimed to have seen a mysterious whirlpool near the lake's outlet. Many people use the campsites around Mystic Lake as base camps for exploring the Curtis Ridge area, and for spectacular views of the Winthrop and Carbon glaciers.

Spray Park Trail

6 miles RT. Moderate. Access: The southeast side of the Mowich Lake Walk-in Campground at the end of Mowich Lake Rd.

Go to Spray Falls at sunset if you want to see the light hit the spray action. Set amid subalpine meadows, Spray Falls is a spectacular sight in the summer when the flowers are blooming, although most of the hike proceeds through forested terrain. The trailhead intersects the Wonderland Trail after a 0.25-mile descent. Follow the Spray Park Trail east for 2 miles, through the woods, across Lee Creek, and eventually to a junction with a spur trail to overlook the falls. The next 0.5 mile to the Spray Park Meadows is a steep climb up a series of switchbacks. Even more extensive meadows are found in another 0.5 mile. The whole trip has an elevation gain of 1,300 feet.

Tolmie Peak

5.6 miles RT. Moderate. Access: The end of Mowich Lake Rd. on the left side of the lake.

This is a hugely popular day hike, with lots of traffic from weekenders and kids, but you know you can't really go that wrong anywhere around here. The trail proceeds gently through 1.25 miles of forested woodland to the junction at Ipsut Pass (elevation 5,100 ft.). Stay left and proceed uphill another 1.75 miles to the subalpine meadows at Eunice Lake for a look at how far you're going to have to climb to Tolmie Peak. *Note:* Tolmie Peak is closed to overnight backpackers. The entire hike has a 1,010-foot elevation gain.

Other Summer Sports & Activities

Biking. There are no trails open to mountain bikes in Mount Rainier National Park. However, there are plenty of trails to ride at nearby **Crystal Mountain** and **White Pass ski areas** during the summer months. Crystal Mountain is by far the most popular and is known for its grueling climbs and brake-turning downhills. Luckily, you can avoid much of the climbing by riding the lifts up. The lifts generally operate only on weekends. A good gravel road for great biking is Westside Road, which you can access through the Nisqually Entrance of Mount Rainier National Park. It is completely closed to motorized vehicles after 3 miles. One of the best reasons to ride this road is the chance to get on some of the little-used westside hiking trails (closed to bikes). Try strapping some hiking boots on your bike; this is a great way to get away from the crowds and access some of the rare, less crowded areas of the park. However, you might want to call ahead for information on the usage of Westside Road.

Boating & Canoeing. Located in the northwest corner of the park, Mowich Lake is a pristine little lake with a peekaboo view of the mountain from its west side. The water is incredibly clear, and it's fun to paddle around gazing down into the deep at the large logs and boulders lying on the bottom. Early morning and late afternoon are particularly good times. You might catch a glimpse of an otter, and in the evening, deer often feed in the meadows by the lake's edge. A walk-in campground beside the lake makes this a great spot for a weekend camping and paddling trip. Yes, there are even a few fish in the lake if you want to try your luck (see "Fishing," below).

Fishing. The good news about fishing in Mount Rainier National Park is that no fishing license is required. The bad news is that the fishing isn't very good. However, there are some fish out there, and you're welcome to try your hand at catching a few. Lots of people do. Just remember that only artificial lures and flies can be used within the park, and some posted waters are closed to fishing. Ask for details.

For the most part, glacial silt keeps Mount Rainier's rivers too cloudy for fishing in the summer. The Ohanapecosh River is one exception. This river in the southeast corner of the park flows clear throughout the summer and is designated fly-fishing only. Anglers are also encouraged to release the trout they catch. Most of the park's many lakes are home to one or another species of trout, but in most cases you're going to have to hike in to do your fishing. Some shorter hikes include Sunrise Lake below Sunrise Point; and Louise, Bench, and Snow lakes, east of Paradise off the road to the Stevens Canyon Entrance.

Horseback Riding. If you'd like to do some horseback riding, you've got a couple of choices in the area. In Elbe, you'll find **EZ Times Outfitters,** 18703 Wash. 706 (© 360/569-2449), which leads rides into the Elbe State Forest. Over on the east side of the park, 19 miles east of Chinook Pass on Wash. 410, you'll find **Chinook Pass Outfitter & Guides,** (© 509/653-2633). East of White Pass on U.S. 12, you'll find **Indian Creek Corral** (© 509/672-2400) near the shore of Rimrock Lake. Horse rental rates start at around $20 per hour.

Mountaineering. Each year, more than 10,000 people set out to climb the 14,410-foot summit of Mount Rainier. That only slightly more than half make it to the top is a testament to how difficult this climb is. Although the ascent does not require rock-climbing skills, the glacier crossings require basic mountaineering knowledge, and the 9,000-foot climb from Paradise is physically demanding.

Also, the elevation often causes altitude sickness. This is not a mountain to be attempted by the unprepared or the untrained, and over the years, dozens of people have died attempting the summit. Because of the many difficulties presented by summit ascents at Mount Rainier, this mountain often serves as a training ground for expeditions headed to peaks all over the world.

The easiest and most popular route starts at Paradise at 5,400 feet and climbs to the stone climbers' shelter at 10,188-foot Camp Muir. From here, climbers, roped together for safety, set out in the middle of the night to reach Columbia Crest, the mountain's highest point. From the summit on a clear day, seemingly all of Washington and much of Oregon stretches below.

The best way for most people to climb Mount Rainier is with **Rainier Mountaineering,** P.O. Box Q, Ashford, WA 98304 (✆ **888/89-CLIMB;** fax 360/569-2982; www.rmiguides.com), which offers a variety of mountaineering classes as well as guided summer climbs. A 1-day basic climbing class combined with the 2-day summit climb costs $771.

White-Water Rafting. The Tieton River, which flows down the eastern slopes of the Cascades to the east of the national park, is one of the state's most popular rafting rivers. The rafting season lasts for the month of September during the annual drawdown of water from Rimrock Reservoir, and the rapids are class III. Rafting companies offering trips on this river include **All Adventure Rafting** (✆ **509/493-3926**), **Alpine Adventures** (✆ **800/723-8386**), and **AAAA River Riders** (✆ **800/448-RAFT**).

Wildlife Viewing. Hunting is prohibited in Mount Rainier National Park; consequently, deer, elk, and mountain goats within the park have lost their fear of humans. Anyone hiking the park's trails in the summer can expect to encounter some of these large mammals. Deer are the most commonly spotted, although it is the park's mountain goats that seem to command the greatest interest. Look for goats on Goat Island Mountain across the White River valley from Sunrise (use binoculars) on the Summerland Trail, on Mount Fremont (5.5-miles round-trip hike from Sunrise), and at Skyscraper Pass (7-mile round-trip hike from Sunrise).

Undoubtedly, the most seen mammals in the park are the marmots, which resemble beavers but have round tails and live in the subalpine meadows. These big, shaggy members of the squirrel family are often seen lying on rocks and soaking up the sun. They often allow people to approach quite closely, but when alarmed, will let loose with a shrill whistle.

Wild animals are fun to see, but they *are* wild. Keep your distance.

Winter Sports & Activities

Cross-Country Skiing. There are several ungroomed cross-country trails around the Paradise and Longmire areas. Perhaps what's equally satisfying in winter is the absence of crowds and cars that haunt these regions during the summer months. Peace and quiet abound when snow covers the landscape, although there is often a threat of avalanches (check at the Jackson Visitor Center or Paradise Ranger Station). The slopes above the Paradise Inn usually stay covered with snow well into June. You can rent cross-country skis at **Longmire** at the National Park Inn (✆ **360/569-2411**). Skis, poles, and shoes will cost you $15 per day.

West of the park, the Mount Tahoma Trails Association Trail System maintains almost 90 miles of easy to difficult trails, which are accessed from Ashford (follow the signs to the snow parks). For information, maps, or hut reservations, contact the **Mount Tahoma Trails Association,** P.O. Box 206, Ashford, WA 98304 (✆ **360/569-2451;** www.skimtta.com), or stop by their headquarters in Ashford, which is usually open on winter weekends.

There are 10 miles of trails at **White Pass** (℃ 509/672-3101; www.skiwhitepass. com for a snow report), which is located about 20 miles southeast of the park.

Outside the northeast entrance of the park, **Crystal Mountain** (℃ 360/663-2265; www.crystalmt.com) offers good backcountry skiing, though there are no maintained trails. Only experienced skiers should attempt backcountry skiing here due to the difficult conditions and danger of avalanches.

Snowmobiling. Snowmobiles are permitted on designated roadways only, and when such roadways are closed by snow to normal traffic. Do not attempt to travel cross-country on trails or on undesignated roads. Obtain a copy of the park's snowmobile regulations.

Snowshoeing. If you've never tried snowshoeing and want to, visit Mount Rainier National Park on a winter weekend or holiday when free, ranger-led **snowshoe walks** lasting about 90 minutes are offered from late December to early April. Call the Longmire Museum for more information (℃ 360/569-2211, ext. 3314). If, after getting a taste for snowshoeing you want to do more, you can rent snowshoes by the day in Longmire at the **gift shop** beside the National Park Inn (℃ 360/569-2411) for $12 per day.

One of the better snowshoeing routes in the park is the marked route from the Paradise parking lot behind the Jackson Visitor Information Center to the Nisqually Glacier Overlook. The Nisqually Vista Trail is only 1.25 miles long and twists and turns as it meanders up and down hills. At the turnaround, you're treated to a great view of the glacier and the rest of the mountain, but don't get too close to the edge!

Lower down on the mountain, at Longmire, snowshoers can make a 4.6-mile loop up Rampart Ridge. This steep trail requires some route finding and the snow level is not always reliable, but if conditions are right, it makes for an enjoyable and rigorous hike. Another

good snowshoeing trail in this same area is the trail to Carter Falls, which starts above Longmire just before the Cougar Rock Campground. This 2.2-mile round-trip trail follows a section of the Wonderland Trail. It's all uphill to Carter Falls and it crosses several avalanche chutes.

Camping

There are over 500 campsites in Mount Rainier in five drive-in campgrounds. Only two of these, Ipsut and Sunshine Point, are open year-round; all others are open seasonally. (All are usually open late June to mid-Sept, though specific opening and closing dates are dependent on weather.) None of the campgrounds in the park have RV utility hookups, nor are there laundry or shower facilities.

You must make reservations at Cougar Rock and Ohanapecosh Campgrounds between the last Friday in June and Labor Day by calling ℃ **800/365-CAMP** or online at http://reservations. nps.gov. Other campgrounds are on a first-come, first-served basis.

Cougar Rock Campground is located 2⅓ miles northwest of Longmire and has an amphitheater for ranger programs. **Ohanapecosh Campground,** 11 miles north of Packwood, Washington, on Wash. 123, also has an amphitheater. **Sunshine Point Campground** is located ⅓ mile from the Nisqually Entrance, and **White River Campground** is 5 miles west of the White River Entrance. **Ipsut Creek Camp Campground** is 5⅓ miles east of the park's Carbon River Entrance.

There are two walk-in campgrounds that often have spaces available even on weekends. **Mowich Lake Campground** is in the northwest corner of the park, at the end of unpaved SR 165, and the sites are only 100 yards from a parking lot. If you're prepared for a longer walk in, consider the **Sunrise Campground,** which is about a mile from the Sunrise parking lot. A backcountry permit is required.

Backcountry camping is free with a permit obtained at any of the ranger stations. A permit is required for all overnight stays in the wilderness. Reservations, which cost $20 per permit, can be made May to September only. Call © **360/569-HIKE.**

When the drive-in national park campgrounds are full, try **La Wis Wis,** a national forest campground on U.S. 12 and the Cowlitz River, near the southeast entrance to the park. There are also numerous unremarkable National Forest Service campgrounds along U.S. 12 east of White Pass and along Wash. 310 east of the park. These campgrounds will be your best chance of finding a campsite on a Friday or Saturday night in summer. The campgrounds along Wash. 410 tend to be less crowded since they are harder to reach and are not near any fishing lakes.

National Forest campgrounds are also located within a few miles of the southwest and northeast entrances.

Where to Stay

For information or reservations at the lodgings inside the park, contact **Mount Rainier Guest Services,** P.O. Box 108, Ashford, WA 98304 (© **360/569-2275;** fax 360/569-2770; www.guestservices. com/rainier).

There are a number of places to stay in the surrounding communities in addition to those reviewed here. For a list, contact the **Seattle and King County Convention and Visitor's Bureau** (© **206/461-5840;** www.seeseattle.org) or the **Enumclaw Area Chamber of Commerce** (© **360/825-7666;** www.enumclaw chamber.com).

INSIDE THE PARK

National Park Inn

At the Longmire Entrance, off Wash. 706 (P.O. Box 108), Ashford, WA 98304. © **360/569-2275.** www.guestservices.com/rainier. 25 units, 18 with bathroom. $87 double without bathroom, $118–$159 double with bathroom. AE, DC, DISC, MC, V.

Located in Longmire in the southwest corner of the park, this rustic lodge was opened in 1920 and fully renovated in 1990. With only 25 rooms and open year-round, the National Park Inn makes a great little getaway or base for exploring the mountain. The inn's front veranda has a view of Mount Rainier, and inside there's a guest lounge with a river-rock fireplace that's perfect for winter-night relaxing. The guest rooms vary in size, but come with rustic furniture, new carpeting, and coffeemakers. In winter this lodge is popular with

Campground	Total Sites	RV Hookups	Dump Station	Toilets	Drinking Water
Cougar Rock	178	No	Yes	Yes	Yes
*Ipsut Creek**	30	No	No	No	No
*La Wis Wis***	90	No	No	Yes	Yes
*Mowich Lake**	30	No	No	No	No
Ohanapecosh	189	No	Yes	Yes	Yes
*Sunrise**	8	No	No	No	No
Sunshine Point	18	No	No	Yes	Yes
White River	112	No	No	Yes	Yes

* Camping here requires a Mount Rainier National Park backcountry permit.
** National Forest site on reservation program.

cross-country skiers; skis and snowshoes can be rented here. The inn's restaurant has a limited menu that nevertheless manages to have something for everyone. There's also a small bar. The Inn offers a B&B package from $118. This is a nonsmoking establishment. You'll need to book reservations well in advance during the summer months. If at first you don't succeed, keep trying because there are often cancellations.

Paradise Inn

Just east of the Henry M. Jackson Memorial Visitor Center (P.O. Box 108, Ashford, WA 98304). ℂ **360/569-2275.** www.guestservices.com/rainier. 117 units, 86 with bathroom. $82 double without bathroom, $123–$169 double with bathroom; $185 suite. AE, DC, DISC, MC, V. Closed early Oct to mid-May.

Built in 1917 high on the flanks of Mount Rainier in an area aptly known as Paradise, this rustic lodge offers breathtaking views of the mountain and the nearby Nisqually Glacier. Miles of trails and meadows make this the perfect spot for some relatively easy alpine exploring. Cedar-shake siding, huge exposed beams, cathedral ceilings, and a gigantic stone fireplace all add up to a quintessential mountain retreat. A warm and cozy atmosphere prevails. The guest rooms vary in size and amenities, so be

sure to specify which type you'd like. The inn's large dining room serves three meals a day, but the Sunday brunch, served from 11am to 2:30pm, is legendary. There's also a snack bar and a lounge. The lodge is entirely nonmoking.

Alexander's Country Inn

37515 Wash. 706 E., Ashford, WA 98304. ℂ **800/654-7615** or 360/569-2300. Fax 360/569-2323. www.alexanderscountryinn.com. 12 units, 2 houses. May–Oct $110 double, $140 suite; Nov–Apr $89 double, $110 suite. Rates include full breakfast. MC, V.

Located just outside the park's Nisqually Entrance, this bed-and-breakfast first opened as an inn back in 1912. Today, as then, it is one of the preferred places to stay in the area, offering not only comfortable rooms but also some of the best food around. Much care went into the interior restoration. The first floor is taken up by the dining room, but on the second floor you'll find a big lounge where you can sit by the fire on a cold night. By far the best room in the house is the tower suite, which is in a turret and has plenty of windows looking out on the woods. After a hard day of

Showers	Fire Pits/ Grills	Laundry	Public Phone	Reserve	Fees	Open
No	Yes	No	Yes	No	$12–$15	Late May to mid-Oct
Yes	No	No	No	No	Free	Year-round
No	Yes	No	No	No	$14–$28	Mid-May to mid-Sept
No	Yes	No	No	No	Free	Late June to mid-Oct
No	Yes	No	Yes	No	$12–$15	Late May to mid-Oct
No	Yes	No	No	No	Free	Year-round
No	Yes	No	No	No	$10	Year-round
No	Yes	No	No	No	$10	Late June to mid-Sept

playing on the mountain, there's no better place to relax than in the hot tub overlooking the inn's trout pond. The entire inn is nonsmoking. The inn also rents two three-bedroom houses (call for details).

The Hobo Inn

Wash. 7 (P.O. Box 921), Elbe, WA 98330. ✆ **360/569-2500.** 8 units. $50–$85 double. AE, DISC, DC, MC, V.

If you're a railroad buff, you won't want to pass up the opportunity to spend the night in a remodeled caboose. Each of the eight cabooses is a little different (one even has its own private hot tub). Though the oldest of the cars dates from 1916, they have all been outfitted with comfortable beds and bathrooms. Some have bay windows while others have cupolas. For the total railroad experience, you can dine in the adjacent Mount Rainier Railroad Dining Co. dining car restaurant (see "Where to Dine," below) and go for a ride on the Mount Rainier Scenic Railroad (✆ **888/STEAM-11**).

Mountain Meadows Inn Bed & Breakfast

28912 Wash. 706 E., Ashford, WA 98304. ✆ **360/569-2788.** www.mountainmeadowsinn. com. 6 units. $135–$149 double. Rates include breakfast. MC, V.

Set beneath tall trees beside a small creek, this B&B was built in 1910 as the home of the superintendent for the lumber mill in the town of National, which was the site of the largest sawmill west of the Mississippi. Today this impressive old home is filled with unique collections, including an outstanding display of memorabilia of John Muir and the national parks, authentic Northwest Coast American Indian basketry, and a 1,000-volume nature library. Each of the attractively decorated rooms has a private bathroom (some with shower only, some with tub only, and some with both). There are three rooms

in the main house, decorated with antiques and American Indian art; plus three rooms in a separate guesthouse, which are more modern. We especially like the Mountain Berry Room in the main house because of its claw-foot tub and handsome early American furnishings. The main house's big front porch overlooks the creek, and there is room to roam on nearby hiking trails through the site of the historic town of National.

Nisqually Lodge

31609 Wash. SR 706, Ashford, WA 98304. ✆ **888/674-3554** or 360/569-8804. Fax 360/ 569-2435. www.escapetothemountains.com. 24 units. A/C TV TEL. $80–$85 double. AE, MC, V.

This modern lodge is well located near the Nisqually Entrance to Mount Rainier National Park, and has a popular restaurant, the Rainier Overland, next door. Rooms are of the modern American motel style, average size, with wood-toned furnishings, upholstered chairs, and a few homey touches, such as flowers. The Nisqually offers a guest laundry, an outdoor hot tub, and satellite TV. You can read or relax by the fireplace in their Great Room.

Stone Creek Lodge

38624 Wash. 706 E., Ashford, WA 98304. ✆ **800/678-3942** or 360/569-2355. www. destination-rainier.com/stone. 10 cabins. $85–$125 double. AE, DISC, MC, V.

Located only 200 yards from the park's Nisqually Entrance, these cabins are set amid green lawns that attract deer throughout the year. These are not the most atmospheric of the cabins right outside the park entrance, but they are the cleanest and most up-to-date. Big picture windows let in plenty of light. Larger cabins have kitchens and fireplaces and sleep up to four people; some smaller ones have microwaves and refrigerators; and all have gas-log fireplaces. Hot tubs have been added. You might even get in on a marshmallow toast over an evening campfire.

Stormking

P.O. Box 126, Ashford, WA 98304. © **360/ 569-2964.** www.stormkingspa.com. 3 cabins. Cabin $155–$175 double. MC, V.

Especially appealing for active, out-doorsy adult couples, the Stormking started out as another hot tub and massage facility similar to the long-established Wellspring. But people enjoyed the setting and experience so much that they kept telling co-owner Deborah Sample that she should build cabins and take overnight guests. That's just what she and her co-owner, Steven Brown, did, and they are gorgeous cab-ins. Two cabins have hot tubs, and so much more. Spa treatments are offered. Breakfasts are "mountain vegetarian style." The Stormking is nonsmoking.

Wellspring

54922 Kernahan Rd., Ashford, WA 98304. © **360/569-2514.** www.wellspringspa.com. 13 units: 3 tent cabins, 6 log cabins, 1 cottage, 3 other; plus larger accommodations for groups. $59–$159 double. $299–$369 group. MC, V.

Billing itself a woodland spa, this rustic and relaxing hideaway more than lives up to its name and is an excellent choice for anyone who enjoys being pampered. Private hot tubs and wood-fired saunas will take the chill out of even the coldest night, while sore mus-cles will benefit from a massage by owner Sunny Thompson-Ward. Accom-modations are an eclectic and fanciful mix. In the modern log cabins, tucked up against the edge of the forest, are feather beds, wood stoves, and vaulted ceilings. In The Nest, you'll find a queen-size bed suspended by ropes beneath a skylight. In the Three Bears Cottage, there's rustic log furniture and a full kitchen; kids are allowed in this cottage. In the Tatoosh Room, there's a large stone fireplace, a whirlpool tub, and a waterfall shower. Want to sleep in a greenhouse with a cedar hot tub and wood-fired sauna? You can—but you can't have the room to yourself until

9pm. Several of the rooms and the cab-ins come with a breakfast basket. Hot tubs and saunas are an additional $5–$10 per person per hour for guests. There are three attractive tent cabins (one permitting children), with four-poster beds; candlelit, but with wood and propane heaters; and stars that appear on the ceiling and then gently fade. That's unique. The facility is non-smoking and pets are not allowed.

OUTSIDE THE NORTHEAST (WHITE RIVER) ENTRANCE

Alta Crystal Resort at Mount Rainier

68317 Wash. (SR) 410 E., Greenwater, WA 98022. © **800/277-6475** or 360/663-2500. Fax 360/663-0728. www.altacrystalresort. com. 24 units. TV TEL. $139–$249 (1–6 peo-ple). AE, MC, V.

This is the closest lodging to the north-east (White River) park entrance and the Sunrise area. The resort has wooded grounds and makes a good base in winter when skiers flock to Crystal Mountain's slopes (just minutes away), but is most popular from late spring through early fall. The resort features suites in chalets and a log honeymoon cabin, all with a mountain lodge atmos-phere and lots of homey touches, such as dried flowers. Accommodations are in one-bedroom units, with a queen bed in the bedroom plus a futon in the liv-ing/dining area; and loft chalets, which have vaulted ceilings, skylights, and two bathrooms and can sleep up to four adults and two children under 12. No matter what size suite you choose, you'll find a full kitchen, fireplace or wood stove, phone with dataport, satellite TV, and VCR. The honeymoon cabin (avail-able for two adults only; no children), set apart from the other buildings, is done in an extremely attractive, moun-tain lodge style, with a gas fireplace, brass bed with a down comforter, lots of large windows, a full kitchen, and a TV/VCR. There is a rustic log lodge for recreation and groups, an outdoor pool and hot tub, with horseback riding, hiking, and mountain-bike trails from your door. Enjoy nightly bonfires, barbecues, and picnic tables.

Cowlitz River Lodge

13069 U.S. 12 (P.O. Box 488), Packwood, WA 98361. © **888/305-2185** or 360/494-4444. Fax 360/494-2075. www.escapetothe mountains.com. 32 units. A/C TV TEL. $50–$75 double. AE, DC, MC, V.

With easy access to Mount Rainier, Mount St. Helens, and White Pass skiing, this lodge offers comfortable accommodations with many amenities. Owned by the same company as the Nisqually Lodge (see above), rooms here are typical of modern American motel style—average size, with woodtoned furnishings, upholstered chairs, and a few homey touches. There's an outdoor hot tub, guest laundry, and a waxing room for cross-country skiers. They also offer a conference room accommodating 60. You may see deer or elk on the lawn, and you can laze by the lobby fireplace.

Hotel Packwood

104 Main St., Packwood, WA 98361. © **360/494-5431.** 9 units, 2 with bathroom, 7 with shared bathroom. TV. $39–$55 double. DISC, MC, V.

Two stories tall with a wraparound porch and weathered siding, this renovated 1912 hotel looks like a classic mountain lodge even though it's right in the middle of this small town. The tiny rooms aren't for the finicky, but are comfortable and most welcome after a day spent traipsing around on park trails. There are iron bed frames in some rooms and a fireplace in the lobby. Packwood is about 10 miles from the southeast entrance to the park.

Where to Dine

In the park, there are dining rooms at **Paradise Inn** (seasonal) and the **National Park Inn** (year-round). (See "Where to Stay," above, for descriptions of the inns themselves.) Operated by the same park concessionaire, both restaurants offer the same interesting menu of American and regional dishes, including trout, salmon, chicken, steak, pasta, and stir-fry. Especially recommended, at least for those who don't mind a bit of boozing at dinner, is the bourbon buffalo meatloaf. Neither restaurant accepts reservations, and because these are the only formal dining options within the park, you may have to wait a bit for a table. But we think the wait is worth it, especially at the Paradise Inn dining room, which has a large fireplace and great views of the surrounding scenery. The National Park Inn is a bit more family oriented; probably a better choice for those with a herd of kids in tow. For quick meals, there are snack bars at the **Henry M. Jackson Memorial Visitor Center,** at **Paradise,** and at **Sunrise Lodge.**

In Ashford you'll find a place that bakes great pies, the **Copper Creek Restaurant,** Wash. 706 E. (© **360/569-2326**), which is one of the closest restaurants to the park's southwest (Nisqually) entrance. Just down the road, another popular spot, **Rainier Overland Restaurant,** 31811 Wash. 706 (© **360/569-0851**), is known for its fresh seafood, trout, and homemade pies. Another interesting dining option in the area has been the **Mount Rainier Railroad Dinner Train** (© **888/RRDINER**), which leaves from the town of Elbe, west of the park's Nisqually Entrance, and spends 4 hours meandering through the foothills. A vintage steam locomotive pulls the restored passenger cars, which include an observation lounge car. The dinner train costs $70 per person, and passengers have the option of prime rib, salmon, or ground ostrich steak. The train did not run in 2003, when the tracks were under repair, so be sure to call ahead to see if the dinner service has been resumed.

Alexander's

37515 Wash. 706 E., Ashford. ℂ **360/569-2300.** Reservations recommended. Full dinners $16–$19; a la carte $11–$14. MC, V. AMERICAN.

Alexander's, which is also a popular B&B, is the best place to dine outside the Nisqually Entrance to the park. Dining is now offered outside during the summer beside the pond and waterfall. Fresh trout from the inn's pond is the dinner of choice here, but you'll also find chicken potpie, steaks, fresh salmon, stuffed pork chops, and pasta. Whatever you order, just be sure to save room for the wild blackberry pie.

Mount Rainier Railroad Dining Co.

Wash. 7, Elbe. ℂ **360/569-2505.** Lunch $5–$15; main dinner courses $5–$21. AE, DC, DISC, MC, V. Mon–Fri 11am–9pm winter weekdays, summer and weekends 8am–9pm. AMERICAN.

You can't miss this unusual restaurant in Elbe—just watch for all the cabooses of the adjacent Hobo Inn. Meals are basic, with steaks and fried seafood the staples of the dinner menu, but the surroundings make this place worth a stop. You'll be dining in an old railroad dining car. Your car won't go anywhere while you dine, but you'll get a sense of being on a rail journey.

NORTH CASCADES NATIONAL PARK

by Jack Olson

THE CASCADE RANGE, IN MANY STRETCHES OF ITS SPAN, RECEIVES SIGNIF-
icant visitation, but here in the northern reaches lies the largest
wilderness in the state of Washington. Here, gray wolves and grizzly bears still roam, and human encroachment is more limited.

The North Cascades National Park
Service Complex is at the heart of this
region. Note the name; this is not just a
park but a complex, which includes not
only the national park itself but also
Ross Lake and Lake Chelan national
recreation areas. In 1988, by act of
Congress, about 93% of the acreage of
the entire complex was designated the
"Stephen Mather Wilderness." Unlike
many national recreation areas, both
Ross Lake and Lake Chelan are wild and
remote, with minimal development.

A trip into this region is a true wilderness experience. Hiking here takes time
and preparation. Although there are
several shorter trails, many attract the
rugged few to take a few days or weeks
to get reacquainted with the natural
state of things. If you're prepared,
though, there's nothing else like it in
the continental United States.

Geologically speaking, the North
Cascades are some of the most complex
and least understood mountains in
North America. These peaks were
formed over millions of years as a

tectonic plate drifting northward from
the South Pacific slammed into the
North American coast, causing the
area's sedimentary rocks to buckle, fold,
and transform. In some areas, the rock
in the North Cascades is obviously the
result of this collision and subsequent
metamorphosis. However, in other
areas, there is rock that predates the tectonic collision—one upthrust of mountain is believed to be 10 million years
old.

Geologic complexity has been further augmented in the North Cascades
by glaciation both past and present. In
past ice ages both alpine glaciers and
the continental ice sheet covered this
region. The visual legacy of this intense
activity today can be seen in the wide
U-shaped valleys carved out by the ice
sheet. The single most fascinating
legacy of this glaciation is Lake Chelan,
which lies in the heart of the North Cascades southern section.

Avoiding the Crowds. Actually, it's not
hard at all to avoid the crowds in the

North Cascades. The lack of roads, the weather, and the ruggedness of the terrain all work in concert to keep this one of the best-kept secrets in the national park system.

If it's true isolation you seek, head north. The northern unit of the national park has the least number of tourists. (Lake Chelan, Ross Lake, and Diablo Lake are all tourist-heavy spots.) But, considering that Stehekin (the developed unit of the southern park section) has a permanent, year-round population of around 100, it's a matter of avoiding the crowds or being absolutely alone, at least for the fall and winter.

In the summer, this park can be like many others in the system, and you're more likely to run into folks on the Big Beaver Trail, or on your way to Hozomeen, than in the fall, which is about the last part of the year in which you can easily get anywhere in the park. Ross Lake is thicker with boaters on summer holiday weekends, and the heaviest load of visitors all year can be found in Stehekin and the Cascade Pass area during July and August. Of course, the deeper into the backcountry you go, the fewer people you are likely to encounter. Winter is not to be underestimated in this park, and remember Wash. State Route 20 will almost certainly be closed.

Just the Facts

GETTING THERE & GATEWAYS

There's only one paved road that goes through the park complex, **Wash. State Route 20.** There are a few unpaved alternatives, though. The **Cascade River Road,** which leaves Wash. 20 at Marblemount, enters the national park proper as an unpaved road. And the gravel **Stehekin Valley Road** above High Bridge also enters the national park. This road, however, does not connect with the outside world; rather, the park and a concessionaire provide shuttle service along this road from mid-May to mid-October.

From **Seattle** on the west side, take the Wash. State Route 20 exit off I-5 and head east, toward Rockport and Marblemount, into the park. From **Spokane** (the major metropolitan area on the east side) it's U.S. 2 West, linking up with U.S. 97 North, to Wash. State Route 153 and finally Wash. State Route 20. And remember, in the winter, these roads could be closed any time from late October to early May. Be sure to call ahead.

The Nearest Airport. The Seattle-Tacoma International Airport (© 206/431-4444) is located 15 miles south of Seattle on I-5. The airport is served by practically all major airlines and car rental companies, whose toll-free numbers are in the appendix.

INFORMATION

Contact **North Cascades National Park Service Complex,** 810 Wash. State Route 20, Sedro-Woolley, WA 98284 (© 360/856-5700; www.nps.gov/noca). The park publishes a newspaper, the *North Cascades Challenger,* which contains much useful information. This newspaper is published once a year, so current information, such as road closures, is best obtained by phone or checking the park's website.

VISITOR CENTERS

The **North Cascades Visitor Center** (mile marker 120, Wash. State Route 20, Newhalem; © 206/386-4495), open daily in the summer and weekends only during the winter, offers exhibits, audiovisual programs, a bookstore, and assistance from rangers. There is also a wheelchair-accessible trail (Sterling Munro Viewpoint) leading from the back of the building that affords excellent views of the surrounding mountains. There are several other universally accessible trails nearby, including the Rock Shelter Trail.

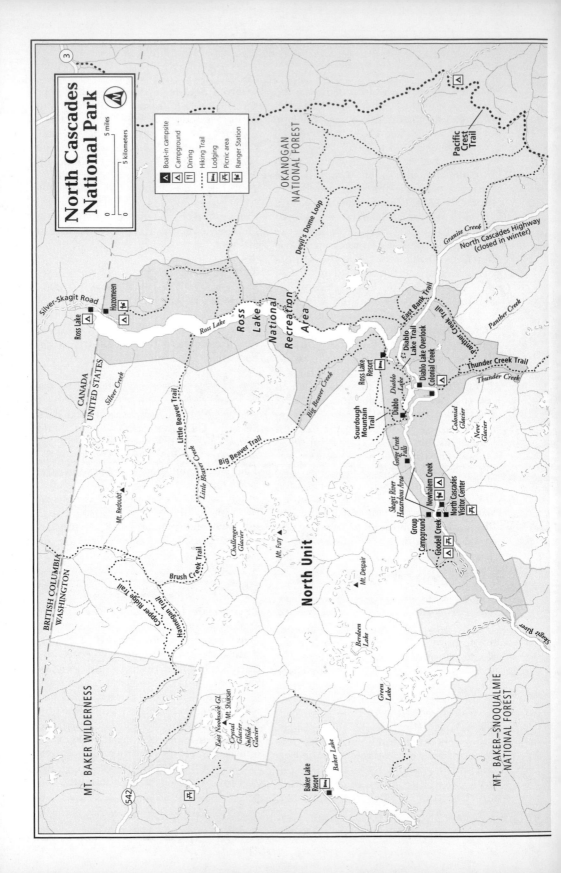

North Cascades
National Park

3

5 miles
5 kilometers
0
0

Boat-in campsite
Campground
Dining
Hiking Trail
Lodging
Picnic area
Ranger Station

OKANOGAN
NATIONAL FOREST

Devil's Dome Loop

Pacific Crest
Trail

Granite Creek

North Cascades Highway
(closed in winter)

Panther Creek

Silver-Skagit Road

Hozomeen

Ross Lake

Ross Lake

Ross Lake National Recreation Area

Ross Lake
Resort

East Bank Trail

Panther Creek Trail

Diablo
Lake Trail

Diablo
Lake Overlook

Colonial Creek

Thunder Creek Trail

Thunder Creek

Big Beaver Creek

Sourdough
Mountain
Trail

Diablo
Lake

Diablo

Colonial
Glacier

New
Glacier

CANADA
UNITED STATES

Silver Creek

Little Beaver Trail

Little Beaver Creek

Big Beaver Trail

Gorge Creek
Falls

Skagit River
Hazardous Area

Newhalem Creek

North Cascades
Visitor Center

BRITISH COLUMBIA
WASHINGTON

Mt. Redoubt

Challenger
Glacier

Mt. Fury

North Unit

Mt. Despair

Group
Campground

Goodell Creek

Skagit River

Copper Ridge Trail

Hannegan Trail

Brush Creek Trail

Bersden
Lake

MT. BAKER WILDERNESS

East Nooksack Gl.

Mt. Shuksan

Crystal
Glacier

Selfide
Glacier

Green
Lake

Baker
Lake

Baker Lake
Resort

542

MT. BAKER–SNOQUALMIE
NATIONAL FOREST

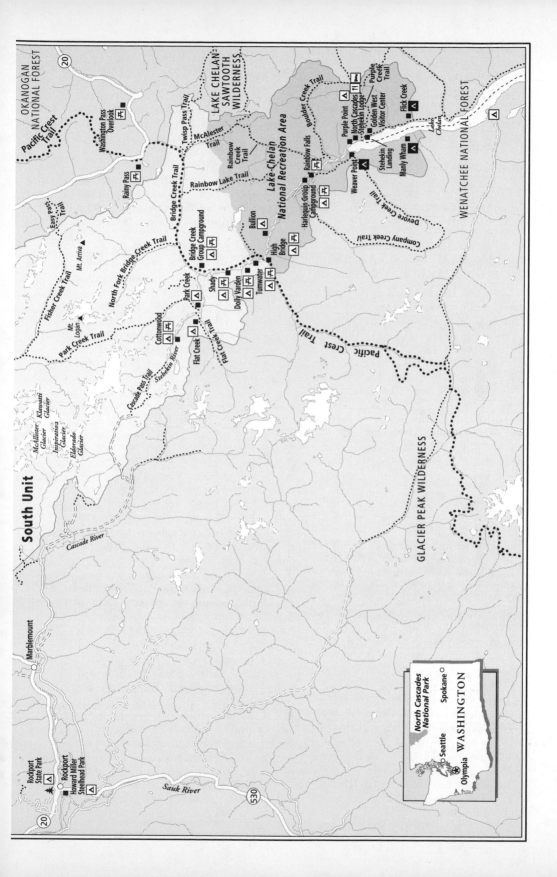

The **Golden West Visitor Center,** P.O. Box 7, Stehekin (℗ **360/856-5700,** ext. 340, then ext. 14), located on the banks of the northern tip of Lake Chelan, provides information on camping, hiking, backcountry permits, and the local environs in general, plus interpretive exhibits and a bookstore. Call for hours of operation. Nearby, you can rent bicycles from a concessionaire.

GETTING AROUND INSIDE THE PARK

By Boat. On Lake Chelan in the spring and summer, the *Lady Express,* the *Lady of the Lake II,* and the *Lady Cat* (a high-speed catamaran) run between the Lake Chelan boat landing and Stehekin at the north end of the lake. In the fall and winter, there's only the *Lady Express.* Rides cost $26 to $90 round-trip, depending on the boat. Contact **Lake Chelan Boat Company** (℗ **509/682-4584**). The **Ross Lake Resort** (℗ **206/386-4437**) operates water taxis to trailheads and campgrounds on Ross Lake, as well as portage service.

By Shuttle Bus. Two different shuttle buses provide transportation up the Stehekin Valley Road.

One, operated by the National Park Service, costs $6 one-way and operates in the Upper Valley from High Bridge to Glory Mountain. Reservations should be made at least 2 days ahead of time (preferably much farther in advance) by calling the **Golden West Visitor Center** (℗ **360/856-5700,** ext. 340, then 14).

Between mid-June and the end of September, another shuttle bus, the Stehekin Shuttle, runs several times a day between Stehekin Landing and High Bridge, the Lower Valley Shuttle. No reservations are required, and the cost is $6 one-way. If you just want to ride as far as the Stehekin Pastry Company, the fare is only $1 each way.

Taxi service is also available from the North Cascades Stehekin Lodge at the boat landing.

By Air. If you want to get to Stehekin in a hurry, you can make the trip by float-plane on **Chelan Airways** (℗ **509/682-5555** or 509/682-5065), which leaves from the dock next to the ferries at Chelan. The fare is $120 round-trip. This company also offers flightseeing trips for between $80 and $169. Rates are per person, two passenger minimum. Children 2 to 11 are half fare.

FEES & PERMITS

There are currently no entrance fees for the park complex itself, though there are fees for camping (see the campground chart, below). The Northwest Forest Pass ($5 per day or $30 per year) is required for Cascade River Road parking and certain trailheads along Wash. State Route 20. A dock fee pass ($5 per day or $40 per year) is required on Lake Chelan from May 1 until October 31. Backcountry permits are required but free.

SPECIAL REGULATIONS & WARNINGS

Beware of the wintertime! Wash. State Route 20 is usually closed from mid-November through mid-April. Call ahead to the park complex headquarters in Sedro-Woolley (℗ **360/856-5700**), or check the park's website, www.nps.gov/noca/cond.htm.

Check in at a visitor center for full details on trail info before you head into the backcountry. Since this is bear and mountain lion (cougar) country, you might want to pick up the free handout on hiking and camping safety.

Other than the general precautions that anyone would take when camping in a wilderness area, keep in mind that the North Cascades National Park Service Complex can be extremely remote for both the backcountry hiker and the midpark driver. Even when day hiking, remember to carry enough water (and all of the 10 essential items; see box, below). Don't forget bug spray—the area has a lot of water (not necessarily to drink), and consequently, lots of insects during some seasons at some locations.

The most pernicious of seasons for people visiting the North Cascades area is the winter, which begins creeping up in October in the upper elevations and mid-November in the lower elevations. It lasts until mid- to late April, and is accompanied by the regular closure of Wash. State Route 20. Closure depends on snow and avalanche conditions.

From April to September, things get pretty temperate, with daytime temperatures ranging from 50° to 80°F (10°C–27°C), depending on the elevation. However, this is a land of extremes: Trails at higher elevations are usually snow-covered into early July (though this varies considerably from year to year), and summer temperatures of 100°F (38°C) are not unusual at Ross Lake and Lake Chelan. As can usually be expected in the northwest, rains arrive westerly from the Pacific in the spring and fall, with summer being the most pleasant all around. At any time, though, expect rain; and bring rain gear. The eastern side of the mountains is less wet than the western though this is nothing to bank on.

In addition, with the extremes in altitude here, it's always good to bring some warm clothing, even in the summer months.

There are several **art exhibits** at the Golden West Visitor Center in the summer. Contact park headquarters for dates.

If You Have Only 1 Day

Considering that this is one of the most rugged wilderness areas in the United States, any attempt to see the park in a day must be made with the understanding that you're not going to see it all.

10 Essential Items

The Park Service considers the following 10 items absolute essentials for hikers—even day-hikers—in the North Cascades National Park Service Complex. Hikers should carry them and know how to use them.

- Navigation (a topographical map and compass)
- Food and water (boiling water can kill *Giardia*, but some treatment pills can't)
- Clothing (including rain gear, wool socks, sweater, gloves, and hat)
- Light (a flashlight with spare bulb and batteries)
- Fire (waterproof matches and a fire starter, such as a candle)
- Sun protection (sunglasses and sunscreen)
- First aid (a kit including any special medications you might need)
- Knife (a folding pocket knife is best)
- Signals (both audible and visual: whistle and metal mirror)
- Emergency shelter (a plastic tube shelter or waterproof bivouac sack)

For most folks with limited time, the choice is a **summer drive** across the park via Wash. State Route 20 (North Cascades Highway, described in the next section).

If You Have More Time

The road into the park is a beautiful drive along the banks of the Skagit River, past the Mount Baker–Snoqualmie National Forest. Your last real connection with civilization, and the last chance to stock up on groceries, is Marblemount, the oldest town in the region. From here, you can head south or east. South is the Cascade River Road, and east is Wash. State Route 20.

The **Cascade River Road** is a 23-mile stretch of mostly gravel road that leads to the Cascade Pass Trailhead. The road, at the very beginning, crosses the Skagit River and then passes near a fish hatchery before terminating at the **Cascade Pass Trailhead** (Northwest Forest Pass required for parking). Many folks take the 3.7-mile one-way trip to the top of Cascade Pass, which leads the hiker up a relatively modest set of switchbacks to beautiful views of glaciers and sub-alpine meadows.

If you're not up to the unpaved twisting of the Cascade River Road, continue on Wash. State Route 20 to **Newhalem,** where the North Cascades Visitor Center has exhibits and regularly scheduled ranger-led walks and talks. This is a good place to get information about the many short walks and hikes that are in the immediate vicinity. You'll find a short, boardwalk trail (Sterling Munro Viewpoint) beginning behind the visitor center that affords beautiful views of the surrounding mountains. In addition, if you're there late enough in the day, check out the trail to **Ladder Creek Falls** (which is not on National Park Service property but rather owned by Seattle City Light), which is fun in a most decidedly touristy manner. There's a hydroelectric dam at the end of the trail that creates a miniature light show on the falls at night, created by James Ross, the master dam builder of the area. It's worth the hike.

The National Park Service recommends the short, accessible, **Newhalem Rockshelter Trail** to an archaeological site near the visitor center, as well as the **River Loop Trail** from the visitor center.

Next up on the route is the little town of **Diablo,** located at the foot of 389-foot-high Diablo Dam, which holds back the blue-green waters of Diablo Lake. A tour operated by Seattle City

Light's **Skagit Tours** (✆ 206/684-3030) takes you on Diablo Lake. Tours last 2 hours and cost $17 for adults, $15 for seniors over 62, $12 youths 6 to 12, 5 and under free. Reservations are recommended.

As the road loops south from Diablo, look for fantastic views of **Neve Glacier.** In fact, there are beautiful views to be had from a plethora of turnouts along the road. Between Newhalem and Diablo there is the new, and universally accessible, **Gorge Overlook Trail,** with great views and interpretive signs.

At the **Ross Lake Dam,** the lake begins its 24-mile dogleg up the eastern side of the park complex to the Canadian border. For views of the lake from the dam, stop the car and take the steep, 1-mile walk down the **Ross Dam Trail** (Northwest Forest Trail pass required for parking). This trail leads over the top of the dam, eventually winding its way to the Ross Lake Resort and the North Cascades backcountry. Another good choice is the accessible **Happy Creek Forest Walk,** a quarter mile past the Ross Dam Trailhead, a ⅓-mile boardwalk stroll through old-growth forest, with interpretive signs. Farther along Wash. State Route 20, take the turnout at the **Ross Lake Overlook,** where you can see the Ruby Arm (leading to Ruby Creek) as well as Ross Lake proper, heading north toward Canada (with Hozomeen Mountain in the distance).

The **Stehekin Area,** at the head of Lake Chelan, is not accessible by car. To get there, you have to either hike in, take a passenger ferry or floatplane up from the southern resort town of Chelan, or take the Cascade River Road from Marblemount to its southern terminus at the **Cascade Pass Trailhead.** From there, you can hike 12 miles over Cascade Pass to Glory Mountain, along the Stehekin Valley Road, where you can catch a shuttle bus to the Stehekin area, if the road is open (usually from early July to mid-Oct). Flood damage has closed the road from Glory Mountain to its terminus 2¾ miles farther at Cottonwood Camp. Be sure to call ahead for up-to-date information and to reserve a seat on the **shuttle bus** (© **360/856-5700,** ext. 340, then ext. 14). A ferry ride up the lake from Chelan is the only quick way to the Stehekin Area. (A floatplane is actually the quickest, though most expensive, option.)

Once you make it to Stehekin, you can rent a bike to ride the roads in the area, but bikes are not permitted on trails. Give yourself enough time and strength for the hike out, though.

If you wish to visit the **northern sections of the park,** there are a couple of options. From the Ross Dam area, park the car and hike the trail in to the **Ross Lake Resort.** You can hike around the general area, or, better yet, catch a water taxi up the shores of the lake. Call the Ross Lake Resort to arrange for **water taxi service** (© **206/386-4437**). The taxis will drop you off at any of the trailheads that intersect both sides of the shores of this lake all the way to Hozomeen, the northernmost part of the lake in U.S. territory. Ross Lake Resort also offers boat rentals (small outboards, canoes, and kayaks) for those who want to fish or explore the lake on their own.

The only practical way to get near the **northwest section of the park** by vehicle is to head east from the Mount Baker Wilderness Area, which is popular and easily accessible because of the Mount Baker Ski Area. Beyond the Mount Baker area, take the **Hannegan Road** (Forest Service Road 32), which is accessible by two-wheel drive. As usual, it's a good idea to call ahead for road conditions. Beyond the end of the road lie the popular **Hannegan Pass, Copper Ridge,** and **Chilliwack trails.** These are popular trails in the summer season, but they are multiday hikes and require a permit for camping overnight. Backcountry permits are available at the Glacier Public Service Center in Glacier. Permits are issued in person only, the day of your trip or up to

a day in advance. Permits are issued on a first come, first served basis. The trails offer beautiful views of glaciers spreading southward through the park, especially the Nooksack Glacier along the ridges overhanging the Nooksack River. The Northwest Forest Pass is required for all trailhead parking on U.S. Forest Service Lands in Washington and Oregon.

Organized Tours & Ranger Programs

For tours of Diablo Lake and Ross Dam, call **Seattle City Light, Skagit Tours** (© **206/684-3030**). Check with them for the new tour program.

Want to track radio-collared mountain caribou? Stalk newts, frogs, and salamanders in Heather Meadows? Learn about Lummi Indian basketry? Delve into the mysteries of mycology? Hang with some bats? You can do any of these things if you sign up for the right class through the North Cascades Institute. Offering around 60 natural history field seminars each year, **North Cascades Institute,** 810 Wash. State Route 20, Sedro-Woolley, WA 98284-1239 (© **360/856-5700,** ext. 209; fax 360/856-1934; www.ncascades.org), is a nonprofit educational organization that offers a wide range of courses each year. Although these seminars, many of which involve camping out, focus on the North Cascades region, there are programs throughout the state. The Institute, in partnership with the National Park Service and Seattle City Light, will open a North Cascades Environmental Learning Center in 2004.

A variety of day trips are operated in conjunction with the three passenger ferries of the **Lake Chelan Boat Company** (© **509/682-4584**). Tours include a popular bus ride to 312-foot Rainbow Falls ($7 adults, $4 children age 6–11, children under 6 free), a bus ride up the valley and a bike ride back down (adults $15–$25, children under 6 are $5), and a narrated bus trip up the valley to High Bridge and then a picnic lunch ($20 adults, $10 children age 6–11, $5 children under 6).

There are a number of **ranger-led hikes** in the park. These often start from the North Cascades Visitor Center, Stehekin Landing, Hozomeen, or the Colonial Creek Campground, but this varies from year to year. Check at the visitor center for a schedule of daily events.

Hikes

Day hikes do not require a hiking permit; however, a Northwest Forest Pass for vehicle parking may be required. Those going into the backcountry overnight must obtain a free permit at one of the visitor centers, the National Park Service Complex headquarters in Sedro-Woolley, or the Wilderness Information Center in Marblemount. In addition to the hikes discussed below, a small section of the famed Pacific Crest Trail, which runs some 2,650 miles from Mexico to Canada, goes through the park (see "Bridge Creek Trail," below). For information on the entire Pacific Crest Trail, contact the **Pacific Crest Trail Association,** 5325 Elkhorn Blvd., PMB no. 256, Sacramento, CA 95842-2526 (② **916/349-2109;** fax 916/349-1268; www.pcta.org).

ROSS LAKE NATIONAL RECREATION AREA

Desolation Peak

9.8 miles RT. Strenuous. Access: Desolation Landing on Ross Lake via the Ross Lake Resort water taxi, or hike north along the East Bank Ross Lake Trail. Northwest Forest Pass required for parking.

This is the peak that inspired Jack Kerouac's *Desolation Angels,* and it's no wonder that people (and in the middle of summer there are often quite a few of them) would be inspired to meditate on desolation after hiking up this steep hillside through alpine meadows. On the way to the top there are spectacular

views of Hozomeen Mountain, Jack Mountain, and below, beautiful Ross Lake. This can be a very hot and dry hike in the summer, however, and the full round-trip takes several days. Carry plenty of water. Desolation Lookout is closed to the public.

Diablo Lake Trail

7.6 miles RT. Moderate. Access: At the end of the road, across Diablo Dam.

This is the "Grand Central" of the Diablo Lake area. You get views of Ross Dam and of the power lines, which the trail intersects, but you'll also see some larger old-growth trees and varied forests. The trail starts at Seattle City Light's power project dock, from where you can also pick up the summer boat for a ride to the base of upstream Ross Dam (call for schedules). Better to follow the trail as it winds along what was once the Skagit River, but is now Diablo Lake. In front of Ross Dam, however, you get a good idea of how well the dams really work. Check out the view as you cross the suspension bridge, which once traversed the Skagit River Gorge but now is part of the system of dams that makes the Ross and Diablo lake areas.

East Bank Trail

0.5–30 miles one-way. Easy to moderate. Access: Several points along the shore of Ross Lake via the Ross Lake Resort water taxi, or from the trailhead on Wash. State Rte. 20 to the terminus of the trail at Hozomeen Campground. Northwest Forest Pass required for parking.

During the summer, this is one of the most popular trails in the whole park because of its plentiful and well-maintained campsites, the easy grade of its path, and its proximity to Wash. State Route 20. To avoid crowds, you might want to wait until late in the season, or hike mid-week. The path, near the eastern perimeter of the park, borders the Pasayten Wilderness and the Okanogan National Forest, from which several trails intersect the East Bank Trail. The highest point along the trail is the Desolation Peak Trail, to the north. Along the way, be prepared for black bears, beautiful fall foliage, and, on the northern section of the trail, the remote possibility of sighting a member of one of the few remaining wolf packs in the Lower 48.

Fourth of July Pass/Panther Creek

10 miles RT. Moderate to strenuous. Access: Hike 1.8 miles up the Thunder Creek Trail to the junction with the trailhead. Northwest Forest Pass required for parking at the Panther Creek Trailhead on Wash. State Rte. 20.

For a day hike through some of the most astonishing country in the Lower 48, this section of trail isn't too shabby. It's a popular summer hike to the top of Fourth of July Pass, which offers views of the ever-majestic Neve Glacier and Colonial Peak to the west. It isn't easy, though—this is a switchback-cursed climb from Thunder Creek up to the 3,500-foot top of the pass. But that's the hardest part. You get to return downhill via the beautiful Panther Creek Valley for 5 miles to the junction with Wash. State Route 20 at the Panther Creek Bridge and the East Bank Trailhead.

Pyramid Lake

4.2 miles RT. Moderate. Access: 1 mile east of Diablo, on the south side of the highway near the creek, close to mile marker 127. Northwest Forest Pass required for parking.

This trail is like many in the park—steep. But it's not so steep as to be avoided. The hike is a beautiful but relatively sharp climb, passing through pine and fir forests. It ends at a pond, fed by the Colonial Glaciers looming above you along the southeast side of Pyramid Peak. You're liable to see climbers descending from the peaks at the end of the day, looking tired but happy after having ascended the 7,000 feet to the top of Pyramid.

Sourdough Mountain

10.4 miles RT. Strenuous. Access: In the town of Diablo, or via water taxi on the West Bank Trail to the Pierce Mountain Trailhead.

From the west, the trail is easily accessible by car. But rest assured, either way, you're going to be doing some serious climbing: Try a 3,000-foot climb from the Diablo direction, and in just 2 miles, too. And then there's the remaining 2,000 feet or so along the next 4 miles. It's a densely forested walk over the first couple of miles. Be sure to take the right fork at the 3-mile mark to get to the summit for spectacular views of the lake and the glaciers that dot the horizon to the north. This area is hot and dry in the summer, so take extra water. Sourdough Lookout is closed to the public.

Stetattle Creek

5 miles RT. Moderate. Access: Take the exit before the green bridge on Wash. State Rte. 20, just before you reach the town of Diablo along Gorge Lake.

This is a pleasant summer hike down a gentle, scenic path along a creek. The trail meanders north for some 2.5 miles before hitting a stretch of giant, moss-hung trees, and finally petering out in the middle of the forest. The waters of Stetattle Creek often flow milky blue-white from the glacial silt that comes down from McMillan Spire and Mount Terror.

Thornton Lakes Trail

10.6 miles RT. Moderate. Access: Take Wash. State Rte. 20 to Thornton Lakes Rd., 3 miles west of Newhalem. The gravel road climbs steeply to the trailhead. The Northwest Forest Pass is required for parking.

Despite the fact that the first part of the trail is basically an old logging road that might remind you of resource-stripping, this trip is not to be missed. It's a moderately steep walk to the lakes, with a scramble route to Trapper Peak, for sublime views of the Picket Range. Even if you don't take the side route, the sight of Mount Triumph's glaciers to the north, from the nestled valleys in which the lakes sit, is worth the hike.

Thunder Creek Trail

Variable distances. Difficulty varies. Access: The trailhead is south of Diablo Lake, at the Colonial Creek Campground parking lot.

There are plenty of things to do if you decide to take the Thunder Creek Trail. You could amble past the Thunder Creek Arm of Diablo Lake to the intersection with the Fourth of July Pass Trail (also called the Panther Creek Trail), then head to the left and make a loop around the hub of ever-looming (and it goes without saying, snowcapped and gorgeous) Ruby Peak. Or you could make an overnight trek through the rugged wilderness that lines the trail north to south on its way to its terminus in the Park Creek Area along the Stehekin River. Along the way, you can intersect with the Fisher Creek Trail, sloping left along the creek toward an intersection with a possible terminus over Easy Pass at Wash. State Route 20.

From Diablo Lake, it's a broad and easy path for the first couple of miles, which then begins to slope upward for the next several miles, through the Panther Creek junction on the way to McAlester Creek Camp. This is the 6-mile mark, and a lot of day hikers head back the way they came at this point. Otherwise, it's off for several days in some of the most gorgeous country in the continental United States, through the rugged and lush valleys in the southern part of the park.

LAKE CHELAN NATIONAL RECREATION AREA

Agnes Gorge Trail

5 miles RT. Easy. Access: High Bridge; it can be reached via the park's shuttle bus.

This is an easy hike along the west-side cliffs of Agnes Gorge, with beautiful views of looming Agnes Mountain above you. This is a good walk for a day visitor to the Stehekin area.

Coon Lake Trail

2.5 miles RT. Moderate. Access: High Bridge, a stop on the shuttle bus up the valley.

This trail, the beginning of the McGregor Mountain Trail, leads to a pretty little lake created by beavers. Wildlife, especially waterfowl, is plentiful on and around the 15-acre lake. On the far side, a waterfall on Coon Creek can be seen. Though forests surround the lake, there are views to the southwest toward Agnes Mountain.

Rainbow Falls

7 miles RT. Easy. Access: Stehekin Landing.

At 312 feet high, Rainbow Falls is among the most impressive falls in Washington and a popular destination for day-trippers who visit Stehekin by boat (see "Getting Around Inside the Park," above). The falls were created when a glacier scraped out the walls of the Stehekin Valley, leaving Rainbow Creek hanging high above the valley floor. The falls are 3.5 miles from Stehekin landing by road and make a good day-hike destination if you are staying at the North Cascades Stehekin Lodge; you get there by walking along the road. The lodge also offers a bus tour of the falls (although it's open to anyone and timed for the convenience of the "day-tripper"). Alternatively, if the shuttle bus is running, you can take it to and from the falls or just one-way.

Rainbow Loop Trail

9.2 miles RT. Moderate. Access: Rainbow Creek Upper Trailhead, 5 miles from Stehekin.

Although trails in the Stehekin area tend to be flat valley-bottom hikes or grueling climbs straight up steep walls, this hike makes a good in-between choice. Views of the Stehekin Valley and Lake Chelan are the payoff. Start the hike from the Rainbow Creek Trailhead, which can be reached from the shuttle bus. From here climb 1,000 feet in 2.5 miles—along the way passing a bluff with a view of the valley—to a bridge over Rainbow Creek. Just before reaching the creek there is a trail junction. If you turn left here and hike up this trail 0.5 mile, you'll find views even more stunning than the ones along the main trail. The creek marks the midpoint of the trail. The lower trailhead is 2.5 miles down a steep trail with more great views.

NORTH CASCADES NATIONAL PARK—SOUTHERN UNIT

The interior of the southern unit of the North Cascades National Park is remote. Most of the trails are concentrated on the northern or southern end. The northern trails are accessed via Wash. State Route 20. The southern trails are accessed via the Cascade River Road, a winding, sometimes rugged stretch of mostly gravel road, which will get you to the Cascade Pass Trail. Call ahead to Marblemount for road conditions; sometimes this is not easily accessible to the average vehicle. Backpackers can take Thunder Creek Trail, an artery through the interior, for access to the Chelan/Stehekin area, but it's not a day hike. The **Wilderness Information Center** in Marblemount can be reached at ℂ **360/873-4500**, extension 39.

Bridge Creek Trail

29 miles RT. Moderate. Access: The trailhead is at the Bridge Creek Bridge on the Stehekin Valley Rd.; the other end of the trail is at Bridge Creek Trailhead, east of Rainy Pass on Wash. State Rte. 20. The Northwest Forest Pass is required for parking at the Wash. State Rte. 20 end.

This backcountry hike steadily ascends to Wash. State Route 20 (never too steeply) through some beautiful valleys, after a short hike along a section of the Pacific Crest Trail (see the introduction to this section, above). There are beautiful views of Goode Mountain and Mount Logan, as well as the massive ice-hangs below Memaloose Ridge.

Cascade Pass/Sahale Arm Trail

11 miles RT. Moderate. Access: From Marblemount on Wash. State Rte. 20, cross the bridge and drive east for 23 miles on the Cascade River Rd. to the trailhead. The Northwest Forest Pass is required for parking along the Cascade River Rd., as well as at the Cascade Pass Trailhead.

This is one of the most popular hikes in the park. Starting high above the valley of the North Fork Cascade River, the trail follows an ancient American Indian trading route over the Cascades to Lake Chelan. Today the trail is popular as a day trip, an overnight trip, a climber's route to some challenging North Cascades rock, and a through trail to Stehekin. For a spectacular day hike, climb to the top of Cascade Pass (3.7 miles), then continue to ascend on a trail to the left until you cross a ridge. Soon, you will be traversing Sahale Arm, far above jewel-like Doubtful Lake. From here, there are sweeping views of the North Cascades.

Park Creek Pass

8 miles one-way. Moderate to strenuous. Access: Park Creek Campground on the Stehekin Valley Rd.

Though this hike is often crowded in the summer with people passing through Stehekin, it's still worth it. Make your way up the steep, forested slopes towards the alpine meadows beyond the logistically named Five Mile Camp. From here on up it's glacier lilies and the cracking of calving glacier ice on the slopes of Goode Mountain. Huge chunks of ice have been known to crash into the valley below the slopes. Look for slabs as big as your average house. Beyond the 6,000-foot Park Creek Pass, you can connect with the Thunder Creek Trail (see above) for a much longer hike to the Ross Lake Area and State Route 20.

NORTH CASCADES NATIONAL PARK—NORTHERN UNIT

The backcountry trails in this region, such as **Hannegan Trail** and **Big Beaver Trail,** aren't easy to get to, but they're worth the effort. Here you'll find some of the most stupendous mountain views in the park complex. This is the most remote wilderness area in the state, home to abundant wildlife. From virgin forests in glacial valleys to high meadows with head-on views of the park's jagged Picket Range, these hikes have everything.

Start at the Mount Baker Wilderness Trailhead in the Mount Baker–Snoqualmie National Forest, near the north section of the North Cascades National Park Northern Unit. From the town of Glacier drive 13 miles to F.S. 32 (Hannegan Rd.), and continue to the trailhead at the Hannegan Camp at the road's end. You can also take a water taxi, which must be arranged in advance, up Ross Lake and start your hike from the Big Beaver Landing. Check with the **Ross Lake Resort** (© 206/386-4437) for fare.

Other Sports & Activities

Biking. Riding off the road is not allowed in the park complex, but there are still several good biking routes. Keep in mind that biking is usually best in late July and August, but even then, bad weather can descend suddenly to ruin the views and soak the riders.

The trip along Wash. State Route 20 through the park and also west of the park between Rockport and Marblemount is strenuous but beautiful. The road has a wide shoulder in many (though not all) places and developed campgrounds. There are some extremely steep stretches.

Mountain bikers will want to try the Stehekin Valley Road route, a 21-mile stretch from the community of Stehekin to Flat Creek, on Lake Chelan. The road parallels the glacier-fed Stehekin River and provides plenty of great views of

the North Cascades peaks. The 312-foot-high Rainbow Falls is a wonderful stop along the way.

Cross-Country Skiing. West of the park complex, the **Mount Baker Ski Area** is where most skiers end up. But if you're looking to do some cross-country skiing away from the crowds, consider **Stehekin.** The chance to ski past 312-foot-tall Rainbow Falls should not be missed.

Fishing. Anglers must have Washington state fishing licenses; these can be obtained at sporting goods stores. Fishing regulations and seasons are listed in the "Fishing in Washington" pamphlet, published by the Washington Department of Fish and Wildlife (© 360/902-2000; www.wa.gov.wdfa).

Ross Lake contains populations of both native rainbow and cutthroat trout, as well as eastern brook trout and a few bull trout (which must be released). Fishing boats can be rented at the **Ross Lake Resort** (© 206/386-4437). Fishing season on Ross Lake is July 1 to October 31.

Lake Chelan, although it looks like an awesome fishing hole, is so large, so deep, and so cold that it doesn't support a large fish population. However, it does have quite a variety, including kokanee; landlocked chinook salmon; cutthroat, rainbow, and Mackinaw trout; and freshwater ling cod (burbot). The **Stehekin River** and its tributary streams offer excellent fly-fishing. Check fishing regulations for season.

If you want to hire a guide to take you where the fish are biting, try **Big 1 Fishing Guide Service** (© 509/682-4647) or **Graybill's Guide Service** (© 509/667-9203).

Hang Gliding & Paragliding. In recent years, Lake Chelan has become one of the nation's hang gliding and paragliding meccas. These activities, however, are not allowed in the national park or the adjacent national recreation area. Strong winds and thermals allow flyers to sail for a hundred miles or more from the Chelan Sky Park atop Chelan Butte, which is located on the outskirts of town. Paragliding lessons are available here through **Chelan Paragliding School** (Alpman@dellepro.com).

Kayaking & Canoeing. Diablo Lake and Ross Lake both offer excellent flat-water paddling and are among the few inland waters in the Northwest with extensive boat-in campsites. However, there is no road access to **Ross Lake** in the U.S. (the unpaved Silver Skagit Rd. enters the park from Hope, British Columbia, leading 40 miles to the north end of the lake). **Ross Lake Resort** (✆ **206/386-4437**) offers a canoe and kayak shuttle service from Diablo Lake (which is accessible by car) around Ross Dam to Ross Lake. Check with the resort for charges per canoe or kayak. You can also rent outboard motorboats, kayaks, and canoes at the resort.

You'll need a backcountry permit to overnight on Ross Lake. These permits are available at the Wilderness Information Center in Marblemount. The permits allow you to stay at the many campsites along the shores of Ross Lake. Backcountry permits are also available at the Hozomeen Ranger Station. Here you can explore the Narrow Ruby Arm using Green Point Campground (1 mile above the dam) as a base camp. Farther north are the Cougar Island (2 miles above the dam), Roland Point (4 miles above the dam), McMillan (5½ miles above the dam), and Spencer's (6 miles above the dam) campgrounds.

Because of the 24-mile length of the lake and the strong winds that often blow in the afternoon, many paddlers stick to the lower end (unless they enter at Hozomeen at the lake's north end).

If you aren't inclined to spend the money for the shuttle, you can have a similar experience paddling on **Diablo Lake,** which is an amazing turquoise color due to the amounts of glacial flour suspended in the water. Diablo also has three boat-in campsites (Thunder Point, Hidden Cove, and Buster Brown) as well

as a couple of small islands to explore. Backcountry permits are needed for boat-in campgrounds on Diablo Lake. Alternatively, you can explore the lake from the drive-in Colonial Creek Campground on the Thunder Arm of the lake.

Snowshoeing. The **Stehekin Valley** makes an ideal snowshoeing destination, with various trails that offer opportunities for exploring the mountain slopes surrounding the valley. The road is plowed to a point 9 miles north of Stehekin Landing. You can rent snowshoes at the **North Cascades Stehekin Lodge** (✆ **509/682-4494;** www.stehekin.com).

Camping

Reservations are available for Newhalem Creek Campground and several group campgrounds through the **National Recreation Reservation Service** (✆ **877/444-6777;** www.reserveusa.com); other campgrounds are first come, first served. Camping in the backcountry requires a free backcountry permit, available at visitor centers or the Wilderness Information Center in Marblemount. The only drive-in campsites are located along Wash. State Route 20 through the Ross Lake area, except Hozomeen, which is accessible by car only through the Silver Skagit Road, 40 miles south of Hope, in British Columbia, Canada.

Backcountry permits are issued in person only, the day of your trip into the backcountry, or up to a day in advance. Permits are issued on a first come, first served basis. There are no advance reservations by phone.

IN ROSS LAKE NATIONAL RECREATION AREA

For information, contact national park offices (✆ **360/856-5700**).

Goodell Creek Campground, just west of Newhalem, is popular with paddlers and anglers. It has a good view of the Picket Range from just across the highway. Drinking water is not available

Campground	Total Elev.	RV Sites	Dump Hookups	Station	Toilets	Drinking Water
Goodell Creek	500	21	0	No	Yes	Yes
Newhalem Creek	500	111	0	Yes	Yes	Yes
Colonial Creek	1,200	162	0	Yes	Yes	Yes
Hozomeen	1,600	122	0	No	Yes	Yes
Rockport State Park	500	90	62	Yes	Yes	Yes
Howard Miller Steekhead Park	400	59	49	Yes	Yes	Yes
Marble Creek	1,000	24	0	No	Yes	No

from late fall through winter. There is a raft and kayak launch adjacent to the campground for white-water runs down the Skagit River. This campground is open year-round.

Newhalem Creek Campground, one of the area's busiest, is at the center of the action near the North Cascades Visitor Center. It's wheelchair accessible and has many short hiking trails nearby. Park rangers present weekend campfire programs in the summer.

Colonial Creek Campground, on the banks of the Thunder Arm part of Diablo Lake, is the largest campground on the highway and also the busiest. It has pleasant sites on the water and access to boat ramps. Park rangers present nightly interpretive programs during the summer.

For the above campgrounds, a fee is charged and all are available on a first come, first served basis.

Hozomeen Campground is a more primitive campground, with no garbage facilities, at the northern tip of Ross Lake. Drinking water is provided. There is no fee, and the campground is available on a first come, first served basis.

IN LAKE CHELAN NATIONAL RECREATION AREA

At the north end of the lake, near Stehekin, there are 11 campgrounds, most of which are served by the shuttle bus

from Stehekin. Purple Point Campground is right in Stehekin and is the most convenient to the boat landing.

For information on campgrounds in the Stehekin Valley, contact the **Golden West Visitor Center,** P.O. Box 7, Stehekin, WA 98852 (© **360/856-5700,** ext. 340, then ext. 14). A free backcountry permit is needed for these campgrounds. Permits are available in person only at the Golden West Visitor Center, on a first come, first served basis.

ALONG THE NORTH CASCADES HIGHWAY

Heading over the North Cascades Highway from the west side, you'll find a very nice campground at **Rockport State Park** (© **360/853-8461**), just west of Rockport. This campground is set amid large old-growth trees. Right in Rockport itself, there are campsites in a large open field at the Skagit County-run **Howard Miller Steelhead Park** (© **360/853-8808**).

East of Marblemount, there are a couple of small National Forest Service campgrounds on the Cascade River Road, which leads to the trailhead for the popular hike to Cascade Pass. Among them, **Marble Creek** is 8 miles east of Marblemount and **Mineral Park** is 18 miles east.

For U.S. Forest Service campground reservations, call © **800/444-6777;** or contact www.reserveusa.com.

Fire Pits/ Showers	Grills	Public Laundry	Phone	Reserve	Fees	Open
No	Yes	No	No	No	$10	Year-round
No	Yes	No	No	Yes	$12	Late May to Oct
No	Yes	No	No	No	$12	Mid-May to Oct
No	Yes	No	No	No	Free	Late May to Oct
Yes	Yes	No	Yes	No	$15	Apr–Oct
Yes	No	No	Yes	Yes	$18	Year-round
No	Yes	No	No	No	$10	May 15–Oct 15

Where to Stay

There aren't a lot of choices for lodging in the park. To the west, along Wash. 20, you can find places in and near Marblemount and Rockport; to the east there's Mazama and Winthrop, also on Wash. 20.

INSIDE THE PARK

North Cascades Stehekin Lodge

P.O. Box 457, Chelan, WA 98816. ℂ **509/ 682-4494** or 509/682-8206 (reservation office). Fax 509/682-5872. www.stehekin.com. 28 units. $79–$110 double. DISC, MC, V.

Located right at Stehekin Landing, the North Cascades Stehekin Lodge is shaded by tall trees and overlooks the lake. There is a variety of rooms ranging from basic ones with no lake view to spacious apartments. The studio apartments, which have kitchens and lake views, are the best deal. Fishing boat and bike rentals are available. Snowshoeing has become popular; Saturday moonlight snowshoe walks are held January to March. Narrated bus tours are also offered.

Ross Lake Resort

Rockport, WA 98283. ℂ **206/386-4437.** www. rosslakeresort.com. 15 cabins. $92–$197 double. 25% off June and Oct most cabins. MC, V.

There may not be another lodging of this type in the United States. All 15 of the resort's cabins are built on logs that are floating on Ross Lake. If you're looking to get away from it all, this place comes pretty close. There is no road to the resort. To reach it, you first drive to the Diablo Dam on Wash. 20, and then take a tugboat to the end of Diablo Lake, where a truck carries you around the Ross Dam to the lodge. Alternatively you can hike in on a 2-mile trail from mile marker 134 on Wash. 20. There is no restaurant or grocery store here, so be sure to bring enough supplies for your stay. All cabins have some cooking facilities, ranging from stovetops to full kitchens. Most cabins have private bathrooms; some share with one other cabin. What do you do once you get here? Rent a boat and go fishing, rent a kayak or canoe, do some hiking, or simply sit and relax.

Stehekin Valley Ranch

P.O. Box 36, Stehekin, WA 98852. ℂ **800/536- 0745** or 509/682-4677. www.courtneycountry. com. 5 cabins, 7 tent cabins. Cabins: $85 per adult, $75 per child 7–12, $60 per child 4–6, $20 per child 3 and under. Tent cabins: $10 less. Rates include all meals and transportation in lower valley. MC, V, if payment made in advance by phone. At the ranch, only cash or checks are accepted.

If you're a camper at heart, then the tent cabins at the Stehekin Valley Ranch should be just fine. With canvas roofs, screen windows, and no electricity or plumbing, these "cabins" are little more than permanent tents. Bathroom facilities are in the nearby main building. For slightly more comfortable accommodations, opt for one of the permanent cabins. Activities available at additional cost include horseback riding, river rafting, mountain biking, kayak tours and instruction.

IN ROCKPORT

Clark's Skagit River Resort

58468 Clark Cabin Rd., Rockport, WA 98283. ℂ **800/273-2606** or 360/873-2250. Fax 360/873-4077. www.northcascades.com. 36 cabins. TV. $59–$129; call for seasonal rates. AE, DISC, MC, V.

The first thing you notice when you turn into the driveway are the rabbits. They're everywhere—hundreds of them in all shapes and sizes, contentedly munching the lawn or just sitting quietly. Although the bunnies are among the main attractions at Clark's, it's the theme cabins that keep people coming back. Western, nautical, Victorian, American Indian, Adirondack, hacienda, and mill are the current choices for interior decor in these cabins. There are also five new chalets named for local wildlife. Other cabins on the property are equally comfortable, but the theme cabins are what make Clark's just a bit different. The cabins are especially popular in winter, when folks flock to the area to watch the bald eagles congregate on the Skagit River. They also have a B&B Lodge with a conference room and patio for groups. Furthermore, they offer two R.V. parks ($20) and tent camping ($12–$20), and there's a restaurant, the Eatery, on the property.

IN MAZAMA

Freestone Inn

17798 Hwy. 20, Mazama, WA 98833. ℂ **800/639-3809** or 509/996-3906. Fax 509/996-3907. www.frestoneinn.com. 38 units. TEL. Summer $140–$215 double, $165–$245 cabin, $275–$485 lodge; winter $120–$190 double, $125–$230 cabin, $250–$435 lodge. Lower rates in spring and fall. AE, DC, DISC, MC, V.

Located at the upper end of the Methow Valley outside the community of Mazama, the Freestone Inn is an up-and-comer. The inn's main building is a huge new log structure complete with a massive stone fireplace in a cathedral-ceilinged great room that serves as lobby and dining room. The lodge sits on the shore of small Freestone Lake and has a superb view of the mountains rising beyond the far shore. Guest rooms are thoughtfully designed with gas fireplaces and sunken tubs that open to the bedroom. All in all, these are some of the most memorable rooms in the state. For more privacy, you can opt for one of the renovated Early Winters Cabins or one of the newly constructed cabins. Families may want to go all the way and rent one of the large lakeside lodges. Meals here are every bit as nice as the rooms. Northwest cuisine is the focus with prices in the $18 to $27 range.

The inn also offers tour arrangements, a heli-ski operation, cross-country ski lessons, ski rentals, mountain-bike rentals, an extensive equestrian program, and sleigh rides. Nearby, there are ski trails and a lake for swimming or ice skating.

The Mazama Country Inn

15 Country Rd., Mazama, WA 98833. ℂ **800/843-7951** or 509/996-2681. Fax 509/996-2646. www.mazamacountryinn.com. 18 units. Summer $80–$135 double; winter (including all meals) $150–$230 double. MC, V.

Set on the flat valley floor but surrounded by rugged towering peaks and tall pine trees, this modern mountain lodge is secluded and peaceful and offers an escape from the crowds in Winthrop. If you're out here to hike, mountain bike, cross-country ski, or horseback ride, the Mazama Country Inn makes an excellent base of operations. They also have a private outdoor tennis court and a newly built athletic facility with a squash court and workout room. After a hard day of outdoor fun, you can come back and soak in the hot tub and have dinner in the rustic dining room with its massive freestanding fireplace and high ceiling. The medium-size guest rooms are simply furnished, but modern and clean. The Inn has recently added four deluxe rooms with king beds, gas fireplaces, and jetted tubs. They also rent out 13 cabins ranging in size from one to five bedrooms.

IN WINTHROP

Hotel Rio Vista

P.O. Box 815, Winthrop, WA 98862. *C* **800/398-0911** or 509/996-3535. www.hotelriovista.com. 29 units. A/C TV TEL. $55–$110 double. MC, V.

The Hotel Rio Vista, ravaged by a 2002 fire that began next door, has arisen from the ashes and been rebuilt with all brand-new units that include more king suites, minisuites, and rooms with single and doubles. The suites offer kitchenettes and DVD and VCR players. Step out onto your private balcony for a view of the confluence of the Chewuch and Methow rivers; guests often see deer, bald eagles, and many other species of birds. A hot tub overlooks the river and there's a riverside picnic area. The hotel is located in downtown Winthrop, so it's an easy walk to shops and restaurants.

Sun Mountain Lodge

P.O. Box 1000, Winthrop, WA 98862. *C* **800/572-0493** or 509/996-2211. Fax 509/996-3133. www.sunmountainlodge.com. 102 units, 13 cabins. Summer $170–$330 double, $220–$360 cabin; winter/spring/fall $130–$270 double, $170–$300 cabin. AE, DC, MC, V.

If you're looking for resort luxuries and proximity to hiking, cross-country skiing, and mountain-biking trails, the Sun Mountain Lodge should be your first choice in the region. Perched on a mountaintop with grand views of the Methow Valley and the North Cascades, this luxurious lodge captures the spirit of the West in both its breathtaking setting and its rustic design. In the lobby, flagstone floors, stone fireplaces, and

wagon-wheel tables combine in a classically Western style. Most guest rooms feature rustic Western furnishings and views of the surrounding mountains. The rooms in the Gardner wing have balconies and slightly better views than those in the main lodge. The newest rooms are in the Mount Robinson wing. If seclusion is what you're after, opt for one of the all-new cabins down on Patterson Lake.

A superb menu that focuses on Northwest cuisine makes the lodge's dining room the region's best restaurant, and the views will definitely take your breath away. Prices range from $25 to $36 for entrees.

The lodge offers ski rentals and ski school; horseback and sleigh rides; guided hikes; and boat, mountain-bike, and ice-skate rentals. Guests can also use the outdoor heated pools, two whirlpools, tennis courts, exercise room, ski shop, children's playground, spa services, and ice-skating pond.

The Virginian

808 N. Cascades Hwy. (P.O. Box 237), Winthrop, WA 98862. *C* **800/854-2834** or 509/996-2535. www.virginianresort.com. 37 units, 7 cabins. A/C TV. $45–$95 double; $95 cabin. DISC, MC, V. Pets accepted.

Located just south of downtown Winthrop, The Virginian is a collection of small cabins and motel rooms on the banks of the Methow River. The deluxe rooms overlooking the river are our favorites. These have high ceilings, balconies, and lots of space. The cabins, though quaint, don't have river views. The rooms and cabins are all lined with cedar, which gives them a rustic feel. There's a heated swimming pool, horseshoe pit, and volleyball court. There's a cross-country ski and mountain-bike trail out the front door.

Where to Dine

Better stock up on the chow before you head into the park, Marblemount, or Winthrop. In most places, including

Ross Lake Resort, there's just no food to be had.

IN STEHEKIN

There are several dining options in Stehekin, but if you plan to stay in a cabin or camp out, be sure to bring all the food you'll need. Otherwise, simple meals are available at **North Cascades Stehekin Lodge** (© 509/682-4494), which is located right at the boat dock in Stehekin. If you just have to have something sweet, you're in luck—the **Stehekin Pastry Company,** which is located 2 miles up valley from the boat landing, serves pastries and ice cream, as well as pizza and espresso.

IN MARBLEMOUNT

Buffalo Run Restaurant

60084 Wash. 20 (mile marker 106), Marblemount. © **360/873-2461.** www.buffalorun restaurant.com. Main dishes $2.50–$33. AE, DISC, MC, V. Sun–Thurs 8am–9pm; Fri–Sat 8am–10pm. AMERICAN.

From the outside this looks like any other roadside diner, but once you see the menu, it's obvious this place is something more. The owners have a buffalo ranch, so it's no surprise that the menu includes buffalo burgers, buffalo chili, and buffalo T-bones. They also serve venison, elk, and ostrich, as well as salmon and mussels, plus vegetarian items. After a day of hiking, enjoy a pleasant meal on their garden patio. They offer beer, wine, and cocktails. Of course there's a buffalo head (and hide) on the wall. They also have a furnished bunkhouse in their barn, which they rent out in the summer for $55 per night for two, and a two-bedroom mobile home renting for $85 per night for two.

IN THE WINTHROP AREA

The best meals in the Winthrop area are to be had at the dining rooms of **Sun Mountain Lodge,** where you'll also enjoy one of the most spectacular views in the state. See "Where to Stay," above.

The Duck Brand

Wash. 20 (Riverside Ave.). © **509/996-2192.** Main courses $6–$17. AE, DC, DISC, MC, V. Daily 7am–9:30pm or later. MEXICAN.

Located across the street from the gas station and partially hidden by trees, the Duck Brand is a casual restaurant with a big, multilevel deck that's a great spot for a meal on a warm summer day. In cold or rainy weather, you can grab a table in the small dining room and order a plate of fajitas or ribs and a microbrew to wash it all down. The Duck Brand's muffins and cinnamon rolls make great trailside snacks.

Winthrop Brewing Company

155 Riverside Ave. © **509/996-3183.** Main courses $5–$17. MC, V. Daily 11:30am–midnight weekends, 11:30am–10pm weekdays (shorter hours in winter). AMERICAN.

Located in a tiny, wedge-shaped building in downtown Winthrop, this local watering hole is by far the liveliest restaurant/bar in town. The walls are covered with the owner's cigarette lighter collection, as well as old rifles and beer coasters from around the world. There's a deck out back overlooking the river, and in summer a beer garden. On weekends there's usually some kind of live music. The menu is typical pub fare—burgers, fish and chips, steaks, sandwiches, chicken, fish, and ribs.

26

OLYMPIC NATIONAL PARK

by Jack Olson

ET READY FOR SENSORY OVERLOAD. OLYMPIC NATIONAL PARK IS AN area of such variety in climate and terrain that it's hard to believe it's just one park. Here you can view white, chilled alpine glaciers; wander through a green, sopping-wet rain forest; or soothe your muscles with a soak in a hot springs pool. Or perhaps you'd prefer to ponder the setting sun from the sandy Pacific coastline, or disappear from the outside world altogether in the deep green forests of its largely untouched mountains.

In the Olympic Mountains, remnants of 2-million-year-old glaciers that once crept northeast toward what are now the Strait of Juan de Fuca and the Hood Canal can still be seen. The 60 glaciers inside the park continue to grind and sculpt the mountains now as they did then, if only a bit more slowly. Farther down some of the steep coastal valleys traversing the peninsula lie the major temperate rain forests in the contiguous United States. In addition, Olympic National Park contains the longest stretch of uninterrupted coastal wilderness area of any park south of Alaska.

Water is serious business here. Precipitation is measured in feet, not inches, with some areas receiving up to 20 feet in a single season. Contrast this with some parts of the drier eastern side of the peninsula, which receive a comparatively paltry 20 inches on average. Again, variety is the rule. If the crystalline, jade waters of the glacier-fed lakes feel a little too cold for comfort, there's always the opportunity to warm your bones in hot springs in the northern section of the park.

Despite its inherent ruggedness, raininess, and mysterious nature, the interior of the park began yielding its secrets in the mid- to late 1800s. Unbridled curiosity and the inevitable desire for timber, mineral, and tourism dollars played a part in its exploration. Homesteads had been established by westward-moving pioneers on the peripheries of the peninsula as early as the mid-1800s. However, the first documented exploration of the interior didn't occur until 1885, and then it was no easy feat. It took one group of explorers a grueling month of hacking through dense brush to get from Port Angeles to Hurricane Ridge. Today, it takes approximately 45 minutes by car.

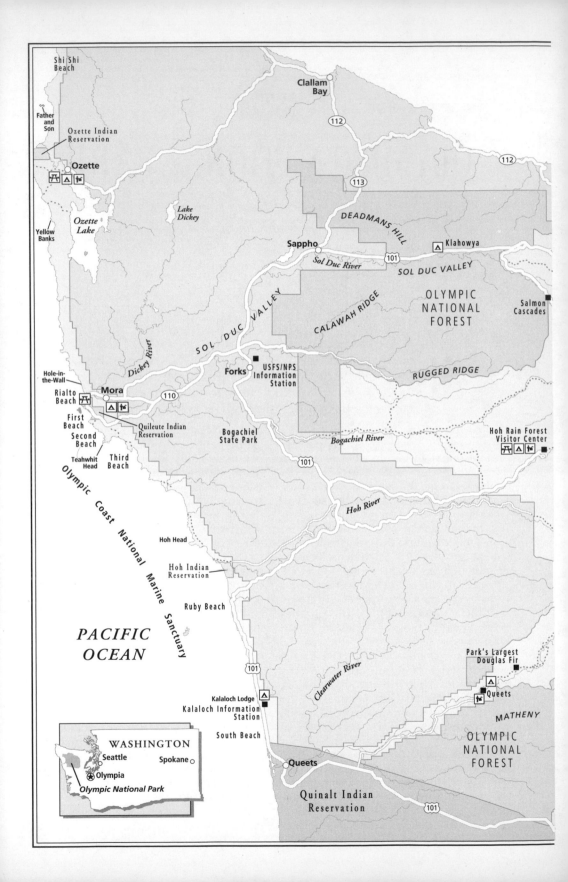

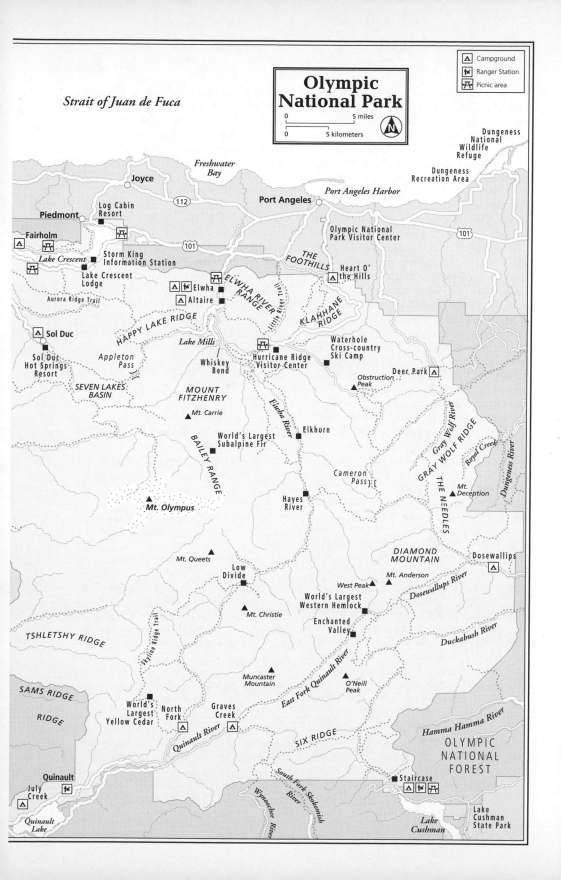

Olympic National Park

Campground
Ranger Station
Picnic area

0   5 miles
0   5 kilometers

N

Strait of Juan de Fuca

Freshwater Bay

Joyce

112

Port Angeles Harbor

Port Angeles

Dungeness National Wildlife Refuge

Dungeness Recreation Area

Log Cabin Resort

Piedmont

Fairholm

Olympic National Park Visitor Center

101

101

Lake Crescent

Storm King Information Station

Lake Crescent Lodge

THE FOOTHILLS

Heart O' the Hills

Aurora Ridge Trail

Elwha

Altaire

ELWHA RIVER RANGE

Little River Trail

KLAHHANE RIDGE

Sol Duc

Sol Duc Hot Springs Resort

Appleton Pass

HAPPY LAKE RIDGE

Lake Mills

Whiskey Bend

Hurricane Ridge Visitor Center

Waterhole Cross-country Ski Camp

Obstruction Peak

Deer Park

SEVEN LAKES BASIN

MOUNT FITZHENRY

▲ *Mt. Carrie*

World's Largest Subalpine Fir

Elkhorn

Elwha River

Cameron Pass

Gray Wolf River

GRAY WOLF RIDGE

Royal Creek

Dungeness River

BAILEY RANGE

▲ Mt. Olympus

Hayes River

▲ *Mt. Deception*

THE NEEDLES

▲ *Mt. Queets*

Low Divide

▲ *Mt. Christie*

West Peak

DIAMOND MOUNTAIN

▲ *Mt. Anderson*

Dosewallips

World's Largest Western Hemlock

Dosewallups River

TSHLETSHY RIDGE

Skyline Ridge Trail

Enchanted Valley

Duckabush River

SAMS RIDGE

RIDGE

Muncaster Mountain

▲ O'Neill Peak

East Fork Quinault River

World's Largest Yellow Cedar

North Fork

Graves Creek

SIX RIDGE

Hamma Hamma River

OLYMPIC NATIONAL FOREST

Quinault River

Quinault

July Creek

South Fork Skokomish River

Staircase

Wynoochee River

Quinault Lake

Lake Cushman

Lake Cushman State Park

On the advice of these adventure-some explorers, Congress declared most of the peninsula a national forest. Then, in 1909, just before leaving office, Pres. Theodore Roosevelt, an avid hunter, established Mount Olympus National Monument, in order to preserve the summer range and breeding grounds of dwindling herds of Roosevelt elk (flatteringly named for the president himself in a brilliant piece of prelegislative public relations). In 1938, Pres. Franklin Roosevelt turned the national monument into a national park, and in 1953 the coastal strip was added. Finally, in 1981, the park was declared a World Heritage Park.

Today, Olympic National Park encompasses more than 900,000 acres of mountains and rain forests, glacial lakes, and Pacific shoreline. It was either a fortunate stroke of planning, or fortunate lack of money, that no roads divide the interior of the park. Consequently, large sanctuaries exist here for the elk, deer, eagles, bear, cougars, and other inhabitants and visitors to its interior.

Avoiding the Crowds. Avoiding the crowds in Olympic National Park is not as simple as it would seem. With easy access from both Seattle and Victoria, B.C., Olympic National Park is a magnet for visitors from around the world. However, there are a few options within your control.

The easiest solution is to go in the off season, especially in the fall. Although the west side of Olympic is often deluged with rain in the fall and winter, the eastern side can actually be fairly dry at the same time. So head east toward **Duckabush** or **Sequim.** Otherwise, strap on your snorkel and try some winter camping in the **Hoh** or the **Queets.**

You might also try getting to the park via the southern route, up the peninsula through Aberdeen. If you choose this route, you can see everything the peninsula offers in a nutshell. Instead of going to the Hoh, try the Queets. Although less traveled, this area affords

the same rain-forest views as the more popular Hoh. On the east side, try a walk into the interior from Duckabush or Dosewallips. Both jumping-off points are less trafficked than the more northerly areas, and the views as you walk through the old growth beside the blue-white rivers are as good as any in the park.

Finally, if you absolutely have to come in the summer and don't want to miss the most popular views, such as those on **Hurricane Ridge,** try heading up in the late afternoon when everyone else is on their way down. You're liable to get spectacular views of the sunset over the Strait of Juan de Fuca as the fog rolls in and the deer make their evening pilgrimage to the parking lot at the Hurricane Ridge Visitor Center.

Just the Facts

GETTING THERE & GATEWAYS

The main travel artery for all visitors to Olympic National Park is **U.S. 101.** This northernmost point of the famous coastal highway encircles and only briefly enters the park. Most of the traffic into and out of the park is on the northeastern side, from Vancouver and Seattle.

If you're departing from **Seattle,** you can take either one of the ferries that run daily/hourly from the same downtown Seattle dock. No reservations are needed for the ferries, which cost about $12 for a standard passenger vehicle and two people one-way. The **Seattle–Bainbridge Island Ferry** takes you for a half-hour ride across the Puget Sound before arriving in Bainbridge Island. From there, take Wash. 305 north through Poulsbo to the Hood Canal Floating Bridge, and then Wash. 104 across to U.S. 101. The **Seattle-Bremerton Ferry** arrives in Bremerton after a 60-minute ride. From Bremerton, take Wash. 3 north to the Hood Canal Floating Bridge. The **Edmonds-Kingston Ferry** is a 30-minute ride to Kingston, where you take Wash. 104 24 miles to U.S. 101. In addition, the **Keystone Ferry** shuttles between Whidbey Island and Port Townsend. It's smaller, but in the off season it can be a good bet for shorter lines.

For all ferry **schedules,** contact **Washington State Ferries,** Colman Dock/Pier 52, 801 Alaskan Way, Seattle, WA 98104 (✆ **888/808-7977** statewide, or 206/464-6400 local and out-of-state; www.wsdot.wa.gov/ferries/current).

If you'd rather drive your car over dry land only, head west from **Tacoma** via Wash. 16 over the Tacoma Narrows Bridge, which connects with the eastern shore of the Kitsap Peninsula just south of Gig Harbor. Drive north on Wash. 16 to Port Orchard and Bremerton. From Bremerton, take Wash. 3 to the Hood Canal Floating Bridge and across to U.S. 101.

To access the park from the south, take I-5 to **Olympia,** where you can connect with U.S. 101 North, or with Wash. 8 West to the other side of the U.S. 101 loop, to access the Pacific Ocean section of the park.

The Nearest Airport. Seattle-Tacoma International Airport (✆ **206/431-4444**) is located 15 miles south of Seattle on I-5. It's served by most major airlines and car rental companies. **Fairchild International Airport** is located in Port Angeles, site of the park's main visitor center, and is served by **Horizon Air** and **Alaska Airlines,** and **Budget Rent-A-Car.** Toll-free numbers for airlines and car-rental companies are listed in the appendix.

INFORMATION

Contact **Olympic National Park,** 600 E. Park Ave., Port Angeles, WA 98362-6798 (✆ **360/565-3130;** www.nps.gov/olym). Several free publications provide a good look at the area, including the *North Olympic Peninsula Visitor's Guide,* published by the *Peninsula Daily News* twice yearly.

VISITOR CENTERS

There are three visitor centers in the park, offering exhibits, maps, guides, and information; plus smaller ranger and information stations that are located at popular trailheads and open only in summer.

The **Olympic National Park Visitor Center** (✆ **360/565-3130**), located on the northern end of the park and within close proximity to Port Angeles, is a good jumping-off station before heading into the northwest part of the park. It's a 45-minute drive from there to one of the most popular spots in the park, the newly constructed **Hurricane Ridge Visitor Center.** Here you'll find beautiful views (free telescopes!) of the Olympic Mountains and alpine meadows blooming with wildflowers each summer. It also has a snack bar, interpretive exhibits, and trails. If you want to avoid the crowds, drive up in the late afternoon, as everyone else is leaving. Wait for sundown, and you might get a beautiful view of the mists coming in, and a visit from some surprisingly tame deer. Those who arrive before 10am will find more elbowroom as well.

The **Hoh Rain Forest Visitor Center,** on the west side of the main part of the park, is some 15 miles off a turnoff from U.S. 101. This is an excellent spot for those who want to experience a temperate rain forest without spending a soaking couple of days hiking. The information center is, like the Hurricane Ridge Observatory, a favorite spot for tourists in the summer season. There are several interpretive trails and the beautiful **Hall of Mosses** nearby, as well as longer trails into the heart of the rain forest. Just remember that this visitor center is in the middle of the rain forest—it gets unbelievably humid when full!

Smaller centers include the **Storm King Information Station,** on Crescent Lake in the northern section of the park, and the **Kalaloch Information Station,** on the south end of the beach section of the park. You can get food and some supplies near the **Sol Duc Ranger Station** at the Hot Springs Resort.

Entrance into the park for up to a week costs $10 per vehicle, or $5 per individual hiking or biking. An annual Park Pass costs $30. There is a $1 per day parking charge at Ozette. A $5 wilderness use fee is charged to camp in the wilderness (for groups up to 12 people) plus $2 per person per night.

Camping in the park campgrounds costs $8 to $16 a night. Dump station use costs $3.

SPECIAL REGULATIONS & WARNINGS

Wilderness use permits, available at the Wilderness Information Center (located just behind the main visitor center in Port Angeles) and at all ranger stations, are required for overnight stays in the backcountry. During the summer, you may also need reservations for certain areas. Call the **Wilderness Information Center** (℃ 360/565-3100) for information.

When hiking, be prepared for sudden and extreme weather changes.

SEASONS & CLIMATE

The climate of the entire peninsula is best described as varied, of the marine type. In the winter the temperatures stay in the 30s and 40s (single digits Celsius) during the day, and 20s and 30s (negative single digits Celsius) at night. At the lower elevations, near the water, there is rarely more than 6 inches of accumulated snow per season, and it melts quickly. However, on the upper slopes, the snowfall can become quite heavy.

Spring is the late half of the rainy season, mostly wet, mild, and windy. Temperatures range from 35°F to 60°F (2°C–16°C), with lingering snow flurries in the mountains.

Summer temperatures range from a low of 45°F (7°C) in the evening to 75°F (24°C) and up to 80°F (27°C) during the afternoons. In the latter half of the summer and early fall, fog and cloud banks drift into the valleys and remain until midday, burn off, and sometimes return in the evening. Thunderstorms may occur in the evening in the upper elevations.

The fall is moderately cold and blustery, and ushers in the rainy season. Snow begins to fall in the mountains as soon as early autumn. Temperatures range from 30°F to 65°F (-1°C–18°C).

Rainfall is varied throughout the Olympic Peninsula, but about three-quarters of the precipitation falls during the 6-month period from October through March, primarily on the Pacific side of the peninsula.

SEASONAL EVENTS

There are seasonal events across the Olympic Peninsula, if not within the park itself. They include salmon cook-offs; classical, jazz, and bluegrass festivals; boat races; light opera; and arts and craft festivals. For a full list, contact the **Port Angeles Chamber of Commerce Visitor Center,** 121 E. Railroad Ave. (℃ 877/456-8372; www.portangeles.org), or the **North Olympic Peninsula Visitor & Convention Bureau** (℃ 800/942-4042; www.northwestsecretplaces.com).

If You Have Only 1 Day

First things first: Decide in advance what you would like to see. This is a big park, and no roads go completely through it. The roads that do venture inside (and they're major tourist attractions) are generally short and pleasant. It's 18½ miles from U.S. 101 to the Hoh Visitor Center, and 17 miles to Hurricane Ridge.

If you want to see the **rain forests and the coastal strip,** drive up from Olympia on U.S. 101 through the coastal region, perhaps stopping at the Kalaloch Information Station and Ruby Beach, and then head to the Hoh Rain Forest Visitor Center, from where you can explore further. To see the **glaciers and the alpine meadows** of the east side of the park, start by driving to the Olympic National Park Visitor Center in Port Angeles, and from there head up to Hurricane Ridge, where you can take in a hike, or drive even farther into the park.

Exploring the Park by Car

THE RAIN FORESTS & THE COAST

If the rain forests are your destination, your best bet would be to drive west and north from Olympia along the western side of the peninsula. (Or, in reverse, west and south from Port Angeles or Port Townsend.) The first opportunity to see a bit of the rain forest is near the south shore of **Lake Quinault,** at the southern end of the main part of the park. If you plan to stay the night, this area is packed with lodges, motels, and campgrounds. From the ranger station on the south shore, there are several interpretive hikes along the lake. The view of the mountains here is quite spectacular on a sunny day, but save the rest of your day for nature trails or longer hikes in nearby rain forests. Lake Quinault serves as a good hors d'oeuvre more than anything.

Drive north on U.S. 101. At this point, you have an option—you can drive east to the **Queets Ranger Station** in the Queets River Valley for a rugged hike into some of the most beautiful (and remote) rain forests on the peninsula. Or you can keep driving northwest to the **Kalaloch Information Station,** where you can enjoy views of the Pacific from Kalaloch to Ruby Beach. It's a tough call. You might get to see elk in some of the former homestead meadows in the early morning or late afternoon on the 3-mile **Sam's River Loop Trail** in the Queets, but understand, it's the least accessible of the rain forests. The road to Queets is unpaved, but it's still a relatively decent gravel road.

Watch for seasonal closures during the winter and late fall.

After leaving the coastal area at Ruby Beach, continue your northward drive on U.S. 101 to the turnoff for the **Hoh Rain Forest Visitor Center.** It's an 18½-mile drive from U.S. 101 to the center, with excellent views of the Hoh River along the way. You could also spend a long day hiking the 9 miles from the Hoh Visitor Center parking lot up to the **Olympus Ranger Station.** In just a few hours, this hike goes from temperate rain forest to alpine meadows with stunning views of Mount Olympus. If you're not feeling so ambitious, take the short **Hall of Mosses** or **Spruce Nature trails,** and get ready to head north again, to Sol Duc.

The last leg of our rain forest excursion takes you to one of the most commercially developed areas in the park, **Sol Duc** and the **Sol Duc Hot Springs Resort.** It might be a nice idea, before you head back down the coast to Olympia, or to sleep in your campsite or hotel room, to have a dip in these famous hot springs (open from late spring to early fall). The hot springs experience costs $6.75 to enter, but packages, including a sauna and a massage, can be purchased as well. You also have your choice of comfort levels, anywhere from 70° to 158°F (21°C–70°C). But be forewarned: There's a resort here, and the springs can be crowded. Still, if you're into luxuriating after a long day of hiking, it could be just the thing.

The area has more than hot springs. Try taking the 1-mile hike from the springs through some wonderfully dense forest to **Sol Duc Falls.** Or take the **Mink Lake Trail** through 2.5 miles of uphill grade and dense forest to get a look at one of the many higher-altitude lakes that dot the Sol Duc region.

THE EAST SIDE OF THE PARK

Seen the rain forests? You could do a lot worse than spending a day seeing the glaciers and the alpine meadows of the east side of the park. This time, the jumping-off point of convenience would probably be **Port Angeles.** First, visit the **Olympic National Park Visitor Center,** to get acquainted with what you're about to see.

As in the rain forest tour, this trip starts with a choice: Head back through Port Angeles for the **Elwha/Altaire area,** or from the visitor center head to **Hurricane Ridge.** Either way, you're going to be treated to a variety of Olympic experiences.

The Elwha area has a small ranger station beside **Lake Mills** (a reservoir), and farther up the road, a very nice observation point for viewing the surrounding hills. In addition, if you don't want to deal with the crowds at Sol Duc, you can hike 2.5 miles from Elwha to the only other hot springs available inside the park. Located on the banks of Boulder Creek, the **Olympic Hot Springs** is not accessible by car, and don't expect amenities or guarantees of sanitation either. In other words, use at your own risk.

Along the way to Hurricane Ridge from Port Angeles, pass the **Heart O' the Hills Ranger Station.** At Hurricane Ridge, one of the most popular spots in the park, there are a number of short interpretive trails, very good for seeing wildflowers, and many larger trails intersect here as well. The visitor center has numerous interpretive exhibits and a snack bar.

Leaving Hurricane Ridge, Port Angeles, or the Elwha area, drive a little farther southeast, and off a turnoff of U.S. 101 is the less crowded **Deer Park Ranger Station,** where you get the same sort of views as Hurricane Ridge without jostling for position. The road to Deer Park is steep and graveled. It's not suitable for RVs and trailers, and prepare to deal with steep inclines, turns, and potholes. In the winter the road may be closed.

Outside Olympic National Park, consider visiting other locations along U.S. 101, such as **Dungeness** or **Sequim Bay** state parks on the northeastern tip of the peninsula, with their beautiful shorelines and views of the strait. As you travel farther south, the **Hood Canal** will appear on your left—there are numerous places here to see seals on the rocks on a good day, especially at **Seal Point.**

Organized Tours & Ranger Programs

A variety of programs are offered in Olympic National Park, including campfire talks, stargazing, and beach walks. You'll find rain forest tours originating from the Hoh and the Quinault ranger stations, alpine wildflower walks from the Hurricane Ridge area, and lakeside and waterfall walks from the Storm King Ranger Station. Contact park headquarters for a current schedule.

Historic & Man-Made Attractions

There aren't many man-made attractions within the park itself, although there are **old homestead sites** scattered throughout the park, such as those found along the **Geyser Loop Trail.** Also, there's an old cabin located behind the Olympic National Park Visitor Center that will leave you wondering how early settlers here managed to maintain their sanity in such a claustrophobic environment.

Hikes

There are a vast number of trails in the park, and it seems like they all connect somewhere. Consequently, it's very easy to tie several trails together to create your own customized route. For a complete listing, write ahead for a free **Olympic National Park map** from the Wilderness Information Center, Olympic National Park, 600 East Park Ave., Port Angeles, WA 98362.

The following is a partial, though representative, list of some of the many wonderful trails within the park. **Backcountry**

permits are required for overnight trips. They're available at the Wilderness Information Center (located just behind the main visitor center in Port Angeles) and at all ranger stations. During the summer, you may also need reservations for certain areas. There is a $5 registration fee for wilderness camping for groups up to 12 people, plus $2 per person per night. Call the Wilderness Information Center (© **360/565-3100**) for information.

> **Warning: Coastal hiking can be treacherous. Tides can trap you. Never round headlands without knowledge of the tide heights and times. Carry a tide chart. Obtain additional information from the Wilderness Information Center.**

COASTAL AREA

Cape Alava/Sand Point Loop

9.1 miles RT. Easy. Access: Ozette Ranger Station.

This loop begins with a stroll over a cedar-plank boardwalk through teeming coastal marsh and grasslands. (Careful! Boards are slippery when wet, which is most of the time.) The trail connects to its second leg on a wilderness beach strip of the Pacific shoreline, the westernmost point in the Lower 48. Camping is permitted on the beach, but beware, it's a popular spot in the summer. Continue south 1 mile past the petroglyphs that can be seen from the rocks along the shore next to the high-tide line. Two miles south, the trail connects to the Sand Point leg, which is an easy stroll back to the Ozette Ranger Station. (There's a permit and reservation required here. Call the Wilderness Information Center.)

Hoh River to Queets River

14.7 miles one-way. Easy to moderate. Access: Ruby Beach parking lot.

The beaches here are wide and flat, the surf fishing is good, and with its proximity to U.S. 101, you can expect to see a lot of people here in the summer. This section, compared to the more northern trails, is fairly tame. Destruction Island Overlook is famous for its whale-watching from March to April and November to December.

Sand Point to Rialto Beach

17 miles one-way. Easy to moderate. Access: Ozette Lake Ranger Station from the north or Mora Campground from the south.

This is a coastline famous for its shipwrecks, the memorials of which dot the beach at many points, along with an abandoned mine. Other than that, though, there's not a lot of man-made activity going on. Enjoy the sand and the mist, enjoy the forests that come down to land's end, and get ready for the storms that visit here regularly.

Second Beach Trail

0.8 mile one-way. Easy. Access: Second Beach parking area on the La Push road, 14 miles west of U.S. 101.

Wander through a lovely forest to a sandy beach, with tide pools and sea stacks. There's a long set of stair steps at the end. For a short hike, this is hard to beat.

Third Beach to Hoh River

17 miles one-way. Moderate to strenuous. Access: Third Beach Parking Area, 3 miles beyond the La Push Rd. left fork.

This trail is not your leisurely stroll. You'll be required to do a bit of inland skirting along old oil company roads to avoid some of the more wicked headlands, and there are some sand ladders (contraptions constructed of cables and wooden slats) just beyond Taylor Point. In addition, there's a slightly treacherous crossing farther south at Goodman Creek. So what's the reward for the intrepid hiker? Toleak Point is located approximately 5 miles down the beach, where there is a sheltered camp-site famous for its wildlife. The entire area is well known for its shipwrecks, wildlife, coastal headlands, and stacks. The trail ends at Oil City, north of the Hoh Indian Reservation.

WESTERN PARKLANDS & RAIN FORESTS

Bogachiel River

Length varies. Easy to moderate in the low-lands, more strenuous farther inland. Access: 5 miles south of Forks, turn left across from Bogachiel State Park onto Undie Rd., and con-tinue 5 miles to the trailhead.

This hike is as long or short as you want to make it, but it is an equally beautiful cousin to the often-crowded Hoh River Trail. The beginning is loaded with rain-forest extravaganza—huge Douglas firs, spruce, cedar, and big-leaf maples, including the world's largest silver fir, some 8 miles from the trailhead. Approximately 6 miles into the trail is the Bogachiel Shelter, and 8 miles in is Flapjack Camp, both good backcountry campsites. This is pretty much the end of the flatland; farther up, the trail begins to get steep.

Hoh River Valley

Up to 17 miles one-way. Easy to moderate in the lowlands, more strenuous farther inland. Access: Hoh Rain Forest Visitor Center.

This is one of the most heavily traveled trails in the park, at least in the lower elevations, and it won't take you long to figure out why. Huge Sitka spruces hung with moss shelter the Roosevelt elk that wander among its lowlands. The first 13 miles, through the massive rain forests and tall grass meadows along the Hoh River Valley bottomlands, are relatively flat. The number of fellow walkers drops

off after the first few miles. Happy Four Camp (6 miles in) and Olympus Guard Station (9 miles in) provide excellent camp or turnaround sites. Continue eastward into the hills for the remaining 4 or 5 miles. If you connect with the Hoh Lake Trail, you can eventually find yourself at the edge of the famous Blue Glacier on Mount Olympus, elevation 7,965 feet. Be careful. After July, hiking near the park's glaciers can be danger-ous because of snowmelt.

Lake Quinault Loop

4 miles RT. Easy. Access: Trailheads located at various spots along the loop, including South Shore Rd., Quinault Lodge, Willaby Campground, Quinault Ranger Station, and Falls Creek Camp-ground. All access originates from the south shore of Lake Quinault.

This trail is easily accessible, is well maintained, and offers beautiful views. Consequently, it's quite crowded in the summer. Elevation changes are gentle, making this an excellent walk for kids.

The trail wanders about the shore of Lake Quinault, past historic Lake Quinault Lodge as well as the adjacent campgrounds and other lakeside attrac-tions, before heading into its most popular section, the Big Tree Grove. Here you can wander among the huge trunks of 500-year-old Douglas firs. Watch for the interpretive signs. In addi-tion, the Big Tree Grove can be accessed via a short, 1-mile loop trail, originating from the Rain Forest Nature Trail park-ing lot.

Maple Glade Rain Forest Trail

0.5 mile RT. Easy. Access: Across the bridge from the Quinault Ranger Station.

This is another beautiful, peaceful little trail with lots of exhibits. Take the kids, or just enjoy it yourself. As you meander, you'll pass through dense trees, open meadows, and an abandoned beaver pond. As usual, keep your eyes peeled for the ever-possible elk sighting.

North Fork of the Quinault

Up to 15 miles one-way. Moderate. Access: End of the North Shore Rd. Alternatively, if a washout has occurred at the trailhead, the trail is accessible from the South Shore Rd. as well.

This is either the end of the Skyline Ridge Trail or the beginning of the North Fork Trail, both of which could conceivably take you 47 miles all the way through the park to Altaire and Elwha on the north side—if you make the right connections and are maniacal enough. The trail is relatively benign for the first dozen miles as it winds its way inward along the river toward its source near Mount Seattle. Campsites are available at Wolf Bar (2.5 miles in), Halfway House (5.3 miles in), and in a gorge in Elip Creek (6.5 miles in). For the last several miles, the trail climbs steeply toward Low Divide, Lake Mary, and Lake Margaret, where you can get beautiful views of Mount Seattle, at an elevation of 6,246 feet. Snow can remain at this elevation until midsummer, so be ready. There's a summer ranger station at Low Divide, and many high-elevation campsites here as well.

Queets River Trail

Up to 16 miles one-way. Moderate to strenuous. Access: Queets River Campground.

This is the trail for the serious rain forest/wilderness lover. Part of its appeal is that it requires a bit of an effort from the average hiker to reach the trail's solitude and quietly majestic scenery. Within 50 yards of your car, you'll be traversing the Queets River. Even on this first of several fords you will have to make across the river, the water can be treacherous if it's up. It's best to visit during the dry season in late summer. An option is to cross the Sams River to the right of the Queets, connecting and crossing the Queets River farther up. At 2.5 miles, gape in awe at the largest Douglas fir on the planet. After 5 miles of hiking through elk and giant fern

territory, you'll arrive at Spruce Bottom, which is a common haunt for steelhead anglers and has several good campsites. The trail ends at Pelton Creek, where campsites are also available.

Sams River Loop Trail

3 miles RT. Easy to moderate. Access: Queets River Ranger Station.

This short loop parallels both the Sams River and the Queets River, providing a view of some old homestead meadows, beautiful spruce trees, and perhaps an elk or two in the meadows in the evening.

NORTHERN PARK REGIONS

Deer Lake

8 miles RT. Moderate. Access: Junction of Sol Duc Falls.

A good choice for those who want to see deer, this trail is a steady climb through beautiful woods to this tree-lined lake. Canada jays await to eat your food, but don't feed them. There are some switchbacks on this trail, and it can get pretty bumpy in spots.

Elwha River Trails

Up to 50 miles one-way. Difficulty varies. Access: Drive just beyond the Elwha Ranger Station to Whiskey Bend Rd. Go past the Glines Canyon Dam, 1½ miles up the road. Approximately 2 miles above the dam is the Whiskey Bend Trailhead, just beyond the Upper Lake Mills Trailhead.

The serious backpacker arranges a pickup car at the Dosewallips or the North Fork ranger districts and heads for a week or so along the trail that was fortuitously blazed by the famed 1889 Press Expedition, the expedition that essentially broke this park wide open. For a good distance, the trail follows the intense blue-green of the Elwha River to its source on the sometimes snow-slushy peak at Low Divide (elevation 3,600 ft.), which is also the head of the Quinault River. You can follow the trail downhill from here to the North Fork of the Quinault.

What can you expect on such a monumental trip?

Old-growth forests, moist valley flatlands, and gently sloping hills appear around you as you explore the Elwha Valley before you begin your ascent towards the sometimes calf-busting Low Divide. Roosevelt elk, black bears, mountain lions, marmots, or a grouse or two might show up. At Low Divide, you're treated to spectacular views of Mount Seattle to the north and Mount Christie to the south. From here, you begin your descent from alpine heights to the deep, dense rain forests along the Quinault.

Geyser Valley Loop

5 miles RT. Moderate. Access: Drive just beyond the Elwha Ranger Station to Whiskey Bend Rd. Go 1½ miles to the Glines Canyon Dam, and continue up the road approximately 2 miles to the Whiskey Bend Trailhead, just beyond the Upper Lake Mills Trailhead.

From the Whiskey Bend Trailhead, hike 0.75 mile down the trail to the Eagles Nest Overlook for a view of the meadows that stretch from valley to valley. You may see an elk or black bear. Head back to the trail and proceed 0.5 mile to the Rica Canyon Trail for a view of Goblin's Gate, a rock formation in the Canyon Gorge that might look like a bunch of goblins' heads staring at you, if you stare back hard enough. The trail to Goblin's Gates drops 325 feet on the half-mile walk to the viewing area. At this point, you can follow a riverside trail for another half-mile to some prime fishing spots, or continue on to the Krause Bottom and Humes Ranch area. The Humes Ranch has been restored, although some of the wood is starting to get moldy. At any one of these points you can return north back to the Whiskey Bend Trail, or continue 0.8 mile northeast past Michael's Cabin, another old homestead.

High Divide Loop

Up to 20 miles RT. Moderate. Access: Sol Duc Ranger Station.

Like many trails in the park, this one gives you a chance to design your own hike. From the Sol Duc Ranger Station Trailhead, climb a relatively easy wooded 0.8 mile to Sol Duc Falls, and keep going. You can take a leg out to the Seven Lakes Basin Area, where you'll find many campsites (crowded in the summer), or toward Appleton Pass, some 14 miles inland. From Appleton Pass, pass nearby Heart Lake, and begin your climb toward Bogachiel Peak (elevation 5,474 ft.), which presents some of the most breathtaking views in the park. On clear summer days, you can enjoy the wildflowers along the slopes of Bogachiel, the view to the south of the glaciers of Mount Olympus, or the brilliant sunsets on the western Pacific horizon. Continue back down toward Sol Duc Trail through the Deer Lake area, and make the final leg back to the Sol Duc Trailhead.

Lovers Lane Loop

6 miles RT. Easy to moderate. Access: Next to site 62 in Loop B of the Sol Duc Campground.

This trail extends a loop that begins just past Sol Duc Falls. Cross the bridge at the falls and continue around on the trail, which will return you to the resort/campground area after taking you through beautiful spruce groves and fern glades. Portions of the trail are narrow and rocky and can get muddy until things dry out in midsummer. Occasionally, you can spot grouse along the trail.

Marymere Falls

2.2 miles RT. Easy. Access: Storm King Ranger Station.

This is one of the most popular hikes in the park. It's well maintained, close to U.S. 101, and has a definite goal: beautiful Marymere Falls. It's a popular trail for kids. Start out on the Barnes Creek

Trail, which leads 0.7 mile through beautiful maples and conifers to the Marymere Trail turnoff. Continue up to the falls, where silvery water drops from a moss-covered outcropping some 100 feet to the basin below.

Mink Lake Trail

5 miles RT. Moderate. Access: Opposite end of the Sol Duc Resort parking lot from the pools.

This is a long climb up to Mink Lake, where herons are known to pursue an elusive trout or two. In late summer, brilliant buckbean flowers fill the marshy edges of the lake, and huckleberries are abundant.

North Fork of the Sol Duc

2.4 miles RT. Moderate. Access: North Fork Trailhead, 3¾ miles down the Sol Duc Rd. away from the resort.

On this trail you climb the ridge between the main and north forks of the river before descending into the North Fork Valley. The trail passes through old-growth forests before arriving at the deep-green pools of the river. The curious can venture upriver for several more miles.

Sol Duc Falls

1.7 miles RT. Easy. Access: Sol Duc Ranger Station.

One of the more popular spots on the peninsula, beautiful Sol Duc Falls is viewed from a bridge that spans the canyon just below the falls. On the way, check out the huge hemlocks and Douglas firs, some of which are 300 years old. This trail is wide, graveled, and level, making it great for kids.

Spruce Railroad

8 miles RT. Easy. Access: 4 miles from the Fairholm Campground, at the end of the North Shore Rd. along Lake Crescent.

This is the trail you want to take for a leisurely, hot summer afternoon stroll. The flat, wide trail wanders gently around the unbelievably blue-green, glacial-fed waters of Crescent Lake, along an old stretch of abandoned railroad. Weather permitting, clamber down the bank and go for a swim, or simply enjoy the views of Mount Storm King. There are two abandoned railroad tunnels (don't go in!) and a much-photographed arch bridge at Devil's Point.

HURRICANE RIDGE AREA

Cirque Rim Trail & Big Meadow Loops

0.5 mile and 0.25 mile RT. Easy. Access: Hurricane Ridge Visitor Center parking lot.

These trails provide a wonderful little taste of alpine meadows, deer, and the spring display of wildflowers, along with excellent views of Port Angeles and the Strait of Juan de Fuca.

Grand Ridge (Obstruction Point to Green Mountain)

11 miles RT. Moderate. Access: From Hurricane Ridge, turn left onto the dirt road to Obstruction Point, and continue 8½ miles to the end of the road.

This is the highest section of trail in the park, a fact you might notice as you gaze out to Victoria, B.C., and the Strait of Juan de Fuca to the north, or to the south, where you'll see the Grand Valley with its string of lakes and the numerous snow-clad peaks of the Olympic interior. There is a shortage of both trees and water on this hike.

From the parking lot, follow the trail to the left. (The right goes to Grand Valley.) In 2 miles you'll find yourself at the breathtaking top of Elk Mountain. Over the next 5.5 miles, you will pass through Roaring Winds Camp (not misnamed), up to Maiden Peak and finally Green Mountain. In late June the air is filled with the smell of Lyle's lupine, which grows amid the loose scree. This is a good turnaround point, unless you want to descend to Deer Park.

High Ridge, Alpine Hills to Klahane Ridge

1–8 miles RT. Easy to moderate. Access: Hurricane Ridge Visitor Center.

You can take the short, paved 1-mile High Ridge Route (which is chock-full of interpretive exhibits) and then return to the parking lot. Or you can proceed along the unpaved portion to Sunrise Ridge, a rocky little backbone of a view point off the High Ridge Trail, providing excellent panoramas of the Strait of Juan de Fuca, Port Angeles, and beautiful alpine glaciers and wildflowers. The rest of the 3.3-mile, somewhat strenuous, walk climbs to the top of Klahane Ridge. As numerous signs warn, beware of the deer and marmots here! They're unafraid, and may hassle people who approach them.

Hurricane Hill

2.75 miles RT. Easy to moderate. Access: 1½ miles from the Hurricane Ridge Visitor Center.

This is a popular trail in the summertime, as it is a broad, easy climb along an abandoned work road up to brilliant alpine meadows, with fantastic views of the Strait of Juan de Fuca and Port Angeles to the north.

EASTERN & SOUTHEASTERN SECTION

Main Fork Dosewallips/ Constance Pass

11 miles one-way. Moderate. Access: Dosewallips Campground and Ranger Station.

Take the Main Fork Dosewallips to the north, and you'll find yourself on a moderate climb through old-growth forests for 7.5 miles before the trail flattens out at Constance Pass. There are fields of wildflowers skirting the edge of Mount Constance. The trail ends in another 3.4 miles at Boulder Shelter in Olympic National Forest. You can also catch the Upper Big Quilcene Trail or the Upper Dungeness Trail here.

Main Fork of the Dosewallips

31 miles RT. Moderate. Access: Dosewallips Ranger Station.

This is a versatile trail. You can catch a lot more of the inland trails from here, including Constance Pass Trail, the Gray Wolf Trail, and the Elwha River Trail. The Dosewallips side of the park sometimes seems like the neglected side—it's not as flashy as a glacial meadow or a rain forest. But the Dosewallips is one of the most beautiful rivers in the country, its jade-green water crashing down among narrow cliffs. And you might skirt some of the crowds.

Staircase Rapids

6.5 miles RT. Easy to moderate. Access: Staircase Ranger Station.

The Staircase Trail is one of the more popular hikes in the park, and once you get to Staircase Falls, you'll see why. Along the way you'll enjoy the sight of the North Fork Skokomish River's white water rushing through stands of huge cedar trees. After the falls, the trail continues for another 1.5 miles, following in the footsteps of the 1890 O'Neil Expedition that named the area.

Other Sports & Activities

Biking. Almost all trails in the park are closed to mountain bikes. The only exception is the **Spruce Railroad Trail,** which was once a railroad grade that ran along the shore of the lake. It is quite flat and easy for its 4-mile length, and there is an additional 1½-mile stretch of road past the North Shore Picnic Area. In the summer there are spots where you can get down the banks for a little dip in Lake Crescent. The highlight of the trail is a much-photographed arched bridge across a rocky cove. There are also a few **dirt roads** for mountain bikers, extending from paved roads, such as the section from Hurricane Ridge to Obstruction Peak.

For road bikers, U.S. 101 can be somewhat treacherous, with eager motorists rubbernecking and all. But if you get through all that, you can find some pleasant rides on any of the roads that poke their way into the park.

Kayaking & Canoeing. Although large and often windy, glacier-carved **Lake Crescent** is a beautiful place to do a little paddling. Lush, green forests rise straight up from the shores of this 624-foot deep lake, giving these waters a fjordlike quality unmatched anywhere on the peninsula. Boat ramps can be found on U.S. 101 at Storm King (near the middle of the lake) and at Fairholm (at the west end of the lake). On East Beach Road, on the lake's northeast shore, there is a private boat ramp at the Log Cabin Resort.

If you launch at Storm King, you can explore around Barnes Point, away from U.S. 101 traffic noise (but in view of the Lake Crescent Lodge). From Fairholm, you can paddle along the north shore; and from the Log Cabin Resort, you can explore the narrow bay that feeds the Lyre River, the lake's outlet stream. When winds blow down this lake, as they often do, the waters can be very dangerous for small boats.

Canoes can be rented at **Fairholm General Store** (© 360/928-3020) at the west end of the lake, or at the **Log Cabin Resort,** 3183 E. Beach Rd. (© 360/928-3325), on the lake's northeast shore.

Ozette Lake, 300 feet deep, nearly 10 miles long, and the third-largest natural lake in Washington, is a fascinating place to explore by sea kayak or canoe. Situated only a mile from the Pacific Ocean, the lake is indented by numerous coves and bays, and surrounds three small islands. Campsites along the shore include the boat-in sites at Erickson's Bay.

The **Swan Bay boat launch,** one of the lake's two, is probably the best choice for paddlers heading out on this large lake. For a leisurely half-day paddle, just explore the shores of this convoluted bay, in the middle of which is Garden Island. For a daylong trip, try

paddling down the lake to Tivoli Island. For an overnighter, head to the lake's western shore and the campsites at Erickson's Bay. From here, you can explore up and down the west shore.

Both Lake Crescent and Ozette Lake are big lakes subject to quick changes of weather and wind. Whitecaps can come up suddenly, and cold waters can lead to hypothermia. Check the weather forecast before leaving, and keep an eye on the sky.

Llama Trips. The park has become a favorite for llama pack trips. Try **Wooley Packer Llama Co.,** 5763 Upper Hoh Road, Forks, WA 98331 (© **360/374-9288**), which offers trips of up to 7 days within the park; or **Kit's Llamas,** P.O. Box 116, Olalla, WA 98359 (© **253/857-5274;** fax 253/857-5141; www.northolympic.com/llamas), which offers day and extended trips.

Snowshoeing & Cross-Country Skiing. Any of the snow-covered roads leading into the mountains will offer a satisfying winter trek. However, if it's views you seek, then head to **Hurricane Ridge** with the rest of the winter crowd and set out on any of the area's trails. Snowshoe rentals are available at the Hurricane Ridge Lodge.

White-Water Kayaking & Canoeing. Although the Olympic Mountains generate an astounding number of runnable rivers, the best are on the west side of the peninsula and along the southern slopes of the range. However, the east and north sides of the peninsula also offer some good runs. As elsewhere in the Northwest, sweepers, strainers, and logjams are always a problem on the steep, narrow rivers. If you're interested in taking a white-water kayaking class or obtaining any other information on local white-water action, contact the **Olympic Outdoor Center,** P.O. Box 2247, Poulsbo, WA 98370 (© **360/697-6095;** www.kayakproshop.com), which focuses on sea kayaking and white-water kayaking classes and rentals.

White-Water Rafting. White-water rafting, scenic floats, and sea kayaking are offered in and around Olympic National Park. Guided trips last approximately half a day, and canoe and kayak rentals are available. Contact **Olympic Raft & Kayak,** 123 Lake Aldwell Rd., Port Angeles, WA 98363 (© **888/452-1443;** www. raftandkayak.com). Rates begin at $42 per person for guided trips.

Camping

Campgrounds at Elwha, Heart O' the Hills, Hoh, July Creek, Kalaloch, Mora, Ozette, Queets, and Staircase are open year-round; other campgrounds are open only seasonally, and their exact schedules are subject to change. Campgrounds at higher elevations may be snow-covered (and closed) from early November to late June; seasonal campgrounds at lower elevations may open earlier. Fees range from $8 to $16 depending on campground amenities.

There are no showers or laundry facilities inside the park, though both are available at the Log Cabin Resort.

The park has no RV hookups, and many sites can accommodate RVs of only 21 feet or less. Use of the park's RV dump stations costs $3. RVs and trailers are prohibited at Deer Park and Dosewallips. July Creek's campsites are all hike-ins. However, the Log Cabin Resort, on the north shore of Lake Crescent at the northern edge of the park, offers RV sites with hookups (see below).

Campground	Elev.	Total Sites	RV Hookups	Dump Station	Toilets
Altaire	450	30	No	No	Yes
Deer Park*	5,400	14	No	No	No
Dosewallips*	1,540	30	No	No	Yes
Elwha	390	40	No	No	Yes
Fairholm	580	88	No	Yes	Yes
Graves Creek	540	30	No	No	Yes
Heart O' the Hills	1,807	105	Yes	No	Yes
Hoh	578	88	No	Yes	Yes
July Creek***	200	29	No	No	Yes
Kalaloch	50	175	No	Yes	Yes
Log Cabin Resort	580	40	Yes	Yes	Yes
Mora**	35	94	No	Yes	Yes
North Fork	7	520	No	No	Yes
Ozette	0	15	No	No	Yes
Queets	290	20	No	No	No
Sol Duc	1,680	82	No	Yes	Yes
South Beach	50	50	No	No	No
Staircase	765	56	No	No	Yes

* Trailers/RVs prohibited.
** Group reservations only (must be made directly through the ranger station).
*** Walk-in sites.

NORTH- & EASTSIDE CAMPGROUNDS

The six campgrounds on the northern edge of the park are some of the busiest in the park due to their proximity to U.S. 101.

Deer Park is the easternmost of these campgrounds (to get there, take Deer Park Rd. from U.S. 101 east of Port Angeles); at 5,400 feet, it's also the only high-elevation campground in the park. Deer Park is reached by a winding one-way gravel road that will have you wondering how you're ever going to get back down the mountain. (Thus, RVs and trailers are prohibited.) Deer frequent the campground, and hiking trails head out across the ridges and valleys.

Because of its proximity to Hurricane Ridge, **Heart O' the Hills** is especially popular. It's located on Hurricane Ridge Road, 5 miles south of the Olympic National Park Visitor Center. Several trails start at or near the campground.

Two campgrounds are located on Olympic Hot Springs Road, up the Elwha River, which is popular with kayakers and anglers. **Elwha** is the trailhead for a trail leading up to Hurricane Ridge. **Altaire** has a boat ramp often used by rafters and kayakers. And, yes, there are hot springs, a 2.5-mile hike away.

The only national park campground on Lake Crescent is **Fairholm,** located at the west end of the lake. This campground is popular with power boaters and could be rather noisy. South of this

Drinking Water	Showers	Fire Pits/ Grills	Laundry	Reserve	Fees	Open
Yes	No	Yes	No	No	$10	Seasonal
Yes	No	Yes	No	No	$8	Seasonal
Yes	No	Yes	No	No	$10	Seasonal
Yes	No	Yes	No	No	$10	Year-round
Yes	No	Yes	No	No	$10	Seasonal
Yes	No	Yes	No	No	$10	Seasonal
Yes	Yes	No	No	No	$10	Year-round
Yes	No	Yes	No	No	$10	Year-round
Yes	No	Yes	No	No	$10	Year-round
Yes	No	Yes	No	Yes	$12–$16	Year-round
Yes	Yes	Yes	Yes	Yes	$31	Seasonal
Yes	No	Yes	No	Yes	$10	Year-round
No	Yes	No	No	No	Free	Seasonal
Yes	No	Yes	No	No	$10	Seasonal
No	No	Yes	No	No	$8	Seasonal
Yes	No	No	No	No	$12	Seasonal
No	No	Yes	No	No	$8	Seasonal
Yes	No	Yes	No	No	$10	Year-round

area, nearby **Sol Duc** is set amid impressive stands of old-growth trees, adjacent to the Sol Duc Hot Springs (and the resort there). Not surprisingly, it is often crowded.

Finally, you'll find RV sites with full hookups at the **Log Cabin Resort,** 3183 E. Beach Rd., on the north shore of Lake Crescent (℗ **360/928-3325**). Because there are no hookups at any of the national park campgrounds, this is a good choice for those with RVs, but tent campers aren't allowed. Major credit cards (DISC, MC, V) are accepted, and the resort is open year-round.

SOUTHEASTSIDE CAMPGROUNDS

At the end of F.S. 2610, which parallels the Dosewallips River and provides access to the Hayden Pass, Anderson Pass, and Lake Constance trails, you'll find **Dosewallips Campground** in a forested setting on the river's banks. RVs and trailers are prohibited.

The remote **Staircase Campground** is located inland from the Hood Canal and is a good base for day hikes or as a starting point for a longer backpacking trip. It's located up the Skokomish River from Lake Cushman on F.S. 24 and is the trailhead for the Six Ridge, Flapjack Lakes, and Anderson Pass trails.

SOUTH- & SOUTHWESTSIDE CAMPGROUNDS

If you want to say you've camped at the wettest campground in the contiguous U.S., head for **Hoh,** a busy campground near the Hoh Rain Forest Visitor Center.

Queets is more off the beaten track and has good hiking and white-water kayaking nearby. This campground is located 14 miles up the gravel Queets Road from U.S. 101.

Other rain-forest camping options include **July Creek,** a walk-in campground on Quinault Lake's north shore. East of Lake Quinault, **North Fork** and **Graves Creek,** reached only by an unpaved road, provide access to several long-distance hiking trails.

COASTAL CAMPGROUNDS

Along the peninsula's west side are several beach campgrounds. One is **Mora,** located on the beautiful Rialto Beach at the mouth of the Quillayute River west of Forks. You can make group reservations (only) here by contacting the ranger station; call the main park number (℗ **360/452-4501**) for more information.

The other coastal campground is the remote **Ozette,** on the north shore of Lake Ozette. It's a good choice for kayakers and canoeists, as well as people wanting to day-hike to the beaches on either side of Cape Alava. There is a designated swimming beach on the lake.

Where to Stay

INSIDE THE PARK

Kalaloch Lodge

157151 U.S. 101, Forks, WA 98331. ℗ **866/525-2562.** Fax 360/962-3391. www.visit kalaloch.com. 20 rooms, $83–$248 double; 44 cabins, $95–$264 cabin for 2, $12 each additional person, children under 6 free. Lower rates Sun–Thurs Oct–May. AE, MC, V.

This rustic, cedar-shingled lodge and its cluster of cabins perch on a grassy bluff. Below, the Pacific Ocean thunders against a sandy beach where huge driftwood logs are scattered like so many twigs. The breathtaking setting makes this one of the most popular lodges on the coast, and it's advisable to book rooms at least 4 months in advance (11 months in advance for July, Aug, and major holidays). The rooms in the old lodge are the least expensive, but the ocean-view bluff cabins are the most popular. The log cabins across the road from the bluff cabins don't have the knockout views. Pets are allowed in cabins only. For comfort you can't beat the motel-like rooms in the Sea Crest House. The dining room serves breakfast, lunch, and dinner, and a casual coffee shop serves from the same menu. Dinner prices range from $10 to $18. The lodge also has a general store and gas station.

Lake Crescent Lodge

416 Lake Crescent Rd., Port Angeles, WA 98363. ℭ **360/928-3041.** www.LakeCrescent Lodge.com. 52 units. $68 double with shared bathroom, $120 double with private bathroom; $113 single cottage, $145 double cottage. AE, DC, DISC, MC, V.

This historic lodge is located 20 miles west of Port Angeles on the south shore of picturesque Lake Crescent and is the lodging of choice for those wishing to stay on the north side of the park. The guest rooms in the main building are the oldest and all have shared bathrooms. If you'd like more modern accommodations, there are also standard motel-style rooms. If you have family or friends along, we recommend reserving a cottage. Those with fireplaces are the most comfortable and the most popular. They are the only rooms available between November and mid-April, weekends only. All rooms have views of either the lake or the mountains.

Wood paneling, hardwood floors, a stone fireplace, and a sunroom make the lobby a popular spot for just sitting and relaxing. The Lodge Dining Room menu includes Continental cuisine with an emphasis on local seafood. Prices are moderate. A lobby lounge provides a quiet place for an evening drink. Rowboat rentals are available.

Log Cabin Resort

3183 E. Beach Rd., Port Angeles, WA 98363. ℭ **360/928-3325.** www.logcabinresort.net. 24 cabins, 8 with bathroom; 4 motel units; 2 chalet units. $59 cabin for 2 without bathroom, $86–$104 cabin for 2 with bathroom; $115 double motel unit; $141 chalet. DISC, MC, V. Closed Nov–Mar.

This log-cabin resort on the north shore of Lake Crescent first opened in 1895 and still has buildings that date from the 1920s. The least expensive accommodations are rustic one-room log cabins in which you provide the bedding and share a bathroom a short walk away. More comfortable are the 1928 cabins with private bathrooms, some of which also have kitchenettes. (You provide the cooking and eating utensils.) The lodge rooms and a chalet offer the greatest comfort and best views. The lodge dining room overlooks the lake and specializes in local seafood. The resort also has a general store and RV sites.

Sol Duc Hot Springs Resort

Sol Duc Rd., U.S. 101 (P.O. Box 2169), Port Angeles, WA 98362. ℭ **360/327-3583.** Fax 360/327-3593. www.northolympic.com/solduc. 32 cabins. $112–$132 cabin for 2. RV sites $20. AE, DISC, MC, V. Open Apr–Oct.

Located at the end of Sol Duc Road, the Sol Duc Hot Springs have for years been a popular family vacation spot. Campers, day-trippers, and resort guests all spend the day soaking and playing in the hot-water sitting pools. The grounds of the resort are grassy and open, but the forest is at arm's reach. The cabins are done in modern motel style and are comfortable, if not spacious. There's an excellent restaurant here, as well as a poolside deli, gift shop, and convenience store. Three hot spring–fed sitting pools are the focal point, and the pools are open to the public for a small fee. Massages are available.

NEAR THE PARK IN PORT ANGELES

Domaine Madeleine

146 Wildflower Lane, Port Angeles, WA 98362. ℭ **888/811-8376.** Fax 360/457-3037. www.domainemadeleine.com. 5 units. TV TEL. $145–$235 double. Rates include full breakfast. AE, DISC, MC, V.

Located 7 miles east of Port Angeles, this B&B is set at the back of a small pasture and has a very secluded feel. Combine this with the waterfront setting and you have a fabulous weekend hideaway—you may not even bother exploring the park. The guest rooms are in several different buildings surrounded by colorful gardens, and all have views of the Strait of Juan de Fuca and the mountains beyond. There are also fireplaces and VCRs in the rooms, and whirlpool tubs in all but one. The breakfasts are superb.

Red Lion Hotel Port Angeles

221 N. Lincoln St., Port Angeles, WA 98362. © **800/RED-LION** or 360/452-9215. Fax 360/452-4734). 186 units. A/C TV TEL. $99–$129 double; $165 suite. Lower rates off season. AE, DC, DISC, MC, V.

If you're on your way to or from Victoria, there's no more convenient hotel than the Red Lion. Located on the waterfront, it's only steps from the ferry terminal. Most rooms have balconies and large bathrooms, and the more expensive rooms overlook the Strait of Juan de Fuca. There's a seafood restaurant adjacent to the hotel. Laundry/valet service is available, and there's an outdoor pool and hot tub.

The Tudor Inn

1108 S. Oak St., Port Angeles, WA 98362. © **866/286-2224.** Fax 360/457-9360. www. tudorinn.com. 5 units. Summer $95–$145 double; off season $85–$135 double. AE, DISC, MC, V.

Located in a quiet residential neighborhood 13 blocks from the waterfront, this 1910 Tudor home is surrounded by a large yard and pretty gardens. Upstairs are five rooms furnished with European antiques. Several rooms have good views of the Olympic Mountains; one room has a balcony and fireplace. On the ground floor is a lounge and library, both with fireplaces that get a lot of use. Wake up to a delicious breakfast served by candlelight in the formal dining room.

Elwha Ranch Bed & Breakfast

905 Herrick Rd., Port Angeles, WA 98363. © **360/457-6540.** www.elwharanch.com. 3 units. $120–$130 double in summer, $90–$110 double in winter. Rates include full breakfast. Call for directions. AE, MC, V.

Although it isn't located within the national park, this cedar-log inn, on a 95-acre ranch high above the Elwha River Valley, has a superb view up the valley into the park. Two of the suites are in the main house, which has a casual Western ranch feel and lots of windows to take in the views. If you're traveling with friends or family, opt for the two-bedroom suite. However, the nicest and most comfortable room here is a sort of modern log cabin outside the front door of the main house. Fresh pies are a specialty of innkeeper Margaret Mitchell.

Eagle Point Inn

384 Stormin' Norman Rd. (P.O. Box 546), Beaver, WA 98305. © **360/327-3236.** www. eaglepointinn.com. 3 units. $85 double. Rates include full breakfast. No credit cards.

Located 10 miles north of Forks, a short drive from milepost 202 on U.S. 101, this rustic B&B is housed in a log home. Although the inn's 5 acres are surrounded by recently planted forest, the inn itself is in a beautiful parklike setting on the bank of the Sol Duc River. The guest rooms are everything the rooms in a log house should be—rustic, romantic, rugged—yet with antiques, down comforters, and private bathrooms. Out in the yard you'll find a hot tub and a covered barbecue area.

Huckleberry Lodge

1171 Big Pine Way, Forks, WA 98331. © **888/ 822-6008.** www.huckleberrylodge.com. 6 units. Summer $90–$135 double; call for rates at other times. Rates include breakfast. MC, V.

Although ostensibly a modern hunting and fishing lodge, this place makes a great base of operations for anyone visiting the area. The lodge is down a gravel road on the edge of Forks and is set on 5 wooded acres adjacent to the Calawah River. In the living room, a moose antler table and trophy heads on the walls emphasize the hunting lodge aesthetics. Guest rooms are comfortable; the room in the main house has a king bed and fine antiques. For greater privacy, there are three cabin units behind the main house. Fishing and hunting packages are available. There are limited RV hookups for $24.

Manitou Lodge

Kilmer Rd. (P.O. Box 600), Forks, WA 98331. ℂ **360/374-6295.** Fax 360/374-7495. www. manitoulodge.com. 7 units. $90–$145 double. Rates include full breakfast. AE, MC, V. Take Wash. 110 west from 1 mile north of Forks; after 8 miles turn right on Mora Rd. and then right on Kilmer Rd.

This secluded B&B is set on 10 forested acres and is only minutes from some of the most beautiful and remote beaches in the Northwest. The largest room in the house is "Sacagawea," which has a wood-burning fireplace and king bed. A separate cabin houses two of the rooms. Guests tend to gravitate to the comfortable living room, where a huge stone fireplace is the center of attention. Breakfasts consist of fruit and a main course, sometimes a seafood scramble with hollandaise sauce or a German apple bake. There's also a Northwest arts gallery on the premises.

Miller Tree Inn

654 E. Division St. (P.O. Box 1565), Forks, WA 98331. ℂ **800/943-6563** or 360/374-6806. Fax 360/374-6807. www.millertreeinn.com. 8 units, all with private bathroom. Peak $90–$175 double; winter $65–$150 double. Rates include full breakfast. DISC, MC, V.

Located just a few blocks east of downtown Forks, this large B&B is on the edge of the country and is surrounded by large old trees and pastures. There's nothing fussy or pretentious about this place—it's just a comfortable, friendly inn that caters primarily to outdoors enthusiasts and, during the winter months, anglers. Three rooms have whirlpool tubs and two have gas fireplaces. A hot tub is on the back deck.

SOUTH OF THE PARK

Lake Quinault Lodge

P.O. Box 7, Quinault, WA 98575. ℂ **800/562-6672** or 360/288-2900. www.visitlake quinault.com. 92 units. June 14–Sept 25 $115–$180 double; Sept 26–June 13 $68–$130 double. Rates vary according to specific accommodation and view of the lake. AE, MC, V. Pets permitted in some rooms.

Located on the shore of Lake Quinault at the southwest corner of the park, this imposing grande dame of the Olympic Peninsula wears an ageless tranquillity. Huge old firs and cedars shade the rustic lodge, and Adirondack chairs on the deck command a view of the lawn. There are small rooms in the main lodge, plus modern rooms with wicker furniture and little balconies, and also rooms with fireplaces. The annex rooms are the most rustic, but they allow pets. There's an indoor heated pool and a sauna. Canoe, Seacycle, rowboat, and kayak rentals are available, as are rainforest tours, led by the Forest Service in the summers. Hiking trails abound. The dining room is a large, dark place as befits such a lodge, with beautiful lake views, and the menu reflects the bounties of the Olympic Peninsula, especially seafood.

Where to Dine

INSIDE THE PARK

Restaurant choices inside the park are slim. On the north side, there are dining rooms at **Lake Crescent Lodge** (open late Apr to late Oct) and the **Log Cabin Resort** (open Valentine's Day to Christmas), both of which are on the shores of Lake Crescent. On Lake Quinault, try the dining rooms at the **Calash Lodge** and the **Lake Quinault Lodge** (see "Where to Stay," above).

One other dining option on Lake Crescent is the **Fairholm General Store & Cafe,** 221121 U.S. 101 (② **360/928-3020**), which is at the west end of the lake and is open from April through October. Although all you'll get here are burgers, sandwiches, and breakfasts, the cafe has a deck with a view of the lake.

IN PORT ANGELES

If you're hit with a craving for something sweet while in town, check out **Bonny's Bakery,** 215 S. Lincoln St. (② **360/457-3585**), which is located in a 1930 fire department building next door to the Port Angeles Library. Both French pastries and American favorites are baked here and soup/salad/quiche lunches are served. For a good cup of fresh-roasted coffee, try **Mombasa Coffee Co. Ltd.,** 113-A W. 1st St. (② **360/452-3238**).

Bella Italia

118 E. 1st St. ② **360/457-5442.** Main courses $8–$20. AE, DC, DISC, MC, V. Mon–Thurs 4–9:30pm; Fri–Sun 4–10pm. ITALIAN.

Located in the basement of a natural foods store in downtown Port Angeles, this restaurant has a rathskeller feel, with heavy wood beams overhead and booths for privacy. The menu, however, is strictly Italian and starts with a basket of delicious bread accompanied by an olive oil, balsamic vinegar, garlic, and herb dipping sauce. Daily specials include fresh local seafood. Also on the menu are local mussels, steamed clams, and smoked salmon fettuccine. There's a wine bar and a retail wine shop, and the Italian desserts are excellent. This is a good choice for families, as well as those who want a private fine-dining experience.

C'est Si Bon

23 Cedar Park Rd. ② **360/452-8888.** www.northolympic.com/cestsibon. Reservations recommended. Main courses $21–$33. AE, DISC, MC, V. Tues–Sun 5–11pm. FRENCH.

Located 3 miles east of town just off U.S. 101, C'est Si Bon is painted a striking combination of English green and sunny yellow that gives the restaurant a sort of happy elegance. Inside, the non-traditional paint job gives way to more classic decor—reproductions of European works of art, crystal chandeliers, and old musical instruments used as wall decorations. Most tables have a view of the restaurant's pretty garden. There is now a large sunroom on the garden side. The menu is limited, which just about ensures that each dish has been perfected. In addition to French cuisine, they try some local dishes as well. Desserts are limited, but rich and creamy. When you call for reservations, you might ask for directions from where you are. As a start, they're on the north side of U.S. 101 just off Buchanan Road, at the top of a hill. Good luck; it's worth the search.

Downriggers

115 E. Railroad Ave. ② **360/452-2700.** Reservations recommended. Main courses $10–$26. AE, DISC, MC, V. Mon–Thurs 11:30am–9pm; Fri–Sat 11:30am–10pm; Sun 11:30–9pm. SEAFOOD/STEAK.

At the back of the Landing Mall on the second level you'll find this large, casual restaurant, convenient to the ferry landing. Walls of glass provide views of the ferries (so you don't miss yours) and take in some great sunsets. A long menu nearly guarantees that you'll find something you like, but just be sure to try the award-winning clam chowder.

Toga's International Cuisine

122 W. Lauridsen Blvd. ℭ **360/452-1952.**
www.togasinternationalcuisine.com. Reservations recommended. Main courses $17–$28.
AE, DISC, MC, V. Tues–Sat from 5pm. Jan
and Sept call for hours. NORTHWEST/
INTERNATIONAL/GERMAN.

Located on the west side of Port Angeles, this restaurant is an unexpected
treat and serves some very unusual
dishes. Chef Toga Hertzog apprenticed
in the Black Forest and has brought to
his restaurant the traditional Jagerstein
style of cooking in which diners cook
their own meat or prawns on a hot rock.
With 24 hours' notice you can also have
traditional Swiss cheese fondue or a
lighter seafood fondue. To start your
meal, try the crabmeat Rockefeller or
the sampler of house-smoked salmon,
scallops, oysters, and prawns. For
dessert, nothing hits the spot like the
chocolate macadamia nut mousse torte.

IN FORKS

The Smoke House Restaurant

U.S. 101 and La Push Rd. ℭ **360/374-6258.**
Main courses $12–$16. DISC, MC, V. Summer
hours every day 11am–10pm; winter 4–10pm.
AMERICAN.

The name says it all here. This place
smokes fish, and their salmon is just
about the best we've ever had. It's got a
good smoky flavor yet is tender and
moist. If you don't feel like sitting down
for the smoked salmon dinner, smoked
salmon salad, or smoked salmon and
cheddar cheese tray appetizer, then consider getting some to go. It's great beach
picnic food.

27

PETRIFIED FOREST NATIONAL PARK

by Don & Barbara Laine

THE FIRST THING YOU'LL NOTICE AT PETRIFIED FOREST NATIONAL Park are the dozens of logs lying atop hills as if on display, many of them pointing in the same direction. Closer up you can see the colors in the wood—reds, greens, yellows, blues, and purples, all of them rich and moist-looking like wet paint. The colors might tempt you to touch the wood, and if you do you'll find that it isn't wood at all, but cold, hard stone.

About 225 million years ago these petrified trees were enormous conifers growing in a tropical forest. Floods swept them into large rivers, tearing off their branches in the process. Eventually the trees bottomed out in the shallow waters of the floodplain, where silt, mud, and volcanic ash buried them. Because almost no oxygen could reach the entombed trunks, they were slow to decay. Silica from the ash gradually permeated the trunks, replacing or filling the wood's cells before eventually leaving quartz in its place. Minerals such as iron and manganese streaked the quartz with colors. The end result: The wood became beautiful rock.

Recognizing the financial value of this rock, early settlers began shipping it out on East Coast–bound trains. When the residents of the Territory of Arizona realized that the "wood" might soon be gone, they petitioned Congress to protect the "forests." Using the Antiquities Act, Pres. Theodore Roosevelt created Petrified Forest National Monument in 1906, and Congress designated it a national park in 1962.

The same sediments that entombed the trees buried other plants and animals, preserving them as fossils as well. Erosion has exposed these clays and sandstones, collectively known as the Chinle Formation. With little or no vegetation to hold them in place, these sediments erode quickly and unevenly, forming mesas, buttes, and furrowed, conical badlands, unearthing thousands of fossils, including bones from some of the most remarkable creatures ever to inhabit the earth. In addition to the 225-million-year-old fossils, there is evidence that the Ancestral Puebloans (also known as Anasazi), ancestors of the modern Pueblo people, once occupied this area. Evidence of other human occupation dates from 10,000 years ago.

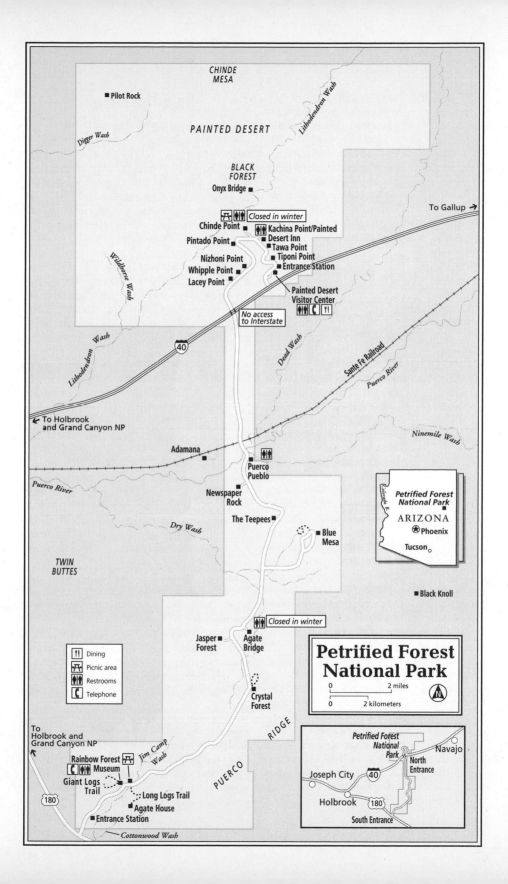

CHINDE
MESA

■ Pilot Rock

PAINTED DESERT

Digger Wash

Litholendron Wash

BLACK
FOREST

Onyx Bridge ■

To Gallup →

⊞ 🚻 *Closed in winter*

Chinde Point ■

🚻 ■ Kachina Point/Painted
■ Desert Inn
Pintado Point ■   ■ Tawa Point
■ Tiponi Point
Nizhoni Point ■   ■ Entrance Station
Whipple Point ■
Lacey Point ■

■ Painted Desert
Visitor Center
🚻 C ❗

*No access
to Interstate*

40

Litholendron Wash

Dead Wash

Santa Fe Railroad

Puerco River

← To Holbrook
and Grand Canyon NP

Ninemile Wash

Adamana ■

🚻

Puerco
Pueblo

Puerco River

Newspaper ■
Rock

Dry Wash

The Teepees ■

■ Blue
Mesa

TWIN
BUTTES

■ Black Knoll

🚻 *Closed in winter*

Jasper ■   ■ Agate
Forest   Bridge

❗ Dining
⊞ Picnic area
🚻 Restrooms
C Telephone

Crystal
Forest

Colorado R.

Petrified Forest
National Park

ARIZONA

★ Phoenix

Tucson ○

PUERCO RIDGE

Petrified Forest
National Park

0   2 miles
⌟───────⌞
0   2 kilometers

Ⓝ

To
Holbrook and
Grand Canyon NP

⊞

Jim Camp Wash

Petrified Forest
National Park

Navajo ○

C 🚻 Rainbow Forest
Museum

North
Entrance

Giant Logs
Trail

Joseph City ○   40

··· Long Logs Trail

■ Agate House

Holbrook ○   180

■ Entrance Station

South Entrance

— *Cottonwood Wash*

Even without these wonders, it would be worth coming here to see the rich red, gray, and maroon colors of the Painted Desert. Shaped like a tusk (with the wider end near Cameron, Arizona), the desert spans from near Holbrook in the south to the Hopi mesas in the northeast to near the Grand Canyon in the west—far beyond the boundaries of the park. Its seemingly barren landscape is home to a rich diversity of plant and animal life: desert grasses; wildflowers, including Indian paintbrush and globemallow; juniper and other trees; mammals, including pronghorns, cottontails, and porcupines; reptiles, including collared lizards and western rattlesnakes; and birds, the most prominent being the raven.

Avoiding the Crowds. About 600,000 people visit the park each year, in part because it is so convenient for cross-country travelers, just a few hundred yards off I-40. Virtually everyone heads down the same 28-mile scenic drive, and the drive's 20 pullouts can get crowded.

Michele M. Hellickson, the park's former superintendent, offers three suggestions for avoiding the crowds. First, arrive early in the day. "There aren't many visitors in the first few hours," she says. "It's also before the heat of the day, and the lighting on the rocks is spectacular." Second, stroll away from the parking areas. "Where there are pullouts, there are going to be people," Hellickson says. "But if you park at some of the pullouts and walk the length of the trails, you'll soon be away from the crowds. This will give you a chance to sit and hear the sounds of the desert and maybe get a picture that's different from everyone else's." Third, day-hike into the Painted Desert Wilderness. "That's the instant answer," says Hellickson. "I think it's relatively easy to do in this terrain. It's a landscape that lends itself to going out and exploring, with less fear involved."

Just the Facts

GETTING THERE & GATEWAYS

Petrified Forest National Park is 117 miles east of Flagstaff and 180 miles north of Phoenix. The north entrance is 25 miles east of Holbrook on I-40; the south entrance is 20 miles east of Holbrook on U.S. 180. From Flagstaff, simply take I-40 east.

The Nearest Airport. Flagstaff's **Pulliam Airport** (℡ **928/556-1234**) is serviced by **America West Express,** and has rental cars from **Avis, Budget, Hertz,** and **National.** Toll-free reservation numbers are in the appendix.

INFORMATION

Contact **Petrified Forest National Park,** P.O. Box 2217, Petrified Forest National Park, AZ 86028 (℡ **928/524-6228;** www.nps.gov/pefo). The **Petrified Forest Museum Association,** P.O. Box 2277, Petrified Forest, AZ 86028 (℡ **928/524-6228,** ext. 239; www.cybertrails.com/~pfma) publishes several excellent books on the park. Written by retired geology professor Sidney Ash, *Petrified Forest: The Story Behind the Scenery* provides a good overview of the human and natural history of the park. Stephen Trimble's colorful book, *Earth Journey: A Road Guide to Petrified Forest,* is almost as good as a guided tour of the park's scenic drive.

For information about area lodging and dining, contact the **Holbrook Chamber of Commerce,** 100 E. Arizona St., Holbrook, AZ 86025 (℡ **800/524-2459** or 928/524-6558; www.ci.holbrook.az.us).

VISITOR CENTERS

The park has a visitor center at each end. Both sell books, videos, and area maps, and offer free brochures on the park's geology, flora, and fauna.

The **Painted Desert Visitor Center,** outside the park's north entrance gate, has general information on the park and offers a 20-minute video on the park, which shows on the hour and the half-hour. Two miles north of the park's south entrance station, the **Rainbow Forest Museum** has displays on the formation of petrified wood, fossilized bones and teeth of ancient animals, and a display of letters from people who stole wood from the park and later regretted it. Both of the above are open daily year-round from 8am to 5pm, except Christmas, and both have bookstores.

Also see the section on the **Painted Desert Inn Museum** under "Historic & Man-Made Attractions," below.

FEES & PERMITS

Entrance to the park costs $10 per vehicle, $5 per visitor on foot or bicycle. Backcountry camping permits are free and are issued at the visitor center.

SPECIAL REGULATIONS & WARNINGS

Because an estimated 25,000 pounds of petrified wood are stolen from the park every year, the National Park Service has adopted a zero-tolerance policy for visitors who remove even the smallest pieces. Violators are subject to fines starting at $275. If rangers suspect you of removing any wood or other resources, they may detain you and search your car.

There are long stretches between water sources at the park, so fill containers at either visitor center before starting on the scenic drive.

SEASONS & CLIMATE

With an average of just 9⅔ inches of precipitation annually, the park couldn't get much drier. Because it averages a lofty 5,800 feet in elevation, however, it's not as hot as many other desert areas. Even in July, daily highs average in the mid-80s (30s Celsius), with nightly lows in the low 50s (10s Celsius). Of course, the park occasionally heats up—temperatures sometimes top 100°F (38°C) in midsummer. The hottest months, July and August, are also the wettest, with afternoon monsoons cutting the morning heat and depositing nearly a third of the yearly precipitation. These storms continue into early fall, but the weather dries out as it cools. By winter it can get very cold, and snowstorms occasionally close the park. In January, daily highs average 42°F (6°C) and lows 19°F (-7°C). Spring tends to be blustery and dry, with daily highs increasing from the mid-50s (lower teens Celsius) in March to about 80°F (27°C) in June—the driest month of all, with just ⅓ inch of rainfall.

SEASONAL EVENTS

During March, special events for **Arizona Archeology Month** are scheduled. Call the park office for details.

For about a week both before and after the June 21 **summer solstice,** rangers meet from 8 to 10am daily with visitors at Puerco Pueblo. The sun shines through a natural crack directing a beam of light onto a smaller boulder beside it. This beam gradually moves down the edge of the rock to a small circular petroglyph, and touches the center of the petroglyph on the summer solstice. Archaeologists believe the Ancestral Puebloans used this petroglyph to monitor the summer solstice.

If You Have Only 1 Day

The most obvious and easiest way to see the park is to first stop at one of the visitor centers and then take the 28-mile **scenic drive,** stopping at the pullouts and taking some of the short trails to get close-up views of the petrified wood. With a bit of extra time, you might consider a hike into the **Painted Desert Wilderness.** Combine this with a pre- or posthike picnic at the **Chinde Point Picnic Area.**

Exploring the Park by Car

The direction you choose for the scenic drive depends on which way you're traveling on I-40. If coming from the west, take U.S. 180 east from Holbrook to the park's south entrance, drive through the park, then rejoin I-40 at the park's north entrance. If coming from the east, do the opposite, driving through the park from the north entrance and exiting onto U.S. 180 in the south. Trails mentioned here are discussed more fully in "Day Hikes," below.

1. If you enter the park from the south entrance, you'll start at **The Rainbow Forest Museum.** Behind the museum is the **Giant Logs Self-Guided Trail,** the first of several easy trails through the forests of petrified wood.

2. Leave your vehicle at the museum parking area. Just past the museum you'll see an access trail to the **Long Logs** and the **Agate House** trailheads. The Agate House Trail ends at a prehistoric pueblo made of petrified wood. Forking to the left, the Long Logs Trail winds among some of the longest and most spectacular petrified trees in the area.

3. Continuing, you'll come to the **Crystal Forest,** where visitors in the late 1800s discovered ground covered with sparkling bits of petrified wood. At that time, the petrified logs in this area were flecked with quartz and purple amethyst crystals. These crystals attracted gem hunters, some of who went so far as to dynamite the trees. Although many crystals and the smaller pieces are gone, some very colorful logs remain.

4. Next comes **Jasper Forest,** an overlook from atop a 150-foot-high bluff. This is a great place to observe the various effects of erosion. Looking downhill, you'll notice that large chunks of sandstone and petrified wood have tumbled from the bluff to the desert floor. Soft clay eroded out from under the harder wood and sandstone, undermining it and eventually sending it downhill. Because erosion continues, someday the rocks underfoot will tumble downhill as well.

5. The first thing you'll notice at **Agate Bridge** is the remarkable bridge itself. With each end firmly embedded in sandstone, a petrified log forms a natural bridge across an arroyo that cuts through the ground underneath its midsection. The next thing you'll probably notice is the concrete span that "supports" it. In 1917, workers who wanted to preserve the bridge as a tourist attraction buttressed it with concrete.

6. Next, a short loop trail takes you to **Blue Mesa.** Like all the badlands in the park, Blue Mesa is made up of soft rocks that can erode at the rate of 3 inches a decade—fast enough to change appreciably in the span of a human lifetime. The Blue Mesa Trail, one of the prettiest walkways in the park, descends from the fourth and last overlook on the spur road.

7. Next comes the turnoff for conical badlands known as the **Teepees.** The flat rocky surface you see is called **desert pavement,** created when strong winds sweep away the fine sands of the desert floor, exposing small stones and petrified wood fragments.

8. From an overlook 2 miles past the Teepees, you can look down on **Newspaper Rock.** Early inhabitants pecked dozens of petroglyphs into the dark surface of the stone. Among them is an image of the famous humpbacked flute player,

Kokopelli. The petroglyphs in this area aren't limited to Newspaper Rock, so be sure to scan the surrounding rocks with your binoculars.

9. With so many petroglyphs around Newspaper Rock, it seems inevitable that a prehistoric dwelling is nearby. Sure enough, a mile down the road is **Puerco Pueblo,** the remains of a 100-room pueblo occupied by the Ancestral Puebloans from 1250 to about 1400. To see this dwelling, walk the easy 0.3-mile loop trail.

10. The remaining stops between Puerco Pueblo and the Painted Desert Visitor Center are overlooks of the Painted Desert. Each one affords a unique view, but the panorama from the hilltop at **Pintado Point** may be most spectacular. Just past Pintado Point is **Chinde Point,** where you'll find sheltered picnic tables, restrooms (open seasonally), and another overlook.

11. A quarter of a mile past Chinde Point is the turnoff for **Kachina Point** and the **Painted Desert Inn National Historic Landmark.** Here, you can descend into the desert on the Painted Desert Wilderness Trail, or, if the drop seems a bit imposing, hike to Tawa Point on the Painted Desert Rim Trail. After hiking, be sure to visit the landmark itself, which has displays on the history of the area (see "Historic & Man-Made Attractions," below).

Organized Tours & Ranger Programs

A changing program of guided hikes and talks is presented at various locations throughout the park, with the greatest number during the summer. Check at either visitor center to see what's on tap on a given day.

Historic & Man-Made Attractions

The **Painted Desert Inn National Historic Landmark,** which overlooks the desert from Kachina Point, once served as a lunch counter and trading post for early travelers on Route 66. After the Park Service purchased the inn from private owners in 1936, workers in the Civilian Conservation Corps (CCC) rebuilt it in the Southwestern style, not so cleverly covering some of the building's original petrified-wood walls with stucco. Inside, they installed oak floors and hand-painted glass ceiling tiles, and added six guest rooms, each with a fireplace. Upon completion in 1940, the 28-room inn became an immediate hit with travelers. It was closed again, however, during the last years of World War II. After the war, the Fred Harvey Company managed the building, using it as a visitor center and restaurant until 1963, when the new Painted Desert Visitor Center opened.

In 1947, Fred Kabotie, the renowned Hopi artist whose work also graces the Desert Watchtower at the Grand Canyon, painted several murals inside, including one that depicted the coming-of-age journey of the Hopi to the sacred Zuni salt lake. Kabotie's murals may have helped save the building, which had severe structural problems caused by expansion and contraction of the clay underneath it. When it was threatened with demolition in the 1960s, preservationists cited the value of Kabotie's art as they called for protecting the building. The Painted Desert Inn was declared a National Historic Landmark in 1987.

Today it houses the **Painted Desert Inn Museum,** which celebrates the area's cultural heritage. Open daily 9m to 5pm, the museum displays American Indian artifacts found in and around the park. Among them is a famous petroglyph of a mountain lion—an image reproduced in contemporary art throughout the Southwest. The building itself is also worth admiring. Several of Kabotie's murals can be seen, and the wood floors and glass ceiling tiles are intact. To the rear of the building, one of the original petrified-wood walls has been exposed. Park crews continue to work on the exterior, but a more significant renovation is on hold, pending an appropriation from Congress.

Day Hikes

Agate House

0.9 mile RT. Moderate. Access: 0.5 mile walk down access trail from Rainbow Forest Museum.

An enjoyable walk takes you to Agate House, a pueblo that archaeologists believe was briefly occupied around A.D. 1100. (Archaeologists suspect a brief occupation because very little "trash" was found in the area.) Colorful bits of petrified wood dot the ground on the way to the eight-room pueblo, which sits atop a knoll overlooking a vast expanse of desert. Made from petrified wood and mortar, Agate House must have been one of the prettiest dwellings anywhere in its time—a house of jewels, on a hill. The pueblo's largest room was reconstructed by workers in the 1930s, and that apparently is how it acquired a window, something the original Ancestral Puebloan dwelling never had.

Blue Mesa Trail

1 mile RT. Moderate to strenuous. Access: Blue Mesa turnoff on scenic drive.

This paved loop trail descends steeply to the floor beneath the blue-, gray-, and white-striped badlands at Blue Mesa—some of the prettiest land in the park. You may notice that it's hard to determine the size of the hills: Because they lack vegetation, there is little to provide a sense of scale. At the bottom, you can observe how the different colors of these hillsides streak and blend where the clay has washed into

drainages. Look for small fossils, abundant in the area. The trail has numerous interpretive panels, spaced to give you a chance to catch your breath as you walk.

Crystal Forest Trail

0.8 mile RT. Moderate. Access: Crystal Forest stop on scenic drive.

This paved trail, which includes a few steep grades, reminds us of why it's important to leave the petrified wood in place. As in other parts of the park, there is evidence here of where visitors have broken off, and continue to break off, pieces of petrified wood. What's left is still lovely, though. Still, it's hard not to wonder what this area looked like before the scavengers arrived.

Giant Logs Trail

0.4 mile RT. Easy. Access: Rainbow Forest Museum.

This paved trail loops past some of the park's largest petrified logs, including "Old Faithful," which spans nearly 9 feet at its base. The trail has 11 stops, each corresponding to a page in a guide (free to borrow, 50¢ to keep) available in the museum. At each stop, you'll find out about the trees or the area's geology. Constructed in the 1930s by the Civilian Conservation Corps (CCC), the trail has some steps, making access difficult for people in wheelchairs.

Long Logs Trail

0.6 mile RT. Easy. Access: 0.5 mile walk down access trail from Rainbow Forest Museum.

This relatively flat, paved loop will give you an idea of the immensity of the Araucarioxylon trees that grew in this area during the Triassic Period. Many of the longest, including one that measures 116 feet, lie alongside the trail on the north end of the loop. You'll see places where these petrified logs protected the softer clay underneath them and prevented it from eroding. The trail also takes you within a few feet of the rugged badlands. The different colored layers are caused by mineral deposits in the clay.

Painted Desert Rim Trail

1 mile RT. Easy. Access: Kachina Point stop on scenic drive.

As this cinder trail meanders along the Painted Desert rim between Kachina and Tawa points, it affords stunning views of the desert, where gray, pink, and red badlands stand out against the green grasses at their bases. The trail is atop the basalt of the Bidahochi formation, which at 8 million years old is much younger than most other rocks in the park. This layer has disappeared in many areas of the park but is widespread in other parts of northern Arizona. Here, it provides fertile soil for a diversity of vegetation, including juniper, Mormon tea, sagebrush, and cliffrose. The trail has wayside exhibits, plant identification signs, and benches.

Painted Desert Wilderness Trail

About 0.5 mile one-way. Moderate to strenuous. Access: Kachina Point.

This trail descends in switchbacks down the face of the badlands below Kachina Point, then follows a wash for a short distance before petering out in the grasslands on the floor of the Painted Desert. You won't find water or shade here, but you will have a chance to experience firsthand the colors and landforms of this desert. Before wandering far, be sure to identify landmarks you can use to retrace your steps. (The Painted Desert Inn makes an especially good landmark.) If you carry a topographical map and plenty of water and sunscreen, you should have few problems in this desert, which has excellent sight lines and few insurmountable obstacles. Walk on the dry streambeds when possible. Besides being easier, this minimizes the damage to the fragile plant life.

It's worth spending the night here just to watch the sun dip below the red sands of the desert. Before bedding down, you must first obtain a backcountry permit at one of the visitor centers, then walk at least a mile into the 43,000-acre Painted Desert Wilderness, which starts on the other side of Lithodendron Wash. The direction you take from the bottom of the wash will depend on which "use area" you sign up for on your permit. You'll find spots smooth enough for camping near many of the mesas and badlands. (Keep in mind, however, that runoff can create problems during storms.) Don't forget to pack insect repellent; in spite of its dry climate, the park has been known to host an unusually active population of no-see-ums.

Puerco Pueblo Trail

0.5 mile RT. Easy. Access: Puerco Pueblo.

This relatively flat loop travels through the 100-room Puerco Pueblo. The 30 excavated rooms hint at the floor plan of the buildings—a trapezoid around an outdoor plaza where most of the activity in the community took place. As you walk, you'll observe places where the rooms were one, two, or three deep around the plaza. Where they were two deep, the rooms on the outside may have been used to store crops harvested from the floodplains below. The inside rooms, which opened onto the plaza, were probably used for sleeping or shelter from inclement weather. Three kivas—ceremonial rooms dug into the ground—were located inside the plaza, and one is obvious alongside the trail. Partway around the loop, a short trail leads down to an overlook from which you can see numerous petroglyphs.

Camping

There are no campgrounds within the park boundaries. Backpackers with backcountry permits can stay in the park after it closes for the evening, but they must hike at least 1 mile into the wilderness before setting up camp. For drive-in camping, head to Holbrook, 25 miles west of the park on I-40, where several commercial campgrounds offer all the usual amenities.

The **KOA Campground,** 102 Hermosa Dr., Holbrook, AZ 86025 (℡ 800/562-3389 reservations, or 928/524-6689), has a large, inviting swimming pool that shimmers like a mirage on sunny days. The 27 grassy tent sites and 109 RV sites are exposed to the sun and wind, as the owners try to grow trees in this unforgiving terrain. The cost is $19 to $22 for tents and RV spaces without hookups, $22 to $28 for RV hookups. Major credit cards are accepted. The campground has a playground, game room, snack bar, public phones, self-service laundry, propane, dump station, and cable TV hookups (with an extra fee). It's open year-round. During the high season, campers feast at relatively inexpensive evening cookouts and all-you-can-eat pancake breakfasts. There are also several camping cabins that share the bathhouse and other facilities, for $35 to $40 double.

Located just 3 blocks south of the KOA Campground, **A-OK RV Park,** 1576 Roadrunner Rd., Holbrook, AZ 86025 (℡ 928/524-3226), is another good spot to set up camp, although it does not have a swimming pool. There are 150 sites; RV sites, at $22, include electric, water, sewer, and cable TV. Tent sites are $19 for two people. The campground offers public phones, a self-service laundry, a convenience store, and a dump station. It's open year-round and does not accept credit cards.

Where to Stay

There is no lodging inside the park.

NEAR THE PARK

The place to get a bed for the night is Holbrook (zip code 86025), 25 miles west of the park. In addition to the fascinating Wigwam Motel, discussed below, Holbrook offers the **Best Western Adobe Inn,** 615 W. Hopi Dr. (℡ 877/524-3948 direct, or 928/524-3948), with rates for two of $42 to $58; **Comfort Inn,** 2602 E. Navajo Blvd. (℡ 928/524-6131), charging $65 to $82 double; **Days Inn,** 2601 E. Navajo Blvd. (℡ 928/524-6949), charging $40 to $80 double; **Econo Lodge,** 2596 E. Navajo Blvd. (℡ 928/524-1448), charging $45 to $55 double; **Holiday Inn Express,** 1308 Navajo Blvd. (℡ 928/524-1466), with rates of $76 to $85 double; and **Super 8,** 1989 Navajo Blvd. (℡ 928/524-2871), charging $44 to $72 double. See the appendix for a list of the national chain toll-free numbers.

Wigwam Motel

811 W. Hopi Dr. (P.O. Box 788), Holbrook, AZ 86025. ℡ **928/524-3048.** www.wigwam gazette.info. 15 units. A/C TV. $40–$45 double. DISC, MC, V. Office opens at 3pm in summer, 4pm in winter. Pets accepted.

You say you're tired of the same boring chain motel rooms? Then it's time for a night at the Wigwam! And even if you don't stay here, the Wigwam Motel makes for a wonderful photo op. Each of the motel's 15 rooms is inside its own 32-foot-high wood-and-concrete wigwam, built during Route 66's glory days in the 1940s by the same family that's running it today. The wigwams are very clean and well maintained, and each is furnished with the motel's original hand-carved hickory furniture. The only drawbacks—which we consider a small price to pay for the experience of this unique motel—are that both the bathrooms and windows are somewhat small by today's standards. The motel's owners have done a good job of preserving this bit of Americana, and also have a small museum on the property containing family items including giant petrified wood slabs, Civil War artifacts, and American Indian items. Also on the property are close to a dozen classic cars.

Where to Dine

INSIDE THE PARK

Harvey's Diner

Next to the Painted Desert Visitor Center. © **928/524-3756.** Most items $1.50–$5.95. AE, DISC, MC, V. Summer daily 7am–4pm; winter daily 8am–3:30pm. AMERICAN/REGIONAL.

This is a convenient but somewhat nondescript family-oriented cafeteria. It serves hot breakfasts, including eggs and pancakes. Specialties for lunch or an early dinner include home-style chili, burgers, Navajo tacos, and a variety of sandwiches. Daily specials, such as spaghetti and meatballs, are also offered. *Note:* In addition to Harvey's Diner, during the summer a small snack bar serves sandwiches and snacks next to the museum at the park's south entrance.

NEAR THE PARK

Butterfield Stage Co.

609 W. Hopi Dr., Holbrook. © **928/524-3447.** Main courses $7.95–$30. AE, MC, V. Daily 4–10pm. AMERICAN.

Named for the famous overland stagecoach line that carried the mail from St. Louis to San Francisco in the mid–19th century, this restaurant is owned, surprisingly, by natives of the former Yugoslavia. But they know how to do American grub right, and we especially recommend the slow-roasted prime rib and barbecued baby-back pork ribs. Seafood lovers enjoy the grilled halibut and the steak and crab legs combo, and everyone likes the soup and salad bar. Tables have historical panels with amusing information to read while you're waiting for your meal.

Joe and Aggie's

120 W. Hopi, Holbrook. © **928/524-6540.** Lunch and dinner items $2.95–$9.95. DISC, MC, V. Mon–Sat 6am–8pm. AMERICAN/MEXICAN.

More than 40 years ago, Joe and Aggie Montano opened this restaurant, and today the Montano family continues to operate this popular eatery at the same Route 66 location. What you'll find is a friendly, down-home sort of place, with plenty of historic Route 66 charm.

Recommended at breakfast are the chili-cheese omelet and the egg burro (scrambled eggs with hash browns and cheese rolled in a flour tortilla). At lunch and dinner you can select from Mexican platters, traditional American dishes, and combinations of both, such as a Mexican hamburger steak with red or green chile. For a sort of Mexican pizza, try the cheese crisp—a deep fried flour tortilla with melted cheese and toppings such as green chile and taco meat.

Mesa Italiana Restaurant

2318 E. Navajo Blvd., Holbrook. © **928/524-6696.** Main courses $8.95–$15. AE, DISC, MC, V. Daily 4–9pm. ITALIAN.

Generally regarded as the best restaurant in Holbrook, Mesa Italiana serves traditional Italian dishes, including baked ziti, stuffed shells, lasagna, linguine, and pizza, at reasonable prices. The Italiana mushrooms (mushrooms stuffed with chicken, spinach, and fresh herbs, all topped with a garlic white-wine sauce) are great. Also highly recommended is the chicken Jerusalem—a chicken breast sautéed with butter, garlic, artichoke hearts, mushrooms, and shrimp, all swimming in a white-wine and lemon sauce.

Picnic & Camping Supplies

Just inside the north entrance to the park you'll find a gas station with a convenience store. In Holbrook, picnic supplies and general foodstuffs are available at **Safeway,** 702 W. Hopi Dr. (© **928/524-3313**).

28

POINT REYES NATIONAL SEASHORE

by Eric Peterson

POINT REYES IS A 100-SQUARE-MILE PENINSULA OF DARK FORESTS, wind-sculpted dunes, endless beaches, and plunging sea cliffs. Aside from its beautiful scenery, it boasts man-made historical treasures that offer a window into California's coastal past,

including lighthouses, turn-of-the-century dairies and ranches, and the site of Sir Francis Drake's 1579 landing, plus a complete replica of a Coast Miwok Indian village.

The national seashore system was created to protect rural and undeveloped stretches of America's coastlines from the pressures of soaring real estate values and increasing population; nowhere is the success of the system more evident than at Point Reyes. Layers of human history coexist peacefully here with one of the world's most dramatic natural settings. Residents of the surrounding communities—Inverness, Point Reyes Station, and Olema—have steadfastly resisted runaway development. You won't find any strip malls or fast-food joints here—just laid-back coastal towns with cafes and country inns where gentle living prevails. The park, a 71,000-acre hammer-shaped peninsula jutting 10 miles into the Pacific and backed by Tomales Bay, is loaded with wildlife, ranging from tule elk, birds, and bobcats to gray whales, sea lions, and great white sharks.

Though the peninsula's people and wildlife live in harmony above the ground, the situation beneath the soil is much more volatile. The infamous San Andreas Fault separates Point Reyes, the northernmost landmass on the Pacific Plate, from the rest of California, which rests on the North American Plate. Point Reyes is making its way toward Alaska at a rate of about 2 inches per year, but there have been times when it has moved much faster. In 1906, Point Reyes jumped north almost 20 feet in an instant, leveling San Francisco and jolting the rest of the state. The 0.5-mile Earthquake Trail, near the Bear Valley Visitor Center, illustrates this geological drama with a loop through an area torn by the slipping fault. Shattered fences, rifts in the ground, and a barn knocked off its foundation by the quake illustrate that the earth is alive here. If that doesn't convince you, a look at a seismograph in the visitor center will.

Avoiding the Crowds. Though the park is heavily visited, crowds are only a problem at a few places and only during

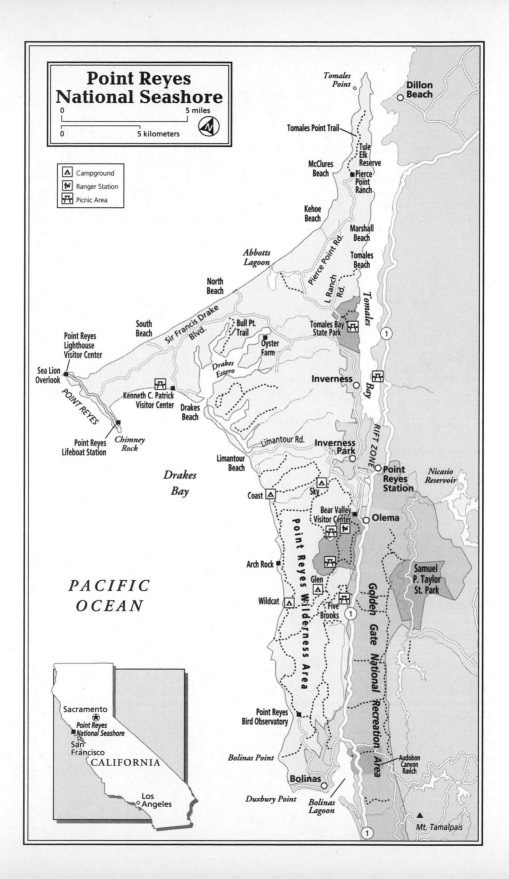

Point Reyes National Seashore

0   5 miles

0   5 kilometers

△ Campground

⊞ Ranger Station

⊞ Picnic Area

Tomales Point

Dillon Beach

Tomales Point Trail

Tule Elk Reserve

McClures Beach

Pierce Point Ranch

Kehoe Beach

Marshall Beach

Abbotts Lagoon

Tomales Beach

North Beach

Pierce Point Rd.

L Ranch Rd.

Tomales

South Beach

Sir Francis Drake Blvd.

Bull Pt. Trail

Oyster Farm

Tomales Bay State Park

Point Reyes Lighthouse Visitor Center

Sea Lion Overlook

Drakes Estero

Kenneth C. Patrick Visitor Center

POINT REYES

Drakes Beach

Chimney Rock

Point Reyes Lifeboat Station

Limantour Rd.

Inverness

Tomales Bay

RIFT ZONE

Inverness Park

Point Reyes Station

Nicasio Reservoir

Drakes Bay

Limantour Beach

Coast

Sky

Bear Valley Visitor Center

Olema

PACIFIC OCEAN

Point Reyes Wilderness Area

Arch Rock

Glen

Wildcat

Five Brooks

Samuel P. Taylor St. Park

Golden Gate National Recreation Area

Point Reyes Bird Observatory

Audobon Canyon Ranch

Bolinas Point

Bolinas

Duxbury Point

Bolinas Lagoon

Mt. Tamalpais

Sacramento

Point Reyes National Seashore

San Francisco

CALIFORNIA

Los Angeles

certain times. If you visit the lighthouse on a weekend or holiday during whale season (Dec–Mar), be prepared for crowds and a wait for the shuttle that operates from Drakes Beach to the lighthouse area. Trails leaving from Bear Valley tend to be more crowded on weekends than others. Try the **Five Brooks** or **Palomarin trailheads** to avoid hordes of backcountry tourists. As a whole, a weekday visitor to Point Reyes will encounter far fewer people than the weekender.

Just the Facts

GETTING THERE & GATEWAYS

Point Reyes is only 30 miles northwest of San Francisco, but it takes at least 90 minutes to reach by car. (It's all the small towns, not the topography, that slow you down.) The easiest route is via Sir Francis Drake Boulevard from U.S. 101 south of San Rafael; it takes its time getting to Point Reyes, but does so without any detours. For a much longer but more scenic route, take the Stinson Beach/Highway 1 exit off U.S. 101 just south of Sausalito and follow Highway 1 north.

The Nearest Airport. San Francisco International Airport (© 650/821-8211; www.sfoairport.com), 14 miles south of downtown San Francisco on U.S. 101, is served by all major airlines and car rental companies, whose phone numbers are listed in the appendix.

INFORMATION

Contact **Point Reyes National Seashore,** Point Reyes Station, CA 94956-9799 (© 415/464-5100; www.nps.gov/pore). The *Natural History of the Point Reyes Peninsula,* by naturalist Jules G. Evens (Point Reyes National Seashore Association, 1993), is a comprehensive and sometimes anecdotal overview of Point Reyes's natural history.

VISITOR CENTERS

As soon as you arrive at Point Reyes, stop at the **Bear Valley Visitor Center** on Bear Valley Road (look for the small sign posted just north of Olema on Hwy. 1), and pick up a free trail map, talk with the rangers about your plans, and check out the natural history and cultural displays. It's open daily year-round.

The **Ken Patrick Visitor Center,** located at Drakes Beach, houses a 250-gallon saltwater aquarium and a 16-foot minke whale skeleton, among other exhibits. It's open weekends and holidays only (except Christmas) from 10am to 5pm. The **Lighthouse Visitor Center,** located at the most westerly point of the Point Reyes Peninsula, offers information on the lighthouse and life-saving services performed over the 125 years of its use, as well as natural history exhibits on whales, seals, and wildflowers. It's open Thursday through Monday from 10am to 5pm; closed Christmas.

FEES

Entrance to the park is free. Hike-in camping is $12 per night (and more for groups of 7–25).

SPECIAL REGULATIONS & WARNINGS

◆ Dogs and other pets are not permitted on trails, in campgrounds, or on beaches that are seal habitats or bird nesting areas. On other beaches they must be leashed. Check at park visitor centers before taking your dog to a beach, to avoid seasonal closures.

◆ Wood fires are prohibited in campgrounds. Use only charcoal, gas stoves, or canned heat. Driftwood fires are permitted only on sandy beaches below the high-tide line, but you must obtain a free permit at a visitor center.

◆ Check the tide tables before walking on the beaches. Rising water can trap you against a cliff with no possibility of escape.

♦ For your safety, sleeping on the beach is prohibited; it can be really dangerous. High tide frequently comes to the base of the cliffs and can trap the unwary.

♦ Do not climb cliffs—they can crumble easily. Your foothold may vanish, leaving you in thin air. Walking or sitting below cliffs is also dangerous due to falling rock.

♦ In wooded areas keep an eye out for poison oak's waxy three-leaf clusters. Also be sure to check for ticks as the Lyme disease–carrying black-legged tick is common here.

♦ The pounding surf and rip currents are treacherous, especially at McClures Beach and Point Reyes beaches, north and south. Stay away from the water.

♦ Don't disturb any abandoned baby seals or sea lions you may encounter on the beach. The mother may be preoccupied with finding lunch, and she won't come back until you leave. In fact, you could be fined up to $10,000 for your good intentions. However, if a pup looks injured or in danger, call the **Mammal Center** at ℂ **707/465-MAML** (6265).

SEASONS & CLIMATE

Weather at Point Reyes is fickle. The seasons here generally reverse expectations: Summer tends to be cold and foggy until the afternoon (the point itself is the foggiest place on the West Coast), while winter is clear and, if not exactly warm, often more tolerable. But these are generalizations at best—winter storms can rage for weeks and sometimes the summer fog miraculously holds off for days. Spring and fall usually see the best weather (that is, little fog, warm temperatures).

To make matters more frustrating, the clearing of fog often signals the onset of strong winds. So, if you are planning to explore the park on foot,

prepare yourself for cool weather, dampness, and wind (*lots* of wind, as gusts have reached up to 133 mph, the highest wind speed recorded on the Pacific Coast). The best plan is to take advantage of variations in local weather by being flexible with your itinerary: Save indoor sightseeing for rainy or foggy days, and hit the beach or go hiking when the sun comes out.

SEASONAL EVENTS

Point Reyes National Seashore hosts an annual **Native American Celebration** on the third Saturday of July. American Indian basket-makers, flint-mappers, singers, and dancers convene at Point Reyes for an annual public celebration at Kule Loklo, an authentic reconstruction of a village of the indigenous Coast Miwok Indian tribe. The **Miwok Archaeological Preserve of Marin** offers classes in traditional California Indian skills in the spring and fall. Call ℂ **415/479-3281** or browse **www.mapom.com** for further information.

If You Have Only 1 Day

First, stop at the **Bear Valley Visitor Center** and pick up the free Point Reyes map, which lists all the trails and roads open to cars, bikes, horses, and hikers. While you're here, spend some time at the nearby **Kule Loklo,** an authentic reconstruction of a village of the indigenous Coast Miwok Indian tribe; and **Morgan Horse Ranch,** a good place to see park patrol horses. Afterward, take a short stroll along the **Earthquake Trail,** an informative 0.5-mile walk along the infamous San Andreas Fault, and, time permitting, the 0.7-mile self-guided **Woodpecker Nature Trail.**

By far the most popular, and crowded, attraction at Point Reyes National Seashore is the venerable **Point Reyes Lighthouse,** located at the westernmost tip of Point Reyes. The drive alone on the **Sir Francis Drake Highway** is worth the trip—a 45-minute, 20-mile scenic excursion through rolling, windswept meadows and working dairy ranches (watch out for cows on the road). When the fog burns off, the lighthouse and the headlands provide a fantastic lookout point for spying common murres, basking sea lions, and gray whales as they make their migration along the coast from December through March.

If there's still some time left, the **Point Reyes Bird Observatory**—an ornithological research organization located at the southeast end of the park—is a must for bird-watchers.

Exploring the Park by Car

The main scenic road in the park is the **Sir Francis Drake Highway** (described above in "If You Have Only 1 Day"). An excellent turnoff on this road is **Mount Vision Road,** which winds its way up to the Mount Vision Overlook for a panoramic view of the entire peninsula.

There are two other major roads within the park. **Pierce Point Road** forks north from the Sir Francis Drake Highway toward Tomales Point, passing Tomales Bay State Park (a popular picnicking area that offers relatively warm and safe waters) and Abbotts Lagoon (a bird-watchers' paradise) before ending at McClures Beach. The other major road is **Limantour Road,** which bisects the park before ending at Limantour Beach, a popular spot for beachcombing, picnicking, and bird-watching at nearby Estero de Limantour. Both these roads are primarily used to access trailheads and beaches, but can also double as scenic alternatives to touring Sir Francis Drake Highway.

Organized Tours & Ranger Programs

Rangers lead programs within Point Reyes National Seashore year-round, including wildlife hikes, local history lessons, and habitat restoration demonstrations. All ranger programs are free, but you'll need to call the **Bear Valley Visitor Center** (© 415/464-5100) for up-to-date schedules.

Oceanic Society Expeditions (© 415/474-3385; www.oceanicsociety.org) runs excursions and outings to the park. During whale season the Oceanic Society takes naturalist-led whale-watching boats from the San Francisco Marina along the Marin coastline to Point Reyes every weekend, weather permitting, from late December to mid-May. The 6½ hour trip costs about $50 per person, but no children under 10 are allowed.

Historic & Man-Made Attractions

Kule Loklo is a re-creation of a Coast Miwok Indian village that often hosts displays of dancing, basket-making, cooking, and indigenous art. Until recently, **Morgan Horse Ranch** was the only working horse-breeding farm in the National Park System. Although breeding is defunct, the ranch remains a good place to see park patrol horses. Also, exhibits here offer an interpretive glimpse into the area's horse ranching past. Both are located near the **Bear Valley Visitor Center** on Bear Valley Road and are open year-round.

But if you really want to escape the crowds and have some stinky man-made entertainment, head to **Johnson's Oyster Farm** (© 415/669-1149), off Sir Francis Drake Boulevard, about 6 miles west of Inverness (open Mon–Sat 8am–4pm and Sun 9am–4pm). Located in the park, right on the edge of Drakes Estero (a large saltwater estuary within the Point Reyes Peninsula that produces about 10% of California's commercial oyster yield), Johnson's may look and smell like a dump, with its cluster of trailer homes, shacks, and oyster tanks surrounded by huge piles of oyster shells, but those tasty bivalves don't come any fresher or cheaper. The typical modus operandi is: 1) buy a couple of dozen (reserve them in advance if you can—they go quick), 2) head for a picnic area along nearby Drakes Beach, 3) fire up the barbecue pit (don't forget the charcoal), 4) split and barbecue the little guys, 5) slather them in Johnson's special sauce, and then 6) slurp 'em down.

Day Hikes

There's a little of everything for hikers here—32,000 acres, crisscrossed by 70 miles of trails, are set aside as wilderness where no motor vehicles or bicycles are allowed. The principal trailheads are Bear Valley, Palomarin, Five Brooks, and Estero. Pick up a free trail map at the visitor center before shoving off.

Abbotts Lagoon Trail

3 miles RT. Easy. Access: Abbotts Lagoon Trailhead parking area on Pierce Point Rd.

If you're looking for a short, easy trail located well away from the masses, this is the one. After climbing a small ridge, you're led down to Abbotts Lagoon, a popular watering hole for migratory birds.

Bear Valley Trail

8 miles RT. Easy. Access: Bear Valley Trailhead south of the visitor center parking area.

This well-worn trail leads through wooded hillsides until it reaches the shore at Arch Rock, where Coast Creek splashes into the sea through a "sea tunnel" (actually the arch of Arch Rock). This is your best bet for a beautiful walk through the woods to the rocky coast.

Coast Trail

7 miles RT. Easy to moderate. Access: Palomarin Trailhead, just off Mesa Rd. at the southern tip of the park.

Recommended by locals, this trek is one of Point Reyes's prettiest. This section of the trail skirts a cliff offering stunning views and then passes several small lakes and meadows before it reaches Alamere

Falls, a freshwater stream that cascades down a 40-foot bluff onto Wildcat Beach.

Easily the longest trail at the national seashore, the Coast Trail continues on for a 15-mile one-way hike along the coast that is usually done in 2 days, camping a third of the way through at Wildcat Beach. (There's another campground at Santa Maria Beach.) The trail ends at the Point Reyes Hostel. You'll need a second car, however, to shuttle you back to the trailhead where you began.

Estero Trail

4.5 miles one-way. Easy to moderate. Access: Estero Parking Area.

A favorite with birders, this mellow trail meanders along the edge of Drakes Estero and Limantour Estero. (*Estero* is the Spanish word for estuary.) The brackish waters here draw flocks of waterfowl and shorebirds as well as many raptors and smaller species. Along the way you cross a dam and a bridge over Home Bay.

Mount Wittenberg Trail

2 miles one-way. Strenuous. Access: Bear Valley Trailhead.

For the Rambo in your group, this huffer-puffer weeds out the weenies due to its steep elevation, peaking at 1,407 feet rather abruptly. Start at the Bear Valley Trailhead, south of the parking area, and turn right on to the Mount Wittenberg Trail after 0.2 mile. The trail up the ridge is steep but rewards hikers with great views back east across the Olema Valley. Instead of turning around directly, if you still have the energy you can loop back along Baldy Trail and take an alternative path such as the Meadow Trail back to Bear Valley Trail, the main route home.

Stewart Trail

9 miles RT. Moderate. Access: Five Brooks parking area.

This trail to Wildcat beach is one of the few unpaved trails in the park open to mountain bikes and is also quite popular with horseback riders. It's quite steep and not nearly as scenic as most other trails.

Tomales Point Trail

4.5 miles one-way. Easy to moderate. Access: Parking lot at the end of Pierce Point Rd.

This trail gives hikers a tour of the park's rugged shoreline and also passes through an elk reserve, home to the park's 400-strong herd of tule elk. Watch for their V-shaped tracks on the trail. About halfway through, you come to the highest spot on Pierce Point, where on a clear day you can see over the bay to the Sonoma Coast and Mount Saint Helena to the northeast.

Beaches

The **Great Beach** is one of California's longest. It is also one of the windiest, and home to large and dangerous waves. You can't swim here, but the beachcombing is some of the best in the world. Tide poolers should go to lonely **McClures Beach** at the end of Pierce Point Road during low tide or hike out to **Chimney Rock,** east of the lighthouse. Swimmers and dog owners will want to stick to **Limantour Beach,** located in the protected lee of Point Reyes. **Kehoe Beach,** in the northwest of the park, is known for its spring wildflower blooms, while **Hearts Desire Beach** at Tomales Bay State Park (© 415/669-1140) has the warmest, safest swimming (as well as a $4-per-vehicle fee).

Sir Francis Drake reputedly landed the *Pelican* (later rechristened the *Golden Hind*) on the sandy shore of Drakes Bay in June 1579, to replenish supplies and make repairs before sailing home to England. **Drakes Beach** is now home to the Kenneth C. Patrick Visitor Center and **Drakes Beach Cafe** (Thurs–Mon 11am–5pm; © 415/669-1297), the only food concession in the park, famous for its great oysters. This beach is good for swimming and beach fires are permitted.

Other Sports & Activities

Biking. As most ardent Bay Area mountain bikers know, Point Reyes National Seashore has some of the finest mountain-bike trails in the region—narrow dirt paths winding through densely forested knolls and ending with spectacular ocean views. A trail map is a must (available for free at the Bear Valley Visitor Center) since many of the park trails are off-limits to bikes. *Note:* Bicycles are forbidden on the wilderness area trails, and plotting a course exclusively on the bike trails can be tricky, so plan your route well in advance. Check at the visitor center to find out which trails are currently open to bikes.

Bird-Watching. During Audubon's annual Christmas bird count, Point Reyes is regularly found to have the largest concentration of diverse bird species in the continental United States—approximately 400. Popular bird-watching spots are Abbotts Lagoon and Estero de Limantour, or you can hang out with the pros at the **Point Reyes Bird Observatory–Palomarin Field Station** (© 415/868-0655; www.prbo.org), one of the few full-time ornithological research stations in the United States, located at the southeast end of the park on Mesa Road. This is where ornithologists keep an eye on the myriad of feathered species that call the seashore home. Admission to the visitor center and nature trail is free, and visitors are welcome to observe the tricky process of catching and banding the birds (open daily 9am–5pm; banding hours vary, as well as other seasonal hours, so call for exact times).

Horseback Riding. Equestrian activities are very popular at Point Reyes, as all of the trails (save Bear Valley Trail on weekends and holidays) are horse-friendly. A good resource is **Fivebrooks Ranch** (© 415/663-1570; www.fivebrooks.com), located at the Fivebrooks Trailhead, 3.5 miles south of Olema on Highway 1. They offer guided trail rides (horses provided) ranging from $35 for an hour-long ride to $165 for a 6-hour beach ride. Horse boarding is available here.

Kayaking. Tamal Saka Tomales Bay Sea Kayaking (© 415/663-1743; www.tamalsaka.com) offers kayak trips, including 3-hour sunset outings, 3½-hour full-moon paddles, yoga tours, day trips, and longer excursions. Instruction and clinics are available, and all ages and skill levels are welcome. Prices start at $65 for tours. Four-hour rentals begin at $35 for one person, $50 for two. Don't worry: The kayaks are very stable and there are no waves to contend with because you'll be paddling through placid Tomales Bay, a haven for migrating birds and marine mammals. The launching point is located on Calif. 1 at the Marshall Boatworks in Marshall, 8 miles north of Point Reyes Station.

Whale-Watching. Each year, gray whales (it's the barnacles that make them appear gray) migrate from their winter breeding grounds in the warm waters off the Baja Coast to their summer feeding grounds in Alaska. You can observe them as they undertake this enormous 10,000-mile journey from just about anywhere within Point Reyes National Seashore, though the most popular vantage point is the Point Reyes Lighthouse.

During peak season (Dec–Mar), you might see dozens of whales from the lighthouse, and the **Lighthouse Visitor Center** offers great displays on whale migration and maritime history. During this period, the Park Service runs a shuttle from Drakes Beach to the **Point Reyes Lighthouse** (a small fee is charged for adults; children 12 and under are free), where watchers have been known to see as many as 100 whales in a single afternoon. Even if the whales don't materialize, the lighthouse itself, a fabulous old structure teetering high above the sea at the tip of a promontory, is worth a visit. Two other spots, **Chimney Rock,** to the east of the lighthouse, and **Tomales Point,** at the northern end of the park, offer just as many whales without the crowds.

Camping

Camping within the park is limited to four hike-in camps. **Wildcat Camp,** near Alamere Falls, is a 6.5-mile hike from Bear Valley Trailhead. **Coast Camp** is on an open bluff, 2.3 beach miles west of the Limantour Beach parking lot. These camps near the sea are often foggy and damp, so bring a good tent and sleeping bag. **Sky Camp** (1.7 miles from Sky Trailhead on Limantour Rd.) and **Glen Camp** (4.6 miles from the Bear Valley Trailhead) are set in the woods away from the sea, more protected from the coastal elements.

In all camps, individual sites hold up to eight people and have picnic tables and food lockers. Pit toilets are available. Stays are limited to 4 days, and sites can be reserved up to 3 months in advance by calling © 415/663-8054 Monday to Friday 9am to 2pm.

Just outside the park is the **Olema Ranch Campground** (© 415/663-8001; www.olemaranch.com), which accommodates tents and RVs and is close to restaurants and a grocery store. It's located about a half-mile north of downtown Olema on Highway 1. Reservations are recommended, and you must be 21 or older to register.

Where to Stay

INSIDE THE PARK

Point Reyes Hostel

Off Limantour Rd., P.O. Box 247, Point Reyes Station, CA 94956. © **415/663-8811.** 44 bunks, 1 family room. $16–$18 per person. MC, V. Reception daily 7:30–10am and 4:30–9:30pm.

Located deep inside Point Reyes National Seashore, this beautiful old ranch-style complex can accommodate 44 guests in dormitory-style bunk rooms. There is also a pair of common areas, each warmed by stoves during chilly nights, as well as a fully equipped kitchen, barbecue, and patio. If you don't mind sharing your sleeping quarters with strangers, this is a deal

Campground	Total Sites	RV Hookups	Dump Station	Toilets	Drinking Water
Coast Camp	12	No	No	Yes	Yes
Glen Camp	12	No	No	Yes	Yes
Olema Ranch Campground (private)	200	Yes	Yes	Yes	Yes
Sky Camp	12	No	No	Yes	Yes
Wildcat Camp	12	No	No	Yes	Yes

that can't be beat. (The family room is available only to families with children 5 years old and younger.) Reservations (and earplugs) are strongly recommended. The maximum stay is 5 nights.

NEAR THE PARK

There are four towns in and around the Point Reyes National Seashore boundary—Olema, Point Reyes Station, Inverness Park, and Inverness—but they are all so close together that it really doesn't matter where you stay, because you'll always be within a stone's throw of the park. Although the accommodations in Point Reyes are excellent, they're also expensive, with most rooms averaging $125 per night. Be sure to make your reservation far in advance during the summer and holidays, and dress warmly: Point Reyes gets darn chilly at night.

Note: If you're having trouble finding a vacancy in Point Reyes, call the **West Marin Network** (✆ 415/663-9543) for information on available lodgings.

Blackthorne Inn

266 Vallejo Ave. (off Sir Francis Drake Blvd., south of Inverness), P.O. Box 712, Inverness, CA 94937. ✆ **415/663-8621.** www.blackthorne inn.com. 5 units. $225–$350 double. Rates include buffet breakfast. MC, V.

This elaborate redwood home, capped by an octagonal "treetop" room and featuring a spiral staircase, turrets, and multiple decks, looks more like a super deluxe tree house than a B&B. The

most delightful, and most expensive, unit is the Eagle's Nest, an eight-sided room enclosed by glass and topped with a private sun deck with a "sky bridge" leading to the private bathroom. The largest room is the Forest View Room, a two-room suite with a deck, furnished with wicker and decorated with floral fabrics and modern lithographs. It can be combined with the much smaller Hideaway Room to accommodate a traveling foursome. The main sitting room in the house features a large stone fireplace, skylight, and stained-glass windows and is surrounded by a huge deck. Guests have use of the hot tub on the top deck until 10pm, when it becomes the domain of the Eagle's Nest guests alone

An English Oak

88 Bear Valley Rd., Olema, CA 94950. ✆ **415/663-1777.** www.anenglishoak.com. 4 units. $95–$120 double, $140–$220 cottage. Rates include breakfast. MC, V.

Originally built by a Swiss dairy farmer in 1919, this venerable two-story farmhouse has survived everything from a major earthquake to a recent forest fire—which is lucky for you because you'll be hard pressed to find a better B&B for the price in Point Reyes. The English-style B&B is loaded with oodles of charm, right down to the profusion of flowers and vines outside and comfy chairs fronting a toasty-warm wood stove inside. The Acorn Cottage, with a kitchen and scads of exotic imports, is a

Showers	Fire Pits/ Grills	Laundry	Public Phone	Reserve	Fees	Open
No	Yes	No	No	Yes	$12	Year-round
No	Yes	No	No	Yes	$12	Year-round
Yes	Yes	Yes	Yes	Yes	$23–$32	Year-round
No	Yes	No	No	Yes	$12	Year-round
No	Yes	No	No	Yes	$12	Year-round

personal favorite; the indoor rooms balance function and style, each evoking a different component of the United Kingdom. The location is great, too, with a couple of good restaurants only a block away, and the entire national seashore at your doorstep.

Manka's Inverness Lodge & Restaurant

P.O. Box 1110, on Argyle St. (off Sir Francis Drake Blvd., 2 blocks north of downtown Inverness), Inverness, CA 94937. © **800/58-LODGE** or 415/669-1034. www.mankas.com. 13 units. $240–$665 double. MC, V.

Nestled in the forest with a certain era of mystery, this immediately lovable, elegantly funky lodge is one of the top places to stay and dine on the entire West Coast. Every room resembles the sort of rugged old mountain cabin you read about in Jack London novels, and the restaurant has that perfect balance of rural charm and refined sophistication. In addition to the standard rooms in the main lodge (which are anything but standard with their tree-limb bedsteads, billowy down comforters, and bucolic furnishings), there are two luxuriously appointed cabins adjacent to the inn (with hot tubs and outdoor showers), and a quartet of smaller, less expensive rooms in the redwood annex.

For the ultimate romantic splurge, inquire about their three secluded guesthouses: Cabin 125, the Boat House, and the Perch. The lodge's reputation is built on its restaurant, which dominates the bottom floor (see "Where to Dine," below).

Motel Inverness

12718 Sir Francis Drake Blvd. (P.O. Box 958), Inverness, CA 94937. © **888/669-6909** or 415/669-1081. www.motelinverness.com. 8 units. $99–$174 double, $300 cottage. Rates include breakfast. MC, V.

Inside, this motel has the feel of a country inn, with a great lobby that overlooks Tomales Bay and features a snazzy pool table. There are comfortable small rooms, supersized family suites with kitchenettes, and the totally unique Dacha, a bayfront cottage built in Russian Orthodox style. The prices are on the low end of the spectrum for the Point Reyes area.

Point Reyes Country Inn & Stables

12050 Hwy. 1 (P.O. Box 501), Point Reyes Station, CA 94956. © **415/663-9696.** Fax 415/663-8888. www.ptreyescountryinn.com. 6 units, 2 studios, 2 cottages. $95–$180 double, $95–$325 studio, $190–$225 cottage. $10–$15 per horse. Rates include breakfast. MC, V.

Are you and your horse dreaming of a country getaway to the Point Reyes National Seashore? Then book a room at Point Reyes Country Inn & Stables, a five-bedroom, ranch-style home on 4 acres that offers pastoral accommodations for two- and four-legged guests (humans and horses only). Each room has a private bathroom, either a balcony or a garden, and easy access to plenty of hiking and riding trails. The innkeepers have also added two new studios with kitchens above the stables, and rent out two cottages in Inverness equipped with decks, stocked kitchens, fireplaces, and a shared dock.

Where to Dine

Manka's Inverness Lodge & Restaurant

On Argyle St. (off Sir Francis Drake Blvd., 2 blocks north of downtown Inverness), Inverness. ℃ **415/669-1034.** Fixed-price dinner $58–$78. A la carte menu items (available only on Mon–Wed) $7–$16. MC, V. One seating daily: Mon–Sat at 7pm, Sun at 4pm. CALIFORNIA ECLECTIC.

The specialties of this fine restaurant are game and fish, including oysters from Tomales Bay. (In fact, almost everything in the kitchen is sourced from within an hour of the lodge.) The menu changes every night, and might feature duck, seared over almond wood and served on a bed of coastal cabbage and locally grown apples; black buck antelope chops with sweet corn salsa; a rich mussel stew; or everybody's favorite, local king salmon.

Station House Cafe

11180 Main St., Point Reyes Station. ℃ **415/ 663-1515.** www.stationhousecafe.com. Reservations recommended. Breakfast $4.50–$8; lunch items $6–$13; dinner main courses $8–$20. DISC, MC, V. Thurs–Tues 8am–10pm. AMERICAN.

A local favorite, the Station House Cafe is known for its good food and animated atmosphere, particularly when the live music fires up on weekends. For breakfast, try a frittata with asparagus, goat cheese, and olives, which always seems to taste better while sitting outside on the shaded garden patio. A lunch specialty is two-cheese polenta served with sautéed fresh spinach and grilled garlic-buttered tomatoes. The menu changes every week, but always features vegetarian selections, locally raised beef, and a good

selection of fresh fish. For dinner, start with a platter of local oysters and mussels, followed by a braised lamb shank (made with Guinness stout) or one of their old standbys such as meatloaf with garlic mashed potatoes or salmon and chips with country fries and coleslaw. Rounding out the menu are homemade turkey chili, calamari, steamed clams, and fresh soup made daily. The cafe has an extensive list of fine California wines, plus local and imported beers.

Taqueria La Quinta

11285 Hwy. 1 (at 3rd and Main sts.), Point Reyes Station. ℃ **415/663-8868.** Main courses $4–$8. No credit cards. Wed–Mon 11:30am–8pm. MEXICAN.

Fresh, good, fast, and cheap: What more could you ask for? Taqueria La Quinta has been a favorite lunch stop in downtown Point Reyes for years. A huge menu of Mexican standards (enchiladas, rellenos, tamales, and the like) is posted above the counter, but those in the know order the standout fish tacos, sheathed in fresh homemade tortillas. Since it's all self-serve, you can skip the tip, but watch out for the salsa—it's *hot.*

Vladimir's Czechoslovakian Restaurant

12785 Sir Francis Drake Blvd., Inverness. ℃ **415/669-1021.** Main courses $12–$18 lunch; $20–$28 dinner. No credit cards. Tues 3–9pm; Wed–Sun 1–9pm. CZECHOSLOVAKIAN.

An Inverness institution, Vladimir's has been dishing out fantastic Czech dishes since 1960 and is still going strong. The menu is dynamic, changing depending on the availability of ingredients; one night, goose or pheasant might be featured; on others, cabbage rolls, kielbasa, or Wiener schnitzel could be among your choices. You can sit inside in the quaint but elegant dining room or outside on the patio, and there is a full bar. *Note:* Call ahead—the restaurant's hours are subject to the unpredictable Point Reyes weather and the annual ski trips of the owner-chef.

29

REDWOOD NATIONAL & STATE PARKS

by Eric Peterson

I T'S IMPOSSIBLE TO EXPLAIN THE FEELING YOU GET IN THE OLD-GROWTH forests of Redwood National and State Parks without resorting to *Alice in Wonderland* comparisons. Like a tropical rain forest, the redwood forest is a multistoried affair, the tall trees being only the

top layer. Everything is big, misty, and primeval; flowering bushes cover the ground, 10-foot-tall ferns line the creeks, and the smells are rich and musty. Out on the parks' crowd-free trails, it's impossible to not feel as if you've shrank, or the rest of the world has grown, or else that you've gone back in time to the Jurassic epoch—dinosaurs would fit in here nicely.

When Archibald Menzies first noted the botanical existence of the coast redwood in 1794, more than 2 million acres of redwood forest carpeted California and Oregon. By 1965 heavy logging had reduced that to 300,000 acres, and it was obvious something had to be done if any redwoods were to survive. The state created several parks around individual groves in the 1920s, and in 1968 the federal government created Redwood National Park. In 1994, the National Park Service and the California Department of Parks and Recreation signed an agreement to manage the four contiguous redwood parks cooperatively, hence the name Redwood National *and* State Parks.

The 105,516-acre park offers a lesson in ecology. When the park was first created to protect the biggest coast redwoods, logging companies continued to cut much of the surrounding area, sometimes right up to the park boundary. Unfortunately, redwoods in the park began to suffer as the quality of the Redwood Creek drainage declined from upstream logging, so in 1978 the government purchased a major section of the watershed, having learned that you can't preserve individual trees without preserving the ecosystem they depend on.

Unaware that the logging of old-growth redwoods in the region is still a major bone of contention between the government, private landowners, and environmentalists, the trees thrive. They are living links to the age of dinosaurs and humble reminders that the era of mankind is but a hiccup in time to the venerable *Sequoia sempervirens*.

Avoiding the Crowds. The parks include three major features—the ocean setting, the old-growth forests, and the prairies. Not many people discover the

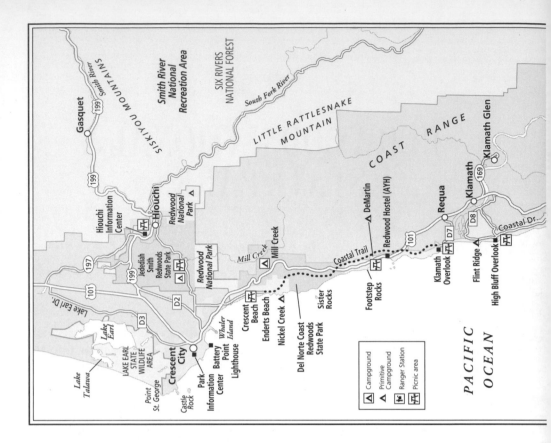

latter. These bald hills (called "prairies" here) offer excellent views over the tops of the redwoods and down to the ocean. And, while the coastal environment and the shade of the redwoods can chill a hiker's bones year-round, these treeless spots are warm and sunny sanctuaries in the summertime. The prairie region also offers many opportunities to explore the park by either hiking to the historic barns used during the ranching days before the park's establishment, visiting the School House Peak Firelook to check out the view, or hiking to the valley bottom along the Dolason Prairie Trail.

Just the Facts

GETTING THERE & GATEWAYS

The parks are located on a narrow strip near the coast in northern California, about 375 miles north of San Francisco. There are three major routes to the Redwood Coast. U.S. 101 travels up from San Francisco and down from Brookings, Oregon, to traverse much of the length of the parks. U.S. 199 takes off from U.S. 101 just north of the parks and heads northeast to Grants Pass, Oregon. The main route to the east is Calif. 299, which goes from Redding, California, to meet up with U.S. 101 south of the park.

If you're heading from the south, you'll want to stop in Orick. If you're heading from the north (Oregon), you'll want to stop in Crescent City. Why? Because both towns have excellent information centers crammed with useful (and important) information about the Redwood National and State Parks, including free maps.

The Nearest Airports. Arcata-Eureka Airport (no phone; call airline directly) is located in McKinleyville, 28 miles south of the Redwood Information Center near Orick. **Crescent City Municipal**

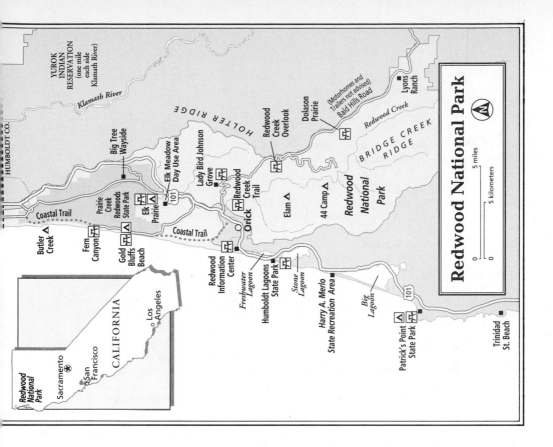

Redwood National Park

Airport (© 707/465-3804) is located in Crescent City, at the north end of the park. Both are served by **United Express;** Arcata-Eureka is also served by **Horizon.** Much farther south, **San Francisco International Airport** (© 650/821-8211; www.sfoairport.com) is located 14 miles south of downtown San Francisco on U.S. 101. All major **car-rental chains** have offices at San Francisco International Airport; some rentals are also available at the Arcata-Eureka and Crescent City airports. Airline and car rental phone numbers are listed in the appendix.

INFORMATION

Contact **Redwood National and State Parks,** 1111 2nd St., Crescent City, CA 95531 (© 707/464-6101; www.nps.gov/redw). The *Visitor Guide* published each summer describes activities taking place in the parks plus information on the wildlife you're likely to see.

VISITOR CENTERS

The southern gateway to the Redwood National and State Parks is the town of Orick, on U.S. 101. You can't miss it: Just look for the dozens of burl stands alongside the road. Here you'll find the sleek **Redwood Information Center,** P.O. Box 7, Orick, CA 95555 (© 707/464-6101, ext. 5265), where you can get a free map and see a variety of exhibits. It's open daily from 9am to 5pm year-round. If you missed the Redwood Information Center, don't worry: About 7 miles farther north on U.S. 101 is the **Prairie Creek Visitor Center** (© 707/464-6101, ext. 5300), which carries the same maps and information. It's open daily from 9am to 5pm in the summer, daily 10am to 2pm in winter.

The northern gateway to the Redwood National and State Parks is Crescent City. The town has its charms, but the face it presents along U.S. 101 isn't exactly alluring. (To combat this, a beautification project is ongoing.) Regardless, it's your best bet for a cheap motel, gas, fast food, and outdoor supplies. Before touring the park, pick up a free guide at the **Redwood National and State Parks Headquarters and Information Center,** 1111 2nd St. (at K St.), Crescent City, CA 95531 (© **707/464- 6101,** ext. 5064). It's open daily 8am to 5pm.

If you happen to be arriving via U.S. 199 from Oregon, the rangers at the **Hiouchi Information Station** (© **707/ 464-6101,** ext. 5067) and **Jedediah Smith Visitor Center** (© **707/464-6101,** ext. 5113) can also supply you with the necessary maps and advice. Both are open daily in the summer months from 9am to 5pm and when staffing is available in spring and fall.

FEES & PERMITS

Admission to the national park is free, but to enter any of the three state parks (which contain some of the best redwood groves), you'll have to pay a $4 day-use fee, good at all three.

Camping fees are $15 for drive-in sites. Walk-in sites are free. Most do not require permits, but free permits, available in person at visitor centers, are required for backcountry camping along the Redwood Creek Trail.

To travel the Tall Trees Trail (see "If You Have Only 1 Day," below) you'll have to get a free permit from the Redwood Information Center near Orick (see "Visitor Centers," above).

SPECIAL REGULATIONS & WARNINGS

Many of the best scenic drives in these parks are on roads not suitable for motor homes or trailers, so if possible those with RVs should consider towing a car; traveling with a friend who is driving a car, pickup, or SUV; or maybe even renting a car near the parks.

◆ **Don't disturb any abandoned baby seals or sea lions** you may encounter on the beach. The mother may be nearby, but will not return until you leave. In fact, you may be fined up to $10,000 for your good intentions. If a pup looks injured or in danger, call the **Mammal Marine Center** at © **707/465-MAML** (6265).

◆ On the beach, **be aware of tidal fluctuations.** Swimming is hazardous because of cold water and strong rip currents.

◆ **Watch for poison oak,** particularly in coastal areas.

◆ **Follow park regulations regarding bears** and food storage; all food and scented personal care items should be secured and hidden from view in vehicles, placed in bear-proof lockers (located at each drive-in campsite), or hung from trees. Roosevelt elk are wild and unpredictable; do not approach them on foot.

◆ **Treat water** from natural sources before drinking.

◆ **Tree limbs can fall** during high winds, especially in old-growth forests.

SEASONS & CLIMATE

Frankly, all those huge trees and ferns wouldn't have survived for 1,000 years if it didn't rain a lot here. Count on rain or at least a heavy drizzle during your visit, then get ecstatic when the sun comes out—it can happen anytime. Spring is the best season for wildflowers. Summer is foggy. (It's called "the June gloom" but often continues into July–Aug) Fall is the warmest and (relatively) sunniest time of all, and winter isn't bad, though it is cold and wet, and some park facilities are closed. A storm can provide the most introspective time to see the park, since you'll probably be alone. And after a storm passes through, sunny days often follow. On an even brighter note, chances are you won't freeze to death in winter or wither and melt in summer because the average annual temperature along the Redwood Coast varies only 16°, ranging from an average low of 45°F to an average high of 61°F (7°C–16°C).

EXPLORING THE PARK BY CAR 471

Annual events include an **Earth Month beach cleanup** in April; the **Smith River cleanup** in May; 7 days of summer seminars with interpretive, ranger-led kayaking tours ($50 per person); the **banana slug derby** in August; and the **Jammin' at Jed concert** in September. Contact the park for exact dates and times. Also, Crescent City holds a **surf contest** in October, and the park holds a **candlelight celebration** through the old growth in December.

If You Have Only 1 Day

First stop at one of the information centers for a free map, which will clue you in to the parks' main attractions.

Next, take the detour along U.S. 101 called the **Newton B. Drury Scenic Parkway,** which passes through dazzling groves of redwoods and elk-filled meadows before leading back onto the highway 8 miles later. Or you can try one of two other spectacular drives: the **Coastal Drive,** which winds through stands of redwoods and offers grand views of the Pacific, or **Howland Hill Road,** an unforgettable journey through an unbelievably beautiful old-growth redwood forest (see "Exploring the Park by Car," below).

The best way to experience the redwoods, however, is on foot, so be sure to fit in time for a short hike or two. The short **Fern Canyon Trail** leads through a fantastically lush grotto of ferns clinging to 50-foot-high vertical canyon walls. **Lady Bird Johnson Grove Loop** is an easy self-guided tour that winds around a glorious lush grove of mature redwoods. However, the best trail of all is **Boy Scout Tree Trail,** through a lush, cool, damp forest brimming with giant ferns and majestic redwoods.

If you prefer to see the park from the water, take a **Klamath River Jet Boat Tour** (© **800/887-JETS** or 707/482-7775; www.jetboattours.com) up the Klamath River Estuary to view bear, deer, elk, and more along the riverbanks, or a **kayak**

tour around the Klamath River Estuary or other nearby waters.

Those determined to see the world's tallest trees should make their first stop the Redwood Information Center near Orick. Here you can get a permit to travel the **Tall Trees Trail.** This 4-hour drive/hike expedition is limited to the first 50 permits each day, so get yours early. It's an experience you'll never forget.

Exploring the Park by Car

A number of scenic drives cut through the park. Steep, windy **Bald Hills Road** (located a few miles north of Orick on U.S. 101) will take you back into the Redwood Creek watershed and up to the shoulder of 3,097-foot Schoolhouse Peak. Don't even think of driving a motor home up here or pulling a trailer. A few miles farther north is the **Lost Man Creek Trail,** a short, unpaved scenic drive through the redwood forest. The 1.5-mile trip leads past the World Heritage Site dedication area and on to a cascade on Lost Man Creek. Again, anyone with a motor home or pulling a trailer can forget this one.

A don't-miss detour along U.S. 101 is the **Newton B. Drury Scenic Parkway,** which passes through dazzling groves of redwoods and elk-filled meadows before leading back onto the highway 8 miles later. While you're cruising along, take the **Cal-Barrel Road** turnoff, a narrow, packed-gravel road located just north of the Prairie Creek Visitor Center off the Newton B. Drury Scenic Parkway. It offers a spectacular 3-mile tour through an old-growth redwood forest (no trailers or motor homes).

One of the premier coastal drives on the Redwood Coast starts at the mouth of the Klamath River and runs 8 miles south toward Prairie Creek Redwoods State Park. The narrow, partially paved **Coastal Drive** winds through stands of redwoods, with spectacular views of the Pacific and numerous pullouts for picture taking (sea lions and pelicans abound) and short hikes. Keep an eye out for the World War II radar station, disguised as a farmhouse and barn. If you're heading south on U.S. 101, take the Alder Camp Road exit just south of the Klamath River Bridge and follow the signs to the Mouth of Klamath. Northbound travelers should take the Redwood National and State Parks Coastal Drive exit off the Newton B. Drury Scenic Parkway. Motor homes and vehicles with trailers are not advised.

The most amazing car-friendly trail in all of the Redwood National and State Parks, however, is the hidden, well-maintained gravel road called **Howland Hill Road** that winds for about 12 miles through Jedediah Smith Redwoods State Park. It's an unforgettable journey through a spectacular old-growth redwood forest—considered by many one of the most beautiful areas in the world. To get there from U.S. 101, keep an eye out for the BP gas station at the south end of Crescent City; just before the station, turn right on Elk Valley Road, and follow it to Howland Hill Road, which will be on your right. After driving through the park, you'll end up at U.S. 199 near the town of Hiouchi, and from there it's a short jaunt west to get back to U.S. 101. Plan at least 2 to 3 hours for the 45-mile round-trip, or all day if you want to do some hiking or mountain biking in the park. Driving a motor home or towing a trailer are not recommended.

Organized Tours & Ranger Programs

The parks run interpretive programs on subjects ranging from trees to tide pools, legends to landforms, at the Hiouchi and Redwood information centers and in the Crescent Beach area during summer months, as well as year-round at the park headquarters in Crescent City. Park rangers lead campfire programs and numerous other activities throughout the year as well. Call the **Parks Information Service** (© **707/464-6101,** ext. 5265) for current schedules.

Day Hikes

Regardless of the length of your hike, dress warmly and bring plenty of water and sunscreen.

Big Tree Trail

0.25 mile RT. Easy. Access: Take the Big Tree turnoff along the Newton B. Drury Scenic Parkway.

For the nonhikers in your group (including those in wheelchairs), this is a short paved trail leading to an impressively large tree.

Boy Scout Tree Trail

6 miles RT. Easy. Access: Ask for directions and a map at the Jedediah Smith Information Center.

After taking this trail through Jedediah Smith Redwoods State Park, you might understand why an activist such as Woody Harrelson would chain himself to the Golden Gate Bridge to protest logging old-growth forests. This is nature primeval, a lush, cool, damp forest brimming with giant ferns and majestic redwoods. It's truly an emotional experience just being here.

Enderts Beach Trail

1.2 miles RT. Easy. Access: End of Enderts Rd. at the south end of Crescent City (about 3 miles south on U.S. 101 from downtown, across from the Ocean Way Motel).

This short trail leads down to Enderts Beach. In the summer, free 1½- to 2-hour ranger-guided tide pool and seashore walks are offered when the tides are right. You start at the beach parking lot, descend to the beach, and explore rocky tide pools at its southern end. For specific tour times, call © **707/464-6101,** ext. 5064.

Fern Canyon Trail

1.5 miles RT. Easy. Access: From U.S. 101, take the Davison Rd. exit (at Rolf's Park Cafe), which follows along Gold Bluffs Beach to the Fern Canyon parking lot. Day-use fee is $2. No trailers or motor homes over 24 ft. long.

This short, heavily traveled trail leads to an unbelievably lush grotto of lady, deer, chain, sword, five-finger, and maiden-hair ferns clinging to 50-foot-high vertical walls divided by a babbling brook. It's only about a 1.5-mile walk from Gold Bluffs Beach, but be prepared to scramble across the creek several times via small footbridges. This short loop connects with a number of trails, allowing the adventurous hiker to get in a 10-mile hike if they so desire.

Friendship Ridge, Coastal Loop Trail

7.5 miles RT. Moderate. Access: Fern Canyon Trailhead on Davison Rd.

This is possibly the most varied and beautiful hike in Redwood National Park. Beginning at the Fern Canyon Trailhead, you'll follow the Coastal Loop Trail north, then veer right and follow the Friendship Ridge Trail. For the next 3 miles you'll walk through a magical fern and redwood forest, then join the West Ridge Trail through old-growth forest to Butler Creek Camp and back south along the Coastal Loop Trail.

Lady Bird Johnson Grove Loop

1 mile RT. Easy. Access: Lady Bird Johnson Grove. Take the Bald Hills Rd. exit off U.S. 101, ½ mile north of Orick.

Here's a self-guided tour that loops around a glorious lush grove of mature redwoods. It's the site at which Lady Bird Johnson dedicated the national park in 1968. The following year it was named for her.

Tall Trees Trail

1.3 miles one-way. Moderate. Access: End of Tall Trees Access Rd., off Bald Hills Rd. Permit required.

To see the world's tallest trees—some 360 feet tall and more than 600 years old—you'll first have to go to the Redwood Information Center near Orick (see "Visitor Centers," earlier in this chapter) to obtain a free map and vehicle permit to drive to the Tall Trees Grove Trailhead. (**Note:** Only 50 permits are issued per day, on a first-come, first-served basis.) After driving to the trailhead—it's a slow, 15-mile one-way drive on a rough gravel road (trailers and motor homes not permitted)—you have to walk a steep 1.3 miles down into the grove, but what a small price to pay to see the tallest trees in the world. By the way, the average time spent gawking at the world's largest trees is 1 minute 40 seconds, but once you figure in the drive and hike to get to the tree, the whole expedition takes at least 4 hours.

Picnickers alert: The Crescent Beach Overlook, along Enderts Road (off U.S. 101 about 4 miles south of Crescent City), is one of the prettiest picnic sites on the California coast. Pack a picnic lunch from Good Harvest Cafe (see "Picnic & Camping Supplies," below), park at the Overlook, lay your blanket on the grass, and admire the ocean view atop your personal 500-foot bluff.

Exploring the Backcountry

The long, beautiful **Coastal Trail,** which runs the entire 37-mile length of the parks' coastal section and as near the ocean as possible, can either be hiked in a day in small segments, or as a great 3- or 4-day trip using several backcountry camps on the route. One of the nicest runs is from Crescent Beach south into the Del Norte Coast Redwoods State Park. A free permit is required if you stay overnight at Butler Creek or along Redwood Creek.

Redwood Creek Trail

16 miles RT. Moderate to strenuous. Access: End of Redwood Creek access road, off Bald Hills Rd.

This hike is a beauty, passing through Tall Trees Grove (where the tallest trees in the world grow on the banks of Redwood Creek), periodic meadows, new-growth forests, and awesome vantage points overlooking the grove. You'll camp along the fine sandbars of Redwood Creek. The bridges on Redwood

Creek are only installed from May 15 to September 15, and from the end of October to the beginning of April heavy rains make creek crossings extremely dangerous.

Other Sports & Activities

Beaches. The park's beaches vary from long white-sand strands to cobblestone pocket coves. The water temperature is in the high 40s to low 50s year-round, and it's often rough out there. Swimmers and surfers should be prepared for adverse conditions.

Crescent Beach is a long, sandy beach just 2 miles south of Crescent City that's a popular destination for beachcombing, surf fishing, and surfing. Just south of Crescent Beach is Enderts Beach, a protected spot with a hike-in campground and tide pools at its southern end.

Bicycling. Most of the hiking trails throughout the Redwood National and State Parks are off limits to mountain bikers. However, Prairie Creek Redwoods State Park has a fantastic 19-mile mountain-bike trail through dense forest, elk-filled meadows, and glorious mud holes. Parts of it are difficult, though, so beginners should sit this one out. Pick up a 25¢ trail map at the Elk Prairie Campground Ranger Station.

There are a few other mountain-bike loops in the 20-mile range, but they are serious thigh burners and make the one above look easy. These loops are the Holter Ridge Trail and Little Bald Hills. Also, mountain biking is available on the old U.S. 101, now the Coastal Trail within Del Norte Coast Redwoods State Park.

The park recently completed the Davison Trail, which connects the Prairie Creek bike trails and the Newton B. Drury Scenic Parkway with U.S. 101. Future plans call for it to connect with Holter Ridge.

Fishing. The Redwood Coast's streams are some of the best steelhead trout and salmon-breeding habitat in California.

Park beaches are good for surfcasting, but you should be prepared for heavy wave action. A California fishing license is required (available at local sporting goods stores). Be sure to check with rangers about any special closures or other restrictions, which seem to change frequently. Rivers West Outfitters (© 707/482-5822; www.riverswestoutfitters.com) offers guide service for around $150 per person per day.

Horseback Trail Rides. Equestrians can go on a variety of guided trail rides, including lunch and dinner trips, with Redwood Trails Horseback Riding (© 707/488-3895 or 707/488-2061), located at the Redwood Trails Campground (5 miles south of Orick on U.S. 101). Riders should be less than 250 pounds. Rates range from $20 for a half-hour ride to $200 for a 6-hour ride with lunch.

Jet-Boat Tours. Tours aboard a jet boat take visitors 22 miles upriver from the Klamath River Estuary to view bear, deer, elk, osprey hawks, otters, and more along the riverbanks. It's about $25 for a 30-mile scenic trip, $45 for a 55-mile morning or evening cruise. (Kids' rates are half-price and those under 4 ride free.) Tours run May through September. Contact Klamath River Jet Boat Tours, Klamath (© 800/887-JETS or 707/482-7775; www.jetboattours.com).

Kayaking. An alternative to exploring the waters of the Redwood parks and vicinity in a jet boat is to take a guided kayak tour on the Smith River. The parks organize a few tours in June and July that include basic lessons, life jacket, and a two-person inflatable kayak. The tour is $50 per person (no children under 12 allowed). Call © 707/464-6101, ext. 5095, for the current schedule and other details.

Whale-Watching & Bird-Watching. High coastal overlooks (such as Klamath Overlook and Crescent Beach Overlook) make great whale-watching outposts during the December/January southern migration and the March/April return migration. The northern sea cliffs also provide valuable nesting sites for marine birds such as auklets, puffins, murres, and cormorants. Birders will also love the park's coastal freshwater lagoons, which are some of the most pristine shorebird and waterfowl habitats left and are chock-full of hundreds of different species.

Wildlife Viewing. One of the most striking aspects of Prairie Creek Redwoods State Park is its herd of **Roosevelt elk,** usually found in the appropriately named Elk Prairie in the southern end of the park. These gigantic beasts can weigh up to 1,000 pounds. The bulls carry huge antlers from spring to fall. Elk are also sometimes found at Gold Bluffs Beach—it's an incredible rush to suddenly come upon them out of the fog or after a turn in the trail. Nearly 100 **black bears** also call the park home but are seldom seen. Unlike those at Yosemite and Yellowstone, these bears are still afraid of people.

Camping

Most drive-in camping is in the state parks. In the southern part of the complex, Prairie Creek Redwoods State Park (© 707/464-6101, ext. 5300), known for its old-growth redwoods and herds of elk, has two drive-in campgrounds. **Elk Prairie Campground,** 5 miles north of Orick on U.S. 101, is near fishing and hiking trails, has a nature center, and offers evening campfire talks. Reservations are available from **ReserveAmerica** (© 800/444-7275, or 916/638-5883 for international callers; www.reserve america.com). **Gold Bluffs Beach Campground** is 3 miles north of Orick on U.S. 101, then 5 miles west on Davison Road. It's somewhat more primitive and offers trail access.

In the northern part of the complex, the campground at **Jedediah Smith Redwoods State Park** (© 707/464-6101, ext. 5113), along U.S. 199 at Hiouchi,

provides easy access to some of the area's biggest and most spectacular redwoods, as well as campsites along the scenic Smith River. Also in the northern section is **Mill Creek Campground,** in Del Norte Coast Redwoods State Park (© 707/464-6101, ext. 5113), located 7 miles south of Crescent City on U.S. 101. It has sites for both RVs and tents, and the walk-in tent sites are nestled among the redwoods. Both Jedediah Smith and Mill Creek take reservations through ReserveAmerica (see above for phone and website information).

Those seeking RV hookups and the usual commercial campground amenities will find several choices in Crescent City, including the quiet, well-maintained **Crescent City Redwoods KOA,** 4241 U.S. 101 North, Crescent City, CA 95531 (© 707/464-5744). Tent sites are among the redwoods, and some RV sites are also shaded. There's a nature trail, farm animals, a recreation room, a Laundromat, a convenience store with RV supplies, propane, and cable TV hookups. The KOA also has 17 rustic cabins ($35–$62 per night for two people) and one modernized cottage that sleeps six ($85–$125) situated among the redwoods.

In addition to the developed drive-in campgrounds discussed above, there are five small primitive hike-in campgrounds located in the national park, which require a walk of 0.25 to 0.5 mile. All are free and have fire rings and toilets. Contact park offices (© 707/464-6101, ext. 5064) for directions and current information.

There are also four campgrounds in the mountains above the park, located along U.S. 199 in the **Smith River National Recreation Area** (© 707/457-3131). We like the Panther Flat campground, with coin-op showers, where sites run $15 per night. The other campgrounds are more primitive, running $8 to $14 per night. Sites at any of the four can be reserved by calling © 877/444-6777, where an actual person can help you make decisions, or go online to **www.reserveusa.com.**

Campground	Total Sites	RV Hookups	Dump Station	Toilets	Drinking Water
Elk Prairie	75	0	Yes	Yes	Yes
Gold Bluffs Beach	25	0	No	Yes	Yes
Jedediah Smith	106	0	Yes	Yes	Yes
Mill Creek	145	0	Yes	Yes	Yes
Crescent City Redwoods KOA	94	42	Yes	Yes	Yes

Where to Stay

A number of bed-and-breakfasts and funky roadside motels are available in the surrounding communities of Crescent City, Orick, and Klamath. **The Crescent City/Del Norte Chamber of Commerce** (© 800/343-8300; www.northerncalifornia.net) can steer you toward a good match. Many of the motels were built in the 1950s and haven't changed all that much, but a number of new properties are slated to open by 2006, including a Hampton Inn, a woodsy lodge near Trinidad, and a casino-resort on the south side of Crescent City.

If you're bringing along the family or traveling in a group along the Redwood Coast, then consider dropping the motel idea and instead renting a fully furnished home on the ocean or river's edge for around $125 a night from **Redwood Coast Vacation Rentals** (© 707/218-7706). **Waterfront Vacation Rentals** (© 877/642-2254 or 707/464-9068) rents a similar array of lodging, including the cozy, funky **Cottage by the Sea B&B** near Battery Point in Crescent City.

INSIDE THE PARK

Hostelling International–Redwood Hostel

14480 U.S. 101 (at Wilson Creek Rd., about 7 miles north of Klamath), Klamath, CA 95548. © 800/909-4776 or 707/482-8265. Fax 707/482-4665. www.norcalhostels.org. 28 bunks, 1 couple's room. $16–$20 per person, $42 couple's room. DISC, MC, V.

The only lodging actually within the park, this turn-of-the-20th-century settler's ranch was remodeled in 1987 to accommodate 30 guests dormitory-style (bunks and shared bathrooms). The minimal privacy is more than made up for by the location—a mere 100 yards from the beach, surrounded by hiking trails leading along the Redwood Coast. One private room that accommodates two is available with advance reservations. Showers and use of a common room, a redwood deck, a kitchen, a dining room, a pellet stove, and outdoor lockers are included in the nightly rate. Reservations (with a credit card) are strongly recommended from March to October.

NEAR THE PARK

Crescent Beach Motel

1455 U.S. 101 S. (2 miles south of downtown on U.S. 101), Crescent City, CA 95531. © 707/464-5436. 27 units. TV. Summer $75–$94 double; winter $51–$72 double. AE, DISC, MC, V.

Crescent City has the dubious distinction of being the only city along the coast without a fancy, full-service hotel. There is, however, an armada of inexpensive roadside motels, the best of which is the Crescent Beach. Near the highway, about a mile south of town, this single-story structure is the only local motel set directly on the beach. The clean, well-maintained rooms are simple and functional; most have queen-size beds and all have remote control color TVs with cable. Four of the units face the highway; try to get one

Showers	Fire Pits/ Grills	Laundry	Public Phone	Reserve	Fees	Open
Yes	Yes	No	Yes	Yes	$15	Year-round
Yes	Yes	No	No	No	$15	Year-round
Yes	Yes	No	Yes	Yes	$15	Year-round
Yes	Yes	No	Yes	Yes	$15	Summer only
Yes	Yes	Yes	Yes	Yes	$20–$32	Year-round

of the others, all of which have sliding glass doors opening onto decks and a small lawn area overlooking the bay. One of the city's most popular restaurants, the Beachcomber (see "Where to Dine," below), is next door.

Curly Redwood Lodge

701 U.S. 101 S., Crescent City, CA 95531. © **707/464-2137.** Fax 707/464-1655. www. curlyredwoodlodge.com. 36 units. TV TEL. Summer $60–$65 double; winter $41–$45 double. AE, DC, MC, V.

This is a blast from the past, the kind of place where you might have stayed as a kid during one of those cross-country vacations in the family station wagon. It was built in 1957 on grasslands across from the town's harbor, and completely trimmed with lumber from a single ancient redwood. Although they're not full of the latest high-tech gadgets, the bedrooms are among the largest and most soundproof in town, and certainly the most evocative of a bygone, more innocent age. In winter, about a third of the bedrooms (the ones upstairs) are locked and sealed. Overall, the aura is more akin to Oregon than anything you might imagine in California.

Historic Requa Inn

451 Requa Rd. (from U.S. 101 take Requa Rd. 2[bf]1/2 miles north of the Klamath River Bridge), Klamath, CA 95548. © **707/482-1425.** www.requainn.com. 12 units. $79–$120 double. Rates include breakfast. AE, DISC, MC, V.

Established in 1914, this two-story charmer, located on the banks of the lower Klamath River, offers 10 spacious guest rooms, each modestly decorated with antique furnishings, all with private bathrooms with showers or claw-foot tubs. Six offer views of the lower Klamath River. The inn's main attraction is the cozy parlor downstairs, where guests bury themselves in the plump armchairs to read beside the wood-burning pellet stove or just relax and watch the river run. There are plenty of enticements just outside, including river access, numerous hiking trails in nearby Redwood National Park, and, of course, fishing. Breakfast is included in the room rate and dinner is served every night except Sunday; the former is limited to the inn's guests only.

Where to Dine

Fresh seafood is plentiful on the redwood coast, especially in Crescent City, and most restaurants are very casual. Microbrewery fans will want to check out the **Surfside Grill & Brewery,** 400 Front St., Crescent City (© **707/464-7962**), serving a terrific dark amber (aka "Da Kine') and a menu of seafood, barbecued ribs, and pub grub. The place is open for lunch and dinner daily with entrees ranging from $5 to $12 at lunch and $5 to $18 at dinner.

Beachcomber

1400 U.S. 101, Crescent City. © **707/464-2205.** Reservations recommended. Main courses $7–$16. MC, V. Thurs–Tues 5–9pm. SEAFOOD.

The decor is as predictably nautical as its name implies: rough-cut planking and a scattering of artfully arranged driftwood, fishnets, and buoys, dangling above a dimly lit space. The restaurant lies beside the beach, 2 miles south of Crescent City's center. Its fans cite it as one of the best restaurants in town. The cuisine is a joy to fish lovers who prefer not to mask the flavor of their seafood with complicated sauces. Proprietor-chef Nancy Bachman grills many dishes over madrone-wood barbecue pits, a technique perfected since she established the restaurant in 1975. The house specialty is Parmesan halibut, a sumptuous dish that accounts for one out of five dinner orders and attracts repeat visitors from across the state line. Pacific salmon, Alaskan cod, oysters, and steamer clams are also favorites, dishes for which visitors line up, especially on Friday and Saturday nights.

Forest Cafe

15499 U.S. 101 (across from Trees of Mystery), Klamath. © **707/482-5585.** Main courses $4–$11 breakfast; $6–$12 lunch; $8–$18 dinner. AE, DC, DISC, MC, V. Daily 7:30am–9pm (shorter winter hours). AMERICAN.

This roadside restaurant's decor is definitely on the kitschy side of the spectrum. Owned by the area's penultimate roadside attraction, the Trees of Mystery, the dining areas are bedecked with nature-oriented murals and oversized, stuffed bears and other beasts. While a bit gaudy, these charms are bound to fascinate kids, and the location is definitely convenient to park visitors, smack-dab in the middle of the redwood forest. Breakfasts and lunches are hearty, running the gamut from black-berry flapjacks to "Bigfoot" cheeseburgers. Dinner portions also fail to disappoint, with fresh seafood, steaks, and a smattering of pasta dishes.

Harbor View Grotto Restaurant & Lounge

150 Starfish Way, Crescent City. © **707/464-3815.** Main courses $4.50–$9 lunch; $8–$22 dinner. DISC, MC, V. Daily 11:30am–10pm (shorter winter hours). SEAFOOD/STEAKS.

Located in Crescent City's harbor, this is the best-established non-chain restaurant in town, specializing in fresh seafood at market prices since 1961. It relocated to a new building in 1995, which features pleasant views of the ocean and harbor from both the dining room and lounge, and is capped with a miniature lighthouse inspired by Crescent City's Battery Point Lighthouse. The "light eaters" menu includes a cup of creamy white chowder (made fresh daily) or salad, a main course, and vegetables; hungrier diners can choose from three different cuts of prime rib or steaks with sautéed prawns. Menu items include a seasonal variety of fresh fish from local fishing fleets, such as Pacific snapper or salmon. Crab (in season) or shrimp Louis, as well as crabmeat or shrimp sandwiches, are perennial favorites.

Rolf's Park Café

On U.S. 101 (about 2 miles north of town), Orick, CA 95555. © **707/488-3841.** Main courses $6–$14 lunch; $9.50–$20 dinner. DISC, MC, V. Wed–Mon 8am–8pm, Tues 5–8pm. Closed Nov–Mar. GERMAN.

Rolf Rheinschmidt, a talented chef who has worked around the world, decided it was time to semiretire, so he opened up his own restaurant in the small town of Orick. For 20 years since, he and his talented sons have wowed the Redwood National and State Parks' visitors with Rolf's tried-and-true versions of bratwurst, Wiener schnitzel, and crêpes Suzettes, as well as his specialty, a marinated rack of spring lamb. He also offers more exotic choices such as buffalo, wild boar, and elk steak. (If you're truly adventurous, get a combo of all three.) Each dinner entree includes lots of extras: hors d'oeuvres, a salad, vegetables, farm-style potatoes, and bread. If you're a big breakfast eater, Rheinschmidt's German Farmer Omelet—an open-faced concoction of ham, bacon, sausage, mushrooms, cheese, potatoes, and pasta, topped with sour cream and salsa and garnished with a strawberry crepe—is guaranteed to fill your tank.

Picnic & Camping Supplies

You can purchase sandwiches and other light fare at the **Good Harvest Cafe,** 700 Northcrest Dr., in Crescent City (© **707/ 465-6028**). They also serve a good hot breakfast, including vegetarian dishes.

Groceries are available in Crescent City at **Safeway,** 475 M St. (© **707/465-3353**), and **Ray's Food Place,** 625 M St. (© **707/465-4045**). Or you might try the **Orick Market,** 121175 Hwy. 101 in Orick (© **707/488-3225**).

Wal-Mart, 900 Washington St. (© **707/ 464-1198**) in Crescent City sells camping supplies and sporting goods.

Trail Ridge Rd · highly suggested
48 mile rd.

p. 486

30

ROCKY MOUNTAIN NATIONAL PARK

by Don & Barbara Laine

S NOW-COVERED PEAKS STAND WATCH OVER LUSH VALLEYS AND SHIMMER-ing alpine lakes, creating the perfect image of America's most dramatic and beautiful landscape: the majestic Rocky Mountains. Here, the pine- and fir-scented forests are deep, the air is crisp and pure, and the rugged mountain peaks reach up to grasp the deep-blue sky.

What makes Rocky Mountain National Park unique, however, is not only its breathtaking scenery, but also its variety. In relatively low areas, up to 9,000 feet, ponderosa pine and juniper cloak the sunny southern slopes, with Douglas fir on the cooler northern slopes. The thirstier blue spruce and lodgepole pine cling to the banks of streams, along with occasional groves of aspen. Elk and mule deer thrive. On higher slopes, forests of Engelmann spruce and subalpine fir dominate, interspersed with wide meadows vibrant with wildflowers in spring and summer. This is also home to bighorn sheep, which have become a symbol of the park. Above 11,500 feet the trees become increasingly gnarled and stunted, until they disappear altogether and alpine tundra takes over. Fully one-third of the park is in this bleak, rocky world, many of its plants identical to those found in the Arctic.

Within the park's 415 square miles are 17 mountains above 13,000 feet. Longs Peak, at 14,259 feet, is the highest.

Trail Ridge Road, which cuts west through the middle of the park from Estes Park, then south down its western boundary to Grand Lake, is one of America's most scenic highways. Climbing to 12,183 feet, it's the highest continuously paved highway in the United States. The road is usually open from Memorial Day into October, depending on snowfall. The 48-mile drive from Estes Park to Grand Lake takes about 3 hours, allowing for stops at numerous view points. Exhibits at the Alpine Visitor Center at Fall River Pass, 11,796 feet above sea level, explain life on the alpine tundra.

Fall River Road, the original park road, leads from Estes Park to Fall River Pass via Horseshoe Park. As you negotiate its graveled switchbacks, you get a clear idea of what early auto travel was like in the West. This road, too, is closed in winter. Among the few paved roads in

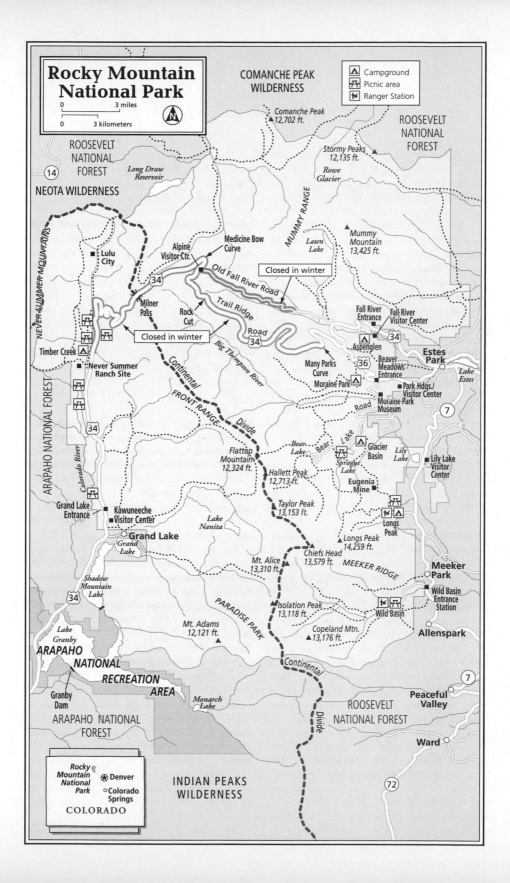

Rocky Mountain National Park

0 — 3 miles
0 — 3 kilometers

N

△ Campground
🛖 Picnic area
👤 Ranger Station

COMANCHE PEAK
WILDERNESS

Comanche Peak
▲ 12,702 ft.

ROOSEVELT
NATIONAL
FOREST

ROOSEVELT
NATIONAL
FOREST

(14)

Long Draw
Reservoir

Stormy Peaks
12,135 ft.

Rowe
Glacier

NEOTA WILDERNESS

Lawn
Lake

Mummy
Mountain
13,425 ft.

Lulu
City

Alpine
Visitor Ctr.

Medicine Bow
Curve

Old Fall River Road

Closed in winter

MUMMY RANGE

(34)

Trail Ridge

Fall River
Entrance

Fall River
Visitor Center

Milner
Pass

Rock
Cut

Road
(34)

(34)

Aspenglen

Estes
Park

Timber Creek △

Closed in winter

Continental

Big Thompson River

Many Parks
Curve

(36)

Beaver
Meadows
Entrance

Lake
Estes

Never Summer
Ranch Site

Moraine Park

Park Hdqs./
Visitor Center

(7)

(34)

FRONT RANGE

Divide

Moraine Park
Museum

Colorado River

Flattop
Mountain
12,324 ft.

Bear
Lake

Bear
Lake

Glacier
Basin

Lily
Lake

Lily Lake
Visitor
Center

Hallett Peak
12,713 ft.

Sprague
Lake

Grand Lake
Entrance

Kawuneeche
Visitor Center

Lake
Nanita

Taylor Peak
13,153 ft.

Eugenia
Mine

ARAPAHO NATIONAL FOREST

Grand Lake

Grand
Lake

Longs
Peak

Longs Peak
14,259 ft.

Shadow
Mountain
Lake

Mt. Alice
13,310 ft.

Chiefs Head
13,579 ft.

MEEKER RIDGE

Meeker
Park

PARADISE PARK

Isolation Peak
13,118 ft.

Wild Basin

Wild Basin
Entrance
Station

(34)

Mt. Adams
12,121 ft.

Copeland Mtn.
▲ 13,176 ft.

Allenspark

Lake
Granby

**ARAPAHO
NATIONAL
RECREATION
AREA**

Monarch
Lake

Continental

ROOSEVELT
NATIONAL FOREST

(7)

Peaceful
Valley

Granby
Dam

Divide

Ward

ARAPAHO NATIONAL
FOREST

Rocky
Mountain
National Park

✹ Denver

○ Colorado
Springs

INDIAN PEAKS
WILDERNESS

(72)

COLORADO

Tips from a Park Insider

The ease with which visitors can experience the many faces of Rocky Mountain National Park helps make it a very special place, according to park spokesman Dick Putney.

There are other alpine tundra areas in the United States, but you usually have to do a lot of hard hiking, Putney says. "What makes Rocky Mountain National Park unique is that Trail Ridge Road takes you up to the tundra—above tree line—in the comfort of your car; you can see plant and animal communities that if not for this park you would have to go to the Arctic Circle to see."

Those willing and able to hike can see plenty of tundra country. Putney suggests having a friend drop you off at the **Ute Trail** turnout on Trail Ridge Road, where you can hike the 6 miles down through Forest Canyon to Upper Beaver Meadows. He says this canyon is among the wildest in the park, adding that the hike along its steep side provides spectacular views of the canyon and Longs Peak, the park's tallest mountain.

Another hike that Putney recommends is the 2-mile (one-way) **Gem Lake Trail,** on the park's east side. "When you're going up that trail, there are several places to look across the Estes Valley to Longs Peak, and the lake is a wonderful spot for a picnic," he says. Those who want to work a bit harder will be well rewarded on another of Putney's favorites, the East Inlet Trail on the west side of the park. "Once you get up there a couple of miles, and gain some elevation, you look back toward Grand Lake and think you're in Switzerland."

Longs Peak, at 14,259 feet elevation, is the northernmost of Colorado's famed "fourteeners" (mountains that exceed 14,000 ft. elevation), and it's a popular hike. "You don't need technical climbing gear once the ice is gone—usually by mid-July," Putney says,

adding that hikers may have some physical problems with the altitude at first. "It's wise to give yourself at least a couple of days to acclimate before tackling Longs Peak." He also recommends that high-elevation hikers drink plenty of nonalcoholic fluids, eat regularly, carry energy bars, take it slow, and listen to their bodies. Another tip he gives backpackers is to spend time discussing their plans with rangers in the park's Backcountry Office before setting out. "We'd much rather spend time with them beforehand to try to get to know their abilities and expectations, and advise them where to go, than be called out on a search-and-rescue mission."

One activity that many visitors miss out on is viewing the night sky, says Putney. He suggests taking a picnic supper and stopping at one of the Trail Ridge Road **view points** after dark, when most park visitors are in their motel rooms or campsites. "We don't have any light pollution here," he says. "You think you can just reach up and touch the Milky Way. You can see satellites, and the Perseid meteor shower in August is something you won't soon forget."

Putney says the easiest method to avoid crowds, even during the park's busiest season, is to take off down a hiking trail, since most visitors remain close to the roads. "The farther you go up the trail, the fewer people you'll encounter," he says. He adds that another sure way to escape humanity is to visit in winter, and explore the park on snowshoes or cross-country skis.

And when would he visit? "Fall—from September through mid-October—is the best time," he says. "Days are warm and comfortable, nights are cool and crisp, there are fewer people than in summer, and the aspens are changing. You can see hundreds of elk, and watch the bulls bugle as they protect their harems from the other bulls. But it might snow!"

the Rockies that lead into a high, mountain basin is Bear Lake Road, which is kept open year-round, with occasional half-day closings to clear snow.

Avoiding the Crowds. The park is only fully accessible for half the year, so few people come in the off season. The very busiest time in the park is from mid-June through mid-August—essentially during school vacation—so just before or just after that period is best. But winter is gaining in popularity, too because it is the quietest time. You won't be able to drive the entire Trail Ridge Road, and the park can be bitterly cold, but it is also beautiful. Regardless of when you visit, the best way to avoid crowds is to head out on a trail.

Just the Facts

GETTING THERE & GATEWAYS

Entry into the park is from either the east (through the town of Estes Park) or the west (through the town of Grand Lake). The east and west sides of the park are connected by Trail Ridge Road, open during summer and early fall, but closed to all motor vehicle traffic by snow the rest of the year. Most visitors enter the park from the Estes Park side. The Beaver Meadows Entrance, west of Estes Park via U.S. 36, leads to the Beaver Meadows Visitor Center and park headquarters, and is the most direct route to Trail Ridge Road. U.S. 34 west from Estes Park takes you to the Fall River Visitor Center, just outside the park, and into the park via the Fall River Entrance, which is north of the Beaver Meadows Entrance. From there you can access Old Fall River Road or Trail Ridge Road.

Estes Park is about 71 miles northwest of Denver, 44 miles northwest of Boulder, and 42 miles southwest of Fort Collins.

The most direct route from Denver is via U.S. 36 through Boulder. At Estes Park, that highway joins U.S. 34, which runs up the Big Thompson Canyon

from I-25 and Loveland, and continues through Rocky Mountain National Park to Grand Lake. An alternative scenic route to Estes Park is Colo. 7, the "Peak-to-Peak Scenic Byway" that transits Central City (Colo. 119), Nederland (Colo. 72), and Allenspark (Colo. 7) under different designations.

Heading south from Estes Park on Colo. 7, you can access two trailheads in the southeast corner of the national park, but there are no connecting roads to the main part of the park from those points. These are **Longs Peak Trailhead**—the turnoff is 9 miles south of Estes Park and the trailhead about another mile, and **Wild Basin Trailhead**—another 3½ miles south to the turnoff and then 2¼ miles to the trailhead.

In summer, a free national park **shuttle bus** runs from the Glacier Basin parking area to Bear Lake, with departures every 15 to 30 minutes.

Those who want to enter the national park from the west can take U.S. 40 north from I-70 through Winter Park and Tabernash to Granby, and then follow U.S. 34 north to the village of Grand Lake and on into the park.

The Nearest Airport. Visitors arriving by plane usually fly into **Denver International Airport** (© **800/247-2336** or 303/342-2000), 90 miles southeast of the park's east entrances. It's served by most major airlines and car-rental companies, whose reservation numbers are in the appendix. From the airport, travelers can also get to Estes Park with **Estes Park Shuttle** (© **800/586-5009** or 970/586-5151; www.estesparkco.com).

INFORMATION

Contact **Rocky Mountain National Park,** Estes Park, CO 80517-8397 (© **970/586-1206;** www.nps.gov/romo). The park's visitor centers (see below) sell U.S. Geological Survey topographical maps. Also available is *Hiking Rocky Mountain National Park* (Old Saybrook, Connecticut: The Globe Pequot Press) by Kent and Donna Dannen, which gives detailed trail descriptions. You'll also find a wealth of detailed information about the park in *Frommer's Rocky Mountain National Park,* which was written by the authors of this chapter.

A great variety of trip-planning tools can be obtained from the **Rocky Mountain Nature Association** (© **800/816-7662** or 970/586-0108; www.rmna.org/bookstore), which sells a variety of maps, guides, books, and videos.

VISITOR CENTERS

The **Beaver Meadows Visitor Center,** on U.S. 36 on the east side of the park (© **970/586-1206**), has a good interpretive exhibit including a relief model of the park, an audiovisual program, a wide choice of books and maps for sale, and knowledgeable people to answer questions and give advice.

Just outside the park, on U.S. 34 and just east of the Fall River Entrance on the east side of the national park, is the new **Fall River Visitor Center,** which was completed in the summer of 2000. Located in a beautiful mountain lodge-style building, it was constructed with private funds but is staffed by park rangers and volunteers from the Rocky Mountain Nature Association. It contains exhibits on park wildlife, including some spectacular full-size bronzes of elk and other animals, plus an activity/discovery room for children, an information desk, and a bookstore. Next door is **Rocky Mountain Gateway** (© **970/577-0043**), a large and somewhat pricey souvenir and clothing shop that also contains a cafeteria-style restaurant with snacks and sandwiches.

The **Kawuneeche Visitor Center** is located at the Grand Lake end of Trail Ridge Road (© **970/627-3471**). In addition to exhibits on the geology, plants, animals, and human history of the park's west side, there is a small theater where films and video programs are shown, and a short self-guided nature trail. By the way, *kawuneeche* (kah-wuh-*nee*-chee) is an Arapaho word that translates as "valley of the coyote."

The **Alpine Visitor Center** (open in summer only) at Fall River Pass has exhibits that explain life on the alpine tundra and a viewing platform from which you are almost certain to see elk. Next door is the Fall River Store, open in summer, with a snack bar and large gift shop that has an especially good selection of souvenirs, gifts, arts and crafts, and clothing, at surprisingly reasonable prices. The **Moraine Park Museum** (open mid-Apr to mid-Oct) is located on Bear Lake Road in a historic log building that dates from 1923. It has full visitor center facilities, in addition to excellent natural-history exhibits that describe the creation of the park's landscape, as well as the plants and animals of the park. There's also a nature trail outside. The **Lily Lake Visitor Center** (open June–Sept) is located along Colo. 7 about 7 miles south of Estes Park. In addition to information on the national park, it has exhibits and information on activities in the adjacent Roosevelt and Arapaho national forests.

FEES & PERMITS

Park admission costs $15 per vehicle for up to 1 week; $5 for bicyclists, motorcyclists, and pedestrians. Camping in developed campgrounds costs $18 per night during the summer and $12 in the off season when the water is turned off, usually from late September to May. Required overnight backcountry permits cost $15 from May through October and are free the rest of the year (see "Exploring the Backcountry," below).

SPECIAL REGULATIONS & WARNINGS

Rocky Mountain National Park's high elevation and extremes of climate and terrain are among its most appealing features, but also its greatest hazards. Hikers should try to give themselves several days to acclimate to the altitude before seriously hitting the trails, and hikers with respiratory or heart problems would do well to discuss their plans with their physicians before leaving home. Hikers also need to be prepared for rapidly changing conditions, including sudden afternoon thunderstorms in July and August. If lightning threatens, stay clear of ridges and other vulnerable high points.

SEASONS & CLIMATE

Even though the park is open year-round, **Trail Ridge Road,** the main east-west thoroughfare through the park, is always closed in winter. Assume that you will not be able to drive clear across the park from mid-October until Memorial Day—even into June it's possible that the road will be closed for hours or even a day or more by snow. That's not to say that intrepid travelers can't enjoy the park in winter. All park entrances are open, trails are open to snowshoers and cross-country skiers, and roads to a number of good view points and trailheads are plowed. Those with the proper skills and equipment can cross-country ski into the high country, although they need to be aware of storm and avalanche dangers and should always check with rangers before setting out.

Weather is a key factor that will affect your trip to the park in any season. In summer, temperatures typically climb into the 70s (20s Celsius) during the day and drop into the 40s (single digits Celsius) at night, but because of the park's high elevation—and range of elevations—you'll find that temperatures vary greatly. The higher into the mountains you go the cooler it gets. Rangers say that for every 1,000 feet in elevation gain, the climate changes the equivalent of traveling 600 miles north. The tree line in the park—the elevation at which trees can no longer grow—varies, but is at about 11,500 feet.

Winters usually see high temperatures in the 20s and 30s (below 0 Celsius) and lows from 10°F below zero to 20°F (-20°C–0°C) above. Spring and fall temperatures can vary greatly from pleasantly warm to bitterly cold and snowy. For this reason, spring and fall

are when you need to be flexible and adjust your itinerary to suit current conditions. Particularly at higher elevations, windchill factors can be extreme, and hypothermia can be a problem at any time, even in summer, when afternoon thunderstorms sometimes occur without warning, causing temperatures to drop dramatically and suddenly.

SEASONAL EVENTS

The elk rutting season in September and October brings hundreds of elk to the lower elevations, where you can often hear the macho bulls bugle and watch them trying to keep other bulls away from their females.

If You Have Only 1 Day

This park simply begs for an extended visit—4 to 7 days would be ideal—but it offers wonderful experiences for visitors who have only a short amount of time, or who are not able or willing to hike.

Those arriving in summer or early fall with only 1 day to see the park will want to stop at one of the visitor centers, and then drive the fantastically scenic **Trail Ridge Road,** described below. Stop at the view points and take the half-hour walk along the **Tundra World Nature Trail** to get a close-up view of the plants, animals, and terrain of the tundra. Those returning to the east or west sides will have time for little else, since it takes about 3 hours each way for the 48-mile drive, but those passing through the park on their way to somewhere else might want to take another short hike.

Exploring the Park by Car

Although Rocky Mountain National Park is generally considered the domain of hikers and climbers, ideal for those who want to leave the crowds behind and head into the backcountry, it's surprisingly easy to enjoy this park without working up a sweat. For that we thank **Trail Ridge Road,** built in 1932 and undoubtedly one of America's most scenic highways, providing expansive and sometimes dizzying views in all directions. This remarkable 48-mile road rises to over 12,000 feet in elevation and crosses the Continental Divide. Along the way it offers spectacular vistas of snowcapped peaks, deep forests, and meadows of wildflowers full of browsing bighorn sheep, elk, and deer. Allow at least 3 hours for the drive, and consider a short walk or hike from one of the many vista points.

To get a close-up look at the tundra, pull off Trail Ridge Road into the **Rock Cut Parking Area** (elevation 12,110 ft.), about halfway along the scenic drive. You'll have splendid views of glacially carved peaks along the Continental Divide, and on the 0.5-mile **Tundra Nature Trail** you'll find signs identifying and discussing the hardy plants and animals that inhabit this region.

Trail Ridge Road is closed by winter snows. In recent years it has usually been clear by late May and closed again between mid- and late October. But even well into June, the road can be closed for snow for hours or even days at a time.

There are two other roads within the park. **Old Fall River Road,** 9 miles long and unpaved, is one-way uphill only. It's usually open from July 4 through mid-October. **Bear Lake Road** is the access road to Bear Lake and is open year-round.

Organized Tours & Ranger Programs

Campfire talks and other programs are offered between June and September. Activities vary from talks on the park's wildlife and geology to photo walks, fly-fishing, and orienteering programs. At night, rangers periodically lead night-sky programs using the park's computerized telescopes, and also give nightly talks during the elk rutting season. Winter visitors will find a variety of activities, including moonlight hikes and snowshoe and cross-country ski trips. Check at visitor centers for current schedules.

Several companies offer van tours into the park, including **Estes Park Shuttles & Mountain Tours** (© **800/586-5009** or 970/586-5151; www.estesparkco.com), which provides 2- and 3-hour guided trips each summer, starting in either Estes Park or Denver. Call for rates.

Historic & Man-Made Attractions

Remnants from the area's mining and ranching days of the late 1800s and early 1900s still persist in the park. Hikers will encounter the ruins of several historic cabins on the Lulu City and Eugenia Mine trails (see "Day Hikes," below). The **Moraine Park Museum** on Bear Lake Road contains exhibits mainly on natural history, but the building itself—a log structure built as a social center in 1923—is listed on the National Register of Historic Places. A half-mile walk from Trail Ridge Road on the west side of the park leads to **Never Summer Ranch,** a preserved dude ranch from the 1920s. It was started as a cattle ranch by Denver saloon owner John Holzwarth after Prohibition began, but Holzwarth soon discovered that it was more pleasant and profitable to take in paying guests (at $11 per week including room, meals, and a horse) than to do the hard work of actual ranching. The ranch buildings contain many of their original furnishings.

Day Hikes

The park contains almost 350 miles of hiking trails, ranging from short, easy walks to extremely strenuous hikes that require climbing skills. Trail difficulty can also vary by time of year—the higher elevations usually have snow until at least mid-July. Many of the park's trails, such as Longs Peak, can be done either as day hikes or overnight backpacking trips. Hikers are strongly advised to discuss their plans with park rangers before setting out. The following are some favorites; there are many more.

Alberta Falls Trail

0.6 mile one-way. Easy. Access: Glacier Gorge parking area.

With an elevation change of only 160 feet, this is an easy and scenic walk along Glacier Creek to pretty Alberta Falls. Along the sunny trail you'll see beaver dams and an abundance of golden-mantled ground squirrels.

Bear Lake Nature Trail

0.5-mile loop. Easy. Access: Bear Lake Trailhead at the end of Bear Lake Rd.

Head out early in the day if you want some quiet time on this very popular walk. From the beginning of the trail, on the eastern side, 12,713-foot Hallett Peak dominates the view; along the lake's north side you'll be looking at the national park's highest mountain, 14,259-foot Longs Peak. Expect to see ground squirrels, chipmunks, and snowshoe hares, while in the clear waters of the lake you may catch a glimpse of a greenback cutthroat trout. (Sorry, no fishing is allowed.) Rocky Mountain Nature Association sells an informative booklet, *Bear Lake Nature Trail* ($2), at park visitor centers that makes a handy companion on your walk. This is an easy stroll, most of which is wheelchair accessible—one section has stairs.

Bierstadt Lake Trail

1.4 miles one-way. Moderate. Access: North side of Bear Lake Rd., 6½ miles from Beaver Meadows.

This trail climbs 566 feet through an open forest of aspen to Bierstadt Lake. From there you'll find good views of Longs Peak from the northwest side of the lake. This trail also connects with several other trails, including one that leads to Bear Lake.

Emerald Lake Trail

1.8 miles one-way. Easy to moderate. Access: Bear Lake.

This trail offers spectacular scenery on its route past Nymph and Dream lakes to its destination of Emerald Lake. The 0.5-mile hike to Nymph Lake is easy, climbing 225 feet; then the trail is rated moderate to Dream Lake (another 0.6 mile) and Emerald Lake (another 0.7 mile), which is 605 feet higher than the starting point at Bear Lake. In addition to the mountain lakes, you'll see the surrounding mountains, which are especially pretty when reflected in the surface of Nymph Lake, or towering over Dream Lake. In summer there's an abundance of wildflowers along the path between Nymph and Dream lakes.

Eugenia Mine Trail

1.4 miles one-way. Moderate. Access: Longs Peak Ranger Station.

This walk to an abandoned mine follows the Longs Peak Trail for about 0.5 mile and then forks off to the right, heading through groves of aspens and then evergreens before arriving at the site of the mine, where you'll see hillside tailings, the remnants of a cabin, and abandoned mine equipment. The trail has an elevation gain of 508 feet.

Gem Lake Trail

2 miles one-way. Moderate. Access: Trailhead on Devil's Gulch Rd., north of Estes Park.

A relatively low-elevation trail, starting at only 7,740 feet, this has an elevation change of 1,090 feet. It offers good views of Estes Park and Longs Peak, and delivers hikers to a pretty lake.

Mills Lake Trail

2.5 miles one-way. Moderate. Access: Glacier Gorge Junction.

This trail leads to a picturesque mountain lake, nestled in a valley among towering mountain peaks. Among the best spots in the park for photographing dramatic Longs Peak (the best lighting is usually in late afternoon or early evening), this is also the perfect place for a picnic. The trail has an elevation change of about 700 feet.

Ouzel Falls Trail

2.7 miles one-way. Moderate. Access: Wild Basin Ranger Station.

This hike climbs about 950 feet and crosses Cony Creek on two bridges before delivering you to a picture-perfect waterfall, among the park's prettiest. The trail passes through areas that were burned in 1978—good spots to see wildlife—and also offers fine views of Longs Peak and Mount Meeker.

Tundra World Nature Trail

0.5-mile loop. Easy. Access: Near Rock Cut parking area on Trail Ridge Rd.

This wheelchair-accessible nature trail has exhibits identifying various tundra plants and animals, and describing how they have adapted to the harsh tundra environment.

LONGER TRAILS

East Inlet Trail

6.9 miles one-way. Moderate to strenuous. Access: West portal of Adam's Tunnel, southeast of the town of Grand Lake.

This trail is an easy walk the first 0.3 mile to scenic Adams Falls. It then wanders along some marshy areas, crosses several streams, and then, becoming more strenuous, climbs sharply in elevation to Lone Pine Lake, about 5.5 miles from the trailhead. It is another 1.4 miles, partly through a subalpine forest, to Lake Verna. The trail continues, unmaintained, after the lake. Total elevation gain to Lake Verna is 1,809 feet.

East Longs Peak Trail

8 miles one-way. Strenuous. Access: Longs Peak Ranger Station.

Recommended only for experienced mountain hikers and climbers in top physical condition, this trail climbs 4,855 feet along steep ledges and through a narrows to the top of 14,259-foot Longs Peak, the highest point in the park. The trek takes most hikers about 15 hours to complete and can be done in 1 or 2 days. Those planning a 1-day hike should consider starting out extremely early, so they will be well off the peak before the summer afternoon thunderstorms arrive. For a 2-day hike, go 5 or 6 miles the first day, stay at a designated backcountry campsite, and complete the trip the following day. Those making the hike in early summer (usually up until mid-July) should be prepared for icy conditions.

Lawn Lake Trail

6.2 miles one-way. Strenuous. Access: Trailhead on Fall River Rd.

This hike, with an elevation gain of 2,249 feet, follows the Roaring River through terrain dotted with ponderosa pine. Along the way you can see all too plainly the damage done by a massive flood that occurred when the Lawn Lake Dam broke in 1982, killing three campers. At higher elevations there are scenic views of Mummy Mountain.

Lulu City Trail

3.7 miles one-way. Moderate. Access: Colorado River Trailhead near the western boundary of the park.

This trail gains just 350 feet in elevation as it winds along the river floodplain, through lush vegetation, past an 1880s mine and several mining cabins, and then along an old stage route into a subalpine forest before arriving at Lulu City. Founded in 1879 by prospectors hoping to strike gold and silver, it was abandoned within 10 years, and little remains today except the ruins of a few cabins.

Timber Lake Trail

4.8 miles one-way. Strenuous. Access: East side of Trail Ridge Rd., 9⅔ miles north of the Grand Lake Entrance.

You'll work hard on this hike but be amply rewarded with views of timberline lakes and alpine tundra. With an elevation change of 2,060 feet, this hike takes you through a forest of lodgepole pines, follows a creek lined with subalpine wildflowers, and then arrives at the lake, surrounded by rocks, tundra, snow, and a few trees.

Ute Trail

6 miles one-way. Moderate. Access: Ute Trail turnout on Trail Ridge Rd.

An excellent way to see the tundra, this moderate hike is really fairly easy if you can get a ride to the top and walk down the 3,300-foot descent. The hike down the side of a canyon provides great views.

Exploring the Backcountry

There are numerous opportunities in the park for backpacking and technical climbing, and hikers and climbers will generally find that the farther they go into the backcountry, the fewer humans they will see. Some of the day hikes discussed above can also be done as overnight hikes; for example, the East Longs Peak Trail, which takes most people about 15 hours round-trip, is often completed over 2 days. Hikers can also combine various shorter trails to produce loops that can keep them in the park's backcountry for up to a week.

The park has well over 100 small **backcountry campsites,** which may be reserved. Backpackers should carry portable stoves, since wood fires are permitted at only a few sites with metal fire rings. In addition to the designated backcountry campsites, there are two dozen cross-country zones, in some of the least accessible sections of the park, which are recommended only for those with good map and compass skills.

The park's **Backcountry Office** should be the first stop for those planning backpacking trips. Rangers there know the trails and camping areas well and are happy to advise hikers on the best choices for their abilities and expectations. Backcountry permits are required for all overnight hikes. Technical climbers who expect to be out overnight usually set up a bivouac—a temporary, open-air encampment that is normally at or near the base of a route or on the face of a climb. Designated bivouac zones have been established; permits are required.

Backcountry and bivouac permits are obtained at park headquarters and ranger stations. They cost $15 from May through October but are free from November through April. For information call © **970/586-1242.**

Other Sports & Activities

In addition to the businesses discussed below, **Estes Park Mountain Shop,** 358 E. Elkhorn Ave. (© **800/504-6642** or 970/586-6548), has an indoor climbing gym and also offers climbing instruction and guided trips both in and near the national park, as well as a kids' outdoor adventure program in half- and full-day sessions and rentals and sales of climbing and camping equipment (call for details).

Biking. As in most national parks, bikes are not permitted off established roads, and here bicyclists will in most cases be sharing roadways with motor vehicles along narrow roads with 5% to 7% grades. However, bikers still enjoy the challenge and scenery. One popular 16-mile ride is the **Horseshoe Park/Estes Park Loop,** which goes from Estes Park west on U.S. 34 past Aspenglen Campground and the park's Fall River Entrance, and then back east at the Deer Ridge Junction, following U.S. 36 through the Beaver Meadows Entrance. There are plenty of beautiful mountain views. A free park brochure provides information on safety, regulations, and suggested routes.

Tours, rentals, and repairs are available at **Colorado Bicycling Adventures,** 184 E. Elkhorn Ave., Estes Park (© **970/ 586-4241;** www.coloradobicycling.com). Rentals are $15 to $30 for a half day, and $21 to $50 for a full day, depending on type of bike, with discounts for multiday rentals. You can also rent child carriers, car racks, and locks. The company offers road trips in the national park (downhill on paved roads) for $46 to $70, and off-road mountain-bike tours outside the park for experienced riders for about $53 per person. Bike rentals are also available at similar rates from **Estes Park Mountain Shop** (see above).

Climbing & Mountaineering. Colorado **Mountain School,** 351 Moraine Ave. (P.O. Box 1846), Estes Park, CO 80517 (© **888/CMS-7783** or 970/586-5758; www.cmschool.com), is an AMGA accredited year-round guide service, and the sole concessionaire for technical climbing and instruction in Rocky Mountain National Park. The school has programs for all ages. The most popular climb is Longs Peak (the highest mountain in the park). It can be ascended by those without experience via the "Keyhole," but its north and east faces are for experts only. Rates vary, and the larger the group the less per person, but the base rate for one person for half- and full-day excursions ranges from $75 to $300. The school also offers lodging in a hostel-type setting (see "Where to Stay," below).

Educational Programs. The **Rocky Mountain Nature Association,** Rocky Mountain National Park, Estes Park, CO 80517 (© **800/816-7662** or 970/586-1258; www.rmna.org/bookstore), offers a wide variety of seminars and workshops, ranging from a half day to several days in duration. Subjects vary but might include songbirds, flower identification, edible and medicinal herbs, painting, wildlife photography, tracking park animals, astronomy, human history, and edible mushrooms. Programs are scheduled from spring through fall,

although most of them are held from June through August. Rates range from $25 to $75 for half- and full-day programs, and $85 to $195 for multiday programs.

Fishing. Four species of **trout** are fished in the park: brown, rainbow, brook, and cutthroat. Anglers must get a state fishing license and are only permitted to use artificial lures or flies. A number of lakes and streams, including Bear Lake, are closed to fishing; a list of open and closed waters plus regulations and other information are available in a free park brochure.

Horseback Riding. Many of the national park's trails are open to those on horseback, and several outfitters provide guided rides, both within and outside the park, usually from spring through fall. Typical prices are $20 for a 1-hour ride, $35 for 2 hours, $45 for 3 hours, $55 for a half day, and $80 for a full day. Highly recommended is the **Sombrero Ranch Stables'** breakfast ride, which runs from March to December and includes a 2-hour ride and an all-you-can eat full breakfast, for about $40. Sombrero has stables on the east side of the park opposite Lake Estes Dam, at 1895 Big Thompson Hwy. (U.S. 34; © **970/586-4577;** www.sombrero.com). The company also offers horseback rides on the west side of the park in the Grand Lake area (© **970/627-3514**). Also in the Grand Lake area, **Winding River Resort** (© **970/627-3215**) offers 1- and 2-hour trail rides plus kids' pony rides at similar rates.

Hi Country Stables operates two stables inside the park that offer similar rides and rates: Glacier Creek Stables (© **970/586-3244**) and Moraine Park Stables (© **970/586-2327**). **National Park Village Stables,** at the Fall River Entrance of the national park on U.S. 34 (© **970/586-5269**), and the **Cowpoke Corner Corral,** at Glacier Lodge 3 miles west of town, 2166 Colo. 66 (© **970/586-5890**), both offer similar rides and rates from May to September.

Cross-Country Skiing & Snowshoeing. A growing number of people have been discovering the joys of exploring the park on cross-country skis and snowshoes, which are conveniently available for rent at area sporting goods stores (see below) outside the park.

If you're headed into the backcountry for cross-country skiing or snowshoeing, stop by park headquarters for maps, information on where the snow is best, and a free backcountry permit if you plan to stay out overnight. Keep in mind that trails are not groomed. On winter weekends, rangers often lead guided snowshoe walks on the east side of the park and guided cross-country ski trips on the west side, starting in February. Participants must supply their own equipment.

Popular winter recreation areas include Bear Lake, south of the Beaver Meadows Entrance. A lesser-known part of the park is Wild Basin, which is south of the park's east entrances, off Colo. 7 about a mile north of the community of Allenspark. A 2-mile road, closed to motor vehicles for the last mile in winter, winds through a subalpine forest to the Wild Basin Trailhead, which follows a creek to a waterfall, a rustic bridge, and eventually another waterfall. Total distance to the second falls is 2.7 miles. Chances are good for spotting birds along the trail, such as Clark's nutcrackers, Steller's jays, and the American dipper. On winter weekends, the Colorado Mountain Club often opens a warming hut at the Wild Basin Ranger Station.

Among shops that rent snowshoes is **Colorado Bicycling Adventures** (see "Biking," above). Daily rental costs $10 per pair, including poles, and the company also offers 4-hour guided snowshoe tours into the park, including equipment, for $25 per person.

Snowmobiling. A recent National Park Service ruling has outlawed snowmobiling within the park, with one exception. On the park's west side, a snowmobile trail leads from the park into the adjacent **Arapaho National Forest.** This trail leaves U.S. 34 just north of the Kawuneeche Visitor Center, and follows County Roads 491 and 492 west into the forest. Contact park visitor centers for current information.

Wildlife Viewing & Bird-Watching. Rocky Mountain National Park is a premier wildlife-viewing area, especially in fall, winter, and spring. Look for large herds of elk in meadows and on mountainsides. During the fall rutting season a group of park volunteers called the **Rocky Mountain National Park Elk Bugle Corps** are stationed at elk-viewing areas in the evenings to help people get the best views while not disturbing the animals—elk are often just 30 or 40 feet away.

Park visitors also often see mule deer, beavers, coyotes, and river otters. Watch for moose among the willows on the west side of the park. In the forests there is an abundance of songbirds and small mammals; particularly plentiful are gray and Steller's jays, Clark's nutcrackers, chipmunks, and golden-mantled ground squirrels. You also have a good chance of seeing bighorn sheep, marmots, pikas, and ptarmigan along Trail Ridge Road. For detailed and current wildlife-viewing information, stop by one of the park's visitor centers and check on the many interpretive programs, such as bird walks. Local wildlife-watching suggestions can be heard on radio at 1610AM.

Camping

INSIDE THE PARK

The park has five campgrounds with a total of almost 600 sites, with nearly half at Moraine Park. Moraine Park and Glacier Basin require reservations Memorial Day through early September. For reservations call © 800/365-2267, or make reservations through the park's website. In summer, arrive early if you hope to snare one of the first-come, first-served campsites. Campsites cost $18 per night during the summer; $12

Especially for Kids

The park offers a variety of special hikes and programs for children, including an especially popular trip to the park's beaver ponds. A ranger-led program for kids from 6 to 12 years old, called **"A Child's View,"** concentrates on the park's geology and wildlife through hands-on activities. The park's **Junior Ranger Program** lets kids earn badges by completing activities that teach them about the park's plants and animals and environmental concerns. Most of the kids' activities are scheduled during the summer; check on schedules at any park visitor center.

in the off season when water is turned off. No showers or RV hookups are available. Camping is limited to 3 days at Longs Peak and 7 days at other campgrounds.

NEAR THE PARK
THE EAST SIDE

Choices on the east side include the **Estes Park KOA,** 1 mile east of Estes Park on U.S. 34, at 2051 Big Thompson Ave., Estes Park, CO 80517 (℘ **800/562-1887** for reservations, or 970/586-2888). Scenically located across the street from Lake Estes and within walking distance of the Big Thompson River, this KOA lacks a swimming pool, but makes up for it with cable TV hookups, a basketball court, and a game room. It also sells LP gas. In addition to the campsites, there are also camping cabins ($46–$54 double). There are fire pits in the tent and cabin areas, but not at RV sites.

The **National Park Resort,** 3501 Fall River Rd., Estes Park, CO 80517 (℘ **970/** 586-4563), is a wooded campground on the border of the park, just across the street from the park's new Gateway Visitor Center. It can accommodate both tents and RVs; all sites have at least water and electricity, while full hookups include electricity, water, sewer, and cable TV. A coin-operated laundry is nearby. Cabins, available year-round, cost $90 to $150.

The most luxurious camping is at **Spruce Lake R.V. Park,** 1050 Mary's Lake Rd., Estes Park, CO 80517 (℘ **970/ 586-2889**), located about a mile west of the intersection of U.S. 34 and Business U.S. 36. Here you'll be pampered with miniature golf, a heated swimming pool, a large playground, a stocked private fishing lake (fee), large sites, cable TV hookups, and numerous scheduled activities such as ice-cream socials. Ground tents are not permitted.

There are links to websites for the above and other commercial campgrounds at **www.estesparkresort.com**.

There are two **Roosevelt National Forest** campgrounds within easy driving distance of the park's east entrances: **Olive Ridge,** 14½ miles south of Estes Park along Colo. 7, has pleasant, shady, well-spaced sites and an amphitheater. A less-developed campground, for those who carry their own drinking water, is **Meeker Park Overflow,** about 12 miles south of Estes Park on Colo. 7. Both campgrounds have vault toilets.

In Estes Park, a **Forest Service Information Center** is located at 161 2nd St. (℘ **970/586-3440;** www.fs.fed.us/r2); it's open daily in summer, and has limited hours for several days a week in winter, depending on staff and volunteer availability. For year-round information, contact the **Forest Service Information Center,** 1311 S. College Ave., Fort Collins, CO 80524 (℘ **970/498-2770**).

For reservations (Olive Ridge Campground only) contact the National Recreation Reservation Service (℘ **877/ 444-6777;** www.reserveusa.com). There is a nonrefundable $8.65 fee per reservation in addition to campground fees.

THE WEST SIDE

Covering more than 36,000 acres along the western edge of Rocky Mountain National Park in Arapaho National Forest, the **Arapaho National Recreation Area** contains excellent fishing lakes (several with boat ramps) and opportunities for hiking, mountain biking, cross-country skiing, snowshoeing, snowmobiling, hunting, and camping.

The recreation area's campgrounds offer shaded campsites plus the usual picnic tables and fire pits. The most developed site, **Stillwater Campground,** is located off U.S. 34 on the west bank of Lake Granby, about 7 miles south of the community of Grand Lake. Stillwater has showers plus water and electric hookups, available only in summer; a limited number of sites are open in winter, although water is then turned off.

Also located in the Arapaho National Recreation Area, south of Grand Lake, are **Green Ridge Campground** (about 4 miles south on U.S. 34 and then 1 mile south on County Rd. 66); and **Willow Creek** (about 10 miles south on U.S. 34 and then about 4 miles west on County Rd. 40). All three are located on lakes with fishing and boat ramps. For information, contact the **Arapaho National Recreation Area office** (© 970/887-4100). Campsite reservations (Stillwater and Green Ridge only) are available from the **National Recreation Reservation Service** (© 887/444-6777; www.reserveusa.com). There is a nonrefundable $8.65 fee per reservation in addition to campground fees.

There are also several commercial campgrounds in the community of Grand Lake, just outside the national park's west entrance, which combine modern conveniences with a forest-camping atmosphere. **Elk Creek Campground,** Box 549, Grand Lake, CO 80447 (© 800/355-2733 or 970/627-8502; www.coloradodirectory.com/elk creekcamp), is located on Golf Course Road, off U.S. 34 on the north side of the village. It has tent and RV sites in a wooded setting, a pond with license-free trout fishing (there is a per-fish charge), a playground, a game room, and a convenience store. There are also 10 log cabins ($39 double). **Winding River Resort,** P.O. Box 629, Grand Lake, CO 80447 (© 800/282-5121 for reservations or 970/627-3215; fax 970/627-5003; www.windingriverresort.com), also offers forest camping with hot showers, full RV hookups, and all the other amenities of a commercial campground. In addition, Winding River offers an abundance of activities, ranging from horseshoes to horseback riding ($20 for a 1-hr. trail ride, $35 for a 2-hr. ride), plus hayrides, ice-cream socials, and chuck-wagon breakfasts. There's also a petting zoo. In addition to campsites there are a variety of cabins that share the campground's bathhouse ($35), plus full cabins and lodge units ($70–$130 double). From Grand Lake head north on U.S. 34 about 1.5 miles and turn left onto County Road 491 (across from the Kawuneeche Visitor Center), continuing for 1½ miles to the resort.

Where to Stay

There is no lodging inside the park.

ESTES PARK AREA (EAST SIDE OF THE NATIONAL PARK)

For help in finding accommodations in and around Estes Park, call the **Estes Park Chamber Resort Association Lodging Referral Service** (© 800/44-ESTES or 970/586-4431; www.estesparkresort. com). National chains here include **Best Western Lake Estes Resort,** 1650 Big Thompson Ave. (U.S. 34), Estes Park, CO 80517 (© 800/292-8439 or 970/586-3386), with rates of $120 to $130 double from mid-June to mid-September, and $50 to $85 double the rest of the year; **Comfort Inn,** 1450 Big Thompson Ave. (© 800/228-5150 or 970/586-2358), charging $85 to $190 double in summer, and $55 to $135 double the rest of the year; and **Holiday Inn,** U.S. 36 and Colo. 7 (P.O. Box 1468), Estes Park, CO 80517 (© 800/803-7837

Campground	Elev.	Total Sites	RV Hookups	Dump Station	Toilets	Drinking Water
Inside the Park						
Aspenglen	8,230	54	0	No	Yes	Yes
Glacier Basin	8,600	150	0	Yes	Yes	Yes
Longs Peak	9,400	26	0	No	Yes	Yes
Moraine Park	8,150	247	0	Yes	Yes	Yes
Timber Creek	8,900	100	0	Yes	Yes	Yes
Near the Park's East Side						
Estes Park KOA	7,500	84	62	Yes	Yes	Yes
Meeker Park	8,600	29	0	No	Yes	No
National Park Resort	8,200	92	88	Yes	Yes	Yes
Olive Ridge	8,350	55	0	No	Yes	Yes
Spruce Lake RV Park	7,622	110	110	Yes	Yes	Yes
Near the Park's West Side						
Elk Creek	8,400	70	33	Yes	Yes	Yes
Green Ridge	8,500	77	0	Yes	Yes	Yes
Stillwater	8,350	129	20	Yes	Yes	Yes
Willow Creek	8,130	35	0	No	Yes	Yes
Winding River	8,672	150	98	Yes	Yes	Yes

* Fees are winter/summer.

or 970/586-2332), charging $129 to $139 double in summer, and $75 to $119 double the rest of the year.

Allenspark Lodge Bed & Breakfast

Colo. 7 Business Loop (P.O. Box 247), Allenspark, CO 80510. ✆ **303/747-2552**. 14 units (7 with private bathroom). $65–$135 double. Rates include breakfast. AE, DISC, MC, V. Children 14 and over welcome.

We especially enjoy the historic ambience of this three-story lodge, built in 1933 of native stone and hand-hewn ponderosa pine logs. The lodge is located 16 miles south of Estes Park at the southeast corner of the national park, and all rooms offer mountain views and original handmade 1930s pine furniture. Guests share the Great Room and its stone fireplace, Ping-Pong and videos in the recreation room, and books in the library. Complimentary afternoon and evening coffee, tea, and

cookies are served. There is also a hot tub, self-service laundry, conference rooms, an espresso coffee shop, and a wine and beer bar.

Alpine Trail Ridge Inn

927 Moraine Ave., Estes Park, CO 80517. ✆ **800/233-5023** or 970/586-4585. Fax 970/586-6249. www.alpinetrailridgeinn.com. 48 units. TV TEL. First 3 weeks of May and mid-Sept to mid-Oct $52–$81; late May to mid-June and mid-Aug to mid-Sept $64–$92; mid-June to mid-Aug plus holidays and special events $81–$108. AE, DC, DISC, MC, V. Closed mid-Oct to Apr.

The Alpine offers a variety of accommodations in a friendly, casual atmosphere. Seven units have shower only, the rest have tub-shower combos; and all have a refrigerator, a table, and upholstered chairs. Largest are the balcony units, with beamed cathedral ceilings, private balconies, and either two queen beds or

Showers	Fire Pits/ Grills	Laundry	Public Phone	Reserve	Fees*	Open
No	Yes	No	Yes	No	$18	May–Oct
No	Yes	No	Yes	Yes	$18	May–Oct
No	Yes	No	No	No	$12–$18	Year-round
No	Yes	No	Yes	Yes	$12–$18	Year-round
No	Yes	No	Yes	No	$12–$18	Year-round
Yes	No	Yes	Yes	Yes	$22–$30	Late Apr to mid-Oct
No	Yes	No	No	No	$6	Memorial Day to Labor Day
Yes	Yes	No	Yes	Yes	$23–$30	May–Sept
No	Yes	No	No	Yes	$12	Mid-May to Oct
Yes	Yes	Yes	Yes	Yes	$33–$35	Apr–Oct 15
Yes	Yes	Yes	Yes	Yes	$18–$24	May–Oct
No	Yes	No	Yes	Yes	$12	May–Oct
Yes	Yes	No	Yes	Yes	$12–$20	Year-round
No	Yes	No	No	No	$10	May–Oct
Yes	Yes	Yes	Yes	Yes	$20–$24	Mid-May to Sept

one king. The modern American decor is underlined with scenic or nature prints on the white walls. Standard units are fairly spacious and quite comfortable, with different combinations of king, queen, double, and twin beds. Even the smallest economy unit doesn't feel cramped, boasting a cabinlike decor with knotty pine and white stucco walls, but the views aren't quite as good as those of the standard and balcony units. Two family units are available.

Complimentary hot beverages are available in the mornings, and the on-site Sundeck Restaurant serves three meals daily, offering American cuisine with specialties such as fresh trout and prime rib. There is a heated outdoor pool (Memorial Day to mid-Sept) and a patio with picnic table. The trailhead for a 0.75-mile hiking/walking trail to the visitor center at the national park is adjacent to the motel. The owners are knowledgeable hikers and love to help with guests' hiking plans.

Aspen Lodge at Estes Park

6120 Colo. 7, Longs Peak Route, Estes Park, CO 80517. © **800/332-6867** (reservations only) from outside Colorado, or 970/586-8133. Direct from Denver © 303/440-3371. Fax 970/586-8133. www.aspenlodge.com. 59 units. June–Aug: 2-day minimum; packages include 3 meals, children's program, entertainment, and recreation (horseback riding extra). 2 days shared room $300 each adult, $180 each child 3–12, children under 3 free; single adult $380. 3 days shared room $450 each adult, $270 each child 3–12, children under 3 free; single adult $580. 7 days shared room $930 each adult, $610 each child 3–12, children under 3 free; single adult $1,345. Sept–May $79–$129 double per night for lodge rooms or 1-room cabins, including full breakfast. Holiday rates higher. Call for 2- and 3-room cabin rates. AE, DISC, DC, MC, V.

Among Colorado's top dude ranches, Aspen Lodge is a full-service Western-style resort, offering horseback riding, tennis, hiking, mountain biking, fishing, cross-country skiing, ice-skating, snowshoeing, and a myriad of other activities. Guests stay in the handsome log lodge, which has a commanding stone fireplace in the lobby, or in cozy one-, two-, or three-room cabins nestled among the aspens. All lodge rooms have balconies, and most rooms and cabins have splendid views of Longs Peak, the tallest mountain in Rocky Mountain National Park. Trails on the lodge's 82 acres of grounds lead directly into the national park. Guests can also enjoy an outdoor heated swimming pool and hot tub, as well as the sports center, which has racquetball, a weight room, and a sauna. Meals are varied and delicious. The lodge also schedules numerous activities to entertain both children and teens. All lodge units are nonsmoking.

Baldpate Inn

4900 S. Colo. 7 (P.O. Box 4445), Estes Park, CO 80517. © **970/586-6151.** www.baldpateinn. com. 13 units (4 with private bathroom), 3 cabins. $85 double with shared bathroom, $100 double with private bathroom; $140 cabin. Rates include full breakfast. DISC, MC, V. Closed Nov–Apr.

This is a good choice for those who seek an old-fashioned, historic lodge experience. Built in 1917, the Baldpate was named for the novel *Seven Keys to Baldpate,* a murder mystery in which seven visitors believe each possesses the only key to the hotel. Guests today can watch several movie versions of the story, read the book, and add to the hotel's collection of more than 20,000 keys.

Each of the early-20th-century-style rooms is unique, with handmade quilts on the beds. Several rooms are a bit small, and although most of the lodge units share bathrooms (five bathrooms for nine units), each room does have its own sink. Among our favorites are the Mae West Room (yes, she was a guest here), with a red claw-foot bathtub and wonderful views of the valley; and the Pinetop Room, which has a whirlpool tub, canopy bed, and gas fireplace. Guests can enjoy complimentary refreshments by the handsome stone fireplace in the lobby, relax on the large sun deck, or view free videos on the library VCR. But it might be difficult to stay inside, once you experience the spectacular views from the inn's spacious porch and see the nature trails beckoning. In summer, an excellent soup-and-salad buffet is served for lunch and dinner daily. Smoking is not permitted.

Big Thompson Timberlane Lodge

740 Moraine Ave. (P.O. Box 387), Estes Park, CO 80517. © **800/898-4373** or 970/586-3137. Fax 970/586-3719. www.bigthompson timberlanelodge.com. 58 units. TV TEL. Summer $99–$335 per unit; off-season rates 20%–40% lower. AE, DISC, MC, V.

You won't find more choices than at this family-oriented facility, which offers cabins, cottages, motel suites, and log homes, with sleeping for from 1 to 10 people. We especially like the cozy historic cabins for 2, including several with VCRs and gas barbecue grills, that were built in the early 1900s. But there are also cabins that sleep up to 6, cottages and motel units that accommodate up to 6, and fully equipped log homes of from 1,000 to 1,200 square feet that can accommodate up to 10. Cabins have knotty pine walls, cottages have pine paneling, the motel suites have painted walls, and the log homes combine rustic-looking logs with painted walls. About half of the units have showers only (no tubs). All units have a refrigerator plus either a stove or a microwave. A few cabins have private hot tubs, and some have decks overlooking the river.

What makes this property especially attractive for families, in addition to family-size units, is the amenities, which include a grassy playground, an outdoor heated pool and a separate wading pool for young children, a large indoor whirlpool tub (there is also a separate "adults only" outdoor hot tub), picnic areas with barbecue grills, a self-serve laundry, and a stocked trout stream. A variety of toys, games, and books for kids are available for children to take to their rooms. Another plus is that it is set back from the highway, with attractively landscaped grounds.

Boulder Brook on Fall River

1900 Fall River Rd., Estes Park, CO 80517. © **800/238-0910** or 970/586-0910. Fax 970/ 586-8067. www.estes-park.com/boulderbrook. 16 suites. TV TEL. $89–$199 double; $129– $229 spa suites. AE, DISC, MC, V.

It would be hard to find a more beautiful setting for a lodging than this. Surrounded by tall pines, all suites face the Fall River, and all feature private riverfront decks and either full or partial kitchens. The spa suites are equipped with two-person spas, fireplaces, sitting rooms with cathedral ceilings, and king-size beds. One-bedroom suites offer king-size beds, window seats, two TVs, and bathrooms with whirlpool tub and shower combinations. There's also a year-round outdoor hot tub. VCRs, in-room movies, and fax service are available, and special-occasion packages can be arranged year-round.

Colorado Mountain School

351 Moraine Ave. (P.O. Box 1846), Estes Park, CO 80517. © **888/267-7783** or 970/586-5758. Fax 970/586-5798. www.cmschool. com. 18 dormitory beds. Per bed, summer $20; off season $17. AE, DISC, MC, V. Open year-round, but office hours are 8am–5pm.

Looking for a cheap, safe place to sleep? Here it is: coed dormitory-style rooms furnished in light woods, clean and well-maintained, with bunk beds, showers, and lockable private storage. Colorado Mountain School also offers a year-round guide service and rock climbing and mountaineering school (see "Climbing & Mountaineering," earlier in this chapter).

The Eagle Manor—A Bed and Breakfast Place

441 Chiquita Lane, Estes Park, CO 80517. © **888/603-3578** reservations, or 970/586-8482. Fax 970/586-1748. www.eaglemanor. com. 4 units. TV TEL. Late May to late Sept and holidays $135 double; rest of year $125 double. Rates include full breakfast. AE, DISC, MC, V.

This Tudor-style carriage house and manor was built in 1917 by Estes Valley pioneer Frank Bond. In the 1960s, a large living room with a gas fireplace, an indoor swimming pool/garden room, and additional living quarters were added. A Great Room links the old and new wings, and has leather-covered overstuffed chairs and sofas. There is a wet bar with complimentary soft drinks, a wood-burning fireplace, a big-screen TV, an antique billiards table, and freshly baked cookies in the evenings. Also on the premises are a sauna and an outdoor hot tub.

Rooms are spacious and comfortable. Three have queen beds and the fourth has two twins. The beds are comfortably firm and the towels are soft. The decor is a coordinated mixture of styles ranging from primitive to classic. A full breakfast of coffee, juice, eggs, breakfast meat, cereals, and breads is served in the formal dining room. Special dietary needs can be accommodated with advance notice.

Named for host Mike Smith's profession—he's a retired army colonel, or "eagle"—and personal interest in eagles, the establishment has magnificent photos of the birds scattered about the walls by noted wildlife photographers.

Estes Park Center/ YMCA of the Rockies

2515 Tunnel Rd., Estes Park, CO 80511-2550. © **970/586-3341,** or 303/448-1616 direct from Denver. 510 lodge rooms (450 with bathroom), 205 cabins. Lodge rooms summer $52–$120, winter $41–$92; cabins year-round $60–$239. YMCA membership required (available at a nominal charge). No credit cards. Pets are permitted in the cabins, but not the lodge rooms.

This extremely popular family resort is an ideal place to get away from it all, and serves as a great home base while exploring the Estes Park area. Lodge units are basic but perfectly adequate, and many were completely renovated in 1998. The spacious mountain cabins are equipped with two to four bedrooms (accommodating up to 10), complete kitchens, and phones; some have fireplaces. The center, which occupies 860 wooded acres, offers hiking, horseback riding, miniature golf, an indoor heated swimming pool and children's pool, fishing, bicycling (rentals available), three tennis courts, and cross-country skiing. Other facilities include conference rooms and a self-serve laundry.

Lake Shore Lodge

1700 Big Thompson Hwy., Estes Park, CO 80517. © **800/332-6867** or 970/577-6400. Fax 970/577-6420. www.lakeshorelodge.com. 54 units. June–Sept $149–$179 double, $239–$279 suite; Oct–May $109–$159 double, $199–$259 suite. Rates include full breakfast. AE, DISC, MC, V.

This handsome, brand-new lodge— it opened in the summer of 2000— produces a dilemma: Which to choose, a room looking out on the lake or one with a view of the mountains? Although there are practically no lodging properties in the Estes Park area that don't have some kind of wonderful view, there are few that offer such a choice. Of course, we want the inside to be nice, too, and the Lake Shore Lodge comes through in that category as well. Decorated in Western Victorian style, with

oak furnishings and rich colors of burgundy and forest green, the rooms are slightly larger than average, and third-floor units with vaulted ceilings feel especially spacious. All units have either two queen-size beds or a king and sofa sleeper, desks, refrigerators, coffeemakers, irons and ironing boards, safes, hair dryers, two phones, dataports, and a free daily newspaper. Second- and third-floor units have decks. The six suites have fireplaces, and two also have whirlpool tubs.

Owing to its role as a conference center, the lodge has an abundance of public areas, from outdoor decks to inside sitting areas with comfortable couches, fireplaces, and, of course, great views out large windows. There's a small indoor swimming pool and a hot tub, two saunas, an exercise room, a game room with video games and a pool table, and a self-serve laundry. The adjacent Lake Estes Marina offers boat rentals, and fishing is available from a boat or the lakeshore. There's a restaurant that serves three meals daily, a lounge, and conference facilities for up to 200. All rooms are nonsmoking. Now, about the dilemma of which room to choose. The first floor units have only limited views, so we'll eliminate those. For a standard room, the best views in our opinion are the third-floor rooms facing the lake. But, if you can afford them, the third-floor corner suites offer views of both the lake and the mountains.

Romantic RiverSong Inn

P.O. Box 1910, Estes Park, CO 80517. © **970/586-4666.** Fax 970/577-0699. www.romantic riversong.com. 9 units. $150–$275 double. Rates include full breakfast. MC, V. Not suitable for small children.

Couples looking for some quiet romance while visiting Rocky Mountain National Park will enjoy this 1920 Craftsman mansion on the Big Thompson River. The elegant bed-and-breakfast has 27 forested acres with hiking trails and a trout pond, as well as prolific wildlife and beautiful wildflowers. Very quiet, the inn is at the end of a country lane, the first right off Mary's Lake Road after it branches off U.S. 36 south. The comfortable bedrooms are decorated with a blend of antique and modern country furniture, and all have fireplaces. Some feature ornate brass beds and claw-foot tubs, and several boast jet tubs for two. Innkeeper Gary Mansfield, a mail-order minister, conducts weddings at the inn, or, for the athletically inclined, on snowshoe treks into the national park. Gourmet candlelight dinners are available by advance arrangement ($69 per couple), but you must supply your own alcoholic beverages. Smoking is not permitted.

Stanley Hotel

333 Wonderview Ave. (P.O. Box 1767), Estes Park, CO 80517. © **800/976-1377** or 970/586-3371. Fax 970/586-3673. www.stanley hotel.com. 135 units. TV TEL. Late May to mid-Oct $159–$209 double, $269–$299 suite; mid-Oct to late May $129–$179 double, $219–$249 suite. AE, DISC, MC, V.

Fans of the automotive, the historic, and the horrific should check out a stay at this hotel. F. O. Stanley, inventor of the Stanley Steam Car, opened this elegant, white-pillared hotel in 1909. The hotel, listed in the National Register of Historic Places, was built into solid rock and run entirely on electric power—including the kitchen. Stanley built a hydroelectric plant and water system to provide power and running water for both the hotel and Estes Park. Heat was the only thing the resort lacked back then, but happily that problem was remedied in 1979. The hotel has also gained fame as the inspiration for Stephen King's masterpiece of horror, *The Shining.*

The entire building, both guest rooms and public areas, was remodeled in 1997. As is often the case in historic hotels, the rooms differ in size and shape, and offer a variety of views of Longs Peak, Lake Estes, and surrounding hillsides. We prefer the deluxe rooms in the front of the hotel that provide

views into the national park. Furnishings are in keeping with the building's Georgian architecture, with 1920s-era mahogany pieces—some original and many reproductions. Amenities include a heated outdoor pool, tennis and volleyball courts, a sun deck, access to a nearby health club, shops, and a business center. And, of course, there's a vintage Stanley Steamer in the lobby.

The hotel has two restaurants. The **MacGregor Room** serves Continental cuisine with a Louisiana flair (dinner prices range from $19–$40), and the less formal **Cascades** serves American cuisine and offers live entertainment Friday and Saturday evenings. All baked goods are prepared fresh daily by the pastry chef. The hotel also has a gift shop and a museum, and tours of the hotel and museum are available by appointment (© **970/577-1903**).

GRAND LAKE AREA (WEST SIDE OF THE NATIONAL PARK)

For a complete listing of lodging and dining choices in the Grand Lake Area, contact the **Grand Lake Area Chamber of Commerce,** P.O. Box 57, Grand Lake, CO 80447 (© **800/531-1019** or 970/627-3372 for the chamber, 970/627-3402 for the visitor center; fax 970/627-8007; www.grandlakechamber.com).

Daven Haven Lodge

604 Marina Dr. (P.O. Box 1528), Grand Lake, CO 80447. © **970/627-8144.** Fax 970/627-5098. www.grandlakecolorado.com/dh. 16 cabins. TV. $78–$185 double; off-season midweek discounts available. DISC, MC, V. 3-night minimum required on reservations mid-June to Labor Day and holidays.

Those seeking seclusion and quiet in a mountain-resort setting will find happiness at this group of cabins, set among pine trees about 1 block from the lake. The lobby has a stone fireplace, some old Coke machines, and several antique jukeboxes—they actually play 78 RPM records! The cabins vary in size, sleeping from two to nine people; each has its own picnic table, and six have stone fireplaces. Decor and furnishings vary, but most have attractive light wood walls and both solid-wood and upholstered furniture. You'll also find a heated swimming pool (open in summer), a volleyball court, horseshoes, a bonfire pit, and a barbecue area. Complimentary morning coffee is served in summer. The **Back-Street Steakhouse** (see "Where to Dine," below) is open for dinner in summer.

Driftwood Lodge

12255 U.S. 34 (P.O. Box 609), Grand Lake, CO 80447. © **970/627-3654.** Fax same. www.rkymtnhi.com/driftwood. 17 units. TV TEL. Summer $70–$85 double, $95 suite; lower rates in winter. DISC, MC, V.

Located 3 miles south of town across from Shadow Mountain Lake, this comfortable and well-maintained establishment is a great bet if all you're looking for are basic motel rooms and suites. It has a swimming pool, sauna, whirlpool, and playground.

E.G.'s Garden Grill & Country Inn

1000 Grand Ave. (P.O. Box 1618), Grand Lake, CO 80447. © **970/627-8404.** Fax 970/627-0118. 3 units. TV TEL. $110–$145 double. Rates include full breakfast. AE, DISC, MC, V.

Located in downtown Grand Lake on the third floor of a 1910 building, this bed-and-breakfast is a good choice for those seeking a bit more personal attention than will be found in the area's standard motels and larger lodges. The three spacious, well-appointed rooms are individually decorated and have some antiques. Each has a whirlpool tub, a gas fireplace, combination TV/VCR units, and one queen- or king-size bed. For a room with a view, you can't do much better than this: two rooms overlook the lake, and the third faces the national park. Room service for lunch and dinner is available from E.G.'s Garden Grill downstairs (see "Where to Dine," below), and a full breakfast is delivered to your room each morning. All rooms are nonsmoking.

Grand Lake Lodge

15500 U.S. 34 (P.O. Box 569), Grand Lake, CO 80447. © **970/627-3967.** Fax 970/627-9495. www.grandlakelodge.com. 56 units. $70–$160 double. Minimum stays apply to most units, and all units on weekends and holidays. AE, DISC, MC, V. Closed mid-Sept to May. Take U.S. 34 north ½ mile from Grand Lake (or ½ mile south of the park entrance) and turn east (watch for their sign) onto the entrance road.

At an elevation of 8,769 feet, Grand Lake Lodge brags about having Colorado's "favorite front porch," and we have to admit that the lodge's veranda offers spectacular panoramic views of Grand Lake—both the town and the lake—and the surrounding mountains. Established in 1921, the Lodge has been owned and operated by three generations of the Ted L. James family since 1953. It offers excellent service and food in a delightful rustic setting, with sleeping quarters in modern cabins scattered among the pines beyond the Main Lodge.

Decor and furnishings vary, but most have Southwest-style bed coverings and upholstery and walls of wood-grain paneling. Units range from single rooms (that sleep two) in a duplex cabin, to two rooms with fully equipped kitchenettes and either gas heat or a Franklin stove (these units sleep four to six). There's a large outdoor heated pool, hot tub, decks, playground, picnic area with grills, riding stables, volleyball, horseshoes, and hiking trails; recreation room with games, Ping-Pong, pool table, and laundry facilities; large gift shop, bar, and restaurant (see "Where to Dine," below).

The Inn at Grand Lake

1103 Grand Ave. (P.O. Box 1590), Grand Lake, CO 80447. © **800/722-2585** or 970/627-9234. 17 units. TV TEL. $60–$70 double; 10%–20% less in spring and fall. DISC, MC, V.

For modern lodging with an Old West feel, stay at this restored historic building, originally built in 1881 as Grand Lake's courthouse and jail. Rooms have a variety of bed combinations, and several sleep up to six. They're equipped with Western-style furniture and have ceiling fans, white stucco walls, and American Indian–motif draperies and bedspreads. Over half the units have refrigerators and microwaves. About half of the units have shower-tub combinations, and the rest have showers only. The best views are on the street side of the building. The inn is located in the center of town, about a half block from the lake.

Where to Dine

There are no dining facilities inside the park.

ESTES PARK AREA (EAST SIDE OF THE NATIONAL PARK)

The Dunraven Inn

2470 Colo. 66. © **970/586-6409.** Reservations highly recommended. Main courses $7–$32. AE, DISC, MC, V. Sun–Thurs 5–10pm; Fri–Sat 5–11pm; closes slightly earlier in winter. ITALIAN.

The eclectic decorations here include various images of the Mona Lisa, from a mustachioed lady to opera posters, plus autographed dollar bills posted in the lounge area. House specialties are scampi; linguine with clam sauce; veal parmigiana, chicken cacciatore; and Dunraven Italiano, which is a char-broiled sirloin steak in a sauce of green, red, and yellow peppers, with black olives, mushrooms, and tomatoes. Fresh fish is served most evenings, and vegetarian plates are also available. There's a good wine list, and a separate smokers' room leaves the main dining room entirely smoke-free.

Estes Park Brewery

470 Prospect Village Dr. © **970/586-5421.** Sandwiches and salads $4.95–$6.95; dinner main courses $9.95–$16. AE, DC, DISC, MC, V. Summer daily 11am–midnight; closes earlier in winter. AMERICAN.

Pizzas, burgers, sandwiches—including meatball and grilled turkey—and bratwurst made with the brewery's own beer are the fare here. Vegetarians can order a veggie burger and a variety of salads. In addition, a number of full dinners are also offered, ranging from barbecued chicken to Rocky Mountain rainbow trout to steak. The brewery offers about 10 fresh beers at any given time, specializing in Belgian-style ales. It also produces an excellent India pale ale and an especially pleasant stout. Even children are welcome in the tasting room, where they can sample the brewery's own root beer and cream soda—on tap, of course.

Grumpy Gringo

1560 Big Thompson Ave. (U.S. 34). © **970/586-7705.** www.grumpygringo.com. $5–$15. AE, DISC, MC, V. Daily 11am–10pm summer; slightly shorter hours in winter. Closed last week of Jan and 1st week of Feb. On U.S. 34, 1 mile east of the junction of U.S. Hwy. 34 and 36. MEXICAN.

Dine in style at this classy Mexican restaurant without breaking your bank. The private booths, whitewashed plaster walls, green plants and paper poppies, and a few choice sculptures provide an atmosphere usually associated with higher-cost dining. And although the food is excellent and portions are large, the prices are surprisingly low. Choose from several different burritos, or order the enchilada olé, a mammoth entree made up of three different enchiladas: cheese, beef, and chicken. The fajitas—either chicken or beef—are delicious. There are six sauces to choose from, each homemade, and rated mild, semi-hot, or hot. Burgers and sandwiches are also offered, and there's a children's menu. The house specialty drink is the Gringo Margarita—made with Jose Cuervo gold tequila from an original (and secret) recipe. The full bar also offers frozen fruit margaritas, about a dozen premium tequilas, a good selection of beer—including Mexican—and wine.

Molly B

200 Moraine Ave. © **970/586-2766.** Reservations recommended for dinner. Main courses $3–$7 breakfast, $5–$8 lunch, $8–$17 dinner. AE, MC, V. Thurs–Tues 6:30am–3pm year-round; plus 4–9pm May–Oct. AMERICAN.

The friendly staff makes you feel right at home in this busy, casual restaurant, which, along with the freshly prepared home-style food, makes this a must-stop for us when we're in Estes Park. Located in an older building, the dining room has light-colored pine walls and tables that help provide a down-home atmosphere. It's especially popular at breakfast, with specialties such as the sunrise stuffer—a large tortilla filled with scrambled eggs, potatoes, cheese, and spicy chorizo. Lunch and dinner selections include vegetarian entrees, fresh seafood, pasta, prime rib, and steak. Desserts are made in-house, and full liquor service was recently added. Patio seating, providing good people-watching along the noisy street, is available in warm weather.

Timberline Family Restaurant

451 S. St. Vrain Ave. © **970/586-9840.** Sun brunch $4.50–$12; dinner main courses $6.50–$21. AE, DISC, MC, V. Sun brunch 10am–2pm; dinner daily 4–10pm. AMERICAN.

Friendly service and good home-style cooking are the hallmarks of the Timberline. The pleasant, light-pine paneled dining room has a mountain-lodge decor, complete with a moss rock fireplace, local and regional artwork, and three-dimensional, petroglyph-like figures. For dinner we particularly recommend the Rocky Mountain trout, one of the charbroiled steaks, or the coconut shrimp served with a spicy marmalade sauce. The menu also includes American standards such as liver and onions and Western favorites such as chicken-fried steak. A local favorite is the Timberline salad—a mixture of fresh garden greens topped with mandarin orange, pear slices, and Parmesan cheese, and served with raspberry vinaigrette dressing. Grilled chicken can be added to the salad if you like. Among homemade desserts we suggest the coconut cream pie. The popular Sunday brunch offers a good selection of breakfast and lunch items including omelets, eggs Benedict, fried chicken, and grilled salmon. The entire property is nonsmoking.

GRAND LAKE AREA (WEST SIDE OF THE NATIONAL PARK)

Back-Street Steakhouse

In the Daven Haven Lodge, 604 Marina Dr. © **970/627-8144.** Reservations recommended in summer and on winter weekends. Main courses $14–$28. DISC, MC, V. Summer and Christmas holidays Sun–Fri 5–9pm, Sat 5–10pm; winter Wed–Sat 5–9pm. Closed Nov and Apr. STEAKS.

This cozy, country inn–like restaurant offers fine dining in a down-home atmosphere. Steaks—from the 8-ounce filet mignon to the 20-ounce porterhouse—are all USDA choice beef, cooked to perfection. We especially like the Jack Daniel's pork chops (breaded, baked, and served with a creamy Jack Daniel's mushroom sauce), which were featured in *Bon Appétit* magazine. Also on the menu are pasta, chicken, and fish dishes, plus slow-roasted prime rib.

Chuck Hole Cafe

1131 Grand Ave. © **970/627-3509.** $2.95–$6.25. No credit cards. Daily 7am–2pm year-round. AMERICAN.

Eat traditional fare while surrounded by historic photos and prints at this small cafe, which offers good, home-style food at reasonable prices. The place has a Western atmosphere and serves breakfast items such as omelets and pancakes, and quick lunches including burgers and deli-style sandwiches.

E.G.'s Garden Grill

1000 Grand Ave. © **970/627-8404.** Main courses $7–$12 lunch, $8–$25 dinner. AE, DISC, MC, V. Summer daily 11am–10pm; call for winter hours. NEW AMERICAN/SOUTHWESTERN.

If you want to experience innovative American cuisine served in a congenial setting, it would be hard to top this eatery. The large stone fireplace, trellised ceiling, and spacious outdoor beer garden give this restaurant a warm and comfortable atmosphere. The menu offers creative variations on traditional American dishes, often with a Southwestern flair. Although the menu changes seasonally, house specialties usually include items such as mustard catfish with jalapeño tartar sauce and jicama slaw, shrimp enchiladas, tortilla crusted ruby red trout, and Barb's babyback ribs with E.G.'s homemade barbecue sauce. There are also pizza, sandwiches, soups and salads, daily seafood specials, and a fairly extensive wine list.

Picnic & Camping Supplies

The **Country Supermarket,** 900 Moraine Ave., Estes Park (© 970/586- 2702), is located ¾ mile from the Beaver Meadows entrance to the park in a small shopping center. The store has a good stock of groceries, including fresh meats and produce; a deli and an ATM machine; ice and firewood; and a large RV-accessible parking lot. Outside the Fall River Entrance Station, adjacent to the new Fall River Visitor Center, **Rocky Mountain Gateway,** 3450 Fall River Rd. (© 970/577-0043), contains a large gift shop; a restaurant; a convenience store with groceries, camping supplies, clothing, ice, and firewood; and a self-serve laundry.

Those looking for camping and outdoor sports equipment should stop at **Outdoor World,** downtown at 156 E. Elkhorn Ave. (© 970/586-2114), which sells all sorts of backpacking equipment and outdoor gear, including hiking boots, outdoor clothing, maps, and supplies. It also rents equipment, such as backpacks, day packs, hikers' baby carriers, sleeping bags, tents, and snowshoes. Another good choice for outdoor gear is **Estes Park Mountain Shop,** 358 E. Elkhorn Ave. (© 800/504-6642 or 970/586-6548), which has a store with sales and rental departments and an indoor climbing gym.

In Grand Lake, on the park's west side, the **Mountain Food Market,** 400 Grand Ave. (© 970/627-3470), and the **Circle D,** 701 Grand Ave. (© 970/627-3210), have good selections of groceries and picnic supplies. You can get picnic and fishing supplies, and almost anything else you might need, at **Grand Lake Pharmacy,** 1123 Grand Ave. (© 970/627-3465).

31

SAGUARO NATIONAL PARK

by Don & Barbara Laine

THE STATELY SAGUARO CACTUS, SYMBOL OF THE AMERICAN SOUTHwest, is the king here, dominating the entire landscape. Although Saguaro National Park preserves a sizable chunk of the Sonoran Desert, it is one of America's few national parks dedicated to protecting one specific plant. Saguaros are plants with personalities. They often look human, standing tall and proud, their arms reaching toward the sky or pointing the way. Though some achieve heights of 50 feet and weigh up to 8 tons, saguaros grow slowly. It usually takes them 15 years to reach 1 foot in height, and they don't flower or produce fruit until they're about 30. They take about 100 years to reach a height of 25 feet. Their maximum life span is about 200 years.

One of the hottest and driest parts of North America, the Sonoran Desert also has an amazing variety of life, more than any other of the continent's deserts. Although the saguaro forests dominate the horizon—and are consequently the first thing we notice here—this desert is home to dozens of other cacti, grasses, shrubs, flowers, and trees, as well as several hundred species of birds, mammals, and reptiles. Many of them are uniquely adapted to the demanding environment of this dry land. For instance, javelinas, those odd-looking piglike animals, have mouths so tough they can bite through prickly pear cactus pads in search of moisture; and kangaroo rats never need to drink—they extract all the water they need from seeds.

The park is composed of two separated sections. The Tucson Mountain District, also called Saguaro West, covers 32 square miles of Sonoran Desert west of the city of Tucson; while the Rincon Mountain District, also called Saguaro East, covers 104 square miles of saguaro forest, desert, foothills, and mountain terrain on the east side of Tucson. The two sections are about 30 miles apart.

Both districts have scenic drives and trails, with good wildlife viewing and bird-watching. When the rain cooperates, there are also spectacular shows of wildflowers and cactus blooms in the springtime.

Avoiding the Crowds. Annual visitation is about 3.3 million people, with Saguaro West receiving the greater number. The park's busiest time is from

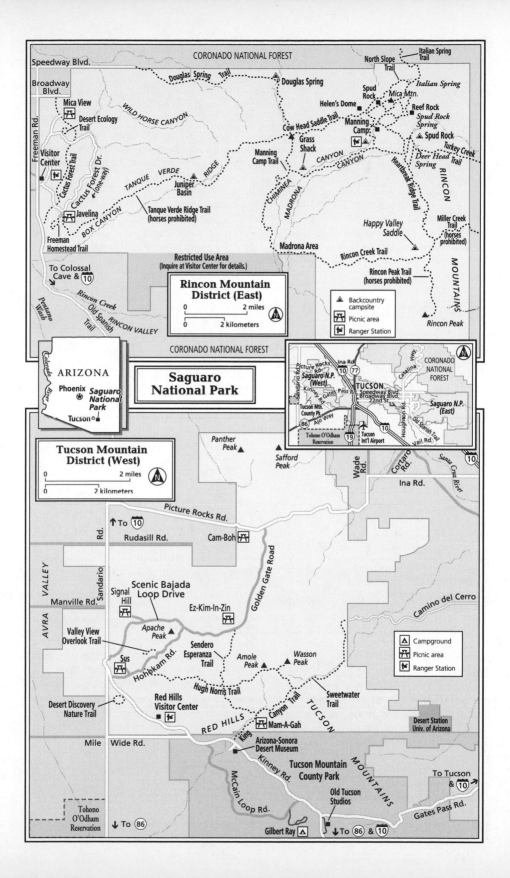

Saguaro National Park

Rincon Mountain District (East)

Speedway Blvd.
Broadway Blvd.
Freeman Rd.

CORONADO NATIONAL FOREST

Douglas Spring Trail
Douglas Spring
North Slope Trail
Italian Spring Trail
Italian Spring
Spud Rock
Mica Mtn.
Reef Rock
Helen's Dome
Spud Rock Spring
Mica View
Desert Ecology Trail
WILD HORSE CANYON
Cow Head Saddle Trail
Manning Camp
Spud Rock
Visitor Center
Cactus Forest Dr. (one-way)
Cactus Forest Trail
TANQUE VERDE RIDGE
Grass Shack
Turkey Creek
Deer Head Spring
Heartbreak Ridge Trail
RINCON
Manning Camp Trail
CHIMINEA
CANYON
MADRONA
CANYON
Juniper Basin
Javelina
Tanque Verde Ridge Trail (horses prohibited)
BOX CANYON
Happy Valley Saddle
Miller Creek Trail (horses prohibited)
MOUNTAINS
Freeman Homestead Trail
Madrona Area
Rincon Creek Trail
Restricted Use Area
(Inquire at Visitor Center for details.)
To Colossal Cave & 10
Pantano Wash
Rincon Creek
Old Spanish Trail
RINCON VALLEY
Rincon Peak Trail (horses prohibited)
Rincon Peak

Rincon Mountain District (East)
0   2 miles
0   2 kilometers

▲ Backcountry campsite
⛱ Picnic area
Ranger Station

CORONADO NATIONAL FOREST

ARIZONA

Colorado River
Phoenix
Saguaro National Park
Tucson

Tucson Inset

Picture Rocks Rd.
Ina Rd.
10   77
Saguaro N.P. (West)
CORONADO NATIONAL FOREST
Santa Cruz River
Sandario Rd.
Kinney Rd.
Gates Pass Rd.
TUCSON
Speedway Blvd.
Broadway Blvd.
22nd St.
Saguaro N.P. (East)
Houghton Rd.
Tucson Mtn. County Pk.
Ajo Hwy.
86
19
Tucson Int'l Airport
Old Spanish Trail
Vail Rd.
Tohono O'Odham Reservation
10

Tucson Mountain District (West)
0   2 miles
0   2 kilometers
N

Panther Peak
Safford Peak
Wade Rd.
Cortaro Rd.
Ina Rd.
10

Picture Rocks Rd.
To 10
Rudasill Rd.
Cam-Boh
Golden Gate Road
Camino del Cerro

AVRA VALLEY
Sandario Rd.
Manville Rd.
Signal Hill
Scenic Bajada Loop Drive
Ez-Kim-In-Zin
Valley View Overlook Trail
Apache Peak
Sus
Sendero Esperanza Trail
Amole Peak
Wasson Peak
Hohokam Rd.
Hugh Norris Trail
Sweetwater Trail
TUCSON
Desert Discovery Nature Trail
Red Hills Visitor Center
King Canyon Trail
Mam-A-Gah
Desert Station Univ. of Arizona
RED HILLS
Mile Wide Rd.
King
Arizona-Sonora Desert Museum
MOUNTAINS
Kinney Rd.
Tucson Mountain County Park
To Tucson & 10
McCain Loop Rd.
Old Tucson Studios
Gates Pass Rd.
Tohono O'Odham Reservation
To 86
Gilbert Ray
To 86 & 10

▲ Campground
⛱ Picnic area
Ranger Station

Christmas through Easter. Those wanting to avoid crowds should visit at other times, although all visitors who plan on hiking will want to avoid summer's extreme heat. Fall through mid-December can offer the best of both worlds: fewer crowds and lower temperatures.

Another way to avoid crowds, even at the busiest times, is to hike. Although the park gets a lot of visitors during the first 3 months of the year, many confine their activities to scenic drives and short walks. Within 15 minutes you can easily leave the crowds behind.

Just the Facts

GETTING THERE & GATEWAYS

Saguaro National Park is located in southern Arizona on the fringes of **Tucson,** about 116 miles southeast of Phoenix. There are two parts to the park: the **Rincon Mountain District (Saguaro East)** and the **Tucson Mountain District (Saguaro West),** each about 15 miles from downtown Tucson. To get to Saguaro East from Tucson, head east on Broadway Boulevard and turn right on Old Spanish Trail, which meanders in a southeast direction to the park. Watch for signs for the park as you go.

To get to Saguaro West from Tucson, go west on Speedway Boulevard, which first becomes Gates Pass Road and then ends at Kinney Road, where you turn right and continue to the park entrance. From Phoenix, follow I-10 southeast toward Tucson and watch for signs directing you to the park.

The Nearest Airport. Located 6 miles south of downtown, **Tucson International Airport** (© 520/573-8000; www.tucsonairport.org) is served by most major airlines and all major car-rental agencies, whose toll-free numbers are in the appendix.

INFORMATION

Contact the **Superintendent, Saguaro National Park,** 3693 S. Old Spanish Trail, Tucson, AZ 85730-5699 (© **520/ 733-5153** for the east side, 505/733-5158 for the west side; fax 520/733-5183; www.nps.gov/sagu). For information on other area attractions and services, contact the **Tucson Convention and Visitors Bureau,** 100 S. Church Ave., Tucson, AZ 85701 (© **800/638-8350** or 520/624-1817; www.visittucson.org).

Those particularly interested in the plants, animals, and geology of the park can get additional information from *Saguaro National Monument* by Doris Evans, published in 1993 by the Southwest Parks and Monuments Association.

VISITOR CENTERS

The park has two visitor centers, one in each district. On the west side of the park, in the Tucson Mountain District, the **Red Hills Visitor Center** contains a museum, an information desk, and a bookstore. The museum offers exhibits on desert life and a 15-minute slide program on the uniqueness and importance of deserts.

On the park's east side, in the Rincon Mountain District, the **visitor center** has similar facilities on a somewhat smaller scale. There's an excellent 15-minute video on the flora and fauna of the park, plus exhibits on saguaro and the world's deserts. Both visitor centers are open daily from 8:30am to 5pm year-round except Christmas.

FEES

Entry into the east district costs $6 per private vehicle, or $3 per person on foot or bike. Entry into the west district is free. Permits for backcountry camping cost $6 per campsite per night, and can be obtained in advance by writing the park, or at the Rincon Mountain District Visitor Center after arrival.

SPECIAL REGULATIONS & WARNINGS

Extreme heat, cactus spines, and poisonous reptiles are the main safety hazards

Tips from a Park Ranger

For those who have not experienced the Southwest's deserts, and particularly the Sonoran Desert of southern Arizona, Saguaro National Park can be an unusual experience, according to Tom Danton, the park's chief of interpretation.

"Many visitors are petrified," he says. "It's essential they stop at the visitor center to learn about the park before going out into it." The park environment, with its extreme heat and forests of saguaro, is alien to most people's experiences. Visitors can be even more frightened, Danton says, when they learn there are rattlesnakes, Gila monsters, and other poisonous creatures.

Among his suggestions for enjoying Saguaro West are hiking the 5.5-mile Hugh Norris Trail. "Within 30 minutes you feel like you're on the top of the world," he says. "You get a tremendous sense of accomplishment." For those with less ambition or time, he suggests the short Valley View Overlook Trail and the Desert Discovery Nature Trail, both also in the western district.

On the east side, he suggests the easy Freeman Homestead Trail, which passes by the site of a historic homestead, and the challenging Tanque Verde Ridge Trail, which, he says, is "steep and rugged, but gives you great views of Tucson and the mountains." To really be alone, he recommends trying some of the backcountry trails, where you'll be hiking from desert up into forests of Douglas fir and ponderosa pine.

The prettiest time at the park is spring, when the wildflowers and cacti are in bloom; but Danton himself would visit in midwinter because the weather is best for hiking. In winter there are also a large number of interpretive programs, such as moonlight walks, and you seldom see any poisonous reptiles.

Danton says that one problem for visitors going to Saguaro East is the lack of parking, even at the visitor center. He suggests that those with recreational vehicles use a smaller vehicle in the park, if they have one, or check with rangers about where to park their big rigs. There are pullouts just inside the Cactus Forest Drive where motor homes can be parked when there's no room in the parking lot.

here. Temperatures that soar to 115°F (46°C) in summer make hiking not only uncomfortable but also often dangerous. Those who insist on hiking in the hot months can minimize the dangers by starting very early in the day, perhaps by 4am, and getting off the trails by noon. Hikers should carry plenty of water and drink it even if they do not feel thirsty.

Cactus spines can be very painful, as anyone who's inadvertently backed into one while trying to line up a photo can tell you. The bites of rattlesnakes, Gila monsters, and various types of scorpions are poisonous. Park rangers recommend that you always look before putting your hands or feet under rocks or in other hidden spots, and that you use a flashlight at night to help avoid unwanted encounters. Weather-related dangers include lightning (stay off exposed ridges during thunderstorms) and flash floods (avoid drainages during rain).

SEASONS & CLIMATE

Summers are hot and winters comfortable, so the best time to visit, especially for hikers, is between October and April. Summer high temperatures are routinely between 100° and 115°F (38°C and 46°C), with lows generally in the

70s (20s Celsius). Visitors should also beware of the occasional torrential thunderstorms in July, August, and September, which bring dangers from lightning and flash floods.

During winter, high temperatures are usually in the 60s and low 70s (upper teens Celsius), with lows dropping into the upper 30s and 40s (single digits Celsius). Occasionally it snows, but the snow is almost always light and melts quickly. Winters are also known for periodic gentle rains, but most of the time it's sunny.

SEASONAL EVENTS

The best wildflower displays are from mid-March through mid-April. Cacti bloom a bit later—some kinds flower from mid-April through September, although the saguaro usually bloom from late April through June.

If You Have Only 1 Day

Because Saguaro National Park is composed of two separate sections, visitors should ideally spend at least a day or two at each district, starting with the visitor centers, then the short interpretive walks, and finally a serious hike or two. Those with only a day can either see a bit of each district or choose to explore one of them more thoroughly.

To see both sections of the park in 1 day, start in the **Tucson Mountain District** at the impressive new **Red Hills Visitor Center,** where you can examine the exhibits and try to get a handle on life in the Sonoran Desert. Check the bulletin board for the schedule of ranger-led activities; if your timing is right you can join a short guided walk on the **Cactus Garden Trail,** just outside the visitor center, which serves as an excellent introduction to the park. You can also take this short walk on your own. Then drive the 9-mile **Bajada Loop Drive** through a thick stand of saguaro, taking time for a short hike along the **Valley View Overlook Trail.** Those interested in early American Indians will want to take a slight detour off the Bajada Loop Drive to ponder the rock art on the **Signal Hill Petroglyph Trail.**

By now it should be lunchtime, so you can stop in one of the picnic areas if you happened to bring food, or at a restaurant in Tucson as you drive through on your way to the **Rincon Mountain District.** Stop at the visitor center as you re-enter the park—by now you may have a few questions for the rangers, such as, "What were those two big eyes staring out at me from a hole in that old saguaro?" (probably an elf owl). Then head out onto the 8-mile **Cactus Forest Drive** for an easy close-up look at a forest of saguaro. About a third of the way into the drive the road crosses the **Cactus Forest hiking trail,** where you can get out of your vehicle, stretch your legs, and walk a short way into the saguaro forest. If time remains, pull off at the Javelina Picnic Area access road and take a walk along the **Freeman Homestead Trail,** which offers good scenic views and a look at the remains of an old homestead.

Exploring the Park by Car

Each section of the park has its own scenic drive. Before you set out on one, consider buying one of the inexpensive booklets discussing the park's terrain and vegetation at the visitor centers. The 9-mile **Bajada Loop Drive** in the western section begins at the Red Hills Visitor Center and proceeds through a dense forest of saguaro cacti, offering scenic views. There are pullouts where you can get out of your vehicle for a close-up view of the saguaro, and a trailhead for the very worthwhile **Valley View Overlook Trail** (see "Day Hikes," below). Because 6 miles of the loop are gravel, those driving low-clearance vehicles or towing trailers should check on current conditions before starting.

In the eastern section of the park, the **Cactus Forest Drive** is a somewhat hilly and twisting 8-mile loop that wanders through a forest of saguaro. This one-way road is paved, and also provides access to picnic areas, several hiking trails, and short walks.

Organized Tours & Ranger Programs

Ranger-led guided walks, hikes, and talks take place year-round, although most occur from December through April. Activities vary, but might include an easy cactus or bird identification walk, a 4-mile hike through the desert, a video program on desert life, or slide shows on wildflowers or bats. Check at the visitor centers for schedules.

Historic & Man-Made Attractions

Both sections of the park contain impressive **rock art** believed to have been created by the Hohokam people, who lived here from about A.D. 700 to 1500. The best and easiest place to see rock art is on the Signal Hill Petroglyph Trail in the Tucson Mountain District. These petroglyphs (a type of rock carving) usually depict figures of humans and animals plus many abstract designs, such as wavy lines and combinations of circles and spirals.

The park also contains reminders of the miners and settlers who arrived in the late 1800s. The remains of the **Gould Mine,** active in the early 1900s, can be seen along the Sendero Esperanza Trail, in the Tucson Mountain District. In the Rincon Mountain District you can see what's left of an **adobe house** built in 1929 on the Freeman Homestead Trail, and several **limekilns,** built in about 1880, along the Cactus Forest Trail. See "Day Hikes," below.

Day Hikes

Desert hiking can be a killer, literally. Those planning to do any serious hiking at Saguaro National Park are strongly advised to talk with rangers about their plans before setting out, and then to carry at least a gallon of water per day per person. Rangers do not recommend hiking at all in the summer, when temperatures frequently reach a scorching 115°F (46°C). Because some of the longer trails are difficult to follow, hikers are advised to carry good topographic maps, available at the visitor centers.

TUCSON MOUNTAIN DISTRICT (SAGUARO WEST)

SHORTER TRAILS

Cactus Forest Trail

.15 mile RT. Easy. Access: Red Hills Visitor Center.

A level nature walk just outside the visitor center, this wheelchair-accessible trail is a good introduction to the park and the Sonoran Desert environment. Interpretive signs identify a variety of desert plants.

Desert Discovery Nature Trail

0.5 mile RT. Easy. Access: Kinney Rd., 1 mile northwest of the Red Hills Visitor Center.

This mostly level wheelchair-accessible trail has signs describing the plants, animals, and ecology of the Sonoran Desert. It also provides panoramic views of the Tucson Mountains.

Signal Hill Petroglyph Trail

0.25 mile RT. Easy. Access: North of Signal Hill picnic area, off Golden Gate Rd., 5 miles northwest of the Red Hills Visitor Center.

This trail zigzags up the side of a small hill to an area containing dozens of examples of American Indian rock art, believed to have been left by the Hohokam people between 500 and 1,300 years ago (see "Historic & Man-Made Attractions," above).

Valley View Overlook Trail

1.5 miles RT. Easy. Access: Bajada Loop Dr., 3½ miles north of the Red Hills Visitor Center.

Built by the Civilian Conservation Corps in the 1930s, this trail passes through cactus forests and two washes before climbing to a ridge for splendid views of the surrounding desert and mountains.

LONGER TRAILS
Hugh Norris Trail

4.9 miles one-way. Strenuous. Access: Bajada Loop Dr., 2½ miles north of the Red Hills Visitor Center.

The longest and most difficult in the park's Tucson Mountain District, this trail begins with a series of switchbacks that lead to a ridge overlooking a huge forest of saguaro cactus. From there it offers good panoramic views and passes old mines and intriguing rock formations. The trail climbs another series of switchbacks before finally making its way to the top of Wasson Peak, at 4,687 feet, from which you generally have spectacular views of Tucson and the surrounding mountains. The trail has a total elevation gain of 2,087 feet.

King Canyon Trail

3.5 miles one-way. Moderate to strenuous. Access: On Kinney Rd., directly across from the Arizona-Sonora Desert Museum, about 2 miles southwest of the Red Hills Visitor Center.

This trail combines with the last 0.3 mile of the Hugh Norris Trail to take you from 2,800 feet in elevation to the top of Wasson Peak, at 4,687 feet, the highest point in the Tucson Mountains. Along the trail are petroglyphs believed to have been created by the Hohokam people, some open mine shafts that you'll want to avoid, and panoramic views once you get to the higher elevations. The trail is rocky in spots so good hiking boots are recommended.

Sendero Esperanza Trail

3.2 miles one-way. Moderate. Access: Golden Gate Rd., about 6 miles northeast of the Red Hills Visitor Center.

There are several steep switchbacks as the trail leaves an old mining road and climbs to a ridge, with spectacular views in all directions, before finally dropping to the Mam-A-Gah Picnic Area and a junction with the King Canyon Trail. Along the way it passes the remains of the Gould Mine, which was enthusiastically but unproductively worked in the early part of the 1900s.

RINCON MOUNTAIN DISTRICT (SAGUARO EAST)

SHORTER TRAILS
Desert Ecology Trail

0.25 mile RT. Easy. Access: Cactus Forest Dr., east of the Mica View Picnic Area.

Interpretive signs along this paved wheelchair-accessible walkway explain how plants and animals of the Sonoran Desert make the most of the limited amount of water available.

Freeman Homestead Trail

1 mile RT. Easy. Access: Off Cactus Forest Dr., on the Javelina Picnic Area access road.

This walk through gently rolling desert terrain offers good panoramic views as well as close-up views of saguaro, ocotillo, and other desert plants. Along the way, you'll find several interpretive signs describing desert life and the remains of the Freeman Homestead, a three-room adobe house built by Safford Freeman in 1929. All that's left now is a mound of sand from the adobe bricks and a portion of the foundation.

LONGER TRAILS
Cactus Forest Trail

5 miles one-way. Easy. Access: Near the east end of Broadway Blvd., just east of Freeman Rd.

This sandy, level trail, which can also be accessed from two points on the Cactus Forest Drive, is simply a very pleasant walk though a forest of cactus, primarily saguaro; a variety of other desert plants, such as paloverde and mesquite; as well as large beehive-shaped lime kilns, dating from about 1880.

Douglas Spring Trail

6 miles one-way (to Douglas Spring Campground). Strenuous. Access: East end of Speedway Blvd.

This trail through the foothills of the Rincon Mountains is considered strenuous, starting off fairly level but gradually becoming steeper, and then alternating between steep and flat sections all the way to Douglas Spring Campground. Along the way you'll find lots of cactus, especially prickly pear, and some interesting rock formations. Signs of damage from a devastating 1989 fire can still be seen here, as well as the results of revegetation. The trail continues beyond the campground, providing access to other backcountry trails. You need a backcountry permit to stay overnight at the campground (see "Camping," below).

Tanque Verde Ridge Trail

6.9 miles one-way (to Juniper Basin Campground). Strenuous. Access: Javelina Picnic Area off Cactus Forest Dr.

This trail offers splendid panoramic views as it follows a ridgeline northeast into the wilderness area. You'll see saguaro, cholla, prickly pear, and other cactus for a while, and then pinyon, juniper, and some oak as you climb higher into the foothills. The Juniper Basin Campground, at 6,000 feet, is 2,900 feet higher than the trailhead. Although the trail continues, this is a good spot for day-hikers to turn around. See "Exploring the Backcountry," below, for information on forging ahead.

Exploring the Backcountry

All the park's backcountry hiking and camping opportunities are in the Rincon Mountain District (the eastern section), which includes the 59,930-acre **Rincon Mountain Wilderness.** Varying considerably in elevation, this area contains both hot desert sprinkled with saguaro and other cacti, and relatively cool forests of pine and mixed conifer. The main access routes into the backcountry are the **Douglas Spring Trailhead** and **Tanque Verde Ridge Trailhead,** which are discussed above. From these two trails you can access more than 100 miles of interconnecting

Especially for Kids

Kids will enjoy the "Please Touch" tables at both district visitor centers. The park also has several **Junior Ranger Programs,** in which children complete a variety of projects and activities to earn Junior Ranger badges and certificates.

trails, as well as the park's six backcountry campgrounds (see "Camping," below). Dirt roads lead to several other trailheads; check with park rangers for directions and current conditions. Rangers strongly suggest that those going into the backcountry carry topographical maps, which can be purchased at either visitor center. Backcountry camping requires a permit (see "Fees," above).

Other Sports & Activities

Biking. Bikes are permitted on the scenic drives in both districts. **Arizona Off-Road Adventures** (© 520/822-9830; www.azora.com) rents front- and full-suspension mountain bikes for $30 to $40 per day, a price that includes delivery and pickup, safety gear, and trail maps. The company also offers guided biking tours, from half-day excursions to multiple-day adventures.

Horseback Riding. Horseback riding is permitted on most trails in both districts of the park, although horses are not allowed off-trail. Horses may be kept overnight in the backcountry campgrounds in the Rincon Mountain District. At Manning Camp there's a corral; at the other backcountry campgrounds, riders should secure horses with a picket rope slung between two trees. Get details from park rangers.

Big Sky Rides, 6501 W. Ina Rd. at Desert Trails Resort (© **520/744-3789**), offers guided horseback riding trips through the park and the Catalina Mountains, including sunrise and sunset tours. A 1-hour ride costs $25; 2-hour trips are $40.

Wildlife Viewing & Bird-Watching. Both sections of the park offer abundant opportunities for wildlife and bird-watching, although because Saguaro East has a greater range of elevations, and therefore climates, you'll see a larger variety of animals there.

In both sections of the park, look for holes punched in saguaro cacti by Gila woodpeckers and gilded flickers. These finicky birds sometimes make several cavities before settling on one as home for the year. They always punch out a new home when they return the following year. The extra holes are taken over by other desert inhabitants, including cactus wrens, Lucy's warblers, and cute little elf owls.

Among other birds you're likely to see in both sections of the park are black-throated sparrows, brown towhees, verdin, brown-crested flycatchers, Costa's hummingbirds, roadrunners, mourning doves, white-winged doves, Gambel's quail, American kestrels, and red-tailed hawks. In the eastern part of the park you'll also see rufous-crowned sparrows, olive warblers, yellow-rumped warblers, solitary vireos, American robins, pygmy nuthatches, Steller's jays, mountain chickadees, violet-green swallows, broad-tailed hummingbirds, and Cooper's hawks.

Mammals commonly seen in the park include desert cottontails, Harris ground squirrels, round-tailed ground squirrels, striped skunks, javelina, mule deer, and southern long-nose bats, which pollinate saguaro flowers while feeding on their nectar. You may also spot white-tailed deer in the higher elevations of Saguaro East. Reptiles commonly seen include zebra-tailed and western whiptail lizards, gopher snakes, and king snakes. In the desert and foothill areas, watch out for the many western diamondback rattlesnakes, which are poisonous.

Camping

INSIDE THE PARK

There are no drive-in campgrounds within the national park, but backpackers will find six backcountry campgrounds in the Rincon Mountain Wilderness. All the campgrounds have three sites each except Manning Camp, which has six. Water is available at Manning year-round, but water availability at the other campgrounds is spotty—ask a ranger. To avoid illness, you must treat backcountry water before drinking. Backcountry camping is permitted only in designated campsites. Pick up the $6 permit at the Rincon Mountain District Visitor Center or by writing to the park.

Campground	Elev.	Total Sites	RV Hookups	Dump Station	Toilets	Drinking Water
Cactus Country						
R.V. Resort	3,300	246	246	Yes	Yes	Yes
Catalina State Park	2,700	48	24	Yes	Yes	Yes
Gilbert Ray	2,600	139	133	Yes	Yes	Yes
Molino Basin	4,370	37	0	No	Yes	No
Rose Canyon	7,200	74	0	No	Yes	Yes
Spencer Canyon	8,000	68	0	No	Yes	Yes

NEAR THE PARK

Four miles south of the park's Tucson Mountain District is **Gilbert Ray Campground,** just off Kinney Road on McCain Loop Road, operated by the Pima County Parks and Recreation Department (✆ **520/883-4200,** or 520/740-2690 in the summer). It offers an attractive desert mountain environment of saguaro, prickly pear, cholla, mesquite, and paloverde, with well-maintained gravel sites. The sites are first-come, first-served. No wood fires are permitted and RV hookup sites offer electricity only.

Convenient for visitors to the national park's Tucson Mountain District, the campground at **Catalina State Park,** 9 miles north of Tucson on Ariz. 77 (✆ **520/628-5798**), has nicely spaced, well-shaded sites, an abundance of rock squirrels, and splendid views of the Santa Catalina Mountains to the southeast.

There are also campgrounds in the Santa Catalina District of the **Coronado National Forest** (✆ **520/749-8700**), to the north of the national park's Rincon Mountain District. Located along the Catalina Highway, they include **Molino Basin,** about 18 miles northeast of Tucson, which has virtually no facilities and can accommodate trailers up to 22 feet only; **Rose Canyon,** about 33 miles northeast of Tucson, which offers fishing at Rose Canyon Lake; and **Spencer Canyon,** located near the top of Mount Lemmon about 39 miles northeast of Tucson, which can accommodate trailers up to 18 feet only. Of these, only a few sites at Rose Canyon can be reserved by calling ✆ **877/444-6777.**

Among commercial campgrounds in the area are **Cactus Country RV Resort,** 10195 S. Houghton Rd. (✆ **800/777-8799**), at I-10 Exit 275, which has large spaces, some shade trees, and attractive desert landscaping. All RV sites have full hookups including cable TV. There are only a small number of tent sites. Campers have access to an outdoor heated pool, a hot tub, modem hookups, a game room, a playground, shuffleboard, and horseshoes.

Where to Stay

There are no accommodations inside the park.

NEAR THE PARK

In addition to the lodgings listed below, you'll find dozens of chain motels along I-10, including the **Days Inn Tucson,** 222 S. Freeway (Exit 258; ✆ **520/791-7511**), charging $55 to $129 double; **Motel 6–Tucson/Congress Street,** 960 S. Freeway (Exit 258; ✆ **520/628-1339**), and **Motel 6–Tucson/22nd Street,** 1222 S. Freeway (Exit 259; ✆ **520/624-2516**), both charging $38 to $55 double; and **Super 8–Tucson/Downtown,** 1248 N. Stone St. (Exit 257; ✆ **520/622-6446**), charging $47 to $92 double. Among

Showers	Fire Pits/ Grills	Laundry	Public Phone	Reserve	Fees	Open
Yes	Yes	Yes	Yes	Yes	$17–$27	Year-round
Yes	Yes	No	Yes	No	$10–$15	Year-round
No	No	No	No	No	$7–$13	Year-round
No	Yes	No	No	No	$8	Oct–Apr
No	Yes	No	No	Yes	$10–$15	Apr–Oct
No	Yes	No	No	No	$8–$12	May–Oct

hotels near the airport are the **Best Western Inn at the Airport,** 7060 S. Tucson Blvd. (© **800/772-3847** or 520/746-0271), with winter rates from $69 to $139 double, $49 to $89 double at other times; and **Super 8–Tucson/East,** 1990 S. Craycroft Rd. (Exit 265 off I-10; © **520/790-6021**), charging $46 to $90 double. See the appendix for a list of the national chain toll-free numbers.

Casa Tierra

11155 W. Calle Pima, Tucson, AZ 85743. © **866/254-0006** or 520/578-3058. Fax 520/578-8445. www.casatierratucson.com. 4 units. $135–$205 double; $200–$325 suite. 2-night minimum stay. Rates include a full vegetarian breakfast. DISC, AE, MC, V. Closed mid-June to mid-Aug.

If you've come to Tucson to really be a *part* of the desert, this is an excellent choice. A modern adobe home surrounded by 5 acres of cacti and paloverde, Casa Tierra is on the west side of Saguaro National Park's Tucson Mountain District, and has fabulous views of a saguaro landscape and the surrounding mountains. Surrounding a central courtyard with a desert garden and a fountain is a candlelit, covered portal—a seating area where guests congregate. The rooms have queen beds, brick floors, and private patios; the family suite includes two bedrooms, a bathroom, a dining area, and a library area. Breakfast here is truly gourmet, ranging from stuffed French toast with prickly pear syrup to green-chile polenta. In terms of facilities, there's an exercise room and a common area with TV, stereo, and games. Another perk: an outdoor whirlpool spa that makes a perfect stargazing spot at night (a telescope is provided)!

Hotel Congress

311 E. Congress St., Tucson, AZ 85701. © **800/722-8848** or 520/622-8848. Fax 520/792-6366. www.hotcong.com. 40 units. A/C TEL. $35–$80 double. Student discount available. Lower rates for shared hostel rooms. AE, MC, V.

Located in the heart of Tucson's downtown arts district, the Hotel Congress once hosted John Dillinger. Today it operates as a youth hostel and budget hotel. Conveniently located near the Greyhound and Amtrak stations, this hotel is especially popular with students and European backpackers. The lobby has been restored to its original Southwestern elegance, and most of the hostel rooms have been recently renovated. Some bathrooms have tubs only and others have showers only. There are computers with high-speed Internet access in the lobby, a restaurant, and an appropriately Western bar. At night the **Club Congress** is a popular and loud dance club. Guests can pick up free earplugs at the front desk if they want to sleep through the noise.

Radisson Suites Tucson

6555 E. Speedway Blvd., Tucson, AZ 85710. © **800/333-3333** or 520/721-7100. Fax 520/886-7968. www.radisson.com. 304 suites. A/C TV TEL. Mid-Sept to mid-Jan $144–$154 double; mid-Jan to mid-May $94–$114 double; mid-May to mid-Sept $75–$85 double. AE, DISC, MC, V. Pets accepted ($25 nonrefundable fee).

With surprisingly reasonable rates throughout the year, this all-suite hotel is a good choice for those who want plenty of space. The five-story brick building is arranged around two lushly landscaped garden courtyards, one of which has a large pool and a hydra-spa (a fixed-jet whirlpool). The pool and gardens, along with the full breakfast and evening cocktail hour, are the best reasons to stay here. The two-room suites feature contemporary furnishings, and all have refrigerators, coffeemakers, hair dryers, and irons and ironing boards (most also have microwaves). Summer 2003 saw the start of a $4.5-million renovation. The hotel has a restaurant (American) serving three meals a day, an exercise room (and access to a nearby health club), room service, valet/laundry service, and a coin-operated laundry.

Smuggler's Inn

6350 E. Speedway Blvd. (at Wilmot), Tucson, AZ 85710. ℂ **800/525-8852** or 520/296-3292. Fax 520/722-3713. www.smugglersinn.com. 150 units. A/C TV TEL. Jan–Mar $99 double, $129 suite; Apr–May $89 double, $109 suite; June–Sept $69 double, $89 suite; Oct–Dec $79 double, $99 suite. Rates include complimentary continental breakfast and welcome cocktail. AE, DC, DISC, MC, V.

Built around an attractive garden and pond, the Smuggler's Inn is a comfortable and economically priced hotel, with neatly trimmed lawns and tall palm trees that provide a tropical look. Guest rooms are spacious, and all have modern furnishings and a balcony or patio. The newly renovated rooms are beautifully appointed. Amenities include coffeemakers, video games on the TVs, a cocktail lounge, golf and health club privileges available, and an outdoor pool, whirlpool, and putting green.

SunCatcher Bed & Breakfast

105 N. Avenida Javelina, Tucson, AZ 85748. ℂ **877/775-8355** or 520/885-0883. Fax 520/885-0883. www.thesuncatcher.com. 4 units. A/C TV TEL. Winter $125–$145 double; summer $80–$100 double. Rates include full breakfast. AE, DISC, MC, V. Located 2½ miles east of Houghton Rd. via Broadway.

Located on the east side of Tucson, about 3 miles from the entrance to the Rincon Mountain District of Saguaro National Park, this stylish, sunny home is set amid 5 acres of picturesque desert that's just a short walk from a trail into the park. Innkeepers Janos Siess and Nicola Young provide lodging that balances modern convenience with refreshing tranquillity. All units have queen beds, refrigerators, and VCRs (guests can borrow from a large video library). The rooms are named after famed hotels from all over the world: the Connaught features a marble-floored bathroom and a fireplace; the Oriental has an in-room hot tub. The decor of the common areas is contemporary Southwestern. The inn's great room

is spectacular, with a majestic mesquite and oak bar and a copper-hooded fireplace. A second-story balcony, a heated outdoor pool, and a whirlpool spa add to the relaxing atmosphere. There's also a corral for those who bring their horses to ride into the park.

Where to Dine

There are no restaurants inside the park.

NEAR THE PARK

Anthony's in the Catalinas

6440 N. Campbell Ave. ℂ **520/299-1771.** Reservations highly recommended. Main courses $7.50–$15 lunch, $20–$38 dinner. AE, DC, MC, V. Mon–Fri 11:30am–2:30pm and 5:30–10pm; Sat–Sun 5:30–10pm. CONTINENTAL.

If you head north on Campbell Avenue up into the foothills of the Catalinas, you'll come to this modern hacienda-style building overlooking the city. Anthony's exudes Southwestern elegance from the moment you drive under the portico and let the valet park your car. The waiters are smartly attired in tuxedos and the guests are almost as well dressed. Quiet classical music plays in the background, and the lights of the city below twinkle through the windows. In such a rarefied atmosphere you'd expect only the finest meal, and that's what you get. Smoked salmon is a fitting beginning, followed by lamb Wellington, baked in puff pastry with pâté and prosciutto. At 80 pages, the wine list is quite likely the most extensive in the city. The pastry selection may tempt you, but, if it's available, don't miss out on the best part of a meal: the day's soufflé (order early).

El Charro Cafe

311 N. Court Ave. ℂ **520/622-1922.** www.elcharrorestaurant.com. Reservations recommended for dinner. Main courses $6–$15. AE, DC, DISC, MC, V. Sun–Thurs 11:30am–10pm; Fri–Sat 11:30am–11pm. MEXICAN.

Located in an old stone building in El Presidio Historic District, El Charro claims to be the nation's oldest family-operated Mexican restaurant that has been continuously open—it's been serving authentic Tucson-style Mexican food for almost 80 years. A porch has been glassed in for a greenhouse-like dining area overlooking the street, and there's also dining downstairs. Look at the roof of El Charro as you approach, and you might see a large metal cage containing beef drying in the sun. This is the main ingredient in *carne seca,* El Charro's well-known specialty, rarely found outside the Tucson area. The chimichangas and enchiladas are also hard to beat, as is the volcanic Tompopo Salad—a conical heap of shredded lettuce, grilled chicken, and black olives on a tostada shell.

Other El Charro branches can be found in the Tucson International Airport (© **520/573-8222**) and at 6310 E. Broadway (© **520/745-1922**).

Evangelo's

4405 W. Speedway Blvd. © **520/792-3055.** Reservations recommended. Main courses $13–$25. AE, DC, DISC, MC, V. Daily 11:30– 9pm. Bar open later. FRENCH/MEDITERRANEAN.

Located near Saguaro West, this restaurant looks a bit like a lost Italian villa searching for the Mediterranean Coast, with saguaros standing next to cypresses out front. Inside, plush carpets, comfortable brocade chairs, and big windows allow diners to enjoy desert views in comfort. There are three menus—lunch, tapas, and dinner—where you'll find everything from lamb to fowl to octopus. Veal remains the specialty of the house—as was the case in the restaurant's previous incarnation as Scordato's—and the veal Oscar, topped with fluffy crabmeat and tangy hollandaise, is simply mouthwatering. There's also an extensive wine list and a cigar room that doubles as a tapas bar.

Little Anthony's Diner

7010 E. Broadway Blvd. © **520/296-0456.** Burgers and sandwiches $4–$7. MC, V. Mon 11am–9pm; Tues–Thurs 11am–10pm; Fri 11am–11pm; Sat 8am–11pm; Sun 8am–10pm. AMERICAN.

This is a great place for kids, although kids-at-heart will also enjoy the 1950s music and decor. The staff is good with children, and there's a video-game room and a rocket ship outside to ride. How about a Jailhouse Rock Burger or Hound Dog Hot Dog with a tower of onion rings? Or an old-fashioned banana split or a hand-dipped shake? Daily specials and bottomless soft drinks make feeding the family fairly inexpensive. Beer and wine are also served. Most nights after 5pm there's a DJ along with the dinner.

The Tack Room

7300 E. Vactor Ranch Trail (off Sabino Canyon Rd., about ½ mile north of Tanque Verde Rd.). © **520/722-2800.** Reservations recommended. Main courses $25–$34. AE, DC, DISC, MC, V. Tues–Sun 6–11pm. Closed Mon. SOUTHWESTERN/AMERICAN.

The Tack Room is Tucson's most prestigious restaurant, and dining here is a very special experience. Housed in an older Southwestern-style hacienda with an atmosphere of casual elegance, The Tack Room has a bevy of tuxedoed waiters who attend to your every need, with service that is both attentive and discreet. Diners are pampered from the time they sit down and taste the little bites of marinated salads to the moment the last bit of dessert is savored. Particularly tasty are the plump Guaymas shrimp subtly seasoned with orange zest and garlic, the perfectly grilled salmon with papaya salsa, and the crisp yet succulent duck. Coffee comes with a condiment tray that includes whipped cream and crumbled Belgian chocolate.

Tucson McGraw's

4110 S. Houghton Rd. ⓒ **520/885-3088.** Reservations accepted for large parties only. Main courses $7–$14. AE, MC, V. Tues–Sat 11am–10pm; Sun–Mon 11am–9pm. Bar open later. AMERICAN.

Owned by Lex McGraw since the early 1980s, this eatery is now a southeast Tucson institution, and a favorite of the Saguaro National Park staff. A friendly vibe exudes from the pastel roadhouse atmosphere, and the menu revolves around meat—ribs, burgers, steaks— and cold beer. (There's a horse trough packed with bottled suds and ice in the bar.) The margaritas are some of Tucson's best, as are the old-fashioned, homemade desserts: The cream puffs and coconut cream pie are standouts. On cooler days, the patio is a great place to enjoy a desert breeze and a nice view.

Picnic & Camping Supplies

Although there are no stores within the park's boundaries, you'll find plenty of places to stock up on supplies in the Tucson area. Recommended for basic groceries are the numerous **Safeway** supermarkets, including the one at 7110 N. Oracle Rd., Tucson (ⓒ **520/575-0949**), which has a deli, bakery, pharmacy, and liquor department, in addition to a good selection of groceries. You'll also find pretty much any food and beverages you need at the area's several **Albertson's Food & Drug Stores,** including the outlet at 6363 E. 22nd St. (ⓒ **520/571-9091**).

For camping, hiking, backpacking, and mountain-biking gear, as well as tips on outdoor recreation locations, stop at **Summit Hut,** 5045 E. Speedway Blvd., Tucson (ⓒ **520/325-1554**), open 7 days a week and offering both sales and rentals. Another good bet for supplies and equipment is **Popular Outdoor Outfitters,** 6315 E. Broadway Blvd. (at Wilmot; ⓒ **520/290-1644**), also open 7 days a week.

32

SEQUOIA & KINGS CANYON NATIONAL PARKS

by Don & Barbara Laine and Eric Peterson

IN THE HEART OF THE SIERRA NEVADA MOUNTAINS, JUST SOUTH OF Yosemite, are Sequoia and Kings Canyon national parks, home to the largest Giant Sequoia trees in the world, vast wilderness areas, and a deep, beautiful canyon. Sequoia and Kings Canyon are separate adjacent parks that are managed jointly, and combined they exceed Yosemite in size. Their peaks stretch across 1,350 square miles and include the 14,494-foot Mount Whitney, the tallest point in the continental United States. The parks are also home to the Kaweah Range, a string of dark, beautiful mountains nestled amid the Sierra, and three powerful rivers: the Kings, Kern, and Kaweah. Despite their size and scenic beauty, these two parks attract less than half the number of Yosemite's annual visitors, making them an appreciated alternative for those looking to avoid huge crowds.

The parks owe their existence to a small band of determined conservationists in the mid-1800s. Alarmed by the wholesale destruction of the region's sequoia forests, these farsighted people pushed to make the area a protected park. Finally, Sequoia National Park was created in 1890, along with the tiny General Grant National Park, which was established to protect Grant Grove. In 1926, the park was expanded eastward to include the smaller Kern Canyon and Mount Whitney, and in the 1960s Kings Canyon was finally protected. In 1978, Mineral King was added to Sequoia's half of the park.

Avoiding the Crowds. Though Sequoia and Kings Canyon national parks receive far fewer visitors than nearby Yosemite, they still get crowded, especially in the summer. Luckily, there's a lot of space here, so it's relatively easy to find solitude. To get the most from the parks, while avoiding traffic, try to visit before Memorial Day or after Labor Day, keeping in mind that snow can limit access in the high elevations. Fall provides some scenic color often missing from the California landscape. As always, a trip to the backcountry will help avoid the crowds.

You can also try taking one of the dead-end roads into the parks. Mineral King, South Fork and, to a lesser extent, Cedar Grove, all lack the through traffic prevalent on the larger highways.

Just the Facts

There are two main entrances to the parks. Calif. 198 via Visalia and the town of Three Rivers leads to the **Ash Mountain Entrance** in Sequoia National Park. Calif. 180 via Fresno leads straight to the **Big Stump Entrance** near Grant Grove in Kings Canyon National Park. There are also three dead-end entrance roads open only in the summer: the Kings Canyon Highway (a continuation of Calif. 180) to **Cedar Grove** in Kings Canyon National Park, and two smaller roads to **Mineral King** and to **South Fork,** both in the south part of Sequoia National Park.

The parks are roughly equidistant (5 hr. by car) from both San Francisco and Los Angeles. The Ash Mountain Entrance is 36 miles from Visalia, or about an hour away. The Big Stump Entrance is 53 miles from Fresno, about 1½ hours.

The Nearest Airports. The closest major airport is **Fresno-Yosemite International Airport** (© 559/621-6699; www.flyfresno. org), 53 miles from the Big Stump Entrance in Kings Canyon. It's served by Allegiant Air, America West Express, American and American Eagle, Delta, Horizon, Skywest, and United Express, and you'll find most major car rental companies here. **Visalia Municipal Airport** (© 559/713-4201; www.flyvisalia. com), 36 miles from the Ash Mountain Entrance, is served by United Express with daily flights to L.A. (direct) and San Francisco (via Fresno).

Toll-free reservation numbers for airlines and car-rental companies are in the appendix.

Contact **Sequoia & Kings Canyon National Parks,** 47050 Generals Hwy., Three Rivers, CA 93271-9651 (© 209/ 565-3341; www.nps.gov/seki).

There are three visitor centers in the parks, open year-round, where you can talk with rangers, see exhibits, and buy books and maps. The biggest is in Sequoia National Park at **Lodgepole,** 4½ miles north of Giant Forest Village, with exhibits on geology, wildlife, air quality, and park history. The **Foothills Visitor Center,** just inside the Ash Mountain Entrance on Calif. 198, includes exhibits on the chaparral region's ecosystem. The visitor center in **Grant Grove,** Kings Canyon National Park, includes exhibits on logging and the role of fire in the forests. Also, the new **Giant Forest Museum,** which opened in late 2001, has exhibits on giant sequoias, and there's also a small visitor center at **Cedar Grove** that's open only during the summer.

It costs $10 per motor vehicle ($5 for individuals on foot or bike) to enter the parks for up to a week. Park campgrounds charge $12 to $20 a night.

The roads in the parks are steep and winding, and those in RVs will find it easiest to come via Calif. 180 from Fresno. All groundwater should be boiled for 3 minutes before drinking. Rattlesnakes are common; look where you step and touch. In the foothills, check your clothes frequently for ticks. Beware also of black bears. When camping, store all food in lockers and put all garbage in bear-proof containers.

Sequoia and Kings Canyon, for the most part, share a climate that varies considerably depending on the region of the park. A good rule of thumb is to remember that the higher you go, the cooler it

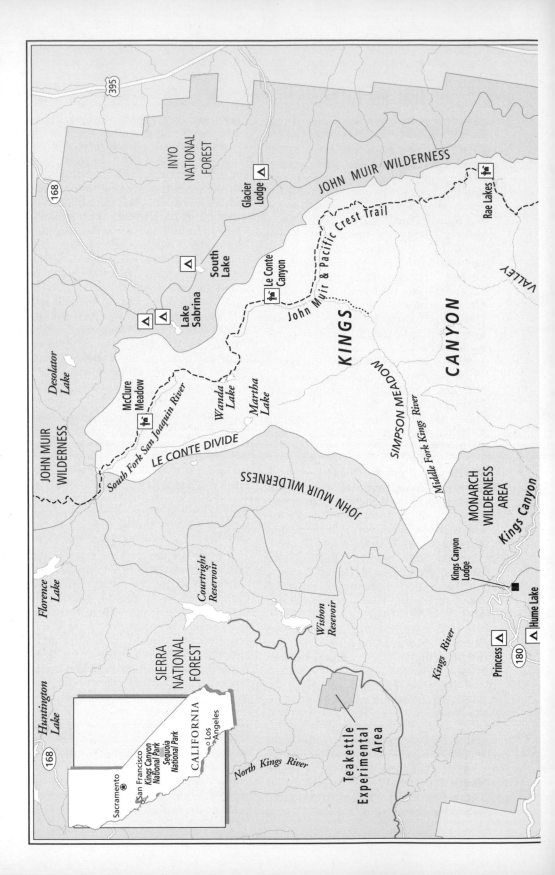

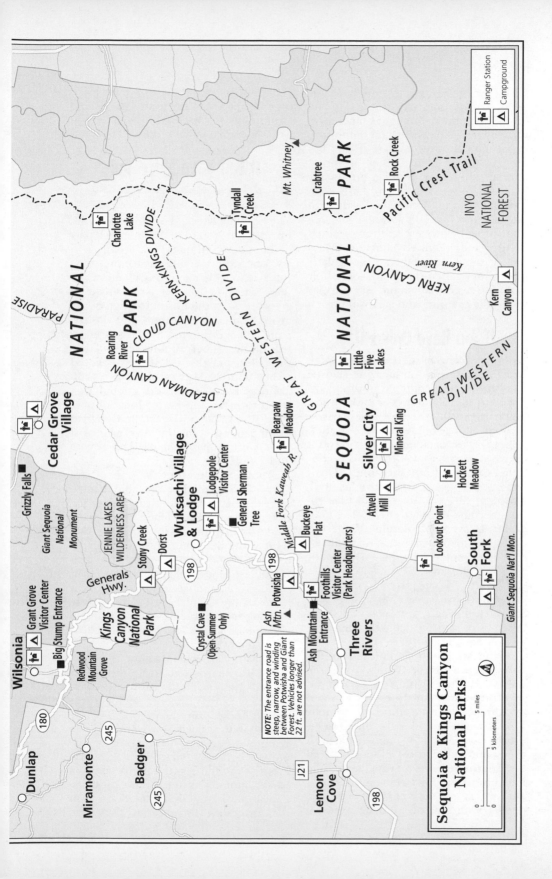

Sequoia & Kings Canyon National Parks

Ranger Station
Campground

INYO NATIONAL FOREST

Pacific Crest Trail

Mt. Whitney
Crabtree
Rock Creek
Tyndall Creek

Charlotte Lake

KERN-KINGS DIVIDE

GREAT WESTERN DIVIDE

Kern River

KERN CANYON

Kern Canyon

Little Five Lakes

GREAT WESTERN DIVIDE

PARADISE

NATIONAL PARK

Roaring River

CLOUD CANYON

DEADMAN CANYON

Bearpaw Meadow

SEQUOIA NATIONAL PARK

Silver City

Mineral King

Hockett Meadow

Cedar Grove Village

Grizzly Falls

Giant Sequoia National Monument

JENNIE LAKES WILDERNESS AREA

Wuksachi Village & Lodge

Lodgepole Visitor Center

General Sherman Tree

Middle Fork Kaweah R.

Buckeye Flat

Atwell Mill

Lookout Point

Stony Creek

Dorst

198

198

South Fork

Giant Sequoia Nat'l Mon.

Wilsonia

Grant Grove Visitor Center

Big Stump Entrance

Kings Canyon National Park

Redwood Mountain Grove

Generals Hwy.

Crystal Cave (Open Summer Only)

Ash Mtn.

Potwisha

Ash Mountain Entrance

Foothills Visitor Center (Park Headquarters)

Three Rivers

NOTE: The entrance road is steep, narrow, and winding between Potwisha and Giant Forest. Vehicles longer than 22 ft. are not advised.

Dunlap

180

Miramonte

245

Badger

121

Lemon Cove

198

245

0   5 miles
0   5 kilometers

gets. During the summer, temperatures at lower elevations can climb into the 90s (30s Celsius) or higher, and drop into the 50s (10s Celsius) at night. Afternoon temperatures average in the 60s and 70s (upper teens Celsius) in spring and fall, and again, evenings are usually cool. Afternoon showers are fairly common year-round. Winter days average in the 40s and 50s (10s Celsius) and seldom drop below zero, although much of the land is buried beneath several feet of snow. Remember, a particularly wet winter often leads to incredibly stunning wildflowers and spectacular waterfalls in spring and early summer.

If You Have Only 1 Day

Eighty percent of park visitors come here on day trips—an amazing statistic considering the geography of this place. Three to 4 days will do the park justice, but it is possible to take a short walk through a grove of big trees in one afternoon. Day-trippers should stick to Grant Grove if possible—it's the most accessible. Coming from the south, Giant Forest is a good alternative as well, although the trip takes some time on the steep and narrow Generals Highway. Cedar Grove and Mineral King, two other destination points, are a bit farther afield and require an early start or an overnight stay.

Consider **driving from Giant Forest to Grant Grove,** or vice versa. It's about 2 hours through the park. Get your bearings by starting at a park visitor center—either the **Foothills Visitor Center** near the Ash Mountain Entrance or the **Grant Grove Visitor Center.** You'll see the varied climate within the park as you pass through dense forest to exposed meadows and then through scrubby foothills covered in oaks and underbrush. In spring and summer, much of the route is dotted by wildflowers, and the southern portion runs along the Kaweah River. This route also passes near two large stands of Giant Sequoias, one at Grant Grove and the other at Giant Forest. Both have easy trails looping through the majestic stands. At Grant Grove, a footpath passes lengthwise through a fallen sequoia.

If You Have More Time

SEQUOIA NATIONAL PARK

The best-known stand of sequoias in the world can be found in **Giant Forest,** part of Sequoia National Park. Named in 1875 by explorer and environmentalist John Muir, this park consists mostly of huge meadows and a large grove of giant trees. At the northern edge of the grove, you can't miss the **General Sherman Tree,** considered the largest living tree on the planet, although it is neither the tallest nor the widest. It is believed to be about 2,100 years old, **and it's still growing.** Every year, it adds enough new wood to make another 60-foot-tall tree. The tree is part of the 2-mile **Congress Trail,** a foot trail that includes groups of trees with names such as The Senate and The House.

Another interesting stop in Giant Forest is **Tharp's Log,** a cabin named after the first non–American Indian settler in the area, Hale Tharp, who grazed cattle among the Giant Sequoias and built a summer cabin in the 1860s from a fallen sequoia hollowed by fire. It is the oldest cabin remaining in the park.

You'll also encounter two kitschy items in the Giant Forest vicinity. **Tunnel Log** is a toppled tree that you can drive *through,* and **Auto Log** is a tree that you can drive *on.*

Nearby **Crescent Meadow** is a pristine clearing dotted with wildflowers and tall grasses. A trail wraps around the meadow. This is also the trailhead for several backcountry hikes.

Also in the area is **Moro Rock,** a large granite dome that offers one of the most spectacular views in the Sierra. From atop the rock, the high-elevation, barren mountains in the Kaweah Range appear dark and ominous. Snow caps the ridgeline throughout the year.

Although the cliffs appear towering and steep, they are actually smaller than the summit of the Sierra, which is obscured from view. The walk to the top takes visitors up hundreds of stairs and requires about a half-hour to complete. At the top is a narrow, fenced plateau with endless views. During a full moon, the mountain peaks shimmer like silver.

South of the Giant Forest is the turnoff for **Crystal Cave,** one of more than 100 caves in the park and one of just 2 in the area that offer guided tours. (Boyden Cavern in the neighboring Giant Sequoia National Monument is the other.) The cave is composed of limestone that has turned to marble, and contains a wonderful array of cave formations, many still growing, that range from sharply pointed stalactites and towering stalagmites to beautiful flowing draperies. To reach the entrance, drive 7 miles down the narrow, winding road (RVs, trailers, and buses are prohibited), and the cave entrance is an additional half-mile walk down a steep path (which you'll have to hike up after your cave tour). The Sequoia Natural History Association conducts 45-minute tours daily between 11am and 4pm from mid-June to Labor Day, and less often in May and late September. Tickets are not sold at the cave, but rather at the Lodgepole and Foothills visitor centers. Cost is $9 for adults, $7 for seniors 62 and older, and $5 for children 6 to 12; admission is free for children under 6. A special **discovery tour** is offered in summer, Sunday through Friday at 4:15pm. It is less-structured, limited to 12 people, has a minimum age requirement of 13, and a fee of $16 per person. Information is available at visitor centers and by telephone (© **559/565-3759**). It gets cold underground, so take a sweater or jacket.

Lodgepole, the most developed area in both parks, lies just northeast of the Giant Forest on the Generals Highway. Here, you'll find the largest visitor center, a large market, several places to eat, the Walter Fry Nature Center (see "Especially for Kids," later in this chapter), a

laundry, and a post office. Nearby is Wuksachi Village, with a restaurant, lodge, and gift shop.

South of Giant Forest about 16 miles is the region of the park known as the **Foothills.** Located near the Ash Mountain Entrance, the Foothills has a visitor center, several campgrounds, and **Hospital Rock,** a large boulder with ancient pictographs that are believed to have been painted by the Monache Indians, who once lived here. Nearby are about 50 grinding spots once used to smash acorns into flour. A short trail leads down to a beautiful spot along the Kaweah River where the water gushes over rapids into deep, clear pools. Hospital Rock also has a picnic area.

Mineral King is a pristine, undeveloped region in the southern part of the park. This high-mountain valley was carved by glaciers and is bordered by the tall peaks of the Great Western Divide. To reach this area, patient drivers must follow the marked highway sign 3 miles outside Sequoia National Park's Ash Mountain Entrance. From the turnoff to Mineral King, it's a 28-mile trip that makes many tight turns and takes 1½ hours to drive. Trailers, RVs, and buses are not allowed. The road is closed in winter.

The rocky landscape in Mineral King is as colorful as a rainbow—red and orange shales mix with white marble and black metamorphic shale and granite. In winter, this area is prone to avalanches. The most prominent point in the area is **Sawtooth Peak,** which reaches 12,343 feet. Sawtooth and other peaks in this region resemble the Rocky Mountains more than the rest of the Sierra Nevada because they are made of metamorphic rocks. The trails in Mineral King begin at 7,500 feet and climb from there. Park rangers sometimes conduct hikes in this area.

KINGS CANYON NATIONAL PARK

With its rugged canyon, huge river, and desolate backcountry, Kings Canyon is a hiker's dream. It consists of Grant Grove and Cedar Grove, as well as portions of the Monarch Wilderness and Jennie Lakes Wilderness. *Note:* Between Grant Grove and Cedar Grove is a stretch of land not in the park, but in Giant Sequoia National Monument (see the sidebar later in this chapter).

Grant Grove is the most crowded region in either park. Not only is it located just a few miles from a main entrance, but the area is also a thoroughfare for travelers heading from Giant Forest to the south or Cedar Grove to the east. The grove was designated as General Grant National Park in 1890, and was incorporated into Kings Canyon National Park when it was created in 1940.

Here you'll find the towering **General Grant Tree** amid a grove of spectacular Giant Sequoias. The tree was discovered by Joseph Hardin Tomas in 1862 and named 5 years later to honor Ulysses S. Grant. It measures 267 feet tall and 108 feet around, and is thought to be the world's third-largest living tree, possibly 2,000 years old. This tree has been officially declared "The Nation's Christmas Tree" and is the cornerstone of the park's annual Christmas tree ceremony.

Two and a half miles southwest of the grove is the **Big Stump Trail,** an instructive hike that winds among the remains of logged sequoias. Since sequoia wood decays slowly, you'll see century-old leftover piles of sawdust that remain from the logging days. Nearby, **Panoramic Point** visitors can stand atop a 7,520-foot ledge and see across a large stretch of the Sierra, and across Kings Canyon. **Grant Grove Village** also has a restaurant, market, gift shop, and visitor center.

The **Cedar Grove** section of the park is known for its lush landscape, tumbling waterfalls, and miles upon miles of solitude. Getting to it is half the fun, as you drive through **Kings Canyon,** with the sheer granite canyon walls towering above you and the wild South Fork of the Kings River racing by. One mile east

of the Cedar Grove Village turnoff is **Canyon View,** where visitors can see the glacially carved U shape of Kings Canyon. Easily accessible nature trails in Cedar Grove include Zumwalt Meadow, Roaring River Falls, and Knapp's Cabin. **Zumwalt Meadow** is dotted with ponderosa pine and has good views of two rock formations, the **Grand Sentinel** and **North Dome.** The top of Grand Sentinel is 8,504 feet above sea level, while North Dome, which some say resembles Half Dome in Yosemite, towers over the area at 8,717 feet. The mile-long trail around the meadow is one of the prettiest in the park. Begin this walk at a parking lot 4½ miles east of the turnoff for Cedar Grove Village.

Roaring River Falls is a 5-minute walk from a parking area 3 miles east of the turnoff to the village. Even during summer and dry years, water crashes through a narrow granite chute into a cold, green pool below. During a wet spring, these falls are powerful enough to drench visitors who venture too close. **Knapp's Cabin** can be reached via a short walk from a turnoff 2 miles east of the road to Cedar Grove Village. Here, during the 1920s, Santa Barbara businessman George Knapp commissioned lavish fishing expeditions. This tiny cabin was used to store tons of expensive gear.

Ten miles west of Cedar Grove, in the national monument and back toward Grant Grove, is the entrance to **Boyden Cavern,** the only other cave in the area to host tours. Boyden is an especially scenic cave, known for a wide variety of formations including rare shields. Highlights include a flowstone formation known as Mother Nature's Wedding Cake, and the aptly named Baby Elephant formation. The cave is open daily April through October. Hours are 11am to 4pm in April, May, and October; and 10am to 5pm from June through September. Cost is $10 for adults and children age 14 and up, $5 for children ages 3 to 13, and free for children 2 and younger. Tickets can be purchased at the entrance. For information, contact

Sierra Nevada Recreation Corporation, P.O. Box 78, Vallecito, CA 95251 (© 866/762-2837 or 209/736-2708; fax 209/736-0330; www.caverntours.com).

In Cedar Grove is a small village with a store and gift shop, restaurant, laundry, showers, lodge, and campgrounds. This region of the park is often less crowded than others. It's closed from mid-November to mid-April.

The **Monarch Wilderness** is a 45,000-acre region protected under the 1984 California Wilderness Act. Part of it lies on the grounds of Sequoia National Forest and it adjoins wilderness in Kings Canyon National Park. It's small, tough to reach, and so steep that it seems more appropriate for mountain goats than human hikers. You're near the wilderness area when you pass Kings Canyon Lodge and Boyden Cave.

The **Jennie Lakes Wilderness,** at 10,500 acres, is tiny enough to hike through in a day, but it exhibits a variety of wilderness features, including the 10,365-foot Mitchell Peak and several wide, lowland meadows. This region lies between the Generals Highway and Highway 180, east of Grant Grove.

Organized Tours & Ranger Programs

Park rangers lead a variety of guided walks and hikes, and present other programs, with the greatest number held during the summer (check at visitor centers for the current schedule). In addition, the **Sequoia Natural History Association,** HCR 89, Box 10, Three Rivers, CA 93271-9792 (© 559/565-3759; fax 559/565-3728; www.sequoiahistory. org), offers a number of field seminars, with topics such as mountain wildflowers, the natural history of bristlecone pines, birding, photography, and an introduction to caving for teens. The programs run from 1 to 4 days, with fees from $45 to $50 for the 1-day seminars to $90 and up for multiday programs.

Day Hikes

NEAR GIANT FOREST

Big Trees Trail

1.5 miles RT. Easy. Access: Start at the Giant Forest Museum.

A scenic loop walk among the sequoias, Big Trees Trail skirts the edge of a pretty meadow and has trailside exhibits that explain why this area is such a good habitat for sequoias. There are usually abundant wildflowers in Round Meadow in early summer. The trail, which has a 60-foot elevation change, is wheelchair-accessible, and is mostly paved with some wooden boardwalk sections.

Congress Trail

2 miles RT. Easy. Access: General Sherman Tree, just off the Generals Hwy., 2 miles northeast of Giant Forest Village.

This walk circles some of Sequoia National Park's most well-known and loved giants. The trail is a paved loop with a 200-foot elevation gain. Here you'll find the General Sherman Tree, considered to be the largest living tree on earth. Other Giant Sequoias along this loop include the President, Chief Sequoyah, General Lee, and McKinley trees. The Lincoln tree is nearby. Several groups of trees include The House and The Senate. Try standing in the middle of these small clusters of trees to gain the perspective of an ant at a picnic.

Crescent Meadow Loop

1.8 miles RT. Easy. Access: Crescent Meadow parking area.

The meadow is a large, picturesque clearing dotted with high grass and wildflowers, encircled by a forest of firs and sequoias. The park's oldest cabin (Tharp's Log) is along this route as well. This is a particularly nice hike in early morning and at dusk, when the indirect sunlight allows those with a camera to take the best pictures.

Hazelwood Nature Trail

1 mile RT. Easy. Access: South side of the Generals Hwy., across from the road to Round Meadow.

Follow the signs for a pleasant, informative walk with exhibits that explain the relationship between trees, fire, and humans while winding among several stands of sequoias.

High Sierra Trail

9 miles RT. Moderate. Access: Near the restrooms at the Crescent Meadow parking area.

This is one gateway to the backcountry, but the first few miles also make a great day hike. Along the way are spectacular views of the Kaweah River's middle fork and the Great Western Divide. The trail runs along a south-facing slope and is therefore warm in spring and fall. Get an early start in summer. From the trailhead, cross two wooden bridges over Crescent Creek until you reach a junction. Tharp's Log is to the left, the High Sierra Trail to the right. Hike uphill and a bit farther on through the damage done by the Buckeye Fire of 1988, a blaze ignited by a discarded cigarette 3,000 feet below near the Kaweah River. After 0.75 mile you'll reach Eagle View, which offers a picturesque vision of the Great Western Divide. To the south are the craggy Castle Rocks.

Continue on to see Panther Rock, Alta Peak, and Alta Meadow. At 2.75 miles is a sign to the Wolverton Cutoff, a trail used as a stock route between the Wolverton trailhead and the high country. A bit farther on are Panther Creek and a small waterfall. At 3.25 miles is another fork of Panther Creek and above is the pink and gray Panther Rock. Follow a few more creeks to reach the last fork of Panther Creek, down a steep, eroded ravine.

Huckleberry Trail

4 miles RT. Moderate. Access: Hazelwood Nature Trail parking area, ⅓ mile east of Giant Forest Village on the Generals Hwy.

This is a great hike with a lot of beauty and not a lot of people. It passes through forest and meadow, near a 100-year-old cabin and an old American Indian village. The first mile of this hike takes you along the Hazelwood Nature Trail. Head south at each junction until you see a big sign with blue lettering that marks the start of the Huckleberry Trail. You pass a small creek and meadow before reaching a second sign to Huckleberry Meadow. The next mile is steep and runs beneath sequoias, dogwoods, and white firs. At the 1.5-mile point is a Squatter's Cabin, built in the 1880s. East of the cabin is a trail junction. Head north (left) up a short hill. At the next junction, veer left along the edges of Circle Meadow for about a quarter mile before you reach another junction. The right is a short detour to Bear's Bathtub, a pair of sequoias hollowed by fire and filled with water. Legend has it that an old mountain guide named Chester Wright once surprised a bear taking a bath here, hence its name. Continue on the trail heading northeast to the Washington Tree, almost as big as the General Sherman Tree, then on to Alta Trail. Turn west (left) to Little Deer Creek. On both sides of the creek are American Indian mortar holes. Some of the largest are 3 feet in diameter. At the next junction, head north (right) to return to the Generals Highway and the last leg of the Huckleberry Trail to the parking area.

Moro Rock

0.25 mile one-way. Moderate. Access: Moro Rock parking area.

This walk climbs 300 feet up 400 steps that twist along this gigantic boulder perched perilously on a ridge top. Take it slow. The view from the top is breathtaking. It stretches to the Great Western Divide, which looks barren and dark, like the end of the world, and mountains are often snowcapped well into summer. During a full moon, the view is even stranger, and more beautiful.

Moro Rock and Soldiers Loop Trail

4.6 miles RT. Moderate. Access: 30 yards west of the cafeteria at Giant Forest Village.

This hike cuts cross-country from the village to Moro Rock. Part of the early trail is parallel to a main road, but the trail quickly departs from the traffic and heads through a forest dotted with Giant Sequoias. A carpet of ferns occasionally hides the trail. It pops out at Moro Rock, and then it's just a quick heart-thumper to the top.

Trail of the Sequoias

6 miles RT. Moderate. Access: The northeast end of the General Sherman Tree parking area.

This trail offers a longer, more remote hike into Giant Forest, away from the crowds and along some of the more scenic points of this plateau. The first quarter mile is along the Congress Trail before heading uphill at Alta Trail. Look for signs that read Trail of the Sequoias. After 1.5 miles, including a 0.5-mile steep climb among Giant Sequoias, is the ridge of the Giant Forest. Here are a variety of specimens, young and old, fallen and sturdy. Notice the shallow root system of fallen trees, and the lightning-blasted tops of others still standing. The trail continues to Log Meadow, past Crescent Meadow and Chimney Tree, a sequoia hollowed by fire. At the junction with Huckleberry Trail, follow the blue and green signs north toward the General Sherman Tree and back to Congress Trail.

NEAR GRANT GROVE

Azalea Trail

3 miles RT. Easy. Access: Grant Grove Visitor Center.

From the visitor center, walk past the amphitheater to Sunset Campground and cross Calif. 180. The first mile joins the South Boundary Trail as it meanders through Wilsonia and crisscrosses Sequoia Creek in a gentle climb. After 1.5 miles is the third crossing of Sequoia Creek, which may be dry in late summer, but the banks are lush with ferns and brightly colored azaleas. Return the way you came.

Big Stump Trail

1 mile RT. Easy. Access: Picnic area near the entrance to Grant Grove from Kings Canyon.

This trail meanders through what was once a grove of Giant Sequoias. All that's left today are the old stumps and piles of 100-year-old sawdust. A brochure available at visitor centers (and at the trailhead during the summer) describes the logging that occurred here in the 1880s. To continue onward, see the Hitchcock Meadow Trail described below, which leads to Viola Fall.

Dead Giant Loop

2.25 miles RT. Easy. Access: The lower end of the General Grant Tree parking area, at a locked gate with a sign that reads NORTH GROVE LOOP.

The Dead Giant Loop and the North Grove Loop (described below) share the first 0.75 mile. The trail descends a fire road and after a quarter mile hits a junction. Take the lower trail. After another half-mile you'll break off from the North Grove Loop and head south around a lush meadow. It's another quarter mile to a sign that reads "Dead Giant." Turn west to see what's left of this tree. The trail climbs slightly as it circles a knoll and comes to Sequoia Lake Overlook. The lake was formed in 1899 when the Kings River Lumber Company built a dam on Mill Flat Creek. The water was diverted down a flume to the town of Sanger. During logging, millions of board feet of Giant Sequoias were floated down that flume to be finished at a mill in Sanger. The lumber company went bankrupt in a few years and sold the operation to new owners who moved it over to Converse Basin. The company then clear-cut Converse Basin, once the world's largest stand of sequoias. Continue around the loop back to the Dead Giant sign, then head back to the parking area.

General Grant Tree Trail

0.5 mile RT. Easy. Access: Grant Tree parking area 1 mile northwest of the visitor center.

The walk leads to the huge General Grant Tree, which is also the nation's only living national shrine. Signs help visitors interpret forest features.

Hitchcock Meadow Trail

3.5 miles RT. Easy. Access: Picnic area near the entrance to Grant Grove from Kings Canyon.

This trail takes you to pretty Viola Falls. The first half-mile mirrors the Big Stump Trail described above. From there, hike another quarter mile to Hitchcock Meadow, a large clearing actually in Sequoia National Forest that is surrounded by sequoia stumps. Notice the small sequoias in this area—these are the descendants of the Giant Sequoias logged in the last century. From here the trail climbs slightly to a ridge, where it re-enters Kings Canyon National Park before descending a short series of steep switchbacks to Sequoia Creek. Cross the creek and look for a sign directing you to Viola Falls, a series of short steps that join into onc fall whcn the water level is high. It is very dangerous to venture down the canyon, but above it are several flat places that make great picnic spots.

North Grove Loop

1.2 miles RT. Easy. Access: Lower end of the General Grant Tree parking area.

The trail follows an abandoned mill road from long ago. It cuts through stands of dogwood, sugar pine, sequoia, and white fir. A large dead sequoia shows evidence of a fire.

Park Ridge Trail

4.7 miles RT. Easy. Access: Panoramic Point parking area, a 2½-mile drive down a steep road from Grant Grove Village.

This hike begins by walking south along the ridge, where views of the valley and peaks dominate. On a clear day, you can see Hume Lake in Sequoia National Forest, the San Joaquin Valley and, occasionally, the coast range 100 miles away. Return the same way.

Sunset Trail

6 miles RT. Moderate to strenuous. Access: Across the road from the Grant Grove Visitor Center.

The hike climbs 1,400 feet past two waterfalls and a lake. After crossing the highway, the trail heads left around a campground. After 1.25 miles, follow the South Boundary Trail toward Viola Falls. You'll reach a paved road where you can head to the right to see the park's original entrance. Return the way you came, or follow the road to the General Grant Tree parking area and walk to the visitor center.

NEAR CEDAR GROVE

Bubbs Creek Trail

8 miles RT. Moderate to strenuous. Access: East end of the parking area at Road's End.

The trail begins by crossing and recrossing Copper Creek. This site was once an American Indian village, and shards of obsidian can still be found on the ground (please leave them in place). After the first mile you'll enter a swampy area that offers a good place to watch for wildlife. The trail here closes in on the river, where deer and bear drink. At 2 miles, you'll come to a junction. The trail to Paradise Valley heads north (left), while the hike to Bubbs Creek veers right and crosses Bailey Bridge, over the South Fork of the Kings River.

Continue hiking east over four small, wooden bridges that cross Bubbs Creek. The creek was named after John Bubbs, a prospector and rancher who arrived here in 1864. The trail will climb on the creek's north side, following a few steep switchbacks, which provide nice, alternating views of the canyon of Paradise Valley and

Cedar Grove. At 3 miles is a large, emerald pool with waterfalls, and far above is a rock formation that was named "the Sphinx" by John Muir. At 4 miles you get to Sphinx Creek, a good area to spend the day or night (with a wilderness permit). There are several campsites nearby. Hike back the way you came or along the Sentinel Trail described below.

Mist Falls

8 miles RT. Moderate to strenuous. Access: Short-term parking area at Road's End; pass Cedar Grove Village and follow the signs.

This is one of the more popular trails leading to the backcountry, but it's also a nice day hike. The first 2 miles are dry, until you reach Bubbs Creek Bridge. Take the fork to the left and head uphill. The first waterfall is not your destination point, although it is a pretty spot to take a break. From here, the trail meanders along the river, through forest and swamp areas before it comes out at the base of Mist Falls, a wide fall that flows generously in spring. There are dozens of great picnic spots here, and along the way up. Return along the same route, or at Bubbs Creek Bridge, cross over and head back on the Sentinel Trail described below. This will add a mile to the hike. From Mist Falls, you can also continue on to Paradise Valley, described below.

Muir's Rock

100 yards RT. Easy. Access: The rock is 100 yards from the parking area at Road's End, along the trail to Zumwalt Meadow.

This level, simple, short stroll takes you to one of the most historically significant spots in the park's modern-day history. From this wide, flat rock, John Muir used to deliver impassioned speeches about the Sierra.

Paradise Valley

12 miles RT. Moderate to strenuous. Access: Short-term parking area at Road's End; pass Cedar Grove Village and follow the signs.

This is a great overnight hike because the valley is so pretty and there's much to explore. But it can also be accomplished as an ambitious day hike. Follow the above trail to Mist Falls and then head up 3 miles of switchbacks to Paradise Valley. The valley is 3 miles long, relatively flat, and beautiful. Hike through the valley to connect with the John Muir Trail and the rest of the backcountry, or return the way you came.

River Trail

5.5 miles RT. Easy. Access: From the Cedar Grove Ranger Station, drive 3 miles to the Roaring River Falls parking area.

The trail hugs the river and can be shortened if you just want to walk to the waterfalls (0.5 mile round-trip), or Zumwalt Meadows (3 miles round-trip; a shorter version is listed below). The waterfalls are 0.25 mile along the trail. The falls are short, but powerful. Do *not* attempt to climb them. Just north of the falls, back toward the parking area, is a sign that reads ZUMWALT MEADOW—ROAD'S END. Take this trail, which initially hugs the highway before breaking off into a beautiful canyon.

At 1.5 miles is the Zumwalt Bridge. If you cross the bridge you'll be a quarter mile from the Zumwalt Meadow parking area. However, to stay on this trail, don't cross the bridge, but continue onward up the canyon for another quarter of a mile to Zumwalt Meadow. From here there's a slight incline. In a half-mile you'll reach a fork; head uphill. The rest of the hike follows the riverbank, which sports plenty of swimming and fishing holes. After 2.5 miles you'll come to another footbridge. Cross over and it's a short half-mile walk back to the Road's End parking area, where you can try to catch a ride. Otherwise, retrace your steps back to your car.

Sentinel Trail

4.6 miles RT. Easy. Access: The trailhead mirrors the hikes to Bubbs Creek, Mist Falls, and Paradise Valley described above.

Essentially what this hike does is encircle a small length of the South Fork of the Kings River. After hiking 2 miles on the river's north side, the trail splits and heads north to Mist Falls and Paradise Valley or east across Bailey Bridge toward Bubbs Creek. Follow the eastern trail, but instead of hiking on to Bubbs Creek, follow a sign that reads ROAD'S END—2.6 MILES. This will take you through dense groves of pine and cedars, with occasional views of Grand Sentinel. You'll cross Avalanche Creek before emerging into a huge meadow and returning near the riverbank. At 2 miles, you can see Muir's Rock, the huge, flat boulder described above. At 2.25 miles, you'll find a footbridge that points back to the parking area.

Zumwalt Meadows

1.5 miles RT. Easy. Access: Zumwalt Meadows parking area, 1 mile west of Road's End, on Calif. 180 past Cedar Grove Village.

Cross the bridge and walk left for 100 yards to a fork. Take the trail that leads right for a bird's-eye view of the meadow before descending 50 feet to the ground below. The trail leads along the meadow's edge, where the fragrance of ponderosa pine, sugar pine, and incense cedar fill the air. The loop around returns along the banks of the South Fork of the Kings River. Grand Sentinel and North Dome rise in the background.

OTHER HIKES

Cold Springs Nature Trail

2 miles RT. Easy. Access: Mineral King's Cold Springs Campground, across from the ranger station.

This easy loop illustrates the natural history and beauty of the region. It passes near private cabins that predate the area's addition to Sequoia National Park in 1978. The walk offers views of the Mineral King Valley and surrounding peaks. It can get hot and dry in summer, so carry additional water.

Deer Cove Trail

4 miles RT. Strenuous. Access: In the Monarch Wilderness, on Calif. 180, about 2¾ miles west of the Cedar Grove Village turnoff. The parking area is on the north side of the road.

This hike in the Monarch Wilderness, maintained by the U.S. Forest Service, starts at 4,400 feet and climbs to 5,600 feet. It follows short, steep switchbacks that climb through bear clover and manzanita. After the first 0.5 mile, it passes above a large spring. Deer Cove Creek is in a steep drainage area at the 2-mile mark. This area is heavily wooded with cedar, fir, and Jeffrey pine. To continue, see the Wildman Meadow Trail below.

Kings River National Recreation Trail

6–10 miles RT. Easy to Spring Creek; strenuous to Garlic Meadow Creek. Access: On Calif. 180, 6 miles below Big Stump Entrance, turn north on F.S. 12S01 (a U.S. Forest Service road), a dirt road marked MCKENZIE HELIPORT, DELILAH LOOKOUT, CAMP 4½ MILES. Drive 17½ miles to the Kings River. Turn west and drive another 2½ miles to Rodgers Crossing. Cross the bridge and turn east, following signs to Kings River Trail. The trailhead is at the east end of a parking lot another 7 miles ahead, at the road's end.

It's a long drive to the trailhead, but after hiking in upper Kings Canyon, this is a great place to see what it looks like from the bottom. The views here rival anything in the park, with peaks towering overhead and the river rushing nearby. The hike cuts through the Monarch Wilderness along the belly of Kings Canyon, although this trail, too, lies in the national forest, not the park. The trail starts along a dirt road but soon departs and follows the river, which is broad and powerful at this point. The first mile alternates between rapids and great fishing pools. At 1.5 miles is a view up Converse Creek and its rugged canyon.

At 3 miles you'll find Spring Creek, a short but pretty waterfall and a good place to rest. You can turn around here for a total hike of 6 miles, or proceed for the 10-mile option. The trail from here ascends the steep Garlic Spur, a ridge that ends suddenly at the ledge of the canyon. The trail above Spring Creek is flecked with obsidian. The nearest source of this rock is the Mono Craters, more than 100 miles to the north. For that reason, many believe this trail was used for trading by the Monache Indians. After the long, steep ascent, the trail heads down to Garlic Meadow Creek. A short way upstream are large pools and wide resting areas. Beyond the creek, the trail is not maintained.

Marble Fork Trail

6 miles RT. Strenuous. Access: Follow the dirt road at the upper end of Potwisha Campground, which is 3¾ miles east of the Ash Mountain Entrance. There is a small parking area past campsite no. 16.

This is one of the most scenic hikes in the Foothills area. The walk leads to a deep gorge where the roaring Marble Falls spill in a cascade over multicolored boulders. From the parking area, begin hiking north up the Southern California Edison flume. After crossing the flume on a wooden bridge, watch for a sign to the trail and head east uphill. The trail crosses some steep switchbacks and near some large poison oak bushes with stems 3 inches wide. Watch out for these bare sticks in late fall and winter.

The trail will begin to flatten out and settle into a slight slope for the rest of the hike up to the waterfalls. Look for large yuccas and California bay along the way. After 2 miles, you can see the waterfalls as the hike cuts through white and gray marble, a belt of the rock that is responsible for seven caves in the park, including Crystal Cave near Giant Forest. Once you reach the falls, it's almost impossible to hike any farther and only very experienced hikers

should attempt a walk downstream. The marble slabs break very easily, and the boulders in the area can get very slick. Be extra careful when water is high. This is a good hike year-round, but can be very hot during summer afternoons.

Potwisha & River's Edge

0.5 mile RT. Easy. Access: From the Ash Mountain Entrance, take the highway to the Potwisha Campground. At the campground entrance (which will be to your left) turn right down a paved road toward an RV dump station. Take the paved road until it hits a dead end at a parking area. Continue toward the river on a footpath to open bedrock.

This was once the site of an American Indian village known as Potwisha, home to the Monache tribe. The main village was just about where the dump station is now, and on the bedrock are mortar holes where the women ground acorns into meal. From here the trail continues above the river to a sandy beach and a good swimming hole. The trail turns east upstream before the suspension bridge, then northward up a short but steep hill. Near the top of the hill you'll run into Middle Fork Trail. Turn west (left) and hike the short distance back to the parking area.

Wildman Meadow

14 miles RT. Strenuous. Access: The trailhead for the Deer Cove Trail, with which this trail connects, is in the Monarch Wilderness, on Calif. 180, about 2¾ mile west of the Cedar Grove Village turnoff. The parking area is on the north side of the road.

This hike through the Monarch Wilderness mirrors the first 2 miles of the hike to Deer Cove. After reaching Deer Cove, it's a steep ascent to 7,500 feet—a 1,900-foot gain in 5 miles. From Deer Cove, hike 3.5 miles to a sandy knoll, from where there is a good view into the rugged canyon drainage area of Grizzly Creek. At 6.5 miles, you'll top the ridge and cross over to the north-facing slope.

A quick drop lands you in Wildman Meadow, where a large stock camp occupies the edge of the clearing.

Exploring the Backcountry

Be aware of bears that frequent these regions, and in the summer take insect repellent for protection against mosquitoes. Stay off high peaks during thunderstorms and don't attempt any climb if it looks as if a storm is rolling in; exposed peaks are often struck by lightning. And finally, many of these routes are buried under snow in winter.

All overnight backpacking trips require a **$15 wilderness permit,** available by mail, fax, or in person at the ranger station closest to the hike you want to take. First-come, first-served permits can be issued the morning of your trip or after 1pm on the previous afternoon. **Reservations** can be made 21 or more days in advance, starting March 1. To reserve a permit, you must provide a name, address, telephone number, the number of people in your party, the method of travel (snowshoe, horse, foot), number of stock if applicable, start and end dates, start and end trailheads, a principal destination, and a rough itinerary. Mail the application to **Wilderness Permit Reservations,** Sequoia and Kings Canyon National Parks, Three Rivers, CA 93271, or fax it to ✆ **559/565-4239.** Reserved permits must be picked up by 9am. If you're delayed, call the ranger station or you risk forfeiting your permit. If your hike crosses agency boundaries, get the permit from the agency on whose land the hike begins. Only one permit is required.

Note: There are eight ranger stations along the John Muir and Pacific Crest trails, and six in the southern part of the park in the Sequoia backcountry. Most are not staffed from fall to spring. To find which ranger station is closest to your trailhead, consult the park map handed out free at all entrances.

Alta Peak–Alta Meadow

16 miles RT. Strenuous. Access: From Giant Village, drive about 3 miles north on the Generals Hwy. and then turn right on the Wolverton Rd. turnoff. Look for the trail at the southeast end of the parking area at Wolverton Creek.

From Wolverton, hike on the Lakes Trail toward the Panther Gap Trail. Head right on the Panther Gap Trail, up through the 8,400-foot gap to Alta Trail. Turn left on Alta Trail and hike past the junction with Seven-Mile Hill Trail and the junction with Alta Peak Trail. Left takes you up Alta Peak, a 2,000-foot ascent in 2 miles that offers spectacular vistas. If climbing isn't your idea of fun, plow straight ahead to Alta Meadow, which also has a nice view and good places to camp.

High Sierra Trail

10 miles RT. Moderate to strenuous. Access: Take Calif. 198 to Giant Forest and proceed to Crescent Meadow Rd. Bear right at the Y, passing the signed parking area for Moro Rock to the road's end and the Crescent Meadow parking area.

This trail is a popular route into the backcountry, and some utilize it as a one-way passage to Mount Whitney. It gets a lot of sun, so begin early. From the parking area, head out on a paved trail to the south, over several bridges to a junction. Turn right onto the High Sierra Trail. You will pass Eagle View, the Wolverton Cutoff, and Panther Creek. Hike at least 3 miles before setting up camp.

Jennie Lakes Trail

12 miles RT. Moderate to strenuous. Access: From Grant Grove, drive about 7 miles south on the Generals Hwy. to the turnoff for Big Meadows Campground. The trailhead and parking area are on the south side of the road next to a ranger station.

This is a nice overnight hike that's not too demanding and that can be further extended into the Jennie Lakes

Wilderness Area. From the parking area, cross through the campground and continue across Big Meadow Creek. From here the trail climbs. At Fox Meadow, there is a wooden trail sign and register for hikers to sign. At the next junction, head right toward Jennie Lakes (left goes toward the Weaver Lake Trail) and up to Poop Out Pass. From here it's a drop down to the Boulder Creek drainage area and on to emerald-green Jennie Lakes. This hike can be combined with a second day hike to Weaver Lake. Just retrace your steps to the Weaver Lake turnoff. Weaver Lake is a relatively warm mountain lake surrounded by blueberry bushes that weigh heavy with fresh fruit in July.

Lakes Trail

13 miles RT. Moderate to strenuous. Access: From Giant Forest, drive north on the Generals Hwy. to the Wolverton parking area. The trailhead is on the left of the parking lot as you enter from the highway.

This trail hikes along a string of tarns, high-mountain lakes created by the scouring action of glaciers thousands of years ago. Heather Lake and Pear Lake are popular destinations along this route. From the trailhead go east, avoiding the Long Meadow Trail. Climb up a moraine ridge and soon you'll be hiking above Wolverton Creek, which darts through small meadows strewn with wildflowers. At a junction with the Panther Gap Trail, head left toward Heather Lake. At a second junction you have to choose. To the right is Hump Trail, a steep but always open trail. Left is the Watchtower Trail, which leads along a granite ledge blasted in the rock with dynamite. With the Tokopah Valley far below, this hike is not for those who suffer vertigo. Both trails wind up at Heather Lake. Camping is not allowed here, but is permitted farther up the trail at Pear and Emerald lakes.

Especially for Kids

The **Walter Fry Nature Center** in Sequoia, located at the Lodgepole Campground, is a fun place for children to visit during the summer months. They can look through a microscope, watch water bugs, and generally have a good time.

Other Sports & Activities

Cross-Country Skiing. Ski rentals, instruction, and trail maps for 35 miles of marked backcountry trails are available from **Sequoia Ski Touring** (© 559/565-3301).

Fishing. Open all year for trout fishing—rainbow, brook, German brown, and golden trout—are a section of the south fork of the **Kings River,** the **Kaweah** drainage, and the parks' lakes. Most other waters are open for trout fishing from late April through mid-November, and open for other species year-round. California fishing licenses (available at stores in the park) are required for anglers 16 and older, and you should also get a copy of the National Park Service's fishing regulations, available at visitor centers.

Horseback Riding. Guided horseback and mule rides and overnight pack trips are offered by concessionaires in both parks and the adjacent national monument during the summer. In Sequoia, one concessionaire (© 559/565-3106) operates a pack station at **Mineral King,** at the end of Mineral King Road. In Kings Canyon, **Cedar Grove Pack Station** (© 559/565-3464 summer, 559/337-2314 winter) is located about 1 mile east of Cedar Grove Village; and **Grant**

A Nearby National Monument

Some of the most beautiful scenery in the Sequoia/Kings Canyon National Park area is not actually in either of these national parks, but in an adjacent section of the Sequoia National Forest now designated a national monument.

Covering 328,000 acres, Giant Sequoia National Monument was created by proclamation by U.S. President Bill Clinton on April 15, 2000. The monument contains 38 groves of sequoias, including some of the most magnificent giant trees to be seen anywhere. In addition, it has towering domes of granite, scenic Hume Lake (a popular destination for boaters and anglers), and the spectacular Kings Canyon—the deepest canyon in North America, with elevations ranging from 1,000 feet to 11,000 feet.

Among hiking trails in the monument is the Boole Tree Trail, a moderate 2.5-mile loop trail that leads to Boole Tree, the largest sequoia in the 1.1-million-acre Sequoia National Forest, and the eighth largest tree in the world. This trail, located off Forest Road 13S55 off Kings Canyon Highway, includes forest and open country, where you'll see sequoias, scenic vistas of the Kings River, and wildflowers in summer.

An easy walk on the quarter-mile (each way) **Chicago Stump Trail** leads to the stump of the General Noble Tree, which was cut down, cut into pieces, and then reassembled and displayed at the 1893 World's Fair in Chicago. Some fairgoers refused to believe that a tree could grow so big, and dubbed it "the California hoax."

Information about other attractions and facilities within the monument are discussed elsewhere in this chapter. For additional information, contact the **Hume Lake Ranger District,** Sequoia National Forest, 35860 E. Kings Canyon Rd. (Calif. 180), Dunlap, CA 93621 (© **559/338-2251;** www.fs.fed.us/r5/sequoia).

Grove Stables (© 559/335-9292 summer, 559/337-2314 winter), is located near Grant Grove Village. In Giant Sequoia National Monument, **Horse Corral Pack Station** is located on Big Meadows Road, 10 miles east of Generals Highway (© **559/565-3404** summer, 559/564-6429 winter; www.horsecorralpackers.com). The pack stations offer hourly rides as well as overnight treks, while the stables offer day rides only. Rates range from $25 to $30 for a 1-hour ride to $75 to $100 for a full day in the saddle; call for current charges for pack trips.

Snowshoeing. On winter weekends, rangers lead introductory snowshoe hikes in **Grant Grove** (© 559/565-4307) and **Giant Forest** (© 559/565-4436). Snowshoes are provided, but a $1 donation is requested.

White-Water Boating. The **Kaweah** and **Upper Kings** rivers in the parks are not open to boating (either kayaks or inflatable rafts), but several companies run trips just outside the parks. **Kaweah White Water Adventures** (© **800/229-8658** or 559/561-1000; www.kaweah whitewater.com) runs class III, IV, and V trips (rated moderate to difficult) on the Merced River. Trips are run in inflatable kayaks or rafts, and are offered from spring through early fall. Prices range from about $50 per person for a 3-hour trip to $120 per person (including lunch) for a full-day trip. Offering trips on the Kaweah, Kings, Kern, and Merced rivers is **Whitewater Voyages** (© **800/400-RAFT;** www.whitewater voyages.com), with rates that range from $22 for 1-hour trips to $100 to $170 (including lunch) for full-day trips, and multiday trips are also available (call for rates). **Kings River Expeditions** (✆ **800/846-3674** or 559/ 233-4881; www.kingsriver.com) specializes in rafting trips on the Kings. For 1-day trips they charge $90 to $150 in spring, and $130 to $225 from mid-May until the season ends. Overnight trips are also available (call for rates).

Camping

There are numerous camping opportunities both within and surrounding Sequoia and Kings Canyon National Parks. It's important to remember that when camping in this area, proper food storage is *required* for the sake of the black bears in the parks, as well as your safety. See local bulletin boards for instructions.

INSIDE SEQUOIA NATIONAL PARK

The only national park campgrounds that accept reservations are Dorst and Lodgepole (✆ **800/365-2267;** http:// reservations.nps.gov), which can be made up to 5 months in advance; the other campgrounds are first-come, first-served.

The two biggest campgrounds in the park are in the Lodgepole area. The **Lodgepole Campground,** which has flush toilets, is often crowded, but it's pretty and near some spectacular big trees and enough backcountry trails to offer some solitude. In summer, you'll find nearby a grocery store, restaurant, visitor center, children's nature center, evening ranger programs, and gift shop. From Giant Forest, drive 5 miles northeast on the Generals Highway. **Dorst Campground,** located 14 miles northwest of Giant Forest via the Generals Highway, is a high-elevation campground that offers easy access to Muir Grove and some pleasant backcountry trails. It has flush toilets and evening ranger programs. Group campsites are also available here by reservation.

In the Foothills area, **Potwisha Campground** is a small campground where the well-spaced sites are tucked beneath oak trees along the Marble Fork of the Kaweah River. However, it does get hot in summer. The campground has flush toilets. From the Ash Mountain Entrance, drive 3 miles northeast on the Generals Highway to the campground entrance. The **Buckeye Flat Campground,** which is open to tents only, is also set among oaks along the Middle Fork of the Kaweah River, and although it also gets hot in summer, is among our favorites due to its scenic beauty. Recently rehabilitated, it has flush toilets. From the Ash Mountain Entrance, drive about 6 miles northeast on the Generals Highway to the Hospital Rock Ranger Station. From there, follow signs to the campground, which is several miles down a narrow, winding road. **South Fork Campground** is the smallest and most remote campground in the park, located just inside Sequoia's southwestern boundary. It is set along the South Fork of the Kaweah River and has pit toilets only. From the town of Three Rivers go east on South Fork Road 23 miles to the campground.

The two campgrounds in the Mineral King area are open to tents only—no RVs or trailers. **Atwell Mill Campground** is a pretty, small campground near the East Fork of the Kaweah River, at Atwell Creek. It has pit toilets. From Three Rivers, take Mineral King Road east for 20 miles to the campground. **Cold Springs Campground,** which also has pit toilets, is a beautiful place to stay—it's just not very accessible. However, once you get there, you'll be rewarded with beautiful scenery. It's also a good starting point for many backcountry hikes, as it's near the Mineral King Ranger Station. From Three Rivers, take Mineral King Road east for 25 miles to the campground.

Additional information can be obtained by calling the general Sequoia/ Kings Canyon information line at ✆ **559/ 565-3341.**

Campground	Elev. (ft.)	Total Sites	RV Hookups	Dump Station	Toilets	Drinking Water
Inside Sequoia National Park						
Atwell Mill	6,650	21	0	No	Yes	Yes
Buckeye Flat	2,800	28	0	No	Yes	Yes
Cold Springs	7,500	40	0	No	Yes	Yes
Dorst	6,700	204	0	Yes	Yes	Yes
Lodgepole	6,700	214	0	Yes	Yes	Yes
Potwisha	2,100	42	0	Yes	Yes	Yes
South Fork	3,650	10	0	No	Yes	No
Inside Kings Canyon National Park						
Azalea	6,600	113	0	No	Yes	Yes
Canyon View	4,600	37	0	No	Yes	Yes
Crystal Springs	6,600	62	0	No	Yes	Yes
Moraine	4,600	120	0	No	Yes	Yes
Sentinel	4,600	82	0	No	Yes	Yes
Sheep Creek	4,600	111	0	No	Yes	Yes
Sunset	6,600	200	0	No	Yes	Yes
Outside the Parks						
Big Meadows	7,600	30	0	No	Yes	No
Hume Lake	5,200	74	0	No	Yes	Yes
Landslide	5,800	9	0	No	Yes	No
Princess	5,900	88	0	Yes	yes	Yes
Stony Creek	6,400	49	0	No	Yes	Yes
Tenmile	5,800	10	0	No	Yes	Yes
Horse Camp	300	80	0	Yes	Yes	Yes
Lemon Cove	300	55	40	Yes	Yes	Yes

IN KINGS CANYON NATIONAL PARK

All of the campgrounds in Kings Canyon are first-some, first-served only (reservations not available), and all have flush toilets.

In the Grant Grove area, there are three attractive campgrounds near the big trees—**Azalea, Crystal Springs,** and Sunset—which have a pleasant, woodsy feeling, are close to park facilities, and offer evening ranger programs. From the Big Stump Entrance, take Calif. 180 east about 1¾ miles.

There are four attractive campgrounds in the Cedar Grove Village area, all accessed from Calif. 180, and all fairly close to the facilities in Cedar Grove Village. **Sentinel,** the first to open

Showers	Fire Pits/ Grills	Laundry	Public Phones	Reservations	Fees	Open
No	Yes	No	No	No	$12	May–Oct
No	Yes	No	Yes	No	$18	Apr–Oct
No	Yes	No	Yes	No	$12	May–Oct
No	Yes	No	Yes	Yes	$20	June–Aug
Yes	Yes	Yes	Yes	Yes	$20	Year-round
No	Yes	No	Yes	No	$18	Year-round
No	Yes	No	Yes	No	$12	Year-round
Yes	Yes	No	Yes	No	$18	Year-round
Yes	Yes	Yes	Yes	No	$18	May–Oct
Yes	Yes	No	Yes	No	$18	May–Oct
Yes	Yes	Yes	Yes	No	$18	May–Oct
Yes	Yes	Yes	Yes	No	$18	Apr–Oct
Yes	Yes	Yes	Yes	No	$18	June–Sept (as needed)
Yes	Yes	Yes	Yes	No	$18	May–Oct (as needed)
No	Yes	No	Yes	No	Free	June–Oct
No	Yes	No	Yes	No	$16	May–Sept
No	Yes	No	No	No	$12	May–Oct
No	Yes	No	No	No	$16	June–Oct
Yes	Yes	No	Yes	Yes	$16	June–Oct
No	Yes	No	Yes	No	Free	May–Oct
Yes	Yes	No	Yes	Yes	$16	Year-round
Yes	Yes	Yes	Yes	Yes	$20–$24	Year-round

for the season, tends to fill quickly; and **Moraine** is the farthest from the crowds. The others generally open on an as-needed basis. These include **Sheep Creek,** located along picturesque Sheep Creek; and **Canyon View,** Kings Canyon's smallest campground.

Additional information can be obtained by calling the general Sequoia/ Kings Canyon information line at ✆ **559/ 565-3341.**

OUTSIDE THE PARKS

The U.S. Forest Service operates a number of campgrounds in **Giant Sequoia National Monument,** a 327,769-acre section of Sequoia National Forest, which was given national monument status in April, 2000. They provide a delightful forest camping experience, and are usually less crowded than national park campgrounds.

In the Hume Lake area, all the Forest Service campgrounds have pit toilets except the beautiful **Hume Lake Campground,** which is set on the banks of the lake and has flush toilets. It's about 3 miles south of Calif. 180 via Hume Lake Road. The largest campground in this area is **Princess,** located along Calif. 180; two smaller campgrounds, both beyond Hume Lake via Ten Mile Road, are **Landslide** and **Upper Ten Mile.**

In the Stony Creek/Big Meadows area, you'll find vault toilets at all U.S. Forest Service campgrounds except **Stony Creek Campground,** located off Generals Highway in Stony Creek Village, which has flush toilets. Among the larger campgrounds in this area is **Big Meadows,** which is set along Big Meadows Creek. Nearby trails lead to the Jennie Lakes Wilderness. From Grant Grove Village, drive 7 miles southeast on the Generals Highway, then turn east on Big Meadows Road and drive 5 miles to the campground.

For additional information on the above and other campgrounds in the national monument, contact **Giant Sequoia National Monument,** Sequoia National Forest, Hume Lake Ranger District, 35860 E. Kings Canyon Rd., Dunlap, CA 93621 (© **559/338-2251;** fax 559/338-2131; www.fs.fed.us/r5/sequoia).

Another great place to camp is **Horse Creek Campground,** operated by the U.S. Army Corps of Engineers. It's located along the south shore of Lake Kaweah, in Lake Kaweah Recreation Area, about 6 miles east of the community of Lemon Cove off Calif. 198. The lake, which is about 5 miles long and a half-mile wide, covers 1,900 acres when full, and is popular with boaters, who take to the waters in kayaks, canoes, personal watercraft, fishing boats, and larger

patio boats. There are several boat ramps, and boat rentals are available at the **Kaweah Marina** (© **559/597-2526**). Call for current rates and availability. This is also a popular fishing lake, where you're apt to catch largemouth bass, crappie, bluegill, catfish, and rainbow trout. The number of campsites varies with the water level, with the fewest usually in spring, when the lake is at its highest. There are some shady sites and some open, and most have good views across the lake. The campground has flush toilets. For information, contact **U.S. Army Corps of Engineers,** Lake Kaweah Recreation Area, P.O. Box 44270, Lemon Cove, CA 93244 (© **559/561-3155** or 559/597-2301). Campsite reservations are available from the **National Recreation Reservation Service** (© **877/444-6777;** www.reserveusa.com).

Those seeking a full service commercial campground with RV hookups and all the usual amenities should head to **Lemon Cove/Sequoia Campground,** on the west side of Lemon Cove at 32075 Sierra Dr. (Calif. 198), P.O. Box 44269, Lemon Cove, CA 93244 (© **559/597-2346;** www.lemoncovesequoiacamp.com). This attractive and convenient campground (22 miles east of Visalia) in the foothills of the Sierra Nevada can handle large rigs with slide-outs and offers cable TV hookups, propane sales, a convenience store, grassy and shaded sites, a recreation room, a playground and volleyball court, and an outdoor swimming pool.

Where to Stay

INSIDE THE PARKS

Lodging inside these national parks ranges from rustic cabins to pleasant and well-equipped motel-style lodging, usually with a mountain lodge atmosphere and great views. There are also several good lodging choices in the nearby Giant Sequoia National Monument and in the gateway towns of Visalia,

Three Rivers, and Lemon Cove (see "Lodging Outside the Parks," below).

Cedar Grove Lodge

Calif. 180, Cedar Grove, Kings Canyon National Park (mailing address: Sequoia Kings Canyon Park Services Company, 5755 E. Kings Canyon Rd., Ste. 101, Fresno, CA 93727). © **866/ 522-6966** or 559/452-1081. Fax 559/452-1353. www.sequoia-kingscanyon.com. 18 units. A/C. $99–$110 double. AE, DISC, MC, V. Closed Nov–Apr.

This motel offers comfortable rooms on the bank of the Kings River. Getting here is half the fun—it's a 36-mile drive down a winding highway that provides beautiful vistas along the way. The rooms are standard motel accommodations—clean, comfortable, but nothing special—but what you're really paying for is the location, surrounded by tall trees with a pretty river. Most of the rooms are above the Cedar Grove Café (see "Where to Dine," below), with communal decks with river views. However, we prefer the three smaller and not-quite-as-attractively appointed rooms on ground level because they have private patios looking right out on the river, and their own refrigerators and microwaves. Although Cedar Grove Lodge has no room phones, a 24-hour pay phone is just outside.

Grant Grove Cabins

Calif. 180, Grant Grove Village, Kings Canyon National Park (mailing address: Sequoia Kings Canyon Park Services Company, 5755 E. Kings Canyon Rd., Ste. 101, Fresno, CA 93727). © **866/522-6966** or 559/452-1081. Fax 559/452-1353. www.sequoia-kingscanyon.com. 53 units (9 with private bathroom). $45–$112 cabins. Register at Grant Grove Village Registration Center, between the restaurant and gift shop. AE, DISC, MC, V.

Although these are all cabins, there's a wide range of amenities and prices to be found here, from handsomely restored cabins with private bathrooms that ooze historic charm, to rustic tent cabins that simply provide a comfortable bed out of the weather at a very low price. Those who want to "rough it" in style should reserve one of the nine cabins, built in the 1920s, that have electricity, indoor plumbing, and full private bathrooms. A bit less modern, but still quite comfortable, are the 43 rustic cabins that have kerosene lanterns for light and wood-burning stoves for heat, and share a bathhouse. Some are rustic wooden cabins; others, available in summer only, have wood floors and walls but canvas roofs. All cabins have full linen service. It's a 10-minute walk from the cabins to the Grant Grove Visitor Center, and they are also near the Grant Grove Restaurant, described under "Where to Dine," below.

John Muir Lodge

Calif. 180, Grant Grove Village, Kings Canyon National Park (mailing address: Sequoia Kings Canyon Park Services Company, 5755 E. Kings Canyon Rd., Ste. 101, Fresno, CA 93727). © **866/ 522-6966** or 559/452-1081. Fax 559/452-1353. www.sequoia-kingscanyon.com. 30 units. $140 double, $240 suite. Register at Grant Grove Village Registration Center, between the restaurant and gift shop. AE, DISC, MC, V.

This handsome log lodge, built in 1998, looks perfect in this beautiful national park setting and is an excellent choice for park visitors who want lodging in a forest atmosphere while still in quiet, comfortable, modern rooms, with full bathrooms and all the other comforts we've all come to appreciate. Standard rooms are simply but tastefully decorated, with a mountain lodge atmosphere, two queen beds, and wonderful views of the surrounding forest. Suites are pretty much two connecting lodge rooms, except that one of the rooms has a queen bed and a queen sofa sleeper instead of two queens. The lodge also has a gigantic and very attractive log-beam lobby.

Silver City Mountain Resort

Mineral King, Sequoia National Park (mail: 2570 Rodman Dr., Los Osos, CA 93402). © **805/528-2730** in winter; 559/561-3223 summer only. Fax 805/528-8039. www.silver cityresort.com. 14 cabins, 7 with shared central bathhouse. $70–$250 double. Discounts June 1–15 and after Sept 18. MC, V. Closed Nov–May. Take Calif. 198 through Three Rivers to the Mineral King turnoff. Silver City is a little more than halfway between Lookout Point and Mineral King.

This is an excellent choice for those who seek a woodsy experience in a handsome cabin. There are three types of cabins here, with a variety of bed combinations (some sleep up to eight) and wood stoves for heat (wood provided). Blankets and pillows are provided, but guests need to bring their own sheets, pillowcases, bath and kitchen towels, paper towels, and tall trash bags. The top-of-the line Swiss Chalets are finished in knotty pine with completely equipped kitchens, full bathrooms, phones with dataports, and an outdoor barbecue. The midlevel units, dubbed "Comfy Cabins," are two-bedroom units with complete kitchens, light from propane wall lamps and kerosene lanterns, small restrooms with toilets but no showers (there is a centrally located bathhouse), and decks with barbecue grills. The "Rustic Cabins," which were built in the 1930s, are the most basic units, with light from kerosene and propane lamps, a camp kitchen with a gas stove and oven and cold-water sink, and outdoor decks with barbecues. Some have refrigerators, and all use the showers and toilets in the shared bathhouse. There is also one small one-room cabin, with a double bed and little else, that sleeps two. These cabins are booked early, with reservations accepted in January for the entire year. There are 2-night minimums for the Swiss Chalets and Comfy Cabins. All units are nonsmoking. On the premises is a breakfast bar, open daily, with homemade muffins and rolls, fruit, and beverages; a full-service restaurant/bakery serving lunch and dinner Thursday through Monday; and a store.

Wuksachi Lodge

Calif. 180 and 198 (P.O. Box 89), Sequoia National Park, CA 93262. © **888/252-5757** or 559/253-2199. www.visitsequoia.com. 102 units. TV TEL. May–Oct and holidays $160–$219; Nov–Apr (except holidays) $89–$123. AE, DISC, MC, V.

The Wuksachi Village and Lodge are the newest development in the park. The handsome lodge has a dining room (see "Where to Dine," below), lounge, gift shop, conference rooms, and registration desk. Guest rooms, however, are located in three buildings separated from the lodge by parking lots. The rooms are attractively but simply decorated, with wood furnishings, light-colored plaster walls, and artwork depicting the area's attractions. Of course, the best views are out the windows, where the forest and surrounding mountains dominate the scene. There are refrigerators, coffeemakers, hair dryers, ski storage racks, and phones with dataports. The standard rooms have one or two queen beds and a small desk; deluxe rooms are larger with two queen beds or a king and a sofa bed, plus a table and two chairs; and "superior" rooms are mini-suites, with two queen beds or one king, plus a sofa bed in an alcove sitting area with a sliding door (a good place for your teenager!). All the rooms are a healthy walk from the parking lots (especially when loaded down with luggage), but bellhops with golf carts are available.

LODGING OUTSIDE THE PARKS

Additional lodging choices are found outside park boundaries, and, in most cases, you'll be passing these facilities as you travel to different sections of the parks.

IN GIANT SEQUOIA NATIONAL MONUMENT

Kings Canyon Lodge

Calif. 180, Giant Sequoia National Monument (mail: P.O. Box 930, Kings Canyon National Park, CA 93633). © **559/335-2405.** 11 units, 2 with shared bathroom. $69–$169 double (including tax). MC, V. Closed Dec–Mar. Take Calif. 180 from Grant Grove toward Cedar Grove. The lodge is at the halfway point, about 15 miles from both locations.

Built in the 1930s, the historic Kings Canyon Lodge offers relatively inexpensive accommodations close to the park, with great scenic views. There are three lodge rooms (two share a bathroom) plus a variety of cabins, all constructed of knotty pine. Although old (and a bit old-fashioned looking, which we don't mean as a criticism), the units are clean and well maintained. Most have showers only, but one cabin has a shower/tub combo. Most rooms have either one or two double beds, and one large family cabin can sleep up to eight and has a full kitchen. On the property is a gas station that uses a 1928 double gravity pump, believed to be one of the few still being used, that is worth seeing; a bar and grill serves breakfast, lunch, and dinner (see "Where to Dine," below). All units here are nonsmoking.

Montecito-Sequoia Lodge

8000 Generals Hwy., Giant Sequoia National Monument (mail: Box 858, 8000 Generals Hwy., Kings Canyon National Park, CA 93633). © **800/227-9900,** 800/843-8667, or 559/565-3388. Fax 559/565-3223. www.mslodge.com. 36 units, plus 13 cabins that share 2 bathhouses. $55–$139 per person. Rates include breakfast and dinner. Special weeklong packages available. AE, DISC, MC, V. Take Calif. 180 into Sequoia National Park, turn right at the fork, and drive 8 miles south to the lodge access road, turn right, and follow the road about ½ mile to the parking lot.

The Montecito offers comfortable rooms in a well-stocked resort that caters to families with children and large groups, although guests of all ages will enjoy this well-run facility. Rooms, which all have private bathrooms, are located in four separate buildings, and another 13 cabins share two bathhouses. Bed types and number vary, with units that sleep from two to eight. The property has a mountain lodge atmosphere, with simple but attractive units that are carpeted, have ceiling fans, and are decorated with photos of the area. Meals are served buffet style, and there is a bar on the premises. A small lake accommodates sailing and canoeing. During winter, guests can also go cross-country skiing, snowshoeing, and ice-skating. There's also a large heated outdoor pool, Jacuzzi, sun deck, two outdoor tennis courts, watersports equipment, nature trails, a game room, children and teen programs, conference rooms, and a self-serve laundry.

Stony Creek Lodge

Generals Hwy., Giant Sequoia National Monument (mailing address: Sequoia Kings Canyon Park Services Company, 5755 E. Kings Canyon Rd., Ste. 101, Fresno, CA 93727). © **866/522-6966** or 559/452-1081. Fax 559/452-1353. www.sequoia-kingscanyon.com. 11 units. $125 double. AE, DISC, MC, V. Closed Sept–May. Take the Stony Creek Village exit off the Generals Hwy., between Grant Grove Village and Giant Village.

This small, pleasant lodge offers comfortable, motel-style accommodations in a pretty setting, in the new Giant Sequoia National Monument, which is located between the Grant Grove and Cedar Grove sections of Kings Canyon National Park. Rooms are simply but attractively decorated and sleep from two to four. The lodge's lobby is especially inviting, with a massive stone fireplace. There's a family restaurant that serves lunch and dinner, a self-service laundry, store, and nature trails.

IN THE NEARBY GATEWAY TOWNS

In addition to the properties discussed below, reliable chains in Visalia include the **Best Western Visalia Inn Motel,** 623 W. Main St., Visalia, CA 93291 (© 877/ 500-4771 or 559/732-4561), which has rates for two of $79 to $84; and the **Super 8,** 4801 W. Noble Ave., Visalia, CA 93277 (© 800/800-8000 or 559/627-2885), charging $50 to $95 double. Options in Three Rivers include the **Best Western Holiday Lodge,** 40105 Sierra Dr. (P.O. Box 129), Three Rivers, CA 93271 (© 888/523-9909 or 559/ 561-4119), which charges $79 to $119 double; and the **Holiday Inn Express,** 40820 Sierra Dr., Three Rivers, CA 93271 (© 800/465-4329 or 559/561-9000), charging $69 to $109 double.

Ben Maddox House

601 N. Encina St., Visalia, CA 93291. © **800/ 401-9800** or 559/739-0721. Fax 559/625-0420. www.benmaddoxhouse.com. 6 units. TV TEL. $85–$130 double. Rates include full breakfast. AE, DISC, MC, V. Closed Nov–Mar. Appropriate for children 13 and older.

Our top choice for an enchanting place to stay in the Visalia area, the Ben Maddox House is named for one of Visalia's most prominent citizens of the late 1800s and early 1900s, who started the local newspaper and the area's first electric company. Located 4 blocks from downtown Visalia on a street with a number of other Victorian homes, the inn is comprised of two historic homes set on an acre of land, with gardens, decks, a small finch aviary, and a citrus orchard that includes a 100-year old lemon tree that is still producing. Large palm trees grace the front yard, and the long covered porch includes a porch swing, where you can sit and watch the world go by.

Both houses are furnished with antiques, and the comfortable and attractive guest rooms boast 14-foot ceilings and white oak floors. One room has a king-size bed; the rest each have one queen bed; all have phones with dataports, refrigerators, irons, ironing boards, and hair dryers. Breakfast, which is served at private tables, is cooked to order from a menu, which might include omelets, waffle or pancake specialties, plus breakfast meats and baked items. There is also an attractive 40-by-20-foot swimming pool (10 ft. deep at the deep end), open April through October. Rooms are appropriate for only two people; and all are nonsmoking.

Buckeye Tree Lodge

46000 Sierra Dr., Three Rivers, CA 93271. © **559/561-5900.** www.buckeyetree.com. 12 units. A/C TV TEL. $58–$130 double; $99–$210 cottage. Rates include continental breakfast. AE, DC, DISC, MC, V. Pets accepted but must be declared when making reservations.

Located just a half-mile from the entrance to Sequoia National Park, this motel is a good choice for almost anyone. Not only does it offers affordable and attractive rooms, but the property has rolling lawns that end at a picturesque river, and every room has a patio or balcony offering splendid views. Rooms are clean, basic motel units, with a king or two queen beds, light-colored wood furnishings, stucco walls, refrigerators, coffeemakers, and VCRs (video rentals available). Some rooms have microwaves. Eight rooms have showers only; the rest have shower/tub combos. There is also a separate cottage that sleeps up to five. The motel has an outdoor swimming pool, and pathways lead down to the river.

Lake Elowin Resort

43840 Dineley Dr., Three Rivers, CA 93271. © **559/561-3460.** Fax 559/561-1300. www. lake-elowin.com. 10 cabins, all with showers only. A/C. $80–$120 double. AE, DISC, MC, V. From eastbound Sierra Dr. in Three Rivers, about 2½ miles before the park entrance, turn left on Dineley Dr. (the street sign says DINLEY) and drive across a bridge. Bear right, and it's less than ½ mile to the resort's driveway.

One of the best places to stay in the Sierra, this 70-year-old resort is the perfect place to get away from it all.

There are no phones and no televisions, just clean rustic cabins nestled under huge trees, all facing Lake Elowin, a small body of water above the Kaweah River. Milton Melkonian purchased the resort in the 1970s with the idea of creating a place to coexist with nature, and he is fastidious about his creation, which now attracts all sorts of creative types, such as writers and artists, as well as others seeking a refuge. Cabins can accommodate two to six people. We especially like cabin no. 1, which sits close to the lake and has a delightful view from the kitchen window; and Master Cabin, which boasts a fireplace, deck, and Jacuzzi. However, we wouldn't turn down any of them. All cabins include linens and towels, pots and pans, kitchen utensils, and barbecues. You bring the food, sunblock, and good attitude. All cabins are nonsmoking and guests must actually sign a contract to not smoke here.

Plantation Bed & Breakfast

33038 Calif. 198, Lemon Cove, CA 93244. ℭ **800/240-1466** or 559/597-2555. Fax 559/597-2551. www.plantationbnb.com. 7 units. A/C. $129–$219 double. Rates include full breakfast. AE, DC, DISC, MC, V. On Calif. 198, 16 miles west of the park entrance.

Step into the Old South at this delightful inn, where rooms are named for and decorated in keeping with characters from *Gone With The Wind*. For a quietly conservative atmosphere request the Ashley Wilkes Room, which has a king bed; and honeymooners might enjoy the luxurious Scarlett O'Hara Room, with king bed, velvet love seat, fireplace, and marble bathroom containing a Jacuzzi tub and separate shower. Our favorite, though, is the Belle Watling Room, done up in elegant bordello style: a king-size bed with a huge mirror alongside, red crystal chandelier, and claw-foot bathtub with a (tastefully done) Renaissance-style nude painted on the side. Several rooms have TVs and VCRs; two rooms have showers only, while the others have showers and tubs.

Secluded in the orange grove, and watched over by an almost life-size statue of a mermaid, are a large swimming pool and oversized Jacuzzi. The wonderful breakfasts include an abundance of fresh fruit, homemade granola, and a hot entree such as mushroom asparagus crepes, croissant French toast, or spinach frittata. The inn is nonsmoking.

Sierra Lodge

43175 Sierra Dr., Three Rivers, CA 93271. ℭ **800/367-8879** or 559/561-3681. Fax 559/561-3264. www.sierra-lodge.com. 22 units. A/C TV TEL. $58–$79 double; $130–$175 suite. Rates about 20% lower in winter. Rates include morning pastries and coffee or tea. AE, DC, DISC, MC, V.

Built to resemble a Swiss chalet, this small motel about 3 miles from the national park entrance offers well-maintained rooms and suites in a very scenic setting along a river and with 150-year-old oak trees. The rooms range from quite small to fairly spacious, and have a lot of homey touches such as decorative plates, artificial flowers, and the like. Most standard rooms have painted block walls and offer a variety of bed options—two doubles, one queen, or one king. The suites are more luxurious. For instance, the VIP Suite would be ideal for two couples traveling together. It has two bedrooms (one queen bed in each), a full bathroom, a kitchenette, a living room with a handsome stone fireplace, and a private balcony with splendid views. All rooms have small refrigerators, and some have fireplaces. Eight units have showers only; the rest have showers and small bathtubs. Guests also have use of barbecues and a small outdoor swimming pool.

Spalding House

631 N. Encina St., Visalia, CA 93291. ℭ **559/739-7877.** Fax 559/625-0902. www.the spaldinghouse.com. 3 suites. A/C. From $95 double. Rates include full breakfast. AE, MC, V.

This Colonial Revival home—built in 1901 by local lumberman W. R.

Spalding—offers only suites, each with a sitting room and private bathroom (one with a shower/tub combo, the others with showers only). The owners restored the entire home themselves, decorating it in the style of the early 1900s with Oriental rugs, antiques, and reproductions. Two suites have queen-size beds; the other has a double. We especially like the Spalding Suite, which has a four-post, colonial-style queen-size bed and a delightful sitting room with wicker furniture and lots of windows. Common areas include the library, which contains more than 1,500 books, and the music room with its 1923 Steinway grand player piano. Breakfast is a major event here, a five-course meal that includes hot entrees such as cheese blintzes, apple crepes, or omelets, and might also include baked grapefruit, sausage or ham, or yogurt dishes. The inn is totally nonsmoking.

Where to Dine

INSIDE THE PARKS

Major improvements and additions to the restaurant scene in these parks in recent years mean that, yes, you can have a really good meal, or, if you prefer, you can find a quick and tasty lunch at a fairly reasonable price. In addition, there are several good possibilities in the communities outside the park and within Giant Sequoia National Monument.

Cedar Grove Café

Cedar Grove, Kings Canyon National Park. Information: ✆ **559/335-5500.** Breakfast $4–$7; lunch and dinner $4.50–$13. AE, DISC, MC, V. Daily 8am–8pm. Closed Nov–Apr. AMERICAN.

Providing the only dining at Cedar Grove, this glorified snack bar offers a simple but adequate menu at affordable prices, although those staying at the lodge here for several days will quickly tire of the limited choices. Breakfasts

include eggs, cereals, fruit, and pastries. Lunch and dinner include burgers and a few sandwiches, plus several meals such as fish and chips. The cafe has a pleasant outdoor balcony seating area that overlooks the river.

Grant Grove Restaurant

Grant Grove Village, Kings Canyon National Park. Information: ✆ **559/335-5500.** Breakfast and lunch $3.50–$8; dinner $7–$20. AE, DISC, MC, V. May–Aug daily 7am–9pm; Sept–Apr daily 7am–8pm. AMERICAN.

This pleasant cafe-style restaurant, located in the hub of activity in Kings Canyon National Park, is a good choice for a sit-down meal, with a simple but very adequate menu, well-prepared food, and good service. Breakfast ranges from omelets and pancakes to cereal or fruit, while at lunchtime you'll find sandwiches, salads, and hot entrees. Complete dinners include our choice—a grilled New York strip steak topped with sautéed mushrooms and served with soup or salad, potato or rice, and the vegetable of the day. Also available at dinner are pastas, chicken cordon bleu, and a tasty trout, which is sautéed in white wine and butter and topped with roasted almonds.

Lodgepole Deli & Snack Bar

Lodgepole, Sequoia National Park. ✆ **559/253-2199.** www.visitsequoia.com. Most items $3–$7. AE, MC, V. Daily 8am–8pm. Snack bar open year-round with shorter hours fall through spring; deli closed Nov–Apr. DELI/PIZZA.

Actually two separate counter-service fast-food restaurants in the Lodgepole Market Center, you'll find kids' favorites such as burgers, hot dogs, pizza, and the like in the snack bar, and less fun but more healthy grown-up fare nearby at the deli, which specializes in made-to-order deli-style sandwiches, salads, yogurt, and fruit. Both the snack bar and deli offer ice cream.

Wuksachi Dining Room

Wuksachi Lodge, Sequoia National Park. © **559/565-4070,** ext. 608. www.visitsequoia. com. Dinner reservations required. Sandwiches and salads $4–$9, dinner main courses $13–$25. AE, DISC, MC, V. Daily 7–10am, 11:30am–2pm, and 5–10pm. AMERICAN.

This upscale mountain lodge–style restaurant, with a high natural wood beamed ceiling, huge stone fireplace, and large windows offering wonderful views of the surrounding forest, make the Wuksachi Dining Room a delightful spot for a refined and relaxing meal. Standard American breakfasts are the morning fare, and a number of salads and sandwiches—such as a half-pound burger or citrus marinated salmon with caramelized onion—are offered during lunch and dinner. The main dinner entrees are quite elegant. We recommend the lavender chicken, with honey-roasted shallots and balsamic syrup; the rib-eye steak, served with portobello-ancho sauce; or for those who can't decide, the triple divide plate, which includes a filet mignon smothered in a sauce of black beans and chiles, plus a chicken breast and grilled shrimp.

OUTSIDE THE PARKS

Anne Lang's Emporium

41651 Sierra Dr. (Calif. 198), Three Rivers. © **559/561-4937.** Most items $2.95–$5.95. MC, V. Mon–Fri 10am–4pm; Sat–Sun 11am–4pm. DELI.

This is a great spot for a quick lunch or to pick up a picnic lunch before heading into the park. Part of a shop that also sells a wide variety of gifts, flowers, cards, coffee beans, teas, and the like, this busy full-service deli has a half dozen or so small tables inside, in a cafelike atmosphere, plus a large deck out back (away from the highway) that overlooks the Kaweah River. You order at the counter and they prepare your sandwich to eat there or as a box lunch. In addition to the usual cold deli sandwiches, there are a few hot items, including burgers and chicken breast sandwiches. There are also several luncheon salads, a soup of the day, fresh baked items, ice cream, and specialty drinks including espressos, smoothies, and Italian sodas.

The Hummingbird

35591 E. Kings Canyon Rd., Clingan's Junction (19 miles west of the Kings Canyon National Park boundary). © **559/338-0160.** Menu items $4.25–$15. AE, MC, V. Daily 7:30am–8:30pm. AMERICAN.

A friendly, folksy, family-run restaurant, the Hummingbird offers hearty, home-made grub, from freshly baked corn-bread and rolls to juicy burgers and steaks, seafood, pasta, and other traditional plates. Breakfasts are dominated by eggs and potatoes and ham—try the country eggs Benedict if you've got a day of hiking and need that extra fuel. The desserts make the place, all fashioned from scratch in-house, including fudge, cakes, and delectable blackberry pies.

Kings Canyon Lodge Bar and Grill

Calif. 180, in Kings Canyon Lodge, Giant Sequoia National Monument. © **559/335-2405.** Sandwiches and plates $3.50–$7.95. MC, V. Daily 8am–8pm. Closed Dec–Mar. AMERICAN.

This Old West–style bar, sitting along the roadside between Grant Village and Cedar Grove, has a small dining room with lots of Western ambience, plus patio dining with views of the nearby John Muir Wilderness Area. The restaurant offers basic American grub—ham and eggs and the like at breakfast, with burgers, sandwiches, soups, salads, and a few complete meals for lunch and dinner. Occasionally on weekends, a locally popular barbecue dinner special is offered for about $12. It's worth stopping here at any time of day for the hand-dipped ice-cream cones, and despite the fact that this is a bar, the atmosphere is very kid-friendly around mealtime.

Vintage Press

216 N. Willis St., Visalia. © **559/733-3033.** www.thevintagepress.com. Reservations recommended at dinner. Main courses $8.95–$15 lunch, $12–$25 dinner. AE, DC, MC, V. Mon–Thurs 11:30am–2pm and 6–10pm; Fri–Sat 11:30am–2pm and 6–11pm. Sun brunch 10am–2pm; dinner 5–9pm. AMERICAN/ CONTINENTAL.

The best place to eat within miles, this is our choice for celebrating a special occasion or just giving ourselves a treat. The restaurant's three dining rooms are all somewhat different, but are all elegant in the spirit of an upscale gin mill in Gold Rush–era San Francisco. There is a handsome old bar imported from the city by the bay, and many antiques and leaded mirrors. There is also patio dining. The menu features a dozen meat and fish selections, including steak, free-range chicken with braised leeks, and crispy veal sweetbreads with a port wine-jalapeño-Roquefort sauce. Those who want a somewhat lighter meal, or who desire to experience this fine restaurant at a slightly lower cost, can make a dinner of one of the exotic appetizers ($8.95–$12). The restaurant's wine cellar, a winner of the *Wine Spectator* Award of Excellence, offers over 1,000 selections.

Picnic & Camping Supplies

Stores throughout the parks stock basic camping supplies, such as flashlights, canteens, and tarps, and enough food that you won't starve, but you'll find better selections in the nearby towns. In the parks, the **Cedar Grove Market** is open from May through September only, as is the **Lodgepole Market,** which has the widest selection available, including a good deli for take-out sandwiches (see above). The **Grant Grove Market** is open year-round, and during the winter a small variety of goods is available at **Wolverton,** in Sequoia.

Outside the parks, **Dixon's Village Market** along Calif. 198 in Three Rivers is a small town grocery store with a fairly good selection. However, for the best selection and prices on foodstuffs, on your way to the parks stop in Visalia at **Save Mart,** in the Mary's Vineyard Shopping Center at Calif. 198 and Ben Maddox Way, an excellent supermarket with a good bakery and a deli with made-to-order sandwiches. Just east of Mary's Vineyard Shopping Center is a **Wal-Mart** discount store, at 1819 E. Noble Ave., where you'll find a wide stock of camping supplies, along with film, clothing, and practically everything else you might need.

33

THEODORE ROOSEVELT NATIONAL PARK

by Jack Olson

WHEN HE BECAME PRESIDENT IN 1901, THEODORE ROOSEVELT pursued his love of nature and the outdoors by creating the U.S. Forest Service and signing the 1906 Antiquities Act, under which he proclaimed 18 national monuments.

He also obtained congressional approval to establish five national parks, as well as set aside millions of acres of land as national forests and 51 wildlife refuges. As a conservationist, Roosevelt is arguably without equal among American presidents. So it seems appropriate that he is the only president for whom a national park has been named, and that Theodore Roosevelt National Park be located in western North Dakota, where many of his early experiences formed his later environmental efforts.

Roosevelt first traveled to the North Dakota badlands in 1883. Before returning home to New York, he became interested in the cattle business and joined two other men as partners in the Maltese Cross Ranch. The following year, Roosevelt returned to North Dakota and established a second open-range ranch, the Elkhorn, which became his principal residence in the area.

During his frequent visits, Roosevelt led what he called the "strenuous life" that he loved. When he wasn't studying botany or herding cattle, he hunted,

fished, and enjoyed the camaraderie of fellow Dakotans, some of whom would later form the nucleus of his Rough Riders.

Roosevelt arrived in the badlands soon after the last of the bison herds had been slaughtered, and he spent much time pondering what was being done to the animals and land around him. He carried those thoughts and convictions, born on the Dakota prairie, into his later political life. He wrote, "I would not have been President, had it not been for my experience in North Dakota."

Badlands & Buffalo. The colorful, broken landscape of the North Dakota badlands provides the scenic backdrop for Theodore Roosevelt National Park. Carved over millions of years by the natural forces of wind and rain and the tireless waters of the Little Missouri River, this land is home to a variety of animals and plant life.

Some 60 million years ago, streams carried eroded materials eastward from

Tips from the Chief of Interpretation

After 16 years at Theodore Roosevelt National Park, a dozen years with the National Park Service in Alaska, and 6 years each in Death Valley and Crater Lake, Chief of Interpretation Bruce Kaye has some insights for prospective visitors.

Kaye encourages visitors to view Roosevelt's two ranch sites—the Maltese Cross, whose ranch house was relocated to the park in 1959 from the state capital in Bismarck; and the Elkhorn Ranch site, located 35 miles north of Medora. Kaye said visitors should check with rangers before traveling to the Elkhorn site, to ensure that road conditions or high water will not impede their progress.

While visiting the park, Kaye says travelers should keep their eyes open for a wide variety of wildlife, including bison, elk, wild horses, mule deer, white-tailed deer, coyotes, antelope, a variety of birds, and the ever-abundant prairie dog.

"The best month to be without crowds at Theodore Roosevelt National Park, yet do the things you want to do in view of the weather, is September," Kaye says. "But even at the height of the summer season, most visitors will not be bothered by overcrowding." Kaye adds, "Summertime is not all that busy—you can still go out into the backcountry and not see people; you can even drive one of the park roads and not be inundated."

Since the park is open every day of the year, Kaye says that hiking, camping, and cross-country skiing are ideal experiences in the off season.

the young Rocky Mountains, then deposited them on a vast lowland, today's Great Plains. During the warm, rainy periods that followed, dense vegetation grew, fell into swampy areas, and was later buried by new layers of sediment. Eventually this plant material turned into lignite coal. Some plant life became petrified.

Even as layers of sediment were being deposited, streams were starting to carve through the soft strata, sculpting the infinite variety of buttes, tablelands, and valleys that comprise the badlands today.

As inhospitable as this land looks, it is home to a large variety of creatures and plants. Rainfall supports an abundance of prairie grasses and wildflowers, and 186 species of birds have been counted. Mule deer and white-tailed deer inhabit the park, and prairie dogs have built their tunnel "towns" in the grasslands. Through careful management, some animals that nearly became extinct in the 19th and early 20th centuries are once again thriving. Bison and elk, for example, have been successfully reintroduced into the area.

The wealth of wildlife that first attracted Theodore Roosevelt and thousands of other avid sports enthusiasts to this area still exists. Bands of wild horses roam in the park's South Unit, just as they did when Roosevelt rode over this land and tended his cattle a century ago.

Avoiding the Crowds. Since the park has 70,000 acres, three spread-out units, and less than a half million visitors per year, avoiding crowds at Theodore Roosevelt National Park is not difficult. In general, you'll see fewer visitors in early morning and evening hours, particularly during the high-visitation months of June, July, and August. Early fall is especially appealing to those seeking a more contemplative experience. But even during the height of the summer season, those enjoying backcountry treks and scenic drives are not likely to encounter throngs of camera-clad vacationers: This

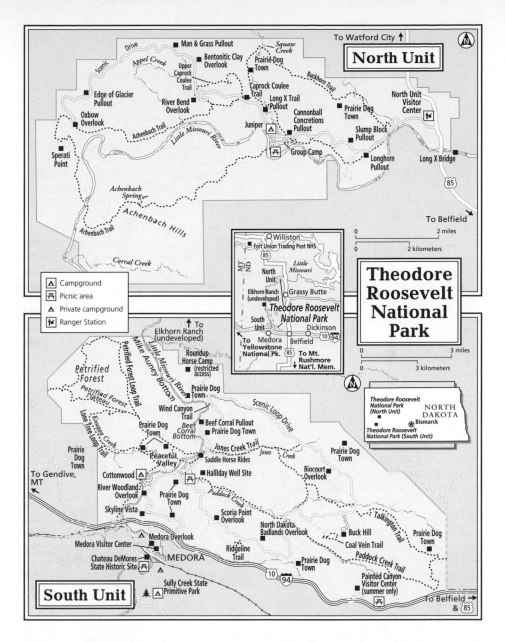

national park is just too big, and visitation too low, to make that occur.

Just the Facts

The park's **South Unit** is located 130 miles west of Bismarck and just north of Medora (Exit 24 or 27 on I-94). The **North Unit** is located near Watford City. From I-94, take Exit 42 (Belfield); then you must continue north on U.S. 85 another 50 miles to the North Unit Entrance. The park also includes **Theodore Roosevelt's Elkhorn Ranch,** which is located between the North and South units, but visitors should ask rangers about road conditions before attempting to go there.

The Nearest Airports. About 130 miles east of the park is **Bismarck Municipal Airport** (✆ **701/222-6502**), served by

Northwest, Big Sky, and United Express airlines plus Avis, Hertz, and Enterprise car rentals. **Dickinson Municipal Airport** (© **701/483-1062**) is 35 miles from Medora and is served by United Express airline and Budget Car Rental. The toll-free numbers for airlines and car-rental agencies are in the appendix.

INFORMATION

Contact the **Superintendent, Theodore Roosevelt National Park,** P.O. Box 7, Medora, ND 58645 (© **701/623-4466** for the South Unit, the main number, or 701/842-2333 for the North Unit; www.nps.gov/thro). The National Park Service has a variety of brochures that explore the park's cultural and natural resources, including a very useful **road log guide,** sold in the visitor center. Information and a variety of publications are available from the **Theodore Roosevelt Nature and History Association,** P.O. Box 167, Medora, ND 58645 (© **701/623-4884;** www.nps.gov/thro/tr_shop.htm), which produces *Frontier Fragments,* an excellent park newspaper. It's updated annually and filled with relevant stories on the park's history, wildlife, interpretive offerings, and visitor services.

For information about the area, contact the **Medora Chamber of Commerce,** P.O. Box 186, Medora, ND 58645 (© **701/623-4910**).

VISITOR CENTERS

The park has three visitor centers. The **Medora Visitor Center** (for the South Unit) is located just inside the park entrance at Medora and is open daily year-round. The **Painted Canyon Visitor Center** is about 7 miles east of Medora and open daily from April to mid-November. The **North Unit Visitor Center,** located at the eastern end of the North Unit, just off U.S. 85, is open daily from Memorial Day through September and weekends and most weekdays the rest of the year.

FEES & PERMITS

Entry into the park for up to 7 days costs $5 per person, or a maximum of $10 per vehicle. Campsites cost $10 per night, plus $1 per horse if you use the group horse-camping site in the South Unit. Group camps cost $2 per person, with a minimum of $20 (reservations required). Backcountry permits are free.

SPECIAL REGULATIONS & WARNINGS

The animals in the park are wild and should be viewed from a safe distance. (Even the prairie dogs can bite.) Watch out for ticks in late spring and early summer. Climbing on the steep, barren slopes of the badlands can be dangerous due to slippery clays and soft sediments that may yield underfoot, so stay on designated trails. Horses are prohibited in campgrounds, in picnic areas, and on self-guided nature trails.

SEASONS & CLIMATE

The climate in the badlands can be extreme (bitter cold and snow in the winter and intense heat in the summer), with high or low temperatures and sudden, violent storms.

If You Have Only 1 Day

If you have only 1 day, you'll probably want to limit yourself to either the North or South Unit. Since it's more accessible from I-94, and more developed, it's likely you'll choose the South Unit.

If you're coming from the east, stop first at the Painted Canyon Overlook and Visitor Center to get a sweeping, panoramic view of the North Dakota badlands, then continue 7 miles west to the Medora Visitor Center. Here, you'll be able to view a film and listen to one or more ranger talks. There's also a museum with some of Theodore Roosevelt's personal effects. Be sure to stop in at the Maltese Cross cabin, behind the visitor center. Take the 36-mile scenic driving loop around the park, stopping at the overlooks (be sure to stop at one of the prairie-dog towns), and stop along the way to explore one of the scenic trails.

Exploring the Park by Car

THE SOUTH UNIT

If you're traveling west on I-94, your first introduction to Theodore Roosevelt National Park is the **Painted Canyon Overlook and Visitor Center,** about 7 miles east of Medora. Here, on the upper ridge of the badlands, is an unparalleled panorama of ragged ridges and colorful hues. Watch for wild horses, the descendants of former domestic ranching stock; you might even see bison grazing.

A highlight of the South Unit is a paved 36-mile **scenic loop road** with interpretive signs that explain some of the park's historical and natural phenomena. The scenic drive is best accessed from the Medora Visitor Center by turning right onto the loop in Peaceful Valley. If you've bought the **road log,** you'll want to travel counter-clockwise around the loop. Descriptions of the shorter interpretive trails are incorporated into the driving tours for the North and South units; for more information on longer hiking opportunities, please see "Exploring the Backcountry," below.

South Unit Scenic Drive. In any season, the South Unit Scenic Drive can take you into some of the most remote areas of North Dakota. When Gen. Alfred Sully traveled through these badlands, he described them as "hell with the fires burned out." In reality, they are teeming with wildlife, wildflowers, and bird life. The South Unit comprises 46,158 acres, of which 10,510 acres are designated as wilderness.

Scoria Point is the first overlook you'll come to. Strictly speaking, scoria is volcanic in origin, but in the badlands, wherever a seam of coal has caught fire and baked the surrounding sand and clay, it's called scoria. You'll see it from this view point, where the topsoil has been stripped away by erosion and the harder material underneath is exposed.

About a mile farther, you'll come to the **Ridgeline Nature Trail.** If you choose to take this very short (0.6-mile loop) hike, you'll learn more about the badlands and their ecology. This is a moderately easy trail, suitable for most people.

Next is the **North Dakota Badlands Overlook.** The view here is over Paddock Creek, and what you'll see is a surreal, striking landscape. This is because erosion has worn away the topsoil, leaving behind only the rocks and harder materials underneath the thin, top layer.

After crossing Paddock Creek, you'll come to the turnoff for the **Coal Vein Trail,** a short (0.8-mile) loop that winds through an area where a fire burned in a coal seam from 1951 through early 1977. The fire baked the clay and soil here, changing both the appearance of the terrain and altering the vegetation patterns. Here, you'll be walking around the scoria (the same kind of formations you viewed from a distance at the Scoria Point Overlook earlier). You must drive down a short, unpaved road to reach the trail.

After returning to the main loop road, you'll next come to the turnoff for **Buck Hill.** It's only a short walk to the hill itself from the end of the road. The hill (at 2,855 ft.) has two very different slopes. On the south side, the slopes are hot and dry, and you'll see only shrubs and small plants. On the north side, which is wetter and cooler, you'll see trees.

Several miles farther will bring you to the **Boicourt Overlook,** which affords one of the best views of the badlands in the South Unit.

The next stop is **Wind Canyon Trail.** This is a very short walk up to a ridge, where you'll have a great view of the Little Missouri River, which did much to create the landscape here. Beyond the river, to the west, is the virtually untouched wilderness of the South Unit. Pause here around sunrise to listen for the call of coyotes in the valley below.

After passing the **Beef Corral Pullout** and a **prairie-dog town,** which is just beyond the pullouts on either side of the road, you'll pass the parking lot for the **Jones Creek Trail.** This is one of two trailheads for the Jones Creek Trail on Scenic Loop Drive. (You passed the other one earlier; it was at the parking area between the Boicourt Overlook and the Wind Canyon Trail pullout.) The trail itself is 3.7 miles and leads into the heart of the badlands.

The final stop on the Scenic Loop Drive is in Peaceful Valley, shortly before you reach the intersection where you turned off onto the loop. The **Peaceful Valley Ranch,** which is on the National Historic Register, was established during the heyday of cattle ranching in the 1880s. The tall central section of the ranch house was constructed about 1885. Today, the ranch offers trail rides from May through the end of September (see "Horseback Riding in the Park," below).

THE NORTH UNIT

Fewer visitors take the time to travel to the park's North Unit, although paved roads provide easy access. There are 24,070 acres in the North Unit, of which 19,410 acres are designated as wilderness. Stop at the visitor center at the entrance to the unit, and the rangers will help you plan your time.

North Unit Scenic Drive. The 14-mile scenic drive (and State Scenic Byway) travels from the entrance station to the **Oxbow Overlook** with plenty of turnouts and interpretive signs along the route.

Keep your eyes open for longhorns on the prairie between the entrance and Juniper Campground; these are the same type of cattle raised by ranchers here during Roosevelt's time. At the Oxbow Overlook, you must double back along the same route.

Since less of the North Unit is developed, the thing to do here is to get out of the car at one of the scenic pullouts and take a hike. Whether you go a long or a short distance, you'll be able to see dramatic scenery populated with many bison, elk, and bighorn sheep but few people.

The **Little Mo Nature Trail,** which starts at Juniper Campground, offers a comfortable, leisurely walk through the Little Missouri River bottom. The trail cuts through woodlands near the river as well as badlands formations and gives you two options. The shorter portion of the loop is only 0.7 mile, paved, and wheelchair accessible. But you can also extend your hike by 0.4 mile and take the unpaved portion. If you're more adventurous, you'll see additional formations and cross some wildlife trails that (mostly) bison use.

Just across the road from the Juniper Campground entrance road, stop at the **Cannonball Concretions Pullout.** A short walk reveals the well-named rock formations. Contrasting formations in the area make this stop a photographer's delight. Light doesn't hit the best "cannonball" until late morning.

The **Caprock Coulee Nature Trail,** 1.5 miles west of Juniper Campground, is another easy, self-guiding nature trail that winds through badlands and dry water gulches, crosses breaks, then finds a welcome interruption in the grassy plains of the park. The total length round-trip is 1.6 miles.

If you want to do something more ambitious, combine the self-guiding nature trail with the Upper Caprock Coulee Trail. Together, they run a distance of 4.1 miles. (The latter portion is 3.3 miles.) You'll go farther into the wilderness this way; it also brings you back to the trailhead so that you don't have to double back over the same route. Bighorn sheep were introduced into the North Unit in 1996. Be on the lookout for these majestic animals.

It's at this point that the North Unit Scenic Drive is closed for the winter. If you continue, you'll end up at the **Oxbow Overlook,** another sweeping panoramic view of the badlands.

The **Sperati Point Trail** can be accessed from the Oxbow Overlook. This is the spur of the Achenbach Trail that leads to the Oxbow Bend Overlook and makes a less strenuous alternative if you want something shorter than the Achenbach's 16 miles. (The length of this trail is 1.5 miles round-trip.) The trail leads to the narrowest gateway in the badlands. The flow of the Little Missouri River once continued north to Hudson Bay. Blocked during the Ice Age, the river was forced to find a new course and finally broke through the gap between this point and the Achenbach Hills on the other side. The Little Missouri now drains into the Gulf of Mexico via the Missouri-Mississippi system. Take this trail for a taste of prairie country and long, sweeping views.

Exploring the Backcountry

If you wish to explore some of the wilderness the park has to offer, you'll need a free backcountry permit from the Medora or North Unit visitor center to do any overnight camping. You can also explore the backcountry on horseback. If you bring a horse, you must camp either in the backcountry or at the group campsite in the South Unit. You can also board your horse at the Peaceful Valley Ranch (see "Horseback Riding in the Park," below). Your stay in the Theodore Roosevelt National Park backcountry is limited to 14 consecutive days.

Special Regulations. You cannot have a campfire in the backcountry due to the possibility of wildfires, so you must bring a self-contained camp stove. You must

pack out what you pack in (no burying of trash). The park requires that those with horses bring certified weed-free hay. Groups entering the backcountry are limited to 10 persons (or 8 persons with 8 horses). Finally, don't drink the water in the backcountry; there are no safe, approved water sources here.

The mother of all trails in the area is the **Maah Daah Hey Trail,** completed in summer 1999. The Maah Daah Hey is a 120-mile hiking, horseback, and mountain biking trail that traverses the scenic and rugged North Dakota badlands. The trail passes through the Little Missouri National Grasslands, as well as state and private land, as it connects the North and South units of Theodore Roosevelt National Park. The north end of the trail begins at the U.S. Forest Service CCC Campground in McKenzie County, located 20 miles south of Watford City off Highway 85. The trail winds its way to its southern terminus at Sully Creek State Park in Billings County, south of Medora. Six fenced overnight campsites with hitching posts, vault toilets, and campfire rings have been constructed along the trail.

For more information about this trail, contact the **U.S. Forest Service,** Medora Ranger District, 161 21st St. W., Dickinson, ND 58601 (© **701/225-5151;** www.fs.fed.us/r1/dakotaprairie); or the **McKenzie Ranger District office** at HC02, Box 8, Watford City, ND 58854 (© **701/842-2393**).

SOUTH UNIT TRAILS

Petrified Forest Trail

16 miles RT (from the east). Moderate. Access: You can get on the trail at the parking area at Peaceful Valley at the trail's eastern end; from the west, the trailhead is located at the end of a dirt road outside the park (ask park rangers for directions).

Pieces of petrified wood are scattered throughout this national park, but the greatest concentration can be reached only on foot or horseback along this lengthy trail. The trail leads up along Petrified Forest Plateau. Just don't take any souvenirs.

NORTH UNIT TRAILS

Achenbach Trail

16 miles RT. Moderate. Access: Juniper Campground.

This route climbs from the river bottomlands up through the Achenbach Hills, drops down to the river again, climbs to the Oxbow Overlook on a spur trail, then returns along the river bottom to the campground. Before departing, ask a ranger about the condition of river crossings. The "spur" trail is the Sperati Point Trail described in "The North Unit," above.

Buckhorn Trail

11 miles RT. Moderate. Access: From the Caprock Coulee Nature Trail (see "The North Unit," above).

About a mile into this loop, hikers discover a large prairie dog town. Of the five varieties of prairie dogs, only the black-tailed variety inhabits Theodore Roosevelt National Park.

Organized Tours & Ranger Programs

From mid-June to early September, ranger programs, including nature walks and longer hikes, are offered at various locations. If snow conditions permit, rangers may conduct ski tours in winter.

Historic & Man-Made Attractions

There are a variety of historic attractions, both in the national park and nearby.

A **museum** housed in the Medora Visitor Center features personal items that once belonged to Theodore Roosevelt,

ranching artifacts, and natural history displays. Tours are conducted (free, about 20 min.) through the **Maltese Cross Cabin** from mid-June through Labor Day; you can take a self-guided tour during the rest of the year. Roosevelt used this cabin, which was relocated to its new home behind the visitor center after a detailed restoration program.

At the **Elkhorn Ranch site,** where Theodore Roosevelt started his second cattle ranch in the area, no buildings remain (save the foundation stones from the main ranch house). To get there, you must take the dirt road that goes north out of the South Unit (its turnoff is at the top of the Scenic Loop Dr.) and drive another 20 miles, but you must cross the river to get to the actual ranch site. Inquire at the Medora Visitor Center about river conditions before attempting this trip. An alternate route accesses the site from the west.

Chateau de Mores State Historic Site (✆ **701/623-4355;** www.state.nd.us/hist), near the town of Medora, is a 128-acre site that contains the Chateau de Mores, Chimney Park, and De Mores Memorial Park. The town of Medora was built by the Marquis de Mores, an entrepreneurial French nobleman, on the Northern Pacific Line and named for his American wife. The Chateau de Mores, a 26-room rustic summer home built in 1883, contains many of its original furnishings. The ruins of the Marquis's meat-packing plant, found in Chimney Park, recall his ambitious plans to revolutionize the meat-packing industry. A young Theodore Roosevelt was a business acquaintance of the Marquis. Admission costs $6 adults, $3 kids 6 to 15, under 6 free; group tour rates are available. Guided tours of the chateau are offered from mid-May to mid-September, hours 8:30am to 6:30pm MDT, and other times by appointment.

Knife River Indian Villages National Historic Site, consisting of three villages along the Knife River in North Dakota, was inhabited by the Hidatsa, Mandan, and later the Arikara from the early 1500s to 1860. Located a half-mile north of Stanton, North Dakota (via County Rd. 37), it offers insights into the life of the Northern Plains Indians. The site is open from 7:30am to 6pm (Mountain time) daily from Memorial Day through Labor Day, 8am to 4:30pm daily the rest of the year. Admission is free. The exhibits and 15-minute orientation video depict life in the villages before and after Euro-American contact. Earth-lodge tours are conducted daily, Memorial Day through Labor Day. The annual **Northern Plains Indian Culture Fest** is held the last full weekend in July.

Special attention has been focused on Knife River Indian Villages due to the Lewis & Clark Bicentennial. This area is believed to have been the home of Sacagawea, her new baby, and her husband before they joined the Corps of Discovery for the arduous trip west.

There are various short trails to the three village sites. Other trails meander through prairie and woodland ecosystems. Check at the visitor center for trail hours. Some trails are wheelchair accessible. For information, contact the **Knife River Indian Villages NHS,** P.O. Box 9, Stanton, ND 58571 (✆ **701/745-3300;** www.nps.gov/knri).

Fort Union Trading Post National Historic Site preserves the restored Fort Union, which was, for nearly 4 decades in the 19th century, a bastion of John Jacob Astor's American Fur Company, which dominated the fur trade in the region of modern-day North Dakota, Montana, and Saskatchewan. Now, as then, the focal point of the historic site is Fort Union's Indian Trade House. Here, goods were traded between the fur company and Assiniboines, Crows, Crees, and Blackfeet. Also called the Bourgeois House (or Manager's House), this facility is now the visitor center and bookstore. In this, the farthest reaches of the Missouri River country, the National Park Service and the Fort Union Association have meticulously restored and refurnished the Trade House to its appearance in 1851. The site is located about 2 hours north of Theodore Roosevelt National Park via U.S. 85 at Belfield, North Dakota; N. Dak. 16 at Beach, North Dakota; or Mont. 16 at Glendive, Montana. The Bourgeois House Visitor Center is open from 8am to 8pm Memorial Day through Labor Day, from 9am to 5:30pm the remainder of the year. The Indian Trade House is open from 9:45am to 5:45pm daily during the summer only. Ranger tours are available from noon to 3:30pm daily during the summer, with self-guided tours the remainder of the year.

Fort Union Trading Post will be a focus of attention during the Lewis & Clark Bicentennial. Lewis & Clark stopped at the confluence of the Yellowstone and Missouri rivers in 1805, near the location where Fort Union was constructed 23 years later. Several events related to the Bicentennial will take place at the Fort.

For scheduled dates of special programs, or for more information, contact the **Superintendent, Fort Union Trading Post NHS,** 15550 Hwy. 1804, Williston, ND 58801 (✆ **701/572-9083;** www.nps.gov/fous).

Horseback Riding in the Park

Many backcountry trails are open to those on horseback, and you can use either your own horse or go on a guided trail ride with a park concessionaire. In the South Unit, contact **Peaceful Valley Ranch,** P.O. Box 308, Medora, ND 58645 (✆ **701/623-4568**). They operate from Memorial Day to Labor Day and have regularly scheduled horseback rides lasting from 1½ to 5 hours. Trail rides run daily from 8:30am to evening, and all scheduled rides include a riding lesson. In the North Unit, the concessionaire is **Little Knife Outfitters,** Box 82, Watford City, ND 58854 (✆ **701/842-2631;** www.littleknifeoutfitters.com). They offer 1- to 5-day trips.

Camping

Cottonwood Campground in the South Unit and **Juniper Campground** in the North Unit are operated on a first-come, first-served basis. You'll find drinking water, flush toilets, public telephones (Cottonwood only), and fire grates in both campgrounds, but no showers or RV hookups. Juniper Campground has an RV dump station, but Cottonwood does not. Camping costs $10 per night. Campgrounds are open year-round, but the availability of water is limited during the winter.

Camping for organized groups is available at the Cottonwood Campground in the South Unit and in part of the Juniper Campground in the North Unit. Groups must have a written reservation from the park superintendent.

Riding groups with their own horses should write the superintendent to make arrangements. It's possible to camp with a horse, but only at the Roundup Group Horse Campground in the South Unit; the cost is additional and reservations are required.

Other privately run and Forest Service campgrounds are located near both units of the park, and you can get a list from park offices.

Where to Stay & Dine

There are no accommodations or dining facilities in the park, but you will find hotels, motels, and bed-and-breakfasts, as well as a variety of modest restaurants in Medora, Belfield, and Beach near the South Unit, and in Watford City near the North Unit. Most are open year-round, but some may close in the winter. Rates are highest in summer.

IN MEDORA

The **AmericInn,** the most luxurious choice, is located at 75 E. River Rd. S., 1 block south of the Medora Community Center (© **800/634-3444** or 701/623-4800; www.americinn.com). It has seasonal rates, ranging in the main tourist season from $99.90 to $149.90 double; American Express, Diners Club, Discover, MasterCard, and Visa are accepted.

The **Badlands Motel,** on Pacific Avenue, and the **Rough Riders Motel,** at 301 Third Ave., both in Medora, charge $89 for a double. The Badlands is open May 1 to September 30 and the Rough Rider's season is June to September. They both take American Express, Discover, MasterCard, and Visa. For reservations, call © **800/MEDORA-1** or 701/623-4444 (fax 701/623-4494; www.medora.com).

Custer's Cottage, located at 156 E. River Rd. S. in Medora, is a medium-sized house with two units, one main floor, and one basement. Each unit has separate private entrances, full kitchens, large living rooms, cable TV, up to four bedrooms, and laundry facilities. It is open year-round by advance reservations (© **800/783-6366,** PIN #0749, or 701/623-4378; www.custerscottage.com); prices range from $45 to $105, depending on how many bedrooms are used and length of stay; one group or party per night per unit. Credit cards are not accepted for payment but may be used to reserve a room. The facility is 2 miles from Maah Daah Hey Trail. This is a smoke-free facility.

IN BELFIELD

The **Bel-Vu Motel** is located west of U.S. 85 on U.S. 10 (© **701/575-4245**). A double costs $37 to $60 depending on the season; MasterCard and Visa are accepted.

The **Trapper's Inn** is located at I-94 and U.S. 85 North, 15 minutes from Medora (© **800/284-1855** or 701/575-4261). Rates range from $70 to $80 double in the peak season; American Express, Diners Club, Discover, MasterCard, and Visa are accepted.

IN BEACH

The **Buckboard Inn** is located at I-94 and N. Dak. 16 South (© **888/449-3599;** fax 701/872-4794, ext. 127). A double costs $46 during the summer; American Express, Discover, MasterCard, and Visa are accepted. Pets are welcome.

IN WATFORD CITY

The **McKenzie Inn** is located on U.S. 85 West (© **701/444-3980**). The year-round rate is $45 for a double, $36 for a single; American Express, Discover, Master-Card, and Visa are accepted. AAA rated.

The **Roosevelt Inn & Suites,** on U.S. 85 West (© **800/887-9170** or 701/842-3686; www.rooseveltinn.com), has a new addition with a swimming pool, spa, sauna, and game room. Rates year-round are $49 for a double; American Express, Carte Blanche, Diners Club, Discover, MasterCard, and Visa are accepted. Continental breakfast and handicapped facilities are available.

34

YELLOWSTONE NATIONAL PARK & LITTLE BIGHORN BATTLEFIELD NATIONAL MONUMENT

by Eric Peterson

YELLOWSTONE HAS SHAPED THE AMERICAN PUBLIC'S DEFINITION OF nature for more than a century, and with good reason: There are more geysers, hot springs, and other thermal features here than the rest of the planet combined. Then there's the pristine snowmelt cascading into dazzling waterfalls of every description, including one that's twice as high as Niagara Falls. Not to mention a canyon deep and colorful enough to fall into the "grand" category. Best of all, a significant chunk of the park's incredible terrain is reachable by a hiker of just average ability.

Then there's the wildlife: Ever focus your telephoto lens on a wild, untamed grizzly bear? Or a bald eagle? What about a wolf? Thousands of visitors have these experiences here every year.

And the park doesn't appeal solely to the visual senses. By one biologist's estimate, Yellowstone has more than 1,100 species of native plants; so when wildflowers cover the meadows in spring, you won't just see them, you'll be overpowered by their fragrances. The mud pots and fumaroles have their own set of odors, though many are less pleasing than a wild lily. Your ears will be filled with the sounds of geysers noisily expelling thousands of gallons of boiling water into the blue Wyoming sky. After sunset, coyotes break the silence of the night with their high-pitched yips.

It's possible to see the highlights of Yellowstone without ever leaving your car—park roads lead past most of the key attractions—but why would you want to? There's so much more to see by actually getting out of your vehicle. And there's even more to see by venturing into the backcountry, something embarked upon by only a small percentage of the park's visitors. You can spend weeks hiking Yellowstone's backcountry or fishing its streams, and the crowds and traffic snarls become faint memories.

Aside from monthlong closures in the fall and spring, Yellowstone's season is year-round. It's not nearly as crowded in the winter, and wildlife is more visible. Mammoth and Old Faithful serve as home bases for the thousands of skiers, snowmobilers, and wildlife watchers.

The beauty of Yellowstone's natural architecture comes from its geology. The area experienced three separate volcanic periods beginning 2.1 million years ago, and occurring every 600,000 to 800,000 years since. The last big bang happened 640,000 years ago, meaning the area is ripe for another massive eruption—if Mother Nature's timetable holds to form.

During the biggest eruptions, thousands of square miles of landmass were blown skyward, leaving enormous calderas (volcanic depressions). This process has repeated itself several times—there is geologic evidence of 27 layers of lava in some areas. Subsequently, glaciers covered the volcanic mountains during the ice ages. The powerful bulldozing caused by the movement of these gigantic blocks of ice shaped the valleys and canyons of the park.

Yellowstone National Park was officially created in 1872, when Pres. Ulysses Grant signed legislation making it the first national park in the world. In the years afterward, it suffered from incompetent superintendents and shortages of cash until at last, in 1886, the U.S. Army took possession and helped reign in poaching and establish a sense of order. In 1916, control of the park was transferred to the newly created National Park Service. Yellowstone became one of the first parks to come under its stewardship.

Avoiding the Crowds. If a few thousand people on the benches in front of Old Faithful is not your idea of a wilderness park experience, then skip Yellowstone's busy summer season, which is in full swing during July and August. Or, if you can't avoid that time of year, head up the trails away from the roads and car traffic. Less than 10% of the park's visitors venture into the backcountry.

Although the beautiful seasons between May and mid-June and after Labor Day are no longer the best-kept secret in the Rockies, they only attract a fraction of the midsummer traffic. Just be careful how far you push it in this unpredictable climate. A beautiful Halloween weekend of rustling leaves and bright sun can become a winter wonderland overnight. Come too early in the spring—which is when most of the region's precipitation falls—and you'll be stuck at lower elevations while walls of snow melt on the higher trails. Try June and September, or, if you like taking chances, go the first 2 weeks in October. Any earlier or later, and you're on your own—truly on your own, because most of the inns in the park will have shut their doors.

Even if your visit is scheduled during the park's busy months, you can still avoid the crowds: Take short hikes in popular spots at times of day when others are eating. Take a sack lunch—you can buy them at the Yellowstone General Stores—and avoid the lines at restaurants.

Better yet, take long walks into this grand wilderness. About 500 yards from a trailhead, the crowd thins rapidly. Strap on a backpack, pick up a backcountry permit, and spend a night in the wilderness. You'll see some of the park's most beautiful landscapes, and there won't be a single tourist in the picture.

Just the Facts

GETTING THERE & GATEWAYS

To get to Yellowstone from I-90 and **Bozeman,** Montana (91 miles), take U.S. 191 south to its junction with U.S. 287 and head straight through the town of **West Yellowstone** to the park's west entrance.

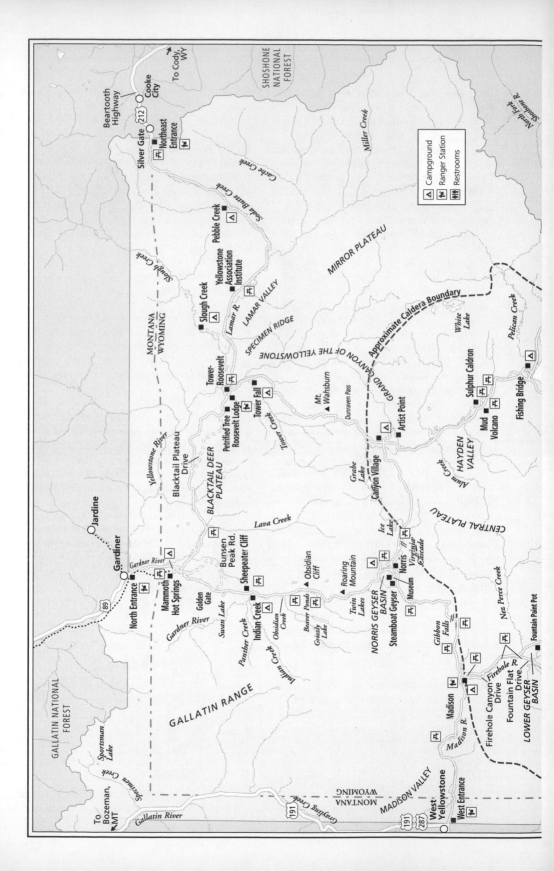

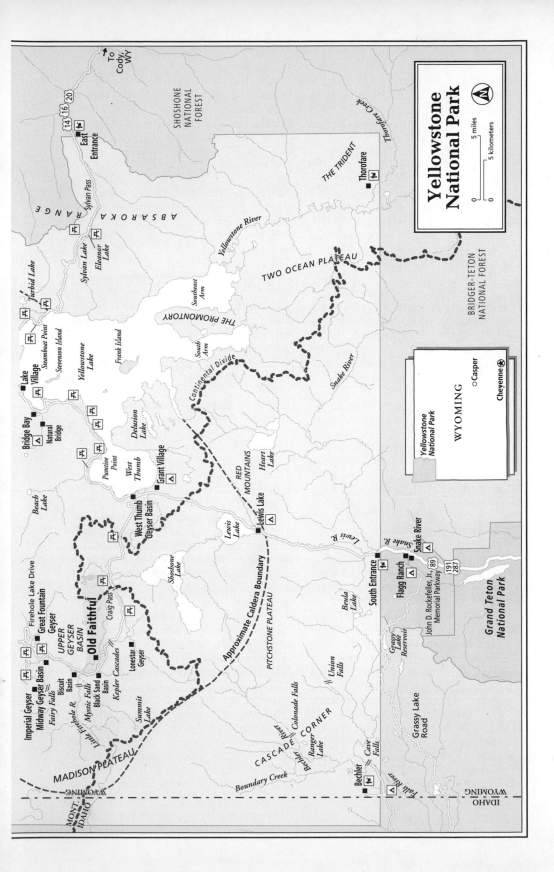

Billings, Montana, is 129 miles from Yellowstone's northeast entrance over Beartooth Pass (closed Oct 15 to Memorial Day). It's a 65-mile drive south from I-94 on U.S. 212 to Red Lodge, then 30 miles on the Beartooth Highway to the park.

Cody, Wyoming, is 52 miles to Yellowstone's east entrance, which is closed from November 1 to April 30, via U.S. 14/16/20. To Yellowstone's northeast entrance, it's 53 miles via Wyo. 120/296 to the Beartooth Highway (closed Oct 15 to Memorial Day) intersection, and 14 miles beyond that to the entrance.

Jackson, Wyoming, is 57 miles south of Yellowstone's south entrance. Take U.S. 89/191 north through Grand Teton National Park. You can also approach this entrance from the east over Togwotee Pass on U.S. 26/287 from **Dubois,** Wyoming (83 miles).

From **Little Bighorn Battlefield National Monument,** an easy detour on the way to or from Yellowstone, take I-90 south from the monument into Wyoming about 50 miles to Exit 9, and then follow U.S. 14 west about 190 miles to Yellowstone's east entrance (closed in winter).

The Nearest Airports. You can fly into Bozeman's airport, **Gallatin Field** (© 406/388-8321), which provides daily service via Delta, Northwest, and United as well as Horizon (© 800/547-9308) and SkyWest (© 800/453-9417) commuter flights. The **West Yellowstone Airport** (© 406/646-7631), U.S. 191, 1 mile north of West Yellowstone, provides commercial air service seasonally, from June through September only, on Delta's commuter service, SkyWest. The airport in Billings, **Logan International** (© 406/238-3420), is the busiest in Montana and is located on the rimrocks 2 miles north of downtown. Daily intrastate service is provided by Big Sky Airlines (© 800/237-7788 or 406/245-2300). America West, Delta, Horizon, Northwest, and United provide regional daily service. Cody's **Yellowstone Regional Airport** (© 307/587-5096) serves the east entrance of Yellowstone National Park with year-round commercial flights via SkyWest, United, and Frontier.

Renting a Car. Most of the major car-rental agencies have operations in the gateway cities. For toll-free numbers for airlines and car-rental agencies, see the appendix.

INFORMATION

To receive maps and information before your arrival, contact **Yellowstone National Park,** WY 82190 (© **307/344-7381;** www. nps.gov/yell).

Information regarding lodging, some campgrounds, tours, boating, and horseback riding in Yellowstone is available from **Xanterra Parks and Resorts,** P.O. Box 165, Yellowstone National Park, WY 82190 (© **307/344-7311;** www. travelyellowstone.com).

For information regarding educational programs in Yellowstone, contact **Yellowstone Association,** P.O. Box 117, Yellowstone National Park, WY 82190 (© **307/344-2293;** www.yellowstone association.org), which operates bookstores in park visitor centers, museums, and information stations, and oversees the excellent **Yellowstone Association Institute,** which conducts a varied curriculum at the old Lamar Buffalo Ranch in the park's northeast corner. They also have a catalog of publications you can order by mail.

The following books are interesting and informative. If you cannot find them in your local bookstore, you can order many of them by mail from the Yellowstone Association (see above). Look for *Yellowstone Trails,* Mark C. Marschall (Yellowstone National Park, Wyoming: The Yellowstone Association) if you're a hiker. If you're traveling with kids, pick up *An Outdoor Family Guide to Yellowstone and Grand Teton National*

Parks, Lisa Gollin Evans (The Mountaineers). For a more comprehensive guide, look for *Frommer's Yellowstone & Grand Teton National Parks,* by the author of this chapter.

VISITOR CENTERS

There are five major visitor and information centers in the park, and each has something different to offer. The **Albright Visitor Center** (© 307/344-2263) at Mammoth Hot Springs is the largest. It provides visitor information and publications about the park, exhibits depicting park history from prehistory through the creation of the National Park Service, and a wildlife display on the second floor.

The **Old Faithful Visitor Center** (© 307/545-2750) is another large facility. An excellent short film describing the geysers' microscopic inhabitants, *Yellowstone Revealed,* is shown throughout the day in an air-conditioned auditorium. Rangers dispense various park publications and post projected geyser eruption times here. Once fundraising efforts net $15 million, the Park Service plans to open a state-of-the-art visitor education center in place of the current architecturally maligned building.

The **Canyon Visitor Center** (© 307/242-2550) in Canyon Village is the place to go for books and an informative display about bison in the park. It's staffed with friendly rangers used to dealing with crowds.

The **Fishing Bridge Visitor Center** (© 307/242-2450), near Fishing Bridge on the northern shore of Yellowstone Lake, has an excellent wildlife display. You can get information and publications here as well.

The **Grant Village Visitor Center** (© 307/242-2650) has information, publications, a slide program, and a fascinating exhibit that examines the effects of fire in Yellowstone.

Other sources of park information are at the **Madison Information Station** (© 307/344-2821); the **Museum of the National Park Ranger** (no phone; open daily in summer 9am–6pm) and the **Norris Geyser Basin Museum** (© 307/344-2812), both at Norris; the **West Thumb Information Station** (no phone; open daily in summer 9am–5pm); and the Public Lands Desk at the **West Yellowstone Chamber of Commerce** building (© 406/646-7701).

FEES & PERMITS

A pass to enter Yellowstone is $20 per vehicle for a 7-day period (no matter the number of occupants), and covers both Yellowstone and Grand Teton national parks. Entering on a snowmobile or motorcycle costs $15 for 7 days, and someone who comes in on bicycle, skis, or foot pays $10. If you expect to visit the parks by car more than once in a year, buy an annual pass for $40.

You must have a backcountry permit for any overnight trip, whether you travel by foot, on horseback, or by boat. See "Exploring the Backcountry," later in this chapter, for more information.

SPECIAL REGULATIONS & WARNINGS

It is unlawful to approach within 100 yards of a bear or within 25 yards of other wildlife. Feeding any wildlife is illegal. Wildlife calls such as elk bugles or other artificial attractants are forbidden. Because of wildlife and thermal activity, staying on the trails here is especially important.

SEASONS & CLIMATE

For general information on seasons and climate in the area, see "Seasons & Climate," in the Grand Teton National Park chapter, p. 283. Keep in mind that nearby Grand Teton is actually a bit lower in elevation than Yellowstone, so snows melt later in Yellowstone and temperatures are slightly lower.

Scheduling a driving trip to Yellowstone during spring months can be a roll of the dice, since openings can be delayed for weeks, especially at higher altitudes. A heavy snowstorm in October can compel early closure of the park gates. Depending upon weather, most other park roads remain open until the park season ends on the first Sunday in November (the Beartooth Hwy. between Cooke City and Red Lodge, Mont., closes mid-Oct). The only road open year-round is the **Mammoth Hot Springs–Cooke City Road.**

Plowing in Yellowstone begins in early March. The first roads open to motor vehicles usually include **Mammoth-Norris, Norris-Canyon, Madison–Old Faithful,** and **West Yellowstone–Madison.** The latter may open by the end of April. If the weather cooperates, the east and south entrances, as well as roads on the east and south sides of the park, will open early in May. Opening of the **Tower-Roosevelt** to **Canyon Junction Road,** however, may be delayed by late season snowfall on Dunraven Pass.

The **Sunlight Basin Road** (which is also called the **Chief Joseph Hwy.**), connecting the entrance at Cooke City, Montana, with Cody, Wyoming, often opens by early May. The **Beartooth Highway** between Cooke City and Red Lodge, Montana, is generally open by Memorial Day weekend.

The road connecting **Gardiner** and **Cooke City,** Montana, remains open year-round, providing the only wintertime access to the latter. This presents late-season travelers with an opportunity to see the northeast area of the park and some of its abundant wildlife during winter months.

Call the park's main information number (*©* **307/344-7381**) for updates on road conditions and closings.

If You Have Only 1 Day

If you'll be coming into Yellowstone for 1 day and leaving the next, here's an itinerary that highlights the best of the best.

If you'll be spending the night, try to reserve a room in one of the park hotels—either Old Faithful Inn or the Lake Hotel—and you'll find yourself minutes from all of the major attractions.

The quickest route to the inner road loops of the park is on the west entrance road, so come in that way, stopping perhaps for a stroll along the banks of the **Madison River,** where you can see the forest recovering from the 1988 fires. You'll likely spot wildlife: ducks and trumpeter swans on the river, and grazing elk and bison near its banks. Turn north at Madison Junction to **Norris Geyser Basin,** where there are two boardwalk tours. Take the southern one if you don't feel there's time for both because there you can wait for the **Echinus Geyser** pool to fill and erupt.

You're now driving the **upper loop,** which goes north to **Mammoth Hot Springs,** east to **Tower-Roosevelt,** south to **Canyon Village,** and west again to Norris, finally returning to Madison Junction, a circuit of about 85 miles. But don't complete the entire loop—at Canyon, continue south on the Lower Loop, which will take you to **Fishing Bridge** and **Lake Village,** then by **West Thumb,** west over Craig Pass to **Old Faithful,** and back to the Madison Junction from the south. If you do the entire loop, it covers 96 miles. Our recommendation: Do one loop the day you enter the park, spend the night, then do the second loop and leave the way you came. If this is part of a longer cross-country trip, you can enter one side of the park and leave the other.

The Upper Loop. The Norris Geyser basin is a major concentration of thermal attractions, including **Porcelain Basin** and the legendary **Steamboat Geyser** (the park's largest, erupting only about once a decade historically but more often in recent years) and has a nice **museum.** Mammoth has one of the park's major attractions, the ever-growing terraces of **Mammoth Hot Springs.** In addition to the natural attraction, the Albright Visitor Center provides excellent historical background for everything you'll see in the park. There is a fine old hotel at Mammoth, and mom-and-pop and chain lodging just north of the park in Gardiner, but we recommend you continue farther around the loop on your first day. From Mammoth the route winds through forested areas that lead to the edge of the **Lamar Valley,** a deep, rounded path for the Lamar River that is prime wildlife habitat. You could stop for the night at nearby **Roosevelt Lodge,** or continue south to Yellowstone's **Grand Canyon,** one of the most dramatic sights in the park, and on to the Lake Yellowstone Hotel, at the north end of **Yellowstone Lake.**

The Lower Loop. This is a better way to go in our opinion. You'll also see the two largest geyser areas in Yellowstone: **Norris** to the north and the park's signature attraction, **Old Faithful,** to the south. On the eastern side of this route, you'll find the **Grand Canyon of the Yellowstone** and **Hayden Valley,** where you'll often see herds of buffalo. Farther south, the **Yellowstone Lake** area is a haven for water-lovers: There's fishing, boating, and places for picnicking on the shore of the lake.

Altogether, this circuit is called the **"Grand Loop,"** and takes you through all the major areas of the park except the road between Norris and Canyon Village. If you have 2 days, then do both loops. You could do it in a day—it's only 120 miles long—but you'd scare a lot of other travelers as you sped by.

If You Have More Time

Stretching your visit to several days will give you time to delve into some of the park's lesser known, but nonetheless impressive, offerings. Since the roads in Yellowstone are organized into a series of interconnecting loops that you can access from any of the park's five entrances, it doesn't really matter where you begin your tour. To simplify things, we will discuss attractions and activities

going clockwise along each section of the **Grand Loop Road,** beginning at **Madison Junction.** But you can enter the loop at any point and pick up our tour as long as you are traveling clockwise. We haven't suggested an optimum amount of time to spend on each leg of the loop since that will depend on your particular interests. *Note:* Road maintenance is a continual process in the park, so expect delays.

WEST YELLOWSTONE TO NORRIS

Since most of Yellowstone's visitors enter at the **West Yellowstone Entrance,** we'll use that as a jumping-off point for an extended tour of the park. As you travel the 14 miles from the gate to **Madison Junction,** you will find the **Two Ribbons Trail,** which offers an opportunity to walk through and inspect the effects of the 1988 fire. Park maps don't identify all the observation points and side roads in the area, so now is the time to begin forming the habit of driving off the beaten path, even when you may not know where you're going. Keep a sharp eye peeled for the poorly marked **Riverside turnout** on the Madison River side of the road; it's a paved road on the north side of the highway about 6 miles from the entrance. This back road takes you along a river, removed from most traffic, with a number of turnouts perfectly situated to look for resident swans, enjoy a picnic, or test your fly-fishing ability.

As you continue toward **Madison Junction,** you'll see vivid evidence of the 1988 fire and, odds are, a herd of bison that frequents the area during summer months. As frightening as the fire was, it had its good points: When temperatures exceeded 500°F (260°C), pine seeds were released from fire-adapted pine cones, which has quickened the rebirth cycle. The thick carpet of tiny trees making their way through the soil is evidence that this forest is recovering very quickly.

The short **Harlequin Lake Trail** offers an excellent, easy opportunity to explore the area and see various types of waterfowl. An alternative hike, the **Purple Mountain Trail,** is more strenuous, but is one of the best in the area. For descriptions of both, see "Day Hikes," later in this chapter.

Madison Junction marks the confluence of the Gibbon and Firehole rivers, two famous trout streams, which meet to form the Madison River, one of three that join to form the Missouri. It's also where you'll enter the northern loop toward Norris Junction, along a windy 14-mile section of road that parallels the **Gibbon River.** At **Gibbon Falls,** which is 84 feet tall, you'll see water bursting out of the edge of a thermal vent in a rocky canyon, the walls of which were hidden from view for several hundred years until being exposed by the fire of 1988. There's a delightful **picnic area** just below the falls, on an open plateau overlooking the Gibbon River. Before arriving at Norris Junction, you'll discover the **Artist Paint Pot Trail** in Gibbon Meadows 4½ miles south of the Norris Junction, an interesting yet easy half-mile stroll. Across the road from the trailhead is **Elk Park,** where you are likely to see a large herd of elk.

NORRIS GEYSER BASIN

Perhaps more than any other area in Yellowstone, this basin is living testimony to the park's unique thermal activity. It changes from year to year as thermal activity and fierce weather create new and different ponds and landscapes. This is the location of one of the park's highest concentrations of thermal features, including the most active geysers, with underground water temperatures that reach 459°F (237°C).

There are two loop trails here, both mostly level with wheelchair access, to the Porcelain Basin and the Back Basin. If you take in both of them, you'll see most of the area's interesting thermal features. If you're pressed for time, take the shorter **Porcelain Basin Trail,** a boardwalk that takes only 45 minutes. To us, this area is especially spectacular on summer days when thermal activity takes place on the ground with thunder and lightning storms overhead.

The **Porcelain Basin Trail** is a 0.75-mile round-trip that can be completed in 45 minutes; on it are Black Growler Steam Vent, Ledge Geyser, and the descriptively named Whale's Mouth.

The 1.5-mile **Back Basin Loop** is easily negotiable in 1 hour and passes by **Steamboat Geyser,** which has been known to produce the world's highest and most memorable eruptions. However, these 400-foot waterspouts occur infrequently, so it will take some luck to see one. (There were only two from 1990 through 2001, but four between Apr 2002 and Mar 2003.) Conversely, **Echinus Geyser** erupts several times a day.

Among the many highlights of the area is the **Norris Geyser Basin Museum,** a beautiful, single-story stone-and-log building with several excellent exhibits explaining the nature of the area. Also nearby is the **Museum of the National Park Ranger,** which is little more than a room full of artifacts in a small building near the campground (see below). Both museums open in mid- to late May, weather permitting, and are open until September; hours vary by season, but you can expect the museums to be open from 9 or 10am to 5 or 6pm during the busiest times (roughly Memorial Day to Labor Day; again, weather is a factor).

NORRIS TO MAMMOTH HOT SPRINGS

From Norris Geyser Basin, it's a 21-mile drive north to Mammoth Hot Springs, past the **Twin Lakes,** beautiful, watery jewels surrounded by trees. During the early months of the park year, the water is milky green because of the runoff of ice and snow. This is an excellent place to call timeout and do some bird-watching.

This stretch of road, between Norris Junction and Mammoth Hot Springs, presents yet another excellent opportunity to see the effects of the 1988 fire.

The large **meadow** on the west (left, if you are traveling north) side of the highway that begins 3 miles from Norris is popular with moose, thanks to water from bogs, marshes, and a creek. As you travel alongside **Obsidian Creek,** you'll notice the smell of sulfur in the air, evidence of thermal vents.

On the east (right, if you are traveling north) side of the road, 4 miles from Norris, is **Roaring Mountain,** a patch of ground totally devoid of brush and plant life, covered with trees and stumps from the fire. Its bareness is attributed to the fact that, as steam vents developed here, the ground became too hot and acidic, which bleached and crumbled the rock, taking the undergrowth with it. Historians say that the noise from the Roaring Mountain was once so loud that it could be heard as far as 4 miles away; these days it is nearly silent.

Just up the road 2 miles is the **Beaver Lake Picnic Area,** an excellent little spot right on Beaver Lake for a snack. It's also a good place to keep an eye out for moose.

As you wend your way a half-mile to **Obsidian Cliff,** across the road from the picnic area the terrain changes quickly, and you'll find yourself driving through a narrow valley bisected by a beautiful green stream. Obsidian Cliff is where ancient peoples of North America gathered to collect obsidian, a hard, black rock that was used to make weapons and implements.

If you didn't stop at Beaver Lake, consider taking time for the 3-minute detour to **Sheepeater Cliffs** (unless you're driving an RV or pulling a trailer). This quiet, secluded spot on the banks of the Gardner River is home to yellow-bellied marmots that live in the rocks, safe from flying predators (such as eagles) and coyotes.

Exiting the valley, head north onto a high plateau, where you'll find **Swan Lake,** which is surrounded by Little Quadrant Mountain and Antler Peak to the west, and Bunsen Peak to the north.

At the northernmost edge of the Yellowstone Plateau, you'll begin a descent through **Golden Gate.** This steep, narrow stretch of road was once a stagecoach route constructed of wooden planks anchored to the mountain by a massive rock called the **Pillar of Hercules,** the largest rock in an unmarked pile that sits next to the road.

From the 45th parallel parking area on the north entrance road north of Mammoth Hot Springs, a short hike leads to the **Boiling River.** Here you can take a dip, during daylight hours, where a hot spring empties into the Gardner River.

MAMMOTH HOT SPRINGS

The large Albright Visitor Center located near park headquarters has more visitor information and publications than other centers. You'll probably want to stop in here.

Though it's possible to see most of the wildlife and the major thermal areas here from behind car windows, your experience of the park will be multiplied tenfold by getting out of your vehicle and expending a small amount of energy. Most people in average shape are capable of negotiating the trails here, a significant percentage of which are level or only moderately inclined boardwalks. Even the more challenging trails frequently have rest areas where you can catch your breath and stop to absorb the magnificent views.

One of Yellowstone's most unique, beautiful, and fascinating areas are the **Upper** and **Lower terraces.** Strolling among them, you can observe Mother Nature going about the business of mixing and matching heat, water, limestone, and rock fractures to sculpt the area. With the exception of the Grand Canyon of the Yellowstone River, this is the most colorful area of the park; its tapestries of orange, pink, yellow, green, and brown, formed by masses of bacteria and algae, seem to change colors before your eyes.

The mineral-rich hot waters that flow to the surface here do so at an unusually constant rate, roughly 750,000 gallons per day, which results in the deposit of almost 2 tons of limestone on these ever-changing terraces. Contours are constantly undergoing change in the hot springs, as formations are shaped by large quantities of flowing water, the slope of the ground, and trees and rocks that determine the direction of the flow.

On the flip side of the equation, nature has a way of playing tricks on some of her creatures: **Poison Spring** is a sinkhole on the trail, so named because carbon dioxide collects there, often killing creatures who stop for a drink. The **Lower Terrace Interpretive Trail** (see "Day Hikes," later in this chapter) is one of the best ways to see this area.

After passing **Palette Spring,** where bacteria create a collage of browns, greens, and oranges, you're on your way to **Cleopatra** and **Minerva terraces.** Minerva is a favorite of visitors because of its brightly colored travertine formations, the product of limestone deposits.

The hike up the last 150 feet to the Upper Terrace Loop Drive is slightly steeper, though there are benches at frequent intervals. From here you can see all the terraces and several springs— **Canary Spring** and **New Blue Spring** being the most distinctive—and the red-roofed buildings of **Fort Yellowstone,** which is now the park headquarters.

MAMMOTH HOT SPRINGS TO TOWER JUNCTION

Heading east from Mammoth on the Tower Road, a 6-mile drive will bring you to the **All Persons' Self-guiding Trail;** this flat, easy, boardwalk stroll is an excellent opportunity to learn about the environmental effects of the fire.

Two miles later is **Blacktail Plateau Drive,** a 7-mile, one-way dirt road that offers great wildlife-viewing opportunities and a bit more solitude. You'll emerge back onto the Mammoth-Tower Road, about a mile west of the turnoff to the Petrified Tree.

Turn right onto this half-mile-long road that dead-ends at the **Petrified Tree,** a redwood that, while standing, was burned by volcanic ash more than 50 million years ago.

TOWER-ROOSEVELT

Just beyond the Petrified Tree, you'll come to **Tower-Roosevelt,** the most relaxed of the park's villages and a great place to take a break from the more crowded attractions. Even if you aren't going to stay, you might want to take a look at the **Tower Soldier Station,** now the ranger residence at Tower Junction, one of three surviving outposts from the era of U.S. Cavalry management of the park. Also here is **Roosevelt Lodge,** a rustic building that commemorates Pres. Teddy Roosevelt's camping excursion to this area of the park in 1903.

At **Specimen Ridge,** 2.5 miles east of the Tower Junction on the northeast entrance road, you'll find a ridge that entombs one of the world's most extensive fossil forests.

FROM TOWER JUNCTION TO THE GRAND CANYON OF THE YELLOWSTONE

A few minutes' drive from the Tower area is the **Calcite Springs Overlook.** A short loop along a boardwalk leads to the overlook at the rim of **The Narrows,** the narrowest part of the canyon. You can hear the river raging through the canyon some 500 feet below, and look across at the canyon walls comprised of rock spires and bands of columnar basalt. Just downstream is the most prominent feature in the canyon, **Bumpus Butte.**

Continuing south, you will travel through the **Washburn Range,** an area in which the 1988 fire ran especially hot and fast. The terrain changes dramatically as the road climbs, as well as along some major hills toward **Mount Washburn.** There are trailheads for the **Mount Washburn Trail,** one of our favorites, on each side of the summit.

As you approach **Dunraven Pass** (8,859 ft.), keep your eyes peeled for the shy mountain sheep, as this is one of their prime habitats.

One mile farther south is the **Washburn Hot Springs Overlook,** which offers sweeping views of the Grand Canyon. On a clear day, you can see 50 to 100 miles south, beyond Yellowstone Lake.

CANYON VILLAGE

You're in for yet another eyeful when you reach the **Grand Canyon of the Yellowstone River.** Compared to the Grand Canyon of Arizona, the Yellowstone canyon is relatively narrow; however, the sheer cliffs are equally impressive, descending hundreds of feet to the bottom of a gorge where the Yellowstone River flows. It's also equally colorful, with displays of oranges, reds, yellows, and golds. You won't find thermal vents in Arizona, but you will find them here, a constant reminder of ongoing underground activity.

You should plan on encountering crowds when you reach **Canyon Village.** The **Canyon Visitor Center** (© 307/242-2550) is the place to go for books and a bison exhibit.

An auto tour of the canyon follows **North Rim Drive,** a two-lane, one-way road that begins in Canyon Village, to your first stop, **Inspiration Point.** On the way, you'll pass a **glacial boulder** estimated to weigh 500 tons that was deposited by melting ice more than 10,000 years ago.

At Inspiration Point, a moderately strenuous descent down 57 steps takes you to an overlook with views of the Lower Falls and canyon. There are several other view points you can stop at along North Rim Drive before you reconnect with the main Canyon Village–Yellowstone Lake road, which will take you down to South Rim Drive.

For the adventurous, an alternative to driving from one overlook to another is to negotiate the **North Rim Trail,** which is slightly more than 2.25 miles long, beginning at Inspiration Point.

Unfortunately, the North Rim Trail is not a loop, so if you take the hike, you'll have to backtrack. The footpath brings you closer to what you want to see, and you won't be fighting for elbowroom, as you will at the overlooks that are only accessible to cars.

Whether you drive or walk, you should go down to the **Upper Falls View,** where a 0.25-mile trail leads down from the parking lot to the brink of the **Upper Falls** and an overlook within splashing distance of the rushing river and the waterfall. At this point you won't just hear, you'll feel the power of the river as it begins its course down the canyon.

The **South Rim Drive** leads to several overlooks and better views of the Lower Falls. The most impressive vantage point is from the bottom of **Uncle Tom's Trail,** a steep, 500-foot steel staircase that begins at the first South Rim parking lot.

South Rim Road continues to a second, lower parking lot and a trail that leads to **Artist Point.** The view here is astounding, one of our favorites in the park, and is best in the early morning.

CANYON VILLAGE TO FISHING BRIDGE

The road winds through the **Hayden Valley,** which is a vast expanse of beautiful green meadows accented by brown cuts where the soil is eroded along the banks of the Yellowstone River. The valley is now a wide, sprawling area where bison and antelope play and where trumpeter swans, white pelicans, and Canada geese float along the river. This is also a prime habitat for the grizzly, so during early spring months pay close attention to binocular-toting visitors grouped beside the road.

Nature is working at her acidic best at the **Sulphur Caldron** and **Mud Volcano** areas, 12 miles south of the Canyon Junction, which were described by the frontier minister Edwin Stanley as "unsightly, unsavory, and villainous." We think he was right on the money, so you'll not want to miss this area. After all, there's nothing quite like the sound of burping mud pots.

At **Dragon's Mouth Spring,** steam and sulfurous gases propel turbid water from an underground cavern to the surface, where it colors the earth shades of orange and green. The belching of steam and the attendant sound, which is due to the splash of 180°F (82°C) water against the wall in a subterranean cavern, creates a medieval quality; hence, the name of the spring.

Nearby **Mud Volcano** is an unappetizing mud spring, the product of vigorous activity caused by escaping sulfurous gases and steam. The youngest feature in the area is **Black Dragon's Caldron,** which is often referred to as "the demon of the backwoods," and rightly so. The caldron emerged from its subterranean birthplace for the first time in 1948 when it announced its presence by blowing a hole in the landscape, scattering mature trees hundreds of feet in all directions. Since then, continual seismic activity and intermittent earthquakes in the area have caused it to relocate 200 feet south of its original position.

The road across the Yellowstone River at **Fishing Bridge** was once the only eastern exit in the park, the route leading over Sylvan Pass to Cody, Wyoming. The bridge, which was built in 1902, spans the Yellowstone River as it exits Yellowstone Lake, and is another prime spawning area for native trout. The **Fishing Bridge Visitor Center** (℃ 307/242-2450) has a first-rate wildlife display. You'll find an excellent hiking trail, **Elephant Back Loop Trail,** leading off the short strip of highway between Fishing Bridge and the Lake Village area.

YELLOWSTONE LAKE AREA

As if the park didn't have enough record-setting attractions: at 7,773 feet, **Yellowstone Lake** is North America's largest high-altitude lake. The lake exhibits its multifaceted personalities daily, ranging from a placid, mirrorlike surface to a tantrum whipped by southerly winds that create 3- to 4-foot waves. Because the lake has the largest population of native cutthroat trout in North America, it makes an ideal fishing spot during the summer.

Lake Village, on the northwest shore of the lake, offers a wide range of amenities, the most prominent of which is the majestic 100-year-old **Lake Yellowstone Hotel** (℃ 307/344-7311), perhaps the most beautiful structure in the park.

Just south of Lake Village is the **Bridge Bay Marina,** the center of the park's water activities. Here you can arrange for guided fishing trips or small boat rentals, or learn more about the lake during an informative and entertaining 1-hour narrated boat tour. The marina is usually open from mid-June to mid-September.

Though the **Natural Bridge,** near Bridge Bay, is well marked on park maps, it's one of the park's best-kept secrets, and you may end up enjoying it by yourself. The mile-long path down to the bridge, a geologic masterpiece consisting of a massive rock arch 51 feet overhead, spanning Bridge Creek, is an excellent bike route.

The **West Thumb** area along the western shoreline is the **deepest** part of Yellowstone Lake. Because of its suspiciously craterlike contours, many scientists speculate that this 4-mile-wide, 6-mile-long, water-filled crater was created during volcanic eruptions approximately 125,000 years ago.

The **West Thumb Geyser Basin** is notable for a unique series of geysers. Some are situated right on the shores, some overlook the lake, and some can be seen **beneath** the lake surface. Three of the shoreline geysers, the most famous of which is **Fishing Cone,** are occasionally marooned offshore when the lake level rises. Fortunately, boardwalks surround the area, so it's easy to negotiate. Maps and details on the area are available in the **West Thumb Information Station** (no phone; open daily in summer 9am–5pm).

As you depart the West Thumb area, you are presented with two choices: either to head south toward Grand Teton National Park or to head west across the **Continental Divide** at Craig Pass, en route to Old Faithful.

GRANT VILLAGE TO THE SOUTH ENTRANCE

In contrast to the forgettable **Grant Village,** the 22-mile drive to **Grand Teton National Park** (see chapter 17), along high mountain passes and **Lewis Lake,** is beautiful. After the lake loses its winter coat of ice, it is a popular spot for early-season anglers who are unable to fish streams clouded by the spring runoff.

Beyond the lake, the road follows the Lewis River through an alpine area and along the **Pitchstone Plateau,** a pile of lava more than 2,000 feet high and 20 miles wide that was created some 500,000 years ago. A high gorge overlooking the river provides views that are different from, but just as spectacular as, those in other sections of the park.

WEST THUMB TO OLD FAITHFUL

The most interesting phenomenon on the Old Faithful route is **Isa Lake** at Craig Pass. Unlike most lakes and streams in the park, it drains into both eastern and western drainages and ends up in the Pacific Ocean and the Gulf of Mexico. Amazingly, as a consequence of a gyroscopic maneuver, the outlet on the east curves west and eventually drains into the Pacific, and the outlet on the west curves east and drains into the Gulf.

Before you reach the Old Faithful geyser area, two additional detours are recommended. Two and one-half miles southeast of Old Faithful is an overlook at the spectacular **Kepler Cascades,** a 150-foot, stair-step waterfall on the Firehole River that is footsteps from the parking lot.

Near that parking lot is the trailhead for the second detour, a 5-mile round-trip to the **Lonestar Geyser** (on the eponymous trail), which erupts every 3 hours, sending steaming water 30 to 50 feet from its 12-foot cone.

OLD FAITHFUL GEYSER AREA

Despite the overwhelming sight of the geysers and steam vents that populate the Old Faithful area, we suggest you resist the temptation to explore until you've stopped at the **Old Faithful Visitor Center** (✆ **307/545-2750**). Check the information board for estimated times of geyser eruptions, and plan accordingly.

The Old Faithful area is generally divided into four sections: **Upper Geyser Basin,** which includes **Geyser Hill, Black Sand Basin, Biscuit Basin,** and **Midway Geyser Basin.** All of these areas are connected to the Old Faithful area by paved trails and roads. If time allows, hike the area; it's fairly level, and distances are relatively short. Between the Old Faithful area and Madison Junction, you'll also find the justifiably famous **Lower Geyser Basin,** including **Fountain Paint Pot** and the trails surrounding it. You can see some of these geysers on Firehole Lake Drive.

Though **Old Faithful** is not the largest or most regular geyser in the park, its image has been said to be the West's equivalent of the Statue of Liberty. Like clockwork, the average interval between eruptions is about 90 minutes, though it may vary 30 minutes in either direction. A typical eruption lasts 1½ to 5 minutes, during which 3,700 to 8,400 gallons of water are thrust upward to heights of 180 feet. For the best views and photo opportunities of the eruption in the boardwalk area, plan on arriving early to assure a first-row view.

An alternative to a seat on the crowded boardwalk is a stroll from the Old Faithful Geyser up the **Observation Point Trail** to an observation area that provides better views of the entire geyser basin. The path up to the observation point is approximately 0.5 mile, and the elevation gain is only 200 feet, so it's an easy 15-minute hike. The view of the eruption of the geyser is more spectacular from here and the crowds less obtrusive.

Accessible by walkways from Old Faithful Village, the **Upper Geyser Basin Loop** is referred to as Geyser Hill on some maps. The 1.3-mile loop trail winds among several thermal attractions. **Anemone Geyser** may offer the best display of the various stages of a typical eruption as the pool fills and overflows, after which bubbles rising to the surface begin throwing water in 10-foot eruptions, a cycle that is repeated every 7 to 10 minutes.

Two other stars of the show in the Upper Geyser Basin are **Castle Geyser** and **Grand Geyser.** Castle Geyser, with the largest cone of any geyser in the park, currently erupts for 20 minutes every 10 to 12 hours, after which a noisy steam phase may continue for half an hour. Grand Geyser, the tallest predictable geyser in the world, usually erupts every 7 to 15 hours with powerful bursts that produce streams of water that may reach 200 feet in height.

The **Riverside Geyser** is situated on the bank of the Firehole River, across from a large viewing area. One of the most picturesque geysers in the park, its 75-foot column of water creates an arch over the river. Just to the south, **Morning Glory Pool** was named for its likeness to its namesake flower in the 1880s, but has since lost some of its beauty. Vandals have tossed so much debris into its core over the years that it now suffers from poor circulation and reduced temperatures, which are causing unsightly brown and green bacteria to grow on its surface.

The **Black Sand Basin** is a cluster of especially colorful hot springs and geysers located a mile north of Old Faithful. It is interesting primarily because of its black sand, a derivative of obsidian. **Biscuit Basin,** located 2 miles farther up the road, was named for biscuitlike deposits that surrounded colorful **Sapphire Pool** until a 1959 earthquake caused the pool to erupt, sending them skyward. Both the Black Sand Basin and the Biscuit Basin can be viewed from flat, interpretive boardwalks.

The **Midway Geyser Basin** extends for about a mile along the Firehole River. The major attractions here are the **Excelsior Geyser,** the third-largest geyser in the world and once the park's most powerful geyser, and the well-known **Grand Prismatic Spring,** the largest hot spring in Yellowstone, and the second largest in the world.

OLD FAITHFUL TO MADISON JUNCTION

Believe it or not, there are more superb geysers and hot springs on **Firehole Lake Drive,** all viewable without leaving your vehicle, along a 3-mile, one-way road. The turnoff for Firehole Lake Drive is about 8 miles north of the Old Faithful area. There are three geysers of particular interest on this road. The largest is **Great Fountain Geyser,** which erupts every 8 to 12 hours, typically spouting water some 100 feet high for periods of 45 to 60 minutes. However, the lucky visitor may see the occasional "superburst" that reaches heights of 200 feet or more.

Estimates are that **White Dome Geyser** has been erupting for hundreds of years. Unfortunately, the age and height of this massive cone are not matched by spectacular eruptions. The vent on top of the cone has been nearly sealed with deposits of "geyserite," so eruptions now reach only 30 feet. However, the cone itself is worth a trip down this road.

Further on, **Pink Cone Geyser** couldn't be closer to the road, since road builders cut into the geyser's mound during construction. The geyser still erupts occasionally, but the 30-foot spray goes mostly skyward and doesn't interfere with traffic.

About a half-mile north of where Firehole Lake Drive rejoins the Grand Loop Road is the **Fountain Paint Pots** area. This is a very popular spot, so you may

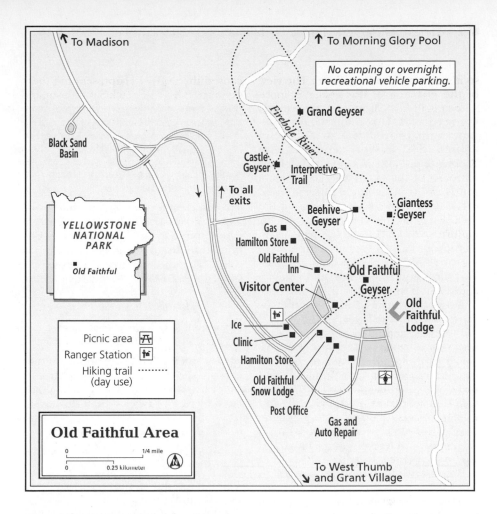

To Madison ↑

To Morning Glory Pool ↑

No camping or overnight recreational vehicle parking.

Firehole River

■ Grand Geyser

Black Sand Basin

Castle Geyser ■
Interpretive Trail

↓ ↑ To all exits

Beehive Geyser ■

■ Giantess Geyser

YELLOWSTONE NATIONAL PARK

■ Old Faithful

Gas ■
Hamilton Store ■
Old Faithful Inn ■

Old Faithful Geyser

Visitor Center

Old Faithful Lodge

Ice —
Clinic —

Hamilton Store —

Old Faithful Snow Lodge

Post Office —

Gas and Auto Repair

Picnic area 🏕
Ranger Station
Hiking trail .... (day use)

Old Faithful Area

0   1/4 mile
0   0.25 kilometer

To West Thumb and Grant Village ↓

be forced to wait for a parking place. All the various types of thermal activity are on display here, so as you stroll along the easy, 0.5-mile boardwalk, you'll be in an area that may have six geysers popping their lids at the same time.

Organized Tours & Ranger Programs

A number of tour companies offer bus tours of the park originating in gateway communities: **Grub Steak Expeditions** (© 800/527-6316; www.grubsteaktours. com) out of Cody has daylong tours; **Yellowstone Alpen Guides** (© 800/523-3102; www.graylineyellowstone.com) takes travelers around the park from West Yellowstone, as does **Buffalo Bus Lines** (© 800/426-7669). If you are

looking for specialized guided trips such as photo safaris or snowmobile tours, contact the chambers of commerce of the gateway community where you want to begin.

Within the park, the hotel concessionaire, **Xanterra Parks and Resorts** (© 307/344-7311; www.travelyellowstone. com) has a variety of general and specialized tours. Three different **motorcoach tours** are available from all of Yellowstone's villages. For $41 you can explore the **Circle of Fire** (Old Faithful, Yellowstone Lake, the Hayden Valley), or, for $45, you can do the whole thing, **Yellowstone in a Day.** These are full-day tours, with stops at all the sights and informative talks by the guides. Specialty trips include photo safaris, wildlife trips up the Lamar Valley (try it in winter), and Yellowstone Lake Sunset Tours in historic buses from the 1930s.

At Bridge Bay Marina, 1-hour **scenic cruises** depart throughout the day from June to the end of September for a trip around the northern end of giant Yellowstone Lake. You view the Lake Hotel from the water, and visit Stevenson Island, while a guide fills you in on the history, geology, and biology of the area. Fares are $9.75 for adults, $5 for children 8 to 11. Guided fishing trips on 22-foot and 34-foot cabin cruisers are also available from Yellowstone National Park Lodge at Bridge Bay, and you can rent smaller outboard and rowboats.

Buses are replaced in the winter by **snow-coach tours.** These are more vans than buses, mounted on tank treads with skis in front for steering. The snow coach can pick you up at the south or west entrances, or at Mammoth, and take you all over the park. You can spend a night at Old Faithful and then snow coach up to Mammoth the next night, or do round-trip tours from the gates or wherever you're lodged in the park. One-way trips range from $49 to $54, while round-trips cost $98 to $108.

Ranger-led programs are held throughout the park during the summer, some at campground amphitheaters, some at visitor centers, some on hikes or at key landmarks. It's the best value in the park: free.

Evening campfire programs are presented nightly in the summer at campgrounds at Mammoth Hot Springs, Norris, Madison, Grant, Bridge Bay, and Canyon. Many of these activities are accessible to travelers with disabilities. There are more tours and evening programs in the **Old Faithful** area than anywhere else in the park. The talks and walks, which can run as long as 1½ hours, usually focus on the geysers, their fragile plumbing, and their role in the Yellowstone ecosystem. Check the park newspaper when you enter the park for a current listing of ranger programs.

Day Hikes

WEST YELLOWSTONE TO MADISON

Artist Paint Pot Trail

1 mile RT. Easy. Access: Gibbon Meadow 4½ miles south of Norris Junction.

This interesting and worthwhile stroll along a relatively level path winds through a lodgepole pine forest in Gibbon Meadows, to a mud pot at the top of a hill. This thermal area contains some small geysers, hot pools, and steam vents.

Harlequin Lake Trail

0.6 mile RT. Easy. Access: West entrance road 1½ miles west of the Madison Campground.

This is an excellent, easy opportunity to explore the area while winding through the burned forest to a small lake populated by various types of waterfowl.

Purple Mountain Trail

6 miles RT. Easy. Access: Madison-Norris Rd. ¼ mile north of the Madison Junction.

This hike requires more physical exertion. It winds through a burned forest to the top of what many consider only a tall hill, with an elevation gain of 1,400 feet.

Two Ribbons Trail

0.75 mile RT. Easy. Access: A turnout on the north side of the road 3 miles east of the west entrance.

This trail offers an opportunity to inspect the effects of the 1988 fire. Along the boardwalk, you'll see evidence of not only the blaze that ravaged the area, but the beginning of a new cycle of life in the dense green shag of lodgepole saplings.

NORRIS GEYSER BASIN

Back Basin Loop

1.5 miles RT. Easy. Access: Norris Geyser Basin.

This level boardwalk is easily negotiable in 1 hour and passes by Steamboat Geyser, which has been known to produce the world's highest and most memorable eruptions. However, these 400-foot waterspouts rarely occur more than twice a year, so it will take some luck to see one.

Porcelain Basin Trail

0.5 mile RT. Easy. Access: Norris Geyser Basin.

This short trail, which can be completed in 45 minutes, is on a level boardwalk that, like the Back Basin Loop, is in a concentration of thermal attractions that may change every year.

MAMMOTH HOT SPRINGS AREA

All Persons' Self-guiding Trail

0.8 mile RT. Easy. Access: Tower Rd., 8 miles east of Mammoth Hot Springs.

This level, easy stroll along a boardwalk presents an excellent opportunity to learn about the effects of fire on the environment.

Bunsen Peak Trail

4.2 miles RT. Moderate. Access: Across the road from the Glen Creek Trailhead, 5 miles south of Mammoth on the Mammoth-Norris Rd.

This trail leads to a short but steep 2.1-mile trip to the 8,564-foot summit, with a 1,300-foot gain in elevation. Park rangers say this is a favorite for watching the sunrise behind Electric Peak, off to the northwest, which glows with a golden hue. At the top of the peak, you will be 3,000 feet above the valley.

Lower Terrace Interpretive Trail

1.5 miles RT. Easy. Access: South of the village on the road to Norris.

This interpretive trail is one of the best ways to see the Mammoth area. The trail starts at 6,280 feet and climbs another 300 feet (an easy climb) along marginally steep grades through a bare, rocky,

thermal region to a flat alpine area and observation deck at the top.

GRAND CANYON OF THE YELLOWSTONE RIVER AREA

Mount Washburn Trail

6 miles RT. Moderate. Access: At the end of Old Chittenden Rd. and at Dunraven Pass.

The Mount Washburn Trail falls into the "If you can only do one hike, do this one" category. The 1,400-foot elevation gain is fairly gradual, and the rises are interspersed with long, fairly level stretches. At this elevation, however, the best method of attacking the mountain is to pace yourself, which has its own rewards: You have time to appreciate the views to the east of the Absaroka Mountains, south to Yellowstone Lake, and west to the Gallatin Mountains. You could see bighorn sheep, since it's a popular summer grazing area for them, as well as yellow-bellied marmots and red foxes. The hike to the summit is an easy 90-minute walk at a steady pace, or 2 hours with breaks. At this elevation, where weather changes quickly, it's always a good idea to bring several layers of clothing. Fortunately, there's a warming hut in the base of the ranger lookout, as well as viewing telescopes and restrooms, but, alas, no hot-chocolate machine.

North Rim Trail

2 miles one-way. Easy. Access: Inspiration Point.

This trail, which is described more fully in the Canyon Village section above, offers better views and less bustle than you'll find at the paved overlooks.

South Rim Trail

3.2 miles one-way. Easy. Access: In the parking lot just beyond South Rim Dr. Bridge.

Like the North Rim Trail, this trail gives you more and better views of the canyon and river than you can see from a vehicle, and you're away from the crowds.

Uncle Tom's Trail

500 ft. one-way. Moderate. Access: South Rim parking lot.

The short trip is down 328 stairs and paved inclines that lead to an incredible perspective on Lower Falls. The staircase (shackled to the canyon's wall) is rather steep but can be negotiated in an hour, though it will be challenging for inexperienced hikers.

YELLOWSTONE LAKE AREA

Elephant Back Loop Trail

4 miles RT. Easy. Access: Just before the turnoff for the Lake Yellowstone Hotel.

The hike is to an overlook that provides photographers with panoramic views of Yellowstone Lake and its islands, the Absaroka Range, and Pelican Valley.

Storm Point Trail

2 miles RT. Easy. Access: Directly across from the Pelican Valley Trailhead (on the lake side of the road), 3½ miles east of Fishing Bridge.

The Storm Point Trail follows a level path that terminates at a point jutting into the lake with panoramic views. During spring months, this is a popular spot with grizzlies, so the trail may be closed; even when it's open, check with rangers regarding bear activity.

OLD FAITHFUL AREA

Fairy Falls Trail

7.6 miles RT. Moderate. Access: Imperial Meadows in Biscuit Basin.

Though considerably longer than the Mystic Falls Trail, the Fairy Falls Trail is equally popular with the park staff because it leads to a taller waterfall. The hike begins at the Imperial Meadows Trailhead, 1 mile south of the Firehole River Bridge on Fountain Flat Drive. It winds through an area populated by elk along Fairy Creek, then past the Imperial Geyser. From here, it joins Fairy

Creek Trail and travels east to the base of the falls. The total gain in elevation is only 100 feet.

Fountain Paint Pot Trail

0.5 mile RT. Easy. Access: Fountain Paint Pot parking lot.

This area is a very popular attraction, so you may be forced to wait for a parking place. All of the various types of thermal activity strut their stuff here, so as you stroll along the easy half-mile boardwalk you'll be in an area that may have six geysers popping their lids at the same time.

Geyser Hill Basin Loop

1.3 miles RT. Easy. Access: Old Faithful boardwalk.

One of the most interesting, and easiest, loops in the area, this trail winds around several thermal attractions. Anemone Geyser may offer the best display of the various stages of a typical eruption as the pool fills and overflows. The Lion Group consists of four geysers that are interconnected beneath the surface, and Doublet Pool is especially popular with photographers, who are attracted by a complex series of ledges and deep-blue waters. Giantess Geyser is known for its violent eruptions.

Lonestar Geyser Trail

4.6 miles RT. Easy. Access: The parking lot opposite Kepler Cascades.

This is another trail that falls into the "Gotta Do It" category, and its popularity is its only disadvantage. Despite the probability that you'll be sharing the territory with others, there are several compelling reasons to give it a go. From the trailhead you'll wend your way through a forested area along a trail that parallels the Firehole River. The payoff for your effort is the arrival at the geyser, though it will not be found in the *Guinness Book of Records*. It sits alone, a vanilla-chocolate ice-cream cone near the middle of a vast meadow partially covered by grass and trees, exposed rock, gravel, and volcanic debris. The geyser erupts about every 3 hours, with the eruption lasting about 30 minutes. Small, bubbling hot springs and steam vents surround it. The trail is popular with cross-country skiers in winter.

Mystic Falls Trail

1 mile one-way. Easy. Access: Imperial Meadows in Biscuit Basin.

This is a favorite of park rangers. The trail leads to a waterfall on the Little Firehole River that drops more than 100 feet, one of the steepest in the park. The trail starts at Biscuit Basin, crosses the river, and then disappears into the forest. The total distance to the falls is only 1 mile; there's a trail to take you to the top.

To make your return more interesting, continue 0.2 mile to the Little Firehole Meadows Trail, which has an overlook that offers a view of Old Faithful in the distance. Best estimates are that the total time for the hike is an easy 2 hours, with an elevation gain of only 460 feet.

Observation Point Trail—Solitary Geyser

2 miles RT. Easy. Access: Old Faithful boardwalk.

This trail leads to an observation area that provides better views of the entire geyser basin. The path up to the observation point is approximately 0.5 mile, and the elevation gain is only 200 feet, so it's an easy 15-minute hike. The view puts the entire Upper Geyser Basin into a different perspective; it is possible to see most of the major geysers, as well as inaccessible steam vents located in the middle of wooded areas. From the top of the boardwalk, continue to the Solitary Geyser on a downhill slope that leads past the geyser, through the basin, and back to the inn, which completes the loop.

Exploring the Backcountry

The backcountry season in Yellowstone is brief but glorious: For just 2 or 3 months, the snow melts off, the streams drop to fordable levels, and you can go deep into a domain of free-roaming wildlife and pristine natural beauty.

You must have a backcountry permit for any overnight trip on foot, on horseback, or by boat, and you can camp only in designated campsites, many of which are equipped with food storage poles to keep wildlife out of your stores. You can pick up a permit for hiking or boating the day before beginning a trip, but if you'll be traveling during peak season, make a reservation in advance. It costs $20 to hold a site, and you can begin making reservations for the upcoming year beginning April 1.

Contact the **Yellowstone Backcountry Office,** P.O. Box 168, Yellowstone National Park, WY 82190 (© **307/344-2160**), and they'll send you the useful *Backcountry Trip Planner* with a detailed map showing where the campsites are, how to make reservations, and how to prepare. Pick up your permit in the park within 48 hours of your departure, at one of the following visitor ranger stations any day of the week during the summer: Bechler, Canyon, Mammoth, Old Faithful, Tower, West Entrance, Grant Village, Lake, South Entrance, and Bridge Bay.

Backcountry Geysers. If you just can't get your fill of geysers, or if you've had your fill of people, several trails lead to more isolated geysers. The **Shoshone Geyser Basin** and **Heart Lake Geyser Basin** contain active geysers, as do **Ponuntpa Springs** and the **Mudkettles** in the Pelican Valley Area, **Imperial Geyser** in the Firehole area, and the **Highland Hot Springs** on the Mary Mountain Trail. If you head in these directions, be careful about walking on unstable surfaces: Many have met their fate this way.

Shoshone Lake. Shoshone Lake is the park's largest backcountry lake and a popular spot for hikers. The shortest route is via the **Delacy Creek Trail,** which begins 8 miles east of Old Faithful on the Old Faithful–West Thumb road. The trail winds 3 miles along Delacy Creek through moose country and the edge of the forest at the lake. From here you can head around the lake (a distance of 18 miles) in either direction. Assuming you take a clockwise track, you'll take the Delacy Creek Trail to its intersection with **Dogshead Trail,** then head west on the **Shoshone Lake Trail** until it intersects with the **North Shoshone Trail** and returns to your starting point.

A detour: At the western end of the lake you'll arrive at the 1-mile-long **Shoshone Geyser Basin Trail,** which loops through a number of geysers, hot springs, and meadows that during spring months are ankle-deep in water and mud.

As you travel the lake's loop trail along the **Delacy Creek Trail,** you'll have views of the lake at the top of a 100-foot rise. Then, on the **Shoshone Lake Trail,** you'll cross the Lewis Channel, which may have thigh-high water as late as July. Beyond that, the trail is a series of rises that are easily negotiable by the average hiker, passing across shallow Moose Creek and through meadows where you may spot deer or moose early in the morning or evening.

The 8.4-mile **North Shoshone Trail** winds through a lodgepole-pine forest, over numerous ridges up to 200 feet high. The best views of the lake are from cliffs on this trail. The loop trail is especially popular with overnighters, since there are 26 campsites on the loop.

The Bechler Region. This area is often referred to as the Cascade Corner because it contains a majority of the park's waterfalls. It offers great opportunities to view thermal features. Many backpacking routes cut through this region, including one that leads to Old Faithful on the **Bechler River Trail.**

To begin your hike, drive into the park from Ashton, Idaho, and check in at the Bechler Ranger Station. To reach the ranger station, drive east 17 miles from Ashton on the Cave Falls Road; 3 miles before reaching Cave Falls, you'll find the ranger station turnoff. The ranger station is 1.5 miles down the gravel road.

The **Bechler Meadows Trail** takes you into this southwest corner, which is rich in waterfalls, cascades, and thermal areas, and is rarely visited. About 6 miles into the journey, the trail fords the river several times as it enters Bechler Canyon, where it passes Collonade and Iris Falls. This is a camping trip—you can cover a good 30 miles, depending on what turns you take—best made late in the summer to avoid high water during creek crossings. For a shorter trip, hike 3.5 miles along the **Bechler River Trail** to the **Boundary Creek Trail,** then return to the station via the **Bechler Meadows Trail,** a round-trip of 7 miles.

The most adventurous, and most scenic, route takes you 30 miles from the ranger station to the end of the trail at the **Lonestar Trailhead** near Old Faithful. Beyond Iris Falls, and then Ragged Falls, you'll reach a patrol cabin at Three Rivers Junction at the 13-mile mark, a popular camping area. If you continue towards Old Faithful, you'll intersect the **Shoshone Lake Trail** at the 23.5-mile mark and exit 6.5 miles later.

Thorofare Area. When you enter this section you're venturing into the most remote roadless area in the Lower 48. You can make a round-trip of around 70 miles deep into the wilderness, or shorter hikes, such as a trip from the park's east entrance road to the Yellowstone River inlet on Yellowstone Lake's southeast arm. The remoteness of this country discourages many hikers, so you'll have it mostly to yourself. The tepee rings and lean-tos that you may see are remnants of the presence of American Indians, who once used this area as the main highway between Jackson Hole and points north.

The trail follows the eastern shore of Yellowstone Lake and then the Yellowstone River into some of the most remote and beautiful backcountry in the Rockies. It's a lot of miles and climbing, but you'll be rewarded with views of the Upper Yellowstone Valley, Two Oceans Plateau, and abundant wildlife. You'll reach the Park Service's Thorofare Ranger Station at 32 miles, and a few miles farther you'll come to Bridger Lake, outside the park, and a gorgeous alpine valley with a ranger station known as Hawk's Rest. Fishers love this area—so do grizzly bears, especially during the cutthroat trout spawning season in early summer. You'll be a good 35 miles from the trailhead at the lake, and even the most capable hikers should consider riding with an outfitter. You can cut 9 miles off the journey by getting a boat shuttle to the mouth of the lake's southwest arm; call the **marina** at *C* **307/242-3876.** Only human-powered boats are allowed into the arm to the Yellowstone River outlet (you can canoe in, a wonderful trip in good weather). Or you can come into Thorofare through Bridger-Teton National Forest up the North Fork of the Buffalo Fork to the south (check with the forest's **Blackrock Ranger Station,** *C* **307/543-2386**).

Aside from grizzlies, the major obstacle to early season trips in the Thorofare is water; you'll encounter knee-deep water at **Beaverdam Creek** and at **Trapper Creek,** as late as July.

The Sportsman Lake Trail. This moderate, 14-mile trail begins near Mammoth Hot Springs and extends west toward U.S. 191 to Sportsman Lake. From the Glen Creek Trailhead 5 miles south of Mammoth Hot Springs, you'll spend 2 miles on the Glen Creek Trail as you traverse a mostly level, wide-open plateau, covered with sagebrush, that is the home of herds of elk and a bear management area. At the **Sepulcher Mountain Trail** at the 3-mile mark, the terrain gets steeper as you continue northwest on the **Sportsman Lake Trail**—the elevation gain is approximately 2,300 feet to the Sepulcher summit (though you don't go to it on this route). The trail eventually enters the forest and descends to a log that is used to cross Gardner River. Then, it's uphill for another 4 miles to **Electric Divide,** another 2,000-foot gain in elevation. From there, the trail descends 2,100 feet in 3 miles to Sportsman Lake. The lake, which sits in a meadow populated by moose and elk, is teeming with cutthroat trout. There are two campsites.

Other Summer Sports & Activities

Biking. Yellowstone's narrow and twisty roads and lack of bike lanes make life difficult for bikers, and off-road opportunities are limited because of the small number of trails on which bikes are allowed. The following trails are available to mountain bikers, but know that you will share the roads with hikers. The **Mount Washburn trail,** leaving from the Old Chittenden Road, is a strenuous trail that climbs 1,400 feet. The **Lonestar Geyser trail,** accessed at Kepler Cascade near Old Faithful, is an easy 1-hour ride on a user-friendly, partly paved road. Near Mammoth Hot Springs, **Bunsen Peak Road** and **Osprey Falls trails** present a combination ride/hike: The first 6 miles travel around Bunsen Peak; getting to the top requires a hike. A hike down to Osprey Falls adds 3 miles to the journey.

Bike rentals are available in the gateway towns of West Yellowstone (**Yellowstone Bicycles,** *C* **406/646-7815**) and Jackson (**Hoback Sports,** *C* **307/733-5335**).

Boating. The best place to enjoy boating in Yellowstone is on **Yellowstone Lake,** which has easy access and beautiful, panoramic views. The lake is also one of the few areas where powerboats are allowed. Rowboats and outboard motorboats can be rented at **Bridge Bay**

Marina (© 307/344-3876). Motorboats, canoes, and kayaks can be used on **Lewis Lake** as well.

Fishing. Seven varieties of game fish live in the parks: native cutthroat, rainbow, brown, brook and lake trout; grayling; and mountain whitefish. Of the trout, only the cutthroat are native, and they are being pressured in the big lake by the larger lake trout, despite efforts to remove the exotic strains by gill-net fishing. As a result, you can't keep any pink-meat cutthroat caught anywhere in Yellowstone, and you **must** keep any lake trout.

The Yellowstone season typically opens on the Saturday of Memorial Day weekend and ends on the first Sunday in November. The exceptions are Yellowstone Lake's slightly shorter season, and the lake's tributaries, which are closed until July 15 to avoid conflicts between humans and grizzly bears, both of which are attracted to spawning trout.

In June, try the **Yellowstone River** downstream of Yellowstone Lake, where the cutthroat trout spawn. In July, fish the **Madison River** near the west entrance, and again in late fall for rainbow and some brown trout. In late summer, you can try to hook the cutthroats that thin out by September on the **Lamar River** in the park's beautiful northeast corner.

You can fish the **Yellowstone River** below the Grand Canyon by hiking down into **Seven Mile Hole,** a great place to cast (not much vegetation to snag on) for cutthroat trout from July to September, with the best luck around Sulphur Creek.

Other good fishing stretches include the **Gibbon** and **Firehole** rivers, which merge to form the Madison River on the park's west side, and the 3-mile **Lewis River Channel** between Shoshone and Lewis lakes during the fall spawning run of brown trout.

Fishing within the park requires a special permit good only within the park. For anglers 16 and older, it's $10 for a 10-day permit or $20 for a season permit. Anglers 12 to 15 need to get a permit, too, but it's free. Children 11 or younger may fish without a permit when supervised by an adult. The permits are available at all ranger stations, visitor centers, and Yellowstone General Stores.

Horseback Riding. People who want to pack their gear on a horse, llama, or mule must get permits to enter the Yellowstone backcountry, or hire an outfitter with a permit (see below). Other visitors who want to get in the saddle but not disappear in the wilderness can put themselves in the hands of the concessionaire, **Yellowstone National Park Lodges.** Stables are located at Canyon Village, Roosevelt Lodge, and Mammoth Hot Springs. Roosevelt Lodge also offers **evening rides** from June into September. Choices are 1- and 2-hour guided trail rides daily aboard well-broken, tame animals. Wranglers refer to these as "nose-and-tail" tours, and an experienced rider is likely to find them awfully tame.

If you're looking for a longer, overnight horse-packing experience, contact the park and request a list of approved concessionaires that lead backcountry expeditions. Most offer customized, guided trips, with meals, horses, and camping and riding gear provided. Costs will run from $200 to $400 per day per person, depending on the length of trip and number of people. In Gardiner, at the north entrance to the park, **Adventures Beyond Yellowstone** (© 406/848-7287) offers horseback trips in the park for groups of 4 or more; rates begin at $90 per day for customized trips, $150 for horseback/fishing expeditions. Coming from the south side of the park, try **Press Stephens, Outfitter** (© 307/455-2250).

Winter Sports & Activities

The average snowfall in a Yellowstone winter is nearly 50 inches, creating a beautiful setting for sightseers, and a wonderful resource for outdoor winter recreation. The steaming hot pools and geysers create little islands of warmth and attract not just tourists but wildlife as well. Nearby trees are transformed into "snow ghosts" by frozen thermal vapors. Bison become frosted, shaggy beasts, easily spotted as they take advantage of the more accessible vegetation on the thawed ground. Yellowstone Lake's surface freezes to an average thickness of 3 feet, creating a vast ice sheet that sings and moans as the huge plates of ice shift. But the ice is thinner where hot springs come up on the lake bottom, and you'll see otter surfacing at the breaks in the ice. Waterfalls become astounding pieces of frozen sculpture.

Only two of the park's hostelries, **Mammoth Hot Springs** and the **Old Faithful Snow Lodge,** provide accommodations from December through March, as does **Flagg Ranch,** just outside the park's south entrance. The only road that's open for cars is the **Mammoth Hot Springs–Cooke City Road.** Most visitors these days come into Yellowstone in winter from the west or south by snow coach or snowmobile.

For additional information on all of the following winter activities and accommodations, as well as snow-coach reservations, contact **Yellowstone National Park Lodges** (© **307/344-7311**). (For more on snow-coach tours, see "Organized Tours & Ranger Programs," earlier in this chapter.)

The **Yellowstone Association Institute** (© **307/344-2294**) offers winter courses based out of its headquarters at the Lamar Buffalo Ranch in the park's northeast corner. Past offerings have included 3-day classes devoted to wintertime photography, cross-country skiing, and wolf ecology.

Cross-Country Skiing. There are 40 miles of cross-country trails in the Old Faithful area, including the popular Lonestar Geyser Trail, an 8-mile trail in a remote setting that starts at the Old Faithful Snow Lodge; and the Fern Cascades trail, which winds for 3 miles through a rolling woodland landscape

on a short loop close to the Old Faithful area. In the Mammoth area, try the Upper Geyser Basin and Biscuit Basin trail, which some say is the best in Yellowstone, though it may take an entire day to negotiate.

Equipment rentals (about $15 per day), ski instruction ($25 per person for a group lesson), ski shuttles to various locations, and guided ski tours are available at the **Old Faithful Snow Lodge** and the **Mammoth Hot Springs Hotel.** A half-day guided excursion (two-person minimum) is around $40 per person.

Ice-Skating. The Mammoth Hot Springs ice rink is located behind the Mammoth Hot Springs Recreation Center. On a crisp winter's night you can rent a pair of skates ($1 per hr., $4 per day) and glide across the ice while seasonal melodies are broadcast over the PA system. It's cold out there, but there's a warming fire at the rink's edge.

Snowmobiling. Roads that are jammed with cars during the summer fill up with bison and snowmobiles during the winter. In deference to these shaggy road warriors, moderate speed limits are strictly enforced, but this is still an excellent way to sightsee at your own pace. A driver's license is required for rental ($170 for a single rider, $180 per day for two at **Mammoth Hot Springs Hotel** or **Old Faithful Snow Lodge**), and a quick lesson will put even a first-timer at ease. A helmet is included with the snowmobile, and you can rent a clothing package for protection against the bitter cold. **Warming huts** are located at Mammoth, Indian Creek, Canyon, Madison, West Thumb, and Fishing Bridge. They offer snacks, a hot cup of coffee or chocolate, and an excellent opportunity to recover from a chill. *A caution:* Keep an eye on snow conditions. Although it's true that snowmobile trails are groomed for travel, when snow cover is scanty, a normally smooth trip can become something akin to riding on a jackhammer. Also, if engine noise is what you came to Yellowstone to escape, this is probably not for you.

Snowmobile rentals are also available in the **gateway communities** of Gardiner and West Yellowstone, Montana, and at Flagg Ranch. Most rental shops accept reservations weeks in advance, so reserving at least a day to 2 weeks ahead of time is a good idea. Plan on making reservations for the week between Christmas and New Year's at least 6 months in advance.

Note: In December 2003 snowmobiling was banned in Yellowstone and Grand Teton national parks. But in February 2004 the ban was overturned; however litigation continues. If you are planning a snowmobiling adventure, you can get up-to-date information by calling © **307/344-2580** or visit www.nps.gov/yell/planvisit/winteruse.

Camping

There are 12 campgrounds in Yellowstone, 5 of them under the efficient management of **Xanterra Parks and Resorts,** the park concessionaire. The other 7 are smaller, less expensive, and often less crowded—our personal favorites are Slough Creek, in the Lamar Valley, and Norris, a shady riverside spot near the Norris Geyser Basin. The 7 campgrounds still run by the **National Park Service** are at Indian Creek, Lewis Lake, Mammoth, Norris, Pebble Creek, Slough Creek, and Tower Fall. They fill daily on a first-come, first-served basis.

Yellowstone National Park Lodges runs the bigger campgrounds at Bridge Bay, Canyon, Grant Village, Madison, and Fishing Bridge. **Same-day** and **advance reservations** may be made by calling © **307/344-7311** (TDD 307/344-5395); by writing to Yellowstone National Park Lodges, P.O. Box 165, Yellowstone National Park, WY 82190; or online at **www.travelyellowstone.com**. The only campground equipped with RV hookups is at **Fishing Bridge RV Park,** and it accepts hard-sided vehicles only (no tents or tent trailers), with electrical, water, and sewer hookups. Though there

are no hookups at the other campgrounds, RVers can be accommodated at any of them.

Camping is allowed only in designated areas and is limited to 14 days between June 15 and Labor Day, and to 30 days the rest of the year. Checkout time for all campgrounds is 10am. Quiet hours are enforced between the hours of 8pm and 8am. No generators, radios, or other loud noises are allowed during these hours. See the chart below for specific amenities and prices at each campground.

INSIDE THE PARK

The **Tower Fall Campground** is near a convenience store, restaurant, and gas station at Roosevelt Lodge and has forested sites; it is located 19 miles north of Canyon Village and 18 miles east of Mammoth.

Slough Creek Campground is located in the Lamar Valley, near the northeast entrance, where there are fewer people, good fishing, and the possibility of a wolf howl to stimulate your dreams; however, restroom facilities are in pit toilets.

Canyon Campground is the busiest in the park, with sites in a heavily wooded area. There's a store, restaurants, visitor center, and laundry nearby at Canyon Center.

Fishing Bridge RV Park is somewhat controversial because of its location in an area where bears feed in the spring; only hard-sided camping vehicles are allowed.

Bridge Bay Campground is near the shores of Yellowstone Lake, offering tremendous views, especially at sunrise and sunset. Unfortunately, though surrounded by the forest, much of the area has been clear-cut, so there's not a whole lot of privacy. It's close to boat launching facilities and the boat rental operation.

The **Madison Campground** is in a wooded area just south of the river. It has good access to fishing and hiking, and is a short drive to the amenities of West Yellowstone.

The attractive, wooded sites at **Norris Campground** are in the heart of the park's east side, close to wildlife activity, geothermal areas, and the Gibbon River.

There are three National Forest Service campgrounds in the **West Yellowstone** area, all located in the Gallatin National Forest. They accommodate both RVs and tents, but there are some periods in late summer where they accept hard-sided vehicles only. All three are first-come, first-serve, so it's best to stake out a spot early. The heavily forested **Bakers Hole,** just 3 miles north of West Yellowstone on U.S. 191, is popular because of its fishing access. Both tents and RVs are accepted, but there are no hookups. **Lonesomehurst,** 8 miles west of the park on U.S. 20, then 4 miles north on Hebgen Lake Road, is only one-third the size of Bakers Hole and fills up quickly in summer. It has tent and RV sites, some of them right on the shore of Hebgen Lake. **Rainbow Point** is reached by driving 5 miles north of West Yellowstone on U.S. 191, then 3 miles west on Forest Service Road 610, then north for 2 miles on Forest Service Road 6954. Tucked away in the forest near Hebgen Lake, it accommodates both tents and RVs (no hookups) and has boating and fishing access. For further information on these campgrounds, call the **Hebgen Lake Ranger District** (*C* 406/823-6961). You can find a wealth of information on the Forest Service website at **www.fs.fed. us/gallatin**.

Where to Stay

INSIDE THE PARK

If you're coming at the height of summer, book ahead! Contact **Xanterra Parks and Resorts,** P.O. Box 165, Yellowstone National Park, WY 82190 (*C* 307/344-7311; www.travelyellowstone. com), for lodging in the park. Accommodations are normally open from early summer to late October. Mammoth Hot

Springs and Old Faithful Snow Lodge then reopen for the winter season beginning in mid-December and running through mid-March.

Another option is **Flagg Ranch Resort** (see chapter 17). Only 2 miles from Yellowstone's south entrance, it's a convenient jumping-off point for exploring the southern reaches of the park.

MAMMOTH HOT SPRINGS AREA

Mammoth's distance from key attractions such as Old Faithful and the Grand Canyon of the Yellowstone makes it one of the last places to fill up. Despite that, it's a good base as home to the park's best visitor center, as well as to colorful limestone terraces.

Mammoth Hot Springs Hotel and Cabins

At Mammoth Hot Springs (P.O. Box 165), Yellowstone National Park, WY 82190. *C* **307/ 344-7311.** Fax 307/344-7456. www.travel yellowstone.com. 212 units. $82–$107 double; $315 suite; $70–$100 cabin; $160 hot tub cabin. AE, DC, DISC, MC, V.

This historic building stands below the steaming, stair-stepping terraces of Mammoth Hot Springs, only 5 miles from the north entrance. It began life as a hostelry in 1911, and was replaced by a lodge in 1937. The hotel's dormer windows and wood floors are attractive, and the high-ceilinged lobby is comfortable and relatively quiet. The only high-end accommodations are the suites. Standard rooms and cabins are arranged around three grassy areas, where elk often graze. If you require a tub, be sure to request one when you make your reservation; otherwise, you could get a cramped, old-fashioned shower stall. The cabins here are cottage-style buildings that are among the best in the park, some with private hot tubs and sun decks. A formal dining room and a fast-food restaurant are both located in a separate building; nearby amenities include a medical clinic, a grocery store, stables, and a filling station.

CANYON VILLAGE AREA

Standing at the center of Canyon Village, you may feel like you're in a mall parking lot. With one of the park's biggest attractions close by, this is one of its busiest areas, and the design of the place adds to it. It's certainly a plus, though, that the Grand Canyon of the Yellowstone is a short walk from the center of the village.

Canyon Lodge and Cabins

In Canyon Village (P.O. Box 165), Yellowstone National Park, WY 82190. ℂ **307/344-7311.** Fax 307/344-7456. www.travelyellowstone. com. 605 units. $155 double; $66–$132 cabin. AE, DC, DISC, MC, V. Closed Oct to late May.

This lodge and cabin complex is one of the newer facilities in the park, but it

can't escape the Disneyland-style atmosphere of Canyon Village. The two lodges are similar, offering tastefully appointed motel-style accommodations (Dunraven is a bit more modern, with an elevator, and nicely positioned on the edge of a woodland area), and cabins that are scattered throughout the village. The motel units have various sleeping configurations designed to accommodate the needs of singles and families. The cabins are single-story duplex and four-plex structures with private bathrooms. They're a bit weathered but livable; given the sheer number of units involved, this isn't the place to "get away from it all."

TOWER-ROOSEVELT AREA

This complex is a cheerful throwback to the early days of car camping in

Campground	Total Sites	RV Hookups	Dump Station	Toilets	Drinking Water
Inside the Park					
*Bridge Bay**	431	No	Yes	Yes	Yes
*Canyon**	272	No	Yes	Yes	Yes
*Fishing Bridge**†	346	Yes	Yes	Yes	Yes
*Grant Village**	425	No	Yes	Yes	Yes
Indian Creek	75	No	No	Yes	Yes
Lewis Lake	85	No	No	Yes	Yes
*Madison**	277	No	Yes	Yes	Yes
Mammoth	85	No	No	Yes	Yes
Norris	116	No	No	Yes	Yes
Pebble Creek	32	No	No	Yes	Yes
Slough Creek	29	No	No	Yes	Yes
Tower Fall	32	No	No	Yes	Yes
Near the Park					
Bakers Hole†	72	No	No	Yes	Yes
Lonesomehurst	26	No	No	Yes	Yes
Rainbow Point†	85	No	No	Yes	Yes

* Reserve through Xanterra Parks and Resorts.
† Accepts hard-sided vehicles only.

Yellowstone: no big complex of shops and services, not a lot of amenities. It's small, out of the way, and less crowded, which is worth a lot. Hiking trails and the beautiful corridor of the Lamar Valley and River that runs to the northeast entrance are nearby.

Roosevelt Lodge Cabins

P.O. Box 165, Yellowstone National Park, WY 82190. © **307/344-7311.** Fax 307/344-7456. www.travelyellowstone.com. 80 cabins (14 with private bathroom). $60–$100 cabin. AE, DC, DISC, MC, V. Closed early Sept to June.

This is considered the park's family hideaway, a low-key operation with primitive cabins and a lodge restaurant that's more like a big ranch house. It's a good choice for budget-conscious, outdoor types interested in exploring the northeast part of Yellowstone. The bare-bones cabins, Roughriders, are furnished with two simple beds, clean linens, a writing table, and a wood stove. Frontier cabins are slightly higher quality. The lodge, which contains a dining area and a small lounge, is a rugged but charming stone edifice with a long, deep porch outfitted with rockers for relaxing. Stagecoach rides, horseback trips, and Western trail cookouts give this place a cowboy flavor that many enjoy, and it's a less hectic scene than other park villages.

LAKE VILLAGE AREA

This resort along the lake is reminiscent of another, less hurried era. The location puts you near the lake's recreational opportunities and hiking trails, and you'll find accommodations in a historic hotel as well as motel and cabin

Showers	Fire Pits/ Grills	Laundry	Public Phone	Reserve	Fees	Open
No	Yes	No	Yes	Yes	$17	Late May to Sept
Yes	Yes	Yes	Yes	Yes	$17	June–Sept
Yes	Yes	Yes	Yes	Yes	$31	Late May to Labor Day
Yes	Yes	Yes	Yes	Yes	$17	Late May to Sept
No	Yes	No	No	Yes	$10	June–Sept
No	Yes	No	No	No	$10	Mid-June to Nov
No	Yes	No	Yes	Yes	$17	Late May to Nov
No	Yes	No	Yes	No	$12	Year-round
No	Yes	No	Yes	No	$12	Mid-May to Sept
No	Yes	No	No	No	$10	Mid-June to Sept
No	Yes	No	No	No	$10	Late May to Nov
No	Yes	No	No	No	$10	Mid-May to late Sept
No	Yes	No	Yes	Yes	$13	Late May to mid-Sept
No	Yes	No	No	Yes	$13	Late May to mid-Sept
No	Yes	No	Yes	Yes	$12.50	Late May to mid-Sept

units and nearby lakeside camping sites. The food at the hotel is as good as any in the park, though low-priced alternatives are in the neighborhood.

Lake Lodge Cabins

On Lake Yellowstone (P.O. Box 165), Yellowstone National Park, WY 82190. © **307/344-7311.** Fax 307/344-7456. www.travelyellowstone. com. 186 cabins. $63 Frontier cabin, $128 Western cabin. AE, DC, DISC, MC, V. Closed mid-Sept to early June.

These cabins, which surround Lake Lodge, stand near the lake just around the corner north of the hotel. The lodge's most attractive feature is a large porch with rockers that invite visitors to sit and gaze out across the water. Accommodations are in well-preserved, clean, freestanding cabins near a trout stream that threads through a wooded area. The cabins come in two grades: Western cabins provide electric heat, paneled walls, two double beds, and bathrooms with tub/shower combinations; while Pioneer cabins are smaller and sparsely furnished, with one or two double beds and small shower-only bathrooms. (Ten of these units were renovated in 2002, making them the freshest and nicest cabins in the park.) There's a small bar area and a cafeteria that serves inexpensive meals.

Lake Yellowstone Hotel and Cabins

On the north side of the lake (P.O. Box 165), Yellowstone National Park, WY 82190. © **307/ 344-7311.** Fax 307/344-7456. www.travel yellowstone.com. 300 units. $128–$200 double; $93 cabin; $451 suite. AE, DC, DISC, MC, V. Closed early Oct to mid-May.

The Ionic columns, dormer windows, and deep porticos of this classic yellow structure recall the year it was built: 1891. The facility was completely restored in the early 1990s, and its better rooms are the park's most comfortable and roomiest. Accommodations are in three- and four-story wings in the hotel, in a motel-style annex, and in cabins. The upper-end rooms here have stenciled walls and

traditional spreads on one queen or two double beds. The freestanding cabins are passable low-priced alternatives, decorated with knotty-pine paneling and furnished with double beds and a writing table. *Note:* If you take a cabin, request a single rather than a duplex, since walls are paper-thin.

When you find yourself sipping a cocktail in a wicker chair in the huge sunroom overlooking the lake while a classical pianist twinkles the keys, you'll appreciate those Victorians' refined tastes. Also elegant, the dining room has rattan furniture and is big enough to feed the busloads that arrive at mealtimes. A take-out delicatessen on the first floor serves ordinary fast food.

GRANT VILLAGE AREA

Though Grant Village is near the south end of beautiful Yellowstone Lake and has a good visitor center, this fairly recent addition to park accommodations lacks the character of the Lake and Old Faithful villages. It's also isolated from other park centers, so guests here are likely to frequent its tiny lounge and eat in one of its two decent restaurants overlooking the lake. Other guest services include a laundry facility, service station, and convenience store.

Grant Village

On the West Thumb of Yellowstone Lake (P.O. Box 165), Yellowstone National Park, WY 82190. © **307/344-7311.** www.travelyellowstone.com. 300 units. $107–$120 double. AE, DC, DISC, MC, V.

The southernmost of the major overnight accommodations in the park, Grant Village was completed in 1984. It's not as architecturally distinctive as the park's historic options, consisting of six condo-style chalets set back from the water's edge, but it's also less touristy and more isolated. Rooms are tastefully furnished, most outfitted with light wood furniture and track lighting. Nicer, more expensive rooms with lake views have mullioned windows and full bathrooms. Midrange rooms are set farther back from the lake and overlook drab grounds.

OLD FAITHFUL AREA

At the Old Faithful area you'll spend a night in the midst of the largest and most famous geyser basin in the world. The park has removed some of the old building clutter, and does its best to protect the geothermal features and control the crowds. Here you have more choices of rooms, restaurants, and services—including a visitor center, gas station, and Yellowstone General Store—than anywhere else in the park.

Old Faithful Inn

At Old Faithful (P.O. Box 165), Yellowstone National Park, WY 82190. © **307/344-7311.** Fax 307/344-7456. www.travelyellowstone. com. 327 units. $107–$197 double with private bathroom; $86–$149 double without bathroom; $293–$390 suite. AE, DC, DISC, MC, V. Closed mid-Oct to mid-May.

When Robert Reamer designed the Old Faithful Inn almost a century ago, he created the perfect blend of rustic and regal, a grand building that blends beautifully with the native timbers and rock. There are three hotels within viewing distance of the geyser, including a very nice new one, but this is undoubtedly the crown jewel of Yellowstone's man-made wonders. Seven stories tall with dormers peaking from a shingled, steep-sloping roof, it looks like a lodgepole jungle gym inside—and indeed, you can climb the stairs to its internal balconies, but seismic activity eventually closed the crow's nest in the rafters to visitors. Only 30 miles from the west entrance and 40 miles from the south entrance, this is the first place visitors think of when they want a bed for the night, so make reservations far ahead during the busy summer months. The dining room is warmed on cool evenings by a fieldstone fireplace. Like other park properties, this lobby also houses a busy fast-food outlet that serves light meals, and there

is a bar and a gift shop. Guest rooms are in the main building, and in wings that flank the main lodge. Original rooms are well appointed with conservative fabrics and park-theme art, but may not have private bathrooms; the wing rooms offer better facilities and more privacy.

Old Faithful Lodge Cabins

At Old Faithful (P.O. Box 165), Yellowstone National Park, WY 82190. © **307/344-7311.** www.travelyellowstone.com. 96 cabins (some without private bathroom). $44–$68 double. AE, DC, DISC, MC, V. Closed mid-Sept to mid-May.

The cabins that once littered the landscape around the world's most famous geyser were hauled off years ago, but those that remain offer an inexpensive albeit no-frills lodging option. Rent one of the budget cabins, just slightly less flimsy than tents, and you'll get basic beds and sinks, and a sense of what it was like to visit Yellowstone half a century ago. Showers and restrooms are a short walk away. Frontier cabins are the better units, adding a private bathroom to other amenities. The lodge has several snack shops and a huge cafeteria dishing up varied fast food. In addition, you're within a short walk of the cafeteria and snack bar at the Old Faithful Snow Lodge (see below).

Old Faithful Snow Lodge

At Old Faithful (P.O. Box 165), Yellowstone National Park, WY 82190. © **307/344-7311.** Fax 307/344-7456. www.travelyellowstone. com. 134 units. $167 double; $85–$128 cabin. AE, DC, DISC, MC, V.

If your last visit to Yellowstone included a stay at the Old Faithful Snow Lodge, put the memory out of your mind. The old dormitory-style lodge was torn down in 1998, and this new, award-winning place could aptly be called the *New Faithful Snow Lodge*. Its contemporary big beam construction and high ceiling in the lobby echo the Old Faithful Inn, and a copper-lined balcony curves above the common area, where guests can relax in wicker furniture. The rooms are spacious and comfortable, and a spacious dining room shares a two-sided fireplace with a lounge. The cabins here are among the park's newest, as many of them were built after the 1988 fires.

See the "Grand Teton National Park" chapter for information about Jackson activities, lodging, and dining.

WEST YELLOWSTONE

West Yellowstone is turning itself into the park's biggest all-season gateway town. It has lots of new motel rooms, but it can still fill up during the peak seasons. **West Yellowstone Central Reservations** (© 888/646-7077) handles booking for many of the hotels.

Moderately priced chains (with prices ranging from $80–$140 double) include the **Marriott Fairfield Inn** (© 800/565-6803) at 105 S. Electric St.; and the **Days Inn** (© 800/548-9551) at 118 Electric St. There are also some Best Western affiliates; the general toll-free number is © 800/528-1234. These include the **Best Western Desert Inn,** 133 Canyon St. (© 406/646-7376); the **Executive Inn,** 236 Dunraven St. (© 406/646-7681); and the **Best Western Weston Inn,** 103 Gibbon St. (© 406/646-7373). Still holding its own is the 88-room **Stage Coach Inn,** 209 Madison Ave. (at Dunraven St.; © 800/842-2882).

Less expensive options (doubles cost $50–$100) include the **Brandin' Iron Motel,** 201 Canyon St. (© 800/217-4613 or 406/646-9411); and the 1912 **Madison Hotel,** 139 Yellowstone Ave. (© 800/838-7745 or 406/646-7745), which also has some historic rooms that go for as little as $37 with a shared bath.

Firehole Ranch

11500 Hebgen Lake Rd., West Yellowstone, MT 59758. © **406/646-7294.** Fax 406/646-4728. www.fireholeranch.com. 10 cabins, each sleeps up to 4. $290–$350 per person per night, double. Rates include all meals. 4-day minimum stay required. No credit cards. Kids under 12 allowed only with prior approval.

Visitors can take a boat ride to Firehole Ranch's location on a mile of private shore along Hebgen Lake, only 16 miles from Yellowstone National Park. The resort is surrounded by thousands of acres of national forest in which guests can ride horses, hike, canoe, and make use of the ranch's mountain bikes. The ranch also offers guided fishing on the area's rivers, streams, and lakes. Lodging is in 10 cabins, most suitable for two guests. The nicest units have separate living rooms complete with wood-burning stoves and private bathrooms with tub-shower combinations. There are no television sets on the property, and telephone service is limited. Cocktails are served in a cozy nook before dinner—exquisite meals prepared by a French chef. Breakfast is buffet style, and there are box lunches at midday.

West Yellowstone Conference Hotel Holiday Inn SunSpree Resort

315 Yellowstone Ave., West Yellowstone, MT 59758. © **800/HOLIDAY** or 406/646-7365. www.doyellowstone.com. 123 units. $79–$144 double; $90–$200 suite. AE, DISC, MC, V.

From its individual rooms to its restaurant, this big, new resort is West Yellowstone's standout offering. Small conveniences such as coffeemakers, plush carpeting, hair dryers, microwaves, a big indoor pool, and laundry service abound. You can arrange fishing and rafting trips, bike and ATV rentals, and chuck-wagon cookouts. Snowmobilers who have been rattling around all day can relax in the Jacuzzi in the king spa suites. Rooms are spacious with bright decor, comfortable furniture, and landscape art on the walls. The Iron Horse Saloon serves regional microbrews, and the Oregon Short Line Restaurant features Western cuisine. At the center of the restaurant sits the restored railroad club car that brought Victorian gents to Yellowstone a century ago.

GARDINER

This little town has character, and it's where the year-round park employees hang out in the winter. Chain motels include the **Comfort Inn** (107 Hellroaring Dr.; © **800/424-6423** or 406/848-7536) and the **Super 8** on U.S. 89 South (© **800/800-8000** or 406/848-7401). Both are open year-round, with high-season rates ranging from $50 to $150 double. The **Best Western by Mammoth Hot Springs,** on U.S. 89 (© **800/828-9080** or 406/848-7311), is another solid option, with doubles for $95 to $105 in the summer.

Absaroka Lodge

U.S. 89 at the Yellowstone River Bridge. © **800/755-7414** or 406/848-7414. Fax 406/848-7560. www.yellowstonemotel.com. 41 units. A/C TV TEL. $40–$100 double. AE, DC, DISC, MC, V.

Every room in this lodge has a balcony, many with nice views of the Yellowstone River. The lodge's riverbank location—with a nice slope of lawn overlooking the river gorge—is just a few blocks from the village center, and the rooms are well appointed with queen-size beds. Suites with kitchenettes cost a little more. The owners have been in business here for decades, but the building is modern and new. Like most other properties in town, the lodge has staff ready and able to assist in arrangements with outfitters for fly-fishing and rafting.

Yellowstone Suites Bed and Breakfast

506 4th St., P.O. Box 277, Gardiner, MT 59030. © **800/948-7937** or 406/848-7937. www.wolftracker.com/ys. 4 units. Summer $85–$110 double; winter $47–$69 double. Rates include full breakfast. AE, MC, V.

This quiet B&B on the south bank of the Yellowstone River is a good alternative to the motels that line U.S. 89. Originally built in 1904, legend has it that the second story's quarried stone exterior is actually a leftover from the Roosevelt Arch. The rooms are frilly and cozy, with a teddy bear motif in the Roosevelt Room and a Victorian theme in the Jackson Room, and the Yellowstone Suite has a television and a kitchenette. The real perks here are the impeccably gardened backyard and the breakfasts, which might feature bread pudding French toast or tomato-and-spinach frittatas.

COOKE CITY

If you choose to spend the night in little Cooke City, you have several options, although none of them includes modern facilities, gourmet dining, or valet parking. Rooms at each of the properties listed below are clean and comfortable, but that's about all lodgings in Cooke City offer. A room for the night will be less expensive than in other gateway towns, anywhere from $60 to $80 a night. The **Soda Butte Lodge** (© **800/527-6462** or 406/838-2251) is the biggest, newest, and poshest motel in town, and it includes the good **Prospector Restaurant** and a small casino; or you can go to the cheaper, bare-bones **Alpine Motel** (© **406/838-2262**), also on Main Street, which accepts pets.

CODY

With some of the showmanship of its founder, William F. "Buffalo Bill" Cody, this town offers more than just a gateway to the east entrance. The night rodeo and the very fine historical center are the big summer attractions.

Buffalo Bill Village Resort: Comfort Inn, Holiday Inn & Buffalo Bill Village Historic Cabins

17th and Sheridan Ave., Cody, WY 82414. © **800/527-5544.** Fax 307/587-2795. Comfort Inn: 75 units. A/C TV TEL. $69–$169 double. Holiday Inn: 189 units. $69–$169 double A/C TV TEL. Buffalo Bill Village Historic Cabins: 83 units. TV TEL. $59–$159 double. AE, DC, DISC, MC, V. Buffalo Bill Village closed Oct–Apr.

This is not exactly a "resort" but an oddly matched cluster of lodgings with a convenient downtown location. The Holiday and Comfort Inns are similar to their chain brethren elsewhere, but the village of aged cabins provides a rustic exterior with a more Western feel and modern conveniences inside. Family units have two bedrooms. There is also a short "Old West" boardwalk where you can shop for curios or sign up for tours and river trips, an outdoor heated pool, and several restaurants.

The Irma Hotel

1192 Sheridan Ave., Cody, WY 82414. ✆ **800/ 745-4762** or 307/587-4221. www.irmahotel. com. 40 units. A/C TV TEL. Original rooms $96–$119 double; motel rooms $69–$92. AE, DC, DISC, MC, V.

Buffalo Bill did a lot for this part of Wyoming, including building this charming old hotel, named after his daughter, in the heart of town. Cody hoped to corral tourists who got off the train on their way to Yellowstone, and one of his lures was an elaborate cherry-wood bar, a gift from straitlaced Queen Victoria. You can still hoist a jar on Her Royal Majesty's slab in the Silver Saddle Saloon. Antique-furnished suites are named after local characters from the town's early days: The Irma Suite, on the corner of the building, has a queen-size bed, a writing table, a vanity in the bedroom area, a small sitting area with TV, and an old-fashioned bathroom with a tub-shower combination. The traditional rooms are more akin to those in a roadside motel. The large restaurant serves excellent prime rib and a summer breakfast buffet. Every summer night except Monday a gang of mustachioed gunfighters draws crowds as they fire blanks at each other on the porch along 11th Street.

Pahaska Tepee Resort

183 Yellowstone Hwy., Cody, WY 82414. ✆ **800/628-7791** or 307/527-7701. Fax 307/527-4019. 48 units. $90–$135 double. DISC, MC, V. Closed Nov and Apr.

Buffalo Bill's hunting lodge, only a mile from the east entrance to Yellowstone, was dubbed with his Lakota name, "Pahaska" (longhair), when he opened the lodge to park visitors in 1905. Near the top of the beautiful Wapiti Valley along U.S. 14/16/20, Pahaska is a popular stop for people visiting the Yellowstone area in both summer and winter. The cabins scattered on the hill behind the lodge close in the winter, while the A-frames by the lodge are open year-round. Accommodations have limited amenities and might best be described as "mini-motels" with two to five rooms, each with a private entrance. Some bathrooms have only showers, some tubs—it's best to ask in advance.

Where to Dine

INSIDE THE PARK

Each of the dining rooms at Mammoth Hot Springs Hotel, Old Faithful Inn, and Lake Yellowstone Hotel has a distinctive ambience, with solid, if none too adventurous, cuisine and servings that are aimed squarely at a hiker's appetite (for reservations, contact **Xanterra Parks and Resorts** at ✆ **307/ 344-7901**). The atmosphere is festive and just elegant enough that you might want to dress up a bit for dinner—put on socks perhaps, and a shirt with a collar. The prices aren't bad, either, and the big halls absorb sound well enough that young children are rarely a bother. Reservations are recommended and sometimes required.

If you're not up for restaurant dining, there is counter-style fast-food service at the **Yellowstone General Stores** and snack shops and cafeterias in the villages at Canyon, Mammoth, Grant Village, Yellowstone Lake Lodge, and Old Faithful.

MAMMOTH HOT SPRINGS

You'll find the **Terrace Grille** at the opposite end of the building in which Mammoth Hot Springs Hotel Dining Room is located. It serves typical restaurant fare in a less formal—and less pricey—dining room, but doesn't take reservations.

Mammoth Hot Springs Hotel

At Mammoth Hot Springs. © **307-344-7901.** Dinner reservations required. Breakfast $4–$8.50; lunch $6–$9; dinner $9–$20. AE, DC, DISC, MC, V. Summer daily 6:30–10am, 11:am–2:30pm, and 5–10pm. STEAK/SEAFOOD.

In this big, high-ccilinged dining room, the breakfast buffet features scrambled eggs, French toast, and muffins. Delicious omelets are served with home fries and toast. Lunch features an array of sandwiches including smoked turkey on Parmesan-crusted sourdough, grilled veggies, and grilled German bratwurst. With a beef- and seafood-oriented menu, dinner is a bit more substantial: The house-smoked entrees are quite good.

CANYON VILLAGE AREA

Arrayed around this busy village parking lot are a casual, soda fountain–style restaurant, a cafeteria, a take-out place, and a conventional dining room.

The **Canyon Glacier Pit Snack Bar,** operated by Yellowstone General Stores, shares a building with a convenience store and souvenir shop, so it's possible to buy a souvenir ashtray as well as a burger. Seating is on stools in the fashion of a 1950s soda fountain, and you can expect to wait up to 30 minutes during peak hours. Breakfast consists of egg dishes, lunch is soup and sandwiches, and dinner is traditional Western food. The snack bar is open from 7:30am to 10pm daily from mid-May to late September.

The **Canyon Lodge Cafeteria** is a fast-food alternative across the parking lot in the Canyon Lodge area. Hours are the same as at the snack bar, and the menu bears some striking similarities— but you may get through the cafeteria line faster than you would get a stool at the soda fountain. The cafeteria is open from June to mid-September.

Canyon Lodge Dining Room

Reservations required. © **307-344-7901.** Open June to mid-Sept. Breakfast $4.50–$8.50; lunch $5.75–$9; dinner $9–$20. Daily in season 7–10:30am, 11:30am–2:30pm, and 5–9pm. AC, DC, DISC, MC, V. STEAK/SEAFOOD.

This spacious dining area, a tad sterile perhaps, gets noisy when it fills up. The salad bar is long and loaded, but otherwise the fare is largely geared to the carnivore, with a wide selection of steaks alongside seafood and pasta dishes. Regardless of the 1950s-style decor, there's a relaxed and unhurried feel to the place that you don't find at some of the other busy areas in the park.

TOWER-ROOSEVELT AREA

Roosevelt Lodge

At Tower Junction. © **307-344-7901.** Breakfast $3.25–$7; lunch $5.25–$9; dinner $9–$19. AE, DC, DISC, MC, V. Summer daily 7–10:30am, 11:30am–4pm, and 5–9pm. STEAK/SEAFOOD.

Advertised as family-friendly and cowboy style, Roosevelt is an alternative to the fancier eateries of the big hotels, but the unadventurous menu will win over only the most naive city slickers. Like the aging cabins that take you back to the early days of auto camping, Roosevelt's dining area is simple and spare, a collection of tables that take up one side of the lodge's big lobby. Our recommendation: Join Roosevelt's Old West Dinner Cookout and ride by horse or wagon through the Pleasant Valley to a chuck-wagon dinner that includes cornbread, steak, watermelon, beans, and apple crisp. It's $49 to $59 for an adult, depending on the route of your horseback ride, or $39 if you go by wagon. Children pay $10 less.

YELLOWSTONE LAKE

For the eat-on-the-run traveler, a **deli** in the Lake Yellowstone Hotel serves light fare in an area slightly larger than a broom closet from 11am to 9pm. Just down the road, the **Yellowstone General**

Store offers three meals in a section of the store that is shared with tourist items; the best bet here is breakfast or a burger. It's open from 7am to 9pm. Inexpensive meals served cafeteria-style are available at the **Yellowstone Lake Lodge and Cabins** from 6:30am to 9pm, with closures in between meals.

Lake Yellowstone Hotel

On the north side of the lake. ✆ **307/344-7901.** Dinner reservations required. Breakfast $4.50–$11; lunch $5.75–$10; dinner $12–$30. AE, DC, DISC, MC, V. Open mid-May to early Oct. Daily 6:30–10:30am, 11:30am–2:30pm, and 5–10pm. CONTINENTAL.

This represents the finest dining Yellowstone has to offer, with a view of the lake stretching south from a big, high-ceilinged dining room that doesn't feel crowded even when it's full. Among the variations here are a generous breakfast buffet with alternatives including a tasty traditional country pan breakfast of bacon, eggs, and home fries; pan-fried trout and eggs; and huevos rancheros. There's also a wide selection of fresh fruit, juices, pastries, and cereals. The dinner menu is equally inviting. Appetizers include duck quesadillas and spanakopitas (a tasty Greek pastry stuffed with spinach and cheese), while entrees include sea scallops, pan-seared yellowfin tuna, and several beef dishes.

GRANT VILLAGE

The casual choice here is the **Lake House,** footsteps away from the Grant Village restaurant. It specializes in less expensive fish entrees, as well as burgers and beer. Dinners are served from 5:30 to 9pm, breakfasts from 7 to 10:30am. No reservations or lunch.

Grant Village

At Grant Village. ✆ **307/344-7901.** Dinner reservations required. Open June–Sept. Breakfast $4–$9; lunch $5.25–$7.75; dinner $9–$20. AE, DC, DISC, MC, V. Summer daily 6:30–10am, 11:30am–2:30pm, and 5:30–10pm. STEAK/SEAFOOD.

Breakfast and lunch at the Grant Village restaurant are much like the other restaurants in the park, though the chef occasionally surprises diners with interesting items that stray from the norm. The lunch menu may include pan-fried trout covered with toasted pecans and lemon butter, Wyoming cheese steak, and a gourmet burger. The dinner menu focuses on trout, but also includes honey-lemon chicken and prime rib. Quality and ambience here are comparable to those of the better dining rooms at the major park hotels.

OLD FAITHFUL AREA

For a quick and inexpensive meal, there is the **Old Faithful Inn** cafeteria, which serves lunch and dinner in a fast-food environment; an ice-cream stand in the lobby is your best choice for dessert. The **Yellowstone General Store** also has a lunch counter.

Obsidian Dining Room

Near Old Faithful (in the Old Faithful Snow Lodge). ✆ **307/344-7901.** No reservations. Breakfast $4.50–$11; dinner $9–$20. AE, DC, DISC, MC, V. Open May to mid-Oct and mid-Dec to mid-May daily 6:30am–noon and 5–10pm. STEAK/SEAFOOD.

In the well-designed new snow lodge, a spacious restaurant provides an alternative to the Old Faithful Inn dining room. It's a little quieter, a little less expensive, and a little less formal, which is reflected in an eclectic menu with such Yellowstone exotics as polenta lasagna. It also has some park standbys on the menu—teriyaki chicken and huge porterhouse pork chops—and the Southwestern eggs are a solid breakfast option. (The room serves breakfast until noon, later than anyplace else in the park.) All in all, it's a huge improvement over the cramped restaurant of the old Snow Lodge.

Old Faithful Inn

Near Old Faithful. ✆ **307/545-4999.** Dinner reservations required. Breakfast $7–$9; lunch

$5–$10; dinner $9–$20. AE, DC, DISC, MC, V. Open May to mid-Oct daily 6:30–10:30am, 11:30am–2:30pm, and 5–10pm. STEAK/ SEAFOOD.

There's nothing wrong with the food here, but the real highlight is the gnarled log architecture of this distinguished historic inn. Breakfast is buffet or a la carte, and there's a lot to choose from. The dinner menu is fairly long, with four cuts of prime rib, fish dishes, and pastas. Two of the highlights: roasted pork loin with a jalapeño cream sauce and a succulent shrimp scampi. Due to the high volume, the service and food here are more inconsistent than other park eateries.

NEAR THE PARK

WEST YELLOWSTONE

Bullwinkle's Saloon, Gambling and Eatery

19 Madison. ✆ **406/646-7974.** Lunch $5–$8; dinner $9–$24. Summer daily 11am–2am. AE, DISC, MC, V. AMERICAN.

Boisterous and noisy crowds, families and fishers, gamblers, and goof-offs fill this restaurant, and they leave well fed. Both luncheon and dinner menus are packed with traditional American entrees: burgers and salads for lunch; huge chicken, rib, and steak plates at dinner. Try the inexpensive and plentiful Bullwinkle's salad, which includes shrimp.

The Canyon Street Grill

22 Canyon St. ✆ **406/646-7548.** Most dishes $6–$12. Mon–Sat in season 7am–10pm, shorter hours in winter. MC, V. AMERICAN.

You gotta like a restaurant whose slogan is: "We are not a fast food restaurant. We are a cafe reminiscent of a bygone era when the quality of the food meant more than how fast it could be served." This delightful, 1950s-style spot serves hearty food for breakfast, lunch, and dinner. Hamburgers and chicken sandwiches are popular, accompanied by milkshakes made with hard ice cream.

A combo of steak, mashed potatoes, and veggies goes for $12.

Eino's Tavern

8955 Gallatin Rd. 9 miles N of town on U.S. 191). ✆ **406/646-9344.** Reservations not accepted. Main courses $5–$20. No credit cards. Daily winter 9am–9pm, rest of year daily noon–9pm. Closed first 2 weeks of Dec. AMERICAN.

Locals snowmobile out from West Yellowstone to Eino's (there's a trail that follows Hwy. 191) to become their own chefs at the grill here. It's a novel concept, and one that keeps people coming back to this restaurant with a fine view of Hegben Lake. At the counter order your meat—steak, teriyaki chicken, hamburger, or hot dog—and don't be surprised when it arrives raw. Go to the grill, slap it on, and stand around drink in hand shooting the breeze with other patrons until your food is exactly the way you like it. Steaks and chicken come with your choice of salad (or twice-baked potatoes in the wintertime); hamburgers come with potato chips. Snowmobilers can purchase gas and oil here, too.

The Outpost Restaurant

115 Yellowstone Ave. (in the Montana Outpost Mall). ✆ **406/646-7303.** Dinner $6–$18. AE, DISC, MC, V. Daily 6am–11pm. Closed Oct 15–Apr 15. AMERICAN.

Tucked away in a downtown mall, this restaurant's food is presented with a family-oriented, home-cooking style—exemplified in the beef stew. There's also salmon, steaks, trout, liver, and an excellent salad bar. For breakfast, if you're really hungry, you can't beat the Campfire Omelette, smothered in homemade chili, cheese, and onions. The menu isn't all that adventurous, and there's none of the vices you'll find in the local taverns (no video poker, beer, wine, liquor, or smoking), but it offers solid fare in a quiet, family-friendly atmosphere.

GARDINER

The Chico Inn

Old Chico Rd., Pray, MT. ℂ **800/HOT-WADA.** Reservations recommended. Main courses $20–$30. AE, DISC, MC, V. Summer daily 5:30–10pm; winter Sun–Thurs 6–9pm, Fri–Sat 5:30–10pm. CONTINENTAL.

It's 30 miles north of Gardiner, but if you're in the area, stop here for some of the best food in the Rockies, and a quick soak in this resort's hot springs. The carnivorous traveler will enjoy the selection of top-drawer beef, and the pine nut–crusted Alaskan halibut is a seafood aficionado's dream. Many of the incredibly fresh veggies originate in the resort's garden and greenhouse, and the menu always includes a vegetarian selection. You'll want to linger over the food, so consider a night's stay.

Helen's Corral Drive-In

U.S. 89 at Yellowstone St. ℂ **406/848-7627.** Reservations not accepted. Menu items $2.25–$10. Credit cards not accepted. Daily 11am–11pm in summer, daily 11am–9pm rest of year. BURGERS.

Okay, so it's not much to look at, and the menu's most adventurous item is a basket of fried shrimp. But proprietor Helen Gould's half-pound hamburgers are the stuff of legend, topping out at 7 inches from top to bottom and featuring all of the fixings. Gould uses both beef and buffalo, earning the nickname "Helen's Hateful Hamburgers" from a local who found the wait staff's ways to be uncouth. A born marketer, Gould seized the nickname and continues to draw in hordes of locals and tourists alike.

Park Street Grill and Cafe

204 Park St. ℂ **406/848-7989.** Main courses $13–$23. MC, V. Tues–Sat 5:30–10pm. Closed mid-Oct to May. ITALIAN/STEAKS.

Adding a dash of zest to Gardiner's staid meat-and-potatoes dining scene, this eatery opened in 1999 to rave reviews. Served in a room with an exposed pine interior, the menu here is a refreshing mix of gourmet Italian entrees, fresh seafood, and good old American chicken, pork, and beef dishes. The Crazy Mountain Alfredo is a good choice from the pasta menu: Reputedly served in Italy's insane asylums, the delectable sauce is spiced with sweet and hot peppers, julienned chicken breast, and Italian sausage. Hearty appetites won't mind the rib-eye steaks or the slow-roasted prime rib, and there's a decent selection of lighter fare as well.

CODY

Cassie's Supper Club

214 Yellowstone Ave. ℂ **307/527-5500.** Main courses $18–$35. AE, DISC, MC, V. Mon–Sat 11am–2pm and 5–10pm; Sun 5–10pm. WESTERN.

Cassie's is the sort of place you might expect and look for in the West, complete with big platters of beef, four bars serving drinks, and ornery roadhouse decor: taxidermy, antelope skulls, and assorted cowboy ephemera. They've got the routine down, having been in business since 1922. Located along the highway west of town in what was once a "House of Ill Fame," Cassie's is now very respectable and very busy. Besides the requisite steaks, there's seafood (including a great rainbow trout dinner), pasta, and chicken, plus a full menu of specialty drinks. In the Buffalo Bar, a 20-foot mural depicts horses, cowboys, and shootouts. Hesitant dancers are lured onto the floor by free Western swing lessons several evenings a week and there's live country music every night in summer.

Tommy Jack's

1134 13th St. ℂ **307/587-4197.** Reservations recommended. Lunch $6–$8, dinner $98–$22. AE, DISC, MC, V. Mon–Sat 10am–2pm and 5–9pm; Sun 10am–2pm. CAJUN.

A geographically unusual eatery right off Cody's main drag, Tommy Jack's dishes up surprisingly authentic Cajun specialties like gator, crawfish, étouffée, gumbo, and fried catfish. Locals love the place; it helps that the eponymous owner is a Louisiana native and fresh crawfish is flown in several times a week. The service here is also excellent, as is the atmosphere, an inviting room done up in brick and glass block.

Maxwell's Restaurant

937 Sheridan Ave. © **307/527-7749.** Lunch $7–$10, dinner $12–$21. AE, DISC, MC, V. Mon–Sat 11am–9pm. ECLECTIC AMERICAN.

A family restaurant in which "family" does not translate to "bland," Maxwell's has some spicy chicken and pasta dishes to go with its salads, seafood, and beef. The gourmet pizzas (especially the garlicky Margherita) aren't a bad choice, nor is the pork tenderloin Marsala, sautéed in a light wine sauce with shiitake mushrooms. You can even order a Philly cheese steak for lunch, uncommon in Wyoming. The low-backed booths and varnished wood tables are sometimes packed with boisterous families, raising the noise level and waitress stress, but it's a friendly crowd.

Stefan's Restaurant

1367 Sheridan Ave. © **307/587-8511.** Reservations recommended. Lunch $5–$9, dinner $10–$23. AE, DISC, MC, V. Summer daily 11am–10pm; off season Mon–Sat 11am–8pm. CONTEMPORARY.

Stefan Bennett is a restless chef, so the menu of his restaurant today is almost completely different from what he began with in 1997—but everything is still made from scratch with an eye for invention. A sign reads, "We don't do giddy-up here," and it's right: This eatery—mild yet sleek in its appearance—serves truly gourmet fare that bears little resemblance to typical Wyoming cuisine. Among the entree survivors are a filet mignon stuffed with Gorgonzola cheese, sun-dried tomatoes, and portobello mushrooms; an "Untraditional Meatloaf" with spicy buffalo; a crustless chicken potpie; and Stefan's delectable honey-soy salad dressing. There are separate lunch and Sunday brunch

menus—for the latter, Stefan smokes his own salmon and even makes hollandaise sauce from scratch—and a "little bites" menu with $4 to $5 children's meals.

Picnic & Camping Supplies

Pick up your food and camping supplies at the ubiquitous **Yellowstone General Stores,** which are in all the park villages.

A Side Trip: Little Bighorn Battlefield National Monument

Even given its importance in American history, Little Bighorn Battlefield will probably not be your primary destination in Montana. But you will find that it is a relatively easy detour on the way west or east if you are passing through this area, and it is worth a trip if you are anywhere close by. Most people who visit the battlefield include it in their trip to Grand Teton or Yellowstone National Park. For driving directions from the monument to Yellowstone, see "Getting There & Gateways," earlier in this chapter.

Like the Revolutionary War battlefield at Lexington, Massachusetts, and Civil War battlefields at Gettysburg, Pennsylvania, and Appomattox, Virginia, the Little Bighorn Battlefield National Monument in eastern Montana presents visitors with an opportunity to immerse themselves in American history. This is where Lt. Col. George Armstrong Custer and the 647 men of the 7th Cavalry were wiped out on June 25, 1876, after Custer and his troops attacked an American Indian village along the banks of the Little Bighorn River. Custer had divided his troops into three companies—he led one while the others were commanded by Maj. Marcus Reno and Capt. Frederick Benteen. Custer expected little resistance from the American Indians, but was surprised by what some have estimated at several thousand Lakota Sioux, Cheyenne, and Arapaho warriors, who surrounded and killed the soldiers.

Until 1991, the battlefield was known as the Custer Battlefield in honor of the soldiers who fought there. However, when 20th-century activists protested that the battlefield recognized only one side of what occurred on its dusty soil, Congress changed the name. Then, in late 2001, Congress approved $2.3 million for construction of a memorial to the American Indian warriors who fought at Little Big Horn to be built at the national monument. Dedicated in June 2003, the memorial includes bronze tracings of three American Indian warriors—a Sioux, a Cheyenne, and an Arapaho—and what is described as a "spirit gate."

JUST THE FACTS

When to Go. The national monument is popular, and visitation is busiest between Memorial Day and Labor Day. The best advice if you wish to avoid crowds is to avoid these months, or arrive early in the morning or late in the day. This is also good advice because summers in eastern Montana can get very hot and there is no shade on the battlefield.

Getting There. If you are coming from the west, from Billings, Montana, take I-90 east 61 miles to the Little Bighorn Battlefield off-ramp at U.S. 212 (Exit 510). If you are coming from the south, from Sheridan, Wyoming, take I-90 north (approximately 70 miles) to the same off-ramp at U.S. 212. If you are coming from the east, from the Black Hills of South Dakota, you will already be on U.S. 212. The battlefield is 42 miles west of Lame Deer, Montana.

The Nearest Airport. Billings is home to the busiest airport in Montana, **Logan International.** For more information, see "The Nearest Airports" in the Yellowstone section, earlier in this chapter.

Information & Visitor Center. Contact the Superintendent, Little Bighorn Battlefield National Monument, P.O. Box 39, Crow Agency, MT 59022-0039 (© 406/638-3204; www.nps.gov/libi).

At the **visitor center** just inside the park entrance, you'll see actual uniforms worn by Custer, read about his life, and view an eerie reenactment of the battles on a small-scale replica of the battlefield.

Park Hours & Fees. The park is open daily from 8am to 9pm from Memorial Day to Labor Day; spring and fall hours are 8am to 6pm; winter hours are 8am to 4:30pm. The visitor center is open the same hours. The park is closed on Christmas, New Year's Day, and Thanksgiving. There is a $10 admission fee per vehicle; $5 for those on foot.

Ranger Programs & A Guided Tour. Hourly **interpretive talks** help visitors understand the battle and its participants. Subjects vary during the day, and include discussion of the culture and life of the Northern Plains tribes that engaged in the battle, army life in the 1870s, weapons and tactics, and the significance of the battle.

For a unique perspective, take a guided tour with **Apsaalooke Tours,** concessionaire at Little Bighorn Battlefield. Contact them at: Little Big Horn College, P.O. Box 370, Crow Agency, MT 59022 (© 406/638-3120). One-hour tours, starting at the visitor center, are led by American Indian guides to the battle sites, at a cost of $8 for adults, $2 for children, or $5 for seniors. The tours have been offered in summer only, three times each day.

EXPLORING THE MONUMENT

It's possible to view the site in less than a half-hour, but you'll shortchange yourself with that approach. Instead, plan to spend enough time to explore the visitor center, listen to interpretive historical talks presented by rangers there, and then tour the site. You'll leave with a greater appreciation for the monument and greater understanding of the history that led up to the battle.

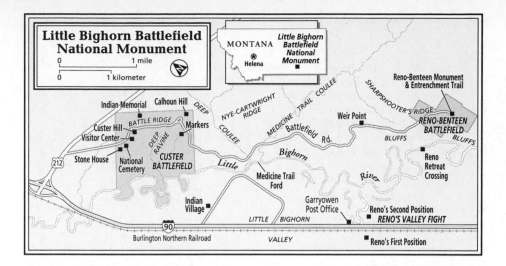

After stopping at the **visitor center,** drive 4½ miles south to the **Reno-Benteen Monument Entrenchment Trail,** at the end of the monument road, and double back. Interpretive signs at the top of this bluff show the route followed by the companies under Custer, Benteen, and Reno as they approached the area from the south, and the positions from which they defended themselves from their American Indian attackers.

As you proceed north along the ridge, you'll pass **Custer's Lookout,** the spot from which the general first viewed the American Indian village. This was the spot at which Custer sent for reinforcements, though he continued marching north.

Capt. Thomas Weir led his troops to **Weir Point** in hopes of assisting Custer, but was immediately discovered by the American Indian warriors and forced to retreat to the spot held by Reno.

The **Medicine Trail Ford,** on the ridge, overlooks a spot well below the bluffs in the Medicine Trail Coulee on the Little Bighorn River, where hundreds of warriors who had been sent from the Reno battle pushed across the river in pursuit of Custer and his army.

Farther north, the Cheyenne warrior Lame White Man led an attack up **Calhoun Ridge** against a company of the 7th Cavalry that had charged downhill into the coulee. When American Indian resistance overwhelmed the army,

troops retreated back up the hill, where they were killed.

As you proceed to the north, you will find detailed descriptions of the events that occurred on the northernmost edges of the ridge, as well as white markers that indicate the places where army troops fell in battle. The bodies of Custer, his brothers Tom and Boston, and nephew Autie Reed, all were found on Custer Hill.

American Indian casualties during the rout are estimated at 60 to 100 warriors. Following the battle, which some say began early in the morning and ended within 2 hours, the American Indians broke camp in haste and scattered to the north and south. Within a few short years they were all confined to reservations.

The survivors of the Reno-Benteen armies buried the bodies of Custer and his slain army where they fell. In 1881, the graves that could be located were reopened, and the bones reinterred at the base of a memorial shaft found overlooking the battlefield. Custer's remains were eventually reburied at the U.S. Military Academy at West Point in 1877.

There are three **walking trails** within the monument for visitors wishing to explore the battle in greater depth.

The adjacent **National Cemetery,** established in 1879, incorporates a self-guided tour to some of the more significant figures buried there.

35

YOSEMITE NATIONAL PARK

by Don & Barbara Laine and Eric Peterson

YOSEMITE'S SKY-SCRAPING GEOLOGIC FORMATIONS, LUSH MEADOWS, swollen rivers, and spectacular waterfalls make it a destination for travelers from around the world. It's home to three of the world's 10 highest waterfalls and the largest single piece of exposed granite anywhere, not to mention one of the world's largest trees and the most recognized rock formation.

The greatest thing about all this is that you don't have to be a mountaineer to enjoy the beauty. Yosemite's most popular attractions are accessible to everyone. No matter where you go, you'll see a view worth remembering. In the span of a mile, you can behold the quiet beauty of a forest, walk through a pristine meadow, observe a sunset from a towering granite cliff, hike to a half-mile-high waterfall, enjoy a moonlit night as bright as day, climb a rock, and eat a gourmet meal before falling asleep, be it under the stars or in a luxurious hotel.

Yosemite Valley, where 95% of park visitors head (more than four million people a year), is just a small sliver of the park, but it holds the bulk of the region's jaw-dropping features. This is the place of record-setting statistics: the highest waterfall in North America and three of the tallest in the world (Upper Yosemite, Sentinel, and Ribbon falls),

the biggest and tallest piece of exposed granite (El Capitan), and stands of Giant Sequoia.

In spite of its beauty, recent years have brought a disquieting sense of foreboding to this wilderness haven, with increasing traffic, litter, and noise. It seems that, in many ways, Yosemite is being loved to death. But the National Park Service has implemented a transportation plan aimed at getting visitors out of their cars, and we can already see improvements. Yosemite has also seen changes due to Mother Nature. In recent years floods and rock slides have altered the face of the valley, destroying campgrounds and some trails.

Avoiding the Crowds. As at most of America's national parks, Yosemite has its highest number of visitors during summer, and especially during school vacations, so the best advice for avoiding crowds is to go when schools are in session. The campgrounds and lodgings are often full from June through August, and you can expect some crowds in late spring and early fall as well. Because of Yosemite's proximity to California's population centers, which results in a lot of weekend travelers, you'll also want to try to avoid weekends—and especially holiday weekends. Winter is a great time to visit Yosemite—not only is the park virtually empty, but there are a number of activities, from skiing at Badger Pass to sledding, ice-skating, and snowshoeing. Keep in mind, however, that the high country along Tioga Pass Road is inaccessible to vehicles from mid-fall to early June, depending on snow levels.

Other ways to avoid humanity, at any time of the year, are to explore the lesser-visited sections of the park—which generally means anywhere outside Yosemite Valley—and to walk away from the crowds by getting out on the trails. The farther you go from the trailheads, the fewer people you'll encounter. Time of day is also important. Since most people are touring the park between 10am and 4pm, early morning, late afternoon, and early evening are the best times to see the park.

Just the Facts

GETTING THERE & GATEWAYS

Yosemite is a 3½-hour drive from San Francisco and a 6-hour drive from Los Angeles. Many roads lead to Yosemite's four entrances. From the west, the Big Oak Flat Entrance is 88 miles from Manteca via CA 120 and passes through the towns of Groveland, Buck Meadows, and Big Oak Flat. The Arch Rock Entrance is 75 miles northeast of Merced via CA 140 and passes through Mariposa and El Portal. The South Entrance is 64 miles north of Fresno and passes through Oakhurst, Bass Lake, and Fish Camp. From the east, the Tioga Pass Entrance is the only option. It is 10 miles west of Lee Vining via CA 120, although this route is usually open only in the summer. To check on statewide road conditions call © 800/427-7623.

Daily bus transportation into the park from Merced, Mariposa, and nearby communities is provided by the **Yosemite Area Regional Transportation System (YARTS),** operated by VIA Bus Lines (© **877/989-2787** or 209/388-9589; www. yarts.com). Buses are not subject to park entrance delays during peak season. From Merced, there are several departures daily from the airport, Amtrak train station, and Greyhound bus terminal. Round-trip fare is $20 adults, $14 for children 12 and under and seniors 65 and older. There are stops in Mariposa at several lodgings and the visitor center, with round-trip rates of $10 adults, $9 for children 12 and under and seniors 65 and older.

The Nearest Airports. Fresno-Yosemite International Airport (© 559/621-6699), located 90 miles from the South Entrance at Wawona, is the nearest major airport, serving over 25 cities with more than 100 flights daily. Airlines include Air Wisconsin/United Express, Allegiant Air, America West/Mesa, American/American Eagle, Continental, Delta, Horizon, Northwest, SkyWest, and United. Major car-rental companies are also represented at the airport. A list of toll-free numbers for airlines and car rentals is in the appendix. **Mariposa Airport** (© 209/966-2143) has a tiny airstrip with space for 50 private planes.

INFORMATION

Get general information from **Superintendent, Yosemite National Park,** P.O. Box 577, Yosemite, CA 95389 (© **209/ 372-0200,** or 209/372-4726 for the hearing impaired; www.nps.gov/yose). A good resource for area information is the **Yosemite Area Travelers Information** (© 209/723-3153; www.yosemite.com). The **Yosemite Association** publishes books and interpretive information (© 209/379-2646; www.yosemite.org).

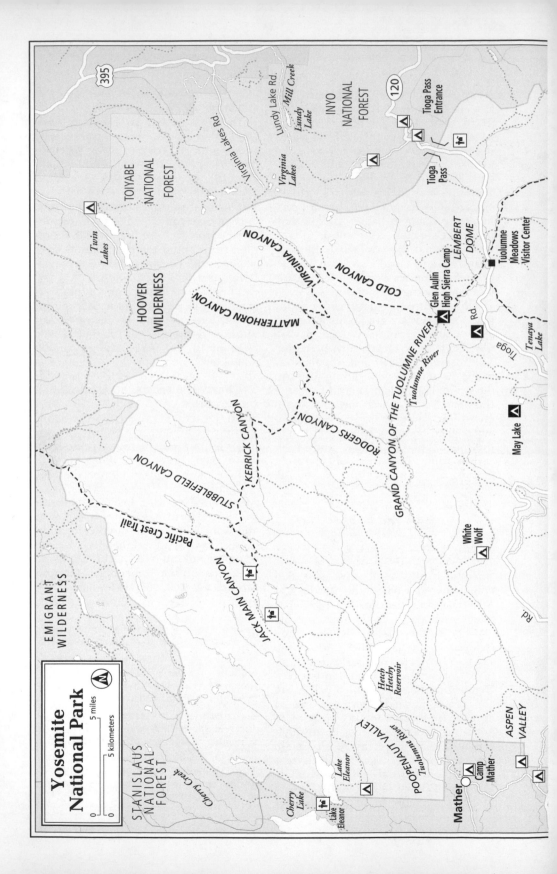

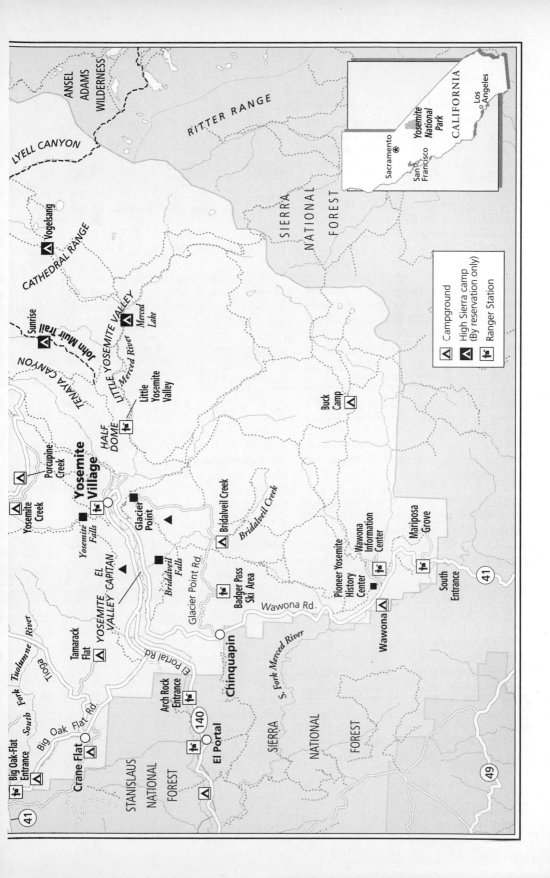

VISITOR CENTERS

In the park, the best and biggest visitor center is the **Valley Visitor Center in Yosemite Village** (© 209/372-0200), open year-round. The center offers tour information, daily ranger programs, lodging, and restaurants. The rangers here are helpful, insightful, and knowledgeable. Inside, information boards update road conditions and campsite availability, and serve as a message board. Maps, books, and videos can also be purchased. There are several exhibits on the park, its geologic history, and the history of the valley. Nearby is **Yosemite Valley Wilderness Center,** a small room with high-country maps, information on necessary equipment, and trail information. A ranger at the desk answers questions, issues permits, and offers advice about the high country. Elsewhere, the **Wawona Information Station** and **Big Oak Flat Information Center** dispense general park information. In the high country, stop at the **Tuolumne Meadows Visitor Center** (© 209/372-0263) for information and advice.

FEES & PERMITS

It costs $20 per vehicle per week to enter the park, or $10 per person per week if arriving on bike or on foot. Camping costs $5 to $18 a night.

Camping in the backcountry and fishing both require permits. See "Fishing" (under "Other Sports & Activities") and "Overnight Hikes," later in this chapter for more information.

SPECIAL REGULATIONS & WARNINGS

In addition to the usual regulations about not damaging the natural resources, staying on established trails, and the like, special regulations at Yosemite are aimed at protecting the park's bear population, which has become much too familiar with the habits of humans. Under no circumstances should food be left in tents, cabins, or cars. There are storage lockers and bear-proof containers throughout the park—use them. Never feed a bear, or any animal for that matter.

SEASONS & CLIMATE

For general information on the climate of Yosemite, see the "Seasons & Climate" section of the chapter on nearby Sequoia & Kings Canyon national parks. The climate there is very similar to Yosemite's.

The high country in Yosemite receives up to 20 feet of snow, and visitors who plan a winter trip should be well experienced in winter travel.

SEASONAL EVENTS

January to February: Chefs' Holidays. Yosemite hosts nationally renowned chefs, who share their secrets with participants. Each session, which includes several talks and demonstrations throughout the day by noted chefs, concludes with a banquet in the Ahwahnee Dining Room. Cost is $140 per person. Packages that include overnight accommodations at the Ahwahnee are available. Call © 559/252-4848 for rates.

November to December: Vintners' Holidays. California's finest winemakers hold tastings in the Ahwahnee Great Lounge. Each session concludes with a Vintners' Banquet. Cost is $140 per person (includes gratuities and wine). Two-, 3- and 5-night packages are also available. Call © 559/252-4848 for rates and information.

December 22, 24 & 25: The Bracebridge Dinner. This event transports diners to 17th-century England, with music, song, and course upon course of delectable dishes. This popular event requires reservations, which are secured by lottery. Applications are available December 1 to January 15 and are due February 15 for the following year. Expect to pay around $275 per person. Call © 559/252-4848 for more information.

If You Have Only 1 Day

This is a park that begs for an extended visit, but those with a limited amount of time will also have an enjoyable experience, especially if they make use of the park's shuttle bus. The bus is free, easy to use, and operates year-round, with fewer stops in winter. For that reason, we've included shuttle bus stop numbers wherever possible throughout the valley sections in this book. Bus stops are well marked and within easy walking distance of all parking lots.

You can get on and off the shuttles at any point, but be sure to stop at the Valley Visitor Center (shuttle bus stop nos. 6 and 9) for an orientation on how the valley was created.

If you're not apt to take off on your own, one of the best ways to spend your time wisely is to take one of the guided tours (see "Organized Tours & Ranger Programs," below). But if group activities aren't really your cup of tea, try the following sites on your own.

The base of **Lower Yosemite Fall** (shuttle bus stop no. 7) is an easy walk from the parking lot across from Yosemite Lodge. The hike is described in greater detail below. From here, you can see a portion of the magnificent water show. During peak runoff, when the force of the falls sends spray in every direction, it's not uncommon to get wet. In late winter and early spring, a huge snow cone caused by freezing water rises up to 300 feet at the base of this fall.

Happy Isles (shuttle bus stop no. 16) is another major attraction. Located at the convergence of several inlets, it's the site of the valley's new nature center. This is also the trailhead for Vernal and Nevada falls, two picturesque staircase waterfalls that can only be reached by foot. Both are described later in this chapter.

Next, we recommend a visit to **Mirror Lake** (shuttle bus stop no. 17), a small lake named for the near-perfect way it reflects the surrounding scenery. It's slowly filling up with silt and is less dramatic and mirrorlike than it used to be, but its shore still offers a beautiful view of Half Dome. This short stroll is well marked and described below.

Exploring the Park by Car or Shuttle

It's relatively easy to find your way around Yosemite. All road signs are clear and visible. You'll soon realize that everything leads to a one-way road that hugs the valley's perimeter. To get from one side to the other, you can either drive the entire loop or travel one of the few bridges over the Merced River. It is, however, easy to find yourself heading in the wrong direction on the one-way road, so be alert whenever you merge.

In addition to the year-round shuttle bus in Yosemite Valley, Wawona and Tuolumne Meadows offer a similar service during summer months only. Driving in any of these places during peak season—or even off season in the valley—is a surefire way to miss important sights and spend too much of your time stuck in traffic.

YOSEMITE VALLEY

Many people come to Yosemite National Park solely to see Yosemite Valley, which can be simply described as a giant study in shadow and light. In spring, after winter snow begins melting in the high country, waterfalls encircle the valley, shimmering like a diamond necklace. There are wide, beautiful meadows, towering trees, and the ever-present sound of rushing water in the background.

Yosemite Valley consists of three developed areas. Just about all the hotels, restaurants, and shops can be found in **Yosemite Village, Yosemite Lodge,** and **Curry Village.** Curry Village (also called Camp Curry) and Yosemite Lodge offer the bulk of the park's overnight accommodations. Curry Village is near shuttle bus stop nos. 1, 13, and 14. Yosemite Lodge is served by stop no. 8. Both locations have restaurants and a small grocery. The lodge has a

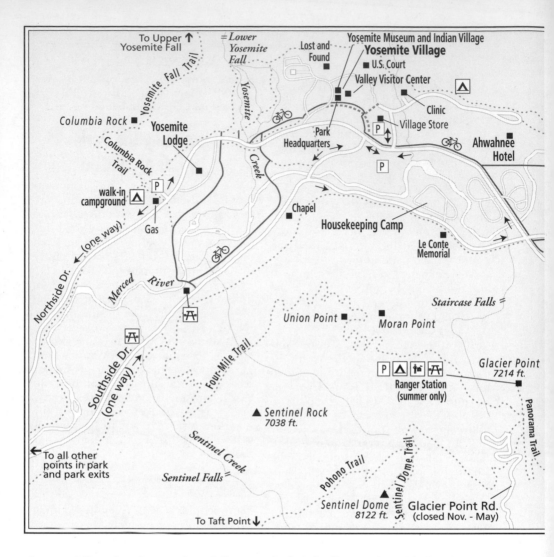

large public swimming pool, and Curry Village has an ice rink open in winter.

Yosemite Village is the largest developed region within the valley and is served by shuttle bus stop nos. 3, 5, 6, 9, and 10. It is home to the park's largest visitor center and the headquarters for the National Park Service in Yosemite, as well as for Yosemite Concession Services, the contractor that runs most of the park's accommodations and restaurants. The village also has a host of stores and shops, including a grocery, restaurants, the valley's only medical clinic, a dentist, a post office, a beauty shop, and an ATM.

Also, check out the **Yosemite Pioneer Cemetery,** a peaceful graveyard in the shade of tall sequoias with headstones dating from the 1800s. (Pick up the self-guiding booklet at the nearby visitor center.) There are about 36 marked graves, identifiable by horizontal slabs of rock, some etched with crude or faded writing. There are some notables in Yosemite history buried here, such as James Lamon, an early settler known for his apple trees—they still bear fruit—who died in 1875. And there's the touching grave of 14-year-old Effie Maud Crippen, who died August 31, 1881, after "she faltered by the wayside and the angels took her home."

Next door, you'll find the **Yosemite Museum** and **Indian Cultural Exhibit.** Both are free and provide a historic

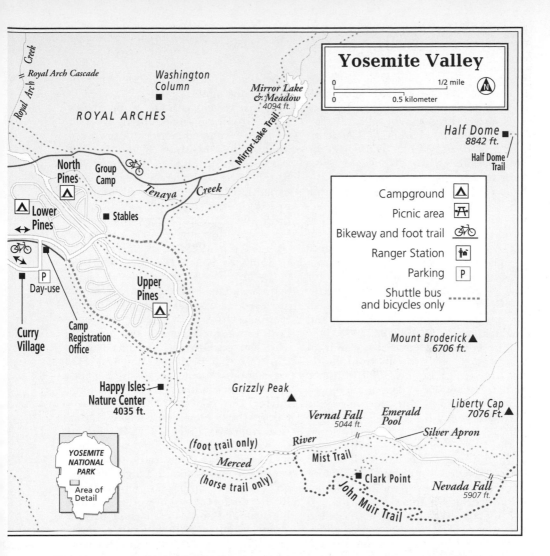

picture of the park, before and after it was settled and secured as a national treasure. The museum entrance is marked by a crowd-pleaser—the cross-section of a 1,000-year-old sequoia with memorable dates identified on the tree's rings. Highlights include the signing of the Magna Carta in 1215, the landing of Columbus in the New World, and the Civil War. The ring was cut in 1919 from a tree that fell in the Mariposa Grove south of the valley in Wawona. The Indian Cultural Exhibit strives to explain the life of the American Indians who once lived here, and members of regional American Indian tribes regularly speak or give demonstrations of traditional arts such as basket weaving. The Yosemite Museum Book Shop is next door (© **209/372-0295**) and sells books as well as traditional American Indian arts and crafts.

The village of the **Ahwahneeche** is behind the museum and Indian Cultural Exhibit, and offers a free self-guided walking tour accessible from the back door of the visitor center. This exhibit guides visitors through the transformation of the Ahwahneeche, the tribe that inhabited Yosemite Valley until the mid-1850s. The village includes a ceremonial roundhouse that's still in use.

The **Ansel Adams Gallery** (© **209/ 372-4413;** www.anseladams.com) sells prints and cards of images made by this famed photographer. The shop also serves as a small gallery for current artisans, some with works for sale.

One mile east of Yosemite Village on a narrow, dead-end road is the majestic old **Ahwahnee** (see "Where to Stay," later in this chapter). Take the shuttle bus to stop no. 4. It's definitely worth a visit for anyone interested in architecture and design.

The **Yosemite Chapel** is located on the south side of the Merced River, shuttle bus stop no. 11. From the bus stop, walk across the bridge and to the left for just under a quarter mile. Schedules for the worship services held in the chapel are posted in the *Yosemite Guide* and available by phone (© **209/372-4831**).

The **LeConte Memorial Lodge** is an educational center and library at shuttle bus stop no. 12. Built in 1903, in honor of a University of California geologist named Joseph LeConte, the Tudor-style granite building hosts a number of free educational programs. Talks are listed in the *Yosemite Guide.*

At the valley's far east end beyond Curry Village is the **Happy Isles Nature Center,** shuttle bus stop no. 16. Summer hours are 9am to 5pm daily, spring and fall hours are shorter, and it's closed in the winter. The nature center offers exhibits and books on the various animal and plant life found in Yosemite, and is a super place for children to explore. This is also where the park's Little Cub and Junior Ranger programs are held. Happy Isles is named for three nearby inlets labeled by Yosemite's guardian in 1880.

NORTH OF THE VALLEY

Hetch Hetchy and **Tuolumne Meadows** are remarkably different regions located on opposite sides of the park. Hetch Hetchy is on the park's western border and can be reached by taking the turnoff just outside the park's Big Oak Flat Entrance. Tuolumne Meadows is on the park's eastern border, just inside Tioga Pass, and is inaccessible by motor vehicle during the winter.

Hetch Hetchy is home to the park's reviled reservoir, one fought over for years by the famed conservationist John Muir. In the end, Muir lost and the dam was built, ensuring water for the city of San Francisco. Many believe the loss exhausted Muir and hastened his death in 1914, a year after a bill was signed to fund the dam project. Construction began on the dam in 1919, and it was completed in 1923.

South of Hetch Hetchy, inside the park, are two large stands of Giant Sequoias. The Merced and Tuolumne groves offer a quiet alternative to the Mariposa Grove of Big Trees in Wawona. Both groves are accessible only on foot. The **Merced Grove** is a 4-mile round-trip walk that begins on Big Oak Flat Road about 4½ miles inside the Big Oak Flat Entrance. Although the trees don't mirror the majesty of the Mariposa Grove, the solitude here makes this a real treat for hikers. The **Tuolumne Grove** of about 25 trees can be reached by a 1-mile hike (2 hr. round-trip).

To get into Yosemite's **high country,** go about 1½ hours east along Tioga Road, which is closed in winter between Big Oak Flat and Tioga Pass. This subalpine region is low on amenities, which makes it a frequent haunt of those who enjoy roughing it, but even cushy-soft couch potatoes can enjoy the beauty up here. Glistening granite domes tower above lush green meadows, which are cut by silver swaths of streams and lakes. Many of Yosemite's longer hikes begin or pass through here.

Olmsted Point, located midway between White Wolf and Tuolumne meadows, offers one of the most spectacular vistas anywhere in the park. Here the enormous walls of the Tenaya Canyon are exposed and an endless view stretches all the way to Yosemite Valley. In the distance are Cloud's Rest and the rear of Half Dome. To the east, easily accessible Tenaya Lake, one of the park's larger lakes, glistens like a sapphire.

About 8 miles east of Tenaya Lake is **Tuolumne Meadows,** a huge subalpine area surrounded by domes and steep granite formations that offer exhilarating climbs. The meadow is a beautiful place to hike and fish, or just admire the scenery while escaping the crowds of Yosemite Valley. To the north of the meadow is Lembert Dome at about 2 o'clock, and then working clockwise, Johnson Peak at 7 o'clock, Unicorn Peak at 8 o'clock, Fairview Dome at about 10 o'clock, and Pothole Dome at 11 o'clock. Up the road is the central region of Tuolumne, where you'll find a visitor center, campground, canvas tent-cabins, and a store. Continue east to reach Tioga Lake and Tioga Pass.

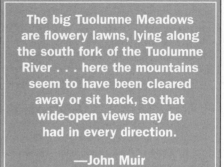

The big Tuolumne Meadows are flowery lawns, lying along the south fork of the Tuolumne River . . . here the mountains seem to have been cleared away or sit back, so that wide-open views may be had in every direction.

—John Muir

SOUTH OF THE VALLEY

This region, which includes Wawona and the Mariposa Grove of Big Trees, is densely forested. There are a handful of granite rock formations here, but none as spectacular as those found elsewhere in the park. En route to Wawona you'll come across several wonderful views of Yosemite Valley. **Tunnel View,** a turnout just before passing through a long tunnel en route to Wawona, provides one of the park's most recognizable vistas, one memorialized on film by photographer Ansel Adams. To the right is Bridalveil Fall, opposite El Capitan. Half Dome lies straight ahead.

Halfway between Yosemite Valley and Wawona is Glacier Point Road (closed in winter past the turnoff to Badger Pass Ski Area), which runs 16 miles to spectacular **Glacier Point.** From the parking area, it's a short hike to an amazing overlook that provides a view of the glacier-carved granite rock formations all along the valley and beyond. At this point you will be at eye level with **Half Dome,** which looks close enough to reach out and touch. Far below, Yosemite Valley resembles a green-carpeted ant farm. There are also some pretty sights of some obscure waterfalls that are not visible from the valley floor.

Glacier Point has a geology hut and a day lodge for wintertime cross-country skiers that is a gift store/snack shack during the rest of the year. It's accessible by both foot and bus (see "Organized Tours & Ranger Programs," below).

Continue south on Wawona Road to reach **Wawona,** a small town located 30 miles from the valley that runs deep with history. It was settled in 1856 by homesteader Galen Clark, who built a rustic way station for travelers en route from Mariposa to Yosemite. The property's next owners, the Washburn brothers, built much of what is today the Wawona Hotel, including the large white building to the right of the main hotel, which was constructed in 1876. The two-story hotel annex went up 3 years later. When Congress established Yosemite National Park in 1890 and charged the U.S. Army with managing it, Wawona was chosen as the Army's headquarters. Every summer, soldiers would camp in what is today the Wawona Campground. For 16 summers, the cavalry out of San Francisco occupied the camp and mapped the park. When Yosemite Valley was added after the turn of the 20th century, the cavalry picked up and relocated to the valley.

As Yosemite grew in popularity, so did the Wawona Hotel and the town itself. When the Wawona Hotel was added to the park in 1932, Section 35 (the number assigned to the plot in its legal description) was allowed to remain under private ownership. The town is still there today, just east of the hotel off Wawona Road.

Near the Wawona Hotel are the Thomas Hill Studio and Pioneer Yosemite History Center. The studio, which keeps sporadic hours that are impossible to pin down but are frequently listed in the *Yosemite Guide*, is the former workspace of noted 19th-century painter Thomas Hill. He came to Wawona in 1885 after his daughter married a Washburn. Hill painted a number of award-winning landscapes, including some recognizable ones of Yosemite.

The Pioneer Center offers a self-guided walking tour of the cabins and buildings moved to this site in 1961 from various locations in the park. Each represents a different time in Yosemite's short history. During the summer, the National Park Service interpreters dress in period clothing and act out characters from the park's past. To reach the center, walk across the covered bridge. An entertaining 10-minute stagecoach ride is offered during the summer for a small fee.

Nearby, the **Mariposa Grove** is a stand of Giant Sequoias, some of which have been around for 3,000 years. They stretch almost 300 feet tall, are 50 feet in circumference, and weigh an average of 2 million pounds. The 500 trees here are divided into the Upper Grove and the Lower Grove. The easiest way to see the trees is from the open-air tram that runs during summer. Cost is $8 for adults and $4 for children; kids under 4 ride free. Trams leave every 20 minutes. A guide provides commentary during the trip, which lasts about an hour. It makes regular stops at the Grizzly Giant, Wawona Tunnel Tree, and Mariposa Grove Museum. It's worth hopping out and walking around as often as possible. Just take the next tram back. All of the area is also accessible on foot. It is an uphill walk to the upper grove, 2.5 miles each way.

The Grizzly Giant is the largest tree in the grove. At "just" 200 feet, it is shorter than some of its neighbors, but its trunk measures more than 30 feet in diameter at the base. A huge limb halfway up measures 6 feet in diameter and is bigger than many of the "young" trees in the grove. Some claim that the limb is larger than any tree east of the Mississippi.

The Wawona Tunnel Tree had a tunnel 10 feet high and 26 feet long cut through it in 1881. Thousands of visitors were photographed driving through the tree before it toppled in the winter of 1968–69, its death caused by heavy snow. (The tree had been weakened by the tunnel and a shallow root system.) No one saw the tree fall.

The Mariposa Grove Museum was the first building constructed by Galen Clark. It was last refurbished in 1981. During the summer there are exhibits, and books and educational materials are sold.

Organized Tours & Ranger Programs

The park offers a number of **ranger-guided walks and hikes** and other programs. Check at one of the visitor centers or in the *Yosemite Guide* for current topics, start times, and locations. Walks may vary from week to week, but you can always count on nature hikes, evening discussions on park anomalies (floods, fires, or critters), and the sunrise photography program aimed at replicating some of Ansel Adams's works. The sunrise photo walk always gets rave reviews from the early risers who venture out at dawn. All photo walks require advance registration. The living history evening program outside at Yosemite Lodge is great for young and old alike.

Several organizations also host guided trips. **Yosemite Guides** (© 877/425-3366 or 209/379-2231) offers excursions to some of the lesser-known areas of the park, and also guides fly-fishing trips for all levels. The **Yosemite Institute** (© 209/379-9511) is a nonprofit organization offering a unique environment for learning about nature and the human history of the Sierra Nevada. Also check out **Incredible Adventures** (© 800/777-8464), which offers 3-day trips and hikes in Yosemite from San Francisco.

Yosemite Sightseeing Tours (© 559/877-8687) conducts scheduled as well as customized trips. Costs range from $48 to $58, depending on the season. Tours are operated on small air-conditioned buses with huge picture windows. The sightseeing includes Mariposa Grove, Yosemite Valley, and Glacier Point. Geology, flora, and fauna are pointed out along the way. Stops are scheduled for lunch, shopping, and photo opportunities. Pickup can be arranged from various motels throughout Oakhurst and Bass Lake.

If you're staying in the valley, the **National Park Service** and **Yosemite Concession Services** present evening programs on the park's history and culture. Past summer programs have included a discussion on early expeditions to Yosemite, the park's flora and fauna, geology, and legends of American Indians who once lived here. Other programs have focused on Mark Wellman's courageous climb of El Capitan—he made the ascent as a paraplegic—and the global ecology and major threats to Yosemite's environment.

Inquire about current programs upon check-in at your hotel or at the information booth outside the visitor center. Although most programs are held in Yosemite Valley, a few campgrounds in other areas of the park offer campfire programs in the summer.

Spring through fall, the **Yosemite Theater** offers inexpensive theatrical and musical programs designed to supplement Park Service programs. They tend to repeat from year to year, and favorites include a conversation with John Muir, a film on Yosemite's future, and singalongs.

A variety of **guided bus tours** are also available. You can buy tickets at tour desks at Yosemite Lodge, The Ahwahnee, Curry Village, or beside the Village Store in Yosemite Village. Advance reservations are suggested for all tours, and space can be reserved in person or by phone (© 209/372-1240). Always double-check at tour desks for updated departure schedules and prices. Most tours depart from Yosemite Lodge, The Ahwahnee, or Curry Village, and prices range from about $18 for adults for a 2-hour tour to about $48 for adults for full-day trips. Children's rates are usually 40% to 50% less, and most tours offer discounts for seniors.

The 2-hour **Valley Floor Tour** is a great way to get acclimated to the park, providing a good selection of photo ops, such as El Capitan, Tunnel View, and Half Dome. This ride is also available on nights when the moon is full or near full. It's an eerie but beautiful scene when moonlight illuminates the valley's granite walls and gives visitors a rare picture of Yosemite. Blankets and hot cocoa are provided. Dress warmly, though, because it can get mighty chilly after the sun goes down.

The **Glacier Point Tour** is a 4-hour scenic bus ride through the valley to Glacier Point. Tours also depart from Yosemite Valley to **Mariposa Grove.** The trip takes 6 hours, and includes the Big Trees tram tour that winds through the grove and stops for lunch at Wawona (lunch not provided). You can combine the trip to Glacier Point and Mariposa Grove in an 8-hour bus ride.

Day Hikes

A nature-lover's paradise, Yosemite has some of the most beautiful scenery you'll see anywhere, and the best way to experience the park is to get out onto the trails. Park rangers lead walks and hikes (see "Organized Tours & Ranger Programs," above), and guided treks are also available from **Yosemite Guides** (© 877/425-3366 or 209/379-2231), with rates from $45 to $200 per person.

IN & NEAR THE VALLEY

Base of Bridalveil Fall

0.5 mile RT. Easy. Access: Drive or walk to the Bridalveil Fall parking area, about 3 miles west of Yosemite Village. Follow trail markers.

Bridalveil Fall measures 620 feet from top to bottom. In the spring, expect to get wet. This walk is wheelchair accessible with strong assistance.

Columbia Rock

2 miles RT. Moderate. Access: Use the trailhead for Upper Yosemite Fall.

This hike mirrors the initial ascent of the waterfall trail, but stops at Columbia Rock, 1,000 feet above the valley. You won't find a valley view, but the sights here are still impressive. The trail is also less likely to get an accumulation of snow because it's on the sunny side of the valley.

Four-Mile Trail to Glacier Point

9.6 miles RT. Strenuous. Access: The trailhead is 1¼ miles from Yosemite Village, at the Four Mile parking area, post V-18; or take the shuttle bus to the Yosemite Lodge stop no. 8 and walk behind the lodge over the Swinging Bridge to Southeast Dr. The trailhead is 0.25 mile west.

This trail climbs 3,200 feet, but your efforts will be rewarded with terrific views of Yosemite Valley's north rim. Check on current trail conditions before setting out; it's usually closed in winter. The trail ends at Glacier Point, but if you'd like to extend the hike, you can connect there to the Panorama Trail (see below). The combined round-trip distance is 14 miles.

Half Dome

17 miles RT. Very strenuous. Access: Happy Isles/shuttle bus stop no. 16.

This long, steep trip, which about 1,000 hikers do each summer day, climbs 4,900 feet. From Happy Isles, take the Mist Trail or the John Muir Trail past Vernal and Nevada falls, and up into Little Yosemite Valley. Leave the John Muir Trail for the Half Dome Trail. Hiking the final 600 feet up the back of Half Dome requires the use of cables, and a strong heart is helpful too. Half Dome has a small level spot on top, at an elevation of 8,800 feet. It's possible to cut the length of the trip by camping in Little Yosemite Valley (you'll need a wilderness permit).

Lower Yosemite Fall

0.5 mile RT. Easy. Access: From shuttle bus stop no. 6 follow the paved path from the Yosemite Fall parking area to the base of this waterfall.

Lower Yosemite Fall reaches 320 feet, but it packs the accumulated punch of the entire 2,425-foot waterfall, and from early spring through midsummer you're likely to get wet. You can also take this trip from Yosemite Village by following the path from the Valley Visitor Center to the trailhead. Add another half-mile or 40 minutes each way. This walk is wheelchair accessible with assistance.

Mirror Lake

2 miles RT. Easy. Access: Shuttle bus stop no. 17.

This paved trail climbs about 60 feet along the west side of Tenaya Creek to Mirror Lake, where you'll likely see overhanging rock formations reflected in the lake's still surface. This trail connects with a delightful 3-mile loop around the lake.

Mist Trail to Vernal Fall

3 miles RT. Moderate to strenuous. Access: From Happy Isles/shuttle bus stop no. 16, walk to the Happy Isles Bridge. Cross the bridge and follow the signs to the trail.

This hike begins on the famous 211-mile John Muir Trail to Mount Whitney in Sequoia/Kings Canyon National Park. From the Happy Isles Bridge, the trail climbs 400 feet to the Vernal Fall Bridge, which offers a good view of what lies ahead, as well as water and restrooms. From this point, you can either take a series of switchbacks along the side of the mountain and come out above the fall, or you can ascend the Mist Trail (our preference), which is a steep climb with 500 steps—it's wet, picturesque, and refreshing. The Mist Trail is so named because the spray from the fall drenches anyone who tackles this route, especially in spring. **Be warned:** It's slick and requires careful placement of your feet. Once you reach the top, you can relax on a series of smooth granite beaches and soak in the cool, refreshing water before hiking back down.

Panorama Trail

9 miles one-way. Moderate to strenuous. Access: The hike begins at Glacier Point, at the east end of the parking area.

From Glacier Point, this trail drops 3,200 feet. At one of its prettiest points, it crosses Illilouette Fall about 1.5 miles from Glacier Point. The path continues along the Panorama Cliff and eventually winds up at Nevada Fall, where it's a straight descent to Yosemite Valley via the Mist or John Muir trails. You can hike this trail in conjunction with the Four-Mile Trail, and it's also possible to take a bus to Glacier Point and hike only one-way.

Upper Yosemite Fall

7.2 miles RT. Strenuous. Access: Shuttle bus to stop no. 8; the trailhead is next to Camp 4 Walk-in Campground, behind Yosemite Lodge.

Climb this 2,700-foot trail and you'll be rewarded with spectacular views from the ledge above the fall. Keep in mind, however, that this hike is not for the faint of heart. Take it slow, rest often, and absorb the scenery as you ascend higher and higher above the valley. One mile up, you'll reach Columbia Rock, which offers a good view. The rest of the trail dips and climbs, and you'll find numerous opportunities to cool off beneath the spray from the fall above. The last quarter mile is rocky and steep, with a series of tortuous, seemingly endless switchbacks that ascend through underbrush before opening at a clearing near the top of the fall, but beware—the view here can induce vertigo. After completing the trail, it's a worthwhile walk upstream to see the creek before it takes its half-mile tumble to the valley floor below. Hikers with the proper permits and equipment can stay here overnight.

SOUTH OF THE VALLEY

Chilnualna Falls from Wawona

8 miles RT. Moderate. Access: From Wawona, take Chilnualna Rd., just north of the Merced River's south fork, until it dead-ends at "The Redwoods," about 1⅓ miles. This is the trailhead.

This trek offers a satisfying glimpse of a stunning waterfall. One of the tallest outside Yosemite Valley, the fall cascades down two chutes. The one at the bottom is narrower and packs a real punch after a wet winter. A series of switchbacks lead to the top fall.

Grizzly Giant

1.6 miles RT. Easy. Access: The trail begins at a sign near the map dispenser at the east end of the Mariposa Grove parking lot.

This is the walking alternative to the Mariposa Grove tram tour described earlier in this chapter. It's a nice stroll to see an impressive tree, and the hike climbs only 400 feet.

Mariposa Grove

13-plus miles RT. Moderate to strenuous. Access: Park at the Wawona Store parking area and walk east ¼ mile to Forest Dr. The trailhead is on the right.

The hike sounds long, but there is a one-way option in the summer that uses the Wawona shuttle bus service for the return trip, cutting the distance almost in half. The trail climbs through a forest, then ascends the Wawona Dome and Wawona Basin, both of which provide excellent views.

Sentinel Dome

2.2 miles RT. Moderate. Access: Take Glacier Point Rd. to the Sentinel Dome parking lot, about 3 miles from Glacier Point.

This hike offers broad views of Yosemite Valley. At the starting point you'll be able to see Sentinel Dome on your left. The trail descends slightly, and at the first fork, bears right. It winds through manzanita and pine before beginning its ascent. It's a steep scramble to the top of Sentinel Dome, and you have to leave the trail on the north side to scramble up. The view from the top offers a 180-degree panorama of Yosemite Valley that includes a host of impressive and recognizable geologic landmarks.

Taft Point

2.2 miles RT. Moderate. Access: The trailhead begins at the same point as the hike to Sentinel Dome. At the fork, head left.

The walk to Taft Point is not demanding, and it crosses a broad meadow dotted in early summer by wildflowers. Near Taft Point, note the deep chasms, known as "fissures," in the rock. Some of the cracks are 40 feet long and 20 feet wide at the top and 100 feet deep. The wall of Yosemite actually overhangs the narrow ravine below, and if you carefully peer over the cliff, you'll notice that your head seems to be on the opposite side of a stream running far beneath you. A small pipe railing farther on marks the 6-by-3-foot Taft Point overlook hanging over Yosemite Valley.

Wawona Meadow Loop

3.5 miles RT. Easy. Access: Take the dirt road through the golf course, and walk about 50 yards to the trail.

This relaxing stroll encircles Wawona Meadow, curving around at its east end and heading back toward the road. It crosses the highway and winds through forest until it returns to the Wawona Hotel. Some cars still use this road, so watch out. This trail is also open to pets.

NORTH OF THE VALLEY

Some of the hikes discussed below can be done either as long day hikes or as overnight backpacking trips; see "Overnight Hikes," later in this chapter.

Cathedral Lakes

8 miles RT. Moderate. Access: The trailhead is off Tioga Rd., at the west end of Tuolumne Meadows, west of Budd Creek.

These lakes are set in granite bowls cut by glaciers, and the views of the peaks and domes around both Lower and Upper Cathedral lakes are worth the hike alone. Lower Cathedral Lake is next to Cathedral Peak and is a good place to stop for a snack before heading up the hill to enjoy the upper lake.

Cloud's Rest

14 miles RT. Strenuous. Access: Take Tioga Rd. to Tenaya Lake. The trail leaves from the parking area on the east side of the road near the southwest end of the lake.

This hike descends through a wooded area, heading toward Sunrise Lake. Ascend out of Tenaya Canyon, and at the junction, bear right (watch for the signposts); the vistas will appear almost at once. The sight line to your destination will be clear—a good thing, since the trail is sketchy at this point. The last stretch to the top is a little spooky, with sheer drops on each side, but your perseverance will be amply rewarded with spectacular views of the park's granite domes. Overnight stays (with a permit) offer the added incentive of beautiful sunrises.

Dog Lake

3 miles RT. Easy. Access: Take Tioga Rd. to the access road for Tuolumne Lodge. Pass the ranger station and leave your vehicle at a parking lot on the left. Walk north (back toward the highway), up an embankment, and recross CA 120 to find Dog Lake Trail.

This easy climb through forests offers great views of Mount Dana. Dog Lake is warm, shallow, and great for swimming.

El Capitan (the back way)

14.4 miles RT. Very strenuous. Access: Take Tioga Rd. to the Tamarack Flat Campground. Turn right and follow the road to the east end of the campground, where you'll see an abandoned road. The trail begins here.

Appropriate only for experienced mountain hikers in extremely good physical shape, this hike takes you along an abandoned road to Cascade Creek, and then along a roadbed to the North Rim Trail. Through a series of switchbacks the trail climbs and climbs and climbs, and a spur trail leads to a summit for wonderful panoramic views. (The main trail heads to Eagle Peak.)

Elizabeth Lake

6 miles RT. Moderate. Access: Take Tioga Rd. to the group camping area of Tuolumne Meadows Campground, where the trail begins.

This popular day hike attracts a slew of people, which can be a bummer, but it's magnificent nonetheless for its beauty—Elizabeth Lake glistens like ice. Don't forget your camera and some extra film—the entire route is one long Kodak moment.

Gaylor Lakes

6 miles RT. Moderate. Access: Take Tioga Rd. to Tioga Pass. The trailhead is on the northwest side of the road.

This trail begins with a climb, then descends to the alpine lakes. It's a particularly pretty hike in summer, when the mountainsides are dotted with wildflowers.

Glen Aulin

10.4 miles RT. Strenuous. Access: Take Tioga Rd. toward Tuolumne Meadows, about 1 mile east of the Tuolumne Meadows Visitor Center and just a few yards east of the bridge over the Tuolumne River. Follow a marked turnoff and take the paved road on your left. The trailhead begins about 0.3 mile ahead, at a road that turns right and heads up a hill toward the stables.

This hike takes you to an impressive waterfall with grand views along the way. Start by heading across a flat meadow toward Soda Springs and Glen Aulin. The trail is well marked, and signs along the way do a good job of describing the area's history. This was once the old Tioga Road, which was built in 1883 to serve the Great Sierra Mine at Tioga Pass. The hike offers a view of the landmarks of Tuolumne Meadows. Behind you, Lembert Dome rises almost 900 feet above the meadow. About 0.4 mile from the trailhead the road forks; head right up a grassy slope. In less than 500 feet is a trail that leaves the road on the right and a steel sign that says GLEN AULIN IS 4.7 MILES AHEAD. Along the way you'll pass Fairview Dome, Cathedral Peak, and Unicorn Peak. The crashing noise you'll hear in early to mid-summer is Tuolumne Falls, a cascade of water that drops first 12 feet, then 40 feet down a series of ledges. There's a hikers' camp nearby if you want to spend the night.

Lembert Dome

2.8 miles RT. Moderate. Access: The trailhead is at a parking lot north of Tioga Rd. in Tuolumne Meadows at road marker T-32. Follow the nature trail that starts here and take off at marker no. 2.

This hike offers a bird's-eye view of Tuolumne Meadows and it's a great vista. A well-marked trail leads you to the top, and from there you'll see the peaks that encircle the valley and get good views of this lovely meadow. It's a great place to watch sunrises and sunsets.

May Lake

2.5 miles RT. Easy. Access: Take Tioga Rd. east past White Wolf; turn off at road marker T-21 and drive 2 miles to the May Lake parking area.

Winding through forests and granite, this picturesque hike offers ample opportunities to fish, but swimming is not allowed. May Lake is in the center of Yosemite National Park and is a good jumping-off point for other high-country hikes. There are numerous peaks surrounding the lake, including the 10,855-foot-high Mount Hoffman, which rises behind the lake. There is a hikers' camp on the south side of the lake.

Mono Pass

8.5 miles RT. Moderate to strenuous. Access: The trailhead is on the south side of Tioga Rd. as you enter the park from Lee Vining. Drive about 1½ miles from the park entrance to Dana Meadows, where the trail begins on an abandoned road and up alongside Parker Creek Pass.

You'll pass some historical cabin sites, then hike down to Walker Lake, and return via the same route. The hike loops into the Inyo National Forest and the Ansel Adams Wilderness, and climbs to an elevation of 10,600 feet. There's a stupendous view of Mono Lake from the top of the trail.

Mount Dana

5.8 miles RT. Very strenuous. Access: The trailhead is on the southeast side of Tioga Rd./CA 120 at Tioga Pass.

This climb is an in-your-face reminder that Mount Dana is Yosemite's second highest peak. The mountain rises 13,053 feet and the trail gains a whopping 3,100 feet in 3 miles. The views at the top are wonderful, and once you catch your breath you can again stand upright. You can see Mono Lake from the summit. In summer, the wildflowers add to this hike's beauty.

North Dome

10 miles RT. Moderate. Access: Take Tioga Rd. east to the Porcupine Flat Campground, past White Wolf. About 1 mile past the campground is a sign for Porcupine Creek at a closed road. Park in the designated area.

This hike offers amazing views of Yosemite Valley. Walk south down the abandoned road toward the Porcupine Creek Campground. A mile past the campground, the trail hits a junction with the Tenaya Creek and Tuolumne Meadows Trail. Pass a junction toward Yosemite Falls and head uphill toward North Dome. The ascent is treacherous because of loose gravel, but from the top you can catch an all-encompassing view of Yosemite Valley, second only to the view from Half Dome.

Polly Dome Lake

12.5 miles RT. Easy to moderate. Access: Take Tioga Rd. past White Wolf to Tenaya Lake. Drive about ½ mile to a picnic area midway along the lake. The trailhead is across the road from the picnic area.

This hike is easily the road least traveled. The trip to Polly Dome Lake is a breeze and you'll find nary another traveler in sight. There are several lakes beneath Polly Dome that can accommodate camping. The trail fades in and out, so watch for markers. It crosses a rocky area en route, then skirts southeast at a pond located just after the rocky section. Polly Dome Lake is at the base of—you guessed it—Polly Dome, a visual aid to help hikers stay the course.

Soda Springs

1.5 miles RT. Easy. Access: There are 2 trailheads. One is at a crosswalk just east of the Tuolumne Meadows Visitor Center. The other leaves from a parking lot north of Tioga Rd. at road marker T-32. Follow the gravel road around a locked gate.

This trail crosses Tuolumne Meadows and then Tuolumne River on a wooden bridge. It's peaceful and beautiful, with the sound of the river gurgling along as it winds slowly through the wide expanse of Tuolumne Meadows. The trail leads to a carbonated spring where you can taste the water, although it gets mixed reviews. For years, the spring was administered and owned by the Sierra Club, which operates the nearby Parsons Lodge, now an activity center. Also nearby is the historical McCauley Cabin, which is used for employee housing in the summer.

Sunrise Lakes

8 miles RT. Moderate to strenuous. Access: Take Tioga Rd. to Tenaya Lake. The trail begins in the parking area on the east side of the road near the southwest end of the lake.

This hike leads through quiet wooded glades while affording occasional glimpses of distant vistas. Look for a sign that says SUNRISE, then follow the level road to Tenaya Creek, cross the creek, and follow the trail to the right. The hike parallels Tenaya Creek for about 0.25 mile, then moves away through a wooded area and climbs gently up a rocky rise. After a while, the trail descends quickly to the outlet of Mildred Lake. There you'll be able to see Mount Hoffmann, Tuolumne Peak, and Tenaya Canyon. At the halfway mark, the trail passes through a hemlock grove, then comes to a junction. Head left. (The trail on the right goes toward Cloud's Rest.) About 0.25 mile from the junction you'll reach Lower Sunrise Lake, tucked into the slope of Sunrise Mountain. The trail climbs past Middle Sunrise Lake and continues upward along a cascading creek coming from Upper Sunrise Lake. The trail follows the lake's shore and opens in less than 0.5 mile onto a wide, bare sandy pass. It's all downhill from here. Before you is the snowcapped Clark Range. The trail begins its descent, sharply switching back and forth in some places. There is a backpackers' camp a short distance above Upper Sunrise Lake.

Tioga Lake to Dana Lake

4.6 miles RT. Moderate to strenuous. Access: Take CA 120 to Tioga Lake. The trailhead is on the west side of the lake, about 1 mile east of the pass.

This is a less-crowded alternative to the above hike to Mount Dana that doesn't top the mountain, although that option is available for experienced hikers on the Mount Dana Trail. The trail is not maintained, although it is fairly visible. This area is easily damaged, so be sure to tread lightly. Mount Dana looms large from the lake's shore.

Vogelsang

14.4 miles RT. Moderate to strenuous. Access: Take Tioga Rd. to Tuolumne Meadows and watch for the signposted trailhead for the John Muir Trail and Lyell Fork.

This hike climbs to a high meadow offering spectacular views. The trail goes south through the woods to a footbridge over the Dana Fork. Cross the bridge and follow the John Muir Trail upstream. Head right at the next fork. The trail crosses the Lyell Fork via a footbridge. Take the left fork a couple hundred feet ahead. Continue onward, and just before you cross the bridge at Rafferty Creek, you'll reach another junction. Veer right and prepare for switchbacks up a rocky slope. The trail climbs steeply for about 0.25 mile, then levels off as it darts toward and away from Rafferty Creek for the next 4 miles. The trail gradually ascends to Tuolumne Pass, crossing many small creeks and tributaries en route. Two small tarns mark the pass. One drains south and the other north. Just south of the tarns, the trail splits. Veer left. (The right fork offers a 2-mile round-trip jaunt to Boothe Lake.) You'll climb to a meadow with great views, at 10,180 feet.

Overnight Hikes

Of the more than four million people who visit Yosemite each year, 95% never leave the valley, but the brave 5% who do are well rewarded. A wild, lonelier Yosemite awaits just a few miles from the crowds where you'll find some of the most grandiose landscapes in the Sierra, and excellent opportunities for backpacking. Check with park rangers for tips on where to go and how to prepare for your backpacking trip.

All overnight backpacking stays require a wilderness permit, available by phone, by mail, or in the park. Permits can be reserved 2 days to 4 months in advance and cost $5 for each individual on the permit. Call © **209/372-0740** or write to Wilderness Permits, P.O. Box 545, Yosemite National Park, CA 95389.

If advanced planning isn't your style, first-come, first-served permits are available up to 24 hours before your trip. Permit stations are located at the Yosemite Valley Visitor Center and Wawona Information Station year-round, and Big Oak Flat Information Station in Tuolumne Meadows in summer. Permits for the popular trails, such as those leading to Half Dome, Little Yosemite Valley, and Cloud's Rest, go quickly. Call © **209/372-0200** for permit station locations and hours.

Other Sports & Activities

About the only thing you can't do in Yosemite is surf. In addition to sightseeing, Yosemite is a great place to bike, ski, rock climb, fish, and even golf.

Bicycling. There are 12 miles of designated bike trails in the eastern end of Yosemite Valley, which is the best place to ride since roads and shuttle bus routes are usually crowded and dangerous for bicyclists. Children under 18 are required by law to wear helmets. Single-speed bikes can be rented by the hour ($5.25) or the day ($20) at Curry Village (© **209/372-8319**) in summer only, or at Yosemite Lodge (© **209/372-1208**) year-round. Bike rentals include helmets for all ages.

Cross-Country Skiing. The park has more than 350 miles of skiable trails and roads, including 25 miles of machine-groomed track and 90 miles of marked trails in the Badger Pass area. Equipment rentals, lessons, and day and overnight ski tours are available from **Yosemite Cross-Country Ski School** at Badger Pass (© **209/372-8444;** www. yosemiteparktours.com/winter/activities _cross_country_skiing.htm).

Fishing. Several species of trout can be found in Yosemite's streams. Guided fly-fishing trips in Yosemite for all levels are available from **Yosemite Guides** (© **877/425-3366** or 209/379-2231) and **Yosemite Creek Outfitters** (© **209/962-5060**). California fishing licenses are required for all those 16 and older; information is available from the **California State Department of Fish and Game** (© **559/222-3761;** www.dfg.ca.gov). **Village Sport Shop** in Yosemite Valley has fishing gear, plus sells fishing licenses. There are also special fishing regulations in Yosemite Valley; get information at the visitor centers.

Golf. There's one golf course in the park and several others nearby. **Wawona** (© **209/375-6572**) sports a 9-hole, par-35 course that alternates between meadows and fairways. Just outside the park, the **River Creek Golf Course** (© **559/683-3388**) is a 9-hole course in the small hamlet of Ahwahnee (not at the hotel); and the 18-hole **Sierra Meadows Ranch Course** (© **559/642-1343**) is in Oakhurst. Call for current greens fees and other information.

Horseback Riding. Several companies offer guided horseback rides in and just outside the national park, with rates starting at about $25 for 1 hour, $40 for 2 hours, and $75 for a half day. **Yosemite Stables** (© **209/372-8348**) offers rides from several locations, including Yosemite Valley and Wawona, and also leads multiday pack trips into the backcountry (call for details). **Yosemite Trails Pack Station** (© 559/683-7611) offers riding just south of Wawona; and **Minarets Pack Station** (© 559/868-3405) leads day trips to Yosemite and the Ansel Adams Wilderness.

Ice-Skating. The outdoor ice rink at Curry Village, with great views of Half Dome and Glacier Point, is open from early November to March, weather permitting. Admission costs $5 for adults and $4.50 for children, with skate rental $2. Check with park visitor centers for the current hours (© **209/372-0200**).

Rafting. A raft rental shop is located at Curry Village (© **209/372-8341**). Daily per-person rental fees are $13 for adults, $11 for children under 13. Fees include a raft, paddles, mandatory life preservers, and transportation from Sentinel Beach back to Curry Village. Swift currents and cold water can be deadly. Talk with rangers and shop people before venturing out to be sure you're planning a trip that's within your capabilities.

Rock Climbing. Yosemite is considered one of the world's premier playgrounds for experienced rock climbers and wannabes. The **Yosemite Mountaineering School** (© **209/372-8344**; www.yosemitemountaineering.com) provides instruction for beginning, intermediate, and advanced climbers in the valley and Tuolumne Meadows from April through October. Classes last anywhere from a day to a week, and private lessons are also available. All equipment is provided, and rates vary according to the class or program.

Skiing. Yosemite's **Badger Pass Ski Area** (© **209/372-8430**; www.yosemitepark tours.com/winter/activities_downhill_skiing.htm) is usually open from Thanksgiving through Easter Sunday, weather permitting. This small resort, located 22 miles from Yosemite Valley, was established in 1935. There are nine runs, rated 35% beginner, 50% intermediate, and 15% advanced, with a vertical drop of 800 feet from its highest point of 8,000 feet. There are five lifts—one triple chair, three double chairs, and a cable tow. Full-day adult lift tickets cost $25 Monday through Friday and $28 Saturday and Sunday, and full-day lift tickets for kids 12 and under are $15 and $16, respectively.

The ski area has several casual restaurants, a ski shop, ski repairs, a day lodge, and lockers. There's also an excellent ski school, thanks to Nic Fiore, a Yosemite ski legend who arrived in the park in 1947 to ski for a season and never left. Fiore became director of the ski school in 1956, and park officials credit Fiore with making Badger Pass what it is today—a family-oriented ski area where generations have come to ski.

Camping

There are numerous camping opportunities both within and surrounding Yosemite National Park. Brief descriptions of individual campgrounds follow; you'll find additional details in the campground chart in this chapter.

It's important to remember that when camping in this area, proper food storage is *required* for the sake of the black bears in the parks, as well as for your safety. See local bulletin boards for instructions.

INSIDE THE PARK

First, the bad news: Yosemite Valley lost half of its roughly 800 campsites during a flood in early 1997. The lost campsites will eventually be replaced elsewhere in the park, but no one's predicting when. Therefore, campsite reservations are a really good idea. Reservations are accepted in 1-month blocks beginning on the 15th of each month and can be made up to 5 months in advance. That said, make your reservations (© **800/436-7275**; http://reservations.nps.gov) as soon after the 15th of the month, 5 months in advance, as you can, especially for sites in the valley. Unless noted otherwise, pets are accepted in the following campgrounds. Additional campground information is available by touch-tone phone at © **209/372-0200.**

Wilderness permits are required for all overnight backpacking trips in the park (see "Overnight Hikes," above), and no wilderness camping is allowed in Yosemite Valley.

The busiest campgrounds in the park are in Yosemite Valley. All four of the following have flush toilets and access to the showers nearby at Camp Curry ($2). Upper, Lower, and North Pines campgrounds require reservations. **Upper**

Campground	Elev. (ft.)	Total Sites	RV Hookups	Dump Station	Toilets	Drinking Water
Inside Yosemite National Park						
Bridalveil Creek	7,200	110	0	No	Yes	Yes
Camp 4	4,000	35	0	No	Yes	Yes
Crane Flat	6,191	166	0	No	Yes	Yes
Hodgdon Meadow	4,872	105	0	No	Yes	Yes
Lower Pines	4,000	60	0	Nearby	Yes	Yes
North Pines	4,000	81	0	Nearby	Yes	Yes
Porcupine Flat	8,100	52	0	No	Yes	No
Tamarack Flat	6,315	52	0	No	Yes	No
Tuolumne Meadows	8,600	304	0	Nearby	Yes	Yes
Upper Pines	4,000	238	0	Yes	Yes	Yes
Wawona	4,000	93	0	Nearby	Yes	Yes
White Wolf	8,000	74	0	No	Yes	Yes
Yosemite Creek	7,659	75	0	No	Yes	No
Outside the Park						
Lumsden	1,500	11	0	No	Yes	No
Lumsden Bridge	1,500	9	0	No	Yes	No
Lost Claim	3,100	10	0	No	Yes	Yes
The Pines	3,200	12	0	No	Yes	Yes
South Fork	1,500	8	0	No	Yes	No
Sweetwater	3,000	13	0	No	Yes	Yes
Jerseydale	3,600	8	0	No	Yes	Yes
Summerdale	5,000	30	0	No	Yes	Yes
Summit	5,800	6	0	No	Yes	No
Big Bend	7,800	17	0	No	Yes	Yes
Ellery Lake	9,500	15	0	No	Yes	Yes
Junction	9,600	13	0	No	Yes	No
Saddlebag Lake	10,000	20	0	No	Yes	Yes
Tioga Lake	9,700	13	0	No	Toilets	Yes
Yosemite–Mariposa	2,400	89	51	Yes	Yes	Yes

Pines is pretty and shady, but you won't find peace and quiet here in the summer. Parking is available, or take the shuttle bus to stop no. 15 or 19. **Lower Pines Campground** is wide open with lots of shade but limited privacy. Still, it's a nice place with clean bathrooms, and is bordered on the north by a picturesque meadow. Parking is available, or take the shuttle bus to stop no. 19. **North Pines,** which we particularly like, is beautifully situated beneath a grove of pine trees that offer little privacy but a lot of shade. It's located near the river,

Showers	Fire Pits/ Grills	Laundry	Public Phone	Reservations	Fees	Open
No	Yes	No	Yes	No	$12	June–Oct
Nearby	Yes	Nearby	Yes	No	$5	Year-round
No	Yes	No	Yes	Yes	$18	June–Oct
No	Yes	No	Yes	May–Sept	$18	Year-round
Nearby	Yes	Nearby	Yes	Yes	$18	Mar–Oct
Nearby	Yes	Nearby	Yes	Yes	$18	Apr–Sept
No	Yes	No	Yes	No	$8	July–Sept
No	Yes	No	Yes	No	$8	July–Sept
Nearby	Yes	No	Yes	Yes	$18	June–Sept
Nearby	Yes	Nearby	Yes	Yes	$18	Year-round
No	Yes	No	Yes		$18	May–Sept
Nearby	Yes	No	Yes	No	$12	July–Sept
No	Yes	No	Yes	No	$8	July–Sept (tent only)
No	Yes	No	No	No	Free	Year-round
No	Yes	No	No	No	Free	Apr–Oct
No	Yes	No	No	No	$10	May to Labor Day
No	Yes	No	No	No	$10	Year-round
No	Yes	No	No	No	Free	Apr–Oct
No	Yes	No	No	No	$12	Apr–Nov
No	Yes	No	No	No	Free	June–Sept
No	Yes	No	No	Yes	$14	June–Oct
No	Yes	No	No	No	$10	June–Oct
No	Yes	No	No	No	$15	May–Oct
No	Yes	No	No	No	$15	June–Oct
No	Yes	No	No	No	$9	June–Oct
No	Yes	No	No	No	$15	June–Oct
No	Yes	No	No	No	$15	June–Oct
Yes	Yes	Yes	Yes	Recommended	$25–$40	Year-round

roughly a mile from Mirror Lake. Parking is available, or take the shuttle bus to stop no. 18. **Camp 4** (also called Sunnyside Walk-In), has tent sites only. It's a small campground that's become a magnet for hikers and climbers taking off or just returning from trips. It's situated behind Yosemite Lodge, near the trailhead for Yosemite Fall, and near rocks frequently used by novice rock climbers. Pets are not permitted. Parking is available about 50 yards away, or take the shuttle bus to stop no. 7.

Elsewhere in the park, **Bridalveil Creek Campground** at Glacier Point has flush toilets. Near beautiful Glacier Point, this campground is away from the valley crowds but within a moderate drive to the valley sights. It's set along Bridalveil Creek, which flows to Bridalveil Fall, a beauty of a waterfall, especially after a snowy winter or wet spring. The campground can accommodate some pack animals; call park offices for information. Take Wawona Rd. (from either direction) to Glacier Point Road. The campground is about 8 miles down the road.

Several campgrounds are located in the vicinity of Big Oak Flat Entrance, roughly 20 to 25 miles from Yosemite Valley. About 1 mile inside the entrance is **Hodgdon Meadow,** which has RV and tent sites, including some walk-in sites, and requires reservations from May through September. It has flush toilets and is located along North Crane Creek and near the Tuolumne River's south fork. The Big Trees are 3 miles southeast. About 8 miles farther and not far from the Tioga Road turnoff is **Crane Flat,** a large but pleasant campground with flush toilets, near the Big Trees and away from valley crowds. **Tamarack Flat Campground** is a bit off the beaten path and therefore more secluded than most, which means fewer folks rest their heads here. Equidistant from Yosemite Valley and Tuolumne Meadows, it has pit toilets and does not allow pets. Head east on Tioga Road about 3 miles, and turn right onto the access road; the campground is another 3 miles down the road.

Campgrounds in the White Wolf area include **Porcupine Flat,** which has lots of shade, shrubs, and trees, although facilities are pretty much limited to pit toilets. It's located near Yosemite Creek; you may find a spot here if you're in a pinch. Pets are not permitted. It's along Tioga Road, 16 miles west of Tuolumne Meadows and 38 miles east of Yosemite Valley. The **White Wolf Campground,** secluded in a forest, is a generally delightful campground where you might want to spend several days. It has flush toilets and offers easy access to nearby hiking, with trails that lead to several lakes, including Grant Lake and Lukens Lake. There's a dirt road to Harden Lake, and beyond that, a trail to Smith Peak, which overlooks the Hetch Hetchy Reservoir. Showers are available at nearby White Wolf Lodge for $2. On the down side, mosquitoes make their presence felt here in summer. From Big Oak Flat Road, head east on Tioga Road for 15 miles to White Wolf Road and turn left. The road dead-ends at the campground.

Among Yosemite's other campgrounds are **Tuolumne Meadows,** the biggest campground in the park and, amazingly, often the least crowded. Its location in the high country makes this a good spot from which to head off with a backpack, and it's also near the Tuolumne River, making it a good choice for anglers. In addition to its standard RV/tent sites, the campground has 25 walk-in spaces for backpackers and 8 group sites that can accommodate up to 30 people each. There are flush toilets, and showers can be bought nearby at Tuolumne Lodge for a fee. From Big Oak Flat Road, drive about 45 miles east on Tioga Road.

Wawona Campground, which requires reservations from May through September, has flush toilets and can accommodate pack animals; call park offices for information. There's not much seclusion here, but the location, shaded beneath towering trees, is beautiful. The campground is near the Mariposa Grove of Big Trees and also close to the Merced River, which offers some of the better fishing in the park. It's about 1 mile north of Wawona. The **Yosemite Creek Campground,** set along Yosemite Creek, has pit toilets and little else, but may have sites available when the park's other campgrounds are full. From Big Oak Flat Road, head east on Tioga Road about 30 miles, turn right on the access road, and it's another 5 miles down the road.

OUTSIDE THE PARK

Yosemite is surrounded by national forests that offer comparable campgrounds to the ones in the park, although often less developed and less crowded. There are also private campgrounds, which usually provide level sites, complete RV hookups, hot showers, coin-operated laundries, convenience stores, and other amenities.

ALONG CA 120

The following campgrounds, located along CA 120 west of the park, are all in the Stanislaus National Forest's **Groveland Ranger District,** 24545 CA 120, Groveland, CA 95321 (© **209/962-7825;** www.fs.fed.us/r5/stanislaus/groveland). They all have vault toilets and can accommodate rigs up to 22 feet long.

Lumsden Campground is along the Tuolumne River, on a scenic stretch between the Hetch Hetchy and Don Pedro reservoirs. It offers fishing in a primitive setting, but can get unbelievably hot in the summer. From Groveland, take CA 120 about 9 miles east to Ferretti Road, turn left and drive about 1 mile to Lumsden Road, where you turn right and travel about 5 miles on a steep, narrow, dirt road to the campground. **Lumsden Bridge Campground** is about a mile and a half past Lumsden Campground (on Lumsden Rd.). Set in a pine and oak forest along the Tuolumne River, it is a favorite of rafters because the location is close to some of the Tuolumne River's best (and most scenic) stretches of white water. The **South Fork Campground,** also located along Lumsden Road, near Lumsden and Lumsden Bridge campgrounds, is a pretty spot near the Tuolumne River. It is recommended that trailers or vehicles with low ground clearance not be taken to any of the above three campgrounds.

The Pines Campground is located about 9 miles east of Groveland via CA 120, and although it's in a mixed conifer forest, it can get hot in the summer. Drinking water is available only in the summer. **Lost Claim Campground,** located about 12 miles east of Groveland via CA 120, offers easy access on a paved road. There are some trees and the river is nearby. Drinking water is supplied by a hand pump. Trailers are not recommended. Pretty **Sweetwater Campground,** located 15 miles east of Groveland on CA 120, is in a mixed conifer forest with shady sites, but it also gets hot in summer.

ALONG CA 140

Jerseydale Campground, located in the Sierra National Forest, 1600 Tollhouse Rd., Clovis, CA 93611-0532 (© **559/297-0706;** www.fs.fed.us/r5/sierra), is a great base for exploring the area, while also allowing you to stay away from the crowds. There are vault toilets and hiking trails, and you can get to the Merced River via a nearby trailhead. From Mariposa, drive about 12 miles northwest on CA 49 to Jerseydale Road, which leads to the campground and adjacent Jerseydale Ranger Station.

A good choice for those who want all the amenities of a top-notch commercial campground is the **Yosemite–Mariposa KOA,** 7 miles northeast of Mariposa at 6323 CA 140 (P.O. Box 545), Midpines, CA 95345 (© **800/562-9391** for reservations or 209/966-2201; www.koa.com). Located 23 miles from the park entrance, this KOA has pines and oaks that shade many of the sites, a catch-and-release fishing pond, pedal boats in the summer, a swimming pool, and a playground. There's also a convenience store and propane sales. A favorite of kids is the train caboose containing video games. There are also a dozen camping cabins (you share the bathhouse with campers), with rates of $48 to $60.

ALONG CA 41

Two Sierra National Forest campgrounds (see contact information under Jerseydale Campground, above) offer pleasant camping, with vault toilets, in a woodsy atmosphere along CA 41, southwest of Yosemite. **Summerdale Campground** is about a mile north of Fish Camp via CA 41, on the south fork of the Merced River, and is often full for the weekend by noon Friday. **Summit Campground,** in the Chowchilla Mountains, about 5 miles west of Fish Camp via a Forest Service Road, is a little campground that's often overlooked.

ALONG CA 120

The Inyo National Forest operates a number of small, attractive campgrounds along CA 120 east of the national park. These include **Big Bend Campground,** with flush toilets, 7 miles west of Lee Vining via CA 120. Located on the eastern Sierra along Lee Vining Creek, this campground is sparse but breathtaking. **Ellery Lake Campground,** which also has flush toilets, is at scenic Ellery Lake, about 9 miles west of Lee Vining via CA 120. **Junction Campground** is near Ellery and Tioga lakes, with easy access to the Tioga Tarns Nature Trail. It has vault toilets and is 10 miles west of Lee Vining along CA 120.

The highest (in elevation) drive-in campground in the state, at 10,000 feet, **Saddlebag Lake Campground** is situated along Saddlebag Lake and near Lee Vining Creek. It's beautiful and is a good place to stay a while, or you can head out from here into the wilderness with a backpack. It has flush toilets. From Lee Vining, drive 10 miles west on CA 120, then turn north on Saddlebag Lake Road and go about 2 miles to the campground. Another high-elevation campground, **Tioga Lake Campground** is a pretty place to camp, and has flush toilets. From Lee Vining, drive 10 miles west on CA 120.

Information on these U.S. Forest Service campgrounds is available from the **Mono Basin Scenic Area Visitor Center,** located on the west shore of Mono Lake (P.O. Box 429, Lee Vining, CA 93541; © 760/647-3044), and the **Inyo National Forest,** 351 Pacu Lane, Suite 200,

Bishop, CA 93514 (© **760/873-2400;** www.fs.fed.us/r5/inyo).

Several primitive campgrounds, with pit toilets and no drinking water, are operated in the Lee Vining area by the County of Mono Department of Public Works (P.O. Box 457, Bridgeport, CA 93517; © **760/932-5252;** fax 760/932-7607). These include **Aspen Campground,** along Lee Vining Creek about 6 miles west of Lee Vining via CA 120. This is a high-country campground near picturesque Mono Lake. The **Lower Lee Vining Creek Campgrounds** includes four campgrounds clustered along Lee Vining Creek. From Lee Vining, drive 4 to 5 miles west along CA 120 to this series of campgrounds.

Where to Stay

There is no lack of choices for accommodations in and near Yosemite National Park. Yosemite Valley is the hub for lodging, dining, and other services within the park, and is usually quite crowded in summer, but it offers the best location, close to Yosemite's main attractions and with easy access to the park's shuttle bus system. A more narrow scope of choices is available outside the valley, but still within the park, during the summer at Wawona, Tuolumne Meadows, White Wolf, and other areas. In addition, there are some delightful (and generally less expensive) accommodations outside the park in the gateway communities of El Portal, Mariposa, Oakhurst, and Groveland.

INSIDE THE PARK

Most lodging in the park is under the auspices of **Yosemite Concession Services Corp.** Rooms can be reserved up to 366 days in advance (© **559/252-4848;** TTY 209/255-8345). You can make reservation requests online at **www.yosemitepark.com.** Reservations are also accepted by mail at Yosemite Reservations, 6771 N. Palm Ave. Fresno, CA 93704.

In addition, more than 130 private homes in the park can be rented through **Redwoods in Yosemite,** P.O. Box 2085, Wawona Station, Yosemite National Park, CA 95389 (© **888/ 225-6666** or 209/375-6666; www.redwood sinyosemite.com). Offerings range from rustic cabins to luxurious vacation homes, and all are fully furnished and equipped with linens, cookware, and dishes. Rates range from $193 a night for a one-bedroom cabin to $500 a night for a five-bedroom spread; there are usually 3-night minimum stays in summer, and 2-night minimums in winter.

The Ahwahnee

Yosemite Valley. © **559/252-4848.** 123 units. A/C TEL. $358 for guest rooms and cottages; 2-room suites from $793; 3-room suites from $1,152. DC, DISC, MC, V. Parking available, or take the shuttle bus to stop no. 3.

The Ahwahnee's accommodations are fit for royalty. Queen Elizabeth has slept here, as have President John F. Kennedy, actor Clint Eastwood, poet Alfred Noyes, and NFL quarterback Steve Young. It's tough to top this hotel, a six-story rock and concrete structure that offers beautiful views from practically every window. The hotel has a number of common rooms on the ground floor. There are three fireplaces large enough to stand in, and the rooms are furnished with large overstuffed sofas and chairs to sink into after a day of hiking. Guest rooms are upstairs, with suites located on the top floor, accessible only by special elevator key. Suites include a pair of rooms: one for sleeping and another for sitting. The Sunroom Suite is a bright pair of rooms in lime and yellow with comfy lounges and floor-to-ceiling French windows that open out onto the valley. The Library Room's rich decor includes a fireplace and walls of books. Standard rooms offer a choice of two double or one king-size bed, with a couch, plush towels, and snuggly comforters.

The Ahwahnee offers a fine selection of food, most notably in its spacious dining room (see "Where to Dine," later in this chapter). The hotel also has a lounge with full bar and limited food service. Amenities include outdoor pool, sun decks, nature trails, in-room massage, limited room service, express checkout, valet parking, dry cleaning, laundry service, babysitting for children out of diapers, VCRs available upon request, complimentary coffee and tea, and tour desk.

Curry Village

Yosemite Valley. © **559/252-4848.** 628 units. Reservations suggested. $59 double tent cabin; $77 double cabin without bathroom; $88 double cabin with bathroom; $110 double motel room. DC, DISC, MC, V. Parking is available, or take the shuttle bus to stop nos. 12, 13, 14, or 19.

Curry Village is best known as a mass of more than 400 white canvas tents tightly packed together on the valley's south slope. It was founded in 1899 as a cheaper alternative for valley visitors at a mere $2 a day, but that rate is long gone. Still, it is an economical place to crash, and gives you something of the feeling of a camping vacation without the hassle of bringing your own tent. One downside is that these units are basically canvas tents, and this is bear country, so you'll need to lock up all foodstuffs and anything that bears might think is food (even toothpaste) in bear-proof lockers (provided free), which may be a healthy walk from your tent cabin. Curry Village also has just over 100 attractive wood cabins with private bathrooms; about 80 wood cabins that, like the tent cabins, share a large bathhouse; and a number of motel rooms. Canvas tents have wood floors, sleep two to four people, and are equipped with beds, bedding, dressers, and electrical outlets. The wood cabins are much more substantial (and comfortable), and the motel units are just that—functional and adequate motel rooms.

There are several food options (see "Where to Dine," later in this chapter); plus an outdoor swimming pool, bicycle rentals, raft rentals, kid's programs, tour desk, mountaineering school, and sports shop.

Housekeeping Camp

Yosemite Valley. © **559/252-4848.** 266 units, all with shared restrooms and shower house. Reservations required. $58 per site (up to 4 people; $4 per extra person). DC, DISC, MC, V. Closed Nov–Mar.

A fun, funky place to spend the night, this is the closest thing to camping without pitching a tent. The sites are fence-enclosed shanties built on concrete slabs, each with a table, a cupboard, electrical outlets, shelves, a mirror, and lights. The sleeping areas have two single-size bunks and a double bed. There is also a self-serve laundry and grocery store.

Tuolumne Meadows Lodge

Tioga Rd., Tuolumne Meadows, Yosemite National Park. © **559/252-4848.** 69 canvas tent-cabins, all with shared bathroom and shower house. $63 double; $8 per extra adult, $4 per child. DC, DISC, MC, V. Parking available in an adjacent lot. Closed in winter. From Yosemite Valley, take Big Oak Flat and Tioga rds. north and east 60 miles (about 1½ hr.) toward Tioga Pass.

This is another group of canvas tent-cabins. Like White Wolf Lodge (see below), these also have tables and wood-burning stoves, and sleep up to four. This is prime hiking territory, with numerous trailheads, plus this is home base for wilderness trekkers and back-country campers. There's a restaurant (see "Where to Dine," later in this chapter), plus a tour desk, small general store, gas station, mountaineering store, post office, and stables.

Wawona Hotel

Wawona Rd., Wawona, Yosemite National Park. © **559/252-4848.** 104 units, 54 with shared bathroom. $87–$161 double; $16 per extra adult. DC, DISC, MC, V. From Yosemite Valley, take Wawona Rd. south 27 miles toward Fresno.

This is a classic Victorian-style hotel made up of six stately white buildings set near towering trees in a green clearing. Don't be surprised if a horse and buggy round the driveway by the fishpond—it's that kind of place—with wide porches, a nearby nine-hole golf course, and vines cascading from one veranda to the next. The entire place was designated a National Historic Landmark in 1987. The 1876 Clark Cottage is the oldest building, and the main hotel was built in 1879. Rooms are comfortable and quaint with a choice of a double and a twin, a king, or one double bed (most of the latter share bathrooms). All rooms open onto wide porches and overlook green lawns. Clark Cottage is the most intimate. The main hotel has the widest porches and plenty of Adirondack chairs, and at night the downstairs sunroom hosts a pianist. Check out the whistling maintenance man who hits every high note in the "Star Spangled Banner" while the American flag is hoisted each morning (leaving many bystanders speechless as more than a few Wawona employees chime in to complete this whistling orchestra).

An adjacent dining room serves great food and an awesome Sunday brunch (see "Where to Dine," below). There is also a lounge, large outdoor pool, two outdoor tennis courts, golf course, grocery store, gas station, and horseback riding.

White Wolf Lodge

Tioga Rd., White Wolf, Yosemite National Park. © **559/252-4848.** 24 canvas tent-cabins, 4 wood cabins. All canvas cabins share bathroom and shower house. $59–$84 double; $10.25 per extra adult in cabins, $8.25 in tents; $4 per extra child in either. DC, DISC, MC, V. Parking available across the road. Closed in winter. From Yosemite Valley, take Big Oak Flat and Tioga rds. north and east 33 miles toward Tioga Pass.

Imagine a smaller, quieter, cleaner Curry Village with larger tents, each equipped with a wood-burning stove.

This small outpost was bypassed when Tioga Road was rebuilt. White Wolf Lodge is not a lodge, but a cluster of canvas tent-cabins, a few wooden ones out front. It's halfway between the valley and the high country, and generally isn't overrun with visitors. It's a popular spot for midweek hikers and weekend stopovers. Though at times crowded, it retains a homey feeling. Maybe it's the fact that there's no electricity after 11pm, when the generator shuts off. Wood cabins all have a private bathroom and resemble a regular motel room, with neat little porches and chairs out front. Canvas cabins beat the Curry Village style by a mile. Each sleeps four in any combination of twin and double beds. The helpful staff will show guests how to work the wood-burning stove. Benches outside give guests someplace to rest their weary feet and watch the stars. Bathrooms here are clean, and guests control access to the facilities except for a few midday hours when nearby campers can pay for showers. There's also a restaurant (see "Where to Dine," below) and a tiny general store.

Yosemite Lodge

Yosemite Valley. ✆ **559/252-4848.** 245 units. Reservations suggested. $110–$143 double. Lower rates Nov–Mar. DC, DISC, MC, V. Parking available, or take the shuttle bus to stop no. 6.

The comfortable and clean motel-type rooms here are popular because of the lodge's location, with some units offering views of Yosemite Falls. Rooms have two double beds or one double with two twins, and most have balconies or patios. It's not uncommon to see deer and other wildlife scamper through this area. Spring mornings offer a wonderful orchestra of songbirds and some stunning views of Yosemite Falls at sunrise. The complex contains a food court (see "Where to Dine," below), lounge, large outdoor swimming pool, bicycle rentals, children's programs, ice-cream stand, general store, tour desk, and babysitting.

Yosemite West Lodging

P.O. Box 36, Yosemite National Park, CA 95389. ✆ **559/642-2211.** www.yosenmitewest reservations.com. A fluctuating number of privately owned cottages and private homes. TV. Most units $99–$265 double. Lower rates early Sept through mid-Dec and early Jan through early May. Take Wawona Rd. 12 miles north of Wawona.

For the unforgettable experience of living in Yosemite National Park (if only for a few nights), rather than just visiting, what could be better than renting a private home, cottage, or condominium unit located right in the park? Yosemite West rents a variety of privately owned accommodations, ranging from fairly simple rooms with one queen-size bed and a kitchenette, suitable for one or two people, to luxurious vacation homes with full-size kitchens, two bathrooms, living rooms, and beds for up to eight people. Kitchens and kitchenettes are fully equipped, all bedding is provided, there are TVs and VCRs, and outdoor decks. All units also have gas or wood-burning fireplaces. The homes are in a forested section of the park, about 10 miles from Yosemite Valley and 8 miles from Badger Pass.

OUTSIDE THE PARK

If you choose to stay outside the park, you'll find a plethora of choices, many of which are less expensive than the lodging in the park.

ALONG CA 120 (EASTBOUND)

Groveland Hotel

18767 CA 120, Groveland, CA 95321. ✆ **800/273-3314** or 209/962-4000. Fax 209/962-6674. www.groveland.com. 17 units, 4 with shower only. A/C TEL. $135–$210 double. Extra person $25. Rates include buffet breakfast. AE, DC, DISC, MC, V. Pets accepted with approval.

There's enough history, good food, and conversation here to give travelers pause before heading into Yosemite. Groveland is about as quaint a town as you can get, and Peggy and Grover Mosley have poured their hearts into making their hotel an elegant but comfortable place to stay. It was vacant for years and on the verge of tumbling down, when the Mosleys decided to forgo a quiet retirement from very interesting careers (you'll have to ask for yourself) to renovate and reopen the hotel. They've done a great job and the hotel is now a historic landmark. The hotel consists of two buildings—one constructed in 1849 to house gold miners and the other built in 1919 for workers constructing the nearby Hetch Hetchy Dam. Standard rooms are spacious, with feather beds, hair dryers, and phones with dataports. Some have TVs. All rooms are filled with antiques, and have thick down comforters, beds you want to sink into, and plush robes. Suites have large spa bathtubs and fireplaces. Many rooms are named after women of the Sierra and local characters, although Lyle's Room is named for the hotel's resident ghost—return patrons swear it's true. Then there's Charlie's Room, named for a harddriving, tobacco-spitting stagecoach driver and farmer. When he died, the townspeople learned he was a she.

The hotel's dining room is small and candlelit, and offers the best food in town (see "Where to Dine," below). There is room service, as well as a safe on the premises, tennis courts, stables, and an 18-hole golf course 1 mile away.

Hotel Charlotte

18736 CA 120, Groveland, CA 95321. © **800/961-7799** or 209/962-6455. Fax 209/962-6254. www.hotelcharlotte.com. 10 units. A/C TEL. $67–$83 double. Rates include continental breakfast. AE, MC, V.

Walking into the Charlotte is like stepping back in time. Built in 1918 by an Italian immigrant of the same name, it's warm, comfortable, no-nonsense, and a good choice for those who enjoy the ambience of a historic Western hotel.

The hotel's rooms—all upstairs—are small and quaint and have the basics, but nothing more. They offer twin, double, and queen beds. Several rooms adjoin each other and have connecting bathrooms (perfect for families). Two units have showers only; the rest have shower/tub combos. There are two common television rooms. The continental breakfast is great—strong coffee, fresh warm muffins, cereals, fruit, and juices. The hotel restaurant is open only during the summer (see "Where to Dine," below).

Inn at Sugar Pine Ranch

21250 CA 120, Groveland, CA 95321. © **209/962-7823.** 12 units; 8 with shower only. A/C. $110–$150 double. Extra person $25. Rates include continental breakfast. MC, V. Children 5 and older welcome.

This whitewashed inn, set among tall pine trees, is just outside of Groveland, toward the park. Its buildings date back to the late 1800s and early 1900s, and underwent an extensive rehab in 2003. The historic main building is an 1860 farmhouse, and there are also separate cottages. Rooms are comfortable, with knotty-pine furnishings, while the three cottages have whirlpool tubs and fireplaces. Some rooms have balconies; all units offer pleasant views. There's an outdoor swimming pool and nature trails over the property's 62 acres. An 18-hole golf course is about 7 miles away. The entire inn is nonsmoking.

ALONG CA 140

Best Western–Mariposa

4999 CA 140, Mariposa, CA 95338. © **800/528-1234** or 209/966-7545. Fax 209/966-6353. www.yosemite-motels.com. 78 units. A/C TV TEL. $84–$89 double. Rates include continental breakfast. AE, DC, DISC, MC, V.

These are typical motel accommodations—clean, comfortable, and attractive, but nothing fancy, and are a good choice for many park visitors who are seeking a comfortable bed and a hot bath for a reasonable price. The motel has an outdoor swimming pool and whirlpool tub, is within walking distance of restaurants and shops, and is near public transportation into the park.

Cedar Lodge

9966 CA 140 (P.O. Box C), El Portal, CA 95318. ✆ **800/321-5261** or 209/379-2612. Fax 209/379-2712. www.yosemite-motels.com. 211 units, some family units, 1 3-bedroom suite with private pool and Jacuzzi. A/C TV TEL. $99–$135 double; $289–$399 suite. AE, MC, V.

Eight miles outside the park, this lodge offers ample-size rooms in a wooded setting, with easy access to the Merced River. Variety makes this property an attractive option for visitors, with units ranging from standard motel-type rooms to luxurious king suites with whirlpool tubs for two, and there are also family units and kitchenettes. There are two restaurants, a large outdoor swimming pool and a smaller indoor pool, plus a whirlpool tub. Rental VCRs and movies are available, and public buses to the park are available from the facility.

Comfort Inn–Mariposa

4994 Bullion St. (P.O. Box 1989), Mariposa, CA 95338. ✆ **800/321-5261** or 209/966-4344. Fax 209/966-4655. www.yosemite-motels.com. 61 units; some suites with full kitchens. A/C TV TEL. $79–$89 double; $189–$359 suite. Rates include continental breakfast. AE, DC, DISC, MC, V.

This well-kept modern motel offers large, clean rooms, an attractive outdoor swimming pool, and a whirlpool tub. It's conveniently located within walking distance of several restaurants and is also close to public transportation to Yosemite.

Highland House Bed & Breakfast

3125 Wild Dove Lane, Mariposa, CA 95338-9037. ✆ **888/477-5089** or 209/966-3737. Fax 209/966-7277. www.highlandhousebandb.com. 3 units. A/C. $85–$140 double. Rates include full breakfast. AE, MC, V. From Mariposa head east (toward Yosemite National Park) on CA 140 for about 4 miles, turn south (right) onto Triangle Road for about 6 miles, and shortly after a 1-lane bridge turn left onto Jerseydale Road. Go 1½ miles and turn right onto Wild Dove Lane, then watch for marked driveway off to the right to the Highland House.

Secluded on 10 forested acres, with easy access to hiking and horseback trails into the nearby Sierra National Forest, this bed-and-breakfast is a wonderful place to relax during a visit to Yosemite National Park. Sort of a mix of Cape Cod and colonial styles of architecture, Highland House is comfortably and tastefully decorated. Common areas include the living room, with a large stone fireplace with a wood stove insert, plus a terrific den, where you'll find a TV/VCR, books, and a pool table.

Rooms include Forest Retreat, with a stone fireplace, a king-size four-poster bed, a TV/VCR/CD player, a tub for two, and a large separate shower with two shower heads: the usual one plus another aimed to soothe your aching back muscles. The other two guest rooms are also inviting, although a bit less elaborate, with more typical shower/tub combos. Spring Creek is blue and white with a king bed that can be split into two twins; and Morning Dove is a cozy dormer room with a queen bed. The big deal, though, is breakfast, with fresh baked goods and a hot entree such as biscuits and sausage gravy or caramel apple French toast. Those who want to get an early start into the park can request breakfast to go. In addition, guests can bring their own horses and use the Highlands House's stables. The inn is completely nonsmoking.

Miners Inn

5181 CA 49 N., Mariposa, CA 95338. ✆ **209/742-7777.** Fax 209/966-2343. 78 units. A/C TV TEL. $50–$139 double. Extra person $6. AE, DISC, MC, V.

Miners Inn is a standard motel in a rustic setting that strives to recapture the Old West. Deluxe rooms include spa tubs and fireplaces, and kitchenette units are available. On-site are a restaurant, lounge, outdoor swimming pool, whirlpool, and public transportation to Yosemite.

Mariposa Lodge

5052 CA 140 (P.O. Box 733), Mariposa, CA 95338. © **800/966-8819** or 209/966-3607. Fax 209/966-5021. 45 units. A/C TV $69–$99 double. AE, DISC, MC, V.

Three generations of the Gloor family have run this top-notch motel on Mariposa's main drag for over 30 years, and their standards are surprisingly high. The place has grown over the years from one building to three, with smaller rooms in the original structure, and larger, more expensive rooms in the newer two. All rooms have refrigerator, microwave, coffeemaker, and iron. The suites here are not truly two-room suites, but oversized rooms with Mission decor, impressive vanities, and many private balconies. Landscaping is also superlative for a roadside motel, especially the garden courtyard around the pool and Jacuzzi. Restaurants and shops are within walking distance. High-speed wireless Internet access (Wi-Fi) is a modern touch.

Poppy Hill Bed & Breakfast

5218 Crystal Aire Dr., Mariposa, CA 95338. © **800/58-POPPY** or 209/742-6273. www. poppyhill.com. 3 units. A/C. $110–$125 double. Rates include full breakfast. AE, DC, DISC, MC, V. Take CA 140 east out of Mariposa (toward Yosemite National Park) 3 miles, turn left on East Whitlock Rd., travel for 1¼ miles, turn right onto Crystal Aire Dr., and go ⅛ mile to the B&B.

This restored country farmhouse, surrounded by large oak and pine trees, provides a delightful escape from the hustle and bustle of the developed areas of the park and nearby communities. The inn is decorated with a variety of antiques, most from the 1800s, but also includes "new" furnishings such as the 1925 Wurlitzer baby grand piano in the parlor. (You're welcome to tickle its ivories.) Each of the three attractive rooms declares its name in its individual decor—Mariposa lily, iris, and, of course, poppy, all area flowers. Rooms have queen-size beds (the Mariposa lily room also has a twin-size day bed), down comforters, bathrobes, and lots of personal touches. The Mariposa lily room has a shower/tub combo; the other two rooms have large showers.

There are outside sitting areas, with a preponderance of rolling lawn and flowers—one hillside bursts into color when the poppies bloom in spring. The second-floor balcony overlooks an ancient spreading oak tree, enticing the birds to entertain you while you relax in the quietude. An aboveground swimming pool and large whirlpool tub nestle in an attractive rose arbor. The full homemade breakfasts are extra special, with a hot entree such as eggs picante, puffed apple pancake, or croissant French toast. The entire inn is nonsmoking.

The Yosemite Bug

6979 CA 140 (P.O. Box 81), Midpines, CA 95345. © **209/966-6666.** Fax 209/966-9667. www.yosemitebug.com. 67 hostel beds, 14 private rooms with private bathrooms, 10 private rooms with shared bathrooms, 12 tent cabins. Hostel beds $14–$16 per person, private room with bathroom (2–5 people) $65–$125, private room with shared bathroom (2–5 people) $40–$70, tent cabin or walk-in campsite (2–4 people) $17–$50. DISC, MC, V.

Much more than a hostel, The Yosemite Bug literally has something for everybody, with accommodations that range from well-maintained dorm rooms and tent cabins to delightful, handsomely appointed private rooms. The dorm rooms (single-sex, coed, or group) are basic, with bunk beds, heat, ceiling fans (no air-conditioning), individual lockable storage boxes, and conveniently located communal bathrooms. The tent cabins have wooden floors and framing, no heat, and different bed combinations, including family units with a double and two single beds. Private rooms are all different, offering a variety of bed combinations and attractive, fun decors ranging from Western modern to Victorian. Private rooms are heated and have swamp coolers, and those with private bathrooms have showers only (no tubs); others share a communal bathroom. There are no room phones; public phones are available on-site. There are also a limited number of campsites (tents only), each with a table and grill and access to restrooms and showers.

Situated in the forest, most of the units have woodsy, national park–like views. There are accessible rooms and cabins for travelers with disabilities, and a kitchen is available for those who are staying in the hostel dorm rooms. In addition, there is a self-service laundry and a computer for checking e-mail ($1 for 10 min.). Mountain-bike rentals are available in summer ($12 per day for guests, $15 nonguests), and in winter you can rent snowshoes ($8 per day for everyone). Nonguests can take a shower for $4. The Yosemite Bug is along the route for the shuttle bus into Yosemite National Park ($10 round-trip). The cafe serves great food (see "Where to Dine," below).

Yosemite View Lodge

11136 CA 140 (P.O. Box D), El Portal, CA 95318. © **800/321-5261** or 209/379-2681. Fax 209/379-2704. www.yosemite-motels.com. 279 units, some with kitchenettes. A/C TV TEL. $109–$179 double. MC, V.

Just outside the national park's Arch Rock Entrance, this lodge offers guests accommodations on the Merced River. Rooms are attractively decorated with dark wood furnishings and floral bedspreads, and many rooms have refrigerators and microwaves. Some units have fireplaces and spa tubs for two. There are two outdoor swimming pools, one indoor pool, three outdoor whirlpool tubs, and two restaurants. Public buses into the park are available.

ALONG CA 41

Château du Sureau

48688 Victoria Lane (P.O. Box 577), Oakhurst, CA 93644. © **559/683-6860.** Fax 559/683-0800. www.chateausureau.com. 11 units. A/C. $350–$550 double; $2,800 guest house. Rates include full breakfast. AE, MC, V.

One of the standout B&Bs in all of California (for that matter the entire U.S.), the lavish Château du Sureau is as close as you get to Europe on the west side of the Atlantic. A world away from the rest of Oakhurst, the 9,000-square-foot inn has an elegant, near-magical ambience to it (which you pay for in spades), radiating from the villa that houses the stylish, uniquely decorated guest rooms, such as the extraordinary Saffron Room with a king-sized ebony and ivory bedroom set from 1834, and the Sweet Geranium Room, with a private balcony overlooking sumptuous gardens and a canopied king. There are details both rustic (fresh fruit and fireplaces) and modern (CD players), and scads of impressive objects of art around every corner. The grounds here are similarly phenomenal—featuring a lawn-sized chessboard with three-foot pawns!—and the restaurant, Erna's Elderberry House, is sublime (see "Where to Dine," below). There's also an outdoor swimming pool, and a bocce court.

Comfort Inn–Oakhurst

40489 CA 41, Oakhurst, CA 93644. © **800/321-5261** or 559/683-8282. Fax 559/658-7030. www.yosemite-motels.com. 113 units. A/C TV TEL. $89–$95 double, $129 suite. Rates include continental breakfast. Lower rates off season. AE, DC, DISC, MC, V.

This attractive Comfort Inn offers standard motel-style accommodations with large, clean, and pleasantly decorated rooms with coffeemakers and refrigerators. There's an outdoor pool and whirlpool. This is one of the larger motels outside the park, and it may have that last-minute room you need.

Hounds Tooth Inn

42971 CA 41, Oakhurst, CA 93644. © **888/642-6610** or 559/642-6600. Fax 559/658-2946. www.houndstoothinn.com. 13 units. A/C TV TEL. $95–$175 double, $225 cottage. AE, DC, DISC, MC, V.

With a Victorian look and but a birth date of 1997, the Hound's Tooth is a good choice for those who want easy access to Yosemite from the south but more intimacy than a motel or sprawling resort can offer. Set a few hundred feet from the highway, the off-white exterior here sheaths a dozen very similar guest rooms, each with the convenience of kitchenette and hot tub, plus the flair of antique reproductions. There's also a private summer house (850 sq. ft.) with a king bed and a kitchenette, plus a Jacuzzi and private patio. The garden area out back is something of a work of art, perfect for whiling away an evening in peace and quiet. The inn is nonsmoking.

Tenaya Lodge

1122 CA 41, Fish Camp, CA 93623. © **800/635-5807** or 559/683-6555. Fax 559/683-0249. www.tenayalodge.com. 244 units. A/C MINIBAR TV TEL. $149–$319 double. Add $20–$80 for suite. Buffet breakfast $30 per couple. AE, DC, DISC, MC, V.

The top-rated Tenaya Lodge seems to have one foot in the Adirondack Mountains and another in the Southwest. This three- and four-story resort opened in 1990 on 35 acres covered with hiking trails. The comfortable rooms are ultramodern with multiple phones and a built-in safe, and the lobby has an impressive fireplace built of river rock that towers three stories. There are three restaurants—a moderately priced deli, a moderate-to-expensive bar and grill (burgers, sandwiches, salads, pizza, and the like), and an upscale and elegant fine dining restaurant that offers fireside dining with regional cuisine. Dinner entrees often include grilled halibut, herb-encrusted pork loin, and tequila chicken, with prices in the $17 to $33 range. The Tenaya also offers room service, indoor and outdoor swimming pools, on-site massage, a health club, a game room, and seasonal sleigh or hay rides. Facilities also include a general store.

Where to Dine

There are plenty of dining possibilities in and near the park, so you certainly won't go hungry. However, you won't find many bargains so be sure to bring a full wallet.

IN THE VALLEY

Ahwahnee Dining Room

Ahwahnee Hotel, Yosemite Valley. © **209/372-1489.** Dinner reservations required. Breakfast $7.50–$17; lunch $7.50–$16; dinner $20–$31; Sun brunch $32 adults, $17 children. DC, DISC, MC, V. Mon–Sat 7–10am and 11:30am–3pm; Sun 7am–3pm; daily 5:30–9:15pm. Shuttle bus stop no. 3. AMERICAN/INTERNATIONAL.

Dining here takes your breath away. Even if you are a dyed-in-the-wool, sleep-under-the-stars backpacker, the Ahwahnee Dining Room is bound to make an impression. This is where the great outdoors meets four-star cuisine, and it's a wonderful place to celebrate a special occasion. With understated elegance, the cavernous dining room, its candelabra chandeliers hanging from the 34-foot-high beamed ceiling, seems intimate once you're seated at a table. Don't be fooled—it seats 350. The walk from the entrance to the table is one long stroll. The menu changes frequently and offers a good variety of creative yet recognizable dishes, such as herb-crusted halibut with lobster risotto, a veal chop with spinach ravioli, and pan-seared filet mignon with forest mushroom ragout, a potato cake, and truffle sauce. The dinner menu includes suggested wines (from its extensive wine list) for each entree. Breakfast includes a variety of egg dishes, hotcakes, and the like, plus specialties such as a thick apple crepe filled with spiced apples and raspberry purée. Lunch choices include a grilled turkey quesadilla and grilled portobello mushrooms on a sun-dried tomato roll, and a variety of plates and salads. An evening dress code requires men to wear a jacket and long pants. (Ties are optional.)

Curry Dining Pavilion

Curry Village. Breakfast $9.25 adults, $5.50 children; dinner $12 adults, $6.25 children. DC, DISC, MC, V. Daily 7–10am and 5:30–8pm. Shuttle bus stop nos. 12, 13, 14, and 19. AMERICAN.

A good spot for the very hungry, this restaurant has all-you-can-eat breakfast and dinner buffets offering a wide variety of well-prepared basic American selections at fairly reasonable prices.

Curry Taqueria Stand

Curry Village. $3–$6. No credit cards. Daily 11am–5pm and Fri–Sun 8–11am. Closed in winter. Shuttle bus stop nos. 12, 13, 14, and 19. MEXICAN.

A good place for a quick bite, this taco stand offers spicy tacos, burritos, taco salads, beans, and rice.

Curry Village Coffee Corner

Curry Village. Most items $1–$3. DC, DISC, MC, V. Daily 6am–10pm. Shuttle bus stop nos. 12, 13, 14, and 19. COFFEE SHOP.

Specialty coffees and fresh-baked pastries are the fare here, and you can also get ice cream after 11am.

Curry Village Pizza Patio

Curry Village. Pizza $8–$16. DC, DISC, MC, V. Daily noon–9pm. Shuttle bus stop nos. 12, 13, 14, and 19. PIZZA.

Need to watch ESPN? If you're a sports fan, one of the park's few big screens makes this the place to be, but you may have to wait in line. The alternative to the big-screen room is the scenic outdoor patio with its large umbrellas, table service, and great view of Mother Nature, plus or minus a hundred kids. The lounge also taps a few brews—nothing special, but a mix aimed to please. This is a great place to chill after a long day.

Degnan's Cafe

Yosemite Village. Most items $1–$4. DC, DISC, MC, V. Daily 7am–7pm. Shuttle bus stop nos. D, 2, and 8. AMERICAN.

Adjacent to Degnan's Deli, this cafe offers specialty coffee drinks, fresh pastries, wrap sandwiches, and ice cream. It's a good place for a quick bite when you're in a hurry.

Degnan's Deli

Yosemite Village. $3–$8. DC, DISC, MC, V. Daily 7am–7pm. Shuttle bus stop nos. D, 2, and 8. DELI.

A solid delicatessen with a large selection of sandwiches made to order, as well as incidentals, this is our top choice for a healthy, quick lunch or supper. The sandwiches are generous. Sometimes the line to order gets long, but it moves quickly. This is half market, half deli, and in addition to the made-to-order sandwiches there is a selection of prepared items—salads, sandwiches, desserts, and snacks—to carry off for a day on the trail. There's also a fairly good selection of beer and wine.

Degnan's Loft

Yosemite Village. Main courses $4.25–$21. DC, DISC, MC, V. Daily noon–9pm. Shuttle bus stop nos. D, 2, and 8. ITALIAN.

This cheery restaurant, with a central fireplace and high-beamed ceilings, adjacent to Degnan's Deli and Degnan's Cafe, is a good choice for families, with a kid-friendly atmosphere. The menu features pizza, calzones, lasagna, salads, and desserts.

Mountain Room Restaurant

Yosemite Lodge. Main courses $17–$29. DC, DISC, MC, V. Daily 5:30–9pm. Shuttle bus stop no. 6. AMERICAN.

The best thing about this restaurant is the view. The food's good, too, but the floor-to-ceiling windows overlooking Yosemite Falls are spectacular. There's not a bad seat in the house. Assuming you're here to fill your stomach as well as your eyes, we suggest the grilled chicken breast, which is flavorful and moist, as is the rainbow trout amandine and the Pacific salmon. Meals come with vegetables and bread. Soup or salad is extra. There are also entrees for vegetarians and an amazing dessert tray. The restaurant also has a good wine list, and the Mountain Room Bar and Lounge (4–10pm Mon–Fri and noon–10pm Sat–Sun) has an a la carte menu available.

Village Grill

Yosemite Village. Most items $3.75–$5.25. No credit cards. Daily 11am–5pm. Closed in winter. Shuttle bus stop nos. 1, 2, and 8. AMERICAN.

The Village Grill is a fast-food joint that's a decent place to pick up a quick bite. It offers burgers, chicken sandwiches, and the like, and has outdoor seating.

Yosemite Lodge Food Court

Yosemite Lodge. Main courses $5–$14. DC, DISC, MC, V. Daily 6:30–10am, 11:30am–2pm, and 5–8:30pm. Shuttle bus stop no. 8. AMERICAN.

You'll find breakfast, lunch, and dinner at this busy restaurant (serving about 2,000 meals each day), which is a vast improvement over the traditional cafeteria. It's set up with a series of food stations, where you pick up your choices before heading to the centralized cashier and then to a table inside or the outside seating area, which offers tables with umbrellas and good views of Yosemite Falls. Food stations specialize in pasta (with a choice of sauces), pizza, deli sandwiches and salads, a grill (offering burgers, hot dogs, and hot sandwiches), meat-based and vegetarian entrees, desserts and baked goods, and beverages. There's also a hot breakfast food station offering traditional American breakfast items.

ELSEWHERE IN THE PARK

Tuolumne Meadows Lodge

Tuolumne Meadows, CA 120. © **209/372-8413.** Reservations required for dinner. Breakfast $3.55–$6.95; dinner $8.65–$19. DC, DISC, MC, V. Daily 7–9am and 6–8pm. AMERICAN.

One of the two restaurants in Yosemite's high country, the lodge offers something for practically everyone. The breakfast menu features the basics, including eggs, pancakes, fruit, oatmeal, and granola. Dinners always include a beef, chicken, fish, pasta, and vegetarian specialty, all of which change frequently. The quality can vary, but the prime rib and New York steak are consistently good.

Wawona Hotel Dining Room

Wawona Hotel, CA 41. © **209/375-1425.** Breakfast $3–$8; lunch $5–$10; dinner $14–$25. Sun buffets $9.95 breakfast; $16 brunch. DC, DISC, MC, V. Mon–Sat 7:30–10am, 11:30am–1:30pm, and 5:30–9pm; Sun 7:30–10am (breakfast buffet), 10:30am–1:30pm (brunch buffet), and 5:30–9pm. AMERICAN.

The Wawona dining room mirrors the hotel's ambience—wide open, with lots of windows and sunlight. And the fare is great. For breakfast choose from a variety of items, including the Par Three, a combo of French toast or pancakes, eggs, and bacon or sausage—just what you need before hitting the golf course. Lunch features a variety of sandwiches and salads. Dinner is delectable. In addition to some exceptional entrees, such as brown sugar–rubbed pork loin with apple-onion relish and bourbon sauce, prime rib, and several seafood and veggie dishes, there are amazing appetizers. The cumin-crusted ahi, roasted whole garlic, and rock shrimp and potato risotto are sumptuous.

White Wolf Lodge

White Wolf, CA 120. © **209/372-8416.** Reservations required for dinner. Breakfast $3.85–$6.95; dinner $7–$17. DC, DISC, MC, V. Daily 7:30–9:30am and 5–8:30pm. AMERICAN.

A changing menu in this casual restaurant, with a mountain lodge atmosphere, offers a variety of American standards, with generous portions. Breakfast choices include eggs, pancakes, omelets, and biscuits and gravy. Dinner always includes beef, chicken, fish, pasta, and vegetarian dishes. Take-out lunches are also available from noon to 2pm.

NEAR THE PARK

In addition to the following restaurants, you'll find an outlet for the reliable **Pizza Factory** chain in Mariposa at CA 140 and 5th Street (© **209/966-3112**), which offers delivery service to downtown Mariposa.

Cafe at the Bug

At The Yosemite Bug, 6979 CA 140, Midpines. © **209/966-6666.** Fax 209/966-9667. www.yosemitebug.com. Breakfast and lunch items $4–$6, dinner main courses $6.50–$13. DISC, MC, V. Daily 7am–9pm. AMERICAN.

Ask the locals what their secret place is to get a great meal at a very reasonable price, and, if they'll tell you, it will likely be this bustling eatery. It's a noisy, somewhat self-service restaurant at the Yosemite Bug, a hostel, lodge, and campground 10 miles from Mariposa on the way to Yosemite National Park. This casual restaurant contains several rooms with knotty pine walls, hardwood floors, wooden chairs, Formica tables, and an open-beamed ceiling which features suspended skis and a kayak. There's a wood stove, some games, and couches where lodgers lounge. You order at a counter and your food is delivered to your table.

The food is great: innovative American dishes with Mediterranean and California influences. Although the dinner menu changes nightly, popular entrees include a 16-ounce broiled top sirloin with pepper sauce, and baked salmon with cantaloupe mango salsa. You also might have baked trout filet with butter pecan sauce, or baked portobello mushrooms stuffed with tomatoes, mushrooms, onions, garlic, basil, and feta cheese. From Memorial Day to Labor Day, smoked and barbecued pork ribs, salmon, beef sirloin kebabs, and half chickens are served on the outdoor deck on Saturdays, Sundays, and holidays from 2 to 6pm. Breakfasts here range from bacon and eggs to pancakes or granola. Lunches, available from 7am to 3pm, include a variety of sandwiches prepared as sack lunches for those heading out into the park.

Castillo's Mexican Food

4995 5th St., Mariposa. © **209/742-4413.** Reservations recommended in summer. Main courses $5.95–$11 lunch; $7.95–$15 dinner. AE, DISC, MC, V. Mon–Thurs 11am–9pm; Fri–Sat 11am–9:30pm. Closes 1 hr. earlier in winter. MEXICAN.

Established in 1955, this cheerful, cozy cantina serves generous portions of well-prepared Mexican favorites. Entrees come with salad, rice, and beans, and can also be ordered a la carte. A house specialty, the *Tostada Compuesta*, fills a hungry belly with your choice of meat plus beans, lettuce, and cheese, stuffed into a bowl-shaped crisp flour tortilla and topped with avocado dip and sour cream. A variety of Mexican combo plates are served. You can also choose several steak specialties or seafood dishes, such as jumbo shrimp fajitas, served in a sizzling skillet with onions, bell peppers, and tomatoes. For those who like their hot food with extra fire, there's *camarones a la diabla*—shrimp sautéed in butter, garlic, and crushed red chile peppers. The outdoor seating in a garden area is delightful.

Charles Street Dinner House

5043 CA 140, Mariposa. © **209/966-2366.** Reservations recommended. Main courses $8.50–$31. AE, DISC, MC, V. Tues–Sun 5–9pm. Closed Jan. AMERICAN.

Locally famous for its charbroiled steaks (marinated and herb-crusted filet mignon and New York steak, 10 oz. each), the Charles Street Dinner House has been the locals' choice for fresh seafood and a variety of other specialties for more than 25 years. We especially recommend the New Zealand rack of lamb, broiled, with mint glaze; and the broiled Peking breast of duck, served with orange sauce. Or try the scallone—abalone and scallops sautéed with lemon butter and toasted almonds. The restaurant is located in a historic building from the 1800s, and decor is straight out of the Old West, with a huge wagon wheel in the front window and touches that include family photos and fresh flowers. Service is excellent.

Erna's Elderberry House

48688 Victoria Lane (at Château du Sureau), Oakhurst. © **559/683-6800.** Reservations recommended. Prix-fixe dinners $82, prix-fixe brunch $33. AE, DISC, MC, V. Daily 5:30–8:30pm; Sun also 11am–1pm. EUROPEAN/CALIFORNIAN

One of the most renowned eateries in the Yosemite area, this elegant restaurant at Château du Sureau is a feast for the eyes, with a contemporary seating area with purple walls and modern prints adjoining a more traditionally elegant room. Likewise, it is a feast for the taste buds, with a nightly changing menu that might include any number of European culinary traditions sculpted into a meal that is definitively Californian. Offerings might range from marinated mussels and chilled carrot-coconut soup to red pepper and prosciutto-wrapped beef tenderloin, spinach gnocchi, and blueberry yogurt terrine. Each menu comes with a list of recommended wines. Proprietor Erna Kubin-Clanin and company also offer regular gourmet cooking classes here.

Groveland Hotel's Victorian Room

18767 CA 120, Groveland. © **209/962-4000.** www.groveland.com. Reservations recommended in summer. Main courses $17–$24. AE, DC, DISC, MC, V. Daily 6–9pm in summer and 6–8pm in winter. CALIFORNIAN.

Top-notch food in a casual atmosphere is what you'll experience at this fine restaurant. The menu has something for everyone and is constantly changing to reflect what's fresh and in season. There's a sumptuous rack of lamb marinated in rosemary and garlic, salmon with fresh cucumber and dill, chicken breast with fresh fruit salsa, and more. The menu usually has fresh seafood and pasta specials, as well as an innkeeper's special. All entrees are served with soup or salad and fresh warm bread. The *Wine Spectator* award-winning wine list—wine being one of owner Peggy Mosley's passions—is fantastic, and in summer there is also courtyard dining.

Happy Burger Diner

5120 CA 140 (at 12th St.), Mariposa. © **209/966-2719.** Menu items $3–$15. AE, DISC, MC, V. Daily 6am–9pm. AMERICAN.

One of the best fast-food joints we've seen anywhere, the Happy Burger offers practically any type of fast food you can think of—it claims to have the region's largest menu—with everything cooked fresh to order. The food here takes a few minutes longer than at your usual chain fast-food restaurants, but it's worth it. Breakfasts (served until 11:30am) include numerous egg dishes, French toast, pancakes, oatmeal, and the like. The lunch and dinner menu, served all day, features a multitude of charbroiled burgers, sandwiches, stuffed potatoes, Mexican dishes, salads, and dinner plates such as chicken fried steak, roasted or fried chicken, and fried fish and shrimp. Delivery to Mariposa motels is provided.

In typical fast-food style, you order and claim your food at the counter; then you can sit inside at booths, among the record album covers from the 1960s and '70s and a vintage pinball game, or go outside to picnic tables next to a children's play area.

Hotel Charlotte

18736 CA 120, Groveland. © **209/962-7872.** www.hotelcharlotte.com. Reservations recommended. Main courses $9–$20. AE, MC, V. Thurs–Mon 5–9pm. Closed Nov–Mar. MEDITERRANEAN.

You'll find generous portions of beef, seafood, and pastas in a fine-dining atmosphere in the small dining room at this historic hotel. A variety of seasonal specials are offered, and staples include charbroiled filet mignon, New York steaks and daily seafood specials. You'll also find delicious artichoke chicken on the menu as well and a several vegetarian choices. All meals include veggies, potato or rice, and bread, and the wine list is quite good.

Meadows Ranch Cafe

5024 CA 140, Mariposa. © **209/966-2239.** Reservations recommended on summer weekends. Breakfast $3–$6; lunch $4–$6; dinner $5.95–$20; pizza $7.95. MC, V. Mon–Sat 7am–8pm; Sun 10am–2pm. AMERICAN.

This cafe is a good spot for a quick bite or a full meal. The food is wholesome and fresh, and the coffee is great. Breakfasts include a variety of egg dishes, omelets, and breakfast burritos—a toss of eggs, meat, veggies, and cheese rolled in a warm tortilla. Lunch includes a selection of more than two dozen sandwiches on a variety of breads. Dinner offers pizzas, pasta, and a few grilled selections, including grilled lemon-herb chicken breast and barbecued beef.

PJ's Cafe and Pizzeria

18986 CA 120, Groveland. © **209/962-7501.** Main courses $3–$7; pizza $5–$15. No credit cards. Daily 7am–8pm. PIZZA/SANDWICHES.

Best known as a pizzeria and burger house, PJ's serves a hearty breakfast with an eye toward helping lower our fat and cholesterol intake. That being said, you can still order bacon and eggs without getting the evil eye. All meat and egg dishes use low-cholesterol cooking oil, and PJ's also uses only lean ground chuck in the chili, taco meat, and meat sauces that are available for lunch and dinner. The taco and Cobb salads are especially tasty. We like the pizzas, too, which range from create-your-own to a yummy pesto-artichoke-tomato combination; and prime rib is featured on weekends.

Savoury's

5027 CA 140, Mariposa. © **209/966-77677.** Entrees $12–$19. MC, V. Tues–Sat 5–9:30pm. INTERNATIONAL FUSION.

In the Art Deco confines of a former California Highway Patrol office, this eatery quickly won the hearts of locals after opening in spring 2003. Not surprising, since proprietor-chef Mirriam Wackerman had catered in the area for years, and customers often urged her to follow her dreams and open a restaurant. Now that she has, the results are top-notch, with a menu of simple, fresh dishes that meld culinary traditions near and far: jambalaya linguini, chipotle pesto chicken, grilled lemon-chive scallops, and the only flat iron steak in town, Cajun-spiced and pan-seared. For dessert, bite into a decadent dish of panna cotta, the Italian equivalent of crème brûlée on a bed of strawberry sauce. There is a cozy but sleek main dining room, as well as a delightful vine-clad patio, sandwiched between historic redbricks, out back.

Picnic & Camping Supplies

If you forget something, chances are you'll be able to get it in bustling Yosemite Valley, but elsewhere in the park it's tough to find equipment. The best place to get supplies and camping equipment in the valley is the **Yosemite Village Store,** which stocks groceries, film, and maps, and has an ATM machine. Nearby, the **Village Sport Shop** has fishing, camping, and other outdoor gear, plus sells fishing licenses. The **Yosemite Lodge Gift Shop** and **Curry Village General Store** stock some supplies. The **Curry Village Mountain Shop** sells clothing and equipment for day hikes as well as for backcountry excursions, and the **Tuolumne Meadows Gift & Mountain Shop** also carries backpacking supplies, including maps

and dehydrated food. The **Badger Pass Sport Shop** (open only during the snow season) stocks ski clothing and other winter supplies. There are also several small convenience stores located throughout the park.

In **Mariposa** you'll find a good selection of groceries plus a deli at **Pioneer Market,** at 5034 Coakley Circle, behind the town rest area (© **209/742-6100**). Our choice for a grocery store in **Oakhurst** is **Raley's** at 40041 CA 41 (© **559/683-8300**). Just outside the park's **El Portal** Entrance, on CA 140, is the well-stocked **El Portal Food Market** (© **209/379-2632**). For a better selection (and better prices) you can stop at the major supermarket and discount chains in **Merced** or **Fresno,** the largest cities in the park vicinity.

36

ZION NATIONAL PARK & CEDAR BREAKS NATIONAL MONUMENT

by Don & Barbara Laine

I T'S NOT HARD TO CONJURE UP A SINGLE DEFINING IMAGE OF MOST national parks, but Zion, a collage of images and secrets, is impossible to pin down. Zion National Park is not simply the towering Great White Throne, the deep Narrows Canyon, or the cascading waterfalls and emerald green pools. You'll discover an entire smorgasbord of experiences, sights, sounds, and even smells here, as you explore everything from the massive stone sculptures and monuments to the lush forests and rushing rivers.

Today, 150 years after the Mormon settler Isaac Behunin named his homestead here "Little Zion," the park still casts its spell as you gaze upon its sheer multicolored walls of sandstone, explore its narrow canyons, hunt for hanging gardens of wildflowers, and listen to the roar of the churning, tumbling Virgin River. The park means different things to different people: a day hike down a narrow canyon, a rough climb up the face of a massive stone monument, the red glow of sunset over majestic peaks. To some degree, each of these experiences is possible only because of the rocks here and the processes that they have been through—uplifting, shifting, breaking, and eroding. The most important of Zion's nine rock layers in creating its colorful formations is Navajo sandstone, the thickest rock layer in the park, at up to 2,200 feet.

Millions of years ago, a shallow sea covered the sand dunes here, causing minerals, including lime from the shells of sea creatures, to glue sand particles together to form sandstone. Later, movements in the earth's crust lifted the land, draining away the sea but leaving rivers that gradually carved the soft sandstone into the spectacular shapes we see today.

But where do the marvelous colors of the rocks come from? Essentially, from rust. Most of the rocks at Zion are colored by iron, or hematite (iron oxide), either contained in the original stone or carried into the rocks by groundwater. Although iron often creates red and pink hues, seen in many of Zion's sandstone faces, it can also result in blacks, browns, yellows, and even greens. Sometimes the iron seeps into the rock, coloring it through, but often it just stains the surface in vertical streaks. Rocks are

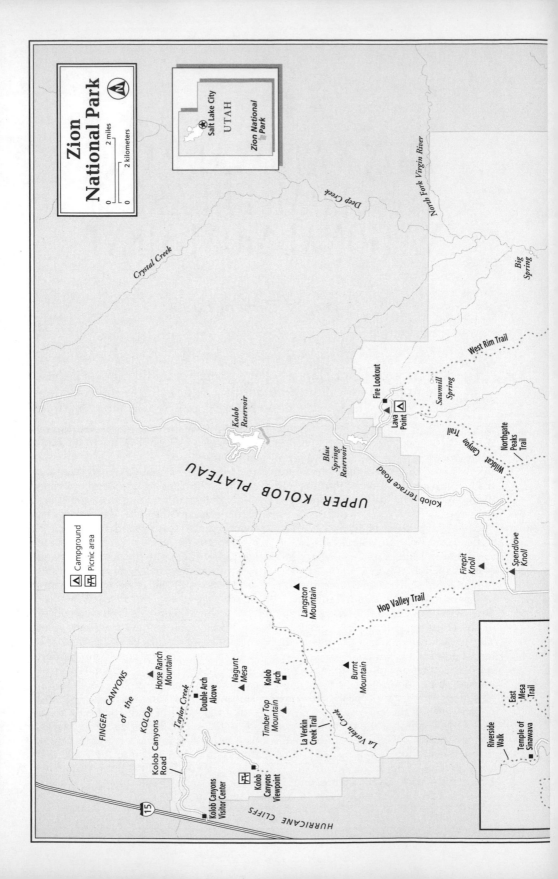

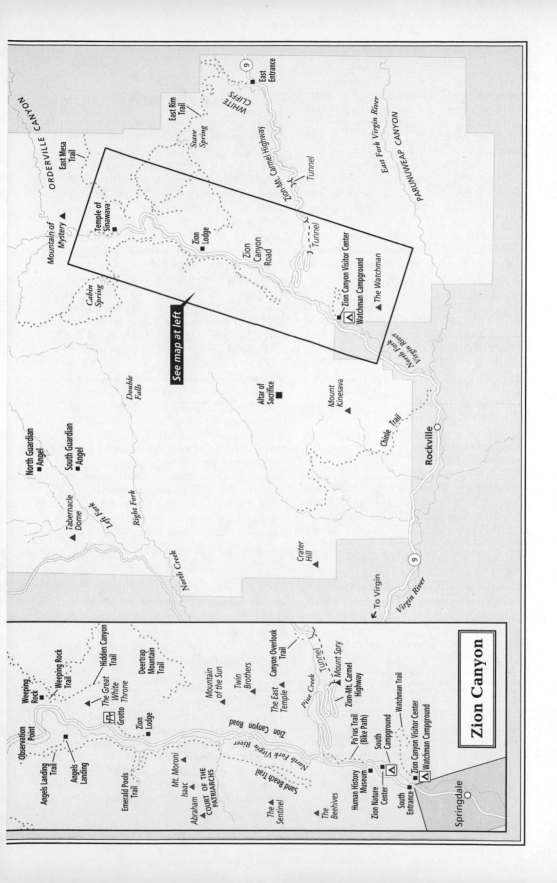

Zion Canyon

also colored by bacteria that live on their surfaces. The bacteria ingest dust and expel iron, manganese, and other minerals, which stick to the rock and produce a shiny black, brown, or reddish surface called desert varnish.

Because of its extremes in elevation (3,666 ft.–8,726 ft.) and climate, Zion harbors a vast array of flora and fauna. Wildlife here includes pocket gophers, mountain lions, hundreds of birds (including golden eagles), and dozens of snakes. As for plants, about 800 native species have been found, including cactus, yucca, and mesquite in the hot, dry desert areas; ponderosa pine trees on the high plateaus; and cottonwoods and box elders along the rivers and streams. Watch for the red claret cup cactus, which has spectacular blooms in the spring, and for wildflowers such as manzanita, which has tiny pink blossoms, and the bright red hummingbird trumpet, sometimes called the "Zion Lily." And don't miss the hanging gardens of plant life clinging to the sides of the sandstone cliffs.

Avoiding the Crowds. Try to avoid the peak summer months of June, July, and August, when temperatures are hot and Zion receives almost half its annual visitors. The quietest months are December, January, and February, but of course it's cold and you may have to contend with some snow and ice. Good times to visit, if your schedule permits, are April, May, September, or October, when the weather is usually pleasant and the park is less crowded than in the summer.

Once in the park, the best way to avoid crowds is to walk away from them, either on the longer and more strenuous hiking trails or on treks into the backcountry. It's sad but true: Most visitors to Zion never bother to venture far from the main view points, and their loss can be your gain. You can also avoid the hordes by spending time in Kolob Canyons, in the far northwest section of the park; it's spectacular and receives surprisingly little use, at least in comparison to Zion Canyon.

Just the Facts

GETTING THERE & GATEWAYS

Zion National Park is in the southwestern corner of Utah, 83 miles southwest of Bryce Canyon National Park and 120 miles northwest of the north rim of Grand Canyon National Park in northern Arizona. It's 309 miles south of Salt Lake City, 42 miles northwest of Kanab, and 158 miles northeast of Las Vegas, Nevada. It's composed of two main parts: Zion Canyon, the main section of the park, and the less-visited Kolob Canyons, in the park's northwest corner. The closest towns with airport service are St. George (46 miles southwest of the park), and Cedar City (60 miles north).

The easiest way to get to the park is to approach from the west on I-15, which runs north to Salt Lake City and southwest through Arizona to Nevada. This route is more direct than the eastern approach, avoids possible delays at the Zion–Mount Carmel Tunnel, and delivers you to Springdale, just outside the park's south entrance, where most of the area's lodging and restaurants are located. From I-15, go east on Utah 9 if approaching from the south, or go south on Utah 17 and then east on Utah 9 if approaching from the north; Utah 9 then continues east to the park's south entrance.

The eastern approach to the park is less direct but far more beautiful. From either the south or the north take U.S. 89 to Utah 9 at Mount Carmel, then go east on Utah 9 for a spectacularly scenic 24-mile drive. However, be aware that this route into the park drops more than 2,500 feet in elevation, passes through the mile-long Zion–Mount Carmel Tunnel, and winds down six steep switchbacks. Oversized vehicles are charged $10 to use the tunnel (see "Special Regulations & Warnings," below).

The Kolob Canyons section, in the park's northwest corner, is reached on the short Kolob Canyons Road off I-15, Exit 40.

Tips from a Park Ranger

"**O**verpowering, but also intimate" is how former backcountry ranger Dave Rachlis sees Zion National Park, adding, "These are some of the highest vertical rock walls that some people will ever see." Rachlis also explains that the Navajo sandstone that forms Zion's walls is one of the thickest sedimentary formations in the world. A good place to see the thickness of the sandstone is in the West Temple formation, just behind the visitor center.

Rachlis says that one of the best aspects of the park, from the visitor's point of view, is its trail system. "The park has a sense of grandeur, but then it also has access—you can go up the West Rim Trail or you can go up the East Rim Trail, and you can get into these narrow canyons, and really experience the park pretty easily."

Most visitors to Zion, according to Rachlis, stay only a short time and see only a small part of the park—essentially only what's visible from the viewpoints. However, Rachlis recommends a visit of at least a full day, preferably more. "In 2 or 3 days you can see most of the major regions of the park and get a chance to get out on the trails a bit for day hikes," he says.

Hikers should keep in mind that they can see the park from two perspectives. "You need to decide what experience you want—to climb to a high plateau and gaze down into the canyons, or to descend into a canyon and look up. I think the West Rim Trail is probably our most scenic trail in terms of getting you up onto the plateau where you can look down into the canyons." He also recommends the La Verkin Creek Trail, which leads to Kolob Arch, believed to be the world's largest freestanding arch. "This trail is very intimate, very colorful—the rock is a little more orange to red than it is in the main canyon. It's just a really magnificent area."

A hike through the Narrows is "the ultimate slot canyon experience," according to Rachlis. "You're following a river drainage, wading or swimming in spots. In summer, it's one of the cooler areas of the park."

One mistake that some park visitors make, Rachlis says, is to downplay the dangers of the easy and moderate hiking trails, where most injuries occur. He says that people understand the hazards on difficult trails such as Angels Landing, where you're inching along a knife-edge ridge, but that you also need to be careful on trails with less-obvious dangers. "Sandstone is slippery, and a 20-foot fall can kill you as easily as a 1,000-foot fall," he says.

As for when to visit, Rachlis says the trails can be hot in summer, so the best time for hiking is probably spring and fall—from April through June and from September through November. The park is also less crowded at those times. But he adds that the park has unpredictable weather, so it's best to call to check on current conditions before showing up.

INFORMATION

Contact the **Superintendent, Zion National Park,** Springdale, UT 84767-1099 (© **435/772-3256;** www.nps.gov/zion) for information. You can purchase books, maps, and videos from the nonprofit **Zion Natural History Association,** Zion National Park, Springdale, UT 84767 (© **800/635-3959** or 435/772-3264; www.zionpark.org). Some publications are available in foreign languages, and several videos can be purchased in either VHS or PAL formats. Those wanting to help the non-profit association can join ($35 single or $50 family annually) and get a 20% discount on purchases, a 10% discount on Zion Canyon Field Institute classes, plus discounts at most other non-profit bookstores at national parks, monuments, historic sites, and recreation areas. Those planning backcountry hikes should purchase a copy of the association's topographical map. The *Zion Map & Guide,* a small free newspaper-format guide, is packed with extremely helpful information.

VISITOR CENTERS

The park has two visitor centers. The new **Zion Canyon Visitor Center & Transportation Hub** (© 435/772-3256), near the south entrance, has outdoor exhibits that provide an introduction to the park. Rangers here can answer questions and provide backcountry permits. You can also buy books, maps, videos, postcards, and posters, and pick up free brochures. The **Kolob Canyons Visitor Center** (© 435/586-9548), in the northwest corner of the park off I-15, provides information, permits, books, and maps. Both visitor centers are open from 8am to 7pm in summer, with shorter varying hours the rest of the year (call to find out when). The new **Zion Human History Museum** now stands at the site of the former Zion Canyon Visitor Center.

FEES & PERMITS

Entry into the park for up to 7 days, which includes unlimited use of the shuttle bus, costs $20 per private vehicle; or $10 per individual on motorcycle or bicycle, or on foot using the pedestrian-only entrance, with a $20 maximum per family. Oversized vehicles (see "Special Regulations & Warnings," below) are charged $10 for use of the Zion–Mount Carmel Tunnel on the east side of the park.

Backcountry permits, available at either visitor center, are required for all overnight hikes in the park as well as slot canyon routes. Permits cost $10 for 1 or 2 persons, $15 for 3 to 6, and $20 for 7 to 12 people. Camping costs $16 per night for basic campsites and $18 to $20 per night for sites with electric hookups (located in Watchman Campground).

SPECIAL REGULATIONS & WARNINGS

The mile-long Zion–Mount Carmel Tunnel was not built for big vehicles. The tunnel is too narrow for two-way traffic involving anything larger than passenger cars and pickup trucks. Therefore, any vehicle more than 7 feet, 10 inches wide (including mirrors) or 11 feet, 4 inches tall (including luggage racks) can only pass by driving down the center of the tunnel after all other traffic has been stopped. Large vehicles can accomplish this feat only from 8am to 8pm daily from March to October; during other months arrangements must be made at park entrances or by calling park headquarters. The charge is $10, good for two trips through the tunnel during a 7-day period.

All vehicles more than 13 feet, 1 inch tall, and certain other particularly large vehicles, are prohibited from driving anywhere on the park road between the east entrance and Zion Canyon.

Bicycles are prohibited in the Zion–Mount Carmel Tunnel, in the backcountry, and on all trails except the Pa'rus Trail.

Backcountry hikers should practice minimum impact techniques and are prohibited from building fires. A limit on the number of people allowed in various parts of the backcountry may be in force during your visit; prospective backcountry hikers should check with rangers before setting out. You can purchase a backcountry permit at the visitor center in advance, and you can reserve permits for hikes in the Narrows at the visitor center. A free booklet on back-country travel, available at the visitor centers, lists all regulations plus descriptions of close to 20 backcountry trails.

Zion experiences all four seasons, although the winters are mild and rarely bring snow. The best times to visit the park are spring and fall, when the temperatures range from lows in the 40s (single digits Celsius) to pleasant highs in the 80s (upper 20s Celsius). Remember that summer daytime highs often soar above 100°F (38°C), with lows in the 70s (lower 20s Celsius). During the summer, do your hiking in the early morning to avoid both the heat and the frequent afternoon thunderstorms in July and August, which can change a babbling brook into a raging torrent in minutes.

If You Have Only 1 Day

Those with only a day in the park should stop first at the **Zion Canyon Visitor Center** to see the exhibits and look through the free *Zion Map & Guide,* which describes the various available options for exploring the park. Then hop on the shuttle bus, which hits the major Zion Canyon roadside viewpoints. When you get to the **Temple of Sinawava,** instead of just taking a quick look and jumping on the next shuttle, hike the easy 2-mile round-trip **Riverside Walk,** which follows the Virgin River through a narrow canyon past hanging gardens. Then take the shuttle bus back to the lodge (total time: 2–4 hr.), where you might stop at the gift shop and possibly have lunch in the lodge restaurant.

Near the lodge you'll find the trailhead for the **Emerald Pools.** Especially pleasant on hot days, this easy walk through a forest of oak, maple, fir, and cottonwood trees leads to a waterfall, a hanging garden, and the shimmering lower pool. This walk should take about an hour round-trip. Those with a bit more ambition may want to add another hour and another mile to the loop by taking the moderately strenuous hike on a rocky, steeper trail to the upper pool.

If time and energy remain, head back toward the south park entrance and stop at **Watchman Trailhead.** Here, a moderately strenuous, 2-mile, 2-hour round-trip hike takes you to a plateau with beautiful views of several rock formations and the town of Springdale. That evening, take in the campground amphitheater program.

Exploring the Park by Car or Shuttle

If you enter the park from the east, along the steep **Zion–Mount Carmel Highway,** you'll travel 13 miles to the **Zion Canyon Visitor Center,** passing between the White Cliffs and Checkerboard Mesa, a massive sandstone rock formation covered with horizontal and vertical lines that make it look like a huge fishing net. Continuing, you'll pass through a fairyland of fantastically shaped rocks of red, orange, tan, and white, and you'll encounter the **Great Arch of Zion,** carved high in a stone cliff by the forces of erosion. At the east end of the Zion–Mount Carmel Tunnel is the **trailhead parking** for the Canyon Overlook Trail, a relatively easy 1-mile walk to a great viewpoint. After driving through the tunnel, you'll traverse a number of long switchbacks as you descend to the canyon floor.

A shuttle bus system has been implemented in the main section of the park to reduce traffic congestion and the resultant problems of pollution, noise, and damage to the park. The shuttle system consists of **two loops:** one in the town of Springdale and the other along Zion Canyon Scenic Drive, with the loops connecting at the transit/visitor center just inside the south park entrance. From April through October, access to Zion Canyon Scenic Drive (above Utah 9) is limited to shuttle buses, hikers, and bikers. The only exceptions are overnight Zion Lodge guests and tour buses connected with the lodge—both have access as far as the lodge. Shuttle stops are located at all the major-use areas in the park, and shuttles run frequently (about every 6 min. at peak times). In winter, when visitation is lowest, visitors are permitted to drive the full length of Zion Canyon Scenic Drive in their own vehicles.

Zion Canyon Scenic Drive: The ride through Zion Canyon is impressive by any standards, with massive stone reaching straight up to the heavens, and the North Fork of the Virgin River threading its way through the maze of rocks. The views in every direction are awe-inspiring. Stops along the road provide access to viewpoints and hiking trails.

The first stop is across from the **Court of the Patriarchs,** where a short paved trail leads to an impressive viewpoint. The next stop is **Zion Lodge.** Across the road from the lodge is the trailhead for the **Emerald Pools Trail system.** The Grotto Picnic Area is about a half-mile beyond the lodge, accessible from the lodge via a trail that parallels Zion Canyon Scenic Drive. Across from the Grotto Picnic Area parking lot is a footbridge that leads to the Emerald Pools, Angels Landing, and West Rim trails.

Continuing north into Zion Canyon, the road passes the **Great White Throne** on the right and then **Angels Landing** on the left, before coming to the turnoff to the **Weeping Rock Trailhead** parking area. From here, the road closely traces the curves of the river, with a couple of stops to allow different views of **the Organ,** which to some resembles a huge pipe organ. Finally the road ends at the **Temple of Sinawava,** where the paved **Riverside Walk** follows the Virgin River toward **The Narrows,** one of the most incredible sights in Zion.

Kolob Canyons Road: To escape the crowds of Zion Canyon, head to the northwest corner of the park. The Kolob Canyons Road runs 5 miles among spectacular red and orange rocks, ending at a high vista. Allow about 45 minutes round-trip, which includes time for stopping at the numbered viewpoints. Be sure to get a copy of the Kolob Canyons Road Guide at the Kolob Visitor Center. Here's what you'll pass along the way:

Leaving **Kolob Canyons Visitor Center,** you'll drive along the Hurricane Fault to **Hurricane Cliffs,** a series of tall, gray cliffs composed of limestone, and onward to **Taylor Creek,** where a piñon-juniper forest clings to life on the rocky hillside, providing a home to bright blue scrub jays. Your next stop is **Horse Ranch Mountain,** which, at 8,726 feet, is the national park's highest point. Passing a series of colorful rock layers, where you might be lucky enough to spot a golden eagle, your next stop is **Box Canyon,** along the South Fork of Taylor Creek, with sheer rock walls soaring more than 1,500 feet high. Along this stretch you'll see multicolored layers of rock, pushed upward by tremendous forces from within the earth, followed by a side canyon with large, arched alcoves boasting delicate curved ceilings. Head on to a view of **Timber Top Mountain,** which has a sagebrush-blanketed desert at its base and a stately fir and ponderosa pine forest at its peak. Watch for mule deer on the brushy hillsides, especially between October and March, when they might be spotted just after sunrise or just before sunset. From here, continue to **Rockfall Overlook;** a large scar on the mountainside marks the spot where a 1,000-foot chunk of stone crashed to the earth in July 1983, the victim of erosion. Finally, stop to see the canyon walls themselves, colored orange-red by iron oxide and striped black by mineral-laden water running down the cliff faces.

Ranger Programs

Park rangers present a variety of free programs and activities. **Amphitheater programs,** which sometimes include a slide show, take place most evenings at campground amphitheaters. Topics vary, but could include subjects such as the animals or plants of the park, geology of the park, or the park's famous slot canyons. Rangers also give short talks on similar subjects several times daily at various locations. **Ranger-guided hikes and walks,** which may require reservations, might take you to little-visited areas of the park, on a trek to see wildflowers, or out at night for a hike under the full moon. Schedules are posted on bulletin boards at the visitor centers and campgrounds.

Historic & Man-Made Attractions

There are no major historic sites in Zion National Park, but there is some evidence of the early peoples who inhabited the area. Hikers with sharp eyes may see potsherds, pieces of ancient stone tools, rock art, and other archaeological objects. Park officials ask that you do not touch these artifacts (skin oils can damage them), but report their location to rangers.

Day Hikes

Zion offers a wide variety of hiking options, ranging from easy half-hour walks on paved paths to grueling overnight hikes over rocky terrain. Hikers with a fear of heights should be especially careful when choosing trails because many include steep, dizzying, and potentially fatal drop-offs. Water found in streams in the park is not safe to drink. Smoking is prohibited on all trails. Shuttle service for backcountry hikers is available throughout the area from **Zion Canyon Transportation** (© 877/635-5993 or 435/635-5993)

and **Springdale Narrows Shuttle** (© 800/776-2099). Those who want to try to arrange rides with fellow hikers can make use of a bulletin board at the visitor center.

SHORTER TRAILS

Canyon Overlook

1 mile RT. Moderate. Access: East side of Zion–Mt. Carmel Tunnel.

This self-guided trail takes you to an overlook with a magnificent view of lower Zion Canyon and Pine Creek Canyon. Be aware that there are some long drop-offs and that the sandy trail can be slippery. Trail guide booklets are available at the visitor center and at the trailhead.

Emerald Pools Trails

1.2–2.5 miles RT. Easy to moderate. Access: Across from Zion Lodge.

This can either be an easy 1-hour walk or a moderately strenuous 2-hour hike with steep drop-offs, depending on how much you choose to do. A 0.6-mile paved path leads from the Emerald Pools parking area through a forest of oak, maple, fir, and cottonwood, to several waterfalls, a hanging garden, and the picturesque Lower Emerald Pool.

From here, a steeper, rocky trail continues 0.25 mile to the Middle Emerald Pool, and then climbs another 0.33 mile past cactus, yucca, and juniper to the Upper Emerald Pool, which has another waterfall. Total elevation gain is 69 feet to Lower Emerald Pool, 150 feet to the Middle Emerald Pool, and 400 feet from the trailhead to Upper Emerald Pool.

Hidden Canyon Trail

2 miles RT. Moderate to strenuous. Access: Weeping Rock parking lot.

A particularly scenic hike, this trail climbs 850 feet through a narrow, water-carved canyon, ending at the canyon's mouth. Those wanting to extend the hike can go another 0.6 mile to a small natural arch. Hidden Canyon Trail includes long drop-offs, and is not recommended for anyone with a fear of heights.

Pa'rus Trail

3.5 miles RT. Easy. Access: From either the entrance to Watchman Campground, near the amphitheater parking area, or near the Nature Center at South Campground.

This paved trail (fully accessible to wheel-chairs) follows the Virgin River, providing views of the rock formations in lower Zion Canyon. Unlike other park trails, this one is open to bicycles and leashed pets. The elevation gain is only 50 feet.

Riverside Walk and the Gateway to The Narrows

2 miles RT. Easy. Access: Temple of Sinawava parking lot.

This paved trail follows the Virgin River upstream to the Zion Canyon Narrows, past trailside exhibits and hanging wild-flowers in spring and summer. Accessible to those in wheelchairs with some assistance, the trail has an elevation change of only 57 feet. At The Narrows, the pavement ends and you have to decide whether to turn around or to continue upstream into The Narrows itself (yes, you will get wet), where the canyon walls are about 24 feet apart in some areas and more than 1,000 feet high. *Warning:* The bottom of a very nar-row slot canyon is definitely not a place you want to be in a rainstorm (common in July–Aug), when flash floods are a serious threat. Before entering The Nar-rows, check the weather forecast and discuss your plans with park rangers. Permits are required for longer treks in The Narrows but not for short day hikes (see "The Narrows," below).

Watchman Trail

3 miles RT. Moderate. Access: Zion Canyon Visitor Center.

This moderately strenuous but relatively short trail gets surprisingly light use,

possibly because it can be very hot in the middle of the day. Climbing to a plateau near the base of the Watchman forma-tion, it offers splendid views of lower Zion Canyon, Oak Creek Canyon, the Towers of the Virgin, the West Temple formations, and the town of Springdale. The trail takes about 2 hours to complete and has an elevation gain of 368 feet.

Weeping Rock Trail

0.5 mile RT. Easy to moderate. Access: Weeping Rock parking lot.

This is among the park's shortest and easiest rambles, although it is steep in spots. A self-guiding nature trail, the route leads to a rock alcove with a spring and hanging gardens of ferns and wild-flowers. Although paved, the trail is rela-tively steep (gaining 98 ft.) and slippery, and not suitable for wheelchairs.

LONGER TRAILS

Angels Landing Trail

5 miles RT. Strenuous. Access: Grotto picnic area.

This strenuous 4-hour hike is most cer-tainly not for anyone with even a mild fear of heights. The trail climbs 1,488 feet to a summit that offers spectacular views into Zion Canyon. *But be prepared:* The final half-mile follows a narrow, knife-edge trail along a steep ridge, where footing can be slippery even under the best of circumstances. Sup-port chains have been set along parts of the trail.

East Rim Trail

8 miles RT. Strenuous. Access: Weeping Rock parking lot.

This strenuous hike takes all day and climbs more than 2,000 feet to Observa-tion Point. But if you can manage it, the incredible views down into the canyon make all the exertion worthwhile. This trail also gives access to other east rim trails: Cable Mountain and Deertrap Mountain.

Hop Valley Trail

13.4 miles RT. Moderate to strenuous. Access: Trailhead on Kolob Terrace Rd.

This backcountry trail loses about 1,000 feet as it meanders through sunny fields and past Gambel oak, partly following an old Jeep road and then a stream, before taking you to La Verkin Creek. Some hikers connect with the La Verkin Creek/Kolob Arch Trail to see Kolob Arch. Hikers should plan on allotting a full day for this trail.

La Verkin Creek/Kolob Arch Trail

14 miles RT. Strenuous. Access: Kolob Canyons Rd. at Lee Pass.

Although there are no drop-offs, this backcountry trail is quite strenuous. Descending almost 700 feet, it follows Timber and La Verkin creeks, ending at Kolob Arch, which, at 310 feet long, may be the world's largest freestanding arch. Some people choose to camp on this hike. You can camp at La Verkin Creek if you have a permit and have been assigned a campsite at the visitor center.

The Narrows

16 miles one-way. Moderate to difficult. Access: Chamberlain's Ranch (outside the park). By permit only.

Hiking The Narrows doesn't really involve hiking a trail at all; instead, it consists of walking or wading along the bottom of the Virgin River, through a spectacular 1,000-foot-deep chasm that, at a mere 24 feet wide, definitely lives up to its name. Passing fanciful sculptured sandstone arches, hanging gardens, and waterfalls, this moderately strenuous hike is recommended for those in good physical condition who are up to fighting sometimes-strong currents. Those who want just a taste of The Narrows can walk and wade in from the end of the Riverside Walk (see above), but more than a short trip will involve a long full- or 2-day trek, which includes arranging a shuttle to the starting point at Chamberlain's Ranch and then transportation from the

Temple of Sinawava, where you'll leave the canyon.

The Narrows is subject to flash flooding, and can be very treacherous. Park Service officials remind hikers that they are responsible for their own safety, and should check on current water conditions and weather forecasts. This hike is *not* recommended when rain is forecast or threatening. Permits ($5) are required for full-day and overnight hikes, and must be purchased at the visitor center the day before your hike.

Taylor Creek Trail

5.4 miles RT. Moderately strenuous. Access: Kolob Canyons Rd., about 2 miles from Kolob Canyons Visitor Center.

This is a 4-hour hike along the middle fork of Taylor Creek—you might get your feet wet fording the creek. The trail leads past two historic cabins to Double Arch Alcove, with an elevation gain of 450 feet.

Exploring the Backcountry

There are numerous backpacking opportunities in the park, and a number of the day hikes discussed above are actually more comfortably done in 2 or more days. In addition to the park's established trails and the famous Narrows, there are a number of off-trail routes for those experienced in using topographical maps—get information at the Backcountry Desk at the Zion Canyon Visitor Center. Backcountry permits, available at either visitor center, are required for all overnight hikes in the park, as well as daylong slot canyon hikes. Permits cost $5 for 1 person, $10 for 2 people, $15 for 3 to 6, and $20 for 7 to 12 people.

The difficult **West Rim Trail** climbs more than 3,500 feet into the high country to a viewpoint overlooking the Right Fork of North Creek Canyon (at 14 miles) and then continues to Lava Point. The round-trip distance is 28.4 miles and access is at the Grotto Picnic

Area. There are striking views from most points on the trail.

Other Sports & Activities

Biking & Mountain Biking. Although bikes are prohibited on almost all trails and are forbidden to travel cross-country within the national park boundaries, Zion is among the West's most bike-friendly parks. The bike-friendly **Pa'rus Trail** runs a little under 2 miles along the Virgin River, from the south park entrance and South Campground to Zion Canyon Scenic Drive. The trail crosses the river and several creeks, and provides good views of the Watchman, West Temple, the Sentinel, and other lower canyon formations. The trail is paved and open to bicyclists, pedestrians, pets on leashes, and those with strollers or wheelchairs, but is closed to cars.

From April through October the **Zion Canyon Scenic Drive,** beyond its intersection with the Zion–Mount Carmel Highway, is closed to private motor vehicles, except to motorists with reservations at Zion Lodge. However, during that time the road is open to hikers and bicyclists, as well as shuttle buses. Cyclists should stay to the right to allow shuttle buses to pass.

Bicycles can also be ridden on other park roads, though not through the Zion–Mount Carmel Tunnel.

Although mountain bikes are prohibited on the trails of Zion National Park (except the Pa'rus Trail), just outside the park—mostly on Bureau of Land Management and state-owned property—are numerous rugged Jeep trails that are great for mountain biking, plus more than 100 miles of slickrock cross-country trails and single-track trails. Talk with the knowledgeable staff at **Springdale Cycle,** at 1458 Zion Park Blvd. (P.O. Box 501), Springdale, UT 84767 (© **800/776-2099** or 435/772-0575; www.springdalecycles.com), about the best trails for your interests and abilities. This full-service bike shop also offers maps, a full range of bikes and accessories, repairs, and rentals

($35–$55 for a full day, $25–$45 for a half day). The company also offers full-day guided mountain-bike trips outside the park, starting at $85 per person (for a group of six), in addition to a variety of multiday excursions. Shuttle service is available throughout the area from **Zion Canyon Transportation** (© **877/635-5993** or 435/635-5993), and **Springdale Narrows Shuttle** (© **800/776-2099**).

Horseback Riding. Guided rides in the park are available March through October from **Canyon Trail Rides,** P.O. Box 128, Tropic, UT 84776 (© **435/679-8665;** www.canyonrides.com), with ticket sales and information at Zion Lodge. A 1-hour ride along the Virgin River costs $20 and a half-day ride on the Sand Beach Trail costs $45. Riders must weigh no more than 220 pounds, and children must be at least 7 years old for the 1-hour ride and 8 years old for the half-day ride. Reservations are advised.

Rock Climbing. Expert technical rock climbers love the tall sandstone cliffs in Zion Canyon, although rangers warn that much of the rock is loose, or "rotten," and climbing equipment and techniques suitable for granite are often less effective here. Permits ($5) are required for overnight climbs, and because some routes may be closed at times, such as during peregrine falcon nesting (from early spring through July), climbers should check at the visitor center before setting out. **Zion Adventure Company,** 36 Lion Blvd. (P.O. Box 523), Springdale, UT 84767 (© **435/772-1001;** www.zionadventures.com), and **Zion Rock and Mountain Guides** 1458 Zion Park Blvd. (P.O. Box 623), Springdale, UT 84767 (© **435/772-3303;** www.zionrockguides.com), offer a variety of guided rock climbing and hiking trips, as well as instruction, near the park.

Wildlife Viewing & Bird-Watching. It's a rare visitor to Zion who doesn't spot a critter of some sort, from **mule deer**—often seen along roadways and in campgrounds year-round—to the many varieties of **lizards** that you're likely to see from spring through fall, including the park's largest lizard, the chuckwalla, which can grow to 20 inches. The **ringtail cat,** a relative of the raccoon, prowls Zion Canyon at night, and is not above helping itself to your camping supplies. Along the Virgin River you'll see **bank beaver,** so named because they live in burrows instead of dams. The park is also home to coyotes, black-tailed jackrabbits, cottontails, chipmunks, several types of squirrels, voles, skunks, porcupines, gophers, and a variety of bats.

The rare **peregrine falcon,** among the world's fastest birds, sometimes nests in the Weeping Rock area, where you're also likely to see birds such as the American dipper, the canyon wren, and the white-throated swift. Bald eagles sometimes winter in the park, and you might also see golden eagles. Snakes include the poisonous **Great Basin rattlesnake,** usually found only below 8,000 feet elevation, as well as nonpoisonous king snakes and gopher snakes. **Tarantulas** are often seen in the late summer and fall.

Camping

INSIDE THE PARK

The best places to camp are at one of the **national park campgrounds,** just inside the park's south entrance. Reservations for **Watchman Campground** can be made through the park website (www.nps.gov/zion) or at http://reservations.nps.gov, or check with park offices for current reservation phone numbers. A fee will be added to the regular camping fee. Reservations are not accepted for **South Campground,** and it often fills by noon in the summer, so get there early in the day to claim a site.

Both of Zion's main campgrounds have paved roads, well-spaced sites, lots of trees, flush toilets, and that national park atmosphere you came here to enjoy. **Lava Point,** located on the Kolob Terrace, is more primitive (vault toilets), but has a delightful wooded setting.

There are no showers in the national park, but the commercial campgrounds listed below offer showers, for a fee, for those camping in the park. Although there are no RV hookups at South Campground, electric hookups are available in two loops in Watchman.

NEAR THE PARK

Just outside the park entrances, on both the east and south sides, are commercial campgrounds with all the usual amenities. Keep in mind that the park's visitor center, campgrounds, and most of its developed attractions are closer to the south entrance than the east.

Mukuntuweep RV Park & Campground, about a quarter mile east of the East Entrance to Zion National Park on Utah 9 (P.O. Box 193, Orderville, UT 84758; © **435/648-3011;** www.expressweb.com/zionpark), has great views of the surrounding rocks. There are some shade trees, grassy tent sites, a fishing pond, a playground, and a game room. Across the street, under the same management, are a store, a restaurant (see "Where to Dine," below), a curio shop, and a gas station. In addition to campsites, there are six log cabins, a hogan, and a tepee, all of which share the campground's bathhouse and cost $25 for two persons.

Just outside the South Entrance to the park is **Zion Canyon Campground,** on Zion Park Boulevard a half-mile south of the park's South Entrance, P.O. Box 99, Springdale, UT 84767 (© **435/772-3237;** fax 435/772-3844; www.zioncanyoncampground.com). It has tree-shaded sites and grassy tent areas, and although quite crowded in summer, the campground is clean and well maintained. On the premises are a store, a restaurant, a swimming pool, and a playground. Dogs are permitted at RV sites but not tent sites. A Quality Inn (42 units; © **435/772-3237**) opened on the grounds in 2003.

In addition to the campgrounds discussed here, there is also camping at Cedar Breaks National Monument. See

Campground	Elev.	Total Sites	RV Hookups	Dump Station	Toilets	Drinking Water
Lava Point	7,900	6	0	No	Yes	No
South	4,000	126	0	Yes	Yes	Yes
Watchman	4,000	168	90+	Yes	Yes	Yes
Mukuntuweep	6,000	150	30	Yes	Yes	Yes
Zion Canyon	3,800	220	102	Yes	Yes	Yes

"A Nearby National Monument," later in this chapter.

Where to Stay

INSIDE THE PARK

Zion Lodge

In Zion National Park. ✆ **435/772-3213.** Fax 435/772-2001. Information and reservations: Xanterra Parks & Resorts, 14001 E Iliff Ave., Suite 600, Aurora, CO 80014. ✆ **888/297-2757** or 303/297-2757. Fax 303/297-3175. www.zionlodge.com. 121 units. A/C TEL. Mid-Mar to Nov motel rooms $120–$125 double; $128–$133 cabin; $143–$148 suite. Discounts and packages available in winter. AE, DISC, MC, V.

The charming cabins on the forested grounds here offer spectacular views of the park's rock cliffs. Each contains a private porch, a stone (gas-burning) fireplace, two double beds, and pine board walls. The comfortable motel units are basic, with one or two queen-size beds and all the usual amenities except televisions. Suites have a king-size bed, a separate sitting room with a queen-size hide-a-bed, and a refrigerator. At the gift shop you can get everything from postcards and T-shirts to top-quality silver and turquoise American Indian jewelry. The lodge's restaurant (see "Where to Dine," below) serves up wonderful views with its three daily meals.

NEAR THE PARK

Most of the lodging listed below is either in Springdale, a village of some 350 people at the park's south entrance, or between Springdale and the nearby community of Virgin, to the west; though there are also several options just outside the park's east entrance.

Best Western Zion Park Inn

1215 Zion Park Blvd. (P.O. Box 800), Springdale, UT 84767. ✆ **800/934-7275** or 435/772-3200. Fax 435/772-2449. www.zionparkinn.com. 120 units. A/C TV TEL. Apr–Oct $95–$109 double, $115–$160 suite or family unit; Nov–Mar $62–$72 double, $85–$125 suite or family unit. AE, DC, DISC, MC, V. Pets accepted, for an extra fee, with management approval.

This is a good choice for travelers seeking an upscale, reliable chain motel with no surprises. Rooms in the handsome two-story complex are tastefully appointed in Southwest style, with two double beds, two queens, or one king-size bed; they also have coffeemakers, hair dryers, irons, and ironing boards. The grounds are beautifully landscaped and offer phenomenal views of the area's red rock formations. Facilities include a heated outdoor swimming pool (Apr–Oct), a Jacuzzi (year-round), a restaurant serving three meals daily, a gift shop, a convenience store, guest laundry, a liquor store, and conference and meeting rooms.

Canyon Ranch Motel

668 Zion Park Blvd. (P.O. Box 175), Springdale, UT 84767. ✆ **435/772-3357.** Fax 435/772-3057. www.canyonranchmotel.com. 21 units. A/C TV. Rates per room (up to 5 people) Apr–Oct $68–$88; Nov–Mar $48–$68. AE, DISC, MC, V.

Showers	Fire Pits/ Grills	Laundry	Public Phone	Reserve	Fees	Open
No	Yes	No	No	No	Free	May–Oct
No	Yes	No	Yes	No	$16	Apr–Sept
No	Yes	No	Yes	Yes	$16–$20	Year-round
Yes	Yes	Yes	Yes	Yes	$15–$19	Year-round
Yes	Yes	Yes	Yes	Yes	$20–$30	Year-round

Pets accepted at management's discretion ($10 per pet, per night).

Consisting of a series of two- and four-unit cottages set back from the highway, this motel has the look of 1930s-style cabins on the outside while providing modern motel rooms inside. Rooms are either new or newly remodeled, and options include one queen- or king-size bed, two queens, or one queen and one double. Some rooms have showers only, while others have shower/tub combos. Kitchen units are also available. Room 13, with two queen-size beds, offers spectacular views of the Zion National Park rock formations through its large picture windows; views from most other rooms are almost as good. The units surround a delightful lawn with trees and picnic tables; an outdoor swimming pool and whirlpool are other perks.

Cliffrose Lodge & Gardens

281 Zion Park Blvd. (P.O. Box 510), Springdale, UT 84767. © **800/243-UTAH** or 435/772-3234. Fax 435/772-3900. www.cliffroselodge. com. 36 units. A/C TV TEL. Summer $119–$189 per unit. Rates 20%–40% lower in winter, except holidays. AE, DISC, MC, V.

With river frontage and 5 acres of lawns that boast shade trees and flower gardens, the Cliffrose offers a beautiful setting just outside the entrance to Zion National Park. The modern, well-kept rooms have all the standard motel appointments, plus unusually large bathrooms with shower/tub combinations. On the lawns, you'll find comfortable seating, including a lawn swing, plus a playground and a

large outdoor heated pool. Guests have use of a self-service laundry.

Desert Pearl Inn

707 Zion Park Blvd., Springdale, UT 84767. © **888/828-0898** or 435/772-8888. Fax 435/772-8889. www.desertpearl.com. 60 units. A/C TV TEL. $78–$125 double. AE, DISC, MC, V.

This imposing property offers luxurious, comfortable accommodations with beautiful views of the area's scenery from private terraces or balconies. Spacious rooms are decorated in modern Southwest style, with either two queens or one king-size bed. Units have dataports on the phone, refrigerators, microwaves, wet bars, and bidets. The grounds are nicely landscaped, and facilities include a huge outdoor heated pool and a Jacuzzi.

Driftwood Lodge

1515 Zion Park Blvd. (P.O. Box 98), Springdale, UT 84767. © **888/801-8811** or 435/772-3262. Fax 435/772-3702. www.driftwoodlodge. net. 47 units. A/C TV TEL. Apr–Nov $82–$96 double, $102–$110 family unit, $109–$119 king suite; Dec–Mar $72–$86 double, $92–$100 family unit, $99–$109 king suite. All rates include continental breakfast. AE, DC, DISC, MC, V. Pets accepted at management's discretion, $10 fee.

Beautiful lawns and gardens enhance this attractive, well-kept motel—a quiet, lush complex that's perfect for sitting back and admiring the spectacular rock formations that practically surround the town. Extensively renovated in 1994, the spacious rooms have white walls and light wood-grain furnishings, and many have patios or balconies. Most standard rooms have two queen-size beds; others have either one queen or a king. The two family suites each have one king-size and two queen-size beds. There's an art gallery, a gift shop, an outdoor heated pool with a sun deck, and a Jacuzzi. There is no restaurant on the premises, but the motel's convenience store has a soup and salad bar, snacks, and drinks.

El Rio Lodge in Zion Canyon

995 Zion Park Blvd. (P.O. Box 204), Springdale, UT 84767. © **888/772-3205** or 435/772-3205. Fax 435/772-2455. www.elriolodge. com. 11 units. A/C TV. Summer $48–$53 double, $60 suite. Lower rates in winter. AE, DISC, MC, V. Pets accepted for a $10 fee.

A good choice for those on a budget, the El Rio is a pleasant mom-and-pop motel with one suite, five rooms upstairs, and another five downstairs, all offering private bathrooms with tub/shower combos. The motel was built in the early 1960s, and although small, the rooms are clean and comfortable, with light-colored walls and simple but attractive decor. There are two double beds in the upstairs rooms, with an outdoor walkway and porch affording terrific views of Zion Canyon. The downstairs rooms each have one queen bed. The suite has its own private parking area, plus a refrigerator, a microwave, an extra large bathroom, and use of a private yard that has a table and chairs and great views of the rock walls of Zion Canyon. Although there are no phones in the rooms, a public phone is available outside.

Flanigan's Inn

428 Zion Park Blvd. (P.O. Box 100), Springdale, UT 84767. © **800/765-7787** or 435/772-3244. Fax 435/772-3396. www.flanigans.com. 39 units. A/C TV TEL. Mid-Mar to Nov and holidays $79–$199 double, $109–$209 suite; Dec to mid-Mar (except holidays) $49–$79 double, $79–$139 suite. AE, DISC, MC, V.

A mountain-lodge atmosphere suffuses this very attractive complex of natural wood and rock, which is set among trees, lawns, and flowers just outside the entrance to Zion National Park. This is a place where you might actually want to spend time relaxing, unlike some other lodgings in the area, which are simply good places to sleep at the end of long days spent exploring Zion. Parts of the inn date to 1947, but all rooms have been completely renovated. Rooms have Southwest decor, wood furnishings, and local art. One room has a fireplace; other units have whirlpool tubs and bidets; and kitchenettes are available. Flanigan's has a heated outdoor swimming pool, a full-service spa, and a nature trail leading to a hilltop vista. An on-site restaurant, the Spotted Dog Café, serves breakfast and dinner (see "Where to Dine," below).

Harvest House Bed & Breakfast at Zion

29 Canyon View Dr. (P.O. Box 125), Springdale, UT 84767. © **435/772-3880.** Fax 435/772-3327. www.harvesthouse.net. 4 units. A/C. $80–$110 double. Rates include full breakfast. DISC, MC, V. Children over 6 welcome.

A good alternative for those seeking something more interesting than a standard motel, this Utah territorial-style (a style similar to Victorian) home was built in 1989. There's a cactus garden out front and a garden sitting area in back, with a koi (Japanese carp) pond and spectacular views of the national park rock formations. Rooms are charming, comfortable and quiet, with private bathrooms. They're furnished with an eclectic mixture of contemporary and wicker items, and original art and photography dot the walls. One upstairs room faces west and has grand sunset views, while the other two have private decks facing the impressive formations of Zion. The downstairs suite can accommodate up to five adults. The gourmet breakfasts are sumptuous yet low fat, and include fresh-baked breads, fresh-squeezed orange juice, granola, fruit, yogurt, and a hot main course that changes daily. Facilities include an outdoor Jacuzzi.

Mukuntuweep RV Park & Campground

¼ mile east of the east entrance to Zion National Park on Utah 9 (P.O. Box 193, Orderville, UT 84758). ℂ **435/648-2154.** www.xpressweb.com/zionpark. $25 double; campsites $15–$19. AE, DISC, MC, V.

For a bed with a roof over it, at bargain rates, this is the place to come. This attractive compound offers six basic but comfortable log cabins, a hogan, and a tepee, which share the campground's bathhouse. There's a fishing pond, a playground, and a game room, plus great views of the surrounding rocks. Across the street, under the same management, are a store, a restaurant (see "Where to Dine," below), a curio shop, and a gas station.

Under the Eaves Bed & Breakfast

980 Zion Park Blvd. (P.O. Box 29), Springdale, UT 84767. ℂ **435/772-3457.** Fax 435/772-3324. www.under-the-eaves.com. 5 units (2 with shared bathroom). A/C. Apr–Oct $70–$135 double. Lower rates off season. Rates include full breakfast. AE, DISC, MC, V.

English owners Steve and Deb Masefield have furnished this lovely 1929 home with many family antiques, creating an inn that is both attractive and comfortable. We especially enjoy the historic ambience. On the first floor are two cheerful rooms decorated in early-20th-century style. Each has one double bed and a private sink, and they share a bathroom (shower only). Upstairs is a 1,100-square foot suite with a vaulted ceiling, a wood-burning stove, a kitchen, and a claw-foot tub in the bathroom. The suite has a queen bed and two single beds, and boasts views of the gardens and national park. The cute Garden Cottage, which was moved here from inside the national park, contains two small but comfortable rooms, each with one queen-size bed. In the backyard is an attractive garden area with seating and a gas barbecue. Massages and facials are available by appointment for an additional fee. Breakfast generally includes home-baked breads, fresh fruit, and a hot main dish such as omelets or pancakes.

Terrace Brook Lodge

990 Zion Park Blvd. (P.O. Box 217), Springdale, UT 84767. ℂ **800/342-6779** or 435/772-3932. Fax 435/772-3596. www.terracebrook lodge.com. 26 units. A/C TV. $49–$63 double, $79–$94 suite. AE, DISC, MC, V.

Reasonable rates for clean, well-maintained rooms are what you'll find here, and there's even an outdoor swimming pool. This comfortable, older motel has Southwest decor with light wood furnishings. Four rooms have shower only; the rest have shower/tub combos. Ten units have phones. There are two barbecue and picnic areas.

Zion Park Motel

855 Zion Park Blvd. (P.O. Box 365), Springdale, UT 84767. ℂ **435/772-3251.** 21 units. A/C TV TEL. $59–$69 double, $79–$119 family suite. AE, DISC, MC, V.

This economical motel, which has recently been remodeled, offers comfortable, attractively furnished rooms. Bathrooms have showers or shower/tub combos. All rooms have refrigerators and microwaves, and two suites have full kitchens. Facilities include a seasonal outdoor heated pool, a picnic area, and a playground. A self-service laundry, a small but well-stocked grocery store with camping supplies and an ATM, and a restaurant are adjacent.

Zion Ponderosa Ranch Resort

2 miles east of the Zion National Park east entrance, then 5 miles north on North Fork Rd. (P.O. Box 5547, Mt. Carmel, UT 84755). ℂ **800/293-5444** or 435/648-2700. www.zionponderosa.com. 28 cabins. $65–$239 per person, all-inclusive lodging packages. $65 per person, all-inclusive camping packages. DISC, MC, V.

Located in a quiet and picturesque area just outside the park, this lodge is a great choice for those who will be spending more than a few days in the area and want everything that a full-service resort has to offer. Lodging is in comfortable but basic cabins, and camp-sites are available. The large cabins have TVs, while smaller cabins do not, and there are no telephones (except in the largest unit) and no air-conditioning. The main reason to come here is for the activities: mountain biking, horseback riding, skeet and trap shooting, fishing, rappelling, climbing, and a myriad of other activities. A summer day camp keeps kids busy for up to 7 hours while adults tackle other activities. There's a pool and Jacuzzi, tennis courts, and other sports equipment. Services also include a shuttle. Rates are complicated and include all activities and meals; there are discounts for children. In the off season, you can just rent the lodgings or camp without buying a complete package.

Where to Dine

INSIDE THE PARK

Red Rock Grill

Zion Lodge, Zion National Park. ☏ **435/772-3213.** www.zionlodge.com. Dinner reservations required in summer. Breakfast $3.75–$6.95; lunch $4.95–$6.75; main dinner courses $9.95–$20. AE, DC, DISC, MC, V. Daily 6:30–10am, 11:30am–3pm, and 5:30–9pm. AMERICAN.

A mountain lodge atmosphere prevails here, with large windows that provide views of the park's magnificent rock formations. Although the menu changes periodically, it's likely to include an excellent slow-roasted prime rib au jus and the very popular Utah red mountain trout. The menu also often includes broiled salmon and several chicken dishes, such as a skinless chicken breast basted with a spicy Caribbean sauce and served with a red onion relish. There are vegetarian items, such as pasta and black bean ragout. At lunch you'll usually find the Utah red mountain trout, barbecued pork ribs, several dinner salads such as chicken Caesar salad and

Greek vegetarian salad, and burgers and sandwiches. The usual American selections are offered for breakfast in addition to an excellent breakfast buffet. The restaurant will pack lunches to go and offers full liquor service.

Zion Lodge's Castle Dome Cafe

Zion National Park. ☏ **435/772-3213.** $3–$8. No credit cards. Daily 7am–9pm. SNACK BAR.

Located at the north end of Zion Lodge, this simple fast-food restaurant offers an outdoor dining patio serving hot dogs, burgers, sandwiches, pizza, ice cream, frozen yogurt, and similar fare. No alcoholic beverages are sold.

NEAR THE PARK

All of the following restaurants, except the Zion Mount Carmel Restaurant, are located in Springdale, just outside the park's south entrance.

Bit & Spur Restaurant & Saloon

1212 Zion Park Blvd., Springdale. ☏ **435/772-3498.** Reservations recommended. Main courses $8.50–$20. AE, DISC, MC, V. Feb–Nov daily 5–10pm (bar open until midnight), and a weekend brunch is offered May–Sept (call for hours); Dec–Jan Thurs–Mon 5–10pm. Closed Christmas. MEXICAN/SOUTHWESTERN.

Rough wood-and-stone walls and an exposed beam ceiling give this restaurant the look of an Old West saloon, but it's an unusually clean saloon that also has a family dining room, patio dining, and original oil paintings on the walls. The food here is a notch or two above what might be expected—the fare is closer to what you'd find in a good Santa Fe restaurant. The menu includes Mexican standards such as burritos, flautas, chiles rellenos, and a traditional chile stew with pork and rice; but you'll also find more exotic creations, such as *pollo relleno*—a grilled breast of chicken stuffed with cilantro pesto and goat cheese, served with pineapple salsa. Also good are the deep-dish chicken enchilada, with scallions, green chilies, and cheese; and the Moroccan spiced lamb—a braised lamb shank with a sweet tamarind glaze, black-eyed pea ragout, and rice. Several vegetarian items are also available. The Bit & Spur has full liquor service and an extensive wine list.

Spotted Dog Café

Flanigan's Inn, 428 Zion Park Blvd., Springdale. ℂ **435/772-3244.** Reservations recommended. Main courses $8.50–$20. AE, DISC, MC, V. Daily 7am–11:30am and 5–10pm. Reduced hours in winter. AMERICAN/REGIONAL.

This restaurant has a greenhouse/garden look and makes the most of the area's spectacular scenery, with large windows for inside diners plus an outdoor patio. The chef uses fresh local ingredients and herbs from the inn's garden whenever possible. Breakfast features homemade granola, fresh fruits and juices, traditional egg dishes including trout and eggs, and wonderful omelets such as smoked salmon and brie. Dinner selections in spring are likely to include fresh vegetable and lamb dishes; in summer look for innovative salads and light entrees, such as local red trout and mesquite-roasted chicken; during fall and winter you can expect rich sauces, Black Angus beef, pork, wild game, and scrumptious desserts. Vegan dishes can be individually prepared. There is an excellent 2,000-bottle wine cellar, and microbrewery draft beers are available along with complete liquor service.

Zion Mt. Carmel Restaurant

Utah 9, ¼ mile east of the east entrance to Zion National Park. ℂ **435/648-3012.** Breakfast $3.25–$5.95; sandwiches $3.50–$5.50; Mexican dishes $2.95–$7.95. AE, DISC, MC, V. Daily 9am–5pm. AMERICAN/MEXICAN.

This is a down-home coffee shop that offers great homemade pies, spicy New Mexico–style Southwest dishes, shakes and sundaes, and burgers and sandwiches. Locals love the green-chile beef and bean burrito, and the enchilada-style burrito, which is smothered with chile sauce. The breakfast menu includes the standards: ham and eggs, omelets, pancakes, and French toast. No alcoholic beverages are served.

Zion Park Gift & Deli

866 Zion Park Blvd., Springdale. ℂ **435/772-3843.** Sandwiches $5–$10. AE, DISC, MC, V. Summer Mon–Sat 8am–9pm; shorter hours in winter. SANDWICHES.

This is our choice for a top-quality deli-style sandwich at an economical price. You can eat at one of the cafe-style tables inside or on the patio outside, or you can carry your sandwich off on a hike or to a national park picnic ground. All baked goods, including the excellent sandwich breads and sub rolls, are made in-house. In typical deli style, you order at the counter and wait as your meal is prepared with your choice of bread, meats, cheeses, and condiments. This is a good breakfast stop for those who enjoy fresh-baked cinnamon rolls, muffins, banana-nut bread, and similar goodies, with a cup of espresso. Locally made candy and 16 flavors of ice cream and frozen yogurt are also offered. No alcohol is served.

Zion Pizza & Noodle

868 Zion Park Blvd., Springdale. ℂ **435/772-3815.** www.zionpizzanoodle.com. Reservations not accepted. Main courses $9.95–$12. No credit cards. Daily from 4pm; call for winter hours. PIZZA/PASTA.

This busy cafe is the place to come for good pizza and pasta in a somewhat funky atmosphere—it's located in a former church with a turquoise steeple. The dining room has small, closely spaced tables and black-and-white photos on the walls. Patrons order at the counter and help themselves to soft drinks while waiting for their food to be delivered. The 12-inch pizzas, with lots of chewy crust, are baked in a slate stone oven. They're very good, though we were initially put off by all the oddly topped specialty pies, such as the Southwestern burrito pizza and the barbecue chicken pizza. But have no fear: You can get a basic cheese pizza or add any of the roughly 15 extra toppings, from pepperoni to green chiles to pineapple. The menu also offers a variety of pastas, such as penne pasta with grilled chicken, broccoli, carrots, fresh cream, and cheese; plus calzones and stromboli. Beer is served.

Picnic & Camping Supplies

You'll find most of the groceries and camping and RV supplies you want in the town of Springdale, which is just outside the park's south entrance. At **Zion Canyon Campground,** on Zion Park Boulevard a half-mile south of the park's south entrance (© **435/772-3237**), is a store with groceries, souvenirs, and RV supplies, plus a restaurant. In downtown Springdale, the **Zion Park Market,** 855 Zion Park Blvd. (© **435/772-3251**), stocks a good selection of groceries and offers video rentals. On the south end of Springdale on Utah 9 (the opposite side of town from the national park), is the highly recommended **Springdale Fruit Company** (© **435/772-3222**), which sells fresh organic fruits, vegetables, and juices (try the fruit smoothies), plus trail mix and baked goods. It also has a picnic area. The **Switchback C-Store,** 1149 S. Zion Park Blvd. (© **435/772-3700**), stocks snacks and pastries and contains the local **state liquor store.** Those in need of outdoor equipment, hiking boots, clothing, and the like will find what they seek at **Zion Rock and Mountain Guides,** 1458 Zion Park Blvd. (© **435/772-3303;** www.zionrockguides. com), which offers both rentals and sales.

Just outside the east entrance to the park, there is a small store and gas station at **Zion Mt. Carmel Restaurant** (© **435/648-2829**).

Nearby Entertainment

Just outside the south entrance to Zion National Park, in Springdale, are two worthwhile attractions.

The **Zion Canyon Theatre,** 145 Zion Park Blvd. (© **435/772-2400;** www.zion canyontheatre.com), boasts a huge screen—some six stories high by 80 feet wide. Here you can see the dramatic film *Zion Canyon—Treasure of the Gods,* which has thrilling scenes of the Zion National Park area, including a hair-raising flash flood through Zion Canyon's Narrows and some dizzying bird's-eye views. Admission costs $8 adults, $6 seniors, and $5 children 3 to 11; the movie is free for children under 3. The theater is open daily year-round except Christmas. Shows begin hourly from April through October from 11am to 7pm (call for winter hours). The theater complex also contains a tourist information center, an ATM, a picnic area, gift and souvenir shops, a deli, an ice-cream shop, a Paiute Indian exhibit, and a bookstore.

The **Tanner Concert Series** presents multidiscipline performing arts in the stunning, 2000-seat outdoor **O. C. Tanner Amphitheater,** just off Zion Park Boulevard. Offerings range from symphony orchestra concerts to dance performances to bluegrass and cowboy poetry shows. Performances begin at 8pm every Saturday through the summer, and cost $9 for adults and $5 for youths (18 and younger). For information, contact **Dixie College,** in St. George (© **435/652-7994;** www.dixie.edu/ tanner/index.html).

A Nearby National Monument

The area surrounding Zion National Park offers a variety of scenic wonders and recreational opportunities. In addition to other nearby national parks, which are discussed elsewhere in this book, you'll discover one relatively unknown gem, Cedar Breaks National Monument, that looks a lot like a small version of Bryce Canyon National Park.

CEDAR BREAKS NATIONAL MONUMENT

A delightful little park, Cedar Breaks is a wonderful place to spend anywhere from a few hours to several days, gazing down from the rim into the spectacular natural amphitheater, hiking the trails, and camping among the spruce and fir trees and the summer wildflowers.

The park forms a natural coliseum more than 2,000 feet deep and more than 3 miles across, filled with stone spires, arches, and columns shaped by the forces of erosion and painted in ever-changing reds, purples, oranges, and ochers. Why the name Cedar Breaks? Well, the pioneers who came here called such badlands "breaks," and they mistook the juniper trees along the cliff bases for cedars.

JUST THE FACTS

When to Go. At more than 10,000 feet elevation, it's always pleasantly cool at Cedar Breaks. At night it actually gets downright cold, so take a jacket or sweater, even if the temperature is scorching just down the road in St. George. The monument opens for its short summer season only after the snow melts, usually in late May, and closes in mid-October. If you happen to have a pair of cross-country skis or snowshoes, you can visit anytime.

Getting There. Cedar Breaks National Monument is 85 miles north of the main section of Zion National Park. From Zion's south entrance head west on Utah 9, then north on Utah 17 to I-15. Then follow I-15 north to Exit 57 for Cedar City, turn and head east on Utah 14, then head north on Utah 148, which goes straight into the monument. From the Kolob Canyons section of Zion, which is off Exit 40 of I-15, it is only 40 miles to Cedar Breaks.

The national monument is 23 miles east of Cedar City, 56 miles west of Bryce Canyon National Park, and 247 miles south of Salt Lake City. If you're coming from Bryce Canyon or other points east, the park is accessible from the town of Panguitch via Utah 143. If you're coming from the north, take the Parowan exit off I-15 and head south on Utah

143. It's a steep climb from whichever direction you choose, so take care, especially if your vehicle is prone to vapor lock or (like many motor homes) to loss of power on hills.

Information & Visitor Center. One mile from the south entrance gate is the visitor center, open daily from early June through Labor Day 8am to 6pm and Labor Day through mid-October 9am to 5:30pm (closed the rest of the year). The visitor center has exhibits on the geology, flora, and fauna of Cedar Breaks. You can purchase books and maps here, and rangers can help you plan your visit. For information, contact the **Superintendent, Cedar Breaks National Monument,** 2390 W. Utah 56, Ste. 11, Cedar City, UT 84720-4151 (© **435/586-9451;** www.nps.gov/cebr).

Fees. Admission is $3 per person for all those 17 and older. Camping costs $12 per night.

Health & Safety Concerns. The high elevation—10,350 feet at the visitor center—is likely to cause shortness of breath and tiredness. Those with heart or respiratory conditions should consult their doctors before making the trip to Cedar Breaks. During thunderstorms you need to avoid overlooks and other high, exposed areas—they're often targets for lightning.

Ranger Programs. During the monument's short summer season, rangers offer nightly campfire talks at the campground; talks on the area's geology at Point Supreme, a viewpoint near the visitor center (daily on the hour from 10am–5pm); and guided hikes on Saturday and Sunday mornings. A complete schedule is posted at the visitor center and the campground.

EXPLORING CEDAR BREAKS BY CAR

The 5-mile road through Cedar Breaks National Monument offers easy access to the monument's scenic overlooks and trailheads. Allow 30 to 45 minutes to make the drive. Start at the visitor center and nearby **Point Supreme** for a panoramic view of the amphitheater. Then drive north, past the campground and picnic ground turnoff, to **Sunset View,** for a closer look at the amphitheater and its colorful canyons. From each of these overlooks you'll be able to see out across Cedar Valley, over the Antelope and Black mountains, and into the Escalante Desert.

Continue north to **Chessman Ridge Overlook,** so named because the stone hoodoos directly below the overlook seem like massive chess pieces. Watch for swallows and swifts soaring among the rock formations. Then get back into your car and head north to **Alpine Pond,** to walk among the wildflowers on the self-guided nature trail (see "Hiking," below). Finally, proceed to **North View,** which offers perhaps the best views of the amphitheater and its stately rock statues.

SUMMER SPORTS & ACTIVITIES

Hiking. There are no trails from the rim to the bottom of the amphitheater, but the monument does have two high-country trails. The fairly easy 2-mile **Alpine Pond Trail** loop leads through woodlands of bristlecone pines to a picturesque forest glade and a pond surrounded by wildflowers, offering panoramic views of the amphitheater along the way. A trail guide pamphlet is available at the trailhead.

A somewhat more challenging hike, the 4-mile **Spectra Point Trail** (also called the Ramparts Trail) follows the rim more closely than the Alpine Pond Trail, offering changing views of the colorful rock formations. It also takes you through fields of wildflowers and by bristlecone pines that are more than 1,500 years old. You'll need to be especially careful of your footing along the exposed cliff edges, and allow yourself some time to rest—there are lots of ups and downs along the way.

Wildlife Watching. Because of its relative remoteness, Cedar Breaks is a good place for spotting wildlife. You're likely to see mule deer grazing in the meadows along the road early and late in the day. Marmots make their dens near the rim and are often seen along the Spectra Point Trail. You'll spot ground squirrels, red squirrels, and chipmunks everywhere. Pikas, related to rabbits, are here too, but it's unlikely you'll see one. They're small, with short ears and stubby tails, and prefer the high, rocky slopes.

Birders should have no trouble spotting the Clark's nutcracker in the campground, with its gray torso and black-and-white wings and tail. The monument is also home to swallows, swifts, blue grouse, and golden eagles.

WINTER SPORTS & ACTIVITIES

The monument's facilities are shut down from mid-October to late May due to the thick blanket of snow that covers it. The snow-blocked roads keep cars out, but they're perfect for snowmobilers, snowshoers, and cross-country skiers, who usually come over from nearby Brian Head ski area. Snowshoers and cross-country skiers have numerous options, but snowmobilers are restricted to the main 5-mile road through the monument, which is groomed and marked.

CAMPING

A 30-site campground in a beautiful high-mountain setting, **Point Supreme,** just north of the visitor center, is open from June to mid-September, with tent, car, and RV sites available on a first-come, first-served basis. The campground has restrooms, drinking water, picnic tables, grills, and an amphitheater for the ranger's evening campfire programs. There are no showers or RV hookups. The camping fee is $12 per night. Keep in mind that even in midsummer, temperatures can drop into the 30s at night at this elevation, so bring cool-weather gear.

USEFUL TOLL-FREE NUMBERS & WEBSITES

Airlines

Air Canada
✆ 888/247-2262
www.aircanada.ca

Airtran Airlines
✆ 800/247-8726
www.airtran.com

Alaska Airlines
✆ 800/252-7522
www.alaskaair.com

Aloha Airlines
✆ 800/367-5250 in
   Continental U.S.
   and Canada
✆ 808/484-1111 in
   Oahu; 244-9071 in
   Maui; 935-5771 in
   Hilo and Kona;
   245-3691 in Kauai
www.alohaairlines.com
Flies between the Hawai-
   ian islands and to/from
   several cities in California, Phoenix, Reno, Las
   Vegas, Vancouver

American Airlines
✆ 800/433-7300
www.aa.com

American Trans Air
✆ 800/225-2995
www.ata.com

America West Airlines
✆ 800/235-9292
www.americawest.com

British Airways
✆ 800/247-9297
✆ 0345/222-111 or
   0845/77-333-77 in
   Britain
www.british-airways.com

BWIA
✆ 800/538-2492
www.bwee.com

Continental Airlines
✆ 800/525-0280
www.continental.com

Delta Air Lines
✆ 800/221-1212
www.delta.com

Frontier Airlines
✆ 800/432-1359
www.frontierairlines.com

Great Plains Airlines
✆ 866/929-8646
www.gpair.com
Flies between Alamo-
   gordo, New Mexico;
   Albuquerque;
   Nashville; Oklahoma
   City; Tulsa (base);
   Taos, New Mexico

Hawaiian Airlines
✆ 800/367-5320
www.hawaiianair.com

Jet Blue Airlines
✆ 800/538-2583
www.jetblue.com

Midwest Express
✆ 800/452-2022
www.midwestexpress.com

Northwest Airlines
✆ 800/225-2525
www.nwa.com

Song
© 800/359-7664
www.flysong.com
Operated by Delta.
  Serves Boston; Hart-
  ford, Connecticut; New
  York; Newark; Wash-
  ington, D.C.; Atlanta;
  West Palm Beach; Fort
  Lauderdale; Fort
  Myers; Tampa; San
  Juan, Puerto Rico; Las
  Vegas; Los Angeles

Southwest Airlines
© 800/435-9792
www.southwest.com

Spirit Airlines
© 800/772-7117
www.spiritair.com

Sun Country
© 800/359-6786
www.suncountry.com

United Airlines
© 800/241-6522
www.united.com

US Airways
© 800/428-4322
www.usairways.com

Virgin Atlantic Airways
© 800/862-8621 in
  Continental U.S.
© 0293/747-747 in
  Britain
www.virgin-atlantic.com

Car-Rental Agencies

Advantage
© 800/777-5500
www.advantagerentacar.
  com

Alamo
© 800/327-9633
www.goalamo.com

Avis
© 800/331-1212 in
  Continental U.S.
© 800/TRY-AVIS in
  Canada
www.avis.com

Budget
© 800/527-0700
www.budget.com

Dollar
© 800/800-4000
www.dollar.com

Enterprise
© 800/325-8007
www.enterprise.com

Hertz
© 800/654-3131
www.hertz.com

National
© 800/CAR-RENT
www.nationalcar.com

Payless
© 800/PAYLESS
www.paylesscarrental.com

Rent-A-Wreck
© 800/535-1391
www.rentawreck.com

Thrifty
© 800/367-2277
www.thrifty.com

Major Hotel & Motel Chains

**Best Western
  International**
© 800/528-1234
www.bestwestern.com

Clarion Hotels
© 800/CLARION
www.clarionhotel.com or
  www.hotelchoice.com

Comfort Inns
© 800/228-5150
www.hotelchoice.com

Courtyard by Marriott
© 800/321-2211
www.courtyard.com or
  www.marriott.com

Days Inn
© 800/325-2525
www.daysinn.com

Doubletree Hotels
© 800/222-TREE
www.doubletree.com

Econo Lodges
© 800/55-ECONO
www.hotelchoice.com

**Fairfield Inn by
  Marriott**
© 800/228-2800
www.marriott.com

Four Seasons
© 800/819-5053
www.fourseasons.com

Hampton Inn
© 800/HAMPTON
www.hampton-inn.com

Hilton Hotels
© 800/HILTONS
www.hilton.com

Holiday Inn
© 800/HOLIDAY
www.basshotels.com

Howard Johnson
© 800/654-2000
www.hojo.com

**Hyatt Hotels &
  Resorts**
© 800/228-9000
www.hyatt.com

Inter-Continental Hotels & Resorts
✆ 888/567-8725
www.interconti.com

ITT Sheraton
✆ 800/325-3535
www.starwood.com

La Quinta Motor Inns
✆ 800/531-5900
www.laquinta.com

Marriott Hotels
✆ 800/228-9290
www.marriott.com

Motel 6
✆ 800/4-MOTEL6
(800/466-8356)
www.motel6.com

Omni
✆ 800/THEOMNI
www.omnihotels.com

Quality Inns
✆ 800/228-5151
www.hotelchoice.com

Radisson Hotels International
✆ 800/333-3333
www.radisson.com

Ramada Inns
✆ 800/2-RAMADA
www.ramada.com

Red Carpet Inns
✆ 800/251-1962
www.reservahost.com

Red Lion Hotels & Inns
✆ 800/RED-LION
www.redlion.com

Red Roof Inns
✆ 800/843-7663
www.redroof.com

Renaissance
✆ 800/228-9290
www.renaissancehotels.
com

Residence Inn by Marriott
✆ 800/331-3131
www.marriott.com

Ritz Carlton
✆ 800/241-3333
www.ritzcarlton.com

Rodeway Inns
✆ 800/228-2000
www.hotelchoice.com

Sheraton Hotels & Resorts
✆ 800/325-3535
www.sheraton.com

Super 8 Motels
✆ 800/800-8000
www.super8.com

Travelodge
✆ 800/255-3050
www.travelodge.com

Vagabond Inns
✆ 800/522-1555
www.vagabondinn.com

Westin Hotels & Resorts
✆ 800/937-8461
www.westin.com

Wyndham Hotels and Resorts
✆ 800/822-4200 in
Continental U.S.
and Canada
www.wyndham.com

FROMMER'S® COMPLETE TRAVEL GUIDES

Alaska
Alaska Cruises & Ports of Call
American Southwest
Amsterdam
Argentina & Chile
Arizona
Atlanta
Australia
Austria
Bahamas
Barcelona, Madrid & Seville
Beijing
Belgium, Holland & Luxembourg
Bermuda
Boston
Brazil
British Columbia & the Canadian
   Rockies
Brussels & Bruges
Budapest & the Best of Hungary
Calgary
California
Canada
Cancún, Cozumel & the Yucatán
Cape Cod, Nantucket & Martha's
   Vineyard
Caribbean
Caribbean Cruises & Ports of Call
Caribbean Ports of Call
Carolinas & Georgia
Chicago
China
Colorado
Costa Rica
Cuba
Denmark
Denver, Boulder & Colorado Springs
England
Europe
Europe by Rail
European Cruises & Ports of Call

Florence, Tuscany & Umbria
Florida
France
Germany
Great Britain
Greece
Greek Islands
Halifax
Hawaii
Hong Kong
Honolulu, Waikiki & Oahu
India
Ireland
Israel
Italy
Jamaica
Japan
Kauai
Las Vegas
London
Los Angeles
Maryland & Delaware
Maui
Mexico
Montana & Wyoming
Montréal & Québec City
Munich & the Bavarian Alps
Nashville & Memphis
Newfoundland & Labrador
New England
New Mexico
New Orleans
New York City
New York State
New Zealand
Northern Italy
Norway
Nova Scotia, New Brunswick &
   Prince Edward Island
Oregon
Ottawa

Paris
Peru
Philadelphia & the Amish Country
Portugal
Prague & the Best of the Czech
   Republic
Provence & the Riviera
Puerto Rico
Rome
San Antonio & Austin
San Diego
San Francisco
Santa Fe, Taos & Albuquerque
Scandinavia
Scotland
Seattle
Shanghai
Sicily
Singapore & Malaysia
South Africa
South America
South Florida
South Pacific
Southeast Asia
Spain
Sweden
Switzerland
Texas
Thailand
Tokyo
Toronto
USA
Utah
Vancouver & Victoria
Vermont, New Hampshire & Maine
Vienna & the Danube Valley
Virgin Islands
Virginia
Walt Disney World® & Orlando
Washington, D.C.
Washington State

FROMMER'S® DOLLAR-A-DAY GUIDES

Australia from $50 a Day
California from $70 a Day
England from $75 a Day
Europe from $70 a Day
Florida from $70 a Day
Hawaii from $80 a Day

Ireland from $80 a Day
Italy from $70 a Day
London from $90 a Day
New York from $90 a Day
Paris from $90 a Day
San Francisco from $70 a Day

Washington, D.C. from $80 a Day
Portable London from $90 a Day
Portable New York City from $90
   a Day
Portable Paris from $90 a Day

FROMMER'S® PORTABLE GUIDES

Acapulco, Ixtapa & Zihuatanejo
Amsterdam
Aruba
Australia's Great Barrier Reef
Bahamas
Berlin
Big Island of Hawaii
Boston
California Wine Country
Cancún
Cayman Islands
Charleston
Chicago
Disneyland®
Dominican Republic
Dublin

Florence
Frankfurt
Hong Kong
Las Vegas
Las Vegas for Non-Gamblers
London
Los Angeles
Los Cabos & Baja
Maine Coast
Maui
Miami
Nantucket & Martha's Vineyard
New Orleans
New York City
Paris

Phoenix & Scottsdale
Portland
Puerto Rico
Puerto Vallarta, Manzanillo &
   Guadalajara
Rio de Janeiro
San Diego
San Francisco
Savannah
Vancouver
Vancouver Island
Venice
Virgin Islands
Washington, D.C.
Whistler

FROMMER'S® NATIONAL PARK GUIDES

Algonquin Provincial Park
Banff & Jasper
Family Vacations in the National
  Parks

Grand Canyon
National Parks of the American West
Rocky Mountain

Yellowstone & Grand Teton
Yosemite & Sequoia/Kings Canyon
Zion & Bryce Canyon

FROMMER'S® MEMORABLE WALKS

Chicago
London

New York
Paris

San Francisco

FROMMER'S® WITH KIDS GUIDES

Chicago
Las Vegas
New York City

Ottawa
San Francisco
Toronto

Vancouver
Walt Disney World® & Orlando
Washington, D.C.

SUZY GERSHMAN'S BORN TO SHOP GUIDES

Born to Shop: France
Born to Shop: Hong Kong, Shanghai
  & Beijing

Born to Shop: Italy
Born to Shop: London

Born to Shop: New York
Born to Shop: Paris

FROMMER'S® IRREVERENT GUIDES

Amsterdam
Boston
Chicago
Las Vegas
London

Los Angeles
Manhattan
New Orleans
Paris
Rome

San Francisco
Seattle & Portland
Vancouver
Walt Disney World®
Washington, D.C.

FROMMER'S® BEST-LOVED DRIVING TOURS

Austria
Britain
California
France

Germany
Ireland
Italy
New England

Northern Italy
Scotland
Spain
Tuscany & Umbria

THE UNOFFICIAL GUIDES®

Beyond Disney
Central Italy
Chicago
Cruises
Disneyland®
England
Florida
Florida with Kids
Inside Disney

Hawaii
Las Vegas
London
Maui
Mexico's Best Beach Resorts
Mini Las Vegas
Mini-Mickey
New Orleans

New York City
Paris
San Francisco
Skiing & Snowboarding in the West
Walt Disney World®
Walt Disney World® for Grown-ups
Walt Disney World® with Kids
Washington, D.C.

SPECIAL-INTEREST TITLES

Athens Past & Present
Cities Ranked & Rated
Frommer's Best Day Trips from London
Frommer's Caribbean Hideaways
Frommer's China: The 50 Most Memorable Trips
Frommer's Exploring America by RV
Frommer's Gay & Lesbian Europe
Frommer's Best RV and Tent Campgrounds in the U.S.A.

Frommer's Road Atlas Europe
Frommer's Road Atlas France
Frommer's Road Atlas Ireland
Frommer's Wonderful Weekends from New York City
The New York Times' Guide to Unforgettable Weekends
Retirement Places Rated
Rome Past & Present

Booked aisle seat.

Reserved room with a view.

With a queen – no, make that a king-size bed.

With Travelocity, you can book your flights and hotels together, so you can get even better deals than if you booked them separately. You'll save time and money without compromising the quality of your trip. Choose your airline seat, search for alternate airports, pick your hotel room type, even choose the neighborhood you'd like to stay in.

Travelocity

**Visit www.travelocity.com
or call 1-888-TRAVELOCITY**